THE AMERICAN CHALLENGE:
A New History of the United States, Vol I
Second Edition

THE AMERICAN CHALLENGE:
A New History of the United States, Vol I
Second Edition

John Moretta
>   Houston Community College System
>   Houston, Texas

Michael Phillips
>   Collin College
>   Plano, Texas

Austin Allen
>   University of Houston
>   Houston, Texas

Doug Cantrell
>   Elizabethtown Technical & Community College
>   Elizabethtown, Kentucky

Norwood Andrews
>   University of Dallas
>   Dallas, Texas

Edited by
Keith J. Volanto
Michael Phillips

Abigail Press　　　　　　　　　　　Wheaton, IL 60189

Design and Production: Abigail Press
Typesetting: Abigail Press
Typeface: AGaramond
Cover Art: Sam Tolia

THE AMERICAN CHALLENGE:
A New History of the United States, Vol. I

Second Edition, 2013
Printed in the United States of America
Translation rights reserved by the authors
ISBN 1-890919-76-4 ISBN 978-1-890919-76-4

Copyright @ by Abigail Press Inc., 2050 Middleton Dr., Wheaton, IL 60189

All rights reserved. No part of the material protected by the copyright notice may be reproduced or utilized in any form or by any means, electronic or mechanical, including photocopy, recording, or any information storage and retrieval system, without permission in writing from the publisher.

Contents in Brief

Chapter One
  THE DISCOVERY OF THE AMERICAS — 1

Chapter Two
  THE SOUTHERN COLONIES — 30

Chapter Three
  THE NORTHERN COLONIES — 72

Chapter Four
  CREATING AN AMERICAN PEOPLE, 1700-1763 — 116

Chapter Five
  ORIGINS OF THE AMERICAN REVOLUTION — 142

Chapter Six
  THE UNITED STATES AND THE AGE OF REVOLUTION — 168

Chapter Seven
  THE STRUGGLE TO CREATE THE CONSTITUTION — 204

Chapter Eight
  THE FEDERALIST ERA: 1789-1800 — 226

Chapter Nine
  JEFFERSONIAN AMERICA, 1801-1815 — 252

Chapter Ten
  ERA OF GOOD FEELINGS, 1815-1829 — 276

Chapter Eleven
  ANDREW JACKSON AND THE "WHITE MAN'S REPUBLIC" — 304

Chapter Twelve
  THE UNITED STATES IN TRANSFORMATION, 1830-1850 — 340

Chapter Thirteen
  AGE OF REFORM — 360

Chapter Fourteen
  AMERICA EXPANDS, 1840-1848 — 382

Chapter Fifteen
  EXPANSION, SLAVERY, AND SECESSION: The Road to War — 404

Chapter Sixteen
  THE AMERICAN CIVIL WAR, 1861-1865 — 430

Chapter Seventeen
  RECONSTRUCTION: The Turning Point That Never Turned — 470

APPENDIX

A. Declaration of Independence	512
B. Constitution of the United States	514
C. Presidential Elections	527
D. Supreme Court Justices	531
E. Admission of States to the Union	534
F. Population Growth	535

GLOSSARY 536

INDEX 563

Contents

CHAPTER ONE
THE DISCOVERY OF THE AMERICAS 1
    The First Inhabitants: Asian Migrations 2
    Great Civilizations of Mexico and South America 3
    North American People and Societies 4
    Europe on the Eve of Exploration 9
    The Renaissance: New Thought and New Technology 11
    European Exploration and Expansion 13
        Exploration Prior to Columbus 13
        Portugal 14
        Spain 15
            "Thursday October 11" 17
            Bartoleme de Las Casas, Brief Account of the Devastation of the Indies (1542) 21
        England 21
        France and the Netherlands 23
    Africans 23
    The Columbian Exchange 24
    New Cultures 26
    Chronology 27
    Review Questions 28
    Glossary of Important People and Concepts 28
    Suggested Readings 29

CHAPTER TWO
THE SOUTHERN COLONIES 30
    The Early Chesapeake Colonies: Virginia and Maryland 32
    Success at Last: The Tobacco Boom 35
        Tobacco and the Changing Nature of Virginia Society and Labor 36
    Toward the Destruction of the Native Americans 38
    Proprietary Maryland 39
    The Caribbean Colonies 41
        Masters and Slaves 41
    Toward African Slavery White Indentured Servitude in the Chesapeake 43
        Bacon's Rebellion 45
        The Rise of Slavery in the Chesapeake Colonies 47
    The Origins of the Atlantic Slave Trade 49
        West Africans 50
        The Middle Passage 52
            Christian Slaves in Muslim Africa 54
    Arrival in the New World 55
    The Impact of the Slave Trade on Africa 56
    Establishing a Slave Society in North America 57
        The Slave Codes 57
    Carolina: A Barbadian Colony on the Mainland 58
        North Carolina 61
    The Founding of Georgia 62
    The Latin South 64
    The Growth of English Colonies 68
    Chronology 69

Review Questions 70
Glossary of Important People and Concepts 70
Suggested Readings 71

CHAPTER THREE
THE NORTHERN COLONIES 72

The Founding of New England 74
The Puritans 74
The Plymouth Colony 77
The Great Migration and the Establishing of the Massachusetts Bay Colony 79
Land and Labor in New England 82
Puritan Family Life 84
New England Prosperity: Fish and Ships 84
Dissension in the Puritan Ranks 86
Roger Williams and Toleration 87
Anne Hutchinson and the Equality of Believers 88

England in Turmoil 90
New Colonies, New Patterns 91
The Dutch Empire in North America 92
From New Netherlands to New York 93
Dutch Colonists 93

Quakerism and the Founding of Pennsylvania 95
The Quaker Faith 95
William Penn's "Holy Experiment" 96

The Northern Colonists and Native Americans 100
Native Americans and Property 101
Tribute 101
The Pequot War 101
Praying Towns 102
King Philip's War 103
North American Survival Strategies 105

Mercantilism, the Navigation Acts, and the Redefinition of Empire 106
The Dominion of New England 107
The Glorious Revolution 108

Witchcraft Hysteria in New England 109
The Salem Witch Trials in Global Perspectives 110

Laying Foundations for the American Nation 112
Chronology 113
Review Questions 114
Glossary of Important People and Concepts 114
Suggested Readings 115

CHAPTER FOUR
CREATING AN AMERICAN PEOPLE, 1700-1763 116

Colonial Economic Development 118
Immigration 119
African Slavery in the Eighteenth Century 120
The Stono Rebellion 121
The European Enlightenment and Colonial North America 122
The Great Awakening 124
George Whitefield: Popular Evangelist and Colonial American Consumers 128
Eighteenth-Century European Conflicts and the North American Colonies 129

New France Crumbles from Within 132
The French and Indian War, 1754-1763 134
Echoes of the French and Indian War 136
Chronology 139
Review Questions 140
Glossary of Important People and Concepts 140
Suggested Readings 141

CHAPTER FIVE
ORIGINS OF THE AMERICAN REVOLUTION 142
Immigration, 1760-1775 144
The Ranks of the Unfree 146
The Evolving Economy 147
The Coming of the American Revolution 147
The Sugar and Currency Acts 147
The Stamp Act 148
Initial Colonial Protests Against the Stamp Act 149
Stamp Act Protests in Boston 149
Stamp Act Resistance Spreads 150
Harbottle Dorr 151
The Townshend Acts 152
The Boston Massacre 153
The Boston Tea Party 154
The Intolerable Acts 155
The Disintergration of Authority 156
The Beginning of the American Revolution 157
Lexington, Concord, and Bunker Hill 157
The Second Continental Congress 158
The Colonists Take the Offensive: The Invasion of Canada and the Siege of Boston 159
George III Throws Down the Gauntlet 160
Common Sense 161
Debating "Independency" 161
Creating Americans 163
Chronology 165
Review Questions 166
Glossary of Important People and Concepts 166
Suggested Readings 167

CHAPTER SIX
THE UNITED STATES AND THE AGE OF REVOLUTION 168
The Balance Sheet: British and American Strengths and Weaknesses 171
The Battle for New York 173
A Surprise Comeback: The Battle of Trenton 175
Another Surprise at Princeton 176
Washington's Brain Trust 178
Seeking Allies 179
Virtue, God and Man in Revolutionary America 180
A Nation of Drinkers 182
Hanging for Pleasure and Education 183
The Battle of the Cupboards 184
The Saratoga Campaign 185
Bruised and Battered 187

    "The Game is Pretty Near Up" 187
        France Enters the War 188
The British Evacuation of Philadelphia 189
The War in the West 190
The War Moves South, 1780-1781 191
        Settling Scores in the Carolinas 193
        The Battles of Cowpens and Guilford Court House 193
        Cornwallis Blunders—The Siege of Yorktown 195
        The Treaty of Paris 197
The "Radicalism" of the American Revolution 198
Chronology 201
Review Questions 202
Glossary of Important People and Concepts 202
Suggested Readings 203

CHAPTER SEVEN
THE STRUGGLE TO CREATE THE CONSTITUTION 204
Chaos Under the Articles of Confederation 206
        The Newburgh Conspiracy 208
        Shays's Rebellion 209
        Western Troubles 209
The Constitution Conspiracy 210
The Constitutional Convention of 1787 210
        "An Assembly of Demigods" 211
        The Virginia and New Jersey Plans and the Connecticut Compromise 212
        The Constitution and Slavery 213
The *Federalist Papers* and the Campaign for Ratification 214
    A Memorial to the South Carolina Senate 216
A Retreat From Democracy 218
The Radical Impact of the American Revolution and the Constitution 219
Chronology 223
Review Questions 224
Glossary of Important People and Concepts 224
Suggested Readings 225

CHAPTER EIGHT
THE FEDERALIST ERA: 1789-1800 226
Establishing the National Government 228
        The "Republican Court" of George Washington 228
        The First Congress 229
Alexander Hamilton 230
        Hamilton's Financial Program 231
        The Federal Excise Tax and the Bank of the United States 233
        The Report on Manufactures 233
The Rise of Opposition 233
        The Birth of the First Party System 233
        Conflicting Visions of Republican Society 234
        A Clash of Titans: Jefferson versus Hamilton 236
The Republic in a World at War, 1793-1800 237
        Americans and the French Revolution 237
        Maintaining Neutrality 238
The Destruction of the Woodland Indians 238

Western Troubles ... 239
Jay's Treaty ... 240
Washington's Farewell ... 241
    The 1796 Election ... 242
The Adams Presidency ... 243
    Troubles with France ... 243
    Crisis at Home, 1798-1800 ... 244
The Virginia and Kentucky Resolutions ... 245
The Politicians and the Army ... 246
"The Revolution of 1800" ... 246
    The Election of Thomas Jefferson ... 246
Transfer of Power ... 248
Chronology ... 249
Review Questions ... 250
Glossary of Important People and Concepts ... 250
Suggested Readings ... 251

CHAPTER NINE
JEFFERSONIAN AMERICA, 1801-1815 ... 252

Jefferson in Power ... 254
    The New President ... 254
    Purging the Government ... 255
    Republican Agrarianism ... 255
    Evangelical Religion and Jeffersonian America ... 256
    Jeffersonians and the Courts: John Marshall and the Advent of Judicial Review ... 258
    The Louisiana Purchase ... 260
    The Lewis and Clark Expedition ... 262
    American Reaction to the Napoleonic Wars ... 263
    The Embargo Act ... 264
The Road to War With England ... 264
    Madison Seeks Peace ... 264
    Native Americans and the Impending War with Great Britain ... 265
    Tecumseh's Vision ... 266
    The Rise of the War Hawks ... 267
The War of 1812: The "Second War of American Independence" ... 267
    The Failed Invasion of Canada ... 268
    Tecumseh's Last Stand ... 269
    The Battles for Baltimore and New Orleans ... 270
    The End of the Federalist Party: The Hartford Convention ... 271
    The Second War of American Independence ... 272
Chronology ... 273
Review Questions ... 274
Glossary of Important People and Concepts ... 274
Suggested Readings ... 275

CHAPTER TEN
ERA OF GOOD FEELINGS, 1815-1829 ... 276

Henry Clay's American System ... 278
The Transportation Revolution ... 280
    Steamboats ... 280
    The Canal Boom ... 280
Judicial Nationalism and the Market Revolution ... 281

The Transformation of the New England Agriculture 282
Migration into the Old Northwest 284
The Beginning of Northern Industrialization 284
    Samuel Slater 285
    The Waltham System 285
    The Antebellum South and the European Demand for Cotton 286
    The Northern Urban Commercial Classes 287
    Urban Industrialization 289
Slavery and the Market Revolution in the South 289
    Southern Planters and Paternalism 290
    The Organization of Slave Labor 290
    Southern Yeoman Farmers 291
    Characteristics of the Market Revolution in the South 292
President Monroe 294
Foreign Affairs Under Monroe 294
    Rapprochement with England 294
    Relations with Spain 295
    The Monroe Doctrine 296
The Missouri Compromise 297
Chronology 301
Review Questions 302
Glossary of Important People and Concepts 302
Suggested Readings 303

CHAPTER ELEVEN
ANDREW JACKSON AND THE "WHITE MAN'S REPUBLIC" 304
"A Speedy Redress": Jackson's Violent, Tumultuous Early Years 306
    Dueling, Politics, and Slaveowning 307
    "Mad Upon His Enemies": Jackson and the "Code of Honor" 308
    "Old Hickory" 309
"The Monster" and the 1824 Presidential Election 310
The John Quincy Adams Presidency and the Long Campaign 313
Jackson's 1828 Triumph 314
    "The Little Magician": Martin Van Buren 314
    "Palsied by the Will of our Constituents" 315
    Poison Pens: Newspapers and the Election of 1828 316
Jackson's First Term 318
    To the Victor Belong the Spoils 318
    The Eaton Affair 318
    "The Tariff of Abominations" 319
    Slave Rebels 320
    The Nullification Crisis 322
    Conspiracy Theories 323
    The Bank War and the 1823 Campaign 324
Jackson's Second Term 325
    The Second American Party System 325
    Killing the Monster 326
    The Heir 326
"Martin Van Ruin" 327
The Wages of Whiteness 328
Indian Removal 329
    Chief Justice Marshall and the Cherokees 330

  The Second Seminole War 331
  The Trail of Tears 332
   Indian Removal Act 333
 The Age of Jackson: An Assessment 334
 Chronology 337
 Review Questions 338
 Glossary of Important People and Concepts 338
 Suggested Readings 339

CHAPTER TWELVE
THE UNITED STATES IN TRANSFORMATION, 1830-1850 340
 New People, New Places: Population Growth, Urbanization, and Immigration 342
  Urban Life 343
  Immigration 344
  Transportation and Communication Innovations 345
  The Transformation of Northern Society 346
  Free Blacks in the Antebellum North 348
  The Changing Life of Women 350
  Popular Culture in the North 350
 The Antebellum South 351
  Cotton and Slavery Expansion 352
  Life Under Slavery in the Old South 352
  Southern Women, Black and White 354
  Slave Labor vs. Free Labor 354
   The Case of the White Slave 355
 Chronology 357
 Review Questions 358
 Glossary of Important People and Concepts 358
 Suggested Readings 359

CHAPTER THIRTEEN
AGE OF REFORM 360
 An Era of Reform 361
  Revivalism and the Second Great Awakening 362
  Moral Reform 363
  Sabbatarians 363
  Temperance 363
  Rehabilitation 364
  Public Education 365
 Writers, Thinkers, and Dissenters 367
  Emerson and the Transcendentalists 367
  Walt Whitman: Songs of America and the Self 368
  The Skeptical View: Hawthorne and Melville 368
 Radical Dissenters 369
  Utopian Communities 369
  The Mormons 370
 The Struggle Against Slavery 371
  The Early Antislavery Movement 371
  Colonization 372
  Militant Abolitionists 372
  Anti-Abolitionist Feeling in the North 373
  Political Abolitionism 373

    The Proslavery Justification 374
    Black Abolitionists 374
The Rise of the Women's Rights Movement 375
    Women and the Antislavery Crusade 375
    The Struggle for Legal Rights 377
    The Women's Rights Movement 377
        The Protest of Lucy Stone and Henry Blackwell Upon Their Marriage 378
    The Impact of Reform 379
Chronology 379
Review Questions 380
Glossary of Important People and Concepts 380
Suggested Readings 381

CHAPTER FOURTEEN
AMERICA EXPANDS, 1840-1850 382
Early Waves of Expansion 384
    Oregon 384
    California and New Mexico 385
    Texas 386
A Surge of Settlers 387
    The Texas Republic 387
    The Trek to Oregon 388
    The Mormon Exodus 389
Manifest Destiny 390
Tyler and Politics of Expansion 391
    The Saga of the Amistad 392
    The Election of 1844 393
The Annexations of Oregon and Texas 393
War With Mexico 395
    Opposition to the Mexican War 397
    Treaty of Guadalupe Hidalgo 397
    Consequences of the Mexican War 398
More Land, More Problems 401
Chronology 401
Review Questions 402
Glossary of Important People and Concepts 402
Suggested Readings 403

CHAPTER FIFTEEN
EXPANSION, SLAVERY, AND SECESSION: The Road to War 404
The Wilmot Proviso and the Politics of Slavery 406
    Political Crisis at Mid-Century 408
The Compromise of 1850 411
The Last Years of Sectional Harmony 413
The Kansas Nebraska Act 415
    The Rise of the Republican Party 415
    Bleeding Kansas 417
The Dred Scott Case 418
    The Crime Against Kansas/The Crime Against Sumner 419
    The Lecompton Constitution 421
The Rise of Lincoln 421
John Brown Returns 423

  The Election of 1860 423
 Chronology 426
 Review Questions 428
 Glossary of Important People and Concepts 428
 Suggested Readings 429

CHAPTER SIXTEEN
THE AMERICAN CIVIL WAR, 1861-1865 430
 The End of Compromise 432
 Preparation and Persistence: The North and South in the Context of a Long War 433
  Economic Development, Population, and the Accident of Geography 434
  A Brothers' War 435
  Executive Leadership, North and South 436
  Diplomacy During the Civil War 438
  The War Begins in Earnest 440
  The First Battle of Bull Run (Manassas) 440
  McClellan Takes Command 442
  The War in the West 442
   The General's Wife 444
  The War at Sea 444
  McClellan and the Peninsular Campaign 445
  Stalemate 446
 Wartime Transformations 448
  The Civil War and State Power 449
  Emancipation 450
  Everyday Life during Wartime 451
  Women on the Home Front 453
  Women on the Battlefield 453
 The Turning Points of 1863 455
  Gettysburg 455
  The Death of Stonewall Jackson 456
  The Vicksburg Campaign 458
 Toward Union Victory 459
  Grant versus Lee 459
  The Election of 1864 460
  General Sherman on the March 461
  The War Ends 462
 Endings, Beginnings, and Continuations 464
  Bioterrorism 466
 Chronology 467
 Review Questions 468
 Glossary of Important People and Concepts 468
 Suggested Readings 469

CHAPTER SEVENTEEN
RECONSTRUCTION: The Turning Point That Never Turned 470
 Confederacy's Defeat 472
 Reconstruction's Overarching Issues 474
 Wartime/Presidential Reconstruction 475
  Abraham Lincoln 475
  Radical Republicans and Reconstruction 477
 Andrew Johnson and Reconstruction 478

    Johnson's Reconstruction Policy 480
    The Black Suffrage Issue in the North 480
    Southern Defiance 480
    The Black Codes 481
Land and Labor in the Postwar South 481
    The Freedmen's Bureau 482
    The Issue of Land for the Landless 484
The Origins of Radical Reconstruction 484
    The Fourteenth Amendment 485
    The 1866 Congressional Elections 486
    The Reconstruction Acts of 1867 487
    The White Backlash During Presidential Reconstruction: The 1866 Race Riots in
    Memphis and New Orleans 488
The Impeachment of Andrew Johnson 490
The Southern Response to the Reconstruction Acts 492
The Completion of Formal Reconstruction 493
The First Grant Administration 494
    The Election of 1868 494
    The Fifteenth Amendment 496
    Grant in the White House 497
    Civil Service Reform 499
    Foreign Policy Issues 499
The White Backlash Continues 502
    The 1872 Presidential Election 503
    The Panic of 1873 504
Retreat From Reconstruction 505
    The 1876 Presidential Election 507
Chronology 509
Review Questions 510
Glossary of Important People and Concepts 510
Suggested Readings 511

APPENDIX

    A. Declaration of Independence   512
    B. Constitution of the United States   514
    C. Presidential Elections   527
    D. Supreme Court Justices   531
    E. Admission of States to the Union   534
    F. Population Growth   535

GLOSSARY   536

INDEX   563

MAPS & TABLES

CHAPTER 1
- Map 1.1 The Bering Land Bridge
- Map 1.2 Location of Native North Americans
- Map 1.3 The Vikings Routes
- Map 1.4 Voyages of Exploration

CHAPTER 2
- Map 2.1 Chesapeake Colonies
- Map 2.2 European Possessions in the Caribbean
- Map 2.3 The Atlantic Slave Trade
- Map 2.4 Carolina Proprietorship, 1685
- Map 2.5 La Salle in Texas
- Map 2.6 Spanish Missions and Presidios 1682-1722
- Map 2.7 North America Before 1763
- Map 2.8 North America After 1763

CHAPTER 3
- Map 3.1 The New England Colonies
- Map 3.2 Colonial Trade Routes
- Map 3.3 Middle Colonies
- Map 3.4 King Phillip's War
- Table 3.1 England's Principal Mainland Colonies

CHAPTER 4
- Table 4.1 Major English Wars, 1689-1763
- Map 4.1 The French and Indian War
- Map 4.2 Proclamation Line of 1763

CHAPTER 5
- Map 5.1 The Thirteen Colonies
- Map 5.2 Lexington & Concord
- Map 5.3 Bunker Hill

CHAPTER 6
- Map 6.1 Battle of Long Island
- Map 6.2 The War in the North, 1776-1777
- Map 6.3 The War in the South, 1778-1781
- Map 6.4 Cornwallis's Campaign
- Table 6.1 Major Battles of the Revolutionary War

CHAPTER 7
- Map 7.1 United States (1787)
- Table 7.1 The Articles of Confederation and the Constitution Compared

CHAPTER 8
- Map 8.1 Pinckney's Treaty, 1795
- Map 8.2 The Election of 1800

CHAPTER 9
- Map 9.1 Louisiana Purchase & Lewis and Clark
- Map 9.2 War of 1812

CHAPTER 10
- Table 10.1 Major Decisions of the Marshall Court
- Map 10.1 Adams-Onís Treaty
- Map 10.2 The Missouri Compromise

CHAPTER 11
- Map 11.1 The Election of 1824
- Map 11.2 The Election of 1828
- Map 11.3 Trail of Tears

CHAPTER 12
- Map 12.1 Railroads in 1860

CHAPTER 14
- Map 14.1 Western Trails
- Map 14.2 Mexican American War
- Table 14.1 Westward Expansion, 1815-1850

CHAPTER 15
- Map 15.1 The Election of 1848
- Map 15.2 Slavery After the Compromise of 1850
- Map 15.3 The Election of 1852
- Map 15.4 Kansas-Nebraska Act
- Map 15.5 The Election of 1856
- Map 15.6 The Election of 1860
- Table 15.1 Overview of the Sectional Crisis

CHAPTER 16
- Map 16.1 Border States
- Map 16.2 The Anaconda Plan
- Map 16.3 The First Battle of Bull Run
- Map 16.4 The Peninsula Campaign
- Map 16.5 The Seven Days' Battle
- Map 16.6 The Second Battle of Bull Run
- Map 16.7 Battle of Antietam
- Map 16.8 Battle of Fredericksburg
- Map 16.9 The Chancellorsville Campaign
- Map 16.10 Battle of Gettysburg, Day One
- Map 16.11 Battle of Gettysburg, Day Two
- Map 16.12 Battle of Gettysburg, Day Three
- Map 16.13 Vicksburg Campaign
- Map 16.14 The Battle of Chattanooga
- Map 16.15 Battle of Chickamauga
- Map 16.16 Sherman's Campaign
- Map 16.17 The Road to Appomattox
- Table 16.1 Major Battles of the Civil War, 1861-1865

CHAPTER 17
- Map 17.1 Reconstruction Districts
- Map 17.2 The Election of 1868
- Map 17.3 The Election of 1876

Preface

Every nation encounters challenges during its existence. Some are common to all countries, some are quite unique. How a people rise to overcome these challenges, or fail in their attempts to address them adequately, engenders much of that country's history. Americans experienced a series of internal and external challenges over the past 500 years even before the creation of the United States: exploration of unknown lands, intense military conflicts, demanding technological problems, divisive political battles, and epic social upheavals, just to name a few. This textbook is an attempt to relay how Americans have risen to their own set of challenges and either prevailed over them or continue to deal with those not yet overcome.

The work's subtitle—"A New History of the United States"—refers to the effort by the authors to synthesize the latest historical scholarship (and borrow, when pertinent, from other disciplines) to provide a fresh account of this country's national story. Unlike many older textbooks originally produced during the Cold War era and simply updated with token changes, the authors of *The American Challenge* have written their chapters entirely from the perspective of the early twenty-first century. At the conclusion of each chapter, the authors have included a list of suggested readings consisting of a few classic works and numerous recent publications that influenced their interpretation of a particular period. These books can also provide an important starting point for students interested in delving deeper into the introduced topics.

Every textbook contains a tremendous amount of information. To guide the retention of material, the authors of *The American Challenge* have emboldened key terms to aid readers in distinguishing the most important persons, events, and concepts appearing in each chapter. A glossary at the end of the book serves as a compilation of all bold terms, providing informative descriptions. To further help digest the information, each chapter also contains a chronology to act as a quick-guide for those wishing to keep track of key events over time, and a set of five summary review questions that students should feel comfortable answering before moving on to the next chapter. To enhance the overall learning experience, all chapters include helpful maps, interesting photographs of noteworthy people and everyday scenes, and other enlightening illustrations relevant to a particular period.

Supplements from Abigail Press are also available for each volume of *The American Challenge*. *Historical Perspectives: A Reader and Study Guide* offers primary source documents and introductory comments designed to help develop an interest in America's past and appreciate the relevance of the course material. Selections cover all periods of United States history, including the Discovery of America, Colonization, the American Revolution, the Civil War, Reconstruction, Westward Expansion, World Wars, the Depression, Cold War, and the Modern Period. *Imperial Presidents: The Rise of Executive Power from Roosevelt to Obama* provides an additional supplement for Volume Two. Transcending the partisan tone of current American debate, authors John Moretta, Michael Phillips, and Carl Luna present a balanced evaluation of the modern presidents. Each essay consists of a biographical portrait of each president, followed by a positive and negative assessment of each man's tenure in office (endeavoring to be as even-handed as possible in their conclusions), and a section devoted to the dramatic expansion of the federal government and the growth of the Executive Branch.

I am very proud to be associated with the fine group of scholars who authored *The American Challenge*. Each professor channeled their broad experiences as academics and classroom educators to produce a book that not only reflects the latest historical scholarship, but also written in a compelling manner which will resonate with today's college students. John A. Moretta earned his Ph.D. in History from Rice University and is currently a Professor of History at Central College, Houston Community College System in Houston, Texas where he has taught for over thirty years. John is currently servings as department chair for the social sciences and humanities for the new Community College of Qatar, which is located on the Arabian Gulf. John has broad historical interests as reflected in his published biographies of William Penn and the Texas statesman William Pitt Ballinger and his numerous contributions to both volumes of *The American Challenge*. John has just finished a book on the Hippies for Oxford University Press, with an anticipated publication date of early fall of 2012. My colleague at Collin College, Michael Phillips, earned his Ph.D. in History from the University of Texas at Austin. His teaching and books on race in Dallas and Texas House Speakers demonstrate his strong interest and expertise in American government as well as race, class, and gender issues. Doug Cantrell holds the rank of Professor of History and chairs the History Department at the Elizabethtown Community and Technical College where he has taught for the past 25 years. Professor Cantrell studied at the University of Kentucky and has authored numerous articles and book reviews in academic journals and encyclopedias in the field of immigration and ethnic history. Norwood Andrews is currently a Visiting Professor of History at University of Dallas. He earned his doctorate at the University of Texas at Austin and specializes in American criminal justice history. Austin Allen received his Ph.D. from the University of Houston and is an Associate Professor of History at the University of Houston-Downtown where he has taught since 2002. A specialist in the legal history of the antebellum United States, Austin has written a book detailing the origins of the Dred Scott Case and is presently working on a book about the Fugitive Slave Law. Finally, I received my Ph.D. in American history from Texas A&M University and currently teach history and serve as Chair of the History Department at Collin College in Plano, Texas. I have taught American and Texas history for the past 15 years and published a book and several articles reflecting my interests in 20th century American politics and race relations. The authors hope you enjoy this effort and welcome feedback from our readers.

Keith J. Volanto

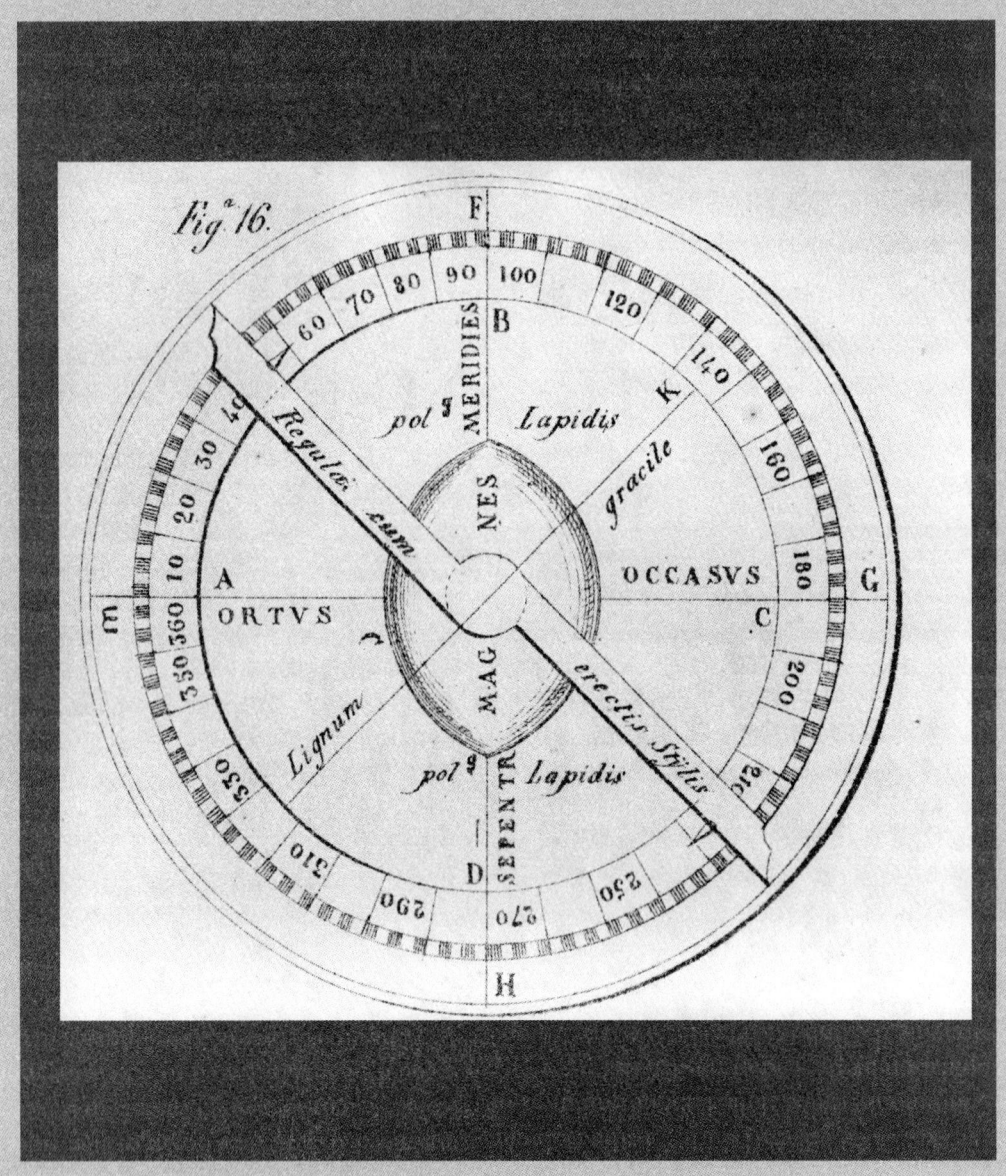

A MARINER'S COMPASS

Chapter One

THE DISCOVERY OF THE AMERICAS

On the morning of October 12, 1492, Taíno men, women, and children awoke to find European ships, with their sun-bleached sails billowing in the light breeze, anchored off the coast of their homeland, one of the many islands making up the Bahamas. Awestruck, these Arawak-speaking people emerged from their homes and walked to the island's sandy beaches to get a closer look at the strange boats, which were much larger than the native canoes they were accustomed to seeing. Suddenly, strange men emerged from the boats. Their skin was light, their dress seemed odd, and they spoke a language the natives could not understand. Following their custom, the Taíno greeted the strangers and brought them food and water. They then gave the newcomers gifts—parrots, balls of cotton, spears, and other items commonly found in the Bahamas. In return, the Europeans, led by a Genoese sailor, Cristoforo Colombo (Christopher Columbus), gave the Arawaks glass beads, hawks' bells, and other trinkets.

After this initial meeting, Columbus described these people in his journal as generous and handsome. He wrote: "...they willingly traded everything they owned.... They were well-built, with good bodies and handsome features...." However, the Spanish did not hold this view for long. Instead of returning the Taínos' hospitality and generosity, Columbus and his men later enslaved them, viewing the natives as ignorant, uncivilized, and fit only for servile roles. In another journal entry, Columbus wrote: "They do not bear arms, and do not know them, for I showed them a sword, they took it by the edge and cut themselves out of ignorance. They have no iron. Their spears are made of cane.... They would make fine servants.... With fifty men we could subjugate them all and make them do whatever we want."

For their part, the Taínos initially seemed to like the Spanish and viewed their first encounter as an opportunity to increase trade. They were puzzled, however, by one question the Spanish repeated over and over: **Dónde está el oro?** (Where is the gold?) Unfamiliar with these words, the Taíno could not understand what the explorers wanted. Finally, the natives were made to understand that Columbus and the others were interested in the small gold earrings, which the Taíno adorned themselves. Although they were willing to give the Spanish these earrings, the Taíno could not satisfy the newcomers' desire to know the source of the gold used to make the jewelry. Promised 10 percent of the profits from all gold and spices that he brought back to the Spanish government by King Ferdinand and Queen Isabella, Columbus began to fantasize about vast gold fields that would make him rich beyond his dreams. Unable to answer to his question, Columbus took many Taínos prisoner aboard his ships. Eventually, Columbus took his captives to Hispaniola (the name Spain gave to the island that today consists of Haiti and the Dominican Republic), all the time insisting that he be shown the source of the gold.

Three years later, on his second expedition to the Caribbean region, Columbus led a party of twelve hundred men who accompanied him to enslave as many natives as could be found. Raiding parties captured approximately fifteen hundred Arawak men, women, and children. These people were then confined in outdoor pens and guarded twenty-four hours a day by vicious dogs and soldiers. Five hundred natives, those considered to be the finest slave material, were eventually chained in the hold of ships and transported to Spain to be sold by an archdeacon in the Catholic Church.

Only three hundred captives survived the trip, the remainder succumbing to poor food, stale air, cramped living quarters, and harsh treatment. The Taínos who remained on the islands fought back, but to no avail. Their forces faced armored Spanish soldiers armed with muskets and steel swords and riding on horseback. Many prisoners that the Spanish captured were either hanged or burned alive. Thousands more fell to smallpox and other diseases inadvertently brought to the New World by the Spanish. When resistance failed, those Taínos who could escape fled from their islands. Still others committed suicide by cassava poisoning, loving their freedom so much they killed their precious babies to save them from captivity.

THE FIRST INHABITANTS: ASIAN MIGRATIONS

The Taíno and other native peoples Columbus encountered probably arrived in North America as a result of a massive migration from central Asia across the Bering Strait into what is now Alaska beginning about 30,000 years ago during the last Ice Age. At that time, a large quantity of water in the form of massive glaciers lay upon the earth's surface, creating a land bridge that nomadic hunters from modern-day Siberia crossed into North America, searching for bison, caribou, reindeer, and other large animals. Geologists generally believe that this land bridge, which was perhaps 600 miles wide, afforded easy passage between Asia and North America. Although paleoanthropologists disagree on the precise timing of this migration, most likely the bulk of it occurred between eleven and fifteen thousand years ago. By about 8,000 B.C. these Asian people reached the southernmost parts of South America. Although scholars disagree, one estimate is that fifty to sixty million people inhabited the Western Hemisphere at the end of the fifteenth century when the Spanish invasion occurred. In comparison, about eighty to ninety million people lived in Europe and about seventy million in Africa at that time.

Recent scholarship indicates that **Amerindians**, a term anthropologists use to describe Native Americans, included approximately 2,000 cultures. These people spoke several hundred different languages and lived in towns and cities scattered throughout North and South America. There was much variety among native peoples in religion, government, economic life, values, and social systems. In fact, the Amerindians were as different from each other as they were from the Europeans they encountered.

Because of their common Asian ancestry and certain physical features, dark skin, straight black hair, and high cheekbones they shared, Europeans disregarded the cultural and linguistic differences among tribes. Europeans usually thought of Native Americans as being alike in most respects. Native Americans, however, had no reason to think of themselves as a singular, undifferentiated people. Each tribe was a separate entity that referred to itself by a different name. For example, the Cherokee called themselves Ani-yun-wiya (the real people), the Mohawk called themselves Kaniengehaga (people of the place of flint), the Pawnee called themselves Chahiksichahiks (men

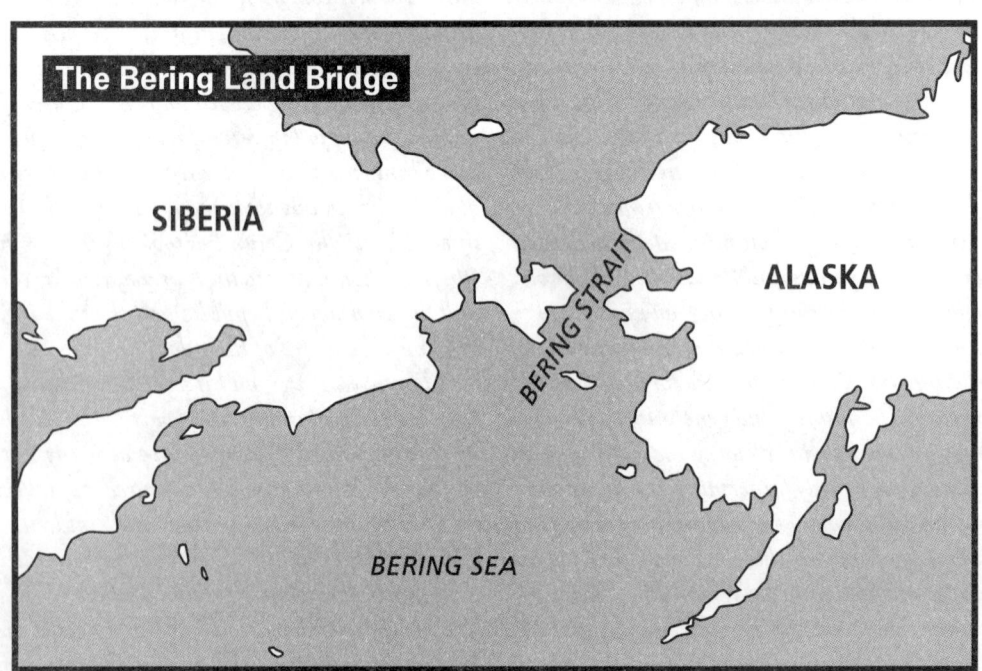

Map 1.1 Location of the Bering Land Bridge

of men), and the Cheyenne called themselves Dzi-tsistas (our people).

Forerunners of modern Native Americans, referred to as Paleo-Indians by archaeologists, lived as nomadic hunters and gatherers of wild plants. Most likely, they moved about the land in extended families called bands. Later, tribes formed when various bands created alliances to protect each other from attacks by other bands. The earliest archaeological evidence of the presence of Paleo-Indians in the Western Hemisphere dates to about 28,000 years ago. At archaeological sites throughout North and South America, artifacts, including stone projectile points attached to wooden shafts used to hunt and butcher wildlife, have been unearthed.

One of the most important technological developments in the hunting practices of Paleo-Indians was the **Clovis point**. Named for the site of its discovery at Clovis, New Mexico in 1923, this tool was far superior to crude choppers and scrapers found at sites in Europe and Asia that date to the same time, indicating that American technology was superior to that of the Old World at the same time. Archaeological evidence suggests that Paleo-Indians in North America began using Clovis points about 12,000 years ago. Clovis points have been discovered at many sites throughout North America, demonstrating that use of this superior technology spread rapidly. Necessity was the mother of invention, as evidence suggests North American Paleo-Indians had to devise a more efficient technology to feed an increasing population. Clovis point users were probably mobile people who traveled in bands of thirty to fifty individuals tied together by kinship. Each band claimed territory as large as several hundred square miles and moved from camp to camp, season after season, returning to previous encampments at different times. Clovis point hunters generally built camps near sources of water that attracted game animals that were driven into swamps and bogs where they could be slaughtered. Houses in Clovis villages were usually arranged in a half circle with doors opening toward the south so inhabitants could avoid the chill from the north wind.

Clovis Points

Paleo-Indians had to change their nomadic lifestyle when the Ice Age ended and large mammals such as the woolly mammoth disappeared. Deprived of their primary source of meat, Paleo-Indians had to find an alternative means of survival. They turned toward agriculture, especially cultivation of maize (corn), beans, squash, and peppers. The development of agriculture was perhaps the most important change to take place among Paleo-Indians, because it allowed the human population to increase and people to establish permanent villages.

Agricultural development seems to have first occurred in Mexico and South America about eight thousand years ago. Paleo-Indians in the highlands of Mexico developed a wild grass into corn. Maize agriculture then became their dominant means of support. The cultivation of corn eventually spread across North and South America, transforming bands of nomadic hunters and gatherers into village farmers. Everywhere the transformation occurred, vast changes in human society took place. More and larger villages were constructed, religious beliefs became ordered around elements of nature such as the sun, moon, rain, and the seasons. Work roles increasingly became separated by gender with men hunting, fishing, and preparing the fields for crops while women engaged in child rearing, planting, weeding, food preparation, and harvesting.

GREAT CIVILIZATIONS OF MEXICO AND SOUTH AMERICA

The development of agriculture enabled Native Americans to create large and sophisticated civilizations that rivaled those in Europe and Asia at the same time period. Residents of these societies were able to produce objects of art, create rituals and ceremonies, and accumulate wealth, because they no longer had to devote most of their energy to acquiring the materials necessary for survival.

Several sophisticated civilizations arose in Mexico and South America. Centered in the Yucatan Peninsula, the **Maya** civilization was the most important early society to develop in Mexico, with archaeological finds placing its origins before 1500 B.C. By the time of the Classic Period (250-900 A.D.), Maya cities were substantial in size, containing large temples and pyramids. A creative people who valued learning, the Maya created the first system of hieroglyphic writing in the Western Hemisphere, enabling scribes to record their history and other aspects of their culture. Interested in science, Maya mathematicians discovered the usefulness of the number zero long before the Arabs and Europeans. Their astronomers could calculate the beginnings of eclipses and track the movement of the moon and major planets in the sky. The Maya also developed the most accurate calendar in the entire world at that time, enabling them to predict the arrival of the seasons among other benefits. Maya craftspeople created jewelry from gold and silver, and merchants developed extensive trading networks throughout Central America.

Maya society (like the later Aztecs) was highly stratified into various classes—kings, priests, merchants, and slaves—and their religious activities made use of blood sacrifices. Unlike other Native American civilizations, however, the Maya did not develop a warrior class. This did not mean that their kings did not engage in warfare; they frequently did. In fact, war brought about the decline of the Maya. About fifteen hundred years ago, leaders of Maya city-states fought each other for dominance. When no king or city-state could defeat all other city-states, the Maya civilization began to decline. Aggravating the decline was overpopulation. When the Spanish *conquistadors* arrived in Mexico, the Mayan civilization had largely disappeared.

A major trading partner of the Maya, the city-state of Teotihuacan (before it was abandoned and later rebuilt by the Aztecs) reached an estimated population of 200,000 at its zenith around 600 A.D. Initially settled 2,200 years ago in the valley of Mexico, the city served as a major center of commerce. Sellers from Teotihuacan traveled hundreds of miles in all directions trading a variety of items, including obsidian—a dark, volcanic glass. Thousands of craft workers in Mexico labored to convert that igneous rock into arrowheads, cutting blades, and decorative items. Teotihuacan also served as a center of religious worship. Native Americans traveled great distances to worship the feathered serpent god, Quetzalcoatl, at the temples of the Sun and Moon.

The most powerful native civilization at the time of European arrival proved to be the **Aztecs** of central Mexico. According to an oral tradition and Aztec chronicles, people who referred to themselves as *Mexica* (hence the word Mexico) migrated into Mexico during the twelfth century. There they found a large city that had been abandoned for almost two centuries. Huitzilopochtli, the most important Aztec god of war, ordered his people to construct their capital city on an island where they saw an eagle eating a snake. This city, which was named Tenochtitlan, was built and became the center of a vast Aztec empire. Tenochtitlan's population surpassed 200,000 by 1500, making it one of the largest cities in the world, rivaling population centers such as Paris, London, and Rome. At the height of Aztec civilization in the fifteenth century, the empire's population numbered about five million. The Aztecs were an aggressive people who dominated neighboring peoples. Those under Aztec domination hated their oppressors because of the frequent demands for tribute, including captives to be used in ritualistic religious sacrifices. Huitzilopochtli demanded a steady diet of human hearts, which were torn from the victim's chest while he or she was still alive. At the coronation of the Emperor Moctezuma II in the year that the Aztecs called Ten Rabbit (1502, according to the European calendar), five thousand humans were sacrificed to Huitzilopochtli, all of them alive and without sedation when their beating hearts were ripped from their bodies. At one temple dedication at a later time, reports indicate that Aztec priests sacrificed twenty thousand victims. When Spanish *conquistadors* arrived, tribes subjugated by the Aztecs, not surprisingly, helped the Spanish destroy their oppressors.

Perhaps the most sophisticated of all Native American civilizations were the **Incas** of present-day Peru. This civilization became prominent about 1100 A.D. in the Andes Mountains. At its height, the Inca Empire contained six to seven million people. The Incas constructed an elaborate system of roads that connected virtually every place in the empire with every other place. Inca craftspeople were extremely skilled metallurgists, fashioning weapons, tools, and jewelry from materials such as gold, silver, copper, and bronze. In fact, the Incas were far wealthier than the Aztecs, at least by European standards. They valued gold and silver, which were mined in large amounts. This made the Incas an attractive target for Spanish *conquistadors* who came searching for precious metals.

Inca society, like that of the Aztecs, was militant. All young males were required to undergo military training to become warriors to protect the empire and Inca emperors who were believed to be gods. Although elites enjoyed the benefits of their privileged states—all riches belonged to the Inca ruler, while chiefs and warriors lived more comfortably than most of the people—Inca society also took care of the less fortunate. Incas believed their government should care for the aged, poor, and ill. Consequently, the Inca government operated a type of welfare system that enabled the physically handicapped, the mentally ill, and individuals suffering from chronic illness to have an adequate lifestyle. Modern society has unknowingly borrowed, to some degree, this Inca idea.

NORTH AMERICAN PEOPLE AND SOCIETIES

Within what is now the United States, a great variety of Native American cultures developed. Differences in climate and geography caused human societies to develop differently in different regions. Native American people were very intelligent and thus highly adaptive: able to change to meet the different environmental conditions they encountered. When Europeans first arrived in the sixteenth century, there were perhaps eight million Native American inhabitants.

Two of the most prominent civilizations that existed in North America prior to the arrival of Europeans were the **Adena and Hopewell Cultures**. The most distinctive feature of these societies was their construction and use of earthen mounds. As a result, these ancient people are referred to as mound builders. Little is known about these early Paleo-Indians. Both cultures developed in the Ohio River Valley about 1000 B.C. and survived until about 700 A.D. Adena and Hopewell people were farmers, traders, craftspeople, and hunters. Their trade networks extended over most of the central United States. Adena and Hopewell trade goods have been unearthed in archaeological excavation sites from the Great Lakes to the Gulf of Mexico. At the center of Hopewell and Adena communities stood relatively small earthen mounds used to inter the dead. Higher status individuals, like chiefs and priests, were generally buried within the mounds along with important personal possessions like ceremonial axes and pipes, while common people were buried around the mounds' periphery. Occasionally, larger burial mounds were constructed. The Great Serpent Mound in Ohio is perhaps the best example of such a mound.

Another mound building culture that developed in North America was the Mississippian. This society, which was heavily engaged in the cultivation of corn, arose about the time Christianity developed in the Middle East and lasted until about 1400 A.D. Mississippian culture existed throughout the Mississippi River Valley. Like the Hopewell and Adena that preceded them, Mississippian people were traders who had contact with most groups of Native Americans on the continent. Mississippian people constructed substantial cities. The largest was at **Cahokia**, in present-day Illinois, where 80,000 people lived. Mississippian people constructed much larger mounds than did the Hopewell and Adena cultures. Mississippian mounds generally had elaborate temples at their top where priests resided. Eighty-five large temple mounds stood at Cahokia, with the largest surpassing the size of the great pyramids constructed in ancient Egypt. For reasons not clearly understood by scholars, Mississippian society disintegrated before significant contact with Europeans occurred. However, several modern Native American tribes appear to be direct descendants of the Mississippian culture, including the Shawnee, Choctaw, Creeks, and Natchez. These tribes built mounds and buried their dead in ways similar to the Mississippians.

Within North America there was a diversity of native life. At the time of contact with Europeans, between five and six hundred different languages were spoken by different tribes. Each tribe developed a life style suited to meet survival needs in its environment. In the Pacific Northwest, for example, the Chinooks, Nez Perce, and Nootka relied primarily upon salmon fishing, whereas in the Great Plains the Kiowa, Comanche, Sioux, Cheyenne, Pawnee, and Arapaho hunted wild animals within set territorial boundaries. In the desert Southwest, the Navaho, Ute, Hopi, Zuni, and Apache farmed the land through use of irrigation because the arid climate created a scarcity of animal life which limited hunting. In the New England and Mid-Atlantic regions, the Micmac, Abenaki, Iroquois, Wampanoag, Patuxet, and Pamunkey relied upon hunting, fishing, and gathering due to their cold, harsh climate and relatively short growing season. Southeastern tribes, including the Cherokee, Chickasaw, Shawnee, Choctaw, Creek, and Tuscarora, were primarily agricultural, because the warm climate, long growing season, and rich, thick topsoil were conducive to farming. Native Americans along the Gulf Coast and Florida, in particular the Natchez and Seminole, like tribes in the Pacific Northwest, largely fished, because the sea offered a bountiful harvest.

Just as there were economic similarities and differences among tribes, there were also cultural, social, and political distinctions. Most native people held a deep respect for nature. Plant and animal life were treated with reverence, and Native Americans, unlike their European counterparts, emphasized cooperation with nature rather than control over it. Native people, for example, generally did not attempt to control flooding rivers with dams or level mountaintops to build cities, as Europeans would do after they took control of the Western Hemisphere.

Since Native Americans lived in harmony with nature, their religions were nature-based. Most believed that every living thing, including plants and trees, contained a spirit, and these spirits governed animal and plant behavior. Humans were only allowed to kill enough animals or gather enough plants for survival. Greed on the part of human beings would anger the animal or plant spirit, which would direct the life form to stop growing and reproducing or cause it to leave tribal lands, resulting in human starvation. It was important, therefore, not to be greedy. Native Americans also did not value the acquisition of great personal wealth because doing so violated the natural balance present in the world.

Within each tribe a medicine man, or shaman, functioned somewhat like priests, ministers, and doctors in European societies. The shaman was called by the Great Spirit and given enormous powers to communicate with animal and plant spirits. In this capacity the medicine man relayed to the people the wishes of the spirits. These wishes eventually developed into rules, values, mores, and taboos regarding the relationship between humans, animals, and plants. For example, Native Americans were forbidden to kill an animal because they wanted a trophy for the lodge wall. Nothing was wasted.

Since Native Americans lived in harmony with nature, individual ownership of land was an alien concept to them. Land was believed to belong to everyone within the tribe. Individuals acted as stewards of the land and, as such, were charged with caring for it. Fencing land to deny people and animals use of it was a concept Native Americans rejected because of their religious views. Tribal boundaries usually consisted of an area large enough to supply the needs of people inhabiting it. Wars to enlarge territory were not part of the Native American mindset; after all, taking more than was needed would bring disaster to the tribe.

Native American society emphasized cooperation over individualism. The achievements of one person were not valued as highly as group accomplishments. Native Americans usually did not seek personal glory but sought instead to bring recognition to their tribe or family. This idea was particularly evident in sporting contests held within various tribes. Events, such as lacrosse matches, were team-centered. Native peoples formed lacrosse teams that competed with teams from different tribes, but the victor was not any individual or team; it was the tribe. The same principle held true for other types of competition. Archery contests, as well as spear and tomahawk throwing events, pitted one tribe against another for tribal glory. Personal glory was not a goal in such competitions.

Native American tribes sometimes waged war against other tribes. However, intertribal warfare was usually short-lived. Two or three small battles between bands of wandering warriors numbering between twenty and forty individuals might occur within the space of several months. Very few lives were lost in these engagements, and tribal chiefs often ended the conflict by negotiating an oral peace agreement. The concept of a long, drawn out war with another tribe for control of a territory was completely foreign to Native Americans.

Among many tribes in North America there existed a division of labor along sexual lines. Hunting and gathering tribes often assigned the hunting to men and the gathering, food processing and preservation, clothes making, and child rearing responsibilities to women. Agricultural societies differed in this regard. Among the Pueblo people in the desert Southwest, for example, men were responsible for planting, cultivating, and harvesting crops, while in eastern farming tribes like the Iroquois women were responsible for raising food crops. In Iroquois society men hunted wild game and cleared the land, usually by burning trees, for agriculture.

Photograph of a Cahokia mound in Illinois, c. 1907

In some agricultural tribes, like the Algonquian, Iroquois, Muskogean, and Pueblo, family lineage was defined matrilineally, and ancestry was traced through female lines of descent. Likewise, kinship was defined along matriarchal lines, and property was inherited through the mother's side of the family. Extended families generally were comprised of a mother, their married daughters, their husbands, and all children produced by the daughters' marriages. At the time of marriage, husbands left the home of their mothers to live with the mother of their wife. These extended families were also linked into clans along matrilineal lines.

More nomadic groups of the Great Plains who lived by hunting and gathering usually traced their lineage patrilineally. The Sioux, Cheyenne, Kiowa, Comanche, Pawnee, and Arapaho lacked permanent villages and constituted themselves into small bands of family members related to the group's father who moved four or five times a year, depending on the availability of game within a given territory. Fathers, sons, their wives, and children usually lived together in extended families. When a move was necessary, each family packed up the belongings and moved together as a unit.

Women in some Native American tribes wielded much political power. Among the Iroquois, the village council, consisting of men, sat in a circle to discuss issues and make decisions relating to war, diplomacy, and other things affecting the tribe. Behind the circle of male chiefs stood the village women who gave advice to the chiefs, often persuading them to vote one way or another. Political influence and power in Iroquois society was often the result of age. The eldest women had much political power. Even though Iroquois chiefs were men, it was the older women in the village who chose the chiefs. Chiefs who displeased Iroquois women were subject to removal by the female council who had appointed the village leader.

In some Native American groups, such as the Algonquian, women served as chiefs. Powerful women chiefs could also be found among tribes dwelling in the area encompassed presently by the southeastern United States. In western South Carolina during the 1550s a female chief, called the Lady of Confitachequi by Spanish explorers, ruled over several villages.

While there was a sexual division of labor among Native American tribes, there was also a degree of sexual equality unknown in European cultures. Divorce existed in tribal societies. Women in matrilineal societies could initiate divorce proceedings simply by setting the husband's possessions outside the lodge door. Among the Cherokee, tribal rulers could be either male or female, and women controlled both household and village life. Cherokee women were influential in the matrilineal clans that linked various settlements with each other as well. Each year different Cherokee villages met in tribal councils that lasted several days or, on occasion, several weeks. At these meetings all tribal members, both men and women, were allowed to speak. No decision was reached until the views of all were considered. Women owned property in some Native American tribes. Pueblo peoples in Arizona and New Mexico, for example, developed an economic system in which women owned the fields, the crops that grew in them, the tools used in cultivation, and the family house. Within this system, men hunted game and worked the corn, bean, and squash fields, which they did not own, coming home to houses owned by their wives.

Government among Native American peoples varied from tribe to tribe. Some societies had governments that were open and democratic, while others had monarchial types of government that were more authoritarian. Generally, tribes that relied upon hunting and gathering had governments in which the power of the ruler derived from the general consent of the population, while groups depending upon agriculture had governments whose rulers were appointed by a small group of influential people. Among the Muskogean people, for example, government consisted of a twenty-to-thirty-man elected council empowered to make all decisions affecting the tribe. In contrast, the Natchez, an agricultural tribe inhabiting lands in the Mississippi River Delta region, were governed by a chief called the Great Sun who ruled more like a dictator. He was treated royally by his subjects, much like the great Pharaohs of ancient Egypt. Believed by his people to be a god, the Great Sun was carried on a litter born by servants whenever in public, with the pathways swept clean before him by an array of servants and wives who accompanied him. Natchez society was not democratic. Noble families, whose position in society was based on heredity, comprised the Great Sun's council. This council appointed village chiefs. Most of the population belonged, however, to a group subordinate to the nobles called Stinkards.

Native American tribal people sometimes exhibited a high degree of political unity and organization. The Cherokee, Choctaw, Chickasaw, Creeks, and Iroquois formed strong confederacies. Among the Cherokee, over sixty villages were united in the Appalachian region of Tennessee and Georgia governed by councils of elderly men and women. Five Iroquois nations, the Mohawks, Oneidas, Onondagas, Cayugas, and Senecas, were united in 1451 by **Chief Deganawida**, the Law Giver, to control violence and warfare and regulate the economy among them. According to oral histories taken during the nineteenth century, Deganawida caused the sun to become dark to demonstrate his power and convince tribal leaders

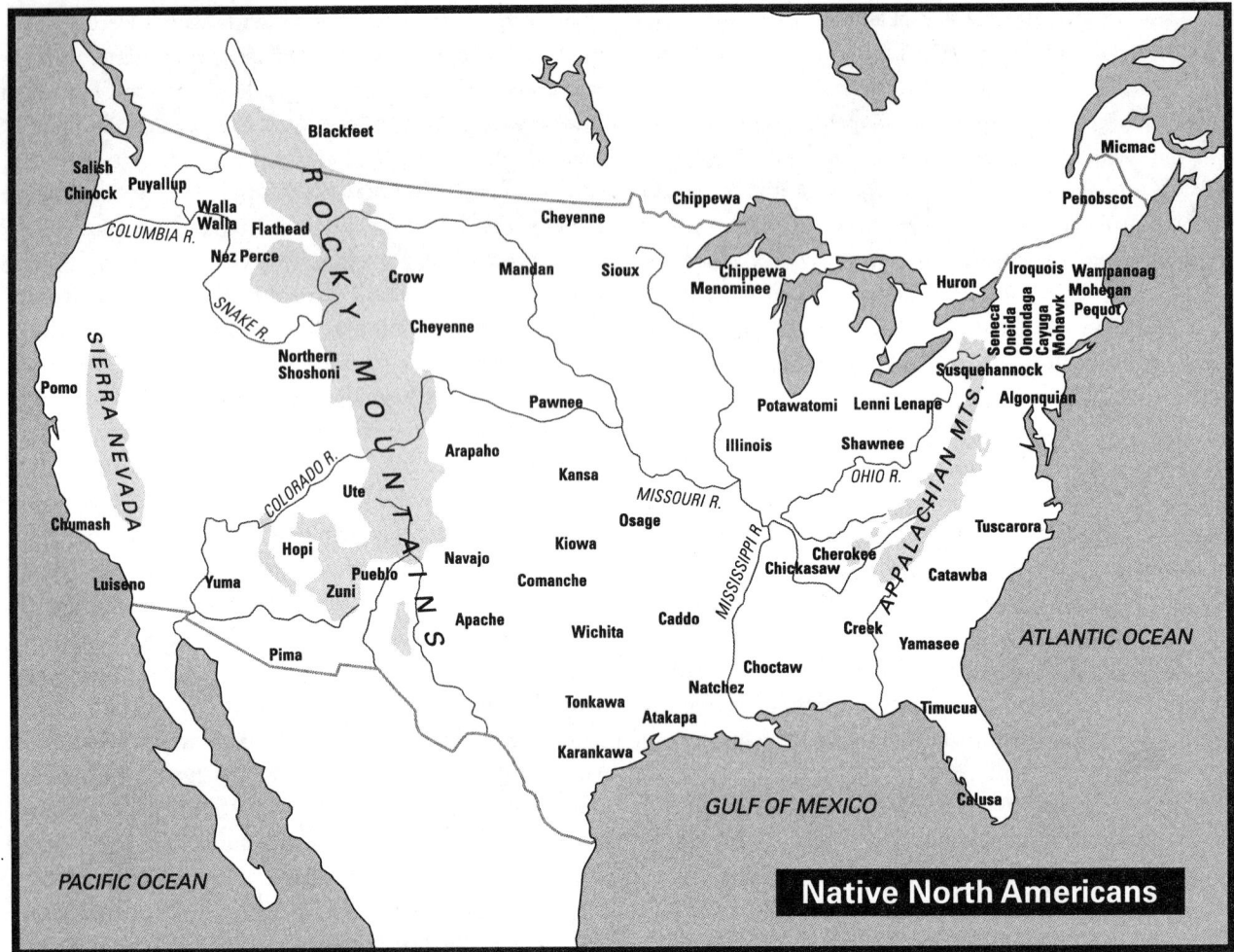

Map 1.2 Location of Native North Americans

to join the confederacy. Assisting Deganawida was the great Iroquois orator Hiawatha. His elaborate words are said to have helped convince various chiefs to support participation in the Iroquois Confederation. Within this alliance, local communities were relatively autonomous, but the central government brokered disputes among member villages and organized the five nations to wage war on enemy tribes such as the Hurons, Petuns, and Eries, who also organized confederacies of their own to defend against Iroquois aggression.

Like governmental systems, housing also varied from tribe to tribe. Generally, housing developed to enable Native Americans to take advantage of resources present within the territory each tribe inhabited. Nomadic tribes of the Great Plains usually fashioned dwellings from animal skins stretched over wooden frames. These "teepees" were light in weight and mobile, enabling inhabitants to dismantle them quickly when it became necessary to move the village after game and plant life became scarce in one location. Despite their ease of construction and weight, teepees were comfortable dwelling structures. A hole at the top enabled light to enter and smoke from fires used to cook food and provide heat in winter to exit.

More settled agricultural tribes constructed houses that were larger and more elaborate than the mobile teepee. The Iroquois built a dwelling structure called a longhouse from tree bark. These houses, measuring about 800 feet long and 25 feet wide, contained five or six fireplaces and provided living quarters for two nuclear families. Pueblo and Navaho tribes in the desert southwest constructed houses from mud and stone called adobe. These structures were stacked on top of each other and interconnected with hallways. Muskogean and Algonquians residing in the present-day American Southeast lived in dwellings consisting of a wooden frame covered with thatch.

During the centuries that North and South America were inhabited before Europeans invaded, Native American cultures, in all their sophistication and splendor, thrived. The hundreds of distinctive societies that developed among native people were designed to suit the particular environment they lived in. These societies continued to develop unimpeded until European nations began to conquer and destroy them after 1492.

EUROPE ON THE EVE OF EXPLORATION

Approximately one thousand years ago, during the time that the Mound Builders in the Mississippi River Valley were constructing elaborate cities at Cahokia and elsewhere, Western Europe began to emerge from a languishing period that historians call the Dark Ages (500 A.D.—1400 A.D.). During this time, political and economic power resided with the Byzantine Empire, which controlled vast territories in Eastern Europe, the Balkan Mountains, and Turkey, and with Islamic civilizations in North Africa and the Middle East. At this time, Western Europe largely consisted of agricultural societies whose populations were dominated by peasants who usually lived in single family dwellings situated in small villages. Politically, Western Europe was controlled by an economic and social system called feudalism. European nations divided land into many small units owned and governed by noblemen who wielded absolute power over peasants living on their land. The nobles demanded labor from the peasant farmers, taking a portion of the crops produced each year as rent, and provided basic protection in return. Within this system, the noble landowners accumulated large estates and much wealth, allowing them to build huge castles overlooking their vast land holdings.

Poor nutrition, overcrowding, and lack of sanitation often contributed to high death rates due to disease. The most devastating epidemic to strike European societies during the Dark Ages, however, the Bubonic Plague, was a bacterial infection spread by parasitic fleas on rats. This disease, which first hit Europe in 1347, most likely originated in China and was carried to Italy by rodents living on trading vessels. The "Black Death," as the Bubonic Plague was commonly called, killed about one-third of Europe's population by the end of the 1370s.

After surviving the Bubonic Plague, Western Europe emerged from the Dark Ages. Several developments occurred that eventually played a role in European exploration of territory lying westward across the Atlantic. During the fourteenth century, trade routes with Asia opened. Products from India and China, including silk, jewels, and spices, were sold in Europe while copper, wood, iron, armor, lead, tin, and other products were carried to Asia along a trade route known as the Silk Road. Chinese, Italian, and Arab traders who handled this trade made vast fortunes, which caused them to be envied by other nations and traders. Spices from Asia proved to be the most important commodity that Europeans received in this intercontinental trade. In Europe, Asian spices were literally worth their weight in gold. Wealthy Europeans believed spices were necessary for a comfortable life. They retarded spoilage, relieved the bland taste of local foods, and hid the poor quality of meat before refrigeration was developed. Most of these spices, like cinnamon, cloves, black pepper, and nutmeg, could only be acquired from Asia.

The European trade with Asia led to development of a new economic system, capitalism, which eventually replaced feudalism. Capitalism overtook most countries within a hundred years. Before the spice trade developed, kings and nobles held merchants in contempt, often using the power of government to suppress them. Trade with Asia changed European attitudes toward money and profit making. Rulers began to rely upon wealthy traders to provide money to pay debts or equip the king's army with weapons. In return for financial assistance, European monarchs ended the oppression of merchants, enacted new laws granting various privileges to them, and used armies and navies to protect trade. This, in turn, caused religious leaders, who had previously declared profit making sinful, to ease their views on lending, interest, and earning money through investment, which led to establishment of capitalism as an economic system.

The Euro-Asian trade also helped end the feudal system. Manorial estates that nobles and peasants resided on were largely self-sufficient before Europeans had economic contact with Asia, producing virtually all items their residents needed for survival. Trade with Asia caused European nobles to desire the wonderful luxuries found by Islam and the Orient. Since silk and spices could not be produced on manorial lands, nobles needed cash, which was difficult to acquire within the feudal economy, because payments were received in the form of goods and services produced locally. Because nobles now needed cash, they began to alter rules governing the feudal system, allowing peasants to leave the land so that it could be sold or leased to others for money.

The growth of urban areas proved to be another factor that characterized Europe on the eve of exploration. The Euro-Asian trade caused new cities to arise and old ones to increase in size and population. As serfs became free, they moved to urban areas and worked as wage laborers. Not only did cities attract former serfs, they also attracted educated people who wanted to enjoy the company of others and take advantage of learning and entertainment opportunities urban areas offered. The migration to urban centers caused problems. As more people arrived in cities, overcrowding became commonplace. This situation led, in turn, to increased unemployment and the spread of diseases, which caused some urban residents to strongly desire to leave the cities. Many such people later moved to European colonies in North and South America to escape chronic unemployment and unhealthy living conditions.

Western Europe also underwent an important political change during the two centuries before the invasion of the Americas began. This change was the rise of the modern nation state. The nation state arose largely because capitalism could not function smoothly in feudal lands. The powerful manor lords who controlled the land made it difficult for merchants to easily move their products. Most lords required merchants to pay extravagant fees to cross their lands, an act which cut into already thin profits. At the same time, nobles refused to pay taxes to monarchs. Able to use peasants as soldiers, nobles often had stronger armies than kings, which meant that rulers could not always enforce their laws or collect taxes. To combat this situation, some merchants and monarchs joined forces. Merchants provided capital that kings used to form larger and stronger armies than any forces that noblemen could raise. In return, merchants wanted protection, stability, and an end to feudalism. Merchants and burghers (town residents) were opposed to the feudal system because it created disorder and chaos that interfered with trade. Capitalistic merchants preferred a centralized government that could protect them and ensure the safety of goods being transported over long distances.

Kings also preferred centralized government. By using merchant capital, monarchs could free themselves from reliance on priests and bishops to carry out administrative tasks and hire professional clerks who were more loyal to the king than the church. Centralized government also enabled kings to impose and collect national taxes, which fattened the coffers of monarchs, enabling them to sponsor national projects such as overseas exploration. By 1500 the modern nation state, complete with its powerful armies and navies and the ability to mobilize vast resources to undertake large projects to promote national interests had replaced the inefficient feudal system throughout Western Europe.

Perhaps the most important nation state formed in Western Europe was Spain. In 1469 the marriage of Ferdinand of Aragon to Isabella of Castile began the process of nationalism. Ferdinand and Isabella had sufficient capital to equip an army powerful enough to subdue defiant nobles. After bringing the feudal lords under their control, these strong monarchs crushed the power of the Moors, a Muslim people from North Africa who had conquered parts of Spain, driving them completely out of the country. At the same time, Isabella and Ferdinand, in conjunction with the Roman Catholic Church, began the infamous Spanish Inquisition, using torture against individuals with questionable Catholic loyalties. By 1500, they succeeded in tying the allegiance of the Spanish citizenry to the monarchs rather than feudal estate owners. All residents of Spain were required to exhibit loyalty to the nation and serve the Crown.

Other European nations underwent nationalistic movements. During the 1380s, John I consolidated power in a divided Portugal. National unification helped to fuel Portuguese exploration. King John had sufficient resources afterwards to support efforts by his son, **Prince Henry the Navigator**, to explore parts of the world unknown to Europeans. Prince Henry established an academy at Sagres, Portugal to train ship captains in the art of exploration. Financed by King John's money, Prince Henry outfitted ships and sent them on exploratory missions. Information from these voyages was used to draw more accurate maps, compose manuals on sailing tactics and navigational techniques, and design ships better suited for transoceanic voyages. Initially, Prince Henry was concerned with learning more about the world. As exploration led to trade opportunities with other nations, Prince Henry and Portugal became less concerned with knowledge and more concerned with profit.

England and France were also changed by nationalism. Louis XI successfully subdued French nobles in the 1460s after ending the Hundred Years War with England. Henry VII (Henry Tudor) united England in 1485 after two powerful manorial families, the Yorks and Lancasters, destroyed themselves in the War of the Roses from 1455 to 1485. Henry VII greatly diminished the power of the English nobility, helping to turn England into a modern nation while also preparing his country for overseas expansion.

The formation of nation states was critical to the beginning of European exploration. Without a centralized government with the power to raise tremendous sums of money through taxation, Christopher Columbus and other early navigators could not have secured sufficient financial backing to undertake long, expensive voyages across the ocean.

Beginning in the early 1500s, Europe was not only impacted by changes brought about by the rise of nationalism, but also felt the effects produced by the **Protestant Reformation**. This religious upheaval shattered the previous unity of Europe provided under the auspices of the Roman Catholic Church, provoking major conflicts across much of the continent. Prior to the Reformation, the Roman Catholic Church reigned as the most powerful and dominant institution in Western Europe. All nations, their rulers as well as ordinary citizens, were Catholic. Those daring to challenge church orthodoxy risked imprisonment, torture, or death if they refused to publicly recant their heretical views.

Circumstances changed in 1517 when an obscure German monk, Martin Luther, openly challenged numerous teachings of the Catholic Church by nailing his "Ninety-five Theses" to a church door in Wittenberg. Luther's actions began a religious revolt against Catholicism that profoundly changed the Western world. Luther believed that the Catholic Church had become corrupt since its creation in the early days of Christianity. He proposed to cleanse the church of its corruption by following Scripture and returning it to a pure form of worship as practiced by first-century Christians.

By the 1520s, another branch of Protestantism also appeared in France, where the Catholic Church persecuted those who observed the teachings of the dissenting theologian Jean Calvin (John Calvin). Fleeing France, Calvin settled in Geneva, Switzerland where he and his followers eventually gained control of the city. A lawyer by profession, he developed a strict set of theological principles for his followers published in his famous *Institutes of the Christian Religion* in 1536. From the 1560s to the late 1590s, France experienced forty years of religious strife between Huguenots (as Calvin's adherents who gained influence and displayed their faith openly came to be called) and supporters of the French government who had become one of the most ardent foes of Protestantism in Europe. A degree of peace returned in 1598 when the Edict of Nantes declared Catholicism to be the official state religion of France but also granted religious and political freedoms to the Protestants.

England, like France and Germany, underwent its own Reformation, but the Anglican reformation was more the result of politics than religious dissent. Henry VIII, the English king from 1509 to 1547, was a devout Catholic with a huge political problem. He had no male heir to assume the throne when he died. Henry and his wife Catherine of Aragon (daughter of Isabella and Ferdinand) had six children, but only one, Mary, survived childhood. Henry needed a son to perpetuate the Tudor line. In 1527, he requested that Pope Clement VII annul his marriage to Catherine. The Pope refused, leading Henry to renounce his Catholic faith and to sever all ties with the Roman church. Henry then created the Anglican Church, making it the official religious denomination of England. Fewer than ten years earlier, Henry had published *Defense of the Seven Sacraments*, which attacked Luther's idea that Christians should only accept two sacraments. For this, the Pope had given Henry the title "Defender of the Faith."

Overall, the effect of the Protestant Reformation was to shatter the unity of the Christian church in Western Europe and break the power of the papacy. Spain, Ireland, France, and the Italian States resisted the Reformation, remaining Catholic, while England, Scotland, Germany, Switzerland, the Netherlands, and

Print depicting Martin Luther nailing his Ninety-five Theses to a church door in Wittenberg, Germany.

the Scandinavian countries became largely Protestant. The Reformation also caused much violence, with Protestants and Catholics slaughtering each other in the name of God. The Reformation also fostered a strong interest in colonization as both Catholics and Protestants established colonies, in North America to escape religious persecution.

THE RENAISSANCE: NEW THOUGHT AND NEW TECHNOLOGY

Contact between Europeans, Asians, and the Middle East sparked a revolution in though, the flowering of knowledge known as the **Renaissance**, which led to important new technological developments in overseas navigation and exploration. While scholars disagree about the exact dates that the Renaissance took place, the period encompassed parts of the fourteenth through seventeenth centuries and began in the Italian cities of Venice, Genoa, and Pisa as a result of the spice trade. Contact with Muslim civilizations gave Europeans access to ancient writings from the Egyptians, Greeks, Romans, and Arabs found in libraries at Alexandria, Egypt and Baghdad, Iraq that had not been read in Europe for several centuries. The rediscovery of these documents sparked an interest in classical antiquity that eventually spread by trade routes throughout Western Europe. In literature, philosophy, science, mathematics, and art much work took place during part of this revival of learning.

Generally speaking, the Renaissance was a celebration of human accomplishment and potential, which can be illustrated in many facets. Artists, for example, used light and shadow techniques to focus on the human body, producing paintings and sculptures showing humans as heroes rather than as the degraded beings common in medieval works. Changes in architecture also reflected the change in thought. Medieval buildings of the Gothic style were gradually replaced with architectural styles heavily influenced by the ancient Greeks and Romans.

The new artistic and architectural styles were part of a broader movement within the Renaissance that revolted against religious orthodoxy known as Humanism. While art, literature, and architectural styles during the Middle Ages focused on religion, depictions of Heaven, and the afterlife, Renaissance art, literary works, and architecture emphasized human life on Earth. Through its inherent arousing of human curiosity, this new outlook on life helped to stimulate overseas exploration.

The development of the printing press helped to spread Renaissance ideas from Italy to other European nations. In ancient and medieval times, books were extremely rare and expensive because each page had to be laboriously copied by hand. Given the high cost of books, it is not surprising that a high degree of illiteracy existed in Europe. With the exception of Catholic priests, church officials, and nobles, most Europeans could neither read nor write. Trade with Asia and the Middle East had, however, created a need for literacy within the merchant class due to the need to keep accurate records of business transactions. Though the high cost of producing the written word prevented the rapid spread of literacy and knowledge, this situation was about to change. Since at least the seventh century, the Chinese used a means of printing an entire page of paper or cloth using a carved block of wood. By 1050, Chinese craftsmen had developed a basic moveable type system. Four hundred years later, the German smith **Johann Gutenberg** independently devised a printing press using moveable type. Pages could now be mechanically printed from individual letter blocks that could be set to form words and sentences then reused. Printing was to change the world forever. In fact, the printing press made possible the Protestant Reformation by rapidly spreading distribution of Luther's writings attacking the Catholic Church and his German-translated Bible.

Printing houses opened everywhere. A new profession had been created; by 1500 about 1200 printers were operating throughout Western Europe. These early printers published about 35,000 different books, issuing a total of eight million copies on subjects including science, history, philosophy, religion, exploration, trade, and travel. Some of the books sparked an interest by Europeans in overseas exploration. The most important was Marco Polo's *Travels*. First published in 1477, this work, which detailed a Venetian merchant's travels in China during the thirteenth century, was widely read by educated Europeans. Polo stimulated interest in oceanic travel by stating that China was bounded on the east by an ocean, convincing many traders that there might be a way to circumvent Arabs who controlled the Silk Road to China and thus European access to Asian products. If Polo was correct about an ocean lying east of China, then it should be possible to navigate directly to Asia by ship. The only problem was that the ocean was largely unexplored.

Engraving of Johan Gutenberg taking the first proof from his printing press.

Before significant oceanic exploration could occur, improvements in navigation and technology had to take place. Prior to the Renaissance, navigational methods were primitive. Viking sailors, the best mariners that Europe had produced by 950, simply calculated their position on the ocean by viewing the sun with the naked eye. They could only guess at the speed their ships traveled and the distance covered. However, all this had changed by the time Columbus made his first voyage in 1492.

By the late 1400s, European sailors had begun to use a myriad of mechanical devices to help with navigation on the open seas. The most important navigational device proved to be the **compass**. First invented by the Chinese, the compass was a simple tool that consisted of a magnetic needle fastened to a piece of wood marked with directions. Since the magnetized needle always pointed toward the earth's magnetic North Pole, navigators could always determine the direction their ship was travelling. All they had to know was that to the right of where the compass needle pointed was east, to the left was west, and directly opposite the needle was south.

In addition to being able to mechanically determine direction of travel, ship captains could also fix their precise location on the ocean's surface by using the astrolabe, quadrant, and sextant. All three instruments enabled navigators to measure the altitude and position of stars in relation to the earth's surface and thus precisely locate a ship's location on a map. Used in conjunction with the compass, ship captains could correctly and accurately record direction, distance, location, and speed.

Not only were improvements in navigation made, but Europeans also benefited from better ships. The medieval ship was a relatively small vessel with one sail, high sides, wide bodies, and a steering rudder on its side. The sail was useful only if the wind blew from behind the ship, because it could not be rotated. For locomotion these ships often relied upon slaves to man oars. Over time, modifications in ship design occurred. Important changes included more, larger, and adjustable sails. By using a sailing tactic called "tacking" and a new type of rigging developed by Arabs called the lateen sail, ships could position various sails to travel into the wind. No longer did ships have to travel in the same direction that the wind blew—now they could even move against it. Not only were there improvements in sails, European ships in the fifteenth and sixteenth centuries became longer, sleeker, faster, and more stable. Also, improved rudder designs made them more maneuverable. Such improvements were first manifest in Portuguese caravels and carracks during the 1400s and in Portuguese, Spanish, French, Dutch, and English galleons in the 1600s. These ships, and the navigational devices incorporated into them, made possible European exploration of North and South America. Without this technology, Europeans would have been stuck on their side of the Atlantic, lacking the equipment, knowledge, and confidence to make long voyages across the ocean.

Another important technological innovation that made possible European exploration was the use of gunpowder. Although its origins are not clear, most likely the Arabs invented gunpowder around 1000 A.D. The Chinese, who had traded with Arabic peoples, were using gunpowder when Marco Polo visited Cathay (the European name for China). Europeans were quick to find a military use for this invention. During the early years of the fourteenth century, gunpowder was used to shoot objects from cannons. Primitive artillery pieces small enough to be operated by an individual were in use by 1360. By 1450, European soldiers widely used a firearm called the blunderbuss. This weapon, which resembled modern shotguns, utilized a trigger mechanism that ignited gunpowder in the barrel. Although heavy and highly inaccurate, these loud and frightening guns further enabled Europeans to defeat Native Americans in combat. Without gunpowder, cannon, and personal firearms, it is doubtful that Europeans could have prevailed in war against Native Americans.

The printing press, nationalism, the end of feudalism, gunpowder, improved ships, navigational instruments, the increase in trade, and the growth of a mercantile class all help to explain why European nations were able to explore, invade, and subdue lands in North and South America, a process begun in 1492 when Christopher Columbus set sail from Spain.

EUROPEAN EXPLORATION AND EXPANSION

Exploration Prior to Columbus

Contrary to popular belief, Christopher Columbus was not the first European to reach the Western Hemisphere. About 1000 A.D. Scandinavian sailors explored portions of modern Canada. These Norse adventurers, often called **Vikings**, were Europe's foremost seafarers. In 984 A.D. a group of Vikings led by Erik the Red sailed westward across the Atlantic from Iceland to a large island. Erik the Red, who had been banished from Norway after committing murder, called the island he reached Greenland, in an attempt to attract settlers to his colony. Greenland was not an appropriate name for this island because it is ice bound for much of the year due to its location in the far northern latitudes. Several years later, Erik the Red's son, Leif Ericson, led an expedition of Norsemen from Greenland to present-day Newfoundland and Labrador.

Ericson had apparently heard about lands that lay west of Greenland from Bjarni Herjolfsson, captain of a Viking ship blown off course en route to Greenland from Iceland. According to Herjolfsson, he sighted land but did not stop on it. Instead, he rushed back to Greenland. Excited by the story, Ericson purchased Herjolfsson's ship and, with a crew of thirty-five, sailed westward in 1001 A.D. The first landing was at a site Ericson named Helluland or Flat Rock Land. Modern scholars believe the site to be Baffin Island in Canada. Sailing south, the Vikings then reached the eastern coast of Canada, which they called Markland or Woodland. From Markland, Ericson sailed southeast for two days, most likely reaching Newfoundland. Since Newfoundland had an abundance of wild grapes, the Vikings called the land Vinland.

Ericson and his Norse mariners established short-lived colonies in Vinland before returning to Greenland. The job of colonizing the land that Ericson reached fell to his

14 / CHAPTER ONE

younger brother, Thorvald. However, things did not go well. The first contact with Native Americans resulted in bloodshed after the Vikings captured and enslaved several natives. One slave escaped and later returned with an armed war party. A battle ensued, and Thorvald was killed when an arrow pierced his heart. He became the first known European to be buried in North American soil. After the battle, the Vikings abandoned their settlement and returned to Greenland.

Norse colonies did not thrive because there was no strong expansionist nation-state supporting them, poor communications with their homeland, political problems in Norway, and hostile encounters with Native Americans. In fact, the Viking explorations were largely forgotten after their North American settlements were abandoned. If not for oral history, saga, and song, record of these accomplishments likely would have been lost.

During the twentieth century, archaeologists unearthed additional evidence of the Norse presence in North America, discovering the ruins of a Viking settlement in 1960 at L'Anse aux Meadows in Newfoundland. At the site, scientists uncovered eight Norse sod houses along with jewelry, tools, slag iron, and coal.

Other Europeans might have visited the Western Hemisphere before Columbus. In the ancient Mediterranean world of the Greeks and Romans, writers speculated about where the fabled continent of Atlantis lay. Supposedly, a great civilization had mysteriously sunk beneath the Atlantic Ocean. This fascination with Atlantis illustrates the mythical appeal lands to the west of Europe had for the continent's residents. According to legend, in the fifth century A.D., the Irish monk, Saint Brendan, discovered islands hundreds of miles west of Ireland in the Atlantic. It was here that he was said to have met a talking whale. A Welsh explorer, Prince Madoc, might also have discovered America. A rock, called the Brandenburg Stone, was found near Brandenburg, Kentucky in the twentieth century that has markings on it that appear to be Welch writing. Many scholars, however, refuse to accept the authenticity of this stone.

Portugal

The modern age of European exploration began with Portuguese explorations during the late fifteenth century. Portugal's exploration began largely as a result of Prince Henry the Navigator's quest to make contact with the nation of Prester John. According to legend, Prester John was a Catholic priest who governed a Christian state somewhere in Africa or Asia. A devout Catholic, Prince Henry wanted to contact Prester John in hopes of forming a Christian alliance that would encircle Muslim nations. To achieve this objective, Prince Henry undertook a major exploration along Africa's western coast. Although he personally did not sail on any of these voyages, his financial assets were critical to their success. Portuguese explorers, who may or may not have believed in the existence of Prester John, realized there were vast profits to be made in Africa. Portuguese ships left Cape St. Vincent, the

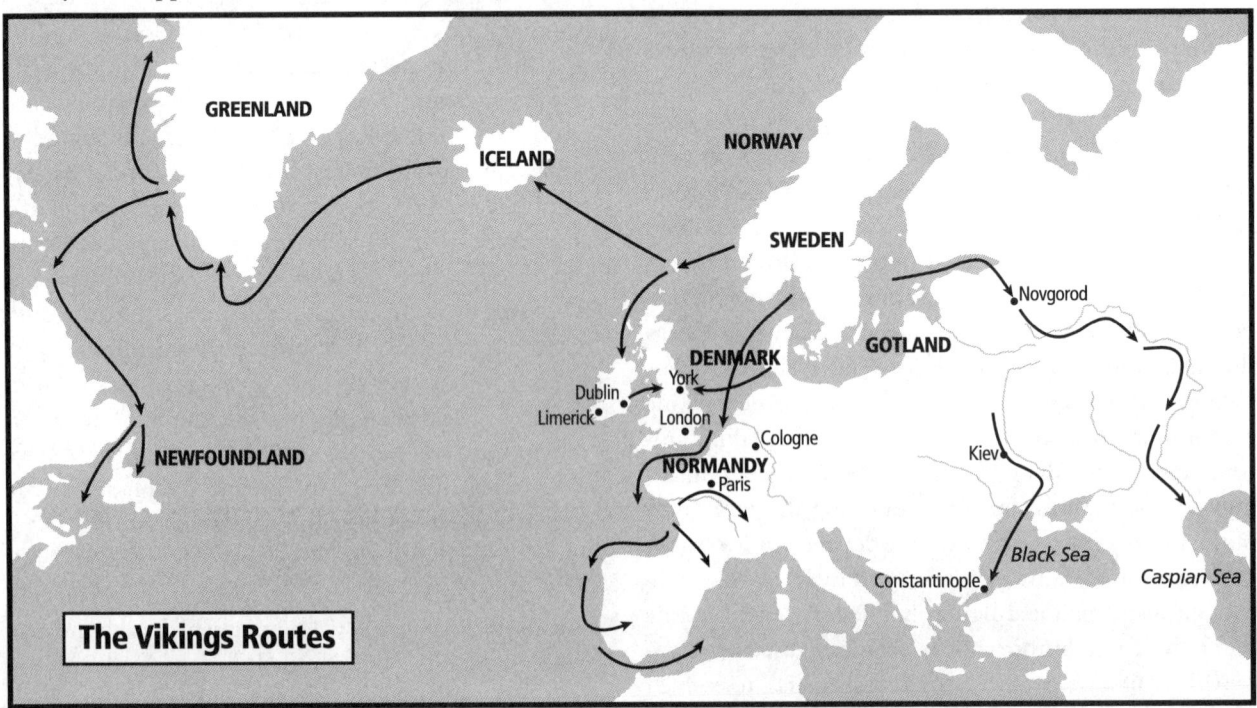

Map 1.3   The Vikings Routes

westernmost point on the European continent, under Prince Henry's guidance. Paid handsomely by their royal benefactor, Portuguese captains pushed farther south and west, discovering the island of Madeira to the southwest of Portugal in 1420 and the Azores archipelago to the west of Portugal in 1427, leading to the establishment of colonies in both locations. On a voyage in 1445, Dinis Dias sailed around Cape Verde and passed beyond the Sahara Desert. Ten years later, Alvise da Cadamosto sailed up the mouth of the Senegal and Gambia Rivers and discovered the Cape Verde Islands.

After Prince Henry died in 1460, his exploration program was continued under various Portuguese monarchs not concerned with contacting Prester John. The new goal became to find the southern tip of Africa, sail around it, and reach India, China, and Japan. Consequently, merchants began to invest in Portuguese exploration, willing to risk large sums on these exploratory voyages upon the promise of trade monopolies granted by the government. If Portugal could discover a water route to Asia, it could control the spice trade, which had been dominated by Italian and Arab traders for centuries. By bypassing Italian and Muslim middlemen, Portugal could reduce the cost of importing silk, spices, perfumes, and other Asian luxuries. Not only would this make Portuguese merchants rich, it would make Portugal one of the strongest nations in Europe.

In 1488 Portugal achieved its goal of sailing around Africa. **Bartolomé Dias** rounded the Cape of Good Hope at the southern tip of Africa and saw the Indian Ocean for the first time. Dias had to turn back before reaching Asia, because his sailors were afraid to go farther. Ten years later Portugal finally found its ocean route to Asia. Vasco da Gama set sail in 1497 intending to go beyond the Cape of Good Hope. The next year de Gama reached India. Later expeditions reached China. Portugal had achieved its goal of dominating the spice trade. After reaching India, Portugal began to build a commercial empire in Africa and Asia by establishing trading posts at São Tomé, the Cape Verde Islands, Ceylon, and Malabar, India. In 1509, the Portuguese solidified control over their Indian Ocean trade route with a decisive naval victory over a Muslim fleet at Diu off the coast of western India. This triumph ensured that Portugal would be the dominant European power in Asia. By 1550, Portugal had a world monopoly on the spice trade with an empire stretching from the Persian Gulf to the Pacific Ocean.

Some Portuguese colonies failed because of diseases such as yellow fever and malaria. Unable to establish colonies, the Portuguese sent Catholic missionaries to convert native peoples to Christianity. In Africa, converted natives sometimes married Portuguese traders. The ethnically mixed society they formed became important in securing captives for the Atlantic slave trade begun by Portugal.

After discovering an oceanic route to Asia, Portugal largely lost interest in further western explorations across the Atlantic. However, in 1500, a storm blew the ships of Pedro Alvares Cabral so far off course that he reached the coast of Brazil, which eventually became a Portuguese colony. With the exception of Brazil, Portugal established few colonies in the Western Hemisphere. Exploration and colonization of North and South America was largely left to other European countries, including Spain, England, France, and the Netherlands.

Spain

Spain eventually emerged as the most important nation involved in the exploration and colonization of the Western Hemisphere. Jealous of Portugal's success and fearful of its power, Spanish monarchs wished to challenge Portuguese mastery of the seas. Like Portugal, Spain sought an ocean route to the riches of Asia but first had to win back its territory from the Moors, a Muslim people from North Africa who had occupied portions of the Iberian Peninsula for 750 years. The Spanish monarchs Ferdinand and Isabella finally removed the Moors in 1492 when their forces conquered the southern province of Granada. With the defeat of the Moors, Spain could focus on challenging Portugal.

An Italian sailor, **Christopher Columbus**, persuaded Ferdinand and Isabella in 1492 that a third trade route to Asia could be discovered. In 1476, Columbus had been shipwrecked near Prince Henry the Navigator's school at Sagres. After being rescued, he lived with his brother who labored as a mapmaker in Lisbon. Columbus later married and lived in the Portuguese colony of Madeira where he worked as a sailor. During this time, his study of maps convinced him that a new route could be found by sailing westward across the Atlantic. Contrary to popular opinion, Columbus was not the only European who believed the earth was round. In fact, most educated Europeans accepted the ancient Greek idea that the world was oval. After all, Aristotle had proven it mathematically. In actuality, Columbus based his theory on false premises, believing that the Earth was far smaller than its actual size, and thus the Asian continent was much closer to the west of Europe than previously believed. These misconceptions convinced Columbus that the Atlantic Ocean was small enough to cross after a short voyage, never suspecting two entire continents lay between Europe and Asia.

At first, Columbus tried to convince Portugal to finance his voyage in search of a westward route to the riches of Asia. When the mariner presented his ideas to

Replica of the *Pinta*, one of Columbus's caravels.

Portuguese government officials in 1484, they politely listened but turned him down because their primary interest lay in finding a southern route around Africa. Columbus then tried to arouse other European monarchs, but all rejected his ideas because royal geographic advisors determined that Columbus had miscalculated the distance to Asia.

Columbus's last hope of achieving royal backing for his scheme lay with Ferdinand and Isabella. At first, the Spanish monarchs were no more interested in his ideas than other European rulers. However, fear of Portugal's increasing power, coupled with Columbus's promises of gold, glory, and colonies, caused the Spanish rulers to change their minds and take a chance on this Italian sailor. Provided with three ships, the *Niña, Pinta*, and *Santa Maria*, Columbus set sail for China in August 1492. After stopping for repairs and supplies in the Canary Islands, he sailed across the Atlantic for just over a month before spotting a small, flat island in the Bahamas, either Samana Cay or San Salvador Island. Erroneously believing that he had found the East Indies near the Asian mainland, Columbus began to call the native peoples that he encountered *indios* (the Spanish term for Indian). He then explored the islands of Cuba and Hispaniola (modern-day Haiti and the Dominican Republic). After capturing several Native Americans to prove that he had reached Asia, Columbus returned triumphantly to Spain. There he was knighted, made governor of the Indies, and given the title "Admiral of the Ocean Sea." For a while, Ferdinand and Isabella believed that Spain now possessed a short route to the wealth of Asia. To resolve potential disputes over the newly discovered lands, Spain and Portugal negotiated the Treaty of Tordesillas in 1494, creating a longitudinal demarcation line 370 leagues (approximately 1,100 miles) west of the Cape Verde Islands with Spain being granted all the lands to the west of the boundary (and thus, most of the Americas) while giving Portugal all the lands in the eastern zone (thus securing exclusive rights to the eastern water route to Asia).

Columbus's first voyage did not produce the wealth that he had promised Ferdinand and Isabella because the mariner found no large hordes of gold, silver, spices, or gems. Columbus did report that natives on Hispaniola wore gold earrings leading him to order the construction of a fort to be manned by a small contingent of men with instructions to find the source of the gold. In fact, the small amounts of jewelry that Native Americans wore

Christopher Columbus

infected Columbus and his sailors with gold fever. Afterwards, the Spanish spent most of their time and energy searching for the precious metal.

In 1493, Ferdinand and Isabella provided Columbus with seven ships and 1,500 men to begin colonization of the islands that he had discovered. Their primary orders were to locate the source of the gold that the natives used to fashion their jewelry. When this expedition reached Hispaniola, the fort that Columbus had erected during his first voyage had been destroyed and his men killed by the Native Americans, unwilling to tolerate Spanish brutality in their pursuit of gold. Columbus responded by destroying villages of the Taíno people, enslaving them, and demanding gold as tribute.

Columbus made two additional voyages to the Americas in 1498 and 1502, respectively, exploring numerous Caribbean islands and portions of the coastal mainland. On his fourth trek, Columbus reached the northern coast of Venezuela in South America. After this voyage, however, Ferdinand and Isabella ordered him arrested and shipped back to Spain in chains for brutality and mismanagement of the colonies while serving as governor. After being cleared of wrongdoing (though never reinstated as governor), Columbus received funding for one final expedition, which reached the eastern coast of Central America, briefly exploring modern-day Honduras, Nicaragua, Costa Rica, and Panama.

Even before Columbus died in 1506, some Europeans realized what he had accomplished: that what he had reached was not Asia but a new continent. One was the Italian adventurer Amerigo Vespucci, an Italian mariner who joined a 1499 Portuguese expedition that explored the coast of South America. In 1500, he published a series of vivid and largely fictional descriptions of the

---

> **"Thursday October 11"**
>
> The course was W.S.W., and there was more sea than there had been during the whole of the voyage. They saw sand-pipers, and a green reed near the ship. Those of the caravel Pinta saw a cane and a pole, and they took up another small pole which appeared to have been worked with iron; also another bit of cane, a land-plant, and a small board. The crew of the caravel Niña also saw signs of land, and a small branch covered with berries. Everyone breathed afresh and rejoiced at these signs. The run until sunset was 27 leagues.
>
> After sunset the Admiral returned to his original west course, and they went along at the rate of 12 miles an hour. Up to two hours after midnight they had gone 90 miles, equal to 22 1/2 leagues. As the caravel Pinta was a better sailer, and went ahead of the Admiral, she found the land, and made the signals ordered by the Admiral. The land was first seen by a sailor named Rodrigo de Triana. But the Admiral, at ten o'clock, being on the castle of the poop, saw a light, though it was so uncertain that he could not affirm it was land. He called Pero Gutierrez, a gentleman of the King's bedchamber, and said that there seemed to be a light, and that he should look at it. He did so, and saw it. The Admiral said the same to Rodrigo Sanchez of Segovia, whom the King and Queen had sent with the fleet as inspector, but he could see nothing, because he was not in a place whence anything could be seen.
>
> After the Admiral had spoken he saw the light once or twice, and it was like a wax candle rising and failing. It seemed to few to be an indication of land; but the Admiral made certain that land was close. When they said the Salve, (Salve Regina) which all the sailors were accustomed to sing in their way, the Admiral asked and admonished the men to keep a good lookout on the forecastle, and to watch well for land; and to him who should first cry out that he saw land, he would give a silk doublet, besides the other rewards promised by the Sovereigns, which were 10,000 maravedis to him who should first saw it. At two hours after midnight the land was sighted at a distance of two leagues.
>
> Source: "Christopher Columbus Discovers America, 1492," Columbus's journal appears in Olson, Julius, *The Northmen, Columbus and Cabot, 985-1503* (1926). EyeWitness to History, www.eyewitnesstohistory.com (2004).

Amerigo Vespucci

lands that he visited. Vespucci was the first European to describe the lands Columbus reached as a *mundus novus*, or "new world." In 1507, a geographer named Martin Waldseemuller published a map depicting lands west of Europe as a separate continent, which he labeled America in honor of Vespucci. Perhaps not having the lands he discovered named after him was the ultimate insult to Columbus. This aside, Columbus paved the way for later Spanish exploration that gave Spain control of much of the Western Hemisphere.

Largely as a result of Columbus's exploration, Spain replaced Portugal as Europe's most dominant nation. One century before the English founded their first permanent colony at Jamestown, Spain already possessed a New World empire. In 1521-22, **Ferdinand Magellan**, a Portuguese navigator sailing for Spain, accomplished what Columbus failed to do—find an Atlantic Ocean route to Asia. Magellan sailed around a passage at the tip of South America into the Pacific Ocean, later named the Straits of Magellan in his honor. Magellan eventually reached the Philippine Islands where he died during a fight with the native people. One of his ships sailed around the tip of Africa and returned to Spain, thus completing the first voyage to circumnavigate the globe.

Other Spanish explorers became part of a group called the *conquistadors*, or conquerors, who began the process whereby Native American peoples and their societies were systematically destroyed over the next four centuries. Before 1510, *conquistadors* generally operated in the Caribbean, where they sought out Native Americans in their attempts to find gold, silver, and spices. To deceive the intruders, Native Americans often lured the Spanish away by enticing them with stories about enormous cities filled with gold somewhere else in the Americas. After 1510, the *conquistadors* moved onto the mainland of North and South America. In 1513, the Spanish explorer Vasco Nuñez de Balboa led an expedition across the Isthmus of Panama, becoming the first Europeans to see the Pacific Ocean. During that same year, Juan Ponce de León, the governor of Puerto Rico, claimed Florida for Spain as an expedition he led trekked across portions of Florida, fighting Native Americans along the way, during a fruitless search for a Fountain of Youth that Taínos on Puerto Rico described to him.

Perhaps the most famous *conquistador* was **Hernán Cortés,** a government official in Cuba, who made plans to lead about six hundred men into Mexico after hearing Native American stories about gold, silver, and precious gems located there. In 1519, Cortés landed in Mexico, finding the great civilization established by the Aztecs. Though greatly outnumbered by Aztec warriors, the Spanish soldiers had gunpowder, muskets, and horses, which gave them a tactical military advantage. Especially terrifying to Aztecs were soldiers mounted on horses, which they believed were four-legged monsters. Native American groups subservient to the Aztecs also helped Cortés in his plans of conquest. Further benefiting the Spanish invaders was an Aztec prophecy predicting that, about the time the *conquistador* appeared, their world would be destroyed by a powerful god arriving on a great white bird. The Aztecs and their emperor Moctezuma II mistook Cortés for the

Lithograph depicting Moctezuma's reception of Hernán Cortés.

old Toltec war god, Quetzalcoatl, who they thought had returned to destroy them. The Spaniards' ships were believed to be the white birds foretold in the divine prediction. Moctezuma responded by trying to bribe Cortés with vast amounts of gold and silver, hoping that the great god would not destroy Tenochtitlan. The sight of vast amounts of gold and silver, however, only whetted the Spanish appetite for more wealth. Rather than withdrawing from the Aztec capital, Cortés attacked and captured Moctezuma, holding him for ransom. In 1520 the Aztecs drove Cortés out of their city (with Moctezuma dying in the process), but the Spanish returned the next year and recaptured Tenochtitlan with the help of other Native Americans and the onset of smallpox among the Aztecs. Soon, the Aztec empire lay in ruins.

Cortés's success in finding riches led other *conquistadors* to search for further gold, with **Francisco Pizarro** proving to be the most ruthless. In 1531, Pizarro commanded an expedition following rumored cities of gold in the Andes Mountains. After a year of searching, Pizarro found the mountain homeland of the Incas. After a forty-five day climb up the high Andes, Pizarro and his force of 168 men reached Peru, encountering the Incas led by Atahualpa. Like the Aztecs, the Incas regarded the Spanish as vengeful gods and thus feared that their empire would be destroyed. Through emissaries, Pizarro told Atahualpa that the Spanish meant the Incas no harm—that they were simply exploring, and intended to remain among the Incas only a few days. Believing what Pizarro said, Atahualpa allowed the *conquistador* to enter the Inca capital of Cuzco. After being welcomed, Pizarro turned on his Inca benefactors, killing more than five thousand Inca warriors and capturing Atahualpa. To gain his freedom, the emperor offered Pizarro a room full of gold and silver. Pizarro agreed to set Atahualpa free once the precious metals were transferred to him, but he lied. Once he had the treasure safely in hand, Pizarro tied Atahualpa to a stake and executed him by strangulation. With the help of traitors in the Inca royal family, Pizarro completely conquered the Inca Empire, destroying a great civilization. All Inca resistance crumbled when the Spanish survived a siege at Cuzco in 1533. After acquiring Inca lands, the Spanish Empire stretched along the entire length of the western coast of South America.

The last great Native American civilization destroyed by the Spanish was the Maya of the Yucatan Peninsula. Spain could not conquer the Mayas as quickly as they had the Aztecs and Incas because there was no centralized seat of authority in the Yucatan. Instead, the Maya Empire consisted of numerous states bound together in a loose confederation. Spanish forces first entered the Yucatan in 1527, beginning a twenty-year fight, which ended with a Maya defeat thus securing Spanish dominance over most of Central and South America.

After taking control over much of the Americas, Spanish rulers began to devise a system to keep order, enforce its laws, and keep other nations from encroaching on its vast territorial holdings. Spain established two agencies in Madrid to control its American colonies. The House of Trade was placed in charge of economic policy, while the Council for the Indies handled governmental administrative duties. To administer the empire, the Council of the Indies created four territorial regions called viceroyalties, governed by viceroys who consulted with a council of appointed officials called *audiencias*. There was no democracy in New Spain. Ordinary citizens did not elect their government officials, while only pure-blooded Spaniards could serve as government officials.

The Spanish who came to New Spain faced a tremendous labor shortage. To overcome this shortage, Spain devised the *encomendero* system, whereby the Spanish government rewarded *conquistadors* by giving them title to vast tracts of land, including Native American villages and the territories surrounding them. As part of the system, the *encomendero*, or landlord, was required to civilize, Christianize, and educate Native Americans living on his land. In return, the *encomendero* was allowed to enslave native people. Under this system, thousands of Native Americans had their freedom taken away and were greatly abused by the Spanish. Execution awaited anyone who resisted. Native people were often bought and sold like livestock. Despite the death penalty, Native Americans occasionally revolted against their enslavement. The Carib people, for example, defended their islands from Spanish invasion until the end of the sixteenth century. In Mexico,

Francisco Pizarro

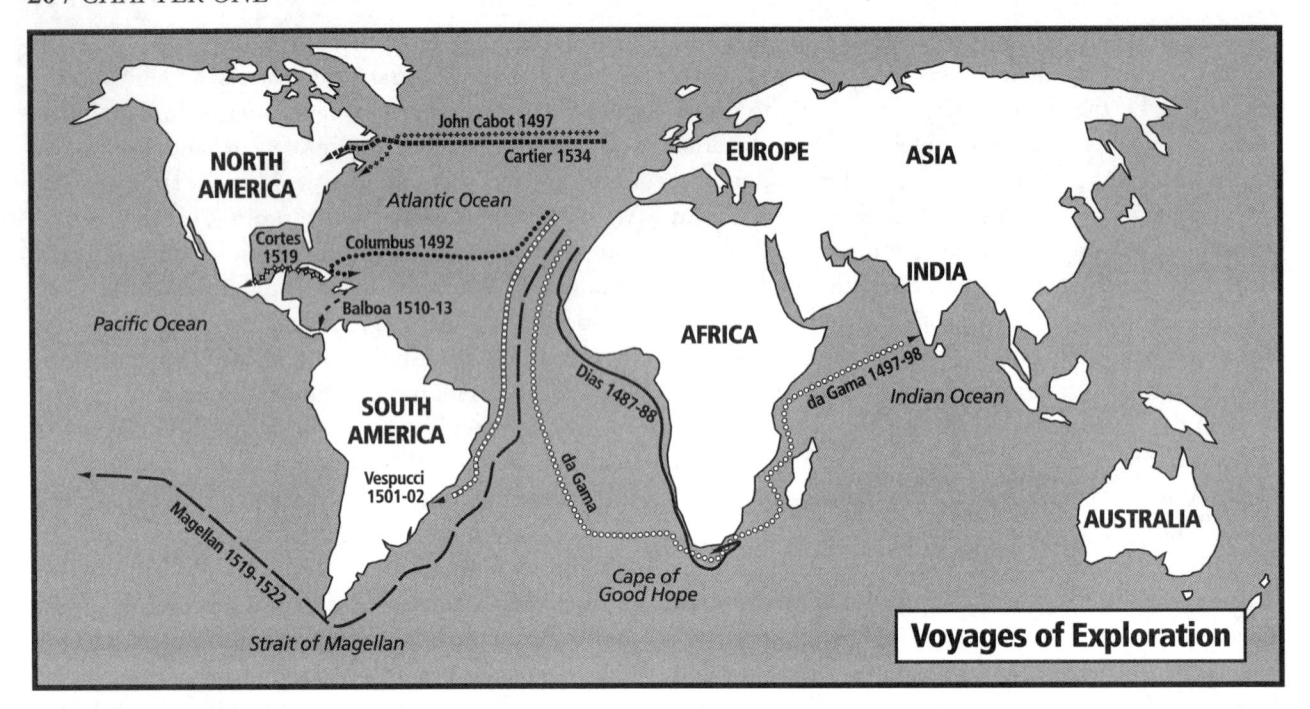

Map 1.4 Voyages of Exploration

the Chichimec people also resisted enslavement for over a hundred years.

A former *conquistador* who rejected his previous ways to become a Dominican friar, **Bartolomé de Las Casas** gained notoriety for his impassioned protests against Spanish rule in the New World. In a book entitled *The Destruction of the Indies*, Las Casas indicted the Spanish for their brutal conquests and subsequent enslavement of the Native Americans, demanding that all people should be treated humanely. Published in 1522, his work was subsequently translated into several languages, earning him a place among the great humanitarian leaders.

In 1542, the Spanish government finally outlawed the ***encomienda* system**. Despite the government's best intentions, things changed little for Native Americans. Government officials simply replaced the *encomienda* system with the *hacienda* system. Spanish settlers were still given large land grants called *haciendas*, where enslavement was replaced with debt peonage. Henceforth, Native Americans had to borrow money from Spanish landlords and were forced to produce crops given to the *hacienda* master to help discharge the debt, which usually grew larger with each passing year. For Native Americans, this system was often little better than slavery.

Because Native American mortality rates were high, the Spanish could not meet their labor needs entirely from the native population. Spain began to import African slaves to American colonies in 1501. In all, about ten million Africans were enslaved in North and South America. Slavery was an evil and brutal institution in New Spain. *Hacienda* owners preferred young males who were often worked so hard they collapsed and died from exhaustion. Slaves did, however, have some protection. Spanish law and Catholic authority forbade brutality, at least in theory. Because the church wanted all souls to be saved, slave marriage was recognized as a sacrament. This meant that slaves could wed, raise families, and their marriages could not dissolve when one party was sold. Under Spanish law, slaves could buy their freedom. While the work was hard, slaves in New Spain certainly had more legal rights than those in the later English colonies located farther north.

The Spanish discriminated against slaves on the basis of skin pigmentation. Those in bondage with lighter colored skin received better treatment than those with darker skin tones. In fact, Spain created a racial pyramid in its American colonies. At the top of society were pure-blooded Spanish natives called *peninsulares*, who had more rights and privileges in society than all other people. Next were the *creoles*, pure-blooded Spanish born in the New World. Beneath the *creoles* was a class called *mestizos*, which consisted of offspring produced by the sexual union of Spanish males and Native American females. Finally, there were the *mulattoes*, products of Spanish males and African females. The lower an individual's position on the racial pyramid, the less status and fewer privileges they retained in society.

The Spanish Empire used slave labor to ensure that wealth flowed to the mother country from the colonies, which existed primarily to benefit Spain. New World wealth made Spain the envy of all European nations and spawned rivalries. Other nations, England, France, and

> ### Bartolomé de Las Casas, Brief Account of the Devastation of the Indies (1542)
>
> *The Indies were discovered in the year one thousand four hundred and ninety-two. In the following year a great many Spaniards went there with the intention of settling the land. Thus, forty-nine years have passed since the first settlers penetrated the land, the first so claimed being the large and most happy isle called Hispaniola, which is six hundred leagues in circumference. Around it in all directions are many other islands, some very big, others very small, and all of them were, as we saw with our own eyes, densely populated with native peoples called Indians. This large island was perhaps the most densely populated place in the world. There must be close to two hundred leagues of land on this island, and the seacoast has been explored for more than ten thousand leagues, and each day more of it is being explored. And all the land so far discovered is a beehive of people; it is as though God had crowded into these lands the great majority of mankind. And of all the infinite universe of humanity, these people are the most guileless, the most devoid of wickedness and duplicity, the most obedient and faithful to their native masters and to the Spanish Christians whom they serve. They are by nature the most humble, patient, and peaceable, holding no grudges, free from embroilments, neither excitable nor quarrelsome. These people are the most devoid of rancors, hatreds, or desire for vengeance of any people in the world. And because they are so weak and complaisant, they are less able to endure heavy labor and soon die of no matter what malady. The sons of nobles among us, brought up in the enjoyments of life's refinements, are no more delicate than are these Indians, even those among them who are of the lowest rank of laborers. They are also poor people, for they not only possess little but have no desire to possess worldly goods. For this reason they are not arrogant, embittered, or greedy. Their repasts are such that the food of the holy fathers in the desert can scarcely be more parsimonious, scanty, and poor. As to their dress, they are generally naked, with only their pudenda covered somewhat. And when they cover their shoulders it is with a square cloth no more than two yards in size. They have no beds, but sleep on a kind of matting or else in a kind of suspended net called bamacas. They are very clean in their persons, with alert, intelligent minds, docile and open to doctrine, very apt to receive our holy Catholic faith, to be endowed with virtuous customs, and to behave in a godly fashion. And once they begin to hear the tidings of the Faith, they are so insistent on knowing more and on taking the sacraments of the Church and on observing the divine cult that, truly, the missionaries who are here need to be endowed by God with great patience in order to cope with such eagerness. Some of the secular Spaniards who have been here for many years say that the goodness of the Indians is undeniable and that if this gifted people could be brought to know the one true God they would be the most fortunate people in the world.*
>
> *Yet into this sheepfold, into this land of meek outcasts there came some Spaniards who immediately behaved like ravening wild beasts, wolves, tigers, or lions that had been starved for many days. And Spaniards have behaved in no other way during the past forty years, down to the present time, for they are still acting like ravening beasts, killing, terrorizing, afflicting, torturing, and destroying the native peoples, doing all this with the strangest and most varied new methods of cruelty, never seen or heard of before, and to such a degree that this Island of Hispaniola once so populous (having a population that I estimated to be more than three million), has now a population of barely two hundred persons.*

the Netherlands, were determined to plant colonies in the New World and gain riches from America for themselves. Among these nations were England, France, and the Netherlands.

England

Five years after Columbus's initial voyage, England sent Giovanni Caboto (**John Cabot**), a Venetian sea captain, on a New World expedition via a northern Atlantic route. From 1497 to 1498, Cabot explored the Atlantic coastline of North America from Newfoundland to Chesapeake Bay. Like Columbus, he sought a westward oceanic route to Asia across the Atlantic—a "Northwest Passage." Cabot's 1497 voyage represented the first recorded transatlantic trek by an English ship, although some evidence indicates that English fishermen might have accidentally landed in Nova Scotia and Newfoundland in the 1480s. Regardless, the English based their territorial claims in the New World upon Cabot's voyages. After Cabot died on his second voyage to America in 1498, his son Sebastian continued England's explorations. In 1508 and 1509, he sailed across the Atlantic attempting to find the elusive Northwest Passage. Along the way, he explored the Hudson Bay area, claiming the region for England.

After the Cabots failed to find a Northwest Passage, England lost interest in the New World for the next seventy-five years. When Elizabeth I assumed the throne, English overseas exploration witnessed a revival, with **Sir Humphrey Gilbert** proving to be a driving force. Originally, he wanted to continue the search for a Northwest Passage, publishing a book on the subject, which included speculations about where such a passage might be located. Gilbert also promised readers, who might be potential investors in an expedition to find a northern route to Asia, that wealth awaited those smart enough to find a new trade route. In 1576, he convinced the Crown that it was in England's national interest to find a Northwest Passage. At this time, England was experiencing economic difficulties due to the Calvinist Dutch rebellion against Catholic Spain. The Spanish crushed this revolt, destroying the city of Antwerp and taking away England's primary marketplace for textiles on the European continent. Consequently, English merchants began to form joint-stock companies to develop trade with other parts of the world. These corporations allowed individuals to invest small amounts of capital to finance huge undertakings with little overall risk. Not only did the joint-stock companies undertake trade expeditions throughout the world, but they also financed English privateers like Francis Drake and John Hawkins. On one particular voyage from 1577 to 1580, Drake sailed around the globe, attacking Spanish ports and ships wherever he found them. Upon his return to England (in which Drake returned a 4,600 percent profit for his investors, including the queen), Elizabeth knighted him for becoming the first Englishman to circumnavigate the Earth.

In addition to facing economic pressure, many among the English gentry sought exploration and settlement because of their concern for their younger sons who could not legally inherit their family estates. They often pressured Elizabeth I to claim land in the New World so their sons would have a place to build estates of their own. A growing population and limited economic opportunities among the poor also fueled a desire to explore and settle North America as an outlet for immigration.

Because of these pressures, Elizabeth was ready to challenge Spain's supremacy in the Americas. In 1576, at the behest of Gilbert, the Queen sent **Martin Frobisher** to seek a Northwest Passage. Sailing to the island of Labrador, Frobisher captured an Inuk and his kayak before returning to England with his captive and what he believed was a small sample of gold ore. After finding assayers to claim that the sample was gold, Elizabeth organized a joint-stock company to construct a fort and begin mining operations in Labrador. This company financed two expeditions by Frobisher in 1577 and 1578.

Sir Francis Drake

During these trips, Frobisher captured three more Inuit and brought back two thousand tons of ore. The Inuit like the first one captured in 1576, died soon after arriving in England. Meanwhile, the ore from Labrador proved not to be gold after all, but only iron pyrite ("fools gold"). This mistake forever ruined Frobisher's reputation.

Distrusting Frobisher, Humphrey Gilbert had refused to invest in his expeditions. After Frobisher's fall from grace, Gilbert took advantage of the explorer's misfortune and persuaded Elizabeth to grant him a charter to explore, settle, and govern all territory in North America not occupied by Christian people. The English charter completely disregarded all claims that Native Americans had upon their land. For some time, Gilbert had tried to convince the queen that England should be more interested in land than gold. Although he probably harbored hopes that he might find another Peru or Mexico, Gilbert convinced Elizabeth that establishing colonies in North America would enable England to relieve population pressures, which had resulted in people crowding into English cities where many often committed crimes out of desperation. Gilbert hoped to settle these people on land in North America.

What Gilbert envisioned was resurrecting a form of feudalism in North America. His plans called for providing settlers with free land and farm tools. Gilbert's plans also provided a governmental framework consisting of a governor and thirteen advisors chosen by settlers. He saw himself and other gentry as manorial lords, ruling colonies of tenants who paid rent by giving the lord a portion of crops they produced.

Depiction of Jacques Cartier's first interview with the Indians of Hochelaga (now Montreal) in 1535.

Gilbert set sail in 1583, reaching Nova Scotia until he aborted the expedition due to bad weather. On the return voyage, Gilbert's ship sank during a storm. His death prompted his stepbrother, **Sir Walter Raleigh**, to attempt to colonize the New World for England. Raleigh received permission from Elizabeth I to explore and establish a colony in North America, resulting in the ill-fated adventures at Roanoke Island. England's next attempt at North American colonization at Jamestown in 1607 would prove to be more successful.

France and the Netherlands

The English had rivals for control of North America. Both France and the Netherlands explored and established colonies in the New World. French claims in North America were based on explorations by Giovanni da Verrazzano in 1524 and Jacques Cartier ten years later. Verrazzano sailed westward across the Atlantic under authority of Frances I, exploring the eastern coastline of North America from present-day South Carolina to New England, claiming the entire territory for France. Following in Verrazzano's wake, Cartier led three expeditions between 1534 and 1542 through the St. Lawrence River Valley, reaching sites where the cities of Montreal and Quebec are located today. Cartier established the first French colony in 1541, but the effort failed due to political upheaval in France. Not until 1608 did the French successfully established a settlement in Canada when Samuel de Champlain built a fort at Quebec on the St. Lawrence River.

Fort Quebec served primarily as a trading post. Unlike the Spanish and English who sought gold and land, the French desired to trade with Native Americans for valuable furs. Champlain realized that he could make a substantial profit from trade. Wealthy Europeans had an almost insatiable desire for furs, especially beaver pelts, used to make stylish hats. Likewise, Native Americans developed a great interest in European products, such as metal tools, firearms, and woolen blankets, which could provide security from rival tribes and improve their quality of life. Following Champlain's lead, French trappers and traders explored vast territories throughout eastern Canada, the Great Lakes region, the Ohio River Valley, parts of New England, and the Mississippi River, claiming the land for France. Because they were primarily interested in trade, the French generally established harmonious relations with Native Americans. Sometimes, French settlers fought alongside favored Native Americans in tribal wars in order to gain and maintain trading partners.

Dutch claims to North American territory were based upon the explorations of **Henry Hudson**, an English sea captain. In 1609, Hudson, in the employ of the Netherlands, was sent to search for a Northwest Passage. Along the way, he explored the Hudson River and Hudson Bay, which were later named in his honor. As the French, Hudson was interested in establishing a fur-trading network with Native Americans. To achieve this objective, the Dutch in 1624 established forts on Manhattan Island and at Albany, which they called New Amsterdam and Fort Orange, respectively. For a time, the two outposts, with the Iroquois people supplying furs in return for Dutch trade goods, prospered until England forcefully seized the colony in 1664.

AFRICANS

Africans imported into North and South America as slaves came from a variety of cultures in different geographical locations, many of which were older than the societies of the Europeans who held them in bondage. The Berbers, for example, were a Muslim people who lived along the

Mediterranean coast of northern Africa and had traded with Europe and Asia centuries before Columbus made his voyage to the Caribbean.

Most Africans who became slaves in the Americas came from the western coast of Africa, a tropical area that Europeans called **Guinea** where native peoples engaged in agriculture for at least twelve thousand years before enslavement. The northern part of Guinea, which Europeans called Upper Guinea, was habituated by peoples who converted to Islam after trade with the Mediterranean region exposed them to the teachings of the Prophet Mohammed. In addition to spreading religious ideas, the trans-Saharan trade proved to be very lucrative for Europe, Africa, and the Middle East. European and Middle Eastern peoples exchanged salt, cotton, silk, olives, and dates for African gold, ivory, and slaves. The African kingdoms of Ghana and Mali controlled this trade, centered in the legendary city of Timbuktu located in the heart of northwest Africa where merchants from Europe, Africa, and Asia flocked.

Enslaved Africans from Lower Guinea generally were not Muslims. They practiced traditional religions similar in some ways to those of Native Americans in that rituals were devised to ensure good harvests. Throughout Lower Guinea, people resided in small villages inhabited by groups of kin. These villages were organized into larger kingdoms.

Europeans divided Guinea into several areas named for the chief products produced in the region, such as the Rice Coast, the Grain Coast, the Ivory Coast, the Gold Coast, and the Slave Coast. Many of the first slaves sold in the Americas came from the thirty small states known as the Akan Kingdom. By the 1700s, slave trading shifted to the Slave Coast. Here, merchants established outposts to supply captives in exchange for European trade goods. At first, most slaves were generally criminals, prisoners of war, or debtors. By the early 1700s, however, the demand for slaves became so high that raiding parties from African coastal towns began to attack interior villages to acquire humans for enslavement.

THE COLUMBIAN EXCHANGE

Contact between Europeans and the New World produced what historian Alfred W. Crosby first labeled the **"Columbian Exchange"** to refer to the biological and environmental impact of Columbus's exploration of America. With the breakdown of the previous isolation of the Eastern and Western Hemispheres, a great exchange of plants, animals, and microorganisms began to take place impacting societies on both sides of the globe. While both Europeans and Native Americans realized advantages and disadvantages from the Columbian Exchange, Native Americans generally suffered more harm and Europeans reaped more benefits from this development.

One consequence of the Columbian Exchange that harmed Native Americans, even when Europeans intended no harm, was the arrival of deadly diseases. Because of their separation from Asia, Africa, and Europe when ocean levels rose following the end of the last Ice Age, Native Americans were not afflicted with diseases that developed in the Old World. Smallpox, measles, pneumonia, influenza, and malaria were unknown in the Americas. Without previous exposure, Native Americans had no antibody resistance to the microbes that caused these illnesses.

As Europeans inadvertently brought these diseases to Native Americans, the results were devastating. Spanish contact with Native Americans triggered the largest population decline in recorded history. When Europeans arrived in the Western Hemisphere, about sixty million Native Americans were scattered throughout North and South America. After contact with foreign microbes, the native population declined by about 90 percent within the span of one century, a short time taken within the wide expanse of human history. By 1600, only about six million Native Americans had survived the biological onslaught. On the island of Hispaniola, for example, there were about one million Taínos when Columbus arrived in 1492. Forty years later, only 14,000 remained alive. In Mexico, about twenty-five million Aztecs were alive when Cortés landed. Within twenty years, 50 percent of the population had died of disease. After the passage of a century, only about one million Aztecs survived. A similar fate befell the Incas of Peru. In all areas where Europeans contacted Native Americans, the same catastrophe occurred. European diseases played a major role in European powers being able to defeat, conquer, and destroy Native American civilizations. In fact, diseases were more important than firearms in the European conquest of the New World. After contact with Europeans, Native Americans spread disease inter-tribally. Economic and social contact among various Native American tribes caused millions of people who had never seen a European to die of smallpox or some other disease in what Native Americans call "the great dying." By the time English settlers arrived at Jamestown, three epidemics had already swept through the Chesapeake region.

Epidemics completely devastated Native American societies. Because of the precipitous drop in population, political, governmental, social, religious, and economic institutions were upended. Native American religion and shamans were hit especially hard. Most religious systems in the Americas depended on priestly mysticism and ability to influence nature, including the ability to cure disease and heal wounds. These talents were called into question after European diseases began to ravage tribal people. Native Americans began to question their religious beliefs and doubted the ability of shamans to heal in the face of devastating disease epidemics. Eventually, entire societies collapsed from lack of people to make institutions within native civilizations function.

Not all Native Americans who died after contact with Europeans were killed by disease. A small number were killed in warfare when they resisted encroachment on their territory; others starved to death because their economies were destroyed when marauding soldiers confiscated their food supplies.

Europeans also lacked immunity to infectious diseases present in the New World but suffered far less devastation than did Native Americans. Perhaps the worst disease Europeans contracted from the intercontinental exchange was syphilis. A few years after Columbus's three voyages, a virulent form of syphilis broke out in Europe, quickly spreading across the continent. Thousands of Europeans contacted this venereal disease, dying a slow death before doctors knew what caused it and how to prevent its spread. Recent scientific evidence has shown, contrary to what scientists previously believed, syphilis did indeed exist in the Old World before 1492. Corpses of individuals in Europe known to have died before Columbus's voyages have now been discovered. What is known, however, is that syphilis, not a common killer before 1492, soon thereafter became a noticeable illness that Europeans began to associate with the New World.

The movement of diseases became only part of the Columbian Exchange. The New World and Europe also experienced a transfer of plant and animal life. Since Europe was separated from the Americas by a great ocean, evolution created vastly different ecosystems. Large, domesticated mammals, such as cattle and horses, were present in Europe but unknown in North and South America. The largest beasts of burden found in the Western Hemisphere were dogs and llamas. When contact occurred between Europe and the Americas, Europeans introduced horses, mules, oxen, sheep, and cows. Horses had a particularly important impact on some Native American cultures. Native Americans acquired horses after Spanish *conquistadors* introduced them into the New World. Nomadic tribes of the Great Plains, including the Cheyenne, Apaches, Comanche, and Sioux, who hunted bison came to rely upon the horse as an essential tool to support their lifestyle. Not only did these tribes use equines for hunting, food, and transportation, but they also used them as a source of exchange. Tribal members counted their wealth according to the number of horses they owned. The nature of warfare among nomadic tribes was altered by use of equines. Rather than fighting on foot, these people, who became skilled equestrians, fought from horseback. Even women's work became easier after introduction of the horse. Females no longer had to carry the tribe's possessions strapped to their backs when villages were moved to better hunting territory; now, they loaded belongings on horses. Great Plains tribes also largely abandoned agriculture after acquiring horses. Prior to introduction of equines, these natives had hunted various animals, gathered food plants, and produced agricultural crops. This traditional mode of subsistence among plains tribes gave way to a lifestyle that was almost totally dependent on hunting buffalo.

Domesticated animals harmed Native Americans in other ways. In parts of the Americas, herds of sheep, cattle, and goats destroyed native agriculture. Usually, Native American farming practices were destroyed because livestock did much environmental damage. European ranchers and farmers often allowed large herds of animals to roam free across the landscape, resulting in overgrazing, which produced erosion and prevented Native Americans from farming this land. Other ranchers and farmers fenced in the land, placed "no trespassing" signs on it, and prevented native tribes from using the land for agriculture.

Not only was European livestock introduced into the Americas, but there was an exchange of agricultural products as well. Vegetable crops that grew in North and South America, such as beans, corn, squash, and potatoes, were high in nutrition and produced greater yields than did traditional European crops such as wheat and rye. As a result, European explorers carried American crops back with them. It became common for European farmers to grow crops native to the Americas. Maize, which was the staple crop for most Native American agricultural tribes, became an important food crop in Mediterranean countries, a feed crop for livestock in Western Europe, and the primary food source for slave ships crossing the Atlantic from Africa. Likewise, New World potatoes became a means of subsistence for peasant farmers in northern Europe, and tomatoes became one of the most important ingredients in Italian cuisine. New World crops enabled Europe to overcome the persistent problem of famine that had plagued the region before 1500. Largely as a result of the introduction of American agricultural crops, Europe's population doubled within the three centuries after Columbus's voyages. A downside existed, however, to the introduction of American agricultural crops in Europe. In some localities peasants became so dependent on New World crops that when these crops failed, starvation occurred. In Ireland during the middle decades of the nineteenth century, for example, the potato crop was wiped out by a devastating fungal blight. The subsequent food shortages led to a million deaths and an outward migration of a million more as the island experienced a 25 percent reduction in population.

One plant that Europeans encountered had a devastating effect on Old World people—tobacco. Native to the New World, tobacco had been cultivated and used by Native Americans for centuries before European arrival. At first, tobacco, called the "stinking weed" by James I of England, was believed to have medicinal effects. Smoking or chewing the plant became popular in Europe during the sixteenth and seventeenth centuries. Tobacco cultivation in Virginia and other southern colonies provided a living for many English settlers, making some of them rich. Only in the twentieth century did medical science discover the link between tobacco use and cancer, heart disease, and other ailments. Presently, tobacco use is responsible for countless deaths annually throughout the world and costs governments and individuals billions of dollars. Tobacco-related deaths since contact between Europe and the Americas have numbered in the millions. Most likely, the number of deaths from tobacco use among Europeans equals those of Native Americans from Old World microbes. King James I of England was correct in 1604 when he published an essay denouncing tobacco use as "loathsome to the eye, hatefull (sic) to the Nose, harmfull (sic) to the brain, dangerous to the Lungs."

European agricultural products also came to the New World. Rice, sugar, coffee, wheat, and rye are examples of crops exported from Europe to the Americas. The introduction of these crops to the Western Hemisphere created new industries. Sugar produced in the Americas became an important crop. Portugal first produced sugar in the lowlands of Brazil in the sixteenth century. By 1570 Brazil produced six million pounds of sugar annually; by 1635 the output totaled 32 million pounds. Sugar production impacted Native Americans negatively. England, Holland, France, Spain, and Portugal all produced sugar on various Caribbean islands. In most places, sugar plantation owners enslaved Native American workers. The few natives who escaped enslavement were scattered, their cultures and societies destroyed by the European sweet tooth.

The New World provided Europe with an influx of gold and silver, mostly plundered from Native Americans or mined by them under forced-labor conditions in Mexico and Peru. The amount of specie circulating in Europe tripled during the first half of the sixteenth century and then tripled again from 1550-1600. European economies faced runaway inflation because so much gold and silver was placed in circulation, causing business profits to increase while simultaneously lowering living standards for common people. The buying power of European workers was depressed by 50 percent due to rising prices during the 1500s. Artisans, laborers, and farmers, who comprised the vast majority of Europe's population, suffered deprivation when wages did not keep pace with inflation. A common complaint voiced by artisans was that despite their skills, the lifestyle they led was hardly better than that of a common beggar. Although European economies were wrecked by the inflation, some economic historians believe American gold and silver was the most important factor in the development of capitalism.

European attempts to export religion harmed Native Americans. Many Christian missionaries tried to force native people to abandon traditional religious beliefs and practices. When such efforts failed, Christian missionaries sometimes launched attacks on Native American religious institutions. Soldiers were sent to destroy American temples and religious artifacts contained within them. Diego de Landa, a Catholic bishop in the Yucatan, burned thousands of Mayan books because he wanted to stop what he viewed as idolatry. Consequently, modern scholars have limited knowledge about the Mayan civilization.

Not all aspects of the Columbian Exchange were intentional. Europeans inadvertently carried germs, seeds, plant spores, and pestilent animals when they came to the New World. The process also worked in reverse when Europeans returned home. The destruction of Native American crafts by the introduction of European manufactured products was also unintentional. European products replaced native products, and tribal craftspeople eventually lost the ability to make traditional items previously common in the Americas.

NEW CULTURES

The European exploration of America began a process in which numerous Native American cultures were almost completely destroyed by the time English American colonists declared their independence in 1776. Within a span of three centuries, Europeans destroyed what it took Native Americans thousands of years to construct. By the end of the sixteenth century, the population of the Americas was less than it had been when Columbus first made contact in 1492. Though the seemingly unlimited wealth of the Aztec and Inca empires amazed the Spanish, the invaders tore down native temples, using the stones to construct churches in which the Christian god was worshipped. Native Americans were enslaved along with Africans and employed to work the fields and mines Europeans established in the Western Hemisphere. It is doubtful that Columbus ever realized the changes his voyage across the Atlantic would set in motion. At the same time Native American cultures were being destroyed, European nations were establishing new societies on their ruins.

Chronology

8000 B.C.E.	Asian migrations reach South America.
2500 B.C.E.	Migration across the Bering Strait begins.
1000 B.C.E.	Olmec civilization appears. Adena and Hopewell civilizations in North America.
300-600 C.E.	Teotihuacan at its height.
600-900 C.E.	Maya civilization reaches its zenith.
1000	Anaszi peoples build cliff dwellings at Mes Verde and pueblos at Chaco Canyon.
1001	Vikings reach North America.
1100-1400	Mississippian culture at its height in North America.
1100	Inca civilizations becomes prominent.
500-1400	Dark Ages in Europe.
1300-1500	Aztecs control Mexico.
1450s	Printing Press invented.
1451	Iroquois Confederacy formed.
1460	Prince Henry the Navigator died.
1469	Ferdinand and Isabella married.
1477	Marco Polo's *Travels* published.
1488	Bartolomé Dias reaches the Indian Ocean by sailing around Africa.
1492	Columbus's first voyage. Beginning of European colonization.
1493	Vasco de Gama reaches India.
1497	John Cabot reaches North America.
1508-09	Sebastian Cabot explores Hudson Bay region.
1513	Juan Ponce de León reaches Florida.
1517	Protestant Reformation begins.
1517-1519	Smallpox epidemic devastates Native American populations in West Indies.
1519	Hernán Cortés invades Mexico.
1521-22	Magellan sails around tip of South America into Pacific Ocean, one of his ships circumnavigates the globe.
1532-1533	Pizarro subjugates the Incas.
1534-1542	Jacques Cartier expeditions.
1540-1542	Francisco Vasquez de Coronado explores southwestern United States.
1536	Calvin publishes *Institutes of the Christian Religion*.
1576	Martin Frobisher reaches Labrador.
1583	Sir Humphrey Gilbert reaches Nova Scotia.
1587-1590	Second Roanoke Island colony vanishes.
1607	Jamestown settlement established.
1608	Quebec established.
1609	Henry Hudson explores area near modern-day New York City.

Review Questions

1. Discuss the impact of the Columbian Exchange on Native American and European societies in terms of diet and the natural environment.

2. Explain the advantages that the Europeans had in their conquest of North and South America, with a focus on technology, disease, religion and conflicts among Native Americans as factors.

3. What events prompted the Portuguese, Spanish, French, English and Dutch explorations of the 1400s and 1500s?

4. How did European attitudes towards Native Americans evolve in the fifteenth and sixteenth centuries?

5. In what ways did the conquests of North and South America undermine the European economy and how did the introduction of horses and European manufactured goods shape the Native American way of life?

Glossary of Important People and Concepts

Adena and Hopewell Cultures
Amerindians
Aztecs
John Cabot
Bartolomé de Las Casas
Bubonic Plague
Cahokia
Clovis Point
Columbian Exchange
Christopher Columbus
Compass
Hernán Cortés
Chief Deganawida
Bartolomeu Dias
Encomienda system
Fort Quebec
Martin Frobisher
Sir Humphrey Gilbert
Guinea
Johann Gutenberg
Henry Hudson
Prince Henry the Navigator
Inca
Ferdinand Magellan
Maya
Francisco Pizarro
Protestant Reformation
Sir Walter Raleigh
Renaissance
Vikings

SUGGESTED READINGS

C. R. Boxer, *The Portuguese Seaborne Empire, 1415-1825* (1972).

Carl Bridenbaugh, *Vexed and Troubled Englishmen, 1500-1642* (1968).

Inga Clendinnen, *Aztecs* (1991).

Alfred W. Crosby, *The Columbian Exchange: Biological and Cultural Consequences of 1492* (1972).

Basil Davidson, *The African Genius* (1969).

Brian Fagan, *The Great Journey: The Peopling of Ancient America* (1987).

Felipe Fernandez-Armesto, *Columbus* (1991).

Melvin Fowler, *Cahokia: Ancient Capital of the Midwest* (1974).

Charles Gibson, *Spain in America* (1966).

Karen O. Kupperman, *Roanoke, the Abandoned Colony* (1984).

Peter Laslett, *The World We Have Lost* (1971).

Paul E. Lovejoy, *Transformations in Slavery: A History of Slavery in Africa* (1983).

Kenneth Macgowan and Joseph A. Hester, Jr., *Early Man in the New World* (1983).

Samuel Eliot Morison, *The European Discovery of America: The Northern Voyages, A.D. 1500-1600* (1971).

——, *The European Discovery of America: The Southern Voyages, A.D. 1492-1616* (1971).

Richard Olaniyan, *African History and Culture* (1982).

William and Carla Phillips, *The Worlds of Christopher Columbus* (1992).

David B. Quinn, *North America from Earliest Discovery to First Settlement: The Norse Voyages to 1612* (1977).

Kirkpatrick Sale, *The Conquest of Paradise: Christopher Columbus and the Columbus Legacy* (1990).

Linda Schele and David Friedel, *A Forest of Kings* (1990).

Zvi Dor Ner and William Scheller, *Columbus and the Age of Discovery* (1991).

Jacques Soustelle, *The Olmecs: The Oldest Civilization in Mexico* (1984).

David E. Stannard, *American Holocaust: Columbus and the Conquest of the New World* (1992).

David J. Weber, *The Spanish Frontier in North America* (1992).

John Noble Wilford, *The Mysterious History of Columbus (1991).*

Nova Britannia.
OFFERING MOST
Excellent fruites by Planting in
VIRGINIA.

Exciting all such as be well affected
to further the same.

LONDON
Printed for SAMVEL MACHAM, and are to be sold at
his Shop in Pauls Church-yard, at the
Signe of the Bul-head.
1609.

Virginia Company pamphlet, 1609

Chapter Two

THE SOUTHERN COLONIES

In 1584, Sir Walter Raleigh, one of Queen Elizabeth's closest confidantes, received her permission and a royal charter to settle the New World. This was to be England's first attempt to establish a permanent settlement in North America. In preparation for his venture, Raleigh sent a preliminary reconnaissance party to explore the Atlantic coast of the North American continent to select an appropriate site for the first permanent English colony. It returned to England and reported to Raleigh that Roanoke Island off the coast of present-day North Carolina was the most suitable for a settlement. The party also brought two Croatoan Indians, Manteo and Wanchese, back to England with them. Ostensibly they had volunteered for the voyage. The Croatoan's gentle demeanor reassured all concerned that Raleigh's expedition had nothing to fear from the native population.

Raleigh now needed to raise money to support his endeavor, and by 1585, he had enough money to set sail. In theory, Raleigh's colony, which he named Virginia after the "virgin queen" Elizabeth, included the entire North American continent. In actuality, only a hundred or so individuals were part of the group that settled on Roanoke Island later that year. The colony included men of different backgrounds like Ralph Lane, a soldier, who served as its first governor and John White, an artist, who had been commissioned by Raleigh to serve as its official mapmaker. Within a year, most of the settlers had grown tired of the experiment. There were food shortages, poor weather conditions, and disputes with the indigenous population. When the privateer Francis Drake, fresh from plundering the Spanish West Indies, docked at Roanoke, the weary colonists were more than happy to go home.

This setback, however, did not deter Raleigh. Unaffected by this initial failure, he immediately organized a new expedition to return to the New World. This time the venture would be under the leadership of White. The second expedition consisted of 89 men, 7 women, including White's pregnant daughter, and 11 children. In August, White's granddaughter, Virginia Dare, became the first white English child born in North America.

White's granddaughter, however, was not born on the coast of Chesapeake Bay where Raleigh and White had planned to establish their second colony. Instead, the unscrupulous captain, Simon Fernandes, and crew that transported the settlers to North America dropped them off at Roanoke Island instead of the Chesapeake region so that they could have time to attack Spanish treasure ships before the weather turned bad. Reluctantly, White agreed to stay with Fernandes while he and his sailors undertook their pirating operations (they came up empty) before returning to England. White immediately found Raleigh and told him about Fernandes' treachery and the fact that the settlers were at Roanoke, quite far to the south of their intended destination. Raleigh organized a relief expedition but its vessels were diverted to the English navy to help defend England from the approaching Spanish Armada. Indeed, Queen Elizabeth forbade all ships from leaving English waters until the danger passed, an order that remained in place through the next year. John White could not return to Roanoke until August 1590, only to find the settlement there deserted.

Few clues remained to testify to the fate of the doomed colony. The condition of the abandoned cabins suggested a hasty evacuation, and the broken locks of five chests, three of them belonging to White himself, led the governor to suspect an Indian attack. The word "Croatoan" was found carved on a post, indicating that the settlers had tried to escape to Croatoan Island (now named Hatteras Island) a hundred miles to the south where the friendly Croatoan tribe would give them refuge. Despite an extensive search led by John White, and subsequent operations conducted in 1595 and 1602, no further sign of the missing 114 colonists was ever discovered.

Speculation abounds as to what happened to the Roanoke colonists. Among the most common theories are that the settlers were either killed by the Native Americans or fearing starvation abandoned their small settlement to live with them in order to save their lives. Later, Jamestown settlers heard rumors that the Roanoke settlers had drowned when their small homemade boat capsized on its way back to England. However, recent research indicates that, possibly, the English settlers from Roanoke Island encountered a group of Portuguese sailors and African slaves that had been shipwrecked nearby, decided to move inland, and eventually reached the Appalachian Mountains. There they mixed with Native Americans, creating an ethnic group known as Melungeons. As early as 1654, English and French explorers in the Southern Appalachians reported encounters with dark-complexioned, brown and blue-eyed people of European descent who spoke proper Elizabethan English, lived in cabins, farmed the land, smelted silver, and practiced Christianity. Stories handed down in Melungeon families from earlier generations indicated that there was a connection to the Roanoke Island colony. How the dark-skinned, English speaking Christians appeared in the Appalachian South is itself something of a mystery. Perhaps they were descendants of the Lost Colony of Roanoke Island.

In the aftermath of the Roanoke disaster, English enthusiasm for overseas colonization diminished. More pressing issues confronted England, such as war with Spain, especially the 1588 attempted invasion of England by the massive fleet known as the Spanish Armada. To the surprise of all in Europe, the English defeated (with help from Mother Nature in the form of heavy storms) the supposedly invincible flotilla. After vanquishing the Spanish, England entered the Elizabethan Golden Age. Along with prosperity, stability, and security came a renewed interest in overseas expansion. Moreover, even before the *Armada*, as witnessed by Sir Walter Raleigh's personal investment of 40,000 pounds sterling in the Roanoke enterprise, there had emerged in England a wealthy, entrepreneurial, moneyed merchant and capitalist class willing by the early seventeenth century to once again look across the Atlantic and resume the effort to establish permanent English colonies. Motivating such individuals and their respective consortiums was the desire for monetary gain, which they believed the New World could provide. They were certain untold wealth in the form of precious metals and rich, abundant land were all there waiting for them to exploit. Perhaps more important was the role of these individuals and private companies leading the vanguard of English colonization and subsequent imperialism. The road to empire, however, did not begin very auspiciously. Indeed, many of the new colonization efforts were very much like the earlier, failed ones—small, fragile, private enterprises with little planning or direction from the English government led by people unprepared for the hardships of life in the wilderness. Unlike the Roanoke experiment, they survived but not before enduring several years of "starving times," which almost brought the English presence in North America to a premature end. Nonetheless, by the early years of the seventeenth century it appeared that the lures of the New World—the presumably vast riches, the abundant land, the promise of religious freedom, the chance to begin anew—were too strong to be suppressed for very long.

Four dynamics in particular shaped the character of these English settlements. First, the colonies were mainly business enterprises, and thus their main purpose was to produce a profit for either their company or proprietary sponsors. Second, because the colonies were only at best loosely tied to the English government through the agency of the Crown, they began to develop their own political and social institutions, which over time led to the emergence of a uniquely colonial or American identity. Third, as witnessed in Ireland, the English colonists made few, if any, efforts to blend their society with that of the indigenous peoples. Indeed, the English tried to isolate themselves from their Native American neighbors and create insulated communities that would remain purely English transplantations. And fourth, as will be seen, almost nothing worked out as they had planned.

THE EARLY CHESAPEAKE COLONIES: Virginia and Maryland

To avoid the mistakes made by Raleigh, a group of London merchant capitalists formed a joint-stock company, the **London Company**, (renamed the Virginia Company in 1609) through which they launched England's second attempt to establish a permanent colony in North America.

THE SOUTHERN COLONIES | 33

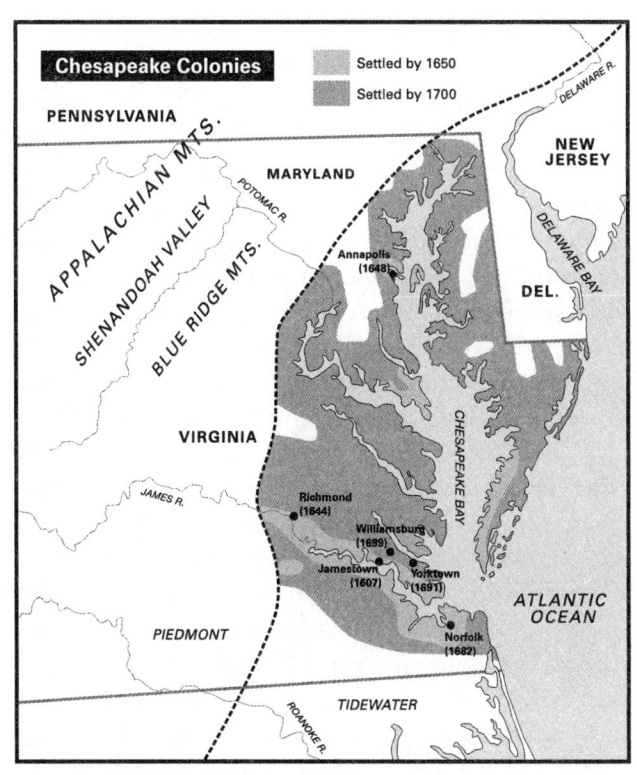

Map 2.1 Chesapeake Colonies

This emerging form of the modern corporation sold stock to small investors to raise the essential funds for their venture. After successfully procuring the necessary capital, an elected thirteen-man "board of directors"—a council, charged with investing and disbursing money and while promoting the company's mission—took charge of the funds. The first step was to petition the king, James I, formerly James VI of Scotland of the **House of Stuart**, and Elizabeth's cousin, who inherited the English throne in 1603 from Elizabeth who never married and died without an heir. Thus began the reign of the Stuart dynasty in English history, a monarchy under whose auspices England established its presence on the North American continent. Under the Stuarts, England experienced some of its most tumultuous and momentous political upheavals and changes, many of which directly impacted the nation's North American colonies.

The Virginia Company had little difficulty persuading James of the enterprise's merits. The king charged the company a hefty fee for his approval (which was the customary practice in the procurement of royal charters for whatever the private undertaking, at home or abroad). Moreover, James was happy to oblige the company because it served the Crown's purposes while not putting the monarchy at any financial risk. From the beginning, the Crown, not Parliament, was involved in overseas expansion and therefore reluctant to extend itself financially to support such endeavors. The Stuarts knew Parliament would not be willing to come to their monetary rescue if such ventures failed. Colonization also appealed to the monarchy because it provided another potential source of royal revenue via taxation and duties levied on trade. National pride also motivated the king, for James did not want England to be excluded from the race for empire in the New World, allowing Britain's rivals to have such an advantage. Finally, James and his heirs hoped the establishment of colonies would help relieve England of potential social, religious, and political problems by providing "a dumping ground" for indigents, criminals, and religious dissenters. For these reasons, James and later Stuart monarchs were willing to grant charters and concessions to individuals and companies who risked their funds in the New World. Ultimately, private enterprise founded England's first twelve North American colonies, and all its West Indian island colonies except Jamaica.

With charter in hand by late 1606, the London Company assembled 144 men to send to North America. However, the Company unwisely failed to recruit enough of the proper settlers—skilled artisans, craftsmen, and experienced farmers. Instead, the majority of settlers on board the three ships—the *Susan Constant*, *Discovery*, and *Godspeed*—were members of the aristocracy or gentry with no skills or experience in wilderness living. They simply paid for their ticket to the New World to experience an adventure—a "grand tour" of North America, similar to what their fathers would do in Europe as part of providing a "gentleman's education." An enterprise composed of such individuals was destined to suffer, if not fail completely.

Only 104 Englishmen survived the journey. After a few weeks of scouting, the reconnaissance party decided on a marshy island in the lower Chesapeake on which to establish their colony, named **Jamestown** in honor of their benefactor, King James I. Though adequate for defense, the settlers chose a poor overall site. The area was low and swampy, perfect conditions for outbreaks of malaria. Surrounded by thick woods, the cultivation of land proved difficult. Moreover, the location bordered the territories of powerful local Indians. The result could not have been more calamitous. Compounding the attempt to survive in the harsh environment, the settlers also had to endure relentless pressure from the London Company to make Jamestown a habitable and profitable colony. Indeed, company demands all but set the colonists up for certain failure. The council maintained that the settlers' primary responsibility involved turning a quick profit for the company's investors. Thus, the colonists had no real incentive to make Jamestown a long-term success for themselves because they simply worked to advance the interests of their absentee stockholders. Since the land was not theirs, and they were not allowed to own any private property, they saw no reason to cultivate the soil, even for their own sustenance. Moreover, since the majority of settlers were "gentlemen," the idea of working to survive rarely entered their minds. Indeed, of the original 104 colonists only ten were skilled artisans.

With few carpenters, blacksmiths, and masons among the original settlers, the situation proved disastrous for both the stockholders and the colonists; the former lost their profits, the latter their lives. The Englishmen spent too much of their time looking for instant wealth, such as gold, which both the settlers and the Virginia Company organizers believed existed in Virginia based solely on the wealth found by the Spanish in Mexico and Peru. When the colonists realized there was no gold in Virginia, they turned their efforts toward exporting lumber, pitch, tar, and iron ore, but these were not the types of commodities that the company wanted from the colony. These products could be fabricated in England or imported more cheaply from other European countries. As a result of such endeavors, the settlers failed to establish any type of community that could sustain itself by producing necessary provisions, such as their own food sources, forcing them to rely on trade with their Native American neighbors to survive. Despite Indian help, some died from diet-related illnesses, as the English were unaccustomed to the native food provided. Many others died from malaria and other sicknesses. After six months, only 53 of the original 104 settlers had survived; by January 1608, when ships appeared with additional men and supplies, all but 38 colonists had died.

At this juncture, with Jamestown on the verge of extinction, a 27-year-old soldier of fortune and famous world traveler, Captain **John Smith**, took charge of the colony. Thanks to his efforts, the settlement survived, allowing England eventually to have an empire in North America. There is a good possibility that such preeminence would not have occurred if John Smith did not emerge to take charge. Had Jamestown failed, it is uncertain how long it would have taken the English to rebound and try again. In the interval, other European powers might have gobbled up the rest of North America, leaving Americans today to be speakers of French or Spanish instead of English. Indeed, England owed a great debt of gratitude to Smith, for he saved their future empire.

When Smith took control of Jamestown, he immediately imposed a harsh regime of work and order on the community. He also made contact with the 20,000 Algonquian-speaking natives living in the area, establishing an uneasy but mutually beneficial trade relationship that lasted for several years. **Powhatan**, leader of the Algonquian Confederacy, had mixed feelings towards the English. He already had suffered at the hands of the Spanish, who earlier had attempted to establish an outpost nearby only to bring conflict and disease, killing hundreds of his people. However, Powhatan hoped that the English would be different and that the Algonquians could establish an effective trading partnership that would benefit both parties. He found a willing Englishman in Smith. Powhatan also hoped to use the English as an ally against rival tribes, helping the chief to subjugate them, thus furthering his dominion in the Chesapeake area. Powhatan hoped to accomplish such objectives by simply providing the colonists with food, thus making them dependent upon his largesse for their survival. When Smith seized control, he was aware of Powhatan's stratagem but had little choice other than to accept the chief's "generosity." By 1609, however, Smith and his men came to resent being at the mercy of a "savage" and began organizing raids on nearby Indian villages, stealing food and kidnapping natives either for ransom or to sell into slavery. Powhatan responded to Smith's raids by cutting off the settlers' food supplies and killing off the livestock recently brought over by another 300 newly-arrived colonists. Smith returned to England in the summer of 1609 after being wounded in a gunpowder accident. During his brief tenure as colony leader, fewer than a dozen colonists in a population of about 200 had died. Nevertheless, the majority of the colonists were glad to see Smith leave, for they resented his forced discipline and rigid behavior. Despite the presence of fresh colonists and a new leader, Jamestown's ordeal was not yet over.

Powhatan's reprisals kept the colonists barricaded within their palisade. Cut off from their food supply, the settlers lived off what they could find within their fortress: "dogs, cats, rats, toadstools, horsehides," and even the "corpses of dead men," as one survivor recalled. The winter of 1609-1610 became known as the "**starving time**" in the settlement, as 440 out of 500 colonists perished from starvation. In May 1610, a ship bound for the colony during the previous spring but had run aground in Bermuda finally arrived. Seeing the pitiful condition of the settlers, the crew took the 60 emaciated survivors onto their vessel, abandoned the settlement, and sailed for England. However, as the refugees proceeded down the James, they met another ship coming up the river, bringing fresh folk, ample provisions, and the colony's first governor, Lord De La Warr (Delaware). The departing colonists agreed to return to Jamestown. New relief expeditions with hundreds of colonists soon began to arrive, and the effort to find a profitable venture in Jamestown resumed.

**Print depicting Captain John Smith with Pocahontas leaning over him, preventing Opechancanough from striking him with a metal weapon.
Powhatan is standing directly behind Smith with his hand raised to stay the execution.**

SUCCESS AT LAST:
The Tobacco Boom

Under the leadership of its first governors—De La Warr and later Sir Thomas Dale—Virginia not only survived but expanded and eventually prospered, though too late to save the Virginia Company. Both De La Warr and Dale imposed strict order on the colony, at times making Smith's regimen seem like a vacation. Indeed, Dale went so far as to march the inhabitants off to work to the beat of a drum. Both men also sent military expeditions against the local Indian tribes in order to protect the new settlements, which began lining the river above and below Jamestown. In the process, Dale kidnapped Powhatan's young daughter Pocahontas. Several years earlier, Pocahontas had played a role in mediating differences between her people and the English and, according to John Smith's autobiography, intervened with her father to save Smith's life after his capture during a foraging expedition. Powhatan refused to pay Dale's ransom for her return. Thus, Pocahontas began to live among the English, eventually adapting many of their ways including conversion to Christianity. In 1614, she married John Rolfe and traveled with him to England. When Rolfe arrived in England with a "native" wife who spoke English and had become a Christian, the couple no doubt raised many eyebrows of both disdain and fascination. Those captivated by her graciousness believed Pocahontas was testimony that Native Americans could indeed become "civilized." (She died of an illness shortly before her return to Virginia.) Although both governors promoted and secured expansion while continuing to stabilize the colony, Jamestown had yet to turn the profit long desired by the Virginia Company and its shareholders. However, a series of events combined to turn this barely functioning outpost into the first step in the founding of an empire. The colonists' cultivation of tobacco as a marketable cash crop proved to be the most important factor in saving Virginia, and perhaps, the English presence in North America.

The wedding of Pocahontas with John Rolfe. 1614

Painting of Pocahontas while in England.

Europeans had become aware of tobacco soon after Christopher Columbus' return from his first voyage to the New World. On the island of Cuba, Columbus first saw natives smoking small cigars (*tabacos*), which they inserted in the nostril. Over the next century, the smoking of tobacco in pipes, as cigars, or consumed by inhalation as snuff became one of the most popular crazes to hit the European continent, especially among the upper classes. Those providing the "jovial weed" (as Sir Francis Drake referred to tobacco) realized substantial profits from growing and curing the plant's leaves. Before cultivation in Virginia, Englishmen imported their tobacco from the Spanish West Indian colonies, thus enriching one of England's most bitter adversaries. However, in 1612, John Rolfe developed a hybrid form of tobacco by crossing an imported West Indian strain with a local variety. Rolfe and others quickly discovered the Chesapeake area's climate and soil was perfectly suited for tobacco cultivation. As more Virginians engaged in tobacco planting, territorial expansion occurred commensurately. Because tobacco exhausted the soil very quickly, growers needed large areas of land upon which to grow their profitable crops, thus the demand for land increased rapidly. As a result, English planters began pushing deeper into the Virginia interior, isolating themselves from Jamestown, while penetrating farther into Native American domain.

Virginia tobacco planters shipped their first cargo to England in 1617, finding it fetched a high price in the London market, three shillings per pound. By the time of the first shipment, many in English society considered the smoking of tobacco a "sinful indulgence," which only added to its growing popularity. Even James I's condemnation of tobacco smoking as "loathsome to the eye, hateful to the nose, harmful to the brain, and dangerous to the lungs," could not prevent Englishmen from smoking. James's detesting of smoking was so great that he even tried to persuade Parliament to ban the weed's importation, but to no avail. Smoking had become too popular of a vice and pastime in English society to prohibit. Moreover, the Virginia Company successfully lobbied Parliament to prevent such an act by convincing its members that a ban on tobacco importation would bring about Virginia's financial ruin.

Thanks to tobacco, Virginia could now sustain itself as the colony established its financial viability. Cultivation had taken off and grew like the weed itself. The tobacco craze became so great in Virginia that colonists were even planting it in the streets and marketplace of Jamestown. In 1618, they planted more tobacco than corn and other food sources. By that same year, Virginia tobacco had captured the English market, with exports to England reaching over 50,000 pounds. In 1624, exports had reached 200,000 pounds; and by 1638, over three million pounds of the jovial weed had been shipped to England. Tobacco became to Virginia what sugar meant to the economy of the West Indies and silver to Mexico and Peru. In London, men joked that Virginia was built on smoke. Suffice it to say, tobacco transformed the colony economically and socially almost overnight into a different sort of venture than originally envisioned by the Virginia Company.

Tobacco and the Changing Nature of Virginia Society and Labor

Tobacco growing in the Chesapeake was an extremely labor-intensive process. A planter first had to clear the field of trees, often only girdling them and cultivating amid the dead trunks. Then, separate from the main fields, a rich bed had to be prepared for the tobacco seeds, taking care to protect the tender plants once they sprouted from the frost by covering them with cloths or leaves. Using a heavy hoe, the grower cultivated the actual fields, mounding the soil into small hills arranged in rows. When the weather was warm enough (usually in late spring or early summer), the slips from the seedbed were transplanted to the hills. Fields then had to be vigilantly maintained, especially to prevent weeds from taking over, or worse, infestation by tobacco worms—green-horned little monsters with voracious appetites, which had to be regularly picked off the maturing tobacco plants. Secondary shoots called "suckers," which grew from the base of the stalks, had to be cut away to keep them from stealing nutrients from the parent plant. Toward the end of the summer (usually late August), the full-grown stalks were cut and hauled to curing barns to be dried. Upon curing, the leaves were picked off and carefully packed into wooden barrels called hogsheads, which could weigh over 500 pounds when fully loaded. The whole process took approximately ten months, with each step requiring tedious labor and exact timing. If off schedule by a few weeks, or even days, the crop could be completely ruined in terms of both quality and quantity. Tobacco cultivation placed a premium on both menial labor and experience. Understanding the role their skill played in producing a profitable crop, successful planters grew in self-confidence and optimism, increasingly sure of their ability to make sound managerial decisions.

The success of tobacco cultivation led to increasing demands for labor. In the first decades of the tobacco craze, the Virginia Company attracted new workers to the colony by establishing what was called the "**headright**" system. Since the company had more land than money, it offered land as dividends to its stockholders. Headrights were fifty-acre land grants given to each individual who came from England to establish a tobacco farm. Those who already lived in the colony received two headrights if they planted tobacco. This system was especially designed to attract family groups to migrate together, for the more family members who came, the more land that the family would receive. In addition, anyone who paid for the passage of immigrants to Virginia would receive an extra headright for each arrival, providing an incentive to the already established planters to import new laborers. Over several years, as a result of the headright initiative, some colonists were able to amass thousands of acres of land. Indeed, two of colonial Virginia's most legendary families, the Carters and Byrds, whose ancestors came to Virginia at this time, eventually owned over 400,000 acres and several plantations by the end of the colonial era in the 1770s. In initiating the headright system, the Virginia Company made an important step in the direction of private enterprise, away from the corporate company-directed economy of the early years.

The Virginia Company also realized the importance of economic diversification and greater colonial self-sufficiency, as shown by the sending to Virginia of ironworkers and other skilled craftsmen to provide tobacco farmers with small manufactured items they needed to sustain the tobacco boom. To keep those workers from returning to England after making money from tobacco, the company sent over 100 English women to Virginia (which was still overwhelmingly male) in 1619 to become the wives of the male colonists. Perhaps the most important incentive that the company offered to keep settlers in Virginia was to end the strict and arbitrary rule imposed by De La Warr and Dale. English common law replaced martial law, guaranteeing all male colonists the full rights of Englishmen. The Virginia Company (much to the English government's subsequent dismay) even allowed the colonists greater rights to self-government than were enjoyed by those living in England. In 1619, the company granted the colonists the right to form a legislative assembly, the **House of Burgesses**—a representative body to be elected by every free adult male colonist. The colony's government now consisted of a governor (appointed by the company), six counselors chosen from the House's members, and twenty-two elected delegates from the colony's various communities. On July 30, 1619, the House of Burgesses assembled for the first time in Jamestown, marking the first meeting in the New World of an elected representative government.

The Virginia Company's concessions attracted 3,500 new settlers to the colony in three years, triple the number who had come in the previous ten years. By the beginning of the 1620s, the Virginia Company, by coincidence more than planning, discovered the formula for establishing a successful colonial enterprise. Indeed, Virginia became a model that all the other colonies would generally follow, offering colonists opportunities to make money and greater political freedoms and rights than they enjoyed at home. These changes came too late, however, to save the Virginia Company from bankruptcy. Although earning substantial profits from tobacco by the 1620s, the many years of having to financially sustain the colony while it struggled through hard times, including protracted Indian wars and an extremely high death rate from disease, proved too much to overcome. In 1624, James I dissolved the company and declared Virginia to be a royal colony, directly under the Crown's control. At this juncture, James also should have disbanded the House of Burgesses, which would have made it clear to the colonists that their true government was located in England. By retaining the House, James and his heirs invited disaster for England. In refusing to dismiss the Burgesses, James allowed the colonists to believe they had been granted the right to self-government, something they had originally received from the Virginia Company, not the Crown." Since the company no longer existed and the colony now came under royal control, James could have easily abolished the company's concession and simply reestablished a more arbitrary form of government directly under a crown-appointed royal governor.

Over time, the colonists grew strongly attached to their colonial assemblies. In the process, they came to believe that from the beginning (Jamestown) they had been granted the right to have such institutions. Such was never the case, but simply assumed. Neither the Crown nor Parliament effectively established their political hegemony over the colonies, allowing the colonies to develop with Americans under the illusion that they had the right to self-government, assuming that any attempt to take away that right would be met with determined resistance. This became the critical issue between the colonists and the British government, leading eventually to the American Revolution. After the French and Indian War, when a financially desperate England needed to more effectively control the colonists, Parliament threatened the colonists with the most serious of reprisals if they did not comply with the new order: the dissolution of their respective colonial assemblies, which by the 1760s the colonists regarded as sacrosanct institutions, bastions of representative government, and the protectors of their individual and collective liberties. Sadly for England, James possessed neither the interest nor the personal longsighted wisdom to have realized such a portent. At the time, all he cared about was the Crown's share of tobacco revenue that he received in lieu of that money going to the Virginia Company. James's shortsightedness in 1624 eventually cost England an empire in North America.

TOWARD THE DESTRUCTION OF THE NATIVE AMERICANS

The English discovery of tobacco dramatically and rapidly changed the relationship between the Chesapeake Algonquians and the English settlers; indeed the dynamic had completely reversed by the early 1620s. As the tobacco craze began to encroach on Indian farmland, "trespassing" occurred on both sides of the James River and further up its tributaries, deeper into Native American territory. Moreover, at the same time, the various Algonquian tribes became increasingly dependent on English trade goods, especially metal tools. Perhaps most impactful for the tribes was the loss of their most important trade item: food, which the English now grew for themselves, breaking their dependence on the Indians for their sustenance. Having lost their once dominant position in the exchange, the Native Americans became more dependent on the English for certain commodities and thus more vulnerable to English reprisals and depredations.

Such was the situation confronting the tribes at the time of Powhatan's death. His more militant brother, **Opechancanough**, succeeded him as chief and was filled with a determination to rid the Chesapeake of the English intruders. On the morning of March 22, 1622, tribesmen entered the white settlements as if to offer goods for sale. Suddenly, they attacked, eventually striking all the plantations along the James River. Over the course of several days, they killed 347 whites (about one-third of the colonists), including John Rolfe. The reason for the uprising was revenge for the English murder of Nemattanew, one of Powhatan's war captains and religious prophet who had resisted arrest under suspicion of involvement in the disappearance of an English settler. The devastating attack bankrupted the Virginia Company. The second Anglo-Powhatan War lasted for ten years and marked the turning point in English-Native American relations. Although some white Virginians admitted that they had provoked the uprising by "our own perfidious dealing," the majority of the surviving colonists concluded that the tribes could not be trusted nor converted to the English way of life. Thus began the process of extermination of the Native Americans in North America. Indeed, John Smith was euphoric when he heard the news of the attacks, for he had long believed that the tribes had to be eliminated from the area if the colony was to progress. "It will be good for the Plantation," Smith declared of the massacre, "because we now have just cause to destroy them by all meanes [sic] necessary." Bolstered by instructions from the Virginia Company to "root out [the Indians] from being any longer a people," the Virginians conducted ruthless annual military expeditions against the native villages west and north of the settled areas. In most instances, the English attacked and killed tribes that had nothing to do with the original 1622 assault on the plantations. Prior to the insurrection, the English were careful only to plant tobacco on the Indians' unused farmland. They now seized territory regardless of Indian ownership. In only 15 years' time, the English and Native Americans in Virginia had become implacable enemies.

With the tobacco economy booming as settlers continued to pour into the colony, plantations continued to spread across the Chesapeake to the Eastern Shore as far north as the Potomac. By the early 1640s, the English had made it clear to the Native Americans that they had become obstacles to be removed from the path of settlement. The aged Opechancanough (believed to be in his nineties) determined one last time to save his people from annihilation, struck again on April 18, 1644, killing 400 English settlers and taking many prisoners. Thus began the Third Anglo-Powhatan War. Uneasy truces were established in the aftermath of the first two conflicts, with

Print depicting Lord Calvert's presentation of the 1649 Act of Toleration establishing civil and religious liberty in Maryland.

the tribes still tenuously holding on to their lands. The third war ended, however, with the Indians' total defeat two years later. English firepower and general ruthlessness, if not outright savagery and butchery, proved too much for the tribes to resist. The Indians had fought to punish the English for their transgressions, not to wipe them out. By contrast, the English went to war to annihilate the Native Americans. During the third war, Opechancanough was captured and killed. The English took complete possession of the land between the James and York Rivers. Henceforth, no Indian could enter this area without wearing a special jacket signifying he was merely bringing a message from the chief. Any English person found providing refuge for a Native American was executed. The land north of the York River was considered to be "Indian territory," making that region the first Native American reservation. However, given the settlers' perpetual need for fresh acreage because tobacco quickly exhausted the soil (usually completely depleted after five years of cultivation), the English moved into that area as well. It would not be the last time that English colonists violated a treaty with the Indians.

PROPRIETARY MARYLAND

By the time Virginia had achieved commercial success in the 1630s, the English had established another colony on the Chesapeake—the proprietary enterprise called Maryland, named in honor of Charles I's Catholic queen, Henrietta Maria. The owner or proprietor of Maryland was an English nobleman, **George Calvert**, honored by James I with a peerage, Lord Baltimore. Calvert was a Catholic, thus a *persona non grata* among the devoutly-Anglican majority of the English aristocracy, but not to the sympathetic Stuart court. In 1628, he received from Charles I, son of James I (who died in 1624), a huge land grant in Newfoundland to serve as a sanctuary for English Catholics. Although not physically persecuted any longer, Catholics nonetheless could not practice their faith openly and were generally a disenfranchised people. Calvert, however, did not find Newfoundland very inviting and convinced Charles I to grant him a more hospitable domain, 10 million acres in what became the colony of Maryland. The charter given to the Calvert family was remarkable not only for the extent of territory granted—an area that encompassed parts of what is now Pennsylvania, Delaware, and Virginia, in addition to present-day Maryland—but also for the powers given to the Calverts who would have true and absolute control over the province for as long as they desired to keep their "gift" from the king. Their only obligation to the Crown was to pay an annual fee. The only other North American proprietor to receive a more generous grant than Baltimore proved to be William Penn. Baltimore found the king's offer much more to his liking and thus Maryland became the first proprietary colony, that is, one owned by an individual and his heirs. As noted earlier, Virginia was originally a charter colony held by a group of private shareholders. Unlike royal colonies, both in charter and proprietary enterprises, financing and management became the sole responsibilities of either the proprietor or shareholders. George Calvert, the first Lord Baltimore, died in 1632 but his son, Cecilius, the second Lord Baltimore, continued his father's efforts.

Cecilius Calvert appointed his brother Leonard to serve as the colony's first governor. In March 1634, two ships—the *Ark* and the *Dove*—carrying Leonard Calvert and about 300 other colonists, entered the Potomac River, turned up into one of its eastern tributaries, and established the settlement of St. Mary's on a high, dry bluff. Fortunately for the settlers, the surrounding Native American tribes, once part of Powhatan's confederacy, had no desire to engage in warfare with these latest English arrivals. Indeed, the Indians befriended the colonists, providing them with temporary food and shelter. Unlike their Virginia counterparts, the early Marylanders experienced no Indian assaults, no plagues, and no starving time. In order for Maryland to survive economically, the Calverts needed to attract settlers as quickly as possible. Although they established the colony as a refuge for Catholics, the Calverts had no choice but to also allow Protestants to immigrate to Maryland. However, much to their disappointment, few of their Catholic brethren came to their safe haven. Meanwhile, plenty of Protestants found Maryland to their liking. Realizing that Catholics would always be a minority in the colony, they wisely adopted a policy of religious acceptance of all Christian denominations. This policy became law in Maryland with the passage of the **1649 Act of Toleration**, guaranteeing civil and religious liberty to all Christians. Maryland soon became one of the most religiously tolerant places in the world at that time.

Although granted extensive powers ranging from dispensing land to making laws, Cecilius Calvert was no autocrat, perhaps because he knew he would have to compete for settlers with Virginia, which already had a representative government. Thus he wisely agreed in 1635 for the creation of a representative assembly—the **House of Delegates**—patterned after both Parliament and the Virginia House of Burgesses. Calvert relinquished much of his political power and prerogatives, particularly exclusive law-making rights, to the assembly but retained absolute authority to distribute land as he wished. Initially, he granted large estates to his relatives and other English aristocrats, both Catholic and Protestant. Baltimore envisioned transforming Maryland into a replication of England's manor-dotted countryside, with huge estates owned by the gentry and the land worked by peasant-like tenants. For a few years, Baltimore's vision appeared to becoming a reality. By 1640, however, fewer family members and English gentry were willing to come to Maryland. Moreover, a severe labor shortage had developed in the colony, forcing Calvert to modify his original plan. Like Virginia, Maryland adopted the headright system—a grant of 100 acres to each male settler, another 100 acres for his wife and each servant brought over, and 50 acres for each of his children. Despite such generosity, by 1650, a distinct upper class of primarily large landholding Catholics had emerged, maintaining power even as the commoner population grew larger and more diverse. Like Virginia, Maryland became a center of tobacco cultivation. Planters worked their land, first with the labor of indentured servants imported from England and then, beginning in the late seventeenth century, with slaves imported from Africa. Although decades transpired before Maryland's population increased substantially (in 1650, its population only reached 600), the familiar political economy emerged early. As in Virginia, attracting colonists required greater opportunities and freedoms than they had in England. Lord Baltimore recognized this reality early on and thus granted these concessions. Unlike their Virginia counterparts, Marylanders maintained generally peaceful relations with the local Native American tribes up through the 1670s. However, despite Baltimore's discernment, Maryland politics remained plagued for years by tensions, and, at times, violence between the Catholic minority and the Protestant majority.

The ongoing rancor and acrimony between the Calverts and their minority Catholic following (about one-fifth of the overall population) on the one hand and the majority Protestant tobacco planters and other settlers on the other, finally escalated into open rebellion in 1689. In that year, the third Lord Baltimore (Charles Calvert), who apparently was not as conciliatory toward the Protestants as his father had been, nor as inclined to make further political concessions to the House of Delegates, decided it was time for his family to assert their full rights and powers as the true and absolute proprietors of Maryland. Such a decision proved disastrous for the Calverts, for it was much too late in the colony's political and religious development to assume such prerogatives. Exacerbating tensions was the decline in tobacco, which planters looked to Baltimore to help remedy by lowering export duties, revenue which still went directly to the proprietor, not the Crown. The colony's best land also remained in Catholic hands and much of it lay fallow as if the Calverts and their Catholic associates still hoped to transform the Maryland landscape into a land dotted with beautiful but non-productive English manors. Protestant planters protested Baltimore's high-handed measures and attitude, and the proprietor responded by imposing a property qualification for voting and appointed increasingly dictatorial governors. According to the Anglican Reverend John Yeo, the Catholic minority in the colony openly disparaged the Church of England. Even Quakers, who Anglicans and other Protestant sects had long despised, were allowed greater religious freedom and protection. Naturally, Yeo accused the Catholic minority of all manner of moral laxity, looking the other way if not condoning debauched and dissipated behavior. "The province of Maryland is in a deplorable condition, for want of an established [Anglican] ministry. Here are ten or twelve counties, and in them at least twenty thousand souls, and but three Protestant ministers of the Church of England. The priests [Catholic] are provided for; the Quakers take care of those that are speakers; but no care is taken to build churches in the Protestant [Anglican] religion. The Lord's day is profaned; religion is despised and all notorious vices are committed; so that it is become a Sodom of uncleanness and a pest-house of iniquity."

When news of the Glorious Revolution, which deposed the Catholic James II (to be discussed in greater depth in the next chapter), reached Maryland in 1689, a group of disgruntled dissidents, led by a former Anglican minister turned militia officer, John Coode, took over the government, proclaimed loyalty to the new Protestant monarchy of William and Mary, getting the new king and queen to revoke Baltimore's proprietorship, and transforming Maryland into a royal colony in 1691. In 1702 Anglicanism became the colony's official faith to which all were required to support financially through the payment of tithes. Religious toleration was still in effect but only for Protestants. Catholics no longer controlled the colony in any capacity. Once again, they became *personae non gratae* even in their former refuge. Coode's Rebellion brought an end to Maryland's experiment with religious toleration.

THE CARIBBEAN COLONIES

Throughout the first half of the seventeenth century, the Caribbean islands and the Atlantic way station of Bermuda rather than the colonies of the Chesapeake Bay region and New England served as the main destinations for English immigrants to the New World. These Caribbean societies, mostly colonized before their North American counterparts, developed close ties with England's mainland settlements, particularly influencing their socio-economic orientations and trading patterns.

Prior to the Europeans' arrival in the late fifteenth century, substantial native populations lived on many of the Caribbean islands. Beginning with Columbus' arrival in 1492 and accelerating after 1496 when the Spanish established their first permanent colony on Hispaniola, however, diseases brought by Europeans decimated the Amerindian population. The Spanish sought only to colonize the largest Caribbean islands—Cuba, Hispaniola, Jamaica, and Puerto Rico, leaving the area's smaller islands available even though the Spanish had claimed the entire West Indies. By the early sixteenth century, English, French, and Dutch settlers occupied many of these smaller islands, though the fledgling colonies were always vulnerable to Spanish attack. In 1621, the West Indies' geopolitics changed as the result of war between Spain and the Netherlands. With the Spanish thus distracted, the English and the French began to pursue Caribbean colonization more aggressively without fear of reprisals. By the 1650s, the English had established several important settlements, most notably on Antigua, St. Kitts, Barbados, and Jamaica (with the latter seized by Admiral William Penn, father of the future proprietor of Pennsylvania).

The English colonists initially tried cotton and tobacco cultivation on these islands, but for a variety reasons they could not sustain profitable production levels. Soon enough, however, they found sugar to be their most lucrative cash crop due to a combination of soil fertility and a substantial and growing European market. Sugar cultivation was extremely labor-intensive. Because European diseases had ravaged the native population, English sugar planters at first found it necessary to import indentured servants from the homeland. The arduous work and the tropical climate, however, proved too much for these white laborers, most of whom died within months after their arrival. Thus, rather rapidly, English West Indies sugar planters, like their Spanish counterparts, began importing Africans as slaves to work their plantations. Soon, African slaves outnumbered whites on the English-held islands by a margin of four to one. Those Englishmen who came to the islands quickly evolved into a tough, aggressive, and ambitious breed. Some became enormously wealthy from sugar. Because the planters' livelihoods depended on their workforce, they quickly put in place one of the harshest, cruelest, and rigid slave systems found anywhere in the New World.

Masters and Slaves

Because African slaves dominated the population of the English sugar islands, whites lived in constant fear of slave rebellion. They thus imposed on their bondsmen a brutal regimen—laws and practices that ensured complete control over their black laborers. As a result, the English

42 / CHAPTER TWO

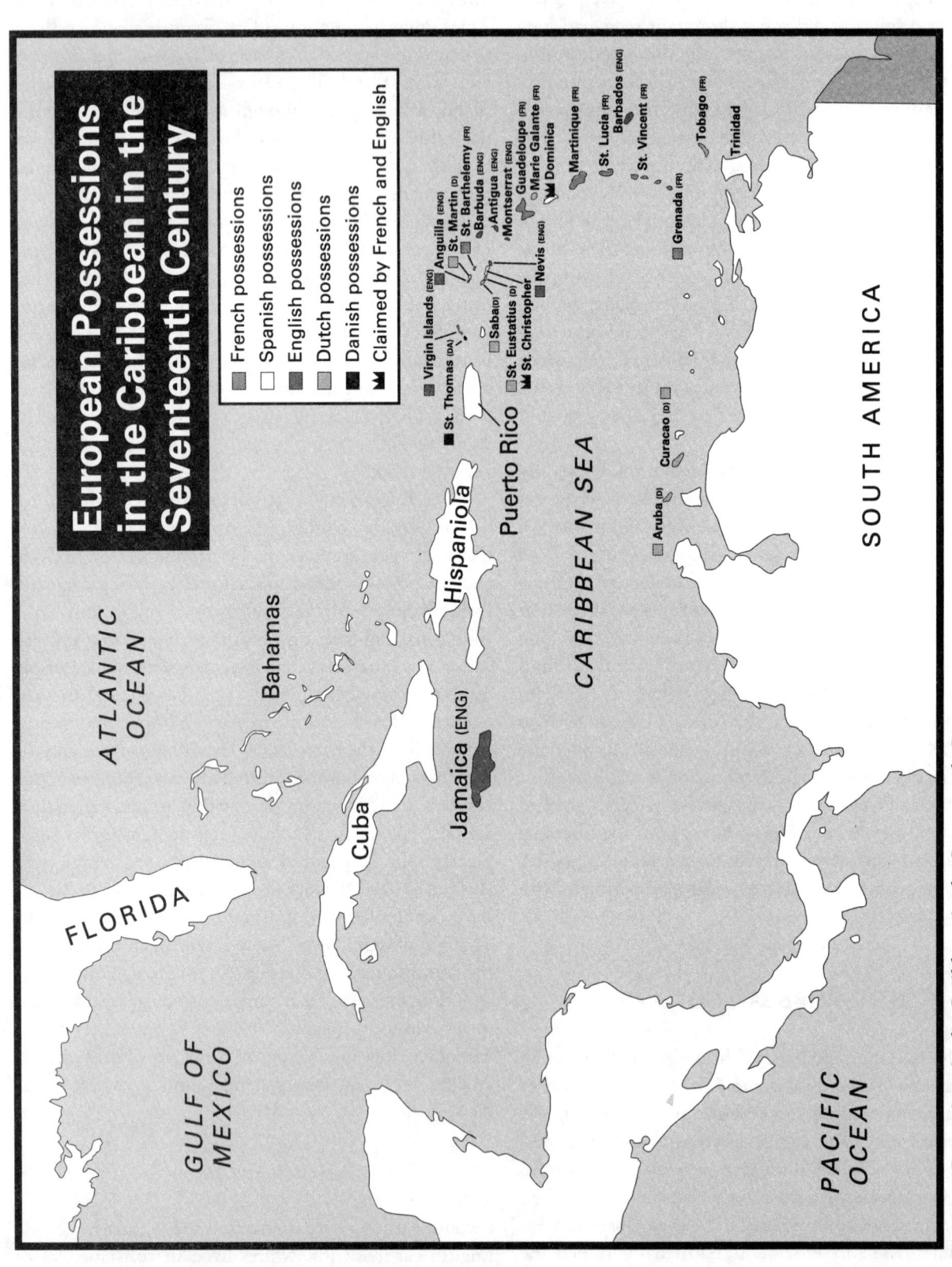

Map 2.2 European Possessions in the Caribbean in the Seventeenth Century

Slaves on a tobacco plantation in Jamaica.

planter elite treated their slaves with little regard for their physical or mental well being. Due to sugar's high profitability, many planters concluded it was cheaper to import more slaves than to take better care of the ones they already owned. Thus, many Englishmen became notorious for literally working their slaves to death. On some plantations, the average life expectancy for slaves was no more than three years after their arrival. Few African workers survived more than a decade in this callous work environment.

Establishing a stable society and culture in such severe, even deadly conditions proved to be extremely difficult. Most of the planter elite were only interested in making quick fortunes in sugar before returning to England as wealthy men. With no long-term commitment to the islands, those who repatriated to England left overseers to manage their estates. These supervisors often dominated the lands in a brutal fashion because they had been instructed by their employer to squeeze as much profit from sugar cultivation as possible. Many overseers received a percentage of the profits as an incentive, providing a reward which resulted in slaves often dying from the effects of overwork. A large proportion of the European settlers either died or left at a young age, leaving the white population a distinct and permanent minority on the islands. Consequently, European society in the West Indies became very transient, dictated and controlled by sugar production and maintained by a rigid slave system. Few social institutions common to the North American mainland settlements, such as churches, families, and stable communities, existed there.

Despite their brutal treatment and low life expectancy, African slaves managed to create communities and cultures of their own. They started families (although many were broken up by death or the slave trade), sustained African religions and social traditions (while resisting Christianity) and, within the rigidly controlled world of the sugar plantations, established patterns of resistance. As the North American settlements developed, the ties between the English West Indies and the mainland grew, becoming part of the Atlantic trading network in which many American colonists participated and profited. Eventually, the mainland tobacco and rice planters turned to African slavery to solve their labor needs, making the Caribbean islands their main suppliers of African bondsmen. Because their West Indian brethren had adopted slavery much earlier, southern planters looked to their Caribbean counterparts to provide models of a successful slave system to be replicated in North America.

TOWARD AFRICAN SLAVERY:
White Indentured Servitude in the Chesapeake

Four factors shaped Chesapeake society in the first half of the seventeenth century: the tobacco market, the availability of land, the demand for labor, and weak government. Neither Virginia's royal governor nor his proprietary-appointed counterpart in Maryland had any real political control in their respective colonies. A wealthy planter oligarchy emerged in both settlements to wield the real power. Motivated by profit, they operated without restraint while the rest of the colonists were forced to survive as best they could with little redress of their grievances from the planter elite. As planters profited greatly, those unable to acquire sufficient land to engage in tobacco cultivation or the requisite skills for such enterprise lived a marginal existence of despair and poverty. Artificial distinctions such as social status counted for little in comparison to willpower, physical strength, and ruthlessness. In this environment, the political economy of slavery took root.

The growing and selling of tobacco affected nearly every aspect of life in the Chesapeake region. Tobacco required much human effort to grow, and planters had to devise a labor system to provide and control the essential work force. For the first four decades of intense tobacco cultivation, Chesapeake planters used white indentured servants from England. These workers made possible the tobacco boom of the mid-seventeenth century that finally proved the area had a viable economic future. However, **indentured servitude** (a system in which those seeking passage to North America sold up to seven years of unpaid labor to pay for transportation costs) had inherent flaws as a labor system. Over time, serious socio-political tensions in Virginia arose between freedmen (ex-indentured servants) and the planter elite, escalating by the mid-1670s into one of the most devastating rebellions to occur in American colonial history—**Bacon's Rebellion**. As a result of that insurrection, Chesapeake planters began shifting to African slaves to solve their labor issues. By 1700, black slaves came to dominate the labor market, changing forever the South's future.

The Chesapeake tobacco boom produced an incessant demand for labor, which the colonial English population could not provide, for it had not grown rapidly enough to meet labor demands. With disease and warfare reducing their numbers rapidly, Native Americans provided no ready source of labor. Although aware of slavery, including African and Indian bondage, Chesapeake planters associated slavery with backward Mediterranean and Catholic societies like Spain and were determined not to succumb to such inhuman practices, even though their Caribbean brethren were already well on their way to utilizing human bondage. Moreover, no need yet existed to ponder the possibility of slavery because England supplied planters with an adequate labor supply. Sustained population growth and an agricultural revolution (the enclosure movement) that had forced hundreds of thousands of English peasants off the manors, had created a surplus population that the planters could employ on their Chesapeake estates. Thousands of such individuals had migrated to England's burgeoning cities searching for work, but few of them had the requisite skills to be reabsorbed into the urban workplace. They were an agricultural people equipped to work only the land. Thus, thousands of young men and women believed several years of labor in the Chesapeake to be an acceptable hardship to bear in order to obtain their own land and a chance to make a better life. The lack of economic opportunity in England proved severe enough to cause young workers to leave the world they knew and risk disease, overwork, potential abuse, and perhaps death in a strange new place.

From 1630 to 1680, approximately 75,000 people migrated to the Chesapeake to start a new life. Three-fourths of them came as indentured servants—individuals and families who had their transportation paid for by a Virginia or Maryland planter. In return for passage, they became the "indenture" of that particular landowner for an agreed upon number of years until the debt had been paid. The servant's age, gender, and skills often determined the number of years owed by the servant. Though legally guaranteed certain basic rights, the planter could set the laborer to work any task he chose until the cost of indenture had been paid off. Tobacco profits in these years were substantial enough that most planters could repay the cost of investment in a servant in two years or less.

For many indentured servants, life in the Chesapeake was worse than they could ever have imagined in England. Death from disease was endemic, with many dying within months of their arrival and a majority before fulfilling their contractual obligations. With many ruthless and unprincipled planters taking advantage of the workers, servants were often worked to death. Servants might be beaten so severely that they died, or find their contracts sold from one master to another. In England, custom and law provided servants with some basic protections, but in Virginia, they suffered brutal working conditions. Such was the existence of Richard Freethorne, a young servant who wrote to his parents in England that "I have nothing to comfort me, nor is there nothing to be gotten here but sickness and death. I have nothing at all—no, not a shirt to my back but two rags, nor clothes but one poor suit, nor but one pair of shoes, but one pair of stockings, but one cap." Freethorne begged his parents to send food: "We must work early and late for a mess of water gruel and a mouthful of bread and beef." Infernally hot and muggy summers and bone-chilling winters, poor food and water, unsanitary living conditions, and loss of contact with loved ones back in England led to an existence filled with loneliness, isolation, despair, all manner of illness, and death. The vastly uneven sex ratio (the majority of servants were young men and teenagers who outnumbered women by a ratio of 4-to-1 for the first two generations), aggravated by the lack of roads and resulting isolation, meant that many indentured servants, even after gaining their freedom, could never find a spouse and gain the comfort and sense of home that a marital partner and children could provide. This situation led to limited population growth, perpetuating the need to import servants to labor in the tobacco fields.

Before 1660, indentured servants who survived their obligation could expect upon gaining their freedom to purchase land, plant tobacco for themselves, and begin sharing in the prosperity of the tobacco boom. If they lived long enough after their servitude, they could even afford to buy the labor of new indentured servants and obtain additional headrights. With more land and tobacco profits, a former servant could begin to move up the social ladder. As long as land along the waterways (the tidewater regions) remained plentiful and cheap, it was still possible for some laborers to make the transition from servant to freeman to planter. Even those unable to rise to such status came to own small farms of modest homes with dirt floors and unglazed windows, but homes nonetheless on their own land—an existence few could have obtained back in England. The more prosperous planters importing indentured servants and acquiring more land were in the process of creating a gentry class separate from the masses of farmers. Service as a local justice of the peace or on the vestry reinforced their sense of community leadership and provided them with the reputation to solidify their status. The economic difference between the wealthy planters and the middling farmers was less than it would ever be again. This relative equality of social condition among Chesapeake whites, along with near universal involvement in a tobacco culture, eventually created a white solidarity that would shape southern society for three centuries.

Comparatively few white indentured servants attained such an existence in the Chesapeake. Most died before gaining their freedom. Of those who did survive, few had the skill, luck, good health, or ambition necessary to succeed. Because the tobacco economy fluctuated greatly, new freemen could not sustain themselves through the learning curve that tobacco cultivation required. The margin of error was tiny—one miscalculation or an unfortunate illness or a fire could ruin a beginning farmer. Once failed, few had the heart or desire to try again. To survive, many had no choice but to become a tenant farmer or wage laborer. Many such individuals and their families came to have an existence of almost unimaginable deprivation.

The Chesapeake of the mid-seventeenth century hardly fits the popular stereotype of the Colonial South, with magnificent brick mansions lining the James and York Rivers, their interiors filled with beautiful furniture and staffed with a retinue of black slaves. Not only were blacks few in number in 1650 (only about 1,000 in the entire Chesapeake at that time), but white planters lived far below what visitors to an eighteenth-century colonial mansions envision. Most so-called planters were in reality large farmers who lived in unpretentious houses or perhaps two ground-floor rooms sparsely furnished with furniture made by someone on the farm. The indentured servants slept in a large attic or in a lean-to attached to the main house, probably taking their meals with the planter and his wife. On smaller farms, women performed very little field work, even if they were indentured servants. On larger plantations, white servant women labored in the fields. Most women, however, devoted the bulk of their time and energy to gathering, washing, and preparing vegetables and fruits for meals. A farmer's wife may have spent as much as two hours a day grinding corn with a pestle and mortar to make meal. Often cider was brewed, and dairying—milking the cows, churning the butter, making cheese—took hours. Men usually slaughtered the hogs and beeves, but women finished the process by rubbing the meat with salt, then smoking the pork in the chimney, and pickling the beef in barrels of brine. Laundry and housecleaning were also strenuous tasks, though seventeenth-century ideas of cleanliness would be considered appalling by today's standards. The making and mending of clothes occupied most evenings. The farmer's wife supervised the servant girl, if there was one, but performed most household chores herself. Certainly the farmer himself supervised the field work of male servants, but he also worked in the field beside them. Homes were small, usually consisting of one 16x20 foot room, with practically no furniture except a table—no chairs, few dishes, and a mattress of sorts lain on the floor serving as a bed. Creature comforts were far less and certainly more spartan in the mid-seventeenth-century Chesapeake than poor farmers had back in England. In short, many indentured servants served their time only to find that scarcity of cheap land deprived them of the upward mobility for which they had come to the New World. Freedom meant working still more years for someone else as a tenant farmer or hired hand; finding a spouse remained difficult. Given the circumstances, these freemen were understandably restless, frustrated, and alienated from the emerging planter elite and farmers who had gobbled up most tidewater lands. Many small and middling growers were also angered at what they considered exorbitant taxation, blaming both the planter oligarchy and the royal governors.

Bacon's Rebellion

Inevitably, the tensions between the planter elite and the freedmen escalated into a violent confrontation. Too many issues and too much resentment had developed over the decades to be improved through compromise or conciliation. By the 1670s, all that was needed was an individual willing to lead the freedmen by articulating and exploiting their grievances, uniting them in a common cause. **Nathaniel Bacon**, an upstart newcomer to the Chesapeake, proved to be such a leader. Bacon was also an unscrupulous, power-hungry young aristocrat who not only inflamed the white colonists' general fear of the "red men" into a frenzy of hatred, but also manipulated the widespread animosity and poor white discontent with the political-economic establishment controlled by the planter elite for his own aggrandizement.

The policies of **Sir William Berkeley**, the imperious 30-year royal governor of Virginia, compounded the growing tension between the Tidewater planters and the freedmen as well as between the established tobacco elite and their frontier counterparts. Over the course of his tenure, Berkeley pursued an aggressive expansionist policy, which opened Virginia's interior all the way to the Blue Ridge Mountains. The governor's ambitions led to constant conflict with the Native Americans, who the colonists crushed in a series of wars during the 1640s. By the 1650s, the defeated Indians had agreed to treaties ceding most of the territory east of the mountains to the English while establishing a western boundary limiting further English settlement. As a result of white population growth in subsequent decades and the concomitant shortage of land in the settled areas, by the 1670s English settlers had violated the treaty, establishing three counties in the territory set aside for the Indians. Not surprisingly, there were frequent clashes between natives and whites in the area.

In the meantime, Governor Berkeley expanded his powers. During Virginia's early decades, voting for delegates to the House of Burgesses had been open to all white men. By the 1670s, however, Berkeley had ramrodded through the assembly various bills restricting the franchise to landowners only, and set the amount of property owned high enough to exclude all but a minority of wealthy **Tidewater** planters. Elections were rare, and the same burgesses, representing the established eastern planters (the Tidewater elite) of the colony and subservient to the governor, remained in office year after year. The more recent settlers, especially those on the frontier (in the western and southwestern regions of the colony) were underrepresented in the assembly or not represented at all. Resentment of the governor's power and the Tidewater aristocrats grew steadily in these newly settled areas (often referred to as the "backcountry").

By the 1670s, the greatest issue for the majority of freedmen was the shortage of land in the settled areas of the Chesapeake, forcing increasing numbers of such individuals to wander further to the west and southwest of the colony in search of virgin land for either tobacco cultivation or for general farming and stock raising. Regardless of the purpose, the remaining Native Americans in the area, such as the Doegs and Susquehannocks, were not about to let any more Englishmen take their land. Thus, as the freedmen entered into native land, the inevitable occurred: red-white reprisals and killings. As the death toll among white settlers on the frontier increased, appeals went out to the governor for a swift and effective response. Berkeley answered by persuading the House of Burgesses to establish a line of forts manned by militia recruited from the Tidewater to protect the settlers but not to exterminate the Indians, which was exactly the policy the frontier folk wanted the governor and the legislature to implement. Berkeley and many Tidewater planters who dominated the legislature believed that friendly Indians benefited the colony in a variety of ways, most importantly, by providing a natural barrier to keep colonists from wandering too far afield, thus preventing Berkeley and his associates on the Governor's Council and the House of Burgesses from controlling the settlers.

Out of this cauldron of fear, hatred, and vengeance toward both Native Americans and the planter oligarchy emerged Nathaniel Bacon, who ignored Berkeley's and the legislature's prohibition against making all-out war against the Indians, and formed his own ragtag army of about 1,000 men from among the disgruntled and Indian-hating frontier settlers. Led by Bacon, this force proceeded to make war against all Indians indiscriminately. Berkeley condemned Bacon's actions, declaring him a rebel and traitor for having usurped both the governor's and the assembly's rightful authority to determine colonial policies. Much to Berkeley's and his supporters' chagrin, Bacon had become a rather popular leader and agitator among not only dispossessed freedmen but also among frontier planters. Despite the governor's official remonstrations, Bacon continued to lead his motley army against the hapless Indians. Backcountry planters complained that their taxes went into Berkeley's and his clique's pockets rather than being used for frontier defense. To the surprise and outrage of Berkeley and the gentry, once the rebel's force believed they had slaughtered enough Indians, Bacon declared himself against the planter elite and the governor, calling upon men of every class to plunder and put back in their proper places those who had prospered at the expense of the common folk.

A small-scale but vicious civil war broke out between Bacon and his followers on one side and Berkeley along with the planter elite on the other. Both forces offered freedom to indentured servants and slaves belonging to their enemies. Bacon's mob killed not only Indians without hesitation but the gentry as well, especially those they considered to be Berkeley's allies. The rebellion's climax occurred on September 19, 1676 when Bacon's forces burned Jamestown to the ground. Fortunately for Berkeley and the planter elite, a little over a month later Bacon died of dysentery. Without his leadership, the revolt diminished, for it had no focus beyond killing Indians, planters, and aggrandizing Bacon's ego. Moreover, a few months after Bacon's death, 1,000 English troops had arrived at Berkeley's behest, ready to put down the rebellion with whatever force necessary. As a result of the insurrection, twenty-three rebel leaders were executed and the controversial governor removed from office. According to Berkeley's estimates, at the insurrection's peak, some 14,000 Virginians had backed the rebel leader, but after his death that support quickly dissipated. As far as the area's Native Americans were concerned (at least among those who were still alive in the aftermath of Bacon's rampages), new treaties were reluctantly signed that opened new lands to white settlement.

Bacon's Rebellion proved to be significant for several reasons. First, the insurrection illustrated the ongoing struggle between Indians and whites to define their respective spheres of existence and influence in the Chesapeake. The conflict also revealed the bitter competition for place and power among rival elites, especially between those of the Tidewater and their backcountry counterparts. More importantly, the revolt revealed the antipathy between landholders and the colony's large population of free, landless men, the majority of whom were former indentured servants. These men formed the bulk of Bacon's followers during the rebellion. Their hatred of both Native Americans and the planter elite drew them to Bacon, who, ironically, was a member of the colony's landed gentry. Although many backcountry landholders initially supported Bacon's cause, especially against the Indians, after he turned his plain folk's rage against the Tidewater elite, many withdrew their support. They saw in that phase of the rebellion the potential for social unrest from below, which they feared just as much as their brethren to the east. As a result, the landed elites of both eastern and western Virginia developed a bond of common interests, especially in their mutual desire to limit tobacco cultivation to themselves as well as reclaim and retain their political control of the colony. In the aftermath of Bacon's Rebellion, it became clear to the planter elite that if they hoped to avoid another insurrection in the future it was time to move away from the use of indentured servants as their principle labor force to an alternative form of labor—one which would never become free and supposedly less inclined to rebel against the status quo. The time seemed to have come to transition to full-scale slave labor. Unlike white indentured servants, African slaves would not be released after a fixed term and thus did not threaten to become an unstable, landless class. By the time the English began to import African slaves into their colonies in the latter seventeenth century, the Spanish and Portuguese had been using enslaved Africans as plantation laborers for well over a century. The English were entering into a global economy that already had come to rely on slave labor.

The Rise of Slavery in the Chesapeake Colonies

Chesapeake Englishmen, for a variety of reasons, avoided the use of African slaves on their plantations for several decades. Blacks from Africa seemed to them the strangest of people; some Englishmen even questioned their humanity. The ethnocentric English, connoting evil and inferiority to black people, did not want themselves surrounded by workers who not only had a different skin color, but spoke incomprehensible languages and behaved in strange ways. Of course, the fact that the Africans were not Christians only added to their alleged inferiority in English eyes. Finally, transportation costs made the use of African slaves prohibitive. The great distance from West Africa to the Chesapeake along with the insatiable demand for black slaves in the West Indian sugar islands drove prices beyond what tobacco planters could afford. In short, cheaper, more familiar, available white servants became the initial laborers of choice for wealthy Chesapeake tobacco growers.

That is not to suggest that there were no Africans in the Chesapeake colonies prior to Bacon's Rebellion; quite the contrary. By 1660, there were approximately 1,600 blacks in Virginia and Maryland with widely varying legal statuses. Some clearly served as slaves for life, while others (the majority) were indentured servants, bonded in the same capacity as their white counterparts, eventually gaining their freedom if they lived long enough. A few even arrived from Africa or the West Indies as free men. Some native-born blacks of mixed parentage enjoyed legal freedom based on the status of their father (in Maryland, for a few years) or their mother (in Virginia). Still other blacks earned enough money to purchase their freedom or were granted such status for good conduct or outstanding service. Until the 1670s, free blacks had the same rights as white colonial Englishmen—property ownership, ability to sue whites and testify against whites in court, voting privileges, service on juries, payment of taxes, access to credit, and even (for a while) ownership of black and Indian slaves and the indentures of whites. The rights extended to free blacks in the first 50 years of their presence in the Chesapeake contrasts sharply with the racial mores of later centuries. Indeed, most white Chesapeake inhabitants paid relatively little attention to their skin color; whether they were slave, indentured, or free, all blacks were simply considered additions to the overall population or to the lower-class work force. Race or color was not yet the salient marker for identity that it later became.

This uncertainty about status is not surprising. Since the English had no experience with slavery at home, a rigid caste system took time to crystallize. When Hugh Davis was whipped in 1630 "for abusing himself to the dishonor of God and shame of Christians, by defiling his body in lying with a negro," his transgression may have been sodomy rather than miscegenation. The record is unclear. Fifty years later when Katherine Watkins, a white woman, accused John Long, a mulatto, of raping her, the neighbors (both men and women) blamed her, not him, for engaging in seductive behavior, which they described in lurid detail. Showing similar ambiguity was the case of Elizabeth Key, a mulatto, a Christian, and the bastard daughter of Thomas Key. In 1655 when Elizabeth claimed her freedom, her new owner fought to keep her enslaved. William Greensted, who had fathered two children by her, sued on her behalf, won, and then married her. One settler had no qualms about keeping her in bondage because of her dark skin, despite the known wishes of her deceased father. Another—Greensted—fell in love with her.

During the pre-Bacon Rebellion decades, because white servants were less expensive than African slaves, they were often worked harder than their black comrades; their skin color did not spare them from the most arduous labor. In fact, white servants and black slaves usually worked together at the same tasks, suffered similar discipline, ate the same food, slept in identical quarters, were subject to the same diseases, played and caroused together, and ran away together. Masters considered both a troublesome lot that needed constant monitoring and disciplining. Black and white laborers tended to regard one another as equals; fellow sufferers and friends. Many Africans became quite Europeanized in the mostly white society. These comparatively benign racial relationships continued as long as the black population remained small, not only between white servants and slaves but also between masters and slaves.

English chauvinism helped Chesapeake whites to embrace the idea of enslaving Africans, which became especially inflated after the Elizabethan era. One of its manifestations became an aversion to non-English cultures and people. Sixteenth-century Englishmen disdained virtually everyone not like themselves—the Irish, Spanish, the Native Americans, and certainly were prejudiced against those considered most foreign of all—the Africans. Throughout most of Western Europe, white Europeans had come to associate the color black with evil and terror, and thus in the English mind, the Africans' skin color made their vast differences from the English more pronounced. Indeed, Englishmen claimed Africans were unattractive, with "dispositions most savage and brutish;" a "people of beastly living," who, "contract no matrimonie, neither have respect to chastity." Northern Europeans considered African women particularly distasteful, sexually promiscuous, and neglectful of their children. One sixteenth century traveler to Guinea thought that African men and women were almost indistinguishable. They "goe so alike, that one cannot know a man from a woman but by their breasts, which in the most part be very foule and long, hanging down like the udder of a goate." Yet, such an automatic predisposition to denigrate Africans was more of an abstract, superstitious dislike of the unknown and the different—a generalized and passive prejudice—than a systematic racism that informed every black-white interpersonal relationship. Although they did not use these views to justify slavery, the English formed the basis for the racism later to develop along with the slave system. In short, this predilection surely made easy the acceptance of perpetual slavery for Africans. Nonetheless, the Chesapeake planters who bought blacks from the Caribbean or directly from Africa justified their actions as purchasing people already in bondage; they were not guilty of enslaving men and women, but merely changing the location of their labor. For almost a half-century, the Chesapeake's handful of blacks were not perceived by the white majority as threats nor were they considered so different to activate the passive prejudice into pervasive racism; that would occur in the aftermath of Bacon's Rebellion.

Prior to the insurrection, the Chesapeake colonies enacted laws categorizing slaves differently from others in society, with the initial changes in one fashion or another all involving slave women. In 1643, a Virginia law declared that slave women (along with slave men and white male indentures) to be titheable, that is, taxable property, while white women servants were considered dependents and thus not taxed. The increase in miscegenation, especially when one of the partners was a black slave, became another issue addressed before the 1670s. Virginia legislated that henceforth all children born of a "mixed" relationship would have the legal status of their mother; thus, if the mother was a black slave woman and her partner was either a free black or white, the children would nonetheless be slaves for life unless manumitted by their master. Maryland passed a similar statute in 1664, declaring that the children of slave women were to serve for life, and those of white servant women who married black slave men would themselves serve as slaves for their husband's lifetime, with any offspring also becoming slaves. Racial intermarriage was not yet made illegal. In practical effect, these laws established that the status of children born of a slave mother as slaves themselves—regardless of their father's status. Thus began the association of slavery with race, with the implication that slavery was the *natural* corollary of being black. Slavery, in other words, became fundamentally a matter of race.

Another factor pushing Chesapeake planters further toward African slavery proved to be the decrease in the supply of readily available white indentured servants of the desired age and gender—young men in their teens or early twenties. By the 1660s, the 200-year population growth in England finally came to an end. Exacerbating this general drop in population was the Great Plague that struck England in the mid-1660s. The resulting labor shortage led to an increase in wages for those who had survived and were healthy enough to work. Job opportunities also opened up in London, especially in construction, in the aftermath of the Great Fire of 1666 that leveled a huge area of the city. As a result of these developments, fewer young English people were desperate for work and thus willing to come to the Chesapeake. Moreover, colonial expansion in the 1670s and 1680s, which saw the establishment of the colonies of the Carolinas and Pennsylvania, presented the Chesapeake with strong competitors for the decreasing numbers of willing white migrants. Servants became harder to procure. When available, they forced masters to grant previously unheard of concessions in order to entice them to the area, such as shortening their time of service, effectively raising the price of indentured servants. By the 1670s, the labor shortage in the Chesapeake became so acute that land-hungry tobacco planters lowered their qualifications and accepted as servants virtually anyone they could find, individuals they would have rejected a decade or so earlier—younger males, more women, Irishmen, the almost totally unskilled laboring poor, and finally, even convicts. In their desperation, they even reconsidered enslaving Native Americans. As these new workers proved to be unsuitable for tobacco plantation work, planters increasingly turned to the enslavement of Africans as their only labor alternative if they hoped to keep their plantations as viable and profitable enterprises.

The chartering of the **Royal African Company** in 1674 helped planters to move in this direction. A joint-stock company authorized by the Crown to engage in the slave trade, the company received a monopoly on all slaves brought into the empire, whether to the West Indies or to North America. The price for slaves dropped sufficiently enough to allow many planters to buy directly from Africa rather than purchasing slaves from the West Indies, though many mainland buyers continued to purchase slaves via the Caribbean. In 1698, the Royal African Company's 26-year monopoly on the exclusive right to import slaves directly from Africa ended by a parliamentary act. By that time, however, numerous individual enterprising merchants in England, the Caribbean, and even North America had built their own fleets of smaller vessels and picked up where the company had left off, either going to Africa or to the West Indies to bring slaves back to the mainland. Most of these smaller slave traffickers went from plantation to plantation in the Chesapeake with their "merchandise" and eventually came to dominate the trade, helping to push slave imports to the region to flood-tide proportions.

In the decades following Bacon's Rebellion, as the cost for white indentured servants increased due to demand exceeding supply, planters increasingly turned to African slaves to solve their labor needs. Not only did Africans become less expensive to purchase, but profitable as well, especially if the slave lived a comparatively long, productive life. Thus, early on, slave life expectancy was much higher in the Chesapeake than in the Caribbean, as mainland planters tended to take better physical care of their slaves than their more ruthless compatriots in the West Indies. Buying slaves came to be seen not just as a necessary solution to a labor shortage, but economically advantageous as well. As planters also made the offspring of their bondsmen slaves, they automatically increased their ready supply and thus were less dependent on continued importation. Moreover, slaves never became free to compete for land or grow tobacco independently. Because the weed had been introduced into Africa by the Portuguese who had brought it from Brazil in the 1550s, an added benefit proved to be the fact that many Africans had prior tobacco cultivating experience. Chesapeake planters found African slavery a solution to many of their economic problems. Beginning in the aftermath of Bacon's Rebellion (the late 1670s), slave imports continued to rise rapidly, with more slaves delivered between 1695 and 1700 than during the preceding 20 years, and more imported between 1700 and 1705 than during the preceding 81 years. By 1700, the Chesapeake became a slave economy with enormous repercussions for everyone involved. At the same time, other southern regions developed a similar labor system, though based on different staple crops.

THE ORIGINS OF THE ATLANTIC SLAVE TRADE

The demand for slaves in North America helped expand the transatlantic slave trade. As slave trading grew more extensive and more sophisticated, the business also grew more barbarous. Before ending in the nineteenth century, the Atlantic slave trade was responsible for the forced migration of approximately 11 million Africans to the Western Hemisphere. Indeed, until the late eighteenth century, the number of Africans transported to the New World was higher than the level of European immigration by a ratio of 6 to 1. The movement of Africans across the Atlantic to the Americas represented the largest forced migration in human history. Of the 11 million Africans bound for slavery in the New World, 76 percent arrived from 1701-1810—the peak period of European colonial demand for labor. Of this vast multitude, about half were delivered to Dutch, French, or English sugar plantations in the Caribbean; one-third to Portuguese/Dutch Brazil, and 10 percent to Spanish America. Only about 5 percent, or roughly 600,000 men, women, and children, were sent from Africa to England's North American colonies.

The Portuguese were the first Europeans to trade for and exploit Africans as slave labor. Moreover, the Portuguese traders found it considerably more efficient (and less dangerous) to leave the procurement of slaves to Africans, who sold captives in exchange for European commodities, such as guns and metallurgical products, which the Africans particularly valued. Thus, by the 1450s, a small but regular traffic in slaves had been established between Europe and Africa. The Portuguese ruthlessly exploited their African slaves, often working them to death on the large sugar plantations they had created on their island colony of Madeira, located off the Atlantic coast of northwestern Africa. The Portuguese did not think twice about inflicting such harsh work upon their slaves because profits were high and replacement costs low. Sugar and slaves had become synonymous since the fourteenth century when Italian merchants first imported sugar cane from West Asia and set up the first sugar plantations on Mediterranean islands. For the luxury of sweet food, Europeans subjected Africans to the sufferings of slavery.

The Spanish followed suit in the New World soon after Columbus' voyages, establishing sugar plantations throughout the Caribbean during the sixteenth century. At first they attempted to capture and enslave the native populations of the islands they conquered, but disease and warfare quickly reduced that potential labor force. Thus, by the middle of the sixteenth century the Spanish too had turned to the enslavement of Africans on their Caribbean island plantations. Desperate for such labor, the Spanish granted their rival, Portugal, an *asiento* (license) to bring slaves to their possessions directly from Africa. In the late sixteenth century, the Portuguese, with the help of Dutch financing, extended sugar production to northeast Brazil, which became the model of the efficient but callous use of African slaves. By 1600 some 25,000 enslaved Africans worked on the sugar plantations of Brazil.

The Dutch, skilled at finance and commerce, greatly expanded sugar production at such little cost with African slave labor that sugar by the middle of the seventeenth century ceased to be a luxury item, becoming readily available for mass consumption by all classes of Europeans. Along with the addictive tropical commodities such of tobacco, coffee, and tea, sugar became what one historian called "a proletarian hunger-killer," helping to sustain people through increasingly long working days. Not to be left out of this sugar boom, both France and England established "sugar islands" in the Caribbean as well. The French first developed sugar plantations on the small island of Martinique, then seized the western half of Hispaniola from the Spanish and created a sugar colony called St. Dominque (present-day Haiti). By the close of the seventeenth century, sugar and slaves had come to define the European colonial system in the West Indies.

West Africans

The overwhelming majority of Africans sold into slavery and brought to the New World came from long-established West African societies. In the sixteenth century, more than a 100 different peoples lived along the West African coast from Cape Verde south to Angola. Northern groups included the Wolofs, Mandingos, Hausas, Ashantis, and Yorubas; to the south, the Ibos, Sekes, Bakongos, and Mbundus resided. Regardless of region, all shared a similar existence centered on the local community, which was organized along hierarchical kinship lines. In each village, clan leaders and village chiefs decided what was best for the good of all inhabitants, ranging from food distribution and production to whether or not to villagers should defend their territory or flee to a safer place. Local tribunals of elders arbitrated internal disputes. Men usually took second and third wives, creating a marriage system known as polygyny, in which large composite families with complex internal relationships developed. Restrictions on sexual relations, however, led West African women to bear fewer children than the typical European female, with many enjoying considerable social and economic independence as tradeswomen.

Economically, West African societies were agriculturally-based, cultivating the land with techniques used for thousands of years. Farmers grew sorghum, millet, and rice on the grassy savannahs and fruits, root crops, and other vegetables in the tropical forests that straddled the Equator. West Africans made iron tools and other implements, but due to the thinness of the region's poor soils, they had no use for iron plows. Like the Native Americans of North America, the Africans practiced "shifting cultivation." Clearing land by burning and using hoes or digging sticks to work in the nutrient-rich ash, they let the old fields lie fallow when the land ceased to be fertile and moved on to virgin soil. Men cleared the land, women worked at cultivation and the sale of surpluses in the markets. West Africans produced enough food and commodities not only to sustain their respective tribes but also to trade with other Africans. Although West Africa remained largely a collection of autonomous villages and rural communities, some large kingdom-states developed, complete with sophisticated, flourishing urban centers. Along the upper Niger River where the grassland gradually turns to desert, sat the city of Timbuktu, one of Africa's most legendary trad-

The Atlantic Slave Trade

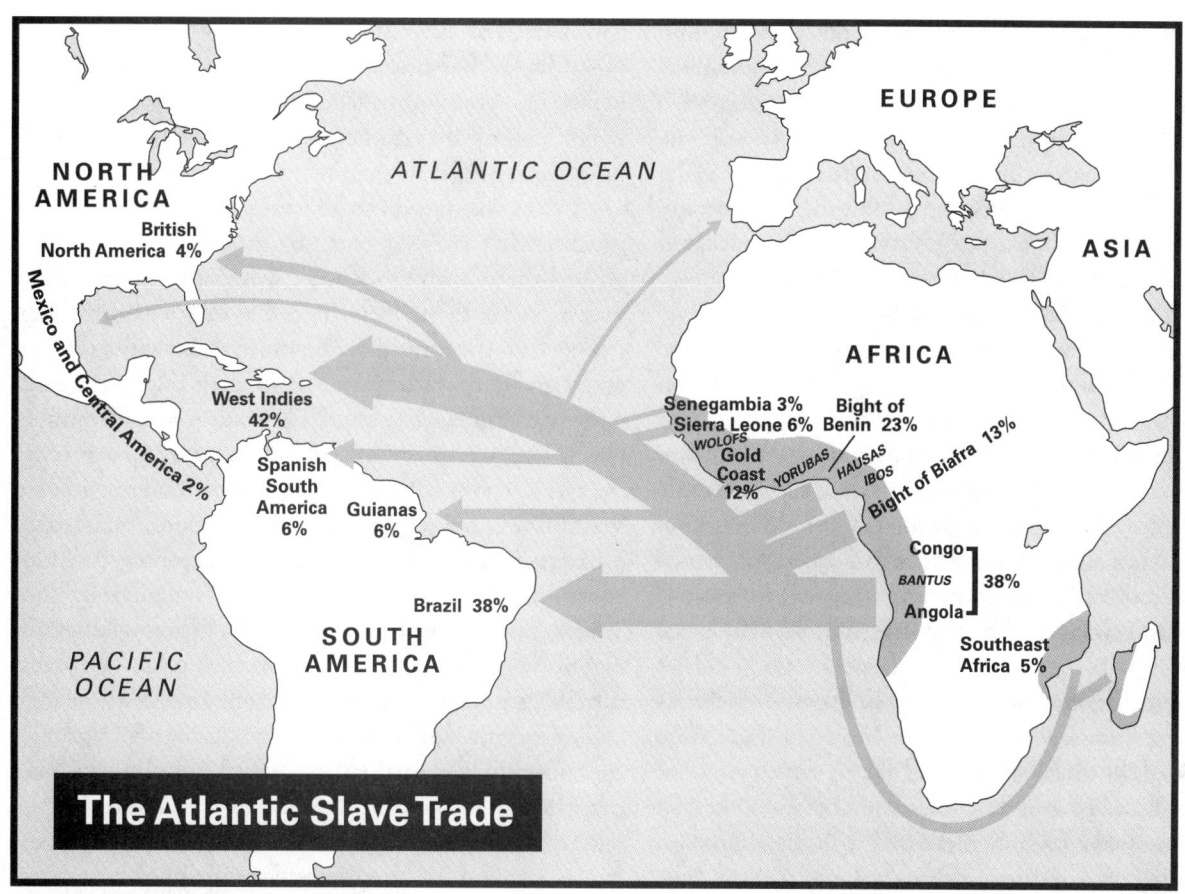

Map 2.3 The Atlantic Slave Trade

ing centers for several centuries. Timbuktu was one of the Old World's greatest marketplaces, where traders exchanged goods from all over the continent and the Mediterranean world, and from where caravans traversed the great Sahara Desert carrying West African metal goods, gold, ivory, textiles, and slaves to the Muslim empires of North Africa and the Middle East.

The more powerful West African tribes competed with each other for control of this trade. In the process, they created a succession of military empires, the most extensive being the Mali Empire, whose greatest king, the Muslim ruler Mansa Musa (1313-1370), transformed Timbuktu into a leading academic and intellectual center as well as a commercial hub. Indeed, during his reign, Timbuktu became a capital of world renown. When the Portuguese first arrived in the fifteenth century, the most important state in the region was the powerful Muslim kingdom of Songhai (today the African nation of Mali). Possessing one of the largest cavalries and armies in the Old World, the Songhai controlled the trans-Sahara trade. Nevertheless, many lesser states and kingdoms also existed along the West African coast with whom the Portuguese first bargained for slaves.

Africans had practiced slavery for centuries and had been involved in a slave trade network with the Muslim empires of the Middle East and south Asia for at least 300 years before engaging the Portuguese in the enterprise. Among the enslaved men and women were war captives, criminals and others socially ostracized, those sold into slavery to pay off the debt of an elder family member, or those who sold themselves into slavery to pay off a personal debt. However, African slavery was not considered a permanent condition; most slaves were eventually incorporated into the families they served or were set free after a certain period of time. Slaves were allowed to marry and their children were born free. "With us they [slaves] did no more work than the other members of the community, even their master," remembered Olaudah Equiano, an Ibo captured and shipped to North America as a slave in 1756, when he was a boy of eleven. "Their [the slaves] food, clothing, and lodging were nearly the same as the others, except that they [the slaves] were not permitted to eat with those who were born free." Most African slave traders believed that would be the treatment and condition of the first slaves they sold to the Portuguese—that European slavery would be similar to that practiced in Africa.

Contrary to popular myth, not until the late eighteenth century did European slave traders penetrate the West African interior and procure slaves directly. The image of Europeans hauling chained retinues of captured Africans to the coast to be transported on ships bound for the New World was not reality. From the beginning of this particular African-European exchange of "goods" until the late eighteenth century, Africans controlled the slave trade. The Europeans were not allowed into the African interior, so slaves were brought by the African traders to designated trading posts along the West African coast for sale. Indeed, only the most audacious of Europeans ventured into the African interior searching for slaves, for few would escape such a foolish endeavor alive. The Africans involved in the trade were determined to protect their interests in this most profitable enterprise. From present-day Guinea to Angola, the African kingdoms involved in the slave trade established trading posts along this 2300-mile coastline. At these flourishing slave marts, which operated two or three times a year (and later on a more regular, year-round basis), native chieftains brought large numbers of blacks, out of the forests and to the ports. Sometimes large armies launched massive attacks, burning whole towns or villages and taking hundreds of prisoners. More common were smaller raids in which small bands of armed men attacked at nightfall, seized everyone they could before the rest of the village awoke, and then escaped with their captives. Kidnapping, or *panyaring*, in the terminology of the slave trade, was also common. One seaman, ashore while his slave ship awaited its cargo, amused himself by peeking at a young African woman bathing. Suddenly two African raiders jumped from the bushes and dragged her off. He later saw them carry her on board and sell her to his ship's captain, no questions asked. Those Africans not involved in the slave trade were not reticent to condemn their fellow African participants. "I must own to the shame of my own countrymen," wrote Ottobah Cugoano, who was sold into slavery in the mid-eighteenth century, "that I was first kidnapped and betrayed by those of my own complexion."

As the slave trade peaked in the middle of the eighteenth century, the European forts or trading entrepots gave way to small coastal clusters of huts where independent European traders set up operations with the cooperation of local headmen or chiefs. The breakdown of formal exchange opened the door for smaller operators, such as the New England slavers, who entered the trade in the early eighteenth century. Often bartering rum, guns, or salt fish for human beings, these Yankees (many of whom came from Puritan ancestry), earned a reputation for shrewd dealing, which they came by honestly. "Water your rum as much as possible," one New England slave merchant instructed his captain," and sell as much by the short measure as you can." Initially, Massachusetts dominated the North American component of the trade, but after 1750, the majority of New Englanders involved in the purchasing of human beings operated out of Rhode Island. Regardless from which colony they came, many Yankee fortunes were built from profits in the slave trade.

In the journey from the interior to the coast, approximately 10 percent of those captured died. Until they arrived there, many had never seen a white man or the ocean, and both terrified them. On the coast, European traders and African raiders assembled their captives. Those about to be purchased waited in dark dungeons or in open pens called *barracoons*. The traders split up families and others within ethnic groups in order to minimize the potential for collective revolt. Most traders gathered their human cargo from a variety of regions, each with a different language, to make sure the captives could not communicate with each other and foment rebellion. Traders also had to be careful not to bring together antagonistic groups who might fight each other. Captains carefully inspected and then selected not only those men and women they deemed physically capable of performing agricultural labor in the New World but also surviving the arduous trip across the Atlantic. Suffice it to say, the selection process was often lewd, invasive, and humiliating, as all about to be enslaved were stripped naked and exposed to the beating sun, the whip, and rough groping hands. Those chosen were then branded on the back or buttocks with the mark of the buyer. Olaudah Equiano remembered that "those white men with horrible looks, red faces, and long hair, looked and acted in so savage a manner; I had never seen among any people such instances of brutal cruelty." Equiano's narrative, written during the 1780s after he had secured his freedom, remains one of the few that provide an African account of enslavement. Equiano and his fellow captives were convinced that they had "got into a world of bad spirits" and were about to be eaten by cannibals. A French trader wrote that many prisoners were "positively prepossessed with the opinion that we transport them into our country in order to kill and eat them."

The Middle Passage

Although being captured or kidnapped for eventual enslavement was undoubtedly brutal and traumatic, for slaves the worst was yet to come: the "**Middle Passage**," as English slavers and sailors in the eighteenth century called the journey to America. After captivity in forts and *barracoons*, those slaves selected were chained in small groups and rowed to the waiting ships. They were then packed into "shelves" below deck only six feet long by two and a half feet high. In most slave ships, these

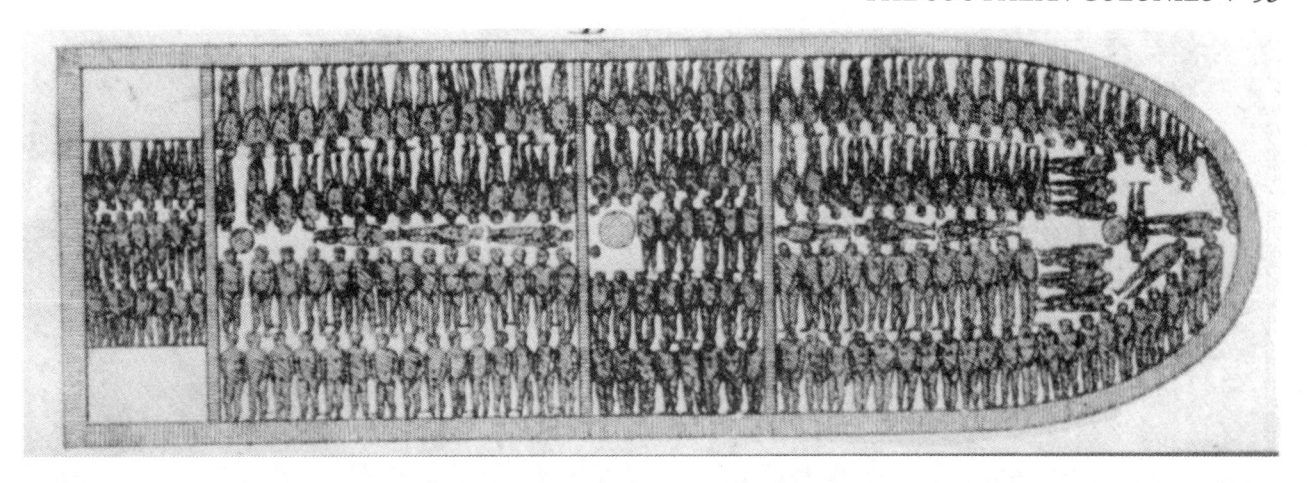

This eighteenth-century engraving shows the horrors of slavery. The slaves were marched to ships and tightly packed below the deck of the vessel.

shelves were tiered one on top of the other several rows deep, sometimes as many as six shelves high. "Rammed like herring in a barrel," wrote one observer, slaves "were chained to each other hand and foot, and stowed so close, that they were not allowed above a foot and a half for each in breadth." People were forced to sleep "spoon fashion" and the tossing of the ship knocked them about so violently that skin over their elbows sometimes was worn to the bone from scraping on the planks. With such little space between the platforms (at most on some ships, four and a half feet), the Africans could not stand up, nor because they were packed so tightly could they move from side to side. Enterprising captains filled every space available with their human cargo, even the smallest spaces by filling them with children. Men and women were kept separate, their portions of the decks divided by partitions. Male slaves were shackled and confined below for most of the trip. The women were often left unshackled, but their relative freedom left them prey to the sailors' lust.

Slavers debated the efficacy of packing strategies, with some arguing that additional room lessened mortality and thus increased profits. Others asserted that because demand was so great for slave labor in the New World, especially by the mid-eighteenth century, and because the cost of transporting slaves across the Atlantic so high (accounting for three-quarters of the price of a slave), that tight-packing should prevail, even if scores of slaves were lost because of such confinement. One ship designed to carry 450 slaves regularly crossed the Atlantic with more than six hundred. Even if one-fourth to one-third were lost, a profit was nonetheless made at the other end. The English were particularly efficient, carrying twice as many slaves per crew member and 50 percent more slaves per ship than other nations, thereby increasing their profits. With their holds filled with human cargo, the ships headed toward Cape Verde to catch the trade winds blowing toward the Americas. A favorable voyage from Senegambia to Barbados might be accomplished in as little as three weeks, but a ship from Guinea or Angola, not able to pick up the trade winds and forced to make way in calm waters or be driven back by storms, might take as much as three months.

Monotonous routine defined the slaves' existence on board. On some mornings, the crew opened the hatch and brought the captives on deck, attaching their leg irons to a great chain running the length of the bulwarks. After a breakfast of beans or gruel, or whatever starch-type food on board they could prepare easily for mass consumption, it was time for exercise or the ritual known as "dancing the slave." While an African thumped an upturned kettle or plucked a banjo, the crew ordered men and women to jump up and down in a bizarre session of calisthenics. The slavers did not want the slaves who survived to lose "muscle tone," because they would fetch a lesser price at auction if they appeared to be physically unfit for work. A day spent on deck was concluded by a second bland meal before the slaves were stowed away for several days before they came on deck again for the same ritual. Although deck time was necessary to prevent muscles from atrophying and to clean out and sanitize the hold and bring out the dead and toss them overboard, captains were nonetheless reluctant to allow too much of such freedom, for many slaves would jump over board the moment they were brought up. To prevent such suicides, captains stretched netting around their ships to catch the slave after he jumped into the water. According to one seaman, nightly he could hear from the cargo hold "a howling melancholy noise, expressive of extreme anguish." Down in the bowels of the ship, the groans of the dying, the shrieks of women and children, and the suffocating heat and stench combined to create, in the words of Equiano, "a scene of horror almost inconceivable."

Christian Slaves in Muslim Africa

While Europeans traded in slaves with the African kingdoms of that continent's West Coast, bringing them to the New World to labor on plantations, the North African suzerainties of the Ottoman Empire were vigorously and profitably enslaving Europeans and dispersing them throughout the Ottoman world. These "Barbary" slave traders captured and sold an estimated 1.25 million Europeans into lifetime bondage. The majority of these poor souls were captives of war and victims of raids between the Hapsburg and Ottoman empires, which were in constant states of conflict during the seventeenth century. International law of that time period established that enemies captured in war could be enslaved for life, and for most of the captives, enslavement was preferable to death. This was the rationale used to justify enslavement, even when the objective of the war for the Barbary chieftains was to obtain more slaves, whom they needed to man the galleys of their corsairs, the pirate ships that preyed upon European commercial vessels in the Mediterranean. The Barbary pirates also raided the coastal towns and cities of southern Europe, searching for young men to enslave. In many ways, these Muslim buccaneers needed slaves to obtain more slaves, and their demand for them was insatiable because the mortality rate was so high among those they had already captured. Indeed, one scholar has estimated that the death rate of galley slaves was as high as 20 percent a year.

Of all the captives, galley slaves were treated the most brutally. In the hulls of the corsairs, as many as five men would be chained together at each oar of the ship. They would row 24 hours a day for days on end, always chained, barely clad and with no protection from the elements, so that their "flesh is burned off their backs." There was enough give in the chain that oarsmen stumbled over each other to make it to the end of the bench, where there was an opening in the ship's hull where they could relieve themselves. However, galley slaves were often too exhausted or depressed even to do that, and as a result, the stench and sanitation in the galleys from sweat and human waste was unimaginable and sickening.

The Muslim pirates seized not only European commercial vessels for slaves but also attacked the Mediterranean islands of Sicily and Sardinia, as well as the coastal settlements of Italy and Spain, where they often found even more plentiful human bounty. In some regions of southern Europe, whole villages were abandoned. Such was the case in large portions of the Italian peninsula, where the governments were too weak to protect their citizens and ordered them to move further into the interior. Although the majority of Christian slaves came from southern Europe, it was not uncommon to see the Muslim pirates on slaving expeditions as far as the North Atlantic, not only seizing English ships, but also raiding along the Irish coast and the western England regions of Cornwall and Devon. It has been estimated that from these areas 7,000-9,000 people were captured and enslaved.

Almost all captives taken from ships were male but coastal areas also witnessed raids resulting in the apprehension of women and children. Nonetheless, 95 percent of all European captives were males who either found themselves chained together as galley slaves, or for the more "fortunate," working in heavy construction or as house servants. Europeans believed that some of the younger men, boys even, were forced into male prostitution or became sex slaves for Muslim potentates. Although North African cities had vibrant homosexual cultures (unlike in Europe at the time), it is difficult to ascertain how widespread young European males found themselves enslaved for the sexual pleasure of their Muslim owners. Interestingly, some of the best-known homosexual men in North Africa were Europeans; quite possibly they had voluntarily migrated to North Africa, attracted by a milieu they found more hospitable.

Although the number of Europeans enslaved by North Africans pales in comparison to the number of Africans forced into bondage in the New World, the Muslim trade in Europeans provides a context for the African slave trade in general. For example, both slave trades developed at the same time and, in both instances, the majority of captives were the losers in battles or raids. Initially the basis for both slave trades was ethnic and religious, not racial; only later was the African slave trade justified in racial terms. Muslim slave traders often engaged in the trade for ransom rather than to obtain slaves, seizing wealthy Europeans in the hope of selling them back for huge sums. Europeans, however, never ransomed Africans. Once Africans were seized either by European slave traders or by their African partners, they lost any hope of returning to their native lands. Finally, the capture and enslavement of Europeans was a pre-modern economic endeavor, neither requiring much capital nor producing much wealth. By contrast, significant capital investment, efficient organization, and the desire for profitable returns defined the African slave trade, a modern business enterprise, which developed new methods of turning human beings into property.

Inadequate sanitary conditions were without question the most appalling of horrors to be endured on board the slave ship. There were "necessary tubs" set below deck, but Africans "endeavoring to get to them, tumble over their companions," one eighteenth century ship's surgeon wrote, "and as the necessities of nature are not to be resisted [urinating, defecating, even vomiting from seasickness], they ease themselves as they lie." Some captains, concerned for their cargoes' well-being relative to profit ordered crews to scrape and swab the holds daily, but so sickening was the task that on many ships it was rarely performed, and thus the slaves were often forced to lie in their own excrement. When first taken below deck, the boy Equiano remembered, "I received such a salutation in my nostrils as I had never experienced in my life," and "became so sick and low that I was not able to eat." Atlantic sailors said you could "smell a slaver five miles downwind." Many slaves sickened and died in these conditions. Among the most common afflictions contracted was "the flux"—dysentery, which often reached epidemic proportions on board many slave ships. As one ship's doctor reported, the slaves' deck "was so covered with the blood and mucous which had proceeded from them in consequence of the flux, that it resembled a slaughterhouse." Frequent shipboard bouts of smallpox, measles, and yellow fever also decimated slave cargoes. Historians have estimated that during the Middle Passage of the eighteenth century at least 1 in every 6 Africans perished; the result of suicide or death from the various diseases noted above.

One should never conclude that these unwilling voyagers resigned themselves to their captivity or were too bewildered or traumatized by the ordeal; quite the contrary. The captives offered plenty of resistance. As long as ships were still within sight of the African coast, hope remained alive and the danger of revolt was great. An historian has found references to 55 slave revolts on English and American ships between 1699 and 1845. With resistance from the slaves being the norm rather than the exception, ship captains used all manner of terror to maintain order. Flogging—a punishment also used on sailors for infractions—was common. Some captains did not hesitate to torture or maim unruly slaves, using such devices as the thumbscrew, "a dreadful engine, which if the screw be turned by an unrelenting hand, can give intolerable anguish." Whipping and torture was not only used on the disobedient but to strike fear in the hearts of their companions. That was surely the intent of the captain and crew of the *Brownlow* after some of the Africans on board rebelled. The captain ordered his crew to use axes to dismember the rebels, "till their bodies remained only like a trunk of a tree when all the branches are lopped away." The slaves' severed heads and limbs were then thrown at the other slaves, who were chained together on the ship's deck and watched as their brethren were murdered in such a gruesome manner.

Such fear of slave rebellion hardened captains and crews of slave ships. Few sailors signed onto a slave ship if they had better options. Thus, only the most desperate or destitute, or most unsavory seamen often signed aboard a slave ship. Indeed, one captain of a slaver described his crew as the "very dregs of the community." Coming from backgrounds of ill-repute, the captain of such a motley crew could count on such individuals to mete out any harsh punishment he deemed necessary to keep the enslaved in line. The life of a seventeenth or eighteenth century sailor was hard enough; service on a slave ship—a floating prison—was even harder. Yet once aboard, even the lowest crew member was superior to the Africans in the hold. After repeated voyages, both captain and crew became practiced in the ways of ruthlessness. Silas Todd, apprenticed to a slave ship captain at the age of 14, believed he was headed down such a barbarous path, and would have someday become a captain of a slaver had he not been "saved" during a Great Awakening revival in 1734. Todd was certain that he would have become, after several years and voyages with the captain, "as eminent a savage" as the man under whom he had served.

ARRIVAL IN THE NEW WORLD

As the ship approached its destination, the crew made their cargo presentable, preparing the slaves for auction or for their single purchasers. All but the most rebellious of Africans were freed from their chains, allowed to wash themselves, and move about the deck under the watchful eyes of armed crewmen. One account describes the ship's surgeon plugging captives' rectums with clumps of hemp fiber to prevent potential buyers from seeing bloody discharges, a symptom of the flux. To impress buyers, slavers sometimes paraded Africans off the ship to the tune of an accordion or beat of a drum, but not until first making them as presentable as possible, whether that entailed simply rubbing them with lotions to make their skin shinier and thus supposedly healthier, or force feeding them to make them appear less emaciated. Slavers also clothed the Africans. For many, it was the first clothing they had worn since their capture, having spent most, if not all, of the Middle Passage naked. They were simply given loin cloth to cover their private parts; for some women that meant only their lower torsos, thus exposing their bare breasts. But the toll taken by the Middle Passage was difficult to disguise, no matter what ruse or cleaning up the traders used. One observer described a disembarking group as "walking skeletons covered over with a piece of tanned leather."

While some cargoes were destined for a single wealthy planter, such as those on Caribbean sugar islands who often bought several hundred at one time, the majority of slaves were handed over to merchant middlemen. These traders either bought the entire cargo from the ship's captain at a wholesale price or bought the slaves on consignment; that is, splitting the profit from the sale of the slaves at auction with the captain at a prearranged percentage. In some cases the slave ship's captain sold his cargo directly to purchasers, eliminating all middlemen, thus garnering all the proceeds from the slaves' sale. To ensure his crew's continued loyalty and diligence, a smart captain would give his shipmates a small percentage of his profits as a bonus. Purchasers, whether at auction or as individuals who had bought the entire cargo, painstakingly examined the Africans, once again subjecting them to the indignity of probing eyes and poking fingers. Those slaves not sold immediately were kept in holding pens until they were purchased. There, they were often killed if the traders concluded that they were too sickly or "deficient" for whatever reason to ever be purchased. South Carolina planters engaged in an interesting method of slave procurement called the "scramble," an activity similar to the "calf scramble" seen at modern rodeos. In the slave scramble, standard prices were set in advance for men, women, boys, and girls. Once the prices were established, the Africans were then "driven" like a herd of cattle into a corral. At a signal, the buyers rushed into the corral, grabbing or roping around the neck, their pick of the lot. Sometimes, to make this particular manner of slave acquisition more fun or entertaining, they allowed the slaves to run away from their prospective captors. No doubt such a game was designed to further dehumanize the Africans, making them appear to be no different than the beasts of burden, which, ironically, many Carolina slaves tended as their main task for the farmer or planter who had "grabbed" or "lassoed" them in the scramble.

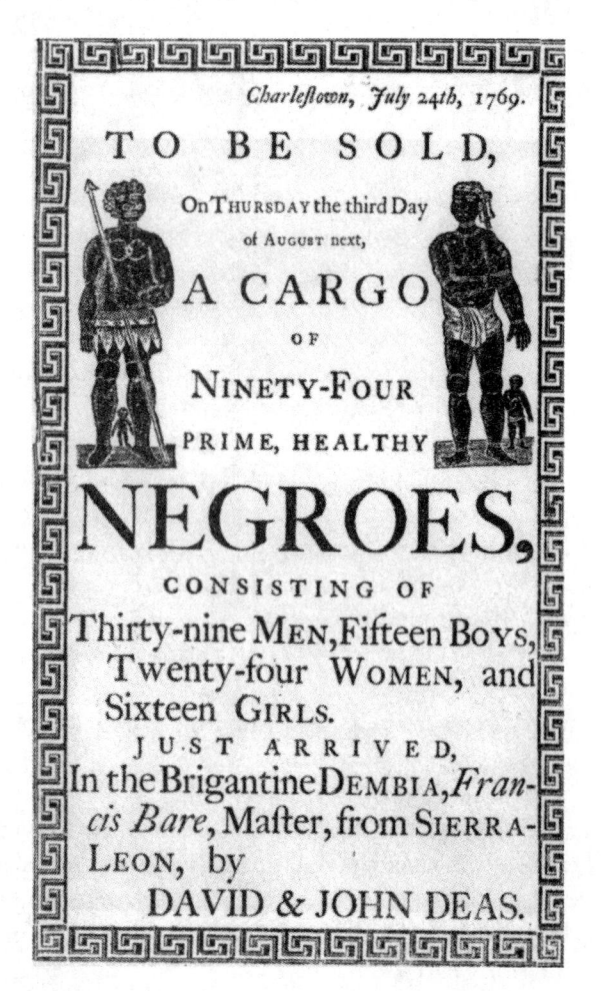

THE IMPACT OF THE SLAVE TRADE ON AFRICA

Down to the present day, West Africa, in particular, still suffers from the legacy of four centuries of the trade in human flesh. Little did sixteenth-century Africans realize when they began the slave trade, first with the Portuguese and then over the subsequent centuries with the other European powers, that six centuries later their continent would still be affected economically, politically, ecologically, and environmentally from such an exchange. The slave trade and the labor of slaves allowed Europe and the eventual United States to grow stronger while weakening Africa. In the short term, the slave-trading kingdoms on the coast increased their power at the expense of the interior states. Thus, the West African state of Songhai gave way to the Gold Coast state of Akwamu. In the Niger Delta, the slaving states of Nembe, Bonny, and Kalabari arose, while to the south the kingdom of Imbangala drew slaves from central Africa. These coastal states, however, soon discovered that they too would eventually be adversely affected by prolonged engagement in the slave trade and that the New World demand for slaves was so great that it would only be a matter of time before the supply to meet that demand would come from their own states. In short, European and American slavers did not care from whom or from where they got the slaves to meet the New World's demand for such labor; the trade was simply too profitable to worry about African sensibilities, protocol, or any other civilized niceties. After all, to both European and American slavers, all Africans were the same—an inferior race that was allegedly suited for enslavement.

As King Dom Afonso of the Kongo, whose country had been involved in the slave trade with Portugal, wrote to the Portuguese King John III in the sixteenth century, "[Your]Merchants [slavers]daily seize our own subjects, sons of the land and sons of our noblemen, they grab them and cause them to be sold, and so great Sir, is their corruption and licentiousness that our country is being utterly depopulated."

The loss of millions of men and women over the centuries caused the West African economy to stagnate, as essential labor for farming and other productive activities was either captured and enslaved or required to help sustain the slave trade in various capacities. West Africa began the sixteenth century self-sufficient and independent, able to adequately produce its food and other products. Participation in the slave trade ended such autonomy as West Africans increasingly became dependent on the European slave traders for their finished goods, such as textiles and metal wares, which they previously manufactured themselves. African slave traders were experts at driving hard bargains, and for several centuries they gained an increasing price for slaves—the result of rising New World demand and increased competition among European slavers. However, even when they appeared to get the best of the transaction, the ultimate advantage lay with the Europeans. In exchange for mere consumer goods—guns, rum, metalwares to name but a few – they received human capital in the form of wealth-producing workers.

For every man or woman taken captive, at least, another died in chronic slave trading. For the new West African states that emerged as a result of participation in the slave trade, most became little more than sources for supplying captives to the European traders. A "gun-slave" cyclical trade network pushed neighboring tribes into destructive arms races and endemic warfare, causing further population contraction, and thus the decreasing ability to remain self-sufficient. Indeed, one of the most serious ramifications of the slave trade became regional starvation, even famine, as the slave trade took so many people out of West Africa that there was not sufficient population left to grow food. The resulting political and cultural demoralization prepared the way for the European conquest of Africa in the nineteenth century. As the Nigerian poet Chinweizu Ibekwe writes, those West African leaders during the centuries of slave trading "had been too busy organizing our continent for the exploitative advantage of Europe, [they] had been too busy with slaving raids upon one another, too busy decorating themselves with trinkets imported from Europe, too busy impoverishing and disorganizing the land, to take thought and long-range action to protect our sovereignty."

ESTABLISHING A SLAVE SOCIETY IN NORTH AMERICA

The Slave Codes

Before 1700, the number of blacks in the Chesapeake and the Carolinas was quite small and scattered among a working class of white indentured servants. Like their white counterparts, they often worked alongside their owners. Although there was a general English predisposition to view blacks—indeed anyone not English—as inferior, a surprising degree of harmony existed between blacks and whites. As long as there were relatively few blacks in the region, and those that were there appeared to be acculturated, the potential for racism was mitigated. Although statutes containing delineation of blacks as different and separate were passed prior to the 1670s, they were few in number compared to laws passed in the southern colonies by 1700. Overall, lower-class white workers and black slaves interacted with apparently little racial consciousness and their respective owners treated all workers—indentured or chattel—essentially the same. This seventeenth-century harmony, however, was short-lived as the denigration of blacks, racism, and white supremacy accelerated in the decades after Bacon's Rebellion. Prompting this dramatic turn of events was the rapid increase in slave imports, which began in the 1690s and reached a torrent by 1700. Not only did more slaves arrive, but they came directly from Africa rather than the West Indies where the majority of slaves had previously spent some time, becoming somewhat acculturated to English ways. The new imports seemed far stranger to the whites and were beginning to dominate the work force. These exotic African slaves were called "outlandish" to distinguish them from the American-born slaves whom whites called "country-born."

As a result of increased slave imports, by 1710, Africans outnumbered whites in many Tidewater counties in Virginia and Maryland and in South Carolina as a whole. Blacks now appeared threatening, and the English predisposition to see slaves as vastly inferior, perhaps even subhuman, went into full force. A spate of laws known as the Slave Codes, passed between 1690 and 1715, significantly altered the slaves' legal status. Slaves were no longer seen legally as individual co-workers, but now as indistinguishable members of a degraded and despised workforce. The codes stripped the slaves of all humanity, relegating them to the status of property. This hardening racial atmosphere made it easier for whites to treat slaves with a harshness and impersonalism almost unthinkable in the mid-seventeenth century. Slavery came to be seen as the natural, almost biologically, determined status of blacks. Virtually no whites understood that their ideology of race reflected a more social construct than a biological reality.

All forms of slavery in the New World had certain common elements: perpetuity, kinlessness, violence, and the master's access to the slave's sexuality. First, unless manumitted, slavery was a lifelong condition. Second, a slave had no legally recognized family relationships. Because kinship was the basis of most societal and political relationships, a slave was considered socially "dead" outside the bounds of the larger society. Third, slavery rested on violence or its threat to keep the slave terrified and oppressed at all times and thus under his master's complete control. Finally, and related to violence, was the master's sexual access to the slave, sustained by law because the slave was his property; thus, slave owners had the right at any time to have sexual relations with their slave women who had no protection from such abuse. In effect, unharnessed personal power characterized the southern colonies' slave codes, which varied in specifics from one colony to another, but displayed underlying similarities. For example, in the Chesapeake colonies as well as in South Carolina, and ultimately Georgia, slaves were forbidden to wander off their plantation without a "ticket" from their owner or overseer. They were never allowed to congregate in large numbers, carry clubs or arms, or strike a white person; this particular offense was punishable by instantaneous whipping, maiming or dismemberment, even death. Masters had license to "correct" (discipline) their slaves as they deemed necessary. If the slave died during punishment, the master was immune from legal prosecution. All white persons were bound to help in the apprehension of runaways or any "Negro unable to give a satisfactory account of himself." If a white person failed to cooperate with this particular code or were found to be harboring any such fugitives, they could be fined and incarcerated. In areas of heavy slave concentration, such as South Carolina, white men were required to serve in the slave "patrols," in order to protect the community from possible insurrections as well as to track down and punish runaways. Slaves committing felonies were tried in specially constituted courts, typically consisting of a justice of the peace and two slave owners. Bondsmen convicted of a felony saw their punishment range from a "specific number of stripes [lashings from a whip] well laid on," all the way, occasionally, to burning at the stake. In short, a slave owner might lash his slaves unmercifully, in full confidence that he was carrying out an obligation to society with the written law to prove it.

CAROLINA: A Barbadian Colony on the Mainland

With the success of the Chesapeake colonies, other Englishmen began looking at the territory southward from Virginia to the northern boundary of Spanish Florida. However the expansionist desire was momentarily eclipsed by the English Civil War fought between loyalists of King Charles I and the Puritan-led Parliament in the 1640s, which resulted in an overthrow of the monarchy. Not until the Restoration, (the ascension of King Charles II to the throne after almost five years of military dictatorship) did England again engage in colonization, both to the north and south of Virginia. Several influential royal supporters led by Sir John Colleton (a wealthy Barbadian sugar planter) and Sir Anthony Ashley Cooper guided the initiative to establish a colony south of Virginia. Also interested in enlarging the empire, Charles II rewarded Cooper and Colleton, as well as six other noblemen, for their roles in the Restoration by granting these men a huge expanse of land in 1663, eventually named Carolina in his honor. Quite generous in his bestowment, the king allowed the men complete political control of the colony. Quick to take advantage of the king's generosity, the "Lords Proprietors" issued the Concessions and Agreements, promising virtually complete self-government to the colony by means of an elected assembly, religious freedom (matched at the time only by Rhode Island), and a most generous land policy that granted 150 acres to every settler and dependent they brought to Carolina. Despite the proprietors' largesse, they simply could not attract sufficient numbers of colonists to get their enterprise off the ground. After several years of trying to entice settlers, by the close of the 1660s the outpost contained only a handful of settlers barely surviving. Dreams of establishing another Virginia seemed delusional.

Advised by his close friend John Locke, Anthony Cooper decided in 1670 that continuing to recruit colonists solely from the British Isles would be senseless; perhaps it would be better to look to the existing English colonies for individuals or groups already seasoned and experienced in New World living. If given the right incentives, they might be enticed to resettle. For such individuals, the proprietors turned to the island of Barbados, a miniscule English-held island in the Caribbean that by the mid-seventeenth century was producing vast quantities of sugar. First settled in 1627, Barbados became a major source of the world's sugar within a decade of its founding. The island's tropical climate and disease-ridden environment had discouraged white servants, but the wealth derived from sugar production made possible the purchase of slave labor. In 1650, Barbados had 15,000 slaves. Ten years

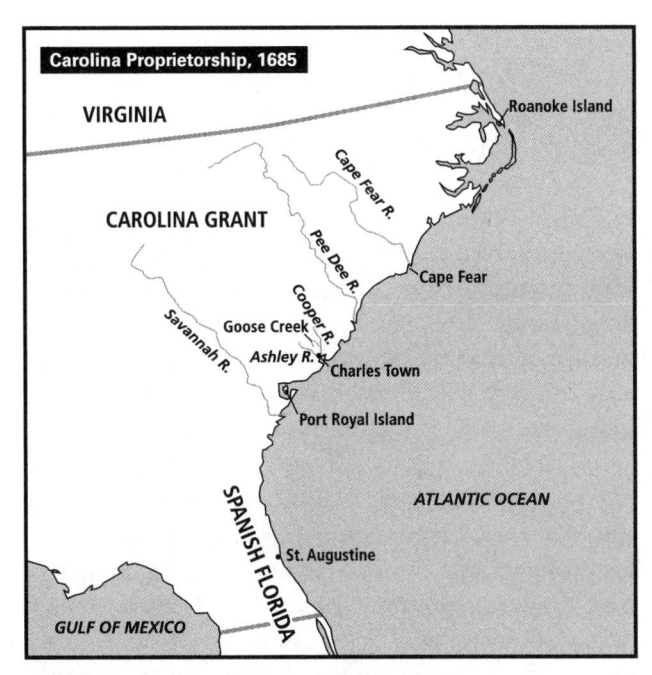

Map 2.4 Carolina Proprietorship, 1685

later, the number of bondsmen had climbed to 34,000 and zoomed to 52,000 by 1670 (with the white population only reaching 40,000). By the end of the seventeenth century, Barbados had become England's most profitable and productive colony, with a per capita income higher than in England. Most important, because of its African majority, Barbados became England's first slave society. The English magnified the differences between themselves and Africans to enhance the distinction between landowners and slaves. Indeed, Barbadians were the first to portray the Africans as beasts, revealing a most intense racism responsible for the harshest slave code in the Atlantic world. These laws prescribed that male slaves convicted of crimes could be burned at the stake, beheaded, starved, or castrated.

A handful of wealthy sugar planters dominated the island's economy, practically owning all the land and squeezing off the island's smaller farmers and freed indentured servants. The proprietors looked for these individuals to come to Carolina, along with those from the older English colonies to the north (the New England colonies discussed in the next chapter), as well as Huguenots from France. Not all Barbadians coming to Carolina had been displaced by the sugar planter elite. Some prosperous planters in search of new opportunities also came, bringing their African slaves with them. Sugar production had become so lucrative by the 1670s that planters had ceased growing foodstuffs, finding it cheaper to import all they needed, including food, from elsewhere. Thus Cooper and the other proprietors believed they could transform Carolina into a profit-making endeavor by providing food and lumber products to their Barbadian brethren. In short, the proprietors' initially envisioned their new Carolina enterprise as a "colony of a colony," in which their profits would come from supplying Barbadian sugar planters with basic necessities grown or produced in Carolina.

The first colonists arrived at Charles Town (renamed Charleston after the American Revolution) in 1670. Most of the original settlers were poor, small white farmers and former indentured servants from Barbados, with a smattering of similar migrants from Virginia, New England, the British Isles, and even France (mostly Huguenots) seeking opportunity or religious freedom. Some wealthy Barbadian planters also arrived portending the future as they came with their slaves, bringing a ready acceptance of the idea of a slave-based economy. Indeed, in many ways, Carolina was born a slave society. Unlike Virginia, there was no gradual, evolutionary process of acceptance and eventual entrenchment. Nevertheless, for the first decade and a half, most Carolina whites could not afford to purchase slaves and there was no lucrative, dominant staple such as tobacco requiring a large labor force. Until such an export crop existed, the necessary wealth required to purchase many slaves was not there.

Carolina grew slowly at first but the settlers never experienced any "starving time" as had their Virginia brethren. Initially, the pioneers experimented with a variety of exotic, Mediterranean-type products such as silk, olives, grapes, and citrus fruits, but all failed, as did surprisingly, early attempts at cultivating rice and indigo. The settlers then set their sights on simply growing mundane foodstuffs such as corn and peas and raising hogs and cattle, all of which proved profitable because they were sold to provision-starved Barbados, according to the proprietors' original intention. Carolina also boasted bountiful forests, from which the colonists developed a profitable extractive industry, producing lumber, shingles, pitch, tar, turpentine, and barrel staves, all of which found ready Caribbean markets. However, the early Carolinians most lucrative endeavor was the deerskin trade with the area's Native American tribes. As occurred frequently when Europeans entered a region, Indian tribes competed to trade with them, and rival groups of Europeans challenged each other to dominate the exchange. During the colonial period, Indian wars usually pitted one group of Europeans and their Native American allies against another group of Europeans and their Native American allies, with the Indians doing most of the fighting. Such conflicts became extensions of Europe's expanding market economy as Native Americans fought for access to European goods while the Europeans struggled with each other to monopolize certain Indian products, most notably furs. In Carolina during the late seventeenth century, the English settlers faced no competition with other Europeans for control of the fur trade. Thus, within little more than a decade, Carolinians exported more than 50,000 deerskins annually to England. Before rice and indigo, Carolina fortunes were made on the skin of the whitetail deer.

The fur trade also introduced the Carolinians to another, even more profitable commodity—Indian slaves. Indeed, until about 1690, enslaved southeastern Native Americans were the most valuable product produced by the colony. One raid against Spanish mission Indians brought back 5,000 captives, comparable in size to a slaving foray in West Africa. In part, this magnification of the Indian slave trade, which had been miniscule in the seventeenth century, was the result of the extensive deerskin trade network. By the early eighteenth century, the English made trade connections through friendly local Indians to Native nations as far away as the Mississippi River, and most of the enslaved Indians came from regions far west of present-day South Carolina. Some Indian deer hunters came to realize that slaves fetched a higher price than pelts, so raids were made against enemy tribes for captives, especially women and children to sell into bondage; the men were simply killed. So lucrative was the Indian slave trade that Carolina traders quickly established their control over the entire Southeast, driving out the Spanish, French, and even their fellow Englishmen in Virginia. In the 1680 Westo War, the Carolinians sent their Indian allies, the Savannahs, to destroy and capture the Westos, who were the Virginians' partner in the Southeastern deerskin trade. The Carolinian marauders, in conjunction with other Indian allies, succeeded in driving the Spanish out of the region as well, destroying the last of their missions in the area and enslaving their natives. Because Indian slaves were dangerous as long as they were near their homelands, most were shipped off to other colonies, most notably New England and the Caribbean.

By the close of the seventeenth century, the Carolinians had come to dominate both the Indian slave and fur trades. They had eliminated all European competitors, including their Virginian neighbors. With the alliance of a few tribes, they were able to bring the rest of the Native Americans of the region under their control. The Carolinians' hegemony, however, did not last long. One of their closest, most loyal trading partners for 40 years, the Yamasees, grew weary of being cheated out of their land and having their women and children enslaved. In 1715, they recruited other Indians in their cause and revolted, taking the Carolinians completely by surprise. The Yamasees got within 12 miles of Charles Town before being stopped. Had their Indian allies not abandoned them along the way, the Yamasees might have been able to penetrate Charles Town. The Yamasee War (1715-1716) claimed the lives of 400 whites, forcing the Carolinians to vacate their frontier outposts and reveal the precariousness of the entire English settlement.

With the trade in deerskins to England and foodstuffs to Barbados, the Carolina economy prospered. The increased need for laborers began to exceed the supply of white immigrants from England and elsewhere. The same demographic late-seventeenth-century developments in England that affected the Chesapeake also impacted Carolina, especially the decrease in the supply of potential indentured servants. Though the Carolinians enslaved local Native Americans, there were not enough to solve the colony's labor needs. Thus, as occurred in Virginia and Maryland, Carolinians during the 1680s and 1690s increasingly shifted from a servant-based economy to a slave economy. However, not until the 1720s rice boom did Carolina become, like the Chesapeake colonies, a slave society. Prior to that time, Carolina society contained slaves set to work in the more open conditions of a mixed economy. Slaves worked with whites of various origins at a variety of tasks: growing food for export to Barbados; cutting timber in the forests for lumber, shingles, barrel staves, working in the infant naval stores industry providing pitch and tar for English shipping, and herding cattle in the woods and rounding them up in cow pens for the beef market at home and in the West Indies. African slave herdsmen served as the South's first cowboys. In this diverse economy of Carolina's pioneer days, blacks and whites worked and socialized together, not as equals, but with a greater degree of harmony than they would for the next two-and-a-half centuries.

From the beginning, the Carolina proprietors had hoped to become rich by discovering a bonanza crop like tobacco or sugar that could be grown there and profitably sold in England. Although the colony thrived by the close of the seventeenth century, Carolina did not become the lucrative colonial venture its proprietors had envisioned until the arrival of extensive rice and indigo cultivation. After several years of experimenting with different techniques, rice farming finally became profitable. In 1700, Carolina rice planters had exported 400,000 pounds of rice; by 1710, they were shipping 1.5 million pounds. By mid-century, Carolinians exported 50 million pounds shipped annually. Increased rice production saw the natural corollary of increased importation of African slaves. Initially, as in the Chesapeake, rice planters purchased most slaves from the West Indies, but the clamor for laborers became so great by the 1720s that the islands could not keep pace with such high demand. Carolina planters thus bought their slaves directly from Africa. Much to their surprise, many of the Africans they purchased (accidentally at first than by planter preference subsequently) came from West Africa's Grain Coast, with expertise in planting and growing rice, helping to expand Carolina's rice production and profitability, which in turn allowed planters to buy even more slaves. Thanks in large part to African expertise, the rice industry matured and became more efficient, shifting from dry-land cultivation to fresh water, swampy regions for irrigation to flood the fields and kill the grass. Finally, after midcentury, it shifted again to tidal-swamp areas in the low country. Rice production required tremendous start-up and maintenance costs, with back-breaking labor which only blacks were thought capable of performing.

Carolinians added another important crop to their economy in the 1740s when a young South Carolina woman named Elizabeth Lucas Pinckney successfully adapted West Indian indigo to the low-country climate. The assistance of Caribbean slaves already skilled in indigo culture was also likely crucial to this development. Native to India, the indigo plant produced a deep blue dye important in textile manufacture. Rice grew best in the lowlands, but indigo could be cultivated on high ground. In addition, the two staples had different seasonal growing patterns, thus the two crops harmonized perfectly. Rice and indigo production rose steadily over the next 30 years. The profits from both crops were enormous. By the 1770s, they were among the most valuable commodities exported from Great Britain's mainland North American colonies. As labor intensive as rice production, Carolina planters believed indigo cultivation was work suitable only for blacks. The old mixed economy with a degree of white-black equality in the workplace disappeared by the 1720s. Coastal Carolina resembled England's Caribbean sugar islands, where black slaves on manorial-sized plantations greatly outnumbered whites, with slaves almost exclusively assigned to agricultural tasks. Moreover, the Carolina slave codes, enacted in the 1690s, were the harshest on the North American continent, reflecting the Carolinians "**Barbadian Connection**." Before the importation of slaves to the United States ended in 1808, at least 100,000 Africans had arrived at Charleston. One of every five ancestors of today's African Americans passed through that port on his or her way to the rice and indigo fields. Like the Chesapeake in the early eighteenth century, Carolina had become a full-fledged slave society. Politically, as in the Chesapeake, the largest, wealthiest indigo and rice planters came to dominate and controlled the colonial legislature, dictating to both the governor and the Carolina plain folk how the colony should be run.

North Carolina

The Lords Proprietors virtually ignored the northern portion of their land grant, the region between Virginia and Cape Fear that became the colony and state of North Carolina. Various factors contributed to this neglect: an inhospitable coastline for shipping, with shifting sand bars, shallow inlets, and no natural harbors such as Charles Town; soil and climate not conducive to staple crop production; and unfriendly Indians such as the Tuscarora. This lack of attention meant that northern Carolina developed with little proprietary assistance. Though sparsely settled until the 1720s, thereafter the area grew through a rich stream of migration from Europe, developing an increasingly profitable mixed economy. By 1790, North Carolina was second only to Virginia in white population among the southern United States.

Even before the proprietors received their grant from Charles II, Virginians had penetrated northern Carolina around Albermarle Sound, searching for virgin tobacco land. One such intrepid individual, Nathaniel Batts, established a home on the western shore of the sound in 1655, becoming the first permanent white inhabitant in all of Carolina. Batts traded with local Indians for deerskins, but word soon spread that the area was perfect for tobacco cultivation and other Virginians began coming to the territory. By the 1660s, the region around Albermarle Sound was more tied to the tobacco economy of the Chesapeake than to the provisioning trade and later rice industry of southern Carolina. In effect, the Albermarle area had become a colony of Virginia, settled by small farmers and servants who had fulfilled their indentures, coming in search of inexpensive, if not free land. Such encroachment by Virginia upset the Carolina proprietors who now took serious interest in the northern portion of their grant.

Although initially hoping to profit from tobacco growing, the Albermarle settlers soon realized that because of the absence of deep-water harbors, tobacco would not be as profitable as originally hoped. Thus, North Carolinians were less committed to trade with England and developed a more diverse local economy. Tobacco was grown as a money crop, but farmers also learned to grow peas, corn, beans, raise livestock and poultry for their own food, trading surpluses to Virginia, the rice farmers to the south, or especially to the West Indies via shallow-drafted boats not suitable for transatlantic commerce. The burgeoning economy saw increases in population, leading by the 1690s to the organization of more counties beyond Albemarle Sound. The development of a growing naval stores industry also helped to promote population growth.

Another lucrative enterprise that some northern Carolinians engaged in during the 1710s was trading with and harboring some of the most infamous Caribbean pirates of the era. The islands of the colony's Outer Banks provided the perfect hiding place and striking point from which the buccaneers' swift, shallow-drafted vessels could attack England's larger, cumbersome, oceangoing ships laden with valuable goods. From 1710 to 1720, these independent maritime opportunists, loyal only to themselves and to their fortunes, plied the waters and raided the cargo ships of any nation. Meanwhile, they also traded with North Carolinians more than happy to purchase or barter with their corsair friends for all manner of exotic goods. The northern Carolinians welcomed the pirates, not only providing them a safe sanctuary, but often publicly advertised when their ships planned to arrive with their latest booty. Of course, when asked by English officials trying to apprehend these outlaws, the North Carolinians declared they never saw such people nor knew where they were hiding. No more colorful and legendary group ever roamed the coastal waters of North America than these sea brigands, whose names are recognizable to this day; men such as the brute Edward Teach, alias "Blackbeard," or Stede Bonnet, the "gentleman buccaneer," who, as a well-educated and wealthy retired British army major, set up his freebooting headquarters along the Carolina coast. The British navy finally dispatched them both, hanging Bonnet in 1718 and killing Blackbeard after a fierce battle the same year. Much to the disappointment of North Carolinians, the heyday of Carolina pirating had ended.

News of northern Carolina's flourishing economy not only brought English settlers to the region from neighboring Virginia and the mother country, but also other Europeans, most notably French **Huguenots**, Swiss merchants from Bern, and Palatine Germans. Along with the English, these three groups gave northern Carolina a rich ethnic and religious diversity along with a devotion to a diversified economy that neither the Virginia tobacco region nor the southern rice-growing district to the south could claim. In short, northern Carolina became a place economically and socially unlike its northern and southern neighbors, in effect, a pluralistic society. Although many North Carolinians owned slaves, particularly those engaged in tobacco cultivation, the northern portion of Carolina did not become a slave society. Indeed, compared to Virginia and South Carolina, African slavery was virtually absent in North Carolina. As late as 1712, when the English government officially granted North and South Carolina, there were only approximately 800 slaves in the region. Thus, in the middle of two slave societies there existed the antithesis; a white community ethnically and economically diversified and tied only in a most marginal and peripheral sense to commercial production and the larger Atlantic trade network. In many ways, colonial northern Carolinians became the prototype for the future American independent, non-slaveholding yeoman farmers, exalted by Thomas Jefferson as the essence of the great democratic, republican experiment called the United States.

THE FOUNDING OF GEORGIA

With the establishment of South Carolina, England worried that Spain and France would resent the presence of an English colony so close to their respective territories that these countries would attempt to drive the British out of the region. Of the two nations, France, not Spain, had become the greater potential menace to English interests in southeastern North America. An unprecedented French encroachment along the Gulf Coast alerted the Carolinians to a potential threat just as it spurred the Spanish to react in Mexico. The French had established garrisons at Mobile (in present-day southern Alabama), Fort Toulouse (in central Alabama), Natchitoches (in western Louisiana), and Natchez (in western Mississippi)—all of which clearly endangered the Carolinians lucrative deerskin trade with the Indians of the Gulf Coast region. The French establishment of New Orleans in 1718 near the mouth of the Mississippi River and the seizing of Pensacola from the Spanish in 1719 caused the Carolinians further alarm. These French initiatives convinced the Carolinians and the English government that the French planned to connect their Gulf Coast settlements with their fur trading empire in Canada. Carolinians thus saw the possible end to one of their most lucrative trading enterprises, not to mention the possibility that Florida could become a viable threat. Such fears came to fruition during the Yamasee War, which the Carolinians believed the French and Spanish helped to instigate in order to drive the English out of Carolina. Although the colonists defeated the Yamasee, they nonetheless continued to feel vulnerable to French and Spanish reprisals. Carolinians thus became convinced that steps had to be taken to establish a buffer between their communities and the enemy, prevent the Gulf and French Canadian settlements from being linked, and safeguard the fur trade routes to the west. All these purposes could be served by establishing another English settlement between South Carolina and Spanish Florida.

The English government took seriously the Carolinians' entreaties, but all attempts at establishing a defensive barrier between Carolina and the European rivals failed. Interestingly, not until the military exigencies of such an endeavor combined with the reform desires of a group of English philanthropists did England successfully establish its 13th colony in North America—Georgia. The individuals most responsible for Georgia's founding were Sir John Perceval, **General James Oglethorpe**, and Dr. Thomas Bray, all of whom were committed to reforming England's penal system, especially how it dealt with debtors. After heading a Parliamentary investigative committee charged with uncovering abuses in the penal system, Oglethorpe became convinced that England needed to establish a charity colony for the poor rather than putting such individuals in prison. He also believed that such a colony in North America could serve as a place to proselytize among slaves and Indians while providing a place of redemption for the deserving poor. Perceval, Oglethorpe, Bray, and other men of such ideals formed a group called the Georgia Trustees and petitioned the king, George II, for a charter to establish their colony. The king granted their request in 1732, with the trustees authorized to govern the colony for 21 years, after which it would revert to the Crown. Originally planned to be a refuge for debtors, Georgia also became a haven for many other economically dislocated Englishmen, "worthy" poor, such as farmers, artisans, and tradesmen who through no fault of their own had become unemployed. Georgia came to be seen as a way of providing all these unfortunates an opportunity for a new life.

Oglethorpe came with the first colonists, arriving with the just over 100 hopefuls at Charles Town in mid-January 1733. Although never officially named governor, Oglethorpe's natural abilities and forceful personality made him the leader of the experiment. After landing at Charles Town, the colonists eventually made their way to the site of present-day Savannah, which became Georgia's first settlement. Illness and death abounded during the first summer, but supplies were sent by the trustees, and friendly Indians, the Yamacraws, also helped provide provisions. Oglethorpe treated the Yamacraws and other local natives fairly. In fact, he became a good friend to Tomochichi, the Yamacraw chief, who helped the Georgians secure peace with the larger Creek confederacy of Native Americans. Georgia experienced no "starving time" and thus the colony quickly proved a success, which attracted more impoverished but "worthy" men and women (though very few debtors). Georgia's reform image spread throughout Europe. Within a year, others seeking a new chance in life requested to come. Driven out by the Catholic Church, 100 German Lutherans from Salzburg, Austria came to Georgia in 1734. After a few years of hardship and disease, the Salzburgers began to prosper, and their presence attracted additional European settlers to Georgia—some transient, most permanent. By the mid-eighteenth century, the colony thus contained a substantial German-speaking population with a cluster of German folkways. Sensing the need for citizen-soldiers who could both farm and fight, the Georgia trustees recruited a group of Scottish Highlanders, known to be aggressive defenders of their property and way of life. By 1740, several hundred had come, most of them settling in Darien at the mouth of the Altamaha River—the accepted boundary between English and Spanish authority. In less than a decade, Georgia's stability and prosperity, along with a reputation for openness to European victims of oppression and poverty, had attracted to the colony people from England, Germany, Switzerland, Wales, Scotland, Ireland, and even a handful of Jews who established one of the nation's earliest Jewish communities in Savannah. About fifty Jews arrived from Eastern Europe in the summer of 1733, and although they had no rabbi, they founded a synagogue, called Mickva Israel, and practiced their faith free from any harassment or persecution. Georgia thus became known for its religious pluralism and toleration, even of non-Christians.

With their numbers increasing, the early Georgians soon felt secure enough to begin to protest Oglethorpe's paternalistic leadership and restrictive policies. Feeling safe from danger, the colonists began to think about their long-term prosperity. The trustees wanted to keep Georgia a charitable preserve for the worthy poor and objected to the idea of individual farmers wanting huge blocks of land for themselves. The trustees compromised somewhat, parceling out land in small amounts to individual farmers that they could hold for their lifetimes. The land could not be sold and could be conveyed only to their male heirs. If there were none, the land reverted to the trustees. In 1735, the trustees also issued decrees prohibiting slavery in Georgia, as well as the consumption of rum and other strong drinks, and restricted trade with the Indians. In the trustees' minds, Georgia should be a moral experiment for those transported persons in unfortunate circumstances, training them in the ways of thrift, sobriety, and morality in order to become upstanding citizens. Such an effort required the prohibition of alcohol, which the trustees believed would lead to intemperance and abuse, and the disallowance of slavery, which they believed would tempt slave owners with idleness, licentiousness, and a hunger for extravagant profits. Good relations with the Native Americans were necessary for security reasons and a sense of fairness, thus the Indian trade had to be closely monitored. By the 1740s, much to the trustees' disappointment, the majority of Georgians chafed under these restrictions. They had come to the colony to have a freer life and simply felt the trustees' mandates impinged upon their right to have a better, more bountiful existence.

Believing that Georgia's climate and soil to be similar to the Mediterranean, the trustees hoped products like wine, olives, and silk could be produced. When it became obvious that neither their colony's climate nor topography was conducive to the growing of such commodities, Georgia farmers sought to adopt the hugely profitable system of rice cultivation pioneered in South Carolina. Recognizing the strenuous work involved in setting up rice fields, those Georgians wanting to engage in such an enterprise demanded an end to the prohibition of slavery. Oglethorpe and his fellow trustees were loath to end the ban on slavery, so Georgians sought ways to circumvent the law, often leasing slaves for 99 years from South Carolina "owners" and paying them the entire "rent" in advance. Others simply bought slaves in flagrant disregard of the law. Opposition to the law became so intense that in 1750 the trustees revoked the 1735 prohibition. Never able to realize a colony of small, contented farmers, the trustees surrendered Georgia back to the Crown in 1752, a year earlier than planned. With Oglethorpe's laws repealed—from outlawing alcohol to land restrictions to the prohibition of slavery—Georgia by mid-century resembled the plantation society of South Carolina. Savannah became a little Charles Town, with its robust civic and cultural life, and slave markets as well. By 1750, Georgia had transformed itself from a fragile new settlement, a buffer between South Carolina and vague enemies to the south and west, to a prosperous colony producing a profitable agricultural export for the world market. In the process, Georgia ceased its noble experiment as a place of charity for the worthy poor. While remaining open to Europeans fleeing from oppression and destitution, Georgia began to enslave large numbers of Africans, becoming a booming plantation society, not much different from its northern neighbors in South Carolina and the Chesapeake.

THE LATIN SOUTH

Colonial American history is often described as the progress of English settlement across a vast continent occupied by decreasing numbers of Indians. French and Spanish settlers only sporadically appear as a prelude to the Louisiana Purchase and the later Anglo-Texan revolt against Mexican authority and the subsequent controversy over Texas annexation to the United States. Yet, the cultures of Spain and France left a deeper imprint on the region from Florida to Texas than the passing mention of their presence that most United States history texts typically devote. European wars and rivalries affected Spanish and French attempts to establish mainland colonies as much, if no more, than homeland problems did. In fact, these Old World antagonisms shaped the timing of both the beginning and the end of Spanish and French control of large portions of the present-day South. By contrast, England, except for the Armada of the late sixteenth century and a few brief forays into continental geopolitics in the early seventeenth century, wisely remained detached from European affairs. As a result, seventeenth-century Englishmen devoted more time and energy to developing and expanding their New World colonial enterprises.

Initially, the Spanish in Florida were little bothered by the English colony at Jamestown. By 1607, Florida had become merely a way-station for Spanish ships carrying silver and gold from Mexico and a mission field for the Franciscan friars whose series of outposts at Indian towns swept across from St. Augustine to the northernmost Sea Islands of Georgia (called Guale after a local Indian chief). Moving westward, the Franciscans had pushed their missions all the way to present-day southern Alabama. By 1674, they had established 32 missions in Florida, ministering to more than 13,000 Christian Indians. Beginning in the 1670s, however, Spanish security and hegemony over the region suddenly became threatened by the English presence in South Carolina. By that decade the Carolinians had begun developing a lucrative fur trade with the area's Native Americans, gaining influence over the Indians who found it hard to resist British goods. English and French pirates also raided the isolated missions in coastal Guale, forcing the Spanish to abandon Georgia and retreat into Florida. Carolinian-armed Indian allies periodically marauded the missions, eventually attacking them full force in 1702 and 1704, when expeditions led by South Carolina governor James Moore invaded Florida with a combined Carolinian-Indian army, devastating the missions near St. Augustine and the Apalachee region—neither the missions nor Spanish authority ever completely recovered in Florida.

At the same time that the English challenged Spanish territory in the east, another European rival, France, had begun to threaten the Spanish presence from the west. Although the sixteenth-century Spanish explorers Hernando de Soto and Francisco Coronado had traveled through present-day Alabama, Mississippi, Louisiana, Texas, and the southern Great Plains, they were each searching for gold and had no intention or interest in establishing any sort of permanent settlements in these areas. Spain supported their sojourns for wealth only to claim new territories. At the western periphery of this tenuous empire, the Spanish beginning in the late seventeenth century began to bring Christianity to the Native Americans by planting a string of missions, with the first established near present-day Santa Fe, New Mexico in

1598. In subsequent decades, they built more near the upper Nueces River and in the Edwards Plateau region of Texas. The oldest permanent settlement in Texas began in 1681 at the mission site of Ysleta near present-day El Paso. Except for this smattering of missions, the Spanish had little success in converting the Plains tribes of the area (which included the Apaches, the Comanches, the Wichitas, and the Kiowas). Spain neglected the entire region from the Rio Grande to the Escambia River in West Florida, seeing neither a military nor an economic reason to become more involved. Then France entered the arena, and the entire geopolitical situation changed.

France did not become a threat to Spanish authority in the old Southwest until the 1670s. Prior to that decade, the French empire in Canada seemed remote to affect Spanish interests. Beginning in the 1670s, however, the French expanded out of Canada, led by their intrepid fur traders and explorers seeking not only to extend the reach of their fur trade deeper into North America, but also to find a warm-water river route southward from Canada. In 1673, the Jesuit priest Jacques Marquette along with Louis Jolliet had come down the Mississippi River all the way to where it joined with the Arkansas River. Nine years later, René-Robert Cavelier, **Sieur de La Salle** floated all the way to the Gulf Coast via one of the Mississippi's several mouths, staking a French claim to the region. La Salle's presence would have been provocation enough for the nervous Spanish, but when he returned from France with an expedition intending to expand France's empire into the Southwest, Spanish authorities became gripped

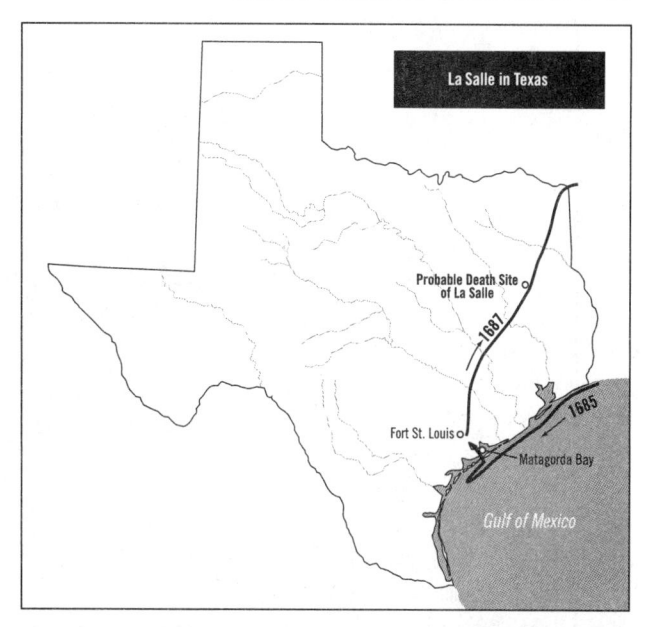

Map 2.5 La Salle was the first to descend the Mississippi all the way to the Gulf of Mexico in 1682. He claimed the entire Mississippi River Valley for France, naming the entire region "Louisiana" in honor of his king, Louis XIV.

with fear. Fortunately for the Spanish, La Salle's attempt to establish a permanent French colony at the mouth of the Mississippi failed, largely due to weather problems compounded by navigational errors forcing his landing on the Texas coast at Matagorda Bay near the Lavaca River. La Salle built a small garrison named Fort Saint Louis, but the outpost soon dissolved due to sickness, poor supplies, and harassment by local Karankawa In-

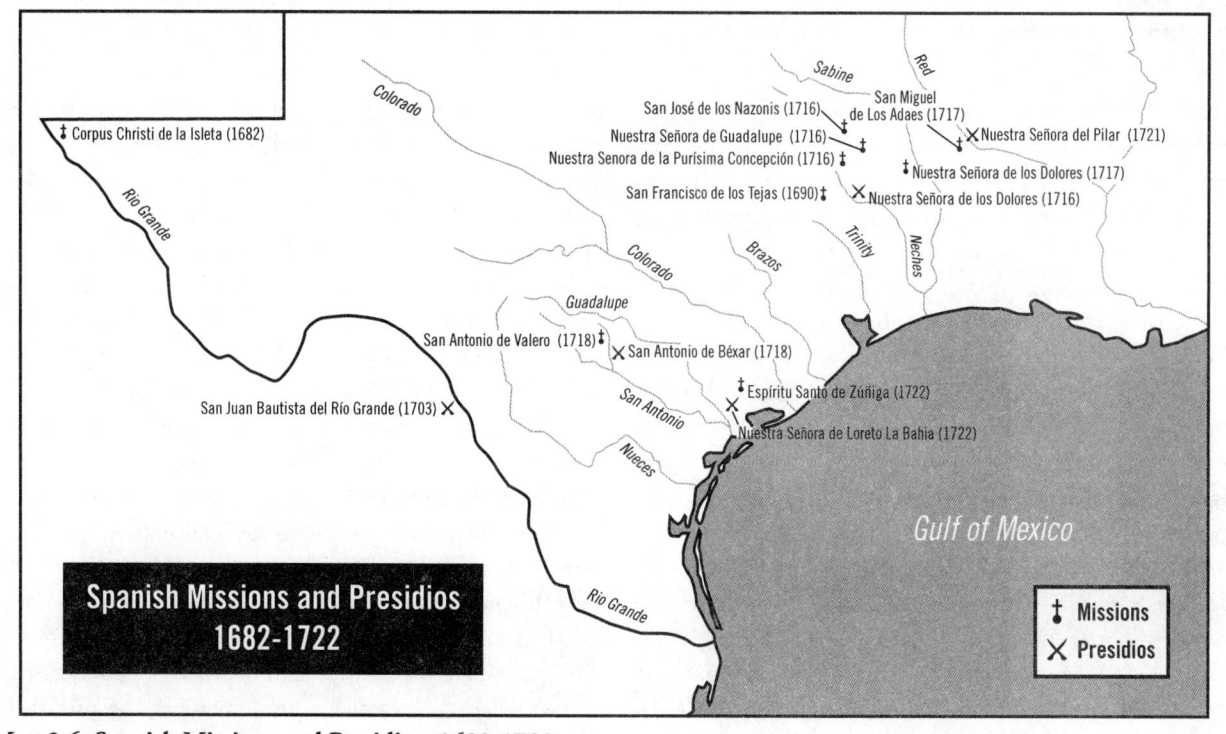

Map 2.6 Spanish Missions and Presidios, 1682-1722

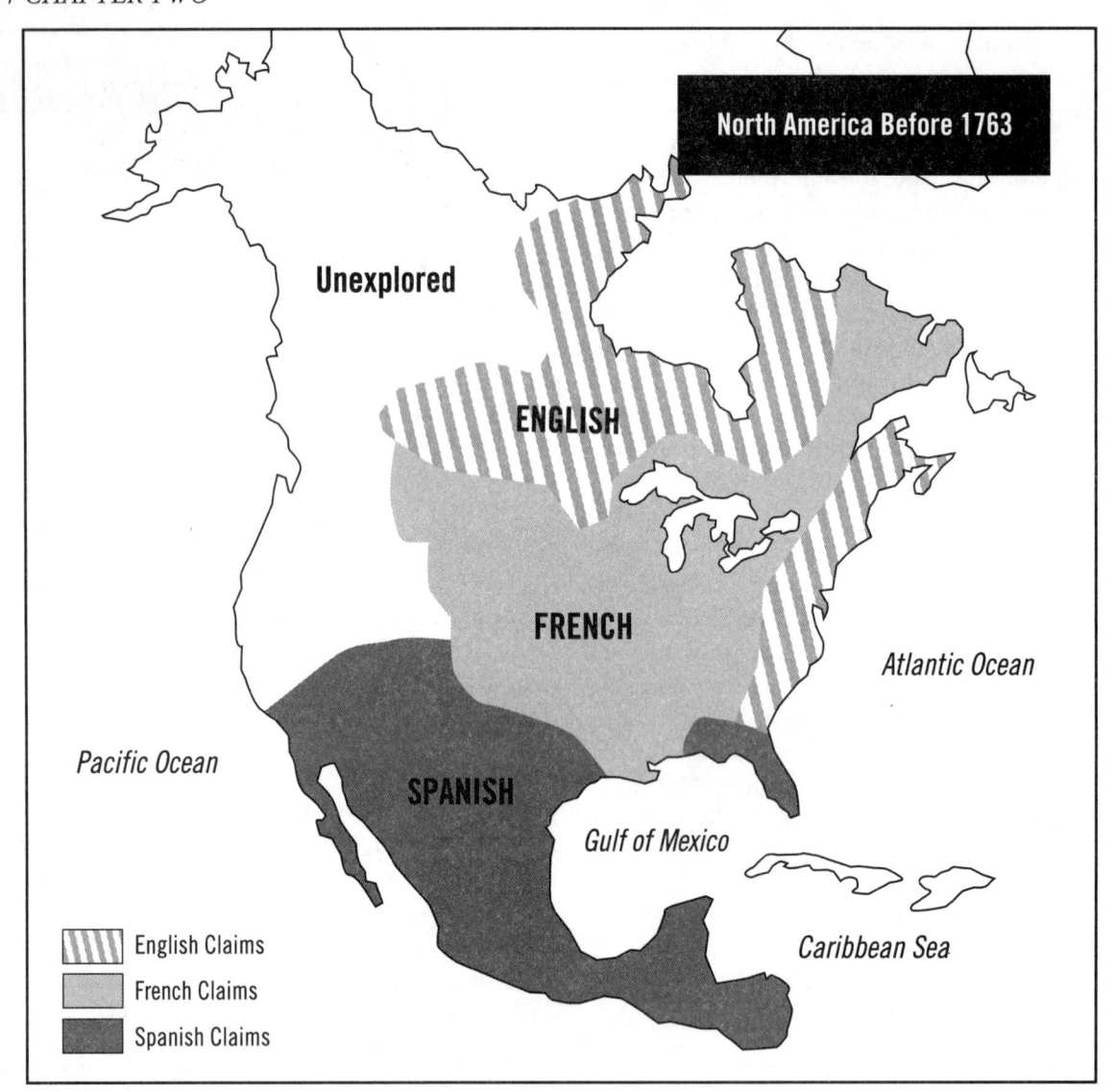

Map 2.7 North America Before 1763

dians. After a storm sunk his last remaining vessel, La Salle decided to return to Canada for reinforcements but was killed by his own men in eastern Texas after an argument over how to share the sparse food supply. After La Salle left, the Karankawas finished off the remnants of Fort Saint Louis, thus ending the French attempt to extend their North American empire to the western Gulf Coast.

La Salle's venture, exaggerated by the Spanish into an "invasion" of the Texas coast, helped to force the Spanish out of their complacency concerning their borderland possessions. Already harassed in the east by the English, the Spanish now put forth a more concerted effort to defend their empire from English and French interlopers. By the time Spanish forces under Alonso de León arrived at the site of Fort Saint Louis, the garrison had already been destroyed. When the Spanish contingent arrived, to de León's shock, a band of Caddo Indians from northeastern Texas arrived and asked the Spaniard to establish a mission for them, which he agreed to do. In 1690, Spanish friars established Mission San Francisco de los Tejas among the Caddo, but the arrival of disease coupled with soldiers' advances upon native women and the Indians' general lack of interest in adopting Spanish ways doomed the mission to failure within three years. With the French threat apparently gone from Texas, Spain once again forgot about this particular borderland province until the French once more appeared on the scene two decades later.

Although foiled in their first attempts to establish a presence along the Gulf Coast, the French renewed their efforts in the late 1690s when Louis XIV authorized another expedition to try to lay claim to the region, now called Louisiana after the great "Sun King." To lead this new venture, the king and his ministers chose two French-Canadian explorers, Pierre Le Moyne (Sieur d'Iberville) and his brother Jean Baptiste Le Moyne (Sieur de Bienville) to establish a settlement at the mouth of the Mississippi and perhaps other outposts along the

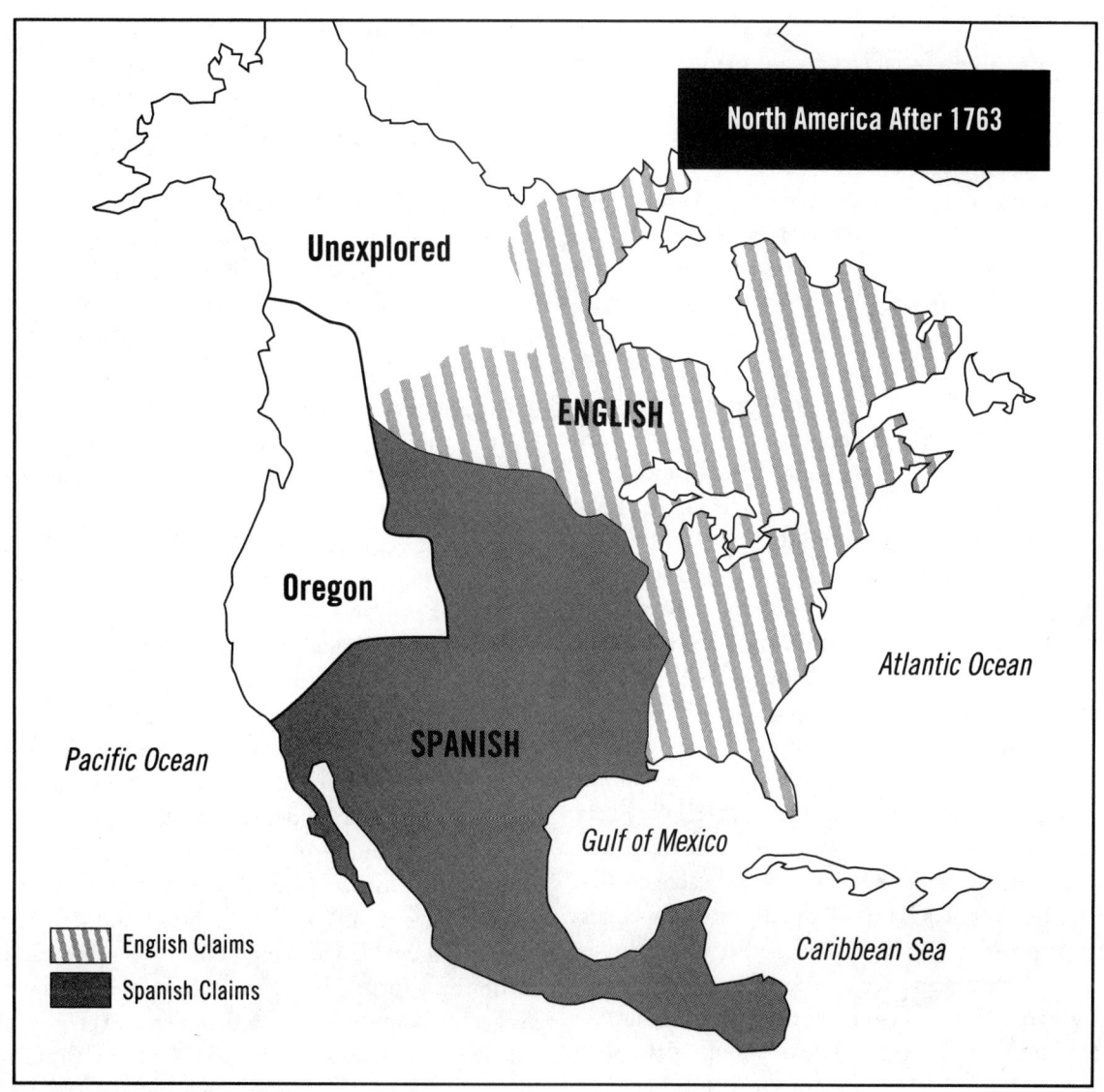

Map 2.8 North America After 1763

Gulf Coast. The brothers sailed from France in October 1698, reaching present-day Mobile three months later. Leaving the bulk of their forces at Mobile, the Le Moyne brothers continued westward until they found the mouth of the Mississippi and made their way upstream all the way to present-day Baton Rouge, Louisiana. After failing to establish settlements along the southern portion of the Mississippi, the Le Moynes brought all settlers to one location at Mobile, officially founded in 1711. Believing in the importance of erecting a barrier against Carolina fur traders and trappers, the French established Fort Toulouse in 1717 at the juncture of the Coosa and Tallapoosa Rivers, just north of the present-day city of Montgomery, Alabama. From their base in Mobile, the French established several other settlements in Louisiana over the course of the next decade. Setting up forts and trading posts to buy furs from the Indians and to stymie the Carolina traders, the French placed trading centers at Natchitoches in 1714; near the Texas border, Fort Rosalie at the site of Natchez, Mississippi in 1716; and the colony's first town, New Orleans, on the bank of the Mississippi south of Lake Pontchartrain in 1718. The local economy depended on trading cheap European goods with a variety of Indian groups in exchange for valuable deerskins. The French displayed little interest in developing any sort of significant agricultural enterprises.

Surprisingly, this strong French presence did not alarm the Spanish until a group of French traders led by Louis Juchereau de Saint-Denis showed up at a Spanish mission and presidio (garrison) on the Rio Grande, asking to open trade between French Louisiana and Spanish Texas. Because peace came between the two nations in Europe after the War of the Spanish Succession, Saint-Denis saw no obstacles preventing such an endeavor, which could benefit both countries' colonial settlements. Though the Spanish authorities were initially hostile to the idea, the wily Frenchman convinced the viceroy in Mexico City of his proposal's merits and Saint-Denis next found himself leading a Spanish expedition to northeast Texas to establish a string of six Franciscan missions and a presidio near present-day Nacogdoches, with the last one, Los Adaes, actually located across the Sabine River in Louisiana. Unfortunately, a year after these settlements had been established (1719), a French force heard that war had resumed in Europe between France and Spain and attacked Los Adaes, causing the entire Spanish population to flee northeastern Texas all the way to recently-established San Antonio. Interestingly, the French did not move into the vacated region, which allowed the Spanish to return in 1721 and reclaim the area. Though actually located in Louisiana, Los Adaes became the Spanish capital of Texas for the next 50 years. This half-century marked the heyday of Spanish Texas with the raising of livestock—hogs, mustangs, and especially cattle. Agriculture, however, did not drive the economy of the entire Spanish Borderlands (which included present-day California, New Mexico, Arizona, parts of Nevada, Utah, and Colorado).

Largely because of the French threat to their dominions, the Spanish during the eighteenth century took the settlement of their borderlands seriously, especially Texas, which by the 1760s had close to 2,500 inhabitants permanently settled in three main locations: Nacogdoches, San Antonio, and La Bahia (Goliad) with the largest concentration in San Antonio. Spanish place names, ranching techniques and terms, the concept of a homestead law exempting a person's property from seizure for debt, the idea that a husband and wife jointly share their property—these and other facets of the Spanish heritage left a permanent legacy and imprint on Texas culture, language, and customs. In 1762, France, as a result of defeat in the Seven Years' War with Great Britain, ceded Louisiana to Spain, removing once and for all the French threat that had worried Spain for close to a century. With the French menace gone, the Spanish abandoned their presidios and missions from eastern Texas and relocated everyone to the area around San Antonio. For the next 50 years, occasional explorers, promoters, pioneers, and scoundrels from Louisiana and the eventual United States came to Texas and settled there. All the while tensions simmered between the *tejano* population and the assortment of Anglo-Americans and other non-Mexican groups. As will be seen in a later chapter, one of the biggest mistakes the Mexican government made was to open Texas's door to immigration, which eventually cost Mexico all of its borderland territory.

THE GROWTH OF ENGLISH COLONIES

Though the English came late to the New World, once fully engaged in overseas expansion, after overcoming initial setbacks born of stupidity, arrogance, and greed, they rapidly developed their southern colonies into commercially successful and profitable enterprises based on the production of staple crops cultivated by slave labor. Had it not been for the perseverance of Captain John Smith and the relationships he established with the local Native Americans, Jamestown would have gone the way of Roanoke and England might not have ever returned to North America. Equally fortuitous were the Virginians' realization of tobacco. Had they not found such an immediately lucrative cash crop, the Jamestown settlement might have economically languished indefinitely, ultimately failing, and again, signaling the end of an overseas empire for England.

Southern colonial prosperity and permanency was founded first on the blood, sweat, tears of indentured servants, mostly from England, then on the backs of over 11 million brutally enslaved Africans forcibly brought to the New World in chains over the course of two-and-one-half centuries. Indeed, one of the great paradoxes of mainland southern colonial history was the initial reluctance of tobacco, rice, and indigo planters to adopt African slavery. Over time, as homeland demographic factors changed beyond their control, staple crop planters not only turned to African slavery to solve their labor needs, but soon embraced a completely segregated black and white society, stripping the slaves of all humanity into valuable chattel. Simultaneously, these black codes elevated lower-class whites while denigrating the slaves, thus turning whites, who once had much in common as laborers with their black brethren, into racists. One of the more insidious purposes of the slave codes was to inculcate a racist mentality in all southern whites, whether or not they actually owned slaves. Although, in retrospect, southern planters of cash crops would have turned to African slavery sooner or later, the inherent flaws of indentured servitude (culminating in the Chesapeake with Bacon's Rebellion), accelerated the process toward the adoption of African slavery. By 1700, the Chesapeake colonies of Maryland and Virginia, South Carolina, and ultimately Georgia by the 1740s had become full-fledged slave societies.

The English also quickly dispensed with the Native American tribes of the Southeast once they required land for tobacco cultivation in the Chesapeake or the Indians themselves for slaves in the Carolinas. Unlike the Spanish, or even the French to a lesser degree, the English had no desire to convert the Native Americans to Christianity. Quickly, the English approach to Native Americans turned genocidal Thus, by 1700, major Chesapeake native groups that inhabited the area when the English first arrived in 1607 were gone. In the Carolinas, the Native American peoples lasted a bit longer, primarily because of the lucrative deerskin trade that developed between the Carolinians and the region's Native Americans.

By the middle of the eighteenth century, the American colonial South was well on its way to becoming a rather distinct region from the colonial North, which developed much differently socially, economically, and politically over roughly the same time period. Indeed, by the time of the American revolt against British authority in the mid-1770s, two rather distinct colonial Americas had emerged, with the differences between North and South only continuing to grow more pronounced in subsequent decades. In effect, many of the foundations for American sectionalism had been put in place by the end of the colonial period.

Chronology

1598 The Spanish establish mission outpost near present-day Santa Fe, New Mexico.

1607 Jamestown established.

1609 Virginia receives sea-to-sea charter.

1613-1614 John Rolfe plants tobacco, marries Pocahontas.

1618 Governor Sandys implements London Company reforms for Jamestown.

1619 First Africans arrive in Virginia.
House of Burgesses first meets.
The headright system is created by the Virginia Company to attract settles to Virginia.

1622 Opechancanough launches war of extermination in Virginia.

1624 The Crown assumes direct control of Virginia.

1632 King Charles I grants Lord Baltimore land for the colony of Maryland.

1644 Opechancanough's second uprising against Virginia colonists.

1649 The Calverts grant religious toleration for all Christians in Maryland to guarantee Catholic security against the majority Protestants in Maryland.

1663 First Carolina charter granted.

1670 First permanent English settlement established in South Carolina.
Charles Town (Charleston) founded in South Carolina.

1675-76 Bacon's Rebellion.

1680 Pueblos revolt in New Mexico.

1689 La Salle attempts to establish a French colony in present-day Texas.

1699 Louisiana established by the French.

1702-04 Carolina slaves destroy Florida missions.

1705 Virginia adopts comprehensive slave code.

1711 The Le Moyne brothers, French-Canadian explorers and traders, establish Mobile in present-day Alabama.

1715 Yamasee War.

1732 Georgia founded.

Review Questions

1. Compare and contrast initial English colonization efforts in the New World with that of the Spanish and French.

2. Discuss the origins of African slavery in England's North American southern colonies.

3. Describe the English colonists' differing relationships with the various Native American nations they encountered in the southern colonies.

4. Discuss the causes and consequences of Bacon's rebellion in Virginia.

5. In what ways did European colonization and exploitation of the West Indies differ from the founding of the colonies on the North American mainland?

Glossary of Important People and Concepts

Act of Toleration (1649)
Nathaniel Bacon
Bacon's Rebellion
Barbadian Connection
Sir William Berkeley
George Calvert (First Lord Baltimore)
Headright System
House of Burgesses
House of Delegates
House of Stuart
Huguenots
Indentured Servitude
Jamestown
René-Robert Cavelier, Sieur de La Salle
London or Virginia Company
Middle Passage
James Oglethorpe
Opechancanough
Powhatan
Royal African Company
John Smith
"Starving Time"
Tidewater

SUGGESTED READINGS

Ira Berlin, *Many Thousands Gone: The First Two Centuries of Slavery in North America* (1998).

Richard S. Dunn, *Sugar and Slaves: The Rise of the Planter Class in the English West Indies, 1624-1713* (1972).

Allan Gallay, *The Indian Slave Trade: The Rise of the English Empire in the American South, 1670–1717* (2003).

Frederic W. Gleach, *Powhatan's World and Colonial Virginia: A Conflict of Cultures* (1997).

Winthrop Jordan, *White over Black: American Attitudes Toward the Negro, 1550-1812* (1968).

Allan Kulikoff, *Tobacco and Slaves: The Development of the Southern Cultures in the Chesapeake, 1680-1800* (1986).

David C. Littlefield, *Rice and Slaves: Ethnicity and the Slave Trade in Colonial South Carolina* (1981).

Gloria L. Main, *Tobacco Colony: Life in Early Maryland, 1650-1720* (1982).

Sidney Mintz, *Sweetness and Power: The Place of Sugar in Modern History* (1985).

Edmund S. Morgan, *American Slavery, American Freedom: The Ordeal of Colonial Virginia* (1975).

Orlando Patterson, *Slavery and Social Death: A Comparative Study* (1982).

David Price, *Love and Hate in Jamestown: John Smith, Pocahontas, and the Start of a Nation* (2003).

M. Eugene Sirmans, *Colonial South Carolina: A Political History, 1663-1763* (1966).

Alan Taylor, *The American Colonies* (2001).

Wilcomb E. Washburn, *The Governor and the Rebel: A History of Bacon's Rebellion in Virginia* (1957).

Richard Waterhouse, *A New World Gentry: The Making of a Merchant and Planter Class in South Carolina, 1670-1770* (1989).

Peter H. Wood, *Black Majority: Negroes in Colonial South Carolina from 1670 through the Stono Rebellion* (1974).

The *Mayflower*, 1620

Chapter Three

THE NORTHERN COLONIES

For fifteen weeks in 1750 Gottlieb Mittelberger sailed aboard the sea vessel **Osgood** *from Rotterdam in the Netherlands to Philadelphia in Britain's Pennsylvania colony in North America. Mittelberger was not a typical passenger on board: he was a paying traveler, having been commissioned to take an organ from Heilbronn in the German states to a Lutheran church in Pennsylvania. As on most ships plying their way across the Atlantic from Europe to British North America in the colonial era, the great majority of the* **Osgood's** *passengers did not pay their own way but instead had already contracted to be indentured servants or would be sold as such upon arrival. They did not have as many provisions nor the security of freedom and a place to go upon reaching America that Gottlieb enjoyed. But for all passengers and the crew as well, the journey was a long and perilous trip full of misery and, for many, death.*

Leaving Holland, ships like Mittelberger's vessel were crammed with stores, provisions, other cargo, and 400 to 600 men, women, and children, "packed densely like herrings," each having a bed space barely two-by-six feet. From Amsterdam, or Rotterdam, these boats had first to go to England, a trip that could with good wind be less than 8 days but might take two to four weeks. Once there, the English checked out the cargo and collected customs duties, a process that might take two weeks or longer. Meanwhile, the passengers had to wait, worry, and use up precious food, water, and money.

After finally leaving England, these ships set out on what in the best circumstances was a seven-week trip. It could take as many as twelve weeks to reach Philadelphia from Cowes in England. With this long voyage underway, Mittelberger observed that "the real misery" began. On the ships there was "terrible misery, stench, fumes, horror, vomiting, many kinds of sea-sickness, fever, dysentery, headache, heat, constipation, boils, scurvy, cancer, mouth-rot, and the like." The food was old and over-salted in efforts to preserve it, and the water was "very bad and foul…so that many die miserably." To this list of sufferings Mittelberger added "hunger, thirst, frost, heat, dampness, anxiety, want, afflictions and lamentations, together with other trouble, as…the lice abound so frightfully, especially on sick people, that they can be scraped off the body." For Mittelberger the ultimate complication was when a gale—an Atlantic storm—continued for two or three days in which cases "the sea rages and surges, so that the waves rise often like high mountains one above the other, and often tumble over the ship…[and] the ship is constantly tossed from side to side…so that no one can either walk, or sit, or lie, and the closely packed people in the berths are thereby tumbled over each other…."

In such an existence, illness was inevitable. As the journey lengthened, circumstances only got worse as the poor quality of provisions caused people to weaken and become easier prey for illness, disease, and death. The meals on board were terrible, according to Mittelberger, and "can hardly be eaten, on account of being so unclean." He remembered that, as stores were depleted near the end of the voyage, they had "to eat the ship's biscuits, which had been spoiled long ago" despite the fact that "in a whole biscuit there was scarcely a piece the size of a dollar [coin] that had not been full of red worms and spiders nests." With disgust he also recalled "the water which is served out on the ships is often very black, thick and full of worms, so that one cannot drink it without loathing, even with the greatest thirst."

On his transatlantic voyage, Mittelberger himself became ill and, knowing how the many others who were sick felt, spent a lot of time trying to ease their sufferings by "singing, praying, and exhorting." He tried to conduct prayer meetings every day out on the deck when the weather was tolerable. Since there was no ordained clergyman on the **Osgood**, *Mittelberger served as a preacher, baptized five children, and "when the dead were sunk in the water, [he] commended them and our souls to the mercy of God."*

Death was an all-too-common event on the **Osgood** *and other such vessels. According to Mittelberger "many hundred people necessarily die and perish in such misery, and must be cast into the sea...." Other sources corroborate such statements: in 1710, the mortality rate for German immigrants to Pennsylvania was 25 percent. Further, in 1738, the sixteen ships reaching Philadelphia suffered a death rate of over 50 percent. In Mittelberger's experience, children and pregnant women were the most likely to die. He saw thirty-two children on his ship die, "all of whom were thrown into the sea." During one "heavy gale," he reported that "a woman in our ship who was to give birth and could not give birth under the circumstances, was pushed through a loop-hole [port-hole] in the ship and dropped into the sea, because she was far in the rear of the ship and could not be brought forward."*

In these desperate circumstances, passengers turned on each other, cursing, cheating, and robbing. They blamed one another or "the soul-traffickers" for having gotten them into their current predicament. Homesickness was common; Mittelberger noted that "many sigh and cry: 'Oh, that I were at home again, and if I had to lie in my pig-sty!'" The ordeal did not end when land finally was sighted and the survivors "weep for joy, and pray and sing, thanking and praising God." The misery continued because unless a passenger had paid his or her own way or "could give good security," they had to stay on the ship until they were bought as a servant. Passengers bought soon after arrival faced an uncertain future of labor for the benefit of others, but at least they had the prospect of eventual freedom for which to hope. Those who were in the worst shape would inevitably be the last purchased, remaining on board in harbor another two or three weeks. Being sickest, many of them died; so close yet so far from their destination—their hopes and aspirations for a new life in a new world ended at the threshold.

Many of the same socio-economic pressures within England during the seventeenth century that led to the establishment of the southern colonies provided the impetus for the establishment of colonies in the regions to the north of the Chesapeake – the New England colonies, Pennsylvania, and, after 1664, New York. Included in this area of English North America were the smaller, colonial entities of New Jersey and Delaware, the latter an outgrowth of Pennsylvania. In New England, a similar process occurred, as the colonies of Connecticut, Rhode Island, and New Hampshire all evolved out of their original parent colony of Massachusetts, which was considered the center of New England life. A dynamic largely missing in the founding of the southern colonies, was religion, which initially drove the settling of both New England and Pennsylvania. Indeed, both Massachusetts and Pennsylvania, two of Great Britain's most commercially successful North American colonies by the middle of the eighteenth century, would not have existed if not for the efforts of the Puritans and Quakers—the persecuted religious dissenters who originally established them as safe havens for their respective followers.

THE FOUNDING OF NEW ENGLAND

The Puritans

No discussion of the founding of the New England colonies would be complete without an understanding of one of the most important of the Protestant faiths to emerge out of the sixteenth-century Reformation: Calvinism, and its English manifestation, Puritanism. Ignited by Martin Luther and completed by John Calvin, the Protestant Reformation dramatically changed forever the face of European Christianity. Those Europeans embracing the new faith found spiritual relief and nourishment in either Lutheranism or Calvinism, with the latter becoming especially appealing to English Protestants. However, with the Elizabethan Settlement of the 1570s, the Church of England had become a "compromise" church; that is, a house of worship that combined Protestant and Catholic doctrines and ceremonies.

Although the majority of Englishmen accepted the Elizabethan Settlement, relieved to be rid of the rancor, divisiveness, and violent persecution that the Reformation had visited upon England during the reigns of Elizabeth's predecessors (especially during the years of her fanatical Catholic sister Mary, alias "Bloody Mary," for her brutal executions of Protestants for heresy), there remained groups who believed that the Church of England had not gone far enough in purging Catholicism from the Church's practice, ritual, and structure. Indeed, the reformed church's ecclesiastical structure of bishops and archbishops remained, except for the substitution of the king for the pope as the head. The king also appointed and commanded close to 9,000 clergy, from the archbishop to parish priests. Those opposed to such a system

John Calvin

came to be known as "**Puritans**" for their desire to purify the Anglican church of *all* appearances and manifestations of lingering popery. To these devout English Calvinists, their duty to God and country was to rid the nation's church of the last remnants of its Catholic past.

Equally important to the Puritans was England's social and political well-being, which they believed the Crown endangered by using the Anglican Church to promote political and religious conformity, as well as obedience to the monarchy, exclusive of Parliament. Church and state were united in England—the law demanded that everyone support the official Church of England through taxes and regular attendance. Because the monarch headed the official church, religious dissent, especially during the Stuart dynasty, became synonymous with treason, not just heresy. One Anglican clergyman declared that "no subject may, without hazard of his own damnation in rebelling against God, question or disobey the will and pleasure of his sovereign." The Stuarts used their position as head of the church to extort revenue and punish dissidents. The early Stuarts often ordered bishops to instruct parish priests to extol particular Crown policies in their sermons. Charles I dictated that the clergy preach that Parliament sinned when it denied new taxes demanded by the monarch. Thus, the Puritans became not only the champions for religious purity, but in the process, also became some of the most outspoken of the Crown's political critics, defending Parliamentary rights and personal liberties against an increasingly arbitrary, despotic, and "papist" (pro-Catholic) monarchy. In short, the Puritans wanted to change both the Church of England and the body politic, which they saw as one in the same, to serve and praise God and to be at all times reflections of His righteousness and will on Earth.

The Puritans believed that a truly reformed Protestant church should be one that reflected the original simplicity and purity of the church of Jesus Christ and his apostles. The church should be a place of worship where individual souls could nurture a more direct relationship with God. Rejecting the intercession of priests administering ceremonial sacraments, the Puritans believed that God's Word, as revealed in the Bible, served as the starting point for a life of righteous living along with prayer groups and heeding learned and zealous ministers who delivered evangelical sermons. Physically, Puritan churches were to be austere, drab and colorless places, stripped of all Catholic "idolatry"—statues, paintings, gold chalices—all were nothing more than distractions and manifestations devised by the lavishly corrupt medieval Catholic Church. There was no need for an elaborate, prolonged Mass filled with formulaic prayers uttered in the unintelligible, foreign, and "popish" language of Latin; no need to venerate saints, praying to them for help or guidance by lighting candles to solicit their attention. Puritan catechism even relegated the Virgin Mother to obscurity; prayers to her would not win divine forgiveness. Salvation through God's saving grace was determined solely by God and only He knew

Puritans going to church

who was saved or damned. No amount of devout supplication, moral living, reading the Bible, or obeying to the letter a minister's preaching could guarantee one's salvation. God alone determined one's fate, and He saved selectively and arbitrarily, rather than universally or as a reward for good behavior. This particular article of Calvinist theology, **predestination**, defined the essence of the Puritan faith. Moreover, their God was the wrathful, vengeful, omnipotent Jehovah of the Old Testament. Mankind was nothing more than a collection of innate sinners, "a stench in God's nostrils," whose only hope for redemption was to prostrate before the Lord and beg for forgiveness and grace, which He might grant.

In seeking reform, Puritans were divided over the details. Most remained within the Anglican Church, relentlessly agitating for its purification, while other, more radical Puritans believed the institution beyond redemption. Thus, it was time to completely separate from such a venal and corrupt entity. These "**Separatists**" determined to withdraw immediately to their own independent congregations. Without any larger authority to enforce orthodoxy, the numerous autonomous Separatist congregations steadily splintered in their beliefs and practices, eventually forming many distinct Protestant sects.

The Puritans were incorrigible doers devoted to God's Word as revealed in the Scriptures, perfecting their morality accordingly. Their prodigious energy reflected their conviction that righteous activity was a sign that they had been elected for salvation. Puritanism reinforced the values of thrift, diligence, and delayed gratification, asserting that men honored God and proved their own salvation by working hard in their occupation—their "calling" bestowed by God. As one Puritan declared, "God sent you unto this world as unto a Workhouse, not a Playhouse."

Puritans strove to live without succumbing to worldliness. Although believing God monetarily rewarded the diligent and godly, a potential sign of one's "election," they nevertheless scorned conspicuous consumption and covetousness, convinced that individuals who pursued such self-aggrandizement would fall prey to carnal temptations, and lose sight of the ultimate purpose of human life— preparation for salvation in the next world. Yet, Puritans often could not escape worldly temptation because their virtues helped them to accumulate money. Thus, within every devout Puritan male, there existed a demanding tension regarding how to reconcile individual prosperity with a faith that condemned personal acquisitiveness and displays of material success. For those Puritans born in North America and with each passing generation, the temptations that abounded in the wilderness proved too overwhelming to resist. By the close of the seventeenth century, the progeny of many of New England's original Puritan settlers had transformed into shrewd, prosperous, and some of the most self-indulgent merchant and professional elites in the British Empire.

The Puritans' zeal and overbearing righteousness dismayed most English people, who preferred Anglicanism and the traditional culture characterized by church ales, Sunday diversions, ceremonial services, inclusive churches, and deference to the monarch. In short, for the moment, most Englishmen were satisfied with the House of Stuart and more than happy with their church, which they believed represented the best of both of England's religious traditions. Thus, they saw no need for further anguish and public rancor over whether the Anglican Church needed further reform or purification. To the majority of Englishmen, that issue had been settled long ago. To continue agitation for a further cleansing of the church of its alleged Catholicism was completely unnecessary, leading many Englishmen to see the Puritans as troublesome zealots.

Puritan agitation alarmed the Stuart monarchy, which wanted a united and quiet realm of unquestioning loyalty. James I recognized the subversive potential in Puritanism's insistence on the spiritual equality of all godly men and on their superiority to all ungodly men. He announced that if the Puritans did not conform to his authority and the Church of England, he would "harry them out of the land." Fortunately for James, and for England, the majority of Puritans were not ready or willing to challenge the king's authority or the church's supremacy, at least overtly. Secretly, they did both, and James reluctantly tolerated their clandestine activities to undermine his power. Although James would have liked nothing better than to "harry them" out of England, purging the pulpits and courts of Puritans was difficult, because the Crown depended upon propertied and educated men to keep and preach order in the counties, and such men were often Puritans.

James's reluctant accommodation with the Puritans collapsed completely in 1625 upon the accession of his son Charles I as king. Married to Catholic princess Henrietta Maria of France (which did not sit well with the majority of Englishmen, not only because of her faith, but also because of the Anglo-French rivalry), Charles hoped to satisfy English Catholics by restoring some church ceremonies previously suspended to mollify the Puritans. Actions such as these infuriated the Puritans, causing them to suspect Charles of being a "closet" Catholic. Charles also elevated the Court favorite William Laud to bishop in 1628 and to archbishop in 1633. In return for such status, Laud and his allies preached that it was the

Christian duty of Parliament and taxpayers to submit to the king. In effect, Charles had no intention of pursuing his father's conciliatory policies, determined instead to enforce strict conformity, to change the Anglican Church any way he deemed appropriate. The monarch was a firm believer in absolutism, an idea that both Puritans and most Englishmen agreed to resist.

During the late 1620s and early 1630s, Laud and most other bishops enforced the new Anglican orthodoxy, which increasingly reflected a Catholic revival. They dismissed ministers who balked at conducting the high church liturgy while ecclesiastical courts prosecuted growing numbers of Puritan laypeople. Laud censored all Puritan tracts and publicly denounced as heretics those opposed to the new regime, raising in the Puritan mind (and the minds of non-Puritan Englishmen), the specter of Bloody Mary and a Catholic revival with mass persecutions complete with torture and execution via burnings at the stake or decapitations. Such fears became reality when Laud had pilloried, mutilated, and branded three Puritans who illegally published their opposition treatises.

Puritan hopes of securing a redress through Parliament dissipated after 1629 when Charles dissolved that body and proceeded to rule arbitrarily for the next eleven years, bringing to fruition his absolutist designs. Charles's many mistakes, ranging from alienating the Puritans to trying to rule England as an autocrat without Parliament, eventually plunged England into several years of bloody civil war, ultimately costing Charles not only his throne, but also his life. Charles's usurpation of power and apparent desire to return England to the Catholic fold convinced many despairing Puritans of the necessity to emigrate across the Atlantic to a "New England," where they would establish the true church and a godly community—a "city upon a hill" for all to behold and serve as an inspiration for their brethren back home to rise up and throw out the anti-Christ Charles, purify the church, and restore God's grace upon England. However, before these particular saints came to North America in 1630, ten years earlier, a group of Separatists, known in American folklore as the Pilgrims, established Plymouth Plantation on the south shore of Massachusetts Bay—the first Puritan settlement in North America.

The Plymouth Colony

Not all Puritans believed that the Church of England could be redeemed from its corruption and popery. For them, the church was beyond further reformation; therefore, no reason remained to stay in such a sinful and venal environment. Indeed, the Separatists believed Satan had begun "to sow errors, heresies, and discords" in England. Consequently, in 1608, several hundred Separatists fled to the Netherlands, a country known for its religious toleration and pluralism. Within a decade of their arrival, however, to the Separatists' dismay, the Netherlands proved just as inhospitable as England. Dutch toleration provided not only a safe haven for all Christians, including Catholics, but also European Jews. Being devout Calvinists, the Separatists concluded they could no longer live in such an ungodly place, fearing that their children in particular would be drawn into and corrupted by the surrounding open and tolerant culture. Many also were not prospering economically. Thus, a small group of the more rabid Separatists decided to immigrate to Virginia, obtaining permission from the Virginia Company, which was still in desperate need of settlers for their Jamestown colony. Carrying 150 colonists and crew (among them many non-Puritans called "Strangers" by the Pilgrims), the *Mayflower* sailed from Plymouth, England in September 1620, bound for Virginia. Originally, two ships took part in the expedition, the *Mayflower* and the *Speedwell*,

The landing of the Pilgrims on Plymouth Rock, 1620.

but the latter turned back due to a leaky hull. Blown off course by storms and contrary winds, the *Mayflower* landed not in Virginia, but Cape Cod, five hundred miles to the north. Here, the 102 survivors established the first Puritan community in New England, which they decided to name Plymouth after the English port from which they embarked on their journey.

These Puritan emigrants had followed French and English mariners, fishermen, and fur traders who had visited the New England coast during the summers. In 1607, some English promoters had established a small settlement at the mouth of the Kennebec River on the Maine coast, but Native American hostility and the hard winter demoralized the colonists who eagerly sailed home the following year. Their reports labeled the region frigid and inhospitable. Determined to improve that image, John Smith (of Jamestown fame) explored the coast in 1614, naming it New England because he claimed the climate and soil resembled that of the mother country. Smith published promotional literature, proclaiming that the land was "so planted with Gardens and Corne fields that I would rather live here than any where. Here every man may be master of his own labour and land and by industry grow rich." Such inviting descriptions greatly intrigued Puritans disgruntled with their Anglican rulers. Although "New England" was not the Pilgrims' original destination, it became one for the thousands who followed them a decade later.

Before landing, the Pilgrim leaders drew up the Mayflower Compact, a response to the non-Puritan single men—the "Strangers" that the Virginia Company had hired—who worried about Pilgrim authority. To assuage these men's fears that they would have no voice in the colony, **William Bradford**, who had assumed the leadership of the Pilgrims, drafted the compact that guaranteed that all men of the expedition would be subject to "just and equal laws" enacted by representatives of their own choosing. The signers also agreed to "covenant and combine [themselves] together into a civil body politic," thus formally creating the first document of self-government in North America. Much has been made over the years about the importance of the Mayflower Compact. Upon closer examination of its immediate purpose and design, it becomes clear that despite all the subsequent nostalgic ballyhoo about its alleged democratic and egalitarian principles, the agreement was a simple deal made by the colonists to obey the decisions of the majority—an essential precaution in a colony with uncertain legal status.

By the time the Pilgrims landed, hundreds of European fishing vessels had been operating along the New England coast for decades, not just fishing for cod, but also landing and trading with the various tribes. Unfortunately these fishermen not only brought trade goods, but also diseases which caused the decimation of the Patuxet and Pokanoket tribes who recently lived where the Pilgrims established Plymouth Colony. Indeed, so soon had the Indians inhabited the area that when the epidemic hit, the Pilgrims were able to supplement their meager supplies by rummaging Indian graves, homes, and hidden stores of grain. Nonetheless, half of the colonists quickly died, reducing their number to around fifty by the beginning of spring. The remaining settlers only survived with the help of local Indians, notably with the assistance of a Patuxet warrior named **Squanto**, who had been kidnapped with twenty other Indians and brought to Spain in 1614 by the English explorer Thomas Hunt, who planned to sell them

The Pilgrims signing the Mayflower Compact, November 11, 1620

This wood engraving shows Massasoit and his warriors marching into the night with early settlers of New England and his warriors visiting the Pilgrims at Plymouth.

as slaves. Rescued by a local priest, Squanto somehow made his way to London where he learned English. He returned to Massachusetts in 1619 only to find his tribe had been wiped out by the recent epidemic. He served as interpreter for the Pilgrims, taught them where to fish and how to plant corn, and helped to forge an alliance with **Massasoit**, leader of the once-powerful Pokanokets. Massasoit and his surviving fellow tribesmen had come under the dominion of the Narragansetts, to whom they were now paying tribute. Squanto persuaded Massasoit that the English might prove effective allies against the Narragansetts.

For both Squanto and Massasoit, the survival and protection of their tribe from the Narragansetts was paramount. If that goal could be accomplished by helping the English to establish themselves while forming an alliance with them, then Squanto and Massasoit were willing to provide needed aid. By the time Squanto died from fever in 1622, he had helped secure the future of Plymouth Colony. In the autumn of 1621, the Pilgrims invited their Indian allies for a large feast to celebrate that year's harvest, establishing the first Thanksgiving.

By 1630, Plymouth Plantation numbered about 1500 souls. By then, the Pilgrims had earned enough money to pay off their London creditors, which provided their political independence from the Virginia Company. They were now free to implement their Mayflower Compact to whatever democratic or restrictive degree they chose. All land had been held in common until 1627 when it was divided among the settlers. Over the next decade, their farms flourished as they sold their surplus crops to their fellow Puritans flooding into Massachusetts during the Great Migration. Plymouth survived independently until 1691 when the Crown merged the colony with its larger, more influential neighbor to north—the Massachusetts Bay Colony. The Plymouth Colony demonstrated that New England could be inhabited by Europeans, with its peaceful, nonviolent longevity based on mutually beneficial relations with the local Native American peoples.

The Great Migration and the Establishment of the Massachusetts Bay Colony

In 1630, a much larger Puritan migration began. Known as the **"Great Migration,"** about 14,000 English Puritans came to New England over a ten-year period. Although certainly significant for the peopling of New England, this migration did not represent the greatest wave of English-

The first Thanksgiving, 1621.

men crossing the Atlantic to North America. Indeed, the departure represented only about 30 percent of all the English coming to England's various New World colonies during the 1630s. Surprisingly, many more emigrated to the Chesapeake and the West Indies. Also, the majority of English Puritans remained at home, waiting to see how God would treat both the mother country and the New England experiment. The Great Migration was also brief, as Puritan emigration declined to a trickle after 1640, amounting to 7,000 for the rest of the century. Consequently, colonial New England became populated primarily by the descendants of the great surge of emigrants who came during the 1630s.

Similar to their Separatist counterparts, those Puritans coming to New England during the 1630s sought a distant refuge where they could live apart from sinners and a persecuting government and church. Unlike the Separatists, these Puritans did not come because they believed the Church of England to be beyond redemption; quite the contrary. The expedition's leaders wanted neither their peers nor posterity to see them as frightened refugees who fled in search of a safe haven from persecution or God's wrath, which many believed was about to descend upon England. Rather, the Puritans of the Great Migration convinced themselves that they were coming to North America, according to historian Perry Miller, on an "**Errand into the Wilderness**" for God, to establish a purified church and godly community. Hopefully, they could inspire their countrymen in England to reform and save the nation: rising, if necessary, in righteous rebellion against Charles I and deliver England up to the Lord. Once accomplished, the Puritans would return to England, having fulfilled their mission for God.

The Puritans believed God held them to far higher standards than other, less religious people. They considered themselves God's favored people—heirs of the ancient Israelites of the Old Testament. Like their ancient forebears, they believed if they honored God's wishes, He would bestow health and abundance upon them in this world. But, should they deviate from His will in any way, God would punish them as rebels more severely than He chastised common pagans, like the Indians. Consequently, Puritan authorities did not hesitate to punish or exile people who seemed bent on the Devil's work of destroying New England: sinners, dissidents, and accused witches. Otherwise, God would withdraw His favor and permit Satan to temporarily triumph by vanquishing New

The Seal of the Massachusetts Bay Colony.

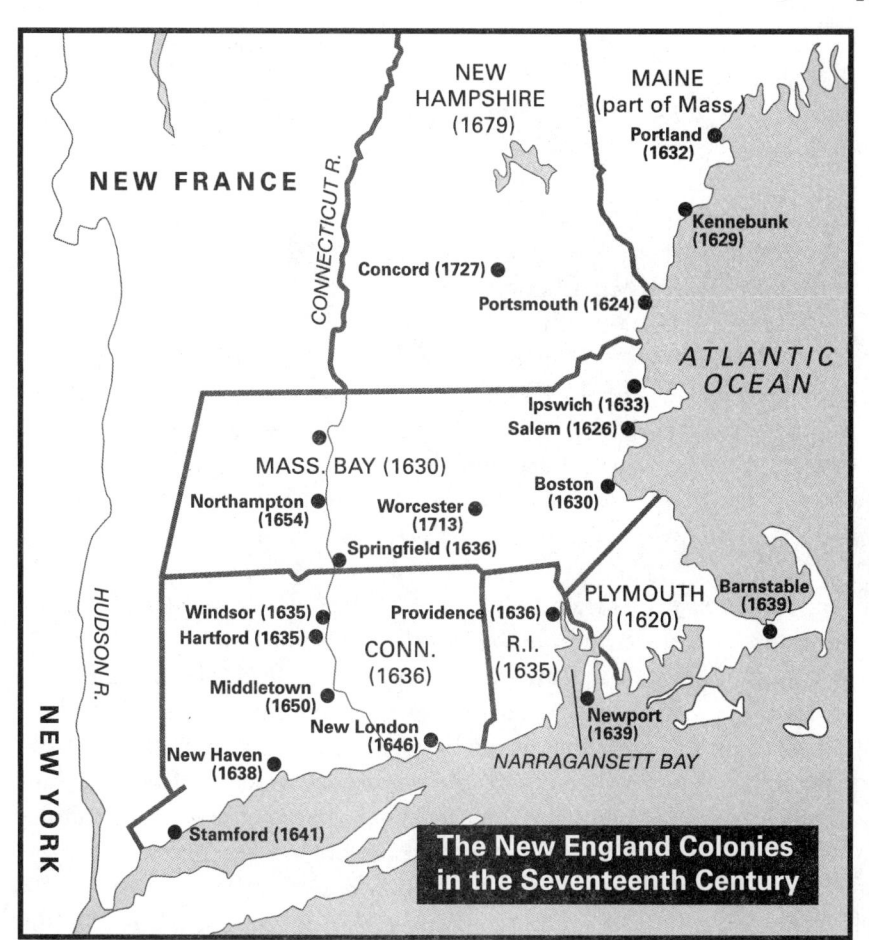

Map 3.1 The New England Colonies in the Seventeenth Century

England. At a minimum, retreat across the Atlantic might save the saints from the divine punishments gathering against the wicked English nation. Indeed, as the colony's leader Winthrop concluded, God had designated New England as "a refuge for manye, whome he meant to save out of the general destruction." At the same time, Winthrop exhorted his fellow colonists to remember their "errand," which was to make Massachusetts a "City upon a Hill [where] the eyes of all people are upon us. So that if we shall deal falsely with our God in this work we have undertaken, and so cause Him to withdraw his present help from us, we shall be made a story and a by-word through the world." In other words, foremost in the Puritan mind should be their mission for God, which was to establish Massachusetts as a beacon of reformed churches and virtuous communities conspicuous to the mother country.

Not all Puritans supported emigration, given its high costs, grave dangers, and uncertain consequences. Moreover, as of 1630, most Englishmen who had migrated to the New World were already dead in either Chesapeake or West Indian graves. Those who had survived had established the most profane societies in those places, at least in the Puritans' view. Many Puritans questioned whether New England would turn out any better. As a result, most English Puritans regarded the migration as premature and dangerous, a foolish weakening of the reform cause at home. As Robert Reyce told his friend Winthrop, "The Church and Commonwelthe heere at home hath more needs of your best abilitie in these dangerous tymes than any remote plantation."

Historians have long debated the Puritans' motivation in coming to North America. Some have asserted that the impetus for migration was purely economic, while others have contended that devotion to their faith prevailed over all other factors. More than likely it was a combination of both dynamics. Puritans came to the New World because of the opportunity to serve God while simultaneously improving themselves, which they believed God wanted them to do.

Despite the opposition of many Puritan leaders to migration, in 1630, under the leadership of the genteel lawyer **John Winthrop**, the Great Migration began. Winthrop, along with a group other wealthy and influential Puritans, formed a joint-stock company, the Massachusetts Bay Company. To the surprise of many, they obtained a royal charter fairly easily. By this time, Charles I strongly desired to rid himself and England of the troublesome Puritans who not only challenged him religiously, but also politically through their defense of

Parliamentary rights. At the moment, Charles simply wanted to remove as many Puritans from England as he could "encourage" by granting a most generous gift: allowing them to take their charter, capital, and records to New England, which, in effect, gave them complete autonomy from the king's authority. Thanks to Charles's haste, the Puritans were able to convert their commercial charter into a self-governing colony 3,000 miles away from bishops and the king. Once in Massachusetts, company leaders established the most radical government in the Western world: a quasi-theocratic republic, where Puritan men elected their governor, deputy governor, and legislature (known as the General Court). Until his death in 1649, whether serving as governor or not, John Winthrop remained the single most powerful Puritan in the colony.

Beginning with a settlement they named Boston, Winthrop's Puritans established the Massachusetts Bay Colony along the coast to the north of Plymouth. After a hungry winter in 1630-31, the colonists raised enough food to sustain themselves and the numerous new settlers coming to the colony throughout the decade. In New England, the starving time of adjustment proved far shorter and less deadly than in the Chesapeake.

New England attracted an unusual group of settlers: the sort of skilled and affluent people who ordinarily stayed at home rather than risk their lives in a hazardous transatlantic crossing and the uncertainties of life in the North American wilderness. Most seventeenth-century English emigrants were poor, young unskilled single men who had limited opportunities in the mother country. Seeking regular meals in the short term and the prospect of land in the long, they indentured themselves to Chesapeake or West Indian planters, with many dying before they had completed their contracts. In sharp contrast, most of the New England colonists could pay their own way and emigrated as family groups. In 1631, a Puritan boasted that the majority of his brethren were "endowed with grace and furnished with means." New Englanders also enjoyed and benefited from a more balanced gender ratio—at mid-century, the New England male-to-female ratio was six males for every four females, compared with four males for every one female in the Chesapeake. Such a balanced sex ratio created a more stable society and faster population growth. Moreover, since the New England climate and topography were unsuitable for staple crop production, no need for large numbers of indentured servants existed. Less than one-fifth of the immigrants came as indentured servants during the Great Migration. Again, in contrast to the Chesapeake and the West Indies, where the majority of servants came in large numbers as single individuals for sale upon arrival to new masters, almost all of the New England servants came with their Puritan families, generally one or two per family. Over time, servant numbers declined in the colony because most New Englanders could not afford to buy replacements. Those servants who came during the Great Migration became free once their term expired, eventually acquiring their own land. By the end of the seventeenth century, servants amounted to less than 5 percent of the New English population.

With a climate and soil not conducive to cash crop production, the Puritans also had little need for African slaves. Though not forbidden in New England, slavery never took hold in the region, not due to Puritan opposition to human bondage, but rather because New Englanders could not grow the requisite staple crop in their rocky soiled, cold-tempered environment. Those Puritans who owned slaves typically had only one or two for use as house servants or farmhands. In 1700, less than 2 percent of New England's inhabitants were slaves, compared with 13 percent for Virginia and 78 percent for the English West Indies. Indeed, compared to the rest of the empire, New England possessed an unusually homogeneous colonial population and culture: free, white, transplanted English.

Land and Labor in New England

In lieu of African slavery and indentured servitude, the Puritans relied instead on the labor of family members, most notably sons and daughters, to sustain their farms. The comparatively healthy climate and good diet allowed for prodigious Puritan families, on average six to seven children, who usually reached maturity. By age 10, boys worked with their fathers in the fields and barn, while daughters assisted their mothers in the house and garden. Most sons did not marry until their middle or late twenties, thus remaining on the family farm, providing continuous, essential labor, and mitigating the need for servants or slaves. Moreover, since arable land was scarce in New England, many sons who stayed at home ensured that they would inherit the estate upon their father's death, and thus avoid competing with other males in the community for town lands.

Land in the Massachusetts Bay Colony was initially owned collectively; that is, belonged to the community which distributed among its inhabitants as equitably as town leaders deemed essential for the welfare of the public. The Puritans in New England desired to replicate their homeland lifestyle. Because the majority came from small towns in southeastern England, they attempted to transplant in the New World as much of that region's culture as possible. They even named the majority of their new hamlets after the villages they had left in England. Since the Puritans were a communally-oriented, corporate people, the New England town came to define their environmental and demographic existence rather than the dispersed settlements and large estates seen in the Chesapeake. In short, Puritan leaders favored relatively compact town settlements to concentrate people sufficiently for defense, to support public schools, to promote mutual supervision of morality, and, most importantly, to sustain a convenient and well-attended local church.

Depending on a town resident's social status, each household received between 10 and 50 acres; the latter amount given to individuals such as ministers or other heads of household responsible for the village's general well-being. As the seventeenth century progressed, land allotments increased, with some families acquiring between 100 and 200 acres of farmland. Although meager in comparison to some Chesapeake plantations, New Englanders owned significant amounts of land compared to landholdings in England. During the seventeenth century over half the men in England possessed no land at all, while those that did considered themselves rich if they owned 50 acres. New England farmers also owned their land outright, a freehold, while in England most land of the common folk was actually leased to them by a larger landholder. The paying of quitrents, an annual fee for the land charged to landowners either by the proprietor or the Crown, also did not exist in New England. Charles I probably would have imposed such a payment on the Puritans had they not wisely taken their charter with them to North America.

New England agriculture was extremely labor-intensive, with farmers performing such tasks as clearing forests, building houses and barns, plowing and planting fields, and the harvesting of crops. Such work was more demanding in cold and rocky New England than in the flatter, warmer, and fertile Chesapeake. New England farms also generated little profit. Because of climate and topography, most were subsistence entities producing no staples in greatest demand in Europe. Instead, New England farmers raised a medley of small crops—wheat, rye, corn, potatoes, beans, and garden plants. Because of the similar climate, all these foodstuffs (except corn) were grown in England, thus the Puritan farmers did not have a profitable export market to the mother country.

The New England family farm also tended to a modest but essential herd of livestock—commonly, two oxen, five other cattle, a horse, two sheep, and six pigs. Because these animals needed grazing land, the New England farm had large pastures and hayfields but small grain fields. Farm families consumed most of their own crops and butchered animals or traded them for the goods and services of local artisans, principally carpenters, blacksmiths, and shoemakers. Since New Englanders were largely self-sufficient subsistence farmers, they were much less vulnerable, if at all, to the boom-and-bust cycle that affected their Chesapeake export-crop producing counterparts.

In contrast to the Chesapeake, the New England environment provided longer and healthier lives. With its long, hot, humid summers and low topography, the Chesapeake proved to be a natural breeding ground for malaria and dysentery. By contrast, New England was a northern and hilly land with a short growing season and faster-flowing rivers and streams, which were less conducive for such diseases. In New England, people who survived childhood could expect to live to about 70 years; in the Chesapeake, only a minority survived beyond 45 years of age. This healthier, longer-lived, and more gender-balanced society sustained rapid growth through natural increase, whereas in the West Indies, the Chesapeake, and the other southern colonies, only continued human imports sustained growth. Beginning with the Great Migration in 1630 through the end of the century, New England received only 21,000 immigrants, a fraction of the total of 120,000 (including African slaves) that went to the Chesapeake. The West Indies received even more human beings, both black and white, about 190,000 during the seventeenth century. However, in 1700, New England's total population of 91,000 exceeded the 85,000 whites in the Chesapeake and the 33,000 whites in the English West Indies. Although not the wealthiest English colonial region, New England was the healthiest, most populous, and most egalitarian in property distribution.

Although wealth did equal power in New England as it did in the southern colonies, fortunes were not concentrated in the hands of the few as occurred in the southern colonies or the West Indies. In New England towns, the larger landholders dominated local politics, but their property holdings were not significantly more substantial than the local average. Such was the case also for the region's major seaport cities—Boston, Salem, and Newport—where the wealthy elite of merchants and professionals congregated, but their collective political power proved to be much less than the South's great planters. This result derived from New England's system of many nearly autonomous towns, which saw political power dispersed throughout the countryside. Because New England had the most decentralized and popularly responsive form of government in the English Empire, royalists denounced the region as a hotbed of "republicanism." James II attempted to destroy such radicalism, but the Puritans ultimately prevailed, keeping intact their cherished autonomy and representative government.

Puritan Family Life

The two most important social institutions for Puritan New Englanders were the church and family. Indeed, Puritans thought of the family as a microcosm of the larger society—"a family is a little Church, and little commonwealth." In the Puritan frame of reference, no sharp distinction existed between home and the wider world. It took a family to establish and maintain a farm, and English culture expected all adults to marry and divide their labors into gender-specific responsibilities. Men did the heaviest outdoor farm work. Women were expected to maintain the home and garden, care for the numerous children, make clothing and soap, prepare the meals, and preserve foods. When a husband was away or incapacitated, the wife also had to assume his labors, becoming a "deputy husband" until he returned or recovered. In all these roles and expectations, the Puritans simply replicated the gender hierarchy of the mother country.

The Puritan faith, especially as it evolved in New England, however, allowed women greater authority, protection, and respect than that enjoyed by their sisters in the Chesapeake or old England. Although no doubt existed about who was "the head of the house"—a mode of thinking strongly reinforced by Puritan ministers—the clergy took equal pains to remind men to behave kindly and generously to Puritan females. Although distrusting of the passion of love because they thought it could lead to impulsiveness and disorder, Puritanism nonetheless preached that love and mutual respect were the foundations of a Christian marriage. Puritans greatly respected the natural affection that grew between a husband and wife over the course of their years together. Indeed, New England Puritans celebrated the sexual expression that took place in marriage. Courting couples were even allowed to lie in bed together with their lower bodies wrapped in an apron, a custom known as "bundling," free to caress and kiss each other. In the words of an old New England ballad: *She is modest, also chaste/While only bare from neck to waist/ And he of boasted freedom sings/Of all above her apron strings.*

Unlike in the Chesapeake or England, where civil or religious authorities rarely intervened in domestic disputes, both magistrates and ministers and church congregations in New England routinely protected women from insult and abuse. New England women could also more easily obtain divorce when abandoned or when their husbands committed adultery. As one historian of the Puritan family has concluded, the effort "to create the most God-fearing society" tended "to reduce the near-absolute power that English men by law wielded over their wives."

New England Prosperity: Fish and Ships

The influx of thousands of Puritan newcomers during the Great Migration allowed for the original settlers to prosper by selling to the new emigrants, at inflated prices, the goods they needed to survive in the wilderness. Consequently, when the Great Migration ended in 1640, economic depression set in, causing many in England who had opposed migration, including the quintessential Puritan leader, Oliver Cromwell, to write New England off as "poore, cold, and useless." Determined not to fail, the Puritans innovated during the 1640s, turning to the sea and developing enterprises that transformed their once largely subsistence economy into one of the most diverse and profitable economies in the empire.

A significant development for Massachusetts proved to be the cod fishing industry, initiated by the residents of coastal towns such as Marblehead and Gloucester. Their main customers were the Catholic countries of Spain and Portugal, to whom the New Englanders sent their better quality cod. The inferior grades of fish went to the West Indies to feed sugar plantation slaves. In 1641, New England fishermen caught 600,000 pounds of fish, a catch that grew tenfold to six million pounds in 1675. By that decade, their fisheries employed 440 boats and more than 1,000 men.

Few New England fishermen were devout Puritans or even Puritans at all. Because fishing was hard, cold, dirty, dangerous, and poorly-paid work, few respectable Puritans left their farms to catch cod. Thus, in New England as in the mother country, fishing attracted desperate, hard-drinking, hard-swearing, and propertyless men. In contrast to the Puritans who came primarily from southeastern England, most fishing folk originated in the English West Country and came to New England with previous experience in the waters around Newfoundland. By promoting the fishing trade, the Puritans took their first step toward economic prosperity, but at the cost of having to tolerate the presence, albeit limited, of the sort of unsavory and defiant folk whom they had hoped would have stayed in England. Suffice it to say, Puritan magistrates constantly hauled fishermen into court, charging them with public drunkenness, assault and battery, blasphemy, Sabbath-breaking, and fornication.

Although important to New England's economic resuscitation, cod fishing never became to New England what tobacco had become to the Chesapeake or rice to the Carolinas—a staple that determined prosperity or ruin. New Englanders wisely refrained from dependency on any one product for their survival, and thus cod became one of many diverse commodities Puritans exported abroad. Although the majority of New England farmers raised

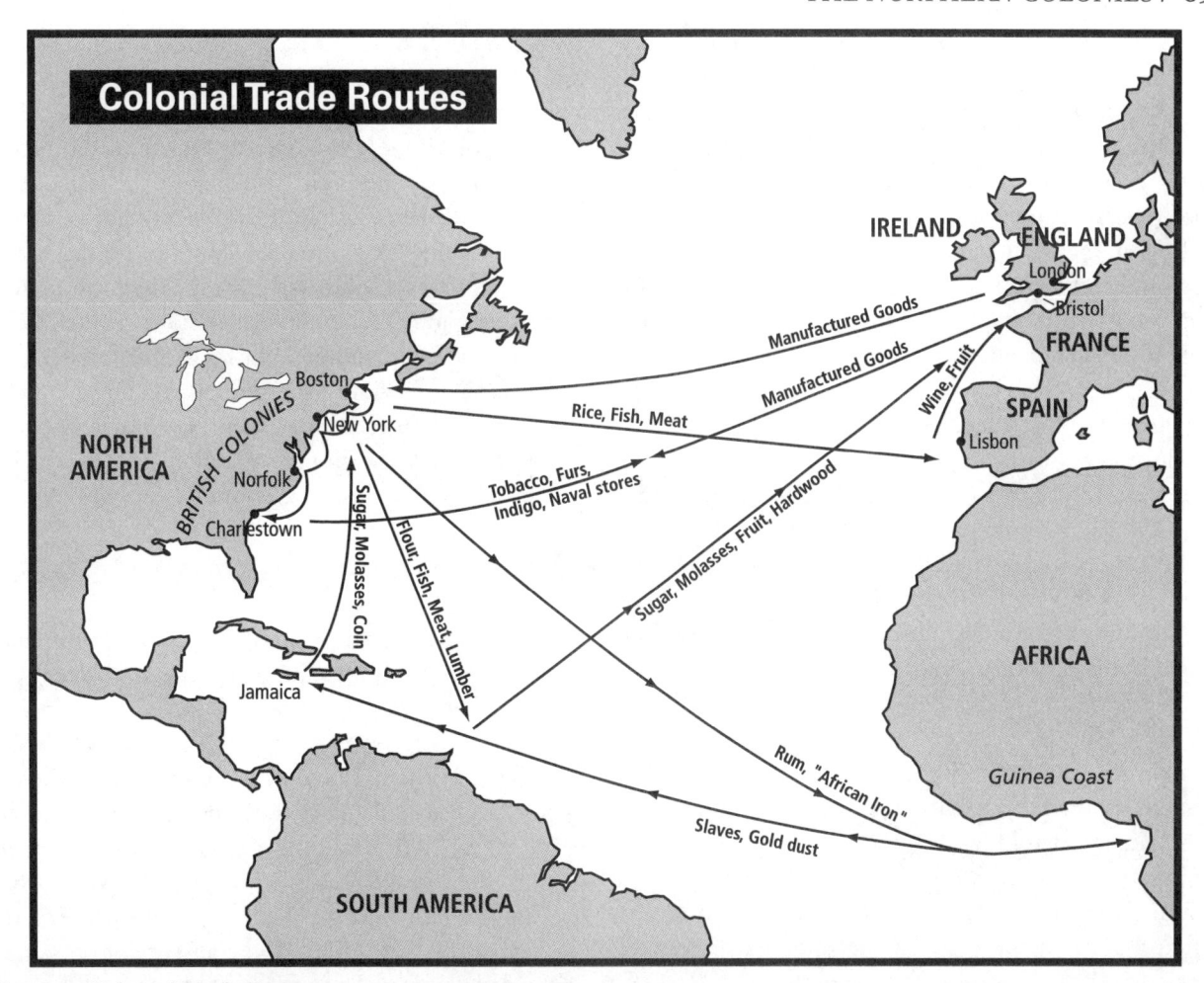

Map 3.2 Colonial Trade Routes

crops for family consumption or local markets, some generated small surpluses that they sold to merchants to obtain West Indian and Chesapeake produce as well as manufactured goods imported from England. Though Puritan frugality or austerity served as a fine virtue initially, as successive generations became more prosperous and less pious and less fearful of incurring God's wrath for their desire for a better material life, imports of sugar, rum, tobacco, cloth, tools, and even fineries such as silk, wine, and chocolate, could be found in increasing numbers of Puritan households.

It became readily apparent to New Englanders engaged in the fishing trade that the West Indies represented their best market, not just for cod but potentially for all their products. Thus early on, a close trading partnership emerged between the West Indies and New England. By the 1650s, New England seaport merchants packed and exported agricultural surpluses along with lumber and fish to the West Indies to help feed and house the indentured servants and slaves working on the sugar plantations. In return, West Indian planters exchanged molasses, rum, and sugar, some for Puritan consumption but most for carrying to other markets in the Chesapeake, the southern colonies, and Europe. As the seventeenth century progressed and New England's carrying trade accelerated, more Puritan products found their way to the West Indies than to England. The mother country did not need what New England produced, but demanded West Indian products, which New England vessels increasingly began carrying to England. During the 1680s, about half of the ships servicing the English Caribbean came from New England.

By the beginning of the seventeenth century, New Englanders began participating in the "triangular trade," of bringing slaves directly from Africa to the English Caribbean and trading for molasses or sugar and then taking those products back to New England to be processed into rum, which the Yankees would then trade with the West African slavers for slaves. This particular trading system proved very profitable for New Englanders because it left out the mother country, benefiting mainly the British West Indies and New England Yankees. In effect, seventeenth-century New Englanders and their English counterparts in the West Indies developed in tandem a mutually beneficial and profitable trade in which New England freedom depended on West Indian slavery.

Both the fishing industry and the carrying trade demanded ships. Thus, by the close of the seventeenth century, New Englanders developed their third most lucrative enterprise—shipbuilding. Not only by the end of the century were Yankees building almost all of their own vessels but also ships as well for a growing number of English merchants. In many ways, ship building was a natural and logical endeavor for New Englanders, for they possessed in abundance all around them the most important ingredient: dense forests full of high-quality timber. The plethora of trees more than compensated for the higher cost of colonial labor, enabling Yankees to produce ships at half the cost of London shipyards. Between 1674 and 1700, New England shipyards built more than 1200 ships, totaling 75,000 tons. By 1700, Boston alone had 15 shipyards, which produced more ships than the rest of the English colonies combined. Indeed, by the beginning of the eighteenth century, after London, Boston had become the second-largest shipbuilding center in the empire. Equally important, the shipbuilding industry provided a boom for the region's job market. The construction of a 150-ton vessel required up to 200 workers, most of them skilled artisans. Shipbuilding also stimulated related industries, such as sawmills, sail lofts, smithies, iron foundries, rope walks, barrel shops, and taverns. Even New England farmers benefited from the enterprise, providing food for the various workers and supplying the timber to build the vessels.

Endowed with quality ships and skilled mariners, New England merchants developed profitable and extensive transatlantic trading networks of growing complexity. New England-made ships manned by Yankee sailors could be seen in every major port-of-call in the empire, earning incredible profits carrying goods they neither produced nor consumed. New England's aggressive foray into the carrying trade not only brought the area into direct competition with the mother country but also diverted the region from performing the preferred (for England) colonial function of producing profitable resources for the homeland. Under the policy of mercantilism, the English government sought to make the colonies economically subordinate to the needs of the mother country, providing essential raw products high in value as well as transformable into finished products for both domestic and overseas consumption. At no time were colonial establishments to be competing with the mother country, but by engaging in fishing, shipping, and shipbuilding, the New Englanders were doing precisely that. By 1700, New England had become a competitor rather than a complement to England's economy. Suffice it to say, English fishermen, merchants, and shipbuilders protested the activities of these Yankee interlopers. As Josiah Child warned the Stuart monarchy, "Of all the American Plantations his Majesty has, none are so apt for the building of Shipping as New England, nor none more comparably so qualified for the breeding of Seamen, not only by reason of the natural industry of the people, but principally by reason of their Cod and Mackeral Fisheries: and in my poor opinion, there is nothing more prejudicial and in prospect more dangerous to any Mother-Kingdom, than the increase of Shipping in her Colonies, Plantations, or Provinces." New England's reputation in the mother country as a den of Puritan heretics and hypocrites would incur not only the wrath of homeland merchants and other economic interests, but also the monarchy, as both called for an end to New England's virtual autonomy within the empire.

Dissension in the Puritan Ranks

The inherent tensions within the Puritan movement, when coupled with the elimination of government persecution due to the vast distance between New England and the mother country, inevitably led to polarization within the Puritan community. Many always had difficulty finding a balance between emotion and intellect, between the individual and the community, between spiritual equality and social hierarchy, and between anxiety over salvation and the self-satisfaction of believing one was saved. In New England, the absence of oppression intensified division. Their migration to a new and strange land populated by people they believed to be savages, as well as the pressure of thinking that the whole world was watching them, only increased the Puritans' desire to maintain strict order. Thus, Puritan magistrates rarely hesitated to invoke the power of government to punish sinners, believing their duty lay in protecting the commonweal from God's wrath.

Inspired by the Old Testament and reinforced by English common law, the Puritans built their religious views into their colonies' legal codes. Residents of Massachusetts and Plymouth could be criminally punished for breaking the Sabbath, worshipping idols, blasphemy, practicing magic and homosexuality The most sensational cases involved sex with animals. In 1642, New Haven authorities suspected George Spencer of bestiality when a sow bore a piglet that resembled him. He confessed, and they hanged both Spencer and the poor sow. New Haven also tried, convicted, and then executed the unfortunately-named Thomas Hogg for the same offense.

The Puritans were especially hostile toward those individuals who publicly promoted an alternative form of Protestantism; that is, those who challenged Calvinist orthodoxy. The Puritans had come to New England to establish the true church and their own ideal of a godly

A portrait of Governor John Winthrop flanked by statues of a Native American on the left and a Pilgrim on the right.

society, not even remotely to promote or sanction religious toleration and pluralism. Puritans denounced liberty of conscience as an invitation to heresy and anarchy, and ultimately, to divine anger and punishment. New England was to be a bastion of orthodox Calvinism—those who did not subscribe to such beliefs must avoid coming to New England. Catholics, Anglicans, Baptists, and especially Quakers were all unwanted and told to stay away. In virtually all the Puritan colonies except Rhode Island, dissenters were prosecuted, tried, convicted, and exiled. After being banished, those who dared to return risked death.

The greatest disputes and general discontent came from within the Puritan community. Without an overbearing church and state to struggle against, Puritans quickly discovered their many differences, ranging from church organization, disagreement over who was saved, to how the Bible should be interpreted, and to complete separation from the Church of England. All these issues came to the forefront within a few years of the Puritans' arrival in Massachusetts. The majority of Puritans condemned such ideas as heresy, fearing that any concession to unorthodox notions would surely damn them as individuals while incurring God's retribution upon their commonwealth. The individual charged with handling such challenges was Governor John Winthrop, who soon realized that his most difficult task in trying to keep community and church unified was to keep his more radical brethren from undermining Puritan orthodoxy and upsetting the population. Winthrop initially feared that trouble would come from the true believers, who in their zeal would become too doctrinal and oppressive. However, much to his surprise, the most troublesome lot were the unexpected and unforeseen radicals, who emerged early in the Bay Colony, wanting to take the Puritan faith and church in completely different directions and down paths that Winthrop and the majority of Puritans believed would destroy the all-important consensus of beliefs and behaviors that had God's blessing.

Roger Williams and Toleration

The first individual to upset Puritan conformity and harmony was **Roger Williams**, a brilliant and obstinate young minister. No sooner had he landed than he announced, to the dismay of Winthrop and others, that he was really a Separatist who would not minister to any congregation unless the commonwealth repudiated all ties to the Church of England. The colony was already suspect in England, for many there felt the Puritans at best only paid lip service to English laws and the English way of life. Winthrop and other magistrates believed any repudiation of the Church of England, no matter how corrupt its current state, meant a disavowal of their "errand into the wilderness," which would be an act of political suicide since English royalist officials looked for any excuse to rescind their charter.

Without a church of his own, Williams began preaching to anyone who would listen to his separatist sermons. Not only did Williams challenge the Puritans' message but also the legitimacy of their charter, claiming that the king had no right to grant land owned by the Indians. He further angered Puritan elders by advocating a strict separation of church and state, as well as segregating those who had been saved from those who remained unconverted; that is, those who had yet to have the conversion experience, a sign from God that they had been "saved." The final straw for the Puritan establishment proved to be Williams's call for religious toleration, with each congregation or sect governing free from state interference. In effect, Williams sought the end of the Bay Colony's quasi-theocratic regime. Winthrop and other Puritan leaders believed Williams's ideas to be heretical and when he violated an order to stop preaching his unorthodox views, the magistrates decided to ship him immediately to England, where he might be imprisoned or even executed for his religious ideals. Winthrop saved Williams from possible death, however, by warning him of his potential fate and giving him time to flee to Narragansett Bay, located outside of Massachusetts Bay's jurisdiction. Some of Williams's faithful followed him to the area where they established the new colony of **Rhode Island,** which received a royal charter in 1644. Rhode Island soon became a refuge for dissenters of all sorts, although the Puritans of Massachusetts referred to it as "the sewer of New England." Although despising their wayward brethren who had fled to Rhode Island, dismissing them as a den of heretics, Williams's colony nonetheless provided Massachusetts and later Connecticut and New Haven (both founded by dissenters, but not for the same reasons that Williams had established Rhode Island), with a place where they could banish their nonconformists. In effect, Rhode Island became a "dumping ground" for discontents who would otherwise have festered in their midst, thus helping Massachusetts, Connecticut, and New Haven to maintain orthodoxy.

Anne Hutchinson and the Equality of Believers

No sooner did Winthrop and the orthodox Puritans of the Bay Colony rid themselves of Williams than an even more controversial and divisive individual emerged in the form of **Anne Hutchinson,** whose religious beliefs were even more radical than those of Williams. Hutchinson was just over forty years old when she, her husband, and their eleven children left England to follow the Reverend John Cotton to Massachusetts Bay. Cotton was a popular preacher who believed that the doctrine of predestination defined the essence of Puritanism. In Massachusetts, Hutchinson pushed predestination to its logical, if disturbing, conclusion. During informal Bible discussion meetings at her Boston home, she claimed that she had experienced several direct revelations from God. At these sessions, Hutchinson challenged the prevailing Puritan concept of "preparation" by proclaiming that if God had truly chosen those he saved, then it was unnecessary for such individuals to prepare themselves for saving grace by leading sin-free lives. To Hutchinson, neither good behavior nor prosperity was a reliable sign that one had been saved. Hutchinson did not advocate any sort of nihilism—she simply believed that her neighbors deluded themselves into thinking that their good works would save them, accusing them of heresy. By claiming that the Holy Spirit spoke directly to her, however, Hutchinson opened herself up to charges of another heresy—"**antinomianism**," (rejecting the legitimacy of religious authorities and believing that God's forgiveness alone and not good behavior results in salvation.)

Depiction of Anne Hutchinson preaching in her Boston home.

To the magistrates' despair, Hutchinson's Bible studies in her parlor attracted a significant number of attendees. Her popularity and self-righteousness emboldened her to claim that certain ministers were "fakirs;" that is, in her view, they were unconverted and preached false doctrine. Such an accusation did not sit kindly with either the clergy or secular authorities who began an intensive campaign against her and her adherents. Indeed, so powerful and influential had Hutchinson become by the time of the 1637 gubernatorial election that leaders moved the election site out of Boston to ensure the return of John to the governorship. Many were certain that had they not ordered a change of venue, the candidate that Hutchinson supported would have won. Winthrop had opposed Hutchinson's radicalism from the beginning but was not governor at the time of her ascendancy. As soon as he reclaimed the governorship, Winthrop made the censuring of Anne Hutchinson his first priority.

Winthrop and his compatriots began their assault on Hutchinson by banishing some of her strongest ministerial allies from Massachusetts. With such individuals gone, no one remained strong enough to protect Hutchinson from the wrath about to descend down upon her as she was put on trial for slandering the ministry. Although certainly unduly critical of some Puritan clergymen, she probably would have been acquitted had she not claimed that God had revealed to her that He would punish her persecutors. Her announcement changed the whole purpose of her trial; slander was bad enough, but to assert that, in effect, God spoke directly to her was plain heresy to orthodox Puritans who believed divine revelations had stopped during Biblical times. Convicted of heresy, Hutchinson and eighty other followers were ordered to leave the colony, finding temporary refuge in Roger Williams's Rhode Island. Eventually, Hutchinson moved to the Dutch colony of New Netherlands where she was killed in an Indian raid. When Winthrop heard the news of Hutchinson's death, he believed that God had dispensed proper justice.

What also alarmed the Puritan establishment about Anne Hutchinson was that such heresy had come from the mind and mouth of a woman. In their view, no woman, unless possessed by the Devil, would dare challenge the sanctity of Puritan orthodoxy. Indeed, Winthrop became so bewildered by Hutchinson's assertions that he suggested that she might be a witch. Without any evidence of sexual misconduct, ministers claimed that the words and actions of Hutchinson and her followers reflected women motivated by lust. Unless punished, their ideas would lead to communal living, open sex, and the repudiation of marriage. Carnal pleasures motivated neither Anne Hutchinson nor her followers, but their banishment revealed the deeper fissures within the Puritan community beginning to come to the surface. Men like Winthrop were determined to combat these pressures by keeping their saintly commonwealth rigidly controlled at all times.

In the minds of men like Winthrop, the radicalism of Anne Hutchinson must be resisted, or else God would surely show displeasure and no doubt punish not just the heretics but the entire community. Perhaps most revealing about the Hutchinson and Williams controversies was that, once in the New World, even the most devout Puritans saw a wilderness not just for their material taking, but a place where they would be free to express themselves without fear of reprisal. Unfortunately for both Hutchinson and Williams, such a notion proved delusional; as the arm of Puritan authority proved to be even longer than that of England's in the Bay Colony. In both instances, Winthrop and his fellow magistrates made it clear that all had to obey the brand of Puritanism they had established in Massachusetts. Dissent in any form would not be tolerated. Those who questioned the sanctity of those tenets with their radical notions would be banished accordingly. Thus, one of the great paradoxes or contradictions of New England Puritanism was the assertion that the Puritans came to North America seeking religious freedom. Massachusetts was to become a refuge for only the right sort of Puritan; certainly not for Separatists such as Williams, or heretics such as Anne Hutchinson. They wanted the liberty to follow their own religion but actively denied that opportunity to others, even among their own kind. Puritan leaders insisted on their right to keep out nonbelievers—anyone who did not embrace their brand of Calvinism. John Winthrop stated his colony's policy succinctly: "No man hath the right to come into us without our consent."

Massachusetts' Puritan leaders were certain that dissension would ruin the colony's reputation at home, for the presence of nonconformists represented a failure to create the inspirational, godly commonwealth that all English Puritans and citizens in general were to behold and emulate, which had been the stated reason for the Bay Colony's existence. News of such suppression and ostracism, however, played into the hands of English critics who denounced New England as a land of religious hypocrites, seditious Separatists, and petty despots. In 1652, an English Puritan warned his colonial friends that, "It doth not a little grieve my spirit to hear what sad things are reported daily of your tyranny and persecutions in New England. . . . These rigid ways have laid you very low in the hearts of the saints, while the enemies [the Anglicans] of the Lord were gloating."

Such chastisement from English Puritans surprised and dismayed Massachusetts Puritans. Indeed, by the mid-seventeenth century, a strain had developed in the transatlantic relationship as Puritans in England began to favor religious toleration for all Protestants—a policy that New England Puritans would never accept, no matter how politically and religiously necessary it might be for the welfare of all English subjects, regardless of their location. This was precisely what occurred in the aftermath of the English Civil War, with New England Puritans, instead of rejoicing in Parliament's victory over the Crown and the eventual execution of Charles I, felt betrayed by the very English Puritans who had led the crusade against Charles's autocracy and popery. Instead of initiating the final cleansing of the Anglican Church, which New England Puritans believed would occur once Charles was gone, English Puritans led by Oliver Cromwell not only left the Anglican Church intact, but proceeded to grant religious toleration to all English Protestants no matter how radical or unorthodox their theology. As a result, New England Puritans concluded that they had failed in their "errand" for God and thus were now stranded and forsaken in the New World. If New England was to be their permanent home, they must turn away from England and create a way of life that still honored God but simultaneously enhanced their material well-being. The Puritans accomplished this by developing their fishing, shipping, and ship building industries. The feeling of being abandoned by England also helped accelerate the transformation from Puritan to Yankee. However, none of these momentous changes would have occurred in New England without the English Civil War of the 1640s and the ensuing Cromwellian Protectorate and dictatorship of the 1650s.

ENGLAND IN TURMOIL

Inevitably, the Stuart monarchy found itself in conflict with Parliament. Beginning with James I and cresting during the reign of his son, Charles I, tensions had been developing between the two institutions. Driving the antagonisms and eventual polarization were the two overlapping issues of sovereignty and religion. Both James and Charles Stuart were devout Anglicans who vigorously opposed any concessions to Puritanism. Moreover, both monarchs believed in absolutism and tried to impose such a system of government on a most defiant Parliament. Although James I accepted limited checks on his power, his son Charles believed the king was accountable to no one but God, thus believing he had the "divine right" to rule England without Parliament's participation. Moreover, Charles sought to impose religious conformity within England and Scotland—that of high-church Anglicanism, which many Englishmen, especially the Puritans, believed was code for the ultimate return to Catholicism. In 1630, Charles I marched troops into Parliament, dissolving the body for the next ten years and began to rule over England as an autocrat.

In the meantime, the Archbishop of Canterbury, William Laud, increasingly moved the Church of England toward a more Catholic orientation in ceremony, liturgy, and structure, which infuriated the Puritans, many of whom served as vocal and powerful members of Parliament. Charles responded heavy-handedly to all opposition but was especially harsh on the Puritans. In 1640, largely as a result of attempting to force the Presbyterian Scots to accept his religious reforms, the Scots revolted, leaving Charles no choice but to summon Parliament in order to raise money to put down the Scottish rebellion.

Before Parliament would vote for the funds that Charles wanted for war, they issued a Petition of Right, which the king had to agree to abide by if he hoped to repel the invading Scots. The document reasserted those freedoms that Englishmen held dear, including no taxation except by act of Parliament, no arbitrary arrests or imprisonment, and no quartering of soldiers in private homes—all rights Charles had violated with impunity during his ten-year autocracy. The king agreed to consider the petition, which was good enough to temporarily satisfy Parliament, so they granted the funds requested by Charles to put down the Scottish rebellion. However, Charles had no intention of accepting any limits on his powers, especially ones dictated by Parliament. For two years he equivocated and procrastinated on signing the Petition of Right. Finally, Parliament's patience wore thin. When it became clear that Charles had no intention of signing the document, Parliament rebelled in June 1642. For the next five years, bloody civil war engulfed England.

From the moment the conflict began, those Englishmen who sided with Parliament became rebels carrying the stigma of treason. The habit of loyalty to God and king remained strong and Parliament had the difficult task of building the machinery of war upon unconstitutional foundations, convincing a doubtful nation that God and justice were on its side. Initially, events appeared to show that God favored Charles, whose royalist forces inflicted several crushing defeats on Parliament's unorganized, undisciplined, and untrained army. However, the right man at the right time emerged to save Parliament from defeat in the form of the fanatical Puritan member of Parliament, **Oliver Cromwell**. Taking charge of the army, he infused it with a passionate devotion to cause and victory. At the decisive Battle of Naseby in the summer of 1645, his New Model Army routed Charles's forces. For the next two years, Charles became more or less a king in exile in his own country, still a monarch, but without any real power.

Charles made one more attempt at regaining power by rallying to his cause fellow Scots and conservative Parliamentarians who had been driven out by the extremists and the military, but Parliament's soldiers routed their forces. In January 1649, Parliament's House of Commons declared itself to "have the supreme power in this nation," and that its dictates "hath the force of law, although the consent of the king or the House of Peers [Lords] be not had thereunto." The newly sovereign House of Commons then declared kingship to be "unnecessary, burdensome, and dangerous," and ordered the execution of Charles I, carried out on January 30, 1649. A week later, the House of Lords was abolished, along with the episcopacy (the top religious office) of the Church of England.

Charles's execution and the inability of the House of Commons to govern England effectively eventually brought Oliver Cromwell to power. Though wisely granting religious toleration to all Protestants except those they regarded as closet Catholics, he imposed a moralistic military dictatorship on England from 1649 to 1659. England officially became a Puritan republic, though for much of that period Cromwell dictated national policy. In 1654, he declared England to be a Commonwealth and himself Lord Protector. As Cromwell's regime became more arbitrary and oppressive, increasing numbers of Englishmen longed for the restoration of the ancient constitution—king and Parliament—which they believed would safeguard property and assure to "the natural rulers of society"—the aristocracy and gentry—their control of local and national government. Cromwell died in 1658. When his son and successor proved to be an inept leader, Parliament, with the military's blessing, restored the monarchy in the form of Charles II, the son of Charles I, who had been exiled in France. With the **Restoration**, the king and Parliament were united in their determination to turn back the clock to 1641. All in attendance at Charles's coronation pretended that twenty years of discord never existed. Two decades of civil war and Cromwellian dictatorship became an interregnum, a limbo between periods of legality. With peace and stability at home, England could once again devote attention and energy to expanding and regulating its North American empire.

NEW COLONIES, NEW PATTERNS

In the first half of the seventeenth century, the English developed two distinct clusters of settlements along the Atlantic seaboard: the Chesapeake to the south and New England to the north. Until the Restoration, England had neglected the mid-Atlantic coast, the area in between Virginia and Maryland and the Massachusetts Bay Colony. The region's temperate climate proved far healthier than both the Chesapeake and New England. Its fertile soil was especially promising for cultivating grain, raising livestock, and reproducing people. The region also possessed three navigable rivers that reached deep into the interior: the Susquehanna, Delaware, and Hudson. English dismissal of the area allowed the Dutch and Swedes to establish their own small colonies: New Netherlands in the Hudson Valley and New Sweden in the Delaware Valley. Although upset by this "usurpation" of land they believed belonged to them, England could do little until the Restoration.

From 1660 to 1700, as the English grew in power and ambition, the later Stuarts, Charles II and his brother, James, the Duke of York, pursued aggressive expansionist policies. They intended not only to extend the English presence in North America, but, in the process, they also wished to augment the Crown's preeminence at home. Along the way, they hoped to consolidate the empire as much as possible under royal control. The Stuart brothers also possessed a violent envy of Dutch wealth, from whom they also learned of the connection between overseas colonies, commercial expansion, and national power. By seeking to conquer New Netherlands, Charles and James meant to strengthen England's commerce by weakening its principal rival, the Dutch empire. The acquisition of New Netherlands (which had annexed New Sweden) would also end the geographical void between the Chesapeake and New England, promoting their mutual defense against other empires and the Indians. Finally, a conquest promised to increase king's control over his own fractious colonies.

Prior to the Restoration, unlike their Spanish or French counterparts, the English monarch exercised little power over the American colonies. Moreover, during the early seventeenth century, the Crown simply did not have the financial resources to launch and administer distant colonies. Reliance upon the proprietary or company system of colonization affected the political relationship between colonists and the English government, indirectly at first, but most discernibly over time. The colonists compelled their distant and weak proprietors to share political power. The proprietors appointed the governor and council, but men of property elected an assembly with power over finances. Throughout the empire, propertied Englishmen believed legislative control over taxation to be their most fundamental liberty. Proprietors did not enjoy having to relinquish so much power to colonial assemblies, but they had little choice if they hoped to attract and retain men of means, those essential to the colony's economic development and thus critical to the proprietor's revenues.

By the Restoration, the liabilities of the proprietary system had become apparent to the new Stuart regime. Noting increasing colonial population growth and prosperity, English government officials sought tighter control to better regulate and tax colonial commerce. They also worried that rival European powers might attempt to take possession of England's scattered, distinct, fractious, but wealthy North American colonies. In a showdown with another empire, one English colony could appeal for help from the others, but because of already bitter intercolonial rivalry, assistance was unlikely. Many imperial bureaucrats thus concluded that the proprietary colonies should first be converted into royal colonies and then consolidated into an overarching government like the Spanish viceroyalty of New Spain. During the second half of the seventeenth century, Crown officials gradually converted a few proprietary colonies into royal colonies. This transformation simply meant that the king, rather than the proprietor, appointed the governor and council, for the monarch felt obliged to retain the elected assemblies. The king's first initiatives in this direction occurred in colonies producing the greatest revenues: tobacco-rich Virginia and the sugar colonies of Barbados, the Leeward Islands, and Jamaica. The Crown was much slower to reorganize the New England colonies, not only because they lacked a lucrative staple beneficial to royal revenue, but also because they knew the region's Puritan majority would make any imperial attempt to command the saints' greater obedience a costly and difficult endeavor.

THE DUTCH EMPIRE IN NORTH AMERICA

The Dutch colony on the Hudson River was in reality nothing more than a frontier trading post and a relatively minor enterprise compared to the rest of the Netherlands' colonial possessions, which by the middle of the seventeenth century, spanned the globe. Dutch ascendancy to military and economic might took place rapidly, completely out of proportion to its confined geography and small population of 1.5 million (compared with 5 million English and 20 million French). By the early seventeenth century, the Netherlands had become the nexus of northern European commerce, dominating the carrying trade of northern and western Europe, the North Sea fisheries, and Arctic whaling. In 1670, the Dutch employed 120,000 sailors on vessels totaling 568,000 tons—more than the combined shipping of Spain, France, and England. By the middle of the seventeenth century, the great Dutch city of Amsterdam (and its port of Rotterdam) had become the center of European shipping, banking, insurance, printing, and textiles.

The Netherlands' liberal government contributed significantly to Dutch commercial preeminence by promoting intellectual freedom and guaranteeing religious toleration for all citizens. Such views were unique in seventeenth-century Europe. While the Netherlands' neighbors proceeded down the paths of centralized, authoritarian monarchies, the Dutch opted for a federal republic dominated by wealthy merchants and rural aristocrats. The seven provinces comprising the Dutch federation enjoyed domestic autonomy, but the most populous and prosperous province, Holland, usually determined the nation's military and foreign policies. The Netherlands also became the safest haven in Europe for a multitude of both religious and intellectual refugees. While the other European powers forced religious conformity upon their countrymen, causing dissidents to flee from persecution, many found safety in the Netherlands. The Dutch welcomed all such outcasts—Jews, Catholics, and Protestants—benefiting from their talents and investments. European intellectuals also gravitated to Amsterdam because the Dutch were more open to new ideas, especially if they helped to improve both the quality and quantity of Dutch life. The great seventeenth-century philosophers René Descartes, John Locke, and Benedict de Spinoza all emigrated to escape censorship in their home countries.

From the 1620s to the 1650s, the Netherlands embarked on an aggressive overseas expansionist agenda, often engaging in wars against either the Spanish or Portuguese in their pursuit of empire. In the Far East, the Dutch took Indonesia and Sri Lanka from the Portuguese, becoming the primary carriers of the especially valuable spice and silk trade from Asia to Europe. To protect that trade route, in 1652, the Dutch established a small colony at the Cape of Good Hope at the southern tip of Africa, the future Capetown, South Africa. However, the most lucrative enterprise that the Dutch usurped from the Portuguese proved to be the export of sugar from New World plantations and the transportation of slaves from West Africa. In 1637, the Dutch captured Elmina Castle, the principal Portuguese fortified trading post on the west coast of Africa. From 1640 to 1660, the majority of slaves sent to the Americas arrived on Dutch ships. In the 1630s, the Dutch seized the northeastern sugar production area of Portuguese Brazil. As a result, by 1650, the Dutch were refining most of the sugar consumed in Europe. To prosecute their attacks and build their empire, the Netherlands developed the most formidable fleet of warships in Europe. In the Dutch navy's most spectacular raid, a flotilla in 1627 led by Holland's most legendary privateer, Piet Heyn, intercepted and captured the entire Spanish treasure fleet homeward bound from the Caribbean. The loss of the ships and 200,000 pounds of silver virtually bankrupted the Spanish Crown while enormously enriching the Netherlands.

In their haste to become a great European and imperial power, the Dutch spread themselves too thin. Their European rivals watched with envy and noted that commerce, colonies, naval might, and national wealth were all interrelated. By mid-century, they faced attacks from their former allies in fights against Spain, France, and England. Their targets included New Netherlands, which was a minor operation on the fringes of an overextended empire with wealthier assets and higher priorities to defend elsewhere in the world.

From New Netherlands to New York

North America attracted the expanding Dutch, though never to the extent of the wealthier East Indies. In 1609, Henry Hudson, an Englishmen in the service of the Netherlands, sailed up the "North River" (the English later renamed it the Hudson), claiming the whole area for the Dutch. "New Netherland," as the colony was called, extended from the trading town of Albany (which seventeenth century ships could ascend for 160 miles, a greater distance than was possible on any other river on the Atlantic seaboard), down the Hudson River to the island city of New Amsterdam (the future New York City). In 1614, Lutheran refugees from Amsterdam built a fort near modern Albany to trade with the Mahicans and Iroquois for furs, but they did not occupy the site on a year-round basis. In 1621, the Netherlands' governing body, the States General, granted a charter to a group of wealthy burghers to form the Dutch West India Company, giving it jurisdiction and monopolistic commercial control over all Dutch interests and enterprises in the New World. Thereafter, colonizing New Netherland in North America became the company's responsibility. The first permanent settlers arrived in 1624, and dispersed throughout the 160 mile-long river valley. The company's plan first involved fortifying the river's entrance at New Amsterdam, which became the colony's most populated town, major seaport, and government headquarters. In the Lower Hudson Valley, the company promoted agricultural development, awarding huge tracts of land to individuals called *patroons*. The company hoped these vast estates would produce grains, cattle, and lumber to supply the fur traders at Fort Orange (Albany) as well the West Indies plantation islands. In effect, New Netherland became a divided colony with a small fur trading outpost upriver and larger agricultural settlements along the lower river.

This interesting system of settlement led to different Indian policies in the two halves of the Hudson River Valley. Upriver, the Dutch were too few and too dependent on trade to intimidate their native neighbors, the formidable Iroquois Five Nations (primarily the nearby Mohawk). Terrifying as enemies but invaluable as trading partners, the Iroquois determined the success or failure of the trading post. Fort Orange became as vital an asset to the Mahicans as for the Dutch. Thus, the Dutch forged a commercial alliance with the Iroquois, who occupied a strategic position between the coast and the interior. The Iroquois sought to channel their furs through the hands of the Dutch, who did not extend the respect shown for the Iroquois to the downriver Algonquian-speaking bands. Compared with the Iroquois, the Algonquians contributed little to the fur trade. Their warriors were fewer and lightly armed. Mostly farmers, the downriver Dutch regarded the Algonquians as a nuisance to be removed as quickly as possible.

Once armed by the Dutch, the Iroquois engaged in a series of military adventures known as the Beaver Wars. In the late 1640s, they attacked and dispersed the Hurons, who had long controlled the flow of furs from the Great Lakes to the French in Montreal. As a result of these wars, the Dutch trading system extended deep into the continent's interior. Assisted by the Iroquois, the Dutch on the lower Hudson in a series of brutal wars beginning in the 1640s succeeded in driving the Algonquians out of the area, opening the way for further Dutch expansion. In 1655, the Dutch also succeeded in overwhelming the small Swedish colony on the lower Delaware River, incorporating that region into their sphere of influence.

Dutch Colonists

Although extending religious toleration to all who came to New Netherland (even to Jews and Catholics), the West India Company proved to be not nearly as magnanimous when it came to the colony's governance. Dutch republicanism remained at home. The company appointed the governor and an advisory council of leading colonists but did not allow for an elected assembly. Governors rarely consulted the council and were legendary for being contentious, arbitrary, and mostly incompetent, reflecting the basic fact that, in the grand scheme of the Dutch Empire, New Netherland was an afterthought.

Although governed by petty despots, the company nonetheless welcomed all religious dissenters from Europe and other North American colonies. Officially, only the Calvinist Dutch Reformed Church could hold public services, but New Amsterdam members looked the other way as private meetings for worship proliferated throughout the settlement among the mix of Puritans, Quakers, Lutherans, and Jews. Indeed, Jewish colonists enjoyed more freedom in New Netherland than any other colony. Thanks primarily to religious toleration, New Netherland became the most religiously and ethnically diverse colony in North America. Indeed, the Dutch were a minority in their own colony. New Netherland attracted emigrants from Belgium (Flemish and Walloons), France (Huguenots), Scandinavia, and especially Germany. The non-Dutch whites composed nearly one-half of New Netherland colonists. Many had migrated first to Holland to live and work but then were recruited by the company to come to America. As in New England, the immigrants were farmers and artisans who came as family groups of modest means; few were unmarried young men, and even fewer were indentured servants. One-fifth of the New Netherlanders were Puritan dissidents who relocated from New England to settle on Long Island (including Anne Hutchinson). About one-tenth of the population were enslaved Africans, mostly owned by the Dutch West India Company living in New Amsterdam where they constructed wharves and buildings and served as longshoremen. The company rewarded favored slaves with a status called "half-freedom," which permitted free movement within the colony and the right to marry and own private property in return for an annual payment in grain, furs, or wampum. Despite an appealing location and a comparatively tolerant society, the Dutch colony failed to attract sufficient settlers to compete with its ever-expanding English neighbors. In 1660, New Netherland had only 5,000 inhabitants—more than the 3,000 in New France, but far behind the 25,000 in the Chesapeake and the 33,000 in New England.

Why did New Netherland fail as a viable colonial enterprise? In part, the colony had difficulty attracting settlers because of its reputation for arbitrary government and Indian wars. In addition, the vast and rich Dutch empire, especially its colonies of Ceylon, the East Indies, and Brazil, were much more alluring to Dutch emigrants than the Hudson River Valley. However, the main reason for New Netherland's failure to thrive simply derived from the mother country's much smaller pool of potential colonists with fewer incentives to leave, compared with the more numerous and discontented English. Blessed with a booming economy and the highest standard of living in seventeenth century Europe, the Dutch had much less reason to emigrate than their English counterparts. Moreover, the Dutch were not suffering through any painful economic transition or bitter religious strife. They also lacked the masses of roaming poor who became indentured servants in the English tobacco and sugar colonies in the Chesapeake and West Indies. Finally, the tolerant Netherlands did not generate a disaffected religious minority such as the Puritans who founded New England.

Beginning in the early 1650s with Oliver Cromwell and over the course of the next two decades, England and the Netherlands fought three wars (in 1652-1654, 1664-1667, and 1672-1674) to establish global economic dominance. These wars were primarily naval engagements fought to a draw. England, nevertheless, ultimately prevailed, supplanting the Dutch as the greatest naval and trading power in the world; a position they held for more than two hundred years During the Second Dutch War of 1664-1667, England conquered New Netherland. Charles II seized New Netherland to eliminate New Amsterdam as a base for Dutch shippers who traded with Virginia, to capture the valuable fur trade of the upper Hudson, to intimidate the wayward Puritans, and to erase New Netherland as an obstruction between the Chesapeake and New England colonies. Charles used the pretext that New Netherland trespassed on land previously explored and claimed by England. But as the Duke of Albermarle stated bluntly, "What matters this or that reason? What we want is more of the trade the Dutch now have." Thus, in 1664, an English fleet sailed into Manhattan harbor and forced the surrender of New Amsterdam without firing a shot. Aided by Puritans from Long Island, the English forces appeared to have the upper hand, convincing the Dutch that resistance would be futile.

Charles named his brother James, Duke of York, proprietor of New Amsterdam. James renamed the colony New York in his honor. New Amsterdam became New York City and the upper Hudson trading posts of Beverwyck and Fort Orange became known as Albany. Victory secured the entire Atlantic seaboard between Florida and Acadia in modern-day Canada to the English. Otherwise, the English government did little to disturb the existing order, preferring simply to reap the benefits of this profitable and dynamic colony. With settlers of various ethnic backgrounds, speaking many different languages and accommodating a wide range of religious sects, New York became the most heterogeneous colony in North America. In 1674, the colonists were granted the status of English subjects. Nine years later, after persistent appeals, James approved the creation of a representative assembly. The Delaware Valley communities of Swedes and Finns, with a spattering of Germans and Dutch, became the proprietary colony of New Jersey in 1665. Initially owned by Sir George Carteret and Lord John Berkeley, a consortium of wealthy Quakers led by William Penn purchased a portion of the colony

(West New Jersey) in 1676 to provide a safe haven for their persecuted brethren.

QUAKERISM AND THE FOUNDING OF PENNSYLVANIA

The move by William Penn and other wealthy Quakers (known as "Weighty Friends" in Quaker parlance) to purchase part of New Jersey served as a prelude to the eventual establishment of a full-fledged Quaker refuge in North America. Greater than the Puritans before them, the Quakers became one of the most persecuted Protestant sects in Restoration England, which saw not only the return of the monarchy but also the resurgence of a more oppressive Anglicanism. Along with English Catholics, the Quakers became the Church's favorite targets for proscription. After several decades of enduring persecution, the Quakers, in the early 1680s, under William Penn finally concluded that it was time to leave England and establish a new colony in North America in order for them to save their followers from further Anglican scorn and punishment.

Similar to the New England Puritans who believed their colony of Massachusetts to be a special place, Penn referred to Pennsylvania in equally righteous terms: "holy experiment." However, in stark contrast to Puritan Massachusetts, Pennsylvania had no tax-supported established church, not even for Friends. Penn certainly wanted his colony first and foremost to be a refuge for persecuted Quakers, but he spoke in universalistic terms of "a free colony for all Mankind that should go hither." Penn thus welcomed (much to the dismay of many Friends) non-Quakers and non-Britons alike, promising all equal rights and opportunities.

The Quaker Faith

Founded in 1640 by George Fox, the Society of Friends (derisively named "**Quakers**" because they allegedly shook or trembled when experiencing a union with the Lord), became one of the many sects that emerged in England after the dismantling of the Anglican Church soon after Charles I's execution. The son of a humble weaver with only the bare rudiments of formal education, Fox nonetheless became one of England's most legendary religious voices and spiritual leaders. The preacher appealed to so many of the religious and spiritually disillusioned because he rediscovered in the Christian faith what the Protestant Reformation had lost—its inner core of mysticism. The essence of Fox's belief was that people's souls communed directly with God, who revealed Himself to the faithful through an "Inner Light"—the Holy Spirit who potentially dwelled within every person. How was one to discover their Inner Light and thus find and know God? Fox asserted

Map 3.3 The Middle Colonies in the Seventeenth Century

that the awakening of this Spirit could come about only by a mystical experience, by an emotional and spiritual exchange and ultimate union between believer and God. Anyone truly awakened by that Spirit could thereafter live in sanctity, for he or she would be filled with God's living grace and constant love.

The Quakers took the Puritan condemnation of elaborate ritual and church hierarchy to the extreme, rejecting all sacraments, liturgies, and paid intermediaries—ministers as well as bishops—who all interfered with the direct communion between the human soul and God. Renouncing formalized worship of any sort, including prayers and sermons, Quakers met together as spiritual equals and sat silently until the divine spirit inspired someone, anyone (including women), to speak. A Quaker service thus consisted of potentially long periods of silence interspersed with brief fits—the "quaking"—of testimony or revelation as a member or several members simultaneously experienced that mystical awakening of their Inner Light. Meetings often lasted several hours and ended when no one felt further compelled to speak.

Although professing to be Christians, the Quakers diminished the concepts of original sin and salvation through Christ; their Jesus was a living symbol of salvation but not a necessary agent of grace, and he certainly was not God. This notion led more orthodox Christians to accuse, condemn, and promote the persecution of Quakers for being Unitarians—those who believed in the humanity of Jesus rather than his divinity, and thus denying that God the Father, Jesus the Son, and the Holy Spirit were one. Although the charge was not completely true, the Quakers' Christ was nonetheless not part of the same trinity of both Catholic and Protestant orthodoxy. Moreover, the Quakers' God was not the wrathful, vengeful, omnipotent Jehovah of the Old Testament. To Quakers, since man was inherently good or at least predisposed to do good rather than evil, especially after accepting God's grace, God must be a forgiving and loving deity who expected the best, not the worst, from mankind.

Quakers also believed they should be practicing, active witnesses and examples for their faith during their daily lives. Humble sobriety was not for Sunday alone; it ought to be part of the daily regimen, along with plain dress and the use of informal, familiar, and sometimes archaic language—the use of "thee" and "thou"—with all people, regardless of their social status, including the king. Deference was not part of the Quaker lifestyle, even regarding something as customary as doffing one's hat in the presence of a supposed social superior. In their faith, only God warranted such submission. Such behavior only reinforced the suspicion that the Quakers were dangerous radicals, intent on subverting the social order. Because Christ had preached the brotherhood of man, Quakers refused to make war. God had also warned against false swearing, so Friends refused to take oaths of allegiance or for testimony. An honest man's word, they insisted, was as good as his oath anyway. In a society that perceived all Europe to be a potential military threat and which regarded all dissidents as subversives, a group that refused military service and rejected loyalty oaths was naturally suspect. Finally, Friends accepted and promoted the democratic implications of their faith. The concept of the Inner Light meant that all men and women were equal before God, and thus all individuals should have the same rights and privileges not only within the Quaker community, but in the larger society as well.

Had the Quakers been content to practice their faith quietly, behind closed doors, they might have been tolerated, although their refusal to swear oaths automatically excluded them from government service, politics, and the universities. Unfortunately for their well-being, they could not remain quiet or passive. True evangelists, they believed God called upon them to spread His word. Their peculiar mannerisms drew attention and aroused suspicion, resulting in physical assaults on many Friends. The previously persecuted Puritans, both in England and in North America, were the most brutal in their treatment of Quakers. Massachusetts in particular treated Quakers most atrociously. There, in towns such as Salem, Friends' ears were lopped off, bodies whipped, tongues bored, fines levied, and people imprisoned. Boston's hostility was almost psychopathic with its cored whips and starvation of prisoners. One Quaker was encased in irons and whipped; when he refused to recant, he was taken out and beaten until the flesh of his back and arms became jelly. In 1658, Boston passed an act against the "pernicious sect" making it possible to arrest them without warrant, imprison them without bail until tried, and if found guilty, banish them. If they dared return, they would be put to death, as occurred to Mary Dyer and three other Quakers in 1660.

William Penn's "Holy Experiment"

Fortunately for the Quaker cause, **William Penn,** the son of one of England's most celebrated naval war heroes, Admiral William Penn, became a Quaker. Because of his father's connections with the Stuarts (both Charles II and his brother, James, Duke of York), Penn was able to obtain a charter to establish a North American colony as a refuge for his persecuted brethren. Since his "convincement" in 1667 at the age of 23, devotion to his faith as well as to liberty of conscience for all Englishmen consumed William Penn's life. He often traveled to the continent

THE NORTHERN COLONIES / 97

William Penn

on behalf of the Society of Friends, winning converts and recruiting potential settlers in the Netherlands and Germany. In England, he was jailed several times for his allegedly scandalous and blasphemous speeches and treatises, all of which simply attempted to explain the Quaker faith and prove to fellow Englishmen that the Friends were not subversives. In the 1670 Penn-Meade trial, which began as another attempt to imprison Penn for having supposedly violated the various acts under the Clarendon Code (a series of laws passed in the early Restoration that forced religious conformity), the proceedings quickly turned on another, more important issue, that of a judge's right to compel a jury to reconsider its verdict. Penn believed a judge had no such power, that a trial by a jury of one's peers was sacrosanct in English common law, thus a jury's verdict had to be honored. Naturally, the jury ruled in Penn's favor. In a landmark decision, a higher court vindicated him.

For years, William Penn believed the Quaker's Truth could transform England. By 1680, however, he no longer had such delusions, believing Friends must now look elsewhere for their own safety. Like the Puritans of Massachusetts Bay, he decided that if the forces of the old order proved intractable in England, then they must turn to virgin territory for construction of a model Christian society. Thus, in June 1680, William Penn formally appealed to the king for a land grant west of the Delaware River between Lord Baltimore's Proprietary in Maryland and Duke James' proprietary in New York.

No doubt the audacity of Penn's request shocked Charles' court, for Penn was one of England's most notorious dissidents. At the same time Penn solicited the Crown for a colonial charter, Charles was attempting to consolidate the empire under tighter royal supervision. Massachusetts began to attract royal attention for its defiance, thus the king was in the process of implementing a plan to deprive the Bay Colony of its charter. Neither he nor his advisers wanted to make the same mistake Charles's father had made in 1630 of letting any future charters leave England; he did not want another Massachusetts in his empire. That either Charles or Parliament would permit another religious visionary to set up a social experiment in the American wilderness seemed highly unlikely.

Penn was fully aware of the controversial nature of his request and therefore had to find some face-saving approach for Charles to allow the king to give Penn his land without causing a political uproar. His tactic lay in exploiting the large sum of money—16,000 pounds—the monarch owed the Penn family for services and outright loans provided by Admiral Penn. William Penn thus suggested a deal in which the king would make restitution for money owed his father with a land grant. Since Charles was chronically short of money, the idea of paying a debt with currently worthless wilderness land that might eventually bring profit to the Crown certainly attracted the king's attention.

To convince his hardcore Anglican Tory court opposed to any concessions to nonconformists such as the Quakers, Charles argued that he would be ridding his realm of troublesome fanatics much the same way his father had relieved himself of the Puritan nuisance. Perhaps the most important issue relative to Penn's grant was strategic in nature. The area requested by Penn was inland from the coast, encompassing lands once held by the Susquehannas, and standing alongside the ancient Iroquois warpath to the south. The new colony would be in position to help New York with frontier defense, and could act as a buffer zone for the Maryland-Virginia frontier. The colony required someone who had experience as well as integrity; Penn proved to be the ideal choice.

When finally approved in April 1681, Penn's charter was generous, declaring him to be the "True and Absolute Proprietor" of an empire encompassing 45,000 square miles to whom the colony's inhabitants were to render total obedience. No private citizen in English history ever possessed as much land or as complete control of all the resources commensurate with such ownership. Charles gave Penn the power to govern in conjunction with an assembly; together they would make the colony's laws. The king could not impose trade duties without the proprietor's or the assembly's consent. Penn could also appoint all magistrates and establish a judicial system. In all cases (excluding murder and treason), he was the ultimate source of appeal, not the king. Penn also had the power to make war on enemies, levy customs, and dispose of lands as he saw fit. Finally, and most importantly, Penn had the right to grant religious toleration to all Christians in his colony, even Catholics.

More thought went into the planning of Pennsylvania than the creation of any other colony. Twenty drafts survive of Penn's First Frame of Government, his 1682 constitution for the province. Upon each revision, the document metamorphosed from a liberal document, the Fundamental Constitutions of Pennsylvania, to the final, more conservative Frame of Government, which placed power firmly under the proprietor's appointee, the governor, who ruled in conjunction with a council chosen from among the colony's wealthy elite. Governor and council would appoint all officials, including judges, and draft the laws. Although concentrating ultimate power in the hands of the few, Penn's Frame of Government in all other areas was far more progressive than his critics were willing to admit. Inviolably secure was the cornerstone of religious toleration, the driving obsession of Penn's life. Indeed, to Penn, his colony was first and foremost a holy experiment in religious toleration. The government would make no effort to dictate matters of conscience. Pennsylvania was to be a safe place for all Christians, including Catholics, but especially for persecuted Protestant sectarians to worship or not to worship as they pleased.

In his new colony, Penn also firmly established an enlightened judicial system and penal code. All courts were to be open affairs conducted in the English language with a person allowed to plead his own case. Penn granted trial by jury and granted bail except in the case of capital offenses. Anyone wrongfully imprisoned could sue for double damages against the informer or prosecutor. Prisons were to be workhouses with inmates provided free lodging and food. Penn's charter gave him the power to pardon individuals for all crimes except murder and treason, the only two crimes subject to capital punishment. At the time, England still had a long list of other crimes punishable by death: piracy, arson, burglary, highway robbery, horse stealing, rape, and kidnapping.

Settlers had been arriving in Pennsylvania for a year when Penn landed in 1682 with his first Frame of Government. On the surface, the colony appeared to be well on its way to becoming the profitable and righteous enterprise that the proprietor envisioned. Indeed, between December 1681 and Penn's arrival, twenty-three ships had brought over 2,000 colonists to Pennsylvania. A year later, twenty more ships brought another 2,000 emigrants. By 1686, Pennsylvania's population exceeded 8,000.

The first settlers were a varied lot—yeomen from Wiltshire in southern England, artisans from Bristol in the west, tradesmen from London, and gentry from Ireland and Wales. The majority of colonists were naturally Quakers, but Penn's guarantee of religious toleration to all Christians attracted English Anglicans, German Pietists, Dutch Calvinists, and even a smattering of English and Irish Catholics. Like the New England Puritans—but unlike the Chesapeake colonists—most early Pennsylvanians came in freedom as families of middling means with a deed of sale, paid for in England, for a freehold in the unchartered expanses of the new "Promised Land" of Pennsylvania. Persons of great wealth were few, and about one-third were indentured servants, bound for a period of service to individuals in better circumstances. Most settled as farmers in the many rural townships, but some lingered in the "instant city" of Philadelphia as artisans and merchants. Whether rich, middling, or poor, word of the new Quaker settlement in the Delaware Valley had sparked yet another wave of European migration to the New World.

Timing also favored Penn's colony, for it was far easier to develop a later colonial enterprise. Learning from their predecessor's mistakes, Quakers came with no golden delusions and thus did not suffer any of the "starving times" which afflicted their Chesapeake counterparts in the early seventeenth century. The Pennsylvanians also benefited from having sufficiently-developed colonies as neighbors who could provision them until their farms and trades became self-sustaining and productive. When Pennsylvania farmers did produce surpluses, they could sell livestock and grain to the large West Indian market, which the older mainland colonies by the 1650s had stimulated into a profitable commercial network. Moreover, Pennsylvania's healthier and more temperate climate (warmer than New England's and certainly more favorable than the hot, humid, malarial Chesapeake as Penn touted in his promotional pamphlets), proved to be a great boon in the colony's economic development and population growth. The invigorating conditions, abundant economic opportunities, and relatively even gender divisions encouraged early marriages with numerous children. In 1698 a visitor reported that he seldom met "any young Married Woman but hath a child in her belly, or one upon her lap." Although immigration slowed during the 1690s, natural increase sustained a population that nearly doubled from about 11,000 in 1690 to 18,000 Pennsylvanians by 1700.

In the 75 years of English colonization of North America, no Englishman did more to pre-establish the structure and functioning of government than William Penn. No other compact compared in comprehensiveness to his 1682 Frame of Government. Yet, for all the preliminary work done in England, Pennsylvania's first years were not marked by political order and stability, but rather by

Unlike the Puritans (and other Christian denominations), the Quakers believed in female equality, even allowing women to speak at their meetings as depicted in this scene.

constant tension and hostility between sections, groups, and individuals, forcing Penn to alter several times over the next 20 years his original Frame of Government. Even before returning to England for the first time in 1684, Penn had to grant the Assembly a greater role in colonial governance. Moreover, from the beginning there had been resentment toward the proprietor for allowing the Free Society of Traders (a group of wealthy Quaker merchants) to basically govern the colony as well as dictate its economy. In effect, Penn became an absentee proprietor, staying away from Pennsylvania for decades at a time. In his absence, anti-proprietary factions emerged, constantly challenging his authority and demanding that Penn give his colonists greater political autonomy; to have the right of complete self-governance. Several factors contributed to his brethren's incessant clamor for greater freedom, but the Friends' inherent anti-authoritarianism became the single most important cause of this ongoing tension. Indeed, even before leaving England, the Quakers were perceived as litigious, uncooperative, and thus ungovernable.

Despite their disclaimers, Quakers exhibited less respect for government authority and for its necessary place in human affairs than any other Englishmen. Being the most persecuted of all dissenters in Restoration England no doubt prompted Quakers to adopt such attitudes as they suffered at the hands of government more consistently and more intensively than any other religious group. As far as they were concerned, the reality of Restoration government blatantly and cruelly negated the notion that governing authority was the word of God. Thus, the government should be obeyed when power was exercised justly and respectfully disobeyed otherwise. The Friends had difficulty believing that governments that ruined them or left them to rot in jail were agents of divine authority.

That Quakers would oppose a government created in conjunction with one of their own is perplexing, especially given that Penn pledged himself to justice in government and his laws were affirmed by elected Quaker representatives. Two factors mitigated these considerations. First, and probably most frustrating to Penn, was the inability of his Pennsylvania brethren to separate his government from England's and to accept his authority as distinct from that of the Crown. Penn compounded this particular issue by sending his colonists mixed messages regarding their allegiance to him and to England. As Penn became increasingly authoritarian because of his colonists' refusals to obey his mandates, he went so far as to contend that his powers as feudal lord of the land and the government of Pennsylvania was greater than those of the English king. Such audacious declarations demanding obedience caused many Pennsylvania Quakers to view Penn no differently than they viewed the distrusted (if not detested) English authorities, including the king. To many North American Friends, Penn became a disappointing manifestation of governmental power; simply another authority to suspect.

Penn had hoped that once Quakers were safely established in their own colony, free from harassment and persecution, they would no longer feel the need to be so combative, a behavior he thought was merely self-defensive. However, much to Penn's chagrin, migration did not affect any change in his brethren's attitude toward authority, even though government officials were of their own choice and religious persuasion. New World Quakers carried a residual anti-authoritarianism to Pennsylvania and were just as inclined to "scurvy quarrels that break out to the disgrace of the Province;"

The second reason for Penn's troubles with his colonists derived from the fact that neither he as a famous "Public Friend" nor the weighty counterparts he appointed to the Council could awe or intimidate the rest of the Quaker colonists into submission. Penn either naively or presumptuously believed that his exalted position within the Quaker community, as well as his title as "True and Absolute Proprietor," warranted his fellows' obedience. Friends believed all individuals were equal in God's eyes and thus no one, not even the king, and certainly not one of their own, was to be respected any differently than the lowliest of society.

In exasperation, Penn appointed a Puritan and former Cromwellian soldier, Captain John Blackwell, as governor in 1688. Penn's choice of a Puritan to manage his colony did not sit well with the majority of his brethren. Still fresh in the Quaker historical memory was the brutal treatment meted out by Puritans, especially in Massachusetts. Such an affiliation did not bother Penn, who became impressed by Blackwell's proven abilities in affairs of government, finance, and administration. As he told Thomas Lloyd, one of the ringleaders of the anti-proprietary faction, "Since no Friend would undertake the Governor's place, I took one that was not, and a stranger, that he might be impartial and more reverenced." Penn instructed Blackwell to "inspect the animosities, to use some expedient; And if no way else, authoritatively to end them, at least suppress them. Rule the meek meekly, and those that will not be ruled, rule with authority." Blackwell was to collect all rents owed Penn and other proprietary revenues without further delay, and most importantly, to silence the Assembly's demand for greater powers. In Penn's mind, here was an individual, stern but devout, who could hopefully establish obedience, harmony, and stability in his colony.

Blackwell lasted 13 months, resigning because Penn believed he had treated the Quakers too harshly. Ultimately, Penn cratered to his colonists' cries of tyranny and prejudice. Penn's gamble with Blackwell proved disastrous, convincing even more Quakers that Penn was an unsympathetic and estranged proprietor. The utopian hopes raised by Penn led to spreading disillusionment, for they elevated hopes to a level that could never be fulfilled.

Instead, Quakers, in their constant battling with one another and in their disregard for Penn's authority, proved they were no different than all the others who had come to the New World; indeed, they became just as land-hungry, aggressive in their pursuit of personal wealth, and covetous of political power and autonomy as the rest of their North American counterparts. Ironically, persecution had forged unity. In Pennsylvania, the absence of oppression intensified internal divisions.

In the end, much to Penn's disheartening realization was the reality that his Quaker brethren could not resist the vast opportunities for individual gain that his colony provided. Continued adherence to Old World creeds would gain only a modest existence in a land of plenty, while the development of more profane standards was better suited for conquering the wilderness. Penn had assiduously planned a godly utopia, delicately balanced between democracy and deference, deeply religious yet utterly tolerant. Sadly, he lived to see his holy experiment vanish in a quarrelsome, commercial metropolis controlled by a self-serving, greedy group of former saints. Indeed, Pennsylvania became one of the most instantly commercially and financially successful colonies in the history of the British Empire. By 1700, the colony was well established in the Caribbean trade as an exporter of wheat, dairy products, and livestock. Quaker families thrived and the colony's policy of religious toleration attracted thousands of outsiders, much to the chagrin of the original settlers. Penn's faith-inspired vision was to create in the wilderness of North America a place where all who came would be guaranteed fundamental human rights and that no one should be denied because of their skin color, gender, or religious beliefs. Over time, as the American character and identity evolved, it became apparent that of all the European people who came to North America in the seventeenth and eighteenth centuries, the Quakers and their leader would leave the most enduring imprint on the shaping of the American creed, which to this day cherishes and espouses the liberties that William Penn first established in Pennsylvania.

THE NORTHERN COLONISTS AND NATIVE AMERICANS

Within less than two decades of their arrival, the English in the Chesapeake were at war with the area's Native American peoples, largely the result of the Britons' insatiable demand for land. In the Chesapeake, they desired Indian land for the production of tobacco. In New England, the same motivation for land precipitated a series of conflicts with Native Americans; in the Puritan case, however, confrontation with local tribes occurred much earlier and with more immediate devastating effects on Native Americans.

Native Americans and Property

In English society, men gained status by accumulating property through market transactions, rather than by redistribution of property as did the Indian chiefs. In the wild plants and animals of New England, the colonists saw potential commodities as particular items that could be harvested, processed, shipped, and sold to make a profit. Consequently, New Englanders disdained the Native Americans as "Lazy Drones who love Idleness Exceedingly." Puritans insisted that the Christian God meant for them to enjoy the land in reward for their godly industry and to punish the Indians for their pagan indolence. Puritan righteousness dictated how much land the Indians needed, which shrank with every passing year. The 1640 resolves of the town of Milford, Connecticut summed up the Puritan view of land ownership: "Voted that the earth is the Lord's and the fullness thereof; voted that the earth is given to the Saints [the Puritans]; voted, we are the Saints."

Perhaps out of guilt, the Puritans felt compelled to legitimize their land titles by buying tracts of Indian land, offering trade goods in return for their marks on paper documents called deeds. To the English, a signed deed represented a legal transaction, protected by the law in which the signatories gave up their right to the land and had to move out; to the Native Americans, who had no concept of private property, they believed they had signed a piece of paper as a gesture to share the land with the colonists. The natives thus expected to continue to hunt and fish on the land and use portions of it as their needs dictated. The Indians were surprised and offended when Puritan property owners shot at them or arrested them for trespassing on the settlers' land. When the Indians responded with their own reprisals, the colonists saw themselves as innocent victims obliged to protect themselves against dangerous brutes who could not keep their bargains.

As the New Englanders cleared the forests with a vengeance, they destroyed the Native Americans' entire ecosystem—the habitat for the wild animals and plants critical to the Indians' diet and clothing, making the natives' land more alien and hostile. The settlers also introduced pigs and cattle that ranged far and wide, beyond an individual's property, into the forests and the Indian cornfields, destroying the natives' food sources. When the Indians reacted by killing and eating the offending livestock, the colonists demanded that the culprits stand trial in their courts for theft.

Tribute

In the early seventeenth century, the arrival of colonial goods, diseases, and people dramatically changed the power relations between rival Indian groups. Welcoming opportunities to trade, the Native Americans competed to co-opt the newcomers in order to make them allies in their conflict with native enemies. During the early 1620s, the Wampanoag Indians had hoped to incorporate the Plymouth colonists into a mutually beneficial network of exchange and alliance. However, much to the Wampanoags' dismay, the Pilgrims regarded their treaty as Indian submission to English domination. As a result of the Great Migration, which augmented the English presence and strength in New England, the Puritans of Massachusetts Bay and Plymouth formed an alliance. With the force of their arms, they bullied the local natives, demanding their formal submission and payment of tribute in wampum—beads and shells Native Americans used as currency in their trade relations with other tribes. Although wampum had little to no value in England, it was "as good as gold" when it came to the fur trade with the Abenaki Indians of Maine who cherished the seashells of Long Island Sound. In effect, the New Englanders extorted wampum from the southern New England Indians and then shipped it to Maine to procure furs for shipment to England. In many ways, the Puritans ran a protection racket that forced local tribes to purchase peace with wampum. The colonists also collected wampum as court fines levied upon individual Indians convicted by colonial courts for such transgressions as killing pigs that had demolished native crops. From 1634 to 1664, New Englanders extorted more than 21,000 fathoms of Indian wampum (nearly seven million beads) worth between 5,000 and 10,000 pounds once converted to furs. This swindling financed the steady expansion of settlements that dispossessed the natives of their lands.

The Pequot War

The first major conflict between the Puritans and local natives erupted in 1636, as the Saints engaged in aggressive expansion into the Mystic River Valley of southeastern Connecticut where the Pequot lived. Colonial leaders demanded that the Pequot pay a heavy tribute in wampum, give up several of their children as hostages, and turn over suspects accused of killing an English trader. The Pequot naturally refused such demands and, in retaliation, the combined militias of Connecticut, Massachusetts, and Plymouth, in conjunction with Narragansett and Mohegan warriors, attacked the Pequot (**Pequot War**). As a reward for their assistance, the Puritans promised their Indian allies that they could have as many Pequot prisoners as they wanted. This appealed to both tribes because they needed to replenish depleted numbers. In May 1637, Narragansett and Mohegan warriors led the Puritan forces deep into Pequot territory. They located a palisaded village beside the Mystic River containing 70 wigwams and 500 inhabitants, mostly women, children, and old men since the warriors had left on a raid. After consulting with their chaplain who told them to remember from the Old Testament that Saul did not spare the women, children, and old men of the Amalekites, the Puritan soldiers under the command of Captains John Mason and John Underhill surprised the village and set it ablaze. The Pequots who did not die in the flames were shot by the Puritan militia as they attempted to flee the inferno with only seven escaping by breaking through the surrounding circle of guns and swords.

The annihilation of one's enemy, especially of women and children, was not the Native American way of warfare. Attacks on enemy tribes took place for punitive reasons only, for transgressions or insults made or to establish boundaries or protect sacred grounds. Natives tended to kill very few warriors. Women and children were rarely the victims. Instead, they were usually captured because prisoners of war were a major way for tribes to replenish themselves. Thus the Puritan slaughter of the Pequot appalled the Narragansett and Mohegan, who had expected to capture and adopt the women and children. They condemned the Puritan mode of war as "too furious and slays too many people." Naturally, the Puritans dismissed their allies' humanity, declaring that the Indian mode of war was "more for pastime than to conquer and subdue." A veteran of European warfare, Underhill sarcastically noted that "they [the Indians] might fight for seven years and not kill seven men." If so, on a single day, Underhill delivered the equivalent of nearly 400 years of Indian warfare. Regarding war as a test of their godliness, the Puritans interpreted their especially bloody victory as a sign of God's blessing upon them.

The Narragansett sachem Miantonomi attempted to unite Indian peoples in the region in 1642, but the Puritans skillfully played the bands against each other. Unable to unite, the individual Indian nations became shrinking minorities in a land dominated by a growing number of English colonists In 1670, the 52,000 New England colonists outnumbered the Indians of southern New England by nearly 3 to 1. Many Indian bands divided over how best to deal with the powerful and aggressive colonists. Should they fight to remain autonomous or should they accept subordination as Puritan wards? Did safety and survival lie in resistance or submission?

Praying Towns

The Pequot slaughter distressed many Puritans, especially those who believed that the time had come to bring God's Word to the Indians. Thus began among some Puritan clergy a movement to evangelize the remaining Native Americans in southern New England. Beginning in the late 1640s, the Reverend John Eliot took the lead along with the Mayhews, Thomas and Thomas Jr., often over opposition from their fellow colonists who preferred simply to destroy the Indians. The missionaries sincerely wished to rescue the natives from future, certain annihilation while saving their souls from damnation. However, the missionary effort demanded that Indians surrender their own culture as the price to be paid for their physical survival. Because the English could not conceive of permitting Indians to remain independent and culturally autonomous peoples, they had to convert or die.

The Mayhews were more successful than Eliot, although he received the greater fanfare for his efforts. The preachers worked with local sachems and only took exception to the tribal powwows, which allowed for prophets or medicine men to perpetuate pagan rituals and beliefs. The Mayhews encouraged Indian men to teach the settlers of Martha's Vineyard and Nantucket how to catch whales, an activity that made them a vital part of the settlers' economy without threatening their identity as males. By contrast, Eliot attacked the sachems' authority as well as the powwows, challenged the traditional tribal structure, and insisted on turning Indian men into farmers, a female role in Indian society. Despite his heavy-handedness and disregard for native folkways, by the early 1670s, Eliot had established more than 1,000 Indians, nearly all of them survivors of coastal tribes that had been decimated by disease, into a string of seven "**praying towns,**" and Eliot was busy organizing five more among the Nipmucks of the interior. In permanent and compact praying towns, the Indians could be kept under close surveillance and under more constant pressure to change their behavior and appearance. There, they could also be removed from friends and relatives who refused to change their traditional ways. Restricting Indians to fixed settlements also freed up additional lands for English acquisition.

By 1675 about 2,300 Indians, perhaps one-quarter of all those living in southeastern New England, were in various stages of conversion to Christianity. Still, only 160 of them had achieved the kind of conversion experience required for full church membership. The Puritan missionaries required from the Indians a thorough conversion, manifest in virtually all aspects of their behavior. They had to give up their Algonquian names and take new English names, and they had to give up wearing body grease, playing traditional native sports, and killing lice with their teeth. The missionaries forced Indian men to cut their hair very short in the Puritan fashion, for the Saints considered long hair as a sign of vanity and pride, sins they were quicker to detect in others than themselves. Short hair and English attire also set the praying Indians apart from their traditionalist brethren. Most important, Indians did not embrace the Puritans' sense of sin. Nor could they grasp why their best deeds made no difference in God's eyes; in other words, they could not fathom predestination. Comfortable in their own culture, most Indians rejected converting to English ways and beliefs.

The praying towns did appeal to small and weak bands like the Massachusett, Nipmuck, and Pennacook, all of whom had been especially devastated by the English invasion. These tribes hoped to find in Christianity a way to make sense of their recent catastrophes. They worked to stabilize their world by seeking new supernatural guides who were superior to their shamans who had failed to stop the epidemics, cattle, hogs, and settlers. In the Englishmen's impressive technology and apparent immunity from diseases, these Indians detected a transcendent form of supernatural power that they desperately hoped to tap for their own use, seeking in the new faith a capacity to recover their numbers and power. Although the progress of their converts pleased the missionaries, most lay Puritans continued to distrust the praying Indians as treacherous savages with a dangerous veneer of insincere Christianity.

King Philip's War

From 1675 to 1676, one of the bloodiest Anglo-Native American conflicts in American colonial history took place in New England, putting to the test the sincerity of both Indians and Puritans. Leading the native uprising was the Wampanoag sachem Metacom, son of Massasoit, who had celebrated the first thanksgiving feast with the Pilgrims. To the Puritans, he became known as King Philip, in reference to one of England's most despised enemies, King Philip II of Spain. For over a year, Metacom quietly prepared for a war that he considered inevitable. One of the larger, more autonomous bands, the Wampanoag had resisted the Puritans' evangelizing, believing that if they succumbed to Puritan proselytizing they would lose their entire way of life. Moreover, by 1675, the Puritans once again engaged in aggressive land acquisition. Determined to resist this latest English attempt at taking more native land, Metacom also tired of seeing his people blamed for everything that went wrong in the colony and being punished for their slightest transgressions of English laws they did not understand nor believe to be fair—such was the incident that precipitated the conflict. In the spring of 1675, the Plymouth colonists provoked the confrontation by seizing, convicting, and executing three Wampanoag for murdering a praying-town preacher and possible spy for the English named John Sassamon. The hanging of their brethren incensed young Wampanoag warriors, who took it upon themselves to avenge their tribesmen's death by attacking isolated Puritan homesteads.

To the Puritans' surprise and horror, the rebellion spread with deadly effect during the summer and fall 1675 as initial Wampanoag victories encouraged other bands with their own grievances to join the fight. Indiscriminate Puritan counterattacks on neutral Indians created additional enemies, including the Narragansett who numbered about 4,000 and were the largest remaining tribe in the region. Although the Puritans quickly labeled Metacom the evil mastermind behind the uprising, in truth, each band fought spontaneously under its own leaders, all driven by a simmering, combustible hatred for the Puritans and their years of self-righteous oppression.

Remembering their easy victory over the Pequot a generation earlier, the Puritans initially believed they would be able to dispense with this latest savage uprising with similar facility. They were quickly proven wrong. Since the 1630s, the Indians had acquired firearms and, perhaps more importantly, they had built forges to make musket balls and repair their own weapons. They had even become marksmen with the smooth-bore musket by firing several smaller bullets instead of a single musket ball with each charge. By contrast, the settlers still tended to be poor shots, even though many had gotten better with a musket since arriving in North America. Most of the time, however, the Puritans usually paid the Native Americans to hunt for them. Moreover, in the tradition of European armies, the Puritans discharged volleys without aiming, which usually resulted in misses with a few kills and maybe a fortunate wounding of the enemy.

To the Puritans' shock, the Indians not only proved effective riflemen but were also organized and purposeful in battle. Most horrifying to the colonists, the natives displayed a newfound willingness to engage in total war, leading to the brutal slaughter of scores of English men, women, and children—a practice the Indians learned from their Puritan nemeses. During the summer and fall of 1675, the Indian rebels assailed 52 of the region's 90 towns, destroying twelve of them while killing entire colonial families in the process. When one settler boasted that his Bible would save him from harm, the Indians disemboweled him and stuffed the sacred book in his belly. When the Puritans counterattacked, the Indians took refuge in the swamps, repelling their foes and inflicting heavy losses. They often surprised and ambushed the Puritans traveling through unfamiliar pathways in the forests. Indian victories bolstered their confidence while shocking and demoralizing the colonists. Hundreds of Puritans abandoned frontier towns, fleeing to the coast for safety. The carnage also made recruitment of men willing to fight increasingly difficult.

For decades, the colonists had labored to remake the New England landscape by constructing churches, houses, fences, and barns, and unleashing their livestock. To reverse their land's alienation, the rebels systematically burned, killed, mutilated, and desecrated all of those symbols of English civilization. The natives regarded every dying colonist, every burning farm or defiled church as accumulating evidence that the English God was no match for their own revitalized spiritual power. Altogether, by war's end, the Indians killed about 1,000 settlers.

Naturally, the Puritans transformed the war from one caused by their own treachery and cruel treatment of the Indians and general disdain for native culture into a sign from God that they had sinned and thus were being punished by the forces of Satan for their transgressions. Such were the sentiments of Increase Mather, a prominent Boston minister, who warned that no victory would come until New England repented and reformed. At first, the Massachusetts General Court agreed, blaming the war on young men who wore their hair too long, on boys and girls who took leisurely horse rides together, on people who dressed above their station in life, and, of course, on the blaspheming dissidents among them. In reality, what Mather truly feared was the fact that by the 1670s, much to his dismay, the hardcore Puritanism of the first generation of emigrants was losing its appeal to succeeding generations born in the New World. In effect, New England society was becoming more secular, less devoted to the original Puritan message and purpose. Thus, in Mather's view, New England had become a sinful place just waiting for God's retribution, which had finally come in the form of Metacom.

To vindicate their God and prove their own worthiness, the Puritans believed it essential to annihilate once and for all their native enemies. Thus, for the Puritans, their struggle to put down the Indian uprising became a holy war—a righteous crusade against the forces of evil and darkness, in which every dead Native American and burned wigwam manifested the resurgent power of the Puritan God and his renewed approval of his chosen people. Unfortunately, in the passion of their crusade, Puritans typically ventilated their rage by attacking and killing Indians who had nothing to do with Metacom and his followers. Among the first victims were the praying-town natives who many Puritans regarded as insidious spies and covert raiders. To protect the praying Indians from the wrath of blood-lusting Puritans or from joining Metacom's forces, colonial authorities relocated them to cold and barren islands in Boston Harbor, where hundreds died from exposure, malnutrition, and disease (or were stolen by slavers) during the hard winter of 1675-1676.

In early 1676, the desperate Puritans realized that they could not win without the assistance of Native American allies, principally the Pequot and Mohegan. The Puritans also recruited praying-town Indians, but required each to prove his loyalty and conversion by bringing in two scalps or heads taken from the enemy. About one-third of the natives in southern New England assisted the colonists, and **King Philip's War** became a civil war among the Native Americans. The Puritans' recruitment of Indian allies proved a smart move; by the summer of 1676, the tide of war turned in the Puritans' favor. The natives taught the allies how to avoid ambushes and how to track down and destroy the rebels in their refuges. Wise colonial commanders abandoned completely inappropriate European military tactics based on masses of men engaged in complicated maneuvers to deliver volleys of fire. Instead, they adopted the Native Americans' "skulking way of war"—stealth, ambush, and small party terrorist raids and individual marksmanship. As summer approached, the rebels had run out of food and ammunition just as they faced a revamped, augmented, and more resolute enemy. Driven from their villages and fields, Metacom's diminishing forces retreated. Desperately hungry, unable to make guns and gunpowder, and cut off from access to colonial traders, they became even weaker. Also aiding the Puritan cause was the entry of the powerful Mohawks (one of the Iroquois Five Nations), who Governor Edmund Andros of New York allowed to participate, even though he had no great love for the Puritans. (Andros was a devoted Stuart royalist and high-church Anglican). With such overwhelming forces arrayed against them, Metacom's rebels' days were numbered.

By the close of summer 1676, resistance collapsed as one demoralized group after another surrendered. In August, Metacom died in battle, shot by a praying-town Indian who served with the Puritan militia. The English cut off his head for display on a post atop a brick watchtower in Plymouth. The bitter and bloody war devastated the Puritan settlements but especially the Native American villages. The conflict killed about 3,000 Indians, a quarter of their population in southern New England. Rather than treat the captives as prisoners of war, the Puritans declared them to be traitors, executed the chiefs, and sold the rest of the survivors into West Indian or Mediterranean slavery. Some of the defeated natives escaped northward, seeking a safe haven among fellow Algonquians, the Abenaki in

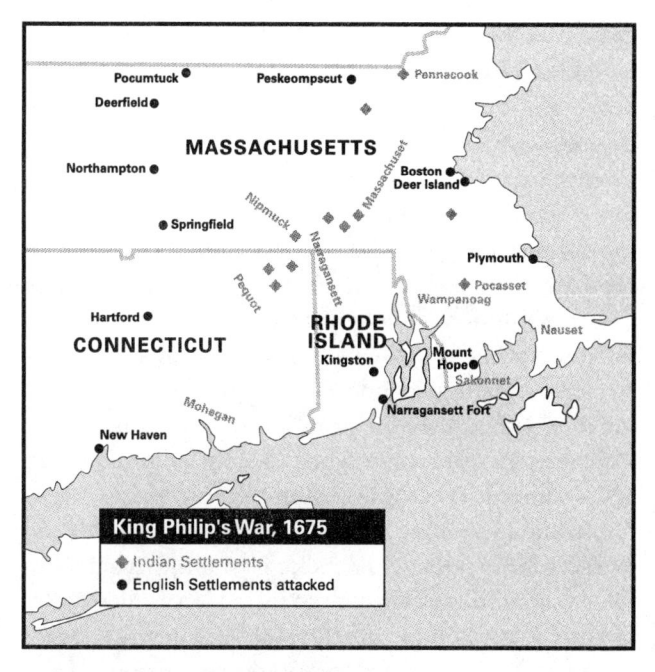

Map 3.4 King Philip's War

northern New England and New France. The refugees carried with them a bitter hatred for New Englanders. In a long series of wars between 1689 and 1760, the remnants of Metacom's rebels and their descendants would guide French raiders on repeated attacks against New England's frontier settlements.

North American Survival Strategies

In some ways, America became as much a new world for Native Americans as for the European immigrants. The Indians welcomed European cloth, muskets, hatchets, knives, and pots, but these goods came at a price. Natives who learned to use them gradually abandoned traditional skills and became increasingly dependent on trade with Europeans, a process not complete until the nineteenth century. Alcohol, the one item always in demand, was also very dangerous. Indian men drank to alter their mood and achieve visions, not for sociability. Drunkenness among Native Americans became a major, if intermittent, social problem.

Settlers who understood that their future depended on the fur trade, such as those in New France, tried to stay on good terms with the Native American peoples. The Dutch West India Company put New Netherland on such a course, and the English governors of New York after the 1664 British takeover followed such initiatives. **Edmund Andros**, governor from 1674-1680, cultivated the friendship of the Iroquois League, in which the five member nations had promised not to wage war against one another. In 1677, Andros and the Five Nations (the Mohawk, Oneida, Onondaga, Cayuga, and Seneca) agreed to make New York the easternmost link in what the English called the "Covenant Chain" of peace, a huge defensive advantage for a lightly-populated colony. Thus, while New England and Virginia fought bitter Indian wars in the 1670s, New York avoided conflict. The Covenant Chain later proved flexible enough to incorporate other Indians and colonists as well, all able to live in peace along the Hudson River Valley for several decades.

Without question, William Penn proved to be the most successful Englishman to develop not only peaceful relations with Native Americans but also profitable and mutually beneficial bonds. By the time of the Quakers' arrival in Pennsylvania, the major Algonquian tribe in the area was the Lenni Lenape (numbering about 5,000), who had already been involved for decades in trade relations with the Dutch and the Swedish settlers. Moreover, by the time of the Quakers' arrival, the Lenni Lenape possessed more land than their reduced numbers could use, and thus welcomed the opportunity to sell some for coveted trade goods. There is little doubt that Penn's sincere yet shrewd policy of cultivating Indian goodwill contributed significantly to Pennsylvania's rapid growth and financial success. Penn's approach allowed his colony to enjoy prolonged peace with the local tribes, avoiding the native uprisings that had devastated Virginia, New England, and New Netherland, as well as South Carolina.

In his first meeting with the natives, Penn laid the foundation for peaceful relations with the Lenni Lenape, telling the tribe that "The King of the Country where I live, hath given me a great Province but I desire to enjoy it with your Love and Consent, that we may always live together as neighbor and friends and not devour and destroy one another but live soberly and kindly together in the world." In this single statement, Penn disassociated himself from the entire history of European colonization in the New World. In contrast to the violent intimidation, deception, and fraud often perpetrated on Native Americans by previous colonial leaders, Penn acknowledged the Lenni Lenape as the land's legitimate owners, and he publicly treated their culture with respect.

Penn was keenly aware of the disintegrative effects that two generations of contact with the Finns, Swedes, and Dutch had perpetrated on the Lenni Lenape. Unlike most of his contemporaries who asserted that the interaction with civilized white Europeans had benefited the savage, Penn contended the opposite: that treacherous Europeans corrupted Native Americans. "The worst is that they are worse for the Christians, who have propagated their vices and yielded them tradition for ill and not for good things." Penn believed that the Lenni Lenape would have been better off had they not established relations with the Europeans, for their inherently "blessed equable temperament" and simple life would not have been altered. As Penn noted, "They care for little because they want but little, and the reason is, a little contents them. In this they are sufficiently revenged [better off than] on us: if they are ignorant of our pleasures, they are also free from our pains. We sweat and toil to live; their pleasure feeds them—I mean their hunting, fishing, and fowling."

Penn also observed the effects of the European "luxury" that had "filled them with anxieties" and "had raised their passions"—alcohol. Penn was certain that "the drinking of strong spirits" insidiously destroyed their idyllic, simple life. "Sober they are extraordinary, sensitive people of high integrity; drunk they are helpless dupes," exchanging for rum, "the richest of their skins and furs." Penn believed Native Americans' addiction to alcohol was not just another manifestation (or confirmation) of their alleged inherent, barbarous nature. To Penn, it reflected something deeper: a need for relief from the intolerable tensions created by the conflict of cultural values in which they were caught.

By the late seventeenth century, Penn's peaceful policy so impressed Native American tribes that Indian refugees began migrating to Pennsylvania, fleeing from abuse and warfare in other colonies. Penn's government welcomed Shawnees from South Carolina, the Nanticoke and Conoy of Maryland, the Tutelo from Virginia, and some Mahicans from New York. As a Conoy explained to the Quakers, "The People of Maryland do not treat the Indians as you & others do, for they make slaves of them & sell their children for Money." Welcoming the refugees was shrewd as well as benevolent. The exiles were relocated along the Susquehanna River, replacing the Susquehannock, thereby giving Pennsylvanians a security screen to the west of their settlements in the Delaware Valley. The outlanders' villages provided a buffer, especially against the French and their Indian allies, who became particularly menacing in the late 1690s. By that decade, England went to war with France, and typically the conflict spilled across the Atlantic to North America. The English government called on its colonies to do their part, expecting them to provide men and arms in defense of the empire. Fortunately, the Quakers' decision in locating the fugitive tribes along their western pale relieved them of having to compromise on their avowed pacifism as their native clients bore the brunt of any frontier warfare. Behind a western rampart of Indian allies, Pennsylvanians enjoyed peace and prosperity until the 1720s, when their desire for land encroached upon their Indian friends, bringing to an end what was perhaps the longest, most amicable relationship between Europeans and Native Americans.

MERCANTILISM, THE NAVIGATION ACTS, AND THE REDEFINITION OF EMPIRE

By the Restoration, **mercantilism** had come to define English imperial policy. Indeed, even before the founding of Jamestown, this economic theory had become the driving force behind English overseas expansion. Mercantilism rested on the belief that the world's wealth was finite, that one person or nation could grow rich only at the expense of another, and that a nation's economic health depended, therefore, on extracting as much wealth as possible from home. The principles of mercantilism spread throughout Europe in the sixteenth and seventeenth centuries, resulting in increased competition among nations. Every European state tried to find markets for exports while seeking to limit its imports. One result of this effort was the increasing attractiveness of acquiring colonies, which would become the source of raw materials and a market for the colonizing power's goods. In effect, colonies became the providers of raw materials for the mother country while absorbing both the mother country's excess finished goods and surplus humanity. In short, colonies acted as the dumping grounds for both "commodities." Perhaps most important, at all times, colonial economic needs were to be subordinate to the needs of the mother country; that is, colonies existed for one single purpose: to enhance the wealth and power of the mother country. At no time were colonies to compete with the mother country, nor were they to produce goods that did not directly benefit either the empire or the mother country. Thus, the European imperial powers all believed colonial trade and other enterprises had to be closely regulated and monitored in order to ensure that colonial wealth, whether personal or collective, advanced not the individual or community, but the interests and power of the sponsoring nation state and empire as a whole. Supporters of mercantile theory were anti-capitalist in that they opposed free trade and individual accrual at the expense of the state.

Although the Restoration's new royalist Parliament rescinded all legislation passed during the Commonwealth period, these Cavaliers promptly reenacted and extended the original 1650s Navigation Act in a series of new measures. The 1660 Navigation Act required that all trade with the colonies be transported on ships made in England or the colonies, commanded by an English or colonial captain, and manned by a crew at least three-fourths English or colonial. The act also created a category of "enumerated" goods, (sugar, tobacco, timber, and naval stores were the most important) that could only be shipped directly to England, the intent being to give England a monopoly over the export of major staples from every English colony to Europe and the rest of the world. The colonists were allowed to export non-enumerated products to other English colonies, so the act did allow for a substantial degree of inter-colonial trade within the empire. In 1663, Parliament passed the Staple Act requiring that all goods sent from Europe to the colonies pass through England on their way, where they would be subject to English taxation. By passing this particular measure, the mother country ensured its monopoly on all colonial trade by guaranteeing that it controlled all products sent to the colonies, even those not "made in England." In effect, English merchants were setting themselves up as middlemen, marking up the price on all exports to the colonies, regardless of their place of origin. Naturally such a procedure forced the colonists to pay higher prices, especially for non-English goods. Finally, an act passed in 1673 imposed duties on the coastal trade among the English colonies as well as providing for the appointment of customs officials to enforce the **Navigation Acts**. These mandates, with later amendments and additions, formed the legal basis of England's mercantile system in America for a century.

The Dominion of New England

Before the Navigation Acts, all the mainland colonial governments (excluding Virginia, a "royal colony" with a governor appointed by the king) had operated largely independently of the Crown, with governors chosen by the proprietors or the colonists themselves and boasting powerful representative assemblies. English officials recognized that to increase their control over their colonies they would have to create a body in London to reign in and monitor the independent-minded colonial governments, which were unlikely to enforce the new laws. In 1675, Charles II created a new agency, the Lords Committee of Trade and Plantations, or simply the Lords of Trade. This body enforced the Navigation Acts and administered the colonies. Although Virginia was the oldest royal colony, the West Indies became the focus of most of the new policies simply because the Caribbean remained a much more important theater of international competition. The instruments of royal government first took shape in the islands and then extended to the mainland with Puritan Massachusetts becoming the first to come under the new royal yoke. In 1679, Charles II stripped the Bay Colony of its authority over New Hampshire and chartered a separate royal colony with a governor he would himself appoint. Charles also began seeking legal grounds for revoking Massachusetts' corporate charter, with designs of making it a royal colony. He soon became convinced that he had found proper grounds when the Massachusetts General Court declared that it would not abide by the Navigation Acts because Parliament did not have the power to legislate for the colony. Such an assertion and usurpation of both royal and Parliamentary authority incensed both the king and Parliament. Thus, in 1684, with Parliament's blessing, Charles revoked Massachusetts' charter.

Matters for the Massachusetts Puritans only got worse in 1685 with the ascension of Charles's brother, James II, to the throne. A devout Catholic consumed with hatred for the Puritans (who, after all, had executed his father), James quickly punished Massachusetts further by incorporating all of New England—New Hampshire, Connecticut, and Rhode Island and later New York and New Jersey—into a consolidated super-colony called the **Dominion of New England**. Modeled along the lines of Spanish viceroyalties, the Dominion extended from the Delaware River to Canada. James dissolved the assemblies in all the respective colonies, administering the Dominion through a governor-general assisted by a lieutenant governor and an appointed council. The new arrangement dramatically and abruptly halted the momentum that colonials had been gathering toward greater autonomy. For the post of governor-general, the king appointed **Edmund Andros**, previously James's imperious New York governor. Francis Nicholson became lieutenant governor, carrying out his duties in New York, while Andros and his Dominion council presided in Boston.

Arbitrary and centralized, the Dominion regime shocked New Englanders. Anglican newcomers replaced Puritan judges and officers. With instructions from James, Andros attempted to destroy Puritanism by defunding it, forbidding the clergy from drawing their salaries from town taxes. Moreover, the Dominion became more expensive than the old charter governments, requiring unprecedented levels of taxation. A good portion of the increased cost of administration covered Andros' lavish salary of 1,200 pounds, an amount that exceeded the entire annual outlay to maintain the former Massachusetts government. Andros also brought along two companies of regular troops, whom he expected the colonists to provision. To raise revenue, Andros levied new taxes without an assembly or even the support of a majority of his own council, composed largely of merchants. The Dominion regime also vigorously enforced the Navigation Acts by establishing in Boston a new vice-admiralty court that operated without juries. The new court greatly depressed the port's business, seizing six merchant ships for violating the acts in the summer of 1686. With their incomes in contraction, New Englanders were hard pressed to pay Andros' increased fees and taxes. Andros' rigid enforcement

Table 3.1 — England's Principal Mainland Colonies

Name	Original Purpose	Date of Founding	Principal Founder	Major Export	Estimated Population c. 1700
Virginia	Commercial venture	1607	Captain John Smith	Tobacco	64,560
New York (New Amsterdam)	Commercial venture	1613 (English Colony, 1664)	Peter Stuyvesant, (Duke of York)	Furs, grain	19,107
Plymouth	Refuge for English Separatists	1620 (Absorbed by Massachusetts 1691)	William Bradford	Furs, fish, livestock	Included with Massachusetts
New Hampshire	Commercial venture	1623	John Mason	Wood, naval stores	4,958
Massachusetts	Refuge for English Puritans	1628	John Winthrop	Grain, wood, fish	55,941
Maryland	Refuge for English Catholics	1634	Lord Baltimore (George Calvert)	Tobacco	34,100
Connecticut	Expansion of Massachusetts	1635	Thomas Hooker	Grain	25,970
North Carolina	Commercial venture	1663	Anthony Ashley Cooper	Wood, naval stores, tobacco	10,720
South Carolina	Commercial venture	1663	Anthony Ashley Cooper	Naval stores, rice, indigo	5,720
New Jersey	Consolidation of new English territory, Quaker settlement	1664	Sir George Cartaret	Grain	14,010
Pennsylvania	Refuge for English Quakers	1681	William Penn	Grain	18,950
Georgia	Discourage Spanish expansion; charity	1733	James Oglethorp	Silk, rice, wood, naval stores	5,200 (in 1750)

of the Navigation Acts and his dismissal of the colonists' claims to the "rights of Englishmen" made him quickly and thoroughly unpopular.

The Glorious Revolution

James II was not only losing friends in America but also alienating powerful Englishmen at home by attempting to Catholicize the country and, as his father (Charles I) tried, ruling as an absolute monarch. By 1688, his popular support had all but evaporated. Determined to avoid another civil war at all costs, Parliament invited his Protestant daughter, Mary, and her husband, William of Orange, ruler of the Netherlands, to assume the throne. Probably remembering what had happened to his father, James offered no resistance and fled to France. As a result of this bloodless coup, which the English called the "**Glorious Revolution**," William and Mary became joint sovereigns.

When news of James's overthrow reached Boston, Puritans were jubilant and quickly moved to overthrow his unpopular viceroy in New England. Andros was arrested and imprisoned. To the Puritans' joy, they were not reprimanded for their actions by the new monarchy; quite the opposite occurred. The new sovereigns accepted Andros' removal and quickly abolished the Dominion of New England, restoring all the colonies to their independent status and granting them all the right of self-government. They did not, however, restore the colonies to their previous state. In 1691, they combined Massachusetts and Plymouth, making it a single, royal colony under the king's sovereignty. The new charter restored the General Court, but the king now appointed the governor. Property ownership also replaced church membership as the basis for voting and office holding.

In New York, the Glorious Revolution took a different turn. Andros had been governing the colony through a lieutenant governor, Francis Nicholson, who enjoyed the support of the province's wealthy merchants and fur traders. Other, less favored colonists—farmers, mechanics, small traders, and shopkeepers—had a long accumulation of grievances against Nicholson and his allies. Leading the dissidents was Jacob Leisler, a German immigrant and prosperous merchant who had married into a prominent Dutch family but had never won acceptance as one of the colony's elite. In May 1689, when news of the Glorious Revolution in England and Andros' fall in Massachusetts reached New York, Leisler raised a militia, captured the city fort, drove Nicholson into exile, and proclaimed himself the new head of the New York government. For two years, he tried in vain to stabilize his power in the colony amid fierce factional rivalry, but the established elite saw him as nothing more than a rabble-rousing parvenu. In 1691, when William and Mary appointed a new governor, Leisler briefly resisted. Although he soon yielded, his hesitation allowed his many political enemies to charge him with treason, leading to his conviction and execution. Fierce rivalry between what became known as the "Leislerians" and "anti-Leislerians" dominated New York colonial politics for many years thereafter.

England's Glorious Revolution of 1688 touched off uprisings, mostly bloodless, in several colonies. Under the new sovereigns, the representative assemblies that had been abolished were restored. However, much to the disappointment of many colonists, the Glorious Revolution in America proved no vindication of Americans' resolve to govern themselves. Particularly in New York and Maryland, the uprisings had more to do with local factional and religious divisions than with any larger vision of the nature of the empire. While insurgents did succeed in toppling the authoritarian regime of the short-lived Dominion of New England, ironically, Massachusetts Puritans lost their previous autonomy and came under greater Crown scrutiny. As the first century of English settlement in America came to a close, the colonists were becoming more a part of the imperial system than ever before.

WITCHCRAFT HYSTERIA IN NEW ENGLAND

By the 1690s, it appeared to many old-line Puritans that the majority of their brethren had become wayward saints who had lost sight or had forgotten completely the original purpose of the Puritan migration to the wilderness of North America. Such refractory behavior, if not outright disdain for Puritan traditionalism, was especially rampant among the younger generations, all of whom had been born in the New World a generation or two removed from Puritan hardships and suffering both in England and North America. To them, "errand" had no meaning or purpose anymore, for they had known only the good life in New England and none of the ordeals of their forebears. As a result of such perceived wantonness, Puritan clergymen feared that God's wrath would inevitably descend down upon New Englanders for their manifold transgressions. To try to bring back the fold, many New England clergymen began delivering a new genre of sermon known as the "jeremiad," named after the grim Old Testament prophet Jeremiah. A jeremiad catalogued the sufferings and sins of New England: Indian wars, the Dominion of New England, earthquakes, fires, storms—all sent by God to punish a region wallowing in immorality and irreligion. Finding the present generation wanting, a jeremiad exhorted listeners to reclaim the lofty standards and pure morality ascribed to New England's founders.

The jeremiads not only warned audiences of impending cataclysm if righteousness and godliness did not return but also that God would cease to protect them from Satan, and thus send among them his most treacherous and insidious agents, witches. Like many Europeans, Puritans believed Satan recruited humans to sign their name in blood in his book. In return, the signers received from the Devil supernatural and magical power, to use for themselves for whatever self-servicing or evil purposes. In exchange for such temporal power, the individual's soul became Satan's upon death for eternity. Since New England's founding, whenever cattle and children sickened and died, Puritans suspected that some in their midst practiced satanic magic. For the community's safety, witches had to be identified, prosecuted, and neutralized. The authorities pardoned witches who confessed and testified against others, but persistent denial consigned the witch to public execution by hanging. Contrary to popular myth and previous European practice, the New England Puritans did not burn witches at the stake.

That a pre-modern, deeply religious people as the Puritans would believe in magic and witches made perfect sense, for they lived in an unpredictable and often deadly

The Salem Witch Trials in Global Perspective

Compared to the witchcraft hysterias that swept through Europe in the sixteenth and seventeenth centuries, the episode that occurred in Salem and other New England towns seems almost uneventful. In the European panic, approximately 110,000 people were accused of witchcraft and put on trial; more than half were convicted and subsequently executed, most commonly by hanging or burning at the stake. Interestingly, the Spanish Inquisition, reputedly for centuries the most vicious in its seeking out of alleged witches and in its punishment, only put to death 2 percent of those tried and convicted. Yet even these realities do not give a full sense of the hysteria's magnitude. Thousands more Europeans, especially in the German principalities, which saw the greatest panics and subsequent trials, convictions, and executions, were harassed, and even more people remained "suspects" until the day they died. It was not uncommon for entire towns or regions, particularly in Germany, to be affected for years. Such was the situation in Wurzberg during one seven-year period, which saw the execution of 900 people, including 133 put to death in one day in 1589 in Quedlinberg.

Although "outbreaks" of the witchcraft hysteria occurred in every European country during the early modern period, certain countries were more affected than others. The most beleaguered by this "phenomenon" was Germany, followed by what is today Poland, Switzerland, and France. It was in those particular countries in which the conflicts of the Reformation and Counter-Reformation occurred most violently and affected the greatest number of people, as Protestant or Catholics lived in states or territories dominated by the other religion. In such areas, the majority feared that their society was being undermined from within by the minority faith, and thus, in most instances, the targets for accusation of witchcraft became either the Catholic or Protestant minority.

It was also during the late sixteenth and early seventeenth centuries that the modern nation-states emerged. As monarchies tried to consolidate their rule over church and state, they often inspired witch hunts in order to impose conformity and unity. Such was the case in France during the sixteenth century, and later in the century many German Protestant princes initiated the same tactic to drive out troublesome Catholics. Witchcraft trials were also common in politically unstable regions, ones where the local prince was relatively weak. In such places, local magistrates, in the prince's name, could generate hysteria and conduct prosecutions with a free hand. Moreover, once the local populace was sufficiently agitated, the hysteria often escalated beyond the immediate locale as mobs searched for more "witches" outside their own area. Such unchecked mania often continued for years, causing even more convictions and executions. In one instance, magistrates in the German town of Rottenburg became concerned that an out-of-control witch hunt might result in the execution of every female in the community. These worries were not unfounded, as two neighboring German villages witnessed the female population being reduced to one woman each.

Without question the main targets of the various witchcraft hysterias were women. The majority of the accused as well as executed were females. In some regions of Europe, women constituted 90 percent of all the accused. Such statistics reveal the incredible misogyny of sixteenth and seventeenth century Western European culture. The **Malleus Maleficarum** *(***The Witch Hammer***), the "guidebook" for witch hunting, first published in 1486 and reprinted many times over the next several decades, declared women to be "naturally" passionate and gullible and thus particularly receptive to the devil's mischief. Female witches were believed to have engaged the devil in "carnal copulation," siring not only minions to do his work in the world but deliver children as well for him to eat. The book made it clear that women were the devil's disciples and for mankind to be ever vigilant for their evil wiles, and that God had "so far preserved the male sex from such crime."*

Such views found a receptive audience in Western Europe. Some historians contend that the witchcraft hysteria reflected the effort by males to reinforce patriarchal controls over women. The majority of women accused were unmarried, either "spinsters" or widows, even younger women, who were not under the "thumbs" of husband or fathers. Constant religious strife that escalated into protracted wars and plagues, especially in Germany, resulted in a significant increase in the number of widows. By the seventeenth century, in some regions as many as 20 percent of the women had never married.

Early modern Europe suffered from many maladies: endemic warfare, religious upheaval, economic depression, and epidemic disease. Such afflictions led many to conclude that God was punishing them for their sins by allowing the devil to come to their communities in the form of his female minions, witches, who were responsible for such calamities. In societies that were organized by gender—rather than other forms of hierarchy—women became

> *the focus of the prosecutions that sought to restore order and security to society by rooting out the subversion that came from within. Russia, interestingly, was the exception. In Russia the targets of the witch hunts were men, because Russian society was still largely medieval and feudal in social structure and thus organized by rank and place. Those suspected of being witches were male vagabonds and itinerants, men who had stepped out of their communities or their societal positions.*
>
> *The New England witchcraft hysteria of the late seventeenth century, though much less sweeping than those that occurred in Europe, nonetheless reflected similar patterns and causes: a time of political and religious instability and uncertainty that made people anxious to reassert control. In their search to regain the familiar, the safe, and the stable, they concluded that all of their personal problems and the ills afflicting their communities was the result of the devil come in the form of a woman—a witch—whom Satan had sent to do his mischief.*

natural world often beyond their control. Seventeenth-century life in the North American wilderness was rife with all manner of inexplicable (to the Puritans) natural calamities—sudden fires, floods, windstorms, droughts, crop blights, and livestock diseases. Especially disturbing were periodic epidemics of measles, influenza, and smallpox that proved especially fatal to children. Since the Puritans had no scientific understanding of the causes of such maladies or natural phenomenon, they naturally called out for an explanation, some attribution of cause, that might protect people from further suffering, or at least console them with resignation to God's will. No Puritan wished to believe that misfortune was purely random and without supernatural meaning, whether the event be a sign from God or Satan, for that would confirm their helplessness and isolation in a world without God. Puritans were certainly more anxious about witches than other English colonists, which hosted very few trials and executions. New England's chief distinction was that the Puritans continued to prosecute and execute witches after 1650, when such proceedings virtually stopped in old England. Puritanism kept New England behind the times in supernatural belief.

Several factors contributed to the most legendary outbreak of **witchcraft hysteria** in the early 1690s in **Salem, Massachusetts**. Many perplexing and anxiety-inducing issues had coalesced by the early 1690s to create the perfect environment for such frenzy. For one, the Puritans were without an effective government because they had not yet received their new charter. The opening battles of King William's War had just begun with the French Catholics of Canada and their Algonquian Indian allies raiding settlements on the northern and eastern frontiers. Slaves reported that the French were planning to recruit New England's Africans to join a force of Indians and French soldiers. Internally, land scarcity by the decade had also become a significant factor, particularly as increasing numbers of young men had no opportunity to inherit their fathers' estate as had been the case in previous decades. Frustrating such individuals was the fact that many widows were in possession of vast amounts of acreage, just holding on to them until they passed. Thus, elderly, widowed women whose land young men coveted became one of the targets of the witch hunts that began in Salem. By accusing such a person of being a witch or by consorting with Satan or engaging in the occult or black magic, young men hoped that such women would not only be convicted of witchcraft but as punishment also lose their land.

One day in late 1691, several adolescent girls ignited the delirium when, in the middle of play and conversation, they threw themselves on the ground writhing in fits and bodily contortions, allegedly speaking in tongues and later awakening at night with nightmares. The girls proclaimed they had been taken over by evil spirits and that witches in the community had cast spells upon them. Hysteria spread throughout the town as people (most of them women) were accused of witchcraft by other townspeople. Since the only way to avoid prosecution was to confess and name others, accusations of witchcraft began to snowball. By the middle of 1692, scores of Salem residents came forward to accuse their

Print depicting a witchcraft trial in Salem, Massachusetts.

neighbors for a variety of reasons, often reflecting the desire to settle old scores within the community. Others accused neighbors, friends, even relatives out of a desire for property or other material aggrandizement. By the time that the investigation and trials ended, 156 people had been jailed and 20 executed by hanging with one man pressed to death (crushed under the weight of stones) for refusing to enter a plea. As in previous witch hunt hysterias, most of the accused were women past the age of 40, and most of the accusers were women in their late teens or twenties. Puritan authorities only ended the madness when they themselves began to be accused of witchcraft. Eventually, the girls who had been the original accusers later recanted and admitted that their story had been fabricated.

In many ways, the Salem witchcraft mania reflected the last-ditch, desperate effort by old-school Puritans to redeem a perceived fallen people and society by returning both individuals and community to the halcyon days of godliness and morality; in effect, to the years prior to 1650 when all Puritans seemed to be unified in their purpose in having come to North America. However, the witchcraft panic also reflected a New England society and a Puritan faith in significant transition, if not transformation. Indeed, many old-line Puritans feared that Puritanism, especially in its original form, had died in the wilderness of New England and along with the faith, the Puritan way of living as well. Whether they liked it or not, life in the wilderness had indeed changed many New Englanders. As this new species of New Englander entered the next century, he became even less Puritan and more Yankee.

Despite the taint of the Salem witch hunts, the Puritans left a prodigious and enduring legacy for English-speaking North America. Compared with other colonial regions, New England was a land of relative equality, opportunity, and thrifty, industrious, and entrepreneurial habits that sustained an especially diverse and complex economy. The region's large, healthy families, nearly even gender ratio, and long life expectancy promoted social stability, the steady accumulation of family property, and its orderly transfer from one generation to the next. Nowhere else in colonial America did colonists enjoy readier access to public worship (except perhaps in Pennsylvania), and nearly universal education. That those ideals remain powerful in our own culture attests to the enduring importance of the Puritan legacy.

LAYING FOUNDATIONS FOR THE AMERICAN NATION

After a period of considerable instability, almost all of England's North American colonies by the beginning of the 18th century had developed societies to be maintained until the American Revolution; some would not change until after the Civil War. For the most part, the colonies were prosperous with a large white middle class. The efforts to replicate a European hierarchical order had largely failed, although manifestations of that system prevailed in the southern colonies. Each region had found a secure economic base: farming and shipping in New England, mixed farming in the middle colonies, and staple crop production in the South. The southern colonies had become slave societies, although every colony had slavery to some extent, including Quaker Pennsylvania. All the colonies had more or less figured out how to control their own populations, whether by granting them (in the case of the Europeans) increased opportunity and political rights, or by exercising tighter control, as was the case for enslaved Africans. When combined with political stability, these strong economic foundations served as the preconditions for the 18th century's rapid population increase when the mainland English population would far surpass that of the French and Spanish colonies. Indeed, by 1750, mainland Spanish and French colonies were still little more than frontier outposts, although both nations still maintained imperial visions for North America. Native Americans remained a strong presence, especially west of the Appalachian Mountains, but the competition among European powers—and even individual colonies—for the tribes' loyalty, their trade, and their land, remained a source of conflict.

Chronology

1620 Pilgrims (Separatists) adopt Mayflower Compact and settle Plymouth.

1621 Dutch West India Company chartered.

1630 Puritans settle Massachusetts Bay.

1635 Peter Minuit founds New Sweden.

1636 Harvard University opens its doors.
Roger Williams founds Providence colony.
Anne Hutchinson banished from Massachusetts Bay Colony.
Pequot War begins.

1637 Puritan militia along with Mohegan and Narragansett warriors slaughter Pequot village of 400 mostly women, children, and old men near the Mystic River.

1638 Pierre Minuit founds New Sweden.

1639 Colony of New Haven founded.

1651 Parliament passes first Navigation Act.

1652-54 First Anglo-Dutch War.
Oliver Cromwell becomes Lord Protector of England.

1660 Parliament passes new Navigation Act.

1662 Charles II grants Rhode Island charter.

1663 Staple Act passed.
Charles II grants Connecticut charter.

1664 England takes New Netherlands from the Dutch and rename it New York.

1675 King Philip's War.

1681-82 William Penn receives charter to establish Pennsylvania

1684-86 Massachusetts charter revoked.
King James II creates the Dominion of New England.

1688-89 The Glorious Revolution begins.

1691 Jacob Leisler, leader of the rebellion in New York, executed.
Witchcraft hysteria begins in Salem, Massachusetts.

1692 Nineteen people hanged in Salem for alleged witchcraft.

1696 Parliament passes Navigation Act.
Board of Trade replaces Lords of Trade.

1701 Iroquois make peace with New France.

Review Questions

1. In what significant ways did English colonization of the northern colonies differ from the founding of the southern colonies?

2. No sooner did Englishmen begin to settle in Massachusetts Bay and other New England locations, than their respective communities became wracked by dissension. What caused such divisions?

3. Discuss William Penn's idea of Pennsylvania as a "Holy Experiment." How did Penn's idea differ from John Winthrop's vision of Massachusetts as a glorious "City upon a Hill"?

4. Why were the Quakers so despised in North America among the Puritans, and in England? What was it about the Quaker faith that made its disciples "suspect?"

5. Discuss the relationship between the Puritans and New England and Native Americans in the region. Why was the relationship so hostile?

Glossary of Important People and Concepts

Edmund Andros
Antinomianism
William Bradford
Oliver Cromwell
Dominion of New England
"Errand into the Wilderness"
Anne Hutchinson
Glorious Revolution
Great Migration
King Philip's War
Mercantilism
Navigation Acts
William Penn
Pequot War
Praying Towns
Predestination
Puritans
Quakers (The Society of Friends)
Rhode Island
Witchcraft Hysteria
Separatists
Squanto and Massasoit
Restoration
Roger Williams
John Winthrop

SUGGESTED READINGS

Victoria D. Anderson, *New England's Generation: The Great Migration and the Formation of Society and Culture in the Seventeenth Century* (1991).

Patricia Bonomi, *Under the Cope of Heaven: Religion, Society, and Politics in the Seventeenth Century* (1986).

William Cronon, *Changes in the Land: Colonists and the Ecology of New England* (1983).

Stephen Innes, *Creating the Commonwealth: The Economic Culture of Puritan New England* (1995).

Edmund S. Morgan, *The Puritan Family* (1944)

———, *Visible Saints: The History of a Puritan Idea* (1963).

Carla G. Pestana, *The English Atlantic in an Age of Revolution, 1640-1661* (2001).

Bernard Bailyn, *The Peopling of British North America* (1986).

Jill Lepore, *The Name of War: King Philip's War and the Origin of American Identity* (1998).

John A. Moretta, *William Penn and the Quaker Legacy* (2007).

Mary Beth Norton, *In the Devil's Snare: The Salem Witchcraft Crisis of 1692* (2002).

Richard R. Johnson, *Adjustment to Empire: The New England Colonies, 1675-1715* (1981).

Perry Miller, *The New England Mind: The Seventeenth Century* (1939).

David D. Hall, *Worlds of Wonder, Days of Judgment: Popular Religious Belief in Early New England* (1989).

Bernard Bailyn, *The New England Merchants in the Seventeenth Century* (1955).

Gary B. Nash, *Quakers and Politics: Pennsylvania, 1681-1726* (1968).

Benjamin Franklin of Philadelphia, between 1763 and 1785

Chapter Four

CREATING AN AMERICAN PEOPLE, 1700-1763

Just as American and European consumers today have become addicted to sugar, coffee, tea, alcohol, and even drugs, addiction to such plantation commodities was just as rampant in the eighteenth century among Europeans and their colonial counterparts. Tobacco was the first of such addictive products. As early as the mid-sixteenth century, European smokers had become "consumed by the weed." However, there were many other staples grown on New World and other colonial plantations that were just as habit-forming: coffee, cocoa, tea, and sugar (as well as its by-product, rum). As European and colonial consumer demand increased for such items and their by-products, colonial plantation agriculture expanded commensurately.

The same phenomenon occurred with coffee, which originated in Ethiopia but was introduced into the Middle East by Arab traders around 1000 C.E. The beverage had made its way to the Ottoman Empire by the middle of the sixteenth century, and although some Muslim religious leaders condemned the drinking of such an "intoxicant," it became popular throughout the Muslim world. European travelers to the major Muslim cities of Constantinople, Cairo, Alexandria, and Aleppo found the taste of coffee appealing (and addicting) and began importing it into Europe. London saw its first coffeehouse established in 1652; 60 years later, at least 500 such establishments existed throughout Europe's urban enclaves. As had developed in the Muslim world, European coffeehouses became places of male sociability.

By 1700, Yemen, which had become the world's largest and most prolific coffee-growing country, could no longer meet the increasing global demand, so Muslim traders introduced coffee cultivation to India. In the late seventeenth century, the European imperial powers—most notable the Dutch and the English—encouraged their colonial planters in Jamaica, Barbados, and Indonesia to grow coffee as well as sugar. Here, the Dutch East India Company played a leading role, introducing both coffee planting and slavery to Indonesia. The French brought coffee cultivation to Martinique in the West Indies, while the Portuguese introduced the crop to Brazil.

The history of tea followed a similar pattern. The beverage was first introduced to England in the seventeenth century by the East India Company, for whom tea became its most valuable export. Tea quickly became more popular in England than coffee, and by the middle of the eighteenth century, tea became not only an item of mass consumption but an integral part of Englishmen's diet. All of the tea drank by the English people was imported, principally from India and China. Both beverages also helped to stimulate sugar production expansion, because Europeans liked to drink their tea or coffee very sweet. New World sugar plantations thus boomed beginning in the late seventeenth and into the eighteenth centuries, with the French West Indies particularly benefiting by providing the bulk of the demand for sugar. Indeed, New World slavery expanded to meet the European desire for tobacco and sugar, luxury products rather than the necessities of life.

The history of opium, the highly addictive drug that also became popular, especially among the European upper classes in the eighteenth century, is somewhat different.

The British East India Company was largely responsible for developing this trade item—the same company that had a monopoly on tea sales to the American colonies. The company made a fortune "pushing" the drug into China to rectify a trade imbalance that had occurred with tea. The British imported substantial amounts of tea from China but the Chinese needed very little in exchange and the British needed something "popular" to send to China to correct the trade imbalance. The Chinese had very little desire for English manufactured goods. They did, however, welcome Indian fabrics. They acquired an even bigger appetite for Indian opium, much to the Chinese government's dismay. China banned the drug's importation. Nonetheless, once the East India Company saw the huge potential profit for the opium trade in China, it secured a monopoly over Indian opium in 1773 and exported as much of the drug as possible to the increasingly addicted Chinese masses.

The trade in addictive substances tied the continents of the world together in the eighteenth century. A global trade network, organized by state-supported companies and in many cases by slave labor, supplied the world's consumers with habit-forming substances that they craved.

By the end of the seventeenth century, the British had established most of the North American mainland colonies that would later become the United States. Primarily within the New England region, religious groups created colonies that institutionalized their doctrine. At the same time, investors fashioned fiscally-focused societies in the South to take advantage of the natural and agricultural resources found there. In both locations, European immigration continued throughout the century as individuals came to the colonies searching for a fresh start in life. Collectively, the British North American colonies had weathered the political unrest generated by the English Civil War and the Glorious Revolution and negotiated a renewed relationship with the English Crown. The colonies were granted greater political and economic freedom in their daily activities, and both sides renewed their commitment to following established strictures, especially in regards to the principles of mercantilism.

The Glorious Revolution ushered in the beginnings of constitutional monarchy in England with certain inalienable rights for all Englishmen guaranteed in the Bill of Rights signed by William and Mary. With political stability at home, both Crown and Parliament could once again devote greater attention to the North American colonies. Although not officially sanctioned by the English government, a degree of autonomy was permitted in the colonies, largely the result of William's preoccupation with war against France. Nonetheless, the relationship between the Crown and the colonies appeared more secure and stable. Colonial tensions with the Native American tribes east of the Appalachians had also eased, but colonists throughout North America remained suspicious and hostile to the native peoples, often looking for the slightest provocation to remove them. Relationships between the different European powers in the New World were similarly stable. By the early decades of the eighteenth century, the colonies no longer existed in sheer survival mode. They were well on their way to developing more complex and sophisticated societies, defining the character and place of their respective inhabitants. The process of growth did not always progress smoothly or peacefully. Nevertheless, during the early-to-mid-eighteenth century, significant changes arose in the colonies' class structure, labor, and religious outlook.

COLONIAL ECONOMIC DEVELOPMENT

The New England, mid-Atlantic, and southern colonies all experienced increased development during the first half of the eighteenth century. In the once religiously-dominated New England colonies, economic growth adhered to mercantile practices. "Yankees" relied almost entirely upon trade with the British Empire for their prosperity while developing strong agricultural and extractive industries such as fishing, timber, and furs. The majority of such products were usually transported back to England in exchange for manufactured goods but just as often they were also traded with other English possessions, most notably the West Indies. The southern colonies were also part of this imperial trade network, but their economies relied almost exclusively on staple crop production—tobacco, rice, and indigo. All three cash crops proved lucrative but were labor intensive and, in the case of tobacco, heavily taxed the soil. The use of indentured servants initially solved the labor problem, followed by the use of forced human bondage in the form of African slaves.

With such a strong reliance upon trade, the English Crown maintained strict trade regulations via the Navigation Acts, which reflected the belief that the biggest profit margins could be made by exporting English-made manufactured goods to the colonies while limiting the colonists' ability to import foreign-made finished products. The Crown also generated additional revenue from the colonies by levying import duties on such commodities as sugar (the 1733 Sugar Act). In addition, the English government wanted to discourage colonial manufacturing enterprises while forcing the colonies to import all their manufactured goods from the mother country; thus, Parliament passed such measures as the Hat Act (1732), the Iron Act (1750), and the Woolen Act (1699). In short, the British government wanted as much control as possible over all aspects of the colonial economy.

IMMIGRATION

As the colonies became more economically prosperous and socially stable, all experienced dramatic increases in immigration. This was especially true in the northern colonies, although the southern colonies also witnessed population growth, though most of that increase came in the form of black slaves. How prodigious was this growth? Total numbers doubled nearly every 25 years after 1670. In 1760, Great Britain's North American colonies had a total population, including slaves, of 1.9 million; by 1775, the number of residents reached 2.5 million. A series of factors were responsible for the rise, including high fertility rates, decreasing infant mortality, young marriages, increased life spans, solid crop yields, and resultant high food availability. In effect, the American colonists lived in better, more stable and healthier environments than their European counterparts. Indeed, the European continent experienced continued geopolitical unrest and unstable economic conditions. Although not as intense nor as passionate and violent as in the decades prior to the Thirty Years' War (an extremely violent war between Catholics and Protestants that raged across Europe from 1618-1648), religious issues continued to affect some European nations, including England, which saw the government and the Church of England enforce uniformity rather vigorously. The **English Test Act of 1704** required all individuals to acknowledge the Anglican faith while stripping non-Anglicans of their political rights. Many such dissidents sought sanctuary in the North American colonies.

Others left Europe because of poor living conditions and limited opportunity. Overpopulation in many countries created an array of socio-economic problems such as food shortages, crowded living conditions, poor sanitation, and high disease rates. High unemployment strained whatever limited resources were dedicated to public programs. Unable to improve their circumstances, the large underclasses decided that their only salvation was to leave Europe for the New World, particularly for Britain's North American colonies. These immigrants hailed from a multitude of regions and encompassed a wide range of ethnicities, including the Scots-Irish, German, French Huguenots (Protestants), Swiss, Scottish, Irish, and Jews.

Upon their arrival in the colonies, these various groups tended to congregate in the same geographic locales, creating ethnic enclaves in the respective colonies where they concentrated, preserving their culture and sense of Old World community. Such attempts by these various groups to sustain their European identity and way of life proved to be a benefit and a detriment. Limited integration allowed these groups to remain culturally unique and vibrant while maintaining the heritage of the community left behind. Simultaneously, such aloofness also fostered negative attitudes and suspicion from the mainstream Anglo-American society who did not understand, nor displayed any desire to embrace, such diversity.

The Atlantic crossing was very expensive, especially for families. While some saved or borrowed the necessary money, others resorted to labor-based loans to finance the trip. For many desiring to start anew in North America, indentured servitude was their only alternative, with many so desperate to come to the colonies that they willingly bonded themselves for up to seven years. For more fortunate bondsmen, the end-of-contract payment included, most importantly, land ownership, which would give the laborers a start toward having the type of life that they envisioned in North America when they left Europe.

Redemptioners were a variation of indentured servants; they received passage based on the guarantee of funds at the point of destination. Such individuals traveled to America without charge, but once reaching port, they agreed to be sold into indentured servitude. The fees secured would pay for the voyage. If unable to secure such a position in short duration, the "redeemer," or transported individual, was auctioned off to the highest bidder. This method allowed many to journey to the colonies and become immersed in the colonial economic system without needing to produce the necessary transportation funds up front. The scheme also supplied low-cost labor in a setting where workers were always in constant demand, allowing the colonists to create a sustainable environment, providing them with the ability to expand and diversify their economic enterprises. Most important, the redemption process contributed labor to the colonial economies while offering redeemers the means to begin acquiring wealth and increased independence.

As beneficial as indentured servitude became for large landowners, the system proved to be far from a perfect labor arrangement. Those imperfections would become increasingly clear as the colonies further developed and greater numbers of individuals completed their terms of service. Individuals who became indentured servants usually understood the reality of the agreement; that their bondage would be tough and arduous, yet the benefits acquired at completion would allow them access to the economic system through land ownership or the acquisition of a specific trade or skill. Unlike their European counterparts, these individuals from the lower classes would finally have a solid opportunity to fully integrate into the economic structure. With each wave of individuals completing their contracts, a large number of men exited the system and overwhelmingly demanded access to land, upon which suffrage or voting rights were granted. When the pseudo-bartering system first began, it worked smoothly as the new underclass did, in fact, integrate into the socio-economic hierarchy. As the number of indentured servants increased, however, colonial landowning elites had a difficult time fulfilling the terms of the freedom dues to their newly emancipated bondsmen.

As the number of freedmen multiplied, Native American attacks on those venturing beyond the established borders became more vicious, and access to available lands diminished. If freedmen could not gain land, they could not, in turn, become self-sufficient land owners, increase their personal wealth, or participate in the political system. This imbalance in the demand for land led to a charged situation, where freed indentured servants grew frustrated at their inability to claim the land they had been promised or to which they felt entitled. Moreover, not every master believed he was obligated to reward faithful bondsmen with land; indeed, quite a few servants got nothing more than a piece of paper signifying they had fulfilled their contractual obligation. Such cavalier dismissal for their former bondsmen's well-being only intensified the servants' mounting grievances against the colonial elites for whom they had sweated, suffered, and labored for several years. These freedmen formed a new class of colonists who eagerly awaited the completion of their servitude and the collection of the freedom dues owed them at term's end. In the Chesapeake, this form of systematic labor abruptly ended in violent confrontation between freedmen and their former owners in the uprising known as Bacon's Rebellion. In the northern colonies disgruntled freedmen searching for unclaimed land west of the Appalachians would help to instigate the French and Indian War.

AFRICAN SLAVERY IN THE EIGHTEENTH CENTURY

During the eighteenth century, African slavery in Britain's North American colonies assumed distinctive northern and southern manifestations. Northern slaves, never great in number at any time during the colonial period, served masters in a variety of capacities, ranging from servants, maids, and nannies to skilled craftsmen and day laborers. Though daily life for these individuals was certainly not desirable, as they were still deprived of their basic freedoms, it was nonetheless better when compared to the struggles, daily misery, and abuse endured by their southern counterparts. The plantation system, driven by tobacco, rice, and indigo production, required intense levels of labor and harsh working conditions.

Prior to Bacon's Rebellion in the Chesapeake and before the arrival of rice and indigo cultivation in the Carolinas, African slavery was not a fully entrenched system. Many slaves had an existence similar to indentured servants where they could often gain complete freedom or live semi-free lives with their masters. In some recorded instances, blacks were treated like indentured servants and released with freedom dues at the end of their term of service. As the availability of indentured servants declined, landowners increasingly desired a permanent labor force. More importantly, planters wanted to avoid dealing with the discontented, landless masses demanding access to the political and economic systems. As employment and living conditions in Europe began improving during the eighteenth century, individuals were less willing to accept the harsh opportunities offered in the colonies. In the absence of negative forces pushing immigration, the number of individuals interested in signing a potential seven-year contract declined. Thus, a marked shift in the labor force developed and the use of slave labor intensified, as did the restrictions placed upon black bondsmen.

Bacon's Rebellion precipitated indentured servitude's final demise in the Chesapeake. In South Carolina, however, white indentured servitude never really took hold. From the beginning, white Carolinians had used African slaves as well as enslaved Native Americans as their principal labor force. Carolina slave owners treated their bondsmen in the late seventeenth and early eighteenth centuries paternalistically; that is, with a degree of civility and respect for them as human beings, a relationship that was non-existent in the Chesapeake by the beginning of the eighteenth century. Such solicitude, however, did not reflect any sort of recognition of the Africans' equality; they were still slaves, but nevertheless property that their masters were willing to allow a modicum of humanity and privilege. The colony's economics largely determined this unusual relationship. Until the discovery of the profitability of rice and indigo cultivation by Carolina slave owners, their black laborers engaged in a variety of non-agricultural, extractive industries, often requiring the learning and utilization of specific skills. Such enterprises were primarily related to timber and naval stores production, which were the main products along with deerskins exported to England until the 1720s. Thus, among the Carolina slave population, there developed a group of highly skilled, proud, privileged, respected, and fairly autonomous community of laborers. Moreover, the majority of these individuals had come directly from Barbados with their masters and thus came to see themselves as valued settlers. In addition, master-slave relations were much more fluid and generous during this pre-rice era; bondsmen not only felt acknowledged for their skills but as human beings as well.

Tragically, this unusual and complex master-slave relationship came to an end beginning in the early decades of the eighteenth century as white Carolinians increasingly discovered the great potential profitability of rice and indigo cultivation. Once engaged in this new enterprise, slave owners not only ended timber and naval stores production but also began bringing directly from Africa thousands of new slaves for purely agricultural work. The new arrivals quickly came to outnumber the original slaves. In the process, they became the dominant group. Initially, the older black Carolinians resented the recently arrived Africans. Over time, however, they bonded with them in rebellion. In fact, many of the uprising's leaders came from the original Barbadian slave community.

With rice and indigo cultivation came the end of the need for as many skilled slaves as was required during the pre-rice decades. Thus, many once-proud, valued, skilled, and autonomous slaves now found themselves stripped of such existence and working alongside recently-arrived Africans in the rice fields, whom the older slaves initially viewed with contempt for their "barbarity." The original black Carolinians no longer felt privileged and respected. They had now become chattel, and along with such degradation came increasing restrictions and harsher treatment. Formerly-benign slave owners no longer believed it necessary to treat their bondsmen as special, because little skill was required for rice or indigo cultivation. Thus, in the minds of rice and indigo planters, all blacks, whether recent arrivals from Africa or from the original Barbadian community, were the same: laborers for profitable staple crop production. It was only a matter of time before such seething discontent at the loss of status would inflame into rage and result in open, violent rebellion against the new order.

The Stono Rebellion

In the fall of 1739, the Carolina planters' worst fears came to fruition in the form of the **Stono Rebellion**. Exacerbating the tensions noted above was the presence of Spanish Florida just a few miles to the south. New Spain, always leery of their aggressive Anglo neighbors to the north, welcomed any event, internal or external, that could remove the English threat to this particular frontier outpost. If inciting or assisting a slave uprising in South Carolina would accomplish the end of the colony, then the Spanish were willing to engage in such an effort. Information quickly spread through the slave communities that any escaped slaves would be given amnesty and freedom upon reaching Florida. If they wanted to kill their masters or destroy property on the journey there, no questions would be asked. Thanks in large part to slave informants, white South Carolinians became aware of this offer and quickly passed slave codes further restricting black mobility, severely punishing defiant slaves. A new law known as the Security Act, required all men to carry arms (even during Sunday morning church services) for the purpose of having a white populous ready and armed to crush any slave insurrection.

The slaves began to sense real, long-lasting changes on the cusp of implementation, knowing that once the restrictions were put in place there would be no reversal of their new conditions. Such fear and alienation was especially felt among the original Barbadian slaves, many of whom were among the first to make a hasty retreat to St. Augustine, Florida. Their attempted flight began on a Sunday morning in September 1739 before the new laws took effect. The fugitives met at an arms store on the outskirts of Charles Town and killed the two shopkeepers working there. They then went house to house, freeing the slaves that they found, adding them to their numbers, and killing close to twenty-five whites. The size of the slave force swelled to almost a hundred before the rebellion collapsed. Initially, the slave rebels had the momentum. Their flight and subsequent attacks surprised many white Carolinians, who naively believed that their repressive new codes would effectively prevent any uprising. Despite the initial shock, white South Carolinians, many of whom had anticipated the event and were ready to respond, ultimately gained the upper hand. The tide turned against the rebels when South Carolina's lieutenant governor, William Bull, eluded the killing spree, reached the center of town, and alerted those attending Sunday services of the rebellion. Bull was not the only individual to escape the massacre. A group of slaves actually hid their masters from the mob because of the kindness they had been shown throughout their servitude. Those slaves would be aptly rewarded. A slave named July, who protected his master Thomas Elliott and his family from certain death, was given "as a reward for his faithful Services and for his encouragement to other slaves to follow his example ... shall have his freedom and a present of a suit of clothes, shirt, hat, a pair of stockings and a pair of shoes." Others among them, including several Native Americans, were rewarded with similar possessions.

Once alerted to the danger, white Carolinians quickly retaliated, determined to hunt down and kill the murderous rebels as rapidly as possible. Outnumbered and outgunned, the escaping slaves stood little chance of successfully making it to the Florida border. Before nightfall, the rebellion was over. Approximately thirty slaves had been shot dead. Of those who had escaped, all but one were captured and executed for their crimes within six months. A single fugitive evaded the law for three years before being arrested. In the slave owners' minds, the Stono Rebellion had made it clear that the slave community was a dangerous entity that had to be completely subordinated to protect the white population and their property from future uprisings. The **Negro Act**, written in direct response to the mayhem of the Stono Rebellion, was designed to eliminate any possibility of future slave revolts or violence. The measure further increased black restrictions, such as limiting free association, the right to possess arms, the ability to grow food for personal consumption, earn money, or become literate. Slaves were now at the complete mercy of their masters and depended entirely upon them for their daily sustenance. Moving forward, these restrictions only intensified in severity.

The aggression displayed by Spain during the Stono Rebellion was not an isolated event. All of the major nations with North American possessions constantly engaged in further territorial aggrandizement as well as control over navigable waterways and ports, and trading relationships with the native populations. Britain had successfully maneuvered the Dutch out of the New York region through a show of military force, and both Spain and Britain engaged in similar confrontations along their respective southernmost frontiers. Each wanted an increased buffer zone in the area between Florida and the Carolinas. The English had sought the region for a long time and had implemented different tactics to secure the territory, including employing coastal pirates to raid the ports and Native American tribes to attack outposts, neither of which succeeded in obtaining control of the area.

THE EUROPEAN ENLIGHTENMENT AND COLONIAL NORTH AMERICA

Not since the Renaissance had Europe experienced a more profound intellectual and creative impulse than that expressed by the Enlightenment *philosophes* of the "Age of Reason." Beginning in the late seventeenth century and extending into the last decade of the eighteenth century, the **Enlightenment** reflected the new thoughts and ideas about society, culture, religion, and science that had been germinating among Europe's creative classes (particularly those from France and England) for decades. Inspired by the Scientific Revolution of the sixteenth and seventeenth centuries, European "social scientists" began to look at the world around them and question the tenets upon which society rested. Politics and religion particularly interested the *philosophes*, as the movement's progenitors liked to call themselves. These individuals believed the time had come to critically analyze the systems and institutions that governed society. If a thoroughly rational and dispassionate investigation found any institutions to be harmful to society by retarding human progress, they should be reformed or abolished. The *philosophes* believed in the potential of human perfectibility, but such progress could only be accomplished by ridding society of those antiquated and repressive institutions and systems that had kept European society backward, superstitious, illiterate, intolerant, and cruel.

This particular intellectual and creative current did not develop from any one individual or single school of thought, but rather an accumulation of new and innovative ideas. In short, men's minds were beginning to embrace the idea of change in all areas of human interest. The hand of God was being pushed back by the mind of man as educated Europeans were coming to believe that everything that happened in the natural world had a rational explanation and that humans were capable of finding it. Man's power over nature, not God's grace, would henceforth be his salvation. Although European in origin and purpose, many members of Great Britain's North American colonial intellectual elite embraced the Enlightenment impulse, finding many of the movement's ideas to be particularly applicable to their lives in the New World.

In the colonies, a fascination with scientific exploration and Enlightenment rationalism flourished. **Benjamin Franklin** became not only colonial America's most outstanding example but an individual respected and honored as an equal among Europe's Enlightenment community. Born into a candle maker's family, Franklin was a newspaper editor and printer by trade, and thus a common man by eighteenth-century standards. Though he lacked the upbringing and schooling of the great European *philosophes*, Franklin fully embraced the impulse, encouraging his colonial peers to join him in the quest for new knowledge. Along with a cadre of his friends, he formed the **Junto Society of Philadelphia**, in which they discussed a wide range of topics, including science. His only expectation was for debates to be "conducted in the sincere spirit of inquiry after truth, without fond-

Cotton Mather

ness for dispute or desire of victory." Outside the group, Franklin personally pursued scientific exploration, most famously through his experimentation with lightning. In his legendary kite and key experiment, he identified the conductive nature of electricity, explaining how and why electricity traveled. His *Experiments and Observations on Electricity* (1751) outlined his discovery. During the next year, he invented the lightning rod to help protect buildings from dangerous lightning strikes. Franklin also created bifocals, an odometer, and the Franklin Stove. For so many new ideas to stem from a common, ordinary man provided a clear indication that Enlightenment thinkers could come from any sector of society, not just from the elite.

Franklin was not alone in his scientific probing. **Cotton Mather**, a Boston pastor, began studying new techniques to prevent the contraction of diseases, particularly smallpox. Although initial death rates had fallen since the early settlements both in the Americas and Europe, the fear remained that a new outbreak could quickly sweep through closely settled populations and exact tremendous death tolls. In 1721, when sailors docked in Boston began showing symptoms of smallpox, Mather began an investigation into the matter. One of his slaves, Onesimus, mentioned that while still in Africa he had been intentionally exposed to a weakened strain of the disease as a means of prevention. Mather wrote to a group of Boston doctors imploring them to begin inoculating the townspeople against the disease. Dr. Zabdiel Boylston took up the charge and looked for healthy volunteers who would allow weakened strains to be injected into them. In total, 287 Bostonians were inoculated, including Mather's son and nephew, with a high level of success. While the procedure was not completely safe (six of the test subjects died), it nevertheless provided the initial steps toward the advancement of modern medical practices.

Unfortunately, Mather's promotion of medical advancement was not well-received by the majority of Bostonians. The reverend had a bomb thrown through his window with a note attached reading, "Cotton Mather, you dog, dam you! I'll inoculate you with this with a pox to you." The bomb did not explode, but the sentiments of the sender and fellow Bostonians were made clear; the increased reliance upon science and the corresponding shift away from providential will and omnipotence would not be immediately or universally accepted regardless of the concrete benefits to be gained from such forward thinking.

The move away from divine determinism naturally led others to question man's capacity to order the universe and all contained within it. For many, the increased concentration on human understanding decreased the role of God to secondary standing. Rationalism elucidated this concept with clarity stating that the human mind was capable of solving all earthly problems, replacing God and His will in deciding mankind's existence and fate. Man could figure out the workings of the world all on his own. In the process, he could also unlock the mysteries of the cosmos and life on Earth. **John Locke** (1632-1704) applied this rationalism to political thought and institutions, as well as the manner in which man learned and acquired knowledge. In one of his seminal works, *Essay Concerning Human Understanding*, Locke asserted that man was born with a *tabula rasa* (blank slate) entirely free of any preconceived opinions or hard-wired behaviors. If properly trained in rational and scientific thought, man could use his insights and reason to their fullest capacity and all problems, (whether social, political, or religious in nature) could be solved and society could attain perfection.

Locke and other political rationalists believed human institutions, or class stratifications, could not constrain rational thinkers. Consequently, many questioned why, if everyone could reach equal levels of understanding, that the common people had to continue supporting a relatively small upper-class society dominated by the monarchy. Why was deference owed to a group that not only mistreated and abused those below them, but did not posses any unique intelligence? These ideas would be advanced further in the coming decades and eventually

John Locke

no aspect of society or government would be off limits to examination and criticism. In Europe and Britain's American colonies, Enlightenment criticism of monarchial autocracy and its repressive institutions gained a foothold in political discourse especially among the North American colonial intellectual elite, who avidly read the political treatises of men such as Locke, the Baron de Montesquieu, James Harrington, John Trenchard, and Thomas Gordon—all of whom wrote on a variety of political issues, mostly focusing on republicanism, individual liberties, and a general criticism to monarchial, aristocratic government. Much of American revolutionary ideology would be informed by this particular group of political *philosophes* who believed that man was capable of representative self-government, guaranteeing each individual certain alienable rights and liberties, such as freedom of speech, religion, and press. These writers' ideas gained greater currency among American colonial elites as well as among many of the common folk. Much of the rhetoric of American resistance to alleged British tyranny and oppression reflected the political theories and ideas first articulated by the European *philosophes*. In short, Enlightenment political theorists and essayists provided the ideological foundation for the American and French Revolutions.

Enlightenment *philosophes* focused particular attention on both the Catholic and Protestant religious establishments. François-Marie d'Arouet (pen name **Voltaire**) of France, among others, displayed a special viciousness for the Catholic Church, questioning how an organization that perpetrated so many evils, superstitions, and repression could possibly provide better solutions for man's existence than rational thinkers. Voltaire wrote extensively of the excesses and abuses of monarchial power and of the self-indulgent and superficial culture of the eighteenth-century aristocracy. In his classic work *Candide*, he wrote one of his harshest critiques of Christian orthodoxy, attacking the hypocrisy of the Catholic Church including its fiscal policies that, he claimed, placed a severe strain on the lower classes. Voltaire did not stand alone in his shunning of organized religion; many both in Europe and the American colonies increasingly adopted a more secular outlook, believing not only in man's inherent capacity to reorder and redefine his place in the world, but that orthodox Christian religion, whether it be Catholic or Protestant, had handicapped individuals' ability to progress both intellectually and materially.

Despite their often vicious criticism of organized Christian religion, surprisingly few *philosophes* were atheists or agnostics. Instead, many gravitated toward **Deism**, a brand of monotheism that gained traction during this period, allowing its primarily rationalist followers to retain Christian morality without the formalism. The faith reflected the fundamentals of Enlightenment rationalism, rejecting the foundational beliefs of traditional Christianity, including Christ's divinity and God's involvement in man's daily life. Instead, Deists remade God into the great "Clockmaker," who set the universe into motion much like a clockmaker who fashioned all the working pieces of a clock, wound the gears, and set it in motion. Once the pendulum pushed forward, however, God simply sat back and watched history unfold without intervention. As a consequence, man had a responsibility to live a good, moral life with respect for fellow human beings, regardless of their position in society. Most important, Deists believed that the best way to honor God's majesty was to use His greatest gift, the human mind, to improve the human condition. In the Deist frame of reference, Jesus represented the perfect example of the good man—an individual who lived to help others find their better selves. Deism found few followers among the colonies' common folk. However, many members of the colonial elite found this religious philosophy appealing. Founding Fathers Benjamin Franklin, Thomas Jefferson, and George Washington were all confirmed Deists.

THE GREAT AWAKENING

Not all individuals in either Europe or the British colonies agreed with the growing emphasis on the rationality of man or the associated withdrawal from the religious foundations that served as society's binding structure. Both within and outside established churches, religious leaders mounted a counteroffensive and began actively proselytizing among the colonial population. As a result, a strong evangelical movement swept through the colonies during the 1730s and 1740s. The New England colonies were especially affected by the increasing secularization of colonial society, as economic enterprises, such as shipping, led many Yankees to embrace broader, more profane vistas, particularly if such a worldview proved profitable. Since the 1690s, New England churches had been experiencing shrinking membership as well as a decline of enthusiasm from those who remained.

The first generation of New England colonists possessed a strong dedication to their faith, fortified by the fires of persecution suffered in England. Subsequent generations born in North America, however, did not display a similar devotion or passion about their faith. Indeed, with each passing generation, fewer individuals were willing to strictly adhere to Puritan orthodoxy. They had not experienced firsthand the persecution or the desperation that had forced their kinfolk to relocate to unknown lands and start a new life. Second-generation colonists overwhelmingly lacked such experiences and desired a worldly existence outside of strict religious beliefs. Puritan leadership initially dealt with the issue of declension (as the perceived decline in religious faith was known) by agreeing to implement the Half-Way Covenant, which had been strongly supported by the influential minister Solomon Stoddard who preached in Northampton, Massachusetts located in the western frontier region of the colony. Under the conditions of the compromise, the children and grandchildren of church members were granted partial membership in the church, which kept them on the rolls but restricted participation in such activities as the taking of communion. Authorities began to keep two sets of rolls to maintain accurate records on full-versus-partial members. Though some churches balked at the compromise, the Half-Way Covenant prevailed among most congregations by the end of the century. Ironically, Solomon Stoddard eventually challenged the Half-Way Covenant due to his growing belief that there was no Biblical justification for allowing only regenerate members to take communion. As a consequence, the minister preached that all Christians should be baptized and become fully-participating members of the church. By 1677, he ceased keeping separate member rolls, thus all members of his congregation openly participated in communion.

From the pulpit, Stoddard's style stressed making emotional connections with his listeners. Viewing the pastor's role as being more than a conduit for bringing God's Word to church members, he also sought to elicit passionate responses ("awakenings") from his audiences through vivid descriptions of eternal bliss in Heaven along with graphic depictions of spending an eternity in the depths of Hell. A Calvinist who firmly believed in divine predestination regarding one's salvation, Stoddard agreed with other Puritan theologians in the concept of "preparation," whereby individuals must first actively prepare their hearts to receive the grace of God. In practice, people were expected to understand their utter helplessness to achieve salvation on their own—good works alone or even devout faith would not produce salvation. Such an understanding then typically generated an intense sense of despair and doubt. While some never emerged from the depths of desolation induced by such preoccupation (even to the point of committing suicide), many others experienced a profound and liberating ecstasy they identified as God's saving grace—the "New Birth"—which confirmed to the individual that they were indeed one of God's "elect." During the sixty years that Stoddard preached, his Northampton parish underwent six sporadic revivals (in 1679, 1683, 1696, 1712, 1718, and 1727, respectively) characterized by large waves of conversions. Other congregations across New England experienced their own revivals, but they occurred less frequently than in Northampton and took place independently from other churches.

The larger inter-colonial religious revival known as the **Great Awakening** began in the 1730s and 1740s as evangelical ministers crossed denominational lines to make contact with each other and publicized their congregation's success in achieving conversions. In New England, the most influential preacher proved to be Solomon Stoddard's grandson, Jonathan Edwards (1703-1758), whose successes promoted the movement with greater force across the region. A student of the Enlightenment who embraced the concept that Christians should awaken from their routine and start living lives that glorified God's righteousness and omnipotence, Edwards believed that if people would do so fully then society would show dramatic improvement and social ills would be eliminated. He compelled his congregation to establish a proper relationship with Christ and to live a life worthy of that calling. If any man chose not to reconcile with God, his or her fate was sealed: an eternity spent apart from God in Hell. His most famous sermon, *Sinners in the Hands of an Angry God*, was a "hellfire and brimstone" lecture reminiscent of his grandfather's style, promising impending doom for those unwilling to turn to God, stating: "The God that holds you over the pit of hell, much as one holds a spider, or some loathsome insect over the fire, abhors you, and is dreadfully provoked. His wrath towards you burns like fire; he looks upon you as worthy of nothing else but to be cast into the fire. O sinner! Consider the fearful danger you are in." Interestingly, Edwards's sermons attracted younger audiences, capturing their attention because of the lack of emotional vitality and passion among too many traditional clergy who tended to deliver long, esoteric sermons filled with high-brow intellectualism.

In the late 1730s, Edwards published *A Faithful Narrative of the Surprising Work of God*, which detailed revival activities in the Connecticut Valley and elsewhere in an attempt to show God's saving grace in action across the colonies. The work enjoyed wide readership in English-speaking America and in England. One English preacher who read Edwards's account was George Whitefield (1714-1770), an ordained minister of the Church of England and colleague of Methodist founder John Wesley. Before coming to the North American colonies as an itinerant (traveling) preacher, Whitefield had built a successful evangelical career in Great Britain, drawing large crowds in outdoor settings among common laborers and the poor. Speaking without notes rather than following a prescribed written text, Whitefield grabbed his audiences' attention with fluid body movements and a booming voice that he altered to fit the mood he was setting and the emotion he wished to elicit from the crowd. A strong believer (unlike Wesley) in predestination, Whitefield agreed with Calvinist theologians who accepted the need for preparation before souls could receive God's saving grace. Thus, Whitefield often directed his message toward waking up sinners from their spiritual slumber to begin that process. In his sermon "The Wise and Foolish Virgins," Whitefield argued: "As for the openly profane, the drunkard, the whoremonger, the adulterer, and such-like, there is no doubt of what will become of them; without repentance they shall never enter into the kingdom of God and his Christ: no; their damnation slumbereth not. . . . Nor is there the least doubt of the state of true believers. For though they are despised and rejected of natural men, yet being born again of God, they are heirs of God, and joint heirs with Christ. They have the earnest of the promised inheritance in their hearts, and are assured that a new and living way is made open for them, into the holy of holies, by the blood of Jesus Christ."

Word of Whitefield's activities spread through English newspapers across the Atlantic, generating huge interest. From 1739-41, he toured the colonies, attracting enormous crowds including an astounding twenty-thousand people during a three-day revival in Boston. While staying in Philadelphia, Benjamin Franklin (not a religious man) befriended Whitefield and wrote admiringly of the preacher's abilities as a performer and his positive impact on the citizenry, at least in terms of improving the morals of the common people: "It was wonderful to see the change soon made in the manners of our inhabitants. From being thoughtless or indifferent about religion, it seem'd as if all the world were growing religious, so that one could not walk thro' the town in an evening without hearing psalms sung in different families of every street."

The Great Awakening ministers, whose followers began to be referred to as the "New Lights," made a tangible difference in the daily life of many spiritually-deprived colonists. Yet, not all colonists were pleased with the increased number of conversions or the ministers that encouraged them. Indeed, many older, more conservative Calvinists and their respective clergy decried the emotionally-charged messages which generated unwelcomed "enthusiasm" (then a term of ridicule implying madness) as little more than crass manipulation of a person's fear of hell to sway listeners. These "Old Lights" defended the traditional belief that the New Birth occurred within an individual gradually over time after patiently studying the Bible and reflecting upon carefully prepared and dispassionate sermons delivered by a learned ministry. As many fresh itinerant New Light evangelists began to appear, many lacking any formalized seminary training, Old Lights denounced them as not possessing the necessary training to teach others about God's true nature or the foundational elements of salvation. Therefore, the masses of converts had not truly come to the point of redemption. Conservative church and political leaders believed that the new evangelism possessed inherent potential for social disturbance, possibly a complete breakdown of the established order. They believed that if men felt empowered in their access to an all-powerful God, they would most certainly lose all deference for community leaders and begin to question all traditional societal norms and mores, especially those that bolstered the status quo.

Old Lights began implementing new regulations in an attempt to keep the ideas of the Great Awakening from taking further hold. Laws were passed prohibiting itinerancy, or traveling preachers; the Connecticut Assembly revoked toleration laws, which had been in place since 1708, as well as threatening with expulsion any student of Yale University who was caught attending a New Light gathering. Either through actual legislation or simple coercion, the colonial governments, intensely intertwined with the religious establishments (especially in the New England colonies), used all techniques at their disposal to prevent the spread of any new religious ideas that threatened not only orthodox Calvinist theology and doctrine but the very nature of the social order.

The New Lights responded quickly to the Old Lights' claims that they were undermining religious orthodoxy. New Lights insisted that formal training was not necessary to understand the mysteries of God; Simon Peter after all was just a fisherman and yet he became one of Jesus' most devoted and prominent disciples and apostles. Rather than being a hoax, displays of emotion were actually critical evidence of salvation. Any person experiencing the saving power of Christ could not help but have a physical manifestation of the event, and the salvation of any person lacking a visible sign of conversion was questionable. The same applied to ministers; only those with an observable conversion experience should be given audience. Gilbert Tennent, a Presbyterian minister whose father William founded the Log College to train evangelical preachers, drew comparisons between Old Light preachers and the Biblical Pharisees. His sermon "On the Danger of an Unconverted Ministry" directly attacked the Old Light ministers, declaring them to be "rottenhearted hypocrites, utter strangers to the saving knowledge of God and of their own hearts."

Radical evangelicals advocated for an increased separation of church and state to prevent a repeat of government involvement in religious affairs that had caused such problems for Protestant dissidents across Europe. Isaac Backus, a minister of the "Separate Baptist" faith, vocally supported such a division, calling on the Massachusetts legislature to allow his and other evangelical congregations to break from the state-backed Congregationalist church and relief from the paying of taxes associated with such a mandated affiliation.

The New Lights also focused attention on the founding of educational institutions capable of training individuals in Great Awakening theology. If the established community was going to denigrate the movement because of limited education, new colleges would remedy the situation and train those wishing to preach the new faith. Although almost all New Light converts came from established Protestant denominations, the schools they established became over time some of the nation's most prestigious educational institutions. The Presbyterians founded the College of New Jersey (Princeton University) in 1747; Baptists founded the College of Rhode Island (Brown University) in 1764; Dutch Reformists founded Queens College (Rutgers University) in 1766. Other non-denominational colleges surfaced during this period

A depiction of Harvard College in 1726.

George Whitefield: Popular Evangelist and Colonial American Consumers

On October 12, 1740, some 20,000 men and women gathered on Boston Common to hear and to hopefully be spiritually re-energized by George Whitefield, the English-speaking world's most popular evangelist during the Great Awakening. On his "American tour," Whitefield drew crowds larger than the cities' populations he visited, such as in Boston, which had a total population of 16,000 at the time. Those who could not attend the revivals read about Whitefield's sermons in the newspapers. If there was one uniting experience for colonial Americans (especially for those living in northern colonies) in the decades before the American Revolution, it was George Whitefield's ministry and his uplifting message for salvation that appealed to many Americans who had become spiritually bereft and disillusioned with their respective mainstream faiths. Further, by the time of Whitefield's visit, a flourishing market economy had emerged between England and the American colonies with citizens on both sides of the Atlantic participating in a consumer culture that offered many ways to spend money and leisure time. To those American colonists reared in traditional Calvinist households, the consumer society was both attractive and frightening, as many wondered if one could serve God while simultaneously enjoying and benefiting materially and pleasurably from the fruits of one's labor.

Whitefield was born in Bristol, England in 1714. At the time of his birth, no one would have guessed that he would not only become the Great Awakening's leading proselytizer but also one of the most influential preachers in the history of Anglo-American Christianity. Ironically, during his youth, he was quite the **bon vivant**, preferring the aesthetic life of the theater, romance novels, and dandyish clothes rather than serious studies, especially those dealing with theology. At the age of 17, Whitefield, who grew up in poverty, discovered that he had no desire to become a tradesmen. He came to believe that there was something else he was supposed to do; that "God intends something for me which we know not of." Finally accepting the notion that God intended Whitefield to become a minister, he set out to prepare himself for his calling. He enrolled at Oxford University, paying his way by working as a servant to wealthy students. He befriended several Methodist students who were planning a mission trip to the new English colony of Georgia. Whitefield found Methodism to be very appealing, and before long, he eschewed his earlier penchant for finery and foppish behavior. Now, "whatsoever I did, I endeavoured to do all to the glory of God." Whitefield believed he had an obligation bestowed upon him by God to share what he had learned with all who would hear.

In the process of spreading God's message, Whitefield helped create a mass public that broke down the boundaries of small communities. Before his visit, each minister or priest typically addressed only his own congregation or parish; rarely, if ever, did they leave their respective locales and spread God's word beyond to larger gatherings. The crowds that Whitefield attracted were far too large for any colonial building to hold, so the only other place big enough to hold his "revivals" were the outdoors. Fortunately for enraptured attendees, Whitefield possessed a booming voice that Ben Franklin calculated could be heard by 25,000 people at a time. In Philadelphia, Whitefield told the crowd, "Did I desire to please natural Men, I need not preach here in the Wilderness." Although he spoke directly to the heart of each individual, he also drew together entire communities in a way no one had ever done before.

Whitefield's faith and preaching reflected the great contradictions of his time without threatening either the political or economic order that sustained them. His appeal was universal; men and women, rich and poor; slaves as well as their masters, and to those who were suffering from the burgeoning capitalist economy as well as those who were reaping the rewards. Whitefield's approach was to call to task the individual, not the system. In Philadelphia, he declared to a crowd of 8,000, "Do not say you are miserable, and poor, and blind and naked, and therefore ashamed to come, for it is to such that this Invitation is now sent. The Polite, the Rich, the Busy, Self-Righteous Pharisees of this Generation have been bidden already, but they are too deeply engaged in going one to his Country House, another to his Merchandize."

He lambasted many traditional but individual Old Lights but never the faith or church itself. He condemned cruel slave owners but not the institution of slavery. Like a modern-day Joel Osteen, he showed men and women who had yet to make it in the new market economy how to acquire the self-discipline that would help them either to succeed in a competitive market or to accept failure with Christian resignation. He helped them embrace religion as an intense personal feeling. He showed people how to find meaning for their lives in a time of rapid economic transformation.

Whitefield died in Newburyport, Massachusetts in 1770. In 1775, a band of Continental Army officers, on their way to fight the British in Quebec, dug up his corpse. The evangelist's body had decayed, but his clothing was still intact. For "good luck" and "God's help," the soldiers snipped pieces of Whitefield's final attire to take with them.

including Dartmouth in 1769, which focused on the education of Native American populations, and King's College (Columbia University) in 1757 which increased the educational training available to increasingly larger percentages of the colonists. Then, as now, education empowered those who possessed it and allowed them to gain an increased stake in the community. Despite the efforts of the Old Lights to squelch the alleged radicalism of the New Lights, the Great Awakening established new religious thought that did not fade from colonial consciousness and, over time, came to change and inform much of American Protestant theology and doctrine. As the colonial elites during the 1760s and 1770s sought to justify their resistance to British laws, inherent in many of their arguments was a degree of egalitarianism and rejection of established authority first expressed by New Light evangelicals.

EIGHTEENTH-CENTURY EUROPEAN CONFLICTS AND THE NORTH AMERICAN COLONIES

Confrontations among the great European powers intensified during the latter decades of the seventeenth century and carried over into the early years of the 1700s. The root cause of such conflicts in Europe and the New World proved to be the aggressive foreign policy of **Louis XIV** of France, resulting in the formation of various European coalitions to stop the French king's ambitious territorial ambitions. As the only nation powerful enough to stop Louis's advances on the European continent, England led the anti-French alliance. Thus, the various wars fought in Europe beginning in the late seventeenth century were in many ways the resurrection of the centuries-old rivalry for European hegemony between England and France. However, that tension by the eighteenth century had assumed a global dimension, with the North American continent becoming a particularly important battleground for empire.

The French had only minimal interest in settling and colonizing their North American territory, despite the efforts of La Salle and others to promote such enterprises. The fur trade dominated French ambitions in North America and thus their settlements in New France were nothing more than frontier trading posts in the Ohio Valley, the Great Lakes region, and along the Mississippi River Valley. Montreal and Quebec in Canada demographically reflected French priorities in North America; they certainly were not cities such as those that existed in Great Britain's North American colonies. Indeed, by 1750, the population of English North America had reached 1.5 million free whites of European origin and another approximately 200,000 white indentured servants and redemptioners scattered throughout the thirteen colonies. In the southern colonies, the number of slaves had increased to over 200,000 by 1750, accounting for 60 percent of South Carolina's overall population. Philadelphia, Pennsylvania had a population of close to 30,000 inhabitants, while Boston was second with 15,000 citizens and New York City, third, with 12,000 residents. Neither Quebec City with a population of 4,600, nor Montreal with 4,200 people, could rival in population Great Britain's North American colonial cities. New France's entire European population reached 50,000 by mid-century. In short, the French never intended to create permanently settled colonies. In fact, religious settlements, which made up a significant foundation for the British colonies, were not permitted in French territory. The primary goal of New France was the development of viable trading outposts and ongoing trading alliances with the Native American populations, not widespread and densely populated colonies. France envisioned the American continent as a buoy to its homeland economic system and concentrated efforts to that end.

As a result, Native Americans were more likely to increase trade with the French because they were less suspicious of any underlying aims of dispossessing them of their lands. The fur trade proved lucrative for both parties and neither wanted or would allow any outside threat to this mutually beneficial partnership. Moreover, intermarriage between French men and Native American women was commonplace, further cementing the bonds between the two groups.

Spain was arguably the weakest of the three major European nations with North American possessions. Spanish territory consisted of Florida, as well as land west and southwest of the Mississippi River. Despite its undisputed control of Mexico and Central and South America, Spain was the least powerful of the three main empires. In addition, outside of the religious settlements manned by Jesuit, Franciscan, or Dominican priests, Spain did not have substantial colonial settlements in North America other than in Mexico. Yet that reality did not discourage the Spanish from attempting to expand their presence in North America or their involvement in the region. With the three nations in relatively close proximity, conflict was inevitable as seen already with Spain's attempt to foment slave rebellion in Great Britain's southern colonies.

As contentious as the relationship between the three nations became in North America, the military aggression between them was often an extension of European geopolitical disputes. At the center of the tension was the escalating animosity between France and England, as Louis attempted to increase his dominance in Europe while Great Britain tried to preserve the continent's balance of power by allying with those European nations resisting French encroachment and hegemony. Although the two powers had maintained a cordial relationship during the Stuart monarchy, the relationship grew sour after the Glorious Revolution replaced James II with William and Mary. The new king, a Dutchman, made the protection of his homeland from French aggression a major priority. Both sides also understood the value of using their empires as extensions of their continental struggles. If either side could be weakened through colonial war, the fiscal, military, and geopolitical consequences could be devastating to the loser. Four inter-colonial wars resulted from such policies. On the whole, the Anglo-French European wars that spread to North America proved to be of little consequence to the colonies; only the last conflict, the Seven Years' War, directly affected Britain's mainland colonists. Indeed, that particular confrontation would eventually force a dramatic change in British colonial policy, resulting in the passage of Parliamentary acts that sowed the seeds of American protest, resistance, and ultimately, armed rebellion.

The first of these conflicts, King William's War (1689-1697), resulted in border raids, including the burning of Schenectady, New York by the French and their Algonquian Indian allies and attacks on Port Royal, Nova Scotia, and Quebec by British regulars aided by colonial militia from some of the New England colonies as well as by the British navy. Although the conflict ended with no territorial adjustments after the signing of the Treaty of Ryswick, the stage was set for further conflagrations between the two powers.

Other wars had slightly larger impacts on the colonial populations. The War of the Spanish Succession (1702-1713) erupted when Charles II, the king of Spain, died without an heir. French King Louis XIV tried to install his grandson, Philip of Anjou, as the new "puppet" monarch, believing Philip would be loyal to him. Louis based his claim on the fact that his wife, Marie Theresa, was an heir to the Spanish throne despite the fact that she had renounced any rights to the throne when she married the French monarch. The major European powers grew concerned because Louis had already demonstrated his desire to dominate the continent. If allowed to "annex" Spain and its New World empire and wealth via the coronation of his grandson to the Spanish throne, France could easily impose its will on the whole of the continent. England quickly responded to Louis's highhandedness by forming an alliance with Holland and the Habsburgs of the Holy Roman Empire, who were long-standing French enemies. Those hostilities eventually crossed the Atlantic, causing renewed, vicious warfare between English and French colonists. The French and Indian forces attacked England's colonial frontier settlements, burning and killing scores of English colonists in the process. In one raid on **Deerfield, Massachusetts**, fifty men, women, and children were massacred, more than one hundred were captured, and the town was burned to the ground. The English in the southern colonies were no less opportunistic. In 1702, South Carolinians invaded Spanish Florida, conquering and burning outposts as they marched toward St. Augustine. Although the English failed to take North America's oldest settlement after a prolonged siege, they managed to render Florida an ineffective Spanish base, neutralizing any threat to the English from that locale.

After eleven years of war, the belligerents negotiated a peace settlement, the Treaty of Utrecht, which confirmed Louis's grandson Philip as king of Spain while transferring Gibraltar to England. Although Philip became Spain's new king (Philip IV, thus beginning the Bourbon dynasty in Spain), the two royal households were never to be united. France also ceded its North American possessions of Nova Scotia, Newfoundland, and the Hudson Bay area to Great Britain. France maintained control of the Saint Lawrence River and the northern portion of Nova Scotia. Spain retained Florida but did grant England the *asiento*, or contract to provide slave labor to the Spanish empire. Traditionally held by Portugal and France, the *asiento* called for the British South Sea Company to supply 4,800 African slaves annually to the regions for a 30-year term. In addition, one British trade ship could enter Spanish ports per year and sell goods to the local population. These limits were closely monitored by the Spanish navy to ensure that black market smuggling was not undermining completely the nation's mercantile trade policies, thereby reducing Spain's financial earnings. Yet maintaining widespread oversight proved difficult in light of the vastness of the Spanish empire, and British merchants exploited the situation when possible. In the process, they were certainly guilty of breaking the Spanish trade limitations, just as they did with similar English trading restrictions, yet these infractions carried substantially more weighty consequences of international proportions.

English sea captain **Robert Jenkins** participated in this trade and often pushed Spanish concessions to their limits. When his illegal activities were discovered in 1731, Spanish authorities apprehended Jenkins and, for his punishment, cut off his left ear as a warning to other Englishmen who might dare to violate Spanish trade regulations. The Spanish official who had ordered such a reprisal allegedly told Jenkins, "Carry this home to the

King, your master, whom, if he were present, I would serve in like fashion." The British had been looking for an excuse for several years to declare war on Spain. Jenkins provided them with the pretext they needed when he dramatically appeared before Parliament with an ugly stump on one side of his head and holding his pickled ear preserved in a jar. Proclaiming Jenkins's treatment to be an insult to their nation, the British government declared war on Spain in 1739 and, once again, Britain's mainland colonists joined in the fray, hoping to be participants in a glorious international endeavor, only to meet disillusionment. In 1741, 3,600 colonists, mostly poor young men lured by the promise of obtaining a share of Spanish plunder, combined with 5,000 British troops in a failed attack on Cartagena, Colombia. More than half of the colonial contingent died.

On the North American continent, fighting broke out once gain along the Georgia-Florida border when a force of South Carolina and Georgia militia with Cherokee and Creek allies led by James Oglethorpe invaded Spanish Florida. Hoping to finally capture St. Augustine from Spain, the expedition failed, leaving the southern border vulnerable. In retaliation the Spanish attacked in 1742 but were repulsed by an Oglethorpe-led force, thwarting Spain's plan to demolish Georgia and South Carolina by fomenting slave insurrections in both colonies. The War of Jenkins's Ear (1739-1744) ended in a stalemate, with the Spanish remaining in control of Florida, British colonials in command of Georgia and South Carolina, and relations between the two empires still raw and explosive.

No sooner did the War of Jenkins's Ear conclude than conflict again erupted among Europe's great powers, this time over succession to the Austrian throne. King George's War (1744-48), as the colonists referred to the contest, pitted Britain and its Austrian ally against a Franco-Prussian alliance. In this conflict, the belligerents fought to decide the heir to the Habsburg Empire of central and eastern Europe. In North America, a French raid on a fishing village in Nova Scotia led to massive retaliation by the British. With the help of the British navy and subsidized by Pennsylvania and New York, Massachusetts militia captured the French fortress at Louisburg. Flushed with success, the English decided to attack Quebec, but such ambitions were dashed when the British fleet failed to arrive with reinforcements. At the war's conclusion, Britain returned Louisburg and warned the colonists that they had to maintain the peace with no more secret raids on French possessions. Events in North America, however, were out of European control. The British blockade of French ports cut off trade to Canada, including the all-important gifts to Native American trad-

James Edward Oglethorpe

ing partners. Without them, the French-Indian alliance began to crumble.

Collectively, these engagements set a tone for the military strife between the three major colonial powers, as the limited nature of the conflicts only increased the likelihood that a full-scale confrontation would occur. The increasing numbers of British and other European immigrants coming to England's North American colonies seeking land threatened to break the French stranglehold on the lucrative fur trade with the Native Americans, making the likelihood of another war among the European powers almost a certainty. Beginning in the 1740s, increasing numbers of British colonists began crossing the Appalachians and the other mountain ranges that had served as the natural boundaries between New France and British North America. The French were naturally alarmed by this swarm of English trespassers and interlopers, who they rightly feared would not only disturb their trade relations with the Native Americans, but also destroy the ecosystem and habitats of the various animals that provided the furs by clearing the forests for farming. The Ohio River Valley, which encompassed much of western Pennsylvania and Virginia, into present-day Ohio, proved to be the area most coveted by the English colonists. The western portion of upper New York, partially claimed by the French, was also penetrated by British colonials.

Table 4.1	Major English Wars, 1689 - 1763			
Dates	European Name	American Name	Major Allies	Treaty
1689-1697	War of the League of Augsburg	King William's War	Britain, Holland, Spain, their colonies and Native American allies against France, its colonies and Native American allies	Treaty of Ryswick (1697)
1702-1713	War of the Spanish Succession	Queen Anne's War	Britain, Holland, their colonies and Native American allies against France, Spain, their colonies and Native American allies	Treaty of Utrecht (1713)
1739-1748	War of the Austrian Succession (War of Jenkins's Ear)	King George's War	Britain, its colonies and Native American allies, and Austria against France, Spain, their Native American allies, and Prussia	Treaty of Aix-la-Chappelle (1748)
1756-1763	Seven Years' War	French and Indian War	Britain, its colonies and Native American allies against France, its colonies and Native American allies	Peace of Paris (1763)

New France Crumbles from Within

In the aftermath of King George's War, the French position in North America became weaker than before the conflict. The war's cost had forced the French to cut back on their gifts to allied Algonquian tribes, especially in the Ohio River Valley. In addition, to raise revenue, the French government sharply increased the prices for their trading post leases, which forced local French traders to raise the prices for the goods they sold to their Indian patrons. These changes negatively affected French trade relations with Native Americans, weakening both their economic and political bonds with their once secure native allies. Such strained relations between the French and Native Americans became the underlying North American cause of the French and Indian War.

The North American region most impacted by this changed dynamic proved to be the Ohio River Valley, where bands of "refugee" tribes such as the Miami began trading with the English settlers (mostly from Pennsylvania) who had recently arrived to take advantage of Indian disaffection with the French. The Miami and other tribes who had trickled into the area welcomed the Pennsylvania traders, finding their goods to be better and cheaper, with less demanding terms than those imposed by the French. The Indians hoped to trade with the English colonists unencumbered by military or political obligations; they were soon to be disappointed.

The Miami's defection angered the French, who unwisely decided to retaliate by using force to return their wayward allies to the French fold. They not only began raiding Miami villages but also those of the other tribes who had migrated to the area in hopes of establishing more beneficial trade relations with the English colonists. The French attacks failed to bring their former Indian allies back into submission. With this change in policy, Native Americans in the region seemed to have two options: return to the French camp or make new alliances with the British colonists. Neither alternative offered the Indians any real security; they were fast becoming the pawns of both European powers. They became increasingly dependent both economically and politically on the Europeans for survival and thus vulnerable to their capricious games of power politics. Interestingly, until the Miami and other tribes migrated to the Ohio River Valley (and before English colonial traders showed up to do business with the Indians), the French had little to no interest in the area. Now, the Ohio River Valley had become a territory that France and England, via their respective colonists, claimed as their own.

Compounding the tension in the area between the Indians and French, as well as between the French and English colonists, was the rivalry to claim the territory between Pennsylvania, Virginia, and New France. Virginia was particularly keen on acquiring the area. By the late 1740s, tobacco cultivation had reached its geographic limits in the colony and planters were seeking virgin soil. The Ohio River Valley seemed to provide that outlet. To that end, a group of wealthy Virginians, among them George Washington (a member of the powerful clan of families residing in the Fairfax area of the colony), sought a charter from the king to form the **Ohio Company,** whose purpose would be to claim and develop the region for British expansionist interests. Virginians and the Crown desired not only to promote land development but also a lucrative trade between colonists and Native Americans. The British government then hoped that the influx of substantial numbers of English colonists would be threatening enough to force the French to abandon the region. To the dismay of the Crown and the Virginia speculators, the Anglo penetration into the Ohio River Valley did not intimidate the French, who responded by constructing a series of forts in the area to assert their hegemony over the territory. The outposts also served the purpose of connecting Louisiana to Canada for a more united and defensible North American empire while serving as an important buffer against aggressive English expansion.

England swiftly responded, informing the French that any trading in the region would violate Virginia's sovereignty and actions should cease and desist. France rejected such claims and built Fort Duquesne (located on the site of modern-day Pittsburgh), in the center of the region. England moved militarily under the field direction of twenty-one-year old George Washington, whose brother was an investor in the Ohio Company. In 1754, Virginia governor Robert Dinwiddie ordered Washington to deliver a request for a French retreat from their defensive position, thus opening the territory to English traders and settlers. Neither Dinwiddie nor the British government sent Washington to provoke a war, instructing the young Virginian to proceed cautiously in his negotiations with the French. However, on their way to visit with the French at Fort Duquesne, Washington and his force, which included some Native Americans, encountered a small French reconnaissance party and foolishly attacked the contingent, killing ten French soldiers in the process. Little did Washington know at the time that the "Battle" of Jumonville Glen would help to ignite one of eighteenth-century Europe's greatest conflicts—the Seven Years' War. After the skirmish, the colonials retreated and hastily built a stockade named Fort Necessity. French forces wasted little time in attacking the palisade, soon forcing Washington and his men to surrender. The French commander allowed Washington and his men to evacuate the area as he reasserted his nation's dominion over the Ohio River Valley.

British colonists now faced a unique experience—not only had Washington failed to secure the territory, but his encounter represented the first substantial conflict between Europe's two greatest powers that did not originate on the European continent. Unlike the previous three inter-colonial wars, the **French and Indian War**, as the struggle would become known in the colonies, resulted solely from issues of American colonization rather than European power struggles. Many colonists recognized the significance of what occurred in the Ohio River Valley, seeing the vast potential for expansion that the territory represented. Thus, a movement arose, spearheaded by New York and Pennsylvania, to try to unite all the colonies in a collective effort to drive the French out, not only from the Ohio River Valley but along the entire trans-Appalachian frontier, all the way to New Orleans at the mouth of the Mississippi River. A meeting was thus called for the colonies to create a plan to accomplish this objective. Representatives from seven of the thirteen colonies gathered in Albany, New York to develop a strategy to meet the challenges of the situation. The **Albany Plan of Union** was intended to "prepare and receive plans or schemes for the union of the colonies, and to digest them into one general plan" among which included proposals for funding the effort, building defensive forts, and establishing Native American alliances. The Albany attendees hoped that the Iroquois Nation, which consisted of the Onondaga, Oneida, Seneca, Mohawk, Cayuga, and Tuscarora, would become colonial allies since all the tribes had once been friendly to the English. Moreover, the confederation's size represented a great military boon to the colonials and, therefore, a real threat to the French-allied tribes. Although willing to accept the bribes offered for an alliance, the Iroquois Nation remained neutral during the conflict until 1758 when an English victory seemed certain. In that year, they joined with British and colonials to defeat the French. In the end, the Albany Plan established a Grand Council presided over by a Crown-appointed President General representing all the colonies, with all colonies being taxed to support the endeavor.

The fear of post-war conditions in the colonies motivated many colonial leaders, such as Ben Franklin, to propose the plan of union. Franklin urged his colonial brethren to take the initiative in every capacity to drive the French out of all of North America, including Canada, without the help of British regulars. He warned that British troops would inevitably be sent to the colonies to do much of the fighting if the colonials did not unite and raise their own army of militia and assume the bulk of the combat, resulting in Britain permanently stationing soldiers in North America. These troops would not only be used to protect the colonists, but also to serve as a possible police force to control the colonists by enforcing the English government's will over them. At the time, Franklin was ignored, with many of his colleagues snickering at such a prospect. In hindsight, the colonists should have heeded Franklin's warning, for his 1754 forecast became reality in the 1760s.

Submitted to the colonial assemblies and the British Board of Trade, the Albany Plan was rejected by both parties. Suspicious of the central taxing feature, the colonial assemblies balked at the proposal. Meanwhile, many British government officials, already distrustful of the growing power of the colonial assemblies, disliked the idea of granting them additional power. Although the Albany Plan never went into effect, the proposal set an interesting precedent. The idea of a colonial governing entity, with the ability to organize a mutual defense force and raise funds for its implementation, would resurface again when the colonies began agitating for independence from the British Empire. On the second attempt, the idea would not be dismissed so easily.

The French and Indian War, 1754-1763

In response to the defeat of the inexperienced Washington and his men in the Ohio River Valley, the Crown ordered Major General **Edward Braddock** to North America to atone for such a humiliation of British sovereignty. Braddock brought with him two regiments (about 3,000 men), which the English government believed was a sufficient force. The Crown also counted on the colonists to carry the load for most of the fighting, though that hope would soon be dashed. The British strategy called for the capture of France's four main forts in North America: Fort Duquesne, Fort Niagara (near Niagara Falls in upper New York), Fort St. Frederic (at Crown Point, on the southern edge of Lake Champlain), and Fort Beausejour (located in Nova Scotia). The British were confident that if they could take these four outposts, France would surrender because all the forts served as vital gateways into the interior of New France.

In July 1755, Braddock took his army of British regulars, accompanied by 2,500 colonial militiamen, into the field for a planned attack upon Fort Duquesne. Marching in full, bright-red regalia, and with drums beating and bagpipes and fifes playing, the British troops made an easy target for the ready and waiting camouflaged French and Indians who ambushed Braddock's force just a few miles from Fort Duquesne. The French and Indians made short work of Braddock's force, killing or wounding over 1,000 British and colonial troops, including Braddock who was slain in the first few minutes of battle. George Washington, serving as a colonel in the Virginia militia, barely escaped the slaughter. The French and Indians lost a total of 39 combatants. Washington said of the encounter, "We have been most scandalously beaten by a trifling body of men." Even though the British troops had been soundly defeated and were now facing an uncertain war, they failed to understand the severity of the situation facing them. On his deathbed, Braddock had trouble acknowledging the gravity of his defeat uttering, "Who would have thought it? We shall do better next time."

That next time would take a while, as the English would spend two years trying to keep the French and their allies at bay while suffering defeat after defeat primarily because of the greater strength of the French and Indian forces. The majority of the northern tribes did not trust the English to honor pledges and keep expansionist aims restrained, so remaining allied with France seemed to be the safer bet. Indeed, the French-allied tribes attacked along the frontier from Maine to South Carolina, killing some 3,000 settlers by the fall of 1756 while pushing back, in some places, the line of settlements almost 150 miles. Additionally, England did not provide any significant military support to the effort as the number of British regulars remained limited. During the first phase of the war from 1754 to 1757, the French dominated the fight with four times as many troops as the British in North America, superior leadership, and no inter-colonial rivalries to burden their war effort.

The overwhelming success of the French military was clearly illustrated with the massacre at Fort William Henry. Lieutenant Colonel George Munro, a seasoned commander, engaged the French forces led by Louis-Joseph de Montcalm and supplemented by the Native American allies, which included the Ottawa, Abenaki, and Potawatomi tribes. Completely undermanned and unable to secure reinforcements, Munro surrendered after a seven-day siege and heavy bombardment. The subsequent negotiated surrender did not end so peacefully. As Munro marched his men and their families (many of whom were sick or wounded) back toward English

Map 4.1 The French and Indian War

territory, the Indians, who felt betrayed by Montcalm for forbidding them to take plunder and captives as was their custom, broke Montcalm's pledge by savagely attacking the battered and beaten British soldiers and settlers. Eager for the opportunity to exact revenge on the English, the tribes rapidly descended on the retreating soldiers and civilians, killing two hundred men, Munro among them, and taking over three hundred hostages. In numbers, allies, and military strategy, the English were outmatched. The situation became increasingly obvious that, without a stronger commitment from the English government to increase support, the colonials had little hope of securing a successful conclusion to the war.

A change of British fortunes of war would come and those of victory beginning in 1757 when **William Pitt the Elder** (1708-1778), became Prime Minister of England. Pitt realized that the key to victory in North America was not only to bolster the number of British troops significantly but also to get the American colonists to fight with equal intensity and devotion to the cause. Pitt further realized that the ultimate triumph lay in attacking France where it was the weakest—in its colonial possessions, not just in North America, but in the Caribbean and as far away as India. In Pitt's view, England had yet to utilize its most obvious advantage over France, a superior navy. Until Pitt's ascension to power, Britain had concentrated on defeating France on the European continent, which was difficult if not impossible; France had a larger army as well as a strong ally in Austria. Pitt also correctly surmised that if Britain concentrated its land and sea power on defeating France in its colonial possessions, the war in Europe would end as well, with a stalemate at the very least. In short, to Pitt, the French and Indian War became a war for empire, with the winner ultimately controlling a global empire, the expanse of which the world had yet to see. The opportunity to implement Pitt's grand vision occurred when Prussia, ruled by the militant and expansionist Frederick II (later known as Frederick the Great), decided to enter the fray on Britain's side against France, Austria, Russia, and many of the German states. When Prussia invaded the territory of Saxony, Pitt funded the Prussian war effort, making the war lengthier and more contentious. Therefore, while entrenched in the European war, France would be unable to match the strength of the British war machine within the colonial theatre.

Pitt also began looking more closely at the regulation of colonial trade. According to the Navigation Acts, the colonies were prohibited from trading with non-English merchants. Part of the reason why the French were able to remain engaged in the war for so long was their access to colonial markets and continued trading with the British colonists. The financial benefits to be acquired through trading exceeded that of patriotism for many North American English colonists. This was especially true for the colonies' non-English settlers such as the Dutch. Consequently, thanks to continued access to colonial goods, the French were able to sustain their presence in North America longer because many colonists had placed self-aggrandizement above their loyalty to king and country. At one point, a hundred British colonial vessels were found trading in Spanish ports. When the prime minister learned of this flow of goods, he immediately tightened regulations on all transactions and issued writs of assistance, or search warrants, which allowed officials to search ships without prior evidence, in order to prevent smuggling. Even these aggressive tactics could not entirely stop all illegal trading, but they temporarily halted the illicit colonial trading. After the war's conclusion, the Crown would continue such ambitious trade regulations much to the colonists' disappointment and agitation.

Pitt's imperial ambitions extended beyond the acquisition of the Ohio River Valley—he set his sights widely as he hoped to divest the French of all their North American holdings and permanently remove the French threat from Britain's North American empire. To accomplish this goal, he amassed a force of 40,000 colonial and British regulars and placed them under the command of General James Wolfe. Young, but militarily brilliant, Wolfe undertook a steady march northward toward Montreal and Quebec through the heartland of New France. Along the way, he engaged one French army after another, defeating them as he rolled toward his Canadian destinations. If the war had to be won one fort at a time, the British were willing to do so, partially because they felt that the French forces, now tied up on European and colonial fronts, would be unable to match Britain's staying power. In this manner, the war would quickly move to a favorable British conclusion.

The strategy proved successful, as key forts fell to the combined British and colonial forces. From the beginning of his grand plan, Pitt had wanted the American colonial militias to concentrate their efforts on defeating France's Indian allies, for Braddock's defeat as well as several British-Indian engagements that had ended in disaster made it clear to the prime minister that British regulars were incapable of fighting "Indian-style" in the wilderness of North America. The American colonials, on the other hand, were experienced Indian fighters who had adopted Native American warfare tactics as their own. Thus, the majority of colonial militias engaged not French troops, but their Indian allies, which often resulted in pitched, brutal and vicious battles, with all manner of barbarity inflicted on combatants from both sides. To further persuade the colonials, Pitt also agreed to pay half their costs of fighting the war as well as promising that, upon Britain's seizure of New France, American colonists would be allowed to cross the Appalachians and occupy and settle the territory all the way to the Mississippi River.

With successive British victories, an end to the fighting appeared imminent. Tied up on several fronts—North America, the Caribbean, India, and Europe—France simply could not sustain its armies and navies against such a broad effort. Still, the British were looking for a decisive victory in North America to force the French to surrender. The decisive victory that they hoped for, and the one that the French feared, came in the summer of 1759 when the cunning Wolfe engaged Montcalm in the Battle of Quebec. Understanding that he lacked superior numbers but desperately desiring a conclusive victory, Wolfe besieged the fort and prevented supplies and reinforcements from gaining entrance to the walled city. Additionally, the British forces attacked the surrounding civilian populations in an attempt to force the French into surrendering. In September, the British and French forces engaged in a fearsome, albeit only fifteen-minute battle on the Plains of Abraham outside Quebec. When the dust settled, both Wolfe and Montcalm lay dead and the French gave up Quebec. The loss of the two leading officers was damaging to both sides, yet the fall of France's two strongest forts was even more devastating than the loss of manpower and the French were unable to recover.

ECHOES OF THE FRENCH AND INDIAN WAR

Although it took until 1763 to bring an official conclusion to the war, the British remained firmly in control

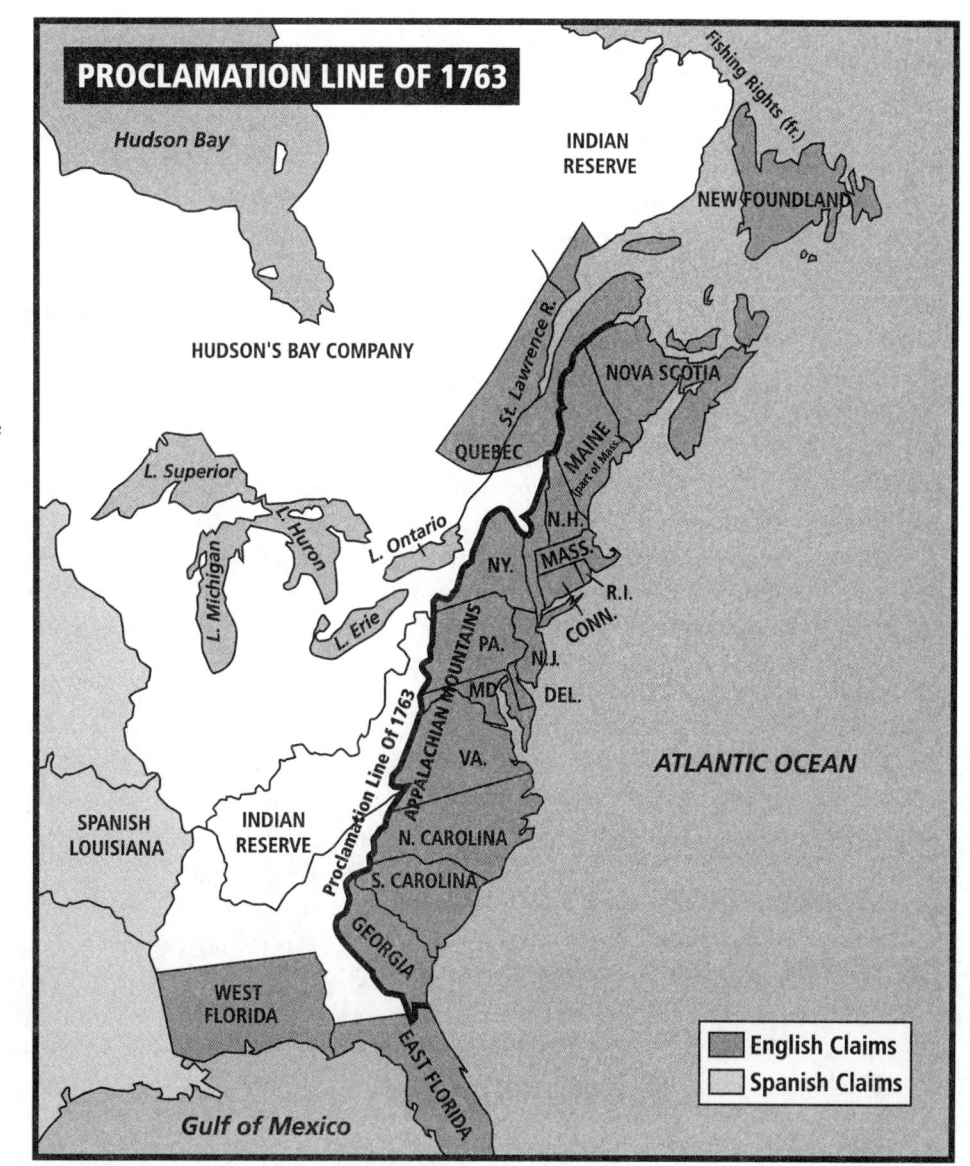

Map 4.2 Proclamation Line of 1763

after the fall of Quebec, and very little doubt remained about who the victor would be. The British continued their acquisition of French territories as Pitt instructed the troops to fulfill his imperial vision and take the Saint Lawrence Valley and the Great Lakes Basin, in addition to several islands in the French West Indies. In 1758, the last bulwark of the French war effort had been removed when the Iroquois Nation officially entered into an alliance with the British upon signing the Treaty of Easton. In exchange for neutrality in the remaining battles, the Iroquois received a promise that future territorial expansion would not extend past the Alleghany Mountains—a promise which resonated strongly with tribes who understood first-hand the threat that the European presence presented to their way of life.

In 1761, France made one last attempt to reverse the tide of war by forming an alliance with Spain. With the Spanish alliance, the French hoped that the infusion of additional funds and men, especially to the area on the British colonies' southern border, would divert British attention away from Canada and the Ohio River Valley and allow France time to regroup in those regions in order to mount a counteroffensive. The French gambit proved futile; both Spain and France were too weakened by the protracted war to help each other, and it was only a matter of time before peace negotiations began. Both the European and colonial stages of the war reached their conclusions in 1763 by two separate treaties. The French and Indian War came to an official end with the Treaty of Paris of 1763, while the larger Seven Years War was concluded with the Peace of Hubertusburg.

When the dust settled, the European landscape stayed relatively unchanged with the exception of Silesia, which remained a part of the Prussian Empire, and the ascension of Frederick the Great who became the most aggressive expansionist and militarist among his contemporaries. In the colonies, the changes were more substantial. As a condition of peace, France surrendered all of its North

American holdings—its lands east of the Mississippi River plus Canada to Britain while its territory west of the Mississippi River, including the all important port of New Orleans, were transferred to the Spanish. (The British also gained control of Florida from Spain). Although France militarily and politically abandoned its North American empire fairly rapidly, thousands of French decided to stay in Quebec and Montreal and grudgingly accepted British rule.

In acquiring such large tracts of land, and more importantly, by removing all serious military threats to their territory, the British Empire was free to expand westward with only Native Americans standing in their way. The colonists were thrilled at the new opportunity to expand borders and acquire lands that had been previously off limits. Though the conclusion of the French and Indian War opened up those vast stretches of land, many British government officials, however, saw in this development an underlying danger —unchecked expansion could possibly create unmanageable chaos, which would consume the resources of the empire. If the Native American tribes still inhabiting those regions decided to create alliances among themselves, they could force the English military back into a protracted war. Yet, the voices of caution were not loud enough to convince the land-hungry colonists of the danger that the newfound victories had secured. Established by the British Prime Minister, George Grenville, the Proclamation of 1763 attempted to prevent further red-white conflicts in the trans-Appalachian regions. As the only concession made by the English Crown at the conclusion of the war, and as an attempt to honor the Treaty of Easton, the dictate limited all further colonial presence past the Appalachian Mountains. The agreement further required any traders traveling west of that established line of demarcation to possess a license issued by the Crown. This would be a major point of contention in the coming years but most certainly not the only one.

At the war's conclusion, the British and the colonials within their North American empire felt pleased with the results. The war had been a long engagement with heavy casualties on all sides, but the process had not necessarily been without rifts between the motherland and the colonists. As both prepared to take advantage of the post-war situations, tensions would begin to mount that would create an insurmountable chasm of resentment and hostility that ended in armed rebellion, independence, and war that ironically might not have come about had Great Britain not been victorious in the French and Indian War. England's triumph resulted in the acquisition of a huge debt that Parliament believed the colonists, who appeared to have benefited most from the war, were to pay. The debt consequently forced a dramatic change in British imperial policy, abruptly ending over a century of "salutary neglect" from which the colonists had most definitely been the beneficiaries. In short, the war had plunged Great Britain into serious financial straits, if not crisis, and both the Crown and Parliament were united in their belief that it was time for the colonists to pay as loyal British subjects. English government expectations of loyalty and obedience proved to be delusional. It was simply too late for such highhanded policies. The colonists had been on their own far too long to accept such desires from the mother country, particularly if such mandates threatened the sanctity of what the colonists believed was their *right* to self-government. In the end, the American Revolution was not about taxation or trade restrictions, but rather about *political* issues and liberties, about *inalienable rights* that the American colonists believed they were entitled to as free-born Englishmen.

Chronology

1690 Spanish begin to settle Texas.

1711 North Carolina founded.

1715 Yanasee War.

1717 Scots-Irish immigration increases.

1721 Bolyston introduces smallpox inoculation in Boston.

1732 Georgia founded.

1733 Molasses Act passed.

1734 Jonathan Edwards promotes Great Awakening.

1739 Stono rebellion.

1740 George Whitefield preaches religious revival in North America.

1741 New York slave conspiracy trials result in 35 executions.

1745 New England militia capture Louisbourg in Nova Scotia on northeastern Canada during King George's War.

1747 Ohio Company of Virginia founded.

1754 George Washington attacks French patrol near the forks of the Ohio River
Albany Congress proposes plan for colonial union.

1755 General Braddock killed and his force devastated by French and Indian forces near Fort Duquesne.

1756 French take Oswego, New York.

1757 French take Fort William Henry.
William Pitt the Elder becomes prime minister.

1758 British take Fort Duquesne.
British take Fortress Louisbourg and Fort Frontenac.
French repel British assault on Fort Ticonderoga.

1759 British take Ticonderoga and Crown Point.
James Wolfe dies capturing Quebec.

1760 Montreal falls.
Canada surrenders to the British.

1763 Peace of Paris ends the Seven Years' War.
Britain acquires France's North American empire.

Review Questions

1. Discuss the causes of the Stono Rebellion in South Carolina.

2. What socio-cultural and religious dynamics gave rise to the Great Awakening "revival" in New England during the 1720s and 1730s? Why did this movement cause a schism in many Puritan churches as well as in Puritan orthodoxy?

3. In what ways did the European Enlightenment impact the American colonies? What were the movement's basic tenets and what did they reflect about 18th century European society?

4. By the beginning of the 18th century, England's North American empire was flourishing in virtually every capacity. How did the British government attempt to "govern" the colonies? What was more important to the English government and its ruling classes—regulation of trade or imposing political control?

5. Discuss the causes of the Anglo-French conflict in North America. Why was the last of the French and Indian wars so important for both Great Britain and the colonies?

Glossary of Important People and Concepts

Albany Plan of Union
Asiento
Edward Braddock
Deerfield, Massachusetts
Deism
Jonathan Edwards
English Test Act of 1704
Enlightenment
Ben Franklin
French and Indian War
Great Awakening
Robert Jenkins
Junto Society of Philadelphia
John Locke
Louis XIV
Cotton Mather
Negro Act
New Lights
Ohio Company
Old Lights
Philosophes
William Pitt
Redemptioners
Stono Rebellion
Voltaire
George Whitefield

SUGGESTED READINGS

Fred Anderson, *Crucible of War: The Seven Years' War and the Fate of Empire in British North America, 1754-1766.* (2000).

Bernard Bailyn, *Voyagers to the West: A Passage in the Peopling of American on the Eve of the Revolution.* (1986);

—— *The Origins of American Politics.* (1968).Richard Bushman, ed., *The Great Awakening: Documents on the Revival of Religion, 1740-1745* (1989).

Tom Hatley, *The Dividing Paths: Cherokees and South Carolinians through the Era of Revolution.* (1993).

Francis Jennings, *Empire of Fortune: Crowns, Colonies, and Tribes in the Seven Years' War in America* (1988).

Frank J. Lambert, *"Pedlar in Divinity": George Whitefield and the Transatlantic Revivals.* (1994).

Ned Landsman, *From Colonials to Provincials: Thought and Culture in America: 1680-1770.* (1998).

Perry Miller, *Jonathan Edwards.* (1949).

Robert C. Newbold, *The Albany Congress and Plan of Union of 1754.* (1955).

James Pritchard, *In Search of Empire: The French in the Americas, 1670-1730.* (2004).

Peter Silver, *Our Savage Neighbors: How Indian War Transformed Early America.* (2007).

Stephanie E. Smallwood, *Saltwater Slavery: A Middle Passage from Africa to American Diaspora.* (2007).

Ian K. Steele, *An Exploration of Communication and Community* (1986).

Alan Taylor, *American Colonies: The Settling of North America* (2001).

W.R. Ward, *The Protestant Evangelical Awakening* (1992).

Richard White, *The Middle Ground: Indians, Empires, and Republics in the Great Lakes Region, 1650-1815.* (1991).

Peter Wood, *Black Majority: Negroes in Colonial South Carolina from 1670 Through the Stono Rebellion.* (1996).

Serena Zabin, *Dangerous Economies: Status and Commerce in Imperial New York.* (2009).

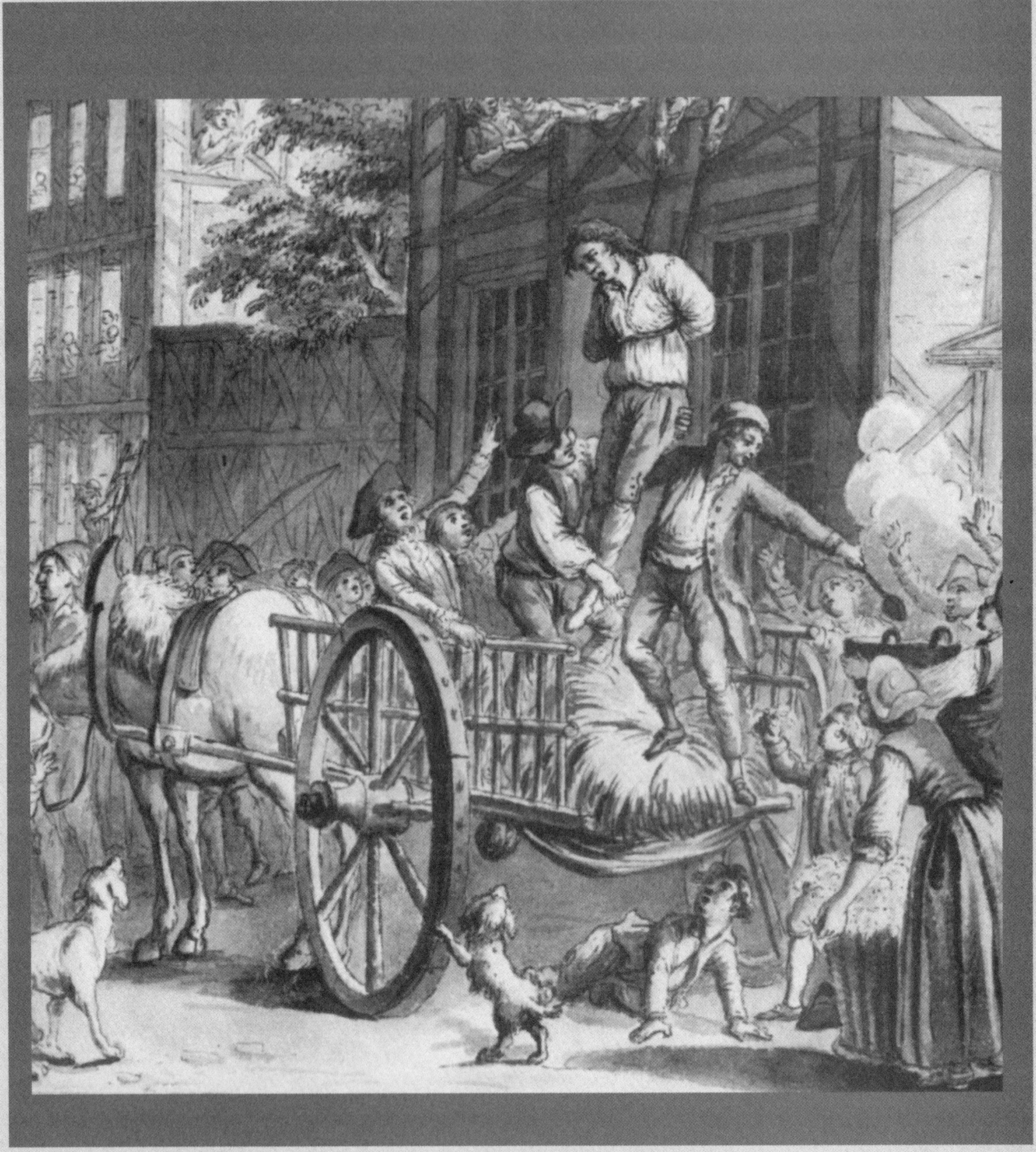

Chapter Five

ORIGINS OF THE AMERICAN REVOLUTION

In 1776, Thomas Jefferson wrote the most famous words of America's revolutionary era. "All men are created equal," he stated in the Declaration of Independence. All men, and women, however, were certainly not treated as equals in America, either in the years leading up to the Revolution or just after its conclusion in the early 1780s. Taught by their ministers that to "spare the rod" was to "spoil the child," parents punished wayward children with physical violence. Husbands were given license to physically discipline wives who they believed acted disrespectfully toward them. During the 1780s, almost one-third of the American population toiled as slaves or indentured servants—they too suffered physical beatings, while the women among them were sometimes raped.

Until the eve of the American Revolution, American schools, the Anglican Church, and the prevailing legal system taught the average person in the colonies that the division of humanity into the nobility and the commoners and the rule of kings was part of the divine order, as historian Gordon S. Wood notes in his book **The Radicalism of the American Revolution**: "[Future leader of the American Revolution] John Adams recalled that in the early 1760s the Massachusetts authorities had . . . introduced new 'scenary' in the Supreme Court —of scarlet and sable robes . . . and enormous tie wigs—in order to create a more 'theatrical' and 'ecclesiastical setting for the doing of justice.' Full-length, gold-framed portraits of [English kings] Charles II and James II, said Adams, were 'hung up on the most conspicuous sides' of the courtroom 'for the admiration and imitation of all men.' 'The colors of the royal ermines and long flowing robes were the most glowing, the figures the most noble and graceful, the features the most distinct and characteristic—these portraits of these particular Stuart kings were designed to overawe.'"

In war and peace, the law treated the rich and the common man differently. "Common soldiers captured in war were imprisoned [where they often died from disease caused by wretched conditions]; captured officers, however, could be released 'on parole,' after giving their word to their fellow gentlemen officers that they would not flee the area or return to their troops," Wood wrote. "Although English law was presumably equal for all, the criminal punishments were not; gentlemen, unlike commoners, did not have their ears cropped or their bodies flogged."

In the decade before the American Revolution, ministers of the Church of England "tended to bolster monarchical authority . . . for example, by preaching from Romans 13 that all were subject unto the higher powers . . . for conscience sake' . . . Even moderate Anglican preachers continually stressed the sacredness of authority and the need for subjects to honor and revere those set over them . . ." Men who would later fight for the cause of liberty against a British tyrant held the lower classes in contempt. As Wood noted, revolutionary leaders typically compared the average American to cattle, with George Washington calling the country's masses "the grazing multitude." Likewise, John Adams referred to the "common herd of mankind" and dismissed the "vulgar, rustic Imaginations" of the working poor, who had "no Idea of Learning, Eloquence and Genius." Elites even assumed that the poor were biologically closer to animals. "Ordinary people were thought to be different physically, and because of varying diets and living conditions, no doubt in many cases they were different," stated Wood. "People often assumed that a handsome child, though apparently a commoner, had to be some gentleman's bastard offspring."

The poor and the working class were expected to show constant deference to their social "betters." The average person had obedience literally beaten into him in some cases. Fear and awe often defined the relationship between rich and poor. A Maryland doctor named Alexander Hamilton (not the one who served as the United States' first Secretary of the Treasury) observed that people of the lower class glanced downward "like sheep" when addressing the powerful and wealthy. One man, George Hewes of Massachusetts, remembered decades later how he trembled and was "scared to death" when he made a visit as a cobbler's apprentice to the stately home of future leader of the Revolution John Hancock. As Wood observes, "Indeed, we will never appreciate the radicalism of the eighteenth-century revolutionary idea that all men are created equal unless we see it within this age-old tradition of difference."

The idea of equality percolated slowly in English society back in the homeland and in the American colonies. In much of Europe the Catholic Church taught its faithful that kings ruled by divine right. "Why, even the hairs of your head are all numbered," said the Gospel of Luke, so it was inconceivable to the Church that God would allow anyone to serve as monarch over a Christian kingdom without divine approval. The king, therefore, ruled as God's representative politically, as the Pope ruled over the church. The English king, however, never enjoyed the absolute rule held by monarchs in France and Spain. However, since Henry VIII established the Church of England, the king ruled not only over an Earthly kingdom, but he also became the nation's religious leader as well. The Church of England portrayed the Pope as the Anti-Christ, an earthly embodiment of satanic evil. This made the English king the defender of the faith. Even the most powerful of the nobility, such as those serving in Parliament, were not citizens but subjects, occupying a lower place on a God-created hierarchy of power.

The idea that God appointed Christian kings and placed them on top of a chain of being in which nobles ruled over commoners, and men over women, began to slowly unravel when the Stuart dynasty assumed the English throne in the 1600s. The Stuarts sought to achieve absolute authority like their European counterparts and to reign without the consultation with Parliament and, through marriage, the Stuart family had many family connections to the Catholic French royal family. Furthermore, James II (who reigned from 1685-1688) proposed that the British government legally tolerate Catholics, which raised the suspicions of the fiercely anti-Catholic Puritan faction in the Parliament. These differences led to violence between the Stuart King Charles I and the Parliament in 1642-1651 (which led to the beheading of the king in 1649) and in the so-called Glorious Revolution in 1688 that led to the overthrow of James II. These anti-royal rebellions posed a major challenge to the idea of the divine right of kings. If God placed the Stuarts on the English throne, then the successful parliamentary rebels had twice made themselves enemies of God. As historian Edmund S. Morgan notes in his book **Inventing the People: The Rise of Popular Sovereignty in England and America**, English philosophers like John Locke turned the concept of Divine Right on its head, arguing that the British people, in some distant, primeval past, had expressed God's will by creating the monarchy. This was a subtle but important change that provided an important rationale for the American Revolution. God had acted through the "people," not the king. The king was obligated to rule in the interest of the people. A king who did not serve the greater interests, whose rule failed to guarantee the life, liberty and property of the people, was no longer legitimate and the people as a whole were morally justified in ending that king's rule. The question now was how to define "the people." When privileged Virginia slave owner and plantation master Thomas Jefferson wrote, "All men are created equal," he certainly wasn't referring to women, the poor, commoners, or African Americans. The common people, Jefferson wrote at one point, "must never be considered when we calculate the national character." Jefferson's words, however, acted as a solvent on the Old World hierarchy. In the coming decades, slavery opponents would insist that the "peculiar institution" made a mockery of Jefferson's words. When women met in Seneca Falls to demand suffrage rights in 1848, they would draft "The Declaration of Sentiments" in conscious imitation of the Declaration of Independence, and paraphrase Jefferson in proclaiming "that all men and women are created equal; that they are endowed by their Creator with certain inalienable rights; that among these are life, liberty, and the pursuit of happiness..." Much of American political history from the 1770s on would be a struggle over how inclusive the United States would be when the nation defined "the people."

IMMIGRATION, 1760-1775

By the 1760s, rapid growth—in population, wealth, economic activity, and settled territory—transformed the British North American colonies. With a population reaching 2.5 million by 1775, the colonists no

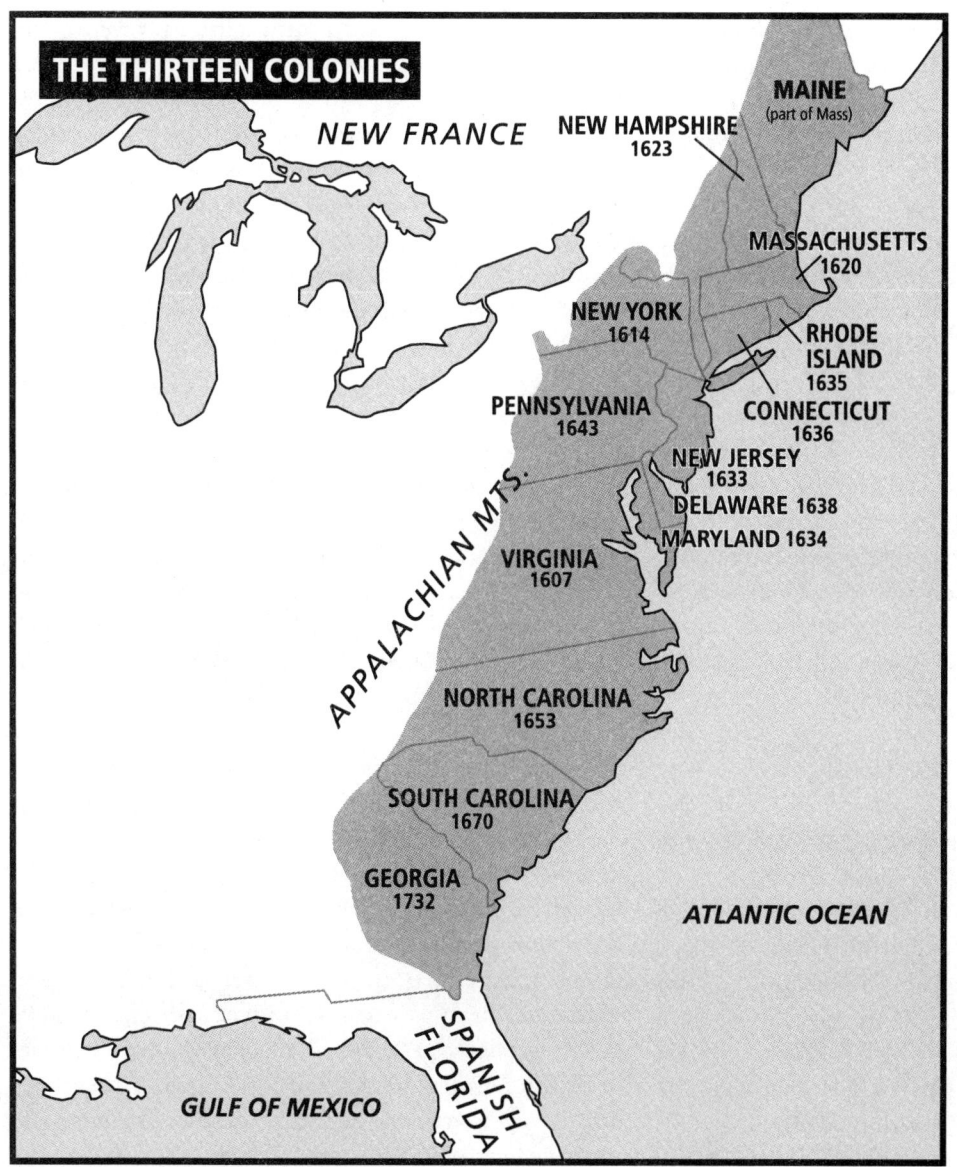

Map 5.1 The Thirteen Colonies

longer saw themselves as remote, isolated frontiersmen dependent upon the mother country's protection nor did they simply view themselves as just New Yorkers or Virginians, but increasingly as part of something larger. In a fiery pamphlet titled *Common Sense*, Thomas Paine exhorted his readers to think of themselves as Americans. "There is something absurd in supposing a continent to be perpetually governed by an island," Paine insisted. "In no instance hath nature made the satellite larger than its primary planet." The island kingdom and its colonies, he claimed, "belong to different systems: England to Europe—and America to itself."

New waves of immigration across the Atlantic further increased the population. Over 55,000 immigrants to America in the mid-to-late 1700s arrived from Ireland—some were native Irish Catholics, but many others were Protestants whose families who originally came from Scotland, the "Scots-Irish," who fled heavy taxes and extortionate land rents. Another stream of immigration, consisting of 70,000 newcomers, brought farming families from rural northern England and Scotland to the frontiers of settlement in western North Carolina and northern New York. Between 1760 and 1775, an estimated 220,000 immigrants poured through colonial ports of entry and spread out across the hinterlands. After the Seven Years' War ended, some 12,000 German-speaking members of various Protestant sects migrated to Pennsylvania. Not everyone welcomed all these newcomers. **Benjamin Franklin,** soon to be a leader of the revolutionary movement in the thirteen colonies, feared the impact of German immigration, viewing the new arrivals as backwards, racial outsiders with an inferior culture. He called for an end to German immigration in a 1751 essay:

> [W]hy should the Palatine Boors [Germans] be suffered to swarm into our Settlements, and by herding together establish their Language and Manners to the Exclusion of ours? Why should Pennsylvania,

founded by the English, become a Colony of Aliens, who will shortly be so numerous as to Germanize us instead of our Anglifying them, and will never adopt our Language or Customs, any more than they can acquire our Complexion.

. . . [T]he Number of purely white People in the World is proportionably very small. All Africa is black or tawny. Asia chiefly tawny. America (exclusive of the new Comers) wholly so. And in Europe, the Spaniards, Italians, French, Russians and Swedes, are generally of what we call a swarthy Complexion; as are the Germans also, the Saxons only excepted, who with the English, make the principal Body of White People on the Face of the Earth. I could wish their Numbers were increased . . . [W]hy increase the Sons of Africa, by Planting them in America, where we have so fair an Opportunity, by excluding all Blacks and Tawneys, of increasing the lovely White and Red?

The Ranks of the Unfree

From Great Britain one group of migrants consisted of young artisans and laboring men who secured passage by signing themselves into indentured servitude, embarking from London and arriving at labor markets in Pennsylvania, Maryland, and Virginia. The indentured servants sold up to seven years of their life to a master in return for the cost of transportation to North America, and their travel here was often miserable. A German musician, Gottlieb Mittelberger, traveled with indentured servants on a ship bound for North America in 1750 and recalled little but horrors:

During the journey the ship is full off pitiful signs of distress — smells, fumes, horrors, vomiting, various kinds of sea sickness, fever, dysentery, headaches, heat, constipation, boils, scurvy, cancer, mouth rot and similar afflictions all of them caused by the age and the highly salted state of the food, especially of the meat, as well as by the very bad and filthy water . . . Add to all that shortage of food, hunger, thirst, frost, heat, dampness, fear, misery . . . as well as other troubles . . . On board our ship, on a day on which we had a great storm, a woman about to give birth and unable to deliver under the circumstances, was pushed through one of the portholes into the sea.

Many indentured servants would not live to see the end of the seventh contracted year of service. Those who did reach the emancipation date traditionally were paid a small amount of money by their former masters, so-called freedom dues. But although they were no longer subjected to beatings by their one-time masters, and the women were no longer sexually exploited by them, life remained incredibly hard for most former servants. Only about 20 percent of former indentured servants ever achieved anything better than miserable poverty. On the other hand, their masters raked in a handsome profit of about $5,000 per servant.

The largest single category of new migrants to America were brought to the colonies in chains, as survivors of the horrors of the "Middle Passage." Slave importations reached peak levels in the early 1760s, as British military successes and the European peace settlement reopened trading routes with West Africa.

Approximately 84,000 Africans disembarked at North American ports during the 1760-1775 period. A large majority of these—over 57,000—were brought to the Lower South colonies of North Carolina, South Carolina, and Georgia, where rice and indigo planters relied on imported Africans to sustain slave labor forces and compensate for high rates of disease and death. In the Chesapeake, by contrast, slave populations had begun to reproduce themselves and grow more rapidly through sexual reproduction. Virginia and Maryland masters reduced their purchases of Africans, encouraged (or claimed to encourage) the formation of strong families among slaves, and in some cases even advocated for an end to the transatlantic slave trade itself. The southern colonies in British North America, and the American states they became represented the only slave societies in human history in which the population increased naturally. In the sugar colonies of Cuba and Brazil, for instance, there was need of constant importation of new slaves because the masters, enjoying huge profits from their cash crop, found it cheaper to work their slaves to death and purchase replacements. Even after the British Navy began suppressing the transatlantic slave trade after the Parliament banned it in 1807, the smuggling of newly captured slaves to Cuba and Brazil continued until slavery became illegal in those countries in 1886 and 1888, respectively. Tobacco and cotton growers enjoyed slimmer profit margins and the skill level in tending these crops required training, so out of self-interest, masters in the southern colonies often provided more food and somewhat better treatment to their slaves.

This difference in slave treatment fails to mitigate the cruelty of American slavery. As slaves would later say in Texas, they worked from "can see to can't see"— from sunrise to sunset, and sometimes beyond. Most masters provided two sets of clothing, one set for the winter that usually provided scant protection against the cold and another set during the warmer months. Slaves received uncomfortable, one-size-fits-all shoes that the servants usually abandoned when the weather got warm enough. Masters generally provided slaves monotonous and sometime unappetizing corn and pork diets. Lucky slaves could supplement their diets by tending small gardens near their slave cabins, or by hunting or fishing. Malnutrition, nevertheless, became commonplace as indicated by the high number of slaves reported suffering from pica, the compulsion to eat dirt as the body craves needed minerals. Slaves who escaped or disobeyed their masters often received cruel punishments ranging from whipping to hobbling, in which a hammer was swung to hit knee joints from the side in order to displace the joint and impair future escape attempts.

A small but significant number of Africans—roughly 6,500—were imported to the northern colonies, where slave labor was well established in larger cities and particular rural areas, such as the Hudson River Valley. In 1770, the slave population in New York was actually larger than in Georgia. Until the Revolution itself, a large majority of transatlantic immigrants—including slaves, indentured servants, and convicts sent into exile—came to the colonies as unfree workers.

AN EVOLVING ECONOMY

Others living in the colonies—such as urban merchants and master craftsmen, plantation gentry and the much larger ranks of middling landowners and small farmers—benefited from North America's economic growth. By the standards of the eighteenth-century world, British North America by the late-colonial period enjoyed extraordinary prosperity, although the wealth was distributed unevenly among regions and between economic classes. From the mid-seventeenth century to the eve of the Revolution, colonial per capita GDP (gross domestic product) grew at twice the rate of Great Britain. Faster economic growth reflected population growth, spread of territorial settlements, and development of new lands as well as increasing trade with the rest of the world. Each of the colonial regions—even New England, with its stony soil, limited arable land, and lack of incoming migrants—grew economically over time, although by far the greatest gains were realized by the masters of southern plantations. As a result of the long-term trend, by the 1770s, per capita wealth in the colonies overall was higher than in Great Britain, and the gap widens when measuring slaves as part of the wealth of their owners. White Southerners were (according to this average measurement) more than twice as wealthy as their counterparts in Great Britain, the middle colonies, and New England.

Yet economic growth was not steady or constant, and even its leading beneficiaries were never very secure. Dependence on exports kept the colonies exposed to the rise and fall of commodity prices. In the late 1750s, the British war against the French and their Native American allies on the western frontier, in French Canada, and in the Caribbean had generated huge orders for new ships, munitions, and other goods and supplies—and lucrative opportunities as well for colonial merchants to undertake "privateering" raids on enemy flag vessels. Meanwhile, Virginia tobacco, South Carolina rice, and New York refined sugar all brought high prices from consumers and their mercantile agents. But after 1760, the boom went bust, and hard times prevailed for most of the decade.

THE COMING OF THE AMERICAN REVOLUTION

The Sugar and Currency Acts

After the French and Indian War, the British government experienced dire financial circumstances. Years of waging war, and the victories in Canada and the West Indies, had added millions of pounds to the national debt. The British sent 10,000 troops to North America to defend their new conquests in Canada and the Ohio Country. Those soldiers had to be paid, fed, clothed, and armed, which added further to the British government's fiscal burdens. Reduced purchases of military supplies, meanwhile, increased colonial unemployment. A post-war recession caused tax revenues to decline, while government expenditures continued to climb. The poor and working class in England rioted in some cases over taxes, high prices, and growing unemployment. Meanwhile, the rich landowners who dominated the Parliament selfishly voted themselves a 25 percent tax cut, worsening the deficit.

The British prime minister, **Sir George Grenville** (in office from 1763-1765), looked for ways to raise revenue and cut expenses, eventually deciding to focus on taxing overseas commerce and the American colonists (who previously never had to pay revenue taxes to the British Treasury). In 1764, he steered through Parliament a series of revenue bills, including the Sugar Act. Previously-existing high tariffs on foreign molasses within the empire, often evaded by smugglers, had originally been intended to protect British sugar producers from foreign competition. The Sugar Act actually lowered these rates, but it tightened procedures for enforcement of the duties by customs officers. The act also allowed customs officers to prosecute smugglers in vice admiralty courts, before royally appointed judges, rather than in local courts under colonial judicial systems. Grenville feared that local judges and local juries would sympathize with the smugglers and find them not guilty, regardless of the evidence. For the smugglers, the days of benign neglect by imperial authorities were at an end. Overall, the British government hoped by reducing smuggling, revenues into the Treasury would increase even though the tax rates had been cut. In so doing, however, the nature of this particular Navigation Act governing molasses had been fundamentally altered from a basic trade regulation controlling the flow of legal trade to a law designed simply to accumulate revenues for the British Treasury.

At the same time, Parliament also passed a new **Currency Act**, which prohibited the colonies from issuing paper money as legal tender. British merchants and lenders had often sought to keep colonial debts from being repaid in depreciated colonial currency, and the new legislation responded to their petitions. It also guarded against inflation. But forcing all colonists to rely on limited supplies of specie (gold and silver) to pay their bills deepened the predicaments of the many debtors in the colonies.

The Stamp Act

Though the Sugar and Currency Acts began to generate sporadic protests in the colonies, the impending confrontation would eventually shake the British Empire to its core, leaving its rule over the North American colonies fatally undermined. A strange paradox began to characterize relations between the king and his subjects in North America. In some ways—economically, socially, and culturally—they were growing ever more closely connected. The rapid growth of the colonies encouraged higher volumes of transatlantic trade, bringing not only goods, capital, and immigrants, but also news, political commentary, fashion trends, and even religious movements—such as the evangelical Great Awakening itself, which began in England and thrived on both sides of the ocean. Wealthy colonial planters and merchants sought to imitate English standards of refined living and sent their sons to London to become socially polished and professionally trained. But were the colonists truly Englishmen? Were they even, as one New Hampshire newspaper editor stated, "British brothers"?

One of Benjamin Franklin's friends observed in a letter to Franklin that the tortured relationship between Britain and the American colonies was based on the fact that neither actually knew much about the other. Great Britain was also a dynamic, changing society. For a recently united kingdom now realizing unprecedented commercial wealth from its command of a global empire, the evolving meaning of "Britishness" was inseparable from the experience of imperial conquest and subjugation of others. By the 1760s, newspapers in England frequently referred to colonists as Americans—a name not yet so widely used by the colonists themselves.

Familiarity gave way to mutual estrangement. First-time colonial visitors to the mother country confronted an array of disorienting spectacles. As much as Philadelphia had grown, by the late-colonial period, London was twenty times larger. England outdid its colonies in terms of the ostentatious wealth, mass poverty, magnificence, and squalor on display. Social networks with elaborate rituals and pecking orders tended to exclude even eminent visiting young colonials. (In 1761, after two years of legal studies at the Inns of Court, Charles Carroll, who would later sign the Declaration of Independence, wrote to his father in Maryland, "I am intimate with nobody.") Colonials in Great Britain often felt they were strangers in a strange land.

The political system was perhaps most alien of all. In theory, the Houses of Parliament embodied the will of the British people—both lords and commoner. While Parliament swore allegiance to the king, its political supremacy supposedly protected the historic liberties of Englishmen from any potential tyrant. In reality, Parliament was anything but a straightforward, well-ordered system of representation. Elections to the House of Commons were held in constituencies that varied drastically in size, population, and qualifications for voting. "Rotten boroughs"—former towns or onetime settlements that still retained ancient charters entitling them to elect members—were controlled by local noble men, or others with cash to spend and a desire for influence in the Commons. Faction leaders wheeled and dealed with bribery the normal means of doing business. Far fewer people enjoyed the right to vote in England than in the colonies. While both the colonies and Great Britain required that a male citizen hold a certain amount of property to vote or run for office, the requirements were much higher in the mother country, effectively disfranchising about two-thirds of the male adult population in Great Britain but only an average of one-fourth in the American colonies.

In early 1765, Grenville moved forward with a proposal for "Stamp Duties" on the colonies. As already existed in the British Isles, all printed materials, including legal documents, books, newspapers, magazines, and playing cards were to be made with special paper stamped in London and distributed in the colonies by authorized tax collectors. As with the Sugar Act, vice-admiralty courts were empowered to handle cases of violation. Meeting

Burning of the Stamp Act in Boston

with a group of colonial agents that included Benjamin Franklin, Grenville gently insisted that the colonies must help pay the costs of their own defense and refused to hear arguments challenging the authority of Parliament to impose any kind of tax on the colonies. The House of Commons also ignored protest petitions from the colonial assemblies. On March 22, Parliament passed the Stamp Act, with its provisions due to start taking effect on November 1, 1765.

Initial Colonial Protests Against the Stamp Act

Within the colonies, the response would not be a quiet one. In Williamsburg, Virginia, news of the Stamp Act's passage arrived toward the end of the spring session of the House of Burgesses, the elected Virginia assembly. **Patrick Henry** was a young, new member but already a successful trial attorney known for his courtroom eloquence. The tobacco planters who dominated the Virginia legislature generally opposed the imposition of taxes by Parliament and had protested the Sugar Act, but Henry's brand of opposition went further. On May 29, he and his allies proposed a set of seven resolutions, and a fiery debate consumed the chamber for three days. Together the "Virginia Resolves" denounced the Stamp Act, not as merely an unfair policy but as unconstitutional, illegitimate, tyrannical, and void.

The colonists were not represented in the Parliament and, therefore, had no direct voice in legislation directly affecting their pocketbooks. Taxation of the people by their own elected officials was "the distinguishing characteristic of British Freedom, without which the ancient Constitution cannot exist," according to Henry. Defenders of the tax, however, would argue that the colonies were "virtually represented" because members of Parliament supposedly represented not only their particular districts but all the citizens of the British Empire. Men like Henry found these arguments unconvincing and "No taxation without representation" became a rallying cry for the growing American resistance. The seventh and last of the "resolves" even deemed any supporter of the Stamp Act to be "an enemy to this His Majesty's colony." Only four of the Resolves were actually approved by the burgesses (and a fifth was passed but rescinded after Henry had left for home), but all seven were printed in the newspapers.

This represented the boldest challenge yet by the colonists to the authority of Parliament. As the shock waves spread, Henry gained fame for his own speech during the Resolves debate. According to one observer, Henry called out names of tyrannical kings and the rebel leaders who overthrew them, noting for instance that "Caesar had his Brutus," and then said he "did not Doubt that some american would stand up, in favour of his Country." Cut off by cries of "Treason," Henry affirmed his loyalty to the King. But Henry maintained that if he had gone too far, it was because of "the Interest of his Countrys Dying liberty which he had at heart." Henry had mastered the hellfire-and-brimstone sermonizing style of evangelical Baptist and New Side Presbyterian preachers that had fired the Great Awakening, and his eloquence won a large audience for the cause of resistance to Parliament.

Stamp Act Protests in Boston

In Massachusetts, a democratic culture was evolving, reflected by the institution of the town meeting where citizens of all walks of life (but not women) gathered together to decide political issues. Town meetings in Boston included the wealthy, the middling, and even some of the "working artificers, seafaring men, and low sorts of people" (as an irate governor of the colony once observed). An organized faction called the Caucus, led by a group of master craftsmen and lesser merchants who called themselves the Loyal Nine, claimed to represent the workingmen and controlled the town meeting with their votes. At the same time, some colonists remained deeply loyal to imperial authority.

The leading example of this was **Thomas Hutchinson**, a successful merchant and a descendant of the same Anne Hutchinson who had challenged the original Puritan leadership of Massachusetts in the 1600s. Never widely popular but always politically ambitious, Hutchinson cultivated connections with successive royally appointed governors of Massachusetts, and he secured many of the colony's other high offices for himself and his relatives. During the early 1760s, Hutchinson repeatedly urged Governor Francis Bernard to abolish Boston's town meeting and establish a local council that he, his relatives, and their friends could control.

Among the local leaders who resisted Hutchinson's efforts was **James Otis Jr.**, an unpredictable but brilliant lawyer and scholar who helped to unify the rest of the opposition. Otis was driven by a private feud with Hutchinson, but he could channel personal grievance into principled arguments. Rising to defend the interests of Boston's merchants, he boldly denounced policies such as the use of broad search warrants to seek evidence of smuggling, and the Sugar Act itself. Like Patrick Henry, Otis put narrow legal arguments aside and characterized the imperial customs laws as unconstitutional, tyrannical violations of the colonists' fundamental rights.

At the same time, he reached out to the Loyal Nine and their followers, attacking Hutchinson as an aristocratic pretender and an enemy of the common folk. Increasingly, the leadership of the town meeting became an alliance of merchants, artisans, and laborers who viewed their elite adversaries as tools of the Parliament who would usurp the self-governing powers of all colonists. By 1765, opposing Parliament, in the minds of many in Massachusetts, equaled supporting the rights of the people.

Boston's response to the Stamp Act was slow in coming but explosive. Newspapers in Massachusetts reprinted the Virginia Resolves. Hutchinson claimed to oppose the law but refused to deny Parliament's authority to pass it. His brother-in-law, Andrew Oliver, was appointed as stamp distributor for Massachusetts. On the morning of August 14, 1765, an ominous sight appeared, under one of Boston's largest elm trees: a figure representing Oliver, hanging by his neck from a branch. Suspended alongside Oliver's effigy was a boot (a symbolic reference to the Earl of Bute, once an adviser to King George III) with its sole painted green (and with a helpful sign bearing the word "Green-ville").

Hutchinson, as lieutenant governor of the colony, ordered the local sheriff to cut down the effigy, but a crowd of workingmen, led by a poor shoemaker named Ebenezer McIntosh, surrounded the tree. That night they took down the figures themselves, carried them through the city streets to the stamp distributor's office, tore down the office building, built a bonfire from its timbers, "stamped" on Oliver's effigy with their own boots, and beheaded it by the light of the flames. Then they stormed through Oliver's own house, leaving its interior partially gutted. Oliver pledged the next day to resign the stamp distributorship. Twelve nights later, McIntosh and the crowd reassembled at the houses of several other officials, including Hutchinson's own grand mansion, intent on destroying everything. Hutchinson and his family fled for their lives. A mob broke into, vandalized and burned his mansion. He lost a fortune in worldly possessions (for which he compiled a detailed inventory, and eventually was compensated) including a draft of an extensive history of the colony that he had been working on for many years, but maintained his dignified composure, as well as his network of political connections.

More than the material losses, the collapse of law and order left Hutchinson, the royal governor, and other respectable men most shaken. Members of local militias given the duty of maintaining crowd control had participated in the violence. Such mobs, however, had long been a local tradition. Crowds, sometimes including well-off men dressed as poor folk, assembled to force the closing down of houses of prostitution and to drive contagious smallpox sufferers out of town. Ritual mobs gave humble men roles in the maintenance of local traditions.

For decades, in Boston, on November 5 ("Pope's Day"), crowds took over the streets, lit bonfires, and paraded with effigies of the Pope as the Devil, to express hatred of the Catholic Church and its minions. (Pope's Day, also known as "Guy Fawkes Day," commemorates an incident in which Catholic conspirators failed to set off a bomb intended to blow up King James I and the Parliament at the start of the 1605 legislative session). A violent routine even developed in which rival mobs from opposite sides of town battled in the streets, seeking to capture each other's effigies. (Ebenezer McIntosh was the elected leader of the South End's Pope's Day Company.) Additionally, at times of grain shortage, crowds in Boston and elsewhere gathered to force merchants to keep the price of bread within financial reach. By the time of the Stamp Act riot, for the struggling mass of people in Boston, the authority of the royally connected, socially condescending, tax-collecting leaders of the colony was no longer legitimate.

Stamp Act Resistance Spreads

Together, Patrick Henry's inflammatory rhetoric and the explosion of the Boston mob helped spread flames of protest across the colonies. In July, Otis had called for a Stamp Act Congress of delegates from all the colonies. Representatives from nine colonies convened in New York in October and issued more resolutions. Like the Virginia Resolves, the Congress invoked the historic rights and liberties of British subjects. Others went about it differently. Local politicians organized demonstrations,

Harbottle Dorr

The back of a hardware store hardly seems an appropriate place to study revolutionary theory. Yet in 1765, a young hardware storeowner with the striking name of Harbottle Dorr began a collection of Boston newspapers that he annotated with detailed and bold comments. These notes hold many clues to the meaning and purpose of American colonial society and the American Revolution.

Little is known of Dorr's personal life. His father died when Harbottle was about 17, and the only inheritance the son managed to salvage from the debt-ridden estate was a small library of books. This may have influenced Dorr's later interest in a newspaper collection. Dorr's mother was probably illiterate since this was the standard of the day for women of the lower class. With this inauspicious start it took a combination of luck, ambition, and the rising economy of colonial Boston to produce a modest life style for Dorr. He eventually did accumulate enough wealth to purchase a hardware shop and earn a constant income. At his shop, during the quiet times and between customers, he collected Boston newspapers, reading them with great interest and making fascinating commentary about the events of the times.

This collection, begun during the Stamp Tax Crisis, was a conscious effort made by a man who saw his community become the object of tyrannical imperial political policy. It ended in 1776 when the publication of Boston newspapers was destroyed by marauding British troops. Dorr chose to collect newspapers to make his case against the English government because he claimed the articles gave a "full Account of the Jealousies, great uneasiness, vast difficulties, and cruel Treatment of the Colonies by the Detestable Acts of Parliament."

It is clear that Dorr believed he was providing an important contribution to the study of the era. Later, during the war years, Dorr organized the papers into four volumes and indexed them to make them useful to readers not familiar with the names and events of his day. There is no doubt he had a wide knowledge of English law, history, and both past and present politicians. He identified names, events, dates, and acts of Parliament only vaguely referred to in the newspapers. His primary object seems to have been to make future readers aware of the "rightness" of the American cause. He did this by pointing out the "goodness" of the American patriots and the "badness" of the British and, even, the King. The presentation was in very moralistic terms with good fighting evil.

The editing was comprehensive. The margin notes were frequently redone and added in a second or third review. The fact that he never referred to George Washington as any more than General, not as Mr. President, seems to confirm that all the editing was done before 1789.

Dorr was more than a literary commentator on the Revolution. He was an early member of the boisterous Sons of Liberty and a proud signer of the agreements to boycott British goods. In 1776 Dorr proved that local newspapers were a good tool for reaching the patriots in the community because he himself advertised in **The Continental Journal and Weekly Advertiser** *for information about the British troops who had allegedly plundered and robbed his shop. The robbery, which he said nearly ruined him, heightened his hatred of the British and added to the tone of his annotations and his belief that the American cause was righteous. From 1777 to 1784, and 1786 to 1791, Dorr was a town selectman, an indication that his opinions were popular enough for him to win at least minor office in his community.*

Harbottle Dorr was not a member of any kind of intellectual or social elite, nor even a prominent member of his community. When he died in 1794, the Boston newspapers mentioned his passing in short lists of others who had died about the same time. There was little that was special about him, but he fully believed the American Revolution to be an idealistic preservation of rights, freedoms, and good leadership qualities. Insignificant as history might treat him, Harbottle Dorr was proud to be an active American patriot.

which turned into riots, in Newport, Rhode Island, in several Connecticut towns, and in New York City, where crowds seized the colonial governor's coach, burned it, and sacked the home of a commander of the local British garrison manning the harbor. In each of the colonies, stamp distributors either resigned their commissions on their own or were forced to do so by mobs.

The spirit of rebellion turned out to be difficult to contain, and even whites leading the opposition to the Stamp Act became nervous as they feared that their slaves might also rise up. In Charles Town, South Carolina, white artisans had marched with their effigies on the local stamp distributor's home, chanting and waving flags bearing the word "Liberty." Whites were a minority in the city; most of the residents were black slaves. Whites began to fear that the African Americans would attempt a revolt of their own. One day in January 1766, as one white resident recalled it, "some negroes, apparently in thoughtless imitation, began to cry 'Liberty,'" and almost simultaneously more than one hundred slaves escaped from plantations outside the city. "The city was thrown in arms for a week," and masters throughout the colony alerted each other and prepared for the worst.

As the protests echoed up and down the Atlantic seaboard, respectable protest leaders sought greater control over the forces they had unleashed. In Boston, shortly after stating their disapproval and regret over the destruction of Hutchinson's mansion, the Loyal Nine rebranded themselves as the "**Sons of Liberty**" (using a phrase from a speech delivered in the House of Commons) and focused on sustaining the opposition movement while calming its penchant for violence. Opposition leaders quickly adopted the name in other colonies. In Boston, the Sons of Liberty claimed some successes. They held mass meetings and mock trials for the Stamp Act under the same elm tree (now renamed the Liberty Tree, or "Liberty Hall") where the demonstrations had begun. With funds contributed by the wealthy merchant **John Hancock**, they bought a general's fine uniform for McIntosh and arranged for him to lead both of the Pope's Day companies in a more orderly celebration. (Several years later, when McIntosh fell into debtor's prison, none of the Sons of Liberty could be found to bail him out.)

Meanwhile, in late 1765, merchants in New York, Boston, and Philadelphia organized a boycott of British goods, which proved crucial in killing the hated Stamp Act. Rising prosperity over the decades had fostered the trade in British-made goods, but with the economic downturn reducing new purchases anyway, merchants were willing to suspend new shipments and focus on selling off their existing inventories. Sons of Liberty enforced the boycott, which proved to be a turning point. In London, Grenville had alienated King George over matters unrelated to the empire and was dismissed from his ministry in July 1765. The incoming government had no commitment of its own to the stamp tax, and it received numerous petitions from hard-pressed British merchants seeking policies that would promote trade rather than discourage it. Franklin, still in London, offered testimony before Parliament that shrewdly emphasized colonial loyalty as well as economic grievances. In March 1766, an act repealing the Stamp Act was passed into law. An accompanying **Declaratory Act**, however, set an ominous tone, insisting that Parliament retained "full power and authority" to make laws binding the colonies "in all cases whatsoever."

The Townshend Acts

The colonists' rejoicing over the death of the Stamp Act proved to be short-lived. The Declaratory Act cast a shadow over their celebrations from the start, with its defiant message that many of the colonists' arguments had been heard but not accepted. The sugar taxes remained in place. Moreover, the budgetary problems facing His Majesty's government had hardly disappeared with the Stamp Act's repeal. Barely a year later, an entirely new tax scheme reopened the entire dispute. Another turnover of ministries placed responsibility for government finances in the hands of Charles Townshend, a clever politician with a short attention span and few visible principles, who became Chancellor of the Exchequer (the British equivalent of Treasury Secretary). He felt forced to seek revenues from America. Townshend's Revenue Act of 1767 placed new import duties on goods for which colonial consumers relied on the import trade: lead, paint, glass, paper, and tea. The revenue yield would not be great, but Townshend viewed it as a first step. Perhaps more important, it would cover salaries for royal governors and magistrates. Townshend packaged his revenue act with other laws aimed at strengthening the authority of royal customs collectors and punishing New York for failing to pay for housing British army forces.

In the colonies, few were truly eager for renewed conflict, and at first the response to the Townshend Acts was muted. For the colonists, the issue remained not the amount of the tax but that the colonies had no voice in the debate about the Townshend duties. The Townshend taxes might be a small burden, but the colonists could see clearly enough how they could create a precedent for future taxes imposed by an unresponsive Parliament across the Atlantic Ocean.

Once again, Boston took the lead. **Samuel Adams**, a longtime member of the Caucus group and one of the Sons of Liberty, stepped forward. Uniquely well suited to the leadership role he created, Adams was respectable yet humble, the son of a prosperous tradesman (and maltster, a provider of malted grains—not a brewer as legend has it, although close). Never successful in business himself, he led an austere life out of both necessity and principle. While the increasingly erratic Otis had connected with the rank and file through bold oratory and shared animosity, Adams treated Caucus followers as social equals and maintained their trust—and votes—through his absolute commitment to the idea of a common cause. Holding a seat in the Massachusetts colonial legislature, Adams secured its approval of a letter to "sister colonies," presenting the case against the Townshend Acts as "infringements of their natural and constitutional rights."

The Massachusetts Circular Letter stirred a renewal of opposition throughout the colonies. In Boston, it led to the suspension of the legislature itself (by Royal Governor Francis Bernard, acting on orders from London). As royal customs commissioners attempted to enforce the duties, ominous crowds again filled the streets. At "Liberty Hall," under the tree branches, the Sons of Liberty convened official town meetings and passed resolutions condemning the governor. The newly arrived customs commissioners appealed for armed support, reporting to London that, "the Governor and Magistracy have not the least Authority or power in this place." Their request was heard. In October 1767, transport ships arrived from Canada carrying four regiments of British army regulars. Boston was now a city under military occupation.

As accounts of strife in Boston spread through the colonies, resistance took on a more urgent character. In London, Townshend and his successors remained intent on asserting imperial authority, and directed governors in all colonies to dissolve legislatures that endorsed the Massachusetts Circular Letter. Cut off from expressing opposition through their established institutions, colonists resorted to more extreme tactics. Non-importation of British goods, the same policy agreed upon by merchants during the Stamp Act crisis, became a crucial means of resistance once again. This time, however, a more resolute imperial policy would test the ability of colonists to mount a sustained opposition. Merchants had suffered economically during previous boycotts, and they wanted to spread the pain of resistance around more broadly. In each of the seaport cities, artisans—often having struggled for years to compete with imported British products—now emerged in a critical role. Under pressure from Samuel Adams and his followers, Boston merchants reluctantly agreed in August 1768 to cease shipments of most British goods. In Charles Town, an alliance of artisans and rice planters put forward similar demands in a series of public meetings. But, as opponents organized, they also began looking beyond the merchants and toward consumers, toward the broader public itself. In Boston, town officials encouraged "Persons of all Ranks" to sign an agreement publicly pledging to "encourage the Use and Consumption of all Articles manufactured in any of the British American Colonies" and to avoid purchasing "Articles from abroad." So-called "Subscription lists" quickly spread beyond Boston as well.

By 1769, while "committees of inspection" in each colony enforced the non-importation campaign among merchants, the consumer boycott movement had extended the resistance movement into colonial communities and households. A decision not to buy imported "Articles"— or a pledge not to do so—made one a participant in the broader struggle against British tyranny. Spending money on luxury items took on a new political meaning, making one a traitor to a virtuous cause. Attempting to discredit the resistance movement, Peter Oliver (brother of Andrew Oliver, the Boston stamp distributor) portrayed the Boston subscription list in what he thought was a ridiculous way: "Among the various prohibited Articles, were Silks, Velvets, Clocks, Watches, Coaches & Chariots; & it was highly diverting, to see the names & marks, of Porters & Washing Women." For Oliver, a statement "signed" by humble and illiterate folk meant that the movement represented little more than a mob action. Unscrupulous boycott leaders, he suggested, had manipulated the lower classes into an act of disloyalty. The class diversity of boycott participants, however, suggested how deep the opposition to British government policies had grown.

The Boston Massacre

In the supercharged political environment of Boston, England's decision to station red-coated troops in the town only raised tensions further. Quartered on private properties seized from the city, guarded by sentries who challenged townsfolk at will, these soldiers inevitably provoked resentment by their mere presence. Poorly paid soldiers seeking work on the side competed with local laboring men. Fights with civilians led to prosecutions of soldiers in local courts, where convictions and fines confirmed the army's sense of being surrounded by enemies. When townsfolk confronted merchants accused of violating the non-importation agreement, soldiers on patrol served as targets of rage and frustration. The explosion finally came on the moonlit night of March 5, 1770, when a detachment of army privates, commanded by Captain Thomas Preston, faced an angry crowd in front of Boston's custom house. The crowd began to throw snowballs, some containing rocks. One of the soldiers was hit by a chunk of ice, slipped to the ground, regained his feet and fired his musket. The soldiers in formation beside him then fired into the crowd, hitting eleven men. Five died, including Crispus Attucks, a mixed-race dockworker of African and Wampanoag descent. (Historians are uncertain whether Attucks was a slave or free.) Hutchinson, then serving as acting governor of the colony, faced the furious crowd the following day, promised justice, and managed to prevent further bloodshed.

The "**Boston Massacre**" had immediate local consequences. The British troops were redeployed to an island fortress in Boston Harbor. Samuel Adams, and others in the thick of the struggle to enforce non-importation, immediately sought to portray the incident as a deliberate attack on helpless civilians—a view illustrated in the famous engraving by local silversmith Paul Revere. Captain Preston and his men were held and later tried in colonial court, defended by **John Adams**, Samuel's second cousin. John Adams was equally dedicated to the opposition movement but, as an attorney, believed in the

Paul Revere's famously skewed version of the Boston Massacre, 1770

principle of a fair trial. Adams secured acquittals of all the defendants on murder charges (although two of the privates were convicted of manslaughter and released after being branded with an iron).

Beyond Boston, the incident coincided with a partial reversal of imperial policy toward the colonies. A new set of ruling ministers in London was willing to modify the Townshend policies, mainly in response to new petitions by London merchants. The original rationale—that modest import duties and firm enforcement could prepare the way gently for future imperial revenue gathering—now lay in ruins. The new prime minister, **Lord Frederick North**, secured the repeal of most of the Townshend duties but kept the tax on tea, which would continue to pay the salaries of governors and other leading officials. North calculated, correctly, that partial concessions would appeal to colonists afraid of further violence and tip the political balance against non-importation. In July 1770, merchants in New York, over the objections of the local Sons of Liberty, declared that they would resume import shipments. Over the months that followed, the resistance movement continued to die down. In October, the Boston merchants gave in as well. On Bowling Green at the tip of Manhattan, a new equestrian statue of George III was raised, to general acclaim. For the time being, as Lord North had intended, peace, order, and normal commerce appeared to prevail once again in the British North American colonies.

The Boston Tea Party

A deceptively quiet pause of three years ensued, a time that encouraged complacency on the part of government ministers in London and frustrated firebrands like Sam Adams. In fact, discontent and frustration with imperial rule continued to fester, sustained by minor incidents in the absence of major provocations such as the Townshend Acts. (In one notable incident taking place in 1772, angry locals burned a British customs patrol vessel—the *H.M.S. Gaspée*—after the anti-smuggling schooner ran aground off the Rhode Island coast.) The relationship between colonies and mother country had already been altered forever, though most in America and Great Britain did not realize it at the time.

The Tea Act shattered the surface calm, and set in motion a final sequence of events leading to war and independence. Lord North really had no intention of demonstrating imperial power over the colonies. His attitude toward the colonies was relatively conciliatory. The British Empire, however, still badly needed revenues to pay its expenses, and the leadership of that Empire remained adamantly opposed to allowing any self-rule for the colonies or their representation in the Parliament. Then, a new fiscal problem arose. The **British East India Company**, a vast commercial enterprise controlling British trade with India and the Far East that heavily impacted the overall British economy, teetered on the edge of bankruptcy. The company wielded great influence in Parliament, and government ministers basically granted the company more favorable terms for the importation of its Indian tea to the American colonies. The company would now be allowed to bypass Britain (where even tea sold for transshipment had been subject to British import duties) and use its own ships and consignment agents to supply colonial markets (where the tea would now be available to consumers at lower prices, even with the Townshend duty included). Americans would pay a lower price, but the East India Company would be able to undersell smugglers and would eventually achieve a monopoly that could come back to haunt the colonies. Again, the colonists continued to object to a tax that had been passed without their consultation, whatever the amount of the duty. Tea represented a major issue. Americans preferred tea to coffee and quaffed gallons of it. North received advice that the existing tea duty remained a sensitive issue, and that the Tea Act risked stirring new controversy if the duty were maintained. But as a continuing source of funds for payment of royal officials, North reasoned that the duty was too valuable to be abandoned.

Responses to the Tea Act in the colonial ports of entry were decisive, reflecting the underlying strength and renewed intensity of the opposition movement. Special circumstances made Boston's response uniquely provocative. As the Tea Act's provisions appeared in the colonial newspapers, the Sons of Liberty insisted that the act was a ruse to "trick" colonists into accepting the Townshend duty and portrayed the East India Company as a rapacious monopoly extending its reach into the colonies—a perfect example of the general corruption that many colonists now associated with the mother country and its government. Merchants now faced the loss of their own profitable trade in smuggled tea, as well as the prospect of seeing the legitimate trade taken over by East India Company consignment agents. On the question of allowing the new law to take effect, merchants were drawn back into alliances with artisans and planters. The Sons of Liberty gently—or not so gently—persuaded local recipients of the company's tea consignment rights to resign their commissions. In New York and Philadelphia, incoming tea ships were warned away and sailed for England with their cargoes. But Governor Hutchinson—who, true to form, had secured company commissions for his two sons—insisted on allowing three Boston-bound vessels to enter the port. As the casks of tea remained on board, a standoff commenced between the ship owner and consignment agents, who wanted the vessels unloaded, and Adams and the other leaders of the Boston town meeting.

Once again, the city was like a boiling kettle. The Boston committee of correspondence appealed to the rest of the colony for support. Mass meetings at "Liberty Hall" and the Old South Church attracted thousands of townsfolk, with thousands more from the surrounding counties demanding that the ships leave for England. Adams and the other Sons of Liberty felt compelled to act before a legal deadline empowered the governor to confiscate the cargo. On the night of December 16, 1773, dozens of men dressed as Indians boarded the ships, smashed open the casks, and threw the tea into the harbor waters. The event, later called the **"Boston Tea Party,"** had one long-term cultural impact on the future United States, marking when Americans would begin to favor coffee to the tea preferred in the British Isles.

The Intolerable Acts

English responses to the Boston Tea Party reflected how much political, economic and emotional distance had grown between Boston and London. Even previous friends of the colonies fell silent, finding the action incomprehensible. A council of ministers summoned Benjamin Franklin, ostensibly to defend a petition from Boston, but instead had to stand silently while his own character was impugned in extravagant terms, obviously in retaliation for Boston's collective action. (Franklin remained in England for another year then left, never to return, and soon became a leader in the revolutionary cause.) For North, at this point, the only issue now involving the colonies was "whether we have, or have not, any authority in that country."

Parliament quickly approved a package of proposals known as the Coercive Acts. (In the colonies, they were derisively referred to as the "**Intolerable Acts**"). These new laws included the Boston Port Act, which closed the port to all commerce until the destroyed tea was paid for; the Massachusetts Government Act, which unilaterally rewrote the colony's charter to strengthen the governor's powers and limited town meetings to once a year; and new procedures for royal officials accused of crimes, allowing their trials to be held in England, which amounted to a grant of impunity, since witnesses for the prosecution were unlikely to be able to afford attending the proceedings. **General Thomas Gage**, a longtime commander of British forces on the western frontier and elsewhere in the colonies, was appointed military governor of Massachusetts and sent to Boston in command of some four thousand regular troops.

Several months later, Parliament passed a separate piece of legislation, the Quebec Act, that colonists associated with the Coercive Acts. Much of the legislation related to the internal governance of formerly French Canada and the rights of French-speaking Catholic residents, but it also included an expansion of the province's boundaries south to the Ohio River and west to the Mississippi River, taking in vast lands previously granted to New York, Pennsylvania, and Virginia. This move did not favor the *Quebecois* as much as the Iroquois nations who occupied these lands and were given new protections against white squatters. The British authorities were already worried about the French and the Spanish; they now hoped that by protecting the Iroquois they would make peace with one of the largest Native American nations dwelling within their empire. By the same token, the act amounted to a new assault on the financial interests of colonial land speculators, whose claims made under the previous colonial boundaries were now rendered invalid. With few exceptions, members of Parliament agreed that the rebellious colonies needed to be cut down to size. In addition, the Quebec Act granted freedom of worship to French Catholics living in the province and ended the requirement that Catholics renounce their faith before they could serve in public office. This expression of religious tolerance infuriated many in the thirteen colonies, especially in Puritan New England, where anti-Catholic prejudice burned the brightest.

The British government could hardly have done anything more to confirm the colonists' worst suspicions. Admittedly, even now, at least some divisions persisted among colonists. A significant minority of Boston merchants, facing the extinction of the city as a trading center, were willing to offer payment for the tea destroyed during the Tea Party and beg for mercy. Others elsewhere remained reluctant to go back to non-importation. But the Intolerable Acts seemed far more of an immediate threat. As the Boston Port Act took effect, with its catastrophic economic consequences for the city, colonists in other places recognized Boston as a martyr in a common cause. In Williamsburg, Virginia, Patrick Henry and a young burgess named Thomas Jefferson proposed a "Day of Fasting, Humiliation, and Prayer" for their fellow colonists facing a "hostile invasion." (John Murray, the Fourth Earl of Dunmore and the royal governor of Virginia, then promptly dissolved the legislature.) Once again, denied a legal framework to express their grievances, the colonists turned to each other and acted outside of the law.

The Disintegration of Authority

In September 1774, the First Continental Congress convened in Philadelphia with delegates from twelve colonies appointed by legislatures when possible and by unofficial conventions when necessary. (Georgia was the one colony that failed to participate.) Behind closed doors, seven intense weeks of debate and committee work resolved differences over tactics and smoothed out differences between boycott advocates and southern planters dependent on British manufactured goods. Ultimately, they found common ground, endorsing a declaration of rights; agreements on non-importation, non-exportation, and nonconsumption of tea; and a network of "committees of safety," to be elected "in every county, city, and town," which would enforce the agreements. A Second Continental Congress was also scheduled for the following year.

Though the meeting of the Congress held much importance, the most crucial developments may have been those assemblages occurring within local communities, particularly those well outside the seaport cities whose merchants, artisans, and laborers had long provided much of the leadership and support for the colonial resistance. In long-settled farming regions and in the backcountry, in small villages and in the sprawling countryside, among the small landowning and tenant families who constituted 70 percent of the white population of the colonies, participation in the resistance developed slowly. Even in rural eastern Massachusetts, Boston's fights with redcoats and customs commissioners seemed distant. Humble farming folk, however, were hardly cut off from the surrounding world. They read newspapers, attended evangelical revivals, and traded surplus crops for consumer goods, some even imported, but compared to city folk, their exposure (as producers or as consumers) to the impact of imperial tax policies was limited.

When the shift finally came, the most important factor proved to be the passage of the Coercive Acts. The extreme punishment inflicted by the British blockade on Boston and that city's masses of impoverished artisans and hungry laborers evoked an emotional response and a tide of donations from throughout the colonies. (In rural Maryland, a member of a relief committee explained that "those who cannot give money, can give corn.") Participation in the charitable campaign created new networks of correspondence and led to further commitments to a common cause. Moreover, for farmers within the colony, the Massachusetts Government Act posed an even more direct threat. Appointments to colonial offices by General Gage under the terms of the act were seen as intrusions into local government by an illegitimate pretender. As villagers began withholding taxes, assembling in crowds to shut down county courts, and disabling other functions of the colonial government, the "committees of safety" mandated by the Continental Congress began filling the vacuum. Farmers began joining the boycotts, watched their neighbors for signs of disloyalty, took charge of local militia units, and sought what one county committee called "a well-ordered resistance." The revolt against the British had moved from the cities to the countryside.

As Gage's appointees and others loyal to his government fled the rural areas for the safety of Boston, the governor recognized that his authority outside the city had disintegrated. An unauthorized Massachusetts Provincial Congress featuring Sam Adams and other resistance leaders now held sessions in Cambridge, across the river from Boston. Other colonial governors found themselves similarly isolated. In New York and Philadelphia, as large-scale "committees of safety" dominated by merchants and artisans asserted power, long-established colonial legislatures adjourned quietly and disappeared. In Virginia, Lord Dunmore grimly acknowledged that local committees of safety were now the acting government of the colony. By early 1775, opposition to British authority, once the distinct preoccupation of merchants, artisans, and leading planters had emerged as a defining feature of American patriots.

The stage was set for war, especially in Massachusetts, where rival governments now confronted each other with military force. Gage kept his regiments in Boston through the winter, pondering his options, appealing to London for reinforcements, and waiting for orders. Across the surrounding countryside, in towns and villages, militia companies held drills, and local volunteers enlisted as so-called minutemen, ready for military duty upon a moment's notice. As they watched and waited, a well-organized network of spies monitored Gage's forces and intercepted his scouts. In the city itself, Paul Revere, William Dawes, and other unemployed artisans kept watch in shifts.

In London, Lord North and his fellow minister William Legge, the 2nd Earl of Dartmouth and the secretary of state for the colonies, fumed over Gage's inaction. In late January, Dartmouth sent new instructions. Without issuing formal orders, and without fulfilling Gage's requests for thousands of additional troops, he demanded some kind of action "to defend the Constitution & to restore the Vigour of Government." Dartmouth was unconvinced that the Massachusetts resistance amounted to anything more than "a rude Rabble" incapable of seriously challenging the king's regular soldiers. In his own view—"in which His Majesty concurs"—the proper next step was to arrest and imprison the leaders of the Massachusetts Provincial Congress.

THE BEGINNING OF THE AMERICAN REVOLUTION

Lexington, Concord, and Bunker Hill

The arrival of Dartmouth's letter in April 1775 forced Gage's hand. The general organized an expedition to seize militia arms and ammunition believed to be held in the town of Concord. Gage's own scouting patrols alerted the patriot militias to the impending action. Late on the evening of April 18, on Boston Common, Gage assembled a detachment of select infantrymen from different regiments. In the middle of the night, they rowed across the bay separating Boston from its hinterlands and advanced along the Concord road.

The British troops intended to arrest Samuel Adams and John Hancock, who they regarded as the leaders of a treasonous movement. Revere ordered associates to hang signal lanterns in the Old North Church steeple to send a warning then made his own crossing to the mainland with William Dawes. The two men scurried on horseback along a designated route through a succession of towns leading toward Concord, rousing the minutemen and sending other riders on their way. In Lexington, he awakened Adams and Hancock, who (after some hours of delay and debate) agreed to head for safety.

Ultimately, a British advance patrol caught Revere before he reached Concord, but not before the alarm system was fully operational. By the time that the redcoated troops reached Lexington shortly after four in the morning, the village militia stood assembled on the green, some seventy men strong. As the regular infantrymen arranged themselves in battle formation, the minutemen attempted an orderly withdrawal with their arms. Just then, a shot rang out—the famous "Shot Heard Round the World," probably fired by a colonist located somewhere off the green. The British troopers responded by exchanging volleys with the militiamen before charging with their bayonets. At the end of the brief skirmish, sometimes referred to as the "**Battle of Lexington**," eight of the Lexington men lay dead and ten were wounded (including the militia commander, Captain John Parker). The war had begun. More than eight years of bloodshed lay ahead.

Marching onward, the British infantry reached **Concord** later in the morning and searched the town. Failing to find any large cache of weapons (they had been long-since removed), they set a few buildings on fire, perhaps by accident. Unwilling to reenact the bloody scene in Lexington, the residents of Concord had initially evacuated to a nearby hillside until they saw the billowing smoke column rising from the town. Arriving on one side of the Concord River across from the main body of British troops, a group of Concord minutemen fired on three isolated companies of infantrymen, which had crossed one of the village bridges, sending them in retreat across the river. Suddenly, the momentum shifted. As the infantry column marched back to Boston, it found itself facing a gauntlet of militiamen along both sides of the road, shooting from behind trees and fences, and attacking stragglers with hatchets and clubs. The British troopers defended themselves with bayonets and return fire, but what had been an intimidating show of force became a bloody ordeal. By the time they reached safety, the British forces had suffered nearly three hundred killed and wounded. Militia casualties numbered less than one hundred.

News of the shots fired at Lexington and Concord resounded across the colonies. "This accident has cut off our last hope of reconciliation," Jefferson wrote in a private letter, "and a phrenzy of revenge seems to have seized all ranks of people." John Adams later wrote that the news of the bloodshed "changed the instruments of War from the pen to the sword." Reflecting the dominance of patriot views in the colonial press, the first published accounts converted the bloody, inconclusive events of the day into a debacle for the British. Believing that Great

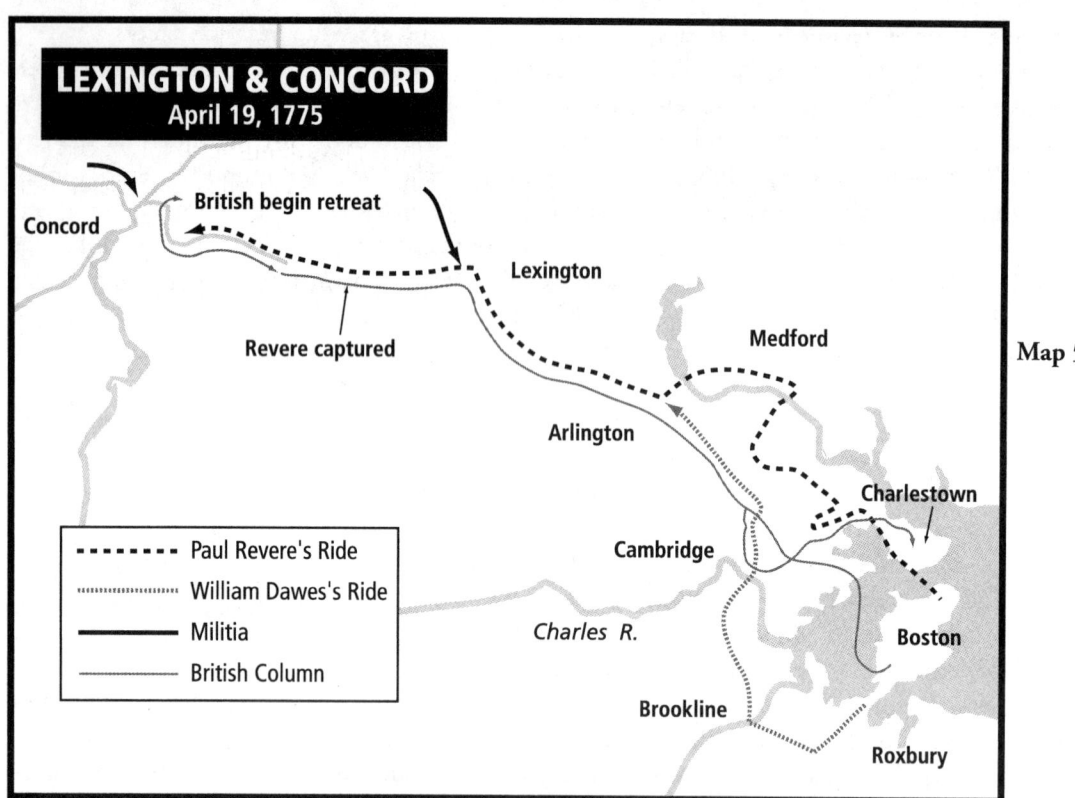

Map 5.2 Lexington & Concord

Britain had started a war on the colonies, new volunteers enthusiastically enlisted in militia companies.

General Gage, still under intense pressure to show results, recognized that militia forces on the ridges overlooking the Boston peninsula and its rivers and harbor might soon encircle his army. With his own reinforcements now arriving, Gage planned to secure the Charlestown Peninsula close to the North End of Boston, but he found himself beaten by a quick deployment of Massachusetts militia forces led by Colonel William Prescott. As Prescott hastily fortified his positions on the high ground above Charlestown—two ridge tops named **Bunker Hill** (the larger, but located further away from Boston) and **Breed's Hill** (where most of the subsequent fighting would take place)—Gage and his lieutenants prepared an assault. On June 17, troops crossed the Charles River from Boston and marched up the hills. General William Howe, entrusted by Gage with the field command of 1,700 light infantrymen, sent his men with bayonets directly against the militia fortifications on Breed's Hill into a devastating volley of musket fire. Howe and his subordinates managed to organize a second advance, but this attack also dissipated in the face of a second patriot volley described by one British officer as "an incessant stream of fire." But with Prescott's militia now out of ammunition, Howe's men overran the top of Breed's Hill on the third attempt. Overall, the fighting (famously mislabeled the "**Battle of Bunker Hill**") produced over a thousand British casualties (226 killed and 828 wounded), including many of Howe's subordinate officers who were sons of members of Parliament. The Americans suffered almost 500 total casualties (140 killed), mostly on Bunker Hill during the retreat to nearby Cambridge. Three days after Gage's report was received in London, Dartmouth wrote a request for the general's resignation.

The Second Continental Congress

Initially the **Second Continental Congress** had been envisioned, like the First, as a kind of inter-colonial treaty conference working out a common response among the colonies to new actions by the British government. But when delegates convened in Philadelphia in May 1775, the colonies were already in a state of undeclared war against the world's leading imperial power. Instead of convening for a brief, intense assembly, delegates prepared for prolonged legislative debates and the difficult task of managing the war. The ultimate objective of the colonial resistance continued to divide the delegates. During its opening months, the new congress attempted, as John Adams put it, "to hold the sword in one hand, and the olive branch in the other."

George Washington, who had commanded frontier troops and militiamen during the French and Indian War, arrived as a uniformed representative for Virginia—the largest colony—and appeared as an indispensable man

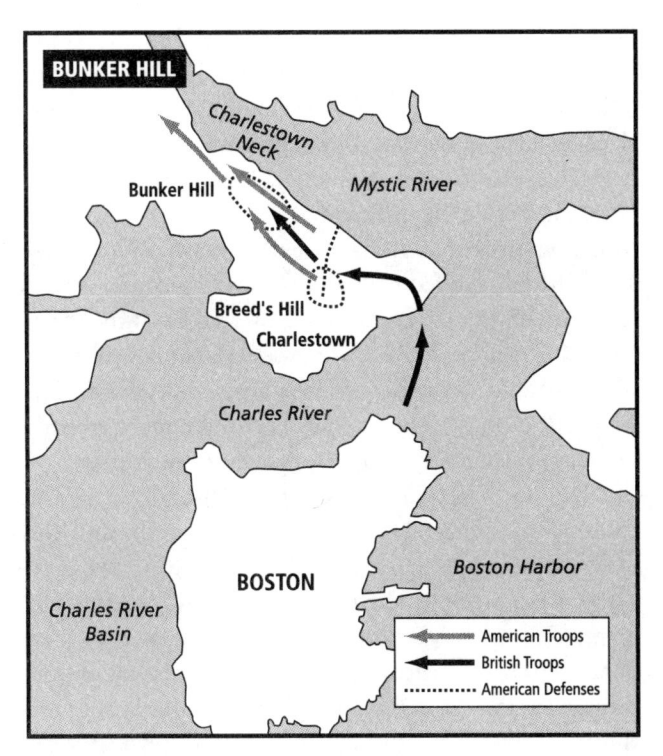

Map 5.3 Battle of Bunker Hill

at a critical moment. On June 14, the Congress created the Continental Army, to be made up of new recruits from Pennsylvania, Maryland, and Virginia, along with the New England militia around Boston. Washington humbly accepted Congress's selection of him to be the Army's commander and immediately left for Massachusetts. The Virginian had earned the trust not only of fierce advocates of independence, such as John Adams (who had nominated him), but also supporters of continued efforts at negotiation with Britain, including **John Dickinson** of Pennsylvania, the leading advocate of reconciliation, who voted in favor of the army's creation and Washington's appointment as commanding general.

Perhaps in return for his cooperation, Dickinson secured the delegates' signatures to an **"Olive Branch Petition"** addressed to King George III, professing their loyalty as faithful subjects. The deferential prose of the petition, which described the conflict between the colonies and Great Britain as painful and blamed the impasse on devious ministers and "artful and cruel enemies," offers a window into the mindset of a colonial moderate who was honestly conflicted, still feeling loyalty to England but sympathetic to colonial complaints. In London, as Adams, Franklin, and other independence advocates could clearly see, none of it mattered. In November, intermediaries on behalf of the colonies presented the Olive Branch Petition to George III. The king refused to receive it.

The Colonists Take the Offensive:
The Invasion of Canada and the Siege of Boston

Waging war brought its own kinds of disappointments. In late 1775, the Congress supported an ambitious effort to expel British forces from Quebec, bring the formerly French Canadians into the common struggle against London, and remove Canada as a source of likely threats to the colonies from the north and west. The opportunity arose from an early victory at Fort Ticonderoga, located on Lake Champlain in northern New York. **Ethan Allen**, a legendary frontiersman, land speculator, self-styled philosopher who commanded a backcountry militia called the Green Mountain Boys, took on the project of capturing the fort along with **Benedict Arnold**, a Connecticut merchant and militia leader who had conceived the same project. Allen and Arnold surprised the token British force and seized the fort without firing a shot.

Having gained the main strategic point between New York and Quebec, the Congress approved an expedition to Canada ultimately led by General Richard Montgomery. Passed over for command, Arnold obtained a separate commission and a detachment of men from Washington. As Montgomery invaded Canada from New York, capturing Montreal and continuing down the St. Lawrence River toward the British stronghold at Quebec, Arnold led his men on an impossibly arduous two-month advance through the Maine wilderness.

Ultimately, both expeditions proved to be wasted effort: by the time both forces converged near Quebec, they were drastically reduced by sickness, hunger, and expiring enlistments. When they attacked the city in the midst of a snowstorm on December 31, the large British garrison repelled them with heavy losses. With Montgomery killed in combat, Arnold maintained a semblance of a siege with his few surviving men. Eventually the American forces wore out their welcome among French-speaking colonists, and the entire venture gradually collapsed. The failure to foster an alliance with French Canadians would prove potentially costly later in the war, as British strategists considered the same invasion route between Canada and New York, but in the reverse direction.

Washington's own work that winter was less adventurous but much more successful. With British forces, now under the command of General Howe, still nursing their wounds in Boston, the Continental Army focused on instilling discipline and building basic skills among the men in its ranks. Lacking an experienced officer corps and trained soldiers, Washington complained, as he had in his previous military career, about their rudimentary state, but tried to work with the materials he had been given. By early March 1776, he felt ready to act. Through a series of careful maneuvers, he successfully occupied Dorchester Heights—like Bunker Hill and Breed's Hill, a site overlooking Boston from a short distance—without exposing his forces unduly to a possible counterattack from the city. Then, to the amazement of the British, he quickly installed artillery, captured at Fort Ticonderoga, behind portable fortifications. Facing the guns, Howe was forced to make a choice and decided not to attempt another uphill attack against fortified positions. Instead, the British forces evacuated Boston for the safety of Nova Scotia, Canada, while Washington and his men watched from above. On March 17, as the Continental Army entered the city, no British armies of occupation remained in the thirteen colonies.

George III Throws Down the Gauntlet

A Congress which could approve a document such as the Olive Branch Petition was clearly not yet ready to declare independence. Indeed, a major reason for the petition was to defend the Congress against accusations of disloyalty. The Adams cousins from volatile, radical Massachusetts continued to bide their time and avoid provoking their colleagues. Yet, the mood in America changed quickly in the months that followed. The experience of being at war, under attack by British soldiers supposedly sent to defend the colonies had a profound impact upon the colonists. If **George III** felt they were behaving disloyally, the colonists themselves felt betrayed. The king's reaction to the Olive Branch Petition also made a lasting impression. In fact, during the closing months of 1775, both king and Parliament added still further insults and injuries. In a speech to Parliament in October, George III charged that the colonial rebellion was "manifestly carried on for the purpose of establishing an independent empire." In December, Parliament passed one more piece of punitive legislation. The American Prohibitory Act closed the thirteen colonies to all legal commerce and empowered the Royal Navy to confiscate not only American ships and their cargoes, but also those belonging to other nationalities found to be trading with the colonies.

For white Southerners, the most serious provocation came at the hand of **Lord Dunmore**, the royal governor of Virginia. After formally dissolving the House of Burgesses in response to its denunciations of the Intolerable Acts, Dunmore, like other royal governors in other colonies, watched helplessly as unsanctioned committees claimed legitimacy and began exercising the powers of government. When he attempted to prevent elections for the Second Continental Congress (again in response to orders from Lord Dartmouth), his own situation became dangerous. Before leaving for the safety of a Royal Navy frigate, he warned that if militia units threatened him, he would "declare freedom to the slaves, and reduce the City of Williamsburg to ashes." In fact, Dunmore was himself a slave owner, but he placed military necessity ahead of his own interests. In May, he sent Dartmouth a proposal to "arm all my own Negroes and receive all others who come to me whom I shall declare free." Then, in November 1775, having landed at Norfolk with two companies of loyal British troops, Dunmore reasserted his authority as Virginia's legitimate governor and declared free all slaves who "are able and willing to bear arms, they joining His Majesty's Troops as soon as may be, for the more speedily reducing the Colony to a proper sense of their duty."

For the Virginia planters now committed to the colonial resistance, Dunmore's proclamation, and the military campaign that followed, could hardly have been a deeper outrage or a graver threat. As in the days of the Stamp Act, as masters debated the defense of their own liberties, slaves listened carefully and watched for opportunities for their own freedom. In fact, Dunmore's initial threats against Williamsburg were not his own idea. A group of local slaves had offered to "take up arms" against Williamsburg in the governor's defense. News of the British government's offer of freedom spread widely among excited Virginia slaves.

In the closing days of 1775, as Dunmore marched inland from Norfolk through Princess Anne County, crowds of escaped slaves, including many women and children, flocked to his standard. With hundreds of new volunteers, Dunmore's officers formed a new "Ethiopian Regiment." Their uniforms included sashes bearing the inscription "Liberty to Slaves." (A second, smaller regiment was composed of white volunteers.) The Virginia "committee of safety" sent a force of militiamen and a Continental Army regiment. In the first major battle of the war in the South, at the hamlet of Great Bridge, on December 9, Dunmore's regular troops and volunteers attacked but failed to overrun the patriot position. Falling back on Norfolk, they were soon forced to withdraw to Royal Navy ships in the harbor. Dunmore attempted to maintain the Ethiopian Regiment offshore, but smallpox swept through the crowded vessels. Ultimately, the surviving members of the regiment were assigned to scattered locations, including Bermuda, Florida, and British regular forces later occupying New York.

Throughout the colonies, slaves spread word about Dunmore, the "African Hero." While gathered in cities or isolated on their own estates, masters active in the patriot struggle lived in fear. In South Carolina, in August 1775, a free black fisherman and boat pilot, **Thomas Jeremiah**, was accused of planning a general slave insurrection, to be supported by Royal Navy ships that he would guide into Charles Town harbor. Jeremiah, who owned slaves himself, had grown rich and probably stood out to white slave owners because of his business success, which made a mockery of the theory of white supremacy upon which slavery rested. Despite flimsy evidence, a kangaroo court quickly convicted Jeremiah, who was hanged. Escape plots, fears of insurrection, and the threat of British forces together preoccupied white Southerners. Even in the North, with significant concentrations of slaves in port cities and a vastly larger proportion of free black residents, rumors of slave conspiracies terrified local elites. Yet, in the seaport cities where artisans actively involved in politics had fostered the resistance movement, free blacks were well represented in the artisanal communities. A substantial number of black militiamen fought with distinction at Bunker Hill and Breed's Hill. When Washington, an extensive owner of slaves, arrived outside Boston, he found himself in the intriguing position of commanding black troops. He worked out his own idea of a judicious policy, which the Congress later ratified: he ordered an end to the recruitment of "Slaves and Vagabonds" into the regular army but would not expel black soldiers already serving. In some regiments, such as in Connecticut, slaves took advantage of an offer of freedom in return for military service from the colonial authorities. Many dropped the slave names imposed by their masters and took new last names like "Liberty" or "Freedman" or even "Washington" to celebrate their new personal independence.

Common Sense

The colonists would long struggle with reconciling a fight supposedly for freedom with the racist practice of slavery. However, a significant number of Americans had traveled a long philosophical distance from when they considered themselves loyal British subjects. Beginning in January, copies of **Thomas Paine**'s pamphlet ***Common Sense*** began to circulate throughout the colonies. Over the year that followed, the pamphlet was reprinted no fewer than twenty-five times, with roughly half a million individual copies made. Paine was a virtually penniless Englishman fleeing to America from a failed career as a corset-maker and tax collector, but along with a letter of introduction from Franklin, he brought a style of written expression that was clear, sharp, elegant, and fearless. In Philadelphia, he found work as an editor, but he would make his mark as an author of one of the clearest arguments for the colonies' political independence.

With his skeptical, scientific turn of mind and his uncompromising temperament, Paine saved no respect for sacred traditions in his blunt pamphlet. His complete lack of deference was breathtaking. "The royal brute of Great Britain" was no guardian of his subjects' liberties. England was corrupt, not as a result of recent missteps or individually bad government ministers, but because kings by their nature tended to be corrupt tyrants. Governments existed to serve the people, not the other way around, and the British regime could not meet that basic requirement. "A government of our own," he proclaimed, "is our natural right." British rule brought no practical benefits, recent British military attacks made reconciliation unthinkable, and independence was no more likely to lead to intervention by foreign powers or civil wars among the colonies. Paine was not only angry at injustice, however, but his pamphlet also offered a vision of an optimistic American future. In his scripture-quoting yet fundamentally secular way, Paine reimagined America, as had earlier Puritans, as a shining city on a hill, a light to the rest of humanity:

> O! ye that love mankind! Ye that dare oppose not only the tyranny but the tyrant, stand forth! Every spot of the old world is overrun with oppression. Freedom hath been hunted round the Globe. Asia and Africa have long expelled her. Europe regards her like a stranger, and England hath given her warning to depart. O! receive the fugitive, and prepare in time an asylum for mankind.

Common Sense captured a growing public mood and helped to seal a permanent shift away from olive branches and petitions to the king to demands for a separate, new American nation.

DEBATING "INDEPENDENCY"

As the summer of 1776 wore on, heat, dust, and the usual unsavory smells permeated the streets of Philadelphia, and even the insides of its grand brick buildings. In the Pennsylvania state house, in a stifling hall filled for a second consecutive summer by weary delegates from thirteen colonies, the windows had to be closed to keep out the biting horseflies.

Some hoped the Congress would launch not just a war of political independence but a more profound social revolution as well. In writing to her husband in March of that year, **Abigail Adams** had playfully instructed him to "remember the Ladies, and be more generous and favourable to them than your Ancestors. . . . If perticuliar care and attention is not paid to the Laidies we are determined to foment a Rebelion, and will not hold ourselves bound by any Laws in which we have no voice, or Representation." John's effort to respond in kind betrayed mild indignation. America's revolution would in many ways be a conservative one, aimed at replacing one government ruled by rich elites with one headed by a different, local set of the privileged. Gender, racial and class inequality were not on the table in Philadelphia.

Some delegates still held out hope for reconciliation at the beginning of this summit, but the day was carried by those who advocated what they called "Independency." In early June, a small committee of delegates to the Second Continental Congress had been assigned to draft a declaration of independence for consideration by the whole. Sequestered in his boarding house, **Thomas Jefferson** of Virginia, diffident in public debate but both meticulous and forceful in written argument, sought to frame a case that would draw upon the delegates' shared experiences of recent years. Taking his wording sometimes directly from the English philosopher John Locke, Jefferson's declaration argued that "life, liberty and the pursuit of happiness" were natural rights possessed by all people and that governments that failed to protect those rights were no longer legitimate. The declaration listed alleged acts of tyranny committed by the British king and the Parliament: the closure of Boston Harbor after the Tea Party protest; the suspension of the right of trial by jury for cases involving smugglers; closing elected colonial assemblies; using foreign mercenaries to attack the colonists, and so on. Jefferson wrote that as a result of these violations of rights, the bonds between the British government and the colonies had been "dissolved."

With minor changes made by Jefferson's fellow committee members (John Adams and Benjamin Franklin),

Depiction of Bostonians tarring and feathering the exciseman.

his draft was brought before the delegates in the airless room on June 28. Eventually, the Congress reduced the length of the Declaration by one-fourth, eliminating Jefferson's more controversial passages condemning King George III for encouraging the transatlantic slave trade. Even though Jefferson himself owned slaves, he frequently attacked the institution of slavery as immoral: "[H]e [the king] has waged cruel war against human nature itself, violating its most sacred rights of life & liberty in the persons of a distant people, who never offended him, captivating and carrying them into slavery in another hemisphere, or to incur miserable death in their transportation thither . . . determined to keep a market where MEN should be bought and sold," read Jefferson's original draft. Jefferson then condemned the king for "suppressing every legislative attempt to prohibit or to restrain this execrable commerce . . ." Southern members of the Continental Congress, particularly from South Carolina and Georgia, disdained the argument that slavery was in any way "execrable" and insisted on deletion of this passage. Meanwhile, some Congressmen did not support slavery per se, but feared Jefferson's words would undermine support for independence on the part of both southern slave owners and New England merchants profiting from the slave trade. Some acknowledged the contradiction of proclaiming the universal right to liberty while holding human beings as property but decided the time to push for abolition of slavery had not arrived and that political independence from Great Britain remained the more important cause. However, they did not remove a reference to Lord Dunmore's offer of freedom to slaves who escaped from their masters and served in the British military or of the recent slave revolt supposedly plotted by Thomas Jeremiah. The final draft of the Declaration condemned the king for "inciting treasonable insurrections of our fellow citizens" and exciting "domestic insurrections among us." Regardless of the arguments it engendered about slavery, the Declaration itself had been improved in many ways from Jefferson's original draft. As historian Pauline Maier has written: "This was no hack editing job; the delegates who labored over the draft Declaration had a splendid ear for language."

Four days later, the delegates unanimously agreed on the core issue—"that these United Colonies are, and of right ought to be, Free and Independent States." Writing to his wife Abigail in Massachusetts, Adams confidently anticipated that "the Second Day of July 1776" would be "celebrated, by succeeding Generations, as the Great anniversary Festival. . . . It ought to be solemnized with Pomp and Parade, with Shows, Games, Sports, Guns, Bells, Bonfires and Illuminations from one End of this Continent to the other from this Time forward forever more." The Congress, however, quibbled about wording for another two days before ratifying a final draft on July 4 and sending the text to a printer. The die was cast. The "American Revolution" would not uproot society, but it would become one of those rare points at which startling new possibilities existed, and the range of possible outcomes stretched the limits of human imagination.

CREATING AMERICANS

Colonial newspapers did not begin to use the term "American" until the French and Indian War (1754-1763). During that conflict, leaders like Benjamin Franklin bemoaned how poorly the colonies cooperated with each other and would urge his peers to form a confederacy like that established by the Iroquois nation in New York. In September 1762, when Bostonians learned of the French surrender in the French and Indian Wars, a wild street party broke out with drunken revelers drinking toasts to King George III and celebrating the joys of being British, which to them meant being the freest people on Earth. It was a short distance geographically from that Boston scene to Lexington Green thirteen years later, but for many, a psychological chasm separated the two events. In Massachusetts and Virginia, in South Carolina and in New Hampshire, commoner and elite alike contemplated a life not as Englishmen. Their new identities remained to be determined.

Only about 40 percent of Americans supported independence while about 20 percent considered themselves British loyalists. The remainder sat nervously in the middle, not opposed to independence, but still hopeful for reconciliation with the throne. Regardless, the pro-independence forces won a rhetorical war. Those rebelling against the British government called themselves the "Patriots," thus making those loyal to the home country traitors or worse. In many ways, the American Revolution became a civil war, with the "Patriots" often torturing their opponents, whom they smeared as "Tories." Many Tories suffered the agonies of tarring and feathering. In these ritual punishments, "The offender was stripped to the waist, sometimes shorn, and daubed with hot tar and pitch," wrote historian Ann Fairfax Withington in her book *Towards a More Perfect Union: Virtue and the Formation of the American Republic*. "Then a pillow of goose feathers (or sometimes turkey or buzzard feathers, which had a stronger smell) was emptied over him, and he was carted through town . . .

One Tory was made to walk from New Milford, Connecticut, to Litchfield, about twenty miles, carrying one of his own geese the whole way. He was then tarred, made to pluck his own goose, feathered, drummed out of town, and forced to kneel down and thank the crowd for its leniency . . . [A tax collector in Pennsylvania was led to a duck hole] . . . where he was dunked for some time. Finally they tied him up with [a] grapevine and forced him . . . to praise the Americans as a generous, spirited, and much injured people.

No punishment for opposition to the Patriot cause was more creative or grotesque than that suffered by Jesse Dunbar of Halifax, Massachusetts. Dunbar had bought cattle from men who had accepted royal government appointments and, thus to some, was a traitor. They sewed him in the carcass of an ox that had just slaughtered and skinned, and carried him in a cart that shook and rattled on a very bumpy four-mile ride. The mob then demanded he pay a dollar to the people of Kingston. He was carted four more miles, Withington notes, to Duxbury where he was made to pay another dollar in ransom. Finally, he reached the house of one of the royal appointees, where he was made to pay one last dollar and was dumped on the roadside. In other cases, Patriots sought to humiliate Tories by chaining them to slaves, implying that they were slaves to the king in the way African Americans were the property of whites. Patriots celebrated liberty, but during the war, there would be little tolerance for pro-British dissent.

Protestants formed an overwhelming majority in the new American nation, but the Revolutionary War still opened up religious fissures. On Guy Fawkes Day on November 5, 1775, George Washington ordered his soldiers to not engage in "the ridiculous and childish custom of burning the Effigy of the Pope." As the author Arthur Goldwag observed in his book, *The New Hate: A History of Fear and Loathing on the Populist Right,* Washington feared that such anti-Catholic merriment would alienate potential allies in the former French colony in Quebec. Even though Catholics were a tiny minority in Revolutionary America (around 35,000 out of the total of just under 4 million), Washington hoped that toleration would win this group over to the Revolutionary cause, particularly in states where Catholics were more numerous, such as Maryland. "At such a juncture, and in such circumstances, to be insulting their Religion, is so monstrous, as not to be suffered or excused," Washington wrote to his officers. Nevertheless, only three of the thirteen colonies granted the right to vote to Catholics, and only in North and South Carolina and Rhode Island could Catholics hold public office. The law banned the opening of Catholic schools everywhere but Pennsylvania, and Virginia law stipulated that priests who entered its borders were subject to arrest. The Patriots celebrated freedom of conscience, but they did not yet embrace religious diversity.

The American Revolution would reveal not only the deep divisions between Tories and Patriots, and Protestants and Catholics, but also blacks and whites. If whites thought they fought for freedom by resisting the crown, many African Americans fought for their freedom by accepting British offers of emancipation in return for service in the royal army. Approximately 50 percent of the slaves in Georgia and 25 percent in South Carolina enlisted with the British. The issue of slavery would not be resolved until after the Civil War, with the ratification of the Thirteenth Amendment abolishing involuntary servitude in 1865. African Americans would be given the right to vote during Reconstruction, but that right for many blacks would quickly be stolen and not returned for another hundred years, until the Voting Rights Act of 1965. The Patriots boldly faced off the king and the Royal Army, but they ducked the issue of slavery and black rights, leaving another generation to fight a war over the issue—a war that would claim about 750,000 lives according to current estimates.

A deep divide separated men and women as well. Women remained without property rights. Any property they brought into a marriage passed to the ownership of their husbands. Laws barred women from seeking divorce even from abusive husbands, and, in the rare cases where divorces were granted (an action that usually required the approval of the state legislature), men almost always gained custody of the children. The Patriot faction answered to the need of merchants and farmers but ignored the pleas of women like Abigail Adams.

The United States in many ways was an accidental nation, the product of a long series of British mistakes. Even though the Parliament was less than representative in England itself, not granting the colonists in North America representation in that body proved to be a fatal mistake. Successive British governments had boxed themselves in, facing riots from the masses in England who already bore a heavy cost for the greatly expanded empire. Unable to raise taxes at home, the British had no choice but to shift some of the burden to the Americans. However, the Parliament proved unwilling to grant representation to the colonies, thus delegitimizing any taxes Parliament would impose, even if the funds went toward the colonies' defense.

Foolish measures by the British government to ensure compliance with the new taxes, like requiring accused tax dodgers to face trial in military courts where they would be denied their accustomed right to a trial by jury, only alienated the colonists further. When the British shut down uncooperative elected assemblies that protested the taxes, as happened in New York, it only granted further credence to the extremists like Samuel Adams who argued that the colonists were treated like second-class citizens and denied basic freedoms guaranteed by Britain's unwritten constitution. As hypocritical as the complaint was when voiced by white Americans, many thought it was no exaggeration that the colonists were being "enslaved" by the crown.

It may be one thing to be opposed to something— across the colonies, the so-called Patriots rose up against British taxes and British military occupation—but it was not always altogether clear for what larger purpose the colonists were pledging "their lives, their liberties, and their sacred honor," to quote the Declaration of Independence. The new nation waging a War of Independence from Great Britain between 1775 and 1783 called itself the "United States," but these former colonies were united in name only. Even militarily, the states would frequently not cooperate, with several refusing to contribute a fair share of soldiers or the tax money requested by the Continental Congress needed to supply Washington's army. Defining what was meant by the word "American" and who constituted "the people" who supposedly held sovereignty in the new republic, remained a work in progress.

Chronology

1764 Parliament enacts the Sugar Act.
Parliament enacts the Currency Act.

1765 Parliament enacts the Stamp Act
Virginia Resolves protesting the Sugar Act.
Hanging in effigy of Americans supporting the British Parliament begins.
Stamp Act Congress convenes in New York.
Sons of Liberty response against British taxes

1766 The Parliament repeals the Stamp Act and passes Declaratory Act.

1767 Parliament enacts Townshend Acts.
Massachusetts Circular Letter stirs opposition to the Townshend Acts.

1770 Boston Massacre.
Parliament repeals most of the Townshend Acts.

1773 Parliament implements the Tea Act.
Boston Tea Party.

1774 Parliament passes Intolerable or Coercive Acts.
Parliament passes the Quebec Act.
Lord Dunmore dissolves the Virginia legislature.
The First Continental Congress convenes.

1775 Paul Revere and William Dawes rides.
Battles of Lexington and Concord.
Second Continental Congress convenes.
The Congress approves the creation of the Continental Army and appoints George Washington its commander.
The Battle of Bunker Hill.
King George rejects Olive Branch Petition.
Parliament passes the Prohibitory Act.
Lord Dunmore proclaims freedom to defecting slaves.
Americans lose Battle of Quebec.

1776 *Common Sense* published.
The British withdraw from Boston.
The Second Continental Congress approves the Declaration of Independence.

Review Questions

1. Why were British laws such as the Sugar Act, the Stamp Act, and the Townshend Revenue Act so controversial in the colonies? What motivated these laws, what arguments did men like Patrick Henry make against such legislation, and what was the response of the British government to these criticisms?

2. What social divisions tore at American society in the 1760s and early 1770s?

3. How did attitudes toward the British monarchy evolve in England and the American colonies during the 1600s and 1700s?

4. What role did slavery play in the early days of the American Revolution?

5. How does the career of John Dickinson reveal the uncertainty Americans felt toward the British government and the possibility of revolution during the 1770s?

Glossary of Important People and Concepts

Abigail Adams
John Adams
Samuel Adams
Ethan Allen
Benedict Arnold
Boston Massacre
Boston Tea Party
British East India Company
Battle of Bunker Hill
Common Sense
Currency Act (1764)
John Dickinson
Declaratory Act
Benjamin Franklin
Thomas Gage
George III
Sir George Grenville
John Hancock
Patrick Henry
Thomas Hutchinson
"Intolerable Acts"
Thomas Jefferson
Thomas Jeremiah
Battles of Lexington and Concord
John Murray, Fourth Earl of Dunmore
Lord Frederick North
Olive Branch Petition
James Otis, Jr.
Thomas Paine
Second Continental Congress
Sons of Liberty

SUGGESTED READINGS

Fred Anderson, *Crucible of War: The Seven Years' War and the Fate of Empire in British North America, 1754-1766* (2000).

Bernard Bailyn, *The Ideological Origins of the American Revolution* (1967).

___, *The Ordeal of Thomas Hutchinson* (1976).

Colin Bonwick, *The American Revolution* (1991).

___, *English Radicals and the American Revolution* (2011).

Robert M. Calhoon, *Revolutionary America: An Interpretive Overview* (1976).

Edward Countryman, *The American Revolution* (1985).

Marc Egnal, *A Mighty Empire: The Origins of the American Revolution* (1988).

Arthur Goldwag, *The New Hate: A History of Fear and Loathing on the Popular Right* (2012).

J. William Harris, *The Hanging of Thomas Jeremiah: A Free Black Man's Encounter With Liberty* (2011).

Merrill Jensen, *The Founding of a Nation: A History of the American Revolution, 1763-1776* (1968).

Pauline Maier, *From Resistance to Revolution: Colonial Radicals and the Development of the American Opposition to Britain, 1765-1776* (1972).

___, *American Scripture: Making the Declaration of Independence* (1997).

Edmund S. Morgan, *Birth of the Republic, 1763-1789* (1956).

___, *Inventing the People: The Rise of Popular Sovereignty in England and America* (1988).

Gary B. Nash, *The Urban Crucible: Social Change, Political Consciousness and the Origins of the American Revolution* (1979).

Thomas Paine, *Common Sense* (1776).

William Randolph Ryan, *The World of Thomas Jeremiah: Charles Town on the Eve of the American Revolution* (2012).

Sharon Salinger, *"To Serve Well and Faithfully": Labor and Indentured Servants in Pennsylvania, 1682-1800* (1987).

Paul Spickard, *Almost All Aliens: Race and Colonialism in American History and Identity* (2007).

Robert W. Tucker and David C. Hendrickson, *The Fall of the First British Empire: Origins of the War of American Independence* (1882).

Ann Fairfax Withington, *Toward a More Perfect Union: Virtue and the Formation of American Republics* (1991).

Gordon S. Wood, *The Radicalism of the Ameircan Revolution* (1991).

George Washington and Marquis de Lafayette at Valley Forge

Chapter Six

THE UNITED STATES AND THE AGE OF REVOLUTION

A "mini ice age" had gripped the Earth by the time of the American Revolution. This period of unusually cold weather began, roughly, in the mid-1300s and lasted until the mid-1800s. Unlike the phenomenon of global warming starting to occur in the late twentieth century, this variation of climate change likely did not result from human causes but derived instead from natural causes such as cycles in solar radiation or increased volcanic activity. The drop in temperatures was one reason that the Delaware River had frozen before General George Washington's famous crossing the night of December 25-26 and his attack on Hessian mercenaries stationed in Trenton. The plummet in temperatures accounted for the unusually harsh weather that tormented Washington's troops at the Valley Forge encampment in Pennsylvania from December 19, 1777 until June 19, 1778.

Many remember Valley Forge as an American low point during the War for Independence. "The Army was undersupplied with almost everything normally considered necessary to sustain life, shoeless feet leaving (as legend emphasizes) bloody footprints in the snow," wrote historian and George Washington biographer James Thomas Flexner. Food was short for man and beast, with the Army's horses starving. For many days at a time, most soldiers had nothing to eat but pieces of "firecake," a thin bread made from water and scant amounts of flour. In this way, the army stretched its limited stores of flour until it finally ran out completely. Resisting calls to ransack grain stores and seize remaining livestock from area farms, Washington sent foraging parties far and wide, into neighboring states, in desperate search of game.

Unable to directly tax the people and not receiving the requested funds from the states, the Congress urged Washington to seize what he needed from local inhabitants by force, if necessary, but Washington refused. The general knew that the British, when they occupied an area, would often seize livestock, food and dwellings, and alienated their civilian neighbors. Washington hoped he could maintain the support of the people by treating them fairly.

The villages near the city of Philadelphia had filled with refugees, so Washington also declined to seize control of buildings to house his soldiers, who were forced upon arrival to construct a series of huts 14 feet wide by 16 feet long by six and a half feet tall. Until they completed construction, the men lived in tents as the ice on the ground alternately melted and froze and kept their threadbare uniforms damp in the bitter winds. Washington himself, in an expression of sympathy, remained outdoors as well and slept in his own tent.

Dr. Albigence Waldo later remembered the miserable scene at the camp.

Poor food–hard lodging–cold weather–fatigue–nasty-clothes–nasty cookery–vomit half my time . . . There comes a bowl of beef soup–full of burnt leaves and dirt . . . There comes a soldier, his bare feet are seen though his worn-out shoes, his legs nearly naked from the tattered remains of an only pair of stockings, his breeches not sufficient to cover his nakedness, his shirt hanging in strings; his hair disheveled; his face meager . . . He comes and cries with an air of wretchedness and despair. "I am sick, my feet lame, my legs are sore, my body covered with this tormenting itch . . . and all the reward I shall get will be–"Poor Will is dead!"

As if witnessing the physical misery of his army were not enough, Washington endured the grumbling of Congress, whose members grew impatient (as Flexner noted) with his failure in three years to defeat the greatest military power in the Western world. Washington had not yet defeated the main British Army, Flexner wrote, but only isolated outposts at places like Trenton and Princeton. The British, meanwhile, occupied New York City and Philadelphia, the two largest American cities, and much of the South. "General George Washington made a dashing figure on horseback and was revered by his troops, but he had little background in the art of military drills and training," wrote author Randy Shilts. Many in Congress wanted to fire Washington and replace him with General Horatio Gates.

Washington himself worried about the poor training of his Continental Army, its lack of discipline when marching in formation, the frequency with which soldiers disobeyed orders and the high desertion rate. Volunteer militias not part of Washington's professional army in particular drove the general to distraction. "Their lack of discipline made them careless of sanitation (disease competes with combat as a killer)," said historian Garry Wills in his book **A Necessary Evil: A History of American Mistrust of Government**. "Their staggered and short enlistment times were interrupted even more by their desertion rate (over 20 percent), which gave Washington grounds for some scathing comments on the militias' performance. As his officers struggled to create conditions of discipline in the Continental Army, the use of auxiliary forces from the militias broke down what had been painfully built up."

Militias occasionally would abandon the field of battle if it were the agricultural growing season or if a professional officer from the Continental Army offended them. As the military historian Don Higginbotham put it, "When required to stay for extended lengths of time in the field far from home, when mixed closely with sizable bodies of Continentals, and when performing against Redcoats [British soldiers] in open combat, the militias were at their worst. Nothing in their modest training, not to mention their normally deficient equipment and supplies, prepared them for [military] . . . duties."

In Paris, the American ambassador Benjamin Franklin believed he had found a solution to the Continental Army's lack of professionalism in the person of **Baron Frederich Wilhelm Ludolf Gerhard Augustin von Steuben**. The Prussian, a self-proclaimed German nobleman, had little working knowledge of English, but with a letter of introduction from Franklin, as well as an entourage that included an Italian greyhound, he made a big impression. In fact, "Baron von Steuben" was a bit of a con artist, and had no title but was an impoverished Prussian army veteran and soldier of fortune who had served in the Seven Years War (1754-1761) in Europe during which Russian troops took him prisoner. He later served in the army of Prussian King Frederick II, reaching the rank of captain. He then served in the military of the prince of Hohenzollern-Hechingen.

Franklin heard stories about von Steuben's military skills. For his part, the Prussian falsely claimed not only that he was a baron, but also that he was a general. Nevertheless, von Steuben possessed a genuine mastery of advanced methods of drill and training. "Franklin was convinced that the Prussian penchant for order and discipline was precisely what the American forces needed if they were to prevail in their uphill fight against the well-trained British Army," Shilts wrote.

Franklin was in communication with the Continental Congress, urging it to offer von Steuben a position on the Army's general staff. Franklin explained to von Steuben that the Americans would be unable to grant him a commission as a top officer or to even pay him a salary, which von Steuben accepted. However, when Franklin informed him that the cash-strapped Congress would not even be able to pay for his transportation to the United States, von Steuben declined the offer.

He planned to work for another German prince in Baden when a letter accusing him of homosexual behavior while in the service of Frederick II was placed in the hands of the prince of Hohenzollern-Hechingen. The relationship supposedly took place while von Steuben served in the Prussian military. This would be the first of many times such accusations dogged von Steuben. This charge represented a possible death sentence in Europe at the time. Even if von Steuben never faced criminal prosecution, the scandal would ruin his military career on the continent. "Whether true or false," John McAuley Palmer wrote, "it is certain the charge was made and that it was the determining influence in sending Steuben to America,"

Washington, who was sensitive about his army's shortcomings but had never been able to solve many of them, accepted the Baron at face value and appointed him as acting inspector general. The German translator who had been provided him was ignorant of military terminology, so von Steuben had to speak in French and rely on men like Washington's chief of staff Alexander Hamilton to relay the messages. "After his first review of Washington's troops, Steuben was discouraged," Shilts wrote in his book **Conduct Unbecoming: Gays and Lesbians in the U.S. Military**. "There was no uniformity among the regiments. Some drilled in the French style, others in the English, others in the Prussian. He set about writing a drill book. Every day, he issued new chapters in French, which were translated and then laboriously hand-copied for each brigade and regiment and company in the Army. Once the first chapter was completed, General Washington ordered one hundred top soldiers selected from the fourteen infantry brigades to form a model training brigade."

Von Steuben quickly earned the affection of his troops. He insisted on leading drills himself, memorizing the English terms such as "fix bayonets" and "charge." Shilts points out that in this era, American officers "did not perform such menial tasks." The troops saw von Steuben as one of them in spite of the language barrier. When troops made mistakes, he peppered his rants with one of the few English words he knew, "goddamn," and asked his translators to transmit his other more colorful curse words in English. "All this made Steuben immensely popular," Shilts said. "This was no effete European adventurer, but a military man who was going to win battles."

Within weeks, the troops were all following the Baron's precise instructions. Soon discipline and morale were improving as well. New recruits arrived during the spring, and news of the French alliance, arriving in May, provided further encouragement. Money from the French finally made it possible to pay von Steuben a salary. The Continental Army that faced the next year's campaign was actually much improved and more nearly equal in technical abilities to its British and Hessian foes.

Having often fled from British and Hessian troops charging forward with bayonets, Americans had never themselves mastered the use of the weapon until now. As they practiced their drills, they also learned to execute complex maneuvers with speed and precision. The Baron became a bona fide major general and also wrote a comprehensive set of training instructions and standard regulations, which was published by Congress in 1779 and served as the U.S. Army's official manual until 1812. Von Steuben's talents probably saved the American struggle for independence, but this did not lead to an acceptance of gays in the military. Just sixteen days after von Steuben's arrival, the army dismissed Lt. Gotthold Frederick Enslin for homosexual conduct after a military court found him guilty of sodomy and perjury. As Enslin stood in front of a formation of drummers, his sword was broken in half over his head as the drummers banged out a slow beat and his signs of rank were torn from his uniform. It could have been much worse for Enslin as military regulations allowed soldiers convicted of sodomy to be imprisoned or hanged. As Shilts notes, "Thomas Jefferson demonstrated his liberalism by proposing a year earlier that sodomy be punished by castration instead of death in the new penal code that would replace Virginia's colonial charter."

Meanwhile, von Steuben retired to a farm in upstate New York, living off a military pension. He wrote a proposal for a military academy that led to the establishment of West Point in 1802. He remained devoted to two young captains who had served as his aide-de-camps during the Revolution, naming them his "adopted children" and only heirs in his will. In Washington, D.C., a monument to his service stands across from the White House in Lafayette Square. A fort in Ohio and the town of Steubenville are also named in his honor.

THE BALANCE SHEET: BRITISH AND AMERICAN STRENGTHS AND WEAKNESSES

Before he signed the Declaration of Independence as the Second Continental Congress wrapped up its business in July of 1776 Ben Franklin, famous for his wit, engaged in a grim bit of literal gallows humor. Urging his Revolutionary comrades to stay united, Franklin said, "We must, indeed, all hang together, or most assuredly we shall all hang separately."

The prospect that the Americans might lose the Revolutionary War to Great Britain, and that the leaders of the revolt like Franklin, John Adams and George Washington might soon be swinging from a rope for treason against King George III must have seemed like a realistic possibility as the momentous year 1776 drew to a close. When Washington assumed command of the Continental Army in the summer of 1775, there must have been times when he questioned his sanity. The British advantages seemed overwhelming.

The British had built a world empire over the past century, repeatedly defeating European powerhouses like France and Spain. They controlled Canada and islands in the Caribbean, and held outposts in West Africa, India and South America. The British enjoyed a 2-1 population advantage over the Americans, with more than 8 million living in England, Scotland and Wales compared to just under 4 million in the 13 American colonies. The British had an existing professional army.

However, in spite of having a larger overall population, the British never turned that into a military manpower advantage. Poor and working class people held military careers in low esteem and were not eager to sign up for a war against their cousins in America. At the start of the Revolutionary War, their standing army was small, and it fell behind in its recruiting goals. In one three-month period during the war, only 200 British citizens enlisted in the armed forces. "The ardor of this nation in this cause has not risen to the pitch one could wish," Lord Frederick North, the head of the British cabinet, said following the battles of Lexington and Concord.

The British government began hiring mercenaries—paid soldiers not part of the regular British army, especially from six German states whose princes received payments for use of their soldiers. (The Prince of Brunswick, for example, got seven pounds for every soldier provided and another seven pounds for each one who died in service.) The largest group, the "**Hessians**," came from Hesse-Kassel. The princes profited from the arrangement, but the soldiers themselves lacked motivation. The 30,000 German mercenaries constituted about one-third of the total British forces during the Revolution. Of these, 12,000 did not survive and 5,000 deserted their posts in order to live permanently in America.

The British use of such a large number of hired guns probably backfired, underscoring the feeling of Americans that the British themselves had become an invading foreign force rather than countrymen. "While employment of mercenaries was customary in England's wars at a time when military service was low in the esteem of the common man, the use of the Hessians did more than anything else to antagonize the colonists, convince them of British tyranny, and stiffen their resolve," historian Barbara Tuchman said. Eventually the British government built its regular army to full, wartime size, fielding 90,000 regulars and mercenaries, but after a while the American armed forces reached a similar size.

The growing empire, connected and maintained by the most powerful navy on Earth, left the British rich in resources. In spite of their debt problems from previous imperial wars, the British also had one of the richest and perhaps the most sophisticated banking system in the world. They had an established, strong currency. The Industrial Revolution had already started in England, and British factories made the Empire's soldiers some of the best equipped in the world. The officer corps of the British Army and Navy had excellent training and extensive wartime experience.

The British also had a strong central government, which could have allowed for a clear chain of command and efficient decision-making. However, the government was financially strapped, and unfortunately for Great Britain, mediocrities filled the nation's leadership positions. When he ascended to the throne in 1760, King George III sought to assert greater royal power than his predecessor on the throne, his grandfather George II. Hampering his efforts, George suffered a major disability as the result of a blood disease, porphyria, which caused fits that his doctors interpreted as madness. At times George would be bound in a straitjacket and tied to a chair so he wouldn't be injured during his ravings. Some report that George suffered an early bout of this disease during the controversy over the Stamp Act in 1765, though he would mainly be afflicted with bouts of irrationality and delusions in his fifties, after the Revolutionary War ended. Doctors today think that medicines George took containing high levels of arsenic may have triggered the porphyria, which usually doesn't affect behavior in men.

George resented strong personalities who challenged his authority, thus he appointed to key government ministries less talented men who paid him deference. Hence, the lengthy tenure of Lord Frederick North, who would reign as prime minister from 1770 to 1782, during the critical final five years before the American Revolution and during the entire combat phase of that war. Throughout his lengthy tenure, North would repeatedly beg King George to relieve him of his duties. North knew he was in over his head. In one letter he wrote to the monarch, he argued that the first minister should be "a man of great abilities, who can choose decisively and carry his determination authoritatively into execution . . . and be capable of forming wise plans and of combing and connecting the whole force and operations of government . . . I am not that man."

Lethargic in temperament, North had developed a habit of falling asleep during debates while he served in Parliament. "Fat-cheeked and corpulent, with bulging eyes, he bore a startling resemblance to George III, which was often made the subject of ribald suggestion . . ." wrote Tuchman. "When appointed chief minister, he was 38, awkward in movement with weak eyesight and a tongue too large for his mouth 'which rendered his articulation somewhat thick though not at all indistinct.'" Though he received a quality education at Eton and Oxford University, had traveled and achieved fluency not just in French, German and Italian, but also classic Greek and Latin, and had a sense of humor, North had a hard time asserting himself in the cabinet and was plagued by self-doubts. He had urged King George to avoid war with the Americans if at all possible. Even as the Parliament debated sending three regiments across the Atlantic to supplement General Thomas Gage's force in New England, North proposed what he called the Conciliatory Proposition, which would have exempted any colony from taxation provided it paid for its own expenses for governance and defense at amounts the Parliament and the King approved. The Parliament rejected the proposed compromise and North, out of unwavering loyalty, backed his king's decision to declare the colonies in a state of rebellion and to respond militarily. Charles James Fox, who served with him in the cabinet, described him as lacking an air of authority. He was "far from leading the opinions of the other ministers that he seldom gave his own and generally slept the greater part of the time he was with them." As Tuchman argued, "This did not conduce to firm collective policy."

Another key player in the British government, **George Germain**, the secretary of state for the American Department, had been court-martialed and kicked out of the military during the French and Indian War when he refused to follow the orders of a superior officer he personally disliked in the Battle of Minden in 1759 in modern-day Germany. Germain would be in charge of promoting and demoting generals and managing logistics, and helped form the British government's war plans. Germain reinforced North in some of his worst miscalculations, including that Britain could win the war by the conventional means that had brought victory previously against European powers. He also poorly communicated his intentions to officers, which would play a major role in the decisive British loss at the Battle of Yorktown in 1781.

Perhaps the most serious British shortcoming in the war was simple overconfidence. The British had defeated several vastly richer and more militarily powerful European rivals like France, the Netherlands, and Spain in the past century, and the British military and government never took George Washington's Continental Army seriously. The British military command had been unimpressed with the performance of the American militias in the French and Indian Wars and had not been particularly awed by George Washington's performance as an officer in that conflict. Unable to conceive that the Americans could win the Revolution, the British never fully committed their potentially vast resources to the war.

While the Americans had gifted leaders like George Washington, John Adams and Ben Franklin, they faced their own extensive challenges. The white American population was thinly stretched along the Eastern seaboard, extending deeply inland, where they faced a threat not only from the vast British military forces, but hostile Indian nations who had seen land confiscated and their peoples slaughtered for almost two centuries by the white conquerors. About 20 percent of the white colonists opposed the revolution, and whites always had to worry, particularly in the South, about the potential revolt of 600,000 abused and exploited slaves, many of whom had already signed up with the British armed forces in exchange for emancipation. The American military was improvised, with many of the soldiers not even professionals but militiamen who came and went as they pleased. The Americans had no navy. The Americans had no banking system to fund the war or even a currency. Gold and silver was in short supply in the 13 would-be independent states. The United States was still overwhelmingly a rural nation, with a microscopic manufacturing base to arm its troops, compared to the British juggernaut.

On top of all, the Americans labored under one of the weakest central governments ever devised by humanity. The American government had no chief executive. The Continental Congress made military decisions by committee. Given no power to tax directly, the Congress could only plead with each state to contribute a proportionate share of the cost and military manpower. The states, however, often functioned like 13 separate republics. Each state had its own financial hardships and was reluctant to send desperately needed funds to the Congress. States also worried about the safety of their own borders and often put local needs ahead of the needs of the embryonic nation. In Vermont, Ethan Allen and his Green Mountain Boys militia ostensibly fought for the American cause, but they were embroiled in a secessionist struggle with New York and during the Revolution secretly negotiated with the British government about the possibility of becoming a separate province of the Empire.

On the plus side of the ledger, the Americans possessed one powerful psychological advantage. The war would be fought on their turf, on familiar terrain. Already deeply in debt, the British would spend a fortune transporting troops and supplies across the Atlantic and from battlefield to battlefield. British soldiers found themselves mostly surrounded by unfriendly locals who gave emotional and material support, and military intelligence, to the American troops. Communications with the British government were slow, with transatlantic voyages taking six or more weeks. Sometimes, months elapsed before officers in the field received orders from the government. American soldiers likely were more motivated throughout the war, because the British threatened their farms and homes. They also saw as fighting for political independence and liberty, which probably meant more to them than maintaining an Empire meant to the so-called "Redcoats." Finally, British victory depended on holding large swaths of American territory. The British lost political control of an area the moment they left. Fighting at home, surrounded by a mostly supportive population, George Washington and other American commanders could afford to avoid major direct battles with the British, striking only when an advantage arose, and then disappearing into the vast American forests. This led to a long war, with mounting costs and casualties ultimately sapping the British will to fight.

THE BATTLE FOR NEW YORK

The Revolutionary War, nevertheless, started out badly. "These are the times that try men's souls," wrote Thomas Paine, in an essay called appropriately *The Crisis*, printed in Philadelphia on December 19, 1776. "The summer soldier and the sunshine patriot will, in this crisis, shrink from the service of his country; but he that stands it NOW, deserves the love and thanks of man and woman." Paine scribbled out his ringing sentences at one of the grimmest junctures in the war. Just months earlier the British had captured New York City, and it appeared that General Washington was on the run.

Following the withdrawal of British troops from Boston in the spring of 1776, Washington relocated his 19,000-man force to New York City. He knew New

Thomas Paine's essays on freedom rallied tens of thousands to the cause of American independence.

York would be a major objective for the British General **William Howe**. The British hoped to put a quick end to the American rebellion that had begun in Lexington and Concord, Massachusetts on April 19 of the previous year by cutting off the colonies from trade with the outside world. They planned to do this by occupying important port cities like New York. Once they strangled the United States economically, overwhelming Washington's disorganized and poorly trained forces would theoretically be easy. Washington felt he had no choice but to make a defensive stand in New York, despite being outnumbered on land and sea. He worried about the general public who might interpret the loss of such a major city as a dangerous blow. Yet Washington was hampered by illness among his soldiers and faulty intelligence. Unable to predict where Howe would strike, he divided his already smaller force, sending one half to fortified positions in Manhattan, most dug in at fortifications in Brooklyn Heights, and the other half to **Long Island**. Washington hoped to re-create the conditions that led to high British casualties when the British tried to scale heights while facing murderous fire in the Battle at Bunker Hill. He tried to draw the British into again trying to seize high ground in Brooklyn Heights from entrenched, well-protected forces.

Even as the Continental Congress put the finishing touches on the Declaration of Independence in Philadelphia July 2, British General William Howe landed an invading force that eventually numbered 30,000 British regulars and hired guns from Germany at Staten Island. As was his custom, Howe waited before his attack. When he moved, he avoided Brooklyn Heights and instead attacked Long Island, an area with strong pro-British sentiment. Later, on August 27, Hessians faked a major frontal assault on the Heights while Howe's main force bypassed the Heights through an unguarded, wooded Jamaica Pass and attacked the Americans from the left and the rear. Fearing they were surrounded, the Americans panicked. Washington uncharacteristically lost control and began beating officers and common soldiers who ran too near to him with his riding crop. He undertook a Herculean effort to restore order as his forces withdrew across the East River to Manhattan. For the first of many times in his career, Washington got a break. The always lumbering Howe failed to pursue Washington's men, or to cut off their path of retreat with his Navy fleet, (commanded by his brother Richard Howe) when they were at their most vulnerable, letting the Continental Army live to fight another day.

Howe had reasons not to take up the chase. "In common with his governmental superiors overseas, Howe believed that the rebellion had been fomented by a few desperate men, who had terrorized the American majority, which still loved their sovereign," Washington biographer James Thomas Flexner wrote. "By making fools of these desperate men—as he had just done—Howe would encourage the well-disposed majority to brush them aside." In fact, during the struggle in New York, secret negotiations had taken place with representatives of the Continental Congress and representatives of the British government, but the talks failed because the Americans insisted on recognition of their political independence. There would be no easy way out of the struggle for either side.

As the British took control of most of New York City, a devastating fire, most likely from accidental causes, raged the night of September 21. High winds and dry weather fed the flames. The blaze obliterated up to a fourth of the city. Both the British and the Americans accused each other of deliberately starting the inferno. The fire forced British troops to quarter themselves in private homes, which caused resentment, especially when **Tories**—Americans loyal to Great Britain—began to pour into the city, which would remain partly in ruins and would suffer from poor sanitation for the rest of the war. In a sign of how badly divided New York—a port city that suffered economically from the colonies' loss of trade with Britain—was over the war, when the Howe brothers offered amnesty to New Yorkers who would lay down their arms and swear allegiance, thousands took up the offer.

Howe again waited, this time until November 16, when he finally forced the rest of Washington's men out of Manhattan but for two encampments, Fort Washington on the highest point in Manhattan overlooking the Hudson River and Fort Lee on the New Jersey side of the waterway. Howe crushed the 3,000-man force in northern Manhattan, attacking the fortress from three sides. He paid for this victory dearly, however, with the loss of

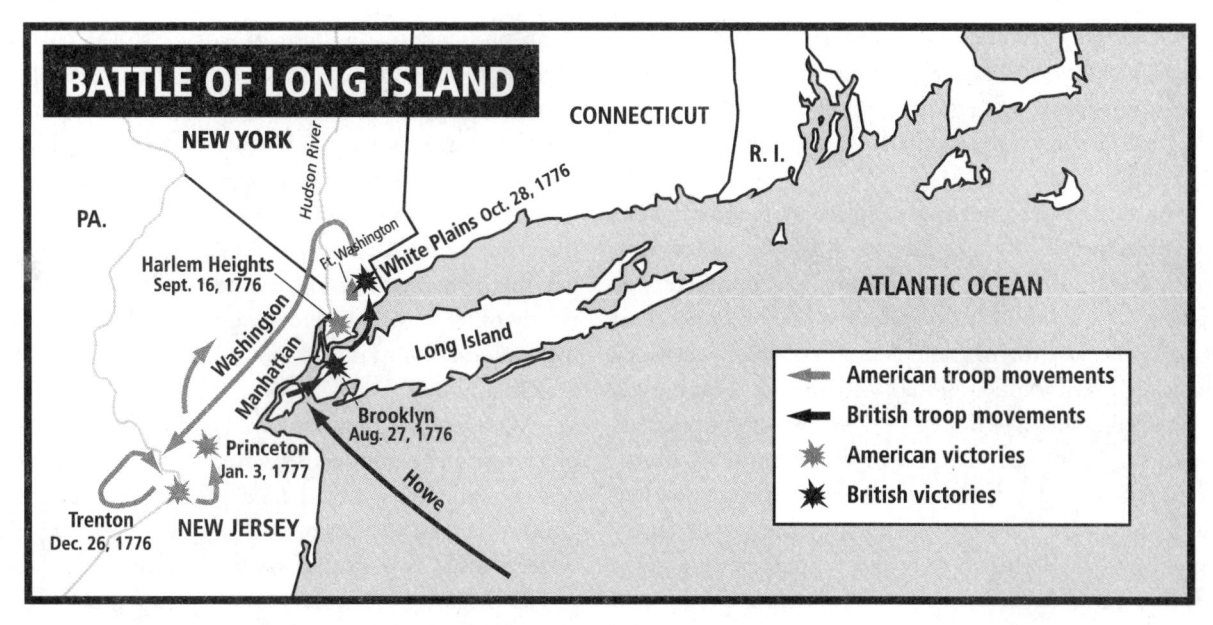

Map 6.1 Battle of Long Island and Washington's Retreat from New York

almost 500 men, though a much heavier cost awaited the Americans. Some Americans who surrendered to the British were killed by resentful soldiers, while others were packed onto prison ships in New York harbor where more than 11,000 imprisoned soldiers and civilians died in horrific squalor during the war. Washington himself, from the New Jersey side of the river, watched helplessly. Self-control was everything to him, even though at times he struggled to keep his temper in check. But now, for once, he lost his composure completely and as one of his aides later admitted "wept, with the tenderness of a child."

A SURPRISE COMEBACK: THE BATTLE OF TRENTON

To many observers, the loss of New York City looked like a grave defeat for the colonial rebels, but Washington soon began to implement his primary strategy: prolonging the conflict. While avoiding direct confrontations with larger and superior British forces, he would instead attack smaller enemy contingents when the opportunity presented itself and gradually reduce England's desire to continue. Washington's army slipped across the Hudson River into the woods of New Jersey, eventually crossing the Delaware River into Pennsylvania. One of General William Howe's chief subordinates, **Lord Charles Cornwallis**, crossed the Hudson with some 5,000 British and Hessian troops and maintained the pursuit. As New Jersey fell under British control, patriots fled, Loyalists re-emerged, and many switched sides. Richard Stockton, a New Jersey delegate to Congress and a signer of the Declaration of Independence, was captured by a Loyalist band, imprisoned in New York, and persuaded to pledge his allegiance to the King as a condition of amnesty.

Meanwhile, Washington's still mostly green, untested army shrank with each mile it marched, men deserting because of the miserably cold weather and poor morale or leaving once their enlistment period ended. On December 2, as Washington's remaining units began arriving at the Delaware River crossing at Trenton, they numbered little more than 3,000 men. Pennsylvania militiamen arriving to help the army across the river were shocked to find the men of the Continental Army staggering onward, covered in sores and clothed in tattered rags.

When the British and Hessians arrived in Trenton on December 8, Philadelphia, a short distance down river, seemed in immediate danger. Among those suddenly fleeing the city was the Second Continental Congress, which reconvened in Baltimore. "'Tis surprising," Paine wrote, "to see how rapidly a panic will sometimes run through a country." Despite Howe's proximity to Washington's disheveled force, the British general once again failed to pursue Washington's men, allowing them to escape and missing an opportunity for a knockout blow.

Howe and Cornwallis planned to end their campaign for the year, without invading Pennsylvania and forcing another battle. The chase had served their purpose well, and they had reason to hope that the Continental Army might keep fading away on its own, but Howe would be disappointed. As news spread about the conditions of Washington's men, Patrick Henry (now Virginia's governor under its new constitution as an independent state) ordered militia leaders in each county to gather blankets from residents "and draw upon me for the Amount of the Purchase." On December 20 and 23, two vessels arrived in Philadelphia from the West Indies loaded with blankets and woolens, as well as arms and munitions. Captained by commissioned officers of the small Continental Navy, they had successfully run the Royal Navy's blockade of the Atlantic coast.

As desperately-needed supplies arrived, brigades of troops previously assigned by Washington to other commanders arrived in Pennsylvania as reinforcements. In fact, new infantry units were also on the horizon, as appeals by Washington and his officers to the various states recruited more men than anticipated. Making use of lessons learned the hard way, Washington reorganized his forces to improve command and control. Colonel **Henry Knox**, a self-taught artillery expert, attached companies with field guns to each of the new infantry brigades. Morale began to recover. Soldiers were given newly printed copies of Paine's "**American Crisis**" and read them out loud to their comrades gathered in small crowds.

Unlike Howe, Washington felt too much political pressure to wait out the winter. The general feared that his tenacious fighting men were doomed unless they could fight and actually win. Many enlistments were also due to expire at the end of the year, which would further reduce his forces. Thus, he decided to make the first of many timely surprise attacks during the Revolution, leading his men in a perilous crossing of the ice-clogged Delaware River on Christmas night to seize Trenton, New Jersey from a Hessian garrison.

Washington's men set out when the bitterly cold winds "blew a hurricane," in the words of one soldier. Arriving at the ferry for the crossing at 6 p.m., Washington divided his men into three groups who crossed at different points along the river. As they crossed, the rain and sleet turned to snow, the temperature dropped sharply, and the waters, roiling at first, became choked with drifting ice. Standing in several inches of freezing water in his boat, Washington was rowed across by Massachusetts infantrymen who worked at home as fishermen and seamen. Then he stood by the shore, watched, and waited as the other boats struggled through the ice, marveling as his men crossed without the loss of a soldier or being discovered by the nearby Hessians.

"Trenton was nine miles away, but there was no turning back," Flexner wrote. ""It was a desperate march. Men who lay down to rest for a moment never rose again." About 2,400 Americans arrived at Trenton in the morning light and found it nearly unguarded. But General Knox positioned the field cannons within the town and began firing at point-blank range. Many of the Hessians' heads ached with hangovers from the previous evening's Christmas celebrations. The shells exploding all around them probably made the pain worse. In the chaos, the Hessian commander could not organize a successful counterattack. "The battle at Trenton was an anti-climax to the army's getting there," Flexner noted. "The Hessians were caught by complete surprise. Awakened from sleep, blinded by driving snow when they tried to look in the direction from which the patriot fire came, they could not get into formation—and they did not know how to fight in any other way. Surrender came quickly. When there was a bloody lump in the snow, it invariably represented a German body . . ."

Washington's men killed 22 of the German soldiers of fortune and wounded 98, while capturing about 1,000 prisoners and laying their hands on badly needed muskets, gunpowder and artillery pieces. In combat, the Americans suffered only five wounded (one of whom was future president James Monroe, who received a musket ball in his shoulder), though a number comparable to the Hessian losses may have died in the coming days from illness brought on from exposure to extreme cold. Nevertheless, Washington described his losses as "trifling." The Battle of Trenton held minimal to no strategic significance, but it greatly improved the spirits of the fighting men and increased the confidence of civilians in the Continental Army's prospects. The psychological impact was electric. Many throughout the states viewed it as providential, a deliverance from evil by the grace of God. Others who had lost faith in the army and its commander, in the midst of defeat and retreat, now gained a lasting confidence in both. Before returning to Philadelphia, John Hancock addressed Washington on behalf of the Continental Congress. "Troops properly inspired, and animated by a just confidence in their leader will often exceed expectation, or the limits of probability," Hancock wrote. "As it is entirely to your wisdom and conduct, the United States are indebted for the late success of your arms."

ANOTHER SURPRISE AT PRINCETON

Washington still worried about the number of soldiers whose enlistment would expire in a matter of days, at year's end. He was aware of his emotional effect on the troops, and their growing devotion to him. The Massachusetts soldiers who had rowed him across the Delaware River were among those whose enlistments were expiring at year's end. Scrambling for cash, Washington managed to pull together a bounty (a cash reward of ten dollars in hard coin) for those who re-enlisted, but he also held a ceremonial meeting with regiments from New England and appealed personally to his men, all of them now veterans, acknowledging their bravery and hardships.

Washington crossing the Delaware

He led his men in a crossing back across the Delaware to return them to the scene of their recent victory in order to add emotional power to his pleas. "My brave fellows," Washington said, "You have done all I have asked you to do, and more than could be reasonably expected, but your country is at stake; your wives, your houses, and all that you hold dear. You have worn yourself out with fatigues and hardships, but we know not how to spare you . . . The present is emphatically the crisis which is to decide our destiny." More than half of his men would re-enlist. Of those who committed to stay on during this pep talk near the Delaware River, nearly half would be killed in battle or by disease without ever making it back home.

Meanwhile, the British made a serious effort finally to battle Washington and his men before winter conditions ended hostilities for the season. General Cornwallis led 8,000 British regulars and Hessians south from New York to, as the British say, "bag the fox." Eager to avenge the embarrassment at Trenton, Cornwallis's troops quick-marched and located Washington's camp right before sundown the evening of January 2. Yet again, a British general paused. Cornwallis waited until sunrise when his men would have light to see their foes, but by the time the British awakened for their assault and reached the American encampment, they found nothing but lonely, burning campfires. Washington had evacuated his troops during the dark hour, muffling the wheels of his wagons and artillery to conceal the noise, and quietly slipped around Cornwallis, heading down a back road toward New Jersey. He left a handful of soldiers behind in the dead of the night to keep the campfires roaring and lull the British into thinking their prey remained nearby.

Washington's unconventional escape, which took him in the opposite direction of patriot-held territory and supplies, flabbergasted Cornwallis. As Flexner wrote:

> This maneuver had not been foreseen as a possibility by the British since for a professional army it would have been utter madness. Washington had left a force that was stronger than his own between his army and all patriot-held territory. The idiot, by God, blocked his possibility of retreat and also cut his own supply lines!

Washington was, in fact, for the first time making complete use of the advantages of his army. Men fighting for their own liberties did not need a perpetual infusion of supplies. Being devoid of heavy equipment and able to think for themselves, they could move twice as fast as a professional army. Unless actually cornered, they were as hard to catch as quicksilver.

"The Fox" was giving his pursuers some harsh lessons in guerilla warfare, difficult for the traditional British military to grasp, so accustomed in the tradition of tightly aligned formations facing each other on open ground. Officers like Cornwallis did not know it, but an older era of warfare had ended and a new one had begun. This the British would learn to their sorrow in other hostile countries they would occupy in the nineteenth century, including Afghanistan.

Washington led his men toward **Princeton, New Jersey**. As the sun rose January 3, Washington's men happened upon another isolated British regiment, commencing a quick battle in which the Continental Army enjoyed a 5-1 advantage. In a closely fought battle, with Washington appearing on horseback at the head of the Pennsylvania infantry, the general rallied the men forward against the British line marching into Princeton to score a second startling victory within two weeks. For a moment Washington got greedy, wishing to plan further attacks, but his lieutenants pointed out "the harassed state of our own troops . . . and the danger of losing the advantage we had gained by aiming at too much." Still keeping clear of Cornwallis's main force, the army set off for the mountains of northern New Jersey, settling there for the rest of the winter.

For many Americans, Washington was already passing into the realm of legend. General Howe, meanwhile, had retreated to New Brunswick, New Jersey, more than sixty miles northeast of Philadelphia, which remained safe for the time being. For Howe and his superiors in London, the year 1776 had ended badly, given the scale and expense of the British effort. The real purpose of the British winning successive battles, and conquering and occupying territory, was to discourage and demoralize the "damned Rebels," and inspire the Loyalists, so that the army, the Continental Congress, state governments, and the patriot cause would all collapse on their own. For a time it had appeared to be working, but no longer.

In American minds, the New York-New Jersey campaign in 1776 captured the agony and the ecstasy of the entire revolutionary experience: humiliating retreats, barely avoided disasters, lucky breaks, inexplicable British blunders, and victories pulled off by Washington like rabbits from a magician's hat. The next six years would be grueling and would indeed try men's souls, but Washington's greatest accomplishment was not any particular successful battle plan, but his ability to keep an army together and its most determined core motivated, until the British will to fight collapsed.

WASHINGTON'S BRAIN TRUST

As indispensable as Washington was, even the leadership of the Continental Army, like the Revolution itself, represented a collective effort. The commander-in-chief was overworked and constantly had to consider the delicate political implications of some of the most mundane tasks. Dealing with the egos of Congress alone could have been a full-time job for the thinly-stretched commander. Some, like John Adams, were jealous. Adams had pushed for Washington's appointment, but he felt flashes of resentment when he saw the adulation showered on the general even at the beginning of the war. On June 23, 1775, when Washington received a big parade to mark his departure from Philadelphia to assume his duties as commander-in-chief in Massachusetts, Adams steamed. "Such is the pride and pomp of war," he wrote privately in his study. "I, poor creature worn out with scribbling for my bread and my liberty, low in spirits and weak in health, must leave others to wear the laurels which I have sown."

Sometimes, the laurels must have seemed like a crown of thorns. Some members of Congress were constant critics, looking for an excuse to sack him. As mentioned earlier, as Washington and his troops suffered the hardships of Valley Forge in the winter of 1777-78, some in Congress grew impatient with the length of the war and the scarcity of Washington battlefield victories, and spoke loudly of dismissing Washington and replacing him with Horatio Gates.

Pressure came not just from his political superiors in the Congress, but sometimes from his fellow officers. Congress offered high-ranking commissions and responsibilities to individuals such as **Charles Lee**, who led a portion of the army in the New York campaign, and Gates, then stationed at Ticonderoga who had little respect for Washington and allowed this to become known. "Charles Lee had the reputation of being a military genius," Flexner observed. "Many patriots regretted that because he was a recent immigrant from England (and was so eccentric), he could not be commander in chief instead of Washington.

After a distinguished service in the British regular army, Lee had adventured to Poland, where he was a major general and accompanied a Russian army against the Turks. Having, on his return to England, written radical pamphlets, and insulted George III to his face, he had settled in America. He was tall and emaciated, dirty of clothes and body, voluble, loudmouthed, seemingly brilliant, best characterized by his Indian name, "Boiling Water." He felt that he was making too big a sacrifice in agreeing to be commanded by the amateur Washington.

Wisely, however, Washington recognized some of his own limitations, and he found subordinate officers who were loyal, capable, listened to advice. Over time, the officer corps became a training ground for future national leaders. One of the most exceptional examples would be **Alexander Hamilton**, a native of the West Indies island of Nevis who was studying at King's College (now Columbia University) in New York at the outbreak of the Revolution. Young Hamilton responded to an appeal for the defense of the city by recruiting a full company of artillerymen with himself as captain.

Hamilton had no prior military training or experience (apart from a great deal of reading), but through the campaign from New York to Trenton and Princeton, he led his men energetically and directed cannon fire with consummate skill. That winter, Washington asked him to join his staff as a personal assistant. Hamilton had a particularly brilliant mind regarding budgets and logistics. As Washington's indispensable aide still in his early twenties, he became notable himself. Able to anticipate the general's own thinking, he was soon relied upon to exercise his own judgment in drafting correspondence and offering advice. Hamilton rarely left Washington's side during the war. A man of enormous political and social ambition, he craved the social acceptance that would come with battlefield victories, but Washington repeatedly reminded him that he was too valuable making all the parts of the war machinery fit in the command center for his life to be risked on the battlefield.

SEEKING ALLIES

As the war progressed, American leaders sought, and sometimes received, assistance from the rest of the world. For the delegates in Congress, a major purpose of declaring independence was winning military and financial aid from foreign powers that would otherwise avoid interfering in what was basically a British civil war. Smuggled shipments of arms and supplies from the West Indies proved vital during the Battle of Trenton and other engagements, but patriot leaders had little hope of prevailing in an extended war without help on a far larger scale. France had fought seven wars with England since 1627, and in the 1700s had been defeated by the English in the War of the Spanish Succession (1702-1713), the War of the Austrian Succession (1740-1748), and the French and Indian War (1754-1763). France and England battled for world supremacy, and their eighteenth-century wars had been global in scale. France might ally itself with the United States not because it supported the ideas of democracy and human equality called for in the Declaration of Independence (France was a monarchy where the king's power was considered absolute), but on the principle of "the enemy of my enemy is my friend."

Early in 1776, the delegates in the Continental Congress dispatched Silas Deane, a purchasing agent, to send out diplomatic feelers in Paris. Deane made little headway, so as the military situation grew more grim, the Congress sent a member who had become a global celebrity, one of the Pennsylvania delegates, Benjamin Franklin. Franklin displayed dazzling diplomatic gifts in France, not only because of his fluency in French, his charm, and his sometimes uproarious sense of humor, but also because a cult had grown up around him across the Atlantic. The French admired his literary skills and his role in the American Revolution thus far. His scientific experiments in electricity fascinated the French, who saw in him a harbinger of a more advanced age.

"Franklin's . . . popularity was so widespread that it does not seem exaggerated to call it a mania," wrote European historian Simon Schama in his epic *Citizens: A Chronicle of the French Revolution*. "Mobbed wherever he went, and especially whenever he set his foot outside his house in Passy, he was probably better known by sight than the King [**Louis XVI**], and his likeness could be found on engraved glass, patterned porcelain, printed cottons, snuffboxes and inkwells . . . In June 1779 he wrote to his daughter that all of these likenesses 'have made your father's face as well known as that of the moon' . . . On one famous occasion his fame even goaded the King into a solitary act of wit for, in an attempt to make [French noblewoman] Diane de Polignac desist from her daily eulogies of the Great Man, he had a Sevres chamber pot painted with Franklin's image on the inside."

Even the French giant of the Enlightenment, the *philosophe* Voltaire thrilled to meet Franklin. The French crowds loved Franklin's frequent affected rusticity, such as when he donned a beaver pelt cap. "Aware that the French idealized America as a place of natural innocence, candor, and freedom, he milked the stereotype for all it was worth," Schama said. ". . . And Franklin knew that this image of the incorruptible, virtuous old fellow went down so well because it threw into unflattering relief the more sybaritically rococo aspects of the court style . . ." In Franklin, many of the educated French, sick of the royal court's intrigues, lavish spending, sexual profligacy and its anachronistic obliviousness got a glimpse of their hoped for, more innovative, forward-looking future.

The seeds of the French Revolution in 1789 had already found fertile soil by the time of Franklin's visit. The French did not immediately commit to support the American Revolution, cautious about another war with their indefatigable nemesis, but Franklin's proposed alliance intrigued them. The French needed to have more confidence that they would not lose yet another expensive war to the British before an alliance with the Americans could be forged. The French court waited on more American battlefield victories.

Outside of government ministries, however, the Declaration of Independence found an audience among French political thinkers and scientists. A well-known scholar of the French Enlightenment, Abbé Guillaume Raynal, found great importance in Jefferson's words, and gave several lectures on the American interpretation of the "rights of man." One audience member was an earnest young nobleman, Marie-Joseph Paul Yves Roch Gilbert du Motier, **Marquis de Lafayette**, who through military service had already become aware of the American struggle. "Lafayette" (as he would become known) now decided that if the American cause was just, and if the rights of man were genuine, then he must do all that he personally could.

Lafayette contacted Silas Deane and was given a major general's commission in the Continental Army (albeit an unpaid one). He bought a ship, only to have it confiscated by agents of the king when his plans became known. Fleeing to Spain, he sailed from there, in disguise, and finally arrived in Philadelphia in July 1777. Delegates in Congress were bewildered by the young nobleman and skeptical of "French glory seekers." Washington, however, had been advised by Franklin to treat Lafayette with respect, as a possible means of encouraging French assistance in the war. When the Marquis presented himself at the Continental Army's headquarters, Washington told him that he could not offer him a position of command but would hold him in confidence "as friend and father." Indeed, like Hamilton, Lafayette saw in Washington a role model and father figure he had yearned for. Lafayette agreed to serve alongside Hamilton on Washington's personal staff.

VIRTUE, GOD AND MAN IN REVOLUTIONARY AMERICA

The leading men of the revolutionary generation loved debating philosophy and religion. As deists, or heavily influenced by deism, and firm believers in science, most of those who became known as the "Founding Fathers"—Franklin, Washington, Hamilton, John Adams—didn't believe in a God who performed miracles. Their God was a divine clockmaker. He put the gears together, wound the cosmic clock, and let it run. The complexity of the universe, its vastness and its dependability, as revealed by Isaac Newton's Laws of Motion, was the miracle, not Biblical tales of water turning into wine or the dead being raised. Many of the Founders revered the Bible as a source of wisdom and saw Jesus as a great philosopher, but no more.

Thomas Jefferson was particularly skeptical of biblical accuracy. " . . . [I]n the book of Joshua we are told that the sun stood still for several hours," Jefferson wrote to his friend Peter Carr ". . . [Y]ou are Astronomer enough to know how contrary it is to the law of nature that a body revolving on its axis, as the earth does, should have stopped, should not by that sudden stoppage have prostrated animals, trees, buildings, and should after a certain time have resumed its revolution, and that without a second prostration. Is this arrest of the earth's motion, or the evidence which affirms it, most within the law of probabilities?"

Jefferson frequently expressed his disbelief in the virgin birth of Jesus, arguing that Jesus was Mary's "illegitimate" son. "And the day will come when the mystical generation of Jesus, by the supreme being as his father in the womb of a virgin will be classed with the fable of the generation of Minerva in the brain of Jupiter," Jefferson wrote in a letter to John Adams dated April 11, 1823. He also had no patience for biblical tales of miracles, which he viewed as fairy tales believed only by the ignorant. In fact, he wrote his own version of the New Testament omitting all tales of the supernatural and included only the moral teachings and precepts of Jesus.

Benjamin Franklin shared Jefferson's refusal to take the Bible literally. Once, Ezra Stiles asked his friend Franklin about his thoughts concerning Jesus' nature. Like many, Franklin doubted whether biblical accounts of Jesus' birth, words, and deeds were reliable. "As to Jesus of Nazareth, my Opinion of whom you particularly desire, I think the system of Morals, and his Religion, as he left them to us, the best the world ever saw or is likely to see," Franklin wrote in a March 9, 1790 letter. "But I apprehend it has received various, corrupting Changes, and I have, with most of the present dissenters in England, some doubts as to his Divinity; tho' it is a question I do not dogmatize upon . . ."

John Adams doubted the accuracy of events described in the Bible or words attributed to Biblical figures like Jesus. "What do you call the 'Bible?'" he once wrote to his son John Quincy Adams, before rattling off the names of various translations of the scripture. " . . . What Bible? King James's? The Hebrew? The Septuagint? The Vulgate? The Bible now translated or translating into Chinese, Indian, Negro, and all of the other languages of Europe, Asia and Africa? Which of the thirty thousand variantia are the Rule of Faith?"

This didn't mean that the force they called "Providence" was unconcerned with morality, unimpressed with good and indifferent to evil. Their clockmaker God structured the universe in a rational, predictable way, and morality was rational. Their god did judge, and he demanded virtue. And even if men like Franklin expressed doubts about the accuracy of biblical stories, it didn't mean the stories of the Bible had no effect on how they saw themselves or the world. Franklin saw something heroic in Americans bringing a modern democratic republic, a nation built not on inherited privileges but on equality before the law, to the world through the revolution. He compared the American people to the ancient Israelites in the Book of Exodus who escaped slavery in Egypt, gifting the world with monotheism (the belief in one God) and the Ten Commandments. Between July 4 and August 13, 1776, the Continental Congress appointed Franklin, Jefferson and Adams to a committee to design a great seal of the United States. Franklin suggested the following:

> Moses standing on the Shore, and extending his Hand over the Sea, thereby causing the same to overwhelm Pharaoh who is sitting in an open

Chariot, a Crown on his Head and a Sword in his Hand. Rays from a Pillar of Fire in the Clouds reaching to Moses, to express that he acts by Command of the Deity.

Franklin suggested, "Rebellion to Tyrants is Obedience to God," as the national motto. Jefferson also wanted to compare Revolutionary America to the Israelites. He proposed the seal portray the children of Israel in the wilderness after their escape from their Egyptian slavemasters, being led by a miraculous cloud by day and a pillar by night. The two proposals, neither of which was ultimately accepted, shared a common theme. Americans were unique, a new "chosen people" who would lead the world out of slavery to kings and other tyrants. American victory in the Revolution would mean victory for all of humanity, just as all of mankind had benefited from the moral principles embodied in the Ten Commandments.

Ever since the Puritan cleric John Winthrop described the Massachusetts Bay Colony in 1630 as a shining "city on a hill" providing a moral example and a path to salvation for the rest of the world, many Americans had come to believe their society had been given the mission to rescue the rest of the planet. The Founders may have mostly been deists, but they believed in America's unique mission in the world as well. This belief would lead Americans to create their own colonies in places as far away as the Philippines in the late 1800s, to constantly intervene in the internal politics of Latin America in the twentieth century, to enter World War I as part of a "war to end all wars" and to make "the world safe for democracy," to engage in a "twilight struggle" to destroy communism in the Cold War in places like Korea and Vietnam, and to envision the struggle against Al Qaeda and the invasion of Iraq in 2003 as part of a global "war on terrorism." America, many in this country believed, had been given the mission to save the world regardless of whether it wanted to be saved or not.

According to the historian Ann Fairfax Withington, before the revolution, the white colonists had told themselves that they were free because they were British. By the time of the Revolution, the colonists believed Great Britain had transformed into a tyranny. To some Americans, British tyranny stemmed from the nation's moral corruption. If America were to prevail and to win God's favor in the revolution, it would have to attain superior virtue to their morally lax advisories.

In one of its first acts, Withington notes, the First Continental Congress in September 1774 drew up a specific code of behavior for the people now known as Americans. The Congress banned cockfighting, horseracing, the theater, and ostentatious displays of wealth at funeral services. These laws had a practical side. By banning excessive spending on weddings, funerals, elaborate banquets and so on, more vital resources like food and cloth used to make high-end clothing were available for the Continental Army. Also, by encouraging more virtuous behavior during wartime, the Congress hoped to turn the public away from selfish indulgence and make the masses more concerned about the country as a whole and its struggle for freedom against Britain.

Obeying these laws of virtue would make everyone feel closer and more supportive of the Revolution because everyone was part of the struggle, even women and children. The poor and the working class, who really had little to gain if either side won, also might see the Revolution as a struggle against their rich exploiters if the war could be linked to a rejection of theater and fancy social affairs.

The Congress, Withington argued, carefully selected the targets of its moral purity campaign. It banned theater, seen as an extravagant hobby only the prosperous could afford. The theater encouraged blasphemy, critics said. Actors played characters who didn't exist and portrayed events that didn't happen, which constituted a form of lying. The cash wasted on tickets could be better spent feeding the poor. Plus, many of the plays depicted men who were seducers or immoral in some other ways. Ministers and moral conservatives worried the vice-ridden characters on stage would expose the audience to temptation. Another banned activity, gambling, derived from greed. The winnings didn't come from hard work but from random luck. This desire to achieve undeserved wealth rotted virtues at a time when true patriots put the good of society ahead of their own individual gain. Popular entertainments like cockfighting and horseracing divided a society by encouraging competition at a time when what was needed was unity against Great Britain. Revolutionary leaders associated virtue with discipline. Resisting temptation, the Congress believed, served as needed practice for fighting the crown.

Members of Congress, however, also remembered the stories in the Old Testament of how God rewarded the Israelites when they obeyed his commandments and harshly punished them with military defeat and military occupation when they violated his laws. They hoped for divine assistance. The Congress, on the other hand, had a narrow view of morality. They worried about gambling, but they looked the other way regarding slavery, the desperate plight of the poor, or the widespread corruption of elections.

In regulating morality, the Continental Congress sought to create a more morally "perfect union," a homogenous and cohesive society, in which a common code of morality would unite people divided by race, class, religion and gender. In the end, the Revolutionary campaign for virtue died a quick, painless death. Americans loved their vices. Once the former colonies achieved independence, the old public indulgences came creeping back.

The ban on cockfighting and the theater ended in many states and again served as popular entertainments by the late 1780s. The legislature decided to allow horseracing again in South Carolina, Virginia, Maryland and New York in the decade following the American Revolution, and the sport enjoyed a renaissance across the nation by the 1790s. In 1789, the Pennsylvania legislature repealed its law banning theatrical performances and, ironically, theater curtains and arches were decorated with paintings and embroidery depicting scenes from the Revolution. Cockfighting arose again as perhaps the most popular sport in the United States by the early 1800s.

A NATION OF DRINKERS

Perhaps it is appropriate that the melody of the National Anthem came from a popular song drunken customers used to belt out at taverns as the evening wore on. John Adams worried that the battle for liberty would turn into an excuse for vice, a moral degeneration that would lead to American defeat in the war. Alcohol consumption particularly concerned him. "Each morning during the meetings of the Continental Congress in 1777, John Adams squeezed his round body into breeches, waistcoat, wood-sole shoes, and powdered wig, and walked stiffly from his residence . . . to the Pennsylvania State House (now Independence Hall) four blocks away . . .," historian Thaddeus Russell observes in his book *A Renegade History of the United States*.

> Along the way, he passed by at least a dozen of the more than 160 licensed taverns in Philadelphia that serviced the city's population of 24,000. There were also scores of unlicensed taverns, which means that there was at least one tavern for every 100 residents. (By contrast, in 2007 there was one alcohol-serving business for every 1,071 residents in Philadelphia.) Other early American cities had even greater tavern densities during the time of the Revolution. In New York in the 1770s, there were enough taverns to allow every resident of the city to drink in a bar at the same time. In Boston, it was estimated that liquor was sold at one of every eight residential houses."

As Adams strolled toward his meeting, his route also would have taken him past dozens of legal "bawdy houses" that dotted the landscape of the national capital. 'When Adams walked to the state house, he was almost certainly propositioned by prostitutes advertising their trade," Russell wrote. "They would have shown him their breasts and asked if he cared for a 'nice romp. . . .' In the taverns, many of the boundaries American elites had built between blacks and whites, rich and poor, immigrant and native born, men and women, dissolved in the glow of liquor-driven friendliness. Had Adams entered one of the drinking establishments along the way to the Continental Congress, as Russell notes:

> "If he was in a typical lower class, eighteenth century American urban tavern, he would have seen white men and black men sitting together and drumming their fingers to the music on long wooden tables. He would have seen white women dancing with black men and black women dancing with white men. He would have seen prostitutes openly and shamelessly selling their services. And, quite possibly, he would have seen a woman behind the bar who not only served the drinks but also owned the place. John Adams would have seen renegade America in all its early glory. And he would have known the enemy.

Americans drank alcohol far more in the last quarter of the 1700s than they do today. There were a lot of reasons. Water supplies were not always safe. Farmers producing the grains alcohol is made from did not always have access to reliable, adequately speedy transportation, so they made the grains into whiskey and other liquors because these libations have an extremely long shelf life. Availability undoubtedly increased usage. Attitudes toward alcohol differed from the modern day. "At the beginning of the eighteenth century, tradition taught, and Americans, like Englishmen and Europeans, universally believed, that rum, gin, and brandy were nutritious and helpful," wrote historian W.J. Rorabaugh:

> Distilled spirits were viewed as foods that supplemented limited and monotonous diets, as medications that could cure colds, fevers, snakebites, frosted toes and broken legs, and as relaxants that would relive depression, reduce tension, and enable hardworking laborers to enjoy a moment of happy, frivolous camaraderie.

Americans not only drank in prodigious amounts, they drank hard liquor in abundance. Favorites were rum, whiskey, brandy, and gin, that were 45 percent alcohol. During the colonial period up through the end of the Revolutionary War, Americans consumed 3.7 gallons of alcohol per capita per year, as opposed to 2.25 gallons per capita consumed today. (Between 1800 and 1830, per capita liquor consumption jumped to more than 5 gallons a year, an all-time high).

Taverns often opened next to churches and courthouses so a shot or two could be enjoyed before a trial or worship. "Before trials, it was common for defendants, attorneys, judges, and jurymen, to gather there to drink, and sometimes matters were settled 'out of court,'" Rorabaugh wrote. "At other times, when a controversial trial attracted a crowd, it was necessary to hold the trial in a tavern, which was the only public building roomy enough to accommodate the spectators." Craftsmen making shoes, furniture, saddles, and wagons had a mug of beer or other drinks beside them at their workbenches. They drank while they worked and took lunch breaks where they drank some more.

The Congress' campaign for virtue never conquered those urban neighborhoods. "Never in America have more 'illegitimate' children been born, per capita, than during the era of independence," Russell wrote. ". . . [In] Philadelphia alone in the years 1767 to 1776, one in roughly 38 adults was parent to an illegitimate child." During the Revolution and just after, social renegades like Russell described, and the restless poor and working class would give men like Adams the jitters. As Rorabaugh notes, Adams quaffed a tankard of hard cider every morning at breakfast, but when he contemplated lower-income drinkers, he moaned, ". . . is it not mortifying . . . that we, Americans, should exceed all other . . . people in the world, in this degrading, beastly vice of intemperance?" The whiskey distiller George Washington fretted that distilled liquor was "the ruin of half the workingmen in this country." Adams worried that widespread vice would lead to the collapse of the American republic. After achieving independence, Adams feared, the Americans would become "a Spectacle of Contempt and Derision to the foolish and wicked, and of Grief and shame to the wise among Mankind, and all this in the Space of a few Years."

HANGING FOR PLEASURE AND EDUCATION

The political leaders of America didn't think all forms of entertainment corrupted public morals. Politicians and ministers often embraced public executions as a form of education, even as those attending seemed to enjoy the drama. The Revolutionary generation's elites didn't want rebellion against the British to translate into a class revolution, so they used the elaborate rituals of executions to teach the masses lessons about obedience. "It should come as little surprise that the overriding civil theme of execution day was the preservation of order," historian Louis P. Masur wrote. "Above all else, authorities designed public hangings as a demonstration of the power of government and a warning to those who violated the law. As one minister put it, "In civil society, the wicked would walk on every side, and the cry of the oppressed would be in vain, the foundations would be destroyed, [and] confusion and misery would prevail were punishment, capital punishment, never executed."

As with today, public executions followed a strict protocol. Often the defendant would be led to a church in the morning where the minister would deliver a lengthy sermon on how the God of the Bible approved of capital punishment and the gift represented by the 10 Commandments. The last part of the sermon would be pointed directly at the prisoner, identified by name. The minister would note the condemned's sins and make clear that their gravity meant that God himself demanded the prisoner's death. After the service, the condemned would be walked or carried by cart to the gallows, his arms bound behind him. Sometimes prisoners rode on top of their future coffins on the way to the execution site. Upon reaching the top of the gallows, the prisoner would stand by while the sheriff or other official read the death warrant, then the prisoner would be given the chance to speak last words. It became common for the condemned to explain how they got to that spot, which temptations turned them to a life of crime, and then to repent.

Oddly, the condemned seemed to have willingly played their part in these dramatic execution productions. Typical were the gallows regrets expressed by two burglars hanged in Worcester, Massachusetts just after the war, June 19, 1783. "We pray that our unhappy fate may be a solemn *Warning* to *Youth* and induce them to forsake the paths of vice and immorality, and seek the road of virtue and happiness," one of the burglars said before his death. Another prisoner, a teenager hanged in Dedham, Massachusetts, warned the crowd, "Do not CHEAT—Do not STEAL—Do not LIE—Do not commit ADULTERY—Especially, do not destroy VIRGIN INNOCENCE—and, above all, do not KILL."

A hood would be placed on the condemned's head, he or she would be put on top of a trap door, and the prisoner's body would drop. The length of the rope was calculated so the condemned's neck would break, but the executioner sometimes made mistakes, which meant that the victim would slowly strangle to death. Often, the prisoner's "confession" would be printed in which the doomed person would beg the readers not to follow the path of sin and end up in a noose.

The condemned tended to be young. According to Masur, the median age of those executed in his study sample was 25. The condemned also disproportionately came from the ranks of former soldiers, immigrants, people of color, and people without longstanding ties to communities. Soldiers suffered executions at a rate higher than average, Masur speculates, because of the practical fear that the low-paid servicemen might desert the Revolutionary Army and live a higher-paid life of crime. Authorities profiled African Americans, immigrants and strangers, probably as a result of the anxiety posed by the Revolution, as the former colonists traded in their status as Englishmen for an American identity not yet clearly defined.

Elites hoped that executions would deter future crimes, but also that the masses would learn, for their own sakes, to obey authority. Leaders worried constantly that the revolution would spin out of control. "The fears over social decay and disorder were intensified by the constant chant of the republican hymn," Masur wrote. "Republican values centered on the idea of public virtue, the belief that an individual's passions must yield to the good of the community and that self-abnegation must come before self-interest." In any case, the public hangings during the revolutionary era failed as a deterrent. There was no appreciable effect on the rate of homicides, robberies, rapes and other crimes then punishable by death—and the confused, crowded, excited atmosphere around the gallows during a hanging proved a magnet for pickpockets and other criminals.

THE BATTLE OF THE CUPBOARDS

As their husbands, fathers, brothers and sons went off to war, American women faced their own series of battles: to keep family businesses going; to manage plantations and workforces; to keep the family budget in the black; to raise children. Their added duties during the Revolution did not mean they could neglect the ordinary housework that had always fallen to wives, mothers and daughters in American society—feeding, bathing, doctoring and educating the children; gardening, milking cows; cleaning the henhouse; gathering eggs; plucking chickens; and gathering fuel and water. Greedy merchants did not make the endless chores any easier. Inflation ran rampant and consumer goods were scarce. Some merchants exploited the uncertainty by outrageously overcharging their customers. Prices rose by 45 percent during one year of the Revolution.

Women sometimes formed their own battalions, sometimes joined by men, and organized attacks on unscrupulous shop owners, looting stores and emptying their shelves. This was a matter of justice and, for the poor, survival. More than 30 times between 1776 and 1779, food rioters confronted rapacious shopkeepers and merchants who were hoarding or overcharging. One such riot was described by historian Barbara Clark Smith.

Wrapped in blankets "like Indians," and with their faces blackened, men gathered in the streets of Longmeadow, Massachusetts in July 1776 to express "uneasiness with those who trade in rum, molasses & Sugar &c." The crowd delivered written ultimatum to Jonathan and Hezekiah Hale, retailers, who had taken advantage of embargo and warfare to raise prices on their increasingly scarce goods:

Sirs, it is a matter of great grief that you Should give us cause to call upon you in this uncommon way . . . We find you guilty of very wrong behavior in selling at extravagant prices . . . This conduct tends to undervalue paper currency which is very detrimental to the Liberties of America. We therefore as your offended Brethren demand satisfaction of you the offender for your past conduct and a Thorough reformation for time to Come.

The mob gave the Hales a list of suggested prices for the goods they sold and gave them an hour to consider. Seeing the anger of the crowd, the retailers complied. Another Longmeadow merchant refused to lower what the crowd saw as excessive prices, so the crowd emptied his stores shelves and refused to return his goods until he repented. A few weeks later, however, the merchant (Samuel Colton) had inflated his prices again. A mob returned, smashed into his store, "carried away his rum, sugar, molasses and salt" and ransacked Colton's house, which was attached to the store. Looters in these incidents accused greedy merchants of acting no different from the British oppressors, and would call them unpatriotic.

The rioters came from all classes. In some cases, the mobs were led by the well-to-do, but it seems this was mostly a revolt of the poor and struggling against much better-off merchants. The longer the Revolution lasted, the more the riots shifted from rural areas to cities. The food riots became more an expression of class struggle as the revolution dragged on. "In the latter years of the war, price riots became more urban and, correspondingly, more expressive of the beliefs and grievances of the cities' lower classes," Smith wrote. "This shift was natural enough. In the early war years, prices for imports rose more quickly than prices for domestic products. Farmers' profits bought less rum or sugar, cloth or hardware than was customary. They also suspected rural storekeepers of making matters worse by seeking inordinate profit. They responded with food riots. By the late 1770s, farm prices outstripped imports, and economic distress and food riots both concentrated more heavily in the cities." As a Philadelphia newspaper reported, "[T]he People have always done themselves justice when the scarcity of bread has arisen from the avarice of forestallers. They have broken open magazines—appropriated stores to their own use without paying for them—and in some instances have hung up the culprits who created their distress."

Soldiers heard the complaints of their wives and mothers about widespread price-gouging, leading the First Company of Philadelphia Artillery to petition the state assembly in May of 1779 to crack down on exploitive merchants. In their petition, they threatened violence to "those who are avariciously intent upon amassing wealth by the destruction of the more virtuous part of the community." Residents of Philadelphia demanded an investigation of Robert Morris, a wealthy merchant and one of the chief American financiers of the Revolution, for reportedly hoarding food to increase the sales price.

Women took a leadership position in these riots. According to Smith, the riots became one of the few means of political expression open to women in the 1770s and 1780s. "Excluded from the vote, unqualified to serve as jurors at courts of law, free women—along with servants, slaves, children, and propertyless men were politically disabled by their dependent status," Smith wrote. "Yet women conducted nearly one-third of the riots. Here, then, were possibilities for political action that resistance and revolution opened for women . . . as social and economic actors within household, neighborhood and marketplace."

Women may have lacked the right to vote, but they successfully pressured New England legislatures to mandate that merchants accept paper currency as legal tender, set caps on the prices merchants could charge for a wide variety of domestic and imported goods, and outlaw hoarding. Meanwhile, average people began to organize boycotts of merchants who overcharged, just as elites had organized earlier boycotts of British goods. Fearing that the legislature would fail to enforce these laws, spontaneous gatherings of protestors continued to take the law into their own hands. In one incident on April 19, 1777, the second anniversary of the Battle of Lexington and Concord, a 500-person crowd in Boston grabbed five "Tory" merchants ("Tory" was the term for those Americans supporting the British), tossed them into a cart and intentionally rode them past a gallows, tipping the cart over to dump them out and warning them to never return to the city again.

One again, elites like Adams worried that incidents like these suggested that the Revolution might spin out of control. "Popular initiative particularly troubled those patriots who sought a simple transfer of power from British to American hands and who saw crowds and even committees as temporary expedients at best," Smith observed. A push-back against price controls began in the Continental Congress at the behest of affluent men like Dr. Benjamin Rush and in state legislatures. The well-to-do urged consumers to take their grievances to court, ignoring the fact that lawyers' fees might be beyond most families' reach. Women continued to press for price fairness. "Eighteenth-century women had little reason to doubt their competence in such matters as equitable pricing and neighborly dealing," Smith wrote.

> In America, as in England and on the [European] continent, women took part in marketing and buying for their households. Women were innkeepers, victualers, greenwomen (supplying urban markets), and storekeepers . . .Female shopkeepers and innkeepers were accustomed to facing profit-seeking wholesalers. Rural and urban housewives participated with men in the exchanges of labor and goods that marked everyday life. Equally important, women were accustomed to responsibility for the welfare of their neighborhoods. "Charity" and mutual support represented relationships between neighbors, a part of community life in which women had long been competent and involved.

Far more powerful male politicians still found it difficult to roll back price controls or to too loudly condemn mob actions at the shop counters. "For some years, popular sentiment proved powerful enough to hold the patriot movement to the ideals of social and economic equality," Smith concludes. However, the riots inspired anxiety in the hearts of elites, who started the Revolution committed to a more radical vision of equality but by the time the Constitution had retreated to defense of the traditional hierarchy.

The Saratoga Campaign

The patriot cause had narrowly survived the 1776 campaign, and the next year promised more grave threats. In New York, General Howe and his brother planned a new attack on Philadelphia, which would drive away the Second Continental Congress and, he hoped, also lure Washington into another defensive battle in which the patriot forces might finally be destroyed. The Howes wanted 20,000 more troops for this campaign, but nothing near this number was available to the military. Nevertheless, in London, King George, the Prime Minister (Lord North), and Lord Germain, the Secretary of State for the colonies, embraced a more ambitious plan involving an invasion route between northern New York and Canada. General **John Burgoyne** proposed to lead an army from Canada to Albany, on the upper Hudson River, where he would fight to establish British control over the full length of the great waterway, cutting off New England from the other rebellious colonies and possibly deal a fatal blow to the patriot war effort. The King and his ministers endorsed Burgoyne's plan, but failed to give Howe clear instructions to cooperate fully with the operation.

Burgoyne, meanwhile, led an army of 7,800 from Montreal toward Albany in early June, moving down Lake Champlain with forces that included British and German regulars and Iroquois allies, 130 artillery pieces, a long supply train extending back into Canada. The general also brought his mistress, servants, feather bed, and other tasteful furnishings and culinary delicacies. ("Gentleman Johnny" was a brave and experienced officer who treated his men with consideration, but it never occurred to him to sacrifice his style of living, or that of his senior officers, even in a remote frontier campaign.) Burgoyne's men began the campaign by capturing Fort Ticonderoga, scene of the Patriots' earliest successes in the war, on June 2, 1777. A braggart, Burgoyne boasted in letters sent back to the rest of the world about his initial victory and proclaimed that his invasion was proceeding according to plan.

After this initial success, British plans went awry. Burgoyne carelessly overextended his supply lines, and his men suffered fatigue. According to plans hatched in London, Howe was supposed to send to Burgoyne men and supplies from New York. Instead, Howe launched his own mission and was leaving by sea for an invasion of Maryland and Pennsylvania.

Burgoyne would have to manage with the supplies he already possessed, or his men would have to forage for food in the wilderness. A further setback came when an expeditionary force led by British Colonel Barry St. Leger made a thrust through the Mohawk River Valley, but his Iroquois allies abandoned him when American General Benedict Arnold's forces confronted them in August, reducing St. Leger's forces in half and forcing a retreat back to Oswego in western New York.

Far from supply depots, Burgoyne split his forces, ordering 700 Hessians to hunt for supplies in the nearby Green Mountains. There, a 2,600-man New Hampshire militia led by John Stark launched a surprise from behind, ambushing the 700 mercenaries and killing or imprisoning almost the entire force. Another exchange between the New Hampshire militia and a different group of Hessians had similar results. Burgoyne's force limped toward Albany, his once considerable army much reduced. The American commander near Albany, **Horatio Gates**, in fact, now enjoyed a three-to-one manpower advantage. Unable to punch through Gates's lines to reach Albany, Burgoyne lost two disastrous battles thirty miles from the town on September 19 and on October 7 (the latter initiated by Arnold against Gates's direct orders). Retreating to nearby Saratoga, Burgoyne surrendered on October 17. The British loss would have huge diplomatic consequences, convincing the French that the Revolution was not a lost cause and that the French could damage their British rivals by forming an alliance with the Americans.

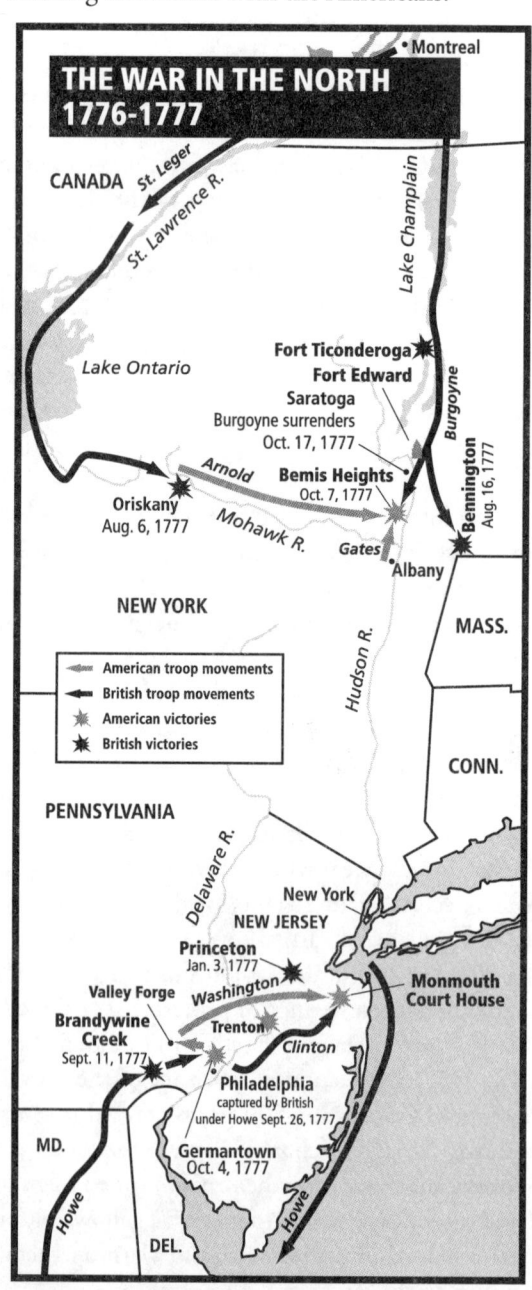

Map 6.2 The War in the North, 1776-1777

BRUISED AND BATTERED

Still thinking in terms of conventional wars in Europe, General Howe placed great stock in capturing cities of economic and political significance rather than pursuing and destroying the enemy's main army. Trained in traditional army tactics, Washington still felt compelled to defend such points, especially a city as symbolically important as Philadelphia, which housed the Continental Congress. As the Saratoga campaign reached its dramatic climax, Washington was left to wage another defensive struggle against Howe's sizeable forces. In July, as Washington watched uneasily, Howe loaded some 18,000 troops onto transports in New York harbor, and then, instead of moving up the Hudson to support Burgoyne, the fleet headed out to the open sea.

Howe sailed to Chesapeake Bay, landing his forces in Maryland in late August. As the British army advanced on Philadelphia from the south, Washington marched from northern New Jersey to the lower Delaware Valley, gathering militia units along the way. Howe correctly surmised that Washington would not surrender the city without a fight and lured him into a direct confrontation that the colonial army could not hope to win.

Washington built defensive fortifications along the main road from Baltimore to Philadelphia at a fording site across Brandywine Creek. Yet despite these preparations, Howe used his superior reconnaissance to find a weakness in the Continental Army's position and utilized the maneuverability of his professional forces to exploit the opportunity. In the **Battle of Brandywine Creek**, on September 11, Howe outflanked Washington's men, forcing them back with heavy losses. Their line of retreat, however, was protected by General **Nathanael Greene**, one of Washington's most trusted lieutenants, and by Lafayette, who kept rallying troops even after he had been shot in the leg. In his report to Congress, Washington cited Lafayette for "bravery and military ardour" as he recommended the Frenchman for command of a division.

On September 26, Lord Cornwallis led a ceremonial entry into Philadelphia. One month previously, Washington had paraded the Continental Army through the city, on their way south. "Much yet remains to be done," John Adams then observed. "Our soldiers have not yet quite the air of soldiers. They don't step exactly in time. They don't hold up their heads quite erect. . . . They don't all of them cock their hats, and such as do, don't all wear them the same way." The occupying army now presented an entirely different spectacle, with British and German regulars in crisp uniforms, brass buttons and polished guns shining in the sunlight, marching to a band playing "God Save the King."

But with the news of Burgoyne's struggles now circulating, even the parade's spectators suspected that military professionalism could do only so much to restore British authority. Congress and many residents were forced to flee the city, but its conquest made far less of an impact on the Patriot cause than Howe had hoped.

"THE GAME IS PRETTY NEAR UP"

A letter sent by George Washington to his brother, Augustine Washington, December 18, 1776, during a low point in the American War for Independence:

Owing to the number of letters I write, the recollection of any particular one is destroyed, but I think my last to you was by Colonel Woodford, from Hackinsac. Since that time, and a little before, our affairs have taken an adverse turn, but not more than was to be expected from the unfortunate measures, which have been adopted for the establishment of our army...

...We are in a very disaffected part of the Province; and, between you and me, I think out affairs are in a very bad situation; not so much from apprehension of General Howe's army, as from the defection of New York, Jerseys, and Pennsylvania...

I have no doubt but that General Howe will still make an attempt upon Philadelphia this winter. I see nothing to oppose him a fortnight hence, as the time of all the troops, except those of Virginia reduced (almost to nothing,) and Smallwood's regiment of Maryland, equally as bad, will expire in less than that time. In a word, my dear Sir, if every nerve is not strained to recruit the new army with all possible expedition, I think the game is pretty near up, owing, in great measure, to the insidious arts of the enemy, and disaffection on the colonies before mentioned, but principally to the accursed policy of short enlistment's, and placing too great a dependence on the militia, the evil consequences of which were foretold fifteen months ago, with a spirit almost Prophetic...

With the Continental Army still attracting recruits, Washington observed the division of Howe's forces into scattered detachments. He attempted to coordinate an attack from different directions against the largest body of British troops under Howe's own command at Germantown, Pennsylvania, on the foggy morning of October 4. Washington's biographer Flexner observed that the general had a bad habit of constructing battle plans far more complex than necessary, and such was the case in Germantown. The baffled Continental Army failed to execute their orders successfully, with some Patriot units accidentally firing on each other. After some initial success, Washington was forced to withdraw, with the army suffering heavy casualties yet again. Still, "the retreat was extraordinary," observed Thomas Paine. "Nobody hurried themselves. Everyone marched his own pace. . . . They appeared to me to be only sensible of a disappointment, not a defeat."

As Paine already recognized, the hard fighting of 1777 had profound consequences, which continued to develop as the battlefields fell silent for the cold season. As the third winter of the war set in, those who were committed to the Patriot cause once again found the reassurance they needed. Having escaped to York, Pennsylvania, the Second Continental Congress proclaimed December 18 a day for "solemn thanksgiving and praise" to Almighty God, seeing "that He hath been pleased . . . to crown our arms with most signal success." Across the thirteen states, village and town churches marked the day of thanksgiving with formal services. Northwest of Philadelphia, in a hilly, forested area known as **Valley Forge**, chosen by Washington for the army's winter quarters, Reverend Israel Evans, the Continental Army chaplain, preached a sermon of thanksgiving. In many ways, it would be a winter of discontent, with Washington's soldiers freezing and barely fed, and members of Congress grumbling about Washington's performance as a general. The criticism of Washington reached a crescendo after the almost simultaneous defeat of the commander-in-chief outside Philadelphia with Gates's smashing victory at Saratoga. A turning point had arrived, however, as Baron von Steuben arrived to professionalize the Continental Army and as a critical diplomatic victory occurred overseas.

Meanwhile, some twenty miles to the southeast, with the occupying British army comfortably settled in the city, English officers surrendered themselves to the strenuous demands of the winter social calendar. (When told that Howe had taken Philadelphia, Franklin was said to have replied, "I beg your pardon, Philadelphia has taken Howe.") In fact, shortly after arriving, Howe sent off a letter of resignation as commander-in-chief. He left in the spring after British officials accepted his offer, but not before one last spectacular, unbelievably costly party thrown for him by his officers (featuring a musical parade of boats and costumed passengers on the Delaware, a medieval joust held in an amphitheatre, a "magnificent bouquet of rockets" and fireworks shaped like "bursting balloons," and a banquet served by slaves in Turkish dress). As he must already have known, Howe would spend the next few years fighting to salvage his own reputation and fend off the blame for Burgoyne's disastrous fate. It would prove to be his last failed campaign, as he never would be able to clearly explain his own crucial errors of judgment.

France Enters the War

The most crucial results of the year's campaigns developed far away, in Paris, in the secret meetings and delicate conversations between the commissioners sent by Congress and the foreign ministry of King Louis XVI. The British occupation of Philadelphia alarmed the French Foreign Minister, Charles Gravier, Comte de Vergennes, because he feared the Americans might surrender and the French would lose a chance to gain an advantage on their English enemy. News of the American victory at Saratoga, however, pleased Vergennes, convincing him that the Americans had a credible army after all. European politics rested upon a zero-sum game. What was bad for England was good for France, and Vergennes hoped to make the situation much worse for the enemy across the English Channel.

On February 6, 1778, the two sides finished negotiations and signed a pair of treaties. One established trade between the two nations, while the other created a military alliance. The French thus committed to American independence for the United States. In an agreement that would pose difficulties for the United States in the 1790s, both nations committed to help each other in the event either was attacked. "Neither of the two Parties shall conclude either Truce or Peace with Great Britain, without the formal consent of the other," stated the alliance treaty, "and they mutually engaged not to lay down their arms, until assured by the Treaty or Treaties that shall terminate the War."

The agreements with France transformed the conflict. What had begun as an American colonial rebellion against British imperial authority had become a global war, with England and France resuming their bloody struggle for supremacy over the Atlantic Ocean and in North America that had been in recess since the end of the French and Indian War fourteen years earlier.

Like France, Spain also eagerly sought a chance to get even for previous military defeats at the hands of

Great Britain. Worried if the United States succeeded in its revolt against England then restless Spanish colonists might follow the example and launch their own revolutions, the Spanish government never entered into a direct alliance with the U.S. government. Instead, Spain fought alongside the French and successfully battled to retake parts of Florida previously lost to England. The British military, already stretched thin, now had to fight in the Gulf Coast, in the Caribbean, and in Europe where the Spanish unsuccessfully tried to recapture the Strait of Gibraltar.

After the French alliance, seasoned European officers volunteered for service and eventually made up 20 percent of all officers in the Continental Army. In London, where the shock of Burgoyne's surrender had scarcely worn off, the announcement of the Paris treaties confirmed the worst fears of virtually everyone in Parliament and the king's cabinet. Great Britain itself was now in peril. With such great commitment of arms, men, and ships already made in North America, and a new, powerful enemy entering the conflict, no light at the end of the tunnel was even faintly in sight. Ironically, as the military and political situations got worse in North America, advocates for peace like Edmund Burke decided to keep their criticisms of the war effort to themselves and joined the call for national unity. The day belonged to George III who, stubborn as always, insisted that his ministers remain resolute.

The American strategy would continue to be to simply outlast the British by keeping the Continental Army intact and avoiding battles with the British when the numbers favored the enemy. Germain proposed the worst possible military strategy in response. He wanted to strike at the French, whom he saw as the greater threat to Britain. If British naval superiority could be maintained in American waters, then parts of the new British commander General **Henry Clinton**'s forces would be redeployed against other targets of opportunity, such as the French islands in the West Indies. However, this meant that Clinton would lack sufficient forces to hold onto Philadelphia, forcing him to withdraw from the American capital.

Meanwhile, Germain gave up on the idea of waging a campaign on land against Washington's army. Instead, after approving Howe's resignation, he instructed Clinton to withdraw from Philadelphia and return to New York. Troops would also be diverted to the southern states on the North American mainland, where ministers believed the British military would find a larger percentage of American Loyalists who would support the troops from the homeland.

THE BRITISH EVACUATION OF PHILADELPHIA

During the Revolution, Washington faced constant trouble from his top officers. General Charles Lee in particular refused to submit to Washington's authority. Lee had never surrendered the idea that he was more brilliant and capable than Washington and every other military commander. While serving as the second-in-command during the Americans' retreat across New Jersey in late 1776, he was captured by the British at a tavern and then held in New York City where, according to later accusations, he offered his expert military advice to General Howe who befriended him. Lee may have entered into a conspiracy to betray the Continental Army. Yet, Washington still felt he needed the benefit of Lee's expertise. In early 1778, Lee obtained his release as part of a prisoner exchange. Lee's arrogance, however, would finally get him fired by his furious commander when he disobeyed battlefield orders after the British evacuated Philadelphia.

General Clinton began his withdrawal by sending shiploads of Loyalists and sick soldiers to New York City by sea. Clinton then transported the bulk of his forces in boats across the Delaware River and began a long march across New Jersey. With the British army and its long baggage train exposed, Washington looked for an opportunity to attack. On June 28, 1778, his troops, now executing maneuvers with precision according to von Steuben's drills at Valley Forge, caught up with Clinton's rear guard, commanded by Lord Cornwallis, near **Monmouth Court House**. Over Lee's objections, Washington ordered his subordinate to mount an attack. Though the assault seemed to be succeeding, Lee mysteriously ordered a retreat. Confused, Lee's men reversed ground and the pullback turned into a panic when Clinton immediately counterattacked. The retreating Continentals ran straight into Washington himself, riding just ahead of the main body of the American army.

Furious, Washington demanded an immediate explanation from Lee, who had little to offer. Washington fired Lee on the spot and gave Lafayette command of Lee's men. Turning his back to Lee, Washington once again personally rallied his forces. The Americans quickly reestablished themselves in an orderly formation while under the fire of the approaching British troops. Their long hours of drill and training paid off in the moment of crisis. An admiring Lafayette later remembered "our beloved chief who, mounted on a splendid charger, rode along the ranks amid the shouts of the soldiers, cheering them by his voice and example, and restoring to our standard the fortunes of the fight."

The British charged the Patriot lines but failed to break through. That night, with both sides having lost hundreds of dead and wounded, and with the American side holding the battlefield, the British troops slipped away and resumed their march to New York City. Monmouth Courthouse would prove to be the last major battle of the Revolutionary War in the North. Though the battle was strategically inconclusive, the Americans claimed victory. "We forced the enemy from the field and encamped on their ground," Washington reported. A court martial later convicted Lee of insubordination and ended his service in the Continental Army.

THE WAR IN THE WEST

The Americans had reached a turning point in the war. Lafayette, who had continued to rise through the ranks of Washington's senior officers, returned to France briefly in 1779, where crowds hailed him as a hero. With his popularity came influence with the French court, and Lafayette worked with Franklin to win new commitments of financial and military assistance for the war effort. The following year, he returned to America, followed by an army of 6,000 troops under an eminent French general, Jean-Baptiste Donatien de Vimeur, **Comte de Rochambeau**.

For nearly three years, Washington kept the main body of his army near New York City, mostly watching and waiting. After the British withdrew from Newport, Rhode Island, Rochambeau established a base there for French land and sea forces before linking up with Washington's army in 1781. The two commanders formed a mutually respectful partnership. Meanwhile, Clinton had few options other than fortifying New York City and hoping the French and Americans would not attack. The British commander had been ordered by North and Germain to send troops to other theaters of combat, so he appealed in vain for reinforcements and never felt he had sufficient numbers on hand to launch an offensive. The hard fighting now continued elsewhere. If the war in the North settled into a long stalemate in late 1779, Clinton was assigned to supervise a new campaign in the southern states even as battles raged on America's western frontier.

After the French and Indian War, the British had tried to draw a line at the Appalachian Mountains that they hoped would serve as the outer border dividing white settlement from "Indian Country." Always worried about France and Spain, the British didn't want to be drawn into Indian wars in the American West. They also hoped to profit from trade with Native American groups. Many of the rebellious colonists, however, assumed they had a limitless right to Indian land and saw British interference as a violation of their rights.

American whites poured over the imaginary border, establishing farms and communities on newly cleared lands and extending the lines of settlement and land claims ever westward. Ruthless land speculators joined them in this creeping conquest. The invaders collided with Native American tribes, many already displaced from their traditional lands farther east. Although many Indian bands tried to remain neutral, when the Revolution started, Native Americans inevitably got caught in the crossfire. The racism of white colonists, and their violence toward indigenous people, drove many Indians into supporting the British. In the West, the British Army was only too happy to ally itself with resisting Native Americans nations. The "War on the Frontier" raged west of the Appalachians, across vast stretches of the Mississippi and Ohio River Valleys (including much of the present-day states of Illinois, Indiana, and Kentucky) populated by Shawnee and other tribes and by isolated French-speaking settlers and soldiers stationed at British-held fortresses.

During the summer of 1778, George Rogers Clark, the young commander of the Virginia state militia in charge of defending the western counties, led some 200 volunteers far down the Ohio River and across hundreds of miles of forest, to Kaskaskia, originally a French colonial settlement and now a British army outpost on the Mississippi. Appearing unexpectedly with his armed company, and proclaiming the news of the Franco-American alliance to the local settlers, Clark occupied Kaskaskia without firing a shot and claimed it for Virginia.

Clark sent some of his men, as well as French settlers, back east to occupy Vincennes, the other main British outpost south of Detroit. Forced to act, the British commander in the frontier region, Lieutenant Governor Henry Hamilton, with a company of British soldiers and Shawnee warriors, retook Vincennes from the small detachment of Virginians, but he still failed to reckon fully with Clark's ability to lead fighting frontiersmen on long, difficult treks. In February 1779, Clark again emerged at Vincennes, having marched through the snow from Kaskaskia with the rest of his militiamen and French volunteers. After Clark ordered the killing of four captured Indians with tomahawks in full view of the British, Hamilton agreed to surrender the fortress and his men.

Clark led repeated campaigns in the Ohio River region, attacking and burning Shawnee villages and cornfields, but he never managed to gather sufficient forces for his ultimate objective, which was crushing Indian resistance. Indian leaders like Mohawk **Joseph Brant** emerged as a threatening force as confrontations between settlers and tribes turned into wars of extermination and elimination. In the North, where most of the Iroquois tribes elected to wage war alongside the British, outrage and fear prevailed among the American settlers of the Mohawk and upper Delaware River valleys. To reassert control of the region, Washington sent an expedition of several thousand Continental troops and militiamen in 1779, giving orders to the commander, General John Sullivan, to "rush on with the war whoop and the bayonet" and "make rather than receive attacks." Brant and other Indian warriors waged guerilla warfare, avoiding set battles. In response, Sullivan and his men focused mainly on the systematic destruction and burning of Iroquois villages and farmlands—literally a "scorched earth" campaign. During the winter of 1779-1780, thousands of homeless Iroquois villagers were forced to migrate to Fort Niagara, where British troops offered shelter. During the next year, however, with Sullivan and his troops reassigned to the war against the British in the south, the Iroquois mounted an equally fierce campaign of retaliation, destroying settlers' homes and farms throughout the Pennsylvania and New York frontier country.

Far to the south, on the Virginia frontier, the destruction was more one-sided. Cherokee communities were deeply split between young militants wanting to battle the Americans who had caused them so much loss and sorrow and older chiefs seeking accommodation with the settlers. However, in 1780 and 1781 Virginia militiamen attacked the friendly villages, destroying the tribe's "beloved town" of Chota and validating the fears of the younger Indian firebrands.

No uglier chapter in the American Revolution took place than the Gnadenhutten Massacre in the Ohio country. A group of Delawares who had been converted to Christianity by the Moravian sect for a time lived in the Moravian-established settlement in modern-day east central Ohio. The band had moved out of Gnadenhutten, but some had returned to harvest crops left behind. They came under attack on March 8-9, 1782 by Pennsylvania militiamen under the command of Captain David Williamson, who sought revenge after Native Americans had recently killed and kidnapped several whites in the region. The Delawares had not been involved, but they would pay the price for these earlier attacks.

When they reached the village on March 8, soldiers forced the men and women to separate at gunpoint and held them in separate buildings. The Pennsylvanians decided to execute the entire village the next morning. Informing them of their fate, women and children cried while the Delawares prayed and tried to rally their spirits with hymns. When morning came, the militia seized two natives at a time and battered the inhabitants' heads with mallets, killing 57 unarmed men and women and 39 children. Only two Delawares survived.

Essentially, the brutal episodes of the "War on the Frontier" were part of a larger pattern of conflict which continued long after the war for independence was settled. After the Revolution, the British ceded control of what they had intended to be Indian Country to the United States. They illegally retained forts in the "Northwest Country" and encouraged the natives living there to attack white settlements, providing them weapons until the end of the War of 1812. Nevertheless, the white conquest of the lands between the Appalachians and the Mississippi River would prove unstoppable. With the British no longer there to hold back the Americans, white invaders pushed into regions such as Kentucky, a favorite hunting ground of the Shawnees, and Indian groups would be forced at gunpoint to resettle farther west. Kentucky became infamous as "a dark and bloody ground" after the Revolution ended, yet, by the time of the first-ever United States federal census in 1790, 74,000 whites and their slaves claimed Kentucky as their home and approximately half that number had made land claims in Tennessee, where the Cherokee had surrendered after defeat in a 1776 battle.

THE WAR MOVES SOUTH, 1780-1781

As the war among the European powers unfolded, the continuing struggle in North America became one piece of a much larger global conflict. British and French ships battled on the high seas, raiding each other's trading routes and imperial possessions around the Atlantic rim, focusing especially on the West Indies and India, where both empires had also established hugely important commercial interests. The Empress of Russia, Catherine the Great, even became involved, organizing on March 11, 1780 the League of Armed Neutrality, which opposed British efforts to cut off trade between the United States and northern European maritime powers. Already battling the Americans, the French and the Spanish, Britain declared war on the Dutch in December 1780 when the Netherlands threatened to join the league. The British now had to maintain naval forces in the North Sea to face a threat from their newest enemy.

Back in London, the global scope of the war stretched Secretary Germain and First Minister North's limited strategic and logistical talents to the breaking point. At the same time, Loyalists from Virginia and the Carolinas, now exiled in London, did what they could to influence the ministers. Encouraged to imagine the southern colonies overflowing with Loyalists patiently waiting for help,

Germain hoped that a campaign there might re-establish royal authority while requiring fewer troops and arms than would a similar effort in troublesome New England.

Optimists like Germain hoped that the capture of Savannah, followed quickly by the rest of the colony, would rapidly lead to British re-conquest of the whole region. Clinton began dispatching his men south, leaving New York in the hands of Hessian troops. A British force of more than 31,000 troops began a siege of the weakly defended port city of **Charles Town, South Carolina** shortly after landing on December 23, 1778. By January, Clinton arrived with an army of 8,000 men. General **Benjamin Lincoln**, the commander of the American southern forces tried to prepare defenses with some 5,000 troops in the city, but Clinton's artillery pounded the city with heavy guns. Sparing the city and his men a blood-soaked finale, Lincoln surrendered on May 12, 1779, giving Clinton the largest British victory of the war.

As John Murray, the Fourth Earl of Dunmore, had done at the beginning of the war in 1775 in Virginia, Clinton tried to exploit the wedge between slave and master in South Carolina as a matter of military convenience rather than humanitarian concern. On June 30, 1779, from his headquarters near New York City, Clinton issued the "**Philipsburg Proclamation**," announcing that slaves who escaped from American rebels were eligible to serve in the British army—and that those captured from American rebels without having escaped would not be freed, but would instead be sold for the benefit of the British. Most important, Loyalists were allowed to keep all their slaves, with those escaping from them were to be returned upon recapture.

Upon arriving in South Carolina, Clinton honored his promise to Loyalists, and sold off many captured slaves of rebels. Even so, the invading army again found that escaped slaves (in the words of one historian) "streamed in like a tidal flood." Overall the war in the South represented by far the largest uprising in the history of North American slavery. In South Carolina, out of a population of 80,000 slaves, perhaps up to 20,000 fled their plantation homes and sought refuge behind British lines. Unlike Dunmore, Clinton refused to set up an "Ethiopian Regiment," but escaped slaves instead provided the British army with a large population of attendants—some acting as servants, others as skilled craftsmen. Perhaps most important, British commanders were able to use refugees familiar with each locale to create effective foraging parties, enabling the army's movements across the countryside. For the refugees themselves, as with Dunmore's black soldiers, most if not all instances of liberation ended in tragedy. Smallpox outbreaks took a drastic toll. When the disease struck Charles Town after the British conquest, hundreds of sick refugees were expelled from the city and left to die in the surrounding woods.

Soon after taking Charles Town, Clinton returned north with 4,000 men, leaving Cornwallis and the rest of his army to occupy the rest of South Carolina. Taking advantage of the ample assistance offered by the escaped slaves, Cornwallis completed the assignment. In one infamous episode, on May 29, 1780, at Waxhaws near the state line, a group of 350 Continental soldiers near Charles Town attempted to retreat to North Carolina but were overtaken by mounted troops made up of enraged Loyalists who had suffered at the hands of the so-called Patriot. They were led by Lieutenant Colonel Banastre Tarleton, one of Cornwallis' officers. As the surrendering soldiers held their hands up in the air, Tarleton coldly ordered his men to gun their captives down. This war crime became a major propaganda coup for the Revolutionary cause as Tarleton's brutality alienated South Carolinians previously uncommitted to the Revolution. The incident also inspired a battle cry. Since Tarleton had given no quarter to his defenseless prisoners, American militias often shouted "Tarleton's Quarter" when they subsequently butchered British or Loyalist troops attempting to surrender. The war turned more vindictive as Patriots destroyed the property of suspected Tories and vice versa, with both sides mutilating the corpses of their enemies.

Trying to restore colonial control South Carolina, General Horatio Gates, the victor of Saratoga, led a hastily assembled army into the state in late July. Cornwallis confronted him at Camden, in the western backcountry, on August 16. When Gates attempted to fight the British in an open European-style battle, the result was a triumph for Cornwallis and another complete disaster for the Americans, as many of Gates's troops panicked leading to the disintegration of his entire army. The bad news continued for the Americans when it was discovered that Benedict Arnold, who had been secretly negotiating with the British, switched sides in the war.

Passed over for promotions, court-martialed, and asked to return money to Congress when accused of misappropriating military funds for personal use, Arnold had grown so bitter against the American government and military command that he began selling military secrets to the British in 1779. After becoming commander of West Point on August 3, 1780, he offered to turn over the fortress to the British. His scheme was exposed when the American military captured a British spy, Major John André, carrying papers detailing the conspiracy. Hearing of André's arrest, Arnold fled and barely escaped arrest by George Washington's forces in New York. A military court sentenced André to death. Hoping to be executed by firing squad, as was the custom in the military for officers, he was hanged instead in Tappan, New York on October 2.

Meanwhile, the British military made Arnold a brigadier general and gave him a cash bonus. Prospects had looked bright for the Americans after the French alliance, but the battle for independence had hit another depressing low. The British had virtually destroyed the Continental Army in the South. "I have almost ceased to hope," Washington privately moaned during this string of disasters.

Settling Scores in the Carolinas

As the British had hoped, Loyalists emerged in significant numbers to support Cornwallis and the crown. Whether Loyalist sentiments were uniquely widespread in the South remains unclear, but the collapse of the Continental Army and state governments brought the Tories out of the underground. The manipulative Philipsburg Proclamation succeeded in encouraging many slaveowners to identify as Loyalists, but it also stoked the rage of Patriot masters against the British. Predating the war for independence were bitter divisions within the region such as the political feud between wealthy coastal planters (who had shaped the Patriot cause) and backcountry settlers (some of whom supported the king because of their grievances against the planters). But ultimately, the war cut across local communities and separated neighbor from neighbor.

Instead of revealing a Loyalist consensus, or enabling a secure re-conquest, British victories created a void in which Patriots (calling themselves Whigs) and Loyalists (or Tories) organized rival militias and paramilitary groups to defend themselves, kill each other, and seize each other's slaves. In this new, grim chapter of the war a new Patriot leader, Francis Marion, led a Whig militia, a fast-moving company of several dozen. "Marion's Men" made deadly surprise raids on larger groups of Tories and British regulars. Determined to eliminate Marion's Men, Tarleton chased them for nearly thirty miles, only to lose them in the swamps covering much of the South Carolina low country. "As for this damned old fox," Tarleton complained, "the Devil himself could not catch him."

Gaining notoriety as "the Swamp Fox," Marion continued to terrorize Tory militias and disrupt British lines of supply and communication. Soon, the Loyalist upsurge was starting to recede. After his victory at Camden, Cornwallis, still trailing a growing population of escaped slaves and taking advantage of their support, continued marching northward, intent on capturing North Carolina. But he could not mobilize the Tories without stirring up Whigs as well. At Kings Mountain, on the border between North and South Carolina, on October 7, converging Pa-

Benedict Arnold, 1741-1801

triot militias attacked a Loyalist detachment led by Major Patrick Ferguson (one of Cornwallis' key officers). After killing Ferguson and winning the battle, the militiamen kept on shooting wounded soldiers and those trying to surrender. "Tarleton's quarter!" they shouted.

The Battles of Cowpens and Guilford Court House

Fierce Whig resistance prevented the restoration of British rule in the South. At the same time, with Lee and Gage discredited, Washington regained momentum with the appointment of a new, vastly more loyal core military leadership. After Gates's calamitous defeat in Camden, with Congress in despair, Washington recommended Nathanael Greene, who had combined field commands with the office of quartermaster general since Valley Forge and had performed heroically in the defeat at Camden. Brigadier General **Daniel Morgan,** the leader of the Virginia riflemen at Saratoga, came out of retirement and offered his services.

Taking the risk of dividing his own outnumbered forces, Greene supplied Morgan 700 men, giving them the mission of disrupting Cornwallis's supply lines, buying Greene more time to rebuild the rest of his army. Cornwallis dispatched Tarleton to destroy Morgan's detachment, now numbering about 1,000. But at **Cowpens**, South Carolina, on January 17, 1781, Morgan gained another measure of revenge for the Whigs and Continentals, striking another damaging blow to British control of the South.

Taking advantage of Tarleton's now-famous ferocity and aggressiveness, Morgan dispatched militiamen

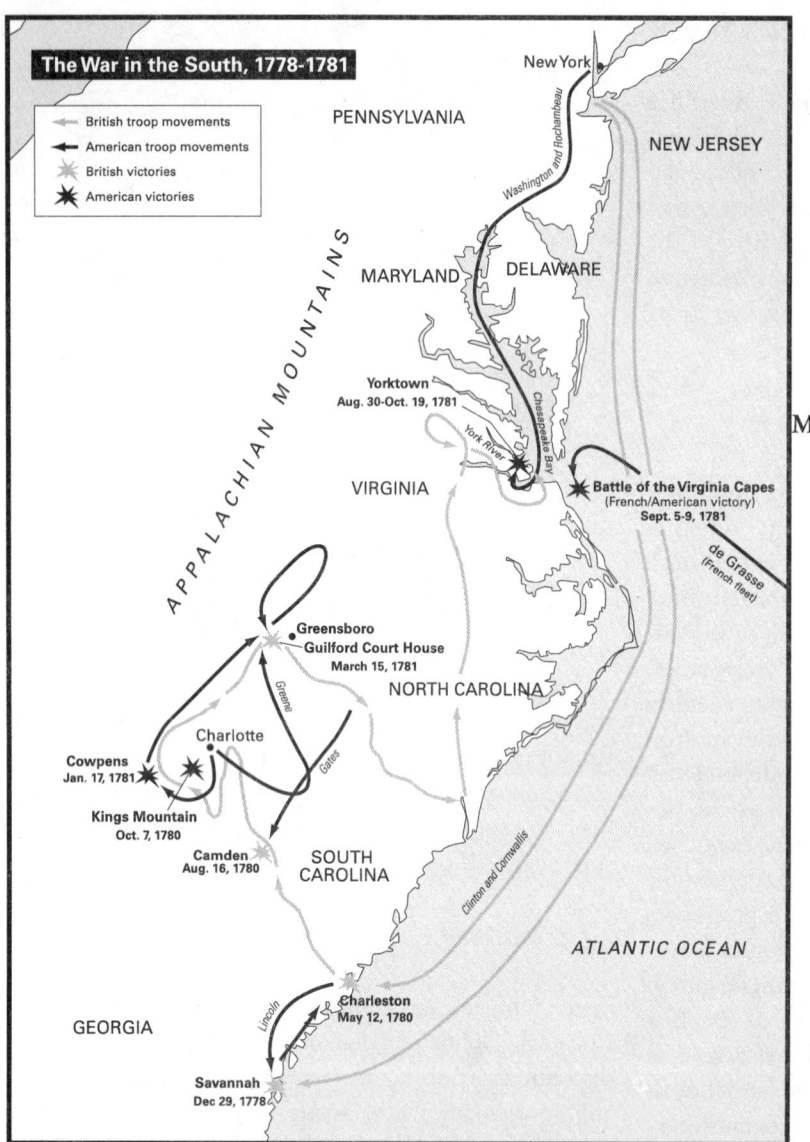

Map 6.3 The War in the South, 1778-1781

to advance against Tarleton. After firing two rounds, the infantrymen fell back. Tarleton unwisely pursued. Morgan had his troops fake a retreat, but with discipline and precision, they wheeled around against Tarleton's unprepared forces, who fell, under the withering line of fire. For the first time in the war, a significant force of British soldiers was almost completely destroyed in battle. Like Gates after Camden, Tarleton fled for his life and escaped with only a few of his men.

Undeterred by this serious setback, Cornwallis plunged into North Carolina, seeking to cut off the supplies that sustained Greene's forces and (he imagined) the rest of the American forces. Greene retreated quickly to the north, maintained his supply lines, and kept gathering reinforcements. At **Guilford Court House** (now in Greensboro), North Carolina, on March 15, the two armies faced off in battle for the only time. Although Cornwallis withstood fierce volleys and continued to advance, Morgan inflicted heavy casualties at a time when the war was becoming increasingly unpopular in Britain. Like Washington in previous battles, Greene kept his own army intact and left his opponent bleeding. "The enemy got the ground the other day, but we the victory," Greene proclaimed. "They had the splendor, we the advantage."

Both armies now turned away from each other and embarked on separate missions. Still searching for a way in which military power could resurrect British authority, Cornwallis looked farther north, toward Virginia, where he imagined uniting his forces with the rest of Clinton's army from New York. Greene envisioned something similarly ambitious but much more practical. Turning south, he set about clearing South Carolina of the occupying forces Cornwallis had left behind. Working closely with Whig militiamen under Marion and others—and taking advantage of collapsing Loyalist support—Greene coordinated a campaign of attacks on British garrisons. Despite several more hard-fought battles in which they held their ground, British unit commanders felt they had no choice but to abandon South Carolina's interior. By September 1781, like Clinton in New York, the British in South Carolina were confined to their stronghold in Charleston.

Cornwallis Blunders—The Siege of Yorktown

Cornwallis yearned for a chance to battle the Continental Army face-to-face with his main army, a confrontation in which he thought British professionalism would prevail. In seeking this showdown, he unknowingly marched into a trap. In May, the general arrived in Petersburg, Virginia and linked up with other British forces under the command of Benedict Arnold. Lafayette now commanded the small army of Continentals based in Virginia while Cornwallis pondered his next move. Tarleton made another of his raids, chasing the Virginia legislature, which had moved from Richmond to Charlottesville. Tarleton and Arnold also staged a raid on Jefferson's estate at Monticello. They almost captured the revolutionary leader, then serving as governor of Virginia. Tarleton celebrated this humiliation of the author of the Declaration of Independence by helping himself to Jefferson's wine cellar.

In New York, Clinton struggled with formulating a plan to end the rebellion, unable to decide between sending the rest of his own forces, as Cornwallis hoped, to fight a decisive battle in Virginia and recalling troops from the South for a campaign in the North. In June, he ordered Cornwallis to find a defensible point on the Virginia coastline and set up a base that would accommodate naval forces. No final decision was ever reached about what purpose this base would ultimately serve, but in August, Cornwallis settled his army at **Yorktown**, a short distance up the York River from Chesapeake Bay—a site isolated on a peninsula between two rivers, but accessible to ships requiring deep-water clearance. As the British army and its trailing mass of escaped slaves began building fortress walls, Lafayette kept watch, reporting back to Washington.

Recognizing a precious opportunity, Washington seized it. Early in the year, he and Rochambeau agreed that any decisive move against British armies would require the participation of the French fleet in the West Indies, now commanded by Admiral François-Joseph Paul, marquis de Grasse Tilly, comte de Grasse. Washington had wanted to launch an operation against Clinton in New York, but Rochambeau suggested to de Grasse that an assault against Cornwallis in the Chesapeake region offered a better option. In mid-August, as word arrived from Lafayette about Cornwallis' base at Yorktown, a message also arrived from de Grasse that the greater part of the fleet was now bound for Chesapeake Bay. Washington's decision had been made for him. The long years of struggle, hardship, training, lessons learned from lost battles, and hard-won improvements in the Continental Army—as well as the arrival of French soldiers—all served as preparation for this moment.

Back in New York, Washington worked to deceive Clinton about his intentions. Within view of the British commander's scouts, American soldiers staged apparent preparations for a move against the British forces in Manhattan. Meanwhile, Washington and his staff wrote detailed instructions for the storage of supplies, repair of roads, and placement of boats along specific routes leading south. As late as the end of August, Clinton still believed Washington was repositioning his forces to attack New York. By then, however, the Continental and French troops had already passed through Trenton and were headed toward Virginia.

Shipping artillery and other heavy equipment on boats down the Delaware, they marched through Philadelphia on September 2, and then onward to the south, almost at running speed. Three weeks later they were in Williamsburg, Virginia, together with Lafayette, as well as French reinforcements from de Grasse and army and militia units arriving from throughout the states. By the end of the month, the expanded American and French armies had marched down the neck of the peninsula toward Yorktown and formed a semicircle around the British defenses. Cornwallis faced French and American troops on three sides on the ground while 300 warships commanded by Admiral de Grasse cut off an escape route by sea. Washington and Rochambeau received one more stroke of luck.

The British naval commander in the West Indies, Admiral George Brydges Rodney, 1st Baron Rodney ordered a squadron led by Admiral Sir Samuel Hood to follow and intercept the French fleet. Hood's men, however, lost sight of the enemy's ships and arrived in the **Chesapeake** ahead of de Grasse's forces. Finding no French ships in Chesapeake Bay on August 25, Hood decided that the French were headed north to attack Clinton's army in New York City, and he directed his ships in that direction, away from the gathering French and American forces in Virginia. Back on Chesapeake Bay, the French fleet arrived unimpeded and landed troop reinforcements for Rochambeau.

On August 28, Admiral Hood arrived in New York and reported to Admiral Thomas Graves, commander-in-chief of the British naval forces in North America, that a French fleet from the West Indies was somewhere in American waters. Graves received intelligence that another French fleet had sailed from Newport, Rhode Island and was headed south. Realizing Graves' mistake, the

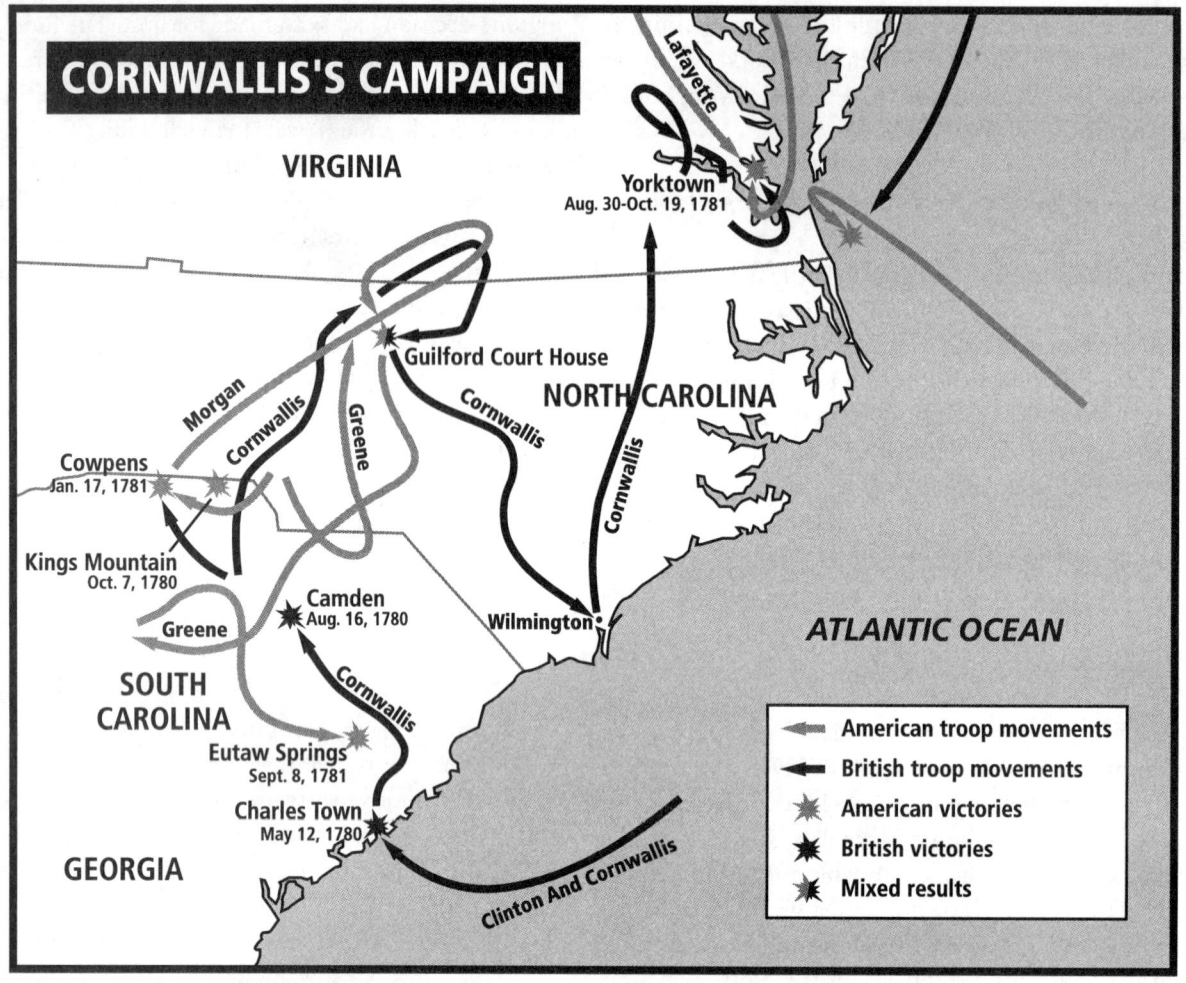

Map 6.4 Cornwallis's Campaign

admiral combined his forces with Hood's and the British fleet took off for Chesapeake Bay for what would be the most decisive naval confrontation of the war. On September 5, the combined forces of Graves and Hood appeared off the Virginia Capes. The French ships sailed hastily out to open water and into battle formation. As much as the outcome of the war depended on Washington's decisions and the Continental Army's abilities, it now rested as well on French naval strength. After long hours in which the opposing lines of ships maneuvered against each other and against the winds and the currents, then raked each other with cannon fire, the French maintained their line and the British failed to break through. As an east wind pushed the fleets farther out to sea, Graves decided to sail back to New York to try to organize a larger expedition. The bay remained under French control. Cornwallis and his army, in their fortress by the bay, remained cut off from the rest of the world.

In the final days at Yorktown, abandoning his headquarters in the city's grandest mansion, the British commander hid in a cave dug underneath a garden. Above ground, shells exploded among his men and smashed against the crumbling fortress walls. In his last messages to Clinton, Cornwallis acknowledged the situation: "Against so powerful an attack, we cannot hope to make a very long resistance." Outside the city, Washington pressed for a rapid end to the siege, before another naval expedition could arrive from New York. (Graves did, in fact, arrive back in the Chesapeake, several days too late.)

Under General von Steuben's supervision, the American and French troops built a tightening ring of earthworks around Cornwallis's forces: parapets for reinforced shelter, batteries for gun emplacements, and redoubts for the massing of troops, all connected by lines of trenches. The network grew quickly once the American and French heavy artillery were fully in position and firing. Washington's right-hand man, Alexander Hamilton, who had spent years coveting battlefield glory, led an infantry brigade that stormed and seized a British redoubt, preparing the way for a final storming of the city. Cornwallis pre-empted the inevitable by asking on October 17 for peace terms. Too proud to capitulate to Washington, Cornwallis sent his deputy to present his sword as a gesture of surrender. Washington and Rochambeau, insulted by Cornwallis' absence, refused it, and directed that the sword be handed to one of the senior American officers, Benjamin Lincoln.

Table 6.1 Major Battles of the Revolutionary War

Battle	Date	Outcome
Lexington and Concord, Massachusetts	April 19, 1975	Contested
Fort Ticonderoga, New York	May 10, 1775	American victory
Breeds Hill ("Bunker Hill"), Boston, Massachusetts	June 17, 1775	Contested
Brooklyn Heights, New York	August 27, 1776	British victory
White Plains, New York	October 28, 1776	British victory
Battle of Fort Washington	November 16, 1776	British victory
Trenton, New Jersey	December 26, 1776	American victory
Princeton, New Jersey	January 3, 1777	American victory
Brandywine Creek, Pennsylvania	September 11, 1777	British victory
Battle of Germantown	October 4, 1777	British victory
Saratoga, New York	September 19 - October 7, 1777	American victory
Monmouth Court House, New Jersey	June 28, 1778	Contested
Savannah, Georgia	December 29, 1778	British victory
Charleston, South Carolina	February 11 - May 12, 1780	British victory
Camden, South Carolina	August 16, 1780	British victory
Kings Mountain, South Carolina	October 7, 1780	American victory
Cowpens, South Carolina	January 17, 1781	American victory
Guilford Court House, North Carolina	March 15, 1781	Contested
Yorktown, Virginia	August 30 - October 19, 1781	American victory

The British taken prisoner numbered over 7,000 soldiers. As they were paraded between lines of American and French soldiers facing each other, a band played "The World Turned Upside Down."

The Treaty of Paris

While the news from Yorktown sparked wild celebrations in Philadelphia and elsewhere across the former colonies, Washington immediately organized a return march to the encampments around New York City, where his forces remained for the next two years. In London, upon receiving the news of Cornwallis' surrender, Lord North cried out, "Oh, God, it's all over!" Determined to cut Britain's losses, the Parliament would not approve any further military attempts to prevent American independence. George III drafted a declaration of his abdication that he decided not to deliver, but he finally allowed North to resign as Prime Minister. A British envoy, Richard Oswald, came to Paris to meet with American and French delegates at a peace conference.

Even though the Congress directed the American peace delegation to follow the instructions of the French, American representative Benjamin Franklin focused on working out terms directly with Oswald. Ironically, British victories in 1782 over Admiral de Grasse in the Caribbean, and over Spanish attempts to reconquer Gibraltar, proved useful to the Americans, in that they persuaded France and Spain to wind down the war as well. On September 3, 1783, treaties were signed in Paris and Versailles by the American, British, and other European delegates. The **Treaty of Paris**, between Great Britain and the United States, not only recognized American independence but also defined American territory as extending west all the way to the Mississippi River. Under the terms of the treaty, the Congress was to "earnestly recommend" that states return confiscated property to Loyalists, or provide compensation for their losses. The states, however, disregarded this provision just as the British disregarded a provision requiring them to abandon military forts near the Great Lakes, which now lay within American territory. The British signed separate treaties with the French and the Spanish.

Cynically, and correctly, the French foreign minister Vergennes observed that the British "buy peace, rather than make it." Ministers in London soon realized that the former colonies would largely retain their traditional dependence on Britain's investment capital and export goods. The restoration of commercial ties between Britain and the newly independent states would restore many of the economic benefits of empire for the British. For the Americans, the uncertainty of the Revolutionary era seemed over. In the summer of 1776, when Howe's army conquered New York, Washington and the Continental Army seemed overmatched, and the war looked like a lost cause. Seven years later, the last British commander-in-chief to occupy Manhattan, Sir Guy Carleton (who had succeeded Clinton the year before), received orders to evacuate. In addition to the remaining British and Hessian troops, the Royal Navy carried away some 29,000 Loyalists and also slaves liberated from Patriot masters (again technically violating the Treaty of Paris). On November 25, the last Union Jack (flag of the United Kingdom) was pulled down from a flagpole over lower Manhattan, and a cannon fired a final shot from one of the departing ships. Roughly 200,000 men (approximately half of those eligible by age) out of a total American population of between three to 4 million served at some point in the Continental Army or in state militia units.

American forces had lost approximately 25,000 dead, only 8,000 directly in combat with another 17,000 dying from exposure, disease and the poor quality of medical care provided. Unaware of the existence of germs, Army doctors performed operations with unclean instruments. Believing that disease derived from an imbalance of body fluids, American medical doctors, like their British counterparts, would bleed patients, deliberately cutting a vein and draining blood to restore the correct ratio of blood, phlegm, and black and yellow bile. This procedure often killed badly dehydrated patients suffering influenza and other serious illnesses. An unknown but surely large number of deaths went unrecorded, among soldiers and camp attendants. The total of deaths and injuries may have amounted to one in four of those who fought. The French lost about 2,000 in North America. Twenty thousand British soldiers died, as well as 7,600 German mercenaries; about 42,000 "Redcoats" and 5,000 Hessians deserted.

THE "RADICALISM" OF THE AMERICAN REVOLUTION

The American Revolution was certainly about battles, but more importantly it was about ideas. As noted previously, in seventeenth century England the concept of popular sovereignty (the idea that governments can rule legitimately only with the consent of the people and that governments existed solely to protect "life, liberty and the pursuit of property") had arisen. This viewpoint suggested that governments failing to meet those ends lacked legitimacy and could be justly overthrown by the people. Such were the explanations offered to explain the overthrow and execution of Charles I in 1649 during the English Civil War, the overthrow and exile of the last Stuart king in England, James II, in 1688, and finally in the American Revolution starting in 1775.

The elites leading the American Revolution sought to create a republic in a world of kings, but the concept of the monarchy was already decaying in England and elsewhere in Europe and the Americas before shots were fired at Lexington and Concord in 1775. As the historian Gordon Wood wrote, "Republicanism seeped everywhere in the eighteenth-century Atlantic world, eroding monarchial society from within, wearing away all the traditional supports of kingship, ultimately desacralizing monarchy to the point were, as [18th century Scottish philosopher] David Hume observed, 'the mere name of king commands little respect; and to talk of a *king* as God's vice-regent on earth, or to give him any of those magnificent titles which formerly dazzled mankind, would but excite laughter in everyone."

The leaders of the American Revolution, however, took the ideas of the enlightenment much further. The years from the French and Indian War in the 1750s and 1760s to the ratification of the United States Constitution in 1788 saw an subtle but important shift in the emerging United States in terms of class, the separation of church and state, slavery, and gender politics. The American Revolution started as a mere shift in who would rule—the British king or wealthy American oligarchs—but opened the door for later more radical change.

After the revolution, inheritance still mattered and the rich still ruled, but the aristocracy became markedly more open-ended. Lineage increasingly mattered less than financial independence and men born to relatively humble means sometimes rose to the social and political top. "There are but two *sorts* of men in the world, freemen and slaves," John Adams declared in 1775. The freemen, as Adams' English contemporary John Toland put it, were "men of property, or persons that are able to live of themselves." Those who derived their living by working for others were the ones Adams called slaves. Adams saw independent farmers, business owners and professionals like doctors, lawyers and the clergy as the freemen. The freemen's supposed independence from political blackmail and manipulation is the excuse the Founders used for limiting suffrage and the right to run for and hold public office to property owners. However, after the revolution, Vermont extended the vote to all adult white men who were not slaves or indentured servants. Kentucky entered the union in 1792 and its state constitution included no property requirements for voting or holding office. Other states generally reduced the property requirements for voting.

The Founders also made tentative steps towards expanding the freeman class. State legislatures began abolishing traditions that limited the number of self-sufficient property owners within families, customs such as primogeniture (in which only the oldest son inherits a father's estate) or entail (in which inheritance is limited to lineal descendents). Before the revolution, widows usually were granted only lifetime use of their husband's estates. New state laws allowed widows to own outright one-third of their deceased spouses' property, giving them the freedom to dispense with this property as they pleased. As Wood puts it, "In a variety of ways the new state laws not only abolished the remaining feudal forms of land tenure and enhanced the commercial nature of real estate; they also confirmed the new enlightened republican attitudes towards the family."

In the late 1700s, a revolution took place within the American family. Even as the just-born United States had severed its connection to the British king, the dictatorial authority of fathers within families noticeably loosened. This process began earlier in the 1700s when more Americans survived childhood, which left more adult children without estates due to primogeniture. As land became more expensive and there were more adults who could not count on inheriting an estate, more adult children moved away from their birth families. The number of marriages arranged by parents as business deals declined and these newly independent young adults began to marry for personal reasons such as romance, sexual attraction or unplanned pregnancies. Early American authors writing advice books urged their readers to have marriages based on affection, and told parents that they should rely less on harsh physical punishments and have more open, affectionate relationship with their children.

Attitudes towards women subtly changed. Before the revolution, women were universally portrayed as physically and morally weak. Sin came to the world and God cursed humanity with mortality because Eve succumbed to temptation by the serpent in the Garden of Eden, ministers insisted. After the revolution, some men acknowledged the role women had played in the success of the war effort. Women had managed the family economy, run farms and businesses and negotiated with merchants while their husbands were off to war. After the revolution, the United States had a new, republican system of government in which the political leaders would not be assumed to hold office because God directly selected them. No one knew if a rotating cast of politicians who could be voted out of office, even (after 1789) the presidency, would command respect. Many men realized that women were the first and sometimes the only teachers children had and it would be up to what were now called "republican mothers" to teach their children respect for the new form of government and loyalty to the new nation.

In sermons and in literature in the post-Revolution period, women were suddenly portrayed as not weaklings without character, but as bedrocks of virtue. Literacy among women in the Northeast skyrocketed. In New England, the literacy rate for women reached 45 percent, one of the highest levels in the world. More affluent women became the chief audience for a wildly popular art form, the novel, which often depicted virginal heroines rejecting the advances of scoundrels and, with grit, holding off marriage proposals until an equally pure hero arrives on the scene. Even as literature depicted women in a more positive light, by the 1790s, female academies began to appear in the United States, creating a better-educated population of women.

This softer attitude towards women, unfortunately, became a double-edged sword. America's patriarchy deemed that these brave, pure "republican mothers" had maintained their virtue precisely because, unlike men, they had been shielded from the supposedly corrupting world of business and politics. This became one more sexist reason for denying women a political voice and keeping them economically subordinate. In 12 of the 13 states women could not vote. In New Jersey, for a time women could vote if they were the heads of households, but by 1807, these women had been disenfranchised.

The revolution, as will be discussed in the next chapter, also ushered in a wave of slave emancipations. Finally, the revolution marked the beginning separation of church and state. In several of the 13 colonies, the officially established faith had been the Church of England, an institution officially headed by the king. This name and this relationship became untenable in the new United States. In the United States, Anglican leaders dubbed their denomination the "Episcopal Church" and severed direct ties to the mother church in England. As the established religion, Anglican churches had been directly subsidized by taxpayers and the Church of England had the exclusive right to conduct marriage ceremonies. After the revolution, across the South the Anglican Church was "disestablished," meaning it lost public funding and its special privileges. This began in Virginia in 1786 where the state passed the Thomas Jefferson-authored Statute for Religious Freedom, which announced in its preamble that, "God hath created the mind free."

The separation of church and state proceeded most slowly in New England, except in Rhode Island, which had established religious freedom for all Protestants in its original colonial charter. In states like Massachusetts, the Congregationalist Church (descended from the Puritan movement) had been established as the state religion by law and ministers and churches still received tax support, a status not changed until 1818 in Connecticut and 1833 in Massachusetts. Most states continued to restrict office holding to Christians, or specifically Protestants, with many, for instance, having so-called "Jew bills" that required elected officials to affirm a belief in Jesus as savior. However, after the revolution, the general public became less comfortable with religious coercion and marginally more tolerant of Jews and Catholics. For instance, just before the revolution, American colonists held ferocious protests upon hearing that the British government had recognized the Catholic Church in the Quebec Act of 1774. A decade later, hardly a voice of opposition was heard when Pope Pius VI consecrated John Carroll of Maryland as the first Roman Catholic bishop in America in the 1780s.

Gordon Wood describes the American Revolution as radical. That might be an overstatement. The leaders of the revolution had ended the rule over the colonies by a king and, as will be noted later, ushered in an era of revolts in France, Haiti and elsewhere that more dramatically altered those societies. But the American founders still created a new government in which Protestant white men of property held a monopoly of power, in which slavery thrived, in which women were disenfranchised and almost all were financially dependent on their nearest male relatives or husbands, and in which Native Americans continued to be the victims of imperialism and genocide.

Nevertheless a door had been opened. In relative terms, "the world turned upside down." Suffocating paternalism had weakened, and the groundwork had been laid for religious diversity and for generations of abolitionists and feminists. It wasn't even the beginning of the freedom revolutions that would mark the period from 1865 with the abolition of slavery to the gay rights triumphs in the early twenty-first century, but it was at least the beginning of the beginning.

Chronology

1776 Siege of New York.
The Continental Congress approves the Declaration of Independence.
Battle of Long Island
The Crisis is published.
Battle of Trenton.

1777 Battle of Princeton.
Vermont abolishes slavery.
Cornwallis's troops enter Philadelphia.
Burgoyne surrenders at Saratoga.
Second Continental Congress approves the Articles of Confederation.

1778 Valley Forge winter.
United States and France agree to a military alliance.
Battle of Monmouth Court House.
Siege of Savannah.

1779 Benjamin Lincoln withdraws from Savannah.
Philipsburg Proclamation.

1780 Pennsylvania passes gradual emancipation law.
League of Armed Neutrality.
Massacre in Waxhaws, South Carolina.
Benedict Arnold given command at West Point and betrays the American cause.
Cornwallis' forces overwhelm Gates' men in Camden, South Carolina.
Benedict Arnold flees.
André is hanged.
Great Britain declares war on The Netherlands.

1781 Battle of Cowpens.
Articles of Confederation ratified.
Battle of Guilford Courthouse.
Slavery of Elizabeth Freeman illegal.
Seige of Yorktown.

Review Questions

1. What strengths and weaknesses of the British and the Americans proved decisive in the American Revolutionary War?

2. What major flawed assumptions did the British military make in its war plans against the Continental Army?

3. How did slavery affect the conduct of the Revolutionary War and what impact did the ideas of the Revolution and the Constitution have on slavery after the war?

4. What role did international diplomacy play in securing a victory for the Americans in the revolution?

5. What major social changes took place in the United States in the late eighteenth century?

Glossary of Important People and Concepts

American Crisis
Battle of Brandywine Creek
Joseph Brant (also known as Thayendanegea)
John Burgoyne
Siege of Charleston
Battle of the Chesapeake
Henry Clinton
Lord Charles Cornwallis
Battles of Cowpens and Guilford Courthouse
Jean-Baptiste Donatien, comte de Rochambeau de Vimeur
Horatio Gates
Lord George Germain
Nathanael Greene
Hessians
William Howe
Henry Knox
Charles Lee
Benjamin Lincoln
Louis XVI
Battle of Long Island
Battle of Monmouth Court House
Daniel Morgan
Treaty of Paris
Philipsburg Proclamation
Battle of Princeton
Battles of Saratoga
Frederich Wilhelm Von Steuben
Tories
Valley Forge
Siege of Yorktown

SUGGESTED READINGS

Carol Berkin, *Revolutionary Mothers: Women in the Struggle for American Independence* (2005).

Jeremy Black, *War for America: The Fight for Independence, 1775-1783* (1991).

Robert M. Calhoon, *Revolutionary America: An Interpretive Overview* (1976).

Colin Calloway, *The American Revolution in the Indian Country: Crisis and Diversity in Native American Communities* (1995).

Stephen Conway, *The War of American Independence* (1995).

Saul Cornell, *The Other Founders: Anti-Federalism and the Dissenting Tradition in America, 1788-1828* (1999).

Edward Countryman, *The American Revolution* (1985).

Gregory Evans Dowd, *A Spirited Existence: The North American Indian Struggle for Unity, 1745-1815* (1992).

Joseph Ellis, *American Sphinx: The Character of Thomas Jefferson* (1998).

___, *Founding Brothers: The Revolutionary Generation* (2000).

___, *His Excellency, George Washington* (2004).

Brian M. Fagan, *The Little Ice Age: How Climate Made History, 1300-1850* (2001).

James Thomas Flexner, *Washington: The Indispensable Man* (1974).

Willim M. Fowler, *An American Crisis: George Washington and the Dangerous Two Years After Yorktown, 1781-1783* (2011).

Sylvia Frye, *Water from the Rock: Black Resistance in a Revolutionary Age* (1991).

Donald A. Grinde, Jr. and Bruce E. Johansen, *Exemplar of Liberty: Native America and the Evolution of Democracy* (1991).

Robert A. Hendrickson, *The Rise and Fall of Alexander Hamilton* (1981).

Don Higgenbotham, *The War of American Independence, Policies and Practices 1763-1789* (1971).

James H. Hutson, *The Founders on Religion: A Book of Quotations* 2007.

Merrill Jensen, *The Founding of a Nation: A History of the American Revolution, 1763-1776* (1968).

Lester D. Langley, *The Americas in the Age of Revolution, 1750-1850* (1996).

Leonard W. Levy and Dennis J. Mahoney, eds., *The Framing and Ratification of the American Constitution* (1987).

Paul Douglas Lockhart, *The Drillmaster of Valley Forge: The Baron de Steuben and the Making of the American Army* (2008).

Piers Mackesy, *The War for America, 1775-1783* (1964).

James Kirby Martin and Mark E. Lender, *A Respectable Army: The Military Origins of the Republic, 1763-1789* (1982.)

Robert Middlekauf, *The Glorious Cause: The American Revolution, 1763-1789* (1982).

Edward S. Morgan, *Birth of the Republic, 1763-1789* (1956).

Robert R. Palmer, *The Age of Democratic Revolution, 1760-1800, Volumes I and II* (1959-1964).

W.J. Rorabaugh, *The Alcoholic Republic: An American Tradition* (1979).

Charles Royster, *A Revolutionary People at War: The Continental Army and American Character, 1775-1783* (1979).

Thaddeus Russell, *A Renegade History of the United States* (2010).

Randy Shilts, *Conduct Unbecoming: Gays and Lesbians in the Military* (1993).

Marshall Smelser, *The Winning of Independence* (1972).

Barbara Clark Smith, "Food Rioters and the American Revolution," *The William and Mary Quarterly*, 3rd Series, Volume LI, No. 1 (January 1994).

Leonard E. Tise, *The American Counterrevolution: A Retreat from Liberty, 1783-1800* (1998).

Barbara W. Tuchman. *The March of Folly: From Troy to Vietnam.* (1984).

JOURNAL

OF THE

PROCEEDINGS

OF THE

CONGRESS,

Held at PHILADELPHIA,

September 5, 1774.

PHILADELPHIA:

Printed by WILLIAM and THOMAS BRADFORD,
at the *London Coffee-House*.

Chapter Seven

THE STRUGGLE TO CREATE THE CONSTITUTION

*A common plot device in science fiction films has been time travel. One of the most popular movies in this genre has been the trilogy that started with the 1985 film **Back to the Future**. In this story arc, the main character, Marty McFly, is accidentally dispatched 30 years into the past where he unintentionally prevents his parents, then teenagers, from meeting and falling in love. Unless he can correct this alteration in history, he and his brother and sister will never be born. In this film and two sequels, McFly continually alters the future in wildly unanticipated ways. As the scientific author Stephen Jay Gould writes, this film accurately captures the progress of history The past is treated as contingent. Nothing is inevitable.*

That is not how most of the public sees American history. The leaders of the American Revolution such as George Washington, Ben Franklin, Thomas Jefferson, and Johns Adams traditionally are imagined by the public to be uniquely far-sighted, with the outcome of the American Revolution and the destiny of the country never really in doubt. In the early twenty-first century, conservative Christian evangelist and amateur historian David Barton argued in a series of bestselling books that God directly inspired the Founders. Many other Americans accepted the idea that the American Revolution, the writing of the Constitution, the republic's increasingly democratic institutions, and the spreading of the United States from coast to coast, were foreordained. Even some of the Founding Fathers convinced themselves of this.

George Washington, writing just after the revolution ended in 1783, concluded that there must have been some divine plan in Americans being "placed in the most enviable condition, as the sole Lords and Proprietors of a vast Tract of Continent, comprehending all the various soils and Climates of the world, and abounding with all the necessaries and conveniences of life . . . [This] seems to be peculiarly designed by Providence for the display of human greatness and felicity." With hindsight, Washington seemed to suggest that the War for Independence could not have turned out any other way than with the United States triumphing over Great Britain.

Washington conveniently forgot about the millions of Native Americans who still lived on the continent when he enthused about whites being the "sole Lords and proprietors" of North America. He also forgot his own deep doubts and fears during the war over how the American Revolution would end, and his own frequent sense that independence was a lost cause. Once the fighting was over, he could pretend that Americans had always been destined for greatness, that it had been part of God's plan from the beginning of time.

That kind of confidence faded once again in the first decade of independence. By the mid-1780s, many American leaders wondered if the new American republic would survive the eighteenth century. As the country languished under its first constitution, the Articles of Confederation, John Adams feared the United States was doomed. With independence less than a half-decade old, Adams reflected on previous republics—the city-states in ancient Greece and medieval Italy, and the short-lived Roman Republic almost 2,000 years earlier. Adams shuddered as he considered how ephemeral those earlier experiments in republican govern-

ment has been and contemplated the vexing complications of governing a vast nation as diverse and complex as the United States. "The lawgivers of antiquity legislated for single cities . . . [but] who can legislate for 20 or 30 states, each of which is greater [in size] than Greece or Rome at those times?" he asked with despair.

Adams was not alone in his pessimism. The Congress, the only branch of the federal government established under the Articles of Confederation, poorly managed the country and commanded little respect overseas. A depression ravaged America after the revolution ended and lasted for most of the 1780s. A farmers' rebellion broke out in Massachusetts. Former Revolutionary War officers grumbled about the need to overthrow the Congress. As the historian Carol Berkin writes, "From his plantation in Virginia, George Washington lamented the steady stream of diplomatic humiliations suffered by the young Republic. Fellow Virginian [and future principle author of the Constitution] James Madison talked gravely of mortal diseases afflicting the confederacy. In New Jersey [Gov]. William Livingston confided to a friend his doubt that the Republic could survive another decade. From Massachusetts, the bookseller turned Revolutionary strategist, Henry Know, declared, 'Our present federal government is a name, a shadow, without power or effect.'"

These men feared for the future, and they floundered for an answer. There were so many different paths American history could have taken. A coup led by former military officers could have installed Washington, if he accepted the post, as king or dictator. Several states could have seceded, asking for readmission to the British Empire or to become part of Spain's imperial realm. Farmers' revolts could have led to a second revolution, this one not managed by a relatively conservative moneyed elite, but by the angry dispossessed. This second revolution could have been a full-scale class revolt and led in a more radical direction as did the French Revolution that started in 1789. Nothing about the future was preordained in the 1780s.

To corral the chaos, the leading men of their times gathered in Philadelphia in 1787 to plot a non-violent overthrow of the existing government and write a new Constitution that would re-establish what they saw as the proper social and economic order. The framers of the Constitution were well off, but still a motley crew—"men of wealth and comfort—landowners, slaveholders, lawyers, merchants, land and securities speculators, and an occasional doctor or clergymen," as Berkin put it. "A few of these self-made men still bore traces of their humble origins in their carriage, in their calluses, or their plain speech. Yet there was no one in the room who might be properly called a man of ordinary means, a yeoman farmer, a shopkeeper, a sailor, or a laborer."

These were not the demigods later depicted in national myth, but deeply flawed and uncertain men, philanderers and rogues like Gouverneur Morris of Pennsylvania, privileged bluebloods like George Mason of Virginia and Preston Butler of South Carolina, and cynical alcoholics like Luther Martin of Maryland. One cliché has it that one should never watch law or sausages being made, because the process is so unappetizing. These often less-than-heroic framers of the Constitution were sausage-makers of the first degree. They cut moral corners and compromised principles, particularly on the issue of slavery, in writing the final document that became the Constitution of the United States.

At several points, the process almost completely fell apart, and several state delegations nearly stormed out of the convention over the issue of slavery and representation in the new two-chamber Congress the delegates debated. It was messy and what would be created in Philadelphia was definitely not inevitable. A misstep at several points and the delegates in Philadelphia would have bequeathed to their descendants a very different future—one in which the new country would have fragmented and failed. Convenience and chance ruled the day as much as inspiration.

CHAOS UNDER THE ARTICLES OF CONFEDERATION

The Americans won the war, but they almost lost the peace. By 1787, six years after the victory at Yorktown secured the independence of the United States, many inside and outside of the country wondered if Americans could actually govern themselves. The country teetered on the edge of economic ruin, the political system lay in chaos, and everywhere lay signs that a second revolution loomed, this time aimed at overthrowing American elites.

Through the years of fighting, the United States lacked a fully functional national government. The Second Continental Congress raised armies, approved officers' commissions, set policies on war and diplomacy, issued paper currency (basically IOU's, promising future redemption in hard cash) to pay for expenses, and declared independence, all in response to immediate practical necessities. Yet the Congress lacked other powers, most important among these the authority to impose taxes. On November 15, 1777, the delegates finally approved the **Articles of Confederation**, which served as the United States' first constitution.

Not until March 1, 1781, did the Articles of Confederation go into effect. Drafted at a time when the American political leadership blamed the American Revolution on a king they believed had assumed dictatorial powers

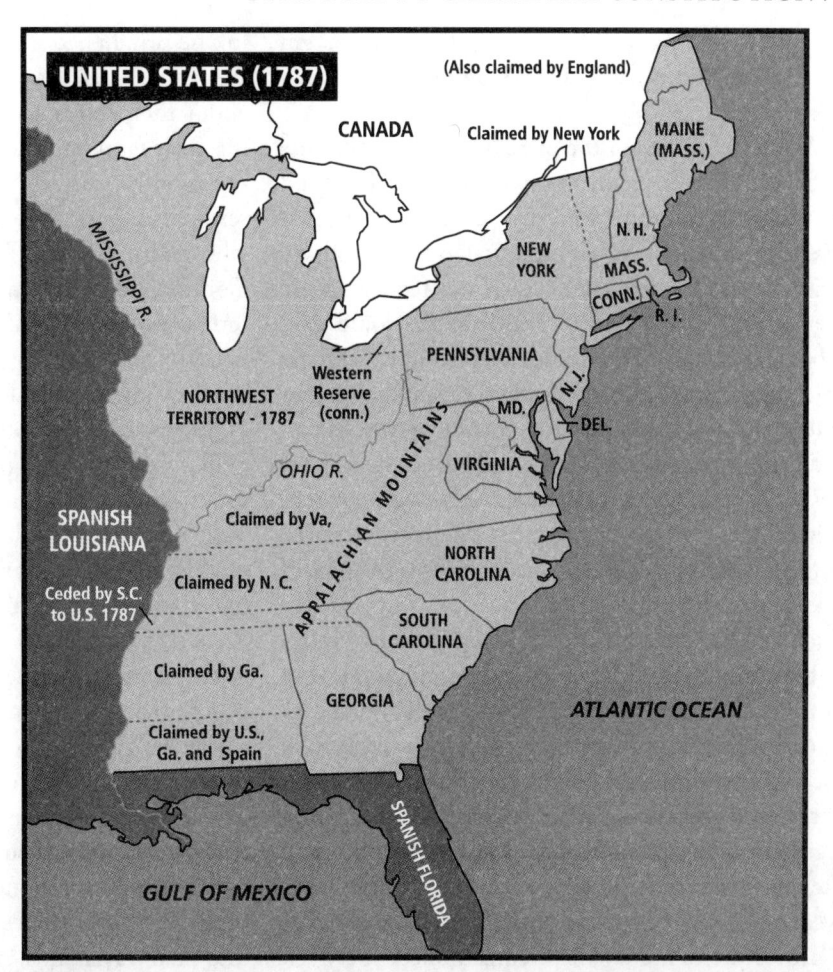

Map 7.1 United States (1787)

and the British Parliament which they thought overruled the authority of local elected governments, the Articles reflected a deep distrust of central government. The national government created under the Articles became one of the weakest in modern Western history.

The delegates in the Continental Congress wrote the Articles with the intention of placing strict limits on the national government's authority. They insisted on a written constitution. Many revolutionary leaders believed the fact that England's "constitution" was unwritten had allowed the Parliament and King George III too much opportunity to claim unchecked power. Not only the Congress, but the states started drafting written constitutions, seen as contracts that spelled out the powers and responsibilities of government.

Under the Articles, the Congress served as the only branch of government. There was no presidency under the Articles, no single executive who could transform into the tyrant George III had supposedly become. The Congress wasn't completely impotent. Each state delegation, regardless of size, got one vote in the Congress. The Articles gave the Congress authority to declare war and make peace, negotiate treaties with other nations and Native American peoples, conduct foreign policy, and formulate military strategy.

The Articles, however, placed severe limits on the Congress, which could not impose a military draft during the Revolution but could only request that the independent-minded states provide a fair share of troops based on their population. The idea of "states' rights"—the concept that state governments were more representative of the voters and should therefore enjoy sovereignty within their borders, granting only limited powers to the federal government—served as the governing principle of the Articles. The drafters of the Articles hoped that state legislatures would see the big picture and put the country ahead of local concerns. Unfortunately, states often worried more about their individual security, and congressional requisitions for troops often went unmet. In a critical error, the Articles provided Congress no power to tax. Again, Congress could only request each state to pay a fair share based on population. Facing financial problems of their own, the states often balked at congressional requests for funds, leaving Washington's Continental Army often underfed, underclothed and under-armed. The Congress paid soldiers and sailors, as well as merchants selling goods to the military, in IOUs to be redeemed at some vague future date. As more IOUs went into circulation, the paper became almost worthless. Washington, who became a bitter critic of the Articles, would say that this system of government almost caused the United States to lose the war.

Lacking the power of the purse also meant that the Congress had limited funds to build roads, bridges, and other infrastructure that not only served citizens, but also were critical for the Continental Army's military operations. The Congress also could not regulate trade between the states. Some states passed burdensome taxes on goods that crossed their borders, leaving consumers in some parts of the country paying substantially higher prices for products than their neighbors. The Articles created no federal judiciary to settle conflicts between states over issues like taxes and boundaries or between citizens living in different states. The "United" States were united in name only and poorly functioned as a loose alliance of 13 independent republics.

Such a weak government could not adequately respond to economic conditions after the combat phase of the Revolution ended in 1781. Following the war, commerce with America's chief trading partner, Great Britain dropped to 40 percent of the pre-war level. The drop in trade created a post-war recession, which caused a big drop in tax revenues. The United States ran up heavy debts to the French, the Dutch, and others during the war, and each year it borrowed more money because the individual states provided less money than requisitioned. Between 1781 and 1786, because of the shortfall of funds requested from the states, the Congress ran up a $2.3 million deficit in addition to the $37 million owed by the Congress for loans taken out to pay for the war (over $1 billion in 2012 dollars). The states owed approximately $14 million, or almost $400 million in today's dollars. By 1787, the Congress faced a day of reckoning as the interest on the foreign debt mushroomed and the principal on foreign loans came due.

Over time, the crushing burden of debt exposed the serious weakness of the American government under the Articles. Unable to tax, the Congress began printing money, which fueled ruinous inflation. By July 1777, the dollar retained one-third of its face value. In other words, it took $3 in Continental currency to purchase $1 in gold coins. By January 1779, $1 in specie required $8 in Continental money. Some two years later, it required $500.

The Newburgh Conspiracy

In 1781, after the successful siege of Yorktown, the French Navy headed back home, leaving the tiny American Navy to defend the long U.S. coastline. Unable to pay their soldiers but afraid to completely disband the armed forces in case Britain had second thoughts about ending the war, Congress refused to discharge enlisted men. Worried about their farms and businesses back home and missing their families, soldiers simmered with resentment in the months after combat ended, inspiring a disturbing series of mutinies. In January 1781, nearly all 500 men who enlisted in the Pennsylvania infantry units of the Continental Army, most of whom had served multiple terms of enlistment and endured occasional hunger and harsh winters rose up in anger and seized control of arms depots. Joined by soldiers from Maryland, on June 20, 1783, the mutineers blocked the exits from Independence Hall, where the Congress met. For a time they refused to let anyone leave unless they received full payment of back wages. With the Philadelphia Executive Council unable to ensure order, the Congress moved its base of operations to Princeton, New Jersey.

But Continental Army officers, not enlisted men, posed a serious threat that the civilian Congress, the new government of the United States, might be replaced with a military dictatorship. By the end of the war, the officer corps was seething over its own grievances, including late pay and the lack of military pensions. Some men had served six years without pay. "Over campfires in the chill autumn, warmed sometimes with rum, the officers fingered the hilts of their swords and talked of taking the law into their own hands," the historian James Flexner wrote. "Only by the most intense persuasion did Washington channel the discontent into a petition to Congress." A committee of officers presented soldiers' grievances to the Congress, without any apparent effect.

Many military officers felt betrayed by a country they recently fought so bravely to establish. On March 12, 1783, in the army's winter quarters in Newburgh, New York, an anonymous letter (actually written by an aide to General Horatio Gates) circulated. Venting fury over the treatment of the military, the author urged fellow officers to "assume a bolder tone" and tell leaders in Congress that if they conveyed disrespect one more time, "you will retire to some unsettled country . . ." Deeply upset by the letter, Washington worried that what became known as the "**Newburgh Conspiracy**" would result in a civil war. "I cannot avoid apprehending that a train of evils will follow of a very serious and distressing nature," Washington wrote at one point as he contemplated the rising anger among his men.

In May 1782, Colonel Lewis Nicola wrote a passionate letter to Washington urging him to assume power as king. A committee of disgruntled officers dispatched Washington's chief aide during the war, **Alexander Hamilton**, to meet with the general to see if he would support a possible *coup d'état* or at least not stand in the way of one. Hamilton sent Washington a letter warning him that the Army could no longer supply the men and "that by June [1782], the troops would have to take everything by bayonet point." Hamilton asked Washington, as Flexner paraphrased it, "in a world of kings, why should not George Washington also be a king?" Washington took months to answer Hamilton, but in his reply he refused to endorse an overthrow of the Congress.

The seditious spirit in the military continued to boil. If Washington would not lead a coup, some officers decided, they would try to persuade him to remain quiet and ask General Horatio Gates to serve as ruler instead. Washington called a meeting of officers in Newburgh, New York, for March 15, 1783, a conference that Flexner called "the most important single gathering ever held in the United States." Washington assured his officers that he loved them and cared about their plight, but tried to assure them that the situation would resolve itself without a second revolution. Republics, he said, act with often frustrating deliberation rather than speed, but the Congress would ultimately do the right thing. A coup would "open the flood gates of civil discord, and deluge our rising empire in blood."

The audience seemed unimpressed until Washington tried to produce a calming letter from a congressman. He seemed disoriented and then pulled out his glasses, saying: "Gentlemen, you will permit me to put on my spectacles, for I have not only grown gray but almost blind in the service of my country." The moment inspired tears of compassion, admiration, and regret from those gathered.

The image of a frail Washington begging his men to not betray the Revolution broke the spell. The officers calmed. The air went out of the "Newburgh Conspiracy" and the coup never took place. As Thomas Jefferson said, "The moderation and virtue of a single character probably prevented this Revolution from being closed, as most others have been, by a subversion of that liberty it was intended to establish." Washington yearned to return to private life, but he knew that the Articles of Confederation provided an unworkable form of government and endangered the future of the United States. He began a quiet campaign to replace the Articles with a new constitution.

Shays's Rebellion

State governments were as weak as the federal government during the Articles period, with many having no governor or one who held only ceremonial duties, unable to veto laws or call the legislatures in sessions in emergencies. Members of many state legislatures had to run for re-election every year, and they proved reluctant to raise taxes to pay off their state's war debts or to fund government operations because taxes were always unpopular, especially during a recession like that gripping the United States in the 1780s.

Struggling to balance budgets, some states went on a spree printing local currency, a policy that worsened inflation. As state-issued bank notes and the Continental currency dropped in value, farmers struggled to pay their tax bills. To prevent a rebellion from the indebted masses, many of whom were war veterans and had not been paid their promised bonuses from the federal government, several states passed laws allowing farmers to delay paying debts. Still many former soldiers and other farmers lost their land because they couldn't pay their debts or state taxes.

The state of Massachusetts harshly rejected any debt holiday, refused to print more money, stepped up collection of back taxes, and raised taxes to record heights. Farmers in western Pennsylvania particularly suffered. In 1786, some began arming themselves and seizing control of courthouses in Hampshire County, stopping judges from foreclosing on farm mortgages. In early 1787, a wounded Revolutionary War veteran, Captain Daniel Shays, led an army of the indebted, who attacked the federal arsenal at Springfield.

Since local militiamen refused to suppress the uprising, Governor James Bowdoin was forced to raise an army with funds donated by his own merchant supporters. In fact, considered as a military episode, **Shays's Rebellion**" quickly dissipated, as the rebels scattered instead of fighting a pitched battle with state forces. But politically, the episode continued to divide Massachusetts and reverberated throughout the states. Shortly afterward, Massachusetts authorities indicted hundreds of rebels and barred thousands more from holding public office. Two convicted ringleaders were hanged, while others, including Shays himself, escaped and were condemned in absentia. But in the gubernatorial elections later that year, John Hancock, a signer of the Declaration of Independence, soundly defeated Bowdoin, sweeping the state's rural votes. Hancock pardoned Shays, reduced payments on state debts, and lightened rural tax burdens. Nevertheless, the uprising became a major topic of discussion among Washington, Alexander Hamilton, and other national leaders. Shays's Rebellion seemed to foreshadow a new revolution, this time aimed at American elites.

Western Troubles

The United States' economic and political standing in the world continued to deteriorate. Unable to get states to deliver sufficient funds, Congress ceased interest payments on debts owed to France in 1785, and two years later defaulted on installments of principal. The likelihood of new foreign loans was now remote. With the navy fully dismantled and the U.S. Army (successor to the Continental Army) reduced to a few hundred men, other imperial powers began to take advantage of the country's military vulnerabilities. Sent to London by Congress to seek more favorable terms of commerce, John Adams found his diplomatic efforts undercut by individual states offering their own concessions. Spanish ministers also saw opportunities to exploit American weakness. Despite the provision of the Treaty of Paris, allowing U.S. access to the Mississippi River, the separate treaty ending England's war with Spain reverted all of Florida, extending across the Gulf Coast west to the river, back to Spanish rule. Having ruled the Louisiana Territory since 1763, Spain now fully controlled the mouth of the Mississippi and, in 1784, closed it to U.S. shipping.

Farmers in Tennessee and Kentucky and other territories near the Mississippi River could not transport their harvests down the Mississippi. Instead, they had to pay high Spanish tariffs, continue using more expensive, difficult overland routes or simply forget participating in global markets. Doubting the ability of the U.S. government to defend their interests, settlers like Daniel Boone began negotiating secretly with the Spanish about handing over control of Tennessee and Kentucky to Spain. Not just rebellion, but treason was in the air.

THE CONSTITUTION CONSPIRACY

Following Yorktown, Alexander Hamilton settled in New York City and served as a member of the state's caucus in Congress. Hamilton had already decided that the Articles were a disaster and wanted to scrap the current government with a new system in which the federal government would take away powers from the individual states, who had plunged the nation into what he saw as anarchy and would provide for a more powerful economy and military. James Madison, a young, quietly effective member of the Virginia legislature, also advocated replacing the Articles with the new constitution. As long as the country languished under the Articles, Madison wrote, "the states will continue to invade the national jurisdiction, to violate treaties and the law of nations, and to harass each other with rival and spiteful measures dictated by mistaken views of interest." Hamilton tried to get the Articles amended to allow the Congress to assess and collect taxes, but his efforts failed, largely because of the requirement that any amendment be unanimously approved by the states.

Washington watched events in the national capital in Philadelphia and the rebellion in Western Massachusetts led by Shays with dismay. His life's work, the establishment of an American nation, seemed in jeopardy. Hoping to start the ball rolling on governmental reform, Washington invited representatives from Virginia and Maryland to his Mount Vernon estate to negotiate a boundary dispute involving shipping along the nearby Potomac River. Meanwhile, Madison persuaded his colleagues in the Virginia legislature to call for a meeting of the states to discuss adoption of "a uniform system in their commercial regulations." Madison and Washington hoped for much more out of this conference, but no one in leadership circles was ready to openly discuss doing away with the Articles of Confederation.

The Annapolis Convention met September 11-14, 1786, with only five state delegations (from Delaware, New Jersey, New York, Pennsylvania and Virginia) attending. Hamilton, representing New York, wrote a resolution urging all the states to appoint delegates to another gathering to be held the following year, "to take into consideration the situation of the United States," and "devise such further provisions as shall appear to them necessary to render the constitution of the Federal Government adequate to the exigencies of the Union." This was the first public hint at the agenda that Washington, Madison and Hamilton shared. The Confederation Congress endorsed the Annapolis resolution several months later. The public still thought the Articles would only be modified. A secret consensus had already formed among the powerful, however, to start from scratch, a genteel conspiracy born of mistrust of the common man.

THE CONSTITUTIONAL CONVENTION OF 1787

In the National Archives building in Washington, D.C., in the "Rotunda for the Charters of Freedom," the **Constitution of the United States**, beginning with "We the People," in its familiar large script, is inscribed on four large pages, spread across a display case underneath the Declaration of Independence. In another glass case is the Bill of Rights or actually a copy prepared for Congress that lists all of the first twelve amendments to the Constitution that were initially proposed, rather than merely the ten which passed.

This shrine reflects the views of politicians, architects, and curators about the civic importance of these pieces of parchment, while their physical condition remains closely monitored by scientists and preservationists. Modern Americans see the Constitution, along with the

A family takes the time to view America's Constitution. It has provided the framework for democracy and freedom for well over 200 years.

Declaration, as secular scripture. However, at the time of its proposal, the Constitution inspired not reverence but heated controversy and even bitter opposition.

Many, like Thomas Jefferson, held profoundly mixed feelings about the document. Jefferson acknowledged the dangerous inefficiencies of the Articles but worried over the new Constitution's shift of powers away from the states to the federal government. Others saw the Constitution as a betrayal of the principles of the American Revolution. They feared that creating the office of the presidency would inevitably lead to tyranny. They did not like the fact that the Constitution would not allow the people to directly vote for members of the newly created Senate (until the Seventeenth Amendment was ratified in 1913, senators were selected by state legislatures) or the president (selected to this day by the Electoral College).

The nation's founders had adopted the Articles of Confederation in a fit of optimism about human nature, believing that the citizens of a free republic would always put the nation's interests ahead of provincial concerns and the needs of the community above selfish desires. Men like Washington, Hamilton, and Madison did not believe that events since the Articles went into effect in 1781 bore out that optimism. They saw states inconsistently contributing to the costs of running the republic and abandoning soldiers who had risked their lives and fortunes to create the nation. They saw events like Shays's Rebellion as the acts of an ungrateful rabble. Furthermore, they saw economic chaos and felt shame at the disrespect shown the United States by powers like Spain. The Articles had ushered in rule by the mob, Hamilton in particular believed. The founders decided to retreat from their experiment in "radical democracy" and create a more hierarchical republic ruled by the supposed best and brightest.

"An Assembly of Demigods"

Once again, Philadelphia, and the assembly room of the Pennsylvania State House, hosted a fateful gathering. Seven of the thirteen states had agreed to attend what would be dubbed the **Constitutional Convention**, before Congress itself endorsed the convention in February. Five states immediately agreed to participate. The sole standout would be tiny Rhode Island, which refused to send a delegation. In mid-May, the Virginia delegation arrived, including George Washington, who had reluctantly agreed to leave his beloved Mount Vernon one more time to represent his state at the convention.

The Convention would be perhaps the largest gathering of some of the most important figures in American history, including not just Washington, already a legend, but fellow icon-in-his-lifetime Ben Franklin, future president James Madison, the man who would soon create the American economic system, Alexander Hamilton, future Senator Gouverneur Morris (who would end up writing the famous Preamble to the Constitution) and scholarly attorney and future Supreme Court Justice James Wilson.

It was a wealthy, well-connected gathering. Of the fifty-five delegates in total, forty-two had served at some point in the Second Continental Congress, or in the Congress created under the Articles. Apart from Washington and Franklin, most of the delegates who had served in the military or in government during the independence struggle had done so as younger men. Nearly all were landowners, although only sixteen made their living

Benjamin Franklin at the Constitutional Convention.

mainly as planters. No fewer than twenty-nine had studied law. Perhaps most important, twenty-five of them, including the sixteen planters, all from the South, owned slaves.

John Adams and Thomas Jefferson were serving abroad as diplomats and so did not attend, while some other leading figures of the older generation, such as Patrick Henry, declined to leave their states. The delegates were not perfectly representative of the elite layer of American society, but they were almost all drawn from it. Jefferson referred to the delegates as "an assembly of demigods" in a letter to Adams.

The Virginia and New Jersey Plans and the Connecticut Compromise

After finally convening on May 25, the delegates quickly made several crucial decisions. Washington was immediately chosen as presiding officer, and for the rest of the Convention he presided, sitting at the front of the room in an ornate Chippendale-style chair with a half-sun and its rays carved into its high back. Washington's chairmanship lent the controversial gathering a measure of credibility with a nervous public. The convention voted to not allow members of the public to observe the proceedings and to keep no official records of the debates. Delegates wanted to be able to debate controversial issues without fear of suffering political harm. The Constitutional Convention met behind closed doors and closed windows. Secrecy was strictly, and successfully, maintained. Several delegates, most notably Madison, kept notes during the Convention, which he amended years after the event and which did not become available to the public until the late 1830s. Robert Yates, a delegate from New York, Rufus King, from Massachusetts, and William Pierce, from Georgia, kept more sketchy records of the proceedings, but none of this material was published until after the participants had died; and no complete, objective record of the convention has ever been found. The creators of the republic were less than enthusiastic about the public's right to know.

By the time the delegates gathered in May 1787, the Articles of Confederation were a dead letter. The Articles could be amended, with unanimous consent of the states, but the convention chose to ignore the Articles' existence. It would be a gentlemanly *coup d'état*. The delegates had lost the fear of executive power that had prevailed at the writing of the Articles, and a consensus formed behind creating a chief executive for the new government, to be called a president. Whatever qualms they might have had that a president could transform into a kingly tyrant like George III, the convention felt confident that the first president at least would respect constitutional limits. Everyone knew the first president would be Washington, a war hero trusted by all factions.

Revealing his distrust of the voting public, Alexander Hamilton proposed that the new office of president and members of an upper house of Congress called the Senate be appointed to lifetime terms. Presidents and senators could rule without worrying about the popular passions of the moment. Hamilton had more faith in the inherent wisdom of the wealthy and powerful who would fill these offices than most of his peers in the convention, who rejected lifetime terms, though the idea would survive for federal judges.

Much of the summer centered on how much power large states and small states would have in a new, re-structured Congress. On May 29, **Edmund Randolph** formally proposed the "Virginia" or "large state" plan, which proposed creation of a Congress with two chambers: a "lower house" elected by the people, and a senate elected by the lower house. In both chambers, the size of the different delegations would be based on each states' population. In short, smaller states faced diminished representation in the Congress under this plan.

The Congress would also enjoy more powers than under the Articles. Under the Virginia Plan, the Congress would appoint the president and also a federal judiciary. The legislature would possess all the powers that the Congress had under the Articles but with enhanced authority over state affairs. In a significant retreat from the concept of "state's rights," the Congress would have gained the ability to legislate in all matters in which the individual states were "incompetent," such as in boundary disputes. In Randolph's scheme, the Congress could have vetoed state laws it considered unconstitutional. A peculiar oversight marked Randolph's "Virginia Plan": he didn't call for giving the Congress the power to impose and collect taxes, perhaps the most serious flaw in the Articles.

On June 15, New Jersey delegate William Paterson proposed the "New Jersey," or "Small State Plan," which retained the basic structure of the Confederation Congress—one single chamber with each state given equal representation—albeit with enhanced powers, such as taxation and regulation of commerce. As different as these proposals were, they shared some basic features: both aimed at vastly expanding the range and scope of federal powers at the expense of the states. Both would have created the office of chief executive not chosen by the voters. The Virginia and the New Jersey plans represented a retreat from the concept of popular sovereignty, the idea that the average person possessed ample civic virtue and could be trusted with a large voice in public matters.

Delegates from small states feared that their voices would be drowned out in the federal government if anything like the Virginia plan won approval, with a Delaware delegate warning that if the convention backed Randolph's proposed constitution, the small states would secede and seek admission into a foreign empire. Delegates from the large states countered that most of the population lived within their borders, so therefore fairness dictated that membership in the Congress should be based on proportional representation. By the end of June, one delegate said that the Convention was "at full stop."

Facing the possibility of collapse, the Convention agreed to settle the dispute. Delegates gave the dispute to a committee made up of staunch small-state partisans (such as the Connecticut delegates) and Virginia Plan advocates (such as Franklin) who were willing to make accommodations. The "**Connecticut Compromise**," introduced July 5, organized the lower house on the basis of population and the senate equally by state, which by then was the position of the small-state delegates. For them, the compromise involved enhancing the power of the lower house, at the expense of the senate, by making the lower house the chamber in which spending bills would originate.

The Constitution and Slavery

By the 1840s, the abolitionist William Lloyd Garrison derided the Constitution as a "covenant with death" and an "agreement with hell." What outraged Garrison was that the framers not only failed to abolish slavery, which he saw as inescapably evil, but that they included provisions in the Constitution that guaranteed the institution's survival for decades.

Even though he owned over a hundred slaves, Madison had been a major advocate for reigning in states' rights and shifting power to the federal government. Many southern delegates, however, feared the North would eventually dominate the new government and would, with expanded powers, be able to limit or even eliminate involuntary servitude. Speaking for increasingly uneasy slaveowners, General Charles Pinckney, of South Carolina, warned the Convention that unless he "received some security against an emancipation of slaves . . . he should be bound by duty to his State to vote against their Report." Despite some objections by northern delegates, the Convention was basically willing to give Pinckney the "security" he demanded.

Thus, six of the Constitution's eighty-four clauses pertained to slavery. Delegates added a provision that prohibited the federal government from passing any laws regarding slavery until 1808, two decades in the future. Big southern slaveowners also worried because the continued importation of slaves from the Caribbean and from Africa, combined with the increase in the slave population from sexual reproduction, threatened to drive the value of slaves down. The bigger slaveowners like Madison, who already had more than enough human property to turn a profit on tobacco and other cash crops, knew they would benefit economically by a slower growth in the slave population. Consequently, delegates to the convention

The Declaration of Independence being fully adopted, John Hancock, President of the Continental Congress took up the pen and signed his name in bold writing.

agreed to a ban on the international slave trade by 1808, a provision that on the surface seems like a blow against slavery but in fact served as a big gift to the wealthiest southern planters.

A heated controversy erupted over the census. The framers of the Constitution sought a nationwide census every 10 years, which would then allow the Congress to apportion the size of each state delegation to the United States House and the representation of each state in the Electoral College.

Southerners, fearing a small but rising tide of anti-slavery sentiment in the North, wanted to guarantee what they hoped would be a permanent strong influence over the new federal government. Southerners insisted that slaves be counted as part of a state's population during future federal censuses, even though slaves had no voting rights or civil liberties and essentially didn't politically exist. Counting slaves, however, would give white Southerners a disproportionate voice in both the new House of Representatives and the Electoral College. Northern delegates wanted slaves to not count, so that only free whites would be considered when apportioning seats in the House and the Electoral College.

As a compromise, delegates agreed to count each slave as 3/5s of a person both when determining representation and in apportioning taxes. By guaranteeing white southern overrepresentation in the House, this **3/5s compromise** would hold profound electoral consequences for the next 70 years. In the first census year, 1790, for instance, even though southern whites made up only 40 percent of the total U.S. population, they held 47 percent of the seats in the U.S. House. Until 1861, when the southern states would secede from the Union over the supposed threat to slavery posed by newly elected President Abraham Lincoln, white southern men held sufficient power in the House of Representatives to stifle any anti-slavery legislation.

The South would also possess sufficient votes in the Electoral College to block any presidential candidate unfriendly to slavery. No candidate could win the White House without substantial southern support until population growth in the North allowed Abraham Lincoln to be elected in 1860 without his name being placed on the ballot in a single southern state. Four of the first six presidents were from what was then the most populous slave state, Virginia. Eight of the first thirteen came from slave states.

Because of the influence Southerners had over the presidency, the South would deeply influence whom the president would appoint, with congressional approval, to the federal judiciary. Southerners and southern sympathizers dominated the Supreme Court for the first seven decades after the Constitution was ratified and usually ruled in favor of slave owner interests until the Civil War changed the regional balance of power.

The Constitution would serve as a shield protecting slavery, yet the authors avoided ever using that word or the word "slave" anywhere in the document. Instead, they employed elaborate euphemisms, such as in the provision regarding how slaves would be counted in the census in Article 1, Section 2 when they direct census takers to count "the whole number of Free Persons" but "three fifths of all other Persons." This cowardly verbal evasion reveals that many of the members of the Constitutional Convention knew that slavery could not be reconciled with the supposed ideals of the Revolution or the proposed new national charter. Winning ratification of the Constitution, however, would require southern support, and that goal, and not liberating millions of humans chained in the South, became the delegates' more pressing objective.

THE *FEDERALIST PAPERS* AND THE CAMPAIGN FOR RATIFICATION

By the middle of September, the substantive decisions were made. One last committee—the Committee of Style—re-edited the proposed preamble and all approved sections and rendered them in polished form. Three delegates who had made important contributions—**George Mason** and Edmund Randolph, from Virginia, and the frequently grumpy Elbridge Gerry of Massachusetts—citing their own reservations about the finished work, pronounced themselves unwilling to sign. But thirty-nine other delegates did add their names to the document. On the day of signatures and adjournment, September 17, 1787, in his final remarks, Benjamin Franklin told his fellow delegates that he had often looked at the half-sun carved on Washington's chair "without being able to tell if it was rising or setting. Now at length I have the happiness to know that it is a rising and not a setting sun."

Writing the Constitution represented one long, difficult political struggle, conducted within the secretive confines of a meeting room. A new and more difficult conflict over the country's future would now unfold in sometimes angry state conventions across the country. The Convention in Philadelphia (with the later consent of the Confederation Congress) ignored the requirement of unanimous ratification for changes to the Articles and set up their own rules for the proposed Constitution. The Constitution specified a threshold of nine states for ratification and required each state to elect special conventions, which were supposed to vote up or down on the text as proposed.

Table 7.1 The Articles of Confederation and the Constitution Compared

	Articles	Constitution
Power to tax	No power to tax	Congress has right to levy taxes on individuals
Source of power	Individual states	Shared through federalism between states and the national government
Representation in Congress	Equal representation of states	Upper house (Senate) with 2 votes; lower house (House of Representatives) based on population
Amendment process	Unanimous consent of the states	2/3 vote of both houses of Congress or a national convention plus 3/4 vote of state legislatures or state conventions
Executive	None	Headed by President with defined powers and potential checks on power of the legislative and judicial branches
Federal courts	None	Federal courts created to deal with issues between citizens and states; potential check on power of the legislative and executive branches
Regulation of trade	None	Congress given power to regulate foreign and domestic trade
Raising an army	Dependent on states to contribute forces	Congress can raise an army to deal with military situations
Sovereignty	Sovereignty resides in the states	The Constitution, federal laws, and U.S. treaties declared the supreme law of the land
Passing laws	9 states out of 13 required to approve legislation	Majority of both houses plus signature of the President

In a clever political move, supporters of ratification named themselves "**Federalists**." The term, implying respect for the division of authority between central and local institutions, minimized the impact of a Constitution that so sharply reduced the power of states. The name also attracted people who distrusted radical change but wanted a more effective government.

The opponents found themselves stuck with the label "**Anti-Federalists**," a negative term that revealed only what they opposed, not what they believed. The Anti-Federalists opposed the Constitution for a wide variety of reasons, but because of these divisions they had problems articulating a clear argument for rejecting ratification. When the convention adjourned in September and presented the brief proposed Constitution to the public, every newspaper in the country printed a copy and invited readers to discuss it. The United States was a nation of newspaper readers, with taverns often providing dozens for their clientele. Literate drinkers would read the newspapers out loud so all could hear the latest developments from Philadelphia. Only twelve newspapers outright opposed the new national charter, and editorial support was generally so enthusiastic that the Anti-Federalists complained that their arguments did not get a fair hearing in the press. Press media coverage increased early support for ratification.

The ratification process at first looked like it would proceed with breakneck speed, with the Federalists winning approval in Delaware, Pennsylvania, New Jersey, Georgia and Connecticut. Ironically, given the initial resistance by small states to early drafts of the Constitution during the convention in Philadelphia, smaller states now

> ### A MEMORIAL TO THE SOUTH CAROLINA SENATE
>
> With the ratification of the U.S. Constitution of 1787, free blacks from Charleston, South Carolina petitioned their legislature for basic civil rights denied them under state law.
>
> *To the Honorable David Ramsay Esquire President and to the rest of the Honorable New Members of the Senate of the State of South Carolina The Memorial of Thomas Cole Bricklayer P.B. Mathews and Mathew Webb Butcherson behalf of themselves & others Free-Men of Colour.*
>
> *Humbly Sheweth*
> That in the Enumeration of Free Citizens by the Constitution of the United States for the purpose of Representation of the Southern States in Congress Your Memorialists have been considered under that description as part of the citizens of this State. Although by the Fourteenth and Twenty-Ninth clauses in an Act of Assembly made in the Year 1740 and entitled an Act for the better Ordering and governing Negroes and other slaves in this Province commonly called The Negro Act now in force Your Memorialists are deprived of the Rights and Privileges of Citizens by not having it in their power to give Testimony on Oath in prosecutions on behalf of the State from which cause many Culprits have escaped the punishment due to their atrocious Crimes, nor can they give their Testimony in recovering Debts due to them, or in establishing Agreements made by them within the meaning of the Statutes of Frauds and Perjuries in force in this State except in cases where Persons of Colour are concerned, whereby they are subject to great Losses and repeated Injuries without any means of redress.
>
> That by the said clauses in the said Act, they are debarred of the Rights of Free Citizens by being subject to a Trial without the benefit of a jury and subject to Prosecution by Testimony of Slaves without Oath by which they are placed on the same footing.
>
> Your Memorialists show that they have at all times since the Independence of the United States contributed and do now contribute to the support of the government by cheerfully paying their Taxes proportionable to their Property with others who have been during such period, and now are in full enjoyment of the rights and immunities of Citizens Inhabitants of a Free Independent State.
>
> That as your Memorialists have been and are considered as Free-Citizens of this State they hope to be treated as such, they are ready and willing to take and subscribe to such oath of Allegiance to the States as shall be prescribed by this Honorable House, and are also willing to take upon them any duty for the preservations of the Peace in the City or any other occasion if called on.
>
> Your Memorialists do not presume to hope that they shall be put on an equal footing with the Free white Citizens of the State in general they only humbly solicit such indulgence as the Wisdom and Humanity of this Honorable House shall dictate in their favor by repealing the clauses the act aforementioned, and substituting such a clause as will effectually Redress the grievances which your Memorialists humbly submit in this their Memorial but under such restrictions as to your Honorable House shall seem proper.
>
> May it therefore please your Honors to take your Memorialists case into tender consideration, and make such Acts or insert such clauses for the purpose of relieving your Memorialists from the unremitted grievance they now Labour under as in your Wisdom shall seem meet.
>
> And as in duty bound your Memorialists will ever pray.
>
> Source: "A Memorial to the South Carolina Senate," Records of the General Assembly, Petitions, 1791, No. 181, South Carolina Department of Archives and History, as reproduced.

appreciated the advantages of a more centralized government. Under the Articles of Confederation, for instance, New Jersey had been squeezed by its neighbors, forced to pay taxes to bordering states on foreign goods imported through New York City and Philadelphia. Under the new Constitution, the federal government would levy a single import duty, thereby reducing the tax bill for New Jersey residents. If smaller states now believed that a more powerful central government would offer them greater protections, residents in larger states like Virginia believed they could survive as separate republics, and became reluctant to surrender control.

The first big ratification battle took place Massachusetts, the birthplace of the American Revolution. Many residents who had fought a war over taxes like the Stamp Act held suspicions about the new federal government they were asked to approve. The Federalists won the Massachusetts convention by a squeaky 187-168 margin in February 1788. That April and May, Federalists also carried the Maryland and South Carolina conventions. Now, eight of the required nine states had ratified the Constitution, but it would be an uphill struggle from there.

Conventions were scheduled almost simultaneously in New Hampshire, New York, North Carolina, and Vermont, and at the outset the Anti-Federalists carried a soft majority in each convention. As the public more closely read the Constitution, its anti-democratic elements became clearer to many. Anti-Federalists insisted that the new government, centered wherever the new national capital would be located (an issue not yet resolved), would be too remote for most voters to influence its decisions. Anti-Federalists contended that the grant of powers to the Congress in the proposed Constitution was dangerously broad. Anti-Federalist writers portrayed the "consolidated" federal government as a kind of successor to Parliament—a distant, uncontrollable authority aiming to invade local jurisdictions and usurp the powers of familiar, established institutions. Anti-Federalists argued that a House of Representatives elected in districts of at least 30,000 people, as mandated by the Constitution, meant that elections would be expensive, guaranteeing that the House would be filled by an aristocracy of wealthy, remote men empowered to impose taxes on the common person and unanswerable to the public will.

Again, the slavery issue erupted, with public figures on both sides finding fault with the Constitution. Yankee abolitionists in Massachusetts and New York pointed to the continuation of the slave trade, and the silence of abolitionist delegates, as damning evidence of moral compromise. Luther Martin, a delegate from Maryland who had left the Convention without signing, actually published the text of a speech from the Constitutional Convention criticizing the failure to limit the slave trade. But, on the other hand, the ambiguity of the Constitution allowed some to criticize it for only weakly supporting slavery. Patrick Henry, after Washington the most respected Virginian revolutionary leader, opposed the Constitution in the Virginia ratifying convention. Its omission of any explicit protection for slave property, in his words, "was done with design." For Henry, a strong central government that had not clearly committed to preserve slavery would inevitably come under pressure to limit or abolish it.

At the convention, George Mason had urged the adoption of a Bill of Rights before the Constitution was submitted to the states, but Madison said this was unnecessary and he carried the day. That decision now haunted the Federalists as the lack of a Bill of Rights stoked much of the opposition. It was obvious that public fears would have to be allayed if the final hurdle to ratification were to be cleared. To get over the hump, three of the most prominent supporters of the new Constitution, Alexander Hamilton, James Madison and John Jay, authored a series of eighty-five eloquent essays supporting the Constitution originally printed in New York newspapers and then republished across the country. The trio addressed criticisms of the Constitution in detail in what came to be known as the "***Federalist Papers***."

Some Anti-Federalists argued that the strong republican government outlined in the Constitution represented a dangerous experiment without historical precedent. The city-state republics of antiquity like Athens in ancient Greece had been small and culturally homogenous, promoting civic discourse and allowing the larger public more direct input to their government. Many feared that a United States ruled as a large republic with a strong central government would be unstable, too vast to be socially cohesive and indifferent to local needs. A powerful federal authority might be forced to impose authoritarian rule in order to preserve law and order.

Madison flipped this argument on its head. He argued in one essay that the greatest threat to freedom came from the tyranny of local majorities. Such majorities formed more easily in small, economically and culturally similar societies. In a republic as massive and diverse as the United States, however, such a majority would have a hard time gaining control, Madison insisted. A large republic encompasses too many competing interests for any one faction to completely dominate. The new, strong central government could intervene in localities where tyrannical majorities reigned to ensure constitutional rights were protected. In addition to these arguments, Madison also promised he would author and propose to the Congress a series of amendments that would provide a Bill of Rights.

If The *Federalist Papers* offered a core argument, it involved the practicality of a large, powerful nation governed by republican institutions. To be strong enough to survive in a dangerous world, the United States would not need to endure at the cost of its guiding principles. Indeed, a powerful national government, rather than a weak confederation of separate states, would offer the best mechanisms for the fulfillment of the highest aspirations of the American Revolution.

The Anti-Federalists were never to mount a case as strong and well-considered. In the end, the multiple problems the Articles had caused, and the support of Washington, Franklin, and other prestigious national leaders for the new Constitution, proved decisive. Following publication of *The Federalist Papers*, the Federalists prevailed over reluctance in the New Hampshire constitutional convention on June 21, 1787. The Constitution had been approved. Madison was able to carry the Virginia convention five days later. New York checked off a month later, then North Carolina by July 1788. On September 13, the Confederation Congress certified that the Constitution had been ratified. The new government assumed authority March 4, 1789. Rhode Island became the last state to ratify, in May 1790. The United States Constitution thus became the law of the land. The controversies surrounding its writing and approval would be forgotten, and the document was on its way to becoming American scripture.

A RETREAT FROM DEMOCRACY

The new Constitution made elected officials less answerable to their constituents. Delegates set the terms for the House of Representatives at two years, instead of the one year required under the Articles of Confederation. Senate terms would last six years. That chamber would not be a democratic body, with senators appointed by state legislatures.

The Constitution's framers sought to limit the influence of the "mob" that had participated in uprisings like Shays's Rebellion, the uneducated voters supposedly swayed by immediate emotions. The framers sought to guarantee rule by men of their education, culture, and class. So they devised an absurdly complicated method of choosing president and vice president, the only two elected officials in the federal government who would represent the entire country. The president would serve for four years, could be re-elected an unlimited number of times, and would not have to grovel for votes from the common person but would be appointed by a body of presumed wise men called the Electoral College. State representation in the Electoral College would be based on the number of representatives and senators each state had in the Congress. The proposed Constitution would allow each state to determine how electors were chosen.

Under the original provisions of the Constitution, each elector would vote for two people in the presidential race. The two could not be from the same state. The candidate with the most votes would gain the presidency, while the one earning the second most ballots would become vice president. This allowed for political opponents to serve in the top two offices in the government. This aspect of the presidential election process would prove troublesome, and electors would begin choosing presidents and vice presidents separately after the states ratified the Twelfth Amendment in 1804.

By dividing powers among executive, legislative and judicial branches, the framers hoped to prevent the dangerous concentration of power in any one part of the government. The Congress no longer represented the only branch of government, but it constituted the heart of the new system. As designed by the Constitution's framers, only Congress could exercise the life-and-death power to declare war. A president could request war, but Congress had to clearly say "yes" or "no," and only Congress could pay for military adventures.

As historian Garry Wills argues, the Constitution placed the Congress at the heart of the government: "The Congress can [through impeachment] remove officers from the other two branches—President, agency heads, judges in district or supreme courts. Neither of the other two branches can touch a member of Congress. Congress sets the pay for the other two and also for itself. It decides on the structure of the other two departments, creating or abolishing agencies and courts. It decides on the number of judges to serve on each court."

Under the Constitution eventually ratified, the Congress approves the president's cabinet appointments and diplomats. As Wills observes, the president can propose a treaty, but the Senate has to approve. Tax bills have to originate in the House. If a president wants legislation, the Congress has to pass it. If the president objects to a law, he can issue a veto, but the Congress can override the veto. If the Supreme Court rules a law approved by Congress violates the Constitution, the Congress can initiate the process to amend the Constitution, can impeach the hostile judges, or expand the size of the court to fill it with friendlier jurists. "No matter what the sequence of action among the three departments, if the process is played out to the end, Congress always gets the last say (if they want it)," Wills notes. If that were not enough, in the so-called "elastic clause" in Article 1, Section 8, the framers would give the Congress a vast mandate to take almost whatever actions, not prohibited by other parts of the Constitution, it deemed necessary. "The Congress shall have Power—To make all Laws which shall be necessary and proper for carrying into Execution the foregoing Powers, and all other Powers vested by this Constitution in the Government of the United States, or in any Department or Officer thereof," the document reads. The Convention had re-created the government in a more aristocratic image, but the issue of slavery threatened to undo all the grand compromises that had allowed the delegates to get this far.

THE RADICAL IMPACT OF THE AMERICAN REVOLUTION AND THE CONSTITUTION

Though a slave-owning oligarch, Patrick Henry was right when he described the Constitution as a retreat from the democracy provided by the Articles of Confederation. With Shays's Rebellion, the leaders of the American Revolution had seen what a democratic future for the United States looked like, and they decided that it did not work. Though the wealthy oligarchs held a great deal of power, they couldn't smother the democratic aspirations of the masses. As the historian Gordon Wood argues, events in America in the 1770s and 1780s represent a real revolution, a true social upheaval and not just the replacement of a government led by British plutocrats with one dominated by American ones.

The struggle for independence transformed race relations in ways subtle but profound. After the Revolution, many whites felt painfully aware of the hypocrisy of a supposedly freedom-loving people embracing slavery. Constitutional protections aside, many masters began to emancipate their slaves. Not long after the Revolution, indentured servitude vanished, with its unmourned death passing almost unnoticed in the 1820s. Within a decade after Yorktown, slavery had virtually disappeared in New England, and in the North would soon be confined primarily to port cities in New York and New Jersey. Vermont banned slavery in its new state constitution in 1777. The Massachusetts Court of Common Pleas essentially ruled slavery unconstitutional four years later. **Elizabeth Freeman**, a slave, had filed a lawsuit arguing that her involuntary servitude violated the new Massachusetts state constitution which read, in part, "All men are born free and equal, and have certain natural, essential, and unalienable rights; among which may be reckoned the right of enjoying and defending their lives and liberties; that of acquiring, possessing, and protecting property; in fine, that of seeking and obtaining their safety and happiness." The court ruled for Freeman and another slave named Brom on August 21, 1781 and ordered them freed. Even though the decision pertained directly only to those two slaves, across Massachusetts and New Hampshire slaves abandoned their masters who, sensing how the tide of history had changed, did not seek to recapture them. Slavery essentially disappeared in those two states. Rhode Island banned slavery completely in 1784. Congress, with its powerful southern caucus, recognized that chattel slavery was likely doomed in the North and voted to abolish slavery in the newly organized Northwest Territory (modern-day Illinois, Indiana, Michigan, Ohio, and Wisconsin) in the Northwest Ordinance passed July 13, 1787.

Quakers openly opposed slavery for the first time and began to insist that their members free their servants. Pennsylvania passed the world's first gradual emancipation law on March 1, 1780. The Pennsylvania law did not emancipate those already enslaved but provided that the children of those slaves would be freed when they reached 28 years of age. Under the law it would potentially take decades for slavery to completely disappear and, tragically, some white masters determined not to lose their financial investment in their chattel auctioned off the slave offspring destined for emancipation to southern buyers before they reached their 28th birthday. Other whites kidnapped free blacks, smuggling them South for auction.

The Pennsylvania Abolition Society became one of the first anti-slavery organizations in the country, forming in 1774 to combat such horrific abuses of the law. By 1800, Philadelphia boasted the largest free black community in the country. The African-American community there had already built many of its own institutions, including political groups, churches, and poverty relief societies. The black community in Philadelphia would establish the African Methodist Episcopal Church in 1818, becoming one of the largest black denominations in the country.

For all its tragic flaws, Pennsylvania's emancipation statue provided a model for other northern states. New York and New Jersey adopted similar laws in 1799 and 1804 respectively, and by 1830 the number of African Americans enslaved north of the Mason-Dixon Line. Even Upper South states like Maryland and Virginia experienced a wave of emancipation, with the legislatures allowing masters to free their slaves. In Maryland, 20 percent of its slaves won freedom by 1820. Idealism did not motivate all these emancipations. The price for tobacco had dropped worldwide, and Southerners had not yet found a replacement cash crop. By the 1790s, British industrialization had given birth to a massive textile industry, which in turn spurred an increased demand for cotton.

Southern planters cultivated long-staple cotton, a fragile species that grew well only on the Sea Islands off Georgia and South Carolina. Long-staple cotton was easy for slaves to remove the seeds, but the crop did not thrive in most of the inland South. The hardier short-staple variety could grow anywhere in the South with at least 200 frost-free days a year, basically anywhere south of

Virginia. The problem for growers was that short-staple cotton had much stickier seeds, making it difficult to remove by hand, a necessary step before the cotton could be processed. On average, one adult slave, working at top speed for an entire day, could clean only about one pound of short-staple cotton, a profit-destroying rate of return for the high labor costs. Absent a technological innovation, it was hard for many planters to see a future for slavery, which, in short, was becoming too expensive and providing too few returns. The loss of profits, most likely, inspired many of the emancipations in southern states like Maryland.

Another ten thousand slaves also received their emancipation papers in Virginia in the aftermath of the Revolution, including the three hundred owned by George Washington. As Washington got older, James Flexner writes, he sought to match his political principles with his personal life. "Washington's growing passion for consistency, combined with his innate inability to separate theory from practice made his horror of slavery increase . . .," Flexner observed. "Although his heart continued to yearn for peace in the world of his forebears and childhood, he began, during his second term as President, an active effort to tear, for the benefit of his blacks, Mount Vernon apart. He proved to be the only Virginia founding father to free all his slaves."

During his presidency, when the capital was located Philadelphia, he penned a letter to the British agricultural expert Arthur Young. He confessed a desire "more powerful than all the rest" to "liberate a certain species of property which I possess very repugnantly to my feelings, but which imperious necessity compels, and until I can substitute some other expedient by which expenses not in my power to avoid (however well disposed I may be to do it) can be defrayed." Washington confided this desire to no one else. When he left the presidency in 1797, however, Washington let several slaves escape. "He slipped into freedom several of his house slaves so quietly, by simply leaving them behind, that no member of the southern opposition [to slave emancipation] even guessed," Flexner wrote.

Washington worried about whether his slaves would be able to thrive as free people and he worried about abandoning his wife, after his death, with a big estate and no slaves to work the fields and provide income. So in his will, drawn up in July 1799, he implemented his own gradual emancipation plan. The slaves he still had would be freed as soon as his wife Martha died. "Having failed to establish a way to assure the adult slaves some employment congenial to their situation and experience, he saw no choice but to free them out of hand," Flexner said.

He did require his heirs to make sure that all who were old and infirm would be "comfortably clothed and fed while they live." And he did his best to protect his former slaves from the harpies who kidnapped free blacks for sale further south or in the Indies. He specified that none be "under any pretense whatsoever" transported out of Virginia. But all this failed to ensure that the black workers, thrown unprepared into freedom, would not be worse off than before.

Children whose parents could not or would not take care of them were to be supported until they were old enough to be legally bound as if they were white apprentices. They were to serve until the age of twenty-five, "be taught to read and write" and be brought up to some useful occupation agreeable to the laws of the Commonwealth of Virginia providing for the support of orphans and other poor children.' They were thus not to be discriminated against but gathered into the white world as if they were not black.

Emancipation was a complicated business, and most slaveowners did not attempt it. A minority of white Americans, however, after the Revolution had already committed to the complete abolition of slavery. Thomas Jefferson, whose words inspired the Revolution, and who often, unlike Washington, publicly condemned the trans-Atlantic slave trade and slavery itself, freed only two of his many slaves in his lifetime. Jefferson had a sexual and possibly romantic relationship with his slave Sally Hemings (1773?-1835), beginning during his diplomatic service in Paris when she was as young as sixteen. Hemings was the half-sister of Jefferson's late wife Martha Skelton. Jefferson and Hemings had as many as six children together, and many remarked on how much the offspring resembled their master. Before his death, Jefferson freed Sally Hemings' older brothers Robert and James Hemings. He also freed five members of the Hemings family in his will, including his three surviving children by her: Madison, Eston, and Harriet. In spite of his familial relationship with African Americans and his apparently affectionate relationship with Sally Hemings, Jefferson demeaned the appearance of blacks and would never believe that "all men were created equally" in terms of intellect. As he wrote in his book, *Notes on the State of Virginia*, published in 1781:

Comparing them [blacks to whites] by their faculties of memory, reason, and imagination, it appears to me, that in memory they are equal to the whites;

in reason much inferior, as I think one [black] could scarcely be found capable of tracing and comprehending the investigations of Euclid; and that in imagination they are dull, tasteless, and anomalous.

Even if he saw blacks as an inferior race, and contended that orangutans were attracted to black women, in the same book Jefferson outlined a plan by which all African Americans born after 1800 would eventually be emancipated. In 1784, Jefferson had proposed legislation to the Confederation Congress that would have prohibited slavery in all Western territories, a plan that failed by a single vote. Already, however, the Revolution had inspired a small minority of white Americans to call for an end to slavery immediately.

As a congregation, the Quakers had begun to discourage their congregants from owning slaves, the first white denomination to take such a position. On February 11, 1790, Quaker delegations from New York and Pennsylvania presented petitions to the Congress asking for an immediate end to the trans-Atlantic slave trade. Many believed the proposal violated the newly ratified U.S. Constitution, which in one section prohibited the Congress from passing any limits on the international slave trade until 1808. The petition outraged southern congressmen like William Loughton Smith of South Carolina, who questioned the patriotism of Quakers whose pacifism had kept them on the sidelines during the Revolution. James Madison, already a leader in the Congress and always a calming influence, gently suggested to Smith that he had overreacted. Madison suggested passing the petition on to consideration by a committee that would let the proposal die a quiet death.

These eighteenth-century Quaker abolitionists would not be silenced so easily. The very next day, the House received another petition, this time from the Pennsylvania Abolition Society. This petition went further, calling not for the end to the international slave trade, but the end of slavery in the United States altogether. The Society called upon Congress to "take such measures in their wisdom, as the powers with which they are invested will authorize, for promoting the abolition of slavery, and discouraging every species of traffic in slaves." The petition made an ingenious Constitutional argument for why the Congress could act on slavery before 1808, according to historian Joseph Ellis in his book *Founding Brothers: The Revolutionary Generation*. "First, it claimed that both slavery and the slave trade were incompatible with the values for which the American revolution had been fought," Ellis wrote, "and it even instructed the Congress on its political obligation to 'devise means for removing this inconsistency from the Character of the American people.

Secondly, it challenged the claim that the Constitution prohibited any legislation by the federal government against the slave trade for twenty years, suggesting instead that the "general welfare" clause of the Constitution empowered the Congress to take whatever action it deemed "necessary and proper" to eliminate the stigma of traffic in human beings and to "Countenance the Restoration of Liberty for all Negroes."

Men like Smith couldn't question the patriotism of one of the petition's signers: Ben Franklin, who had been present at the drafting of the Declaration of Independence and the Constitution. At the Constitutional Convention, the Founding Fathers had agreed, in order to get the charter approved by southern states, to not only ignore slavery but strengthen it, and to cover their shame by not mentioning it directly. By 1790, one year after ratification, the consensus among the Founders had cracked.

Contrary to the myth, however, the Revolutionary generation more often responded to pragmatism than high-minded beliefs. Slavery would not be abolished until a bloody civil war seven decades later, because most slaveowners demanded financial compensation for their human property and would never agree to peaceful abolition without compensation. "[The]census of 1790 provided unmistakable evidence that those antislavery advocates who believed that the future was on their side were deluding themselves," Ellis concluded.

For the total slave population was now approaching 700,000, up from about 500,000 in the year of the Declaration of Independence. Despite the temporary end of the slave trade during the war, and despite the steady march of abolition in the North, the slave population in the South was growing exponentially at the same exploding rate as the American population as a whole, which meant it was doubling every twenty to twenty-five years... Estimate [of compensation costs for slave owners] vary according to the anticipated cost of each freed slave, which ranges between one hundred and two hundred dollars [between $2,500 and $5,000 in 2012 dollars.] The higher figure produces a total cost of about $140 million to emancipate the entire slave population in 1790 [about $3.5 billion today]. Since the federal budget that year was less than $7 million [$175 million today], the critics seem to be right when they conclude that the costs were not just daunting, but also prohibitively expensive

As with Shays's Rebellion and the ratification of the Constitution, the Founders battled to contain the radicalism they had unleashed. This would be one of their signal failures. The American Revolution would inspire other major revolts in the coming decades. Bad harvests, widespread hunger, staggering national debt from their involvement in the American Revolution and the rise of Enlightenment ideas that questioned the absolute power held by the their monarchs led to the French Revolution, an epoch of violence, chaos and war beginning in 1789. The French revolutionaries sent King Louis XVI and his wife Marie Antoinette to the guillotine. By 1793, the French Convention and its "Committee of Public Safety" ruled France. With good cause, the committee believed that the Catholic Church had allied itself with the foreign power trying to overthrow the government. The Convention ordered church property seized, and priests and nuns executed, along with much of the French nobility. Soon, even former leaders of the revolution fell under the suspicion of the government and were executed during what came to be known as the "Reign of Terror." As many as 50,000 died at the hands of the revolutionary government by the time the Terror ended in 1794.

In 1804, Haiti saw the conclusion of first-ever successful slave revolt in the history of the world. Formerly the French colony of Saint-Dominque, the island had been converted into a giant sugar plantation dependent on African slave labor. Conditions were so horrific that deaths from malnutrition, exhaustion, and exposure exceeded births each year. The uprising began in 1791. Within weeks, slaves avenged themselves against their abusive former masters, torturing some of their one-time tormentors, killing 4,000 whites and setting to the torch 180 sugar plantations and scores of coffee and indigo plantations. Haiti achieved independence but started its existence as a republic with a shattered economy and ruled by a narrow band of elites who had achieved freedom before the revolution. The Haitian rebels had been inspired in part by the French Revolution, just as the French had drawn inspiration from the Americans. The United States, however, would try to ignore its sister North American republic.

The Haitian Revolution set a frightening example for American slaves. The United States would place an embargo on Haiti, causing much economic damage, and would not recognize its government until the Civil War in 1862. Jefferson once famously advocated repeated revolutions as healthy for societies, suggesting that one was needed every 20 years. "The tree of liberty must be refreshed from time to time with the blood of patriots and tyrants," he famously said. He didn't feel that way about slave revolts. The Haitian Revolution seemed to him to be a frightful prophecy of the United States' future. He saw only a racial Armageddon if blacks were to be free. As he wrote in *Notes on the State of Virginia*, "Deep rooted prejudices entertained by the whites; ten thousand recollections, by the blacks, of the injuries they have sustained; new provocations; the real distinctions which nature has made; and many other circumstances, will divide us into parties, and produce convulsions which will probably never end but in the extermination of the one or the other race." A racial revolution, one dreaded by many of the Founders of the American Republic and would unfold in ways they never anticipated, coming slowly and sweeping away the world inhabited by the Revolutionary generation. Revolutions, once started, are hard to stop.

Chronology

1782 Gnadenhutten Massacre.

1783 A letter threatening the Congress is sent by aide to General Gates.
Washington meets with dissatisfied officers and persuades them to not pursue a scheme to overthrow the government.
Soldiers block the exits of Independence Hall to protest the government's failure to pay servicemen.
Treaty of Paris end war.

1784 Spain closes the Mississippi River to use by American ships.

1785 Confederation Congress suspends interest payments on a wartime loan from France.

1786 Shays's Rebellion begins.
The Annapolis Convention is held.
Virginia adopts Statute of Religious Freedom.

1787 Constitution convention meets in Philadelphia.
Randolph proposes "large state plan" at the Constitutional Convention.
Paterson proposes "small state plan" at the Constitutional Convention.
Shays's Rebellion ends.
Connecticut Compromise introduced.
Northwest Ordinance.
Delaware provides manumission law.

1788 United States Constitution ratified.

1789 United States government assumes authority.
Slavery ends in Massachusetts by judicial decision.

Review Questions

1. What was the Newburgh Conspiracy and what was its significance?

2. What were the major flaws in the Articles of Confederation, why were they written that way, and what political and economic problems were caused by these flaws?

3. What different proposals regarding representation in the Congress were made at the Constitutional Convention and how was the issue resolved?

4. In what ways did the United States Constitution represent a retreat from democracy, and in what way did it address the flaws of the Articles of Confederation?

5. In what ways did the Constitution strengthen and protect slavery and what were the political impacts of the so-called 3/5s rule?

Glossary of Important People and Concepts

Anti-Federalists
Articles of Confederation
"Connecticut Compromise"
Constitutional Convention
Constitution of the United States
Federalist Papers
Federalists
Elizabeth Freeman
Alexander Hamilton
George Mason
Newburgh Conspiracy
Edmund Randolph
Shays's Rebellion
Three-Fifths Compromise

SUGGESTED READINGS

Akhil Reed Amar, *The Bill of Rights: Creation and Reconstruction* (1998).

Charles A. Beard, *An Economic Interpretation of the Constitution of the United States* (1913).

Carol Berkin, *Revolutionary Mothers: Women in the Struggle for American Independence* (2005).

Ron Chernow, *Alexander Hamilton* (2005).

James Thomas Flexner, *Washington: The Indispensable Man* (1974).

Robert A. Hendrickson, *The Rise and Fall of Alexander Hamilton* (1981).

John P. Kaminski, ed., *A Necessary Evil? Slavery and the Debate Over the Constitution* (1995).

Michael Kammen, *A Machine That Would Go By Itself: The Constitution in American Culture* (1986).

Richard H. Kohn, *Eagle and Sword: The Federalists and the Creation of the Military Establishment in America, 1783-1802* (1975).

Louis P. Masur, *Rites of Execution: Capital Punishment and the Transformation of American Culture, 1776-1865* (1989).

Jon Meacham, *American Gospel: The Founding Fathers, and the Making of a Nation* (2007).

Jack N. Rakove, *Original Meanings: Politics and Ideas in the Making of the Constitution* (1996).

Robert A. Rutland, *The Ordeal of the Constitution: The Anti-Federalists and the Ratification Struggle of 1787-1788* (1966).

Simon Schama, *Citizens: A Chronicle of the French Revolution* (1989).

Garry Wills, *Explaining America: The Federalist,* (1981).

___, *A Necessary Evil: History of the American Distrust of Government,* (2002).

Ann Fairfax Withington, *Toward a More Perfect Union: Virtue and the Formation of the American Republic,* (1991)

Gordon S. Wood, *The Radicalism of the American Revolution,* (1991).

George Washington

Chapter Eight

THE FEDERALIST ERA, 1789-1800

Soon after the deal between Alexander Hamilton and Thomas Jefferson and James Madison had been consummated to build the Republic's capital on the Potomac River, Congress commissioned the French architect and engineer Pierre Charles L'Enfant to plan the city. The Americans dismissed L'Enfant's suggestions for ornamentation and for a national church at the center of the city, but with these modifications the Frenchman's overall blueprints became the plan for the nation's future capital. L'Enfant inscribed the Constitution on the landscape: Congress sat in the Capitol Building, situated on high ground looking down on what would become the Capitol Mall; the President's House (the White House) stood a mile and a half away (neither could be seen from the other), and the building in which the Supreme Court would reside was equidistant between them. Most striking to those who had seen European capitals, the city had no function other than to be the home of republican government. No mercantile or financial establishments were part of the plan; no theaters and no military fortresses were to be built. Broad, straight streets stretched beyond the developed areas of the town; visually as well as politically, the capital was dependent upon and vulnerable to the countryside—the complete antithesis of European court cities. Foreign diplomats would complain for decades that Washington was a swampy, congested, haphazardly planned, unpleasant city with few amusement or divertissements for either its visitors or residents. As late as 1842, the English writer Charles Dickens, who visited Washington in that year, believed the city to be in a constant state of construction and "uncivilized." "It is sometimes called the City of Magnificent Distances, but it might with greater propriety be termed the City of Magnificent Intentions. Spacious avenues that begin in nothing, and lead nowhere; streets, mile-long, that only want houses, roads and inhabitants; public buildings that need only a public to be complete." What Dickens and earlier visitors missed, however, was that American republicans had built precisely the capital city that most of their fellow citizens wanted and believed reflected the nature of their democratic rustic simplicity and virtue.

George Washington became the nation's first president almost by acclamation, having received a vote from every member of the Electoral College in 1789. Washington and his closest advisors thought that the delicate balance between liberty and power had almost tipped toward anarchy during the "Critical Period" of the Confederation years. The Constitution's purpose was to redress this imbalance and restore power to the young nation's elite, many of whom had retreated from public service in the Revolution's aftermath, believing if they had taken power at that moment, they risked the horrors of counterrevolution. By 1787, when the people had come to their senses, realizing that they did not possess the republican requisite of public virtue, the elites seized the opportunity to regain control of the republic. In the process, they countered the democratic excesses of the Confederation period and came into national office determined to make the federal government powerful enough to command respect abroad and to impose order and stability at home. They succeeded for the most part, but in the process they engendered an equally resolute opposition who wanted to grant greater liberty and power to the common folk, via a more limited government. These self-styled **Democratic-Republicans** (led by Thomas Jefferson and James Madison, and often referred to simply as "Republicans") were as devoted to the revolutionary ideals of limited government and the yeoman republic as the **Federalists** were tied to their agenda of an orderly commercial republic with a powerful national state. The rivalry that emerged between the nation's first two political parties reflected in many ways the revolutionary conflict between liberty and power. This time, however, the struggle was purely domestic, though within a backdrop of international intrigue and war between France and England. Only when this age of democratic revolution ended in 1815 with Napoleon Bonaparte's defeat could Americans survey the kind of society and government that their revolution had created.

ESTABLISHING THE NATIONAL GOVERNMENT

The "Republican Court" of George Washington

George Washington left his plantation estate, Mount Vernon, for the temporary capital of New York City in April 1789. In every city, town, or hamlet that he passed, throngs of people turned out to cheer their hero. Militia companies and local dignitaries escorted him from place to place, church bells marked his progress, and lines of girls in white dresses waved demurely as he passed. At Newark Bay, he boarded a flower-bedecked barge, and surrounded by scores of boats, crossed to New York City. The crowds there were even larger, more energized, and jubilant, as he made his way to the president's house. He arrived on April 23 and was inaugurated first president of the United States of America seven days later.

No sooner was Washington inaugurated than he found himself embroiled in a controversy over what title should be bestowed upon the presidential office. Vice President John Adams wanted a title of honor for the president, one that would reflect the power of the new executive. The Senate rejected "His Excellency," for it reminded them of their colonial past when that was the term used to address royal governors and other British officials. After several proposals, ranging from "His Highness," to "His Mightiness," to "His Majesty," which the Senate debated for a full month, it became clear that none of titles would sit well with the more democratic House of

George Washington, First President of the United States

Representatives, which in the end declared that it preferred the austere dignity of "Mr. President." Thomas Jefferson, not yet a member of the government, pronounced the whole affair "the most superlatively ridiculous thing I ever heard."

Although dismissing the whole debate title as "ridiculous," Jefferson learned that much was at stake over what the president should be called. The Constitution provided a blueprint for the republic, but Washington would be responsible for translating that vision into a working state. The new president knew that his every action, behavior, and decision would be precedent-setting. He believed it mattered very much what citizens called their president, for that was part of the huge constellation of laws, customs, and forms of etiquette and protocol that would give the new government either a republican or a more regal tone. Many of those close to Washington wanted to make the office as exalted as possible in order to remove presidential power and prestige from the plebian localism and democratic excesses they believed had nearly killed the republic during the 1780s. Washington's stately inaugural tour, the high salaries paid to executive appointees, the endless round of formal galas and presidential dinners, the appearance of Washington's profile on some of the nation's coins—all were meant to promote the power and grandeur of the new government, especially its head of state. When Jefferson became Secretary of State, he chafed at all the pomp and circumstance and aristocratic pretensions that seemed to surround Washington at official social functions. Jefferson felt isolated at such events "unless there chanced to be some democrat from the legislative Houses." The matter proved to be a revealing episode in the arguments over how issues of liberty and power would be addressed in the new republic.

The Congress' immediate task was to organize the new executive branch of the federal government. Through legislation, the Congress first created four cabinet departments: State (to conduct diplomacy), Treasury (to manage the budget), War (to manage military affairs); and Justice (to handle legal affairs.) The Congress also created the United State Post Office. The president assigned specific duties to the departments and appointed a cabinet secretary to head each one. For all his cabinet posts, Washington chose individuals he knew and trusted personally for their experience and expertise. Washington wanted the best and brightest among the elite to serve in his cabinet, and thus he chose fellow Virginian Thomas Jefferson to serve as Secretary of State and another Virginian, Edmund Randolph, to be his Attorney General (the head of the Justice Department). For Secretary of War, Washington bestowed that honor upon his old friend and fellow comrade-in-arms during the War for Independence, General Henry Knox. Finally, for the Secretary of the Treasury, he chose his brilliant aide-de-camp, Alexander Hamilton, who quickly emerged as the most powerful man in the administration. Initially, Washington did not meet with his department heads as a group, but gradually moved toward establishing the precedent that the president meet on a regular basis with his entire cabinet to discuss and formulate administration policy.

George Washington viewed his responsibilities as president dramatically different than modern chief executives. Washington did not believe it was the president's job to govern the country on a daily basis—that was Congress' responsibility, because they represented the branch of the government closest to the citizenry. He believed his most important role relative to governance was to administer and to uphold all laws passed by Congress. In his frame of reference, if a bill passed both houses of Congress, the people had spoken. In that context, Washington also felt that he could not negate the people's will by vetoing legislation passed by Congress. In effect, he thought that his most important role as president was to bring honor, prestige, integrity, and power to the national government—qualities that he was confident he could deliver.

Although willing to relinquish power when it came to domestic policy, Washington believed the president should be directly responsible for foreign policy and diplomacy. Though foreign affairs fell under the purview of the State Department, Washington nonetheless asserted presidential authority in that area (which also included relations with Native Americans), often acting like his own Secretary of State, much to Jefferson's chagrin. Finally, Washington served no more than two terms as president. Though he had grave reservations about serving a second term, he established the tradition (later to become law by constitutional amendment during the 1950s) that the president can only be elected to two four-year terms. A "hands-off" president during his tenure, especially when it came to domestic affairs, Washington nonetheless laid the foundation for presidential conduct and expectations that subsequent generations followed with reverence. Not until the presidencies of John Quincy Adams and Andrew Jackson, both of whom were members of the post-Revolutionary generation, did executive leadership challenge the precedents for presidential conduct first established by George Washington.

The First Congress

Nicknamed the "Father of the Constitution," James Madison of Virginia came to dominate the nation's first Congress. Under his auspices, the legislative branch strengthened the new national government in a variety of ways. To secure the federal government's chief revenue source, Congress passed a tariff on imports before turning its attention to the proposed constitutional amendments that had been demanded by the state ratifying conven-

Edmund Randolph

tions. Madison proposed twelve amendments, which were sent to the states, though only ten were ratified, the **Bill of Rights**. All ten amendments reflected the fears of a generation that had struggled both ideologically and physically with the idea of centralized power. The First Amendment guaranteed the freedoms of speech, press, and religion against governmental interference; these were to be liberties protected by the government as "inalienable rights" for all citizens. The Second and Third Amendments, prompted by the fears of a standing army, sanctioned the continuation of a militia of armed citizens, the republican ideal of a constabulary of virtuous citizen-soldiers to maintain domestic peace and order and to defend the country if necessary from foreign threats. These amendments also stated the specific conditions under which soldiers could be quartered in private homes. The Fourth through Eighth Amendments protected a citizen's right in court when under arrest—rights whose violation had been central to the rebels' list of grievances. The Ninth Amendment stated that the enumeration of specific rights in the first eight amendments did not imply a denial of other rights, while the Tenth Amendment stated that all powers not specifically relegated to the national government by the Constitution were reserved exclusively for the states and their citizenry.

A devoted nationalist, Madison had performed skillfully and shrewdly as he assuaged his more states rights-oriented colleagues' fears that the Constitution created an overpowering national government. Madison assured his associates that the Bill of Rights would mitigate any potential for the central government to descend into tyranny. In short, Madison constructed the Bill of Rights to guarantee those personal liberties that the majority of American citizens believed the Revolution was fought for and that most directly affected their daily lives, while not weakening the integrity and strength of the national government.

Congress then created the federal courts that were mentioned, though not specified, in the Constitution. The 1789 Judiciary Act established a Supreme Court with six members along with thirteen district courts and three circuit courts of appeals. The act made it possible for certain cases to be appealed from state courts to federal circuit courts, which would be presided over by traveling Supreme Court justices, thus elevating federal power. As James Madison and his more nationalist congressional compatriots of the First Congress surveyed their handiwork, they could congratulate themselves on having augmented national authority in a variety of important capacities.

ALEXANDER HAMILTON

Without question, **Alexander Hamilton** was one of the most brilliant of the Founding Fathers. Washington entrusted his former senior aide-de-camp with the herculean task of creating the new nation's economic and financial foundations. While serving as Washington's military chief of staff during the Revolution, Hamilton and the general became very close friends and confidantes. Indeed, a filial relationship developed between the two men, which, by the war's end, led to Hamilton's emergence as Washington's most favored officer. Thus, few were surprised when the president named Alexander Hamilton to be his Secretary of the Treasury. Since Washington made it clear to his cabinet that he would be in charge of the nation's foreign policy initiatives, thus relegating Thomas Jefferson as Secretary of State to minor cabinet status, such an arrangement allowed for Hamilton to become the most powerful man in the administration. More than any other cabinet member, and perhaps more than even Washington himself (he later referred to Washington's presidency as "my administration"), Hamilton directed the formation of the national government. Because the president gave him *carte blanche* to stabilize the country's economy, Hamilton used such license to create the economic system that he believed would best serve the national interest while simultaneously increasing the power of the national government. To Hamilton, the relationship between the

Alexander Hamilton

economy and the national government had to be symbiotic if the great republican experiment called the United States was to succeed and someday become the most powerful and emulated nation in the world. He believed that was America's destiny, and he was determined to put the country on the path toward greatness and power from the moment he assumed his cabinet position.

An adopted New Yorker, Hamilton had no deeply-felt devotion to any particular state, which fostered his national outlook. Born out of wedlock on the West Indies island of Nevis, the son of a local woman with the traveling son of a Scottish nobleman, the young Hamilton proved to be a voracious reader. A hard worker, he helped his mother run her small shop before her death, then clerked and handled the account books for a merchant company. Ambitious for a life beyond his small island, his boss and local residents raised money to send the able young man to New York City for a formal education at King's College (now Columbia University), where Hamilton was studying when the American Revolution began. He soon became a rabid patriot for the rebel cause.

Hamilton's yearning for the national government's success was not purely personal. Along with many other Founding Fathers, their sense of fulfillment was tied to the nation's success. If the Republic failed, then they had faltered as well. Men like Hamilton saw the United States as extensions of themselves, out of which emerged an often rabid, single-minded nationalism. Indeed, for many of the Founding Fathers, including Hamilton, their larger objective was to use the central government as an agency to inculcate fellow citizens with a sense of nationalism in order to prevent the localism and parochial thinking they believed endemic at the time among the majority of Americans. Finally, and much to Hamilton's subsequent undoing (and despite his humble beginnings), he was an elitist who simply disdained the common people, believing them wholly unfit to participate in government or to provide any input whatsoever in determining national policy. He dismissed the people as plebian rabble, certain that if they ever gained political power the United States would become a "mobocracy." The public was very aware of Hamilton's contempt for them. Despite Washington's unequivocal support for his secretary and his agenda, Hamilton became one of his generation's most reviled men in American popular politics.

A successful lawyer by training and profession, Hamilton read extensively on a variety of topics, including **Adam Smith's** seminal work, *The Wealth of Nations*, as well as the works of the French physiocrats and the other political economists of the Scottish Enlightenment. Hamilton discerned from his reading that what was best for the country's economy was a form of "mixed capitalism;" that is, the powers of the national government should be used to help foster a more balanced economy among trade, manufacturing, and farming. What worried Hamilton was the dependence of 90 percent of American citizens on agriculture for their livelihoods. He believed that as long as the United States remained such an overwhelmingly agrarian economy, the country would have to import all its other commodities from other nations (most notably England), especially manufactured goods. In Hamilton's mind, the United States would be a colonial economy, dependent on a "mother country" for essential products and thus vulnerable to foreign market conditions. He did not want to tip the economic scales in the completely opposite direction, with the United States completely dominated by industry and trade while curtailing agriculture. The Treasury Secretary knew that, first and foremost, a nation must have the ability to feed itself—needing to import food would be worse than dependence on foreign nations for manufactured goods. He simply believed that no nation would be truly politically independent until it had become economically self-sufficient, and that goal became the overarching purpose of his economic agenda and vision for the United States.

Hamilton's Financial Program

In 1789, Congress asked Hamilton to investigate the current state of the public debt. The Treasury Secretary responded with a report stating that the national government owed a total of $54 million. He found that $11.7 million dollars of the liabilities were owed to foreign creditors, with the lion's share owed to France, and a lesser extent to Spain and the Netherlands. Congress agreed with Hamilton's proposal to pay off the foreign debt in full since the young country's financial credibility abroad was at stake. Moreover, nations that loaned the United States money during wartime might be even more inclined to extend credit during times of peace and stability if they had been fully remunerated with interest. By paying its foreign debt, the U.S. government could establish itself as a good "credit risk" in the future. With congressional approval, Hamilton paid foreign creditors, liquidating that portion of the nation's debt and positioning the government for future foreign loans. Controversy ensued because Hamilton compensated the foreign creditors in dollars; not in their respective currency—livres, guilders, or pesetas. At first, the French, Dutch, and Spanish were outraged, claiming that the American dollar was a worthless currency. Hamilton agreed, stating that the dollar had little value in Europe, but in the United States, dollars were as "good as gold" and redeemable at full face value.

Here we see just a glimpse of Hamiltonian wisdom, and even a bit of guile. By paying them in dollars, foreign creditors had no choice but to spend their currency in the United States if they hoped for any return on their money. Such investment and spending helped stimulate American economic expansion, which, from the beginning, was Hamilton's principal objective in paying off the foreign debt.

With regard to the domestic debt, Hamilton reported that the national government owed $42.4 million (or almost four times the level of foreign debt) to American citizens who had dutifully supplied food, arms, and other resources to the Continental Army and the independence movement in general. Paying the domestic debt, however, raised troublesome questions. The obligations represented the amount owed to all those citizens—merchants, farmers, and soldiers—who had received government compensation for wartime contributions or for services rendered. They were paid with paper scrip or bonds and were told at the time to keep all such "money" until the day they would be able to redeem their certificates at face value plus interest. However, during the Confederation period, hundreds of speculators went about the country and bought up as many of the notes as they possibly could at only a fraction of their face value. These men could hoodwink the original holders out of their bonds easily because so many believed that they would never receive compensation from a government as weak and chronically short of funds as the Confederation Congress. When news began circulating throughout the country that the Constitution would create a new national government likely to pay its debts, speculators and their agents coveted the bonds even more. By 1790, about 80 percent of the bonds wound up in the hands of northeastern speculators who often bought the notes for as little as 10 percent of their original value. If the rumor proved true, that the new government was ready to make good its obligations of full payment plus interest to all holders, the speculators stood to make enormous profits.

Equally contentious were the war debts incurred by the individual states. Hamilton and his nationalist supporters wanted the central government to assume all state debts (totaling $25 million), thus adding them to the federal government's foreign and domestic obligations to create an even larger public debt. Such consolidation would fuse individual interests with those of national government, creating in the process a citizenry whose loyalty was first and foremost to the government and the nation. A public debt would also create the need for taxation to reduce the deficit while simultaneously expanding the civil service, for government workers would be needed to monitor the debt and collect the tax revenues.

In short, the nationalists hoped to use the creation of a public debt as a means to expand the power and presence of the national government deeper into Americans' daily lives. Often the same holders of the government bonds, speculators possessing the majority of state certificates now stood to benefit from a double windfall. Local officials whose respective states had paid off most of their notes in the 1780s were especially upset by the "assumption" idea. Such was the case for all the southern states except South Carolina. Meanwhile, none of the northern states had paid their obligation. Thus, if the federal government assumed the state debts and paid them off at face value with interest, money would flow out of the southern, middle, and western states into the Northeast, whose citizens would hold fully four-fifths of the national debt.

Hamilton hoped that his funding and assumption proposal would lead to this scenario. He knew that the majority of the bonds had been bought up by mainly northeastern speculators, and he intended for his bill to make them very wealthy men, tying their wealth and individual self-interest directly to the success and longevity of the national government. Hamilton envisioned using his initiatives to promote the government's role as an agent through which a capitalist and entrepreneurial class would emerge. These businessmen would invest their newfound money to develop and grow the nation's manufacturing and commercial sectors. Hamilton believed that without the initial stimulation from the federal government, these enterprises would never be undertaken. In his view, such policies were imperative if the country was to become economically self-sufficient. The alternative would be the nation's economy languishing indefinitely in an agrarian malaise and the United States remaining a weak, vulnerable country, dependent on foreigners for their economic survival.

In his *Report on Public Credit*, Hamilton stated that the foreign debt should be paid promptly and in full, but he insisted that the domestic debt could be a permanent, tax-supported fixture of government. Under his plan, the government would issue securities to creditors and would pay them an annual interest rate of 4 percent. Hamilton's funding and state debt assumption plans announced to the international community, government creditors, and future investors that the United States would pay its bills. Politically, Hamilton's agenda sought to create a new financial elite, dependent on (and thus loyal to) the federal government. This coterie of wealthy financiers would not only become the capitalist vanguard of industrial entrepreneurs, but also the new ruling class—the privileged successors to the Founding Fathers ensuring that power remained securely in the hands of the best and the brightest, and not in the hands of the people. Indeed, Hamilton's worse nightmare was that after his generation had passed, the common folk would seize power. To prevent such a disaster, Hamilton believed his generation had to establish programs and policies at the national level that would ensure the orderly transfer of power from one generation of elites to the next. In short, the national debt lay at the center of Alexander Hamilton's plan for a powerful national state firmly under the control of the nation's upper classes.

The Federal Excise Tax and the Bank of the United States

To help fund the national debt, Hamilton called for a federal **excise tax** on whiskey. The tax on spirits would fall especially hard on frontier whiskey producers, who were mainly farmers who supplemented their incomes by using their excess grain to make whiskey. Hamilton's whiskey tax would not only raise revenues but also establish the government's power to tax and to collect money even in the most remote regions of the republic. As will be seen later in this chapter, much to the surprise of the Washington administration, western farmers protested the measure, ultimately rising in a "**Whiskey Rebellion**." The president would threaten the use of force to quell the uprising.

As part of his overall agenda and vision for the nation's economy, Hamilton believed it essential to establish a national bank, which he aptly called the **Bank of the United States**. According to the Treasury Secretary's plan, the government would deposit its revenue in the Bank and supervise its operations, but the Bank would also exist as a semi-private institution under the daily charge of a board of directors drawn from the private sector. The Bank would print and back a national currency and informally regulate other banks in the country. Hamilton also made the national bank's stock payable in government securities, thus adding to their value, and giving the Bank a powerful interest in the government's fiscal stability while binding the holders of the securities even closer to the national government. Once again, Hamilton was attempting to use the powers of the national government to create institutions designed to ensure the elite's loyalty to the government, vesting their interests with the new government's success. In this particular case, private individuals would not only have a direct, controlling interest in a quasi-government institution but would also be financially rewarded by the government for their participation in helping to secure and stabilize the nation's economy. Hamilton also desired the Bank to become a source of loans for those individuals interested in starting manufacturing enterprises. One did not have to look too closely to see that Hamilton had replicated, almost exactly, the Bank of England.

The Report on Manufactures

In December 1791, Hamilton issued his *Report on Manufactures*, which proposed government aid to business in order to stimulate the economy and promote the development of American industry. The two main pillars of his plan involved high tariffs on foreign imports and government "bounties," or subsidies, to America's young industries. In addition to providing funds for the federal government, Hamilton argued that raising tariff levels would boost the U.S. industrial base by artificially raising the prices of foreign imports, thereby encouraging the purchase of cheaper domestically-manufactured goods. The tariff monies would also be used for the payment of subsidies to innovative inventors and factory owners who manufactured needed commodities. He believed this form of aid to American industry would lessen the country's dependence on agriculture while further tying the industrial and entrepreneurial class to its primary benefactor, the federal government.

In Hamilton's mind, his program to consolidate the government debt, levy a federal excise tax, and create a national bank sought in a bold fashion to solve the government's immediate financial problems, while his *Report on Manufactures* offered a means for the government to promote industrial growth. His growing number of opponents, however, viewed his program with suspicion, believing Hamilton wished to establish a carbon-copy of Great Britain's Treasury-driven government.

THE RISE OF OPPOSITION

The Birth of the First Party System

In 1789, every branch of the federal government was under the control of the Constitution's most fervent supporters. The most radical Anti-Federalists had either found sanctuaries in the state governments or retired from politics altogether. Nearly everyone serving in the national government was committed to making the new government work. In particular, Alexander Hamilton and James Madison (representing his Virginia district in the House of Representatives) were certain they would be able to continue the personal friendship and amicable collaboration they enjoyed during the Constitutional Convention and the ratification process. Much to Hamilton's dismay, however, his old friend quickly

Conflicting Visions of Republican Society

The Founding Fathers and the American people had difficulty agreeing on the structure of their new republican government. It had taken free Americans thirteen years (1776-1789) to frame the government: a year to propose the Articles of Confederation, four years to ratify the document, and eight more attempting to govern under its provisions. Once the American people realized the weaknesses of the Articles, they sent the Founding Fathers to Philadelphia to devise an alternative (the Federal Constitution), which then took two years to ratify, and in the process, the public debate became very acrimonious if not outright bitter and divisive among many groups of citizens. Even after the Constitution went into effect, many Americans continued to oppose the document, and two states (North Carolina and Rhode Island) had not yet ratified the Constitution when George Washington took his oath of office.

Nonetheless, the majority of white Americans did believe in a core of fundamental republican assumptions that united them sufficiently enough for the new nation to succeed, despite some bitter and potentially perilous moments during the Republic's first decade of existence. Most free Americans believed that the nation's success depended on the citizens' political and public virtue, which meant the various characteristics that would enable citizens to protect themselves against either would-be tyrants or lawless mobs. The requisite "republican persona" had to be self-sufficient, industrious, and, most important, possess a public-spiritedness and mindedness that put the welfare of the country above self-interest. Americans tended to associate these qualities not only with what one did for a living but how one used or benefited from the fruits of one's labor. When people became too wealthy and accustomed to luxury, Americans believed that they became lazy and lost their sense of public virtue, resulting in their support of corrupt, tyrannical governments that not only oppressed the majority of citizens but catered to the interests of the privileged few. Such individuals and the corrupt government officials caused impoverishment and despair on the people, ultimately causing such a society to implode into riots and anarchy. In short, in the minds of the majority of white Americans, there was a "natural" correlation between how one earned their livelihood and public virtue. If that was the case, who in particular constituted the majority opinion that determined what a republican society should look like?

In 1790, 97 percent of free Americans lived in nuclear households on farms or in rural villages where they produced much of their own food, clothing, tools, and furnishings. For this great mass of people, republican virtue was to be found in those who cultivated the land, the nation's independent yeoman farmers. In **Letters From an American Farmer** *(1782), J. Hector St. John de Crevecoeur had identified the new nation as "a people of cultivators scattered over an immense territory, animated with the spirit of industry that is unfettered and unrestrained because each person works for himself." Thomas Jefferson, who actually managed his lands rather than physically putting his hands in the dirt, reinforced and ideologically exalted this view in his* **Notes on the State of Virginia** *(1785): "Those who labor in the earth are the chosen people of God, if ever he had a chosen people, whose breasts He has made His peculiar deposit for substantial and genuine virtue." Jefferson was convinced that only the independent farmer could achieve true self-reliance and from that sense of autonomy, sprang public virtue. "Dependence begets subservience and venality, suffocates the germ of virtue, and prepares fit tools for the design of ambition."*

Farmers, small shopkeepers, landless settlers, and craft workers saw the wealth accumulated and inherited by large landowners or by large merchant families as the moral equivalent of theft. "No person can possess property without laboring," farmer and tavern keeper William Manning declared, "unless he get it by force or craft, fraud or fortune, out of the earnings of others." Manning viewed this distinction between "those that labor for a living and those who get one without laboring—or as they are generally termed, the Few and the Many"—as "the great dividing line" of early Republican society.

Not surprisingly, the merchant class and wealthy landowners saw things differently. They agreed with their bucolic fellow citizens that republican virtue did indeed reside in labor, which they defined as commercial labor—the work of opening markets and expanding trade, of nurturing invention and innovation, all of which brought new wealth to the larger community. Alexander Hamilton was one of the most passionate and determined propagators and promoters of this view. Born in the West Indies, he was raised by his single mother, Rachel, a shopkeeper, who died when he was thirteen years of age. Hamilton then entered the merchant firm of Beekman and Cruger as a clerk, eventually proving to be so valuable that Cruger sent him to New York to attend King's College (present-day Columbia University) to

> *pursue a university education and degree, which he did in law. By the time of the Revolution, he had already gained quite a reputation not only as a first-rate lawyer, but also a "sharp" businessman. These experiences convinced Hamilton that the merchant class (traders, investors, and financiers who risked their own incomes to generate new wealth, new markets, and new ideas) best embodied the qualities needed in republican citizens.*
>
> *Just as yeoman farmers were wary of merchants and financiers, wealthy merchants and large landowners were just as suspicious of middling and laboring Americans. To businessmen, the mass of the people were undisciplined and gullible, thus vulnerable to the deceptions of fanatics and demagogues. The only individuals capable or qualified to control such "passions" were men of property and proven wealth—whether in the form of large, profitable commercial estates or thriving trade or business enterprises. Urban elites dismissed their rural compatriots as "yahoos" and "clodpoles." To the wealthy, the crude homes of farmers, their barefoot children, and their meager diets of beans, potatoes, and corn bread, all reflected not the hardships born of such an existence but rather inherent laziness and slothfulness. Merchants and proprietors especially despised the casualness with which country folk treated debt. Farmers and other rural citizens conducted trade in a combination of barter, cash, and promissory notes, with records kept haphazardly and payments constantly renegotiated in terms of the goods, services, or whatever paper money might be available. Working on a national and international scale, merchants and large landowners needed timely payment, preferably in hard currency, to pay off their own debts, make new investments, or arrange long-distance transactions.*
>
> *These tensions existed between the majority yeoman farmers and the urban commercial elites over who possessed sufficient public virtue to not only lead the nation politically, but determine its social fabric as well. However, the ideology of the yeoman farmer would prevail, as the Republic remained a predominantly agrarian economy and rural society until after the Civil War.*

turned into an adversary, the result of the Virginian's opposition to Hamilton's fiscal and economic policies. Thomas Jefferson joined Madison's crusade to defeat the Hamiltonian agenda, certain that the Treasury Secretary's program was designed to dismantle the Revolution. By the end of Washington's first term, the consensus of 1789 had completely unraveled, largely because of Hamilton's proposals and the bitter ideological debate they engendered. More than 25 years later, Jefferson still insisted that the battles of the 1790s had been "contests of principle between the advocates of republicanism and those of kingly government." In short, to the day he died, Jefferson believed that his war with Hamilton during the 1790s represented a conflict between the forces of elitism and democratic republicanism.

Hamilton challenged his opponents, declaring that his national debt proposal was a solution to specific problems of government finance and did not reflect in any way an attempt to establish a British-style state. In the House, Madison and his supporters (the majority of whom were fellow Southerners) asserted that the funding and assumption bill was unfair; that it concentrated wealth not only in the North (to the South's disadvantage) from where the majority of speculators had originated, but also in hands of an elite, privileged few at the expense of the majority of citizens. These were men, Madison railed, who benefited from associations with government insiders to reap fortunes from government notes bought at rock-bottom prices from soldiers, widows, and orphans. Madison branded Hamilton's plan "public plunder." Hamilton retorted that, regardless of who held the original bonds, when they sold them to speculators their actions reflected someone possessing little faith in the government to make good its obligations. Such people should not be rewarded for such infidelity.

Madison, Jefferson, and the other members of the opposition knew that Hamilton's argument not only had merit but also the support of George Washington, who they knew would never challenge Hamilton on such policies. Thus, the opposition concluded that, since they did not have the president's support or a majority in Congress, perhaps it would be best to compromise with Hamilton. In exchange for accepting his proposals on the debt, they secured his endorsement for locating the nation's permanent capital at a site along the Potomac River between Maryland and Virginia. The compromise reflected the essence of American revolutionary republicanism. Hamilton intended to tie northeastern commercial interests to the federal government. If New York City or Philadelphia became the permanent capital, Hamilton's opponents feared that political and economic power would be concentrated there as in Paris and London—court cities where power, wealth, and every kind of privilege were in league against a plundered and degraded countryside. Benjamin Rush, a Philadelphian but a hardcore republican, condemned the "government which has begun so soon to ape the corruption of the British court, conveyed to it through the impure channel of the City of New York." Holding the same suspicion of Philadelphia and Boston, Madison and enough of his agrarian allies in the Congress agreed to not strongly oppose the Hamilton's funding and assumption bill, letting it pass, on the condition that the Congress designate the U.S. capital's location be placed in the South, between Maryland and Virginia, in the present-day District of Columbia. The compromise would distance the commercial power of cities from the federal government while ending the "republican court" that had formed around Washington. This radically republican maneuver ensured that the capital of the United States would be, except for purposes of government, a place of no importance.

A Clash of Titans: Jefferson versus Hamilton

Personalities as much, if not more than ideology, dominated the first party system. Indeed, one of the most passionate and divisive personal feuds in American political history occurred during this time—the intense rivalry between Alexander Hamilton and Thomas Jefferson, whose antagonisms dictated and determined much of the history of the Republic's first decade. The personal dislike between the two men began during the bank bill controversy. Jefferson opposed the bill on the basis of its constitutionality, believing that Congress did not have the power to charter a national bank. Unlike Madison's earlier attacks on funding and assumption in which he argued about the unfairness of such a measure, Jefferson cleverly used a more sophisticated argument, the bill's supposed illegality, to stop the Hamiltonian legislative effort. Hamilton agreed with Jefferson that the Constitution did not explicitly state that Congress had the right to establish a national bank. However, Hamilton asked Jefferson to find in the document where it stated that Congress did not have such authority expressly stated to implement its enumerated powers, in this case, regulating interstate commerce. He asserted that the Bank's creation reflected the application of the clause in the Constitution empowering Congress "to make all laws which shall be necessary and proper" to carry out its assigned duties. In other words, Hamilton argued that the creation of a national bank was "necessary and proper" for the country's present and future economic stability and security. President Washington and a majority in Congress ultimately sided with Hamilton.

The Hamilton-Jefferson contest over the Bank reflected the larger issue of constitutional interpretation. Specifically, should the document be interpreted literally, leaving no room for "elasticity" as domestic or foreign (and future) exigencies may demand? Led by Jefferson, advocates of such a view became known as strict constructionists, insisting that the government had no powers beyond those specified in the Constitution. Jefferson took exception to all of Hamilton's financial proposals. He was certain that the excise tax would arouse public opposition and that funding the debt would reward speculators and penalize ordinary citizens. Even more threatening, Jefferson asserted, Hamilton was using government securities and stock in the Bank of the United States to buy the loyalty of merchants, speculators, and even members of Congress. Thirty Congressmen owned stock in the Bank of the United States and many others held government securities or had close ties to men who did. Jefferson charged that Hamilton's "corrupt squadron" of "paper men" in Congress was, in the classic fashion of evil ministers, enabling the Treasury Secretary to control Congress from his non-elective seat in the executive branch. In every attack on Hamilton's programs, Jefferson portrayed his rival as an Anglophile, working to bring about the end of republicanism and to transform the United States into another European-style monarchy and aristocracy. Jefferson insisted that, "The ultimate objective of all this is to prepare the way for a change, from the present republican form of government to that of a monarchy, of which the English constitution was the model."

Though Hamilton openly admired the British system, the labeling of him as an outright Anglophile was purely partisan and false. Hamilton's alleged Anglophilia was born of his desire to make the United States a self-sufficient and powerful nation. Indeed, that passion served as the driving force behind all of his proposals and ideas. In the Hamiltonian frame of reference, Great Britain was the undisputed power in the world, possessing a booming, industrializing economy second to none. If the United States hoped to become a powerful country in the future, the young nation could learn much from the British economic system. Moreover, he believed that it was in the United States' best interests to forge strong economic ties with Great Britain.

Hamilton and his supporters, who by 1792 had organized the Federalist Party, insisted that the centralization of power and a strong executive were necessary to the republic's survival. They pointed to the provincialism, selfishness, and disorder that plagued the nation during the 1780s, when revolutionary public virtue degenerated into democratic excesses. They feared all such wantonness and dissipation would return if the Jeffersonians had their way and the Revolution would be destroyed. The argument drew its urgency from the understanding of both Hamilton and Jefferson that the United States was a small revolutionary republic in a world governed by kings and aristocrats, and that republics had a long history of failure; they all knew that it was still very possible for Americans to lose their revolution. Until late 1792, the Hamilton-Jefferson feud was largely confined to members of the government, especially Congress. Hamilton and his supporters tried to mobilize the commercial elite on the government's side, while Madison and Jefferson struggled to hold off the perceived monarchial plot until the citizens could be aroused to defend their liberties, waiting for the perfect political time to take the issues directly to the people to rally them to their crusade against Hamilton's policies. For the most part, Hamilton got his way during Washington's first term, though Madison temporarily stifled the proposals contained in the *Report on Manufactures* (as will be seen in subsequent chapters, Hamilton's ideas in the *Report* would later become a reality). As both sides began mobilizing popular support, events in Europe came to dominate the politics of the young republic.

THE REPUBLIC IN A WORLD AT WAR, 1793-1800

In late 1792, French revolutionaries rejected the idea of a constitutional monarchy and proclaimed a republic. To show the world that the *ancien regime* was dead in France, radicals beheaded Louis XVI, his queen Marie Antoinette, and as many members of the royal household as they could round up. The monarchy's end marked the beginning of the "Reign of Terror" in which radical republicans, in the name of the revolution and for the suppression of counterrevolution, executed over 50,000 Frenchmen from all classes during the next two years. As the other European powers watched the events unfolding in France with horror, they became concerned that if not checked, French revolutionary passion and ideas would soon infect their countries. Thus, in 1792, Austria and Prussia declared war on France. A year later, France declared war on Britain.

Americans and the French Revolution

The French Revolution reverberated across the Atlantic and impacted society and politics in the United States. In 1778, American ambassador Benjamin Franklin negotiated treaties with the French monarchy that pledged U.S. support if France should go to war with England. However, by the beginning of the president's second term, the Washington administration argued that the 1778 treaties were no longer binding—they became null and void the moment the king's executioner held up Louis's head for the crowd to cheer. In other words, the United States made a treaty with a government that no longer existed. This argument became the basis of Washington's neutrality declaration.

When the French Revolution began in 1789, the overwhelming majority of Americans supported the cause. For the first three years, it appeared that was exactly what was happening in France. However, with the king's execution and the advent of the Reign of Terror, increasing numbers of Americans began to disassociate themselves from such a bloodbath. Even in its most violent days, the American Revolution never approximated the terror and bloodletting the French were inflicting upon each other. The execution of thousands of citizens from all classes horrified Americans, and when the French threatened the sovereignty of nations by declaring a war of all peoples against all monarchies, such a proclamation proved to be the final straw for many American supporters. To defend their country, the French created a true citizen's army, hundreds of thousands of men and even women committed to the revolution's slogan of "liberty, equality, and fraternity." Through their army's members saw themselves as the vanguard of revolutionary change for all of Europe and thus after repelling the Austro-Prussian forces, the French decided it was their duty to mankind to liberate all the rest of the oppressed European peoples in the name of the French Revolution. The French army, filled with a *rage militaire* and an *esprit d'corps* unprecedented in European military history, would soon become an undefeatable force of revolutionary passion and commitment that rampaged its way across the European continent for the next several years, conquering other nations in the name of liberation. The argument between Jeffersonian republicanism and Hamiltonian centralization was no longer a squabble within the United States government. National politics was now caught up within the struggle over international republicanism.

No sooner did all-out war begin in Europe than President Washington declared American neutrality. The announcement outraged the French who felt betrayed. Without French help in 1778, they believed, there might not have been a United States of America. Moreover, the French could not understand why a revolutionary people, such as the Americans professed to be, would not come to their aid without hesitation because France was fighting for the same righteous and glorious purpose for which the Americans had fought in 1776. Unfortunately for the French, by 1795, few Americans still believed the two events were even remotely similar.

Washington and most of his advisers realized that the United States was in no condition to fight in another war. They also wanted to maintain peaceful relations with Great Britain. Ninety percent of American imports came from England, with 90 percent of federal revenue coming from customs duties on those imports. In short, the nation's economy, as well as the government's stability and financial health, depended on good relations with Great Britain. Moreover, Hamilton and his Federalist colleagues genuinely sympathized with the British in the war with France and believed that the conflict offered a golden opportunity for the United States to strengthen ties with Great Britain, which they were convinced would prove to be of great economic benefit for the republic. The Federalists regarded the United States as a "perfected" England and viewed Great Britain as the defender of hierarchical society and ordered liberty against French homicidal anarchy.

Jefferson and his followers saw the French Revolution differently. They applauded the French for carrying on the spirit of the American Revolution, as well as being the harbingers of republicanism in Europe. The Jeffersonians condemned the Federalists' alleged monarchial politics and their desire to keep the United States in a neocolonial status relative to Great Britain. Led by Madison and Jefferson, they wanted to abandon the English mercantile system and trade freely with all nations. They did not care if that course of action hurt commercial interests (most of which supported the Federalists) or impaired the government's ability to centralize power in itself. While they agreed that the United States should try to maintain neutrality, the Jeffersonians sympathized as openly with the French as their Federalist counterparts did with the English.

Maintaining Neutrality

Persuading other countries to honor American neutrality proved to be very difficult for the Washington administration, as the president discovered soon after issuing his neutrality proclamation. Neither France nor England showed any intention of respecting American neutrality. As the years progressed, both Britain and France engaged in all manner of intimidation, harassment, even threats of war, to get the United States to abandon its isolationism and become an ally. Eventually, as will be seen in the next chapter, the United States opted for war with England in 1812 rather than succumb to continued economic and political extortion.

In April 1793, the new French government sent **Edmond Genêt** as minister to the United States. Genêt's ruling Girondists were the revolutionary faction that had declared war on all the monarchies. They ordered their minister to enlist American aid with or without the Washington administration's approval. After the president's neutrality proclamation, which the French blatantly disregarded, Genêt proceeded to openly recruit American privateers to harass British shipping and enlisted Americans to become part of a filibustering expedition with designs on Spanish New Orleans. Genêt then opened France's Caribbean colonies to U.S. shipping, providing American merchants with a choice between French free trade and British mercantilism. However, before Genêt could do more to undermine American neutrality, the Girondists fell from power in France in 1793. Learning that he would be guillotined if he returned to France, Genêt decided to obtain asylum in the United States, which was granted. He eventually married a daughter of George Clinton, the old anti-Federalist governor of New York, and lived out the rest of his life as a country gentleman.

Although furious with the French minister's underhanded activities, Washington found the British efforts of insulting and undermining American neutrality to be even more egregious and threatening to American security than Genêt's actions. As soon as British government officials found out about France's free trade declaration, they immediately ordered the seizure of any ship trading with France's West Indian possessions. These "**Orders in Council**" resulted in 250 American ships falling into British hands. Even more outrageous, the Royal Navy began stopping and searching United States merchant ships, allegedly looking for English deserters who had "jumped ship" for safer, better-paying work in the American merchant marine. Inevitably, some American seamen were kidnapped and drafted, or "impressed," into the British navy, a practice the Royal Navy had engaged in for many years, especially during time of war when their manpower needs were the greatest. **Impressment** infuriated the Washington administration, who saw the practice as a flagrant and contemptuous violation of U.S. neutrality as well as an assault on American sovereignty. Meanwhile, to add insult to injury, British agents operating from Canada and their still-garrisoned forts in the Northwest began promising military aid to the Native Americans north of the Ohio River. Thus, while the French ignored United States neutrality, the English engaged in both overt and covert acts of war.

THE DESTRUCTION OF THE WOODLAND INDIANS

Although many of the Woodland tribes were still intact and still living on their ancestral lands, by 1790 they were in serious trouble. The members of the old Iroquois Federation had been dismantled and confined to reservations in New York and Pennsylvania, with those who refused to be relocated fleeing to Canada. The once-powerful Cherokees had been severely punished for allying with the British allies during the Revolution, forced to cede three-fourths of their territory to the United States. Like the Iroquois, they were nearly surrounded by white settlements.

In the Old Northwest (the present-day states of Illinois, Indiana, Michigan, Ohio, and Wisconsin), the Shawnee, Miami, and other tribes—with the help of the British who still occupied seven forts within United States territory—continued to trade furs with the British and to attack encroaching white Americans. Skirmishes with frontier Americans, however, brought U.S. government reprisals. In the Ohio Country, expeditions led by General Josiah Harmar and General Arthur St. Clair failed to defeat the Indians in 1790 and 1791—the second engagement ending in a disastrous and humiliating defeat for the U.S. Army, which saw 630 soldiers killed. In 1794, President Washington sent a third army under General "Mad Anthony" Wayne, which defeated the Indians at **Fallen Timbers** near present-day Toledo. The ensuing **Treaty of Greenville** forced the Native Americans to cede two-thirds of present-day Ohio and southeastern Indiana. At this juncture, the British decided to abandon their forts in the Old Northwest. Following the victory at Fallen Timbers, American settlers flooded into the remaining Indian lands. In 1796, President Washington, who had reluctantly sent the army on all three occasions because he respected Native Americans and wanted peace with them and not their destruction or removal, threw up his hands and announced that "I believe scarcely any thing, short of a Chinese Wall, or a line of troops, will restrain Land Jobbers and the encroachment of settlers upon the Indian Territory." Five years later, Governor William Henry Harrison of the Indiana Territory admitted that frontier whites "consider the murdering of the Indians in the highest degree meritorious."

Relegated to smaller lands but still dependent on the European fur trade, natives in the Old Northwest now fell into competition with settlers and other Indians for the diminishing supply of game. The Creeks, Choctaws, and other tribes of the Old Southwest (Alabama, Arkansas, Louisiana, and Mississippi) faced the same problem: even when they chased whites out of their territory, the Americans managed to kill or scare off the deer and other wildlife, thus ruining the hunting grounds. When the Shawnee sent hunting parties further west, they discovered that they were not welcomed by their western brethren. The Choctaws also sent hunters across the Mississippi River only to find that the Osage and the other tribes of Louisiana and Arkansas considered them to be trespassers and drove them out. The Native Americans of the interior now realized that the days of the fur trade, on which they depended for survival, were numbered.

Faced with shrinking territories, the disappearance of game, and dwindling opportunities to be traditional hunters and warriors, many Indian societies plunged deeply into despair. European epidemic diseases (especially smallpox, measles, and influenza) ravaged people who were sedentary and vulnerable. Longstanding internal frictions grew nastier. In the Old Southwest, full-blooded Native Americans came into conflict with "mixed bloods"—who often no longer spoke their native language and who wanted their people to adopt white ways. Murder and clan revenge plagued many tribes. Depression and suicide became more common. The use of alcohol, which had long been a scourge on Indian societies, became more prevalent. Indian males spent more time in their villages and less on the hunt, and by most accounts they drank more and grew more violent. Although Washington sought to make peace with the Native Americans of the interior a priority for his administration, the president simply could not stop the white onslaught into the Old Northwest and Southwest during the 1790s, marking the beginning of the end for the majority of the region's native peoples and their way of life.

WESTERN TROUBLES

Problems with Native American tribes were not the only issues confronting the Washington administration concerning the nation's western territory. Frontier whites grew increasingly angry at a national government that could neither pacify the Indians nor guarantee their free use of the Mississippi River (controlled by the Spanish by virtue of their possession of New Orleans). The president learned that 2,000 armed Kentuckians were ready to attack New Orleans—a move that would have started a war between the United States and Spain. Meanwhile, Georgia settlers continued to make advances against the Creeks, which could have easily escalated into a full-fledged U.S.-Creek conflict. However, to the Washington administration, the most alarming "western disturbance" had nothing to do with Native Americans but rather with the president's own citizens—the refusal of western grain farmers to pay the federal excise tax on whiskey, which Washington considered to be a direct challenge to his administration and federal authority. In western Pennsylvania, mobs tarred and feathered tax collectors and burned the property of distillers who paid

Home of Thomas Gaddis, one of the principal leader of the "Whiskey Boys." During the short-lived revolt, Gaddis erected a "Liberty Pole" next to this cabin carrying a banner inscribed with the slogan "Liberty and No Excise," to rally support for the rebel cause.

the tax. In July 1794 near Pittsburgh, 500 militiamen marched on the house of General John Neville, one of the most hated of the federal excise collectors. Neville, his family, and a few federal soldiers fought the militiamen, killing two and wounding six before they abandoned the house to be looted and burned. Two weeks later, 6,000 "Whiskey Rebels" met at Braddock's Field near Pittsburgh, threatening to attack the town. Faced with serious international and domestic threats to his new government, Washington was not about to let "mobocrats" make a mockery of federal authority or the sanctity of the Constitution, which gave the government the right to tax with the people's consent. Since the excise tax had passed Congress, in Washington's view, it was settled law, and his job as president was to enforce the nation's laws—a responsibility he took very seriously. Spurred on by Alexander Hamilton, he was determined to end the **Whiskey Rebellion** with force if necessary. In September 1794, Washington ordered 12,000 federalized militiamen from eastern Pennsylvania, Maryland, Virginia, and New Jersey to quell the tax revolt. Intent on upholding federal authority, he personally donned his old uniform to review the troops before they were sent out to western Pennsylvania. Washington promised amnesty to rebels who pledged to support the government and obey its laws and prison terms for those who did not. When the army arrived in western Pennsylvania, the troops found defiant liberty poles but no armed resistance—the rebels quickly dispersed knowing that they would be fired upon if they did not disband. Arriving at Pittsburgh, the army arrested 20 suspected rebels—none of them leaders—and marched them back to Philadelphia for trial. In the end only two rebels, both of them feeble-minded, were convicted. President Washington pardoned them and the Whiskey Rebellion was over. Though federal authority and the office of the president had been vindicated, many citizens in western Pennsylvania resented the sending of troops into their midst. Thomas Jefferson and his allies would soon use such resentment to seek political support in the area.

JAY'S TREATY

Although President Washington had success in dealing with Indians and frontier rebels, when it came to negotiating with the British, the president found them to be a much more challenging adversary. By 1794, tensions between the United States and Great Britain over the violation of American neutrality, impressments, the military forts in the Northwest still occupied by the British in violation of the peace treaty ending the Revolutionary War on American soil, and British military aid to Native Americans had reached a dangerous level. Washington believed it was time for diplomacy to try to ease these disputes before they reached the point beyond which they could not be resolved without violence. Above all, Washington wanted to avoid war with Great Britain—a conflict for which he knew the country was not prepared. If defeated, Washington and other American leaders knew such a calamity would not only mark the end of the Republic but the possible reoccupation of North America by England.

To avoid such a prospect, Washington sent John Jay, chief justice of the Supreme Court, to Great Britain in 1794 to negotiate some sort of rapprochement with Great Britain. Armed with the news of Wayne's victory at Fallen Timbers, Jay extracted a promise from the British to remove their troops from the Northwest Territory. However, that was the sole concession Jay got from the

British, and even that condition was only met when Jay promised to have the U.S. Treasury compensate English merchants owed pre-Revolutionary debts by American citizens. On all the other contentious issues, Jay found the British government officials unyielding. He returned home with a treaty that made no mention of impressment or other violations of American maritime rights, nor did it refer to the old issue of British payments to slaveholders for slaves carried off during the War for Independence as many Southerners had hoped. The treaty did allow small American ships to trade again with English West Indies islands, but anything short of the allowance of large American trading vessels guaranteed a Senate rejection of that provision. Washington knew that given Great Britain's overwhelming military power, this was the best Americans could expect. Indeed, even before Jay left for England, Washington had told his ambassador that he would be operating from a position of weakness and that British officials would be in a most disrespectful and intractable mood and thus unlikely to consider any of America's positions on the issues. Obliged to choose between an unpopular treaty and an unwinnable war, Washington reluctantly passed **Jay's Treaty** on to the Senate, which in June 1795 ratified the document by a bare two-thirds majority.

The ratification of Jay's Treaty became the final straw for the Jeffersonian Republicans. The seaport cities and much of the Northeast reacted favorably to the treaty, for this section of the country was fast becoming a Federalist stronghold and increasingly dependent on British trade for their economic livelihood. The treaty ruled out war with England and cemented an Anglo-American trade relationship that strengthened both Hamilton's national state and the established commercial interests that supported it. Moreover, there was little enthusiasm for the French Revolution in the Northeast—particularly in New England, with its long history of colonial wars with France. The South, on the other hand, viewed Jay's Treaty as a blatant attempt to provoke British and Federalist designs to subvert republicanism in both France and the United States. The South by this time was fast becoming a Republican base. The Virginia legislature branded the treaty as unconstitutional, and Republican congressmen demanded to see all documents relating to Jay's negotiations. Citing "Executive privilege," Washington responded by telling his fellow Virginians that their request could be legitimate only if the House was planning to initiate impeachment proceedings—thus tying approval of the treaty to the president's enormous prestige. Virginia promptly rescinded its demand.

Washington knew that Jay's Treaty was an American capitulation to British intimidation. However, it did avert a war, at least for the foreseeable future. To somewhat atone for the Jay Treaty mishap, Washington announced in early March 1796 the details of a treaty that Thomas Pinckney had negotiated with Spain. In this agreement, Spain recognized American neutrality and accepted the border between the United States and Spanish Florida on American terms. Most important, **Pinckney's Treaty** put an end to Spanish claims on territory in the Old Southwest and gave Americans the unrestricted right to navigate the Mississippi River, including the use of the Spanish port of New Orleans. When coupled with the victory at Fallen Timbers, the British promise to abandon their posts in the Northwest, and Washington's personal popularity, Pinckney's Treaty helped lessen the furor over the unpopular Jay Treaty.

WASHINGTON'S FAREWELL

Reluctant to run for a second term, Washington was adamant about not serving a third. He thus set the tradition of a two-term limit observed by every president until Franklin Roosevelt in the 1940s. Washington could be proud of his accomplishments as president. He had presided over the creation of a national government, and established U.S. control over the Trans-Appalachian region up to the Mississippi River by ending British and Spanish military threats and by securing free use of the Mississippi River for western farmers and their right to deposit their goods in New Orleans. Although going to war against Native Americans on three occasions, Washington nonetheless remains one of the few American presidents to have as his official policy not removal or extinction but respect for Indian culture and recognition of their rights as a free and independent people who he hoped Americans could live alongside in peace. Unfortunately, Washington's noble and sincere attempt to establish peaceful coexistence with Native Americans was constantly challenged and undermined by his fellow citizens' complete disregard for Native American rights, forcing Washington to put down Indian uprisings, which he knew had been provoked by the white onslaught into Indian territories. Those policies, together with quelling the Whiskey Rebellion in western Pennsylvania, made it clear that the government could and would assert its dominion over the nation's most distant regions. Washington had also avoided war with Great Britain, although not without overlooking assaults on American sovereignty on the high seas. Most important, Washington gave the office of the president what it needed most—dignity, honor, integrity, prestige, respect, and power. In the end, these contributions proved to be his most lasting legacy.

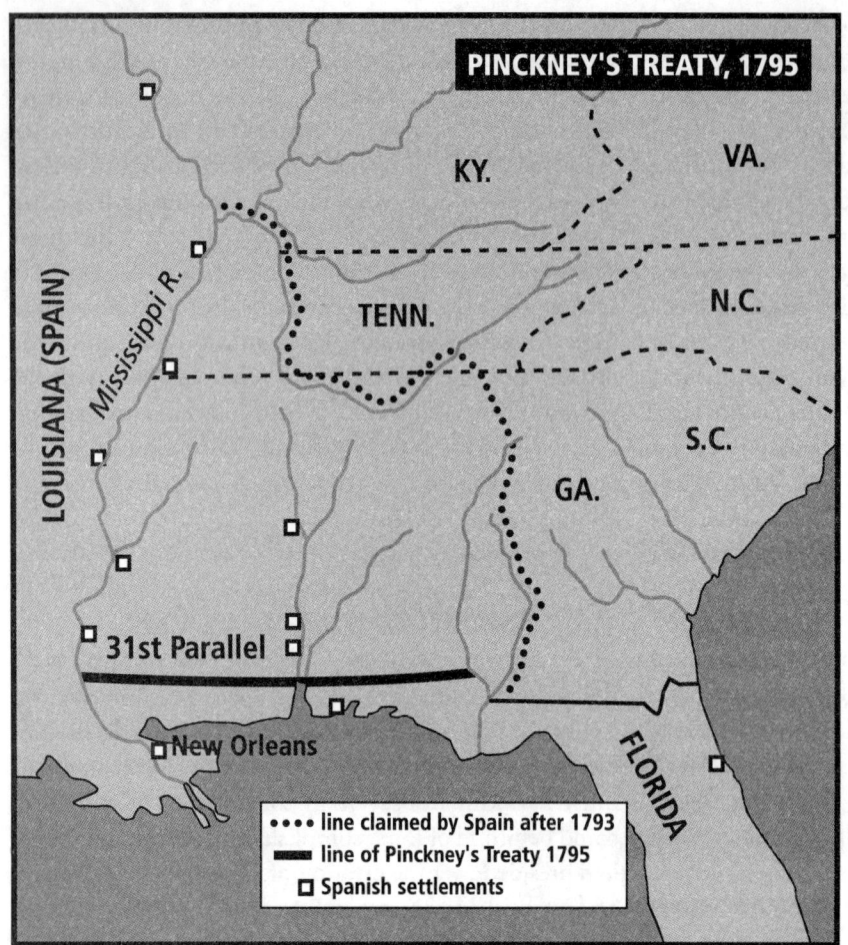

Map 8.1 Pinckney's Treaty, 1795

As Washington prepared to leave office, he wrote his farewell address (with substantial help from Hamilton). In this farewell letter, published in newspapers across the country, he warned against long-term "entangling alliances" with other countries. He expressed the belief that the United States should stay free to operate independently in international affairs—an ideal that many felt had been betrayed by Jay's Treaty. Washington also cautioned against internal political divisions, which by the end of his presidency were becoming more partisan. Interestingly, the outgoing president did not regard his own supporters as a "party" but rather as simply "friends" of the government. Although more ideologically in tune with the Federalists than the Jeffersonian Republican opposition, Washington nonetheless succeeded in remaining detached from the partisanship unfolding before him. Neither a "political" president nor a politician, Washington saw himself, and wanted posterity to regard him, as a statesman who had placed the nation's security and the government's success above all other interests. Meanwhile, he saw the **Democratic-Republicans** (the name by which Jefferson's allies called themselves by 1796) as a self-interested, irresponsible "faction."

The 1796 Election

Washington's retirement opened the door to the fierce competition for public office that he had feared. In 1796, Americans experienced their first contested presidential election. The Federalist Party chose Vice President John Adams of Massachusetts to be their standard-bearer, although he did not have Alexander Hamilton's endorsement because the former Treasury Secretary believed Adams to be too independent-minded and thus neither personally nor ideologically committed to the Federalist vision and agenda for the country. Thomas Pinckney of South Carolina ran with Adams (prior to the Twelfth Amendment's ratification in 1804, the Constitution specified that electors would cast two ballots for president, with the candidate receiving the most electoral votes becoming president and the candidate with the second-highest tally becoming vice president). The Democratic-Republicans nominated Thomas Jefferson and **Aaron Burr** of New York. According to the gentlemanly custom of the day, none of the candidates campaigned in person—a practice that would have to wait for a new generation of political leaders to emerge. Jefferson stayed home at Monticello, while Adams retired to his farm outside Boston. For the candidates' respective friends, relatives, supporters, newspaper editors, and even certain European dignitaries, however, all were free to engage in whatever partisanship they deemed essential for victory.

In 1796, the election would be decided in the state legislatures because (as the case in Washington's previous two victories) they chose their states' presidential electors. Only after 1796 would an increasing number of state legislatures begin to transfer selection of presidential electors to eligible voters among the general public. Since it was clear that Adams would carry New England and that Jefferson would sweep the South, the election would be decided in Pennsylvania and New York. The votes in the legislatures of Pennsylvania and New York proved the key to the election. John Beckley, clerk of the House of Representatives, devised the Republican strategy in Pennsylvania. He secretly circulated a list of prominent and respected candidates for the state legislature who were committed Jeffersonians. Discovering the Republican slate only when it was too late to construct a similar list, the Federalists lost the election. In December, Beckley delivered all but one of Pennsylvania's electoral votes to Jefferson. In New York, however, there was no John Beckley. Adams took the state's electoral votes, which proved decisive to winning the national election. The distribution of electoral votes revealed the bases of Federalist and Republican support: Adams received only 2 electoral votes south of the Potomac River, while Jefferson received only 18 electoral votes (all but 5 of them in Pennsylvania) outside of the South.

The voting was over, but Alexander Hamilton, who since his retirement from the Treasury in 1795 had directed the Federalist Party from his New York law office, was still one of the most powerful men in the country and the undisputed leader of the Federalists. Much to his chagrin, Hamilton knew he could not manipulate the independent and almost perversely upright Adams. Moreover, Adams was almost as apolitical as his predecessor, and consequently had no intention of becoming a Hamilton lackey or engaging in the nitty-gritty of partisan politics. In a secret ploy, Hamilton instructed South Carolina's Federalist electors to withhold their votes from Adams, which would give the presidency to his running mate, the South Carolinian Thomas Pinckney, relegating Adams to the vice presidency. Like some of Hamilton's other schemes, this one also backfired. New England electors somehow heard of the plan, and some angrily withheld their votes from Pinckney. As a result, Adams was elected president and his opponent, who received the second most electoral votes, Thomas Jefferson, became vice president. Adams narrowly won the election, but he took office with a justifiable mistrust of many members of his own party and with the leader of the opposition party as his

John Adams, Second President of the United States

vice president. It was not a promising beginning for the second president of the United States.

THE ADAMS PRESIDENCY

Troubles with France

An international crisis was already in full swing when John Adams assumed his office. As a result of Jay's Treaty, France recalled its envoy and broke off all diplomatic relations with the United States. The French government interpreted the treaty as an Anglo-American alliance, which was incorrect, but the French were still smarting from the American refusal to join them in their revolutionary cause. Indeed, the French were so outraged by Jay's Treaty that they hinted they intended to do all they could to overthrow the Adams administration, which they viewed as a continuance of Washington's allegedly anti-French government. They announced, however, that they would postpone such action in the hope that their "friend of the Revolution," Thomas Jefferson, would replace that "old man in Washington" in 1796. In order to ensure Jefferson's victory, French privateers seized American ships trading with Britain, giving Americans a taste of what would happen if they did not elect an administration friendlier to France. When the election went to Adams, the French gave up on the U.S and set about harassing

British shipping as best they could in the Atlantic and Caribbean. In 1797, France expelled the American minister, refusing to reestablish relations until the U.S. addressed French "grievances," which was code for becoming a French ally. The French government ordered that American ships carrying "so much as a handkerchief" made in England be confiscated without compensation and announced that American sailors serving in the British navy would be summarily hanged if captured.

President Adams, of course, wanted to protect American commerce from French plunder. He knew, as his predecessor had realized, that the United States could not win a war against the greatest military power in Europe at the time. Like Washington in his dealings with England, Adams too had to play the diplomatic game. He thus sent to France three respected statesmen: South Carolinian Charles Cotesworth Pinckney, Virginian John Marshall, and the Boston Yankee, Elbridge Gerry, in hopes of negotiating a settlement of grievances between the two countries. By 1797, the Reign of Terror had ended two years prior and, because of international war, the revolutionary fervor of the earlier years had subsided at home. By the time of the American entourage's arrival, the revolution had begun its move to the right. The radical republicans, the Jacobins and Girondists, had been purged from power, with most of them executed by the increasingly more conservative middle-class leaders who had taken control of the government. By 1797, what was left of the aristocracy had also reclaimed much of its earlier status and power. Nonetheless, the new government, the Directory—a committee of five men representing each of France's estates or classes—still believed the United States had betrayed their country by reneging on their 1778 treaty agreements. Thus, when the American emissaries arrived in Paris, they were left cooling their heels in the outer offices of the Directory. Three French officials (the diplomats' correspondence identified them only as "X, Y, and Z," leading the ensuing diplomatic debacle to become known as the "**XYZ Affair**") then approached the American officials and declared that France would "receive them"—open negotiations—if they paid a bribe of $250,000, arranged for a U.S. loan of $12 million to the French government, and apologized for unpleasant remarks that John Adams had made about France. The delegates steadfastly refused to succumb to extortion, telling the French, "No, not a sixpence," and returned home. There, a journalist transformed their remark into "Millions for defense, but not one cent for tribute."

Adams asked Congress to prepare for war, and the French responded by seizing more American ships. Thus began in April 1798, an undeclared "Quasi-War" with France on the high seas, mostly taking place in the Caribbean. While the French navy dealt with the British in the North Atlantic, French privateers inflicted costly blows on American shipping. After nearly a year of fighting, with the British providing powder and shot for American guns, the U.S. Navy chased the French privateers out of the West Indies.

Crisis at Home, 1798-1800

The troubles with France precipitated a crisis at home. The disclosure of the XYZ correspondence, together with the Quasi-War with France in the Caribbean, precipitated a surge in popular antipathy for France and even clamors for all-out war. Just three years earlier, the American public displayed a similar temperament and outrage toward England because of Jay's Treaty. In both instances, cooler minds prevailed, and a full-scale war was avoided. Of greater importance, the tensions with France produced serious political ramifications absent during the earlier Jay Treaty controversy. Republicans, for example, incurred public hostility for their continued support for France. Many Federalists (in particular the anti-Adams "High Federalists" led by Alexander Hamilton) wanted to use the crisis to destroy their political opponents. Without consulting President Adams, the Federalist-dominated Congress passed a series of wartime measures, even though the country was not officially at war with either Great Britain or France. The first was a federal property tax—graduated, spread equally between sections of the country, and justified by military necessity, but a direct federal tax nonetheless. Congress then passed four laws known as the Alien and Seditions Acts. Designed by the **High Federalists**, these measures' purpose was to destroy the Democratic-Republican Party; in effect, by means of political proscription. The first three were directed at immigrants, who at this time were flooding into the United States, fleeing the war in Europe. The more politically savvy Democratic Republicans were often at the docks greeting them, hoping that when they became naturalized citizens and had the right to vote, they would remember who had first shook their hand and welcomed them to the United States. Thus, the purpose of the **Alien Acts** was to curtail immigrant voting potential by extending the naturalization period from 5 to 14 years and empowered the president to detain enemy aliens during wartime and to deport those he deemed dangerous to the United States. The fourth law, the **Sedition Act**, set jail terms and fines for persons who advocated disobedience to federal law or who wrote, printed, or spoke "false, scandalous, and malicious" statements against "the government of the United States, or the President of the United States"

(Vice President Jefferson was not included), and "with intent to defame or to bring them or either of them, into contempt or disrepute."

The design of the Sedition Act—to censor Republican criticism of Federalist policies and ultimately by such acts of proscription, to demolish their party, thus removing any challenge to Federalist hegemony of the national government—seemed obvious. To the High Federalist sponsors of this bill, a Republican such as Thomas Jefferson in the White House (John Adams was the first occupant of the new presidential mansion, though it was barely completed) would be disastrous for the nation, for they were certain he would give power back to the very "rabble" who almost destroyed the country in the 1780s. To ensure the nation's future security and survival, the Federalists believed their Republican opponents had to be crushed then and there.

Adams never used the powers granted under the Alien Acts, but the Sedition Act resulted in the prosecution of fourteen Republicans, most of them journalists. William Duane, editor of the *Philadelphia Aurora*, was indicted when he and two Irish friends circulated a petition against the Alien Act on the grounds of a Catholic Church. James Callendar, editor of a Jeffersonian newspaper in Richmond, Virginia was arrested, while another prominent Republican went to jail for statements made in a private letter, criticizing Federalist policy. Jedediah Peck, a former Federalist from upstate New York, was arrested when he petitioned Congress to repeal the Alien and Sedition Acts. Matthew Lyon, a vulgar and crude Republican congressman from Vermont, had brawled with Federalist congressman Roger Griswold in the House chamber. He went to jail for his criticism of President Adams, Federalist militarism, and what he called the "ridiculous pomp" of the national administration. To Republicans, it seemed obvious that not only were the Federalists out to obliterate their party, but they were also blatantly violating the First Amendment rights of citizens. To defend their party and save it from possible extinction while also protecting the sanctity of freedom of speech and press as guaranteed in the Bill of Rights, they decided to counterattack—not through armed rebellion, but through passionately felt words in which they hoped to rally effective political opposition to toss out the Federalists in the next election.

THE VIRGINIA AND KENTUCKY RESOLUTIONS

In their political counteroffensive, Republicans turned to the states for help. Southern states, which had provided only 4 of the 44 congressional votes for the Sedition Act, took the lead. Jefferson anonymously provided the Kentucky legislature with draft resolutions for their consideration, with Madison doing the same for Virginia. These **Virginia and Kentucky Resolutions** reiterated the constitutional fundamentalism that had informed Republican opposition to the Federalists through the 1790s. Jefferson's Kentucky Resolutions reminded Congress that the Alien and Sedition Acts gave the national government powers not specified in the Constitution and that the Tenth Amendment made it clear that such powers are reserved for the states. He also argued that the Constitution was a "compact" between sovereign states, and that states could declare that federal laws they deemed unconstitutional were "void and of no force" within their boundaries. (In his original draft, Jefferson used the term "nullification" to describe this type of state action, but the legislature voted to keep that language out of the final version.) In the Virginia Resolution, Madison stated his belief that a state government had the right to "interpose" on behalf of its citizens in order to shield them from an unconstitutional act by the federal government.

In their respective resolutions, Jefferson and Madison established the states' rights theories that many Southerners would come to embrace as their gospel, arguing that the government was not a union of people but of individual states. Such a disposition seems especially disingenuous for Madison, whose contributions to the writing of the Constitution were manifold, especially the preamble, which clearly affirms that the people, not the states, created the Union. The Resolutions, however, need to be viewed within their proper context—as vague party propaganda and a political call to arms against Federalist oppression rather than a justification for secession as future radical states' rights advocates would assert.

The Virginia and Kentucky Resolutions had few immediate effects. Opposition to the Sedition Act ranged from a few popular attempts to obstruct the law to occasional fistfights in Congress. No other states, however, went as far as Virginia and Kentucky in directly asserting their opposition to the acts. A year earlier Adams had let the acts "pass" by simply not signing them. Jefferson and Madison hesitated to challenge the Alien and Sedition Acts in the Supreme Court, because the Court was then dominated by Federalists and they did not want to set a precedent for giving the Supreme Court the power to rule on the constitutionality of laws.

Nevertheless, the political damage had been done to the Federalist Party, upon which the measures backfired. Instead of the Alien and Sedition Acts destroying the Republicans, they ended up contributing to the end of the Federalists, who the people increasingly regarded as the party of elitism, reaction, and oppression. Ironically, by passing such laws, the Federalists contributed greatly to the Republican victory in 1800 and their own subsequent elimination from power in the national government. In short, the Alien and Sedition Acts proved to have been political suicide for the Federalists. Over the course of the next decade, they would slowly disappear from the nation's political landscape, ending the Republic's first party system.

THE POLITICIANS AND THE ARMY

Federalists took another ominous step by implementing President Adams' request that Congress bolster the military in preparation for war. Adams wanted a fortified navy because of the undeclared naval war with France and the general Federalist belief that America's future as a commercial nation required a strong navy. Hamilton and other High Federalists also preferred a strong standing army. At Washington's urging and against his own judgment, Adams appointed Hamilton inspector general, making the New Yorker the de facto commander of the U.S. Army. Congress authorized the creation of a twenty thousand-man army, which Hamilton proceeded to raise, and also approved funds for a greater enlargement of the army in the event of a declaration of war. When he expanded the officer corps in anticipation of such an army, Hamilton excluded Republicans and commissioned only his political friends. The High Federalists made it known that they intended to use the standing army to enforce the Alien and Sedition Acts and to put down any rebellion in the South. Beyond that, there was little need for such a large force. The Quasi-War with France was a conflict at sea, and most Americans believed that the citizen militia could hold off any land invasion until an army was raised. The Republicans, President Adams, and even many Federalists now became convinced that Hamilton and his High Federalist coterie were determined to destroy political opponents by force, enter into an alliance with Great Britain, and impose Hamilton's statist designs on the nation with the army ready to be used to effect such policies. By 1799, Adams and many of his Federalist friends were certain that Hamilton and his supporters were dangerous anti-republican militarists.

President Adams was both fearful and angry. First, the Hamiltonians had tried to rob him of the presidency. Then, they passed the Alien and Sedition Acts, the direct tax, and plans for a standing army without consulting him. None of this would have been possible had it not been for the crisis with France. Adams, who had resisted calls for a declaration of war, began looking for ways to achieve peace. He decided that even though it would split his party and probably cost him reelection in 1800, it was time to try to reopen negotiations with France. He also procrastinated on creating Hamilton's army. The Federalist-dominated Senate initially refused to authorize the sending of an envoy to France but relented when Adams threatened to resign, which would have left the presidency to Thomas Jefferson—a prospect even the least partisan Federalists were not ready to accept. An emissary was sent to France and successfully achieved a rapprochement. The French released the United States from their 1778 treaty commitments, but they refused to pay reparations for attacks on American ships since 1793—the very point over which many Federalists had wanted to declare war. Peace with France took the wind out of the sails of the more militaristic and repressive Federalists, intensifying the growing rift within the party between the High Federalists and their more moderate counterparts, ensuring a split by the time of the next presidential election.

"THE REVOLUTION OF 1800"

The Election of Thomas Jefferson

"Jefferson and Liberty" became the Republican campaign slogan for the 1800 presidential election. By this time, the Republicans had developed effective techniques for mobilizing voters, such as printing pamphlets, handbills, and newspapers—all of which contained information not only about their candidate, but their party's platform and ideology as well. In many ways, the Republicans had become a modern political party machine, complete with staff workers at a variety of levels to individuals who organized mass meetings and rallies to promote their cause. In four short years, Republicans had learned that if one wanted political power in a democratic republic, they had to go out and convince the electorate that they were the people's party and would deliver what the people wanted once in power. The Federalists, meanwhile, continued to view mass politics and campaigning as beneath them, and thus they found it difficult to match their opponent's mobilization.

In their campaign speeches, Republicans charged that the Federalists' actions during the past four years were not only expensive, repressive, unwise, and unconstitutional but they reflected the classic means by which despots destroyed liberty. The Republicans presented themselves as the party of traditional agrarian purity, liberty, states' rights, and "government rigorously frugal and simple," in the words of Jefferson. They were optimistic, convinced that they were riding the wave of the future. Divided

THE FEDERALIST ERA / 247

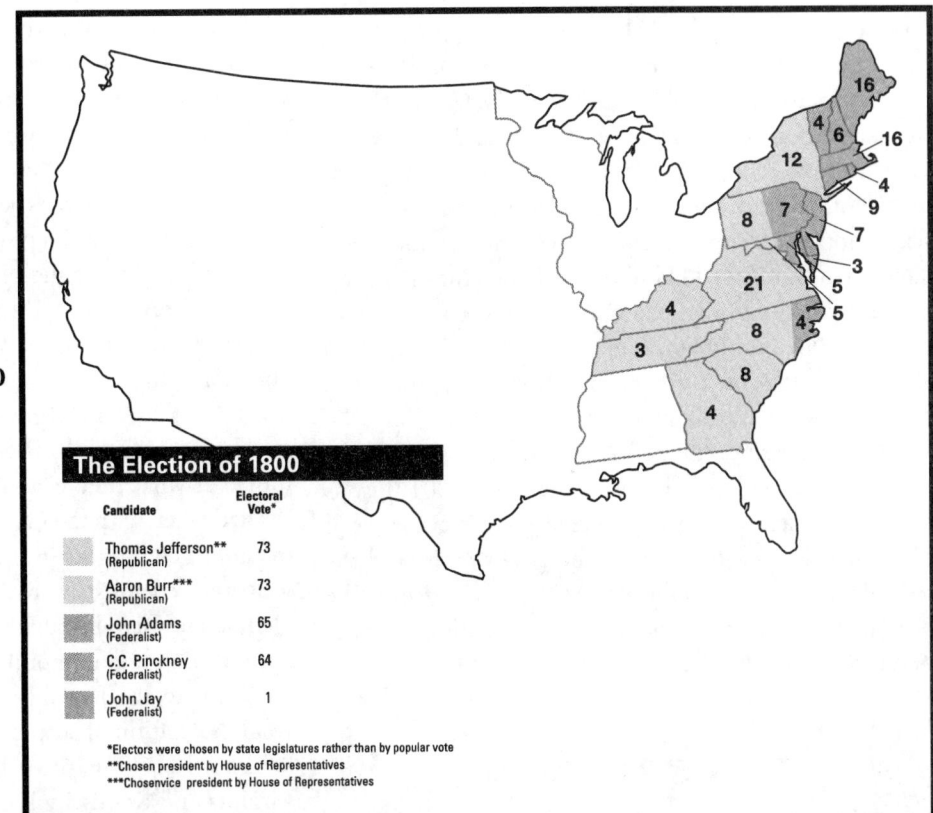

Map 8.2 The Election of 1800

The Election of 1800

Candidate	Electoral Vote*
Thomas Jefferson** (Republican)	73
Aaron Burr*** (Republican)	73
John Adams (Federalist)	65
C.C. Pinckney (Federalist)	64
John Jay (Federalist)	1

*Electors were chosen by state legislatures rather than by popular vote
**Chosen president by House of Representatives
***Chosen vice president by House of Representatives

and bitter, the Federalists waged a defensive struggle for strong central government and public order, and resorted frequently to negative campaigning. They denounced Jefferson as an atheist, a Jacobin, and the father of mulatto children—the first two charges were without foundation, while the last was probably true, as implied by recent DNA tests involving Jefferson descendants. The Federalists also warned that the election of Thomas Jefferson and his radical supporters would release the worst horrors of the French Revolution onto the streets of American towns and cities. Each side believed that defeat in the election would mean the end of the Republic.

The 1800 presidential campaign marked the first time the Republicans and Federalists operated as two national political parties. Caucuses of congressmen nominated respective slates: John Adams and Charles Cotesworth Pinckney of South Carolina for the Federalists; Jefferson and Aaron Burr of New York for the Republicans. The balloting for presidential electors took place between October and December 1800. Adams and Pinckney took all the New England states while Jefferson and Burr captured the South, the West, and (due to Burr's tireless efforts in his home state) New York. Party discipline was so effective that one of the provisions of the Constitution was shown to be badly outmoded. By this clause, the candidate receiving a majority of electoral votes became president and the runner-up became vice president. However, to the Republicans' shock and subsequent quandary, by casting all their ballots for Jefferson and Burr, Republican electors created a tie between the two men, with each receiving 73 ballots. Adams finished "third" with 65 and Pinckney with 64.

Because the ambitious Burr refused to step aside and grant Jefferson the victory outright, such an outcome forced the election into the House of Representatives. Though the Republicans had won control of the House, Congress was not set to reconvene until March 1801. Thus, the Federalists in the lame-duck session were given a last chance to impact the election. Each state delegation in the House cast one vote. To be elected, a candidate had to receive a majority of the votes from the state delegations (at least 9 of the 16 total). For many days, the vote deadlocked at eight votes for Jefferson, six for Burr, and two states tied. Alexander Hamilton, still the Federalist Party's most influential and powerful member, finally exerted his influence to determine who would become the nation's third president. Though not intervening until 35 rounds of balloting had taken place, Hamilton decided it was time to break the impasse. Fortunately for the Republicans, and the United States, if there was one individual Hamilton hated more than Jefferson, it was Aaron Burr. After a long history of personal clashes with Burr, Hamilton concluded he could never stand for the man to become president. He warned Federalist congressmen that Burr was obsessed with power, "an embryo Caesar," and finally convinced some Federalist representatives to submit blank ballots, thus shifting their state's votes to Jefferson, electing him on the 36th ballot. To avoid a repetition of the crisis, Congress and the states soon adopted the Twelfth Amendment to the Constitution, requiring electors to cast separate votes for president and vice president. The election of 1800 also set in motion a chain of events that culminated four years later when Burr killed Hamilton in a duel, the crescendo of the hatred each man had built up for each other over the years. No doubt Hamilton's intervention in the 1800 election, which cost Burr the presidency, contributed to the challenge that took Hamilton's life.

Before retiring, the Federalist Congress got off one more shot at the Republicans. In January 1801, just as the session expired, Congress passed the Judiciary Act of 1801, which gave John Adams the power to expand the federal judiciary by appointing new judges, justices of the peace, attorneys, clerks, and marshals—positions that the outgoing president filled with loyal Federalists.

TRANSFER OF POWER

The events of the 1790s demonstrated that a majority of Americans believed the common people had a right to play an active role in politics, express their opinions freely, and to contest the policies of their government. Samuel Goodrich, a prominent Connecticut Federalist, wrote that his party was overthrown because democracy had become "the watchword of popular liberty." To their credit, the Federalists never considered resistance to the election result. Adams's acceptance of defeat established the vital precedent of a peaceful transfer of power from a defeated party to its successor.

The first decade of the federal government's existence under the Constitution demonstrated that the love of liberty and the love for order and stability sometimes led in different directions, giving rise to very different visions of what constituted "good" citizenship. Republicans fumed at what they viewed as the liberties that Federalists had taken with the Constitution and their willingness to abolish civil rights in the name of order, stability, and security. Federalists were convinced more than ever that Democratic-Republican ideology was a dangerous scourge upon the land, tantamount to lawlessness, and the greatest threat to the Republic. The 1790s had witnessed a steady escalation of suspicion and mistrust, of which the Whiskey Rebellion, the Alien and Sedition Acts, and the Virginia and Kentucky Resolutions had been striking illustrations. The political parties organized that fractious spirit, but they did little to defuse it. Meanwhile, even as Americans fought over the terms of the new Republic's founding, those very terms soon began to change.

Chronology

1789 George Washington inaugurated first president.
Judiciary Act establishes the Supreme Court and federal circuit courts.
French Revolution begins.

1790 Hamilton issues his Report on Public Credit.

1791 States ratify Bill of Rights.
Ohio Indians defeat General Arthur St. Clair.
Congress passes whiskey tax.
Hamilton issues Report on Manufactures.

1793 Napoleonic Wars break out between French and Britain.
General "Mad" Anthony Wayne commander of American forces to subdue the Indians in the Northwest.
Eli Whitney invents cotton gin.

1794 Battle of Fallen Timbers.
Whiskey Rebellion.

1795 Treaty of Greenville.
Jay's Treaty.

1796 John Adams elected second president.
Thomas Jefferson becomes vice president.
First Party System established.

1797 XYZ Affair.

1798 Alien and Sedition Acts.
Virginia and Kentucky Resolutions.

1799 Slave revolt in Haiti results in the overthrow of French rule and declaration by ex-slaves of the Republic of Haiti.

1800 Thomas Jefferson elected third president.

Review Questions

1. Assess the presidency of George Washington. Why is he considered by most historians to be one of the United States's greatest president?

2. Discuss Alexander Hamilton's political and economic philosophy. What was his vision for the United States? Why did many of his policies arouse opposition and hostility, even among some members of the elite such as Thomas Jefferson?

3. Explain the rise of the first party system. What caused such factionalism among the first generation of Americans?

4. Why was it difficult for the United States to maintain neutrality during the French Revolutionary Wars? Why did President Washington originally declare American neutrality?

5. Why did the United States's great democratic republican experiment almost unravel between the years 1798 and 1800? What were the main issues that caused such bitter rancor and partisanship?

Glossary of Important People and Concepts

Alien Act
Bank of the United States
Battle of Fallen Timbers
Bill of Rights
Aaron Burr
Democratic-Republicans
Excise Tax
Federalists
Edmund Genêt
Hamiltonianism
High Federalists
Impressment
Jay's Treaty (1795)
Orders in Council
Pinckney's Treaty (1795)
"Revolution of 1800"
Sedition Act
Adam Smith/*The Wealth of Nations*
Treaty of Greenville
Virginia and Kentucky Resolutions
Whiskey Rebellion
XYZ Affair

SUGGESTED READINGS

Catherine Allgor, *Parlor Politics: In Which the Ladies of Washington Help Build a City and a Government* (2000).

Joyce Appleby, *Capitalism and a New Social Order: The Republican Vision of the 1790s* (1984).

Alexander De Conde, *The Quasi-War: Politics and Diplomacy of the Undeclared War With France, 1797-1801* (1966).

Stanley Elkins and Eric L. McKittrick, *The Age of Federalism* (1993).

Joanne B. Freeman, *Affairs of Honor: National Politics in the New Republic* (2001).

Frederick Hoxie, Ronald Hoffman, and Peter J. Albert, eds. *Native Americans and the Early Republic* (1999).

Stephen G. Kurtz, *The Presidency of John Adams* (1957).

Drew McCoy, *The Elusive Republic: Political Economy in Jeffersonian America* (1980).

John C. Miller, *Crisis in Freedom: The Alien and Sedition Acts* (1952)

___, *The Federalist Era, 1789-1801* (1960).

Jeffrey Pasley, et.al. eds., *Beyond the Founders: New Approaches to the Political History of the New Republic* (2004).

William Stinchcombe, *The XYZ Affair* (1981).

Wiley Sword, *President Washington's Indian War: The Struggle for the Old Northwest, 1790-95* (1985).

David Waldsteicher, *In the Midst of Perpetual Fetes: The Making of American Nationalism, 1776-1820* (1997)

Phillip Ziesche, *Cosmopolitan Patriots: Americans in Paris in the Age of Revolution* (2009).

Thomas Jefferson

Chapter Nine

JEFFERSONIAN AMERICA, 1801-1815

Although the Atlantic world informed much of the commercial history of the early republic, in terms of trade the Pacific Ocean and the Orient were also important arenas for American ambitions. As early as the 1780s, American traders such as Robert Morris had sent ships to the Far East. In 1784, Morris's vessel, **Empress of China**, sailed out of New York harbor and around the southern tip of Africa headed for the port of Macao, China. With the end of the War for Independence, wealthy Americans were eager to purchase Chinese goods (boycotted during the war) such as tea, porcelain, silk, and spices. American merchants were just as keen to find new markets, especially after Morris's ship returned from China realizing a $30,000 profit.

The China trade, however, presented several obstacles. First, although the Chinese were willing to trade with foreigners, they did not want such "barbarians" in their country, and thus traders were confined to designated trading posts called hongs. From there, Chinese merchants would bring their wares to trade or would come to discuss possible transactions. Fearing the settlement of foreign families, the Chinese barred any women on board (not entirely uncommon at the time) from coming to the trading places; they were to wait on the Portuguese island outpost of Macao. The second problem was a lack of interest among the Chinese merchants for American products; there were simply very few commodities the United States produced or had to offer, either manufactured or natural, that the Chinese needed or wanted. American traders eventually found that the Chinese did have an "appetite" for furs, so these were obtained by sailing around the tip of South America and along the Pacific coast to trade with the Indians of the Pacific Northwest. From there, Yankee vessels sailed across the Pacific, frequently stopping in the Sandwich Islands (Hawaii) to pick up sandalwood for the Chinese market.

Among the American merchants who eventually earned a fortune from this trade was the German immigrant John Jacob Astor, who migrated to the United States just after the War for Independence, settling with his wife Sarah (a shrewd businesswoman and fur expert) in New York City. Initially, the Astors dealt mainly in furs from the Great Lakes region, but after Astor sent his first ship to China in the early nineteenth century and made $50,000 from the venture—a staggering sum for the time—he exclusively focused on the China trade, envisioning a route that would carry New England manufactured goods to Northwest Indians to be exchanged for furs traded with China. For such purposes, in 1811, Astor established a trading post in the Oregon Country, present-day Astoria, Oregon on the Pacific coast.

The most valuable commodity the Americans found that the Chinese readily accepted, especially for payment, was silver. This was a difficult product for American traders to procure. Because the U.S. was a specie-starved nation and had yet to discover silver (which would in abundance in the latter nineteenth century in the Rocky Mountain West), obtaining the metal required either trading for silver with Spanish South American colonies or acquiring specie bit by bit in complex trading patterns among Europeans. However, ever resourceful, American traders soon found a *most lucrative and easily procured trade item: opium. The drug had long been chewed in parts of southern Asia as a general analgesic, but the far more additive practice of smoking opium became increasingly popular among the Chinese masses, especially after they had been introduced to tobacco by the Europeans. The opium trade served as one reason why the Chinese had barred Europeans from their country. Although England dominated this particular aspect of the China trade, Americans were finding ways to enter the opium business by the first decade of the nineteenth century. Indeed, Yankee shipbuilding companies built special craft to carry opium from India to Canton, and eventually some of the early republic's greatest merchant fortunes, including those of Stephen Girard of Philadelphia and the Perkins brothers, James and Thomas of Boston, were amassed in part on the profits of drug trafficking in Southeast Asia. From the days of the early republic to the present, many Americans found wealth by engaging in less than savory, self-aggrandizing activities, often to the detriment of others.*

JEFFERSON IN POWER

The New President

On the morning of March 4, 1801, President-elect Thomas Jefferson left his room at Conrad and McMunn's boarding house to walk to his inauguration as the third President of the United States. He refused to ride in a carriage and was attired in the clothes and unpretentious appearance of the common people—pants, not knickers; boots not buckled shoes; a plain shirt and jacket, not a ruffled blouse and fancy coat; and perhaps most revealing, no powdered wig, just his own reddish-brown hair, which he wore almost down to his shoulders. There were military salutes along the way—Jefferson forbade all the pomp and ceremony that had surrounded Washington's inaugural. Accompanied by a few friends and escorted by a company of Maryland militia, Jefferson walked up the street and into the unfinished capitol building (the central dome and the wing for the House of Representatives were only half completed.) Jefferson joined Aaron Burr, other members of the new government, and a few foreign dignitaries in the recently completed Senate chamber where he took the oath of office administered by John Marshall, the newly appointed Chief Justice of the Supreme Court who was a distant relative and political opponent.

In a voice barely audible to those seated at a distance, Jefferson delivered his inaugural address. Referring to the political contentiousness that surrounded the election, he began with a call for unity, insisting that "every difference of opinion is not a difference of principle. We have called by different names brethren of the same principle. We are all Republicans, we are all Federalists." With that statement, Jefferson hoped that he could eradicate the political animosity and factionalism that had almost brought down the Republic during the Alien and Sedition Acts crisis, and return to some semblance of consensus. Most importantly, Jefferson was optimistic that within a short time, the Federalist Party would simply dissolve, already having committed political suicide with their passage of the Alien and Sedition Acts. Jefferson believed that he could speed up that process by inviting moderate Federalists into a broad Republican coalition in which there would be no room for the statist designs of Alexander Hamilton and his High Federalist friends.

Jefferson continued by outlining the type of republican government that he envisioned. Grateful for the Atlantic Ocean, which separated the United States from "the exterminating havoc" of Europe, he stated that his countrymen were the possessors of "a chosen country, with room for our descendants to the thousandth and thousandth generation." He declared that Americans were a free and virtuous people, capable of sustaining republicanism with no need to build a national state based on European models. In such a statement, Jefferson clearly was taking the Federalists to task for having so mistrusted the inherent rectitude of the American people and for having attempted to impose on them such an antithetical and loathsome form of government. A people blessed with isolation, bountiful resources, and liberty needed only "a wise and frugal Government, which shall restrain men from injuring one another, shall leave them otherwise free to regulate their own pursuits of industry and improvement, and shall not take from the mouth of labor the bread it has earned. This is the sum of good government, and this is necessary to close the circle of our felicities."

Jefferson's "wise and frugal" government was code for his states' rights views. The phrase also meant that he intended to shrink the government's size and presence in Americans' daily lives by gutting the federal bureaucracy, cutting taxes, and paying its debts without incurring new ones, thus ending the need for taxation. Such a program would greatly curtail the burgeoning Federalist state. Jefferson also promised a national defense policy based on "a disciplined militia" that could fight invaders while regular troops were being trained—thus ridding the nation of Hamilton's standing army. The "citizen's army" would protect republican liberties from domestic enemies and from the European nations. Most importantly, Jefferson promised to promote an agrarian republic with "commerce as its handmaiden," which meant he would work assiduously to keep the United States on an agriculturally-based economy while attempting to dismantle the Federalist manufacturing and commercial agenda.

Beyond the fostering of an agrarian republic and reducing the size and expense of government, Jefferson promised very little else. He was fortunate that he became president at a most favorable time relative to European affairs. By the time of his inauguration, the French Revolution had come full circle. Napoleon Bonaparte, with the aid of conservatives, aristocrats, and monarchists, had just taken over the government by a military *coup d'etat*. His immediate priority became the consolidation of his power at home rather than expanding France's empire on the continent. In effect, each major belligerent, France and England, were temporarily exhausted after eight years of war. With momentary peace in Europe, Jefferson could implement his domestic agenda without having to worry about international events intruding upon his initiatives. Moreover, Jefferson faced little opposition to his agenda at home, for the Federalist Party was becoming a leaderless and defunct organization, especially with the High Federalists becoming powerless within their own party. Jefferson was thus confident that during his presidency he could bring about the fulfillment of his version of the republican ideals of 1776.

The unpretentiousness of Jefferson's inauguration set the social tone for his administration. Because Jefferson despised the formality and aristocratic pomp and ceremony of the Washington and Adams administrations, there were few elaborate balls, receptions, and dinners. In the manner of English kings and his Federalist predecessors, he sent his annual State of the Union addresses to Congress to be read by a clerk rather than delivered in person. He refused to ride about Washington, D.C. in a carriage. Instead, Jefferson either walked or rode a horse when venturing out on his errands. Abandoning the grand banquets favored by Washington and Adams, Jefferson preferred to entertain senators and members of the House at small dinner parties where attendees sat at a round table without formal seating, a reflection of his more egalitarian temperament. As noted above, Jefferson preferred to dress in the common man's attire—old homespun and, when not at work in the White House (and sometimes when he was), the president would wear a pair of worn bedroom slippers. At his intimate dinners, brilliant conversation was the order of the day, a nicety Jefferson perfected while serving as diplomat and a visitor to the salons of Paris. His dinners set examples of modest excellence through which this cultivated country squire hoped to govern the republic that he claimed to have saved from monarchists.

Purging the Government

As promised in his inaugural address, Jefferson made his first priority of business the curtailing of the size and expense of government. During his first year in office, Jefferson reduced the diplomatic corps and replaced incompetent, corrupt, or avowedly anti-Republican office holders. To the surprise and anger of many of his more fanatical and vengeful Republican compatriots, not all those purged from federal office were Federalists. Jefferson realized that to do so could cripple the government's daily functioning. Because the Federalists had been running the government for eight years, eliminating all individuals with such experience and expertise simply based on their political affiliation would be foolish. Moreover, by keeping moderate Federalists in the bureaucracy, Jefferson was making good his inaugural promise of conciliation and unity. Many of the replacements were not the vindictive revolutionaries that Federalists had warned against, but rather, Republicans cut from the same elite cloth as the departed Federalists. Jefferson only slightly altered the status and politics of the federal bureaucracy—while its size was reduced, its shape remained intact.

Jefferson made more substantial cuts to the military, which he feared more than a Federalist-laden bureaucracy. The Federalists had built a sizeable army and navy to prepare for war and, if necessary, to put down insurrections at home. Legislation passed in March 1802 reduced the army to two regiments of infantry and one of artillery—a total of 3,350 officers and men, most of whom were assigned to western frontier posts far from civilian population centers. Similar cutbacks were made in the navy. The goal, Jefferson asserted, was to rely mainly on the militia for national defense while maintaining a small, well-trained professional army. (Interestingly, the same bill that reduced the army created the United States Military Academy at West Point, New York.) Jefferson let expire all taxes except the tariff, including the hated whiskey tax of 1791 and the property tax of 1798. Meanwhile, the national debt fell during Jefferson's two terms from $80 million to $57 million. Finally, Jefferson also pardoned all those imprisoned under the Sedition Act, repaying with interest the fines levied against them. Thus, with a few deft strokes, Jefferson greatly altered the Federalist state.

Republican Agrarianism

More than either of his predecessors, Jefferson brought to the presidency a clearly defined political philosophy. Behind his actions was an ideology that embodied Jefferson's interpretation of American republicanism. His years as an American envoy to France during the 1780s had greatly

Evangelical Religion and Jeffersonian America

Reminiscent of the passionate preaching of the Great Awakening as well as the prospect of redemption for all who sought God's grace, "the Second Great Awakening," which coincided with the advent of the Jeffersonian Era, brought to the common people of that time a similar message of salvation and hope. Even more so that the First Great Awakening, the evangelism of the Second Great Awakening's propagators delivered to the faithful and the hopeful a religion in tune with its secular, democratic, and republican beliefs and institutions. Americans rightly prided themselves on the sanctity of the separation of church and state; however, in many a rural or "backcountry" community during the early national period, Protestant evangelicals preached a religion that was far more "democratic" than that found in the nation's urban areas, reflecting perfectly the Jeffersonian political and economic philosophy of agrarianism and egalitarianism. Jeffersonian evangelicals dispensed with the notion of original sin, which for centuries had declared that all humans were born inherently sinful beings and thus unable through good acts or deeds to absolve themselves of such "depravity" and earn through righteous and noble action their way to God's grace, forgiveness, and heaven. Salvation, hardcore, orthodox Protestants believed, came completely through God's grace. However, with the advent of Jeffersonian democracy and its expression of faith in the common man's ability to participate fully in the state, increasing numbers of dissenting Protestant ministers carried over to American religion a similar democratic notion: that God had imbued humans with the capacity to yearn toward salvation and required fervent belief and longing as condition for grace. Religion without that longing seemed lifeless and cold. If Thomas Jefferson had faith in the common person to govern, to determine one's own political "future," then reasoned the new evangelicals, so could one decide their own path to salvation.

Such were the beliefs of Barton W. Stone, pastor of the Presbyterian Church of Cane Ridge, Kentucky. Particularly disturbing Stone about his congregation was its members' deadness to God's grace, which he saw not only in his own pews but in the backcountry in general. Stone assumed his position as pastor in 1801, the same year as Thomas Jefferson took his oath of office to become third president of the United States. The majority of Stone's congregants and neighbors were newcomers to the area, migrants from Virginia and Maryland who were busy settling new farms, slaves recently taken from their families in the East, and drifters who had broken free of families and community bonds. Most had few formal church ties, and in Stone's view, little interest in religion in general.

By 1801 something was stirring backcountry folk as revivals and mass prayer meetings were attracting thousands of rural participants throughout eastern and central Kentucky. Stone attend one such gathering in Logan, Kentucky, and was astounded by what he witnessed: "Many, very many fell down in an apparently breathless and motionless state," their catatonic states broken only "by a deep groan, or piercing shriek, or by a prayer for mercy most fervently uttered." When they finally returned from their trances, they rose up "shouting deliverance; men, women, and children declaring the wonderful works of God."

So impressed by what he had seen, Stone set about changing his entire ministry to replicate in his own church the revival he had attended. Calling his meeting "a sacramental communion" to be held on August 6, 1801, he sent out invitations by word of mouth for all in the area to come to his church. Stone did not know what the response would be, but to his rapturous delight, according to one participant, "about 12,000 persons, 125 wagons, 8 carriages, and 900 communicants" showed up at his church in Cane Ridge and for five straight days, all day and deep into the night, the prayer meetings continued. News of the events at Cane Ridge spread "like fire in dry stubble driven by a strong wind," as "between twenty and thirty thousand" people—men, women, and children—whites and blacks, from all Protestant sects, as well as nonbelievers and anguished sinners, hurried to the scene as fast as they could get there. The revival was more than ten times the size of the population of Lexington, the state's capital.

The Cane Ridge revival proved to be the largest and most climatic event of the western revivals of 1800-1801, inspiring other evangelical ministers to continue the spiritual longing and fervency among rural folk that Stone seemed to have tapped into. Interestingly, although evangelical revivals continued in the south and west during the Jeffersonian era, the most intense and legendary occurred in the North, especially in upstate New York, which after experiencing such ferocity, was dubbed "the burned-over district." Throughout the opening decades of the nineteenth century, religious enthusiasm flamed brightly in the republic, reflecting the concomitant equally passionate devotion of Americans to the ideals of Jeffersonian democracy. The rejection by pastors such as Stone of old Calvinist orthodoxies and hierarchical religious styles complimented the Jeffersonian call for the greater democratization of both society and the country. The revival ministers preached this message either from their church pulpits or to the throngs who attended their revival meetings. In either locale, they delivered a "theology" of self-striving and egalitarianism; that salvation was open to all; all one had to do was accept God's grace and forgiveness and proceed to be a "believer" for the rest of their lives, which of course would be temporally better now that God was part of their daily life. They preached such a message with incredible passion and commitment, directness and intimacy, spontaneously as if the Holy Spirit had taken them over and was communicating through them. Such a delivery could not have been more in contrast to the stern, intimidating, foreboding formality of the more traditional Protestant churches and their conservative pastors. Especially remaining tradition-bound were the Congregational and Presbyterian churches, both of which remained committed to preaching the fire and brimstone Puritan message of a vengeful, wrathful God from whom you must prostrate yourself before and beg for his mercy and grace. By contrast, the Baptists and Methodists embraced the evangelical style and the new theology, and consequently benefited the most with significant increases in their respective sect's membership.

Religion had always played an important role in American history, most often on an individual basis, but episodically for the masses of citizens as seen from the above description of the beginnings of the Second Great Awakening during the Jeffersonian era. It only seemed "natural" that a resurgence of evangelism and a new, more dynamic and inclusive American Protestant theology would emerge, reflecting not only the vagaries and exigencies of American frontier life, but perhaps, more importantly, the larger ideological ramifications of Jeffersonian democracy.

influenced Jefferson's political thinking. Affected by the extremes of wealth and poverty that he witnessed there, and the violent revolution such conditions unleashed, he felt that it was impossible for Europe to achieve a just society that could guarantee its citizens the "life, liberty, and pursuit of happiness" of which he had written in the Declaration of Independence. Jefferson was equally disdainful of British industrialization, which produced squalor, poverty, and misery among the working classes in England's factory towns. He believed that the laborers would ultimately rise up in revolt, not only against factory owners, but also against the government that supported the oppressive economic system. Such were the reasons why he opposed the Hamiltonian agenda, for he saw such initiatives creating the potential for the same conditions to arise in the United States. In Jefferson's mind, large-scale industrialization would only bring about bitter class divisions and ultimately class warfare because of the inherent inequities and disparity of wealth produced by the Industrial Revolution. Not completely against manufacturing, Jefferson simply preferred small-scale production of needed goods (not luxuries) performed by independent mechanics rather than wage employees working in factories.

Jefferson believed that only America provided enough fertile earth for a citizenry to maintain republican form of government. To him, what the U.S. possessed and Europe lacked—an abundance of land—was republicanism's necessary prerequisite. As long as there was room to grow, republicanism would flourish in America. In the Jeffersonian frame of reference, if the United States was to remain the bastion of republicanism, it was imperative for the nation's economy to remain predominantly agricultural. Jefferson thus envisaged a nation of small family farms clustered together in rural communities—an agrarian republic. He believed only a country of roughly equal yeoman farmers, each secure in his own possessions and not dependent on anyone else for his livelihood, would exhibit the concern for the common good—public virtue—essential for a vibrant republic. In other words, only in a society in which the majority of its members (in the early Republic that meant white males only) believed themselves to be equals could republicanism flourish. Thus, from the Jeffersonian perspective, egalitarianism and republicanism were symbiotic. More romantically, Jefferson also believed that those who earned their living from the soil were more in tune with the cycles and rhythms of nature—an important ingredient in the formation of the republican character. Indeed, Jefferson said that "those who labor in the earth are the chosen people of God," and so he viewed himself as one of the "chosen," even though his "farm" was the large slave-owning plantation of Monticello.

The Englishman **Thomas Malthus**'s publication in 1798 of his seminal and deeply pessimistic *Essay on the Principle of Population* also influenced Jefferson's thinking. Warning of an impending population explosion, Malthus predicted that the British populace would soon outstrip their country's food supply. Unless checked, England's population growth would lead to misery and poverty soon engulfing the island nation. Malthus's prediction alarmed many Americans, who had taken great pride in

The East Portico of Monticello, Thomas Jefferson's home

having one of the fastest rates of population increase in the world (close to 40 percent per decade), but Jefferson was not worried. He used the English scholar's work to highlight the opportunity to avoid such a catastrophe America's vast land resources provided. Americans need not worry about Malthus's dire predictions because they had at their disposal millions of acres of potential farm land.

Jefferson's vision of an expanding agrarian republic remains one of Americans' most compelling ideas about their uniqueness and special destiny. Indeed, Jeffersonian **agrarianism** informed much of the national creed and became one of the most enduring ideological legacies in American history. However, expansionism also contained negative aspects. The lure of western lands fostered constant mobility, restlessness, and dissatisfaction rather than the stable, settled communities envisaged by Jefferson. Expansionism caused environmental damage, soil exhaustion in particular—a consequence of abandoning old lands, rather than conserving them, and moving on to new ground. Finally, and perhaps most devastating, expansionism bred a ruthlessness toward Native Americans violently pushed out of the way by encroaching white settlement and decimated by the diseases that accompanied the Anglo-American advance. Jeffersonian agrarianism thus engendered some of the best and some of the worst traits of the developing nation.

Jeffersonians and the Courts: John Marshall and the Advent of Judicial Review

Although Jefferson succeeded in rolling back much of the Federalist agenda, he could not completely eradicate all of the initiatives, especially those pertaining to national authority. Such was the challenge that confronted Jefferson in his battle with the federal court system, which at the time was dominated by Federalist appointees. Jefferson and his party wanted to correct such an imbalance and believed the best way to accomplish that was to repeal the 1801 Judiciary Act, passed by the lame-duck Federalist Congress just before the new president's inauguration. Moreover, just before leaving office, John Adams had appointed and signed the commissions for a group of new judges, marshals, federal attorneys, clerks, and justices of the peace (all of whom were staunch Federalists), and expanded the number and levels of federal courts. In this manner, Adams sought to preserve and protect the federal judiciary as a Federalist bastion from Republican retrenchment.

Republicans disagreed about what to do with the Federalist-packed judiciary. A minority distrusted the whole idea of an independent judiciary and wanted to pass legislation and a constitutional amendment to make all judges popularly elected. Such an idea was too democratic even for Jefferson, who surprisingly wanted courts shielded from popular control. However, all Republicans, including the president, deeply resented the fact that the entire federal judicial system lay in Federalist hands. He replaced the new federal marshals and attorneys with Republicans and dismissed some of the justices of the peace, but federal judges were appointed for life. If they did not resign, they could only be removed by impeachment. Jefferson believed the best way to relieve his administration of these men was to simply abolish their jobs by repealing the 1801 Judiciary Act, which Congress did, thus doing away with all of Adams's appointees.

Emboldened by repeal of the Judiciary Act, House Republicans next attempted to reduce the Federalist presence on the Supreme Court by impeaching and removing Associate Justice Samuel Chase for alleged "high crimes and misdemeanors." The move was purely partisan and vindictive. Chase was a hardcore, abusive, openly hostile High Federalist who, during the Sedition Act crisis, prosecuted sedition cases with great relish, handing down the maximum sentences and fines that act allowed for its Republican violators. He was also incredibly arrogant and impolitic, delivering anti-Jeffersonian diatribes from the bench. In short, Chase was an unpleasant, overbearing, and unashamedly partisan member of the bench. Though competent, knowledgeable, and upright, he simply could not keep his political thoughts to himself or his antipathy for the Jeffersonians quiet. However, whatever his personal flaws, no legal grounds existed to justify his impeachment. In their quest to impeach Chase, Democratic Republicans evolved into loose constitutional constructionists, a reversal of their earlier interpretations during the debate on the chartering of the Bank of the United States. In their defense of Chase, Federalists became the strict constructionists, arguing that the power to impeach had been narrowly drawn and should be used only in cases of clear criminal behavior, and Chase's outspoken partisanship was no criminal act. The Senate (the body assigned impeachment trials by the Constitution), acquitted Chase and the Supreme Court remained Federalist by a 5-to-1 margin. Jefferson's desire for a Democratic-Republican Supreme Court would have to wait for unforced vacancies in 1804 and 1807 and the creation of a new western circuit in 1807.

Of greater significance than the Chase controversy was the establishment of judicial review by the Supreme Court under the leadership of one of the most influential chief justices of all time, **John Marshall**, a Federalist appointed by John Adams. The Marshall Court's first landmark decision came in 1803, in the case of *Marbury v. Madison,* when it ruled against the constitutionality of a law passed by Congress for the first time. As previously noted, President Adams named a number of justices of the peace for the District of Columbia on the eve of leaving office. James Madison, Jefferson's new Secretary of State, refused to deliver the commissions (the official documents entitling them to assume their posts) for many of these "midnight appointments." Four appointees, including William Marbury, promptly sued Madison for their offices, seeking a *writ of mandamus* (or judicial order to compel a government official to comply with a law) from the Supreme Court, which Congress had authorized to issue such writs in the Judiciary Act of 1789. In his decision, Marshall ruled that Marbury had a legal right to his appointment, but he surprised many by declaring that the section of the 1789 Judiciary Act which granted the power to issue *mandamus writs* to the Supreme Court to be unconstitutional. Citing Section III of the Constitution, Marshall determined that the Supreme Court lacked jurisdiction to issue such orders. While the High Court had limited original jurisdiction in certain specified matters, this case did not apply. (Though the Court possessed appellate jurisdiction to hear the case if it had come through the lower federal courts, Marbury decided against pursuing his case further.) Thus, the particular provision of the Judiciary Act of 1789 authorizing the Supreme Court to issue *mandamus writs* was null and void because it exceeded the powers granted to Congress as outlined in the Constitution. At first glance, the Jefferson administration appeared to have won the battle over Adams's last minute appointees since Marshall conceded that the Supreme Court could not force the executive branch to appoint Marbury. In the long run, however, Marshall proclaimed that the courts had a duty to "say what the law is," thus unequivocally defending the independence of the judiciary and the principle of "judicial review." Marshall firmly established the principle that only the federal judiciary could decide the constitutionality of laws passed by Congress.

Seven years later, in *Fletcher v. Peck*, the Court extended judicial review to state laws. In 1794, a corrupt Georgia legislature (most of whom were on the payroll of the Yazoo Land Company) had given the company the right to purchase land claimed by Georgia in present-day Alabama and Mississippi. The Yazoo Company then sold the land to individual buyers, mostly New England speculators, for

LOUISIANA PURCHASE AND EXPLORATION

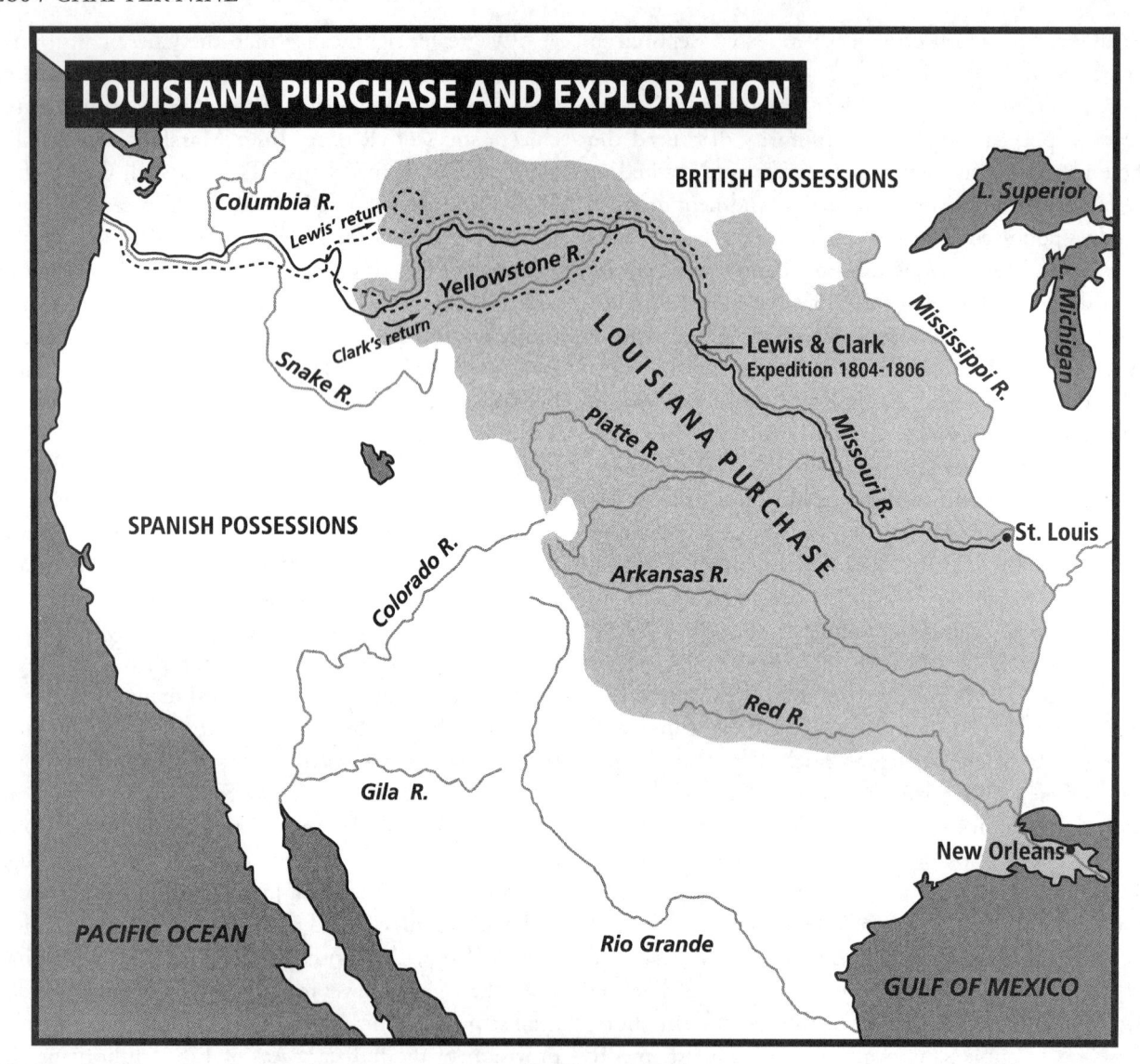

Map 9.1 Louisiana Purchase and Exploration Route of Lewis and Clark

a huge profit. Two years later, challengers defeated many of the corrupt lawmakers' bids for reelection and members of the new Georgia legislature rescinded the land grant and the subsequent sales. The legislature also turned the land over to the federal government, whereby Jefferson agreed to pay off the investors' claims with federal funds. John Marshall, however, interpreted the entire exchange differently. Whatever the circumstances of the legislature's initial action, Marshall argued, the Constitution forbade the states from undertaking any action that impaired a contract. Therefore, the individual purchasers (the New England speculators) could keep their land, and the new Georgia legislature could not repeal the original grant.

Marbury v. Madison and *Fletcher v. Peck* were both vital steps in realizing the three-way balance of power among the branches of the federal government—executive (president), legislative (Congress), and judicial (federal courts)—envisioned by the Founding Fathers in the Constitution. Equally important, during his long tenure as Chief Justice from 1801 to 1835, Marshall would consistently lead the Supreme Court in a series of decisions favoring the power of the federal government over state governments, the sanctity of contracts, private property rights, and the protection of private enterprise from both state and federal encroachment. Under Marshall's direction, the Supreme Court established itself as a powerful nationalizing and unifying force.

The Louisiana Purchase

One of the greatest ironies of Jefferson's presidency involves his most noteworthy accomplishment: the **Louisiana Purchase**. The largest land deal in U.S. history did not result from astute American diplomacy but, rather, from a consequence of international events in Europe and the Western Hemisphere that allowed a vast amount of foreign territory to fall into Jefferson's lap. The one area that posed a possible threat to the United States, Louisiana, eventually became the source of great triumph with the area's acquisition from France in 1803.

The vast Louisiana Territory stretched from the Gulf of Mexico to Canada bounded by the Mississippi River and the Rocky Mountains. According to the Treaty of Paris, which reshuffled colonial possessions at the end of the French and Indian War, Louisiana (ceded by France to Spain in 1762) was never to be returned to French control. In the intervening decades, however, power politics had changed dramatically in Europe. By the beginning of the nineteenth century, France had emerged as the continent's greatest land power while Spain continued its declension. By 1800, Spain was in no condition to reject or resist the French demands for Louisiana to be returned to its "rightful" owners. Napoleon's request was straightforward: Spain either returned Louisiana or France would invade Spain. The Spanish king soon agreed to Napoleon's demands in exchange for some lands in Italy and a promise from France not to transfer Louisiana to a third power.

Napoleon wanted Louisiana returned so he could resurrect the French empire in America, centered on the sugar island of Saint Dominique (present-day Haiti and the Dominican Republic) with food from the mainland colony used to feed the island's slave population, which would tend a sugar crop that would finance the French army. Late in 1802, the Spanish, who had retained control of New Orleans, closed the port to American trade, giving rise to rumors that they would soon transfer the city to France. To forestall such a move, which could threaten the very existence of American settlements located west of the Appalachian Mountains, Jefferson dispatched envoys to France in early 1803 to offer to purchase the city from the French government.

By the time the delegates reached Paris, French plans for a resurrected New World empire had collapsed. To Napoleon's utter dismay and humiliation, slaves on Saint Dominique led by Toussaint L'Ouverture revolted, defeating not only French forces attempting to regain control, but also a later British expeditionary force sent to seize the island. At the same time, war between France and Great Britain seemed imminent. Napoleon (reputedly raving "Damn sugar, damn coffee, damn colonies!") decided to abandon America and concentrate his resources on Europe. Needing money for such ambitions and with his dreams of American empire in ruins, Napoleon's representatives astonished Jefferson's delegation by announcing that France would not only sell New Orleans, but all of the Louisiana Territory to the United States for the bargain price of $15 million—a purchase that would roughly double the size of the United States.

To the shock of his Republican colleagues, Jefferson initially hesitated to authorize the deal, worrying about the constitutional repercussions of his actions due to the fact that the Constitution did not specifically lay out a legal process for acquiring new territories. The only way to maintain the Jeffersonian Republican commitment to strict constructionism seemed to be ratification of a constitutional amendment specifically authorizing the federal government to acquire new lands. Jefferson faced an incredible dilemma. If he followed this procedure, it could take months, perhaps longer, for the amendment to be accepted by the necessary three-quarters of the states, with no guarantee that Napoleon would wait around while the Americans debated his offer.

After pondering his options, Jefferson concluded that the most prudent avenue to pursue was to draw up a treaty with France to include a provision containing the purchase. Such a back-door method troubled Jefferson and traditional Republicans, while Federalists lambasted the president for exhibiting hypocrisy by abandoning strict constructionism in favor of tactics that he and Madison had criticized Hamilton for employing during the controversy over the bill authorizing the Bank of the United States. In the final analysis, the fostering of an agrarian republic was Jefferson's paramount objective. If adopting a loose construction approach furthered those ends, then so be it. Jefferson's devotion to strict constructionism had always been more political than principled. With the Federalists safely out of power, he became more comfortable adopting some of their methods. He concluded that the acquisition of Louisiana was simply too good to pass up on a variety of levels. The purchase would double the size of the country, assure Americans access to interior rivers, eliminate a serious foreign threat on the nation's western border, and give farmers enough land to sustain the agrarian republic for centuries to come.

Republican senators who shared few of Jefferson's reservations quickly ratified the treaty over Federalist objections that the purchase would encourage rapid settlement, leading to more Indian wars, while incorporating into the country thousands of "foreigners"—Spanish, French, "new" Indians (the Plains Indians of the Midwest), and whoever else had taken up residence in the territory over the past several decades. Such a motley assortment of people, the Federalists argued, would only increase backcountry barbarism, making it impossible to govern a large country now inhabited by "strange" peoples totally unfamiliar with American ways. The Federalists also opposed western expansion for selfish reasons—additional lands incorporated into the country would dilute the remaining national political strength of New England where the Federalist Party still had some degree of local supremacy. Despite these protests, the treaty sailed through Congress and met with overwhelming public approval nationally.

The Lewis and Clark Expedition

Within a year of the Louisiana Purchase, President Jefferson dispatched one of the most important domestic expeditions in American history. Led by **Meriwether Lewis and William Clark**, two Virginia-born veterans of Indian wars in the Ohio Valley, the "Corps of Discovery" was charged with the task of exploring the new territory with great attention to detail. The mission was both scientific and commercial—to study the area's plants, animal life, native peoples, and geography in order to assess the region's economic potential. Jefferson hoped the explorers could establish trade relations with western Indians and locate a water route to the Pacific Ocean, still believing in the possibility of a Northwest Passage that could facilitate commerce with Asia.

In the spring of 1804, Lewis and Clark's 50-member expedition set out from St. Louis on their famous journey across half a continent. They spent the winter in present-day North Dakota, then resumed their travels in April 1805. By this time, they had been joined by some western Plains Indians, most notably a fifteen-year-old Shoshone Indian woman, Sacagawea, the wife of a French fur trader who served as their interpreter. After crossing the Rocky Mountains, the expedition reached the Pacific Ocean near present-day Astoria, Oregon, only to find a host of British, French, and Russian fur traders and whalers already there. Lewis and Clark returned to St. Louis in 1806, bringing with them a wealth of detailed information about the region's landscape, topography, mountains, rivers, lakes, flora and fauna, and, of course, about the people who inhabited the territory, including the European fur traders who had established outposts on the Oregon coast. Although failing to find the nonexistent Northwest Passage, Lewis and Clark demonstrated the possibility of overland travel to the Pacific coast. To their surprise, they found Native Americans in the Trans-Mississippi West accustomed to dealing with European traders and already connected to global markets. Their journey's success helped to strengthen the idea that the American dominion was destined to reach all the way to the Pacific.

Although the Lewis and Clark Expedition was undoubtedly one of the most important explorations in American history, delivering invaluable information to the Jefferson administration, the trek across the continent also provided the president with some disappointing assessments. By far the most important was their negative appraisal of the land's suitability for farming. Lewis and Clark dashed Jefferson's hopes that he had purchased millions of acres of "green pastures" for farming. In their evaluation, the complete opposite was true—most of the territory was completely unsuitable for agriculture. Indeed, the explorers believed the entire Great Plains region to be a desert, for they had crossed the area in the summer when the heat and lack of rain turned the earth brown. In their frame of reference, such a topography reflected barren soil. Disappointed at hearing such news, Jefferson became somewhat relieved when told that the Oregon Country was green and fertile. On American maps made after the expedition, the present-day Great Plains region was designated as "The Great American Desert." Not until after the Civil War would American settlers venture into the area, and only because they were given free land from the federal government via the 1862 Homestead Act. Only at the close of the nineteenth century did Jefferson's dream of purchasing an agrarian paradise, "an empire of liberty," begin to come true. By 1900, thanks to the "Hamiltonian" Industrial Revolution that produced the requisite machinery to cultivate the harsh land, American farmers had transformed the Great American Desert into the bread basket of the world.

As Jefferson stood for reelection in 1804, he could bask in many first-term accomplishments. The president had calmed the bitter partisanship that had divided the country prior to his presidency and ended the potential for militarism by curtailing the size and expense of the armed forces. He also greatly reduced the national debt while cutting taxes and doubling the size of the United States at remarkably little relative cost. Jefferson was more confident than ever that the Republic could preserve itself through peaceful expansion. The "wise and frugal" government he had promised in 1801 was becoming a reality.

The combination of international peace, territorial expansion, and inexpensive and unobtrusive government left the Federalists without a campaign issue in the 1804 election. Knowing they would lose because they had no issues on which to attack the Jefferson administration and that they were fast becoming a leaderless and ideologically irrelevant party detached from the mainstream of popular politics, the Federalists nevertheless went through the motions of nominating Charles Cotesworth Pinckney of South Carolina as their presidential candidate. They then watched as Jefferson captured the electoral votes of every state except Delaware and Connecticut. Jefferson even won such Federalist "heartland" states as Massachusetts, Vermont, and New Hampshire. As he began his second term in 1805, Jefferson could safely assume that he had ended the Federalist threat to the Republic.

American Reaction to the Napoleonic Wars

No sooner did Napoleon receive his payment from the United States for Louisiana then he used the money to resume the war in Europe, determined to crush Great Britain, that "nation of shopkeepers," once and for all. This eleven-year war, like the conflicts of the 1790s, dominated national politics. By this time, the majority of Americans favored neutrality. Few Republicans championed Napoleon as they had defended the 1789 French revolutionaries, and none but the most rabid Federalists wanted to intervene on the side of Great Britain. However, neither belligerent would permit U.S. neutrality. The **Louisiana Purchase** demonstrated that despite its vaunted isolationism from the Old World, the United States continued to be deeply affected by events throughout the Atlantic world. At a time when Americans still depended upon British manufactured goods at home as well as English markets as an outlet for their farm produce, European wars directly influenced the livelihood of the country's farmers, merchants, and artisans. Jefferson hoped to avoid foreign entanglements, but he found it impossible to keep from being drawn into European wars. Even as the president sought to limit the power of the national government, foreign relations compelled him to expand it.

Interestingly, because their rural economies had been exhausted by the previous eight years of fighting, both France and Great Britain initially encouraged Americans to resume their role as neutral carriers and suppliers of food. For a time, Americans made huge profits. Between 1803 and 1807, U.S.-exported foodstuffs and plantation staples rose from $66.5 million to $102.2 million. Re-exports (those goods produced in the British, French, and Spanish West Indies, picked up by American ships and taken to American ports, then shipped out on American vessels) rose even faster—from $13.5 million to $58.4 million. However, in 1805, the result of geopolitical changes in the European war, both Great Britain and France ended their lax trade policies with the United States and resumed their harassment of American shipping. Because of their superior navy (solidified by their great victory over combined French and Spanish fleets at Trafalgar off the southwestern Spanish coast), the British were in a far better position to impose their will. France remained invincible on land, however, as exemplified by Napoleon's decisive victory over Austria and Russia at the Battle of Austerlitz near Vienna in December 1805. The war then reached a stalemate: Napoleon had effective political and military control over much of Europe while the British navy controlled the seas.

At this juncture, in hopes of starving the French into submission, Great Britain decided to enact such a plan they could not allow any neutral countries to trade with France. Thus, beginning in 1805, the British Royal Navy implemented a blockade of French ports and once again began seizing American ships engaged in the re-export trade with France. The Jefferson administration decided it was time to get tougher with the belligerents, especially England. In the president's view, the diplomatic approach of his predecessors had failed, so he explored other means to garner respect for American neutral rights. In the spring of 1806, an angry Republican Congress passed the Non-Importation Act, which forbade the importing of British goods that could be purchased elsewhere or manufactured in the United States. The law hurt Americans across the nation because the U.S. was dependent on England in particular for most of its manufactured goods. Moreover, Great Britain was still the United States' best trading partner; if Americans could not trade with England, the economic impact on the United States, especially on New England whose entire economy was commercially-oriented, would be disastrous. The French issued decrees in rebuttal that, in conjunction with Great Britain's Order in Council, virtually outlawed all American commerce with Europe. The British also resumed the impressment of American sailors. By the time of the War of 1812, an estimated 6,000 American citizens had been impressed into the Royal Navy. As in the past, Great Britain remained the most egregious violator of American neutrality and potentially the greatest threat to U.S. security. By 1807, war with Great Britain appeared imminent as anti-British rallies and demonstrations took place in American cities and towns in which war cries were heard constantly. Jefferson responded by barring British ships from American territorial waters and by ordering state governors to call up as many as 100,000 militiamen. The United States in 1807 stood at the brink of war with the most powerful nation in the world.

While dealing with the British, Jefferson also had to contend with other maritime issues, especially those caused by the "**Barbary Pirates**" of North Africa, who had been harassing European shipping in the Mediterranean and the Atlantic for several years by attacking ships directly or demanding tribute, which several countries paid to protect their vessels. Until Jefferson's presidency, the United States had paid tribute as well, but he refused demands for increased payments so the pasha of Tripoli declared war on the United States. Jefferson ordered a large U.S. naval squadron to North Africa. After three years of blockading and raiding North African ports,

American sailors finally won a decisive victory at Tripoli Harbor in 1804, bringing an end to the conflict.

The Embargo Act

The defeat of the Barbary Pirates demonstrated Jefferson's resolve to use force when necessary to defend American sovereignty and honor. However, he knew that war with either Great Britain or France would be a completely different conflict, one which the United States could easily lose. Thus, like his predecessors, the president ignored the public clamors for war with Great Britain and continued to pursue neutrality. Indeed, Jefferson wanted to avoid war at all costs, believing it would lead to high taxes, government debt, repression of dissent, and the creation of a bloated military and civil service—the very evils that he had vowed to eliminate.

Jefferson had one more card to play: suspending U.S. trade with Europe. At the president's urging, Congress passed the **Embargo Act** in December 1807, forbidding American ships from leaving U.S. ports. The law also indirectly limited imports because foreign vessels were not allowed to leave American ports with cargo on return voyages. In effect, the Embargo Act cut off all U.S. trade with the outside world. What prompted Jefferson to push for such a drastic measure? Certainly he wished to keep American ships out of harm's way on the high seas, but the president also long believed that access to American farm products and U.S. markets for exports had become crucial to the economies of many European nations. Thus, a trade ban, especially involving the denial of American food, might apply effective leverage to get a change of behavior from the European belligerents.

Despite Jefferson's high hopes, within less than a year's time it became clear that the United States was more dependent on foreign trade than either of the belligerents. France had access to sufficient foodstuffs on the continent to withstand the embargo (and the ongoing British blockade), while England simply found new markets, especially in Latin America. For the year and a half that the legislation was in effect, the Embargo Act proved to be one of the most economically disastrous laws ever passed in U.S. history. Before its passage, American exports had stood at $108 million. By the end of 1808, they had dropped to $22 million. The economy slowed in every section of the country, but the hardest hit area was, of course, New England, whose entire economic orientation was based on shipping and shipbuilding. With such enterprises shut down, the entire New England economy felt the impact. While the ocean-going merchant fleets rotted at anchor, unemployed sailors, dockworkers, and other maritime workers and their families sank to levels of despair that had seldom been seen in British North America. New England Federalists were especially outraged, convinced that although Jefferson had not overtly sought revenge on them for the Alien and Sedition Acts during his first term, his actions were doing so now by economically ruining them. The Federalists accused Jefferson of plotting an end to commerce and reversion to rural barbarism, often taking the lead in subverting the embargo through smuggling and other means. In short, the Federalists saw the Embargo Act as Jefferson's last attempt to destroy them once and for all.

As a result of the Embargo Act, the Federalists, who but three years earlier appeared to be a party on the brink of extinction, found themselves temporarily resuscitated. In the 1808 presidential election, their candidate, once again Charles Cotesworth Pinckney of South Carolina, received 47 electoral votes to 122 for Jefferson's chosen successor, his old ally and best friend, James Madison. Four years earlier, Pinckney had received only 14 electoral votes to Jefferson's 162. Although the Republicans retained control of both houses of Congress, Federalists made significant gains in Congress and won control of several state legislatures, especially in New England and the Mid-Atlantic states—those commercial regions of the country most adversely affected by the Embargo Act. Federalist opposition to the act, and the supposed southern agrarian stranglehold on national power that stood behind it, seemed to be gaining ground.

As it became obvious that the Embargo Act was devastating the American economy and politically aiding the Federalists while having little effect on the belligerents, Jefferson asked Congress to repeal the legislation before leaving office in early 1809. Congress obliged, replacing it with a new law, the **Non-Intercourse Act**, which banned trade with only Britain and France, but stipulated that commerce would resume with either nation if that country simply rescinded its edicts against American shipping.

THE ROAD TO WAR WITH ENGLAND

Madison Seeks Peace

James Madison became the first president in American history to assume the nation's highest office during a time of intense crisis. At home and abroad, the new president inherited serious issues unleashed by international events beyond his control. If not carefully and skillfully managed, these tensions could escalate into war with grave domestic consequences. The new president was aware of the potential ramifications of his actions and made the avoidance of war with Great Britain a priority. In the end, foreign and domestic pressures proved too overwhelming for him to avoid a conflict of arms, thus Madison became the first president to lead the country during a foreign war. To his credit, down to the eleventh hour, Madison did all he could to avoid a fight. However, neither the British government nor many of his own people would allow him any alternative.

When Madison took office in the spring of 1809, the embargo legislation clearly had failed to coerce the British into stopping their seizure of American ships and men. The act had devastated the U.S. economy and led to the loss of 90 percent of the government's revenue. The Non-Intercourse Act, which had replaced the Embargo Act, proved equally ineffective, as neither England nor France complied with its terms. Determined to preserve peace but still seeking a change of policy from the European powers, Madison asked Congress to consider a bill known as Macon's Bill No. 1, which allowed Americans to export once again but banned imports from any country adhering to trade restrictions on American shippers. Believing the president's proper role to be one who suggested laws rather than forcefully pushing for their passage, Madison left the debate to the congressmen who stopped the measure. He eventually settled for another proposal, **Macon's Bill No. 2**, which passed Congress in 1810. A strange piece of legislation, the law rescinded the ban on trade with France and Britain but then authorized the president to re-impose trade bans with either belligerent if the other did not agree to respect American neutral rights of trade.

In September 1810, the wily Napoleon decided that he would lift his decrees against American shipping, hoping that such a display of magnanimity would lead the United States into conflict with Great Britain, for he knew the likelihood of his enemy accepting anything short of American support for the British cause was remote. Madison accepted the French pledge, then issued a proclamation declaring that the British had three months to follow suit. The president believed his position was "at least an extrication from the dilemma, of a mortifying peace, or a war with both the great belligerents." The British, however, refused to revoke their Orders in Council and told the Americans to withdraw their restrictions on British trade. The United States would either have to obey British trade mandates (thus making American exports and the American merchant marine a part of the British war effort—a neocolonial status utterly repugnant to most Americans) or go to war. When Congress reconvened in November 1811, representatives voted military measures in preparation for war with Great Britain.

Native Americans and the Impending War with Great Britain

The growing crisis with Great Britain took place against a backdrop of deteriorating U.S.-Indian relations in the West, a circumstance which also drove the United States down the path toward war. Thomas Jefferson had long advocated removing those Native Americans who refused to cooperate in "civilizing" themselves to the lands east of the Mississippi River. The Louisiana Purchase made Jefferson even more determined to pursue a removal policy. "The acquisition of Louisiana," he wrote, "will, it is hoped, put in our power the means of inducing all the Indians on this side [of the Mississippi River] to transplant themselves to the other side." In other words, Jefferson wanted to completely eliminate, by removal, all the native peoples located east of the Mississippi River—to force them, in effect, to migrate to the territory west of the river. To put this policy into action, Jefferson purchased as much land west of the Appalachian Mountains as possible from Native Americans, hoping that such a scheme would give the Indians the ability to move further west with their money, buy land somewhere else, and thereby transform themselves in the process into civilized yeoman farmers. Such an expectation was delusional. Few Native Americans had any intention of purchasing land, or of settling down and becoming simple farmers. Jefferson even encouraged traders to lend money to Indians in hope that accumulating debt would force them to sell some of their holdings, thus freeing up more land for "our increasing numbers." Clearly Jefferson believed

President James Madison

the United States should be for white people only. All other inhabitants had to adapt to American ways or step aside and move somewhere else. Yet, at the same time, Jefferson's administration continued George Washington's policy of promoting settled farming among the Indians. Benjamin Hawkins, a friend of Jefferson's who served as the U.S. agent for Indian affairs south of the Ohio River, encouraged African-American slavery among the tribes as one of the signs that Native Americans in the region were becoming civilized by adopting one of white America's more salient manifestations of property ownership.

By 1800, nearly 400,000 white American settlers lived west of the Appalachian Mountains, far outnumbering the remaining Native Americans. The Indians' seemingly irreversible decline in numbers and power led some leaders to rethink their opposition to assimilation. Such sentiment was strong among the Creek and Cherokee, whose respective chiefs, Major Ridge for the Creeks and John Ross for the Cherokee (both partially-white "mixed bloods") enthusiastically supported the federal policy of promoting "civilization." Many mixed-bloods, who had become more present as a result of white advancement into the Old Southwest, established businesses as traders and slave-owning farmers with the help of their white fathers. Their assimilationist views infuriated full-blooded natives who wished to root out European influences and resist further white encroachments on Indian lands.

The period from 1800 to 1812 became an "**age of prophecy**" among many Native American peoples. Movements for the revitalization of Indian life arose among some Creeks and Cherokees, Shawnees, Iroquois, and many other tribes in the Old Northwest. Most leaders of these native groups were accommodationists, however, believing that continued armed resistance to the white onslaught into their lands would be futile. None of them advocated joining a unified inter-tribal movement to better defend their rights. Handsome Lake of the Seneca, who had overcome an earlier addiction to alcohol, for example, preached that Indians must refrain from fighting, gambling, drinking, and sexual promiscuity. He believed that Native Americans could regain their autonomy without directly challenging whites or repudiating all white ways, urging his people to take up farming and to attend school.

Tecumseh's Vision

A more militant and prideful message than Handsome Lake's was propagated by two Shawnee brothers, **Tecumseh**, a chief who had refused to sign the Treaty of Greenville in 1795, and Tenskwatawa ("The Prophet"), a shaman who called for the complete separation from whites, the revival of traditional Indian culture, and

Tecumseh

resistance to U.S. government policies. "The Prophet" preached that whites were the source of all evil in the world, and Indians should abandon their ways—alcohol, clothing, food, and manufactured goods. The Prophet was a mesmerizing, charismatic speaker who acquired a huge following among several tribes in the Northwest, many of whom after hearing his exhortations were ready to unite and repel the white invaders. His disciples became so numerous that they built a town specifically for them and their leader, Prophetstown, along the Wabash River in the Indiana Territory.

Meanwhile, Tecumseh traversed the Mississippi River Valley attempting to unite all the tribes of the region into a Pan-Indian military alliance, which he believed to be imperative if Native Americans had any chance of surviving the continuing white onslaughts. The alternative to resistance, Tecumseh declared, was extermination. "Where today are the Pequot?" he asked. "Where are the Narragansett, the Mohican, the Pocanet, and other powerful tribes of our people? They have vanished before the avarice [greed] and oppression of the white man, as snow before the summer sun." He asserted that Indians must recognize they were a single people and unite against the common enemy, the United States, to claim "a common and equal right in the land." He repudiated the accommodationist and assimilationist chiefs who had sold land to the federal government and believed that white Americans were willing to integrate Native Americans into their culture. To Tecumseh, all such hopes were delusional and, in the end, would lead to the complete annihilation of the Native American peoples. "Sell a country! Why not sell the air, the great sea, as well as the earth? Did not the Great Spirit make them all for the use of his children?" In 1810, Tecumseh succeeded in uniting several thousand Native Americans in the Mississippi Valley into a confederated alliance and began attacking white frontier settlements. In November 1811, while Tecumseh was absent, American forces under William Henry Harrison, attacked and destroyed Prophetstown after the Battle of Tippecanoe.

The Rise of the War Hawks

While President Madison tried to avert conflict with Great Britain, he simultaneously faced strident and sometimes insulting clamors for war in Congress. Leading the charge for war against Great Britain were the **"War Hawks"**— newly-elected ultranationalist, jingoistic, expansionist young lions, mostly from the South and West. These new political leaders had come of age after the winning of independence and thus were imbued with a fervent nationalism. Their leaders included the newly-elected Speaker of the House of Representatives Henry Clay of Kentucky; John C. Calhoun and William Lowndes from South Carolina; George M. Troup of Georgia; and Peter B. Porter representing the Niagara district of New York. The War Hawks spoke passionately about defending national honor against British insults, but they also had more specific goals in mind, such as the annexation of Canada. "Agrarian cupidity [greed], not maritime rights urges the war" declared Congressman John Randolph of Virginia in opposition. "We have heard but one word, Canada, Canada, Canada!" Many southern War Hawks were equally expansionist-minded, agitating for the conquest of Florida, long a source of harm of southern slave owners because it served as a haven for fugitive slaves. Members of Congress also spoke of the necessity of upholding the principle of free trade and liberating the United States once and for all from European infringements on its independence. The Republic's future prosperity, they believed, depended upon unimpeded access to overseas markets.

The many fissures in both the Republican and Federalist Parties aided the War Hawks' efforts to take control of Congress. United against Madison, the Federalist minority was joined on many issues by northeastern Republicans who followed the pro-British Federalist line on international trade, and by those Republicans who wanted a more powerful military than desired by their other compatriots. Led by John Randolph, the self-styled "Old Republican" Southerners also often opposed the president. Under Henry Clay's leadership, however, the Republican divisions disappeared as Clay and his fellow War Hawks imposed order and unity on their congressional compatriots. As House Speaker, Clay controlled debate, packed key committees with like-minded individuals, and worked tirelessly behind the scenes to bring his colleagues together on the issue of war with Great Britain. In the winter and spring of 1811-1812, the War Hawks led Congress toward a declaration of war. In November 1811, they voted military preparations. In April 1812, they enacted a 90-day embargo—not to coerce the British, but to get American ships safely into port before war began.

On June 1, 1812, Madison finally sent a war message to Congress. As was his typical practice, the president stayed out of congressional domain by not asking specifically for a declaration of war. He did, however, present a list of American grievances that could be interpreted in no other way: the enforcement of the Orders in Council, even within U.S. territorial waters; the impressment of American sailors; the use of spies and provocateurs within the United States; and the wielding of "a malicious influence over the Indians of the Northwest Territory." Madison concluded that war had, in fact, already begun: "We behold on the side of Great Britain a state of war against the United States; and on the side of the United States, a state of peace toward Great Britain."

Congress declared war on June 18, 1812 with a vote that was far from unanimous, despite the War Hawks' assiduous attempts to make it so. In the House, the vote was 79 to 49; in the Senate, 19 to 13. All 30 Federalists voted against the declaration, along with one-fifth of the Republicans, nearly all of them from the Northeast where anti-war sentiment was loud and strong. Thus, the conflict became a Republican war, more particularly a southern and western Republican war, with the Northeast, whose commercial rights were supposedly the main issue, adamantly opposed to the declaration.

THE WAR OF 1812: The "Second War of American Independence"

In retrospect, it seems remarkably foolhardy that the leaders of a disunited and militarily unprepared nation chose to fight one of the world's major powers. The nation proved also to be financially unprepared for the conflict. With the expiration of the 1811 charter of the Bank of the United States and the refusal of northern merchants and bankers to loan money because they opposed the war (with many outright sympathetic if not supportive of the British), the government found it extremely difficult to finance the war. Before the conflict ended, the nation was essentially bankrupt. Despite the inherent problems, national pride and expansionist ambitions made the War of 1812 all but inevitable. The War Hawks had pushed the Madison administration into a fight to defend the country's sovereignty and honor by protecting its maritime rights and to secure America's western territories. However, no sooner did the shooting start than the war that they planned ended up reflecting not the larger issues noted above, but rather, the more chauvinistic interests of southern and western Republican expansionists.

The Failed Invasion of Canada

Federalists and their northeastern Republican allies expected a naval war. After all, the British had committed their most egregious violations of American rights on the high seas. Many remembered the U.S. Navy's successes in the Quasi-War against France and believed that American sailors were capable of producing the same results in this conflict. Many of the War Hawks, however, had a different purpose for this conflict. They saw the war as the perfect opportunity for American expansion, especially northward, with an invasion and conquest of Canada, followed by its annexation. Because of their priority,

Map 9.2 The War of 1812

they believed that the army rather than the navy had to be strengthened. Reasoning that no American naval force could challenge British control of the seas, they preferred to make preparations for a land invasion of Canada. This decision outraged Federalists and the Old Republicans, who charged that Madison and the War Hawks deceived them about the war's purpose, accusing them of planning a war of territorial expansion. In spite of these protests, the invasion of Canada was a given. With England engrossed in the **Napoleonic Wars,** the War Hawks believed Canada to be ripe for the taking. Despite its immense land area, the province was lightly garrisoned and only had a population a half million, with many of them French.

As occurred during the Revolutionary War, American ambitions for taking Canada quickly turned into a humiliating defeat. Among other problems, U.S. leaders miscalculated the overall British defensive strength. True, the number of British troops in Canada was relatively small, but the Americans underestimated the number of Indian allies the British had at their disposal, which numbered several thousand. In July 1812, General William Hull, governor of the Michigan Territory, led an invasion force consisting of rag-tag militia and volunteers rather than professional soldiers into Canada only to be easily defeated. The combined British-Indian forces not only drove the Americans out of Upper Canada (Ontario), but proceeded under the leadership of General Isaac Brock to invade the northern United States. The British and their Indian allies occupied many of the remaining American military outposts in the Northwest, transforming the U.S. invasion of Canada into a British occupation of the Northwest. Another American foray from the east fared no better—its 6,000-man force of mostly New York and Ohio militia along with a small contingent of U.S. regulars were routed at the **Battle of Queenston Heights** in western Ontario near Niagara Falls on October 13, 1812. The Canadian debacle made it clear that Jefferson's beloved republican militia was completely incapable of fighting outside of their home areas or standing up against trained, disciplined, professional soldiers. As the winter of 1812 arrived, Canada clearly would not fall as easily as the Americans had assumed. Not only had U. S. forces been militarily defeated and humiliated, but much to their chagrin, the supposedly apathetic Canadian population failed to greet the American invaders as "liberators," instead viewing them as uncouth, ramshackle, wild-frontier misfits and interlopers. The American loyalist émigrés were not about to welcome the very people who had driven them from their homes in the aftermath of the Revolutionary War. Indeed, by the time of the war, the assortment of Tory expatriates, discharged British soldiers, and even American-born settlers who had migrated to Canada had become a self-consciously British-Canadian people who simply did not like Americans. Even the French Catholics of Quebec and Montreal viewed the Americans as invaders and refused to come to their assistance. Indeed, for these particular *Canadiens*, this was a war between two groups of *Anglais*, who French Canadians saw as no different than all the rest of the English-speaking people around them.

Tecumseh's Last Stand

Like the American Revolution, the War of 1812 became a two-front struggle—one against the British and the other against Native Americans. Tecumseh's Indian confederacy, bruised but not broken in the Battle of Tippecanoe, allied itself with the British in 1812, with the warrior offered a brigadier general's commission in the British army (which he refused). On a trip to the southern tribes, Tecumseh found the traditionalist wing of the Creeks—led by natives who called themselves **Red Sticks**—willing to join his Pan-Indian alliance. The augmented confederacy provided stiff resistance to American forces throughout the war. The Red Sticks drove most Americans out of Tennessee before advancing on a stockade surrounding the house of a southern Alabama plantation owner named Samuel Mims where a large group of white and mixed-blood settlers had taken refuge. In what whites soon called the **Fort Mims Massacre**, the Red Sticks overwhelmed the makeshift garrison defended by local militia and then brutally slaughtered at least 250 men, women, and children before leaving with 100 captives (mostly slaves). In the Northwest, Tecumseh's warriors, fighting alongside the British, spread terror throughout scores of white settlements.

Although routed on land, U.S. forces ironically fared better on water against the nation reputed to have the greatest navy in the world. However, it must be remembered that until Napoleon's defeat in 1814, the British were forced to fight the United States with only those troops and ships already stationed in North America. Preoccupied with defeating Napoleon, they simply could not spare the manpower or ships to reinforce their army or navy in North America until France had been defeated.

This strategic situation, of course, proved a great boon to the United States' chances for victory. Such was the scenario that played out on Lake Erie where an American naval victory over the vaunted British navy not only boosted American morale, but proved to be one of the United States' greatest and most important triumphs in the war. On Lake Erie, the British and Americans engaged in a frenzied shipbuilding contest through the first year of the war that the Americans ultimately won.

Death of Tecumseh at the Battle of the Thames, October 18, 1813

In September 1813, **Commodore Oliver Hazard Perry** cornered the British fleet at Put-in-Bay and destroyed it. Control of Lake Erie enabled the U.S. to cut off supplies to the British in the Northwest. As a result, an American army under William Henry Harrison reestablished control over the area before advancing into Canada in search of Tecumseh's Indian forces, which they found on October 5, 1813. In the ensuing **Battle of the Thames** River, Tecumseh was killed. American soldiers ravaged his body, with many taking as souvenirs pieces of his hair, clothing, and swatches of skin torn from his corpse. With Tecumseh's death, the Pan-Indian alliance that he had worked so hard to forge soon dissipated. The following spring, in March 1814, General Andrew Jackson's Tennessee militia aided by pro-assimilation Choctaw, Creek, and Cherokee defeated the hostile Red Stick Creeks at the **Battle of Horseshoe Bend** in eastern Alabama. Although called a battle, the confrontation became a massacre of over 800 Creek Indians, many of whom were women and children. Jackson sought revenge for the Fort Mims attack, showing no mercy on the Creeks. In dictating the surrender terms, he required the Indians, hostile and friendly alike, to cede more than half their land (over 23 million acres) to the federal government. With the Battles of the Thames and Horseshoe Bend, the military power of the Native American peoples east of the Mississippi River was broken forever.

The Battles for Baltimore and New Orleans

In 1814, having finally defeated Napoleon, thus ending the larger conflict of which the War of 1812 was a "sideshow," English forces could now concentrate on the American war. Already blockading much of the Atlantic coastline from Georgia to Maine, the British began raiding the shores of Chesapeake Bay during the summer of 1814. Emboldened by the weak American resistance they encountered, they decided to attack the major port of Baltimore, Maryland. Along the way, the British made a feint toward Washington, D.C. with a detachment of marines who, once again, met surprisingly weak defenses. After a fight outside the city (the Battle of Bladensburg), the British troops entered the capital, chased the politicians out of town, then quickly burned down the Capitol, the president's mansion, and other important government buildings. The British sacking of Washington served as an act of retribution for an earlier American attack that resulted in the burning of the Canadian capital of York (Toronto). The marines then reunited with the larger British forces headed toward the much larger city of Baltimore. This time, however, the British fleet proved unable to push their way past the determined garrison occupying Fort McHenry, finally withdrawing after a 24-hour bombardment. One of the battle's spectators was a Federalist lawyer named Francis Scott Key who viewed the shelling from the British flagship while trying to negotiate a prisoner exchange. Key became so inspired by the determined American resistance that he wrote "The Defence of Fort McHenry"—a poem retitled "The Star-Spangled Banner" and later set to music, becoming a popular patriotic song officially recognized as the national anthem in 1931. By the close of 1814, the war had reached a stalemate: Britain had repulsed American attempts to conquer Canada and had blockaded the American coast, but neither side could capture and hold the other's territory.

The British now shifted their attention to the Gulf Coast, especially New Orleans, which they deemed of vital importance to the United States because it was the hub of the nation's Trans-Appalachian trade and communication networks. With peace negotiations underway in Ghent, Belgium, the British wanted to capture the city and hold it as a bargaining chip if no settlement could be reached. However, from behind an impregnable palisade of cotton bales constructed by conscripted slaves at the outskirts of the city, Andrew Jackson waited for the British to attack with an armed force consisting of U.S. regulars, Tennessee and Kentucky militiamen, clerks, workingmen, free blacks, and French pirates under the leadership of the legendary Jean Lafitte, who had received a general pardon for past transgressions from Jackson in exchange for his men's contribution (and more importantly, their ships' cannons) to the city's defense. The British landed near New Orleans in late December 1814, and for several days exchanged artillery barrages with the Americans. Finally, on January 8, 1815, the British launched their offensive, hurling 8,000 men in a frontal assault across open ground toward the 4,000 defenders concealed behind the cotton-bale breastworks. The withering fire devastated the British troops, whose charge lasted only half an hour. When the smoke of the **Battle of New Orleans** cleared, two thousand British soldiers were killed, wounded, or captured while American losses numbered only one hundred.

Two weeks before the climactic battle had even taken place, representatives for the United States and Great Britain signed the **Treaty of Ghent** officially ending the war. With neither side wishing to continue, both agreed to end the conflict without addressing any of the issues that had caused the war. At the moment, neither cared about the details, especially the English, exhausted from almost twenty years of fighting in Europe. The Americans too were anxious for war's end, also tired of fighting with so little to show for the effort. Considering that the war had not been a military success for the United States, the Treaty of Ghent was about as good an outcome as could be expected.

The End of the Federalist Party: The Hartford Convention

Ultimately, both Jefferson and Madison succeeded in accomplishing what they considered to be their paramount objective: the extinguishing of the Federalist Party. With antiwar sentiment at its peak in 1812, Madison won re-election by the relatively narrow margin of 128 electoral votes to 89 over his Federalist challenger, New York City mayor DeWitt Clinton. Although losing the presidential election for the fourth straight time, many Federalists were nonetheless optimistic the war had rejuvenated their party to the point that victory in the next presidential election was a real possibility. However, the Federalists Party's penchant for self-destruction soon took over. In December 1814, a group of New England Federalists assembled at Hartford, Connecticut to vent their party's long-standing grievances, especially the Republicans' economic proscription policies, the domination of the federal government by Virginia presidents, and their own region's declining influence as new western states entered the Union. Dominating the gathering were remaining High Federalists, many of whom were abolitionists calling for a constitutional amendment eradicating the Constitution's three-fifths clause, which disproportionately strengthened southern political power. They also called for a two-thirds vote of Congress before authorizing the admission of new states, declarations of war, and laws restricting foreign trade. Contrary to later myth, the **Hartford Convention** did not call for secession or disunion. However, the delegates did affirm the right of a state to "interpose" its authority (nullify federal laws) if the federal government "violated" the Constitution (according to that state's interpretation). New England's public antiwar stance added to Federalist Party woes. During the war, New England states seldom met their quotas of militiamen for the war effort while some Federalist leaders had openly encouraged resistance to the war. The British encouraged such obstruction by not extending their naval blockade to the New England coast. Throughout the first year of the war, New England merchants and farmers traded freely with the enemy. Forty years earlier, New Englanders were in the forefront of American colonial protest against alleged English tyranny. At the time, many Southerners saw them as wild-eyed radical Republicans. Times had obviously changed since the 1770s—early nineteenth-century New Englanders, led by the Federalists, were now perceived by Southerners and Westerners as reactionaries bent on destroying republicanism either by proscription (the Sedition Act) or by betraying the country by aiding and abetting its enemy.

The Hartford Convention had barely adjourned when news of Jackson's victory at New Orleans electrified the nation. "Rising Glory of America," one newspaper exulted. In speeches and sermons, political and religious leaders alike proclaimed that Jackson's triumph revealed, once again, that a divine hand oversaw America's destiny. The Federalists' antiwar convention caused many Americans to believe that they were unpatriotic, if not traitors. Within a few years, their party no longer existed. Their stance on the war, however, was only one cause of the party's demise. The urban commercial and financial interests that the party championed had represented only a small minority in an expanding national agricultural economy. Their elitism and distrust of the common people placed Federalist leaders increasingly at odds with the new country's growing democratic ethos. Yet, in their dying moments, Federalists had raised an issue—southern domination of the national government—that would long outlive their political party. Ironically, beginning in the immediate postwar decades, a profound social and economic transformation would occur that strengthened the very forces of commercial development that the Federalists had championed and the Republicans had so disdained and feared.

The Second War of American Independence

A number of contemporaries referred to the War of 1812 as "The Second War of American Independence." Despite widespread opposition, the conflict confirmed the ability of a republican government to conduct a war without sacrificing its institutions. Jackson's victory at New Orleans not only made him a national hero, but the general also became a celebrated example of virtuous citizen-soldiers rising to defeat the forces of despotic Europe. The war also completed the conquest of the area east of the Mississippi River, which had begun during the Revolution. Never again would the British pose a threat to American control of this vast region. Native American resistance to the American advance ended, leading to large numbers of settlers engulfing the Old Northwest and Southwest in the years following the conflict. In the war's aftermath, Americans poured into Indiana, Michigan, Alabama, and Mississippi, bringing with them their distinctive forms of social organization. "I have no doubt," Jackson wrote to his wife, "but in a few years the banks of the Alabama will present a beautiful view of elegant mansions and extensive rich and productive farms." Jackson did not mention that slaves would build those estates and cultivate much of the land.

Britain's defeat of Napoleon inaugurated a long period of peace in Europe resulting in Americans no longer having to worry about European affairs intruding upon their daily lives. Thus, Americans' sense of separateness from the Old World grew ever stronger in the decades after the war. Perhaps the most important repercussion of the War of 1812 was its impact on Jefferson's dream of agrarianism, which he concluded by the war's end must be sacrificed. Throughout his political life, Jefferson envisioned American yeomen trading farm surpluses for European manufactured goods—a relationship ensuring rural prosperity while preventing the growth of industrial cities and sustaining the landed independence on which republican citizenship rested. Westward expansion, he had believed, would guarantee the yeoman republic for generations to come. However, by 1816, Jefferson sadly realized that he had deluded himself, for the war revealed the flaws of his thinking. His policies had made the United States vulnerable and almost unable to sustain itself in times of crises. As Jefferson lamented, his own party began taking steps to atone for Jeffersonian republicanism's shortcomings—measures that would help transform the yeoman republic into a market society and a boisterous capitalist democracy in the decades ahead.

Chronology

1803 *Marbury v. Madison.*
United States purchases Louisiana Territory

1804 Twelfth Amendment passed by Congress.

1806 Essex Decision.
Non-Importation Act.

1807 Embargo Act
British attack and search *Chesapeake*.

1808 James Madison elected president.

1809 Non-Intercourse Act.

1810 Congress passes Macon's Bill No. 2.

1811 Henry Clay elected Speaker of the House.

1812 Congress declares war on Great Britain.

1813 U.S. forces burn Canadian capital of York (Toronto).
Perry defeats British fleet at Put-in-Bay.
Battle of the Thames.

1814 Battle of Horseshoe Bend.
British marines burn Washington, D.C.
Francis Scott Key writes "The Star-Spangled Banner."
Hartford Convention held.
Treaty of Ghent.

1815 Battle of New Orleans.

Review Questions

1. Discuss Jefferson's philosophy of republican agrarianism.

2. Discuss the importance of Chief Justice John Marshall in establishing the precedent of judicial review.

3. Assess the significance of the Louisiana Purchase. Why did Jefferson initially hesitate to authorize the acquisition? What were his concerns and how did he eventually come to embrace such a dramatic expansion of the United States?

4. How did Jefferson respond to England and France's violations of American neutrality during his presidency? How did his policies differ from those of his predecessors?

5. What disadvantages did American forces have in the War of 1812 that ultimately made impossible a decisive victory by the United States?

Glossary of Important People and Concepts

"Age of Prophecy"
Barbary Pirates
Battle of Horseshoe Bend
Battle of New Orleans
Battle of Queenston Heights
Battle of the Thames
Embargo Act
Fort Mims Massacre
Hartford Convention
Lewis and Clark Expedition
Louisiana Purchase
Macon's Bill Number 2
Thomas Malthus
John Marshall
Napoleonic Wars
Non-Intercourse Act
Commodore Oliver Hazard Perry
Red Sticks
Republican agrarianism
Tecumseh
Treaty of Ghent
War Hawks

SUGGESTED READINGS

Stephen Ambrose, *Undaunted Courage: Meriwether Lewis, Thomas Jefferson, and the Opening of the American West* (1996).

Lance Banning, *The Jeffersonian Persuasion: Evolution of a Party Ideology* (1978).

Gregory Evans Dowd, *A Spiritual Resistance: The North American Indian Struggle for Unity, 1745-1815* (1992).

Joseph J. Ellis, *American Sphinx: The Character of Thomas Jefferson* (1997).

Donald R. Hickey, *The War of 1812: A Forgotten Conflict* (1989).

Richard Hofstadter, *The Idea of a Party System: The Rise of Legitimate Opposition in the United States, 1780-1840* (1969).

Ralph Ketcham, *James Madison: A Biography* (1971).

Drew McCoy, *The Elusive Republic: Political Economy in Jeffersonian America* (1980).

Peter S. Onuf, *Jefferson's Empire: The Language of American Nationhood* (2000).

Bradford Perkins, *Prologue to War: England and the United States, 1805-1812* (1961).

James P. Ronda, *Lewis and Clark Among the Indians* (1984).

Adam Rothman, *Slave Country: American Expansion and the Origins of the Deep South* (2005).

Marshal Smelser, *The Democratic Republic, 1801-1815* (1968).

J.C.A. Stagg, *Mr. Madison's War: Politics, Diplomacy, and Warfare in the Early Republic, 1783-1830* (1983).

John Sugden, *Tecumseh's Last Stand* (1985).

Robert W. Tucker and David C. Hendrickson, *Empire of Liberty: The Statecraft of Thomas Jefferson.*

Steven Watts, *The Republic Reborn: War and the Making of Liberal America, 1790-1820* (1987).

Chief Justice John Marshall

Chapter Ten

ERA OF GOOD FEELINGS, 1815-1829

Born in 1793 on the island of Nantucket in Massachusetts, Lucretia Coffin Mott would become one of the antebellum period's most influential and powerful voices for social justice. In the vanguard of the pre-Civil War women's rights movement, she also became one of the most fervent and revered leaders of the antislavery movement. Her Quaker faith and ideals strongly influenced her activism, but so did the evidence all around her—including the actions of her own family members—of slavery's impact on the young Republic.

Reared in a devout Quaker household, Mott spent the first eleven years of her life exposed to the passionate Quakerism of her parents (Thomas and Anna Folger Coffin) while growing up in Nantucket's tight Quaker community. Both constantly urged her to embrace the dignity and quality of all people, male and female, black and white. Perhaps most important, by the late eighteenth century, the Quakers had emerged as the most outspoken critics of human bondage in the young nation. Indeed, as early as 1774, some Quaker meetings had begun expelling members who owned slaves. Lucretia Coffin was educated in Quaker schools, including the Friends Boardinghouse School at Poughkeepsie, New York, where she began as a student before becoming an assistant teacher. While working at the Friends Boardinghouse School, that she met fellow Quaker and future husband James Mott who shared Coffin's passionate devotion to human justice. Before marrying Mott, Lucretia returned home to her parents' house in 1809. By that time, the elder Coffins had moved to Philadelphia, into the heart of Quaker activism in the United States.

Although the Coffins were devout Quakers, Thomas Coffin earned his livelihood within the northern economy, which had numerous ties, direct and indirect, to slavery. He captained of a whaling ship that also engaged in the China trade. Coffin neither owned nor directly trafficked in slaves. Nonetheless, he almost certainly carried food supplies to the Caribbean slave islands (a trade that Quakers had engaged in since the founding of Pennsylvania in the early 1680s and a relationship William Penn had actively encouraged and promoted) and to the West African slaving ports he passed on his way to China. Lucretia's mother, Anna, maintained a family store where she sold goods acquired on Thomas' voyages, many of which were either made by slaves or Africans involved in the slave trade, or were passed along from slave captains to other seafaring men such as Thomas Coffin. Prior to moving to Philadelphia, the elders Coffins had moved from Nantucket to Boston in 1804. Beginning in that year, Thomas had expanded his business to include the burgeoning southern cotton trade. Even before the War of 1812, some of the most prosperous New England merchant families already began experimenting with textile mills (using southern cotton) that would soon power the northeastern manufacturing economy. After moving to Philadelphia, Thomas opened a hardware store with Lucretia's husband James, and the two men most certainly had southern planters as customers.

Lucretia Mott later recalled that her "sympathy was early enlisted for the poor slave, by the class-books read in our schools, and the pictures of the slave-ship," but it may have been in Philadelphia, under the influence of the radical Quaker preacher Elias Hicks and others, that Mott began to reflect on her own personal involvement with slavery. By this time within Philadelphia's Quaker community, there had emerged members, such as Hicks, who insisted that opposing slavery meant more than just speaking out against the institution, refusing to own slaves, or helping to emancipate and educate them. It also included cleansing one's own life of all the luxuries made possible by slave labor. Lucretia embraced Hicks' exhortations, as well as those of the English Quaker Elizabeth Heyrick, whose **Immediate, Not Gradual Abolition** *advocated the same position. After the War of 1812, Lucretia and James began boycotting commodities produced by slave labor, chiefly cotton and sugar. Substitutes for such staples were hard to procure, but the Motts persevered. James severed all business ties with southern planters and any Yankee merchants involved in the slave trade, no matter how peripherally. The move adversely affected his hardware business, but like his wife, he was committed to the antislavery cause and thus willing to make the sacrifices essential to bring about slavery's end in the United States. In 1826, the Motts helped form the Philadelphia Free Produce Society to help not just Quakers, but all abolitionists find alternative choices to slave products.*

Lucretia Mott fought slavery all her life. However, much to her disappointment, the free produce movement she helped establish did not prove a very effective tool in the antislavery campaign. The organization suffered from lack of internal support. Many members simply didn't consider a boycott strong enough or a direct enough measure against the towering crimes of slavery. Although free produce advocates opened additional stores in the middle and northeastern states to sell goods manufactured from cotton grown by free labor (which at the time proved to be a monumental effort because most of the world's cotton was grown by some sort of slave, or indentured, or serf labor), most Northerners understood that it would take political action, not consumer boycotts, to abolish slavery in the United States. Nonetheless, people like Lucretia Mott remained in the forefront of the antislavery crusade in the antebellum United States.

In the post-War of 1812, white Americans, North and South, became a briefly united people as feelings of good will and national pride appeared to bond all behind a common purpose: to develop their country economically while creating a uniquely American identity, reflecting their democratic and republican ideals of egalitarianism, self-reliance, and public virtue. Helping to sustain such sentiments was the security that Americans now felt after having stood up to the greatest power in the world, Great Britain, for a second time. No longer fearing the possibility of England re-conquering its lost "colonies," Americans demanded that their country be respected as a legitimate nation. The British accepted this reality and displayed a willingness to establish a rapprochement with the United States which, over the course of the next century, proved beneficial to both countries. Meanwhile, the United States began a drive toward dominance in Latin America via the Monroe Doctrine, first declared during the 1820s, leading to U.S. economic preeminence over much of the Western Hemisphere by the turn of the twentieth century.

Political divisions and the rancor of party politics that had caused such tension and hostility among the ruling elite during the 1790s also momentarily left the national landscape. By the 1820 election, the first party system had ended with the dissolution of the Federalist Party, allowing the creation in the immediate postwar years of a democratic republic free from the self-serving partisanship that had polarized the American people. Causing much of the party heat and factionalism had been the ideological and personal conflict between Thomas Jefferson and Alexander Hamilton, which became a titanic struggle to determine the nation's political and economic direction. Even before Hamilton's death in a duel with Aaron Burr, Jeffersonianism had prevailed as the majority of the American people, especially outside of New England, embraced the Jeffersonian agrarian agenda. However, much of the Hamiltonian vision and initiatives would be resurrected during the subsequent "Era of Good Feelings" in the form of Henry Clay's American System. Like Hamilton, Clay sought to create a self-sufficient U.S. economy free from dependence on primarily British manufactured goods. In the process, he hoped to develop a sense of economic nationalism and unity based on mutual, regional interdependence and specialization that would mitigate the potential for sectionalism caused by slavery's rejuvenation in the post-1815 period.

HENRY CLAY'S AMERICAN SYSTEM

Among the most prominent members of the nation's second generation of political leaders, **Henry Clay** of Kentucky was perhaps the most passionate. He was also determined to see the United States become economically self-sufficient at home, as well as the most dominant country in the Western Hemisphere. A fervent expansionist for both economic and imperialistic reasons, Clay was a **neo-Federalist** who believed in the necessity of implementing the Hamiltonian vision and agenda. Thus, beginning in 1816 from his position as Speaker of the House and during the course of his public service (he held every major office in the national government except the presidency, for which he ran unsuccessfully three times), Clay formulated the revival of the Hamiltonian agenda. Calling his version of Hamilton's program the "**American System**," he believed his plan would foster national economic growth and self-sufficiency within a salutary regional interdependence that would minimize sectional tensions while further promoting a nationalist spirit. Clay's program called for the same government-sponsored initiatives that Hamilton had conceived during the 1790s: protective tariffs, internal improvements, and a national banking system. Like Hamilton, Clay believed such policies were imperative for both domestic economic development and political stability, as well as for national security, and was confident that, over time, the American System would create a self-sufficient U.S. economy.

In the aftermath of the War of 1812, Clay believed the stabilization of the nation's currency and financial institutions should be Congress' first order of business. Thus, in 1816, largely the result of Clay's persistent lobbying, Congress initiated the first program toward establishing Clay's American System by chartering the **Second Bank of the United States** to be headquartered in Philadelphia. Congress empowered the new bank with even greater monetary and financial control over the nation's economy than given the first bank 25 years earlier. The new bank's charter was similar to the original in that the government would be its main depositor, and the Bank's notes would circulate within the nation as legal tender, acceptable as legitimate payment for the purchase of government land and payment of taxes. The federal government would own one-fifth of the Bank's notes. The bill also authorized the establishment of national bank branches as the need arose relative to regional economic development. Clay believed it was time for the nation to move toward a stable national currency and to centralize control of money and credit.

Much to the dismay of Clay and his supporters, the number of state banks grew astronomically during the Era of Good Feelings, which not only challenged Clay's attempt to establish a uniform currency and federally-controlled banking system, but also competed with the national bank for customers by printing "cheap money"—unregulated and grossly inflated notes—that could easily upset Clay's efforts to stabilize the nation's financial institutions and threaten to plunge the post war economy into chaos. For over a decade, the Second Bank of the United States was able to mitigate the potential for financial disaster that the state banks represented. However, from the moment Congress chartered the national bank, the institution found itself engaged in a running battle with state banks and local interests in an effort to impose direction on the economy. The conflict between the Second Bank of the United States and the state banks would later reach a climax during the presidency of Andrew Jackson, who made the destruction of the national bank, for both political and personal reasons, his own personal mission.

Protective tariffs and federally-funded internal improvements provided the two other cornerstones of Clay's American System. In 1816, with the help of John C. Calhoun of South Carolina (soon to be one of the most powerful second-generation national leaders), Congress passed the first overtly protective tariff in U.S. history. The **Tariff of 1816** raised duties on foreign (primarily English-made) manufactured goods by an average of 25 percent in order to safeguard the nation's infant industries from foreign competition, which meant the prevention of English-made products from dominating American consumer markets. Like Hamilton, Clay believed high protective tariffs essential for the promotion of domestic industrial development. Without them, American manufacturers simply could not survive, let alone compete with British-made commodities. Americans living in the Northeast and West embraced protectionism, arguing that wartime privations demonstrated the folly of depending on imported manufactures. Most Southerners, however, viewed the tariff with disdain, believing it hampered their ability to export crops because nations would often retaliate with tariffs of their own on American cotton.

Although the bank and tariff bills sailed through Congress in 1816, supporters of a federally-funded national infrastructure system experienced much greater difficulty as members of Congress surprisingly divided along sectional or regional lines. All agreed that the nation's transportation system was woefully underdeveloped. The issue became who should build the network—the individual states, who wanted such systems in place primarily for their own benefit, or the national government, which could prevent any one region from dominating such enterprises. Congressmen discussed and debated a variety of undertakings. Some urged the completion of the National Road (started before the war) linking the Chesapeake with the Trans-Appalachian West. Others promoted an inland canal system to connect the northern and southern coastal states. Still others pushed for a federally-subsidized turnpike from Maine to Georgia. Congress agreed to finish the National Road, but President James Madison and his Republican successor, James Monroe, both refused to support further projects without a constitutional amendment, which they believed was necessary to build any infrastructure across state boundaries. Much to Henry Clay's disappointment, the "transportation revolution" that began during the Era of Good Feelings did not become part of his federally-sponsored American System. Rather, the network emerging after

1815 reflected the designs of the most ambitious states, particularly those of the Northeast that, by the end of the 1820s, possessed the most advanced and expansive infrastructure in the nation.

THE TRANSPORTATION REVOLUTION

In 1815, transportation facilities ranged from the primitive to the non-existent as Americans despaired of the difficulty in traveling or communicating with one another over long distances, not to mention trying to do business or trade on a national scale. So many obstacles existed to transporting goods overland over long distances that farmers and craftsmen could ship their commodities more cheaply across the Atlantic Ocean than moving those same goods only 30 miles inland. The cost of transporting wheat from the new settlement in Buffalo to New York City was three times greater than the selling price of wheat in New York. Profitable farming only existed for those farmers near urban markets or with easy river access to the coast. In the Trans-Appalachian West, farmers and merchants made use of the tributaries of the Ohio-Mississippi River system to transport their goods on homemade flatboats to New Orleans, and then shipping their commodities to New York or other eastern seaports. After selling their goods, the boatmen (including a young Abraham Lincoln) knocked down their flatboats, sold the lumber and then walked home to Kentucky or Ohio on the dangerous path known as the Natchez Trace.

Transporting goods between western settlements proved even more difficult, with most keelboat men like the legendary Mike Fink having to navigate upstream using eddies and back currents. Most of the time, however, they had to pole their way upstream or sail if they could catch a rare wind. Skilled crews averaged only 15 miles a day, and the trip from New Orleans to Louisville took three or four months. Downstream, the trip took about a month. Either way, the cargo sizes of keelboats were quite limited.

Beginning with the conclusion of the War of 1812, dramatic improvements in transportation—more and better roads, steamboats, canals, and finally railroads—started to appear, tying old communities together more firmly while penetrating previously isolated neighborhoods for the first time. These positive developments made the transition to a market economy physically possible. In 1815, the United States was an overwhelming rural and agrarian nation. When the Civil War began 45 years later, the country remained so despite the establishment of significantly improved transportation and communication systems in the intervening decades. Nonetheless, the growing nation, especially in the North and West, promoted advancements that greatly enhanced and accelerated economic development.

Steamboats

While the construction and completion of roads and turnpikes made the transport of goods inland easier and less time consuming, the majority of farmers living in the interior of the country still found river use to be the most efficient way to move their products as the cost over the roads remained prohibitive. The economic life of western farmers changed dramatically for the better, however, when the inventor and entrepreneur **Robert Fulton** launched the steamboat *Clermont* on a 150-mile upstream trip along the Hudson River from New York City to Albany in 1807. Fulton's successful introduction of this new mode of river transportation ignited a steamboat craze as scores of individuals and companies built steamboats and offered their services to farmers, craftsmen, and merchants in need of river transport for their wares. Over the next few years, steamboat builders developed flat-bottom craft that could navigate rivers at even low water. By 1817, seventeen steamboats plied the western waterways. In that year, the *Washington* made the New Orleans to Louisville run in 25 days. Thanks to Fulton and other steamboat men, western farmers and merchants could transport their products at much cheaper rates up and down the nation's interior river systems with few restraints. "Fulton's Folly," as many labeled the *Clermont*, proved to be one of the most important innovations of the post-war transportation revolution, transforming the nation's interior from an isolated frontier into a busy commercial region trading farm and plantation products for manufactured goods. The steamboat reduced the total cost of river transport of goods per ton-mile from 6.1 cents to a third of a cent by 1830. By the close of the 1820s, steamboats traveled from Cincinnati to New Orleans, then passed goods on to coastal ships that finished the trip to New York City in a total of 28 days. Prior to the advent of steamboat, the same journey took at minimum 58 days. Such improvements in speed and economy made a national market economy possible.

The Canal Boom

The best example of "Yankee ingenuity" and northern entrepreneurship was New York's construction of the Erie Canal. Begun in 1819 and completed in 1825, the canal was the brainchild of DeWitt Clinton. With other state boosters, Clinton promoted the canal with the design of capturing the farm trade of the Old Northwest by linking the Hudson River with Lake Erie in western New York. Northwest farmers and tradesmen would transport their products to the Hudson River via the canal then ship their goods downriver to New York City. They could also receive goods in the reverse direction.

The **Erie Canal** was the most impressive engineering feat of the antebellum period. Designed by self-taught engineers and built by gangs of Irish immigrants, local farm boys, and convict laborers, it stretched 364 miles between Lake Erie and Albany. Passing over eighteen rivers on stone aqueducts, the canal required a complex system of eighty-three locks. With revenues generated from usage fees, New York's investment of $7.5 million eventually would be repaid many times over. The canal transformed the previously-isolated region, bringing a host of market towns into existence along its route, including Buffalo, Rochester, and Syracuse.

The Erie Canal inspired other northern states to build similar projects, igniting a canal boom that lasted for 20 years. When New Yorkers began construction on their canal, fewer than 100 miles of canals existed in the entire country. By 1840, there were 3,300 miles, nearly all of them in the North. Ohio engaged in the most ambitious canal-building frenzy, linking frontier areas to Erie Canal. In 1835, Pennsylvania completed a canal from Philadelphia to Pittsburgh, although at one point goods were shifted onto an unwieldy railroad that crossed a mountain. Canals greatly reduced both costs and travel time for their users. For example, the Ohio canal system allowed Cincinnati merchants to send goods northward through Ohio, across Lake Erie, over the Erie Canal, and down the Hudson to New York City, an all-water route that took 18 days. By 1830 improved transportation had created made a market revolution.

Though imports and exports increased after the War of 1812, America's dependence on foreign trade declined noticeably in the postwar years. Exports, which had driven American economic growth up to 1815, continued to expand, reaching over $100 million by 1830, (largely due to southern cotton, which had replaced northern food crops as the nation's leading export). Imports also rose, especially of European (primarily British) manufactured goods, rising to almost $200 million by the close of the 1820s. Although foreign trade increased during the postwar period, the number of foreign countries with which the United States traded actually decreased, representing less dependency on foreign market activity to sustain the nation's economy. Before 1815, Americans had exported about 15 percent of their total national product; by 1830, exports accounted for only 6 percent of total production. The reason for this shift was simple: the United States had finally developed self-sustaining domestic markets for farm produce and manufactured goods. The great engine of economic growth—particularly in the North and West—was not the colonial relationship with Europe, but rather a burgeoning internal market.

JUDICIAL NATIONALISM AND THE MARKET REVOLUTION

The transition to a market economy generated some of the most important Supreme Court decisions in U.S. history, often resolving cases in ways that tended to promote the entrepreneurial use of private property, the sanctity of contracts, and the right to do business protected from provincial restraints and the vagaries of democratic politics. As noted in the previous chapter, no Chief Justice did more to promote and protect the concepts of an independent judiciary, including the prerogative of judicial review, than John Marshall, who served from 1801 to 1835. From the moment he put on his black robe, Marshall made it his mission to establish the High Court as a conservative bulwark against the excesses of democratically-elected state legislatures. From 1816 onward, Marshall focused on encouraging and protecting private enterprise, particularly from encroachments by state governments, while simultaneously continuing to strengthen the power of the national government at the expense of the states. Marshall's most important decisions in this capacity protected the sanctity of contracts and corporate charters against state legislatures who, in the name of democracy, wanted them revised or abolished.

In *Dartmouth College v. Woodward* (1816), the school found itself having to defend its original 1760s royal charter against a Republican-dominated New Hampshire legislature determined for political reasons to transform Dartmouth from a perceived Federalist bastion of privilege and elitism into a more "democratic" or egalitarian state institution. Specifically, when the Federalist-dominated board of trustees fired the college's new president, John Wheelock, a Republican, the legislature attempted to modify Dartmouth's charter by allowing the governor to add new board members and creating a review board with the power to veto trustee decisions. By such actions, the legislature basically sought to convert Dartmouth from a private to a public educational institution. Daniel Webster, another of the second generation's stalwart leaders and a Dartmouth alumnus, defended his alma mater passionately against the state's usurpation. By one account, possibly apocryphal, Webster ended his plea after a long dramatic pause by simply stating: "It is, sir, as I have said, a small college. And yet, there are those who love it," which reputedly moved the Chief Justice to tears. Regardless of the story's validity, Marshall ruled with the majority that Dartmouth's original charter of incorporation could not be altered by a state legislature. Although in this case the Court was protecting Dartmouth's independence and chartered privileges from state infringement, Marshall and Webster (both Federalists) knew that the Court's decision went beyond simply Dartmouth College—that the decision also applied to other private universities chartered before independence (the majority of the Ivy League schools) and to the hundreds of private companies engaged in canal, road, bridge, and turnpike construction holding privileges under corporate charters granted by state governments. According to the *Dartmouth* decision, once such charters had been issued, the states could neither regulate the corporations nor cancel their immunities. Thus, for a time, corporate charters acquired the legal status of contracts beyond the reach of democratic politics, though many states later inserted statements specifically declaring that charter provisions could be subject to modification. Further, by the end of the nineteenth century, future Supreme Courts would determine that certain situations existed to permit the states to revise corporate charters to advance the public interest. In early the years of the Market Revolution, however, Marshall's ruling in the *Dartmouth* case protected the nation's expanding corporations from political interference.

Two weeks after the *Dartmouth* decision, Marshall handed down the majority opinion in another landmark case, *McCulloch v. Maryland*. The Maryland legislature, dominated by Jeffersonians who questioned the Bank of the United States' constitutionality, attempted to destroy the national bank by taxing bank notes issued by its Baltimore branch. Marshall understood that the tax was simply a clever ploy to try to destroy the Bank, which had challenged the legislature's right to impose such a burden. Marshall wrote for a unanimous Court declaring that the Bank was a legal institution under the Constitution's implied powers. Further, because the Bank existed as a federal agency, it was exempt from all forms of state control, including the right to be taxed. The case represented Marshall's most direct assault on Jeffersonian strict constructionism and states' rights ideology. Americans, he stated, "did not design to make their government dependent on the states." Interestingly, many disagreed with Marshall's assertion. Among the many decrying national sovereignty were those from Marshall's native South who remained certain that the Founders had intended precisely what the Court was challenging—the supremacy of state government power over the national government.

In an important case involving federal government regulation of interstate commerce, *Gibbons v. Ogden* (1824), the Marshall Court dissolved a monopoly granted by the New York state legislature to control the steamboat traffic across the Hudson River to New Jersey. The original receivers of the privilege, Robert Fulton and Robert Livingston, had transferred the monopoly to Aaron Ogden and Thomas Gibbons. After a falling out between the two partners, Ogden held the monopoly grant, but Gibbons soon received a permit to conduct steamboat traffic across the Hudson under the federal Coasting Licensing Act. After Ogden sued Gibbons, the case eventually reached the Supreme Court, where Marshall contended that the state-granted monopoly interfered with federal jurisdiction over interstate commerce. As with his decisions in the previous cases, the Chief Justice used *Gibbons v. Ogden* to reaffirm federal authority over the states while simultaneously encouraging private entrepreneurialism. Marshall was a firm supporter of Clay's American System, believing as a Hamiltonian that a natural and beneficial link existed between federal power and the market economy.

THE TRANSFORMATION OF THE NEW ENGLAND AGRICULTURE

By the outbreak of the War of 1812, millions of trees had been stripped from the New England countryside as Yankee farmers converted from mixed farming to livestock raising. Other New Englanders had tried growing grain on rocky, worn-out soil but could not compete with farmers from western New York and the Old Northwest who had access to more fertile land and distant markets. However, those Yankee farmers who had turned to raising cattle for meat or dairy production found ready consumers for their products in the Northeast's burgeoning factory towns and cities. Many New England farmers also transitioned to poultry and egg farming as well as tending fruit orchards. The growing shoe industry bought leather from cattle growers and wool from sheep raisers. By 1830, there were 4.75 times more sheep than people in Vermont.

The rise of livestock specialization reduced the amount of land under cultivation. Prior to the war, most New Englanders tilled their few acres in the old three-year rotation: corn the first year, rye the second, and fallow the third. By the 1820s, as farmers transitioned from grain farming to livestock raising, the remaining crop land became cultivated more intensely. Farmers saved manure and ashes for fertilizer, plowed more deeply and systematically, and tended their crops more carefully. These improved techniques, along with cash from livestock sales and the increasing availability of food at stores, encouraged Yankee farmers to allocate less land to

Table 10.1 — Major Decisions of the Marshall Court

Date	Case	Significance of Decision
1803	*Marbury v. Madison*	Introduced the doctrine of judicial review
1810	*Fletcher v. Peck*	Protected sanctity of legal contracts from impairment by the states; first time a state law ruled unconstitutional by the U.S. Supreme Court
1819	*Dartmouth College v. Woodward*	Held that private corporate charters are protected from state government interference
1819	*McCulloch v. Maryland*	Upheld the constitutionality of the National Bank, accepting the principle of implied powers; forbade the states from impeding valid constitutional exercises of federal power
1821	*Cohens v. Virginia*	State supreme court decisions in criminal law issues subject to High Court review; asserted the supremacy of federal law over state law, citing the Supremacy Clause of the Constitution
1824	*Gibbons v. Ogden*	States denied concurrent power to regulate interstate commerce with the federal government

growing food crops. The move to livestock transformed woodlands into open pastures. As farmers cleared the forests, they sold the wood to fuel-hungry cities and factories. In 1829, a cord of wood that sold for $1.50 in Maine fetched as much as $7 in Boston. Over the next decade, manufacturers began marketing cast-iron stoves to heat houses more efficiently than open hearths, and canals brought cheap Pennsylvania anthracite coal to the Northeast. Farmers who needed pastureland could garner a substantial one-time profit from the sale of wood. The result was the massive deforestation of New England. In 1790, in the central Massachusetts town of Petersham, forest covered 85 percent of the town lands; by 1830 the forested area had been reduced to 30 percent, the result of the creation of pastureland through commercial woodcutting. The pattern proved the same throughout New England. At the beginning of English colonization in the early seventeenth century, forests encompassed 95 percent of the region; by 1830, they covered only 35 percent of Connecticut, 32 percent of Rhode Island, 40 percent of Massachusetts, 45 percent of Vermont, and 50 percent of New Hampshire.

On such denuded landscape, poor families with many children continued to supplement their incomes with small-scale industrial "outwork," or household manufacturing performed for large distributors who paid for the finished products. Before the 1820s, outworkers used local raw materials like wool, leather, and flax and had spent only their spare time on such work. The days for this so-called "putting-out system," however, were numbered. Beginning in the 1820s, shoe and textile production increasingly occurred in factories, thus outworkers found themselves without an outlet for their hand-made finished goods. Merchant middlemen or wholesalers began providing factories with the raw materials to be converted to finished products. Although outwork still helped poor families to augment their income and maintain a degree of independence, control of their labor had passed to merchants and other agents of the regional economy.

With the shift to specialized market agriculture, New England farmers became customers for necessities that their forbears had produced themselves or acquired through barter. They began to heat their houses with coal dug by Pennsylvania miners, wore cotton cloth and shoes made by factory women in Lowell, Massachusetts, and donned straw hats produced by New Hampshire farm girls. By 1830, many farmers were even buying food. The Erie Canal and the western grain belt sent flour from Rochester into New England communities where grains were no longer grown. Many farmers found it easier to produce specialized crops for market (such as orchard fruits) and to buy butter, cheese, eggs, and vegetables at country stores. Indeed, by the close of the 1820s, general stores stocked with all manner of merchandise, ranging from local farm products to sugar, salt, and coffee to bolts of New England cloth to sacks of western flour, to little "luxuries" such as silverware, dishes, and wall paper, dotted the New England countryside. Such goods were better and usually cheaper than could be made at home. The price for finished cloth, for example, declined six-fold between 1815 and 1830. As a result, spinning wheels and handlooms disappeared from rural households. Farm families preferred pies and bread made from western white flour to the old "Injun" mix of rye and corn meal, and gladly turned their woodlands and unproductive grain fields into cash-producing pastures. Coal replaced wood as fuel and cast-iron stoves replaced the family hearth. By the 1820s and 1830s, northeastern farmers depended on markets in ways that their fathers and grandfathers would have considered dangerous, not only to family welfare, but also to the well-being of the Republic.

MIGRATION INTO THE OLD NORTHWEST

One reason for the Market Revolution's success in the Northeast proved to be the ability of young people, who had little hope of inheriting land in the older settlements, to leave the region for the greater opportunities of owning property and prospering as a farmer in the more fertile Northwest. Between 1815 and 1840—the same year in which Northeastern agriculture transitioned to agribusiness—migrants transformed the Northwest Territory into a bountiful agricultural landscape. In 1789, no American settlers lived in the entire territory. However, in the aftermath of the Treaty of Greenville, white migrants, now safe from Indian attacks, poured into southern and eastern Ohio. By 1800, the populations of Ohio, Indiana, and Illinois reached 267,562. In the postwar years, settlement skyrocketed; by 1830, over 1.4 million residents lived in those three states.

Before 1830, the majority of emigrants to the Old Northwest were southern yeoman farmers, primarily from the upper southern states of Kentucky and Tennessee, as well as the Carolinas and the Chesapeake region. They moved along the Ohio River and up the Muskingum, Miami, Scioto, Wabash, and Illinois Rivers to set up farms in the southern and central areas of Ohio, Indiana, and Illinois. The Northwest's fertility and availability of abundant land attracted these settlers, but so did the absence of slavery, which many wished to escape for moral and economic reasons. To these white yeomen, slavery had blocked their opportunities to improve their lot in the Old South, thus they flooded into the Northwest in the years between 1815 and 1830. As the Methodist preacher Peter Cartwright of Kentucky declared upon arriving in southern Indiana, "I am now clear of the evil of slavery and I can now raise my children to work where work is not thought a degradation." Similar hopes drew thousands of other southern yeomen north of the Ohio River.

Although the majority of the newcomers rejected slavery, they nonetheless maintained their southern folkways, which included a racial disdain for blacks. Like their kinfolk in Kentucky and Tennessee, the farmers of southern Illinois, Indiana, and Ohio remained tied to the river trade and a mode of agriculture that favored free-ranging livestock over cultivated fields. Typical farmers from these regions fenced in a few acres of corn (his principal food staple) and left the rest of his woodland to be roamed by southern hogs known as "razorbacks" and "land sharks." Pork and corn thus remained the two main staples in these farmers' diets.

THE BEGINNING OF NORTHERN INDUSTRIALIZATION

Prior to the War of 1812, Jeffersonians held fast to the idea of keeping the young Republic a rural and agrarian society. In their minds, the Louisiana Purchase helped to secure for generations to come that the United States would indeed remain an agrarian republic. The acquisition of such a vast amount of territory guaranteed that there would be more than ample land available for yeoman farmers to sustain the Jeffersonian ideal. Citizens could expand westward into the rich, new agricultural lands and trade their farm surpluses for European manufactured goods. In this manner they could avoid creating industrial cities, which they were certain would engender all manner of socio-economic tensions among its inhabitants, resulting in class conflict threatening the stability of republican government. However, Jeffersonian economic policies and sanctions against the European belligerents before the war graphically illustrated the inherent flaws of Jeffersonian agrarianism. Federalists had argued in the pre-war period that if the United States did not manufacture its own products and relied on foreign trade to survive, the nation would become vulnerable to the unpredictable occurrences of international conflict and general European economic condition. Manufacturing advocates argued that the nation's abundant water power, particularly the Northeast's fast-running streams, would enable Americans to build their factories across the countryside rather than in urban areas. Such decentralized manufacturing enterprises would provide employment for country women and children, helping to augment the incomes of struggling farmers. On such premises, the Republic's first factories—New England textile mills—were built during the 1820s.

Samuel Slater

The American textile industry originated from a case of industrial espionage—the result of Englishman **Samuel Slater** committing to memory the construction of a water-powered spinning machine invented by another Englishman, Richard Arkwright, in 1769. Arkwright's invention spun yarn and thread, allowing for the mass production of cotton and woolen textiles. As the number of these time- and labor-saving machines proliferated from the minds of English and Scottish inventors during the late eighteenth and early nineteenth centuries, the British government, to protect the nation's lead in industrialization, forbade the machinery or the people who operated such devices from leaving the country. Scores of textile workers, however, defied the law, making their way to North America where they hoped they could sell or apply their knowledge and expertise for much higher pay. One such individual was Samuel Slater, who had served an apprenticeship under Jedediah Strutt, a partner of Arkwright's who had improved on the original machine. Slater arrived in the United States in 1790 and soon found employment with Moses Brown, a Providence, Rhode Island merchant who paid Slater to reconstruct the Arkwright spinning machine.

Slater's first mill in Pawtucket, Rhode Island was a small frame building tucked among the town's houses and craftsmen's shops. Although of limited capacity and confined to spinning cotton yarn, the factory provided work for children in the mill and paid women to weave yarn into cloth in their homes. Slater's mill fulfilled the neo-Federalist vision of avoiding factory towns while providing supplemental income to farm and artisan households. However, as news of the employment opportunities in Slater's mills spread through Rhode Island, he soon found himself inundated, not by children or widows, but by landless, poor male heads of households. As a result, by the early 1800s, Pawtucket had grown into a disorderly, congested, grimy, and semi-impoverished mill town.

To escape having to employ such a desperate workforce, Slater and other mill owners moved out of the towns. In the countryside they created the "**Rhode Island System**" of complete factory villages, which allowed them better control over their operations and their workers. At Slatersville, Rhode Island, Oxford, Massachusetts, and other locations in southern New England, mill owners built whole villages surrounded by company-owned farm land that they rented to the husbands and fathers of their female and child mill workers. Supervisors closely monitored the workplace—activities such as gambling, drinking, and other such "vices" were forbidden. Fathers and older sons either worked on rented farms or as laborers in the mills. By the late 1820s, Slater and other mill owners had dispensed with the putting-out system and were buying power looms, thus transforming the mill villages into disciplined, self-contained factory towns that turned raw cotton into finished cloth. Household independence was fast disappearing for many New Englanders. When President Andrew Jackson visited Pawtucket in 1829, he remarked to Samuel Slater: "I understand you taught us how to spin, so as to rival Great Britain in her manufactures; you set all these thousands of spindles to work, which I have been delighted in viewing, and which have made so many happy, by a lucrative employment." "Yes sir," replied Slater, "I supposed that I gave out the psalm and they have been singing to the tune ever since."

The Waltham System

Samuel Slater was not the only individual who stole British industrial secrets and brought them to the United States. **Francis Cabot Lowell**, a wealthy, cultivated Bostonian, also engaged in such clandestine activity. In 1811, he visited England and toured of British factory towns. Lowell expressed "curiosity" about what he saw in the plants, asking plant managers an assortment of questions. At night, he made secret drawings of the machines he witnessed. Upon returning home, Lowell immediately applied all that he had seen. Joining with other wealthy Bostonians, Lowell formed the Boston Manufacturing Company, popularly known as the **Boston Associates**. In 1813, the Associates built their first mill at Waltham, Massachusetts, and then expanded during the 1820s into Lowell, Lawrence, and other new towns near Boston. The "**Waltham system**" differed from the Rhode Island system in two ways: first, the Associates' mills were heavily capitalized and as fully mechanized as possible; they turned raw cotton into finished cloth with little need for skilled workers. Second, their machines' operatives were exclusively young, single women recruited from the farms of northern New England—farms that had switched to livestock raising and thus had little need for a daughter's labor. The company provided carefully supervised boardinghouses for the young ladies and enforced rules of conduct both in the workplace and in the larger community. The young women worked steadily, never drank, adhered to a curfew, and attended church faithfully. They dressed neatly, often stylishly, and were taught to read and write if they came illiterate. Management encouraged girls already literate to read newspapers and books, and to attend public lectures.

The neatly-built brick mills and prim boardinghouses set within landscaped towns and occupied by sober, well-behaved farm girls reflected the Boston Associates' desire

The Antebellum South and the European Demand for Cotton

Westward expansion in the aftermath of the War of 1812 was mainly propelled by the cotton boon, and in turn motivating white Americans, especially planters with their slaves to move southwestwardly, was the insatiable (primarily English) European demand for cotton, particularly for the more durable short staple variety grown in the southern United States in the antebellum period.

The American South was not the only supplier of cotton for British mills. India, "the gem" of the British Empire, also grew cotton in large quantities, but it was a much finer, less hardy staple that required more intense cultivation. Nonetheless, until the boom in the American South during the 1820s, India was Britain's main source for this most precious commodity—a product serving as the mainstay of the first phase of England's industrial development, providing a finished product they sold world-wide for incredible profit. Without cotton and its bountiful financial returns, British entrepreneurs and textile manufacturers would not have been able to expand as rapidly into other manufacturing enterprises. Cotton was the single most important imported raw resource (along with an abundance of indigenous coal) that catapulted England to the forefront of the 19th century industrial revolution, which Great Britain dominated globally for most of that century. The American South emerged as the single most important foreign player in that development, for by the end of the 1820s, England bought 80 percent of its cotton from southern plantations.

Not only was southern cotton more durable than that grown in India, it was also cheaper for British textile manufacturers to import because of slave labor. Thus, to southern cotton planters, slavery had become an inextricable part of a larger global economy of which they played a most determining role. By 1800, American planters were producing 36 million bales of cotton (compared to the meager 1.5 million in 1790, three years before Eli Whitney's invention of the cotton gin). By 1830, total production had reached 366 million bales, ten times what it had been thirty years earlier. By that year, cotton accounted for roughly half of all U.S. exports. Over the course of the next thirty years, the white fiber would end up responsible for close to 80 percent of all American exports.

Cotton and slaves went hand in hand. As the foreign demand for American cotton increased, so did the requisite number of slaves and the expansion of territory for cotton production. In 1790, there were approximately 700,000 enslaved people in the United States; by 1830 that number had nearly quadrupled to 2 million, and by 1860 the number of slaves would double again to 4 million. As the number of slaves increased commensurate with demand, so did the price for slaves. "Seasoned" field hands could be purchased for about $250 in 1790; by 1830, the first peak year of southern cotton production, a veteran field hand was worth between $1500-1800. In 1790 the majority of slaves lived in Virginia, South Carolina, Maryland, and North Carolina in that order; by 1830 the number of slaves in Maryland had declined while having increased in the newer "cotton" states of Georgia and Alabama, and would continue to do so, along with Mississippi over the next 30 years.

Former slave Charles Ball later recalled that the explosion in the British demand for American cotton not only bolstered the internal slave trade but also determined the kind of slaves planters looked for to purchase. In 1805, Ball overheard another white man advising Ball's owner to take his coffle of slaves to Columbia (South Carolina) or Augusta (Georgia). "The landlord assured my master that at this time slaves were much in demand" in those places. "Purchasers were numerous and prices good; Cotton he said had not been higher for many years, and as a great many persons especially young men, were moving off to the new purchase in Georgia, prime hands were in high demand, for the purpose of clearing the land in the new country—that boys and girls, under twenty, would bring almost any price at present, in Columbia for the purpose of picking the growing crop of cotton, which promised to be very heavy; and as most persons had planted more than their hands would be able to pick, young niggers, who would soon learn to pick cotton were prime articles in the market. As to those more advanced in life, he seemed to think the prospect of selling them at an unusual price, not so good, as they could not so readily become expert cotton pickers. . . . "

Despite the potential profitability for cotton planters, the international market continued to experience boom-bust cycles throughout most of the antebellum period. Price declines could be triggered by any number of factors beyond the control of southern planters: the War of 1812, the collapse of credit in 1819, the volatility of world markets—any of these could and did precipitate dramatic shifts in cotton prices. In the two-month period between October and the end of December 1818, for example, the value of cotton ready for export dropped 26 percent. As the steady growth of cotton cultivation indicates, however, the planters' response to declining prices was not to cut back on cotton cultivation, but to plant even more of the staple.

to build a profitable textile industry without creating a permanent working class. The system established that the young women would work for a few years in a carefully controlled environment and send their wages back to their family. When their tenure ended, the girls were expected to return home and live as country housewives. These young farm women did, in fact, become an efficient, decorous workforce, but the women themselves imposed the propriety, not the mill owners. In order to protect their own reputations, they punished misbehavior and shunned fellow workers with questionable character. Only a few sent their wages home. Instead, most saved their money to use as dowries that their fathers could not afford while others spent their wages on themselves, particularly on books and clothes.

The factory owners believed that the young women's sojourn would simultaneously reinforce the paternalistic positions of themselves and the girl's fathers. To the owners' surprise, their system produced a self-respecting sisterhood of independent, wage-earning women who twice in the 1830s went out on strike, proclaiming that they were not wage slaves but the daughters of free men. A decade later, the girls were in the forefront of the region's nascent labor movement. After their time in the mills, many remained in these burgeoning factory towns, married local men, and became active participants in various antebellum reform movements, reflecting an independence and self-worth not seen in their mothers or in their rural counterparts. Those who returned home to rural neighborhoods remained single longer than their sisters who had stayed at home. They married men about their own age rather than much older men, as young rural women typically wed during the antebellum period. Moreover, the spouses of the "Waltham Girls'" tended to work at something else besides farming. Thus, through the 1830s, the Boston Associates kept their promise to produce cotton cloth profitably without creating a permanent working class. They failed, however, in their concept of shuttling young women from rural to urban paternalism and back again. Wage labor, the ultimate degradation for agrarian-republican men, became a liberating dynamic for thousands of young women from both rural and urban patriarchy.

The Northern Urban Commercial Classes

The Market Revolution greatly impacted American cities—the old seaports as well as the newer inland manufacturing and commercial towns. In such enclaves, the concern for creating a classless industrial society disappeared. Vastly wealthy financiers, along with an emerging middle class of merchants, craftsmen, small shopkeepers, and professionals, lived and worked amidst the impoverished men and women who produced the ever-expanding range of consumer goods. The richest men in the old seaport cities proved to be merchants who had survived and prospered during the European wars. They continued their various import-export enterprises, with many using their profits to diversify into banking, insurance, and urban real estate, becoming even richer in the process. By the 1820s, this new capitalist elite had solidified their socio-economic and political power, becoming an entrenched, privileged class. In Boston, an extended network of well-educated, urbane, and responsible families known as the Brahmins took control of the city, holding power for the rest of the century. The elite in New York and Philadelphia were less cohesive patriarchs and became more legendary for their self-serving, acquisitive, and ostentatious lifestyles than their Boston counterparts. Nonetheless, they were just as wealthy (if not more so) as their Boston brethren and just as embedded in their power. Regardless of locale, these families earned the bulk of their incomes from international commerce, profiting mainly from cotton exports and a vastly expanding range of imports.

Below the old mercantile elite were the various members of the burgeoning middle class of wholesale and retail merchants, the master craftsmen who had transformed themselves into manufacturers, and an army of lawyers, salesman, auctioneers, clerks, bookkeepers, and accountants who took care of the paperwork for the new market society. The wholesale merchants in the seaport cities who

Located in Pawtucket, Rhode Island, Slater Mill was the first cotton mill in the United States.

bought hardware, crockery, and other commodities from importers and then sold them in smaller lots to interior storekeepers proved to be the most prosperous and affluent members of this new middle class. Slightly below them were the large processors of farm products, such as Cincinnati's meatpackers and Rochester's flour millers, as well as the large merchants and realtors in the interior's growing cities. Another step down the middle-class ladder appeared the specialty retailers—storeowners who dealt in books, furniture, crockery, or other consumer products. Alongside this array of merchants stood the master craftsmen who had become larger-scale manufacturers of shoes, crockery, leather goods, and an ever-increasing number of consumer products once produced by a single individual helped his apprentice helpers. With their workers busy in backrooms or in household workshops, they now called themselves shoe dealers and merchant tailors. At the bottom of this commercial world were the hordes of clerks, most of them young men who hoped to rise in the world by providing their much-needed services. Both in numbers and in the nature of the work, these white-collar workers formed a new class created by the Market Revolution.

In the 1820s and 1830s, the work of these various commercial classes changed the look and feel of northern cities. Indeed, the Market Revolution not only stimulated antebellum northern urbanization but also redefining and re-oriented the physical landscape of the cities themselves. With the number and variety of new enterprises proliferating, many cities witnessed the concentration of similar businesses in specific locales. As retailing and manufacturing became separate activities, the merchants, salesmen, and clerks now worked in quiet downtown offices. In New York City, wholesalers began to congregate in one district along Pearl Street while meatpackers in Cincinnati operated in a stipulated city-space along the Ohio River. The capitalist proprietors also began to differentiate their respective businesses' activities. Seaport merchants, for example, had "counting rooms," marketing or advertising rooms, and some even had a display room for their products. In such particularized areas, workers specialized in the business-related activity for which the room had been named. These new bourgeois classes also took great pride in their enterprises' physical appearance, with many wanting to make their store fronts, warehouses, or places of business as pleasing to the eye as possible. Decorating one's endeavor became the rage among many urban businessmen, such as the seaport merchants of Philadelphia and Baltimore who adorned their warehouses in the new counting-house style. Both in the nation's older cities and in the newer interior towns, impressive brick and glass store fronts appeared on the main streets. Perhaps the most striking monuments of the self-conscious new middle class were the handsome new retail arcades (in many ways the nation's first shopping malls) that began to appear in the 1820s. Boston's Quincy Market (1825), a two-story arcade on Philadelphia's Chestnut Street (1827), and Rochester's four-story Reynolds Arcade (1828) pro-

The putting-out system could not match the productivity of the new factories.

vided consumers with comfortable, gracious spaces in which to shop.

Urban Industrialization

In 1815, wealthy Americans wore tailor-made clothing; everyone else wore clothes sewn by women at home. However, by the 1820s, as a result of the availability of cheap manufactured cloth and an expanding pool of cheap labor (largely female) along with the creation of the southern and western domestic markets, New York City became the center for the manufacturing of ready-made clothes. The New Yorkers' first big clients were southern planters who bought "Negro cottons"—graceless, hastily-assembled shirts, pants, and sack dresses for their slaves. Within a few years, however, New York manufacturers were sending similar low-grade clothing—dungarees and hickory shirts—to western farmers while supplying shoddy, inexpensive attire to the growing ranks of northeastern urban workers. By the 1830s, many New York tailoring houses, including the storied Brooks Brothers, offered fancier ready-made clothes to the more affluent members of the new middle class.

High rents, costly real estate, and the absence of water power made it impossible to establish large factories in cities. However, the nature of the clothing trade and the availability of cheap labor, both rural and urban, gave rise to an outsourcing system that transformed needlework into the nation's first "sweatshops." New York clothing merchants kept a few skilled male tailors in house to take care of their more affluent customers. They also retained a few semi-skilled workers to cut cloth into patterned pieces for ready-made clothing. The merchants then gave work to subcontractors, who then hired female needleworkers to sew the cloth together in their homes. Thus the labor done on the cheap goods sent South and West was performed by women who worked long hours for piece rates that ranged from 75 cents to a $1.50 per week. By 1860, Brooks Brothers, which by then dominated the high end of the trade, kept 70 workers in its shops (mostly male) and used two to three thousand outworkers (mostly women) to produce their less expensive attire. Along with clothing, women in garrets and tenements also manufactured items which adorned middle-class homes such as embroidery, doilies, artificial flowers, fringe, tassels, fancy-bound books, and parasols. All such work provided employment and income, albeit meager, for legions of female workers. By 1860, female workers made up one-fourth of the total workforce employed in manufacturing jobs in New York City, with two-thirds of them laboring in the clothing industry.

During the antebellum period, shoe production followed a similar pattern. Like tailoring, shoemaking was divided into skilled operations and tedious unskilled tasks. Men performed the relatively skilled and highly paid task of cutting and shaping the uppers while low-wage female workers undertook the drudgery of sewing the pieces together. In the shops of Lynn, Massachusetts, the shoemaker's boarding houses in Rochester, and the cellars and garrets of New York City, subcontractors hired and controlled the production of poorly paid, unskilled workers. A skilled "cobbler" could earn as much as $2 a day making custom boots and shoes, while men shaping uppers in boarding houses made a little more than half that amount. Women binders could work a full week, 10 hours a day, and earn as little as 50 cents for their labor. In the shoe industry, as in other trades, wage rates and gendered tasks reflected the old family division of labor, based on the assumption that female workers lived with an income-earning husband or father thus no need existed to pay them a livable wage. In reality, the majority of women who sought such employment were young, single women, living alone, or older women who had been widowed, divorced, or abandoned—often with small children.

In their offices, counting rooms, and shops, the range of members of the new middle class sought to identify and separate themselves according to how they earned their living, with most of them priding themselves on the fact that they earned their livelihoods not with their hands but with their heads. Even lowly clerks, most of whom earned less than a skilled shoemaker or tailor, felt superior to such individuals. In short, as early as the 1820s, American society already distinguished between "white" and "blue" collar workers, with the former certain that their entrepreneurial and managerial skills, along with their education, drove the Market Revolution. Manual or blue collar workers simply performed the tasks envisioned by the middle class. The old distinction between proprietorship and dependence—a delineation that placed master craftsmen and independent tradesmen, along with farm-owning yeomen, among the respectable middling sort—disappeared. The men and women of the emerging working class struggled to create dignity and a sense of public worth in a society that hid them from view and defined them as "hands."

SLAVERY AND THE MARKET REVOLUTION IN THE SOUTH

The southern cotton belt expanded dramatically in the decades after the War of 1812. The resumption of international trade, the revival of British and continental textile manufacturing, the emergence of factory production in the northeastern United States, and the removal of Indians from the southwest encouraged southern planters to extend the short-staple cotton lands westward across the Old Southwest and beyond the Mississippi into Texas and Arkansas. The speed at which this expansion occurred startled contemporaries.

Southern Planters and Paternalism

The owners of the South's largest plantations were among the richest men in the Western Hemisphere. In 1860, the twelve wealthiest counties in the United States were located in the South, with the richest being Adams County along the Mississippi River in western Mississippi. However, in the years before the Civil War, southern wealth became increasingly more concentrated in fewer households. The slaves whose labor created such extravagance owned nothing, and one-third of southern white families lived in poverty. In 1830, 36 percent of southern white households owned at least one slave.

Most antebellum southern historians recount that a growing belief in the virtues of "**paternalism**" increasingly took hold among many masters after 1820. The term describes the attitude of masters who believed that holding the slaves was in their best interest, often referring to their slaves as children needing constant protection, supervision, and discipline. Because cotton required a more intense focus than other crops, masters and overseers rigorously scrutinized the slaves' labor. Masters or overseers became more inclined to "correct" (punish) slaves whose work they believed was sloppy or slow. At the same time, however, slave owners disguised the harsher discipline within a larger image that they wanted to project to the outside world—that American slavery was a system of labor concerned with the slaves' physical well-being as well as their emotional and psychological welfare. Thus, beginning in the 1820s, the quality and diversity of slave clothing and food appeared to improve on many plantations, and individual cabins for slave families became standard. Many southern states passed laws protecting slaves from brutal physical abuse as punishment or discipline (though rarely enforced), and many owners granted slaves the Sabbath as a day free from work in order to dedicate time for religious instruction (Christian indoctrination). Indeed, the 1820s marked the decade in which an evangelical fervor swept through the South, affecting many planters. Wanting their slaves to feel spiritually uplifted, planters often invited evangelical preachers to their plantations to preach the Gospel.

The systemic paternalism resulted from both planter self-interest and, for the majority of slave owners, a genuine desire to develop a more benevolent system of control over their slaves who they began to refer to as "our people," or "our family, black and white." As recorded in his diary, Louisiana planter Bennet H. Barrow professed a belief that masters must make their slaves "as comfortable at home as possible, affording them what is essentially necessary for their happiness—you must provide for them yourself and by that means create in them a habit of perfect dependence on you." Thus, according to Barrow (and other slave-owning paternalists), masters should improve the slaves' quality of life and overall treatment, which would then hopefully instill in slaves greater loyalty to their masters. Slaves would no longer view their condition as harsh and brutal if they experienced a life in which they enjoyed a modicum of humane treatment and respect for their dignity. For many slave owners, paternalism became a more effective means of controlling their slaves through benevolent care and solicitude rather than through the use of the whip or other forms of punishment. In reality, paternalism often served merely as a justification (either conscience or subconscious) for holding slaves and profiting from their labor. Barrow's diary, for example, contains almost daily references to the beating and torturing of his slaves, accompanied by moral platitudes pronouncing why such treatment, in his opinion, was necessary.

The Organization of Slave Labor

The South's cotton plantations were among the most commercialized farming communities in the world. Many of them grew nothing but cotton, a practice that produced huge profits in good years but sent planters into debt, often forcing them to sell land and slaves during periods of bad weather. Other plantations grew supplemental cash crops and produced their own food. Regardless of size or orientation, all cotton planters who used slave labor—from the proudest grandee to the ambitious small farmer with a few slaves—organized their workers in ways that maximized production while simultaneously asserting and reinforcing white dominance and control.

Cotton cultivation required a long growing season with constant care. Slave labor, along with the Deep South's hot, humid climate, proved well-suited for the crop's profitable production. After clearing the land and planting the seeds, laborers weeded the fields with hoes throughout the warm summer months. In the fall, the cotton ripened unevenly. In a harvest season that lasted two months, pickers swept through the fields repeatedly, selecting only the ripe bolls. Meanwhile, slaves laboring on plantations growing their own food cultivated large cornfields and vegetable gardens and tended to the ample numbers of hogs.

Planters established complex labor regimens to cope with diverse growing seasons and killing times that overlapped with the cotton-growing cycle. Many northern and European visitors to the large plantation operations were amazed by how systematized and regimented slave labor had become. First came the hoe gang: "Forty of the largest and strongest women I ever saw together; they were all in a single uniform dress of bluish check stuff, and skirts reaching little below the knee; their legs and feet were bare; they carried themselves loftily, each with a hoe sloping over their shoulder and walking with a free powerful swing." Following the hoe gang was "the cavalry, thirty strong, mostly men, but some women, two of whom rode astride, on the plow mules." Although this slave force was larger than most, its organization was familiar to every Southerner: gangs of women wielded the hoes and men did the plowing, accompanied, especially during the busiest times, by strong women who rode "astride" (not like white ladies, who rode sidesaddle). The division of labor by sex was standard. Even at harvest festivals, teams of men shucked the corn while women prepared the meal and planned the after-supper dance. During the harvest, when every slave was in the fields, men often worked beside men, and women beside women. Female field hands often worked under the plantation mistress' direction, tending to the dairy cattle, chickens, geese, vegetable gardens, and orchards.

While black women routinely worked in the fields, their white counterparts did so only on the more marginal farms during the busiest times of the year. Like their northern cousins, white farm women took care of the poultry and cattle and the vegetable gardens rather than the profit-oriented fields. As the larger farms grew into plantations, white women took on the task of the household management of slaves (usually females), parceling out the different chores many once did themselves. According to northern visitors, southern whites were becoming "lazy" because they increasingly associated most manual labor with "slave" or "Negro work," thus work in the South was losing the dignity that it enjoyed in other parts of the nation.

Southern Yeoman Farmers

The Market Revolution commercialized southern agriculture, but as the antebellum period progressed, fewer southern whites shared in its benefits. The result was not just an unequal distribution of wealth but the creation of a dual economy: plantations at the commercial center and white small free-holding farmers. There were, of course, small farmers living in the plantation belts, with most living on poor, hilly land far from navigable rivers. They engaged in small-scale commercial cotton planting, producing a few bales with family labor and maybe a couple of slaves. Many were the poor kinfolk of prosperous planters. Because of their family ties, they voted for the great planters, used their cotton gins, and tapped into their marketing networks. Some worked as overseers for their wealthier relatives, sold them food, and served on local slave patrols. The economic gap between planters and farmers in the cotton belts widened during the antebellum period, but the smaller farmers nonetheless remained tied to the cotton economy and its socio-cultural imperatives.

The majority of southern plain folk lived in the "Upcountry—the eastern slopes of the Appalachians, the western slopes of the Kentucky and Tennessee mountains, the pine-covered hill country of northern Mississippi and Alabama, and most of the Ozark Plateau in Arkansas and Missouri—far away from the plantation belts. These areas were too high, cold, isolated, or heavily-wooded to support cotton cultivation. In these regions, farmers built a yeoman society that shared many of the characteristics of the eighteenth century countryside. However, with the rise of the cotton kingdom in the 1820s, small southern farmers found themselves unable to commercialize their farms as many Northerners had begun doing. They continued in a household- and neighborhood-centered agriculture through the Civil War. Indeed, many of these farmers stayed out of the market entirely. The mountain folk of the southern Appalachians sent a trickle of livestock and timber out of their neighborhoods, but the mountains remained isolated from the market until the coming of corporate coal mines in the late nineteenth century. Moreover, most upcountry plain folk preferred to raise livestock than to grow cotton or tobacco. They planted cornfields and let their hogs or pigs run loose in the woods and unfenced private land. In late summer and fall, they rounded up the animals and sold them to drovers who traversed the South with the animals, ultimately selling them to flatland merchants and planters. These hill-country yeomen lived a way of life that sustained some of the most fiercely independent communities in the country.

Most southern yeomen practiced mixed farming for household subsistence and community exchange, with the surplus sent to market. A majority of these farmers owned their land and worked it without slave labor, practicing a "subsistence plus" agriculture tied to southern cash-crop production. Cotton, like tobacco, was not food, thus contributing nothing to family subsistence, so they played it safe, putting most of their land into subsistence crops and livestock, cultivating only a few acres of cotton. As transportation improved, they planted more cotton, but few southern yeomen devoted much effort to the growing of cotton because they did not want to become dependent on fluctuating markets. With the income from a few bales of cotton, they could pay their taxes, retire their debts, and buy coffee, tea, tobacco, sugar, cloth, and shoes. They entered and left the cotton market at will, thus serving interests but not dictating their livelihoods.

Unlike the great cotton planters of the plantation belt, southern yeomen were far less acquisitive and ambitious. Since few farms were self-sufficient, the exchange of labor and goods was part and parcel of their existence. In the plantation counties such interaction tended to reinforce planter power as the elite used their more bountiful resources as a means of gaining the loyalty and support of their poorer neighbors, especially politically. In the upcountry, mutual dependence strengthened the bonds of neighborliness; borrowing became "neighboring." Debts contracted within the network of kin and neighbors were generally paid in kind or in labor, and creditors often allowed yeomen debts to go unpaid for years.

Perhaps the most important symbol of the upcountry yeomen's neighborly ethos was the fence. Northerners never tired of comparing their neatly fenced farms with the dilapidated or absent fences of the South. In the bourgeois North, well-maintained fences were a sign of ambitious, hard-working farmers. Yankees thus considered poorly-maintained southern fences as a manifestation of the landowner's laziness. In reality, the absence of, or lack of attention to, fence maintenance in the South (especially in the upcountry) resulted from local custom and state law, not to mention the necessity for the subsistence of families and neighborhoods in the upland South. In rural areas where families fished and hunted for food and where livestock roamed freely, fences restricted land use in a variety of capacities essential for survival. In short, the southern yeomen's concept of private property differed from that of Northerners who used and maintained their fences, not only to designate their land, but also as symbols of personal ambition and acquisitiveness. To southern yeomen, the land, in all its manifestations, was to be used by all with few constraints.

Characteristics of the Market Revolution in the South

In economic terms, the concentration of wealth in the hands of a few planters had profound effects on how the Market Revolution impacted the South. Much of the white population remained outside the market economy. A South Carolina yeoman who raised cattle claimed, "I never spent more than ten dollars a year, which was for salt, nails, and the like. Nothing to wear, eat, or drink was purchased, as my farm provided all." By contrast, in the North, where rural demand for credit, banking facilities, farm tools, clothing, and other consumer goods fueled a revolution in commerce, finance, and industry, the South remained a poor market for manufactured goods. Slaves wore cheap northeastern-made cloth while rich planters furnished themselves and their households with finery from Europe. In the North, the exchange of farm produce for finished goods created a self-sustained economic growth by the 1840s. By comparison, the South had become a completely export-oriented economy based on its plantation staples, only building those factories, commercial institutions, and cities necessary to serve planter interests and needs. In the North, the Market Revolution produced commercial agriculture, a specialized labor force, and technological innovation. In the South, it simply spawned more slavery.

Not that the South resisted or was opposed to innovation in their agricultural orientation. Southerners developed Eli Whitney's hand-operated cotton gin into a technology capable of performing milling operations. They also made many significant improvements to steamboat design. Among other items, Southerners invented the cotton press, a machine with a huge wooden screw powered by horses or mules that compressed ginned cotton into tight bales for shipping. Jordan Goree, a slave craftsman in Huntsville, Texas, gained a reputation for being able to carve whole trees into perfect screws for these apparatuses. Yet, such innovations were few and far between in the antebellum South, with virtually all such devices either directly or indirectly tied to the processing and shipping of cotton, not to the fiber's production. As far as southern planters were concerned, cotton cultivation was a labor-intensive crop that only slave labor was capable of performing—a perception that discouraged innovation. Moreover, plantation slaves often resisted their enslavement by sabotaging expensive tools, scattering manure haphazard ways, and passively stymying innovations that would have added to their drudgery. So the cotton fields continued to be cultivated by clumsy, mule-drawn plows that barely scratched the soil, by women wielding hoes, and by gangs who harvested the crop by hand.

Not only did antiquated, needless, time-consuming labor practices handicap southern agricultural innovation but so did the lack of **internal improvements**, which frugal state governments spent very little money to develop. A Virginia canal did link the Richmond flour mills with inland grain fields, while another connected Chesapeake Bay with the National Road. Nevertheless, most cotton belt planters already enjoyed access to the South's magnificent system of navigable rivers, while largely self-sufficient upland yeomen saw little need for expensive, state-supported internal improvements. The South also placed little value on urbanization. In 1800, about 82 percent of the southern workforce and about 70 percent of their northern counterparts engaged in some form of rural agricultural work. By 1860, only 40 percent of white Northerners were so employed, while the proportion in the South had risen to 84 percent. Southern infrastructure, such as it existed, had been developed around the plantation economy to move cotton or other staples to seaports for shipment out of the region. Indeed, what urban centers existed in the antebellum South, such as Charleston, Mobile, and New Orleans, were essentially service centers for the region's cotton planting elite. River cities like Louisville, Memphis, and St. Louis were little more than stopping points for steamboats.

While the North became more urbanized, southern cities remained few in number and continued to perform the colonial functions of eighteenth-century seaport towns. Southern businessmen turned to New York City for credit, insurance, and the shipping of goods. Affluent Southerners also bought their finished goods from northern cities like New York, Boston, or Philadelphia, or directly from Europe (primarily Great Britain). *De Bow's Review*, the South's premier business journal, reported that South Carolina storekeepers often concealed the fact that they sometimes bought goods from Charleston wholesalers, claiming instead they had bought them directly from New York City because it was well known that New York provided better goods at cheaper prices than any southern supplier. James De Bow himself testified to the superior skill and diversification of the North, when after trying several New Orleans sources, he awarded the contract for his review to a Yankee printer—not surprising given the fact that three-fourths of his income came from northern advertisers. In all, Southerners estimated that 40 cents of every dollar that their cotton produced ended up redirected towards the North.

The South's commitment to cotton and slavery would not only isolate the region politically during the antebellum period but would also deepen the South's dependence on European, and eventually northern, financial and industrial centers. In the years after 1815, the North and West underwent a qualitative Market Revolution—a transformation that enriched both regions and changed the Northeast from being part of the old colonial periphery (the suppliers of food and raw material) into a part of the core (the suppliers of manufactured goods and financing) for the world market economy. In contrast, the South, by its dependency on cotton production and the exporting of such staples for its economic sustenance, while importing all its manufactured, sank ever deeper

Wood engraving of slaves using the first cotton gin. Dec. 18, 1869

into economic colonialism—a status not only controlled by the fluctuations of European markets, but also by an ever-increasing reliance on northern processors, manufacturers, and financiers.

PRESIDENT MONROE

In the 1816 presidential election, everyone knew that another Jeffersonian Republican, Secretary of State James Monroe, would easily prevail over his Federalist Party rival Rufus King. Monroe's selection by President Madison to lead the party also ensured that another Virginian would serve as president. Indeed, Monroe would become the third president in a row (and fourth overall) from the Old Dominion, causing many to hail the presidency as a "**Virginia Dynasty**." As predicted, Monroe routed Rufus King, the last member of his party to run for president. In the wake of the Hartford Convention and the flush of euphoria over the return of peace, Monroe dominated the Electoral College vote by a 183-34 margin, taking every state but Maine, Massachusetts, Rhode Island, and Delaware (the last Federalist bastions). Four years later, when Monroe ran for a second term, he faced no Federalist opponent. The first party system dissolved as its leaders either quit politics or became Republicans. No doubt many were hopeful that a consensus among the nation's leadership could finally occur, ending the bitter partisanship that had divided them during the Republic's early years. However, their celebrations proved premature and delusional. By 1824, some of the same issues had resurfaced, as well as the emergences of new ones, causing the same rancor and polarization among the nation's political elite that had affected the Founding Fathers in the years before the War of 1812.

For the moment, however, all of the nation's earlier troubles seemed in the distant past, as Americans believed that James Monroe's election was the harbinger of a genuine "Era of Good Feelings." Indeed, in his inaugural address, Monroe echoed themes that were both Federalist and Republican. On the one hand, he asked Americans to be vigilant in their efforts to avoid corruption, greed, and the usurpation of power by the Republic's foes. On the other hand, he called for a more vigorous national defense, by which he meant an expansion of the armed services and a more aggressive foreign policy toward Europe. "Our distance from Europe," Monroe declared, "and the just, moderate, and pacific policy of our Government may form some security against these dangers, but they ought to be anticipated and guarded against." Monroe also endorsed federally-subsidized internal improvements, which he believed essential for sustaining the nation's prosperity and current political cohesion. He qualified his support, however, by intimating that a constitutional amendment might be necessary for such an initiative. "Other interests of high importance will claim attention, among which the improvement of our country by roads and canals, proceeding always with a constitutional sanction, holds a distinguished place. By thus facilitating the intercourse between the States we shall add much to the convenience and comfort of our fellow citizens, much to the ornament of the country, and what is of greater importance, we shall shorten distances, and, by making each part more accessible to and dependent on the other, we shall bind the Union more closely together." Throughout his speech, Monroe naturally exalted the virtue of the American people. Perhaps no one in the audience that March day was as euphoric with Monroe's inaugural address as Henry Clay, for the president's words foreboded his American System.

FOREIGN AFFAIRS UNDER MONROE

Rapprochement with England

Once in office, Monroe governed more like a Federalist nationalist than a Jeffersonian Republican, especially in foreign policy. To help him implement his agenda, which called for the United States to play a more assertive role in the Atlantic world, Monroe passed up other deserving contenders and asked the former Federalist son of John Adams, John Quincy Adams, to serve as his Secretary of State (the cabinet position then seen as the stepping stone to the White House). Monroe and Adams proved to be quite a formidable combination of diplomatic and foreign policy acumen. Together they resolved a variety of issues peacefully and in ways beneficial for the United States. They also undertook initiatives that helped to establish respect for the nation in Europe while making the United States the self-declared protector of the Western Hemisphere.

Monroe and Adams made a rapprochement with Great Britain their first priority. The former enemies shared the 3,000-mile-long Canadian border, thus whether either liked it or not, they had to find a way to live with each other. To the British government and its citizenry, the dream of some day reacquiring their North American colonies was gone—the War of 1812 proved all such hopes to have been delusional. British government officials wisely concluded that henceforth it would be better for the empire's interests in the New World to make peace with the Americans. Thus, in a series of treaties and negotiations with the United States,

Great Britain pursued policies designed to achieve détente with its former colonies. For its part, the United States was equally interested in improving relations with its former nemesis, especially if such arrangements better secured the nation while promoting its expansionist impulses. From 1815 onward, both countries realized it would be mutually beneficial to undertake policies of accommodation. By the close of the nineteenth century, not only had all previous tensions disappeared from Anglo-American discourse, but feelings of mutual respect, admiration, and ethno-cultural solidarity had replaced a relationship that for decades had been marked by mistrust and violence. Due to the efforts of the Monroe administration, Americans would have little to fear from their former arch-enemies.

The first initiatives in this direction were a series of agreements that defined the boundaries between the United States and British Canada as well as defusing other potential border disputes. In the 1817 **Rush-Bagot Agreement,** the U.S. and Great Britain agreed to demilitarize the Great Lakes region; that is, neither country's warships or fortifications of any kind would be allowed on the lakes without the other's consent. The following year, the **Convention of 1818** established the Great Lakes as the natural boundary between British Canada and the United States and extended the non-militarized border along the 49th parallel all the way to the Pacific Ocean. The emissaries also formally acknowledged American fishing rights off the Labrador and Newfoundland coasts and declared that the Oregon Country (the present-day states of Oregon and Washington plus the Canadian province of British Columbia) would have the status of "joint occupation," whereby the citizens of both countries had free and unlimited access to the territory while the United States and Great Britain bore mutual responsibility for governing the area. The representatives from the U.S. and Great Britain took actions that transformed the Canadian-American frontier from a battleground into the peaceful border existing ever since.

Relations with Spain

After Thomas Jefferson purchased Louisiana in 1803, Jefferson as well as his successors tried in vain to define U.S. borders with foreign powers located adjacent to the vast territory. Jefferson attempted unsuccessfully to buy Florida, which since its founding had been nothing more than a neglected Spanish outpost often serving as a haven for brigands, outlaws, runaway slaves, pirates, and Seminole Indians who crossed the border to raid Georgia and South Carolina settlements. With Americans along the border wanting the Monroe administration to remove the Indian threat, Secretary of War John C. Calhoun authorized War of 1812 hero Andrew Jackson in 1818 to lead a punitive expedition into Florida if necessary to secure the border. Secretary of State John Quincy Adams had encouraged Monroe to send Jackson into Florida, certain that a display of American military force would finally convince the Spanish of the futility of trying to maintain order there, resulting in the sale of their colony to the United States.

In early 1818, Jackson led a foray of 2,000 federal soldiers, local militia, and Creek allies into Florida, ostensibly to deter the Seminoles from attacking white settlers across the border. His army destroyed Seminole settlements and captured a Spanish fort (contrary to explicit orders) along with two British subjects who he promptly executed for allegedly selling arms to the Indians and runaway slaves. Jackson then seized Pensacola in western Florida before withdrawing. Jackson did not conquer all of Florida, but there was no need. It became clear to both the American and Spanish governments that Florida was incredibly vulnerable, that Spanish authority there was a sham, and that the U.S. could take the province any time at will. In a show of false bravado, however, Spanish officials displayed outrage at Jackson's invasion, as did British diplomats for Jackson's execution of the two English citizens; nevertheless, the British government had no intention of going to war with the U.S. over the incident, and the Spanish, preoccupied with troubles elsewhere in the hemisphere, certainly were not about to engage the Americans over a troublesome territory of little value. This was precisely the scenario Adams foresaw and he proceeded to wrest Florida from Spanish control. In the Transcontinental Treaty or **Adams-Onís Treaty** of 1819, Spain transferred all of Florida to the United States in return for the U.S. government's agreement to assume private American claims against Spain for the damage done (including the loss of slaves) by the Seminoles and other "outlaws." The amount of compensation awarded was $5 million. While at the table, Adams also pushed his Spanish counterpart to address or "clarify" the border between the United States and the Spanish Borderlands west of the Mississippi River. During the negotiations, the U.S. gave up its claims to both California and Texas (the latter many believed was part of the original Louisiana Purchase). In return, the two countries agreed to a boundary line running along a series of ascending steps from Louisiana to the Pacific Ocean. This treaty defined the United States as a nation spanning across the continent. American expansionists should not have been too upset by the loss of legal claims to Texas. While John Quincy Adams was busy at the treaty table, an American named Moses Austin had begun negotiations with the Spanish government in Mexico City to bring 300 American families into Texas. Though Austin died before his *empresario* contract could be finalized, Mexicans soon revolted against Spanish rule, winning their independence in 1821. In that year, his son, Stephen F. Austin, formalized his father's contract with the new Mexican government, granting him the right to bring 297 families into the Mexican state of Coahuila y Tejas and thus establishing an American presence in the Southwest.

The Monroe Doctrine

In 1808, Napoleon made a military mistake that greatly damaged his ability to defeat the British in Europe and would deeply change politics in the Western Hemisphere: the invasion of the Iberian Peninsula to punish both Spain and Portugal for having violated his 'Continental System," which aimed to cut Great Britain off from trade with Continental Europe. By that year, large portions of mainland Europe had come under French control. However, none of the European nations adhered to the trade sanctions against the English. Spain and Portugal became the first nations to break the decree. To punish these wayward countries, Napoleon unwisely decided to invade the peninsula. Much to his surprise, the Spanish fiercely resisted the occupation of their country, engaging French troops in a successful guerrilla campaign (with British aid), ultimately weakening Napoleon's control over the rest of Europe. While Spanish guerrillas made life miserable for the French troops, other European powers formed the Third Coalition with England to defeat the once-invincible French *Grand Armée* and bring about Napoleon's downfall.

Even before Napoleon invaded Spain, independence movements had appeared throughout much of Spain's Latin American empire. With the Spanish monarchy dislodged and French troops occupying the country, full-fledged rebellions against the mother country occurred in Spain's New World viceroyalties, from New Spain (Mexico) to the Rio de La Plata (present-day Argentina, Uruguay, and Paraguay). Led by New World-born *criollos*, the insurrections eventually succeeded in toppling the viceroyalties governed by the Spanish-born *peninsulare* elites. By the time of Napoleon's final defeat at Waterloo, Belgium in 1815, the rebel governments formally declared their independence from Spain and turned to the United States for recognition and support. However, no sooner did the Third Coalition defeat Napoleon than they turned their attention to the New World. The new French king, Louis XVIII, not only helped his Spanish-Bourbon counterpart, Ferdinand VII, crush a republican movement in Spain, but also endorsed Ferdinand's proposal to form a large European armada to reclaim Spain's lost Latin American colonies while preserving, and possibly extending, the other European powers' New World empires. At this juncture, the Monroe administration correctly worried that if Great Britain, the greatest power

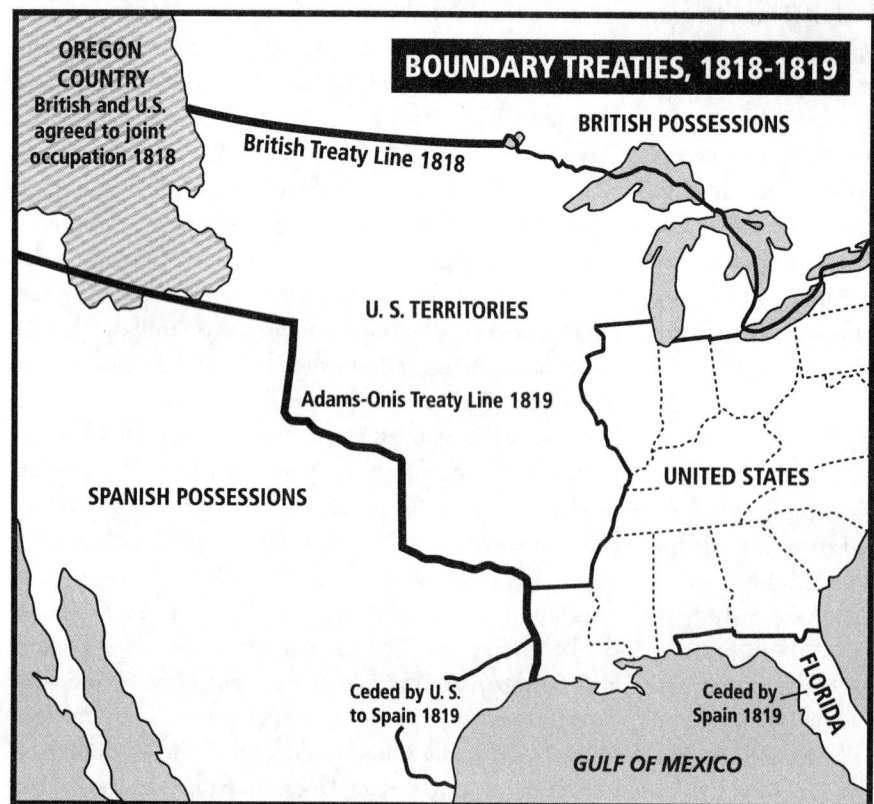

Map 10.1 Adams-Onís Treaty

in the world at the time, were to join such an effort, the combined military and naval force would be difficult for the newly-independent nations of Latin America to defeat.

To the surprise and relief of both the United States and its Latin American neighbors, and to France and Spain's dismay, Great Britain not only rejected the proposed invasion of the Western Hemisphere but also declared that it disavowed any future territorial ambitions for itself in the Americas. What prompted the greatest power in the world into such a conciliatory move toward the United States and an antagonistic one toward its former European allies? Several factors came into play. First and foremost was economics. The newly independent Latin American republics represented great trade opportunities for British merchants and manufacturers, which a Spanish reoccupation would jeopardize. The British surmised that no sooner would Spain reclaim its New World possessions then it would implement mercantilist policies, which, as in the past, had closed off its Latin American markets to all outsiders. The potential for huge profits and domination of new markets was simply too lucrative for the British to pass up. (Indeed, Great Britain would monopolize the Latin American market into the early twentieth century.) Also motivating British policy was its recent rapprochement with the United States, essential to British interests in North America. Great Britain thus offered to make a joint declaration with the United States, warning other nations against intruding in the internal affairs of Western Hemisphere countries. No doubt an alliance with Great Britain would have enhanced U.S. diplomatic credibility, but many Americans suspected that once England established its right to have the Royal Navy patrolling Western Hemispheric waters, Britain would no longer act as an equal partner and gradually squeeze the United States out of Latin American markets. Still, the belief among Americans at the time that they would be able to penetrate Latin American markets and compete with British manufactured products proved delusional. Not until the 1920s would Latin Americans begin to see the "Made in the USA" label on large quantities of finished goods.

Secretary of State John Quincy Adams convinced Monroe to reject the British overture of a joint declaration, persuading the president to issue a unilateral statement of support for the new republics, including an assertion that the United States would consider an attempt by any European power to reclaim its lost colonies or to try to expand elsewhere in the Western Hemisphere as a direct threat to the security and sovereignty of the United States and its Latin American neighbors. Adams also wanted it strongly intimated that any such designs would encounter harsh reprisals from the United States.

The Secretary argued it would be far better to act boldly and independently than for the United States to "come in as a cockboat in the wake of the British man-of-war." Personally, Adams also hoped such a bold declaration would help erase the Anglophile image of him and other former Federalist New Englanders that many Republicans had fostered over the years. Monroe embraced Adams's declaration, enunciating in his 1823 annual address to Congress what has since become known as the **Monroe Doctrine**. The president proclaimed a special relationship existed between the United States and all parts of North and South America. Because of that supposed bond, he insisted, "we are of necessity more immediately connected. We owe it to candor and to the amicable relations existing between the United States and those [European] powers," he continued, "to declare that we should consider any attempt on their part to extend their system to any portion of this hemisphere as dangerous to our peace and safety." The Monroe Doctrine marked an important milestone in the development of American nationalism and internationalism. Indeed, the policy reflected the confidence, pride, and general exuberance Americans felt about their nation and its Democratic-Republican ideals in the aftermath of the War of 1812. Many Americans viewed the Latin American wars for independence as confirmation that the historical "spirit" had passed from the Old World to the New World, and now rested in the United States whose citizens' destiny was now to spread the "Spirit of 1776" across the continent and throughout the Western Hemisphere. For many Americans, the Monroe Doctrine represented the first step toward the realization of that mission.

THE MISSOURI COMPROMISE

Because of its apparent abundance, especially in the West, land hunger fueled much of the new market economy. By 1819, land ownership had come to define national as well as individual prosperity for many Americans. However, as American settlers poured into the Old Northwest and planters into the Old Southwest, the slavery issue reemerged—reigniting a tension that had been stagnant for many years. During the War of 1812, the calls for unity momentarily silenced belligerent Southerners and their equally determined northern antislavery foes. But when peace returned along with the cotton explosion of the Southwest, proslavery expansionists resurfaced, more aggressive than before the war in their determination to protect by expansion their "peculiar institution." Proslavery rhetoric was naturally met by an equally revitalized antislavery crusade in the North. Indeed, the beginnings of the abolition movement took shape in the late 1810s and early 1820s. Although the international slave trade had been abolished in 1808, slavery expansion had given rise to a very active, and in many Northerners' minds, despicable domestic slave trade. By 1819, when Missouri applied for admission to the Union as a slave state, antislavery politicians were outraged and determined to prevent the slaveocracy from gaining any more power in Congress.

The **Missouri Crisis,** although legally framed in terms of national politics on the federal level, was inextricable from the larger dispute over the morality of slavery. Many Northerners had long been disturbed by the unfair political advantage that the Constitution's Three-Fifths Compromise had given white Southerners. They believed that with the apparent rise in slave population faster than the rate of increase for whites, white Southerners would become a minority people in their own region, yet they would continue to wield political power far in excess of their actual numbers. Missouri's proposed admission as a slave state would extend that egregious pattern of representation in the House and create a new imbalance in the Senate, where each state enjoyed equal representation regardless of population. In 1819, twenty-two states (eleven free and eleven with slavery) comprised the Union. Missouri's entry as a slave state would give the latter an upper hand in any purely-sectional disputes. Florida, certain to apply for admission as a slave state at some future point, would add to the disparity. Meanwhile, the South continued to dominate the executive branch. As noted earlier, four out of the nation's first five presidents had been Virginia slaveholders.

Other potentially divisive issues existed over the admission of Missouri as a slave state. Northerners feared that Missouri would set a precedent for extending slavery into new areas carved out of the Louisiana Purchase. By 1819, the hope that slavery would die out on its own had proved to be an illusion. If anything, slavery appeared to be on a revitalized southwestern march poised to veer northward. Far from withering away, the institution seemed to be thriving. Indeed, during the colonial period, American slave owners had imported only about 5 percent of all the Africans brought to the New World; by 1819, slaves in the United States constituted one-third of all people of African descent in the Western Hemisphere. Even some of the new western states such as Illinois passed "black codes" that limited the economic and civil rights of free blacks residing in the state.

No sooner had Missouri requested admission as a slave state than the bitterness began. During the House debate, New York representative James Tallmadge proposed that Missouri be admitted with two caveats: first, no additional slaves would enter the state after admission; and second, after being admitted to the Union, Missourians would enact legislation putting slavery on a path toward eventual extinction. Southern representatives united against the amendment, while Northerners unanimously voted in favor of the provision. The more populous North carried the vote, but when the bill reached the Senate, the committee in charge of consideration reversed the vote. The **Tallmadge Amendment** died in committee, to be taken up in the next session.

By the time Congress reconvened, both sides had become uncompromising. Northern congressmen insisted that Congress had the power to prohibit slavery from a territory just as the Congress had exercised during the Articles of Confederation period when it prohibited slavery from the Old Northwest Territory. They believed the federal Congress had to act quickly in a similar manner to ban slavery in the remaining Louisiana Purchase area. Southerners argued that the Constitution delegated no such power to Congress. In their view, the states had preserved their equality and autonomy on issues such as personal property rights, which the Constitution must uphold and protect at all times as stipulated in the Fifth Amendment. Since slaves were property, owners had the right to take their slaves unmolested into any territory or state of the Union. To deny them this right violated slave owners' constitutional rights of life, liberty, and property.

The struggle over Missouri quickly became more divisive than any previous issue befalling the nation since the volatile 1790s. The Missouri controversy foreshadowed with chilling accuracy the congressional debates to come over slavery and foretold the use of racial politics as a weapon of silencing antislavery Northerners—a pattern that would prevail into the 1850s. Senator Nathaniel Macon of North Carolina reminded his northern colleagues that nowhere in the Union were free blacks truly welcome; that the United States was, in effect, a racist nation and that most whites believed blacks to be inferior. No one rose to dispute him. Indeed, racism had been codified in numerous ways in northern state constitutions. Most northern states denied African Americans voting rights, militia service, or appearing as witnesses against whites, while all barred blacks from holding public office or marrying whites.

The Missouri firestorm finally abated when Maine (then a part of Massachusetts) was encouraged to apply for statehood as a free state. Speaker of the House Henry Clay cleverly linked the two applications to preserve the Senate balance of 12 slave states and 12 free states. Most importantly, the deal created a boundary drawn at the 36°30' parallel aligned with Missouri's southern border that represented a congressional line of demarcation.

The Missouri Compromise

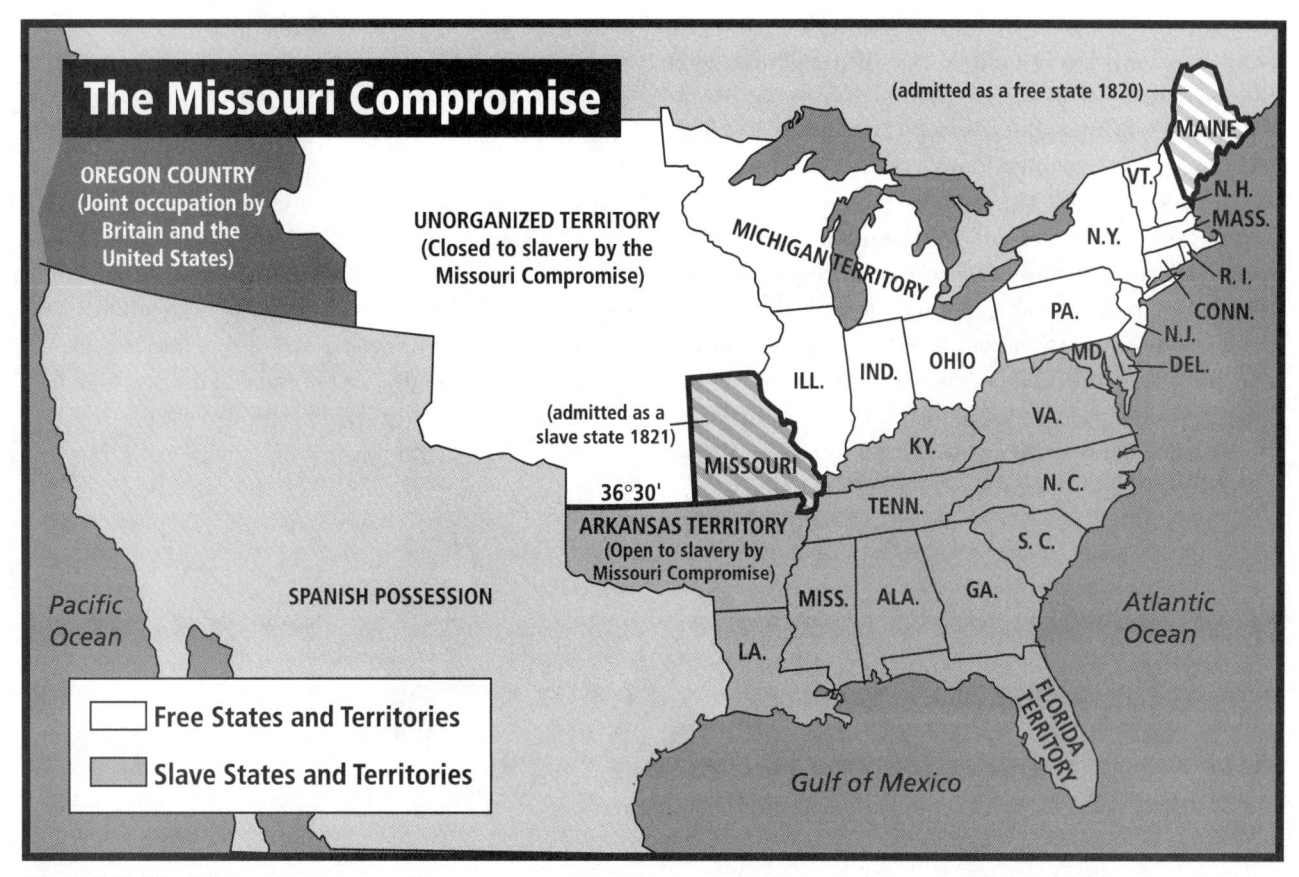

Map 10.2 The Misssouri Compromise

Slavery was permitted in the Arkansas Territory (which included present-day Oklahoma, soon to become Indian Territory) located south of the borderline, but banned north of the line, thus excluding the institution from the remainder of the Louisiana Purchase lands.

A cursory look at the **Missouri Compromise** (map 10.2) reveals that, in terms of the relative size of land granted to each side, the agreement seemed to favor antislavery Northerners. If so, then why would the South and the proslavery forces accept such a settlement when clearly the bulk of the Louisiana Purchase would be free? It must be remembered that by the 1820s in the southern slaveholding mindset, slaves and cotton had become symbiotic; that is, if cotton could not be grown in a certain geographic region, then planters saw no need to take their slaves there. Such was the manner in which southern planters viewed the Louisiana Purchase lands north of 36°30'—a "desert" not at all conducive to cotton cultivation. Thus, a ban on slavery north of 36°30' became moot to southern slaveholders. Southerners, however, believed that Mexican territory including modern-day Texas, New Mexico, Arizona, and California, might one day become part of the United States and would enter the Union as slave territory. When that day arrived, slavery would be allowed in those territories because they were all below the compromise line. With such visions in their minds, enough southern congressmen voted in favor of the bill, which narrowly passed in March 1820. On August 21, 1821, President James Monroe greeted Missouri as the 24th state of the Union.

The Missouri Compromise proved to be a devastating defeat for the antislavery movement. For several years, abolitionists had struggled to halt slavery expansion and thus put a check on the slaveocracy's growing power in national politics. Disgusted and shocked by pro-slavery politicians' increasing belligerence, antislavery Northerners mounted a campaign to keep slavery out of Missouri, hoping to stop slavery expansion once and for all. They believed that the most expedient way to bring about slavery's ultimate demise was to stop its expansion, and Missouri proved to be the initial battleground for their agenda. However, the majority of the nation's new postwar leaders, a different generation politically than the Founding Fathers, were politicians, not statesmen. As such, they believed that the only way the slavery issue could be reconciled, without sectional conflict, was to seek compromise—civil war must be averted at all costs. Indeed, as distasteful as a compromise might be, they believvved that inflaming sectional passions over the institution to the point that all negotiating ends and violence begins would be far worse.

Slavery's defenders had always used racial politics to try to stop antislavery politics, but their successes were limited and local until the 1820s. Impressed by the strength of antislavery sentiment during the Missouri crisis, Southerners joined an emerging coalition with Westerners and some Northeasterners soon to be known as the Democratic Party, which became, in effect, a quasi-proslavery party. Its members sought to keep the slavery issue out of national politics by creating a racial consensus among white Americans in all sections of the country that blacks, regardless of status—slave or free—were an inferior people not entitled to the rights of citizenship or to participate fully in mainstream American life. African Americans were to be an invisible, marginalized people. Such a strategy seemed to have worked.

With the defeat of antislavery forces and the triumph of racial politics, radical abolitionism emerged to fill the void. Absent the discipline of party politics, the abolitionists would reveal themselves to be a contentious lot. Through the 1830s and 1840s, they were the lonely voices of antislavery idealism in America. From the start, they made it their *raison d'etre* to break through the racial consensus and put opposition to slavery back on the national political agenda. In the wake of disastrous defeat, and in the face of overwhelming proslavery forces, the abolitionists persevered.

Chronology

1790 Samuel Slater builds his first spinning mill.

1793 Eli Whitney invents the cotton gin.

1807 Robert Fulton launches first steamboat.

1813 Waltham System.

1816 Second Bank of the United States
Congress passes the nation's first protective tariff.
Dartmouth College v. Woodward..
McCulloch v. Maryland.
James Monroe elected president.

1817 Rush-Bagot Agreement.

1818 National Road completed to Ohio River at Wheeling, Virginia.
Convention of 1818.
Andrew Jackson invades Florida.

1819 Panic of 1819.
Adams-Onís Treaty.

1820 Missouri Compromise.
James Monroe re-elected president.
Federalist Party disbands

1822 Denmark Vessey slave conspiracy.
President Monroe vetoes National Road reparations bill.

1823 Monroe Doctrine asserted.

1824-25 John Quincy Adams elected president by the House of Representatives.
Adams appoints Henry Clay as Secretary of State
Jacksonians charge corrupt bargain.
Second Party System begins.
Gibbons v. Ogden.

1825 Erie Canal completed.

1827 Georgia Cherokees declare themselves a republic.

1828 Jackson elected presidency.

Review Questions

1. Describe the changes in transportation in the United States after the War of 1812 and the impact of these changes on the American economy.

2. Why is the post-war decade referred to as the "Era of Good Feelings?"

3. What caused the Missouri Crisis and how was the matter resolved?

4. What changes took place in American foreign policy following the War of 1812, particularly regarding Great Britain and Latin America?

5. What caused the end of the First Party System and what issues gave rise to the Second Party System in the aftermath of the presidential election of 1824?

Glossary of Important People and Concepts

The American System
Boston Associates
Erie Canal
Henry Clay
Convention of 1818
Corrupt Bargain
Dartmouth College v. Woodward
Robert Fulton
Internal improvements
Francis Cabot Lowell
Missouri Compromise
Missouri Crisis
Monroe Doctrine
Neo-Federalist
Panic of 1819
Paternalism
Rhode Island System
Rush-Bagot Agreement
Second Bank of the United States
Samuel Slater
Tallmadge Amendment
Tariff of 1816
Adams-Onís Treaty of 1819
"Virginia Dynasty"
Waltham System

SUGGESTED READINGS

Samuel Flagg Bemis, *John Quincy Adams and the Foundations of American Foreign Policy* (1949).

Stuart Blumin, *The Emergence of the Middle Class: Social Experience in the City, 1760-1860* (1989).

Christopher Clark, *The Roots of Rural Capitalism: Western Massachusetts, 1780-1860* (1990).

George Dangerfield, *The Awakening of American Nationalism, 1815-1828* (1965).

Daniel Walker Howe, *What God Hath Wrought: The Transformation of America, 1815-1848* (2009).

Gerard Koeppel, *Bond of Union: Building the Erie Canal and the American Empire* (2010).

John Lauritz Larson, *The Market Revolution in America* (2001).

Bruce Laurie, *Artisans into Workers: Labor in Nineteenth-Century America* (1989).

Matthew Mason, *Slavery and Politics in the Early American Republic* (2008).

Ernest R. May, *The Making of the Monroe Doctrine* (1975).

Glover Moore, *The Missouri Compromise, 1819-1821* (1953).

Robert V. Remini, *Henry Clay: Statesman for the Union* (1991).

Charles G. Sellers, *The Market Revolution: Jacksonian America, 1815-1848* (1991).

Francis N. Stites, *John Marshall: Defender of the Constitution* (1981).

George Rogers Taylor, *The Transportation Revolution, 1815-1860* (1951).

Sean Wilentz, *Chants Democratic: New York City and the Rise of the American Working Class, 1788-1850* (1984).

Andrew Jackson

Chapter Eleven

ANDREW JACKSON AND THE "WHITE MAN'S REPUBLIC"

To some of the nation's wealthy and most sophisticated, the event looked like the end of American civilization. The nation's capital had never seen a presidential inauguration as emotional or as chaotic as when on March 4, 1829, Supreme Court Chief Justice John Marshall swore in the man who would soon be his political enemy, Andrew Jackson, as the seventh president of the United States. Jackson had promoted the idea that his ascension to the president represented a new era. His supporters decorated the steamboat he rode up the Ohio River with brooms to symbolize how Jackson was going to "clean up the mess in Washington." It would be, Jackson supporters promised, a new age of the common man. Approximately 20,000 people had trekked to Washington, D.C., temporarily more than doubling the size of the city, to watch their hero grab the presidential reins. Some voyaged more than 500 difficult miles using primitive roads to reach the capital, where they paid $20 a week for rooms at boarding houses, about three times the normal rate, for the privilege of witnessing history.

Many visitors dressed in humble or even shabby clothes, used uneducated and even coarse language and lacked the manners of the well-to-do. The crowd was like "an invasion of the northern barbarians into Rome," groused Senator Daniel Webster, who had supported Jackson's opponent, the departing president John Quincy Adams. To accommodate the crowds, the inauguration moved outdoors to the more spacious grounds near the east portico of the Capitol. When Jackson finally became visible to the audience at noon, the historian Donald D. Cole observed, a giant roar went up. Jackson paid homage to the ordinary folk who had helped him reach the White House, removing his hat and bowing to the audience before taking his seat, inspiring another big round of applause. A master of the populist gesture, he would bow again after finishing his speech and his oath of office.

Following the ceremony, the audience wanted to get closer, and they broke through the rope separating them from the new president, forcing Jackson to retreat back inside the Capitol. One wealthy Washington matron would later mourn that "The Majesty of the People had disappeared," pushed aside by an unruly "rabble, a mob of boys, of negroes, women, children scrambling, fighting, romping. What a pity. What a pity." An audience turned into a mob as hundreds followed Jackson, riding a white charger, with the bearing of a military hero, to his new residence, the White House. Once at the executive mansion, the crowd then, in Cole's words, "stormed through the building, soiling carpets and sofas, and destroying several thousand dollars worth of cut glass and china. Men and women received bloody noses as they fought for the refreshments and had to be lured from the house by tubs of punch placed on the lawns. The president, almost crushed by the mobs, escaped out the back way." He ended up retreating to the boarding house room he had rented for the week's festivities while the White House staff cleaned the mud stains on the rugs and drapes and dried up the pools of liquor spilled everywhere.

The inaugural madness symbolized for many in the American upper crust a disturbing trend in the country's politics personified by Jackson. He had defeated John Quincy Adams, a scion of the eastern establishment and the Harvard-educated son of a former president, in a rematch of their bitter, controversial 1824 presidential contest. A Tennessee planter, Jackson represented the loosening monopoly on economic and political power held by northeastern cities like Philadelphia, New York and Boston and by the largest Atlantic seaboard southern state, Virginia. Of the first six presidents, four had been from Virginia and two from Massachusetts. This east coast dominance no longer reflected the vastness of the country. As Cole observed, as the population of the United States almost tripled from about 5 million in 1800 to around 13 million in 1830, the percentage of the population living west of the Appalachian Mountains grew rapidly, from 7 percent to 28 percent.

Jackson represented the rise of the west, but he also embodied the advance of what political reformers liked to call "universal manhood suffrage"—the idea that all white men, age 21 and older, should have the right to vote, whether or not they held property. In the early years of the republic, states had restricted voting and the right to hold public office to those who owned land or held a certain level of financial assets. The first generation of American politicians justified this by arguing that any man without property had no vested interest in the success of the nation and, lacking economic independence, could be bullied or manipulated by his social superiors when voting. An economic metamorphosis in the country between 1800 and 1830, however, had made this ideology untenable.

America had slowly become urban, and by the time Jackson won election in 1828, more Americans worked for wages and rented their homes than in the time of Jefferson. In 1800, there had been only six cities with a population of 10,000 or more. By 1830, that number had jumped to 23, and one city, New York, became the first to exceed a population of 200,000. As bridges, steamboats, and canals interconnected the growing country and sped the transportation of farm goods, improved transportation and the growth of the economy also allowed the speedy spread of American manufacturing. Older states like Massachusetts filled with mill towns. These mill workers owned little or no property, but—inspired by Thomas Jefferson's claim in the Declaration of Independence that "all men are created equal," they demanded the right to vote, insisting that the ballot was their right because they were producers—men who generated wealth for the country—and that they deserved rights as white men.

By 1821, three states that had been created out of the Northwest Territory—Ohio (1803), Indiana (1816), and Illinois (1818)—had adopted state constitutions that dropped all property requirements for voters and office holders. Between 1815 and 1830, a dozen states out of the twenty-four had adopted or revised constitutions to eliminate religious qualifications for voting (for instance, limiting suffrage to Protestants), lowered or dropped property or taxpaying qualifications for voting, and allowed voters to choose for electors for the Electoral College during presidential elections in place of leaving that power to state legislatures. By 1840, Rhode Island alone in the northern states still required voters to own property.

With that exception, universal white manhood suffrage had been achieved in the Northeast by the time Jackson left the White House in 1837. This dramatic expansion of eligible voters came to be known as "Jacksonian democracy," but the expansion of voting rights for white men came at the expense of free African Americans. Those new white voters saw their ballots as a matter of racial privilege. After the American Revolution, black men who owned property could vote in states in New England like Maine, Massachusetts, New Hampshire, and Vermont while New York and North Carolina gave suffrage rights to "all men" who met **property qualifications**. But as suffrage for white men spread in the first four decades of the nineteenth century, free African Americans lost access to the ballot in Connecticut, Maryland, New Jersey, New York, North Carolina, Pennsylvania, Maryland, and Tennessee.

As the historian Leon F. Litwack documented, by 1840, 93 percent of African Americans in the North lived in states that had either reduced or completely eliminated the right to vote for blacks. Jacksonian Democracy had no place for African Americans or Native Americans. This was to be, as the historian Alexander Saxton called the United States in this time period, "a white man's republic."

That republic was put on full display the day Andrew Jackson became president. White or not, to the wealthy and privileged on the Atlantic coast, and to their elected spokesman in Washington and in the media, this rabble was undesirable. As Supreme Court Justice Joseph Story described the scene after the inaugural mob had partly demolished the White House, "I never saw such a mixture. The reign of King Mob seemed triumphant."

"A SPEEDY REDRESS": JACKSON'S VIOLENT, TUMULTUOUS EARLY YEARS

Historians have struggled to understand Andrew Jackson for more than a century. His first biographer, James Parton, described him in 1860 as "a writer brilliant, elegant, eloquent without being able to compose a correct sentence, or spell words of four syllables . . . a most law-defying, law-abiding citizen. A stickler for discipline, he never hesitated to disobey a superior. A democratic autocrat. An urbane savage. An atrocious saint." Parton might have added that Jackson, the only president known to have fatally shot another person, also spoke loudly of state's rights but would stop cold the first attempt by a southern state to secede from the Union on a states' rights pretext.

Andrew Jackson shaped his era, and the era molded him. He was a violent man in a violent time, and a virulently racist one in a period defined by white supremacist dogma. Aggressive, he led the nation in an expansionist age. Impulsive and tumultuous, he perfectly reflected a transformative, unstable historical epoch. His parents, Scots-Irish immigrants Andrew Jackson, Sr., and Elizabeth Hutchison Jackson, were squatters, frontier people who settled on land for which no one held a legal title in the frontier Waxhaws region so undefined by British colonial authorities that it is still unclear whether the future president was born on the North Carolina or South Carolina side of the border.

Andrew Jackson, Sr., died either just before or shortly after the birth of his namesake son, as the result of a freak accident, a falling log slaying him while he cleared land surrounding the Jackson home. Elizabeth gave birth to Andrew on March 15, 1767 and raised him as a single widow.

As Jackson's biographer Andrew Burstein notes, Jackson seems to have been rambunctious and not particularly studious during his early childhood. Nevertheless, Elizabeth's religious faith deepened after her husband's death and, perhaps hoping he would become a minister, she scrimped and saved her meager earnings to pay for tutors who, according to the historian Charles Sellers, taught him "to read, to cipher, to write crudely, and to spout a few tags of Latin. A precocious reader, he was soon being called to read to assembled neighbors the occasional newspaper that reached the backcountry." During the American Revolution, Jackson's mother and elder brothers supported the patriot cause. One brother, Hugh, died supposedly from heat exhaustion in the Battle of Stono Ferry fought near Charleston in 1779.

The Waxhaws would provide one of the most violent settings during the War for Independence. Using a force made up partly of Tories—Americans loyal to King George III—British Lieutenant Colonel Banastre Tarleton fought a brutal war of vengeance against the American rebels in the South Carolina countryside, gunning down captured soldiers. Elizabeth Jackson, along with her surviving sons Andrew and Robert, nursed wounded patriot soldiers, and the two young boys ran errands for the American forces in the area. British forces including Tories launched a surprise attack on the Waxhaws region in April 1781, taking eleven patriot soldiers prisoner along with Andrew and Robert.

A British officer confronted Andrew, then 14, and demanded that the boy clean his muddy boots. Andrew refused, demanding proper treatment for a prisoner of war. The officer struck Jackson with his sword, Andrew protecting himself with his left hand. Jackson suffered gashes on his hand and head, wounds that would scar him for the rest of his life. The same officer then demanded that Robert Jackson clean his boots and the older brother refused as well. The officer struck Robert on his head. Robert never recovered from the resulting injuries, dying within a matter of days. More tragedy stalked the future president. His mother volunteered to care for prisoners of war held on ships moored in Charleston Harbor and contracted cholera. Elizabeth Jackson died in November 1781, leaving Andrew an orphan at age 14. "I felt utterly alone," Jackson later recalled. He moved from the home of one relative to another, often departing after an ugly argument. He spent his later teenaged years as a drifter, gambling, swearing, drinking and racing horses.

Dueling, Politics, and Slaveowning

Jackson apparently received little formal education, but after his mother's death he relocated to North Carolina where he taught school in the town of Salisbury in 1787. He then apprenticed for a lawyer, read legal books, and was admitted to the bar. When a friend was named Superior Court judge for the western district of North Carolina (later to become the state of Tennessee in 1796) by the legislature, Jackson secured an appointment to be the court's public prosecutor. Moving first to Jonesborough then to Nashville, Jackson practiced as a country lawyer and began a lifelong custom of responding to perceived insults with violence or threatened violence. An opposing attorney named Waitstill Avery challenged Jackson in a way that offended him. "My character you have injured," Jackson wrote in a misspelled letter, "and further you have insulted me in the presence of the court and large audience. I therefore call upon you as a gentleman to give me satisfaction for the same."

Jackson had challenged Avery to a duel and demanded a "speedy redress" for his supposed injury. Jackson would engage in several duels in his life with far more serious consequences. In this case, both parties satisfied honor by firing their pistols in the air.

By this time, Jackson already owned his first slave, a woman between the age of 18 and 20. Undereducated but sharply intelligent, Jackson plowed his legal earnings into land, becoming a successful speculator, with one of his big land investments eventually leading to the establishment of Memphis. He began living with **Rachel Donelson**, the estranged wife of Captain Lewis Robards, a man subject to violent rages. Robards still lived in Kentucky. At that time, divorces had to be approved by state legislatures. Robards filed a request with the legislature charging Donelson with adultery and abandonment, and he placed an article in a newspaper declaring he no longer held any financial responsibility for Rachel. Based on this, Jackson and Donelson believed that Robards had obtained a divorce, and they married in 1791.

The Jacksons only later found out that the divorce had not been approved. Donelson was still legally married to her first husband, thus making the Jacksons bigamists. The relationship between Andrew and Rachel, however, resulted in eventual approval for Robards' divorce petition, and the Jacksons remarried in 1794. The complicated beginning to their relationship would later politically haunt Andrew Jackson and his wife.

Rachel rose from an extensive clan, and this family network boosted Andrew's business and political career. Even though he struggled with a lifelong problem of drooling when he spoke, and he had a weak voice, Jackson would cast a giant shadow on the nation's political life from 1815 until he left the White House in 1837. His success as a lawyer and a businessman led to Jackson's election as a delegate to the 1796 Tennessee state constitutional convention. When Tennessee became a state later that year, he won election to the United States House. He won appointment by the Tennessee legislature to a United States Senate seat in September 1797, but, wishing to stay close to his business interests in Tennessee, especially after he encountered severe financial troubles after passing notes to business associates from a bank that soon failed (an incident that permanently soured Jackson on all banks and paper money), he resigned less than seven months later and accepted a post as a justice on the Tennessee Supreme Court, a position he held until 1804.

Establishing a successful general store in Gallatin, Tennessee in 1803, he also developed a sprawling plantation he named the Hermitage, where eventually as many as 150 slaves at a time tended his cotton fields and maintained his household. "He was insistent in the belief that liberty-loving white Americans had every right to own slaves, and to prosper from their unpaid exertions," Burstein writes. Like other white men of his era, Jackson loved to speak of his own natural right to freedom, but responded with cruelty when African Americans sought liberty themselves. Years later, taking out an advertisement for a runaway slave, Jackson offered a $50 award for anyone capturing the escaped man (more than $800 today) plus "ten dollars extra, for every one hundred lashes any person will give him, to the amount of three hundred." Jackson didn't blink at encouraging crippling and possibly lethal punishment for any black man who dared defy his will.

"Mad Upon His Enemies": Jackson and the "Code of Honor"

For all his success in business and politics, Jackson seemed to derive the most pleasure from military service, and particularly in battling Native Americans. Jackson saw Indian lands as a potential source for vast white wealth, and like many of his countrymen he desired their removal, through conquest and slaughter if necessary. Indians became a target of obsessive hatred for Jackson. He accused the natives of "savage murders & depredations," charged them with being deceitful and tricky and (ironically given the relentless white theft of Indian land and other resources) accused them of "avarice." In his wars against Indians, he saw himself as an avenging angel, punishing Natives in the name of "our beloved wives and little prattling infants, butchered, mangled, murdered, and even torn to pieces by savage bloodhounds, and wallowing in their gore." In his career as a military officer and a politician, Jackson would more than make up for these often imagined offenses with a breathtaking record of genocide against Native Americans.

Jackson headed the Tennessee militia for a decade, leading battles against overwhelmed and demoralized Natives, fighting with a rage that one observer described as "mad upon his enemies." His Indian encounters, however, gave him little opportunity for the martial glory he deeply desired. Jackson became more deeply engaged in personal combat with Tennessee Governor John Sevier, a popular leader of a secession movement among western counties in North Carolina in the 1780s that briefly declared the creation of the never-officially-recognized state of Franklin. These counties later became the eastern part of Tennessee. Sevier was a war hero, having defeated the British at the Battle of King's Mountain during the American Revolution and gaining a reputation as a ruthless Indian fighter.

By the turn of the century, Jackson and Sevier saw each other as rivals. Sevier moved against Jackson's selection as commander of the Tennessee state militia. After Sevier left the office of governor, the two men competed for election as major general, and this time Jackson won the post. Now the bitter opponent of Sevier, Jackson helped circulate the story that Sevier had engaged in land fraud in North Carolina, a charge that had some apparent merit. Sevier challenged Jackson face-to-face and made reference to Jackson's earlier adulterous relationship with Rachel. Jackson challenged Sevier to a duel. Though illegal in some states, duels were everywhere governed by an informal but strict code of honor. To refuse to respond to a challenge was widely seen as a sign of gutlessness. Since Tennessee had outlawed dueling, Sevier insisted that they meet in Virginia or another location where the practice was still legal, but Jackson refused to wait and demanded the faceoff take place illegally in Indian Territory. When Sevier did not respond, Jackson fired off a letter to a newspaper calling the ex-governor a coward. The two later encountered each other in the Tennessee woods, and weapons were drawn, but both men survived the faceoff.

Charles Dickinson would not be so lucky. A 25-year-old attorney, he had been overheard in May 1806 saying something unpleasant about Rachel Jackson and her sexual behavior after Jackson accused him of reneging on a horse race wager, predictably resulting in a duel challenge from Jackson. During their challenge, Jackson (wearing a large overcoat to distort his frame) allowed Dickinson to fire the first shot. Dickinson's men later claimed it was a misfire, which should have ended the duel. The bullet hit Jackson in the chest, as Sellers put it, "splintering several of the general's ribs." Jackson survived, reeling for a time, but steadying himself, and holding one hand to his torso to slow the bleeding. According to dueling rules, Dickinson had to stand still while Jackson took a shot. Jackson cocked his pistol and squeezed the trigger, jamming the first time, but effectively executing his enemy on the second attempt. The bullet that hit Jackson landed close to his heart and could not be removed safely, so the general carried this reminder of his encounter with Dickinson in his body the rest of his life.

This was only the beginning of a career of gun battles. Later on, in September 1813, an argument over another duel in which Jackson served as a second for one of his friends led to a Nashville barroom shootout between Jackson and future Missouri Senator Thomas Hart Benton and his brother Jesse, a brawl in which a bullet struck Jackson in the shoulder. This injury almost resulted in the amputation of his left arm, leaving the future president in considerable pain for the rest of his life. Doctors would not successfully remove that bullet until 1832.

More than twenty years later, on January 30, 1835, toward the end of his presidency when Jackson was 67 years old, Jackson would survive an assassination attempt by Richard Lawrence, a mentally unbalanced out-of-work house painter, who believed that Jackson had prevented the U.S. government from paying money owed him. Once paid, Lawrence believed, he would be crowned King Richard III of England. As Jackson left a funeral just conducted in the Capitol, Lawrence aimed a gun at the president, but the weapon misfired. It was the first attempted presidential assassination in U.S. history. Enraged, Jackson repeatedly beat Lawrence with his cane. Desperate, Lawrence wrestled another gun from his pocket and shot once again, only to have that weapon also misfire. Several people witnessing the fracas jumped in to protect the elderly president, including Representative Davy Crockett of Tennessee, who would die the next year battling the Mexican Army at the Alamo in San Antonio, Texas. Crockett and others tackled Lawrence and seized his weapons. It would be Jackson's last gun encounter. Battered by a childhood sword wound and bullet entry points, Jackson also suffered debilitating bouts of smallpox, exposure, dysentery, malaria, and likely lead poisoning from the bullets lodged in his body and mercury poisoning from folk remedies he took as a laxative. For most of his life, enough shot filled his torso that he supposedly "rattled like a bag of marbles" when he moved.

"Old Hickory"

Jackson had achieved wide fame in Tennessee but rose to national prominence as a result of his role in the War of 1812. Jackson never forgot the death of his brother and his mother's death nursing POWs on a prison ship during the American Revolution, and he had only to look at the wound on his hand to remember his near murder at the hands of the British military, so he fought the War of 1812 against the hated English enemy and their Native American allies with particular relish.

In January 1813, Jackson led an army of 2,000 Tennessee volunteers who marched toward New Orleans with the goal of defending the lower Mississippi Valley, reaching Natchez, Mississippi, but Jackson received instructions from Madison's Secretary of War John Anderson to cancel the mission. Jackson disobeyed an order to immediately disband the force, and instead led them on a march back to Nashville. His resilience on this physically difficult journey earned Jackson the nickname "Old Hickory," in reference to the hardness of the tree so common in Tennessee, and the difficulty in cracking the tree's nuts.

In autumn 1813, Jackson finally received a command, receiving orders to secure the border that Alabama and Georgia shared with Florida (then under Spanish control). After the horrific Fort Mims Massacre of over 250 settlers by Red Stick warriors (discussed in the previous chapter), he needed little to encourage his genocidal longings towards Native Americans. Indians in the region would submit to his authority or face terrible consequences. At one Muskogee village near Huntsville, Alabama, called Tallushatchee, about 1,000 of Jackson's men surrounded the 200 inhabitants and killed all the men. "We shot them like dogs," one of the soldiers, a not-yet-famous Davy Crockett, later recalled. Jackson's men then force-marched the Native American women and children back to the American camp, where they were held as prisoners. Jackson's men then slaughtered another 300 Red Sticks at Talladega, Alabama followed by a decisive victory against the Creeks at the Battle of Horseshoe Bend, in which his 4,000-man army, bolstered with pro-American Muskogee and Cherokee allies, thrashed 1,000 Red Sticks, ending in another massacre in which about 800 Red Sticks died.

Jackson, acting on behalf of President Madison, forced a peace agreement in which all Muskogees—friends and foes—surrendered 23 million acres of territory to the United States, more than half of all they possessed in Alabama and Georgia. This was typical of how Jackson would treat his Indian allies. The land would now be opened to white conquest. In most of his battles he received Native American help but that never mitigated Jackson's harshness toward Indians. "Their struggle to survive never seemed to move him," Andrew Burstein noted with devastating understatement. As a reward for his victory, Jackson received a commission as a major general in the U.S. Army. He already enjoyed a national reputation for his military prowess, which Sean Wilentz suggested was grossly exaggerated:

> His foe, although formidable, . . . had only limited contact with white settlers, and were ill-prepared to undertake a full-scale woodlands war against the Americans. Lacking muskets and ordnance, they proved to be easy targets whenever Jackson was able to outnumber them, which Jackson regularly proved capable of doing. Jackson did perform well on the field for an inexperienced commander, deploying his men skillfully and redeploying them swiftly in the heat of battle . . . [His victory] . . . made Jackson look like a military genius. But the reality was more prosaic: Jackson, when provoked, was an unterrified and accomplished killer.

Jackson's successful defense of New Orleans in January 1815 made him a national hero, enhancing his largely undeserved military reputation, and provided a launching pad for his three presidential bids in 1824, 1828, and 1832. "Old Hickory, although a physical wreck, basked in the adulation," Wilentz observed. "He had risen from next to nothing to become the most renowned American general since George Washington—the greatest hero of what some were calling the second American Revolution. He had wreaked his vengeance on the British Army and their Indian and Spanish friends. As he neared the age of fifty, he knew he would have to sustain the honor he had won, lest his fame, unlike Washington's, disappeared." He need not have worried. From this moment on, Jackson would never be out of the national spotlight.

"THE MONSTER" AND THE 1824 PRESIDENTIAL ELECTION

Like millions of Americans, Andrew Jackson suffered a big financial hit during the **Panic of 1819.** This economic downturn was caused in part by the rebound of European agriculture after economic chaos and trade disruptions caused by the Napoleonic Wars in Europe from 1803-1815. Officers in the Second Bank of the United States, just chartered in 1816, made the wobbly economy worse, with these men deeply in numerous shady corporations that quickly went belly-up, promoting a series of criminal investigations. Langdon Cheavis, the president of the Bank of the United States, tried to tame inflation by tightening the availability of credit and demanding that all notes from other banks deposited with the national bank be paid back in precious metals.

State banks forced to pay back loans from the Bank demanded repayment from their customers, severely shrinking the money supply, suppressing consumer demand, and prompting a tide of businesses to go bankrupt. Businessmen filed more than 500 suits for debt in just one term of the county court in Nashville. Cities such as Philadelphia, where unemployment reached 75 percent, suffered the most from this economic downturn. Almost 2,000 unemployed workers there were jailed for not paying off their debts. A total of a half-million workers nationwide lost their jobs, out of a population of nine million. Tent cities sprang up all over the United States. As Sellers wrote, "Philanthropic groups distributed soup to the starving and passed out recipes for a 'cheap, wholesome, and savory' concoction of rice and mutton suet gravy that could feed a family of six for three cents."

Bankers were seen as the villains behind the financial collapse, and the Bank of the United States itself came

Battle of New Orleans and the defeat of the British by General Andrew Jackson. 1815

to be referred to as "The Monster." Jackson co-wrote a manifesto in 1820 that blamed the economic disaster on "the largest emissions of paper from the banks." Back in Tennessee, Jackson ran again for the U.S. Senate on the issue of the bank in 1822, winning his seat, which he saw as a springboard for a presidential campaign in 1824.

The Panic of 1819, and the earlier slavery-induced controversy over Missouri statehood, opened fissures within the Republican Party. The Federalist Party's frank elitism, opposition to increased white male suffrage and to immigration, and loud criticisms of the War of 1812 had killed the party by 1820, leaving the Republicans with a brief monopoly on power. Many former Federalists like John Quincy Adams joined the Republican ranks. Traditionally, Republicans had supported states' rights and an extremely limited role for the federal government—primarily providing for the national defense, conducting diplomacy and foreign policy and delivering the mail. New Republicans such as Adams (soon to call themselves "National Republicans") believed the federal government should promote economic development by building turnpikes and canals, and creating institutions like the Second Bank of the United States that they believed would promote economic development and business growth.

More traditional Republicans like Jackson blamed the Panic of 1819 on Federalist-style big government represented by the chartering of the Second Bank of the United States three years earlier. The bitter 1819-1820 battle over the admission of Missouri as a slave state and the drawing of the Missouri Compromise line barring slavery in all new states north of the 36°30' parallel also alarmed southern slaveowners like Jackson as a sign that power had shifted from the states to Washington, D.C.

These factions clashed in the highly contested 1824 presidential campaign, in which four Republican candidates – Monroe's Secretary of War William Crawford of Georgia, Secretary of State John Quincy Adams of Massachusetts, Speaker of the House Henry Clay and a dark horse, General Andrew Jackson —faced off against each other in one of the most complex and hotly disputed White House races of all time. The Missouri crisis of 1819 still fractured the country regionally. Crawford's status as a southern slave owner dampened his appeal in the North. Adams's position as an elite Northerner made Southerners suspicious of him. Henry Clay's lead role in the Missouri Compromise, which admitted Missouri to the Union as a slave state but limited the growth of slavery elsewhere, damaged his standing in both the North and the South.

Jackson had the least governmental experience of any candidate, but in 1824, this was more an asset than a handicap. The Panic had led voters to see Washington as run by corrupt insiders willing to bankrupt the ordinary person in order to enrich themselves. As John C. Calhoun of South Carolina, then the Secretary of War, observed, voters throughout the nation believed that there was something "radically wrong with the administration of government" and the public was "ready to seize upon any event and looking out anywhere for a leader." The largest number saw that leader in Jackson, whose victories over the British in the Battle of New Orleans, his defeat of the Seminoles, and his role in making Florida a U.S. territory led many to admire him as a hero, regardless of region.

The democratic revolution in American politics over the previous 24 years played a major role in the 1824 presidential election. Initially, a caucus of Republican congressmen selected Crawford to be their choice for president. While this method was the traditional procedure by which the party chose its nominee, many balked at the idea of Crawford, or any president, being selected in this manner. Without a Federalist Party opponent, whoever the congressmen selected would win the Electoral College vote by default without any consultation with the people. Thus, multiple candidates emerged to challenge Crawford's bid. Further, while six states still left the selection of members of the Electoral College in the hands of their state legislatures, sixteen states began to assign electors based on the popular vote. In the 1824 election, Jackson carried a clear plurality, 43 percent of the vote in those states compared to his nearest rival, Adams, who won only 31 percent. Clay got only 13 percent of the vote and Crawford, who remained on the ballot even though he had suffered a stroke that left him half blind and temporarily paralyzed, won only 13 percent of the popular vote.

The regional lines that would divide the country during the Civil War were already solidifying, with Adams carrying states only in his native New England and isolated electoral votes in other states in the North, Crawford's victories limited to the southern states of Georgia and Virginia, and Clay prevailing only in Ohio, Kentucky and Missouri. Jackson proved to be the only national candidate, carrying 84 percent of the votes in the southwest while winning outside of his home region victories in Pennsylvania, New Jersey, Indiana and Illinois. Yet, no candidate had earned enough Electoral College votes to win the presidency. The election would have to be decided by the House of Representatives.

Since he had won both the most popular votes and the most Electoral Votes (99), and also enjoyed the widest geographic base of support, Jackson assumed he would prevail in the House. Under the Twelfth Amendment, the House would select the president from any of the top three candidates with the highest numbers of Electoral College votes (Jackson; Adams, who had 84; and Crawford, who had 41). Each state delegation would get one vote.

Clay, who finished fourth in the Electoral College, was ineligible, but as Speaker of the House, he carried considerable influence and threw enough support to Adams to win him the presidency. Adams won thirteen state delegations and Jackson won seven. Clay backed the candidate he most agreed with, and Adams believed that Clay's diplomatic skills, in evidence during the Missouri crisis, made him the most qualified person to be the nation's top diplomat. Upon assuming the presidency,

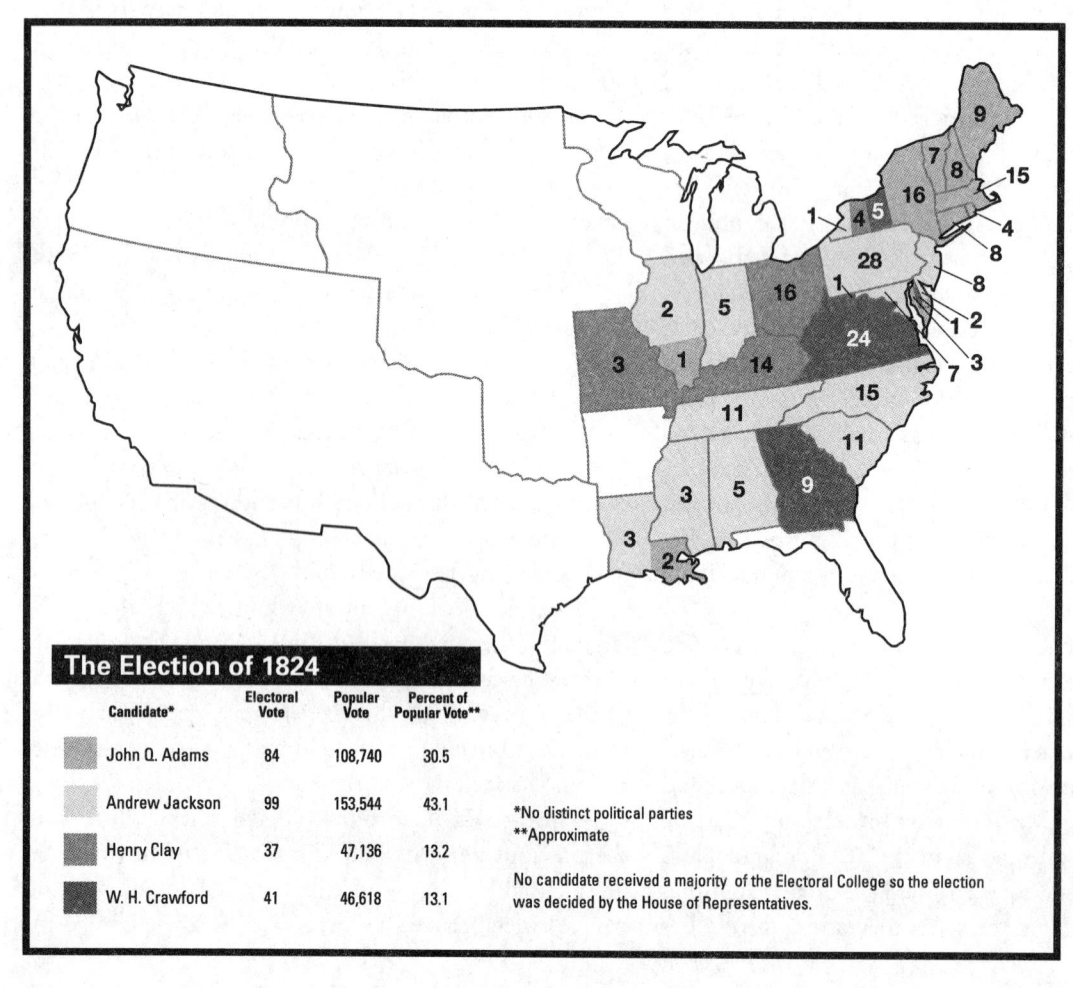

Map 11.1
The Election of 1824

The Election of 1824

Candidate*	Electoral Vote	Popular Vote	Percent of Popular Vote**
John Q. Adams	84	108,740	30.5
Andrew Jackson	99	153,544	43.1
Henry Clay	37	47,136	13.2
W. H. Crawford	41	46,618	13.1

*No distinct political parties
**Approximate

No candidate received a majority of the Electoral College so the election was decided by the House of Representatives.

Adams appointed Clay as Secretary of State. In the early nineteenth century that office was seen as a steppingstone to the White House—Thomas Jefferson, James Madison and James Monroe had served in that office. Certain that he deserved the White House and that the election had been stolen from him, Jackson furiously charged that Clay and Adams had made what Jackson called a "corrupt bargain." Clay had sold his support, Jackson charged, in return for his cabinet post. Referring to the disciple who betrayed Jesus in return for payment and then, in guilt, hanged himself, Jackson said of Clay, "So you see, the Judas of the West has closed the contract and will receive the thirty pieces of silver—his end will be the same."

THE JOHN QUINCY ADAMS PRESIDENCY AND THE LONG CAMPAIGN

Jackson never stopped running for president between his loss in 1824 and his eventual triumph in November 1828. Jackson relentlessly repeated the corrupt bargain charge and, with the help of crafty New York politician Martin Van Buren, a supporter of Crawford in 1824, built a formidable national political machine that would turn into the first modern American political party. Meanwhile, Adams's presidency was doomed at its inception. In a time of rising democratic sentiment, the ascension of Adams, the son of an unpopular former president, to the White House even though he had lost the popular vote, gave his inauguration the air of a coronation and undermined his moral credibility. Senator John Randolph so loudly repeated the corrupt bargain charges that Clay challenged the Virginian to a duel. They met at Pimmit Rim in Virginia. Clay fired his pistol, the shot passing through Randolph's coat without causing any damage to the senator. Randolph had already confided to friends that he had no intention of harming Clay, who was married and a father. Randolph fired his gun harmlessly into the air above his head, ending the dangerous encounter. Clay's reputation, however, suffered permanent damage after the 1824 election and would shadow his unsuccessful presidential campaigns in 1832 and 1844.

John Qunicy Adams had never strayed from the nationalist vision of his father (who died little more than a year into his son's presidency). In his annual message to Congress in December 1825, Adams asked for an ambitious federal program, including building a canal the would link the Potomac River that ran by Washington D.C. with the Ohio River, and the construction of a national road that would link the capital to New Orleans. He called for the creation of an Interior Department to handle public lands, a federal bankruptcy law, and the establishment of a national university, a naval academy, and a national observatory to make the United States a leader in astronomical sciences. Adams's vision was modern, would have stimulated the economy, improved commerce by easing the transportation of goods from one region to another, linked alienated regions more closely together, and provided a great boost to American education, but it was completely out of step with the mood of the times.

After the bank failures of 1819 and the corruption charges surrounding the Second Bank of the United States, too many Americans distrusted the federal government and big institutions and had little appetite for new, ambitious programs coming out of Washington. Congress approved none of Adams's proposals. The hostile reaction to his ideas, Adams later said, caused him "protracted agony." The new president was largely miserable during his term. "I can scarcely conceive a more harassing, wearying, teasing condition of existence" Adams wrote in his diary about the agonies of being the president. "It literally renders life burdensome." The final *coup de grâce* to his administration came with his unsuccessful support of higher tariffs (taxes on foreign-made goods) as a means of aiding American manufacturing, a policy fiercely opposed in agricultural areas like the South where voters wanted access to cheaper foreign goods. His opponents called the proposal, the "Tariff of Abominations," and it proved deeply unpopular in the South and the West when passed by the Congress in May 1828.

John C. Calhoun

Henry Clay

After this, Adams made no effort to prepare for a re-election campaign. The 1828 presidential campaign, one of the sleaziest in American history, would be a rematch between Adams and Jackson, but even before the contest started there was little doubt, even on the part of the incumbent president, how it would turn out.

JACKSON'S 1828 TRIUMPH

"The Little Magician": Martin Van Buren

The historian Lynn Hudson Parsons calls the 1828 presidential election "the birth of modern politics." The contest featured opposing sides that would form the nucleus of the second American two-party system—the Whigs (consisting of the National Republicans, who backed Adams) and the **Democrats** (Jackson's supporters).

Martin Van Buren, a clever and ambitious New York politician, became the architect of the Democratic Party. The son of a New York slave-owning tavern-keeper, Van Buren started his career in politics while still a teenager even as he built his law practice. Elected to state attorney general in 1815 and the New York state Senate in 1821, he became a leader of the so-called "Bucktail Faction" that successfully challenged the dominance of the state by forces allied to DeWitt Clinton (who served as governor and senator). In an era with only one national political party, Van Buren sought to redraw the line between the old Republicans and the former Federalists.

Unlike the Founding Fathers, who disdained political parties and believed that they only served to divide the country into uncompromising, bitter factions, Van Buren saw parties as healthy and vital for democracy. Parties, he wrote, "rouse the sluggish to exertion, give increased energy to the most active intellect . . . and prevent the apathy that has proved the ruin of Republics." Van Buren sought to re-create what he had accomplished with his Bucktails in New York—a tightly organized, disciplined political machine with a clear message, whose members could be counted on to loyally support a slate of candidates. Such an organization had never existed in the American Republic.

Van Buren was never explicitly pro-slavery, but not until later in his life did he become a critic of the institution. After the Missouri crisis he feared that the slavery controversy would block any national party from gaining traction and would eventually tear the nation apart. Van Buren, however, believed he could unite old-style, states'-rights Republicans and farmers in the North (who often opposed tariffs) with southern planters by emphasizing their shared opposition to the supposed increasing power of the federal government. Van Buren urged his party to, whenever possible, avoid the issue of slavery altogether.

More subtly, Van Buren and his allies sought to link slavery with democracy. Van Burenites would argue that because of slavery, white people would not have to do the least-respected, hardest work and even the poorest white would never be the "mudsill" of society. Slavery and black inequality meant that all whites, theoretically, could be equal to each other, and the presence of slaves, supposedly, meant that all whites could possibly climb up the economic ladder. The Van Buren faction, which would in a few short years become the Democratic Party, supported expanding the franchise for white men. The old Federalists like Adams, on the other hand, tended to be suspicious or even hostile to expanding the number of eligible voters and also consistently supported barriers to granting immigrants citizenship rights. The poorer voters and naturalized immigrants would gravitate toward the emerging Democratic Party, not just because that faction was perceived as friendlier to their interests, but also because of its perceived hostility to the African Americans, whom poor native whites and immigrants saw as economic rivals. Even before abolitionism became a major movement, already many poor whites in the North opposed any move toward slave emancipation because free blacks might compete for the same low-wage jobs that poor whites and immigrants filled in northern society.

In spite of the dominance of wealthy southern slave owners within the Van Buren faction, the Democratic Party created in the 1830s would also position itself as the party of the white working man, a party of the producers who toiled in the fields and in the factories against parasites who made money off of trading paper, such as the bankers who engineered the Panic of 1819. The early nineteenth century marked one of the widest gaps between rich and poor in American history. Since the American Revolution, the share of the natural wealth held by the richest 10 percent climbed from almost 50 percent to nearly 75 percent by 1860. The economy, fueled by population growth and the transportation revolution, became supercharged during what came to be known as the "Market Revolution." Business profits raced far ahead of workers' wages.

The genius of Jackson, Van Buren and others within the movement was to sell the Democratic Party, an institution controlled by slaveowners like Jackson, as the voice of these frustrated working men, and to deflect their anger primarily toward even more powerless African Americans and Native Americans. The votes of working class white voters would be crucial to the 1828 election, as the percentage of eligible voters participating leaped from 27 percent four years earlier to 57 percent. As the historian Lynn Hudson Parsons notes, the era of "mass politics" had begun, and Van Buren was ahead of the curve.

The Democratic Party that Van Buren would be creating, the party that would throw its support to Andrew Jackson in 1828, would therefore be pro-states' rights, usually anti-tariff (because its large farmer constituency wanted the lowest prices for manufactured goods), pro-expansionist (because more land taken from Indians and placed under white control meant more farm land available for white farmers), and, just as important, anti-black. Such a coalition would dominate American politics from the 1828 election until Abraham Lincoln's election as president in 1860.

"Palsied By the Will of Our Constituents"

Jackson had resigned from the United States Senate in 1827 so he would not be forced to vote on controversial issues. He returned to the Hermitage and followed the custom of presidential politics of the time and pretended to not be running for office. Starting in 1827, Van Buren tapped wealthy donors and began establishing pro-Jackson newspapers across the country and organized pro-Jackson political clubs across the country, with Jackson keeping close tabs on each development. John Quincy Adams thought such grubbing for votes was beneath the office of the president. He refused to use his power of appointment to reward friends and potential allies, or fire political enemies, from the executive branch, insisting that character and qualifications were all that mattered. While this was admirable, his stance also showed obliviousness to the new politics of the day and the ability of the White House to use its powers to expand a political base.

Adams rarely went out to speak and, following the tradition begun by Jefferson, he didn't deliver his annual messages to Congress, the speeches that later came to be known as "The State of the Union Address." (Jefferson was shy and hated public speaking, so he would send a written message each year that would be read aloud by the House of Representatives clerk. Other presidents followed this example until Woodrow Wilson in the early twentieth century). As carefully considered as his words usually were, the intellectual Adams only proved how out of touch he was when he spoke to the public through the written word. In his controversial first annual message to the Congress, when he called for building a national university and other projects that came to be ridiculed, he—unintentionally or not—insulted the voting public, urging members of Congress to not be "palsied by the will of our constituents." Adams was asking the Congress to not worry about the priorities of voters when considering big projects, a comment that only solidified his image as an arrogant, maybe monarchial, elitist who held the average person in disdain. It was exactly the wrong image to project in a era of expanded suffrage.

John Quincy Adams's father, the second president of the United States, John Adams, died, it seemed providentially, on July 4, 1826, the 50th anniversary of the Declaration of Independence, on the same day as his Revolutionary peer Thomas Jefferson. The younger Adams did not take this time to remind the nation of his family's role in founding the nation. Jackson, on the other hand, gladly took part in a celebration in New Orleans on January 8, 1828, the 13th anniversary of Jackson's defeat of the British army there. When Jefferson died, Jackson and his supporters forcefully depicted the Tennessee general as the rightful heir to the "Sage of Monticello." Meanwhile, the network of pro-Jackson newspapers that Van Buren helped create proved devastating to Adams' re-election efforts.

Van Buren also meticulously organized committees of Jackson supporters within the Congress and on the state level and within congressional districts, or even school districts. No campaign had ever so focused on the grassroots. Jackson organized nationally, whereas Adams had few advocates or even defenders in the South and the West. Jackson's men requested that friendly members of Congress raise funds for the campaign within their districts. With Van Buren at the helm, Jackson benefited from a sophisticated campaign structure that became a model for other presidential bids throughout the nineteenth century.

Poison Pens:
Newspapers and the Election of 1828

Newspapers became cheaper, printed news more quickly, and reached a broader audience by the 1820s and 1830s. Newspapers in the 1820s and 1830s relied on each other for content, with editors simply copying stories from publications they received from across the country. The development of steamships, railroads, telegraph lines, and better roads from the 1820s to the 1840s increased the speed by which news traveled and reduced the costs, which promoted the birth of even more periodicals. Meanwhile, printing a paper became considerably cheaper. Publishers developed a process of making cheap newsprint from wood pulp to replace the more expensive recycled rags that had been used to make paper previously. Printers used new steam-operated web presses that allowed printing at higher speeds on continuous rolls of paper that were then cut into sheets. These reductions in production costs allowed the rise of what came to be known as the "penny press," newspapers at affordable costs aimed at the broadest possible audience.

Van Buren realized the value of this new media market. In the late eighteenth and early nineteenth centuries, newspapers were often directly owned by political parties, or by supporters of particular candidates, and they made no pretense of objectivity. Newspapers assisted in organizing political party conventions and rallies, mobilized voters, promoted the view of candidates and demonized opponents. Amos Kendall's newspaper *Argus of Western America* in Frankfort, Kentucky, promoted the image of Jackson as a man who rose from humble circumstances to become a financial success and a war hero and farmer who hadn't forgotten his rural roots. Jacksonian-era editors rarely felt restrained in attacking the political opposition, with public figures often denounced harshly as cowards, traitors or possibly insane.

In the lead-up to the 1828 election, pro-Jackson newspapers accused the exceedingly prudish president of having engaged in premarital relations with his wife and, when serving as ambassador to Russia, having acted as a pimp for the Czar and procuring American women for the Russian emperor. The Jackson papers made a big issue of a mistaken report filed by Adams's son, John Adams II, who worked as the president's secretary. The younger Adams accidentally reported the purchase of a billiard table, balls and cues as a White House expense when it had actually been paid for by the president himself. Jackson's critics accused the president of misspending the public's money and suggested that pool playing, often associated with drinking and gambling, raised doubts about Adams' morality. Such a pastime, said a North Carolina Congressman, could only "shock and alarm the religious, the moral and the reflective part of the community."

The pro-Adams newspapers probably hurt their cause more than they helped. The *New York Advocate* fully bared the anti-immigrant bigotry of the Adams faction with an ill-timed attack on the Irish. "When we look at the population of some districts of our country, mixtd [sic] up with the dregs of all nations; when we are told that we have among us half a million of Irishmen, and when we know that they are all linked, together and move in a phalanx, we are constrained to say, that the character of our country is being degraded with the connexion [sic]," one issue complained. Needless to say, with such sentiments expressed by Adams' surrogates, few citizens of Irish descent supported the president's re-election efforts.

The ugly attacks on Adams's character no doubt shocked and offended the proper New Englander. No doubt Adams had no direct involvement in the anti-Jackson smear campaign that followed; he hardly could have been unaware of it and he didn't stop it. One of his allies in the press, Charles Hammond, editor of the *Cincinnati Gazette*, began publishing stories in 1827 claiming that Jackson had deliberately lured his wife, Rachel, while she was still married to Lewis Robards, and that the two had deliberately lived in adultery. It got worse. Hammond then charged in his paper that "General Jackson's mother was a COMMON PROSTITUTE!" Hammond wrote that Jackson's mother had been "brought to this country by the British soldiers! She afterwards married a MULATTO [mixed-race] MAN, with whom she had several children, of which number General Jackson is one!!!" Another pro-Adams newspaper compared Rachel Jackson to a "dirty, black wench." Jackson's political advisors immediately worried because their candidate had already killed a man for making similar comments, and they feared that another homicide might prove a political liability for Jackson as a presidential candidate. They managed to convince Jackson to keep his pistol holstered even as Adams' men launched another assault, this time on his military reputation.

Another Jackson foe, John Binn, published a campaign brochure decorated with boldfaced letters, a solemn, black border and coffins under the title of "Some Account of some of the Bloody Deeds of General Jackson." The coffins referred to six Tennessee militiamen whose terms of service were extended in 1814 and who then went AWOL, and were executed under signed orders by Jackson. The infamous "coffin handbill" portrayed Jackson as a cold-

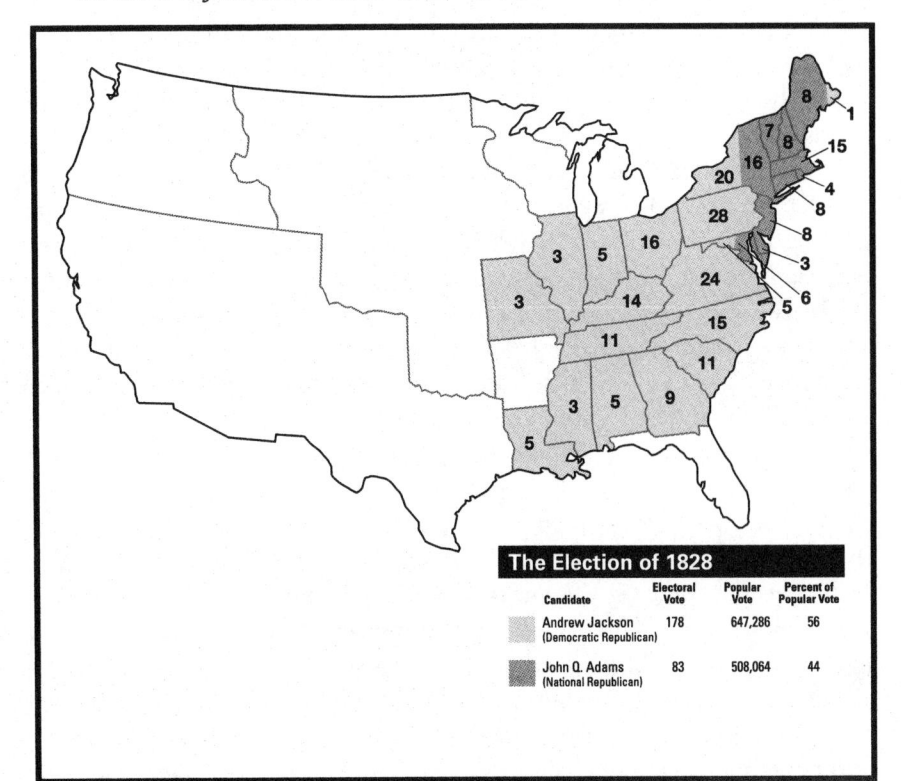

Map 11.2 The Election of 1828

blooded killer, as did other Adams campaign literature that brought up the execution of Robert Ambrister and Alexander Arbuthnot, his duel with Charles Dickinson, and his shoot-out with the Benton brothers.

The Adams campaign's election strategy backfired. For not the last time, the public reacted with hostility when a politician tried to make the private life of an opponent a public issue. Andrew and Rachel Jackson's marriage had survived for almost 40 years by the time of the 1828 campaign, and Jackson supporters believed that their candidate had rescued an honorable woman from a cad of a first husband. They thought it was unmanly for the Adams forces to attack a candidate's wife. Most voters saw Jackson's many violent episodes as evidence of his bravery and virility. Jackson carried 80 percent of the popular vote in the South. Adams carried only New England, New Jersey, Delaware, and Maryland, plus 16 of New York's 36 Electoral College votes. Jackson won everywhere else, sweeping the Deep South and the West as well as Pennsylvania and New York, and even picking up an electoral vote in Maine. Jackson prevailed in the Electoral College 178 to 83.

Unlike 1824, with Jackson scoring well almost everywhere in the country, this was an election shaped more by class than by region. It appears that lower-income voters battled as foot soldiers in the Jacksonian Revolution. These rank-and-file supporters "would include both isolated frontiersmen and working class city dwellers," Parsons said. "His greatest success outside of the South was in economically undeveloped regions . . ." As one bitter friend of Henry Clay stated, "The ignorant and degraded class of our population are all against us." Such

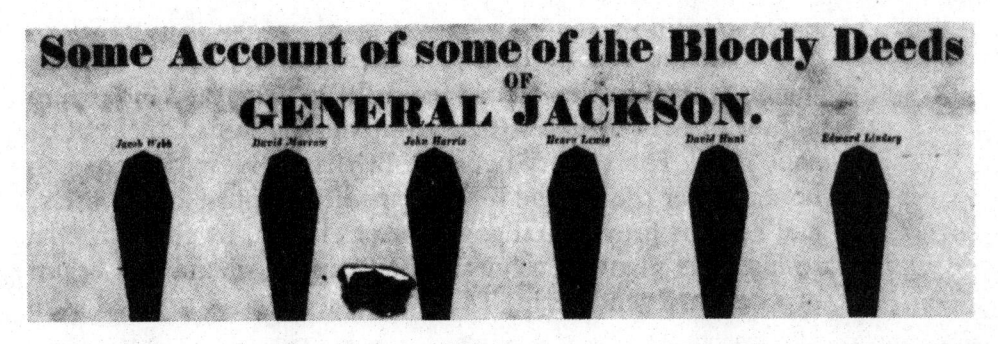

The Coffin handbill was propaganda distributed by the followers of Adams that told of Jackson's brutal shooting of six militiamen.

voters undoubtedly found allure in a party explicitly committed to the cause of white supremacy, a party that ostensibly made even the poorest white worker part of an aristocracy of color. Many whites might be poor and might have limited influence over their nation's politics, the Democratic appeal went, but no white was worse off than the most privileged Native American or African American.

Jackson's joy in his victory was short-lived. Rachel Jackson took the attacks on her husband during the campaign personally, and it seemed to affect her health. During the fall she suffered a heart attack. Still, she bought a gown for the Inaugural Ball. Reportedly, she had been shielded from the accusations regarding her personal life until after the election, but read some newspapers repeating the charges while on a shopping trip. She died a few days later, on December 22, 1828. Andrew Jackson entered the White House a heartbroken widow and wore mourner's black the day he was sworn in for his first term. The new president would always blame his political enemies, like Clay, who was friends with the editor Hammond who had published the bigamy stories, for killing his wife. Much of his time in office, Jackson's relationship with his opponents was barely more civil than the Benton gun brawl.

John Quincy Adams, meanwhile, left the White House a bitter man, but his political life enjoyed a second act as Massachusetts voters returned him to Washington, D.C., this time as a member of the United States House of Representatives, where he served from 1831 to his death in 1848. He became the first and only former president to become a member of Congress.

JACKSON'S FIRST TERM

To the Victor Belong the Spoils

Few doubted that Andrew Jackson would enthusiastically embrace presidential power. As a military commander he had often gone beyond or ignored the commands of his civilian superiors, but Jackson always expected his edicts to be followed. Dealing with Congress and a strong-minded opposition would not be so easy, but Jackson would successfully assert his authority more often than not.

No president had used his veto power so generously before Jackson Washington first used the presidential veto to reject an appropriations act in 1792, and since then, the six previous presidents had directly vetoed legislation passed by Congress eight times or "pocket vetoed" bills (by refusing to sign a bill when the Congress is in recess) twice. Jackson would directly veto five bills and pocket veto seven, more than all his predecessors combined.

If Adams had refused to exploit the patronage power of the presidency to extend his political influence, Jackson had no such scruples. He instituted what came to be derisively known as the "**spoils system**," the term derived from the phrase delivered in a speech by a Jackson supporter, Senator William L. Marcy of New York, who proclaimed "to the victors belong the spoils." Jackson, certain that bureaucrats in the small executive branch might block implementation of his policy, began dismissing some federal employees and filling those posts with Jackson partisans. When government officers retired they would also be replaced with Jackson loyalists. The federal government began to function more like the political machines that ran big cities, like New York. Political advisors such as Martin Van Buren believed that federal patronage was a way to create an army of political activists personally loyal to the president and, when it was formally organized and held its first presidential nominating convention in 1832, to the Democratic Party.

Newspapers at the time claimed that the Jackson White House sacked hundreds of government workers in the first year the new administration took power, but that number most likely is partisan propaganda. Scholars estimate that the administration fired or accepted the resignations of 10 percent of the federal workforce. Qualifications for a particular federal job mattered less under this system than did devotion to Jackson and his ideas, campaign contributions to Jackson's political operations, and effectiveness at campaigning for the president and his allies. In spite of Jackson's devotion to small government, the executive branch would grow after the institution of the spoils system, in some cases jobs being created so they could be dispensed to political loyalists. Between 1832 and 1860, the number of positions in the executive branch increased threefold. The dispensing of jobs to supporters became both a burden and an instrument of political power for future presidents until civil service reforms in the 1880s.

The Eaton Affair

Suspicion and resentment shaped the Jackson White House. In 1824, former Secretary of War and U.S. House Representative John C. Calhoun of South Carolina considered a campaign for president but doubted he could prevail in the crowded field and instead ran for vice president, serving in that office under John Quincy Adams. Calhoun worked behind the scenes to undermine Adams, backing Jackson, but still hoping to one day win the White House himself. Jackson never trusted the vice president, nor many of the political insiders he appointed to his cabinet. This internal dissension only grew worse in the wake of a Washington soap opera surrounding the wife of Jackson's friend, Secretary of War John H. Eaton.

Eaton married Margaret "Peggy" O'Neale Timberlake, the daughter of a tavernkeeper, less than a year after her first husband, a sailor, died. Rumor in Washington had it that John B. Timberlake had committed suicide after he learned of an affair between Eaton and Margaret. One rumor suggested Peggy had miscarried while her husband had long been out to sea. In any case, Washington society frowned upon such a hasty romance in what was supposed to be a time of mourning. Stories spread about Margaret's alleged sexual promiscuity. The marriage took place little more than two months before Jackson's inaugural. The wives of numerous cabinet officers, and particularly Floride Calhoun, the wife of the vice president, shunned her and refused to be introduced to her at inaugural festivities.

The rumors surrounding his close friend's wife provoked Jackson's famous temper and poured salt on some very fresh wounds. The president had just lost his wife, Rachel, who had been slandered as an adulteress and bigamist during the presidential campaign, and Jackson, drawn to Eaton because of her beauty and charm, rushed to her defense. Jackson also felt kinship, given his and Peggy Eaton's shared humble backgrounds and the privileged status of women like Floride Calhoun. Jackson also suspected that the whispered attacks on the Eatons constituted a subterranean attack on him launched by an ambitious Calhoun, who sought to undermine the president to serve his own political ambitions.

Jackson organized an investigation into the Eaton Affair (which also came to be known as the "Petticoat Affair") and proved, to his own satisfaction, that the charges against the Eatons could not be true. He called a cabinet meeting, minus Eaton, to present the evidence. "She is chaste as a virgin," he declared to the stunned officials. The scandal didn't die down, but the president presented an ultimatum, insisting that anyone who doubted John Eaton's honor was personally insulting Jackson and "had better withdraw" from the cabinet. Between May and August of 1831, Jackson's attorney general and secretaries of state, the treasury, and the Navy, as well as Eaton himself, all resigned. Jackson's advisor Van Buren, serving as governor of New York, had played both ends against the middle during the scandal, but convinced the president that he stood firmly behind the Eatons. Jackson appointed Van Buren as the next secretary of state and, with John C. Calhoun as *persona non grata* as a result of the affair, the Little Magician became Jackson's heir apparent. Van Buren became a power within the administration. From that point on, Jackson would largely shun his official cabinet, except for Van Buren, and would heed the counsel primarily of his so-called "**kitchen cabinet**," consisting of longtime friends and confidants.

"The Tariff of Abominations"

In spite of conflicts within his cabinet, by 1832, the movement around Jackson had already coalesced into the Democratic Party. That year, Van Buren cribbed an idea from the minor Anti-Masonic Party and helped organize the first-ever Democratic National Convention, which would nominate the party's presidential and vice presidential candidates, and where delegates would deliver dramatic speeches singing the praises of their nominees, and hammer out an official platform. For the first time, the nomination of a presidential candidate by a major political party became a definable, galvanizing event, replete with pagentry.

More important for the future, the Democrats instituted a rule requiring that two-thirds of the delegates at the national convention support a candidate before he could become the nominee. This threshold required future Democratic presidential candidates, until the Civil War, to support slavery or at least passively accept it, in order to get the party's nomination. After the war, it would require Democrats to be, at a minimum, passive partners in southern disenfranchisement of African Americans, segregation, and lynching.

Van Buren had few doubts that white Southerners would remain loyal to Jackson, who was one of their own, but he wanted to more firmly tie Dixie to states' rights advocates in the North. Van Buren tried to do so by pushing through the Congress a policy most old-fashioned Jeffersonian Republicans would have abhorred: a higher federal tariff on foreign goods. When Jackson became president, the Congress was in the hands of his allies, and opposition to him had not yet become organized.

By 1830, the South had become an agricultural giant, growing cotton tended by slaves. That year, cotton exports were worth $30 million ($623 million today). It was the United States' top export. The high profitability of cotton meant the South had invested little in manufacturing and relied on the North and industrialized nations like England for its factory-produced products. White Southerners, therefore, preferred low tariffs (taxes) on foreign-made goods, because the competition between European and northern manufacturers guaranteed them lower prices for goods.

In 1828, Van Buren served as U.S. senator from New York and, as part of his national strategy to secure Jackson's victory in the presidential election, he convinced his allies in the Congress to pass a tariff bill that would heavily tax foreign-produced wool, flax, distilled spirits, iron, and hemp, giving aid to those industries in the North. Van Buren calculated Jackson's indirect support for the measure would increase his popularity in the northeast while Southerners would support him anyway, since they detested Adams. Van Buren underestimated the anger the law would stir in the South, where the package of duties came to be known as "The Tariff of Abominations." That anger reached a boiling point when Jackson failed, contrary to the expectations of the southern delegation, to even mention the tariff in his first two annual messages to Congress. The issue particularly resonated in South Carolina, which faced fierce competition from other cotton-growing states in the South, paid high tariffs on finished products made with cotton it produced, and had been badly hit by the economic slump of the 1820s. South Carolinians like Vice President Calhoun saw the tariff as a serious roadblock to the state's recovery.

Lurking in the back of Calhoun's mind, and the minds of other Southerners, was fear of what the passage of the tariff meant concerning the power of northern states in the Congress and the implications this held for the future of slavery. Northerners now were a clear majority in the House of Representatives. The northern population was increasing faster than that of the South by reproduction and immigration. Immigrants from Ireland and elsewhere found the North, with its wider availability of jobs, more attractive and were turned off by the South's dependence on slavery. More than 7 million people lived in free states by the 1830s, compared to 5 million in the slave states, and many of the Congressmen from free states began to openly oppose slavery if for no other reason than because slaves represented a threat to white jobs. To men like Calhoun, the so-called Tariff of Abominations illustrated the power of the federal government to impose laws on the South, a power that might eventually be used to abolish slavery.

Slave Rebels

Slavery had turned South Carolina into an armed camp by the 1820s, and state leaders turned to extreme measures to protect it. In 1822, a freed black in Charleston named Denmark Vesey concocted one of the most ambitious slave revolts in American history. A talented slave from the Caribbean, Vesey had convinced his owner to rent him out for work, with the earnings split between him and the master. Vesey used these earnings to purchase a city lottery ticket in 1799. He spent his winnings to buy his freedom, but he lacked the funds to purchase his wife and children. He went to work as a carpenter.

He became a lay preacher at the local African Methodist Episcopal Church, which had approximately 6,000 members, mostly slaves.

Vesey's congregation became fascinated with the story in the Book of Exodus in the Christian Bible, which related how God led Moses and the children of Israel out of slavery in Egypt. Vesey believed God hated slavery and would save African Americans from bondage. One night, Vesey saw a comet in the sky, and he believed that this was a sign from God that a miracle of deliverance would soon unfold in South Carolina. Vesey's congregation believed that God would destroy the city of Charleston just as he had the pagan city of Jericho in the Book of Joshua. The congregants were not content to passively wait for their earthly salvation, however, and they laid plans for an armed uprising in 1822. According to the plan, the plotters would seize the state arsenal, distribute the arms to what they hoped would be a growing army of liberated plantation slaves who would then slay slavemasters and spread the revolution. Vesey and his cohorts planned to kill Charleston's white men including the governor, and, after gaining control of the city, seize control of naval vessels in the harbor and escape the United States, setting sail for Haiti, a republic which had been established by rebellious slaves in 1803.

One of the conspirators, Gullah Jack, an African conjurer, provided the slave rebels with special amulets and cast spells he said would render the slave rebels invulnerable to bullets. However, frightened slaves aware of the plot feared it would fail and that they would be executed as a result. They revealed the conspiracy to white authorities. As expected, a roundup of slaves ensued, with suspected rebels tortured into confessions, though many refused to name their co-conspirators. Vesey was captured June 22. Officials hanged Vesey and five other men on July 2, with Gullah Jack killed a few days later. In all 35 conspirators were hanged, with 22 killed in a single day.

Stories circulated that between 600 to 9,000 slave conspirators remained at large. The event terrified white South Carolinians. They had convinced themselves that their slaves were childlike and wanted the firm guidance of their supposedly loving white masters. Slaveowners had sometimes spoken of their chattel as members of the family and convinced themselves that their black property loved them much as a pet might love its master. The news that a coachman he trusted had entered the Vesey conspiracy rattled one wealthy Charleston slaveowner. Visiting the slave who always seemed obedient but who now awaited punishment in a jailhouse, the hurt master asked, "What were your intentions?" The slave looked coldly at his tormentor and announced to the white man that he planned "to kill you, rip open your belly, and throw your guts in your face."

White South Carolina armed itself and increased nighttime slave patrols, which roamed the woods to catch escaped slaves or those who might be carrying word of another slave revolt from plantation to plantation. In Charleston to this day, antebellum homes are ringed with fences topped with sharp spikes, a defensive measure against slaves who might climb over the fence to kill their masters. At night, many slaveowners became prisoners in their own homes. Convinced that foreign black sailors had conspired with Vesey, the South Carolina legislature passed the Negro Seaman Act, which prohibited free black seamen from leaving their ships, thus imprisoning them when docked at Charleston. Supreme Court Justice William Johnson, presiding over the federal circuit court that included South Carolina, overturned the law, noting it violated naval treaties between Great Britain and the United States. The South Carolina state senate declared it would ignore the court ruling and would enforce the law anyway.

To justify this flagrant violation of a court ruling, the state of South Carolina dusted off a legal theory first proposed by Thomas Jefferson during the controversy over the Alien and Sedition Acts in the 1790s—a concept that came to be known as nullification. According to Jefferson, in his *Kentucky Resolution* (written to protest a law passed during the Adams administration that essentially criminalized criticism of the White House's handling of political tensions with France), Jefferson argued that states were sovereign entities that had voluntarily entered the Union and they retained their power to not comply with federal laws they deemed unconstitutional. The South Carolina Senate nullified Judge Johnson's decision, and the Madison administration made no attempt to enforce it, giving the Palmetto State politicians a *de facto* legal victory.

Slavery continued to poison everything it touched, reducing African Americans to abused property and filling southern whites with dread fear of their human property. This paranoia only deepened in August 1831 when the deadliest slave revolt in southern history broke out in Southampton County, Va., a would-be revolution led by another black preacher, Nat Turner. Turner led 60 slaves who shot and hacked to death about 60 white men, women and children.

Turner, a self-appointed Baptist preacher who conducted faith healings and preached to whites and blacks, saw himself as a prophet of God sent to Earth to bring divine wrath upon white slave owners. Since childhood, Turner claimed, the Holy Spirit regularly spoke to him and assured him that God would give him an important mission. Around 1830, Turner saw visions of a violent, bloody final struggle between good and evil, the Battle of Armageddon described in the Book of Revelation, but Turner saw combat between black angels and white demons. Turner saw a vision of the crucified Christ set against a dark night sky and the next day encountered red spots dotting a cornfield, which he interpreted as Christ's blood. Turner took a solar eclipse in February 1831 as a sign from God that he must lead slaves in that final battle against the forces of Satan, and he started sharing his prophecies with other slaves. The uprising began August 21. The state militia aided by U.S. Naval forces and units from North Carolina obliterated the rebellion within two days. The state of Virginia executed 56 blacks, including Turner who died November 11. After the hanging, Turner's body was skinned, beheaded and quartered (tied to four horses that were made to run in different directions, pulling the body apart.)

A panic swept through the state. Whites murdered as many as 200 African Americans. Whites realized as never before that their slaves were not grateful children, but people who burned with the desire for freedom, many of whom would murder their overlords in an instant should a convenient opportunity ever arise. In the aftermath of the Vesey and Turner revolts, the South transformed into a primitive police state in which mail was opened by postal authorities to search for anti-slavery literature, armed slave patrols roamed the woods at night in search of escaped slaves, and states built their own small armies in preparation for possible revolts.

The rise of a more vocal abolitionist movement in the North, backed by Quakers and by men like the journalist and activist William Lloyd Garrison of Massachusetts and the evangelist Theodore Weld of New York only intensified white southern suspicions, not just of their possibly rebellious servants but also of northern whites who might incite them to violent resistance.

In 1835, abolitionists initiated a "postal campaign" in which they blanketed the North and South with anti-slavery tracts. Southern slaveowners worried that this literature might end up in the hands of their servants and incite rebellions. The Jackson administration and Democrats in Congress contemplated passage of a federal censorship law that would ban such literature from being distributed in the mail but, concerned about the constitutionality of such laws, the Jackson administration quietly gave the green light to local postmasters to ignore federal postal regulations, to remove suspected anti-slavery material, and to destroy it. From 1836 on, abolitionists also bombarded the Congress with petitions calling for the abolition of a speedy end to the domestic slave trade in Washington, D.C. Slave auctioneers sold human beings within hearing distance of the U.S. Capitol, which even some whites not committed to abolitionism considered a national disgrace.

The Democratic majority in the Congress required such anti-slavery petitions to be automatically tabled at the beginning of each session, thus silencing debate on the issue. This became known as the "Gag Rule." By this point, John Quincy Adams was serving in the House and he began a long crusade to end the practice. He would not succeed until 1844.

The Nullification Crisis

Slave revolts and the fear that Northerners were encouraging the overthrow of the "peculiar institution" provided the context for the explosive reaction to the 1828 tariffs. Calhoun and others were not eager to hand any powers to a federal government that might fall into the hands of abolitionists. Even as he served as Adams's vice-president, Calhoun had recruited opposition to the tariffs, constructing a complicated legal argument for defying the tariffs based on the Jeffersonian concept of nullification articulated in the Kentucky Resolution of 1798 challenging the Sedition Act. In 1828, Calhoun anonymously penned and self-published an explosive pamphlet, the *Exposition and Protest*, which echoed and expanded upon Jefferson's treatise, suggesting that the Constitution, effectively, was a treaty between nations and that it was up to each sovereign state, and not the federal courts, to determine whether a federal law violated the Constitution. Calhoun argued that a state could nullify within its borders any national law it deemed unconstitutional. The federal government could only force a state to comply at that point, he insisted, if it incorporated the law into a new constitutional amendment and convinced the states to ratify the provision, a rather arduous process for legislation as mundane as taxes on foreign goods. If such an amendment passed, Calhoun said, an objecting state would still reserve the right to secede from the Union. His concept of federalism had no basis in constitutional history and would have shattered the country into a crazy-quilt of conflicting laws and crippled the ability of Congress to regulate commerce and promote the general welfare, duties given it by the Constitution, thus destroying any chance of effective government at the national level. But for Calhoun, resistance to the tariff and in the future—the defense of slavery—had become paramount, even above national unity.

When Jackson, a fellow Southerner, became president in March 1829, Calhoun banked on Jackson to oppose the tariff, expecting him to propose a repeal, but the vice president miscalculated. The *Exposition*, meanwhile, sparked a fierce debate in Congress in January 1830 between Senator Daniel Webster of Massachusetts and Robert Y. Hayne of South Carolina. The initial debate centered on the issue of sale of public lands but soon centered on the doctrine of nullification. Webster powerfully argued that a nation built upon nullification had entered into a suicide pact. Only a strong union, bound together with respect for the authority of the federal government and national law, he argued, could guarantee liberty for all American citizens, in whatever state they lived. "Liberty and Union, now and forever, one and inseparable!" he proclaimed. Webster's Senate speech would be published across the country, in newspapers and other periodicals and political pamphlets. Meanwhile, South Carolina election season in 1830 focused on the tariff issue and candidates across the state called for a nullification convention to declare the 1828 tariff null and void.

Jackson had on various issues been an advocate of states' rights, but he also embodied fierce nationalism. He despised challenges to his authority as chief executive of the federal government. When he found out that Calhoun—a man he despised as a potential rival in a future presidential campaign and whom he held responsible for the Eaton affair—had authored the *Exposition*, and had been organizing opposition to the tariff, Jackson boiled over. Jackson would brook no further disloyalty from the vice president. The president attended a gala dinner April 13, 1830 held by Democratic Congressmen honoring the late Thomas Jefferson's birthday. The event had become an annual affair, part of Van Buren's party-building efforts. Jackson sat quietly as Calhoun's allies made speech after speech defending the extreme states' rights position articulated in the *Exposition*.

After the heated oratory, the president rose to make a toast and he sent a chill through the room as he made clear his disdain for the previous speakers. "Our federal union," he said, "It must be preserved." Someone in attendance later said those at the table turned absolutely quiet and that, "An order to arrest Calhoun where he sat could not have come with more blindingly staggering force." Shaken, Calhoun knew he had been outed as the instigator of the nullification movement, and he sensed the president's rage. Calhoun calmed himself and responded with his own icy toast. "The Union," he said. "Next to our liberties, most dear."

To Jackson, politics were always a matter of personal honor, and Calhoun's campaign for nullification served, in the president's mind, as an act of personal betrayal. "I had too exalted an opinion of your honor and your frankness," Jackson wrote to him. Then, referring to a scene in William Shakespeare's play *Julius Caesar* where the Roman general realizes that his friend Brutus has joined a circle of assassins stabbing him to death and says, in Latin, "You too, Brutus?" Jackson wrote, "I had a right to believe you were my sincere friend, and until now, never expected to have occasion to say to you, in the words of Caesar, *Et tu Brute*." The relationship between Jackson and Calhoun turned bitter and the vice president resigned in December 1832 in order to serve as South Carolina senator.

A few days later, a South Carolina congressman visited Jackson at the White House, told the president he would be visiting his home state, and asked if Jackson had any messages for the Congressman's constituents. "Yes, I have," Jackson said. "Please give my compliment to my friends in your state and say to them that if a single drop of blood shall be shed there in opposition to the laws of the United States, I will hang the first man I can lay my hands on engaged in such treasonable conduct, upon the first tree I can reach."

In order to appease South Carolina, Congress passed lower tariffs in 1832, but the rates were not cut enough to appease Calhoun's allies. Nullifiers dominated the state elections in 1832. In October 1832, the South Carolina legislature authorized the convening of a nullification convention. The convention met in November 1832 and nullified not only the tariff of 1828, but also the duties approved in 1832. The convention approved an Ordinance of Nullification that declared that the state would not collect duties at its ports beginning February 1, 1833. Many politicians in South Carolina spoke of using their militia to prevent the federal government from collecting the tariffs.

Many had heard of Jackson's violent temper and knew him to be impulsive and thin-skinned, but in the **Nullification Crisis**, he would surprise even his critics with his political skills. Jackson's position was clear: nullification and secession violated the United States Constitution. He issued a statement in which he declared that, "The laws of the nation must be enforced." Speaking in a message directly to South Carolinian voters, he said, "Their object is disunion. But be not deceived by names. Disunion by armed force is *treason*. Are you really ready to incur its guilt? If you are, on the heads of the instigators of this act be the dreadful consequences; on their heads be the dishonor; but on yours may fall the punishment. On your unhappy state will inevitably fall all the evils of the conflict you force upon the Government of your country . . ."

Unchecked, the crisis could have led to civil war. Jackson, however, cleverly took a two-sided approach that would assert the right of the government in Washington to enforce federal laws but also diffuse the potentially dangerous controversy over the tariff in South Carolina. He asked the Congress for a "Force Bill" that would empower him to dispatch federal troops into South Carolina to end resistance to the tariff and restore the authority of the executive branch. At the same time, the president backed another bill reducing tariffs over a long duration to levels acceptable to the South Carolina nullifiers, what came to be known as the Compromise Tariff of 1833. South Carolina rescinded its nullification of the tariff but at the same time declared the force bill to be unconstitutional. The issue, however, had become moot since the lower tariffs began to be collected at South Carolina ports. Both sides claimed victory. Jackson believed he had demonstrated the power of the federal government to enforce laws in the state, but nullifiers believed their threats had forced the federal government to capitulate.

Yet, the nullification doctrine was alive and well and would be used when southern states claimed a right to secede when Abraham Lincoln won the presidency in 1860. Meanwhile, Calhoun's national political ambitions had been destroyed, and he had no chance of ever securing the Democratic Party's presidential nomination in the future. Calhoun was dropped as Jackson's running mate in the 1832 re-election campaign and replaced with the ever-ambitious Martin Van Buren.

Conspiracy Theories

By the 1830s and 1840s, Americans began to distrust each other like never before. Slaveowners started convincing themselves that Northerners had become so anti-slavery that they were willing to incite slaves to murder whites. Northerners, witnessing South Carolina willing to tear up the Union in order to oppose tariffs, began to speak about a conspiracy of slaveowners who controlled the country. Later, they would argue that these slaveowners wanted to spread the peculiar institution to every corner of the country, even where it had long disappeared. A political party formed in 1828, the **Anti-Masonic Party,** focused on a conspiracy theory.

The party rose after an incident in upstate New York, in a region of the state known for its intense religious fervor called the "Burned Over District," in which William Morgan, a disgruntled former member of the Masonic fraternal order mysteriously disappeared in 1826 after he planned to publish a tell-all book revealing the shadowy organization's secrets. The issue became a statewide scandal, with Governor De Witt Clinton, himself a high-ranking Mason, offering a $2,000 reward (about $40,000 in today's dollars) for any information on his fate or his whereabouts. A year later, a corpse washed up on the shores of Lake Ontario and was presumed to be Morgan. A handful of Masons would eventually be arrested and prosecuted for his kidnapping, but no homicide charges were filed because no body had been positively identified. A court convicted the five defendants but gave them lenient sentences, outraging a public because so many judges, lawyers, others in law enforcement, and politicians were Masons themselves. Masonry had always been popular with influential elites such as George Washington and Benjamin Franklin, and publications arose that suggested the organization secretly controlled the world and sought to use that power for nefarious purposes. By 1830, 140 anti-Masonic newspapers were published across the country. The Anti-Masonic Party, which called for the abolition of secret societies and secret oaths, started as a New York organization and became the chief opposition to the reigning Democrats in the state.

The party spread, and William A. Palmer won the gubernatorial race in Vermont in 1831 on the Anti-Masonic ticket. Joseph Ritner also won the governor's mansion in Pennsylvania as an Anti-Mason. The party would hold the first presidential nominating convention in the history of the United States in 1832 when it gave the nod to William Wirt, a Virginian and former U.S. Attorney General, for the president. Former President John Quincy Adams joined the movement and ran unsuccessfully for governor of Massachusetts as an Anti-Mason. These panics over conspiracy theories and the intense religious devotion of the era, which saw the rise of doomsday sects and new religions like Mormonism, reflected anxieties over the rapidly rising market economy in which more skilled artisans found themselves replaced by machinery, and more went from economic independence as small farmers to being wage laborers. Many sought an explanation for their uncertainty, their sense of powerlessness, and their anxiety over the future and Masons provided an easy scapegoat. The panic over Masons eased and the party disbanded by 1838, many of the former members joining the Whig Party, which formed after the 1832 election.

The Bank War and the 1832 Campaign

Jackson helped increase the political paranoia in the land with his constant complaints against the "Monster" Second Bank of the United States. No issue more polarized political elites than the so-called "**Bank War**" of the 1830s. Jackson blamed the Second Bank for investment losses in the Panic of 1819 and held a rigid belief in a specie-based currency (actual gold or silver coins, or paper money supported by precious metals). He had no trust in purely paper currency, which the Second Bank of the United States had issued in abundance at the time of the Panic.

"The Bank of the United States was perfectly well managed," as Burstein wrote. "It regulated the availability of credit through its practical control over the loan activities of the state banks. But to Jackson, the national bank was a morally suspect institution, a symbol of secret manipulation. His combined ignorance and excitement led to a personal war against the bank's recharter and removal of federal deposits. 'Divorce the government from the banks,' as Jackson put it often."

The 20-year charter for the Second Bank was due to expire in 1836. However, Jackson's old nemesis Henry Clay, serving as senator from Kentucky and yearning to challenge Jackson in the next presidential election, and Senator Daniel Webster (his ally from Massachusetts) wanted to make the bank a political issue in the 1832 White House campaign. They prodded **Nicholas Biddle**, the president of the Bank, to apply for a new charter in 1832. Clay suspected that support for the Bank, which could be used to finance transportation projects, might win support for his presidential bid in the largely undeveloped northwest. Knowing Jackson's volatility, Clay and Webster hoped that Jackson might emotionally respond to the issue and make a fool of himself. With Clay and Webster at the helm, Congress voted to re-charter the bank in 1832, but Jackson vetoed the legislation.

The involvement of Clay, whom Jackson saw as the "Judas" who arranged the "corrupt bargain" in the 1824 election, in the bank issue only intensified Jackson's opposition to rechartering the bank. Once again, Jackson's political opponents underestimated him and his nonstandard, but nevertheless eloquent, command of the language. Jackson's veto message became a classic of political rhetoric, seen by his followers as a stirring hymn to the beauties of Jacksonian democracy. The Second Bank of the United States, Jackson insisted, was illegitimate, "unauthorized by the Constitution, subversive of the rights of states, and dangerous to the liberties of the people."

Jackson attacked the Bank as being a creation of manipulative insiders, owned by shareholders from the American Northeast and British investors. "Already is almost a third of the stock [shares in the bank are] . . . in foreign hands . . . Is there no danger to our liberty and independence in a bank that in its nature has so little to bind it to our country?" Jackson wrote. The Bank, Jackson suggested, robbed the West and the South in order to enrich the eastern cities and British businessmen. People are born with unequal talents, Jackson admitted in his message, and these differences produced wealth and poverty, but he wrote the government must not play any role in exaggerating those differences. The president opposed "any prostitution of our government to the advancement of the few at the expense to the many."

Clay, Webster and Biddle received the veto message with delight. In their minds, the message revealed the president to be addled and unstable, the message itself incoherent. Biddle himself published 20,000 copies of the veto message as a campaign pamphlet, assuming it would hurt the president. Clay and his backers would be sorely disappointed. Jackson had deftly touched on all the anxieties, resentments and hopes of the 1832 electorate. Jackson posed the bank issue as a battle between the average person and Washington insiders, rich vs. poor, hardworking farmers vs. vulture-like financiers, the virtuous South and West vs. the corrupt Northeast, and patriots vs. foreign plutocrats. Once again Jackson, the slaveholding overlord of a vast plantation, successfully portrayed himself as a voice of the ordinary people battling democracy-hating aristocrats.

Clay emerged as the candidate of the anti-Jackson National Republicans, soon to evolve into the Whig Party. The bank issue and American policies towards Native Americans would emerge as the key issues in the campaign. Jackson had supported legislation mandating the removal of Indians to west of the Mississippi, a position particularly popular in the southeast and the old northwest (the region around the Great Lakes). Van Buren and other allies again organized an 1832 campaign ahead of its time, maintaining card files of potential supporters to enlist their help in the campaign and their votes, creating campaign buttons, and organizing pro-Jackson clubs to run the campaign at the grassroots level. Jackson buried Clay in a landslide, beating Clay in the popular vote by 16 points, 54 percent to 38 percent. The president also carried almost all of the Electoral College, winning 219-49, with William Wirt of the Anti-Masonic Party winning seven electoral votes. Jackson, however, won fewer popular votes than in 1828, and his majority in the House of Representatives slid from 59 seats to 46. He also lost control of the Senate, where he had enjoyed a narrow four-seat advantage. His allies there now were in a minority by eight seats. Jackson's divisive, often autocratic leadership style had completely divided the electorate and led to the rise of a major opposition party.

JACKSON'S SECOND TERM

The Second American Party System

By 1833, the opposition to Andrew Jackson congealed into an organized political party, a group that shared many beliefs with their Federalist forebears, including support for the federal government as a positive force that could promote American economic development. Men like Henry Clay, Daniel Webster, and John Quincy Adams formed the core of the party, whose members saw Jackson as uneducated, erratic and destructive in his opposition to programs like building federal roads. The party's name, Whig—derived from that of a major British party that supported greater parliamentary authority vs. that of the monarchy—served as a sarcastic reference to the reign of King Andrew in the White House. Whigs supported the Second Bank of the United States as a force that had, save for the Panic of 1819, stabilized the American economy and encouraged business development. Whigs backed protective tariffs, which they felt helped infant American industries get off the ground while competing against their richer and more advanced competitors in England and elsewhere in Western Europe.

Whigs supported Clay's "American System," which, as discussed in the previous chapter, called for the aggressive construction of turnpikes, bridges, canals and, starting in the 1830s, railroads. Improved transportation, they believed, would modernize the economy, create jobs and

Jackson's political opponents pictured him as a King.

tie the different regions more closely together financially and culturally. Whigs also tended to draw reform-minded evangelicals who supported, on the local level, the expansion of public education, more humane prisons and better treatment for the insane and the disabled. Many Whigs would join the temperance movement, which sought to ban alcohol because of its role in crime and other social problems, and the movement for women's voting rights. Whigs won their strongest support in the Northeast and the Old Northwest (states like Ohio and Illinois, where Abraham Lincoln won election as a Whig Congressman, serving from 1847-1849). Whigs prevailed in regions marked by industrial production and by farms owned by whites producing for the national and global market.

A chief weakness of the party was its inability to come to a consensus on slavery, with northern Whigs favoring a limit to slavery expansion west into new territories, with even a minority favoring abolition, and southern Whigs defending slavery. They generally tried to avoid discussions of slavery altogether, seeing the subject as harmful to national unity. The party would splinter over the slavery issue in the 1850s but it served as the chief competition to Jackson's Democrats for two decades.

Killing the Monster

Jackson won, but the Second Bank of the United States still had a four-year lease on life and, with the president's support eroded in the Congress, the White House worried that the Congress might try to re-charter the bank and might be able to override a veto this time. Jackson sought to hasten the bank's demise and, ignoring his supposed insistence on strictly adhering to the Constitution, he defied the will of Congress by illegally transferring federal government deposits to a collection of state banks whose officers had supported him in the 1832 race, the so-called "pet banks." He completed the transfers by October 1, 1833.

Biddle faced a legitimate crisis with the loss of the federal deposits and struggled to keep the Bank of the United States' books in balance. He called in all of the bank's loans to state banks, and those state banks then demanded immediate repayment from their private and business customers. Biddle also hoped that by provoking a crisis he might turn the public against Jackson and create pressure to reverse his policies. Biddle's actions caused a ripple effect, pulling money out of circulation and provoking an economic panic in 1833-1834 that forced businesses across the country into default. The bank president again showed a knack for political miscalculation. The public blamed him and not Jackson for the economic slowdown. After the panic, however, business activity picked up and a boom followed, particularly as a flood of silver export from China and Mexico caused a flow of these precious metals into the United States. For this, Jackson got the credit.

Meanwhile, the circulation of federal funds in state banks enabled those unregulated institutions to make irresponsible loans, often to reckless land speculators. Inflation reared its ugly head. In the South, cotton and slave prices climbed. Wholesale prices jumped 50 percent between 1832 and 1836. Inflation only worsened as a result of the Deposit Act of 1836, which required the federal government to distribute $30 million of the $35 million budget surplus (the equivalent of $604 million of $706 million today) to the states when the Jackson administration retired the federal debt that year. The wild escalation of food prices led to New York City food riots near the end of Jackson's tenure in February 1837. In New York, the cost of flour had doubled. According to one eyewitness, the angry poor broke into stores.

> Barrels of flour, by dozens, fifties and hundreds were tumbled into the street from the doors, and thrown in rapid succession from the windows, and the heads of those which did not break in falling, were instantly staved in. Intermingled with the flour, were sacks of wheat by the hundred, which were cast into the street, and their contents thrown upon the pavement.

To combat inflation, on July 11, 1836, Jackson and Treasury Secretary Levi Woodbury issued the "Specie Circular," which required payment for government land to be made in silver or gold. This policy would later have disastrous consequences. For the well-off, at least, the economy still seemed to be booming, yet sicknesses lay underneath the surface, a problem Jackson bequeathed his successor, Martin Van Buren, when he left office in March 1837.

The Heir

Jackson gave Van Buren, one of a series of surrogate sons, his full blessing when the vice president sought the presidency in 1836. The Whig Party, in its infancy, lacked a single national candidate. Van Buren instead faced a number of Whig regional candidates, such as Senator Daniel Webster, expected to make a powerful showing in New England; General William Henry Harrison of Ohio, who held political strength in the old northwest; Senator Hugh Lawson White of Tennessee, who represented the Whigs' best hope in the South; and Senator Willie Person Magnum to compete in the south Atlantic states. Whigs hoped they could deny an Electoral College majority to Van Buren and throw the election to the House. Worried about whether Southerners would back him, Van Buren, a New Yorker, supported a change in postal regulations that would allow states to censor abolitionist literature.

Van Buren lacked Jackson's charisma, war record, and popularity, and so the Democrats won less support in 1836 than they had under Old Hickory, but none of the regional Whig candidates posed a serious challenge. The worst side effects of Jackson's Bank War and his economic policies had not yet made themselves apparent. Van Buren won just over 50 percent of the popular vote in a five-candidate field, but he carried states in the West, the South, the North and even in Webster's stronghold in New England. Webster turned out to not be a factor. Harrison fared the best of Van Buren's opponents, getting almost 37 percent of the popular vote and 73 Electoral College votes. The election turned out to be the last time a sitting vice president has won a presidential election.

Because 23 electors from Virginia refused to cast their ballots for Van Buren's running mate, Richard Mentor Johnson of Kentucky, he fell one vote short of the Electoral College majority needed to become vice president. Johnson's open relationship with Julia Chin, a mixed-race slave woman by whom he fathered two children, had become a campaign controversy. This would mark the only time so far in history that the Senate, under the provisions of the Twelfth Amendment, had to select the vice president. In the Senate, Johnson prevailed. At the inaugural, Jackson and Van Buren appeared together. The old general got much louder cheers than his successor. It was an ominous sign for the incoming leader. Van Buren could inhabit the White House after Jackson, but he could never assume Jackson's stature in the public mind.

"MARTIN VAN RUIN"

Jackson boosted Van Buren's rise to the White House, but he also burdened the next president with a deeply troubled economy, an unresolved diplomatic challenge posed by the successful Texas War of Independence in 1836, a strengthening and growing institution of slavery and the regional tensions it provoked, and management of the final and homicidal stages of Jackson's brutal Indian removal policies. Committed to a rigid belief in limited government in all circumstances, Van Buren rendered himself incapable of responding to a brewing economic depression. His white supremacist thinking and his desire to build the Democratic Party as a national force propelled the nation further toward civil war and bloodied the nation's hands with one of its worst acts of genocide.

Martin Van Buren

In his inaugural address, Van Buren's proposals for the future could be summarized as more of the same. "There was not, in his mind, all that much to do," according to historian Joel H. Sibley. "The most pressing issues of the era had been confronted and dealt with during his predecessor's years as president. The hated and dangerous national bank was dead, Indian removal [the policy of forcing Indians to move west of the Mississippi River] was in its last stages, the tariff issue remained dormant, and under control, and the American scene was prosperous and forward looking." Van Buren stated his clear intention to do as little as possible, insisting that the "wisest course is to confine legislation to as few subjects as is consistent with the well being of a society and to leave as large a proportion of the affairs of man as is possible to their own management."

Van Buren, however, would be a victim of bad timing, and his administration would be primarily remembered for a severe depression that would ravage the country from 1837 to 1843. Jackson's Specie Circular, and his restrictions on paper currency, contributed to severe deflation. The money supply shrank dramatically. Forced to lower prices for their goods, farmers and businessmen saw their profits drop. Wages dropped as well, which aggravated the downward cycle. Runs on banks—in which panicked depositors raced to withdraw their uninsured deposits, emptying those institutions' vaults and driving them to close—broke out all over the country. About 40 percent of the banks in the United States shuttered their doors permanently during this depression, with customers losing all they held in deposits. States defaulted on their loans, and construction halted in much of the country.

A half-million workers lost their jobs nationwide, with 50,000 jobless and the unemployment rate in New York City in the winter of 1837-38 peaking at a shocking 33 percent. Many of the unemployed found themselves homeless, shivering on the streets, and without assistance as churches ran out of money to offer assistance and no government aid was available. One New York worker, Asa Shipman, recalled he had been able to support his widowed mother and six brothers and sisters before the depression started.

> I was then making good wages every cent of which was spent in the family so of course I had nothing ahead . . . After a time work with me began to get short. First I had only half of the time and finally I was told there was no work . . . We had food enough in the house to last perhaps a week and my last wages lasted perhaps another week. In the meantime I spent every day in search of some kind of employment but all in vain. Nothing could be got . . . Starvation looked us in the face . . . We often went with one meal a day and that was of the plainest kind. How we ever lived six weeks that way I cannot now imagine.

Across the country, tens of thousands of workers went on strike and the wealthy began to loudly worry about a revolution. Unwilling to see the government play any role in relieving the poor or stimulating the economy, during the economic crisis Van Buren called for the government, already doing little, to do even less. Throughout the depression, Van Buren called for the government to maintain "severe economy," claiming that, "To keep the expenditures within reasonable bounds is a duty second only to the preservation of our national character and the protection of our citizens in their civil and political rights." Van Buren wasn't responsible for the policies that led to the depression. But the so-called magician who so innovatively guided Jackson's political fortunes and created the Democratic Party lacked the imagination to end or even relieve the economic misery. The voters would blame the president personally for this depression and during his term he came to be known as "Martin Van Ruin."

THE WAGES OF WHITENESS

There is no biological basis for the concept of race. Based on random traits such as skin color and hair texture, racial categories rest on the incorrect notion that different human groups have clearly distinct biological histories, i.e., that blacks, whites and others branched off into very clearly marked, separate family trees. In fact, millions of so called whites have relatively recent supposedly black ancestors, and vice versa. The concept of race rests on the mistaken idea that superficial features like color imply more important differences between these vaguely defined racial categories in terms of intelligence, work ethic, and character. The idea of race seems to have first developed as Europeans began their conquest of the rest of the world at the start of the 1500s and rationalized the enslavement of supposedly inferior, or even subhuman, Africans and the genocide of Native Americans.

By the time of Jacksonian America, race completely defined American society. Only whites were deemed intelligent and independent enough to function in a democracy. So-called non-whites, such as African-American slaves or Native Americans, possessing what Anglo-descended Americans considered animal-like natures, could not be allowed to participate in American life politically. Even in northern states where slavery had become illegal, African Americans were denied the right to vote; and when Illinois became a state in 1818, it prohibited African Americans from living there.

By the 1820s and 1830s, white society had long puzzled over where black skin came from. Many believed that Africans were the descendants of Ham, one of the sons of Noah described in the Book of Genesis. Noah cursed Ham's descendants to be "servants of servants" because the son had disrespected his father. Many white Christians in the United States argued that Africans' and African Americans' dark skin was a sign of that curse. Black slavery, basically, was God's will, they argued.

Some Americans sought scientific explanations for perceived racial differences. From the 1500s to the early 1800s whites speculated on whether the descendants of Africans would eventually get lighter-skinned the longer they lived in more northern zones. As late as the first decade of the 1800s, Dr. Benjamin Rush, one of the signers of the Declaration of Independence, suggested that blackness represented a type of leprosy. He claimed blackness even infected southern whites who were surrounded by slaves. Rush, however, believed that over the decades, blackness would be cured because of what he thought was the healthier environment of North America, and he made note of cases of blacks gradually losing their dark skin color over a lifetime. Undoubtedly, Rush was referring to cases of vitiligo, a skin condition in which the body in different spots stops producing pigment. Dr. Rush experimented on African Americans to "cure" them of their blackness, and he claimed he had achieved positive results in lightening skin by bleeding test subjects and subjecting them to enemas.

By the Jacksonian era, some ministers and scientists, still accepting the Bible as the source of all scientific knowledge, struggled with answering how blacks and whites could supposedly be so different and yet both be descended from the first two humans, Adam and Eve. Many proposed the theory of polygenesis, the idea that the creation story in Genesis only referred to the origins of white people. Adam and Eve were white, according to the believers in this theory. God had created blacks, Indians and other groups separately. This idea clearly implied that only whites were truly human and that people of color were separate species and could thus be justly used as farm animals.

This rationalization for vicious exploitation came at a convenient time. Since the invention of the cotton gin, slavery had never been more important to the American economy. Southern slaveowners had always argued that slavery was a "necessary evil." While slavery was regrettable, the vast lands of America could not be put to a productive use unless a large workforce was forced to do the labor. By the Jacksonian era, southern slaveowners began to argue that the peculiar institution was a positive good. It kept whites from having to do the most degrading work. It also, the argument went, was good for blacks, who allegedly had been saved from African savagery through slavery and now enjoyed living in safer, healthier white civilization. Blacks were permanently childlike, the white supremacists of the era insisted, and would be doomed forever to hunger, cannibalism, and the most primitive of existences unless placed under the firm, parent-like control of their white masters.

Van Buren was a man of his times, fully accepting the fashionable racist ideas regarding African Americans. Even though he voted against admitting Missouri as a slave state while serving as a U.S. senator from New York, he consistently accommodated slaveholders as vice president and president, not wanting to offend them for fear this might shatter the Democratic Party he had so carefully constructed. In his inaugural address, Van Buren condemned abolitionists and as president he vowed to veto any legislation that would outlaw slavery in the District of Columbia. He supported Democrats in the House who defended the gag rule prohibiting consideration of anti-slavery petitions. When Florida statehood came up for consideration, he vigorously resisted any attempts to restrict slavery there or any other U.S. territory.

INDIAN REMOVAL

Few aspects of American history are as shameful as the treatment of Native Americans, and a low point in that bloody relationship came during the 1820s and 1830s. By then, when much of the land west of the Mississippi was relatively uninhabited by whites and the biggest chunk of that land still lay within Mexican borders, the American government committed to a policy of Indian removal, bribing and forcing Native Americans within U.S. borders to settle west of the Mississippi River. Andrew Jackson and Martin Van Buren didn't initiate Indian removal, but they saw it through to its bloody end.

John Quincy Adams' Secretary of State Henry Clay insisted that Indians were a people "destined to extinction." He dismissed indigenous people as a race "not worth preserving," "essentially inferior to the Anglo-Saxon race," and not an "improvable breed." Contemplating their possible extinction, Clay felt no sorrow but believed that "their disappearance from the human family would be no great loss." During the Adams administration, it became clear that a treaty with the Creek (Muskogee) Indians in Georgia to swap land there for territory farther west had been drawn up under fraudulent circumstances, with representatives of the Creeks bribed by both state and federal agents to make the agreement. The Creeks assassinated the corrupt representatives who made the deal and then declared they were not obligated to follow it. The State of Georgia acted like nothing had happened and began surveying the Creek land in preparation for selling it to whites. The Adams administration allowed it to happen, ignoring previous treaties between the federal government and the Creek people guaranteeing the integrity of their lands.

The Creeks, along with the Cherokees, Chickasaws, Choctaws, and Seminoles, stood as one of what whites called **"The Five Civilized Tribes."** Federal and state government officials and Christian missionaries had previously insisted to Native Americans that as long as they remained supposed savages, they could not live peacefully alongside whites. Anglos, however, had made an implied promise to the Indians that if they "civilized," that is if they abandoned their traditional cultures and strictly conformed to white norms regarding land ownership, political organization, family structure and religion, they might win acceptance as a distinct but still welcomed people within the American nation.

Under the guidance of leaders like Guwisguwi (**John Ross**), the Cherokees in particular represented assimilation with the white majority in the extreme. They adopted a constitution based on the American model. Many within that community converted to Christianity,

Sequoyah, inventor of the Cherokee alphabet

mastered English, and adopted Western-style clothing. Another Cherokee, **Sequoyah**, invented an alphabet for their native language, and Cherokee-language Bibles were widely distributed in Cherokee territory. Land ceased to be seen as a source of identity and increasingly as a mere commodity. Instead of holding land as a community, the Cherokees began, like their white neighbors, to divide their homeland into privately owned lots.

Like white Southerners, they started buying and selling black slaves, and some absorbed the whites' beliefs in black inferiority. They passed laws forbidding interracial marriage with those of African descent. Some Cherokees became wealthy cotton planters running large plantations. They farmed in the same style as whites and married white women. Some cultural traditionalists within the nation bitterly complained that they had so completely adopted white ways that they ceased to be real Cherokees. The nation also published a bilingual newspaper, *The Cherokee Phoenix*, and they produced goods traded on the world market, including cloth, grain, and lumber. Cherokees had accomplished what whites supposedly wanted. But to whites, no technology, no modern businesses, and no accommodation to the dominant culture would ever be enough. The Cherokees remained in white eyes congenital savages—racial inferiors who stood in the way of progress.

By Jackson's first month in the White House in March 1829, Indian removal had become largely a fact in much of the North. New York State's Iroquois mostly struggled to live on tiny reservations while technologically and numerically mismatched, and after the War of 1812, the bands in the Old Northwest struggled as a scattered and demoralized people. In the Southeast, the demands for Indian resettlement only intensified as the white populations of Alabama and Georgia increased and cotton prices rose, making land more expensive for whites and harder to obtain. Then, gold was discovered on the Cherokee land as well. About 10,000 white miners flocked to the Georgia hills within the Cherokee domain.

Always hostile to claims of sovereignty as a nation within a nation, a unique relationship with the United States government ratified through a treaty, Jackson fumed that American progress would not be sacrificed in the interests of people he dismissed as "a few thousand savages." Indian lands, he believed, belonged to whites by right of racial superiority. At the president's prompting, Congress passed the **1830 Indian Removal Act**. The law required an involuntary "exchange of lands with the Indians residing in any of the states and territories, and for their removal west of the river of Mississippi."

Chief Justice Marshall and the Cherokees

The state of Georgia began implementing Indian removal almost immediately, often at gunpoint. Cherokee leaders still retained faith in the American system and turned to the federal courts to challenge the legality of the Indian Removal Act, their lawyers arguing that previous treaties the nation had signed with the United States government (in which Washington recognized Cherokee sovereignty and control of their traditional lands in Georgia) rendered the new land moot. Uncertain of the commitment of the federal government to removal, the state of Georgia, in a series of laws, stripped Cherokees of the right to their traditional lands and invalidated laws the Cherokees had implemented to govern their territory.

Meanwhile, another legal case, involving the right of white men to live in Cherokee lands and to marry Cherokee women, without licenses from the state of Georgia, worked its way through the federal courts. The two cases, ***Cherokee Nation v. Georgia*** (1831) and *Worcester v. Georgia* (1832), reached the United States Supreme Court. The majority opinions, written by Chief Justice John Marshall, sought to define Indian rights and the political relationship between Indian bands and the state and national governments.

In *Cherokee Nation v. Georgia*, the Supreme Court ruled that it did not have jurisdiction in the case because the Cherokees were not, as they claimed, a separate "foreign" nation within U.S. borders. Marshall wrote, instead, that the Cherokees constituted a "domestic dependent nation." Marshall noted that the Cherokees still retained rights to their land until they voluntarily surrendered such property. In *Worcester vs. Georgia*, the state had arrested and sentenced to four years of hard labor seven missionaries who had refused to get required state licenses before living on Cherokee lands. At least two of the missionaries were targeted for prosecution because of their strong opposition to Georgia's Indian removal policies. The missionaries' lawsuit contended that the State of Georgia had no authority to pass laws over tribal lands.

In his majority opinion, Marshall argued that the federal government, not state governments, had the sole authority to deal with domestic, dependent nations such as the Cherokee peoples. He acknowledged that the exercise of conquest and purchase can give political dominion, but those are in the hands of the federal government and not the states. The Cherokees held a special status as a "distinct community" in which "the laws of Georgia can have no force." The U.S. Constitution gave the federal government alone the power over Indian affairs, Marshall wrote.

The Supreme Court decisions outraged Jackson, who was happy to let Georgia expel the Cherokees. Three years earlier, at his first inauguration, Jackson raised his right hand and swore to faithfully execute the laws of the United States. Now he refused to honor that oath and announced his decision to not execute the Supreme Court's decision in the *Worcester* case. "(Chief Justice) John Marshall has made his decision," Jackson reportedly said. "Now let him enforce it." Jackson would let Georgia proceed in its expulsion of Cherokees and other natives, regardless of the Supreme Court ruling or standing American treaties with native peoples. In 1832, he ordered U.S. Army troops to aid the Georgia militia in forced expulsion of Native American tribes.

The Second Seminole War

Across the South, troops forced Indians westward at bayonet point. Not just the Cherokees, but the Creeks as well became victims of white greed. "White squatters and speculators crowded into Creek territory [in Georgia], frequently evicting natives from their homes before they had a chance to gather their belongings," wrote Robert Remini. "Angry exchanges triggered shootings." These violent incidents exploded into a full-scale war between Creeks and the Georgia militia in the Chattahoochee Valley in May 1836. It ended with the Georgia militia routing Creek resistance. "Enforced removal began with 14,609 Creeks carried off to the Indian Territory [modern day Oklahoma], some of them handcuffed and in chains," Remini wrote. In 1837, 5,000 more Creeks had been forced westward.

After armed forces expelled his people, one Creek leader pleaded with a military officer. "You have been with us many moons. Our road has been a long one . . . on it we have laid the bones of our men, women, and children . . . you have heard the cries of our women and children . . . Tell General Jackson if the white men will let us we will live in peace and friendship." This offer was not to be heard.

Afraid of his influence, the United States Army in 1835 arrested a Seminole leader in Florida, named **Osceola**, who loudly objected to removal and urged local Native Americans to hold onto their lands. After soldiers placed him in chains and locked him in a cage, Osceola, sensing the fate awaiting his people, tore out his hair and raged until he foamed at the mouth, according to white witnesses. After he calmed down, authorities eventually released him, but he would lead an uprising that came to be known as the Second Seminole War. This Jacksonian exercise in genocide proved a costly campaign in dollars and blood. Lasting seven years, from 1835 to 1842, this war against the Seminoles took place mostly in murky swamps unfamiliar to American troops. The war dragged on, with the Seminoles adopting guerilla tactics. Jackson told his commander, General **Winfield Scott**, to march toward the place where the "Indian women were collected" in order to draw Osceola and his men into an open battle and destroy his forces.

The Seminoles, women, children and all, refused to fall into a trap, and kept constantly on the move. The war,

Osceola of Florida

Map 11.3 The Cherokee "Trail of Tears"

lasting through the entire term of Jackson's successor Van Buren, eventually cost the U.S. government up to $40 million and the deaths of 1,500 American soldiers. A larger number of Seminoles died, some from starvation. Osceola died after a fierce battle in the Everglades. Political disunity, hunger, exhaustion and disease eventually forced the Seminoles to capitulate, and the Army would force 3,000 of them to flee west of the Mississippi River, with one-fifth of the original group of refugees dying from physical hardships during the brutal march to the distant Indian Territory.

The Trail of Tears

Even though many Cherokees and other Indians started abandoning Georgia because of the fear of white violence, bribery or discouragement, John Ross, the leader of the Cherokees, still refused to lead his people from their Georgia homeland. Van Buren now occupied the White House, but Jackson's bloody handprints were all over the tragedy that came to be known as the **Trail of Tears**, beginning in 1838. General Scott, also busy with the Seminole War, sent 7,000 white soldiers to Georgia to round up the remaining Cherokees. The soldiers were ordered to use any means, including whole-scale violence, to complete the ethnic cleansing. As with the Creeks earlier, soldiers arrived and allowed no time for the Cherokees to collect their personal effects before they were coerced into a long wintertime exodus. One of the survivors, Rebecca Neugin, would be 100 years old when she was interviewed in 1932:

> When the soldiers came to our house my father wanted to fight, but my mother told him that the soldiers would kill him if he did and we surrendered without a fight. They drove us out of our house to join other prisoners in a stockade. After they took us away, my mother begged them to let her go back and get some bedding. So they let her go back and she brought . . . bedding and a few cooking utensils she could carry and had to leave behind all of our other household possessions.

Cherokees would have little time to gather clothing that would protect them from the bitter cold they would encounter in the coming weeks. "Families at dinner were startled by the sudden gleam of bayonets in the doorway," one witness later said, "and rose to be driven with blows and oaths along the many miles of trail that led to [a] stockade. Men were seized in the fields, or going along

Indian Removal Act

U. S. Government, 21st Congress, 2nd Session

Chapter CXLVIII - An Act to provide for an exchange of lands with the Indians residing in any of the states or territories, and for their removal west of the river Mississippi.

Be it enacted by the Senate and House of Representatives of the United States of America, in Congress assembled, That it shall and may be lawful for the President of the United States to cause so much of any territory belonging to the United States, west of the river Mississippi, not included in any state or organized territory, and to which the Indian title has been extinguished, as he may judge necessary, to be divided into a suitable number of districts, for the reception of such tribes or nations of Indians as may choose to exchange the lands where they now reside, and remove there; and to cause each of said districts to be so described by natural or artificial marks, as to be easily distinguished from every other.

Section 2 - And be it further enacted, That it shall and may be lawful for the President to exchange any or all of such districts, so to be laid off and described, with any tribe or nation within the limits of any of the states or territories, and with which the United States have existing treaties, for the whole or any part or portion of the territory claimed and occupied by such tribe or nation, within the bounds of any one or more of the states or territories, where the land claimed and occupied by the Indians, is owned by the United States, or the United States are bound to the state within which it lies to extinguish the Indian claim thereto.

Section 3 - And be it further enacted, That in the making of any such exchange or exchanges, it shall and may be lawful for the President solemnly to assure the tribe or nation with which the exchange is made, that the United States will forever secure and guaranty to them, and their heirs or successors, the country so exchanged with them; and if they prefer it, that the United States will cause a patent or grant to be made and executed to them for the same: Provided always, hat such lands shall revert to the United States, if the Indians become extinct, or abandon the same.

Section 4 - And be it further enacted, That if, upon any of the lands now occupied by the Indians, and to be exchanged for, there should be such improvements as add value to the land claimed by any individual or individuals of such tribes or nations, it shall and may be lawful for the President to cause such value to be ascertained by appraisement or otherwise, and to cause such ascertained value to be paid to the person or persons rightfully claiming such improvements. And upon the payment of such valuation, the improvements so valued and paid for, shall pass to the United States, and possession shall not afterwards be permitted to any of the same tribe.

Section 5 - And be it further enacted, That upon the making of any such exchange as is contemplated by this act, it shall and may be lawful for the President to cause such aid and assistance to be furnished to the emigrants as may be necessary and proper to enable them to remove to, and settle in, the country for which they may have exchanged; and also, to give them such aid and assistance as may be necessary for their support and subsistence for the first year after their removal.

Section 6 - And be it further enacted, That it shall and may be lawful for the President to cause such tribe or nation to be protected, at their new residence, against all interruption or disturbance from any other tribe or nation of Indians, or from any other person or persons whatever.

Section 7 - And be it further enacted, That it shall and may be lawful for the President to have the same superintendence and care over any tribe or nation in the country to which they may remove, as contemplated by this act, that he is now authorized to have over them at their present places of residence.

John Ross

the roads, women were taken from their spinning wheels and children from their play." As Remini wrote, "In many cases, turning for one last look as they crossed the ridge, they [the Cherokees] saw their homes in flames, fired by the lawless rabble that followed on the heels of the soldiers to loot and pillage." One Georgia militiaman who would later fight for the Confederacy compared the Trail of Tears to what Southerners called the War Between the States. "I fought through the Civil War and have seen men shot in pieces and slaughtered by the thousands, but the Cherokee removal was the cruelest I've ever seen."

Rousted from the only homes they ever knew, these families shivered as they groaned with hunger. White men speaking a language they didn't understand yelled at terrified Cherokee children separated from their parents in the chaos. According to a white witness, John G. Burnett, soldiers forced a Cherokee couple to abandon the body of their child, who had just died.

For various people, the Trail of Tears started in different places at different times but was an approximately 1,000-mile forced march from Georgia, Alabama and Mississippi to what is now Oklahoma. Chocktaws, Chickasaws, Creeks, and others joined the Cherokees on this torturous trail. As the winter of 1838 started, some of the Indians began to freeze. Some began to starve and, when allowed to pause, ate raw corn or pumpkins growing in the fields owned by cooperative whites. Government agents had stolen supplies meant for the Indians, with some Natives marching barefoot on ice and snow. Armed whites left the Natives with nothing, according to one witness, than "the sky for a blanket and the earth for a pillow."

Pregnant women were forced to march alongside the others, and when they couldn't keep up in the death march, they faced terrible consequences. A white man, Daniel Butrick, recalled seeing a soldier stab a pregnant Cherokee woman in the stomach. Other soldiers forced Native America women to drink until they became intoxicated, and the men would then gang-rape them. Along the way, when soldiers decided it was time to halt the relentless drive to the Indian Territory, the soldiers forced Indians into hastily constructed stockades, which became hellholes of hunger and thirst, breeding grounds for cholera, diarrhea, dysentery and smallpox as the removal campaign stretched into the summer. One-third of the Chocktaws forcibly moved died, some from starvation. Of the 15,000 Cherokee victims of Indian removal in the 1838-1839 Trail of Tears, about 4,000 died.

In his farewell address of 1837, Andrew Jackson piously rationalized his homicidal Indian policy. The civilized tribes, he insisted, had been "placed beyond the reach of injury or oppression, and that [the] paternal care of the General Government will . . . watch after them and protect them." It was one more lie to the continent's native peoples. Indians knew better than to rely on the tender mercies of the new, rising marketplace and an increasingly racist white society. Removed west of the Mississippi, they faced another six decades in which their lands, and the lands of natives west of the Mississippi, would be stolen by fraud and warfare, and in which their peoples would be destroyed through disease, malnutrition, alcoholism stemming from despair, and deliberate extermination. The Cherokees and others would be forever insecure, wherever they dwelled.

THE AGE OF JACKSON: AN ASSESSMENT

If you were a southern white man of modest means during the 1820s and 1830s, Andrew Jackson represented the swell of democratic forces that lowered property requirements and probably resulted in you gaining the right to vote. If you were Henry Clay, Daniel Webster, or Nicholas Biddle, Jackson embodied the primitive forces afoot in the land, the unwashed ignorant who didn't understand the rising market economy and feared it, the man who stood in the way of making the country an economic and political giant on a par with England.

If you were a white Georgian with the money to buy land, Jackson was the man who enhanced your wealth by destroying Indian nations residing within your state and opening their lands to theft. If you were a Cherokee or a Creek, Jackson was nothing less than an American Hitler, a man who guided wars of elimination, and who pursued one of the most ferocious genocides ever directed against your people. To you, Jackson was a hardhearted ruler who forced your people off of rich, fertile land and made your nation march a thousand miles to a much harsher climate, with soldiers raping and killing unarmed civilians and letting your brothers and sisters shiver and starve in a dark, deadly winter.

In spite of a lifetime of serious injury and poor health, Jackson refused to die, writing furious letters of advice to his admirer, President James Polk, and not giving up until he was a sickly 78-year-old man at his Hermitage Plantation in Tennessee on June 8, 1845. Perhaps aware of his grave sins as a slave owner and Indian killer, Jackson summoned his black servants to his bedside and said, "I want all to prepare to meet me in Heaven . . . Christ has no respect for color." When he died, someone asked one of his slaves where he felt the iron-willed former master had gone. The black servant paused then said, "If General Jackson wants to go to Heaven, who's to stop him?"

Upon hearing of Jackson's demise, one of his many detractors, the New York merchant Philip Hone caustically noted in his diary, "Now, to my thinking, the country has greater cause to mourn on the day of his birth than on that of his decease. This iron-willed man has done more mischief than any man alive." Others denounced Jackson as a dictator. Even to this day, however, mostly white men have written American history, and most of those white scholars have depicted Jackson as one of the giants of his age. Harvard historian and Kennedy family friend Arthur Schlesinger, Jr., in his Pulitzer-Prize winning *Age of Jackson* (published in 1945), saw in Jackson an early Franklin Roosevelt, a mostly benevolent force spreading the blessings of the franchise to poor and struggling whites and leveling the privileges of the well-to-do. Schlesinger, like so many establishment historians of his era, completely ignored Native Americans and slaves in his 523-page account. As an inconvenient truth, the Trail of Tears vanishes from Schlesinger's story of the Jackson years. In three polls of historians held by his father, Arthur Schlesinger, Sr., in 1948 and 1962, and by Arthur Schlesinger, Jr. in 1996, as well as other major surveys of historians in those years, Jackson generally ranked as one of the 10 best presidents, rating as the fifth or sixth greatest in the three Schlesinger rankings.

His image adorns the $20 bill. New Orleans named Jackson Square after him. The seventh president's name also adorns a state park in South Carolina; the city of Jacksonville, Florida; the city of Jackson, Mississippi, that state's capital; and suburbs, towns, high schools, junior highs and elementary campuses all across the country. However, more recent historians, who came of age in the wake of the 1950s and 1960s Civil Rights Movement and the American Indian Movement, have been much more critical, and Andrew Jackson is as likely to be portrayed as an Indian killer as a force for democracy. To the general public, among presidents, Jackson may not be as revered as George Washington or Abraham Lincoln, or have the passionate partisans like Franklin Roosevelt or Ronald Reagan, yet, like Thomas Jefferson, Jackson remains a polarizing but almost universally acknowledged figure of deep historical significance. Not many presidents have ages named after them.

"More than any other American, Jackson oversaw the decline and fall of the elitist gentry order established by the Framers, and its replacement with the ruder conventions and organization of democracy," wrote Wilentz. "More than any other president before him, he made the office of the presidency the center of action in national politics and government . . . Jackson and his supporters also created the first mass democratic national political party in modern history." Yet, Jackson had a very limited view of which people had a right to participate in that democracy: the white "planter, the farmer, the mechanic, and the laborer . . . [T]hese classes of society form the great body of the people of the United States; they are the bone and sinew of the country," as he put it.

Jackson's economic policies, however, including his war with the Second Bank of the United States and his policies tightening the money supply, injured those very same classes, triggering one of the worst depressions in American history and concentrating wealth in the hands of those same wealthy elites he supposedly despised. Meanwhile, Jackson pretended to care for people of color only in the most paternalistic way. He claimed that his Indian removal policies were designed to protect Indians from extinction, but in fact that approach only opened the door to racial mass murder.

His close associate Van Buren would in his later years not be a believer in racial equality but would at least acknowledge the dangers slavery posed to American democracy. Van Buren would run for president in 1848 as the nominee of the Free Soil Party, which opposed the spread of slavery to the western territories taken in the Louisiana Purchase and the Mexican American War. Jackson never entertained any doubts about the rectitude of slavery.

The Democratic Party that Jackson and Van Buren created would remain a force for white racial domination, for slavery, black disenfranchisement and segregation, for decades. The two-thirds nominating rule guaranteed a white southern veto of party presidential nominees until the 1930s. Jackson appointed five southern slaveowners to the Supreme Court, men such as Roger Taney of South Carolina. As Supreme Chief Justice, Taney would write the majority decision in the infamous 1857 *Dred Scott* decision that would declare that the writers of the Constitution saw blacks as "beings of an inferior order, and altogether unfit to associate with the white race, either in social or political relations, and so far inferior that they had no rights which the white man was bound to respect." Jacksonian Democracy, in the end, was a fraud. White democracy in the 1830s and 1840s rested on the cruel foundation of racial dictatorship.

Chronology

1824 Andrew Jackson led in the balloting for the presidential elections, with John Quincy Adams second, William H. Crawford third, and Henry Clay fourth, but no man won a majority.
Gibbons v. Ogden upheld.

1825 Completion of the Erie Canal in New York.
U.S. House of Representatives elected John Quincy Adams president.
Adams appointed Clay secretary of state, prompting charges of "corrupt bargain."

1828 Tariff of Abominations.
Jackson elected president.
Baltimore and Ohio Railroad chartered.

1830 Indian Removal Act.
Maysville Road Bill vetoed.

1831 Nat Turner slave revolt.
First issue of *Liberator* published.
Alexis de Tocqueville wrote *Democracy in America*.
Cherokee Nation v. Georgia.

1832 Jackson vetoed the recharter of the Bank of the U.S.
Jackson signed the Tariff of 1832.
South Carolina nullified the Tariffs of 1828 and 1832.
Jackson reelected to the presidency.
Worcester v. Georgia.

1833 Compromise Tariff.
South Carolina rescinded its Ordinance of Nullification.
Roger B. Taney as Secretary of the Treasury.
New York Sun, the first penny newspaper.

1834 Cyrus McCormick patented the reaper.
First strike by the women at the Lowell mills.
Whig Party organized.

1836 Charter of the second Bank of the U.S. expired.
Jackson sent out the Specie Circular.
Martin Van Buren elected president.
Texas declared independence from Mexico.

1837 Economic panic began a depression that lasted until 1843.
Cotton prices plummet.

1840 Harrison ("Old Tippecanoe") defeated Martin Van Buren.

Review Questions

1. What changes in election laws expanded the number of eligible voters in federal, state and local elections, and who continued to be disenfranchised?

2. Describe the rise of the "Second Party" system and the ideologies of the Democratic and Whig Parties from the 1830s to the 1850s and the way Andrew Jackson changed the way American politics was practiced.

3. What led to Andrew Jackson's opposition to the Second Bank of the United States, what was the viewpoint of the bank's defenders, and what was the economic impact when the bank closed down?

4. What events led to the Nullification Crisis of 1832, what were the constitutional issues at stake and how did personal antagonisms shape the controversy?

5. Describe the relationship between Native Americans and the federal government during the presidential administrations of Andrew Jackson (1829-1837) and Martin Van Buren (1837-1841).

Glossary of Important People and Concepts

Anti-Masonic Party
Bank War
Nicholas Biddle
John C. Calhoun
Cherokee Nation v. Georgia (1831)
Henry Clay
Democratic Party
Five Civilized Tribe
Indian Removal Act of 1830
Rachel Donelson Jackson
Kitchen Cabinet
Nullification Crisis
Osceola
Panic of 1819
Eaton Affair
Property Qualifications
John Ross
Sequoyah
Winfield Scott
Spoils System
Trail of Tears

SUGGESTED READINGS

H.W. Brands, *Andrew Jackson: His Life and Times* (2006).

Andrew Burstein, *The Passions of Andrew Jackson* (2003).

Randolph Campbell, *An Empire for Slavery: The Peculiar Institution in Texas, 1821-1865* (1991).

Joan Cashin, *A Family Venture: Men and Women on the Southern Frontier* (1991).

Donald B. Cole, *The Presidency of Andrew Jackson* (1993).

Arnoldo de León, *They Called Them Greasers: Anglo Attitudes Towards Mexicans in Texas, 1821-1900* (1983)

John Ehle, *Trail of Tears: The Rise and Fall of the Cherokee Nation* (1997)

Daniel Feller, *The Jacksonian Promise: America, 1815-1840* (1995).

Kenneth S. Greenberg, *Nat Turner: A Slave Rebellion in History and Memory* (2004).

Michael F. Holt, *The Rise and Fall of the American Whig Party: Jacksonian Politics and the Onset of the Civil War* (1999).

Nancy Isenberg, *Sex and Citizenship in Antebellum America* (1998).

Mark E. Kann, *The Gendering of American Politics: Founding Mothers, Founding Fathers, and Political Patriarchy* (1999).

Dale T. Knobel, *America for the Americans: The Nativist Movement in the United States* (1996).

Leon F. Litwack, *North of Slavery: The Negro in the Free States, 1790-1860* (1965).

John F. Marszalek, *The Petticoat Affair: Manners, Mutiny, and Sex in Andrew Jackson's White House* (1997).

Joanne Pope Melish, *Disowning Slavery: Gradual Emancipation and "Race" in New England, 1780-1860* (1998).

Dana D. Nelson, *National Manhood: Capitalist Citizenship and the Imagined Fraternity of White Men* (1998).

Lynn Hudson Parson, *The Birth of Modern Politics: Andrew Jackson, John Qunicy Adams and the Election of 1828* (2009).

Theda Perdue and Michael D. Green, eds. *The Cherokee Removal: A Brief History with Documents* (1995).

Robert Remini, *The Jacksonian Era*. 2nd ed. (1997).

——*Daniel Webster: The Man and His Time* (1997).

——*Andrew Jackson and His Indian Wars* (2001).

David Robertson, *Denmark Vesey: The Buried Story of America's Largest Slave Rebellion and the Man Who Led It* (2000).

David R. Roediger, *The Wages of Whiteness: Race and the Making of the American Working Class* (1991).

Mary P. Ryan, *Civic Wars: Democracy and Public Life in the American City during the Nineteenth Century* (1997).

Alexander Saxton, *The Rise and Fall of the White Republic: Class Politics and Mass Culture in Nineteenth Century America* (1990).

Laura J. Scalia, *America's Jeffersonian Experiment: Remaking State Constitutions, 1820-1850* (1999).

Charles Sellers, *The Market Revolution: Jacksonian America, 1815-1846* (1991).

Joel H. Silbey, *Martin Van Buren and the Emergence of American Popular Politics* (2002).

Ronald Takaki, *Iron Cages: Race and Culture in 19th Century America* (2000).

Julie M. Walsh, *The Intellectual Origins of Mass Parties and Mass Schools in the Jacksonian Period: Creating a Conformed Citizenry* (1998).

Harry L. Watson, *Liberty and Power: The Politics of Jacksonian America* (1990).

Sean Wilentz. *Andrew Jackson*. (2005).

Major L. Wilson, *The Presidency of Martin Van Buren* (1984).

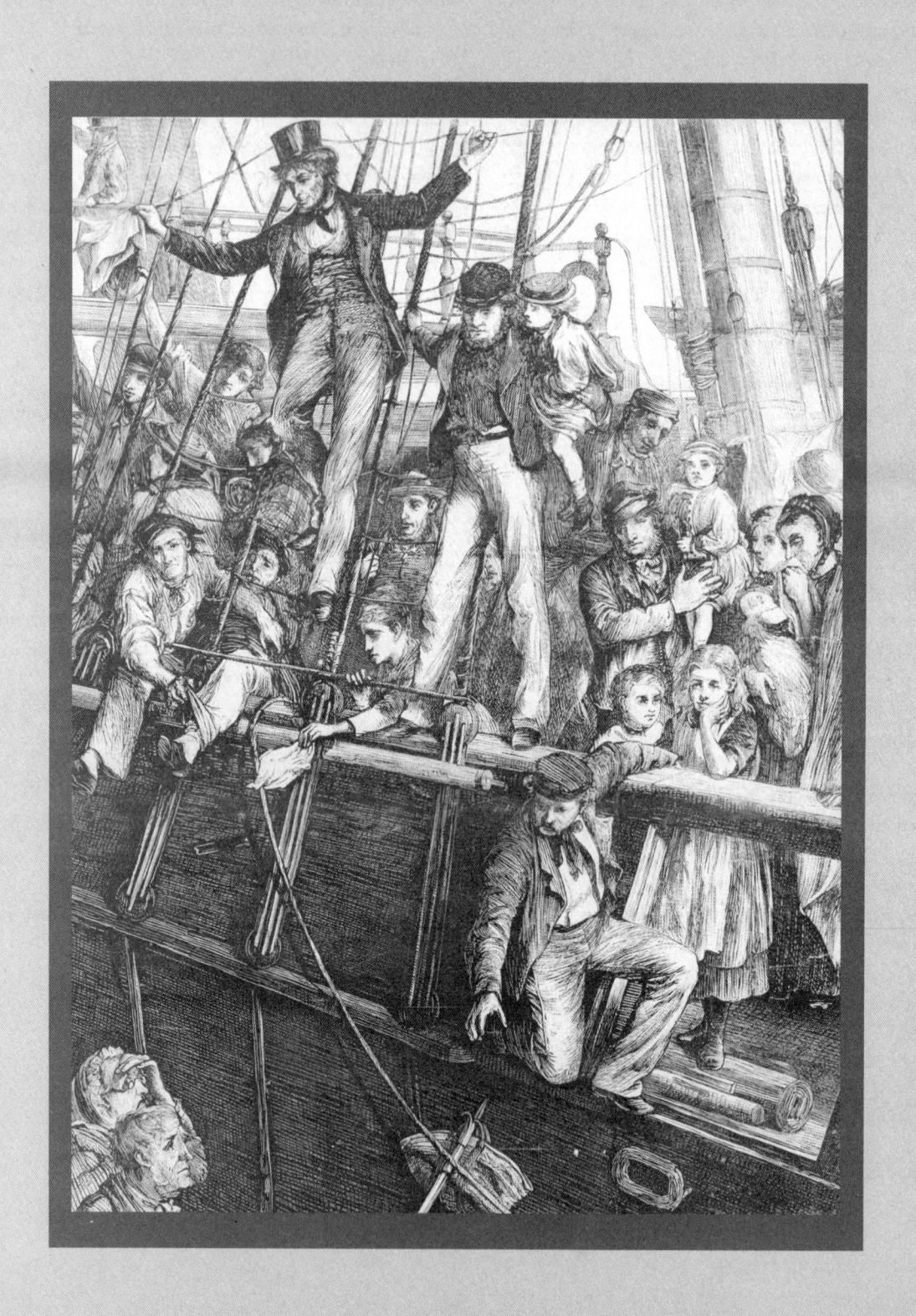

Chapter Twelve

The United States in Transformation, 1830-1850

One of the favorite side trips of proper English travelers in nineteenth century America was to the backcountry South and West to witness "rough-and-tumble" fighting. These brutal struggles by working class men often ended in the backwoods equivalent of the modern knockout punch: the gouging out of the loser's eye by the victor's thumb. One such tourist watched with mesmerized horror as one combatant kept his opponent down with his knees and "fixing his thumb on his eyes, gave them an instantaneous start from their sockets. The sufferer roared aloud.... The citizens again shouted with joy." These renowned local heroes hardened and sharpened their fingernails and oiled them for slickness.

The backcountry heroes bragged with great exaggeration about their abilities and accomplishments. Mike Finn, legendary boatman, daring hunter, and victorious gouger, boasted: "I'm half wild horse and half cock-eyed alligator....I can out-run, out-jump, out-shoot, out-brag, out-drink, an' out-fight, rough-an'-tumble. No holts barred, any man both sides the river...." This "spread eagle" rhetoric represented the young nation and its aggressive expansion.

The "rough and tumblers" lived in isolated, pre-modern areas in kin-based societies where subsistence agriculture was the norm. Their hard lives, limited opportunities, and uncertain futures pushed them into heavy drinking and violent sports in a competitive all-male society. In a world in which slave holding was the mark of honor and standing, poor whites sought to confirm their status as equal and free men through unbridled brutality. They could contrast their unwillingness to allow the slightest insult with the enforced submissiveness of the slave.

By the middle of the century eye gouging incidents began to decline as the modern world intruded on the backcountry. Bowie knives finished off more of the rough and tumbles. The invention of the inexpensive modern revolver, which easily fit into a pocket, changed the nature of frontier contests. Violence became neater and even more deadly.

In the growing cities organized spectator sports developed to counter the loneliness of urban life and preserve traditional pleasures. Steamboats and, later, railroads could carry fans to events and promote inter-city rivalries. Rising literacy and new printing technologies created the popular penny newspapers that reported sporting events. Despite the opposition of religious moralists, both workers and "slumming" upper class men flocked to "low sport" halls. There, they could watch and bet on a dog killing a pit full of rats or a sparring match between "two women who were nude above the waist."

Although it was illegal everywhere, during the 1840s and 1850s, prize fighting became the most popular spectator sport. These bare-fisted matches were almost as brutal as the frontier rough and tumbles. In one epic 1842 contest, the two fighters thrashed each other for over two and a half hours until one collapsed and died when he drowned in his own blood. Irish working class men, who honed their skills in street survival, dominated boxing. (Jews, then Italians, then blacks would replace them in the twentieth century as each group attempted to rise from the slums.) John "Old

Smoke" Morrissey, an Irish immigrant, earned enough from his matches to open his own gambling house and was famous enough to win two terms in the House of Representatives. Newspapers publicized the 1860 match of his successor, John Heenan, against the English champion, as the ultimate test of national superiority. (The match ended in a bloody two-hour draw.) The event stirred up wider publicity than the growing sectional conflict.

Organized team sports also began to capture the public fancy. Cricket clubs, spurred by English immigrants, grew rapidly. Over 24,000 attended an 1859 cricket match in Hoboken, New Jersey between an all-star American team and touring professionals. Others argued that Americans should support "a game that could be termed a 'Native American Sport.'" Boys had long taken part in impromptu bat-and-ball games in empty lots. Lower middle class men began to form clubs to play baseball, touted as "the national game." When the Brooklyn all-stars met the New York all-stars in an 1858 series, excitement reached new heights. One newspaper reported that spectators included, "a galaxy of youth and beauty in female form, who...nerved the players to their task." (New York won two of three: 22-18, 8-29, 29-18.)

The new sports, like the old, tended to encourage drinking, betting, and an absence of self-restraint, much to the dismay of religious critics. These sports, however, reflected the important changes in northern American life at a time of urbanization, immigration, beginnings of industrialization, and increased population growth.

During the first half of the nineteenth century, the United States experienced a series of rapid and often bewildering social, cultural, and economic transformations. As one of a growing number of distinguished American authors whose career became possible due to the dramatic changes occurring in everyday life, Washington Irving captured the spirit of the alterations being made to the social fabric in his 1819 short story, "Rip Van Winkle"—a tale involving a man who falls asleep before the American Revolution, awaking two decades later to discover everything had changed. A prominent local portrait of King George III had been replaced with the image of someone named George Washington. Rip's friends had died or moved away. The pace of life was now bustling.

Unlike Rip Van Winkle, Americans did not have the luxury of sleeping through the swift developments overtaking their society. From 1800 to 1860, the country expanded tremendously. In 1803, the Louisiana Purchase doubled the size of the United States. The country nearly doubled in size again in 1848 with the acquisition of northern Mexico after the Mexican War. Before 1850, the U.S. also took possession of Florida and the Pacific Northwest before completing its continental expansion with the 1853 Gadsden Purchase of southern Arizona and New Mexico. During these intervening years, the nation's population exploded. In 1790, the first U.S. Census counted 3.9 million Americans. By 1860, that number had increased nearly tenfold to 31.4 million people. Northerners frequently moved to newly-established farming areas further west or to the growing urban areas, indulging themselves in a variety of market activities. Meanwhile, Southerners also migrated westward to take advantage of fresh land and to cultivate cotton—a profitable crop whose labor demands were satisfied through the exploitation of enslaved African Americans. Facilitating the movement of people and goods during these years of rapid territorial and demographic growth were the new steamboats, canals, and, ultimately, the railroads. Only the arrival of the Civil War in the early 1860s could temporarily stymie these revolutionary changes to American life.

NEW PEOPLE, NEW PLACES: Population Growth, Urbanization, and Immigration

Tremendous population increases took place during the period between 1790 and 1860, as every decade witnessed no less than 30 percent growth. Before the 1840s, the population consisted mainly of young, restless, and mobile native-born residents (the median age in 1820 was 16.7 years.) **Alexis de Tocqueville,** a French aristocrat touring the United States to observe its experiments in prison reform who later wrote an analytical account of his travels, described a "strange unrest of so many happy men, restless in the midst of abundance," noting:

> In the United States a man builds a house in which to spend his old age, and he sells it before the roof is on; he plants a garden and lets it just as the trees are coming into bearing; he brings a field into tillage and leaves other men to gather the crops; he embraces a profession and gives it up; he settles in a place, which he soon afterwards leaves to carry his changeable longings elsewhere.

The distribution of population growth varied from state to state, with those lacking significant quantities of unsettled land (Delaware, Maryland, and most of New England) experiencing much slower population increases than older ones still possessing large amounts of undeveloped land, such as New York, Pennsylvania, and Georgia. Growth in those states, however, likewise slowed, as new states and territories further west opened for settlement.

Table 13.1

LARGEST U. S. CITIES

	1820			1860	
	City	Population		City	Population
1	New York, NY	123,706	1	New York, NY	813,669
2	Philadelphia, PA	63,802	2	Philadelphia, PA	565,529
3	Baltimore, MD	62,738	3	Brooklyn, NY	266,661
4	Boston, MA	43,298	4	Baltimore, MD	212,418
5	New Orleans, LA	27,176	5	Boston city, MA	177,840
6	Charleston, SC	24,780	6	New Orleans, LA	168,675
7	N. Liberties district, PA	19,678	7	Cincinnati, OH	161,044
8	Southwark district, PA	14,713	8	St. Louis, MO	160,773
9	Washington, DC	13,247	9	Chicago, IL	112,172
10	Salem, MA	12,731	10	Buffalo, NY	81,129
11	Albany, NY	12,630	11	Newark, NJ	71,941
12	Richmond, VA	12,067	12	Louisville, KY	68,033
13	Providence, RI	11,767	13	Albany, NY	62,367
14	Cincinnati, OH	9,642	14	Washington, DC	61,122
15	Portland, ME	8,581	15	San Francisco, CA	56,802
16	Norfolk, VA	8,478	16	Providence, RI	50,666
17	Alexandria, DC	8,218	17	Pittsburgh, PA	49,221
18	Savannah, GA	7,523	18	Rochester, NY	48,204
19	Georgetown, DC	7,360	19	Detroit, MI	45,619
20	Portsmouth, NH	7,327	20	Milwaukee, WI	45,246

Source: U.S. Bureau of the Census

Urban Life

From 1830 to 1860, Americans continued to flock to the cities, with the rate of population growth there far exceeding the overall increase for the total population. In 1790, only 5 percent of the country lived in urban areas. By 1860, nearly 20 percent had moved into the cities, mostly after 1830. Older cities swelled with new inhabitants. The number of people in Charleston, South Carolina increased from 16,359 in 1790 to 40,522 in 1860, but that growth proved to be quite slow relative to other cities. During the same period, Baltimore's population increased from 13,503 to 212,418; Philadelphia's from 28,522 to 565,529; and New York City's from 33,131 to 813,669. New urban centers also emerged. Of the twenty largest cities in 1860, nine were either not yet part of the United States in 1790 (New Orleans, St. Louis, and San Francisco) or simply did not yet exist (Rochester, Buffalo, Milwaukee, and Chicago). All of these cities boasted populations over 40,000 by 1860, and nearly half containing more than 100,000 people.

The rapid movement of people to the cities created a host of new social challenges. What modern urban dwellers now assume to be the basics of city living—police and fire departments, regular waste removal, sewage disposal—had not yet been developed. City folk casually dropped trash in their neighborhoods to be picked over by wandering pigs and dogs. In the absence of sewage systems, people and animals urinated and defecated in the streets, which made cities foul-smelling and disease-ridden environments. Fire companies existed to put out fires, but these groups often had connections to street gangs, and rivalries among various gangs sometimes resulted in violence while buildings burned in the background. Crime became a persistent problem in the absence of professional police forces, and riots by urban crowds remained a persistent danger. Vast disparities in wealth became visible within urban populations. Although economic inequality was not by any means new, city residents increasingly became segregated along class lines. Poor people concentrated in dilapidated slums, such as New York City's notorious **Five Points**—a neighborhood famous for its poverty, brothels, and violence.

By mid-century, a number of cities initiated efforts to deliver public services designed to improve the quality of urban life In response to outbreaks of disease—such as an epidemic of yellow fever 1849—city governments began to build water systems to convey fresh water and to

> Table 13.2
>
> **Immigration: 1820 to 1860**
>
> In thousands, except rate (152 represents 152,000)[1]
>
> | Period | Number | Rate |
> |---|---|---|
> | 1820 to 1830[2] | 152 | 1.2 |
> | 1831 to 1840[3] | 599 | 3.9 |
> | 1841 to 1850[4] | 1,713 | 8.4 |
> | 1851 to 1860[4] | 2,598 | 9.3 |
>
> Footnotes
> [1] Annual rate per 1,000 U.S. population. Rate computed by dividing sum of annual immigration totals by sum of annual U.S. population totals for same number of years.
> [2] October 1, 1819, to September 30, 1830.
> [3] October 1, 1830, to December 31, 1840.
> [4] Calendar years.
>
> Source: U.S. Department of Homeland Security, Office of Immigration Statistics, 2005 Yearbook of Immigration Statistics.

allow (for those who could afford to do so) to pipe water directly into their homes. Rudimentary sewer systems were developed, though service remained limited. In 1860, for example, only about 25 percent of New York City streets tied into the municipal sewer system. Cities also established formal fire departments and professional police forces, primarily to bring crowd violence under control and to patrol the neighborhoods of wealthy citizens. Along with these changes came innovations in urban transit. Animal-powered transportation—at first large horse-drawn wagons and later horse-drawn rail cars—allowed cities to begin expanding in ways not previously possible. Because these transportation services were not free, such developments accelerated class segregation within urban areas. Poor folk remained in downtown neighborhoods within walking distance of their places of employment while wealthier residents began commuting into and out of the inner cities. Some aspects of urban life common to modern Americans were thus beginning to take hold.

Immigration

As native-born Americans moved to the cities, they often reduced the number of children they had in response to the reduced need for family labor (from 1820 to 1860, the national median age increased from 16.7 to 19.4). This decline in birth rates, however, did not slow national population growth because of a large influx of foreign immigrants. Between 1790 and 1840, the United States experienced relatively little immigration when compared to the colonial period or to the decades immediately preceding the Civil War. From 1820 to 1840, only 750,000 immigrants had arrived. After 1840, however, the first of a succession of immigrant waves occurred. Over the next decade, 1.7 million migrated to the United States, followed by the arrival of another 2.6 million people during the 1850s.

The largest group of new immigrants, the Irish, accounted for half of the new arrivals. Fleeing a potato famine that struck in 1845, most Irish arrived in the United States with practically nothing. They clustered in urban slums—Five Points was a predominately Irish neighborhood—and disrupted labor markets through a willingness to work for near starvation wages. Many Americans greeted the Irish with hostility. Those forced to compete with them in the labor market treated the Irish with disdain, and the Irish responded in kind. Protestants, especially in New England, expressed concern that Roman Catholic peasants would not be suited to American democracy. School reformers insisted on instilling Protestant values in the schools, leading the Irish to campaign for **parochial schools**. In politics, the Irish became an influential force within the Democratic Party, primarily because they rejected the evangelical leanings of the Whig (and later Republican) Party. In many cities, the Irish became a major force in local politics.

Prompted by a variety of push and pull factors, large numbers of Germans also immigrated to the United States between 1840 and 1860. Some left for religious reasons, while others fled their homeland after the failed democratic revolutions of 1848. Still more came for economic opportunities. Unlike the Irish, German immigrants were largely Protestant and generally arrived with some monetary resources. Their relative wealth allowed them more options—some established themselves in cities, while others purchased farm land. German settlements rose throughout the country—from Texas to Wisconsin in the center of the country, as well as many northeastern states.

Not all the immigrants to the United States came from Europe. In California, Chinese immigrants arrived to participate in the Gold Rush of the late 1840s. Like the Irish, the Chinese faced considerable hostility from native-born Americans who closed the mines to the Chinese (and other non-whites), forcing many into service industries such as cooking and laundry work. State laws harassed the Chinese, while government officials often overlooked crimes committed against them (including murder).

The hostility experienced by the Irish and the Chinese, which reflected emerging tensions resulting from increased racial diversity and economic competition, greatly complicated American politics. In the North, politicians learned to navigate within an environment charged with ethnic hatred, seeking to attract immigrant voters while also appealing to native-born voters who expressed deep hostility to the newcomers. Moreover, because foreign immigration was largely a northern affair (8 out of every 10 new immigrants settled in the North), these tensions would eventually muddle American sectional politics.

Transportation and Communication Innovations

The emergence of new modes of transportation after 1830 contributed greatly to the period's extensive population movement and economic development, while improved communication systems connected Americans nationally and internationally like never before. As noted in the previous chapter, overland travel in the United States improved after the War of 1812 with an increase in the quantity and quality of roads and bridges. Such projects, however, tended to be overshadowed by innovations in water transportation. Robert Fulton's 1807 invention of the steamboat permitted the transportation of more people and goods along navigable rivers at greater speed, and, most importantly, upstream. Canals soon helped to solve another major limitation posed by the country's river network by carving "artificial rivers" where natural ones did not exist. Completed in 1825, New York's **Erie Canal** led the way, running 364 miles from Buffalo on the eastern bank of Lake Erie to Albany on the Hudson River, thus creating a pathway connecting the Great Lakes to New York City and transforming upstate New York from a sparsely settled frontier region into an area characterized by bustling towns with a burgeoning middle class. Other states tried to replicate New York's success, but generally fell short, facing crushing debts as the new canals failed to pay for themselves with the same speed as the Erie had. Despite these problems, however, a growing network of canals built in the North during the 1830s and 1840s began to restructure the way in which goods and commerce flowed through the country. Canal construction did not bypass the South, but new projects there tended to be relatively limited in scope and generally reinforced existing commodity flows—that is, they moved crops like cotton to port in larger quantities and with more speed than before. Southern transportation projects thus tended to accommodate growth, but relative to those in the North, did not really foster development.

Though the full potential of the most significant transportation innovation before 1860, the railroad, would not be felt until after the Civil War, steam-powered locomotives began to greatly impact the antebellum economy in significant ways by accomplishing what steamboats and canals could not—the ability to traverse steep grades, travel through tunneled hills and mountains, run in areas with little water, and (with the temporary exception of severe blizzards) work under harsh wintry conditions. The world's first commercial railroad began operations in England in 1825, the same year that workers completed construction of the Erie Canal. Three years later, Baltimore business interests chartered the United States' first railroad company, the Baltimore and Ohio (B&O) Railroad, designed to link their city with the Ohio River. Within four years, the line reached 75 miles west of Baltimore. A flurry of lines subsequently began to appear before the Panic of 1837 and the resulting economic depression tempered the financing of new rail projects. New construction, however, reemerged with a fury during the 1850s. By 1860, the United States would lead the world in total railroad mileage, though the lack of a standard track gauge (the length between the rails, of which over a dozen regional variations existed in 1860) belied the notion that the country had yet achieved a unified national rail network. Nevertheless, the combination of improved roads, steamboats, canals, and railroads allowed for the shipment of goods and movement of people between settled areas of the country in time spans that were inconceivable to Americans before the War of 1812.

The postwar period also witnessed great improvements in ocean-going transport and communication. In early 1818, a transatlantic packet line began providing regular mail, freight, and passenger service between the United States and England. By the mid-1840s, close to fifty sailing lines had followed suit and followed set routines of weekly departures along established routes. At the same time, so-called "clipper ships" began to ap-

Railroads in 1860

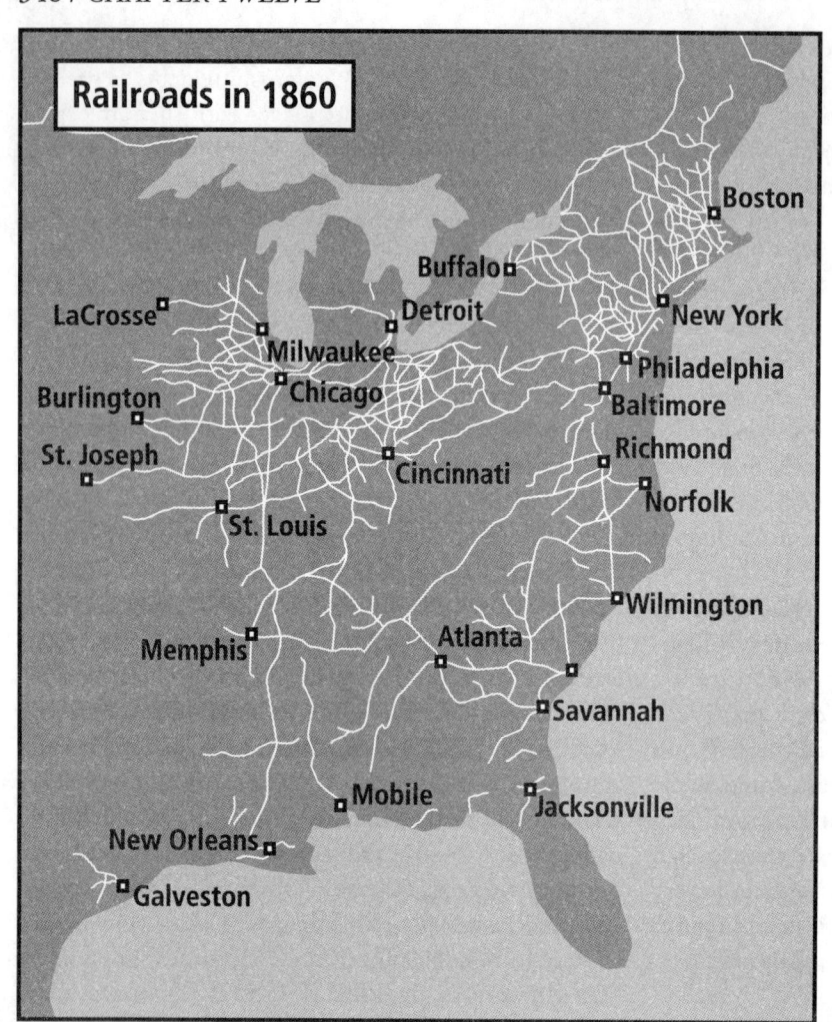

Map 13.1 The network of railroad growth, established by 1860, reinforced economic ties between the Northeast and the West.

pear. Built for speed rather than large cargo capacity, the clippers could cover the same distance as older merchant ships in half the time. Though the clipper ships operated for less than three decades before being supplanted by the steamship, these sleek, tall-masted vessels with abundant sails provided valuable service in their heyday, delivering news more quickly, providing perishable tea from China in record time, and supplying the large numbers of prospectors pouring into California as the result of the late-1840s Gold Rush.

While faster water craft and improvements in overland travel accelerated communication times, **Samuel Morse**'s invention of the **telegraph** in 1836 soon allowed Americans to spread information across many parts of the nation almost instantaneously. The inventor's system involved the transmission and reception of electrical impulses along a connected wire using a standard code. By 1844, congressional funding and years of experimentation with improvements allowed Morse to prove the telegraph's long-distance feasibility by transmitting the first intercity telegraph message from Washington, D.C. to Baltimore: "What hath God wrought!" Less than three years before the start of the Civil War, on August 16, 1858, the first telegraph message sent along a transatlantic cable linked Newfoundland in eastern Canada with Ireland, thus reducing the communication time between North America and Europe from the travel time by ship (usually ten days) to mere seconds.

The Transformation of Northern Society

The tremendous changes made possible by increased mobility, foreign immigration, and growing urbanization, coupled with the impact of new manufacturing methods deeply shaped the development of northern social life. Although European observers such as Alexis de Tocqueville commented on Americans' dedication to equality, often portraying the United States as a "classless" society because it lacked the landed aristocracy so characteristic the Old World, the French aristocrat also relayed his belief that the social changes produced by the rise of factories in the North threatened to create a new aristocracy:

> As the conditions of men constituting the nation become more and more equal, the demand for manufactured commodities becomes more general

and extensive, and the cheapness that places these objects within the reach of slender fortunes becomes a great element of success. Hence there are every day more men of great opulence and education who devote their wealth and knowledge to manufactures and who seek, by opening large establishments and by a strict division of labor, to meet the fresh demands which are made on all sides. Thus, in proportion as the mass of the nation turns to democracy, that particular class which is engaged in manufactures becomes more aristocratic.

This process had major social implications, de Tocqueville noted. "The workman is generally dependent on the master, but not on any particular master; these two men meet in the factory, but do not know each other elsewhere; and while they come into contact on one point, they stand very far apart on all others." The result was a situation in which neither party had any obligations to one another beyond work. "The manufacturer asks nothing of the workman but his labor; the workman expects nothing from him but his wages."

De Tocqueville observed a very real phenomenon taking place in the North—the creation of a new class structure. Although Americans never enjoyed economic equality, urbanization brought the issue into sharp relief, with the shift to new divisions of labor accelerating the trend. In New York City, a mere 4 percent of the population controlled two-thirds of the city's wealth by 1845. Meanwhile, the poor shared much less: 80 percent of Philadelphia's population in 1860 controlled a scant 3 percent of the city's wealth (the top 1 percent controlled over half of the remainder). The result was the emergence of class-segregated cities with the wealthiest families constructing lavish homes in opulent neighborhoods as destitute families scraped by on near starvation wages in households where everyone—men, women, children—had to work.

Americans' assessments of this divide varied. Universalist minister, Jacob Frieze, considered the emerging economic separation to be a form of oppression, as did numerous groups of striking workers. Frieze noted that even though he believed that laborers had a right to ne-

Samuel Morse's invention of the telegraph in 1836

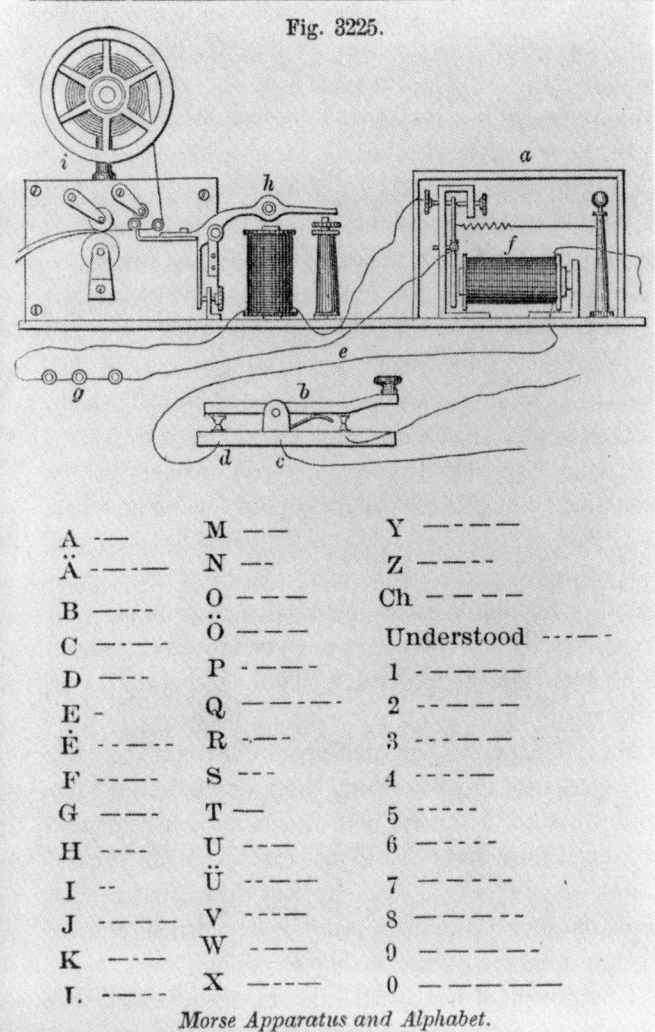

gotiate wages, their ability to do so bargain proved to be more theoretical than actual.

> This is the manner in which *bargains* are made. The employer pays what he pleases, and no more, and will not deviate from the price he has fixed. And the laboring man, with this pittance, is also under the necessities of paying the prices made and demanded for whatever he consumes. Should he venture to complain that he cannot live comfortably, he is accused of extravagance in expending the enormous sum of *seventy-five cents a day*, and told that he should live within his income.

In a 1860 speech defending the right of factory workers to strike against their employers, presidential candidate Abraham Lincoln emphasized his belief that these new labor relations were the essence of freedom. "I am glad to see that a system of labor prevails in … which laborers can strike when they want to, where they are obliged to work under all circumstances, and are not tied down." The system, he continued, offered social mobility. "I take that it is best for all to leave each man free to acquire property as fast as he can. Some will get wealthy." "When one starts poor," Lincoln went on, "free society is such that he knows that he can better his condition; he knows that there is no fixed condition for his whole life."

Both Frieze and Lincoln made valid points, but Lincoln's focus on social mobility pointed to a significant feature of life in the American North—many Americans were moving into a new middle class. The previously-cited numbers for Philadelphia in 1860 again provide a case in point. As noted, at the top of the wealth distribution, 1 percent of the population controlled 50 percent of the wealth, while the bottom 80 percent controlled 3 percent. However, between these two extremes lay the middle class—19 percent of the population that possessed 47 percent of the city's wealth. While they did not match the great wealth of the truly rich and faced very real prospects of being financially ruined in the boom-and-bust economy of the nineteenth-century, these individuals lived with great affluence and privilege not widely available in the eighteenth century. Members of this emerging class built private homes, featuring separate bedrooms for children and specialized rooms for entertaining guests. They prioritized the education of their children, experimented with new forms of non-corporal punishment, and placed a heavy emphasis on the values of self-control in financial transactions and sexual behavior—values that shaped the various reform movements then emerging.

Members of the middle-class identified themselves in relation to the very wealthy and against the emerging urban poor, many of whom flatly rejected their values. They often had come from small towns where they lived under considerable supervision from parents, elders, and ministers. In the cities, employers cared little about what they did while off the job, and they amused themselves with activities frowned upon by the moralists of the emerging middle class. Young workers drank heavily, fought frequently, attended theaters, watched cock-fights, consumed pornography, and patronized brothels. These activities rendered urban life morally dangerous in the eyes of the middle class who soon sought to rein in such activities. These cultural conflicts became basic features of American life, showing no sign of dissipating.

Free Blacks in the Antebellum North

Along with new dimensions of class conflict, the North faced challenges on the racial front. The process of gradual emancipation begun in Pennsylvania in 1780 had generated a small class of free African Americans (one percent of the North's total population). During the colonial period, slaves in the North had been spread thinly throughout the region, a practice that had inhibited African American community development. With the slow emergence of freedom, free blacks found urban life to be appealing because of the opportunities to build families, find work, and develop community ties. These facets of life often occurred, however, in the face of fierce hostility from local whites. Violent urban mobs occasionally targeted Africans Americans, such as the crowd in Cincinnati that tried to drive blacks from the city in 1842. In the same year, an Irish mob in Philadelphia attacked parading black celebrants commemorating the abolition of slavery in the West Indies, setting off a three-day race riot.

Such violent actions reflected extreme manifestations of the prevailing racist attitudes of a majority of northern whites during this period. The gradual abolition of slavery in the antebellum North occurred largely due to economic arguments against slavery (competition and depressed wages for free white laborers) rather than moral concerns over the institution, let alone any belief in racial equality. Free African Americans in the North were subsequently relegated to a second-class status by law and custom. All northern states, for example, barred interracial marriage, African-American office holding, and black testimony in cases involving white litigants. Most prevented blacks from legally voting. Ohio and many other northwestern states also passed laws making it illegal for African Americans not born within their borders to migrate into their states. In addition to these legislative restrictions, simple custom denied blacks numerous liberties across the North, such as the ability to serve on juries, attend most colleges, and enjoy the same public accommodations as whites. Even Massachusetts—one of the most racially liberal states in the Union—permitted separate schools for blacks and whites until the late 1850s.

African Americans thus faced a hard life in the North—legally free, but by no means treated as equals. Most members of the black community found their employment options limited to menial labor. Men worked in low status jobs as teamsters and on road construction crews. Many went to sea, serving as sailors. Women tended to work as laundresses or domestic "help" (Americans of all races preferred not be called servants). Not all African Americans labored at menial jobs. Black communities established churches whose ministers became civic leaders. Organizations like the **African Methodist Episcopal Church** and other denominations provided education and social support. Black communities also supported their own businesses, including newspapers. Even though African Americans represented a relatively small element within the northern population, their organizations magnified their voice.

Some prominent former slaves residing in the North achieved national notoriety through their anti-slavery efforts. A brilliant speaker and charismatic leader, **Frederick Douglass** (discussed more extensively in the next chapter) had taught himself to read while a bondsman in Maryland before escaping to freedom. By the early 1840s, he established himself as a popular lecturer, wrote an autobiography which indicted slavery for its violence and corrosive impact on morality, and published his own abolitionist newspaper, *The North Star*. Adopting the name "Sojourner Truth," Isabella Baumfree became one of the most popular and compelling speakers for antislavery and women's rights groups after escaping slavery in New York with her infant daughter and winning a legal challenge in state court to free her son who had been illegally sold in violation of New York's gradual emancipation statute. Tall and gaunt, she impressed Harriet Beecher Stowe, the author of the abolitionist novel *Uncle Tom's Cabin*, with her dignity and demeanor: "I do not recall ever to have been conversant with anyone who had more of that silent and subtle power which we call personal presence than this woman." **Harriet Jacobs**, a fugitive from slavery, began writing newspaper articles in the 1850s and ultimately published her own narrative, *Incidents in the Life of Slave Girl in 1861*. Her account contained harrowing (and by the standards of the time, frank) depictions of sexual abuse inflicted upon her by her master. Her work also criticized the North for its unequal treatment of African Americans.

No African American woman of the antebellum period has received more renown than **Harriet Tubman**. A tiny woman who suffered from sudden, frequent fainting spells resulting from an overseer's blow to her head when she was a teenager, Tubman escaped from slavery in 1849, bravely following a route from Maryland to Philadelphia with stops at the homes of free blacks and sympathetic whites that she heard might be helpful during her flight. Not content with her personal freedom, she fearlessly returned southward on numerous daring missions to ferry her parents, two children, and her brother's family northward. After reuniting with her relatives, Tubman

These African Americans are arriving at church.

determined to become a full-time conductor of the "Underground Railroad" which channeled hundreds of slaves to freedom. Though the price on her head eventually reached $40,000, she always eluded capture, crediting God for her exceptional courage and luck: "Jes so long as He wants to use me, He'll take ker of me, and when He don't want me any longer, I'm ready to go." (She died in 1913 at the age of 93).

The Changing life of Women

Harriet Jacobs wrote *Incidents in the Life of Slave Girl* with a particular audience in mind: middle class women. Her purpose was to demonstrate that enslavement violated what they considered proper gender roles and sanctions on sexual behavior:

> [I]n slavery the very dawn of life is darkened . . . . Even the little child . . . will learn, before she is twelve years old, why it is that her mistress hates such and such a one among the slaves. . . . She listens to violent outbreaks of jealous passion, and cannot help understanding what is the cause. She will become prematurely knowing in evil things. Soon she will learn to tremble when she hears her master's footfall. She will be compelled to realize that she is no longer a child. If God has bestowed beauty upon her, it will prove her greatest curse. That which commands admiration in the white woman only hastens the degradation of the female slave.

Jacob's account played on an emerging ethos of domesticity that prioritized modesty and female morality as the cornerstone of the domestic sphere.

Gender roles, as the case with class and racial relations, were also going through a series of transformations. In the eighteenth century, people tended to live and work in the same place (either on farms or urban artisan households). The unity of work and home ensured that men and women labored together and socialized with one another. The breakdown of artisan households in urban areas, however, effectively separated work from home. Men increasingly left the house to go to work, and (middle class) women stayed home. Popular writers and moralists characterized this domestic sphere as the exclusive province of women and charged them with creating a morally uplifting environment in which to raise children and support their husbands. Writers, along with the demands of urban life, encouraged women to have fewer children. Women complied by abstaining from sex, using available methods of birth control (male withdrawal mainly), and resorting to chemically induced abortions. Most likely, they used a combination of such methods over the course of their lifetimes. As birthrates for native-born women declined, families became increasingly child centered. Mothers were encouraged to take the primary role in child rearing, and childhood increasingly became seen as the period in which a person's moral character was formed.

Although nineteenth-century writers tended to portray the male sphere of the market and politics and the female sphere of domesticity as completely separate worlds, the division was never so stark in reality. Women never stopped participating in the market, for example. Many middle-class women handled the finances of the household, and poor women, immigrant women, and women of color routinely worked outside the home in jobs ranging from factory work, to laundering, to sewing, housekeeping, to prostitution. Many middle-class women—an increasingly well-educated segment of society—also found employment as teachers as northern states enacted compulsory education laws in the 1850s. The overlap between the spheres, however, did not stop there. If women were truly the moral stewards of society, many believed that they had a obligation to influence the moral character of their family as well as society in general. Consequently, numerous women became involved in all manner of reform movements such as temperance advocacy, anti-prostitution efforts, and the antislavery crusade.

Popular Culture in the North

New technologies in printing, the expansion of literacy, and the emergence of cities also transformed American popular culture. The print media offered a whole new world to American readers. The combination of steam powered presses and the telegraph left Americans awash in information, which generally came in the newspaper. New presses capable of printing thousands of pages per hour forced down production costs to levels making the sale price of newspapers affordable for most people. New journals also proved remarkably easy to set up. Over three thousand papers circulated in the U.S. by 1860 (more than today), covering a wide range of subjects including politics, religion, reform, and literature. Many papers, especially in urban areas like New York City, reported on crimes, especially murder, in a manner generally more escapist than informative.

Print, however, did not offer the only means of entertainment. Americans also patronized a wide array of lectures, theatrical performances, and other amusements. Reformers like Frederick Douglass and Theodore Dwight Weld (an abolitionist and temperance advocate) could earn a decent living on the lecture circuit detailing the horrors of slavery and alcohol. Noted politicians such as

Daniel Webster, Stephen Douglas, and Abraham Lincoln also attracted large audiences to hear their speeches and debates, which could last for hours. Intellectuals like Ralph Waldo Emerson offered public lectures seeking to explore the meaning of the new world in which Americans found themselves. Alongside reformers, politicians, and philosophers were also a number of others who later generations would dismiss as cranks. **Spiritualists** promised to help communicate with the dead, while **phrenologists** claimed that they could predict whether an individual had a predisposition to criminal behavior or laziness by measuring the bumps on an individual's skull. Curious Americans sometimes paid to have their own heads measured. One person who took advantage of this curiosity was **P.T. Barnum** who unabashedly sought to enrich himself by providing the opportunity for Americans to see unusual things. His museum and traveling show gave Americans a chance to see "George Washington's Nurse" (an African-American woman who Barnum claimed was 145 years old) or the "Fiji Mermaid" (probably a monkey torso stitched to a fish's tail). Perhaps more than anyone else Barnum captured the spirit of the commercial bustle and insatiable curiosity that gripped Americans in the pre-Civil War North. The region was morphing into a much different place when compared to life in 1800, standing increasingly sharp contrast to the South, which itself was undergoing fundamental changes.

THE ANTEBELLUM SOUTH

When northern observers looked at the South, they tended to see a backward region. Compared to the North, the southern United States quantitatively lagged in almost every economic category. The South possessed few banks and factories, laid down far less railroad mileage, and contained a small number of cities (and the largest ones—New Orleans, St. Louis, and Baltimore—situated

P. T. Barnum decided to collect real and fake oddities and display them to the public. People came from all over the United States and foreign countries to view his collection of freaks. Popular amusements were now becoming big business. The memory of P. T. Barnum as the "Father of Entertainment" will linger on.

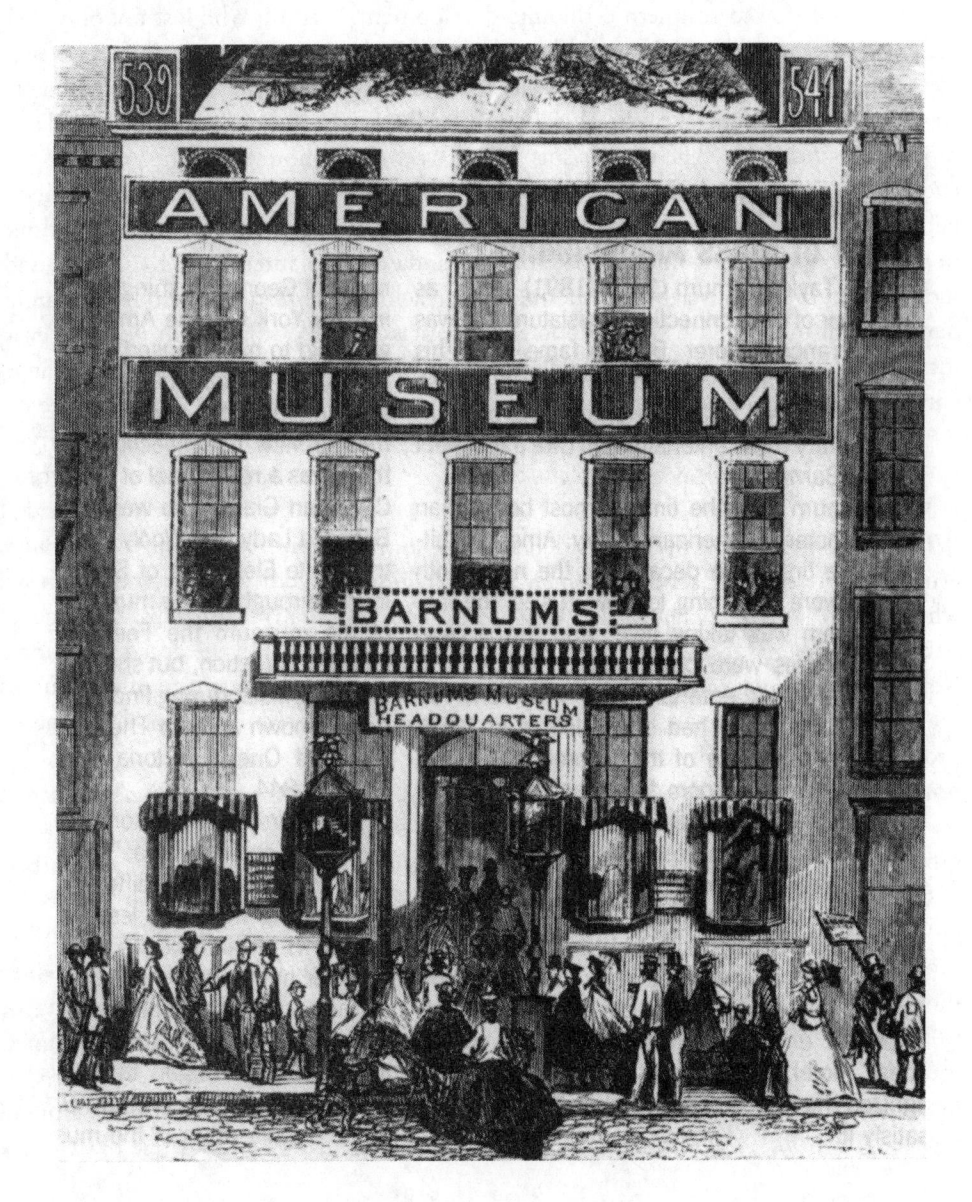

on the region's fringes). **Ralph Waldo Emerson** expressed a common sentiment when he identified the reason for what he perceived to be the South's laggard development in one of his lectures.

> Slavery is no scholar, no improver; it does not love the whistle of the railroad; it does not love the newspaper, the mail-bag, a college, a book or a preacher who has the absurd whim of saying what he thinks; it does not increase the white population; it does not improve the soil; everything goes to decay.

A few Southerners echoed these concerns. "[H]ow is it that the North . . . has surpassed us in everything that is great and good," North Carolina's Hinton Rowan Helper asked in 1857, "and left us . . . an object of merited reprehension and derision?" Helper, a Republican and an outspoken critic of slavery (both rare sights in the South), offered an atypical answer to his own question. Slavery distorted and slowed southern economic development. Other Southerners, like the New Orleans editor and early secession advocate J.E.B. DeBow, contended that slavery was central and beneficial to the South, but pleaded for more diversification. These criticisms may have been overblown. Relative to the North, the South seemed far behind, but by global standards the region ranked highly in terms of per capita income, railroad mileage, and even industrial output. Nevertheless, the most far reaching development in the South was undoubtedly the massive increase in lands under cotton cultivation along with the corresponding spread of slavery.

Cotton and Slavery Expansion

When the United States declared independence, southern slavery remained largely confined to the regions where it had emerged in the eighteenth century. In Virginia and Maryland, a growing number of enslaved Americans worked on tobacco plantations as their masters wrung their hands over their crop's declining profitability and wondering how they would keep their bondsmen employed. Rice planters in the Low Country of South Carolina and Georgia, however, kept large groups of slaves working in the coastal rice swamps. While highly profitable, rice growing required particular growing conditions that made prospects for expansion limited. By 1860, however, slavery had spread beyond the Chesapeake and the Carolinas, reaching eastern Texas to the west and Missouri to the north. Slaves in these southern sub-regions grew new crops such as sugar (in limited amounts), hemp (for making rope), and most especially cotton.

Cultivation of the white fiber transformed the South. Interest in allowing slavery to die out faded away as plans for compensated emancipation faltered in the face of rising prices for enslaved workers. (Congress's decision to outlaw participation in the international slave trade also contributed to inflated prices.) Geographical growth became a central element to the new southern economy. Unlike rice and tobacco, which had reached the limits of their ability to expand, cotton could potentially grow into numerous untapped sections of the South. Ambitious planters thus loaded up their property and migrated westward. Approximately one million enslaved African Americans participated in this process—generally by being ripped from established communities in Virginia and the Carolinas and forced through what some historians term the Second Middle Passage to work on a cotton plantation somewhere in the emerging Deep South. This population movement altered everything it touched. Those enslaved people forced to migrate were overwhelmingly young adults who lost not only their communal and family ties but also any claim to customary rights such as private farm plots, shorter workdays, and more holidays worked out between planters and enslaved workers in the South's more established regions.

This expansion was itself a consequence of a central feature of cotton cultivation: its profitability. Successful planters took their gains and reinvested them back into cotton production by purchasing more land and slaves. Cotton output doubled every ten years, accounting for 50 percent of all American exports by 1860. Southerners' tendency to prioritize cotton production over other forms of economic activity proved quite rational as they resided on some of the world's best cotton land at a time of increasing world demand. Doing anything else seemed counterproductive, although, in hindsight, the South's overdependence upon cotton led the Confederacy to have many distinct disadvantages to the Union during the Civil War. In the decades leading up to the war, however, cotton agriculture offered successful planters a reliable way of securing a good income.

Life under Slavery in the Old South

For the majority of Southerners before the Civil War, slavery was simply a fact of life. Human property had become deeply ingrained into the basic functioning of the Old South. Southern business transactions routinely involved the buying, selling, deeding, willing, mortgaging, and hiring of enslaved human beings. Social mobility in the Old South, moreover, depended more or less directly on the ownership of human beings as the possession of land. All of these practices deeply shaped the life of the

South's black population, which numbered around four million people by 1860. The majority of these slaves lived on plantations (planters comprised only 12 percent of slave owners, but held over half of the slaves in the region) which served as home for the vibrant enslaved communities that shaped African American life in the antebellum South.

Dictated by unrelenting labor, the lives of the slaves remained harsh. On cotton plantations, men, women, and children over the age of ten labored in the fields under constant supervision. Work days for field hands could be as long as eighteen hours during harvest time. Masters and their overseers, at times inflicted harsh punishments, often by whipping—a brutal practice that cut deeply into a person's back and often left deep scars. Not every slave endured such torture, but the mere threat often worked to instill discipline through terror. Material conditions, while perhaps improved relative to the eighteenth century, were by no means lavish. Entire enslaved families lived together in small, one-room buildings that lacked wooden flooring. Clothing consisted of one or two outfits, which were increasingly made out of the cheapest cloth produced by New England cotton mills. The slave diet was usually sufficient in calories but low in nutrients or variety, with pork and corn consistently served. The threat of disease (though not just for enslaved people) remained ever-present. Crowded slave quarters and the use of traditional means for disposing of human waste contributed to a host of medical maladies.

In the midst of these conditions, the slaves coped through a variety of mechanisms. They forged deep bonds within their families and their fellow bondsmen. Although the vast majority of enslaved southerners had been born in the United States, they also found ways to retain aspects of African heritage. By the mid-nineteenth century, many of these "cultural carryovers" consisted of such subtle practices as hair styling or rhythm patterns incorporated into music. Folklore told in enslaved communities passed down lessons that taught strategies for survival, with "trickster" characters often celebrated. Religion also swept through the communities, although it did so in two basic forms. One involved the version of Christianity offered by slaveholders, who (perhaps as part of their effort to defend their institution) had come to view their slaves' religious development as part of their responsibility. What the planters offered, however, was a message based on Biblical passages advising that one should accept their lot in life or stressing that slaves should obey their masters (as St. Paul stated in his epistle to the Ephesians). The other manifestation consisted of the type of Christianity that most enslaved people actually embraced. Self-taught (or at least informally educated) preachers emerged in the slave communities to lead late-night meetings that emphasized freedom and deliverance. Indeed, Moses, the prophet who guided the Israelites out of Egypt, became an inspiring figure in the theology that emerged among the slaves.

Such practices and beliefs within the enslaved community formed part of a resistance strategy by which they turned back their master's claims to absolute control over their minds and bodies. Most resistance took place in covert fashion in order to avoid punishment, such as playing dumb, subtly stealing, deliberately breaking tools, or purposefully performing tasks incorrectly. Enslaved people could also attempt to slow down their work pace and pressure masters to respond to their demands. Some historians argue that these tactics represented a form of negotiation between planters and slaves through which both parties came to agreement about the conditions of work. These strategies, however, carried an unintended consequence. Planters frequently claimed that slavery was a form of moral uplift that took "uncivilized" Africans and disciplined them so that they could survive in modern society. By disposition, they said, slaves lied, stole, and shirked work. Enslavement, therefore, would correct these alleged traits. Although these forms of passive resistance probably worked as negotiating tactics, they did so at the expense of reinforcing racial stereotypes.

Although some slaves "snapped" and undertook individual acts of violence against their master or overseer (or committed suicide), few outright slave revolts took place in the United States, due to the known futility of undertaking such an endeavor rather than any acceptance of bondage. The major exception was the 1831 revolt led by **Nat Turner** in South Hampton, Virginia. A spiritual leader among local slaves, the charismatic Turner claimed to have received visions instructing him to lead a violent upheaval to exact vengeance for his people. Perceiving a solar eclipse to be the final signal, Turner led a group of slaves on a two-day rampage through the county, resulting in the deaths of sixty white men, women, and children. Local militia, however, reacted quickly to suppress the uprising. Turner escaped, but was captured within a month. After his trial, the preacher was hanged, with his body ceremonially cut into pieces. Fifty-six other blacks were executed for participation in the rebellion. Across the South, extreme defensiveness characterized the region's response to the revolt. Fearing the next major violent outbreak, many states passed laws prohibiting education of slaves and free blacks (Turner had been taught how to read by a former master), and requiring white ministers to be present at all black worship services. Masters tightened discipline and supervision to guard against further uprisings. Any public questioning of the institution of slavery met with reprisals by authorities and the white populace.

Southern Women, Black and White

As experienced in the North, women's lives in the South were also transformed during this period, though the changes manifested themselves quite differently. In the North, an ideology of separate spheres had emerged, in some ways enhancing female claims to power within the household. In the South, however, planter claims to paternalism had implications for gender relations primarily because it stressed the organization of a household as a unit of dependents under the authority of a father figure. Women in elite families, which were genuinely large households, did wield real power. They supervised a wide range of activities—cooking, sewing, cleaning, and childrearing—and they could mete out punishments as effectively as any male. Planter women, however, did not achieve the level of public influence beginning to emerge in the North.

Planter mistresses faced additional unique challenges. One was isolation. Plantations were spread out from one another, rendering difficult any regular interaction with other women beyond the household. Another trial stemmed from the tendency of males on the plantation to use their power to take sexual advantage of enslaved women. Harriet Jacobs built much of her narrative about her experience around this issue. Frederick Douglass, who did not spend much time on the subject, hinted in his autobiography that his father also may have been his master. These observations were not just confined to slave narratives. Frances Kemble, an English actress who had been married to the wealthy Georgia planter Pierce Butler during the 1830s who later published her journal as an antislavery tract, noted upon her arrival to her husband's island plantation that she was immediately struck by the large proportion of mulattoes present, asking why there were so many mixed-race people in such an isolated area. In her journal, she noted:

> While we were still on this subject, a horrid-looking filthy woman met us with a little child in her arms, a very light mulatto, whose extraordinary resemblance to driver Bran (one of the officials, who had been duly presented to me on my arrival, and who was himself a mulatto) struck me directly. I pointed it out to Mr. [Butler], who merely answered, "Very likely his child." "And," said I, "did you never remark that driver Bran is the exact image of Mr. K [Butler's overseer Roswell King]?" "Very likely his brother," was the reply; all which rather un-

pleasant state of relationships seemed accepted as such a complete matter of course, that I felt rather uncomfortable, and said no more about who was like who, but came to certain conclusions in my own mind as to a young lad who had been among our morning visitors, and whose extremely light color and straight handsome features and striking resemblance to Mr. K had suggested suspicions of a rather unpleasant nature to me, and whose sole acknowledged parent was a very black Negress of the name of Minda. I have no doubt at all, now, that he is another son of Mr. K, Mr. [Butler]'s paragon overseer.

Mary Chestnut, a elite South Carolina women and unlike Kemble no abolitionist, also reported similar occurrences. "Any lady is ready to tell you who us the father of all the mulatto children in everybody's households but their own."

Most white women in the South, however, did not face these problems. The majority of southern white women lived on small farms, receiving little or no education. Like rural women throughout the nation, they bore a large number of children (six, on average, by 1860) and engaged in work similar to the tasks performed by farm women during the colonial era. They also increasingly labored in new locations since numerous households participated in the process of western expansion.

Enslaved women faced a hard life. In addition to the possibility of being subjected to sexual abuse, they faced expectations, especially on cotton plantations, to do the exact same field work as males. (Other crops, like rice, however, utilized assigned roles and responsibilities assigned by gender.) Work requirements extended through the last month of pregnancy, with responsibilities resumed shortly after the birth of a child. Work responsibilities resumed shortly after the birth of a child. These practices resulted in a disproportionate number of miscarriages and infant deaths. In addition to labor demands, enslaved families constantly lived with the one of the most horrific aspects of slavery—the threat that they might be broken up with their members sold in the domestic slave trade, either as a disciplinary measure or the result of a master's accumulated debts.

Slave Labor vs. **Free Labor**

During the first half of the nineteenth century, the United States was manifesting stark sectional differences as Americans confronted the new challenges represented by economic and territorial expansion. Some contend that the North and the South had become separate and mutually

The Case of the White Slave

James White, a New Orleans slave trader, bought Jane Morrison in the slave market in Jefferson Parish in January 1857. Shortly thereafter, she ran away, and White did not see her again until October of that year when he encountered her in a courtroom in answer to her suit for freedom. Her case, considered by three juries and the Louisiana Supreme Court, created an enormous stir and shook the foundations of race and slavery in the South. The reason for this was that the fifteen-year-old girl, who claimed her real name was Alexina, had blond hair and blue eyes. She claimed that she was from Arkansas and had "been born free and of white parentage" and was "entitled to her freedom and that **on view this is manifest**." She was white, her lawyers argued, because she clearly looked white. The slave trader countered that she was a runaway who had been "harboured" and encouraged by abolitionists. The case brought up the troubling question, in the words of one historian, "Could slaves become white? And could white people become slaves?"

Slave buyers looked for "blackness" in their agricultural laborers, since they believed that dark skin provided immunity to disease. They also probed for strength in men and the ability to bear children in black women. There was a premium, however, on light-skinned, slender women who could serve in the households of the wealthy or fulfill the sexual fantasies of the masters. The trade of "fancy girls" in New Orleans was notorious throughout the country. Still, it was believed that "black blood" could distinguish "nearly white" woman from genuinely white women. Louisiana, like many slave states, attempted to define suppositions of freedom by fractions of "black blood," down to one-sixteenth. If the slave was "too white," however, she (or he) might be tempted to escape to freedom and cross over the color line. Perhaps with that in mind, James White had curled the girl's hair and died it black when he first brought her home from the slave market

The witnesses for Alexina Morrison testified that the "flaxen haired blue eyed" young woman "conducted herself as a white girl. She is so in her conduct and actions. She has none of the features of an African." Southern racial ideology held that there were demonstrable behavioral differences between white and black women. Others contended that they could spot the race of a person, even in "the fourth or fifth degree," but there were no such telltale signs in Morrison.

The witnesses for the slave trader tried to convince the jurors that they could not believe their own eyes. A few argued that "she has African Blood," judging by "the shape of her cheek Bones." Her lawyers, pointing to spectators in the court, implied that if Alexina Morrison was black, it was possible that almost anyone else could also be so. James White's lawyers responded that "black blood" could disappear into ostensible whiteness without an obvious trace but still be there. They also tried to establish her extramarital sexuality to place her in the category of "quadroon mistress."

The jury was largely composed of nonslaveowners. Some came from the class of white laboring men who did such hard work as draining swamps, digging canals, and laying railroad tracks, work usually considered too dangerous for valuable slaves to do. Their wives and daughters often worked in the homes of prosperous neighbors. Morrison's lawyers were able to paint for them the alarming image of a defenseless white servant sold as a slave. This jury was unable to reach a verdict.

James White later claimed that, when he rode out with one of his witnesses to look at Alexina Morrison, he was "surrounded by a lawless mob" that threatened "personal violence because he dared to assert his property in his own slave, who said mob declared to be a white person." The court convinced that White could not find an unbiased jury in Jefferson Parish, transferred the case to New Orleans. In May 1859, a jury there unanimously declared Morrison free. The Louisiana Supreme Court overturned the verdict. A third jury in 1862 failed to agree but announced it had voted 10 to 2 in her favor. White's lawyers appealed once again, but the case was delayed during the Civil War and never considered again. Alexina Morrison and her little daughter, Mary, listed as a free white woman and child in the 1860 census disappeared in the 1870 census.

The case had raised troublesome issues in a society predicated on racial slavery. Could a slave act so white that she became white? Did that mean that there was no inherent difference and that distinctions were rather products of education and socialization? Could the whiteness of workers and their wives and daughters really protect them from being enslaved? Could slaveholders be sure that their property rights would always be protected? The case of **Morrison v. White** demonstrated the complexity of slavery and its alliance with white supremacy.

antagonistic social orders. Others posit that the two sections were substantially similar with the single exception of slavery. Though historians will probably never agree on this issue, a growing number of Americans living in the early nineteenth century certainly concluded in the nineteenth century that the North and the South were developing fundamentally different cultures. Moreover, they argued that their section represented the Founding Fathers' true vision of the United States.

Southern partisans viewed the changes taking place in the North as a sign of moral declension. "Oh! That vile North!" wrote Supreme Court Justice Peter V. Daniel of Virginia as he complained of the cold weather in a letter to his daughter, "it infects and spoils even that atmosphere we breathe!" In another letter, he asked, "I wonder when *the North* . . . would produce anything like these oranges! or indeed anything else that is good or decent." One of Daniel's main complaints was the incessant hustle and bustle of northern life combined with what he saw as an unseemly materialism. But beneath that criticism, Southerners generally portrayed the North's embrace of factory work and wage labor as an abdication of social responsibility. No longer were workers part of a household of a more established and powerful person who provided support and protection. They were thrown onto the mercies of the market. Worse still, those workers possessed the vote, and with every passing year carried the growing possibility that they would vote private property out of existence. Like slavery, southern partisans contended, unfree labor was not just the southern way of life—it was the foundation of all civilized social order.

Northern partisans rejected those arguments as self serving—as indeed they were—and portrayed three developments taking place in the North as the consequence of freedom. Poet Walt Whitman captured the sentiment in his 1855 poem "A Song for Occupations": "Neither a servant nor a master I, \ I take no sooner a large price than a small price, I will have my \ own whoever enjoys me, \ I will be even with you and you shall be even with me." The absence of slavery—the "evenness" of which Whitman wrote—meant that workers were free to choose their own employers, to negotiate their own wages, to stay, quit, or even strike when they wished, to speak their minds, or to move on to somewhere else. That freedom produced material benefits. More banks, more cultivated land, more canal and railroad mileage, more factories, more immigrants—more of everything, except cotton and slaves. Like the Southern counterargument, this one was self-serving. Praising **free labor** often meant overlooking real disparities in power and wealth developing in the North, where free labor really meant little more than the freedom to choose between starvation and a collection of essentially identical offers from employers for low wages, long hours, and dangerous conditions.

Yet along with the developments in the North came a growing number of calls to reform American society. Urbanization placed certain familiar social behavior such as drunkenness and crime into new perspective. New developments in religion, particularly among Protestant evangelicals, fed this reexamination, as did antebellum Americans' general willingness to experiment with new ideas. The consequence was a surge of new reform movements targeting almost every aspect of American society. This development, especially when activists addressed the question of slavery, further increased the gulf between the North and the South.

Chronology

1793	Eli Whitney invents the cotton gin, reviving slavery.
1808	Congress bans importation of slaves to the U. S.
1820	Lowell mills opened.
1822	Denmark Vesey's attempt at slave rebellion in Charleston is crushed.
1825	Erie Canal is completed.
1830	Baltimore & Ohio Railroad commences operation.
1831	Nat Turner leads violent slave revolt in Virginia.
1832	Restrictions on slaves increase in the South.
1834	Cyrus McCormick patents his mechanical reaper. Women workers strike at Lowell mills.
1837	Mt. Holyoke college for women opens. Oberlin college admits women and blacks.
1842	Knickerbocker baseball club organized.
1844	Samuel F.B. Morse sends first telegraph message.
1845	Irish potato famine starts, leading to massive immigration to America.
1845	Invention of the rotary press makes rapid printing of newspapers possible.
1847	John Deere manufactures steel plows.
1848	Failure of German revolutions increase immigration to America.
1849	California Gold Rush stimulates growth of West Coast.
1850s	Cotton boom sweeps the South.

Review Questions

1. What new social challenges were created by the rapid movement of people to the cities?

2. What were the largest groups of immigrants that came to the United States between 1830 to 1860?

3. Explain changes in transportation in the first half of the nineteenth century,

4. Explain the differences between the male sphere and the female sphere.

5. How did Northerners view the South? In what ways did the South differ from the rest of the country in terms of economics, education, and culture?

Glossary of Important People and Concepts

African Methodist Episcopal Church
The American System
antebellum
P.T. Barnum
cotton
Alexis de Tocqueville,
John Deere
Frederick Douglass
dueling (*code duello*)
Ralph Waldo Emerson
Erie Canal
Five Points
free labor
Harriet Jacobs
Cyrus McCormick
Morrison v. White
Samuel Morse
Parochial schools
Patent medicines
phrenology
Planters
Spiritualism
telegraph
Nat Turner

SUGGESTED READINGS

Melvin Adelman, *A Sporting Time: New York City and the Rise of Modern Athletics, 1820-1870* (1986).

Ira Berlin, *Slaves Without Masters: The Free Negro in the Antebellum South* (1974).

Janet Farrell Brodie, *Contraception and Abortion in Nineteenth Century America* (1994).

Victoria Bynum, *Unruly Women* (1992).

Catherine Clinton, *The Plantation Mistress* (1982).

Hasia Diner, *Erin's Daughters in America: Irish Immigrant Women in the Nineteenth Century* (1983).

Paul Escott, *Slavery Remembered: A Record of Twentieth Century Slave Narratives* (1979).

Timothy Gilfoyle, *City of Eros: New York City, Prostitution and the Commercialization of Sex, 1790-1920* (1992).

Herbert Gutman, *The Black Family in Slavery and Freedom, 1750-1925* (1976).

Joan Hoff, *Law, Gender, and Injustice: A Legal History of U.S. Women* (1991).

Julie Roy Jeffrey, *Frontier Women: The Trans-Mississippi West 1840-1880* (1979).

Alice Kessler-Harris, *Out to Work: A History of Wage-Earning Women in the United States* (1982).

Jacqueline Jones, Labor *of Love, Labor of Service* (1985).

Lawrence Levine, *Black Culture and Black Consciousness* (1977).

Leon Litwack, *North of Slavery: The Negro in the Free States, 1790-1860* (1961).

Louise Mayo, *the Ambivalent Image: Nineteenth Century America's Perception of the Jew* (1987).

Patricia Morton, ed., *Discovering the Women in Slavery* (1995).

Lillian Schissel, *Women's Diaries of the Westward Journey* (1982).

Ann Firor Scott, *The Southern Lady* (1970).

Carol Smith-Rosenberg, *Disorderly Conduct: Visions of Gender in Victorian America* (1986).

Christine Stansell, *City of Women: Sex and Class in New York, 1789-1860* (1986).

Stephen Thernstrom, *Poverty and Progress: Social Mobility in a Nineteenth Century City* (1964).

John Unruh Jr., *The Overland Emigrants and the Trans-Mississippi West, 1840-1860* (1979).

FREDERICK DOUGLASS

Chapter Thirteen

THE AGE OF REFORM

At the anti-slavery meeting in Indiana in 1858, she was a very imposing figure— a tall (almost six foot) gaunt black woman. Despite being illiterate, Sojourner Truth spoke with eloquence and passion. Her voice was powerful and low, almost masculine. As usual, she accompanied her talk with songs, pleasing to her audience.

As the meeting drew to a close, however, a sizable group of pro-slavery hecklers charged that Truth was, in reality, a man in a dress. They demanded that she show her breasts to the women in the audience who would verify her sex. After much "confusion and uproar," one particularly obstreperous man expressed loud doubts about her sex. Truth responded with words and actions that shamed her questioners. She informed them that "her breasts had suckled many a white babe, to the exclusion of her own offspring." Then, "in vindication of her truthfulness," she uncovered her breast to the entire audience. After asking her astounded tormentors whether "they too wished to suck," she concluded, "it was not to her shame that she uncovered her breast before them, but to their shame."

Sojourner Truth was born in the 1790s as Isabella, a slave in rural New York. When New York ended slavery, she heard the voice of God in 1826 urging her to live as a free woman. She had been overworked, beaten and even sexually abused when she was a slave. Now she turned to an evangelical Christianity that made her feel sanctified, a woman with a friend in Jesus who she compared to "a soul-protecting fortress." She became a dynamic and moving preacher.

In 1843 she experienced a rebirth. She believed that the Holy Spirit wanted her to become Sojourner Truth—a seeker after truth who, in the words of a popular spiritual, "ain't got long to stay here." In her new persona, she was an enormously effective witness to the evils of slavery on the abolitionist circuit. She also became active in the inter-related struggle for women's rights. "If colored men get their rights and not colored women theirs," she told one gathering, "the colored men will be masters over the women, and it will be as bad as it was before."

AN ERA OF REFORM

Excited gatherings of fervent believers were commonplace in an era when armies of reformers earnestly sought to transform American character. They sincerely believed in a nation in which continuous progress was ensured by the absence of barriers such as fixed social classes. As in contemporary America, these activists were troubled by what they saw as the American preoccupation with the pursuit of wealth and influence. The growing disparity between great wealth and grinding poverty, between religious revival and moral decline, and between freedom and slavery disturbed them.

Despite their concerns, most of these reformers were optimists who believed that human nature could be molded like potter's clay. If society was degraded, it could be uplifted by revivals to recreate a moral social order. The Northeast, particularly New England and northwestern New York State, was "burnt over" by the fires of reformist sentiment. Saints and missionaries have appeared throughout human history. The development of highly organized generally Christian reform associations that stirred up popular opinion and influenced government actions, however, was an innovation of the pre-Civil War era. These groups pursued clear objectives such as banning alcoholic beverages, building public schools, aiding widows, orphans and the mentally ill, and even abolishing slavery.

Middle class women formed many of these voluntary associations. What had begun as charitable and religious societies in the early 1800s had expanded to the broader goals of eliminating social evils. In the first third of the nineteenth century religious revivals, like the **Second Great Awakening**, led to the formation of female associations dedicated to Sunday schools, charity, and missionary work. Eventually, members began to "visit" the poor to distribute aid. This led to the development of institutions to help the "worthy poor," such as widows and orphans. Although these pious activities never challenged the boundaries of women's proper sphere, they led inevitably to wider social activism.

Most reformers continued to believe in the possibility, indeed certainty, of human progress. The **Benevolent Empire** was the name given to an informal association of missionary and reform societies that shared a common goal: to re-establish "the moral government of God." Wealthy humanitarians, who funded these organizations, looked with alarm on the "lawless multitude" with its unbridled appetite for violence, sex, liquor, and coarse amusements. Public morals seemed to these reformers to be in great need of purification. Crusades were required to create a chaste, sober, and responsible society.

Camp meetings brought religion to the frontier.

Revivalism and the Second Great Awakening

A major source of the impetus for reform came from Protestant revivalism that began with the Second Great Awakening. The leaders of this movement in the North stressed that anyone could choose salvation. God's grace could come to all who rejected and fought against sin. Foreign commentators like **Alexis de Tocqueville** noted that in the 1830s there was no other nation in which the Christian religion held "a greater influence over the souls of men." Throughout the nation, people flocked to revival meetings to declare their repentance for their sins, their rebirth, and, in the words of a popular hymn, to "stand up, stand up for Jesus."

The leading evangelical preacher of the Second Great Awakening was the charismatic, spellbinding Presbyterian minister, Charles Grandison Finney. Each person, he thundered, possessed within him or herself the ability to achieve personal salvation and spiritual rebirth. Finney argued that the "great political and other worldly excitements" of the time distracted Americans from achieving true soul searching. Those excitements could "only be counteracted by religious excitements." The expanding economy and its accompanying materialism gave the evangelists an obvious target to attack. The resulting growth of methods of communication and transportation—the railroad, steamship, and telegraph—also, however, made it possible to spread evangelical ideals more rapidly through the country and the world. Revivals, in the words of another preacher, prepared the nation "to lead the way in the moral and political emancipation of the world."

The great economic depression of 1857 led to "the event of the century," a massive wave of urban revivals in 1857 and 1858. In cities throughout the Northeast, workers and wealthy businessmen sat side-by-side in spontaneous midday prayer. Public high schools held exuberant revival meetings. Northerners experienced a new sense of unity in helping to bring about a better world.

The wealthy merchant bankers, Arthur and Lewis Tappan, were among Finney's most ardent followers. They became the major financial supporters of the Benevolent Empire. Finney also had great success appealing to women who found his message of personal control and responsibility to be liberating. Finney's revivalism evolved into activism in the form of a crusade against immorality. "The church," he declared, "must take the right ground on the subject of Temperance, the Moral Reform, and all the subjects of practical morality which come up for decision from time to time."

The Ohio Whiskey War

These ladies in Logan, Ohio, are singing hymns in front of a barroom to aid the temperance movement. 1874.

Moral Reform

The moral reform movement that swept the nation from the 1830s to the early 1840s was basically a woman's campaign. By 1840, the **American Female Moral Reform Society** had 555 chapters and thousands of members. Its goal was to end the sexual double standard by enforcing a single standard of moral purity on both men and women. The reformers sought to end prostitution by gathering in front of brothels where they sang hymns, prayed, looked for runaways, and threatened to publicize the names of patrons. They founded homes and employment services for "fallen women." They even lobbied, with some success, for laws that made seduction a crime. Eventually the movement sputtered out. It fell apart over the issues of the propriety of public discussions of sexual matters and of militant women moving beyond the sphere of their homes.

Sabbatarians

When Congress passed a law to deliver mail seven days a week to meet the needs of business interests for better communication, a movement developed to enforce the Christian Sabbath. The "serious Christians" involved in this crusade had gone from distributing Bibles and building Sunday schools to involvement in direct political action. Not only did they attempt to boycott businesses that opened on Sundays, they also launched a giant petition drive to convince Congress to end Sunday mail. "If this nation fails in her vast experiment, the world's last hope expires; and without the moral energies of the Sabbath, it will fail," one earnest supporter warned.

The Sabbatarians did not succeed at that time. Congress accepted a report of a Kentucky senator declaring that it was not "a proper tribunal to determine the laws of God." Many Americans were suspicious of people who claimed to know the will of God. In addition, divisions over slavery shattered the united front of evangelical reformers.

Temperance

The temperance crusade was the largest reform movement by far. Drunkenness, reformers argued, was responsible for poverty, crime, and abuse of wives and children. Businessmen worried that alcohol misuse lowered workers' productivity. One evangelical preacher declared, "Intemperance is a sin upon our land and with boundless prosperity is coming in upon us like a flood."

In fact, alcoholism was a real social problem. The supply and demand for whiskey, hard cider, beer, and rum grew rapidly. Drinking eased the loneliness of farm life and was the principal pastime of most city workingmen. It has been estimated that, by 1830, the average American male consumed about three times as much alcohol as his modern counterpart.

Temperance societies used the techniques of religious revivalism to persuade people to abstain from alcohol consumption. Reformed alcoholics organized "Washington Societies" to urge people to "take the pledge" of total abstinence. They drew huge crowds to dramatic meetings where they described their past sins and even re-enacted the miseries of delirium tremens before enthralled audiences. Their efforts resulted in more than a million pledges to forgo alcohol.

364 / CHAPTER THIRTEEN

Alcohol, Death, and the Devil

Medusa with a skeletal head, dressed in a tunic, and holding aloft a goblet of wine is exhorting a crowd of people. Behind her stands a devil who joins in the exhortation. The illustrator, Geo. Crikshank, was a popular satirist who began campaigning against alcohol, especially gin, in the 1830s. In 1847, he renounced alcohol and became an enthusiastic supporter of the Temperance Movement in Great Britain.

Reliance on "moral suasion" to solve this problem, however, was undermined by the influx of hundreds of thousands of Irish and German immigrants who disdained these moralistic appeals. The reformers feared these new populations caused the disorder they believed to be prevalent. Some began to demand legislation to restrict alcohol or even prohibit it entirely. In 1851, Maine passed a law that banned the manufacture and sale of alcoholic beverages. Faith in individual moral self-improvement gave way to attempts to remove the temptation through legislation. One temperance advocate noted sadly that the only force that drunkards could understand was "the instrumentality of the law."

Rehabilitation

The same impulse that tried to restrain "the passions of men" through public schools, moral reform, and temperance led to another effective reform movement to create institutions for criminals, the mentally ill, and the handicapped. The Benevolent Empire was active in establishing such charitable institutions as the Perkins School for the Blind in Boston, the first such school in the nation. When he visited the school, the great English novelist, Charles Dickens, was impressed to learn about a blind, deaf, and mute girl who had been taught to communicate through sign language. Her teacher noted

Dorothea Lynde Dix

that, though the "darkness and silence of the tomb were around her, the immortal spirit which had been implanted within her could not die, nor be maimed nor mutilated." Other such institutions were built to provide education and moral structure for orphans, "friendless" women, and other disadvantaged members of society.

One of the most conspicuous evils of society was throwing criminals, debtors, mentally challenged, mentally ill people, and even senile old people together in overcrowded jails. Some of these facilities were quite literally holes; one Connecticut prison was an abandoned mineshaft. As early as the 1820s, some states began replacing these dilapidated facilities with new "penitentiaries," so named since they were to provide an opportunity for inmates to do penitence for their crimes. Reformers succeeded in gradually ending imprisonment for debt or poverty. Public hangings became increasingly rare.

Dorothea Dix, teaching a Sunday school class for prisoners in 1841 in Massachusetts, was appalled to discover the insane mixed in with, and often mistreated by, the other inmates. In the next eighteen months, she surveyed most of the jails and almshouses in the state. She recorded the terrible conditions in which she found "lunitics" and "idiots" restrained "in cages, closets, cellars, stalls, pens! Chained, naked, beaten with rods, and lashed into obedience." She presented her findings about "the condition of the miserable, the desolute, the outcast" to the Massachusetts legislature. The result was increased funding for "asylums" to treat the mentally ill and mentally challenged.

Her success led her to travel 30,000 miles through the United States investigating facilities and presenting her well-known "memorials" to state legislatures. She was directly responsible for the creation of thirty-two state mental asylums and influenced the founding of many more in America, Europe, and even Japan. Eventually, unfortunately, most penitentiaries and many mental institutions became overcrowded and more like warehouses than facilities for rehabilitation or treatment.

Public Education

Both male and female reformers believed that education was the key to molding American character. Teaching the Bible to the uneducated poor and the immigrants would help create a moral and virtuous society. One missionary preacher passionately declared: "We must educate! We must educate! Or we must perish by our own prosperity." This rationale was reinforced by the Jeffersonian idea that education was essential to maintain and extend democracy. Only an educated populace could protect true democracy.

Despite the fact that literacy rates were far higher in America than Europe, educational reformers worried about the state of American education. In rural areas, the one-room schoolhouse, the subject of much romantic nostalgia in a later era, was overcrowded, dirty, ill heated, and undisciplined. Unruly older children occasionally beat up male teachers, and some women teachers kept pistols in their desks. In the rapidly growing northern cities, middle-class citizens could not help noticing growing armies of child beggars, gangs of juvenile delinquents, and increasingly younger prostitutes. Workingmen's parties, representing skilled workers, demanded more equal educational opportunities. Reformers argued that free tax-supported schools would make it possible to tap the innate capacity of even the lowliest person. Others maintained that schools could inoculate students with desirable social values to prevent the lower class disease of disorder and rebelliousness. Nevertheless, as of 1830, no state had instituted a system of universal public education.

Many parents who were wealthy enough to be able to afford private education for their children were hostile to the idea of paying taxes to educate poor children. Many working class parents worried that they could not afford to sacrifice the income that their children added to families that barely were able to make ends meet. One historian studying working-class families in a Massachusetts town of that era has shown that children under fifteen earned 20 percent of these families' incomes. In addition, by the 1840s, these workers in the northeastern cities were increasingly Roman Catholic, as Irish immigrants poured in. They resented the Protestant nature of public schools where Protestant hymns were sung and Protestant prayers recited. The New York Catholic Church even decided to build its own religious school system.

Harvard University, Cambridge, Massachusetts

Public school reformers were successful in overcoming these obstacles. **Horace Mann**, the first secretary of the Massachusetts Board of Education, established in 1837, was the most influential of these reformers. He believed that the public school was "the greatest discovery ever made by man." Schools, more effectively than even the home or church, could preserve the precious values of American democracy. Mann and other reformers contended that women were best suited to inculcate such values as cooperation, righteousness, and deference. Since women worked for wages well below those paid to male teachers, local school boards accepted that point of view, and women soon dominated the field of elementary school teaching. Some observers have argued that the availability of large numbers of "cheap" women teachers made the extraordinary growth of the public school system possible.

Public school curriculum was designed to encourage those character traits (responsibility, honesty, punctuality, and obedience to authority) most valued by the leaders of a newly competitive capitalist society. The unleashing of the human talent inherent in all had its limitations. Most Americans, even reformers, were unconvinced that those in society who were not white Christian males could benefit from the advances of education. Even in the North, most public schools excluded African Americans. When **Prudence Crandall** opened her Female Boarding School in Canterbury Connecticut to "young ladies and little misses of color" in 1833, a storm of controversy erupted. The state responded with a "Black Law," making it a crime to teach or board "any colored person who is not an inhabitant of any town" of Connecticut. Eventually, a mob, under cover of night, completely destroyed the school. The local authorities refused to investigate or guarantee future protection. Reluctantly, the courageous Ms. Crandall was forced to close her school. A few cities, such as New York and Boston, established substandard segregated schools for African Americans. Massachusetts in 1855 became the only state to declare that no child could be excluded from public schools because of "race, color, or religious opinions."

Gradually, and with some reluctance, girls were included in the new formal public education system. Some reformers argued that the young republic required an educated, informed, and moral citizenry. The young men who would become the leaders in the great experiment of liberty would be raised and nurtured by their mothers. How could women fulfill this important role if they were ignorant? Secondary academies or "seminaries" for women began to appear in New England in the 1820s and spread to other parts of the nation, largely in the North, in the next forty years. **Emma Willard** opened the successful Troy (New York) Female Seminary in 1821. She asserted that advanced education, including science, mathematics, history, and languages, as well as domestic science, would enable women to achieve "the greatest possible use to themselves and others." Her seminary not only catered to the ambitious middle class, it also became a leading institution in the new field of teacher training. Mary Lyon founded the Mt. Holyoke Female Seminary in 1837. She included selective admission standards and course offerings that reflected the curriculum of men's colleges. Her institution later became a full-fledged college, the first women's college in the nation.

In 1837, Oberlin College in Ohio became the first coeducational college in America, although women were not given a completely equal education. Oberlin, as well as Harvard, Dartmouth, and a few other private colleges, also admitted a handful of African-American students. The number of colleges grew from 16 in 1799 to 182 in 1860. A system of informal educational institutions known as "lyceums" also flourished. They sponsored public lectures on a dizzying variety of topics ranging from the scientific to the philosophical to the practical. By 1860, more than three thousand lyceums flourished, mainly in the Northeast.

Despite the many limitations, school reformers had made remarkable strides by the end of the 1850s. Massachusetts had developed the parts of a modern educational system all the way up to "normal schools" for the training of female teachers. A boy in New York City could go from elementary "infant" school all the way through college without having to pay tuition. The United States had the highest literacy rate in the world: 94 percent of the population of the North and 58 percent of the South could read and write. More than half of all American women were literate, in startling contrast to the rest of the world of that era. The public school movement strengthened the American ideal that determined effort and democratic morality could eliminate the flaws that remained in American society.

WRITERS, THINKERS, AND DISSENTERS

In the forty years before the Civil War, an enormous growth in serious American literature took place fueled, at least in part, by the dramatic increase in literacy. The growing democratization of American culture led many to question the dependence upon European cultural life. In spite of this, many American artists and writers continued to be fascinated by European sophistication and romance. Others found Europe to be a refuge from the ills of an American society they believed to be obsessed by the search for material rewards and personal power. By the end of this era, a true American literature had been created. The remarkable artistic output of the 1850s has led some historians to describe the decade as the "American Renaissance."

Emerson and the Transcendentalists

More than any other single individual, **Ralph Waldo Emerson** was America's unquestionable philosopher of the nineteenth century. His essays and lyceum lectures had an enormous influence on American culture and ideas and helped activate the literary rebirth of the 1850s. His essays inspired a generation of reformers and ordinary people.

Emerson was an idealist who was drawn to humanitarianism and a philosophy that would bridge the gap between mind and matter. He introduced Americans to German idealist philosophy known as Transcendentalism. He defined the latter as a search for "perfect freedom...for progress in philosophy and theology" that appealed to those "who sympathize with each other in the hope that the future will not always be as the past." He proclaimed that "who so would be a man, must be a nonconformist." He criticized Americans' quest for material things, fame, and power. The American people, according to Emerson, were most endangered by a fragmentation within each individual soul: "The reason why the world lacks unity and lies broken in heaps is because man is disunited with himself." Self-reliance (one of Emerson's favorite concepts) meant that man could stand up against the tyranny of public opinion and achieve a wholeness flowing from unity with God, "the Oversoul." Americans were inspired by Emerson's view that ordinary people could demonstrate unlimited and godlike potential.

Henry David Thoreau, like Emerson, a Harvard man from Massachusetts, carried the ideas of the transcen-

Ralph Waldo Emerson (left) and. Henry David Thoreau

dentalists to their extreme in rejecting social conformity. As an abolitionist and advocate of self-improvement, he considered the state a threat to individual independence. In *Civil Disobedience* (1849), he argued that the just man would refuse to pay taxes to support an unjust government (in this case the United States of the time, which was fighting, in his view, the reprehensible Mexican War). In *Walden or Life in the Woods* (1854), he described his decision to live by himself to achieve self-improvement, free from the distraction of an artificial society where most men were uncertain about life, "whether it is of the devil or of God." Little known in his own lifetime, Thoreau has come to be regarded as one of the most original minds produced by the literary flowering of the nineteenth century.

Walt Whitman: Songs of America and the Self

Emerson had once decried the lack of a true American poet. "Yet America is a poem in our eyes; its ample geography dazzles the imagination," he maintained, "and it will not wait long for metres." Walt Whitman, a New York editor, journalist, and printer, became the poet Emerson hoped for. Whitman's first book of poetry, *Leaves of Grass*, first appeared to great controversy in 1855. Like Emerson, Whitman embraced human progress and celebrated the unlimited possibilities of America. He also defied the traditional limits on poetic language and espoused "what is vulgar," a frank celebration of his own body and sexuality. This led to attacks by conservative critics who characterized him as the "dirtiest beast of his age." Emerson, however, recognized in Whitman's poems "incomparable things, said incomparably well."

Nathaniel Hawthorne

Walt Whitman

The Skeptical View: Hawthorne and Melville

Both Emerson and Whitman had a basically optimistic view of American society, despite any criticisms they made. Whitman declared that the American people retained "a miraculous wealth of latent power and capacity." Other American authors of the period were far less certain.

Nathaniel Hawthorne, who made his living as a government employee while "scribbling women" wrote best selling romances, depicted a somber world in his short stories and novels. In *The Scarlet Letter* (1850), *The House of the Seven Gables* (1851), and *The Blithedale Romance* (1852) human progress is undermined by human vice, and the dreams of reformers are nothing more than illusion.

Herman Melville, Hawthorne's friend, rejected transcendental optimism even more powerfully. After writing two best sellers based on his adventures in the South Pacific, Melville destroyed his popularity by turning to studies of the nature of good and evil. Although he celebrated "the great democratic God," Melville described the destruction that results when humans reject boundaries on their actions. In *Moby Dick* (1851), the greatest American novel of the era, Captain Ahab relentlessly pursues a great white whale, a symbol of the beautiful, evil, and ultimately unfathomable forces of life. Ahab cannot admit that there are forces beyond his control or that he might be wrong. His obsession dooms himself and his ship to annihilation. Transcendentalists contended that humans were close to divine, and most Americans were firmly convinced that God would guarantee the inevitable triumph of democracy. Melville warned of the disaster

Herman Melville, c. 1944

Americans might face if they ignored limits in a quest to penetrate the unknowable.

RADICAL DISSENTERS

Some critics of American society despaired of its future. Simple reforms did not appear to them to be an adequate response to the evils of unbridled capitalism. Far more radical solutions seemed to them to be in order.

Utopian Communities

The horrors of the early Industrial Revolution led some Americans to search for the same kind of cooperative alternatives that European reformers were proposing. They sought to escape the changes in American society by creating separate and idealistic utopian communities. Robert Owen, a Scottish manufacturer and reformer, had built an industrial cooperative in New Lanark, Scotland. He came to America in 1825 and founded a utopian cooperative community in New Harmony, Indiana. His socialist community attracted some outstanding European scholars, as well as nine hundred Americans in search of a more perfect life. Within two years, the Owenite experiment had failed. Owen's attacks on "marriage...private or individual property...and absurd and irrational systems of religion" contributed to its decline by antagonizing the American public and its faith in social norms.

A young Scottish Owenite, Frances Wright, used part of her inheritance to buy 320 swampy acres in Tennessee to carry out an ambitious cooperative experiment. The new community, called Nashoba, a "city of refuge in the wilderness," would be a model of shared labor for white idealists and slaves gradually earning their emancipation. Frances Wright gave lectures to the slaves to explain Owenite philosophy and to "develop their sense of individual responsibility." The slaves, however, found it difficult to differentiate between their former slavery and the forced labor at Nashoba. One of her supporters published an account of the community's "free love" relationships in a popular magazine. To the reading public, Nashoba seemed to be nothing more than a "great brothel." They were not reassured when Wright defended "unlegalized connections" and the rights of unmarried mothers. She went on to denounce matrimonial law as a form of tyranny that kept women in servitude. She further scandalized the public by declaring that her commune was committed to racial amalgamation.

Wright turned to lecturing as a means to further her ideals. Her free lectures and eloquence attracted huge crowds. But, since public speaking was considered deviant behavior for a woman, many came out of curiosity to view the "female monster whom all decent people should avoid." Her denunciation of organized religion, espousal of women's rights, and plans for universal free boarding-school education brought a cascade of public criticism. One newspaper declared that she was "a bold blasphemer and a voluptuous preacher of licentiousness." She eventually ran out of most of her money and ruined her reputation, while demonstrating a singular example of sexual emancipation. One perceptive listener noted, "Simple minded men were out of their wits lest their wives should learn from her example...to question male supremacy." Eventually, Frances Wright abandoned both her lecture career and Nashoba. She chartered a ship and brought the thirty-four Nashoba slaves to freedom in Haiti where they were given land by the government.

Other communal projects drew on the beliefs of the French philosopher, Charles Fourier. Fourier assumed that the wasteful and humiliating competition of capitalism could be replaced by communal "phalanxes," an ancient Greek term for the military formation where the men worked in unison and protected one another. New England transcendentalists were particularly attracted by the idea of combining idealistic cooperation and the dignity of labor. More than forty phalanxes were set up between 1840 and 1850. The most famous was Brook Farm, immortalized in Nathaniel Hawthorne's *Blithedale Romance*. Despite attracting more than four thousand admiring visitors a year, the community was abandoned by 1847.

The most successful communities were run by religious sects like the Shakers or under the discipline of strong leaders like John Humphrey Noyes. There were more than twenty Shaker communities with six thousand members in the 1840s. Their name came from a rapturous dance-like ritual in which chanting members could "shake" themselves free of sin. Shakers were committed to a simple life-style, sexual equality, and total celibacy. They tried to create a disciplined society, immune to the unbridled disorder they felt was characteristic of American life.

Noyes espoused "perfectionism," declaring that the time had come for "renouncing all allegiance to the government of the United States and asserting the title of Jesus Christ to the throne of the world." Americans, he believed, were enslaved by the possessiveness of private property and monogamous marriage. Noyes set up a community in Oneida, New York that owned property cooperatively and practiced "nonexclusive" plural marriage and "mutual criticism." The radical **Oneida** alternative to accepted economic and sexual norms lasted from 1847 to 1879 but continued as a cutlery producer into the early twenty-first century. Ultimately, however, it failed just like the earlier attempts at cooperative communities. Perhaps Americans were too individualistic to be able to sustain these group ventures.

The Mormons

Mormonism, founded in New York in 1830 by **Joseph Smith** was America's first native religion of the nineteenth century. The Church of Jesus Christ of Latter Day Saints (the Mormons) attempted to create a new, more orderly society. In many ways it was also an extreme example of radical dissent, of people who believed in a higher moral law and resisted the secular and religious society of the time.

Smith, the son of a family of poor drifters, was only twenty-four when he published an extraordinary document—the Book of Mormon. It was the translation of golden tablets whose location had been revealed to him by an angel of God in one of his many religious visions. The book contained the history of an ancient Christian civilization in America whose vanished empire was the model for a new Kingdom of Christ in the United States. It also foretold the coming of an American prophet who would re-establish that kingdom with his community of "saints." Mormonism appealed to people who had been left out of the social and economic changes sweeping through America and England at the time. Most were small farmers and artisans whom expanding capitalism had bypassed. The poet, John Greenleaf Whittier, commented that Mormon services "speak a language of hope and promise to weak, weary hearts, tossed and troubled, who have wandered from sect to sect, seeking in vain for the primal manifestation of the divine power."

In the face of persecution, Smith attempted to find a sanctuary for his saints where he could build a "New Jerusalem." They were driven out of settlements they attempted to set up in Ohio and Missouri. In Missouri a band of vigilantes massacred nineteen of them. Smith escaped, although he was convicted of treason and sentenced to be executed. Finally, he and some fifteen thousand of his followers built the model city of Nauvoo in Illinois.

Its carefully laid out squares, spacious streets, mills, factories, schools, and hotel, as well as its magnificent, almost completed, stone temple, impressed visitors to the city in the 1840s. Smith dressed as a general and commanded a legion of two thousand troops. He had a revelation justifying polygamy (the right of a man to have more than one wife). He also established a secret Council of Fifty to prepare for the Kingdom of Christ. These actions led to public suspicions about Mormon international conspiracy and sexual depravity. Neither the state nor the federal government would defend the Mormons against Missouri outlaws who seized many of their buildings. Instead, Illinois charged Joseph Smith with treason and imprisoned him and his brother in the Carthage jail. In 1844, an angry "mob," created from a state militia group and including many leading non-Mormon men, stormed the jail and lynched the two Mormon leaders.

A new leader, **Brigham Young**, arose to replace the martyred prophet. Like Smith, he was a product of a modest New England family. Although he had limited education, he was an outstanding leader and organizer. Young evacuated Nauvoo, selling Mormon property at below bargain prices. He traveled across prairies and desert with 3,700 wagon teams containing 12,000 of his followers. The weary voyagers finally settled in their new Zion in the Great Salt Lake Valley of Utah. There, they created the State of Deseret, which had its own army and even currency. Although they declared their loyalty to the United States, they tended to ignore federal government attempts to control their actions. Scandalized ministers and reformers denounced polygamy and declared that the Mormons were a menace to society. In 1857, President Buchanan actually sent a 2,500-man regular army force to put down the "rebellion." The troops were delayed by winter storms in the Rockies. They finally entered a Salt Lake City that had been evacuated by the Mormons. After an indecisive confrontation with squads of Mormon police, the troops were withdrawn. A few years later, when Abraham Lincoln was asked what he proposed to do about the Mormons, he responded, "I propose to let them alone."

A Latter Day Saint (Mormon) with five wives and his mother. c. 1885.

Like other dissenters, the Mormons believed in human perfectibility. Since God had once been a man, every person could aspire to become a kind of god. The Mormons rejected American secular values of individualism and permissiveness. Against disorder and uncertainty, they created an organized, centralized structure, resting on absolute confidence in divine authority. Although they followed such accepted Protestant ideals as a strong work ethic and temperance, they seemed to represent a radical challenge to American secular ideals. Even worse, they threatened to resist persecution with force. They sorely tried American tolerance and were only able to find their refuge of security and order by moving to the outer edge of America's geographic frontier. They eventually did achieve respectability and grudging acceptance by compromising to accommodate the larger civilization.

THE STRUGGLE AGAINST SLAVERY

The issue of black slavery exposed the limitations of the work of the Benevolent Empire. By 1830, the gap between the optimism of humanitarian reformers' belief in inevitable human perfectibility and the hard realities of human slavery had become apparent. Although federal law prohibited the African slave trade after 1808, the unexpected natural increase of America's slave population made the problem ever more noticeable. In the decade from 1820 to 1830 alone, the slave population grew from 1.5 million to more than 2 million. From the early 1830s on, the crusade against slavery increased in significance until it occupied the center stage in the reform movement.

The Early Antislavery Movement

Before the eighteenth century, few whites had challenged the morality of enslaving blacks. By the end of that century, however, antislavery sentiment emerged in the United States and Europe. One base for this movement was the growth of radical Protestant denominations that opposed slavery, particularly the Quakers. As early as 1775, the Quakers founded the first American antislavery society. Other Protestant sects, such as the Congregationalists and the Methodists, turned the traditional view of sin as a kind of slavery (in which the sinner was enslaved by his own moral limitations) to the idea that slave ownership was a sin. New secular philosophies produced by the Enlightenment also led to questioning the basis of slavery in terms of social justice and economic viability.

The Age of Revolutions in America and France reinforced beliefs in human equality (at least, in equal opportunity). As a result, slavery was abolished in the states north of Maryland, in the French West Indies, and in most of the Latin American countries that won their independence from Spain. In 1808 Britain joined the United States in prohibiting the international slave trade and was active in utilizing its naval power to enforce this restriction. In 1833 Britain abolished slavery in its West Indian colonies. These efforts succeeded in limiting the slave trade and led to the freedom of almost 2 million slaves in the world. Increasing production of cotton, coffee, and sugar, however, entrenched slavery even more solidly in the southern United States, Brazil, and Cuba. Illegal slave ships continued to do a flourishing business in Brazil and Cuba and even smuggled some African slaves into the United States after 1808.

Colonization

As the ideals of the Revolution receded, the push to end slavery on the part of southern Jeffersonians began to lose steam. Many feared that "letting loose" great numbers of black slaves with their "savage instincts" would pose a menace to an orderly society. Jefferson himself remarked in 1820 that the South had "the wolf by the ears" and could not let go. In 1817, a group of prominent Virginians, including Henry Clay and George Washington's nephew, organized the **American Colonization Society**. The Society proposed gradual emancipation of slaves with masters receiving compensation from private charities or state legislatures. The newly freed blacks would be transported out of the country in order to prevent racial war in the North and terror in the South. "We must save the Negro," remarked one adherent of colonization, "or the Negro will ruin us."

The Society bought land in West Africa. There, they established the nation of Liberia to be a refuge for free American blacks whose transportation and settlement they had underwritten. Liberia did become an independent republic in 1847. Colonization societies, however, succeeded in sending fewer than ten thousand freed slaves there by 1860. This was only a small percent of the increase in the population of American blacks over that time period.

Proslavery advocates in the lower South resented even this modest effort to interfere with their "peculiar institution." African Americans, themselves, resisted the Society's efforts. Many were generations removed from Africa and insisted that they were Americans, not Africans. Another source of opposition came from newly militant abolitionists who denounced as racist the preconception that America's race problem could only be solved by shipping black people out of the country.

Militant Abolitionists

The crusades against "sin," arising from the Second Great Awakening, led many to believe that each man was, indeed, his brother's keeper. It seemed obvious to these reformers that black slavery was, by far, the greatest national sin. As long as any American held slaves, all Americans must be held accountable for this sin. Followers of the preacher **Charles Grandison Finney,** such as the wealthy Tappan brothers and the famous lecturer Theodore Weld, along with the uncompromising **William Lloyd Garrison,** helped found the **American Anti-Slavery Society** in 1833. By 1838, it had 1,350 chapters and 250,000 members. The society and its auxiliaries launched an activist campaign against slavery. They sponsored lectures, published newspapers and books, and collected signatures for anti-slavery petitions that were sent to Congress.

These younger abolitionists rejected the moderation of the earlier anti-slavery groups. Colonization, they argued, was nothing more than a trick to strengthen slavery by ridding the country of free blacks. Compromise with slavery was impossible since the righteous person does not compromise with sin, but rather destroys it. William Lloyd Garrison, the leader of the militants, proposed a simple but genuinely revolutionary solution: the unconditional, universal, and immediate abolition of slavery. In 1831 Garrison founded an abolitionist newspaper, the *Liberator*. In its first issue, he announced the manifesto of the new militancy: "I will be as harsh as truth, and as uncompromising as justice. On this subject, I do not wish to think, or speak, or write with moderation. . . . I am in earnest—I will not equivocate—I will not excuse—I will not retreat a single inch—AND I WILL BE HEARD."

Garrison *was* heard, despite the fact that the *Liberator* had only a small number of largely black subscribers in the Northeast. Southerners published impassioned rebuttals. The Georgia legislature even offered a $5,000 reward to anyone who would capture Garrison and bring him south to be tried. The new steam printing press and other technological advances made mass publications possible. The abolitionists were among the first to realize the potential for mass communications. In 1835 alone, the Anti-Slavery Society distributed 1.1 million pieces

William Lloyd Garrison, the leader of the militants, proposed the unconditional, universal, and immediate abolition of slavery. He founded the abolitionist newspaper, the *Liberator*.

of literature. Angry mobs stormed southern post offices and set fire to the *Liberator* and other abolitionist tracts. Declaring that abolitionist books and pamphlets might lead to a slave rebellion, President Andrew Jackson ordered the postmaster general to prevent them from being delivered through the mails. Abolitionists found other ways to spread their propaganda. These included posters, candy wrappers, children's books, medals, and songs.

Abolitionists did not think of themselves as advocates of violence or civil conflict. They viewed their societies as part of the reform movement. Surely slavery and racial prejudice were at least as harmful to the community as drunkenness. Just like other reformers, they were trying to encourage the potentials of the human spirit. Who could possibly be more in need of help in fulfilling their possibilities as human beings than slaves? Theodore Weld clearly stated this position. Slavery, he wrote, was a terrible sin because, "no condition of birth, no shade of color. . .can annul the birthright character, which God has bequeathed to every being upon whom he has stamped his own image, by making him a free moral agent."

Anti-Abolitionists in the North

Most Northerners did not accept this abolitionist message. In a deeper sense, abolitionists seemed to be at war with the established values and institutions of American life. They were a more radical threat to the social order than even the Mormons were. Abolitionists, it seemed to many, were ignoring the rights of private property by urging uncompensated emancipation of the slaves. If the state could do that, whose property would be safe? Their crusade might lead to greater conflict between the sections. Newly freed blacks might flood the northern cities where black men would intermingle with white women. This was yet another threat to the order and stability of society at a time of great disorienting social change.

Anti-abolitionist violence and riots spread through the North in increasing waves in the 1830s. A Philadelphia mob in 1834 burned down the abolitionist headquarters and launched a murderous attack on free blacks. The wealthy Tappan brothers were widely condemned by other businessmen for encouraging radicals like Garrison with their financial support. A crowd of prominent New Yorkers laughed and cheered as they watched a mob of laborers demolish Lewis Tappan's house and burn his belongings

Garrison, himself, barely escaped lynching by an angry crowd in Boston. Three times, enraged mobs in Alton, Illinois smashed the printing presses of abolitionist editor, **Elijah Lovejoy**. Each time, he rebuilt his newspaper. In 1837, in a fourth attack, Lovejoy tried to defend his press. This time the mob set fire to the building and murdered Lovejoy. Most of this mob violence was carefully planned and organized. While the mobs consisted largely of lower class whites who feared job and social competition from freed blacks, some, particularly the leaders, included "gentlemen of property and standing." These leading citizens felt they were protecting the social order. They also used their influence to insure that the forces of law and order did nothing to protect the besieged abolitionists and free blacks.

Political Abolitionism

Garrison, as a result of all this violence, came to believe that American society itself was fatally infected with the virus of brutality. The entire body of the nation was contaminated. The only sane response was to repudiate all coercion represented by the oppression of nonwhites, women, and dissenters. Majority rule simply enforced repression, so Garrisonians withdrew from all political activities. In one of his more dramatic gestures, Garrison would set fire to the Constitution in front of shocked audiences. The Constitution, with its protection of slavery, was nothing more, in Garrison's estimation, than "a covenant with death, and an agreement with Hell."

Most other abolitionists, however, did not agree with Garrison's total moral withdrawal from a corrupt society. They hoped that they could achieve their goals through political action. They collected thousands of antislavery petitions against the slave trade in the District of Columbia and for the abolition of slavery. In 1836, southern congressmen, with the support of many northern sympathizers, passed the "**Gag Rule**," ordering any petitions relating to slavery "in any way" to be tabled and, therefore, ignored. The petitions were an effective way of challenging this rule. John Quincy Adams, the only former president to become a member of the House of Representatives, led an energetic campaign against the gag rule. Since the First Amendment of the Constitution guaranteed "the right of the people. . . to petition the government for a redress of grievances," the rule seemed a clear example of southern attempts to tyrannize free white Northerners just like slaves. To many Northerners, the Gag Rule provided further evidence that slavery was a danger to the rights of all Americans. In 1844, the resolution was repealed.

Some abolitionists decided that it was essential to enter politics directly. In 1840, they formed the Liberty Party and nominated James G. Birney, a reformed slaveholder, for president. The Libertymen attributed the depression of 1837 to machinations by the "Slave Power." This initial attempt had minimal impact since Birney only got seven thousand votes—a mere 0.3 percent of the votes cast. The Liberty Party was ultimately successful, however, in getting the idea of Slave Power conspiracy imprinted on the consciousness of northern public opinion.

Garrisonians rejected the efforts at political action, arguing that it would lead to compromising basic principles. They also attacked organized religion as a "den of thieves" for its refusal to unequivocally condemn slavery. This angered religious abolitionists. Other supporters were upset at the Garrisonian advocacy of equal rights for women. The consequence of these actions was a split in the Anti-Slavery Society. The Tappan brothers and others who withdrew from the society founded the Liberty Party and set up other political antislavery efforts. The most famous of these was the successful struggle to gain freedom for the Africans who had revolted and won control of the **Amistad**, a ship taking them to slavery in Cuba. John Quincy Adams actually represented the rebellious Africans in their victorious appeal to the Supreme Court.

Despite this split, the antislavery movement continued its varied activities after 1840. Political abolitionists narrowed their focus to restricting the spread of slavery in the territories, rather than calling for its immediate abolition throughout the nation. They believed that, as new territories entered the union, preventing the expansion of slavery would cause its inevitable collapse. This political push became most evident in the formation of the Free Soil Party in 1848 and, more importantly, in the Republican Party in 1854. Now, however, more concern was expressed for the rights of free white men who had to compete with slaves than for the rights of black people. Free Soilers insisted that, "slavery withers and blights all it touches.... It is a curse upon the poor white laboring men." A Free Soil newspaper announced, "We are opposed to the extension of slavery because it diminishes the productive power of its population." The antislavery movement became more acceptable to northern voters by accommodating itself to white racism. Garrison contemptuously described free soilism as "white-manism." But the free soil argument was finally able to achieve what abolitionism could never manage: to gain the support of large numbers, eventually the majority, of white northern voters.

The Proslavery Justification

For some time after the Revolution, many planters in the Upper South followed the Jeffersonian tradition of aristocratic distaste for the institution of slavery. They expressed the cautious hope that one day a way could be found to rid the South of its "burden" or "curse." Some non-slaveholding whites seemed to agree that slavery was "ruinous to the whites." Even many supporters apologetically characterized slavery as a "necessary evil" that would one day, in the distant future, disappear.

The 1830s, however, seriously undermined this genteel viewpoint. The extraordinary growth of the cotton kingdom, coupled with a defensive reaction to the increasingly active antislavery movement, led to a defensive counterattack by Southerners. They argued that slavery was, in fact, a "positive good." All great societies of the past, from Biblical Israel and ancient Greece to the medieval empire of Charlemagne, they declared had rested on a foundation of slavery. The South, in their estimation, was superior to a chaotic North like the "ism-smitten people of Massachusetts" prey to such heresies as feminism and utopianism. In the South, society was stable as women and slaves alike understood their established places.

Black Abolitionists

The racism inherent in the arguments of the supporters of slavery and the hypocrisy of many antislavery reformers in accepting the racism of northern society increased the appeal of militant abolitionism to free blacks in the North. These free blacks, numbering around 250,000 by 1850, often lived under conditions of misery and intolerance. The bigotry directed at these African Americans in the North led Tocqueville to observe that "the prejudice which repels the Negroes seems to increase in proportion as they are emancipated." Most worked as domestics or in menial jobs. It was difficult for them to get any kind of formal education. Only a few states granted the vote to black citizens. Nevertheless, these blacks were very conscious of the importance of their freedom and of the danger slavery posed to their precarious position in society.

From the earliest days of organized abolitionism, blacks worked with antislavery groups. The lectures and printed accounts of the lives of escaped or freed slaves like Sojourner Truth, Solomon Northup, and **Frederick Douglass** put a human face to northern images of slavery. Their dramatic accounts succeeded in weakening any feeling there may have existed in the North that slaves were carefree "darkies" who were well treated by kindly masters. Their intelligence and eloquence undermined stereotypes of black inferiority.

Black abolitionist speakers endured far more harrowing dangers on the lecture tours than whites. They were continually threatened, harassed, insulted, humiliated, and attacked. Most of the conductors on the "Underground Railroad" were black. They succeeded in aiding a relatively small number of fugitive slaves in escaping to the North or the greater security of Canada. Black abolitionist groups also hoped to secure the repeal of discriminatory laws in the North. Outside of Massachusetts, they had little success in challenging northern racism. Their white abolitionist allies urged them to remain in the role scripted for them in dramatic shows designed to attack slavery in the South while remaining quiet about discrimination in the North. Abolitionist leaders felt that it was important not to frighten northern audiences with talk of violence or racial equality.

Many northern blacks supported Garrison. But militant black leaders developed who asserted their own authority. David Walker, a Boston free man, as early as 1829, expressed a combativeness that terrified many whites. In his pamphlet: "Walker's Appeal. . .to the Colored Citizens," he proclaimed, "America is more our country than it is the whites—we have enriched it with our blood and tears." Whites who wanted to keep blacks as slaves "will curse the day they ever saw us." Walker counseled slaves to cut their masters' throats, to "kill or be killed."

By the 1840s, other black leaders began to affirm their own leadership and ideas. At a Convention of Free People of Color held in Buffalo in 1843, **Henry Highland Garnet**, an articulate activist, endorsed slave rebellion. He maintained that it was a sin to passively surrender to the bonds of slavery. Another black militant, Charles Lenox Remond, to the deep regret of the pacifist Garrison, openly declared "that slaves were bound, by their love of justice, to RISE AT ONCE, en masse, and THROW OFF THEIR FETTERS."

Most black antislavery leaders, however, were far less fierce in their orations. The greatest of these leaders was Frederick Douglass, one of the most thrilling speakers of an era renowned for its eloquence. Douglass was born a slave in Maryland where he illegally learned to read and write and taught himself intellectually challenging subjects like higher mathematics and Greek. In 1838, he escaped to Massachusetts where he became an outstanding lecturer for the abolitionist movement. He mesmerized audiences with his descriptions of his life under slavery. He published one of the great American autobiographies, *Narrative of the Life of Frederick Douglass*. After that, he spent two years lecturing widely throughout Britain where he was glorified by that nation's flourishing antislavery movement. On his return to the United States in 1847, he continued to speak throughout the North. Although an advocate of nonviolent resistance, Douglass broke with many white abolitionists by demanding full civil, political, and economic rights, as well as freedom for slaves. In 1847, he split with Garrison over his idea of founding a black abolitionist newspaper, *The North Star*. Douglass continued his battle for reform, supporting women's rights, as well as black equality.

Many black abolitionists believed gaining the right to vote would be the best route to greater influence and freedom. They, therefore, supported the efforts of the Liberty and Free Soil Parties in the 1840s. Unfortunately, antislavery politics seemed to be increasingly focused on partitioning off western territories. The partition would keep out free blacks, as well as slaves. By the 1850s some disillusioned black leaders were talking of creating a separate black nation or even of voluntarily emigrating to Haiti or Africa.

By this time, however, increasing numbers of northern whites had become convinced that there was a Slave Power conspiracy. Enforcement of the Fugitive Slave Act, including seizing blacks in the streets of northern cities, led to growing anger, demonstrations, and civil disobedience. Moderates grew more receptive to Garrisonian militants. Wendell Phillips, the most electrifying abolitionist speaker, exulted that, "every five minutes gave birth to a black baby." In that infant's cry he detected a voice that would "yet shout the war cry of insurrection; its baby hand would one day hold the dagger which should reach the master's heart." Thus, black and white antislavery groups both came to an understanding that only extreme measures could destroy the "Slave Power."

THE RISE OF THE WOMEN'S RIGHTS MOVEMENT

Women had played a crucial role in many of the reform movements of the era, particularly in abolitionism. Women gained useful experience in public speaking, organizing, and raising funds in hundreds of female charitable and reform associations. As they labored to correct the ills of an imperfect society, they became increasingly aware of the problems that they, themselves, faced in a male-dominated community. This led to the founding of America's first feminist movement and the beginning of a prolonged struggle for women's rights.

Women and the Antislavery Crusade

Female antislavery societies began forming almost immediately after William Lloyd Garrison launched his movement in 1831. By 1838, there were over one hundred such associations throughout the Northeast and Midwest. At first, they devoted themselves to raising funds for the cause with "antislavery fairs" where homemade goods were sold. Soon, however, they became involved in more activist and controversial ways. Since middle-class women had more time to devote, they were the ones who canvassed door-to-door to collect signatures for abolitionist petitions in the drive to challenge the gag rule. This meant moving out of their traditional sphere—the home.

Their role as antislavery speakers on public platforms was even more problematic. This included speaking to "mixed" or "promiscuous" audiences, an activity considered totally improper for a respectable woman. In the face of mounting criticism, a women's national antislavery convention resolved: "The time has come for woman to move in that sphere which providence has assigned her, and no longer remain satisfied in the circumscribed limits which corrupt custom and a perverted application of scripture have encircled her."

Sarah and Angelina Grimké, two of Garrison's most important converts, best exemplified this exciting new role for women. They were the daughters of an eminent slave-holding South Carolina family whose members included judges and legislators. They deserted their father's plantation to move to Philadelphia where they converted to the Quaker faith, which preached human equality. They then embraced the ideals of abolitionism and became the first official female antislavery agents. As such, they launched a lecture tour, speaking at first to female audiences. Soon, however, they were shamelessly addressing mixed audiences. These clearly upper class and "proper" southern women, who could lecture about the evils of slavery from personal experience, quickly became a sensational attraction for the abolitionists. They drew crowds of thousands of curious spectators, converting many to the antislavery cause.

Clergymen and conservative reformers were outraged that two women had usurped "the place and role of man as public reformer." One minister charged that the Grimkés had abandoned "that modesty and delicacy. . .which constitutes the true influence of women in society." He implored them to return to "the appropriate duties and influence of women."

Sarah Grimké responded with an attack on the male domination of society, drawing an analogy between the treatment of women and that of slaves. "Men and women are CREATED EQUAL. They are both moral and accountable beings," she declared. "All I ask our brethren is that they take their feet from off our necks and permit us to stand upright on the ground which God destined for us to occupy."

This stand angered those abolitionists who believed that the spectacle of women challenging their traditional roles would harm the antislavery cause. Garrison became the main defender of the Grimkés. He drew a parallel between the condition of women and slaves, announcing in the *Liberator*: "As our object is universal emancipation, to redeem women as well as men from a servile to an equal condition—we shall go for the rights of women to their utmost extent." Garrison had persuaded the Grimkés that Christian "principles of peace" were the heart of all reform. In turn, the Grimkés convinced Garrison and his followers that these principles applied to the "domestic slavery" of women as well.

A number of black women were also actively involved in the abolitionist movement. Both the Boston and Philadelphia Female Antislavery Societies had black women as members, and even one officer. In general, however, northern racial segregation led most black women abolitionists to form their own societies. Once women began to speak in public gatherings, African-American women who had once been slaves proved to be particularly effective in describing the harmful effects of slavery on black family life. Sojourner Truth and, somewhat later, Harriet Tubman were especially popular speakers.

The controversy over women's participation caused a final split in the American Anti-Slavery Society. The more conservative faction left the Society to Garrison and his radicals and founded its own organization. The issue

Angelina Emily Grimké (left) and
Sarah Moore Grimké (right)

Elizabeth Cady Stanton (left) and Susan B. Anthony (right) as elderly women. c. 1908.

spread to the World Antislavery convention in London in 1840. The men who controlled the proceedings refused to allow female American delegates to actively participate. Relegated to the balcony as observers (accompanied by a supportive William Lloyd Garrison), Lucretia Mott and Elizabeth Cady Stanton came to the conclusion that improving the status of women should become their major goal as reformers.

The Struggle for Legal Rights

During the 1840s, a sustained campaign was launched to end legal discrimination against wives. Under the law, in all states, married women were considered legal possessions. They could not control their own property and had no rights to their own earnings or even to their children. Attempts to remedy this situation met with some success in the 1840s. Some state legislators, who owned property themselves, reacted favorably to measures to preserve their estates from the hands of greedy sons-in-law when daughters were the sole heirs.

In New York a women's pressure group was formed under the leadership of the fiery **Ernestine Rose**. She was the daughter of a Polish rabbi who fled the restrictions of her home to go to England. There, she became a follower of **Robert Owen**. Rose had recently immigrated to the United States. Her group argued that married women should be allowed to keep their own property and earnings and should be given joint guardianship over their children. In 1848, New York passed a bill providing married women with some control over their property. Gradually, other states passed similar legislation. To some extent, these laws were designed to provide a legal loophole to protect property from husbands' creditors. As one historian notes, however, "In the context of the nineteenth century, the right of wives to own property entailed their right not to be property."

The Women's Rights Movement

After 1848, the battle against legal inequality continued increasingly under the standard of the women's rights movement. After their disillusioning experience at the world antislavery convention, **Elizabeth Cady Stanton** and **Lucretia Mott** resolved to convene a convention to call for action to eliminate the many inequities women faced.

This first women's rights convention was held in 1848 at a Methodist Church in Seneca Falls, New York (Stanton's hometown). The manifesto that emerged from this meeting was called the "Declaration of Sentiments and Resolutions." It was patterned on the Declaration of Independence, proclaiming that "all men and women are created equal," and that women also have certain inalienable rights to life, liberty, and the pursuit of happiness. Just as the original Declaration listed grievances against the King of England, the women's Declaration identified the adversary as the "absolute tyranny" of man and then listed "his repeated injuries and usurpations." These included exclusion of women from better jobs, higher education opportunities, and the professions; the deprivation of property rights; and the imposition of a sexual double standard. In oppressing woman, man had also tried "to destroy her confidence in her own power, to lessen her self respect, and to make her willing to lead a dependent and abject life." After a list of demands to rectify these grievances, the declaration concluded with a claim that women were entitled to the right to vote, a major assault on the long-cherished view that women did not belong in the public sphere.

This demand for women's suffrage was the most controversial of all. Even women's rights activists were unsure. At Seneca Falls, the call for the vote was the only resolution not approved unanimously by the delegates. It only gained a slim majority after Frederick Douglass gave it his eloquent endorsement. Women who were willing to sign petitions calling for legal rights refused to support petitions demanding the right to vote. One woman wrote her suffragist sister, "I am sure I do not feel burdened by anything man has laid upon me, to be sure I can't vote, but what care I for that, I would not if I could." In spite of these difficulties, the struggle for women's suffrage continued until women finally gained the constitutional right to vote in 1920.

The **Seneca Falls** meeting led to a whole series of conventions throughout the North and Midwest to restate and embellish its sentiments. The press greeted these meetings with animosity and ridicule. Despite this, Elizabeth Cady Stanton, joined by **Susan B. Anthony**, persisted in her efforts. Although Stanton and Anthony pressed for more radical changes, most of the conventions held in the 1850s emphasized legal and economic inequality. Many directly challenged the statements of clergymen that the Bible decreed that the "weaker sex" remain in a dependent "sphere." Lucy Stone, a militant feminist, told them, "Leave woman to find her own sphere."

Only moderate progress was made in meeting the goals of women's rights activists by the 1850s. Limited advances occurred in the area of legal rights for married women. Some individual women, like Elizabeth Blackwell, the first licensed female physician, began to break down some barriers to advancement. Blackwell's sister-in-law, Lucy Stone, took the radical step of keeping her maiden name after marriage. (For years after, women who followed her lead were known as "Lucy Stoners.") Some women demonstrated their feminism in their choice of clothing. They wore an outfit that combined a short skirt with long pantaloons. Although a famous English actress first introduced the costume to Americans, it came to be called "bloomers," after Amelia Bloomer, its most ardent advocate. In the face of a rising turmoil over women seeking to "wear the pants" in the family, leading feminists abandoned it. They worried that the bloomer issue was overshadowing their more serious activities.

Attempts to enlarge the following of the women's rights movement by combining with the much larger, more conservative, temperance community did not succeed. In New York State, a Women's Temperance Asso-

---

The Protest of Lucy Stone and Henry Blackwell Upon Their Marriage

The minister who married Lucy Stone and her husband, the Reverend Thomas Wentworth Higginson, an abolitionist reformer, published their statement in the Worcester Spy. It was reprinted in newspapers and journals across the nation. Married women who kept their given names became known as Lucy Stoners.

While we acknowledge our mutual affection by publicly assuming the relationship of husband and wife, yet, in justice to ourselves and a great principle, we deem it a duty to declare that this act on our part implies no sanction of, nor promise of voluntary obedience to, such of the present laws of marriage as refuse to recognize the wife as an independent, rational being, while they confer upon the husband an injurious and unnatural superiority, investing him with legal power which no honorable man would exercise, and which no man should possess. We protest especially against the laws which give to the husband:

1. The custody of the wife's person.
2. The exclusive control and guardianship of their children.
3. The sole ownership of her personal and use of her real estate, unless previously settled upon her, or placed in the hands of trustees, as in the case of minors, lunatics, and idiots.
4. The absolute right to the product of her industry.
5. Also against laws which give to the widower so much larger and more permanent an interest in the property of his deceased wife than they give to the widow in that of the deceased husband.
6. Finally, against the whole system by which 'the legal existence of the wife is suspended during marriage,' so that, in most States, she neither has a legal part in the choice of her residence, nor can she make a will, nor sue or be sued in her own name, nor inherit property.

ciation with Elizabeth Cady Stanton as president quickly split up over Stanton's idea that drunkenness should be grounds for divorce.

In many ways feminists benefited from their association with other reform movements, particularly abolitionism. These reform groups provided women's rights advocates with a ready-made sympathetic audience and conduits to communicate their ideas. On the other hand, this relationship could also be a hindrance. Women's rights, even in the eyes of most of the women involved in both abolitionist and feminist movements, was always secondary to the more pressing need to emancipate the slaves. Until the slave had achieved his or her freedom, the women's rights movement could not advance due to its dependence on an antislavery foundation.

The Impact of Reform

The antebellum (pre-Civil War) period was characterized by an unprecedented burst of reformist sentiment. Organizations struggled to tackle all the perceived ills of society including alcoholism, prostitution, moral laxity, violation of the Sabbath, oppression of women, and, above all, enslavement of human beings. It is important to remember that reform, like dynamic economic changes, was basically a product of northern life. Southerners were largely untouched by the push to create a better society. Although relatively few Americans shared the abolitionist view that slavery must be immediately and completely eliminated, the struggle over slavery ultimately dominated American political life before the Civil War settled the issue once and for all. While some reform goals, such as ending all consumption of alcohol and making seduction illegal, may seem extreme and puritanical to us today, others including racial and sexual equality eventually became the shared ideals of most Americans.

Chronology

1830 Joseph Smith founds the Mormon Church
Charles Finney's religious revival meetings (through 1831).

1831 Nat Turner leads slave revolt in Virginia.
Garrison first publishes *The Liberator.*
Alexis de Tocqueville begins his travels through America, the basis for *Democracy in America.*

1833 American Anti-Slavery Society founded.

1834 New York Female Moral Reform Society founded.

1837 Sarah Grimké writes *Letters on the Equality of the Sexes.*
Horace Mann appointed secretary of the Massachusetts Board of Education.
Ralph Waldo Emerson delivers his "American Scholar" address.
Mt. Holyoke opens women's college.
Oberlin becomes the first coed college.

1840-1 Transcendentalists start utopian communities Hopedale and Brook Farm.

1843 Dorothea Dix issues her report on the treatment of prisoners and the insane.

1844 Joseph Smith murdered in Illinois.

1845 Publication of the *Narrative of the Life of Frederick Douglass.*

1846-7 Mormon migration to the Great Salt Lake.

1847 Frederick Douglass' *North Star.*

1848 First women's rights convention held in Seneca Falls, New York.

1850 Nathaniel Hawthorne's *The Scarlet Letter* is published.

1851 Herman Melville's *Moby Dick* is published.

1852 Harriet Beecher Stowe's *Uncle Tom's Cabin* is enormous best seller.

1854 Thoreau's *Walden* appears.

1855 Massachusetts becomes first state to end public school segregation.
Walt Whitman's *Leaves of Grass* is published.

Review Questions

1. What view of human nature did the reformers of the 1830s and 1840s share, and what social problems did they seek to address?

2. What controversies arose in the first half of the 19th century concerning public education for immigrants, African Americans, and women?

3. Describe the beliefs of Transcendentalism and the philosophy of its leading exponents, like Ralph Waldo Emerson and Henry David Thoreau.

4. Describe the evolution of anti-slavery thought in America in the early 19th century, including consideration of "colonizers," and advocates of immediate emancipation. What was the white southern response to slavery's critics?

5. What was the relationship between the anti-slavery and the women's rights movement, and what reforms were sought by 19th-century feminists?

Glossary of Important People and Concepts

American Anti-Slavery Society
American Colonization Society
American Female Moral Reform Society
Amistad
Susan B. Anthony
Benevolent Empire
Prudence Crandall
Alexis de Tocqueville
Dorothea Dix
Frederick Douglass
Ralph Waldo Emerson
Charles Grandison Finney
"Gag Rule"
Henry Highland Garnet
William Lloyd Garrison
Grimké Sisters
Nathaniel Hawthorne
Elijah Lovejoy
Horace Mann
Herman Melville
Mormonism
Lucretia Mott
Oneida Community
Robert Owen
Ernestine Rose
Second Great Awakening
Seneca Falls Convention of 1848
Joseph Smith
Elizabeth Cady Stanton
Emma Willard
Brigham Young

SUGGESTED READINGS

Robert Abzug, *Cosmos Crumbling: American Reform and the Religious Imagination* (1994).

Barbara Berg, *The Remembered Gate: The Woman and the City, 1800-1860* (1978).

Fawn Brodie, *No Man Knows My History: The Life of Joseph Smith, Mormon Prophet* (1945).

Frederick Douglass, *Life and Times of Frederick Douglass* (1881).

David Brion Davis, *The Problem of Slavery in the Age of Revolution, 1770-1823* (1975).

George Frederickson, *The Black Image in the White Mind, 1817-1914* (1971).

David Gollaher, *Voice for the Mad: The Life of Dorothea Dix* (1995).

Elizabeth Griffith, *In Her Own Right: The Life of Elizabeth Cady Stanton* (1984).

Carol Kolmerten, *Women in Utopia: The Ideology of Gender in American Owenite Communities* (1990).

Aileen Kraditor, *Means and Ends in American Abolitionism* (1967).

Gerda Lerner, *the Grimke Sisters of South Carolina: Rebels Against Slavery* (1967).

William McFeely, *Frederick Douglass* (1991).

Nell Irvin Painter, *Sojourner Truth: A Life, A Symbol* (1996).

Leonard Richards, *"Gentlemen of Property and Standing": Anti-Abolitionist Mobs in Jacksonian America* (1970).

David Rothman, *The Discovery of the Asylum: Social Order and Disorder in the New Republic* (1971).

Shirley Yee, *Black Women Abolitionists: A Study in Activism, 1828-1860* (1992).

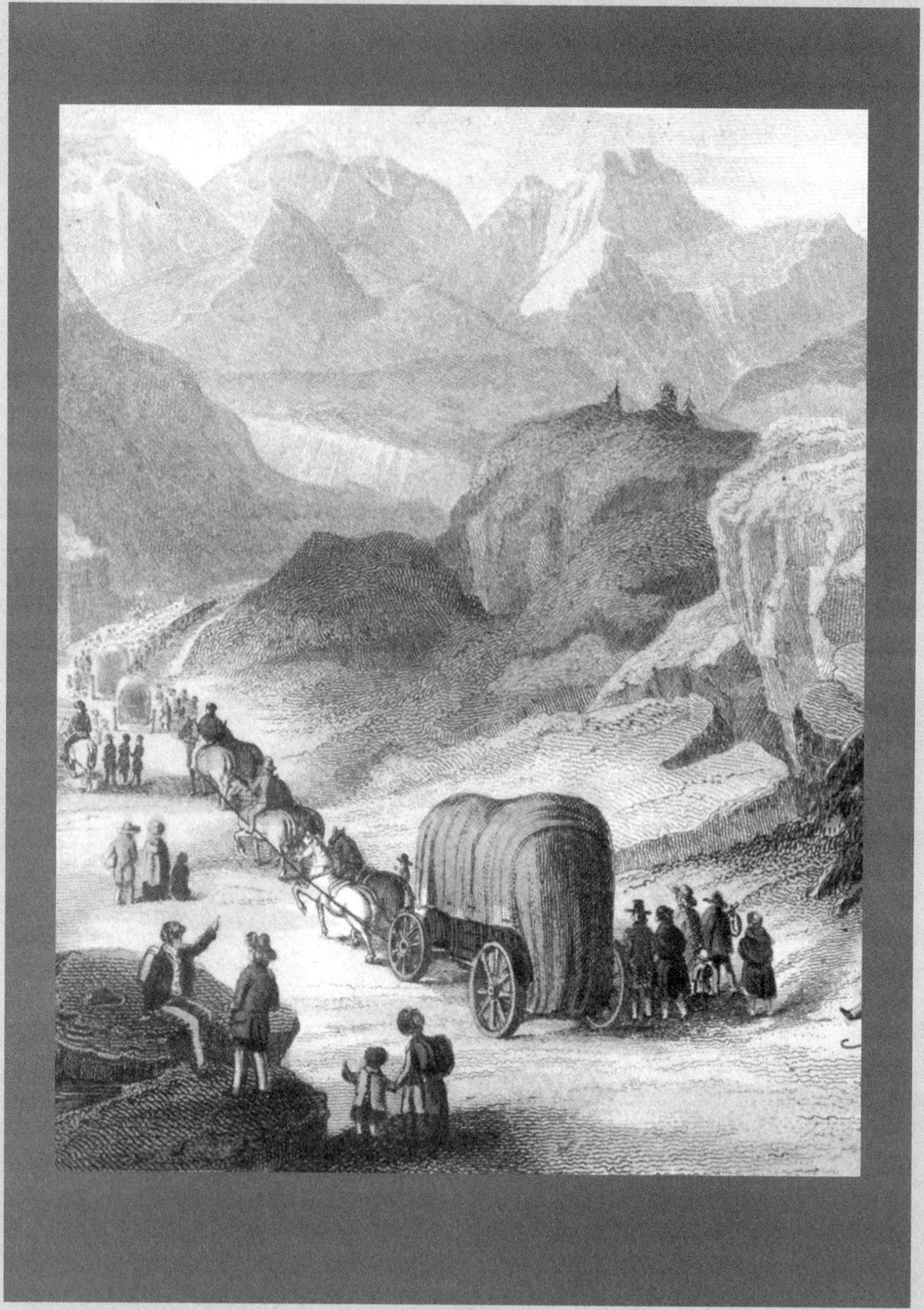

Chapter Fourteen

AMERICA EXPANDS, 1840-1850

"We feel that we cannot do our work too fast to save the Indian . . . from extinction," the missionary Narcissa Whitman wrote her mother in an 1840 letter that revealed much conflict in her attitude to those she professed to be saving. She rightly sensed that there was not much time. "A tide of immigration appears to be moving this way rapidly. What a few years will bring forth we know not." Narcissa and her husband Marcus were among the handful of American missionaries to settle in the Oregon Country, a region in the Pacific Northwest that the United States and Great Britain jointly occupied from 1818 to 1846. When the Whitmans arrived in 1834 and established their mission near the confluence of the Snake and Columbia Rivers (close to what is now Walla Walla, Washington) and along what would become known as the Oregon Trail, the region was dominated by a diverse array of Native American groups who had been interacting regularly with fur traders and Catholic missionaries for decades. That contact had brought new economic activities, new belief systems, and new diseases that together had disrupted previously established patterns of hunting and gathering and left many Native Americans dependent on a fur trade that had gone into decline. The Whitmans planned to remedy that dependency by encouraging the adoption of farming along with Protestant Christianity. Narcissa reported progress to her mother: "they are becoming quite independent in cultivation. . . . Great numbers of them cultivate . . . and do their own plowing."

But in the same letter, Narcissa also expressed frustration. She described her charges as "an exceedingly proud, haughty and insolent people," and she noted that they constantly demanded food and resisted what the Whitmans considered to be true Christian teachings. Narcissa also expressed shock about Native American gender roles, especially the suggestion made by one that her husband, Marcus, travel without his wife, as the local Indians did. Narcissa had no intentions of going native: "[the Indians] are so filthy they make a great deal of cleaning wherever they go, and this wears out a woman very fast. We must clean after them, for we have come to elevate them and not to suffer ourselves to sink to their standard." In short, Narcissa and Marcus Whitman believed that their work of saving Native Americans required remaking them in the image of Protestant Christian farmers before the inexorable tide of American settlers displaced or exterminated them.

Although the Whitmans believed themselves to be on a civilizing mission to save the Indians, they in fact served more as the first wave of the thousands of American settlers who would begin flooding the region after 1840. These newcomers expected the regions into which they moved to conform to the political, economic, and social values that had come to dominate the United States. For the Whitmans, those expectations did not work out. The Native Americans they settled among—the Umatillas, the Walla Wallas, and especially the Cayuses—proved resistant to their teachings, partly because the new missionaries did not meet the Indians' expectations. Previous missionaries, Catholics brought in by the British Hudson Bay Company, worked in a system that had encouraged Indians to become dependent on trading posts and linked religious instruction to trading. Those expectations may have been part of the reason behind the constant demands for food that so troubled Narcissa. Although the Whitmans reported success with the introduction of farming, local Native Americans adopted farming as only a supplemental activity and planned to continue their practices of hunting and fishing. They had little interest in becoming year-round farmers as the missionaries had hoped. They also proved unwilling to reject practices like polygamy simply because the Whitmans claimed they were sinful.

As more settlers passed through the region, tensions increased. Epidemic diseases ravaged the population, and the Cayuses blamed Marcus Whitman, who was a physician by profession, for bringing the sickness. They also increasingly regarded the new missionaries—and especially the Whitmans, who provided lodging to travelers on the Oregon Trail—as agents of conquest. For his part, Marcus Whitman came to accept that the Native Americans' unwillingness to embrace his definition of civilization justified their displacement, and he increasingly turned his attention to the spiritual needs of the American settlers. Tensions came to a head in September 1847 when some Cayuses attacked the mission and killed Marcus and Narcissa Whitman along with twelve others. They also took another fifty-three people captive. Americans responded by pushing Indians off their lands. The United States, which secured exclusive control of the area in 1846, established a fort on the site of the mission. By 1855, American pressure had forced all Native American groups in the area to cede their lands and move to reservations, although fighting between Indians and settlers would continue through the 1850s and beyond. By then, however, Americans had established unquestioned control over the region.

The Whitmans' experience in the Oregon Country illustrated some of the central features of the United States's expansion in the 1840s. Narcissa's insistence that she and Marcus were on a civilizing mission, for example, was a sentiment toward expansion that was by no means unique to her. Numerous politicians and newspaper editors expressed similar sentiments, although they at times made more sweeping claims. John O'Sullivan, editor of the **Democratic Review**, provided one of the most famous formulations when he described American expansion in 1845 as "our manifest destiny to overspread and to possess the whole of the continent which Providence has given us for the development of the great experiment of liberty and federated self-government." In other words, God had given the United States a mission to expand throughout the western hemisphere and to carry its political institutions and moral values to the rest of the world. But the Whitmans' experience demonstrated how Americans lived out that mission. American settlers, like the missionaries, expected the populations living in the areas into which they moved to conform to their standards—not just in Oregon, but also in places like Texas and California. Settlers, moreover, arrived in such large numbers that they quickly overwhelmed and then displaced local populations throughout western North America. From their own vantage point, then, the Whitmans experienced one of the central developments in the mid-nineteenth-century United States: the aggressive expansion of American settlers into areas west of the Mississippi River and beyond the exclusive control of the United States. How to address the consequences of that expansion would become the central issue of American politics in the 1840s, and the choices made to address it would lead to war with Mexico and place the United States in control of an immense amount of new territory filled with rapidly changing populations.

EARLY WAVES OF EXPANSION

As late as 1845, the area of North America between the Mississippi River and the Pacific Ocean fell under the formal political control of Mexico in the present-day American Southwest, Great Britain in the present-day Pacific Northwest, or the United States, whose western boundary extended in stepped fashion from the borders of Mexican Texas to the Pacific Northwest (a claim that overlapped with Great Britain.) Most of this area, however, remained sparsely settled by people of European descent, and effective control of many regions remained in the hands of Native Americans, like the Comanche on the southern Great Plains or the Sioux on the northern ones. After 1820, however, Americans began moving into some of these regions—usually in small numbers and often as merchants, traders, and missionaries rather than settlers. These folk, as the Cayuses said of the Whitmans, tended to function as an advance guard for later groups of settlers because they sent back word of prospective sites for future settlement. By 1840, these initial waves of American migrants had established a presence in places like California and New Mexico, Oregon, and especially in Texas.

Oregon

The Oregon Country, a territory that included the present states of Washington, Oregon, Idaho, parts of Montana and the Canadian province of British Columbia, attracted only a handful of fur traders and missionaries before the 1840s, although the presence of those settlers introduced significant changes into the region. Both Great Britain and the United States claimed Oregon by right of discovery—the latter through the Lewis and Clark expedition of 1804-1806—but the two nations agreed to a joint occupation for an indefinite period of time. Great Britain's

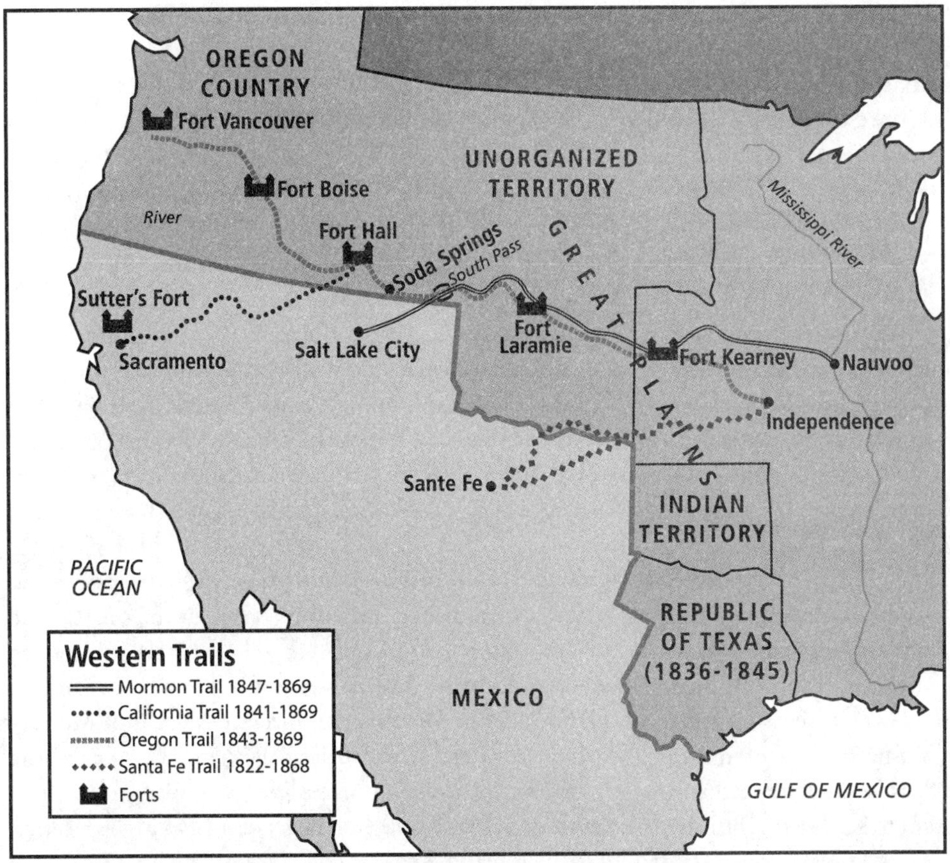

Map 14.1 Western Trails

presence centered on the Hudson Bay Company, which from its headquarters at Fort Vancouver (a location on the Columbia River relatively close to what would become Portland, Oregon) dominated the fur trade in western North America. The first Americans in the region likewise tended to be fur traders who had married into local Native American kinship networks and then settled in the region as their careers wound down.

In the 1830s, Protestant missionaries from the United States (Marcus and Narcissa Whitman among them) moved into a region that had already experienced wrenching transformations. Native Americans in the region, such as the Cayuses, were already participating in a trade network that extended into the North American interior and along the coast of western North America when the Lewis and Clark expedition arrived in 1804. Trade with the interior brought horses; the coastal trade brought new European goods. Both brought epidemic diseases that would reduce the indigenous population from an estimated 180,000 to 40,000 over the course of the nineteenth century. The Hudson Bay Company's fur traders also introduced the region to (generally Catholic) Christianity, which Native Americans incorporated into their own belief structures. By 1840—on the eve of the first wave of expansion of American settlers into the region—Oregon had become an area rife with tension among Native Americans stressed by diseases that nei-

ther traditional belief structures nor Christianity could adequately explain or remedy.

California and New Mexico

Portions of the present-day American Southwest also came into increasing contact with the United States in the decades before 1840. Before the 1820s, the Spanish government had regarded its colonial holdings in northern Mexico as little more than buffer zones protecting its valued possessions south of the Rio Grande from invasion by European competitors or from raids by Native American groups like the Comanche who mastered horseback riding and had developed into a significant military force on the southern Great Plains. Spain worked diligently to keep its territory closed to outsiders—even pursuing and apprehending American explorers on occasion. Spanish settlements in California, New Mexico, and Texas remained relatively isolated as a consequence. Mexican independence in 1821, however, reversed that trend, as the new government liberalized its laws, opening its northern territories to trade and, in some cases, settlement. In California, Mexico secularized a mission system that had extracted the labor of 30,000 Native American converts, a change that mainly resulted in a shifting of the primary claim to Indian labor from the missionaries to the ranchers who sold cattle to New England merchants and businessmen in San Diego and San Francisco. American traders also worked their way into New Mexico along the **Santa Fe Trail**, a route whose harsh environment coupled with hostile Native Americans such as the Comanche rendered quite dangerous and highly profitable for the caravans making the trek.

Texas

Although California and New Mexico received the attention of American merchants, Texas attracted settlers whose migration fundamentally transformed the relationship between Mexico and the United States, contributing decisively to the latter's aggressive expansion in the 1840s. Under Spanish rule, Texas had been a sparsely settled area primarily serving as a buffer zone against Comanche raiders and foreign interlopers. The Republic of Mexico organized the region as part of the state of Coahuila y Tejas, permitting entry to settlers under an 1824 immigration law. Even before that point, however, settlers from the United States were taking up residence in Texas. **Stephen F. Austin**, who had inherited a substantial land grant from his father, negotiated with the Spanish and then Mexican governments to secure permission to settle a few hundred families along the Brazos River. Austin was the first of twenty-four **empresarios**—those persons authorized by the Republic of Mexico to recruit and accept responsibility for settlers in exchange for extensive land grants in Texas. Mexico offered favorable terms to immigrants. Farmers could claim just over 4400 acres (more if they claimed to be ranchers), although they were supposed to become Mexican citizens, and covert to Roman Catholicism (the state religion).

Along with some Mexicans and Europeans, Americans and their slaves (legally classified as indentured servants to comply with official Mexican law which banned slavery) flooded into the region, challenging Mexican control of Texas. By 1830, over twenty-thousand people had settled in eastern Texas, with another ten thousand arriving by 1835. The immigrant population far exceeded the Mexican population in the region. Meanwhile, newcomers often showed little interest in adopting the practices of their hosts. Despite the requirement that they do so, few immigrants converted to Roman Catholicism. Meanwhile, Texas's population of 5,000 African-American slaves by 1835 had moved the cotton frontier into the Mexican Republic, and the area seemed in many respects an extension of the southern United States rather than a part of Mexico.

These developments concerned Mexican officials. In 1828, General Manuel de Mier y Terán undertook an extensive inspection tour. He acknowledged that American settlers were industrious and were rapidly developing the region, but he also noted that a large number of settlers paid no heed to Mexican law (which he admitted had not been rigorously enforced). "Official documents that I have obtained," Terán wrote to Mexico's President, Guadalupe Victoria, "prove that more than two thousand foreigners are living on the best lands on the border. None of them has requested permission." "If it is bad for a nation to have vacant lands and wilderness," he wrote in another part of the letter, "it is worse without a doubt to have settlers who cannot abide by some of its laws. . . . They soon become discontented and thus prone to rebellion." Terán's statement proved prescient. In 1830, the Mexican government responded to his report by instituting a prohibition on American immigration and renewing its laws against slavery. Settlers still came by the thousands, and tensions mounted between the settlers and their Mexican hosts. Relations between the settlers and the Mexican government reached a breaking point when **General Antonio López de Santa Anna** seized power. In 1834, Santa Anna named himself dictator of Mexico, replaced a federal constitutional system that had allowed significant autonomy to states like Coahuila y Tejas with a centralized governance, and began crushing his opposition in many rebellious regions of Mexico with brutal military force.

Anglo settlers in Texas, along with a number of *Tejanos* (Mexican Texans) showed their willingness to resist by first refusing to pay customs duties, then by skirmishing with Mexican troops, and finally by declaring independence on March 4, 1836. By this time, Santa Anna had arrived in Texas to suppress the rebellion personally. His force of several thousand troops laid siege to the Alamo (Mission San Antonio de Valero) in San Antonio where 187 rebels resisted for two weeks until they were wiped out in a final assault. Near Goliad, Mexican troops captured and then executed another 350 rebels under orders from Santa Anna. **General Sam Houston**, a protégé of Andrew Jackson and a relative newcomer to Texas, turned around the bleak string of defeats and retreats at the Battle of San Jacinto, an engagement in which Houston took advantage of Santa Anna's decision to split his forces and managed to capture the Mexican leader. To gain his release, Santa Anna signed agreements acknowledging Texas independence, with the entire Rio Grande serving as the national border. After removing Santa Anna from power upon his return to Mexico City, a new group of Mexican government officials rejected these audacious claims. Since the Spanish period, the border of Texas had always been viewed as the Nueces River, which meets the Gulf of Mexico at Corpus Christi. The Republic of Texas's claim, however, extended the border about 300

The Alamo. San Antonio, Texas

miles further south and encompassed a large slice of New Mexico including the important trading town of Santa Fe. Regardless of border considerations, the Mexican government refused to recognize Texas independence in the first place, though financial constraints and the need to suppress other revolts closer to the capital precluded mounting another major military expedition into Texas.

A SURGE OF SETTLERS

After Texas declared independence, and especially after 1840, emigration from the United States into regions like Oregon and Texas accelerated. A number of factors contributed to the increase. Growing population density combined with a depressed agricultural economy made areas within the United States seem relatively less appealing to farmers throughout the Union. President Andrew Jackson's war with the Second Bank of the United States had in part contributed to a major financial crisis in 1837, which had reduced the national money supply by about one-third and placed enormous pressure on debtors (many of whom happened to be farmers). A collapse in the price of cotton in 1839 followed hard on the heels of the Panic of 1837 and pulled the entire agricultural economy into a deep depression that did not end until 1843. Any pressures that farmers felt after the Panic of 1837 generally became more intense after 1839. Reports from early settlers made regions outside the United States seem especially attractive. An account written by two Oregon missionaries noted that the Willamette Valley, which became the primary area of American settlement in the region, was highly fertile and well suited for growing a wide range of crops. They even hinted that one farmer had managed to grow a crop of potatoes by accident, when some of the buds of his previous year's crop had fallen on the ground during harvest. Although such accounts were overblown, the more modest reports were attractive enough for prospective emigrants. "I came to this place with my wife and two children," read a letter by a new resident of Oregon that appeared in an 1843 Congressional report. "We have settled ourselves, and have got plenty around us to eat and to wear, and our produce bears a good price." Pushed out of the United States by hard times and drawn by favorable reports to places like Oregon, Texas, and other areas of northern Mexico, settlers went on the move. These migrants—with one notable exception—were by no means abandoning the United States and would be within a few years clamoring to be annexed by the country they had (briefly) left behind.

The Republic of Texas

Texas experienced a flood of immigration. Between 1836 and its annexation in 1845, over 100,000 settlers arrived in the **Republic of Texas** (mostly from the United States). Some of these immigrants were surely drawn by reports of good farm land in the region. "What can the husbandman desire more," asked an English observer. Texas had plentiful wood, water, and land well suited for both farming and livestock. "Nature has lavished her [Texas's] bounties with the munificence of an indulgent parent; it only remains for man to show himself worthy of her favors by the due application of his energies, mental and corporal, and the temperate use of the means of enjoyment placed it his disposal." The government of the new republic, however, made Texas appealing by offering land on favorable terms. White heads of households settling in Texas could receive a grant of 1,280 acres of land, and the relative proximity of the new republic to the United States rendered this offer even more enticing.

Despite the influx of new settlers, the Texas Republic faced a host of challenges. Mexico refused to recognize its independence generally and its claim to a border at the Rio Grande specifically. In 1842, Santa Anna (now back in power) launched two raids into Texas to probe the Republic's defenses, twice capturing San Antonio before withdrawing. Continuing hostilities with Mexico contributed to a growing distrust of the Tejano population. Although some prosperous families managed to intermarry with Anglo families and thereby retain their status in the region, other families lost their land holdings and other economic resources either by intimidation or fraud. Relations with Native Americans, especially the Comanche, remained tense. The republic's first president, Sam Houston, sought to establish peaceful relations by marking a border between his constituents and the Comanche. Houston's successor, Mirabeau B. Lamar, rejected that approach and sent troops deep into Comanche territory, an act that led to a war that lasted from 1838 to 1841. Just as Texas's leaders were divided over how best to deal with the Comanche, they split over the prospect of annexation by the United States. Houston's faction supported the idea; Lamar's faction favored an independent Texas expanding westward into California. Texas voters strongly favored annexation, but concerns within the United States about the prospects of war with Mexico and especially the sectional dispute caused by the slavery expansion issue delayed annexation until 1845.

The Trek to Oregon

American migrants also made their way to Oregon. In 1840, only about 500 Americans had settled in the area, but more poured into the region over the next decade. Prospective migrants back east organized Oregon societies early in the decade and planned for the difficult trek across the continent. In 1843 alone, one thousand migrants hit the trail. By 1845, Oregon's settler population reached 5,000—a number that far exceeded the some 750 British inhabitants in the region. Five years later, the 1850 Census reported a population of over 13,000. Compared to the thousands of settlers rushing into Lone Star Republic at the same time, the numbers for Oregon may seem small, but journeys to the Pacific Northwest were exceedingly difficult compared to the relatively shorter sojourns to Texas, either overland or by water transportation via the Gulf of Mexico. Oregon's settlers, meanwhile, had to undertake an expensive, six-month trip across two thousand miles of rugged terrain. The trip along the **Oregon Trail** began in Independence, Missouri and led them across the Great Plains and through the Rocky Mountains before reaching their destination. Settlers generally traveled in large wagon trains, which sometimes contained as many as one hundred wagons. Large groups provided safety during the arduous journey. The migrants had to bring everything they needed with them, often discovering that they had to abandon much of what they toted to lighten their loads. Life on the trail exposed travelers to all sorts of hazards. Attacks by Native Americans were always a possibility, but the settlers generally faced more mundane dangers. Animals and wagon wheels threatened to crush children. River crossings brought the danger of drowning. Moving through the mountains brought the danger of falling. Exposure to the elements remained a constant challenge. The trip was simply hard, especially for women, whose work on the trail stacked with their already daunting expectations for cooking, cleaning, and child-rearing. Despite these challenges, thousands of settlers successfully navigated the trail and established themselves in Oregon.

As their more numerous counterparts in Texas, settlers in Oregon expected that their new home would become part of the United States. Relations with Native Americans in the region deteriorated as they had in other areas of settlement. Some of the Protestant missionaries who believed that they had arrived in the 1830s at the request of the indigenous population expressed frustration with their charges. Local natives rejected critical concepts like human depravity and refused to give up practices like polygamy. By the mid-1840s, they had also concluded that the missionaries were little more than the enablers of conquest. Missionaries did not help themselves in this regard. As settlers moved into the region, they turned their energies toward converting the newcomers and accepted the displacement of the local Native Americans. "When a people refuse or neglect to fulfill the designs of Providence," Marcus Whitman wrote to one of his relatives, "then they ought not complain at the results . . . they have in no case obeyed the command to multiply and replenish the earth [sic], and cannot stand in the way of others doing so." Settlers also clamored for annexation by the

United States. Joint occupation created a very practical problem for the new settlers: they could not establish a legal claim to the land they held while the area remained under the control of two nations. Although the director of the Hudson Bay Company, John McLoughlin, proved to be helpful and accommodating to the new settlers—despite his orders from Great Britain to discourage American settlement—the issue became increasingly urgent by the mid-1840s, and the U.S. government would respond by annexing a portion of the region.

The Mormon Exodus

Although settlers in Texas and Oregon hoped that their new homes would be annexed by the United States, **Mormons** took to the trails in the hope of leaving the nation permanently. Since their emergence in upstate New York in the 1820s, adherents to the Church of Jesus Christ of Latter-Day Saints had experienced resentment and harassment from their non-Mormon neighbors. Mormon communities under the leadership of the church's founder and prophet, **Joseph Smith**, had emerged in Ohio and Missouri, but many values of the Latter-day Saints ran counter to those of their neighbors. Under the stewardship of patriarchal church leaders, Mormon settlements practiced economic cooperation, which allowed them to undercut the prices of nearby farmers. On election days, Mormons voted in a bloc for candidates favored by church leaders. Most controversially, Smith's religious teachings, including polygamy (publicly condemned by early Mormons, but privately practiced as many suspected), were unacceptable to most non-Mormons. When coupled with the economic and political power of their tight-knit communities, Mormon religious and cultural practices bred deep resentment among non-Mormons. The resulting conflicts ultimately drove them to western Illinois where they established a new settlement at Nauvoo along the Mississippi River. The city quickly boasted over ten thousand inhabitants and featured an impressive temple. Nauvoo's time as one of the fastest growing towns in the nation proved to be short-lived. Tensions over Smith's (autocratic) leadership emerged within the Latter-day Saint community, while recurring friction with non-Mormons produced a series of crises that culminated in 1844 with Smith's murder by a violent mob.

Mormon leaders concluded that they needed to leave the United States, ultimately selecting Utah's Great Basin region, a remote area in Mexican territory that had been essentially ignored. The region's remoteness made it especially attractive to Mormon leaders who sought to build their own society free from the interference of hostile neighbors. In 1847, the Mormons' new leader

Joseph Smith's original temple, Nauvoo, IL.

and prophet, Brigham Young, led a group of more than 2,000 settlers along what became known as the Mormon Trail, which branched off the Oregon Trail and terminated between the shores of the Great Salt Lake and the foothills of the Wasatch Mountains. Thousands of additional Mormons arrived each year thereafter. Under church direction, settlers divided land and water rights while building a community centered on their religious values, which by this time included the open practice of polygamy. Though the goal of the Mormon migration was to leave the United States, the nation they fled annexed their territory in 1848 along with the rest of northern Mexico after the Mexican War.

The surge of settlers pouring out of the United States transformed the balance of political and diplomatic power in the region. Native Americans who had managed to accommodate small numbers of settlers found themselves pushed off the land. Great Britain and Mexico found that the growing number of settlers—combined with the certainty that more would surely come—rendered their claims to territory in western North America more tenuous with each passing year. Outside of Utah, the demands of settlers to be annexed by the United States would be embraced by a number of politicians, particularly within the Democratic Party. Their responses would transform American politics and ultimately lead to war with Mexico.

MANIFEST DESTINY

During the 1840s, territorial expansion became the central issue of American politics. The movement of settlers into Texas and Oregon created a new set of pressures that turned politicians' and voters' attention away from the disputes over banking, tariff rates and funding infrastructure projects that had dominated party politics in the 1830s. (These issues did not go away, of course, they just became relatively less pressing concerns.) By the middle of the decade, the parties divided primarily over the speed and scope of American expansion. Democrats favored a rapid expansion, calling at times for the annexation of substantial portions of Canada and Mexico—some of them even advocated expansion throughout the entire hemisphere. Whigs, who themselves accepted the inevitability of American expansion, favored a more cautious approach that they hoped would avoid conflict with other nations and reduce the prospect for political instability at home. The Whigs lost this struggle. In 1844, the Democrats regained the presidency and endorsed a series of aggressively expansionist policies that ultimately led the United States into a war with Mexico.

Part of the Democratic Party's political strength rested on the ability of its partisans to articulate the expansionist impulse emerging in the early 1840s. Foremost among Democratic ideologues was John O'Sullivan, editor of the *Democratic Review*. "[O]ur country," he wrote in 1839, "is destined to be the great nation of futurity." By that awkward phrase, he meant that the United States had broken decisively with the past. The American population came from a multitude of European nations, and it had no legacy of aristocracy and no history of bloody conflicts with other countries. Indeed, the United States essentially had no past; it only had a future. Freed from the historical baggage carried by other nations, Americans enjoyed the opportunity to build a country on the principle of political equality. That principle represented more than simply a formal foundation of government. Equality was a universal value—"a self-evident dictate of morality"—and the United States held an obligation to share it with the rest of the world. For O'Sullivan, fulfilling that obligation entailed expansion. "[W]ho will, what can, set limits on our outward march," he asked. "Providence is with us." All of this led to a sweeping conclusion:

> [T]he boundless future will be the era of American greatness. . . . [T]he nation of many nations is destined to manifest to mankind the excellence of divine principles; to establish on earth the noblest temple ever dedicated to the worship of the Most High. . . . Its floor shall be a hemisphere. . . , and its congregation an Union of many Republics, comprising hundreds of happy millions. . . governed by God's natural and moral law of equality, the law of brotherhood of peace and good will amongst men.

In his later writings, O'Sullivan would coin the phrase "**manifest destiny**" to convey his sense of a God-given American right to expand throughout the Western Hemisphere and to carry political institutions and moral values to the rest of the world.

Very little of what O'Sullivan said, however, proved to be new. Americans already believed strongly that the founding of the United States represented a major break with the past. Thomas Paine had made that point on the eve of independence. The conflict with Britain, he wrote, "[t]is not the concern of a day, a year, or an age; posterity are virtually involved in the contest, and will be more or less affected even to the end of time." O'Sullivan's words in some ways echoed those of Thomas Jefferson's First Inaugural Address (1801), which noted that Americans possessed "a chosen country, with room enough for our descendants to the thousandth and thousandth generation." And Jefferson's own vision of the United States as an expanding "empire of liberty" was hardly unique to him. The idea of mission stretched deep back into the American past. John Winthrop, the first governor of Massachusetts, hoped that his colony would become a "city upon a hill" as an example for others to emulate. Winthrop, of course, did not share the relatively more secular, expansionist vision articulated by O'Sullivan, but the latter built on the theme pronounced on the *Arabella* more than two-hundred years before.

What O'Sullivan and his fellow writers added to this sense of mission and expansion was a sense of ethnic and racial destiny. Speaking of the possibility that California may be annexed, O'Sullivan made the point bluntly: "The Anglo-Saxon foot is already on its borders. Already the advance guard of Anglo-Saxon immigration has begun to pour down upon it, armed with the plough and the rifle, and marking its trail with schools, colleges, courts and representative halls, mills and meeting houses." In a later essay, O'Sullivan cautioned against the annexation of Mexico because he believed its population to be ill suited for republican government. "Are there probably as many men in the whole Mexican Republic competent to exercise the elective franchise with the intelligence of the average American citizen as there were righteous men in Sodom when she was destroyed?," O'Sullivan asked, referring to the story from Genesis in which God promised not to destroy the Sodom if it contained ten righteous persons (it did not). "If so, the number of the righteous in that fated city must have been exaggerated. Beyond a question, the entire Mexican vote would be substantially below our national average both in purity and intelligence." Incorporating Mexicans into the Union, he asserted, would require a much stronger government than that which Americans were accustomed, and establishing that would undermine American values. His discussion in some ways echoed the sentiments of Narcissa Whitman who saw herself as coming "to elevate" the Indians in a way that would not require her "to sink to their standard."

Even if not entirely new concepts, and despite their being chauvinistic by modern standards, these ideas struck upon a powerful chord in American politics. As Americans poured into Texas and Oregon, settlers in these regions and politicians back home clamored for annexation. The process, however, would play out in a way more convoluted and far more violent than O'Sullivan envisioned.

TYLER AND POLITICS OF EXPANSION

Despite the calls of ideologues like O'Sullivan, expansion as a political issue developed quietly in the early 1840s catching a number of political leaders by surprise when it finally burst upon the scene toward the middle of the decade. National politics in the early 1840s revolved around many of the same issues that had dominated the previous decade, especially banking. Taking advantage of the national economic depression, Whig nominee William

President John Tyler

Daniel Webster

Henry Harrison and his party finally won the presidency and control of Congress in 1840 with a solid victory over Martin Van Buren and the Democrats. In an effort to counter the charges of critics that he was too old to serve, the 68-year-old Harrison delivered a two-hour-long inaugural address on a frigid morning without a hat or overcoat. Perhaps weakened by the speech and definitely worn down by the constant demands of office seekers at the beginning of his presidency, Harrison contracted a cold that developed into pneumonia. Within a month of taking office, he was dead, introducing a number of complications into domestic politics. Harrison's successor, **John Tyler,** quickly came into conflict with Henry Clay and other Whig leaders in Congress. A Virginian with a political career as a state legislator, governor, and congressman before election to the U.S. Senate, Tyler had been a supporter of Andrew Jackson before breaking with Old Hickory over the nullification crisis. In the 1830s, he joined a faction of southern Whigs who rejected what they perceived as the president's hostility to states' rights. Party leaders selected Tyler as the vice presidential nominee in 1840 to balance the ticket geographically (though born in Virginia, Harrison had long resided in the Old Northwest and thus considered a Northerner by the general public). No one expected Tyler to become president. The new chief executive soon showed that he did not share the priorities of other Whig leaders. Henry Clay, believing that Tyler would either follow his lead or could be forced into doing so, led a repeal of the Independent Treasury Act—a law passed in 1840 with the support of the Van Buren administration to manage the national money supply in the wake of the destruction of the Second Bank of the United States—and shepherded a new national bank bill through Congress. Tyler vetoed it. All but one member

> ### The Saga of the Amistad
>
> On February 22, 1841, the Supreme Court began hearing arguments in a remarkable case involving mutiny on a Spanish slave ship, **Amistad**, off the coast of Cuba. Although the African slave trade was illegal, the ship held fifty-three captives, including four children and a 26-year old man from Sierra Leone who had been given the name Joseph Cinque. Cinque led a brief, bloody struggle on the ship, killing its cook and captain. After 60 days sailing up and down the Atlantic coast of the United States, American sailors seized the ship. They found forty-three malnourished Africans (the others had died of disease or exposure) and two Spanish officers who demanded the return of their "property."
>
> Louis Tappan and other abolitionists saw the case as an opportunity to expose the slave trade and its brutality. They even found two Africans working on the docks in New York who could translate the language of the mutineers, enabling them to tell their side of the story. Roger S. Baldwin, the Africans' lawyer, argued that they had been illegally kidnapped from their homeland and, thus, were entitled to resist their abductors by any means necessary. Observers were divided into those who saw Cinque as a strikingly handsome black folk hero and others who felt he was a murderous barbarian who deserved to be executed.
>
> The Van Buren administration, citing diplomatic necessities, attempted to return the Africans to Spanish Cuba. Van Buren's blatantly pro-southern **Amistad** policy may well have contributed to his defeat in the 1840 election by alienating northern Democrats. Meanwhile, the case worked its way to the Supreme Court. Abolitionists persuaded the cranky, nearly deaf 73-year old former president, John Quincy Adams, to take the case. The cause became a crusade for the crusty old congressman when he received a powerful letter from Kale, one of the children who had learned English and served as the groups' spokesperson. The letter concluded with the eloquent words, "All we want is to make us free."
>
> After Adams's passionate eight-hour argument, Justice Joseph Story read a decision that freed the mutineers on the grounds that they were "kidnapped Africans" who possessed the innate right of self-defense according to the "eternal principles of justice." Eventually, abolitionists raised funds that enabled the captives, on November 25, 1841, to return to Sierra Leone. What happened to each of them thereafter is not certain. But what is certain is that this was the only time in American history that Africans captured by slave dealers and shipped to the Americas won their freedom in the American courts. This contributed to the continuing struggle against slavery.

of his cabinet resigned in response, A stalemate between a Whig-dominated Congress and the president over economic policies such as banking and tariffs consumed the remainder of Tyler's presidency.

In foreign policy, Tyler proved more successful. Secretary of State Daniel Webster, the only member of Harrison's original cabinet not to join the 1841 mass resignation, completed negotiations on the **Webster-Ashburton Treaty** in 1842. Uncertainty over the border between the U.S. and Canada had generated a number of conflicts in the late 1830s, including the burning of a U.S. steamship by Canadians, a retaliatory arrest of a Canadian in New York, and a related refusal by British officials not to return a group of American slaves who had mutinied on board a New Orleans-bound ship that sailed to the Bahamas. The resulting treaty settled the border between the United States and Canada in eastern North America (from Maine to what is now the state of Minnesota), provided for the extradition of the jailed Canadian, and secured American cooperation in suppressing the African slave trade. With his work finished, Webster resigned in 1843.

Tyler also pushed for the admission of Texas, although without much initial success. A substantial number of Texans, most notably Sam Houston, had favored annexation since the Lone Star Republic's declaration of independence in 1836. President Andrew Jackson, who extended diplomatic recognition to the fledgling nation, opposed annexation on the grounds that doing so would likely lead to war with Mexico. With the certainty that Texas would enter the Union as a slave state ensuring that annexation would be a politically sensitive issue that threatened to intensify sectional divisions, neither party exhibited much interest in the annexation issue. Looking for a way to revive his political fortunes and exploiting rumors that Great Britain planned to use its influence and financial support to entice Texas to end slavery and thus block the institution's expansion, Tyler entered into secret negotiations with the Lone Star Republic. John C. Calhoun, Tyler's newest Secretary of State and one of the South's most outspoken defenders, completed negotiations on an annexation treaty in 1843. He then promptly poisoned the issue with a public letter to a British official

James K. Polk

extolling the virtues of slavery, stating that protecting the institution required that the United States incorporate Texas. Calhoun's outspokenness alienated Northerners in both parties, and a Whig-dominated Senate happily rejected the treaty.

The Election of 1844

Despite the defeat of his Texas annexation efforts, Tyler displayed a keen sense of the direction of American politics. The 1844 presidential election would soon demonstrate that expansion had become the dominant issue. Henry Clay received the Whig nomination, running on a platform that did not mention expansion and focusing instead on the party's signature issues: support for a new bank, a protective tariff, and the belief that the chief executive should defer to the will of Congress. Tyler thought his push for Texas annexation would provide him with enough support to build a third party, but his hopes did not materialize. Democrats ultimately embraced the issue, but they found a relatively unknown candidate from within their own ranks to run for office. Former President **Martin Van Buren** had expected to secure the party's nomination and return to the office he had lost in 1840, but, like Tyler, his hopes were dashed. Van Buren had strongly opposed Texas annexation, especially after the issue had become linked with the expansion of slavery. Southern Democrats successfully pushed for a rule requiring that the party's nominee receive the support of two-thirds of the convention delegates. Van Buren could not generate enough support, and the nomination eventually went to **James K. Polk** of Tennessee.

A former Speaker of the House and governor of Tennessee, Polk unified the Democratic Party around the expansion issue by calling for the annexation of more territory than just Texas. In addition to standard objections to protective tariffs and national banks, the party's platform called for the annexation of Texas and exclusive occupation of the entire Oregon Territory. Polk's linking of Texas and Oregon removed expansion from the realm of sectional politics (for a brief while) and provided the Democrats with a winning political strategy. Expansion's resonance with voters caught the Whigs off guard and even forced Clay to switch positions on Texas annexation, stating that he could support the incorporation of Texas if the act could be accomplished without war. The election results were very close, with Polk edging Clay by less than 40,000 votes while carrying 15 of 26 states. Historians still debate the factors that produced the narrow margin of victory, but most point to Clay's changing position on Texas annexation which alienated some key voters, especially anti-slavery abolitionists who bolted to support James Birney, the nominee of the **Liberty Party**—a third party that grew out of abolitionist church congregations primarily in New York and New England. In western New York, Birney siphoned enough abolitionist support from Clay to allow Polk to narrowly win a plurality and thus all of New York's electoral votes. This result became the difference in the national election, which had far-reaching implications as Polk would soon lead the country into a morally questionable war with Mexico, triggering a series of political crises that a dozen years later culminated in the outbreak of the American Civil War.

THE ANNEXATIONS OF OREGON AND TEXAS

Pledging to serve only one term as president, James Polk carried out his agenda with a single-minded tenacity. By the time he left office, Polk had secured the exclusive occupation of a substantial portion of the **Oregon Territory,** completed the annexation of Texas, and taken possession of one-third of Mexico through military conquest. The new president moved quickly to secure Oregon. In his 1845 Inaugural Address, Polk asserted that the United States' claim to Oregon "is 'clear and unquestionable,'" and he noted that American settlers were "preparing to perfect that title by occupying it with their wives and children." Polk thereby gave public support to an issue that had become dear to expansion-minded northern Democrats who had rallied around the slogan **"54-40 or Fight!"**, insisting that Great Britain must cede all of Oregon (which meant giving up basically what is the entire west coast of Canada) or go to war. Polk never intended to go that far. In late 1845, he asked Congress to terminate the joint occupation agreement while notifying Great Britain that he would be willing to work out a compromise. The British government, which had already concluded that Oregon would be difficult to hold should the situation escalate, agreed to open negotiations. Discussions proceeded quickly, and by mid-1846, the Senate voted by a large margin to ratify a treaty setting the border between the United States and Canada at the 49th parallel. Polk's willingness to compromise—especially when compared to the lengths he would go to secure Texas—left some northern Democrats disappointed, and they accused him of duplicity. But Polk had kept his campaign promise of securing the United States' claim to Oregon, and his willingness to negotiate allowed him to focus on the more challenging matter of Texas.

The annexation of Texas was actually underway before Polk took office. Tyler read the 1844 election results as an endorsement of his policy and bypassed a two-thirds vote in the Senate by asking Congress for a joint resolution accepting annexation. Congress complied a few days before Polk delivered his inaugural address, which portrayed annexation was a peaceful process that involved only Texas and the United States. American expansion, he stated, would simply "extend the dominions of peace over additional territories and increasing millions." Other nations, he continued, should view annexation "not as the conquest of a nation seeking to extend her dominions by arms and violence, but as the peaceful acquisition of a territory . . . with the consent of that member, thereby diminishing the chances of war and opening to them new and ever-increasing markets for their products." Polk's statement echoed the sentiments of writers like O'Sullivan who insisted that the United States represented a break from a past marred by bloody wars of conquest.

Not surprisingly, Mexico's government rejected this assessment of American intentions, believing peaceful expansion felt like aggression. Although deeply divided, Mexican leaders proved determined to resist, so Polk let the conflict escalate. A few weeks after his inauguration, Mexico broke off diplomatic relations. The Mexican ambassador issued a public denunciation of annexation before returning home. A month later, Mexico's president, José Joaquín de Herrera, announced that a state of war existed. Texas's annexation continued despite the increasing tensions. In July 1845, Texas voters overwhelmingly voted to join the United States, and Polk ordered General **Zachary Taylor** and his troops to Corpus Christi to defend American claims. The president also moved a naval squadron to the Gulf of Mexico and sent a diplomat, John Slidell, to Mexico City on the pretext of a peaceful settlement. Slidell's offer from Polk only raised tensions further because it asked Mexico to give up even more territory. Polk offered to give Mexico $25 million in exchange for Texas as well as Mexico's territorial holdings in New Mexico and California. The land for which Polk asked amounted to around one-third of Mexico's territory and included what would become the future states of Texas, California, Utah, and Nevada along with parts of what would become New Mexico, Arizona, Colorado, and Wyoming. Mexico's leaders considered the deal flatly unacceptable. Beleaguered by press rumors that he intended to sell out the country and cede territory, President Herrera refused to meet with Slidell. By January 1846, one of Herrera's Generals, Mariano Paredes, had driven Herrera from office and taken the presidency. Paredes would be the first of four presidents to take power in 1846, a sign of political instability that underscored the divisions among Mexico's leadership.

Despite the divisions, however, Mexico's leaders agreed that ceding territory was unacceptable, though Polk continued to press the issue. In March 1846, General Taylor, on orders from Polk, marched his troops into what is now Brownsville on the northern bank of the Rio Grande. Taylor had now moved some three hundred miles into land claimed by Mexico. A tense standoff between Mexican and United States troops then ensued, ending when Mexican cavalry, responding to American efforts to block access to the Rio Grande, crossed the river and engaged American troops, killing 16 and capturing 49. War with Mexico had begun. Word of the incident, known as the Thornton Affair, reached Washington in early May. A few days later, Polk secured a declaration of war from Congress. Although he informed Congress that Mexico's decision to attack American troops on American soil forced his hand, Polk had already received word from Slidell that Mexico would not give up any territory without a fight, leading him to prepare his war message.

Congress greeted Polk's assertion that a state of war now existed between the United States and Mexico with enthusiasm, and the body promptly passed a bill authorizing the president to call for as many as 50,000 volunteers to carry out the war effort. Despite the large margins of the votes (173 to 14 in the House and 40 to 2 in the Senate), questions about the legitimacy of Polk's actions remained. A number of Whigs wondered whether the president's aggression forced Mexico into a position in which its leaders would feel compelled to go to war. That concern raised the issue of whether the president could use his authority as commander-in-chief to take Congress' power to declare war by maneuvering troops in a manner that made armed conflict all but certain. Democrats proved willing to gloss over this issue. One Representative summed up the position well: "a state of war exists. . . . I hold it to be no part of my duty to inquire how this war originated. . . . It is enough for me . . . to know that it exists. . . to arrive at the conclusion. . . that our only course is to conquer peace by a vigorous prosecution of the war just commenced." Whigs proved more conflicted. All but 14 of 78 Whigs voted for the War Bill because they did not want to follow the example of the Federalists whose opposition to the War of 1812 had left them open to charges of disloyalty. But Whigs gave qualified support that continually questioned the wisdom and propriety of the conflict. A Kentucky Whig expressed the point well in the course of the debate. After expressing his willingness to vote for the War Bill, he protested against "the unfounded statement that Mexico began this war." He then recounted the events leading up to the Thornton Affair and concluded that "our own President. . . began this war. He has been carrying it on for months. . . ." And the war—a conflict that grew directly out of the politics of Manifest Destiny—would last for another two years, fundamentally transforming the United States.

WAR WITH MEXICO

Although overshadowed by the American Civil War, which occurred less than fifteen years later, the Mexican American War remains a highly significant event as the first major conflict fought by the United States on foreign soil, and the first war—thanks to the invention of the telegraph and developments in printing technology—to become the subject of regular, daily reporting. News of the latest developments allowed American readers to experience the war in new ways and fueled continuing debates about the legitimacy of the conflict or the wisdom of its management. Numerous military officers, including Robert E. Lee and Ulysses S. Grant who later opposed each other as commanding generals during the Civil War, received their first real combat experience fighting against Mexico. The war also radically redrew the border between the United States and Mexico, but the peace settlement ultimately reached in 1848 represented only one of a number of possible outcomes shaped by domestic political considerations as well as with social and political developments inside of Mexico.

The war's initial phases proceeded swiftly. By February 1847, less than a year after the conflict began, the United States had taken effective control of the territory that Polk had offered to purchase from Mexico. New Mexico and California fell quickly. General Stephen W. Kearny, upon receiving orders to invade northwestern Mexico, marched the troops under his command from Missouri to Santa Fe. When his force arrived in August 1846, Mexican soldiers retreated, allowing Kearny to take control of the city unopposed. The general then split his forces into three groups. One force remained to occupy New Mexico. Another marched southward with orders to take El Paso before joining up with other American units. The final, and smallest group, rode with Kearny to California. After a grueling trek lasting from September 1846 to December 1846 requiring travel through the harsh Mojave Desert, Kearny arrived in California with one hundred worn-out troops just in time to participate in the final stages of military operations there.

Events in California had moved rapidly in the months before Kearny arrived. In June 1846, a small group of American settlers, upon hearing about the declaration of war, staged the Bear Flag Revolt by capturing a small Mexican garrison in Sonoma and declaring California a republic. A few days later, a small force of American troops under the command of Captain John C. Frémont arrived to claim California for the United States. When American naval forces under the command of Commodore Robert F. Stockton learned of the revolt, they began operations against Monterey, the capital of Alta California. By August 1846, the United States had taken control of northern California. Capturing southern California proved a bit more difficult. In Los Angeles, *Californios* (people of Mexican descent born in California) organized and, for a while, managed to push back the advancing American forces. Nevertheless, Kearny's beleaguered troops arrived just in time to assist in the capture of Los Angeles. By January 1847, the United States had gained control of California.

In contrast to commanders in New Mexico and California, General Zachary Taylor faced significant resistance as he pushed his troops deeper into Mexico. In May 1846, Taylor moved his forces to break the Mexican army's siege of Fort Texas at what is now Brownsville. A larger contingent of the Mexican Army of the North, under the command of Mariano Arista, intercepted him. The two sides engaged on May 8, 1846 at the Battle of Palo Alto. Taylor's troops' use of highly mobile artillery units outmaneuvered Arista's forces, which withdrew to a more defensible location and received reinforcements. On the next day, the two sides engaged again at the Battle of Resaca de la Palma, which largely involved hand-to-hand fighting. The battle ended in a rout when U.S. cavalry troops captured the Mexicans' artillery. Taylor followed up these victories by crossing the Rio Grande and invading Mexico. Command of the Mexican military was again under the control of General Antonio Lopez de Santa Anna, who had been in exile but had returned promising

Map 14.2 Mexican American War

to reverse Mexican losses and claiming (insincerely) that he had no interest in retaking the presidency.

Santa Anna ordered the Mexican Army of the North, now led by General Pedro de Ampudia, to retreat to Saltillo where it would become part of a line of forces defending the nation's interior. Eager for a victory and commanding troops tired of retreating, Ampudia opted instead to hold the fortified city of Monterrey, located fifty miles northeast of Saltillo. On September 21, 1846, Taylor attacked the city with a force of 6,000 troops who lacked experience in urban warfare. The 9,000 Mexican defenders inflicted heavy casualties as Taylor's forces attempted to move through the city on streets exposed to fire from all directions. By the third day of the Battle of Monterrey, however, American troops learned to move from building to building by cutting through walls. These tactics forced Ampudia to seek a cease-fire, leading to an eight-week truce followed by the evacuation of Mexican troops. Neither Polk nor Santa Anna was happy by this turn of events. Polk ordered Taylor to break the truce, and the general complied by capturing Saltillo. Santa Anna relieved Ampudia of his command and marched with 20,000 troops (many of whom deserted along the way) northward from central Mexico. On February 22, Santa Anna's assembled force of 15,000 men attacked Taylor's 4,700 troops who had entrenched themselves in a mountain pass. During the resulting two-day Battle of Buena Vista, Taylor's forces were almost routed. Both sides suffered heavy casualties. The battle might have continued beyond February 23, but Santa Anna received word of political instability in Mexico City, leading him to withdraw his forces so he could reclaim the presidency. Taylor's victory left the United States in control of northern Mexico and established the general as a national hero.

Meanwhile, the war continued. Despite the occupation of New Mexico, California, Monterrey and Saltillo, Mexico's leaders remained determined to resist the invasion, although they remained divided among themselves. Mexico's presidency changed hands nine times during the course of the war, which rendered negotiations even more difficult. Mexican leaders also had to contend with popular uprisings as well as U.S. forces invading central Mexico when Polk ordered General Taylor to capture the capital Mexican City. In March 1847, General **Winfield**

Scott landed 12,000 troops and supplies near Veracruz, Mexico's primary port, safely outside the range of the city's defenses without suffering any casualties, completing the first major amphibious landing in U.S. military history. With the assistance of fire from naval vessels, the general laid siege to the city, which surrendered twelve days later.

Leaving behind garrison troops and many incapacitated by a yellow fever outbreak, General Scott advanced on Mexico City with 8,500 men. His forces outmaneuvered and routed Santa Anna's army to capture, Puebla, the country's second largest city, on May 1, 1847. The general's experience with Puebla underscored the complexity of the central Mexico invasion. Hostility to Santa Anna within the city led its leaders to surrender without any opposition, and Scott wanted to ensure that his troops' actions did not turn that hostility against them. The general remained careful throughout his entire campaign not alienate the local populace. "The people," he ordered, "must be conciliated, soothed, or well treated by every officer and man of this army, and by all of its followers." Scott required that the army pay for any supplies it took, worked to ensure that his largely Protestant soldiers did not disparage Roman Catholicism, and harshly disciplined soldiers who refused to comply with his orders. Despite these efforts, guerrilla units continually harassed the American supply lines between Veracruz and Puebla. Rather than stretch his supply lines further, Scott opted in August 1847 to purchase supplies from non-hostile locals and proceed with his mission. After a few battles fought in the outskirts of Mexico City, including an assault on Chapultepec Hill against a force which included valiant teenage cadets defending their military academy located on the site, Scott's army triumphantly entered the Mexican capital on September 13, 1847. A month later, Scott's forces defeated Santa Anna's effort to cut off their supply lines at Puebla and brought an end to major combat operations between regular forces. Scott and Taylor then maintained the occupation while U.S. and Mexican diplomats worked out a treaty, a process that would not be completed until May 1848. In the meantime, fighting continued as the forces of both generals faced regular attacks by guerrillas.

Opposition to the Mexican War

As the war dragged on, opposition to the conflict in the United States grew. In Congress, opposition from Whigs remained relatively tempered. Antislavery Whigs such as Ohio's Joshua Giddings, denounced the war as a murderous land grab fought by the government on behalf of slaveholders. Most Whigs, however, continued the line of criticism they had employed at the beginning of the war, blaming Polk for starting the conflict and usurping Congress's war making power. A young Abraham Lincoln, then serving his only term in the House of Representatives, proposed a set of "spot resolutions" demanding that Polk prove that the Thornton Affair took place on American soil. The resolutions went nowhere. The Whigs tread carefully for a number of reasons. They drew lessons from the experiences of the Federalists, of course. The fact that Generals Taylor and Scott were Whigs also muted their criticism of the war's progress. Questions remained, however, about the war's objectives. Northern Democrats took the lead on this front, when they expressed their frustration with Polk and their party's leadership by trying to prohibit slavery in any territory acquired from Mexico. Their efforts would reopen the sectional conflict and move the nation toward civil war.

Outside of Congress, intellectuals and antislavery advocates opposed the war. Transcendentalist Henry David Thoreau spent a night in a Concord, Massachusetts jail because he expressed his opposition to the war by refusing to pay his taxes. He would have stayed longer, but a relative paid his fines. Thoreau used his experience to write one of his most significant essays, "Resistance to Civil Government," where he argued the best way to challenge unjust laws was to withdraw one's support for the government and suffer the consequences. "If a thousand men were not to pay their tax bills this year, that would not be a violent and bloody measure, as it would be to pay them, and enable the State to commit violence and shed innocent blood." Following this course, Thoreau noted, would likely lead to imprisonment, but "the true place for a just man is . . . a prison." Thoreau's ideas would later be embraced by the likes of Mohandas Gandhi and Martin Luther King, Jr. Opposition to the war went beyond small circles of intellectuals. A set of resolutions passed in 1847 by large margins of the Massachusetts legislature echoed the rhetoric of numerous antiwar publications: "such a war of conquest, so hateful in its objects, so wanton, unjust and unconstitutional in its origin and character, must be regarded as a war against freedom, against humanity, against justice, against the Union."

Treaty of Guadalupe Hidalgo

The war and occupation continued while both sides worked out a treaty. Over the course of the conflict, Polk increased his demands for territory. He now wanted all Mexican land north of the twenty-sixth parallel, proposing to draw a straight line from the mouth of the Rio Grande across Mexico. Others in his party were advocating taking the entire country. Whigs like Henry Clay and Daniel Webster advised taking no territory beyond the Rio Grande. Polk eventually backed away from his larger demands and settled for the portions of northern Mexico that he had originally offered to purchase. This would achieve one of his main objectives—to secure ports on the west coast of North America to gain better access to Pacific markets. Racist concerns that the United States could not absorb a huge mass of Spanish-speaking Catholics considered by Anglo-Americans to be inferior also entered his decision. So did the inability of the U.S. Army to stop guerrilla attacks, convincing Polk that the densely populated areas of Mexico would be exceedingly difficult to hold. The main reason, however, may have been that Polk took what he could get when his envoy, Nicholas Trist, sent him a draft of the **Treaty of Guadalupe Hidalgo**. At one point, Polk became so frustrated with the slow pace of the peace talks that he recalled Trist, but the diplomat ignored his orders and completed his negotiations. In the treaty, Mexico, in exchange for $15 million, ceded one-third of its territory, giving up claims to Texas as well as land that would later become the future states of California, Nevada, Utah, and portions of what would become New Mexico, Arizona, Colorado, and Wyoming. (Five years later, the United States would secure the area of New Mexico and Arizona south of the Gila River through the Gadsden Purchase.) Polk sent the treaty to the Senate for ratification. After efforts to expand or reduce the size of the Mexican Cession were defeated and a provision protecting the validity of Mexican land grants in the ceded territory was removed, the Senate ratified the treaty officially ending the Mexican War.

Consequences of the Mexican War

James Polk served only four years in office (he pledged to serve just one term and took pride in keeping his promises), but the war he pursued against Mexico had many far-reaching consequences. His actions had a decided human cost, as the war brought 13,000 American and 16,000 Mexican casualties. Meanwhile, the conflict set the stage for another 600,000 American deaths because disputes over whether slavery would expand into the newly-acquired territories contributed greatly to the American Civil War. For people west of the Mississippi, however, life changed drastically as a consequence of the Mexican Cession.

Mormons, for example, found their effort to abandon the United States by moving to Utah compromised by the Mexican Cession, which included almost all of what they claimed as the Kingdom of Deseret. Mormons petitioned Congress to make their territory, which claimed parts of California, Arizona, New Mexico, Colorado, Wyoming, Iowa, and Oregon. Congress refused and created a smaller, but still sizable, Utah Territory in 1850. **Brigham Young**, leader of the church, received appointment as governor of the new territory, and other officials in the church also received high posts. Utah, although expected (and required) to have a republican government, ran more like a theocracy in which elected officials rubber stamped decisions made by Mormon leaders. Federal judicial officials, "gentiles" (non-Mormons) appointed by the president, complained that Young and his followers had established a Mormon court system that allowed them

Contemporary American cartoon boasting over Mexico's defeat in the Mexican War.

to evade following federal law. Tensions between Latter-day Saints and the federal government escalated as eastern politicians continued to denounce Mormonism as a "relic of barbarism." Then, in the 1857 Mountain Meadows Massacre, a group of Mormons and Native American allies killed 120 migrants from Missouri and Arkansas who were passing (although not entirely peacefully) through the region. By the time of the assault, President James Buchanan had already sent 2,500 troops along with a new territorial governor. Young vowed to resist, but the troops moved slowly and winter slowed them even more. The delay provided time for negotiations, and the two sides worked out a tense accommodation in which Young stepped down from the governorship, federal troops would maintain a continuous presence, and the Mormon Church and its practice of polygamy would be left alone (at least for a while).

Life in California changed almost overnight. In May 1848, the same month that the Mexican American War officially came to an end, news of a gold strike in California reached San Francisco and spread rapidly through press reports. A few months later, people began pouring into California from all over the world. They came from the United States, Europe, Latin America, and even China. The non-Native American population increased from 15,000 in 1848 to over 92,000 by 1850 to nearly 224,000 by 1852. Many of these newcomers soon realized that gold prospecting offered few people the opportunity to get rich. A few early prospectors could make their way panning for gold individually, but the opportunities for making the most lay in the hands of people who could mobilize the labor required to build sluices that could redirect rivers so miners could dig in exposed river bottom. More opportunity for profit lay in the hands of people (or more likely corporations) that could use hydraulic mining to blast away hillsides to access the gold stored within. Most miners had no access to these resources and either moved on or became employees of these emerging enterprises. Others found ways to profit in selling supplies to miners, as the rapid increase in population sent the prices of basic goods and services skyward. American attitudes toward race also influenced a person's ability to mine for gold. American miners excluded Chinese and Mexicans (including *Californios*) from working in the mines, even as they forced some Native Americans to work for them as essentially slaves.

The flood of settlers exerted a harsh impact on both Native Americans and *Californios*. In 1845, California's Indian population may have been as high as 150,000. By 1855, that population had been reduced to around 50,000, and it would ultimately decline to about 30,000. A number of factors explain the losses. Disease, of course, extracted a terrible toll. Early California law expressed great hostility toward Native Americans, establishing a system of indentures and a network of legal triggers designed to ensnare them in forced labor. Other laws permitted the killing of Indians who ran away, and extant records demonstrated that white Californians killed at least 4,500 Native Americans between 1845 and 1880. By 1860, most surviving Indians had been driven out of the areas of white settlement.

Meanwhile, numerous *Californios* found themselves stripped of their land. Although the Treaty of Guadalupe Hidalgo originally contained a provision stating that the United States would honor land grants made by the Mexican government, the Senate struck it out. Consequently, numerous landholders, who although of Mexican descent were U.S. citizens by the treaty, found themselves beset with problems. Migrants, especially those who opted for farming rather than mining, moved on to *Californios*' lands with impunity and forced them to defend their claims in court. American common law, however, demanded a level of precision in the delineation of property lines than Mexican land grants employed, and even successful legal defenses, which took years and were expensive, tended to eat away at an estate's value. As a group of *Californios* petitioners to Congress explained, "some, who had at one time had been the richest landholders today find themselves without a foot of ground, living as objects of charity—and even in sight of the many leagues of land, which . . . they once called their own." So in California a process of dispossession quite similar to what was already occurring in Texas was beginning to play out.

The increasing movement of people from the eastern United States to the nation's new holdings in California and Oregon also transformed life on the Great Plains, which lay between the East and the new West. This largely unanticipated development undermined the Indian Removal policy established in the 1830s. Federal policy makers had generally assumed that the majority of territory west of the Mississippi—an area that included the present states of Oklahoma, Kansas, and Nebraska but also extended far beyond the borders of those areas—would be permanently, or at least indefinitely, Indian Country. The new policy drew a sharp line between United States and Native American sovereignty, provided for the federal regulation and supervision of trade between whites and Indians, and assigned territory with clear boundaries to Indian nations among whom the federal government kept peace.

This arrangement began to fall apart in the 1840s when the Indian Territory became a corridor for Americans headed for Oregon, Utah, or California. As the

Table 14.1 — Westward Expansion, 1815 - 1850

New Free States	New Slave States	Territories (1850)
Indiana, 1816	Mississippi, 1817	Minnesota
Illinois, 1818	Alabama, 1819	Oregon
Maine, 1820	Missouri, 1821	New Mexico
Michigan, 1837	Arkansas, 1836	Utah
Iowa, 1846	Florida, 1845	
Wisconsin, 1848	Texas, 1845	

number of migrants increased, they disrupted game migrations and trampled the crops of Native American farmers. Such actions increased tensions on the Plains, but Native Americans contributed to the escalation by demanding tolls and raiding wagon trains for livestock. The federal government tried to manage the situation in the early 1850s by negotiating a series of treaties. Negotiators hoped to establish a system of roads along the Oregon and Santa Fe Trails, providing safe passage for American migrants while delineating the boundaries of Indian Territory. The effort failed. Native Americans had little interest in ceding land that they had been told belonged to them forever, and migrants and settlers tended to disregard the demarcation lines anyway.

Tensions between settlers and Native Americans were by no means confined to the Great Plains. Texas claimed all Indian land within its borders and then worked at removing or exterminating its native population. In Oregon, Washington, and Utah, settlers claimed land before Indians had ceded title to the federal government, a step required by federal law. By the 1850s, policy makers began discussing new solutions to what was often termed the Indian question: reservations. In the words of Commission of Indian Affairs Edwin Lea:

> There should be assigned to each tribe for a permanent home, a country adapted to agriculture, of limited extent well-defined boundaries within which all . . . should be compelled to remain until such time as their general improvement and good conduct may supersede the necessity of such restrictions. In the mean time, the government should cause them to be supplied with stock, agricultural implements, and useful material for clothing; encourage and assist them in the erection of comfortable dwellings, and secure to them the means of facilities of education, intellectual, moral, and religious.

In the 1850s, this new policy went into effect unevenly. Native Americans who moved to reservations either faced problems with encroaching settlers or found could not eke out a living on the land they were assigned. Another two decades and no small amount of warfare would pass before the federal government would achieve full compliance with its new policy. But the new direction of the federal Indian policy was clear shortly after the Mexican American War. Lea summed up the trajectory in 1852. "When civilization and barbarism are brought in such relation that they cannot coexist together, it is right that the superiority of the former be asserted and the latter compelled to give way." Lea, in words that could have been written by the disillusioned missionary Marcus Whitman, saw "no matter of regret that so large a portion of our territory has been wrested from its aboriginal inhabitants and made the happy abode of an enlightened and Christian people."

Following the conclusion of the Mexican-American War, therefore, the process of settling the Trans-Mississippi West by Anglo-Americans proceeded at full pace, and the new inhabitants reshaped their new homes in the image of the East. They established farms and started mines— gold, silver, copper, and zinc among others. They took over the cattle industries that had been dominated by *Tejanos* and *Californios* as well as New Mexico's sheep industry. These activities would fuel American economic and industrial development and help transform the nation's economy in a matter of decades. But before then, American politicians would have to confront the immediate political problem presented by the conclusion of the war: what was the status of slavery in the Mexican Cession.

MORE LAND, MORE PROBLEMS

Narcissa Whitman wrote to her mother on the eve of the United States emergence as a continental republic. In the space of a decade, the United States would double its territory and spread across the North American continent. New settlements emerged rapidly in Texas, Oregon, Utah, and California, and the United States aggressively pursued these claims even to the point of war. Although the United States made war against both Mexico and Native American groups, the United States established a vision of itself as a peaceful actor on the world stage. American expansion did not happen out of a desire for conquest—and defenders of the war can point to the fact that the United States paid for the territory it acquired in 1848—expansion stemmed from a desire to spread American political and social values that had something to offer the rest of the world. But those values contained an expectation that others would conform to them and accommodated the displacement of those people unwilling or unable to do so. The rapid expansion proved to be a major economic boon to the economy, but in the short term the acquisition of new territory opened up a new conflict over slavery that would ultimately split the Union.

Chronology

1818 United States and Great Britain agree to joint occupation of the Oregon Country.

1819 Adams-Onís Treaty.

1821 Mexico gains independence from Spain.

1824 Mexico opens Texas to immigrants.

1830 Mexico prohibits further immigration to Texas and reaffirms its antislavery laws.

1834 Antonio López de Santa Anna becomes dictator of Mexico.

1836 Texas declares independence from Mexico. General Sam Houston secures Texas independence by defeating Santa Anna at the Battle of San Jacinto.

1840 Harrison (Whig) is elected to the presidency.

1841 John Tyler (Whig) becomes president following the death of William Henry Harrison.

1842 Webster-Ashburton Treaty.

1843 The Senate rejects a treaty for the annexation of Texas.

1844 Joseph Smith, founder of the Church of Jesus Christ of Latter-Day Saints (Mormons), is killed.
James K. Polk defeats Henry Clay.

1845 The United States annexes Texas.
Polk sends General Zachary Taylor to Corpus Christi, Texas, to defend the U.S. new claims.

1846 United States and Great Britain end joint occupation of the Oregon Country and establish a border at the 49th parallel.
Thornton Affair.
Bear Flag Revolt.
Taylor pushes captures Monterrey.
U.S. troops occupy New Mexico.

1847 U.S. troops gain control of California.
Battle of Buena Vista.
General Winfield Scott invades Mexico takes Veracruz, Puebla, and then Mexico City.
Brigham Young leads the first group of Mormon migrants to Utah.

1848 Treaty of Guadalupe Hidalgo.
News of a gold strike in California.

Review Questions

1. Describe the idea of manifest destiny. How did this idea shape American expansion in the mid-nineteenth-century United States.

2. How did the experience of Mormon migrants differ from that of other migrant groups? What did the other emigrants from the United States have in common?

3. Discuss the significance of Texas annexation to American politics. Why did the annexation of Texas become such an important issue?

4. What was the significance of race in American expansion?

5. Evaluate American expansionism in the mid-nineteenth century. Do you believe that the territory gained through expansion justified the costs, moral or otherwise?

Glossary of Important People and Concepts

"54-40 or Fight!"
Stephen F. Austin
Empresario
Sam Houston
Liberty Party
Manifest Destiny
Mormons
Oregon Territory
Oregon Trail
James K. Polk
Republic of Texas
Antonio López de Santa Anna
Santa Fe Trail
Winfield Scott
Joseph Smith
Tejanos
Treaty of Guadalupe Hidalgo
Zachary Taylor
John Tyler
Martin Van Buren
Webster-Ashburton Treaty
Brigham Young

SUGGESTED READINGS

Randolph B. Campbell, *An Empire for Slavery: The Peculiar Institution in Texas, 1821-1865* (1989).

John Mack Faragher, *Women and Men on the Overland Trail*, 2d. ed. (2001).

Michael Golay, *The Tide of Empire: America's March to the Pacific* (2003).

Thomas R. Hietala, *Manifest Design: Anxious Aggrandizement in Late Jacksonian America* (1985).

Reginald Horsman, *Race and Manifest Destiny: The Origins of American Racial Anglo-Saxonism* (1981).

Stephen G. Hyslop, *Bound for Santa Fe: The Road to New Mexico and the American Conquest, 1806-1848* (2002).

Robert W. Johannsen, *To the Halls of the Montezumas: The Mexican War in the American Imagination* (1985).

Irving Levinson, *Wars within War: Mexican Guerrillas, Domestic Elites, and the United States of America, 1846-1848* (2005).

James M. McCaffrey, *Army of Manifest Destiny: The American Soldier in the Mexican War, 1846-1848* (1992).

Laton McCartney, *Across the Great Divide: Robert Stuart and the Discovery of the Overland Trail* (2003).

Frederick Merk, *Manifest Destiny and Mission in American History: A Reinterpretation* (1963).

Michael A. Morrison, *Slavery and the American West: The Eclipse of Manifest Destiny and the Coming of the American Civil War* (1997).

Richard H. Patterson, *Manifest Destiny in the Mines: A Cultural Interpretation of Anti-Mexican Nativism in California, 1848-1853* (1975).

David M. Pletcher, *The Diplomacy of Annexation: Texas, Oregon, and the Mexican War* (1973).

Paul W. Reeve, *Making Space on the Western Frontier: Mormons, Miners, and Southern Paiutes* (2006).

Joel H. Silbey, *Storm over Texas: The Annexation Controversy and the Road to Civil War* (2007).

Anders Stephanson, *Manifest Destiny: American Expansionism and the Empire of Right* (1995).

William E. Unrau, *The Rise and Fall of Indian Country, 1825-1855* (2007).

William Earl Weeks, *Building the Continental Empire: American Expansion from the Revolution to the Civil War* (1996).

Richard White, *"It's Your Misfortune and None of My Own": A New History of the American West* (1991).

Steven E. Woodworth, *Manifest Destinies: America's Westward Expansion and the Road to Civil War* (2010).

John David Uhruh, *The Plains Across: The Overland Emigrants and the Trans-Mississippi West, 1840-1860* (1979).

Depiction of John Brown before his Execution

Chapter Fifteen

EXPANSION, SLAVERY, AND SECESSION: The Road to Civil War

In 1835, Harriet, an enslaved woman from Virginia, arrived on the edges of American settlement with her master, Lawrence Taliaferro. Taliaferro brought her to the environs of Fort Snelling (present-day St. Paul, Minnesota) to wait on his family while he worked as an Indian agent for the United States. Although the area in which she settled was included in the territory closed to slavery under the Missouri Compromise, Harriet was not the only enslaved person living at the post. She met her husband, Etheldred (or Dred) Scott, an enslaved man bound to John Emerson, one of the post's surgeons. Life at Fort Snelling for the enslaved couple proved different from residence on a plantation. Although Emerson purchased Harriet from Taliaferro, Dred and Harriet Scott seemed to have an atypical level of autonomy. After marrying in a civil ceremony, their master would frequently leave them alone at the post, sometimes for weeks at a time. Yet, they were not free. Emerson ultimately moved Dred, Harriet, and the couple's two children back to St. Louis.

When John Emerson died in the mid-1840s, Dred and Harriet Scott sued his widow, Irene Emerson, for their freedom. Missouri's judicial system had been relatively accommodating to slaves who had been taken into free territory. Previously, judges had recognized the freedom of slaves who had resided with their masters in Illinois (where Dred had lived with John Emerson for a few years prior to living in Minnesota), and had even freed an enslaved woman named Rachel who had lived at Fort Snelling. By the time their case reached the state supreme court in 1852, however, the judicial attitude toward freedom for slaves taken by their masters into free territory had changed. In the words of the judge speaking for the court:

> Times now are not as they were when the former . . . decisions on this subject were made. Since then not only individuals, but States, have been possessed with a dark and fell spirit in relation to slavery, whose gratification is sought in the pursuit of measures, whose inevitable consequence must be the overthrow and destruction of our government. Under such circumstances it does not behoove the State of Missouri to . . . gratify this spirit.

Dred and Harriet Scott's case had become caught up in the growing rift between the North and South over slavery, and the presiding judge said that he was overturning the court's previous practice because he did not want to give any encouragement to antislavery sentiment. This moment proved to be just the beginning of the politicalization of their case. Five years later, when the United States Supreme Court heard the Scotts' appeal, the judges and lawyers involved used the decision to strike at the antislavery movement and to rule the Missouri Compromise unconstitutional, an act that helped move the United States closer to secession and civil war.

THE WILMOT PROVISO AND THE POLITICS OF SLAVERY

Victory in the war with Mexico greatly increased the United States' total area, but also resulted in renewed conflict over the expansion of slavery. Tensions between the North and South began escalating soon after the war began and became unmanageable by the end of the 1850s. The renewed sectional conflict, in fact, fulfilled the predictions of two of the war's critics. South Carolina Senator **John C. Calhoun**—the South's most prominent proslavery spokesman—likened Mexico to a forbidden fruit, which would bring death to those who consumed it. Ralph Waldo Emerson, a preeminent New England intellectual and opponent of slavery, sounded a similar note. "Mexico will poison us," he wrote in his journal. The war would undermine the Union's stability by shattering a network of legislative compromises and political alliances that had contained the Union's sectional tensions since the 1820s.

Before the war, mainstream politicians, both Whigs and (especially) Democrats, managed sectional conflict in two ways. First, they worked to maintain a balance of power between slave states and free states by ensuring that the Union contained an equal number of both. The admission of Missouri set the pattern. That state (a slave state) entered the Union alongside Maine (a free state). Congress also prohibited the expansion of slavery into federal territory north of Missouri's southern border (36°–30' latitude). The next six states fit the pattern: the admission of Michigan in 1837 (free) followed on the heels of Arkansas's (slave) admission in 1836. Florida and Texas, both slave states, joined in 1845; the next two states—Iowa and Wisconsin—prohibited slavery.

Admitting states in this manner preserved the South's political power, even though its relative share of the Union's population declined steadily. As late as 1800, about half the total population lived in the South. By 1820, its share had fallen to 45 percent. In 1860, its share dropped to 35 percent. These percentages, in fact, overstate the South's share because the Constitution's Three-Fifths Clause reduced the number of enslaved persons that could be counted when determining a state's representation in the House. But the Constitution also gave each state two senators, and the policy of maintaining an equal number of slave and free states allowed southern politicians to protect their section's interests in that chamber.

The second way politicians managed sectional conflict came through their efforts to keep the slavery issue off the national agenda. Both the Democrat and Whig Parties consisted of national political coalitions that depended on the cooperation of their northern and southern wings to remain competitive. Sectional issues like slavery undermined the alliances on which that cooperation rested, and politicians thus had an incentive to keep slavery out of national politics. Democrats worked feverishly, if ultimately ineffectively, to do so. One of that party's founders, Martin Van Buren of New York, described one of his coalition's key alliances as one struck "between the planters of the South and the plain Republicans of the North." Indeed, Van Buren and his numerous northern allies supported purging the mail of antislavery literature and the "gagging" of abolitionist petitions in Congress, and party leaders pressured rank and file members to keep any antislavery leanings they may have had under wraps. Whigs, whose organization contained outspoken opponents of slavery like Ohio's Joshua Giddings and New York's **William Seward,** as well as committed defenders of slavery like Georgia's Robert Toombs and Alexander Stephens, proved more tolerant of diverse views, but their need to work together created an incentive to push slavery out of national politics.

Together, the practice of admitting an equal number of slave and free states and the dynamics of party politics combined to give the South a disproportionate amount of political power. The section provided more than half of all appointed federal officers. Southerners, for example, provided over 60 percent of the men appointed to serve as Supreme Court justices between 1789 and 1860. And that Court, perhaps not coincidentally, stated on a number of occasions in the 1840s and 1850s that slavery was, in almost all cases, a matter of local, and not national, concern.

The South's entrenched political strength, however, appeared to critics as less a way to protect valid minority interests than a way for a **"Slave Power"** to use its lock on the federal government to protect and expand slavery. From the perspective of disgruntled northern politicians, both Whigs and Democrats, the South seemed always to prevail, winning on Indian Removal and the admission of Texas. Now, Southerners threatened to extend slavery into all of the territory acquired from Mexico.

On August 8, 1846, David Wilmot, a first-term congressman from Pennsylvania, provided his discontented northern colleagues with a rallying cry when he attached a rider to a war funding bill. The **Wilmot Proviso**, as it became known, stated "as an express and fundamental condition" that "neither slavery nor involuntary servitude" would be permitted in any territory acquired from Mexico. The bill, with Wilmot's attached amendment, passed through the House with an 85 to 80 vote that split along sectional lines, but the bill died in the Senate. Martin Van Buren's allies, who had grown weary of

EXPANSION, SLAVERY AND SECESSION

Southerners agreed and responded with horror to the Wilmot Proviso. Free soil advocates like Delano spoke as if the South blighted the nation, as if Southerners (or at least slaveholders) were unworthy of reaping the full benefits of American citizenship. That attitude offended their sense of honor as much as the policy threatened their section's political and economic interests. Their politicians countered by insisting that all federal territory should be open to slavery.

In February 1847, South Carolina's John C. Calhoun, then serving in the Senate, provided a forceful articulation of this position, which has been cumbersomely labeled "the **common property doctrine**." Because federal territory had been acquired through the participation of all the states, Calhoun argued, it belonged to them in common. Moreover, because all citizens possessed equal rights under the Constitution, citizens from every state had a right to enter that territory and bring their property with them. Calhoun and his allies argued that the Wilmot Proviso was unconstitutional because it deprived a portion of U.S. citizens of the right to enter federal territory with their (human) property. If Northerners refused to respect the South's rights under the Constitution, then secession might be the appropriate response. Georgia's Robert Toombs made the point clearly in 1849, as a House divided deeply along party and sectional lines struggled to nominate a speaker:

David Wilmot

southern demands, promptly reintroduced the proviso in the next session. Wilmot articulated what became known as the **free soil position**—the argument that all federal territory should be closed to slavery. Northern politicians who became free soilers did so for a variety of reasons stemming from a combination of sincere opposition to slavery, discontent with southern domination of the political system, a desire to protect northern family farms from economic competition with slave-based plantations, and simple, vulgar racism.

Whatever the motivations, the emergence of the free soil position signaled that the consensus for handling slavery at the national level had broken down. Columbus Delano, an Ohio Whig, expressed the sentiment on the House floor in January 1847:

> Let me say . . . to the South, in all kindness and candor. . . . Never, never shall you extend your institution of slavery one inch beyond its present limits. . . . Go on. . . . Conquer Mexico, and add to the territory, but we will make it free. . . . If you drive on this bloody war of conquest to annexation, we will establish a cordon of free States that shall surround you; and then we will light up the fires of liberty on every side, until they melt your present chains, and render all your people free. This is no idle boast. . .

> I do not . . . hesitate to avow before this House and the country and in the presence of the living God, that if by your legislation you seek to drive us from the territories . . . purchased by the common blood and treasure of the whole people, and . . . thereby [attempt] to fix a national degradation upon half the states of this Confederacy, I am for disunion. . . . From 1787 to this hour the people of the South have asked nothing but justice—nothing but the maintenance of the principles and the spirit which controlled our fathers in the formation of the Constitution. Unless we are unworthy of our ancestors, we will never accept less as a condition of union.

Between these irreconcilable positions, moderate politicians struggled to find a middle ground. President Polk, Secretary of State James Buchanan, and Senator Stephen A. Douglas of Illinois advocated extending the Missouri Compromise line (36°–30' latitude) to the Pacific. The position had a number of merits. It represented a (literal) extension of existing policy toward slavery in the territories that had functioned effectively since 1820s, and it lacked ambiguity by clearly laying out the areas open and closed to slavery's expansion. Sectional partisans rejected the suggestion. Under the terms of the common property doctrine, the policy was unconstitutional and therefore unacceptable (although a number of proponents of this position had supported the **Missouri restriction** in the past). Free soil adherents rejected the policy because much of the territory acquired from Mexico would fall on the southern side of the line, thus excluding their constituents from the fruits of any victory.

A potential extension of the Missouri Compromise line also competed with a second option, the so-called "**popular sovereignty** doctrine." Senator Lewis Cass of Michigan, an aspirant to the 1848 Democratic presidential nomination, put forth this final position, which called for letting settlers decide for themselves the future of slavery in the territories. Cass contended that democratic, self-governing territorial legislatures should regulate their own internal affairs (including slavery). Three aspects of Cass's position made it especially appealing to Democratic politicians. First the emphasis on territorial self-governance meshed well with their belief that most policy should be made locally. Second, popular sovereignty had the added benefit of getting the question of slavery out of Congress and giving responsibility for its solution to someone else. Finally, the policy had a useful amount of ambiguity. Cass purposely refused to state precisely when a territorial legislature would make its decision concerning the future of slavery, and his reluctance enabled Democrats who might disagree sharply over the timing of the crucial vote to rally around him.

Each of these four positions (free soil, common property, extension of the Missouri Compromise line, and popular sovereignty) had emerged in fully articulated form by the end of 1847, before the war with Mexico had even ended. Congress achieved very little in the course of this debate. The war appropriations bill, which had been defeated after Wilmot attached his rider, squeaked through Congress (without the proviso) at the close of the next session. An effort to organize the Oregon Territory had stalled because it had become enmeshed in the debate over slavery's expansion. No one seriously thought this area in the present-day Pacific Northwest would become slave territory, but politicians used the issue to position themselves for the real struggle that would occur when the war with Mexico finally ended.

Political Crisis at Mid-Century

The war officially ended with the Treaty of Guadalupe Hidalgo in February of 1848, but Congress proved too divided to act on the slavery expansion issue. As the months dragged on, the situation unraveled until politicians faced what they believed to be a crisis that threatening the Union's continued existence. The deadlock that emerged in the previous Congress created time that nurtured sectional animosity and allowed debate to spread from the future of slavery's expansion in the territory acquired from Mexico, to its status in the District of Columbia, and to include argument over the reach of the Constitution's Fugitive Slave Clause. Politicians faced those issues within a context that simultaneously pushed them to move quickly (because settlers were pouring into California) while encouraging them to drag their feet (because of the impending presidential election). These factors further intensified the deadlock, leading a significant number of southern leaders to respond by seriously contemplating secession. With these prevailing pressures, the stage was set for a potentially great political compromise.

By 1848, slavery had become a problem for Congress in no fewer than three ways. One aspect of the problem involved slavery's legality in the District of Columbia. Under the Constitution, Congress possessed vast authority over the District. Many Northerners had long advocated that Congress contemplate outlawing the institution there—slavery in the capital of a government professing to be devoted to freedom tended to make the United States

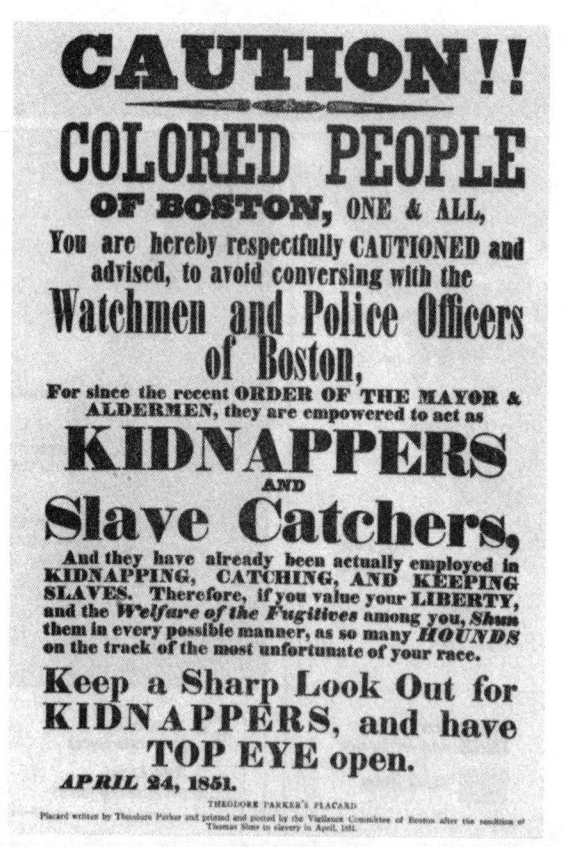

CAUTION!!
COLORED PEOPLE
OF BOSTON, ONE & ALL,
You are hereby respectfully CAUTIONED and advised, to avoid conversing with the
Watchmen and Police Officers of Boston,
For since the recent ORDER OF THE MAYOR & ALDERMEN, they are empowered to act as
KIDNAPPERS
AND
Slave Catchers,
And they have already been actually employed in KIDNAPPING, CATCHING, AND KEEPING SLAVES. Therefore, if you value your LIBERTY, and the *Welfare of the Fugitives* among you, Shun them in every possible manner, as so many HOUNDS on the track of the most unfortunate of your race.
Keep a Sharp Look Out for KIDNAPPERS, and have TOP EYE open.
APRIL 24, 1851.

Professional slave catchers arrived in northern cities where they were denounced as criminal "kidnappers." In several northern cities, particularly Boston, angry mobs harassed slave hunters and attempted to rescue their quarry.

appear hypocritical in the eyes of the world. Abolitionist petitions on this subject had occasioned the House Gag Rule during the 1830s, but the House had since lifted that rule. As sectional tensions intensified, some northern politicians revealed their willingness push the issue.

Another problem centered on the capture of fugitive slaves. Under the Constitution, slave holders and the slave catchers they hired had a right to pursue runaway bondsmen into the free states and to return them to slavery. Congress passed a law regulating this practice in the 1790s, but that legislation provided no procedures for proving whether a captured runaway was the actual person being sought. With some justification, critics argued that the law provided cover for kidnappers. Northern states responded with legislation requiring slave catchers, among other procedures, to prove the status of the people they captured in a jury trial. In 1842, the Supreme Court in *Prigg v. Pennsylvania* ruled those laws unconstitutional, but the Court also said that the federal government could not require state officials to participate in the apprehension of fugitive slaves. A number of northern states responded by ordering their officials not to comply, which effectively made apprehension of alleged fugitives impossible. Southerners considered these actions to be a breach of constitutional obligations and demanded that Congress pass legislation to fix the issue.

Of course, the major issue remained the future of slavery's expansion into the federal territories. The matter was already complicated by the four competing solutions, and became further muddied by politicians in the various camps who did not trust one another. At one point, a group of senators labored hard to push a bill organizing the Oregon, California, and New Mexico territories through their chamber. The bill allowed the Supreme Court to settle the issue of slavery in those territories, and the compromise it embodied represented the product of months of false starts and weeks of deliberation. In the House, however, northern and southern representatives united to kill the bill without debate. No one knew how the Court would have ruled, but both proslavery and antislavery advocates found common ground in not trusting the justices.

A further complication came with the discovery of gold in California, which had occurred a few weeks before the Treaty of Guadalupe Hidalgo had reached Washington. At war's end, California's population (excluding Native Americans) reached 15,000. Two years later, the U.S. Census reported a population of over 92,000, as gold hungry settlers and those who supplied and serviced the miners flocked into the area. The province's stunning growth meant that it could bypass the territorial phase and enter the Union as a state. If that occurred, California would, without question, enter as a free state given the strong anti-slavery feelings of a majority of its inhabitants. This development would break the sectional balance in the Senate because no corresponding pro-slavery area existed to become a slave state. Southerners, therefore, pushed for delay.

Stalling, in fact, proved to be the order of the day in 1848, as politicians positioned themselves for the upcoming presidential election. Although Congress managed to pass a bill organizing the Oregon Territory, it failed to do so for California and New Mexico. Some of this failure resulted from Whigs and Democrats not wanting to work together as the election neared because a solution would have deprived them of issues while helping the other side. Unfortunately, the election brought little clarity. The Democrats nominated Lewis Cass, which seemed to indicate that they had embraced the popular sovereignty position. At the same time, however, President Polk began pushing extension of the Missouri Compromise line as the only solution. Thus, the favored position of Democrats remained unclear.

Whigs also cloaked themselves in ambiguity. They ran without a platform position on slavery and passed over their most prominent national figure, Henry Clay of Kentucky, in favor of General Zachary Taylor. Although he had distinguished himself as a commander of the American forces during the Mexican War, Taylor was an unknown in politics—he belonged to no political party and had never cast a vote in an election. The circumstances of his nomination added little clarity. A Louisianan whose family owned more than one hundred slaves, Taylor received most of his support in the nominating convention from southern Whigs, but his principal advisor was William Seward of New York—an open and forceful advocate of abolition. Exactly how Taylor would come down on the issue of slavery's expansion thus remained open to wishful thinking.

A number of northern politicians had grown weary of this ambiguity and bolted in favor of a new organization—the **Free Soil Party**. Formed in August 1848, the new party attracted three very different groups of antislavery politicians. New York's "Barnburner" Democrats—a faction led by former President Martin Van Buren—formed one of these groups. Barnburners, who had received their name from a story about a farmer who solved a rat infestation by setting his barn on fire, nursed a list of grievances against the national party. Van Buren's loss of the 1844 Democratic nomination and President Polk's subsequent favoring of the "hunkers"—a rival faction in state politics—symbolized southern domination of the party. Barnburners embraced the Wilmot Proviso and looked for like-minded allies. They found support among the "Conscience Whigs," a Massachusetts political faction that had formed around Van Buren's nemesis, former president (and recently deceased) John Quincy Adams. Conscience Whigs had long squared off against rivals they found to be too conciliatory toward the South—a group including so-called "Cotton Whigs" as well as the majority of Democrats. However when Taylor's nomination began to appear likely, they bolted and followed Adams's son, Charles Francis Adams, into an alliance with the Barnburners. Members of the Liberty Party, which had run in 1840 and 1844 on a platform of abolishing slavery in the District of Columbia, stopping the expansion of slavery into the western territories, and ending the interstate slave trade and racial discrimination, rounded out the Free Soil Party's membership.

In the 1848 election, the Free Soil Party received 10 percent of the popular vote but no electoral votes. Such a performance doomed the party's prospects to become a permanent, competitive organization, but its impact proved decisive in the election. The party overperformed in New York where it captured over 25 percent of the popular vote, helping Taylor win a plurality with 48 percent of the state's vote. Victory in New York provided "Old Rough and Ready," as Taylor was known, with enough electoral votes to win the election.

Not only did Taylor prove to be no better than Polk in solving the issues before Congress, the situation only unraveled further on his watch. Southerners, especially Whigs like Robert Toombs, had hoped that the new president would take their position on the sectional issues before them. After all, Taylor was a Southerner who owned a substantial number of slaves. Such a hope, however, proved to be misplaced. William Seward, one of the party's strongest opponents of slavery, assumed a role as unofficial advisor within Taylor's administration, and his influence soon became apparent. To quickly end the issue, he made a bold proposal that only worsened sectional discord. In addition to the prompt admission of California as a free state, he wished to create a large second free state ("New Mexico") out of the remaining lands acquired from Mexico. Southerners felt betrayed. Before and immediately after the election, John C. Calhoun had tried to build a southern political alliance, but his efforts failed for a variety of reasons—a general distrust between Democrats and Whigs, a specific distrust of the ambitious Calhoun, and the Whigs' hopes for Taylor. As Taylor's views became clear, Southerners became united in outrage. Talk of secession became widespread across the region, as historian David Potter noted: "From the pulpit, from the editorial sanctum, from state legislatures, from party conventions, from mass meetings, there poured out a steady stream of sermons, editorials, resolutions, speeches, and joint statements, all warning of the immediate possibility of disunion." Taylor promised to resist all challenges to

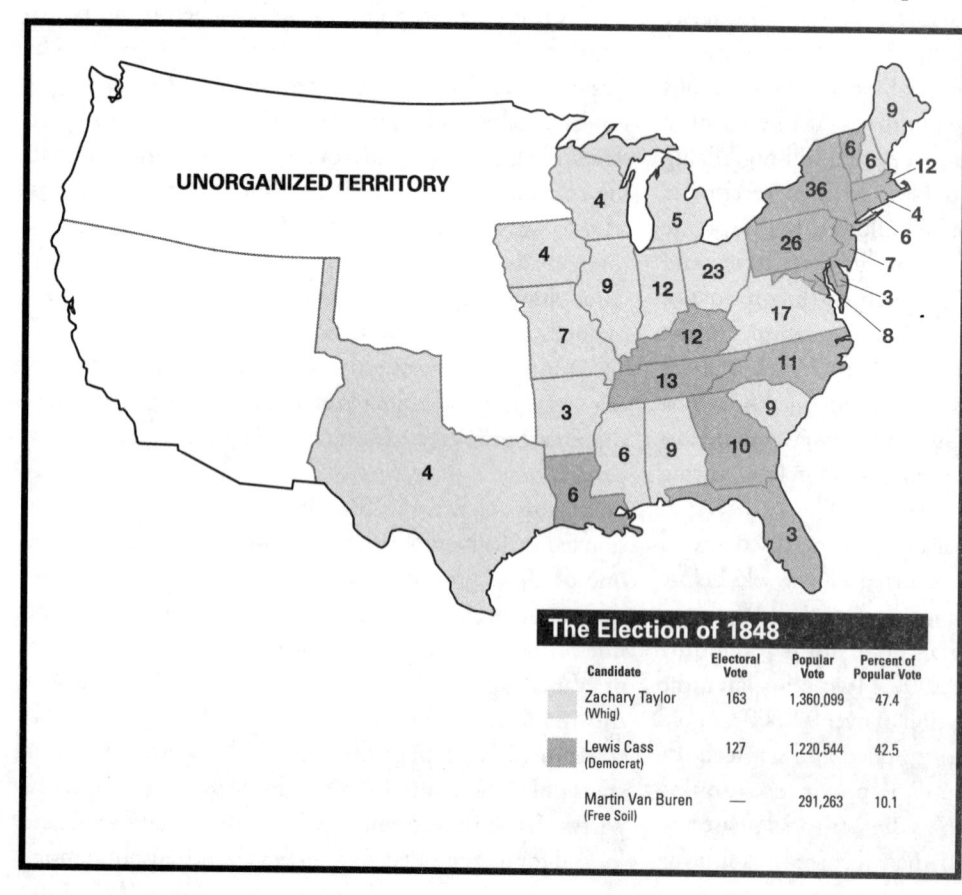

Map 15.1 The Election of 1848

The Election of 1848

Candidate	Electoral Vote	Popular Vote	Percent of Popular Vote
Zachary Taylor (Whig)	163	1,360,099	47.4
Lewis Cass (Democrat)	127	1,220,544	42.5
Martin Van Buren (Free Soil)	—	291,263	10.1

the Union, but numerous observers were concerned that the nation might soon fall apart.

THE COMPROMISE OF 1850

In January 1850, Senator **Henry Clay** of Kentucky embarked on an ambitious plan to solve the crisis. Over the years, Clay had developed a reputation as the Great Compromiser (this term did not carry the same negative connotations in the mid-nineteenth century that it does now). His record supported that image. Clay had engineered the Missouri Compromise and brokered the agreement that reduced tensions between South Carolina and the Jackson administration during the Nullification Crisis. Now, in January 1850, he proposed a set of resolutions that would address all of the outstanding sectional issues. Clay proposed eight resolutions, which boiled down to five basic points:

1. California would join the Union as a free state;
2. Congress would organize the remaining Mexican session lands as federal territories (Utah and New Mexico) with popular sovereignty to decide the fate of slavery in each territory;
3. Congress would amend the Fugitive Slave Law to satisfy southern complaints about its effectiveness;
4. Congress would abolish the slave trade—but not slavery—in Washington, D.C.;
5. Texas would cede much of its western territorial claims in exchange for assumption of its public debt by the U.S. Treasury.

By April 1850, Congress had bundled Clay's resolutions into a single, or omnibus, bill, which meant that accepting any one proposal required compromise on others. Northern partisans who wanted the prompt admission of California as a free state, for example, would also have to accept a revised fugitive slave law. Many Northerners considered that law unconscionable. If the proposed law passed, alleged fugitives would be brought before a federal magistrate to decide whether they would be released to the custody of a slave catcher. The law contained none of the safeguards that many northern states deemed essential to determining whether person was, in fact, a runaway slave, such as a jury trial with the opportunity for alleged fugitives to testify or at least a habeas corpus hearing that required masters to prove their case. To make matters worse, under the proposed law, judges would receive ten dollars in compensation for court costs if they returned a person to slavery, but only five dollars if they did not. Critics charged that the difference amounted to a symbolic bribe. Also troubling to many Northerners was a provision enabling federal marshals to compel citizens to participate in posses to hunt for alleged fugitives. Refusals to do so could result in a $1,000 fine. The fugitive slave provision of Clay's bill represented a significant concession to the South, which would greatly increase the power of the federal government at the expense of the states (in this case, the northern states), thus attacking the principle of states' rights in order to protect the institution of slavery from outside interference. In order to receive that concession, southern partisans would have to accept California's admission as a free state, breaking the sectional balance of power in the Senate that had served as an important element of the South's power within the federal government.

The bill's remaining provisions fell into a similar pattern of compromise. Clay's proposal on the District of Columbia shut down slave markets in the nation's capital, but otherwise left the institution untouched. Clay's handling of Texas did much the same thing. The Lone Star State became smaller, but Texas would be relieved of its public burden in exchange for reduced borders. Because so few citizens lived in the Utah and New Mexico Territories, the matter of slavery's potential expansion into these areas was delayed by adopting the principle of popular sovereignty. The location of the border between those two territories, however, may have hinted at a future settlement, for it ran roughly along the same latitude as the Missouri Compromise line and created the impression that the North may get Utah and the South, New Mexico.

Congress debated the omnibus bill for another four months before voting it down in July 1850. A number of factors explained the result. President Taylor, who thought the Wilmot Proviso should provide the basis for settling the issue of slavery in the territories, opposed the bill and thus left Clay deprived of crucial administration leadership. Clay had also built up a large number of enemies over the decades, and they saw defeat of his omnibus bill as their last opportunity to extract revenge. Further, a general unwillingness to compromise existed among sectional partisans in Congress. A significant number of both northern and southern politicians believed the bill gave up too much to the other section, so they decided to vote against the elements they opposed rather than vote for what they may well have supported in different circumstances. All of these factors ensured that Clay's compromise effort would fail. After months of fierce debate, the sectional issue remained unresolved, secession still remained a viable threat. In fact, nine southern states sent 175 delegates to a convention in Nashville, Tennessee in June 1850 to discuss the appropriate response to the sectional crisis. Although some delegates to the Nashville Convention called for secession, more moderate attendees stifled their efforts. The convention eventually endorsed an extension of the Missouri Compromise line and resolved to meet again in November to discuss the South's options in case Congress failed to act as they wished.

Almost immediately after the defeat of the omnibus bill, however, a series of events worked to diffuse the crisis. In July 1850, President Taylor died after contracting cholera. His successor, **Millard Fillmore,** supported Henry Clay's compromise bill. Congress also experienced changes in its leadership, as the three figures who had dominated the institution passed from the scene. John C. Calhoun had died in March 1850, the same month in which he left his deathbed to hear his speech against the compromise delivered on the Senate floor (he was too weak to read it himself). Clay left Congress shortly after the defeat of the omnibus bill to recover from exhaustion and the effects of tuberculosis (which eventually killed him in 1852). Daniel Webster, who had supported the compromise from the beginning, became Fillmore's Secretary of State, a position from which he would enforce the elements of compromise after it was passed. As these congressional veterans left the scene, new leaders emerged. Some were sectional partisans determined to defend their regions' interests at all costs. Others were dealmakers, including Senator **Stephen Douglas** of Illinois. Like Fillmore, Douglas was eager to put the sectional crisis to rest—largely because he thought the political furor distracted from issues that he considered to be more important, especially railroad construction and the economic development of the western territories.

With Clay and Fillmore's blessing, Douglas used his considerable knowledge of legislative process to work around the sectional impasse. He broke up the omnibus bill into five separate bills (one for each of the numbered points discussed on the previous page), and then he built a different majority around each bill. Douglas's strategy allowed him to rely on a combination of northern Democrats and Whigs to pass the bill for California statehood, while he found enough northern Democrats to join with Southerners to pass the Fugitive Slave Bill. Douglas repeated this process for the other three components of the compromise. As each of them passed, the senator believed that he had achieved a lasting agreement. A more accurate interpretation would be that he found a way for his colleagues to stop arguing for a while. As historian David M. Potter noted, Douglas had not achieved so much of a compromise as he had engineered an armistice.

But in 1850, the temporary nature of the Compromise of 1850 was not evident. Douglas, Fillmore, and their allies considered it to be a final settlement. The Fillmore administration certainly worked hard to enforce it. In his new role as Secretary of State, Daniel Webster ensured that anti-compromise Whigs received no patron-

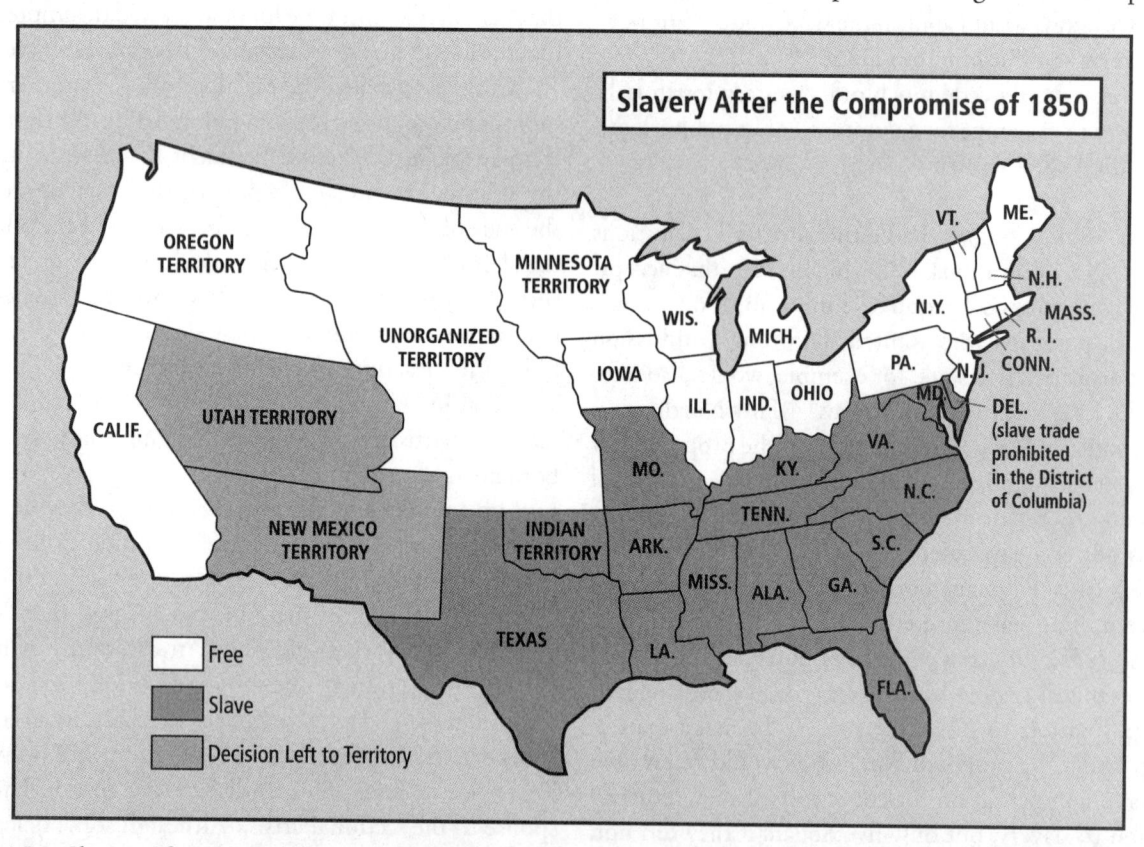

Map 15.2 Slavery After the Compromise of 1850

age from the administration. Abolitionists railed against the Fugitive Slave Law of 1850, urging people to resist. Some abolitionists even advocated violence. When an early attempt to enforce the law in Christina, Pennsylvania produced a riot that left a slave owner dead and a few others seriously wounded, the administration responded by issuing forty-one indictments for treason. The government's case ultimately fell apart—opposition to the Fugitive Slave Law, even when violent, hardly amounted to the constitutional definition of treason as war against the United States—and no one was convicted. In 1851, the administration ensured that Thomas Simms, a Georgia runaway who had been apprehended in the abolitionist stronghold of Boston, Massachusetts be returned to his owner. Court proceedings took place under guard, with Simms being surrounded the entire time by nine armed men. A force of three hundred men surrounded Simms as he was moved from the courthouse to a waiting ship bound for Georgia. In the long term, these incidents convinced many Northerners that the federal government had fully committed itself to the defense of slavery. In the short term, however, these events tended to make the antislavery movement, or at least its more radical elements, appear to be the enemies of law and order—a perception that tended to leave them marginalized. Southern secessionists likewise found themselves isolated. The sequel to the Nashville Convention failed to materialize. By 1851, sectional tensions for the first time since 1846 had subsided, and Americans hoped they could turn their attention to other matters.

THE LAST YEARS OF SECTIONAL HARMONY

Stephen Douglas quickly capitalized on the emergence of sectional peace. His faction within the Democratic Party—the "Young America" movement—took the initiative in setting the agenda for the nation. Young America advocates sought aggressive territorial expansion, free trade, and support for internal improvements. They succeeded in getting one of their own, **Franklin Pierce** of New Hampshire, the Democratic Party's nomination for president in 1852, after which he crushed the Whig candidate, General Winfield Scott. Pierce received nearly 51 percent of the popular vote, carrying 27 of 31 states and captured 254 of 296 electoral votes. Democrats also picked up 30 seats in the House, which secured them a two-thirds majority. The Election of 1852 demonstrated that the Whigs had ceased to be a nationally competitive party. Divisions that had emerged during the crisis that led to the Compromise of 1850 had torn the party apart.

Franklin Pierce

Its northern and southern wings no longer trusted one another, while its northern ranks were also riddled with internal conflict over how to deal with slavery. Yet, the sudden decline of the Whigs was just one signal that U.S. politics were moving in a new direction, one that tended toward continued sectional conflict. Indeed, Pierce would ultimately find himself mired in it—and the developments taking place during his term ensured little prospect existed for a long-term settlement between the North and South.

One development that undermined the Whig Party reflected the changing face of the northern electorate. For most of the first half of the nineteenth century, the vast majority of the American population had been native born. During the 1840s, however, large numbers of immigrants arrived in American port cities. (Nearly three million arrived between 1845 and 1854, more than triple the number of immigrants coming in the preceding ten-year period.) By 1850, nearly 10 percent of the U.S. population was foreign born; by 1860, that number would increase to 13 percent. Most of these migrants settled in the northern states. Massachusetts's foreign-born population increased from 16 percent in 1850 to 21 percent in 1860. Illinois jumped from 13 to 18 percent in the same period. By 1860, New York alone held 25 percent of the nation's foreign-born population. The foreign-born population also increased in the South, but the proportion was

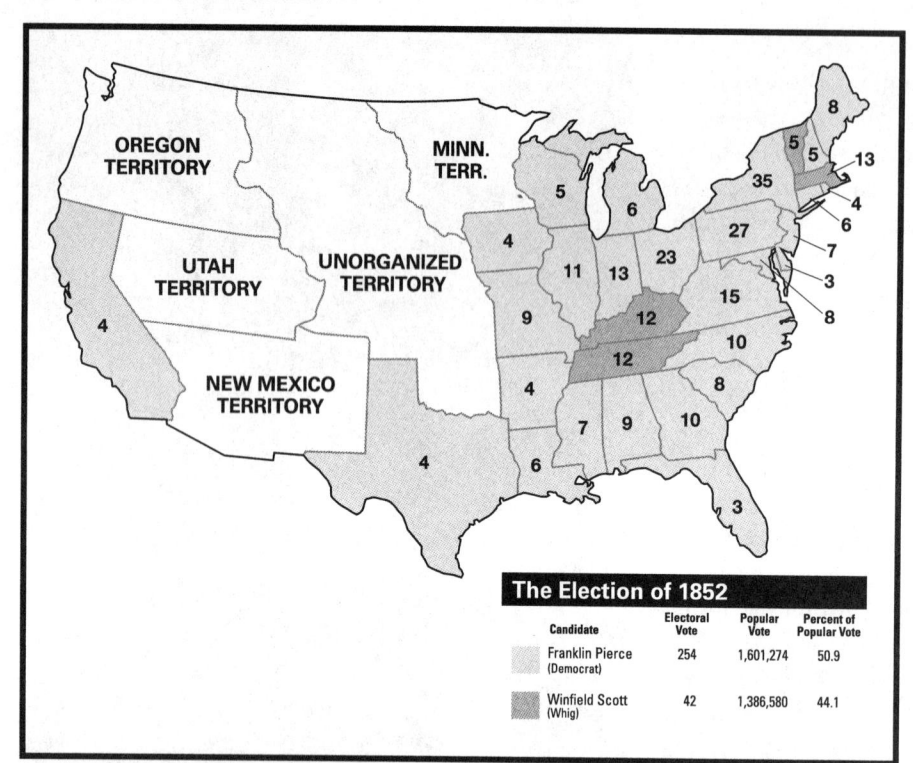

Map 15.3 The Election of 1852

The Election of 1852			
Candidate	Electoral Vote	Popular Vote	Percent of Popular Vote
Franklin Pierce (Democrat)	254	1,601,274	50.9
Winfield Scott (Whig)	42	1,386,580	44.1

small in comparison with the North. Arkansas, Florida, Georgia, Mississippi, Virginia, and both Carolinas each had foreign-born populations under 3 percent. Indeed, nearly 40 percent of the native-born population lived in the South in 1860. These currents of immigration brought large numbers of impoverished, Irish Catholics (along with other migrants, especially Germans) into areas previously dominated by Protestants primarily of English descent. Many Protestant voters felt culturally and economically threatened by these demographic changes and demanded greater restrictions on immigration.

The new political dynamic introduced by immigration competed with continuing concerns over slavery within substantial segments of the northern electorate. Although Douglas, Fillmore, Pierce and others believed that the Compromise of 1850 had settled the matter, the slavery issue remained salient. One sign confirming this was the northern public's reaction to **Uncle Tom's Cabin**, an immensely popular novel published by Harriet Beecher Stowe in 1852. A daughter of the influential, reform-minded minister Lyman Beecher, Stowe found inspiration for her book in the Fugitive Slave Law of 1850, which horrified her and fellow abolitionists. The novel contains two storylines. One subplot involves Eliza, a slave who fled from a Kentucky plantation upon learning that her infant son had just been sold to a slave trader. Her story includes a dramatic escape across the frozen Ohio River (with her child in her arms), meetings with politicians who become moved to renounce their support for the Fugitive Slave Law, and confrontations with armed slave hunters. The second storyline involves Uncle Tom, a loyal, deeply Christian slave sold to the same trader who had purchased Eliza's child, though he refused to run away. Tom's initial sale took him deeper into the South as he was transferred from owner to owner. Along the way he meets a variety of masters and enslaved people who recount their experiences. At one point, Tom is almost set free—his freedom being the dying wish of a girl he had befriended during his travels—but his prospects of freedom end when the girl's father is killed in a drunken brawl. Instead, the man's widow sells Tom, and he eventually lands on the plantation of the abusive Simon Legree, who kills him when he tries to protect two exploited enslaved women. Tom dies in the arms of the son of his original master who had tracked him down with the intent of purchasing him and bringing him home. Throughout the novel, Stowe emphasizes that, although there may have been examples of decent slaveholders, the system of slavery offered no protection from the worst ones—and the entire institution was therefore morally bankrupt.

After being published in serialized form in the *National Era*, Uncle Tom's Cabin sold 300,000 copies in its first year of release as a single volume book. Not all readers embraced her goals, as numerous minstrel shows produced racist, bastardized versions of her narrative. Nevertheless, her novel effectively took arguments that abolitionists had been making for years and presented them in a narrative framework that northern readers found more accessible. The success of her work contributed greatly to a further transformation of northern attitudes toward slavery, clearly demonstrating that there remained a significant amount of interest in the subject.

Harriet Beecher Stowe, author of *Uncle Tom's Cabin*

Southern expansionists had also not lost their interest in the slavery issue, wishing to secure more territory for slaveholders. In 1854, three pro-expansion American diplomats to Europe appointed by the Pierce administration met in Belgium and composed the **Ostend Manifesto**—a diplomatic dispatch supporting the view that the United States should annex the Spanish colony of Cuba, which in the early 1850s was experiencing yet another in a recurrent series of uprisings. Cuban instability, the diplomats argued, posed a threat to the United States, to which the nation should respond by either purchasing the island for no more than $120 million or by "wresting it from Spain if we possess the power." Such an acquisition would have provided the United States with more slaveholding territory since the institution had long been legal in Cuba. The proposal went nowhere, but it did carry some intended consequences when its contents became public. First, the interest in Cuba created an impression that American expansion had now been linked specifically to the expansion of slavery. Second, the Pierce administration had demonstrated its susceptibility to political pressure from proslavery Southerners determined to protect and extend their institution. By the time that the Ostend Manifesto came to light, however, American politicians were concluding that the compromise effort had failed as they had begun to square off over the expansion of slavery into Kansas.

THE KANSAS NEBRASKA ACT

The Rise of the Republican Party

Although the success of *Uncle Tom's Cabin* and the controversy over the Ostend Manifesto hinted that the sectional crisis had not been resolved, Stephen Douglas remained convinced that the compromise measures he ushered through Congress in 1850 had settled the dispute between the North and the South. In 1854, however, he inadvertently reopened the conflict through his effort to secure a railway route that would link San Francisco, California, to Chicago, Illinois. As a leader of the Young America faction of Democrats, Douglas held a deep interest in expansion and economic development. The construction of a transcontinental railroad route furthered both of those goals. As an ambitious politician based in Chicago, he knew this project would benefit both his home state and his own prospects for higher office. But the "Little Giant" did not operate in a vacuum, and the concessions that he made along the way moved the United States' sectional conflict to a level never before seen.

The main challenges that Douglas faced involved beating back competing corridors favored by other politicians while dealing with the fact that much of his route passed through unorganized territory—the remaining Louisiana Purchase lands north of the 36°30' latitude where Congress had banned slavery as a result of the 1820 Missouri Compromise. Before he could move forward, Douglas needed to convince Congress to organize this area. Getting such a bill approved required him to court leading southern Democrats who demanded that the proposed legislation explicitly repeal the Missouri Compromise's prohibition on slavery's expansion. Realizing that such a drastic shift would alienate northern supporters of his plan, Douglas proposed dividing the region into two separate federal territories—Kansas Territory to the immediate west of Missouri, and the larger Nebraska Territory encompassing the lands to the north of Kansas—with popular sovereignty to determine the fate of slavery in each territory. Douglas expected trouble, predicting that the change would raise "a hell of a storm," but he also fully expected Kansas to become a free state.

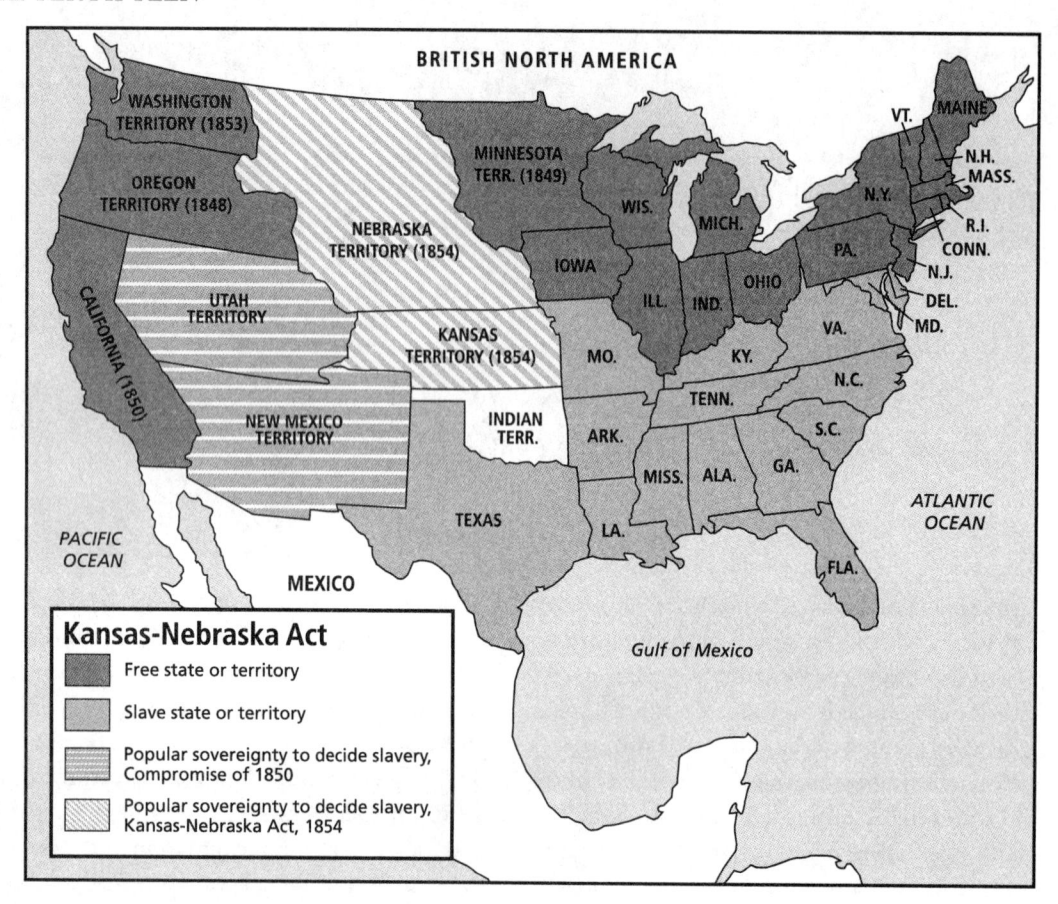

Map 15.4 Kansas-Nebraska Act

The senator believed that the flow of northern settlers combined with the local soil and climate would retard widespread cotton cultivation, thus preventing slavery from taking hold In Kansas.

As Douglas predicted, the introduction of his bill produced a major uproar in the North. Ohio's **Salmon Chase** and Joshua Giddings, along with Charles Sumner of Massachusetts, released "an Appeal from the Independent Democrats" to the press. The three politicians accused Douglas of violating a sacred pledge to stop slavery's expansion and warned that the proposed **Kansas-Nebraska Act** would cut the Union's free territory in half. The "Appeal" shifted the terms of the sectional debate by linking both Douglas and popular sovereignty to the expansion of slavery—a charge from which the "Little Giant" (who personally opposed slavery's expansion) never fully recovered. Douglas moved the bill through the Senate by a 37 to 14 vote, before future Vice President of the Confederacy, Alexander Stephens, guided the measure through the House by a 113 to 100 margin. President Pierce signed the Kansas-Nebraska Act into law a few days later, further cementing his image as a tool of slaveholding interests.

The passage of the Kansas-Nebraska Act transformed American politics. Its passage severely weakened the Democratic Party's northern wing. Before 1854, northern and southern Democrats had been roughly balanced with neither section dominating the party. The House of Representatives that passed the Kansas-Nebraska Act, for example, contained 67 southern Democrats and 91 northern Democrats. After the 1854 congressional elections, however, Northerners made up only 25 of the 88 House Democrats. Although the party regained a majority in the House by 1856, Democrats would remain numerically dominated by Southerners for years to come. The declining number of northern Democrats coincided with larger shifts in the northern electorate. By 1854, northern voters shifted their allegiances as they looked to organizations capable of responding to new concerns that now seemed to be most important.

One of these concerns grew out of the reaction against the growing number of immigrants moving into the North. Anti-immigrant sentiment—or nativism—had spawned its own political movement by 1854, finding its vehicle in the **American (or Know-Nothing) Party**. Founded in New York in 1843, the Know-Nothings transformed nativist concerns into ballots. Taking advantage of the declining power of both the Whigs and northern Democrats, and building on the anxieties generated by the increasing number of immigrants that had arrived in the last decade, the Know Nothings captured 62 seats in the House during the 1854 congressional elections. The party proved to be an ineffective national force for two reasons. First, nativism's strength faded as it moved westward from states like New York, Pennsylvania, and Massachusetts and toward states like Illinois and Indiana, which were hungry for settlers. Second, the party faltered on the slavery issue. The Know-Nothings' leadership sought to build a southern wing, often identifying abolitionists as a threat to the Union. By 1855, however, the party fragmented when its leaders refused to take a stand against slavery's expansion. The renewed fear of slavery's expansion, in fact, competed with nativism for the attention of northern voters. The political organization that best responded to that angst proved to be the new Republican Party, which formed in the North from the ashes of the Whig Party and attracted a growing number of northern Democrats. Politically shrewd, Republican leaders accommodated nativist voters by focusing their critique on immigrant groups who were not likely to vote Republican anyway. (Republicans, for example, wrote off the Irish who generally distrusted the party's Anglo-Protestant orientation and support for issues like temperance.) But the issue that motivated the Republicans overall was antislavery, although they were by no means an abolitionist organization. Some of the new party's members, like William Seward and Salmon P. Chase, favored immediate emancipation, but they also labored alongside members like Abraham Lincoln who could tolerate slavery's continued existence for an indefinite period as long as the institution was not allowed to expand. Opposition to slavery's expansion, in fact, became one of the core principles around which all Republicans rallied.

The key element in Republican Party's opposition to slavery expansionism lay in their conviction that the absence of slavery had made the North's "**free labor**" system superior to the South in every way. To Republicans, the phrase "free labor" denoted workers' ability to labor for employers of their own choosing, to earn and save their wages, to move at will, and to speak their minds. Freedom in the North had produced a society that had more railroad mileage, banks, land under cultivation, investment capital, cities, manufacturing than the South. In highlighting this contrast, Hinton Helper of North Carolina, a rare southern Republican, wrote in his book, *The Impending Crisis of the South*, that "if eight entire slave States . . . and the District of Columbia . . . were put up at auction, New York could buy them all, and then have one hundred and thirty-three millions of dollars left in her pocket! Such is the amazing contrast between freedom and slavery." Continued progress, however, depended on the continued expansion of free farmers into fresh land, and slavery's expansion stood in the way.

The Republicans' vision proved remarkably influential as it came together in the mid-1850s. The party attracted northern Whigs looking for a new political home, such as Abraham Lincoln and William Seward who brought with them a Protestant sensibility and an admiration for Henry Clay. A great many northern Democrats also joined the new party. Voters in New Hampshire, which had been a Democratic stronghold since the days of Jackson, transformed their state into a Republican stronghold in 1854, and they never looked back. Former Democrats like Salmon Chase rose to positions of leadership within the **Republican Party**, whose receptiveness further contributed to the decline of northern Democrats.

The emergence of the Republicans, combined with the growing dominance of the South within the Democratic Party, intensified the sectional conflict. Southerners saw Republicans as a revolutionary force that would destroy the Union. They considered free labor to be little more than a mask for all sorts of radical reform—free love, abolition, socialism. Free labor also accommodated the brutal exploitation of white workers, since employers hired and discarded them at will. This system of "wage slavery" kept people mired in poverty, even as it gave those same people the right to vote. Southern propagandists argued that the electorate would one day vote private property out of existence. Slavery, they continued, provided a fundamental stability that the North lacked. Thus, by the mid-1850s, northern and southern views of their sections had hardened into mutually antagonistic worldviews.

Republican electoral strategy further intensified this dynamic because the party's strategists determined that they could win a national election by carrying the North. Their plan began with their portrayal of the federal government in general, and Stephen Douglas in particular, as a tool of a Slave Power conspiracy to expand slavery into both the West and the North. Republicans only needed to convince a majority of northern voters to believe them. Events over the next few years would give their theory an increasing air of truth, especially since southern politicians feeling increasingly embattled took actions perceived to be increasingly aggressive.

Bleeding Kansas

Events in Kansas soon provided Republicans with an opportunity to develop their narrative. Land-hungry settlers poured into the new territory when it opened in 1855. Most of these folk cared little for sectional politics; they came to farm, but sectional partisans cared deeply about the future of Kansas. William Seward predicted that the North's advantage in population would deliver a free state. Other leaders took affirmative steps to

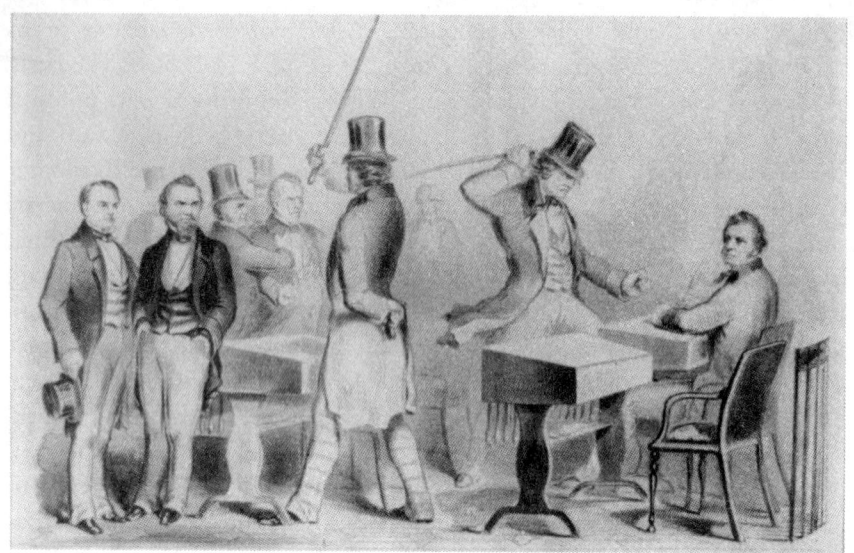

This print is a dramatic portrayal, clearly biased toward the northern point of view, of an incident in Congress. The artist recreates the May 22 attack and severe beating of Massachusetts Senator Charles Sumner by Representative Preston Brooks of South Carolina. Brook's actions were provoked by Sumner's insulting remarks against his cousin, Senator Butler, and against Illinois Senator Stephen Douglas. Illinois Senator Stephen Douglas is standing (hands in pockets) looking vindicated by the event. 1856.

ensure they did so. The New England Emigrant Aid Company settled a few thousand antislavery activists. Proslavery interests met the challenge. Thousands of "**Border Ruffians**"—proslavery activists from neighboring Missouri—spilled into Kansas to cast illegal ballots and intimidate northern settlers. Within months, both factions had organized their own governments. By 1856, the two sides were engaged in open warfare.

Republicans labeled this turn of events "**Bleeding Kansas**," even if the fighting itself up to this point tended to be relatively bloodless. They effectively highlighted selected events to make their case that the "Slave Power" was restraining democracy with violence. Two incidents, in fact, made their job easy. On May 21, 1856, border ruffians attacked Lawrence, Kansas, which free-state settlers claimed as their capital, setting fire to the Free State Hotel (a fortified structure used by the Massachusetts Emigrant Society to welcome arriving anti-slavery settlers) and destroying two printing presses. That act, according to Republicans, showed proslavery advocates' willingness to squelch free speech to protect their institution. Further an event taking place the next day in Washington, D.C., revealed that the violence was not limited to Kansas. During congressional debate over the events in Kansas, three days earlier, Republican Senator Charles Sumner of Massachusetts had delivered a vitriolic speech denouncing slavery while lambasting slaveholders and pro-slavery politicians, specifically insulting South Carolina Senator Pierce Butler, who had no opportunity to respond because he was home recovering from a stroke. Representative Preston Brooks, one of Butler's relatives, avenged his kinsman by savagely beating Sumner on the Senate floor while he worked at his desk, knocking Sumner unconscious. Brooks soon resigned his seat, but the voters in his district easily reelected him. Not only did his constituents look favorably upon his actions, people from across the South sent him new canes to replace the one he broke on Sumner. Meanwhile, Senator Sumner left Congress for three years to recover, with Massachusetts keeping his seat vacant to remind onlookers of the "Slave Power's" quick resort to force when challenged. The Republicans' developing narrative required them to downplay the violent tendencies on their own side. For example, Henry Ward Beecher, an influential minister and brother of Harriet Beecher Stowe, sent rifles to Kansas in boxes labeled Bibles ("Beecher's Bibles"). Meanwhile, **John Brown,** a white abolitionist who concluded that violence offered the only means of ending slavery, led his sons to the banks of Pottawatomie Creek, Kansas, where they killed five proslavery settlers with machetes, setting off a guerilla-style war for the remainder of the year until President Pierce stationed over a thousand federal troops in Kansas to restore order.

THE *DRED SCOTT* CASE

Republican electoral strategy began showing dividends in the Election of 1856, although the new party still fell short of victory. John C. Frémont, a noted explorer and veteran of the Mexican American War, secured the Republican presidential nomination, running on a platform opposing the expansion of slavery and embracing as its slogan: "free speech, free press, free soil, free men, Frémont, and victory!" Pennsylvania's **James Buchanan,** an established politician whose foreign assignments had allowed him to sit out most of the sectional controversies, took the nomination for the Democratic Party, which supported popular sovereignty and the proslavery faction in Kansas. Buchanan won the presidency with 45.3 percent of the popular vote and 174 votes in the Electoral College; Democrats also regained 48 seats in the House, which

The Crime Against Kansas / The Crime Against Sumner

On May 19, 1856, Senator Charles Sumner of Massachusetts, a leader of the anti-slavery forces, rose on the floor of the Senate to deliver a passionate speech he called, "The Crime Against Kansas." He decried, "the rape of a virgin territory, compelling it to the hateful embrace of slavery. . . ." to a gallery crowded with anti-slavery representatives from the House as well as the Senate. "Even now while I speak," he warned darkly, "portents lower in the horizon, threatening to darken the land, which already palpitates with the mutterings of civil war." During his tirade, which lasted two days, Sumner reserved some of his strongest language for Senator Andrew Butler of South Carolina. Butler's mistress, he charged, was the "harlot slavery." All decent and just men must work "to dislodge from the high places that tyrannical sectionalism of which the Senator from South Carolina is one of the maddest zealots." Sumner concluded his "last appeal" in the name of "the Constitution outraged, of the laws trampled down. . . of humanity degraded. . . of freedom crushed to earth," and, finally, "in the name of the Heavenly Father whose service is perfect freedom. . . . ."

Even in an era of unrestrained oratory, Sumner's speech was unusually bitter and provocative in its sexual allusions in a prudish age. Northern Democrats, like Stephen Douglas, rose to denounce Sumner's words as "unfit for decent young men to read." "Is it his object," Douglas inquired, "to provoke some of us to kick him just as we would a dog in the street, that he may get sympathy upon just chastisement?" The speech, however, was rapidly reprinted for distribution in the North where it gained the admiration of many. The poet, Henry Wadsworth Longfellow, for one, wrote to Sumner to congratulate him on his "brave and noble speech," which was "the greatest voice on the greatest subject, that has been uttered since we became a nation."

Preston Brooks, a young congressman from South Carolina, who was a relative and protégé of Senator Butler, resented the personal attacks upon the ailing older man. Brooks, a tall handsome man with "sparkling eyes," was considered "amiable and friendly" by his colleagues. But he decided that "family honor" demanded that he "punish" Sumner. On May 22, he entered the Senate chamber and came up behind Sumner, denouncing the "libel on South Carolina and Mr. Butler." He grasped his gold-headed walking stick and beat Sumner over the head with it until the cane broke. Unable to defend himself because his legs were pinned under his desk, Sumner slumped to the floor, bleeding and unconscious, seriously injured.

Not a single southern Senator condemned the attack. The vote to expel Brooks from the House failed to receive the necessary two-thirds majority when the Southerners all voted against it. Brooks resigned but was unanimously reelected by his

district and exultantly returned to Congress. The South rejoiced in Brooks' defense of southern honor, showering him with praise and hundreds of new walking sticks sent by admiring constituents to "whip some more Yankees."

The North, however, saw the incident as evidence of southern brutality rather than nobility. The New York **Evening Post** bitingly asked, "Are we too, slaves, slaves for life, a target for their brutal blows, when we do not comport ourselves to please them?" George Templeton Strong, a conservative New Yorker who believed "antislavery agitators" to be "wrong in principle and mischievous in policy," nevertheless added, "But the reckless, insolent brutality of our Southern aristocrats may drive me to abolitionism yet." Northerners, he noted, were busy making money and were "law abiding and peace loving." Southern aristocrats claimed to be highly civilized, gallant, chivalrous gentlemen, "whereas I believe they are in fact a race of lazy, ignorant, coarse, sensual, swaggering, sordid, beggarly barbarians. . . ."

The distaste generated in the North, in reaction to Brooks' assault, drove thousands of undecided voters into the fold of the new Republican Party. In the 1856 election campaign the party's banners included "Bleeding Sumner" alongside "Bleeding Kansas." In January 1857, the Massachusetts state legislature unanimously reelected Sumner as Senator and party martyr. For three years, as he slowly recovered, his Senate seat remained empty, a mute reminder of the nation's bitter divisions and a valuable addition to the anti-slavery cause. Sumner was eventually able to return to the Senate and to continue his fight for racial justice until his death in 1874. Ironically, it was the 37-year-old Brooks who died seven months after the attack of suffocation caused by "acute inflammatory sore throat." While Southerners eulogized the "gallant defender" of southern rights, less charitable northern correspondents saw Brook's death as evidence of God's judgment and quoted scripture, "Vengeance is mine saith the Lord: I will repay."

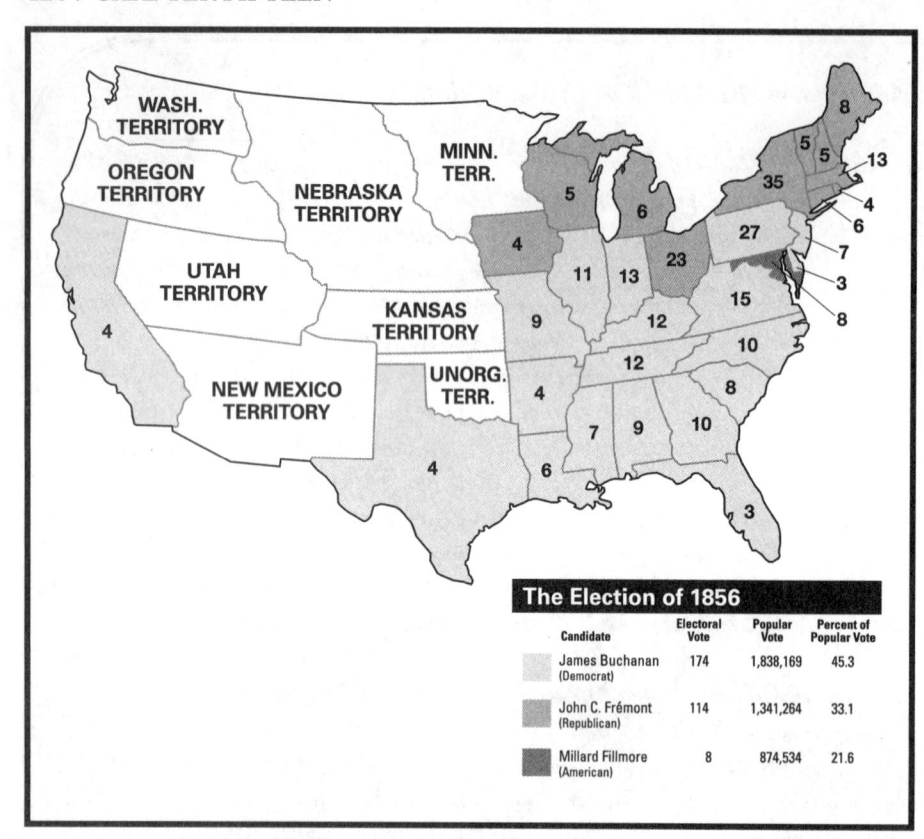

Map 15.5 The Election of 1856

The Election of 1856			
Candidate	Electoral Vote	Popular Vote	Percent of Popular Vote
James Buchanan (Democrat)	174	1,838,169	45.3
John C. Frémont (Republican)	114	1,341,264	33.1
Millard Fillmore (American)	8	874,534	21.6

placed them back in the majority. Although Frémont lost the election, the returns gave Republicans hope. Frémont won 11 of the 16 free states. Meanwhile, in the House of Representatives, Republicans established themselves as the major opposition party, claiming 44 seats and nearly absorbing the American (Know Nothing) Party's loss of 48 seats. In fact, if the anti-Democratic vote had not been split between the Republicans and Know Nothings, Buchanan may well have lost the presidency. The new party, therefore, pushed on, soon benefiting from the actions of overreaching proslavery Democrats.

Within days of Buchanan's inaugural address in which the new president predicted the end of sectional controversy, the Supreme Court renewed the conflict. Buchanan remarked in his speech that the Court was about to issue a ruling that would settle the question of slavery in the territories. The case, **Dred Scott v. Sandford** (1857), grew out of lawsuits filed by Harriet Scott and her husband, Dred, initiated in the 1840s to secure their family's freedom on the basis of being brought into the free territory of Minnesota despite the congressional ban on slavery there as part of the 1820 Missouri Compromise. After losing in Missouri state courts, the Scotts moved their case into federal court where their suit became transformed from a relatively straightforward freedom claim into a case that would finally define Congress's power over slavery in the territories. In early March 1857, Chief Justice Roger B. Taney issued the Court's official opinion. His sprawling, confusing, and decidedly proslavery opinion contained two major rulings. First, since African Americans historically "had no rights which the white man was bound respect," the Constitution did not recognize any African American, whether enslaved or not, as a citizen of the United States, and consequently the federal courts could not take jurisdiction. Nevertheless, Taney continued to issue a second major ruling: that the portion of the Missouri Compromise restricting slavery north of the compromise line was unconstitutional because Congress had no right to ban slavery in any federal territories.

Republicans led the attack against the ruling, linking the Court to the "Slave Power conspiracy," emphasizing the fact that southern Democrats dominated the tribunal. Of the Court's nine justices, seven belonged to the Democratic Party, five were Southerners, and four were slaveholders (though strongly proslavery, Chief Justice Taney had not personally owned slaves for decades). Yet, only the Court's two non-Democratic members—John McLean (a Republican) and Benjamin Robbins Curtis (who remained a devoted Whig)—dissented. The remaining justices all agreed with Taney that Dred Scott and his family should remain enslaved, although they did not agree on exactly why. Some even wrote elaborate opinions that contradicted Taney's reasoning, if not the Chief Justice's conclusions.

Republicans decided, therefore, that the *Dred Scott* decision was, in the phrase of modern lawyers, "result-oriented" and not based on a fair reading of constitutional law. Indeed, they contended that Taney willfully distorted the Constitution into a proslavery document rather than one committed to the eventual ending of the institution. Republican editor Horace Greeley described the ruling "as entitled to just so much moral weight as would be the judgment of those congregated in any Washington bar-room." Both Southerners and northern Democrats pronounced the issue of slavery's expansion to have been settled by the Supreme Court, and they chided Republicans for their continued criticism of the decision. The new party's refusal to accept the idea that the High Court's ruling declared its platform to be unconstitutional, along with its desire to capture the government during the next election, they believed, would lead to anarchy.

The Lecompton Constitution

The bonds between Southerners and northern Democrats became severely strained at the next crisis point, emerging only a few months after the *Dred Scott* decision. Kansas once again became the source of the trouble. Although free-state settlers outnumbered them by at least two to one, proslavery settlers, thanks to votes cast illegally by border ruffians in both 1855 and 1857, controlled the officially recognized government in the territory. In 1857, the legislature called for a convention (held in Lecompton, Kansas) to draw up a new state constitution, provided for the election of delegates through a process that all observers knew to be rigged, and permitted the finished product to advance without a referendum. All of these moves guaranteed that Kansas would have a proposed state constitution favored by the territory's proslavery minority. (The territorial governor, who was not an abolitionist, resigned in disgust.)

President Buchanan appointed Robert J. Walker (a respected Unionist Democrat born in Pennsylvania but who long resided in Mississippi) to be the territory's new governor. Walker urged free-state settlers to participate in the election of delegates, but they refused, thus all the convention's seats fell into the hands of proslavery settlers. Believing he had Buchanan's support, Walker also insisted that any constitution be subject to a referendum, which, he knew, would have doomed a proslavery document in any fairly conducted process. The Lecompton Convention drew up a constitution that explicitly protected slavery. Although initially hesitant, the delegates authorized a public referendum on their work, but in a contrived manner that ensured that the process would not be fairly conducted. Rather than subject the constitution to the usual method of an up-or-down vote, the convention forced voters to choose between two constitutions. Both versions explicitly protected slavery, the only significant difference was that one permitted Kansas to participate in the interstate slave trade while the other did not. Free-state Kansans denounced the process as a sham; Walker resigned in protest; and Kansas voters chose the option allowing participation in the interstate slave trade. (An investigation later concluded that close to half these votes were cast illegally.)

Northern observers, both Democrat and Republican, agreed that the entire process producing the **Lecompton Constitution** was pure folly, and they reacted with disgust when Buchanan proposed that Congress accept the document and admit Kansas as a slave state. Stephen Douglas argued that the Lecompton Constitution reduced popular sovereignty to little more than a joke and led the opposition. Buchanan warned him that Democratic administrations enforced party discipline by crushing those who broke ranks, citing examples as far back as Andrew Jackson's administration. Before storming out of the White House, Douglas told Buchanan "to remember that General Jackson is dead." Douglas could not stop the bill's passage in the Senate, but his supporters in the House of Representatives joined with Republicans to defeat the bill after a fierce debate that included an open brawl on the House floor. Southerners, who had regarded Douglas as an ally, now treated him as a traitor. The Senate stripped him of his leadership positions, and Buchanan tried unsuccessfully to replace him as a candidate for his seat in the upcoming 1858 election.

THE RISE OF LINCOLN

Although some Republicans toyed with the idea of embracing Douglas as one of their own—he was after all the most prominent politician in the North—Illinois Republicans understood that the Little Giant would remain a committed Democrat so instead they nominated **Abraham Lincoln**, a successful lawyer and frustrated politician, to run against Douglas. A former Whig who had retired from politics after serving a single term in the House of Representatives, Lincoln reentered politics as a Republican when the Kansas-Nebraska Act reopened the issue of slavery's expansion. During his famous 1858 "House-Divided" speech in which he accepted his party's nomination for the Senate, Lincoln argued that the Democratic Party's leadership (specifically naming Douglas, along with Franklin Pierce, James Buchanan, and Roger B. Taney) had conspired to force slavery into the territories and perhaps into the North. Their plan had begun with the Kansas-Nebraska Act, and, abetted by the *Dred Scott* decision, would continue until stopped by organized Republicans opposition. In Lincoln's words:

> [T]his government cannot endure permanently half slave and half free. I do not expect the Union to be dissolved.... It will become all one thing, or all the other. Either the opponents of slavery will arrest the further spread of it, and place it ... in the course of ultimate extinction; or its advocates will push it forward, till it shall become alike lawful in all the States, old as well as new—North as well as South.

Douglas, of course, rejected Lincoln's charge that he was a chief architect to transform slavery into a national institution, although he had no moral qualms about slavery's continued existence in the South or the institution's expansion into places where settlers genuinely wanted it. He would have many opportunities to defend himself because he and Lincoln engaged in a series of seven joint debates across the state before voters went to the polls (to choose their state legislators who would actually decide who the next U.S. Senator from Illinois would be).

The 1858 **Lincoln-Douglas Debates** did little to aid Lincoln's short-term prospects—the Democrats would narrowly retain control of the Illinois legislature and reelect Douglas—but they played a powerful role in establishing Lincoln as a national political figure while also intensifing the post-Lecompton divisions in the Democratic Party. Using a common accusation against antislavery politicians, Douglas tried to portray Lincoln as an advocate of racial equality. An end to slavery, Douglas predicted, would place black and white Americans on equal footing and even permit interracial marriage. Lincoln responded that he did not intend to "introduce political and social equality between the white and the black races." He agreed with his opponent that African Americans were "not my equal in many respects—certainly not in color, perhaps not in moral or intellectual endowment." Yet Lincoln insisted that accepting inequality did not therefore mandate slavery: "[I]in the right to eat the bread, without the leave of anybody else, which his own hand earns, [a black American] is my equal and the equal of ... Douglas, and the equal of every living man." By modern standards, Lincoln took a racist position but his stance in 1858 established him as a moderate figure within the Republican Party capable of appealing to a wide range of voters across the northern electorate who detested slavery while holding no great sympathy for African Americans.

Lincoln also pushed Douglas to reconcile his position on popular sovereignty with the Supreme Court's ruling in *Dred Scott* case. The answer Lincoln received further undermined Douglas's already weakened southern support. Although Taney's opinion on the territories dealt primarily with Congress' ability to regulate slavery in the

Stephen Douglas

Abraham Lincoln

territories, the ruling also contained a line stating that if Congress could not regulate the territories, then logically territorial legislatures could not do so either. Whether Taney spoke for the Court or just for himself was not clear, but Lincoln argued that *Dred Scott* had declared popular sovereignty unconstitutional and that Douglas had therefore no mechanism to stop slavery's expansion. Douglas's answer became known as "the **Freeport Doctrine**"—although he had made similar statements a few times before his debates with Lincoln. In short, Douglas contended that, although a territorial legislature could not explicitly prohibit slavery, it could refuse to pass any laws protecting slavery and thereby render slaveholding impossible. Southerners rejected Douglas's position, but fearing its implications, they would eventually demand a uniform federal slave code for all territories. Although Lincoln did not win election to the Senate, his efforts further divided the Democratic Party and set the stage for the national Republican victory in 1860.

JOHN BROWN RETURNS

Over the next two years, relations between the North and South continued to deteriorate. The Panic of 1857, a short but severe economic downturn, forced businesses to close, threw hundreds of thousands of workers onto the streets, and pushed crop prices down. Yet the crisis confined itself to the North; the southern economy remained relatively unscathed. Southerners took their uninterrupted prosperity as a sign of the superiority of "King Cotton" and the institution of slavery that sustained it. In Congress, Southerners blocked a tariff bill that Republicans believed would have boosted the economy and put people back to work. Southerners also blocked bills supported by both Republicans and northern Democrats. Southern maneuvers—supported at times with Buchanan's veto—killed a proposed railroad to the Pacific, grants of land to agricultural and mechanical colleges, and a Homestead Act that would have provided free land to settlers. These actions gave the South some short-term victories, but they further alienated northern voters in a way that would benefit the Republicans in 1860.

Just how distant the North and South had moved from each other became clear in late 1859, when John Brown resurfaced to lead an attempted insurrection among the South's enslaved population. Brown planned to capture the federal arsenal in Harpers Ferry, Virginia (now West Virginia), arm the slaves who he believed would flock to join him, and grow his force as he pushed further into the South. Although he received financing backing from a group of wealthy white abolitionists inspired by his actions in Kansas, Brown received little support from northern blacks. Frederick Douglass, who befriended Brown, thought the plan was suicidal and that the attack would "array the whole country against us." Brown attacked with a force consisting of eighteen men, capturing the nearly unguarded arsenal before armed locals and state militia pinned them down. U.S. Marines, under the command of future Confederate generals Robert E. Lee and J.E.B. Stuart, captured Brown after storming the building near the arsenal where he and the others were held up. Within a few months, Virginia had tried and hanged Brown and six of his comrades for treason against the state.

The reaction to Brown's execution in December 1859 underscored the Union's growing sectional divisions. Southerners welcomed the hanging. Believing that Brown had attempted to open a race war within their section, they feared his effort would not be the last by radical abolitionists. In the North, however, concerns about Brown's sanity gave way over the course of his trial to a portrayal of the man as a martyr for the cause of freedom. His execution triggered the ringing of church bells, gun salutes, and commemorative sermons across the North. This behavior horrified Southerners, who considered Brown to be little more than a murderer, and politicians responded by maneuvering for advantage. Democrats condemned the mourning of Brown's death as the product of minority sentiment and organized anti-Brown meetings. Republicans distanced themselves from Brown's violence, but compared him to the southern "filibusters" who had emerged during the 1850s seeking to expand slavery by capturing territory in Latin America. One of them, William Walker, took over Nicaragua for a while. Brown had simply changed the focus from slavery to freedom.

The Election of 1860

Increasing sectional tensions finally split the Democratic Party in 1860. By that point, most other national institutions had already divided along sectional lines. In 1844, the Methodist and Baptist churches both separated into northern and southern branches. Nearly ten years later, the Whig Party fell apart, leaving some Southerners politically homeless and creating an opportunity for the Republican Party to emerge during the mid-1850s. Northern and southern Democrats, however, had managed to hold their party together until they met in April 1860 to nominate a presidential candidate. Stephen Douglas had established himself as the frontrunner by the time the convention opened, but southern delegates, who controlled enough votes to deprive Douglas of the two-thirds majority required to secure the nomination,

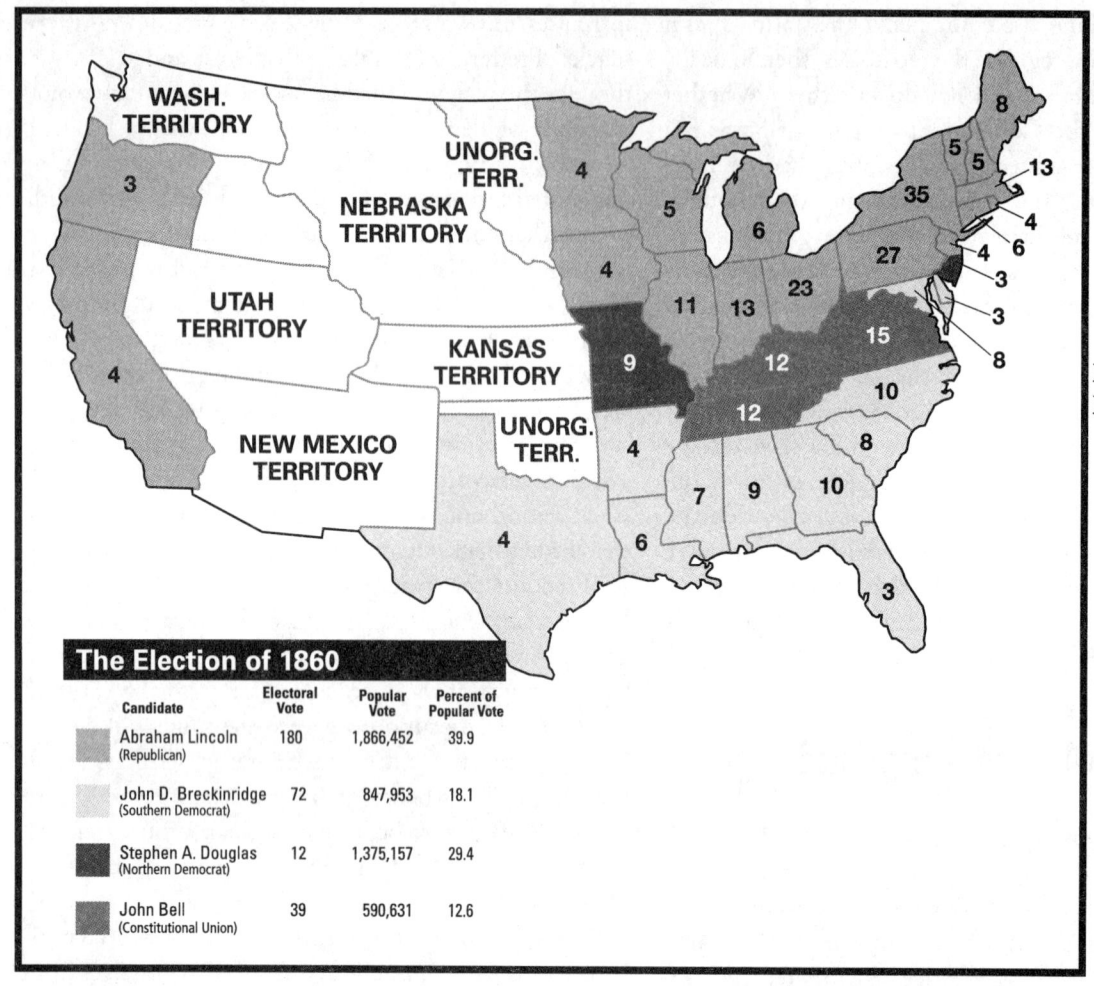

Map 15.6 The Election of 1860

The Election of 1860

Candidate	Electoral Vote	Popular Vote	Percent of Popular Vote
Abraham Lincoln (Republican)	180	1,866,452	39.9
John D. Breckinridge (Southern Democrat)	72	847,953	18.1
Stephen A. Douglas (Northern Democrat)	12	1,375,157	29.4
John Bell (Constitutional Union)	39	590,631	12.6

demanded that the party include in its platform a uniform federal slave code for all U.S. territories. Douglas and his supporters, however, refused to consider the request. Southern delegates promptly walked out, eventually forming their own convention to nominate John C. Breckinridge of Kentucky (Buchanan's vice president) for the presidency on a platform that included the federal slave code provision. Before adjourning, the remaining northern Democrats nominated Stephen Douglas on a platform endorsing popular sovereignty as the best approach to the issue of slavery in the territories.

Republicans emerged from their Chicago convention in May 1860 more unified than their opponents. The main problem leading into their meeting involved the public's perception that some of their leading candidates were too radical. William Seward, for example, an avowed abolitionist who argued that the existence of a higher law trumped the Constitution. Democratic Senator Jefferson Davis of Mississippi charged that John Brown had found his inspiration in such talk, and the charge resonated with many voters, especially those supporting one of Seward's many Republican rivals. Ohio Senator Salmon P. Chase, who had built his reputation by challenging the Fugitive Slave Law, likewise seemed too radical for a national electorate. Other candidates proved too affiliated with the Know-Nothings, too willing to compromise with the South on slavery matters, or seemed too openly opportunistic to secure the nomination. As the convention worked through the list of potential nominees, Abraham Lincoln emerged as a figure worthy of serious consideration. Although his debates with Douglas had given Lincoln some national exposure, few observers thought he had much of a chance going into the convention. After performing well on the first ballot, his managers effectively sold him to the delegates as a self-made man who had worked hard to transform himself from a poor farm boy to a successful lawyer. Most importantly, he was a moderate on the slavery issue who nonetheless would not waver in his opposition to the extension of slavery into the territories. By the third ballot, Lincoln had secured the nomination, and the party rallied behind him with enthusiasm.

Lincoln, however, ran for election only in the North. Most southern states refused to put his name on the ballot. Indeed, the Election of 1860 proved to be nearly two separate elections. In the South, John C. Breckinridge

Table 15.1 — Overview of the Sectional Crisis

Event	Year	Effect
Wilmot Proviso	1846	A rider to an appropriations bill proposed by Representative David Wilmot of Pennsylvania at the beginning of the Mexican-American War. The Proviso stated that any territory acquired from Mexico should be closed to slavery. The Wilmot Proviso was never approved.
Compromise of 1850	1850	The Compromise of 1850 was a series of five bills dealing with the spread of slavery to the territories and other lingering national issues dealing with slavery. California was entered as a free state, New Mexico and Utah were allowed popular sovereignty, and a new stronger Fugitive Slave Act was established. It satisfied neither North or South and planted the seeds of future conflict.
Election of 1852	1852	Franklin Pierce of New Hampshire crushed the Whig candidate, General Winfield Scott. The election of 1852 demonstrated that the Whigs had ceased to be a nationally competitive party.
Kansas-Nebraska Act	1854	A law drafted by Stephen Douglas, passed by Congress, and signed by President Franklin Pierce that organized the territory that became the states of Kansas and Nebraska. Controversy surrounded the law because it repealed the Missouri Compromise restrictions on slavery in the northern Louisiana Purchase lands, and the reaction against that repeal brought about the organization of the Republican Party.
"Bleeding Kansas"	1855 to 1856	A term describing the violence surrounding the settlement of Kansas. The term encompassed the activities of the border ruffians of Missouri, the actions of John Brown, and the attack by Preston Brooks on Charles Sumner on the floor of the U.S. Senate.
Election of 1856	1856	Presidency won by Democrat James Buchanan of Pennsylvania, but a surprisingly strong showing by John C. Fremont, the nominee of the recently formed Republican Party in the North, set the stage for the 1860 election.
Dred Scott Case	1857	An 1857 Supreme Court decision that held African Americans were not citizens of the United States and that Congress possessed no power to limit slavery's expansion into the federal territories. Republicans used the case as evidence that a Slave Power Conspiracy had captured the federal government.
Lecompton Constitution	1857	A document that tried to bring Kansas into the Union as a slave state. The entire process was riddled with fraud, and the effort was defeated – despite the support of President Buchanan – by the combined efforts of Stephen Douglas and the Republicans. Kansas would ultimately enter the Union as a free state in 1862.
John Brown's Raid	1859	John Brown unsuccessfully attempted to start a slave revolt by capturing the federal arsenal at Harpers Ferry, Virginia. He was captured and executed for treason, but many Northerners regarded him as a martyr.
Election of 1860	1860	Abraham Lincoln received around 40 percent of the popular vote. He had carried every free state – seventeen in all. Lincoln's name was not on a ballot in a single southern state, however population growth in the North allowed Lincoln to be elected. The election was a decisive victory for Lincoln and the Republicans.
Fort Sumter	1861	Fort Sumter is best known as the site upon which the shots initiating the American Civil War were fired.

squared off against John Bell of the **Constitutional Union Party**, an organization consisting of former Whigs from the Upper South whose main goal was to seek further compromise between the two regions. By helping to deprive Republicans of enough electoral votes to win the election, they hoped Bell would emerge victorious in the House of Representatives. In the North, Lincoln and Douglas faced off. Douglas nearly worked himself to death during the election campaigning for himself (an unprecedented move in 1860), traveling through the North and South to tell voters that he was the only national candidate with the prestige and ability to end the sectional crisis. Republicans and southern Democrats both rejected this argument; his support for the Kansas-Nebraska Act led Republicans to believe that he was a tool of the Slave Power while his opposition to the Lecompton Constitution and his articulation of the Freeport Doctrine made him appear duplicitous to Southerners. A rash of corruption scandals in the Buchanan administration simply added to Douglas's troubles. Republicans in contrast unified behind Lincoln. William Seward, Lincoln's main rival for the nomination, and his supporters campaigned vigorously for Lincoln. His supporters delivered an estimated 50,000 stump speeches during the campaign.

Despite the crowded field of candidates, Abraham Lincoln emerged victorious in the presidential race. Though he received slightly less than 40 percent of the popular vote, Lincoln carried every free state—seventeen in all—to win a majority (58 percent) of the Electoral College votes. John C. Breckinridge (18 percent of the popular vote) carried eleven of the fourteen slave states. (Bell won the other three slave states, all located in the Upper South). Meanwhile, Stephen Douglas received nearly 30 percent of the national popular vote, but only won Missouri. Coinciding with the Republicans securing control of the Senate and maintaining their advantage in the House, these results all added up to a decisive electoral victory for Lincoln and his party.

Lincoln's triumph, however, moved the sectional crisis into a new phase. Southern partisans had long warned that the election of an antislavery president would lead to secession. Within weeks of Lincoln's election, South Carolina made good on the threat. Mississippi, Florida, Alabama, Georgia, Louisiana, and Texas followed suit over the next two months. By January 1861, these states had organized the Confederate States of America, with Jefferson Davis of Mississippi chosen to be its first (and only) president. The Confederacy's new vice president, former U.S. Senator Alexander Stephens of Georgia, minced no words about the immediate cause of the tumult. Debate over "the proper status of the negro in our form of civilization" had brought the South to this point, he noted, but the new government made possible by secession rested "upon the great truth, that the negro is not the equal of the white man; that slavery . . . is his natural and normal condition." Secession mania did not sweep the entire South. Citizens outside of the Deep South, in states such as Virginia, North Carolina, Maryland, and Kentucky, waited to make their decisions, as Lincoln had not yet taken office. Before his inauguration (not to take place until March 1861, five months after the election), Lincoln kept a low profile but signaled his willingness to bargain on some issues, including endorsement of a proposed constitutional amendment forever guaranteeing the legality of slavery in states where it already existed. He would not, however, compromise on the question of slavery's expansion into the territories; neither would the leaders of the new Confederacy, resulting in the impasse that would ultimately lead to civil war.

Chronology

1793 First Fugitive Slave Law passed by Congress.

1836 Harriet Scott arrives at Fort Snelling (in present-day Minnesota) where she meets her future husband, Dred.

1821 Congress enacts the Missouri Compromise Restriction.

1842 Supreme Court upholds the Fugitive Slave Law.

1843 The American (Know Nothing) Party emerges in New York.

1844 Methodist and Baptist churches split over the slavery issue.

1845 Immigrants to the United States begin increasing in numbers.

1846 Wilmot Proviso.

1847 Alternatives to the Wilmot Proviso, the common property doctrine, popular sovereignty, or extension of Missouri Compromise line, emerge in Congress.

1848 Treaty of Guadalupe Hidalgo.
News of a gold strike in California.
Free Soil Party organizes and nominates Martin Van Buren for president.
Zachary Taylor wins the election of 1848.

EXPANSION, SLAVERY AND SECESSION

1850 Henry Clay proposes a sectional compromise an omnibus bill.
Southern delegates meet in Nashville, Tennessee, to discuss a response to the sectional crisis.
Clay's omnibus bill fails to pass Congress.
President Zachary Taylor dies.
Millard Fillmore becomes president.
Stephen Douglas shepherds five separate bills through Congress and achieves sectional "compromise."
Christina Riot against the Fugitive Slave Law of 1850.

1851 Thomas Simms, a fugitive slave, is led out of Boston, Massachusetts.

1852 Missouri Supreme Court rules against freedom case of Dred and Harriet Scott.
Franklin Pierce defeats Millard Fillmore in the presidential election.
Harriet Beecher Stowe publishes *Uncle Tom's Cabin*.

1854 Ostend Manifesto.
Kansas-Nebraska Act.
Whig Party collapses.
Republican Party organizes.
Anti-immigrant sentiment allows the American (Know Nothing) Party to capture 62 House seats.

1855 Efforts by the American (Know Nothing) Party to become a national political force fall apart over the slavery issue.
Kansas Territory opened to settlement.

1856 Lawrence, Kansas, attacked by "Border ruffians."
Representative Preston Brooks of South Carolina uses a cane to assault Senator Charles Sumner on the floor of the U.S. Senate.
Abolitionist John Brown kills a family of proslavery settlers in Kansas.
James Buchanan defeats John C. Frémont in the presidential election

1857 President James Buchanan uses his Inaugural Address to predict the Supreme Court will end the sectional crisis
The Supreme Court's *Dred Scott* decision intensifies the sectional crisis.
Proslavery politicians try and fail to make Kansas a slave state.
A financial panic briefly grips the North.

1858 Stephen Douglas defeats Abraham Lincoln for a seat in the U.S. Senate.

1859 John Brown attacks the federal armory at Harper's Ferry, Virginia, and is hanged for treason.

1860 Democratic Party splits along sectional lines.
Abraham Lincoln defeats Stephen Douglas in presidential election.
South Carolina, Mississippi, Florida, Alabama, Georgia, Louisiana, and Texas secede from the Union

1861 Seceding states organize the Confederate States of America

Review Questions

1. Discuss the significance of the Wilmot Proviso. Why did the debate over slavery's expansion become the central question of American politics in the 1850s?

2. Discuss the compromise of 1850. What were the components of the compromise and why did it fail to produce a lasting peace between the North and the South?

3. Why did the Kansas-Nebraska Act transform American politics?

4. Republican politicians argued that the federal government had been captured by a conspiracy of slaveholders who were determined to force slavery's expansion. Based on your reading of this chapter, defend or refute this view.

5. Evaluate the South's decision to secede from the Union. Based on your reading of this chapter, why did states of the Deep Southern decide to secede and were they justified in doing so?

Glossary of Important People and Concepts

American (Know Nothing) Party
"Bleeding Kansas"
"Border Ruffians"
John Brown
James Buchanan
John C. Calhoun
Salmon Chase
Henry Clay
Common Property Doctrine
Constitutional Union Party
Stephen Douglas
Dred Scott Case
Millard Fillmore
"Free Labor"
Free Soil Party
Free Soil position
Kansas-Nebraska Act
Lecompton Constitution
Abraham Lincoln
Missouri Compromise Restriction
Ostend Manifesto
Franklin Pierce
Popular Sovereignty
Republican Party
William Seward
"Slave Power"
Uncle Tom's Cabin
Wilmot Proviso

SUGGESTED READINGS

Austin Allen, *Origins of the Dred Scott Case: Jacksonian Politics and the Supreme Court, 1837-1857* (2006).

John Ashworth, *Slavery, Capitalism, and Politics in the Antebellum Republic, 2 vols.* (1995-2008).

Jonathan H. Earle, *Jacksonian Antislavery and the Politics of Free Soil, 1824-1854* (2004).

Nicole Etcheson, *Bleeding Kansas: Contested Liberty in the Civil War Era* (2004).

Don E. Fehrenbacher, *The Dred Scott Case: Its Significance in American Law and Politics* (1978).

Eric Foner, *Free Soil, Free Labor, Free Men: The Ideology of the Republican Party before the Civil War* (1970).

William W. Freehling, *The Road to Disunion, 2 vols.* (1990-2007).

C.C. Goen, *Broken Churches, Broken Nation: Denominational Schisms and the Coming of the American Civil War* (1985).

Holman Hamilton, *Prologue to Conflict: The Crisis and Compromise of 1850* (2005).

Stanley Harold, *Border War: Fighting over Slavery before the Civil War* (2010).

James H. Huston, *Calculating the Value of Union: Property Rights and the Economic Origins of the Civil War* (2003).

Bruce Laurie, *Beyond Garrison: Antislavery and Social Reform* (2005).

Bruce Levine, *Half Slave, Half Free: The Roots of Civil War* (1992).

William A. Link, *The Roots of Secession: Slavery and Politics in Antebellum Virginia* (2003).

Russell McClintock, *Lincoln and the Decision for War: The Northern Response to Secession* (2008).

Michael A. Morrison, *Slavery and the American West: The Eclipse of Manifest Destiny and the Coming of the American Civil War* (1997).

David M. Potter, *The Impending Crisis, 1848-1861* (1976).

Leonard Richards, *Slave Power: The Free North and Southern Domination* (2000).

Brian Schoen, *The Fragile Fabric of Union: Cotton, Federal Policies, and the Global Origins of the Civil War* (2009).

Joel Silbey, *Storm over Texas: The Annexation Controversy and the Road to Civil War* (2007).

Elizabeth R. Varnon, *Disunion! The Coming of the American Civil War, 1789-1859* (2008).

CHARLESTON
MERCURY
EXTRA:

Passed unanimously at 1.15 o'clock, P. M. December 20th, 1860.

AN ORDINANCE

To dissolve the Union between the State of South Carolina and other States united with her under the compact entitled "The Constitution of the United States of America."

We, the People of the State of South Carolina, in Convention assembled, do declare and ordain, and it is hereby declared and ordained,

That the Ordinance adopted by us in Convention, on the twenty-third day of May, in the year of our Lord one thousand seven hundred and eighty-eight, whereby the Constitution of the United States of America was ratified, and also, all Acts and parts of Acts of the General Assembly of this State, ratifying amendments of the said Constitution, are hereby repealed; and that the union now subsisting between South Carolina and other States, under the name of "The United States of America," is hereby dissolved.

THE
UNION
IS
DISSOLVED!

Chapter Sixteen

THE AMERICAN CIVIL WAR 1861-1865

Future United States Supreme Court Justice Oliver Wendell Holmes, Jr. was twenty years old when he enlisted to fight in the Civil War. He would emerge from the conflict physically scarred by his experiences. He took a bullet to the chest at the Battle of Bull's Bluff in October 1861. Returning to service after recuperating from his wound, Holmes was shot in the neck and left for dead at the Battle of Antietam in September 1862. He recovered again and returned to his unit only to be shot in the foot at the Battle of Chancellorsville in May 1863. Although originally wishing to have his foot amputated so he could go home, he bravely finished out his commission. In addition to his physical wounds, the war left a lasting impact on Holmes mentally. Each year until his death in the 1930s, he drank a glass of wine to observe the Battle of Antietam—the single bloodiest day of the war. Other soldiers, who may not have shared Captain Holmes's wish for amputation, returned home from the conflict with missing limbs. Jonathan M. Allison, a Union corporal who lost his right arm at the Battle of Resaca in May 1864, described himself and others like him as "living monuments of the late cruel and bloody Rebellion." A New Hampshire minister, speaking decades after the conflict had ended, reminded his listeners that one need only "count the empty sleeves" to know the cost of the conflict. Southerners, of course, suffered as well, and they would have to cope with the fact that they had lost the war. John Sitgreaves Green, a quartermaster in the Confederate army, was wounded by a "sabre-cut of excruciating, continued agony." He suffered for the rest of his life, becoming addicted to both opium and alcohol. His family ultimately placed him in an asylum, where the doctors had become quite familiar with veterans struggling with the war.

Just as the conflict altered the lives of Holmes, Allison, and Green, the Civil War transformed and, in many cases, devastated the United States. Although few expected the fight to last as long as it did, the Civil War pulled a huge number of Americans into its vortex. Around half of the North's military-age population entered the army. Somewhere between 75 and 85 percent of draft-age, white men fought for the South. Many of these men died—perhaps as many as three-quarters of a million. The war also left the South significantly damaged; the region lost two-thirds of its wealth, including nearly half of its livestock. The former Confederate states also lost their central economic institution: slavery. The North, by contrast, emerged from the conflict significantly stronger. The Civil War did not begin as a war to end slavery. Indeed, President Abraham Lincoln labored hard in the early phases of the war to present the conflict as one devoted solely to saving the Union. When the war stalemated, however, ending slavery became a major northern military objective. The war did, in fact, preserve the Union, but the country also emerged from the conflict an emancipated land. The nation that survived was by no means the nation as it was.

THE END OF COMPROMISE

Although by early 1861 seven southern states announced they had seceded and formed the Confederate States of America, political leaders on both sides still hoped for compromise. President James Buchanan, who believed that secession was unconstitutional but also held the view that the federal government had no legitimate authority to compel a state to stay in the Union against its will, did little to increase (or to decrease) tensions. He refused to recognize the Confederacy and supported the continued occupation of federal property in rebel states where possible, but also let such holdings go where they were not tenable. Federal troops, for example, continued to control **Fort Sumter** in South Carolina because its commander, Major Robert Anderson, remained loyal to the United States. Anderson moved his soldiers into the fort, whose location in Charleston harbor made it inaccessible without a fight. By contrast, General David Twiggs, the commander of the federal troops stationed in Texas, promptly surrendered his headquarters in San Antonio and the forts under his command when pressed by Confederate agitators, in exchange for the peaceful departure of his men from the state (Twiggs later became a commissioned officer in the Confederate army).

Abraham Lincoln also kept a low profile during this period. Not yet holding office, the president-elect did not wish to make the sectional tensions worse, especially since he had not power yet to respond. The situation in the winter of 1860-1861 looked bleak. Along with the states that already announced that they were leaving the Union, a number of others lay on the brink of secession. Virginia, North Carolina, Tennessee, and Arkansas—all slave states—rejected the initial call for disunion, but voters in those states who remained deeply wary of Lincoln and the Republicans could be turned rather easily. Many voters in the border states of Kentucky, Maryland, and Missouri were also sympathetic to secession. Political leaders moved cautiously, but tensions escalated, nonetheless, especially in the vicinity of Fort Sumter.

As the winter dragged on, compromise efforts failed. Neither side could agree on the future of slavery's expansion. Senator John J. Crittenden of Kentucky, a former Whig and Know-Nothing who most recently supported the Constitutional Union Party, brought forward the most notable conciliatory proposal. The so-called **Crittenden Compromise** offered to end the secession crisis with a package of constitutional amendments and congressional resolutions designed to entice the South back into the Union peacefully: "Unrepealable" amendments would have permanently guaranteed the existence of slavery in the states where it currently existed while extending the Missouri Compromise line to the California border, allowing slavery south of that boundary. Other proposed amendments would prohibit the abolition of slavery in Washington, D.C. and provide compensation to owners of fugitive slaves. The congressional resolutions pledged fidelity to the federal Fugitive Slave Law and condemned northern state laws that impeded the return of runaway slaves, but also took into account northern criticisms by suggesting a modification of the national law so judges received the same compensation regardless of their decisions in fugitive slave cases. The compromise failed. Congress tabled the proposal in December 1860, about two weeks after being introduced.

Many of Senator Crittenden's proposals reemerged at a Peace Conference that convened in Washington in February 1861. This convention proposed a constitutional amendment that, like the Crittenden Compromise, permitted the expansion of slavery (again below the Missouri Compromise line). For President-elect Lincoln and most Republican leaders, some of the proposals were open to negotiation but not the continued expansion of slavery. If they made such a concession, their victory in the 1860 election (a mandate against the further expansion of slavery, in Republican eyes) would be meaningless. Without such a concession, however, the seceded states would not willingly rejoin the Union.

Lincoln summed up the impasse in his First Inaugural Address (March 4, 1861): "One section of our country believes slavery is right and ought to be extended, while the other believes it is wrong and ought not to be extended. This is the only substantial dispute." Lincoln professed, likely in all honesty at the time, "no purpose . . . to interfere with the institution of slavery in the States where it exists." He also accepted the Fugitive Slave Law, but he reasserted that secession was the immediate issue, not slavery's future: "I hold that in contemplation of universal law and of the Constitution the Union of these States is perpetual." The Constitution, Lincoln argued, did not contain a "provision . . . for its own termination." No state had the right to break with the Union on its own. "Secession," Lincoln's stated, was "the essence of anarchy." He thus pledged to hold on to the federal property, including Fort Sumter, to assure mail delivery, and to maintain the Union. "In doing this there needs to be no bloodshed or violence, and there shall be none unless it be forced upon the national authority."

Lincoln made two crucial rhetorical moves in this address. First, his portrayal of the conflict as one over the perpetuation of the Union rather than the future of slavery allowed him to push federal claims in a way that would not instantly alienate voters (and potential secessionists) in the Upper South and the Border States. He also gave

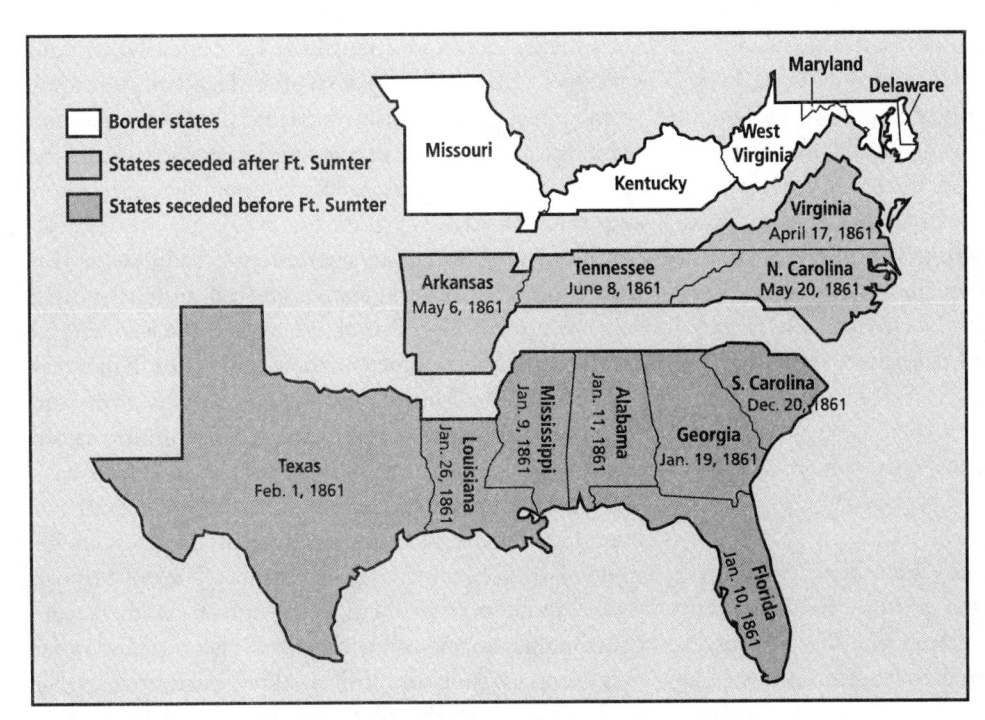

Map 16.1 Border States

assurances that the Union would not be the aggressor if violence broke out: "In your hands, my dissatisfied fellow-countrymen, and not in mine, is the momentous issue of civil war. The Government will not assail you. You can have no conflict without being yourselves the aggressors. You have no oath registered in heaven to destroy the Government, while I shall have the most solemn one to 'preserve, protect, and defend it.'"

Lincoln's words were immediately put to the test. Shortly after he delivered his address, the new president received word that Fort Sumter was running out of supplies. Control of this well-fortified outpost located in Charleston's harbor had been a point of contention ever since South Carolinians claimed they were leaving the Union. Buchanan refused to give it up, and the garrison's commander, Major Robert Anderson, had ratcheted up the tension when he moved his forces into the fort in December 1860. Before Lincoln took office, an effort in January 1861 to reinforce the garrison had failed. Confederate officials then indicated that further efforts would be considered an act of war. Lincoln's most obvious options were not desirable. He could send reinforcements, but that move would precipitate war and make the federal government appear to be the aggressor, despite assurances in his just-delivered inaugural address. He could also authorize the fort's surrender—an action that would certainly be read as a sign of weakness as well as a tacit admission of the legitimacy of secession. These alternatives put Lincoln in a box, and neither choice was desirable to him.

Lincoln demurred for a few weeks until he could find a preferred solution to his predicament. Eventually, he brilliantly opted to resupply the fort, but without reinforcements. He notified the governor of South Carolina of his intentions, assuring the official that only provisions, and not armed men, would be arriving on supply ships. This plan removed Lincoln from his bind while placing the ball squarely into the Confederacy's court. If the southern leadership allowed supplies to land, the action would be interpreted as an acknowledgement of federal control of the fort, not to mention allowing the federals to maintain possession of the fort for several months into the future. If they ordered an attack, the Confederacy would basically assume responsibility for starting the war. The Confederate national government, under pressure from the press and prominent secessionist politicians, opted for the latter course. After 33 hours of bombardment, Major Anderson surrendered Fort Sumter. The Civil War had begun.

PREPARATION AND PERSISTENCE: THE NORTH AND SOUTH IN THE CONTEXT OF A LONG WAR

Nothing about the outcome of the American Civil War was inevitable. Although the North won, emerging from the conflict as a major industrial world power while the South faced the end of slavery and decades of economic dislocation, the outcome was far from clear in April 1861. Hindsight allows observers to focus on particular features of the North and South and identify them as strengths or weaknesses explaining the Union victory or the Confederate defeat. None of these factors alone explained the way that the war transpired. Both the North and the South possessed an array of advantages and disadvantages that may have changed the course of the war had events broken in a slightly different way. Indeed, both sections possessed a set of strengths and weaknesses in terms of their economic development, populations, executive leadership, and diplomatic capabilities. In the short term, a great many of these factors benefited the South. As the war dragged on, however, the North's sizeable material advantages came into play to contribute greatly to the ultimate outcome.

Economic Development, Population, and the Accident of Geography

Economic productivity had increased significantly over the first half of the nineteenth century, fundamentally transforming many aspects of American life. These developments, of course, did not play out in a uniform way across the United States. By 1861, a host of economic changes had left the North better positioned for a prolonged military conflict. Economic historians have noted that the South, if considered as an independent country and measured on a per capita basis, actually ranked in the top ten of the world's nations in railroad construction, pig iron production, and textile manufacturing—placing the region on par with such industrializing contemporaries as France and Germany. Nevertheless, the South's manufacturing sector remained far less developed than the North's. Though approximately 110,000 people worked in southern factories, northern factories employed about 1.3 million people. On the eve of secession, workers in the North produced over 90 percent of the iron, textiles, and firearms produced in the U.S. Northern economic advantages did not end with manufacturing; the section also held three-quarters of the nation's farm acreage and around four-fifths of its wheat production. By war's end, these advantages allowed the Union to field some of the best equipped soldiers in the history of the world.

Despite being outproduced by their northern counterparts, southern manufacturers worked diligently to sustain the war effort. Virginia's secession gave the Confederacy control of the Tredegar Iron Works, one of the largest iron manufacturers in the country. Iron producers in states like Georgia and Alabama emerged as well. These companies, supported by the Confederate Ordinance Bureau under the leadership of a transplanted northerner, General Josiah Gorgas, ensured that Confederate soldiers remained adequately supplied with weapons and ammunition throughout the war. Other supplies, however, proved harder to access. Worn out (or non-existent) shoes and irregular uniforms were common among Confederate soldiers. Food also ran short for both civilians and soldiers. Plantation managers proved slow to shift away from cotton production to foodstuffs. Moving supplies from one part of the South to another, moreover, proved difficult, increasing the burden of sustaining the war effort over the long term.

None of these factors guaranteed certain victory for the Union. The North's greater industrial and agricultural capacity became a significant asset only as the war dragged on. In the earliest phases of the conflict, the Union experienced difficulties in distributing what its farms and factories produced. Consequently, the military relied upon private contractors who gouged the government on everything from railroad rates to firearms. Merchants and manufacturers fulfilled unprecedentedly large orders for military equipment by cutting corners. Cavalry troops took shipments of sick and dying horses. Soldiers were issued poorly-made uniforms, shoes, blankets, and other items (popularizing the term "shoddy" for cheap materials made with scraps) that wore out after a few weeks of use. Many months passed before Edwin M. Stanton, Lincoln's second Secretary of War, and the Union's quartermaster general, Montgomery Meigs, could master the logistical challenges involved in turning the North's productive potential into a definite military asset.

Another economic challenge faced by governments in both the North and the South centered on how to pay for the conflict. Citizens in both regions were adverse to taxes, and neither side possessed a national banking system. The response in both sections was to resort to printing paper money, a policy choice that threatened to foment ruinous inflation. The Union tempered this tendency by backing the value of its "**greenbacks**" with an income tax on certain salaries. The Confederacy never adequately dealt with the issue, and by the end of the war, its currency had become essentially worthless.

The Union also possessed an advantage in numbers. Around nine million people lived in the South (less than one-third of the total U.S. population in 1860). More than three million of those Southerners were slaves and thus ineligible for military service. The North, by contrast, had a population of twenty-two million people, and it would ultimately field an army of over two million soldiers, including 200,000 African Americans.

Sheer numbers, of course, did not ensure victory. Entire communities existing in the North, in fact, preferred (or even openly supported) the Confederacy, especially in the border states of Missouri and Kentucky. New soldiers also needed to be organized, trained, and led. As the Union mobilized, the number of raw recruits swelled from 186,000 to over 500,000. The regular army in 1861, however, had a force of only 13,000, and it was quickly

> ### A Brothers' War
>
> John and James Welsh were brothers, raised together in Virginia's beautiful Shenandoah Valley. In 1853, James, seeking more opportunities, moved to Illinois. There he became a Republican and supported Lincoln for president in 1860. When the southern states seceded after having fired on the American flag at Fort Sumter, James Welsh fired off a letter to his brother still in Virginia, declaring that, "Jeff Davis and his crew of pirates," were guilty of "treason and nothing more or less." John responded that he was "very much pained to find . . . that I have a brother who would advocate sending men here to butcher his own friends and relations." He also announced, "I don't intend to submit to black Republican rule." John angrily informed his brother that becoming a Republican meant renouncing, "home, mother, father and brothers . . . to sacrifice all for the dear nigger." James replied with equal venom that he never imagined a brother of his could "raise a hand to tear down the glorious Stars and Stripes, a flag that we have been taught from our cradle to look on with pride." He concluded by proclaiming, "I would strike down my own brother if he dared to raise a hand to destroy that flag. We have to rise in our might as a free and independent nation and demand that law must and shall be respected or we shall find ourselves wiped from the face of the earth . . . and the principles of free government will be dashed to the ground forever."
>
> James and John Welsh never communicated with each other again. John volunteered for the Confederate army. He served with the 27th Virginia and was killed at Gettysburg. James marched in Sherman's campaign through Georgia as a member of the 78th Illinois. He survived. The Civil War has often been called a "Brother's War." In this case and many others, that was literally true. In a deeper sense, it was symbolically true as the now dysfunctional family of the Union had become, as Lincoln had suggested, a "house divided."

overwhelmed. A lack of experienced, capable officers severely plagued the North. The development of an officer corps that could decisively defeat the Confederate military—particularly in the politically essential eastern theater—took years of bloody trial and error. Even with training and effective leadership, the North's larger population did not translate into overwhelming numbers on the battlefield, since some troops needed to be deployed in the Far West to manage tensions with Native Americans and significant numbers of soldiers were needed to garrison areas under Union control. The Union's sizeable population, however, did allow the Union army to fulfill those tasks while consistently outnumbering Confederate forces on the battlefield by about a third (a significant but not overwhelming advantage).

As with its manufacturing capacity, the South utilized its limited manpower resources effectively. By the end of the war, the Confederacy fielded 900,000 soldiers, a number that included nearly all of the men eligible for military service (about half of the North's eligible men served in its armies). The South's forces also enjoyed the advantage of excellent military leadership. A majority of the U.S. Army's most talented and experienced officers during the antebellum period happened to be Southerners. When their states joined the Confederacy, most resigned their commissions to command Confederate forces. Some of these commanders became legendary. Robert E. Lee, who eventually led the main Confederate army based in the politically critical Virginia region, would batter larger Union forces so soundly and repeatedly that many of his northern counterparts believed him to be unbeatable. General **Thomas "Stonewall" Jackson**, one of Lee's subordinates, became known for his bravery and his ability to outmaneuver larger enemy forces. Because of their previous military service, these men were well placed to move into critical leadership positions early in the war. By contrast, Ulysses S. Grant, the Union general who would ultimately defeat Lee and secure the North's victory, was not even in the army when the war began. Along with other emerging officers who helped him win the war, Grant had to work his way through the ranks before being given an important field command.

Another advantage that the Confederacy possessed came from its geography. The South comprised 750,000 square miles of territory including the Appalachian Mountains and immense woodlands. Preventing Confederate secession meant invading and conquering this territory, a strategy that also threatened to stoke Confederate morale since soldiers would be fighting in their home territory. Moving through the South also proved to be a challenge. Although the amount of railroad construction measured on a per capita basis was second only to the North (who led the world in this area), the South's 9,000 miles of rail proved to be woefully underdeveloped compared to the North. While the North had built an extensive network consisting of 22,000 miles of railway that interconnected most of the region, southern rails basically ran from cotton planting districts to coastal and interior ports. Its rail system had not been designed to move people and products from one part of the South to another. This situation inhibited the distribution of food within the South, but it also complicated the movement of invading armies who found the rails to be of limited usefulness. Travel along roads likewise proved difficult, especially in wet weather that quickly transformed dirt roads into mud pits that bogged down soldiers on the march. Both the roads and railroads remained vulnerable to guerrilla attack throughout the conflict. The difficulties involved in invading the South provided Confederate forces with the advantage of merely holding out until the North's leadership (or populace) concluded that conquering the South was not worth the trouble. That strategy, however, ran counter to the notion of a short war.

Executive Leadership, North and South

Presidential leadership shaped the war effort in crucial ways for both sides. At first glance, the Confederacy appeared to have the man best suited to the occasion. Mississippi's **Jefferson Davis**, the first (and only) president of the new government, brought a great deal of experience to his post. A successful cotton planter, Davis had served a brief stint in the House of Representatives, two terms in the Senate, and as Secretary of War under President Franklin Pierce. He also possessed military experience, having graduated from West Point and serving briefly under his future father-in-law, Zachary Taylor, near the end of the Black Hawk War. Although he left the army to become a planter, Davis later gave up his House seat to serve in the Mexican War. Attaining rank of colonel, he commanded troops during the siege of Monterrey and the Battle of Buena Vista, where he received a bullet wound to the foot. Davis later turned down a promotion to brigadier general, returned to civilian life and resumed his political career. **Abraham Lincoln**, in contrast, came into office with little political or military background. He served briefly in the army during the Black Hawk War but claimed no special knowledge from the experience. Unlike Davis, Lincoln had failed to translate his professional success—as a lawyer—into political office. He served only a single term in the House of Representatives during the late 1840s and was an outspoken opponent of the war with Mexico.

Once in the White House, however, Lincoln proved himself to be flexible, patient, and a tenacious leader. Partisan politics—except perhaps for a brief moment following the attack on Fort Sumter—continued unabated throughout the war years, and Lincoln faced a constant barrage of criticism from both enemies and allies. Democrats, despite the secession of the region that had provided the party's dominant wing in the 1850s, remained a political force, and the party offered consistent opposition to Lincoln and the Republicans. Even so, secession and war left the party internally divided. Moderate Democrats opposed secession and supported the war, even as they bitterly second-guessed nearly every aspect of the manner in which Lincoln handled the conflict. A smaller faction of largely border-state Democrats, the so-called "**Copperheads**," loudly opposed the war. Although they were not generally disloyal, Copperheads pushed for a negotiated settlement and would willingly accept an independent southern republic. For the most part, Lincoln regarded such opposition as legitimate and never moved to suspend elections or to restrain speech or actions that were not openly disloyal. Although he showed little tolerance for disloyalty, Lincoln usually just endured the charges that he was an "ape" or a "tyrant," pressing forward to achieve his goals.

Republicans did not refrain from criticism of the president even though he came from their ranks. Like the Democrats, Republicans split over the best way to conduct the war. One faction, the **Radical Republicans** led by Senator Charles Sumner of Massachusetts and Representative Thaddeus Stevens of Pennsylvania, demanded that the war result in both emancipation and the establishment of racial equality. Moderate Republicans, on the other hand, were willing to stop well short of those goals. Some of them questioned whether emancipation was a legitimate war aim. Lincoln thus had to maneuver among these factions along with opposition Democrats and a rebellious South.

Lincoln's capacity to lead an often divided North emerged early in his presidency as he worked with a cabinet that contained members with deep connections to both major factions within the Republican Party. Salmon Chase, Secretary of the Treasury, was an Ohio politician who spoke for the Radicals and repeatedly pressed the president to move quickly toward ending slavery. Secretary of State William Seward of New York, although outspoken in his opposition to the peculiar institution, represented moderate Republicans who urged the president to move cautiously, if at all, toward emancipation. Both Chase and Seward possessed far more political experience than Lincoln; they had both been senators and state governors. Most of their colleagues in the cabinet could boast more experience than the new president. Seward, in fact, planned to be the real power within the administration and thought he could reduce the inexperienced Lincoln to a figurehead. Immediately upon taking office, Seward began working toward a settlement of the secession crisis and even promised his southern contacts that Lincoln would abandon Fort Sumter. As his intrigues fell apart, he proposed that Lincoln start a conflict with Mexico as a way to reunify the country around a foreign

Lincoln's cabinet including (left to right) Postmaster General Montgomery Blair, Secretary of the Interior Caleb B. Smith, Secretary of the Treasury Salmon P. Chase, President Lincoln, Secretary of State William H. Seward, Secretary of War Simon Cameron, Attorney General Edward Bates, and Secretary of the Navy Gideon Welles. 1861.

enemy. Lincoln declined but did so in a way that allowed Seward to save face while definitely affirming that he, as president, would be the one making the major policy decisions. Seward soon became one of the president's most loyal supporters, and Lincoln became without question the dominant figure in his administration. He also proved willing to replace appointed officials whose performance inhibited the war effort. Lincoln removed his first Secretary of War, Simon Cameron, who had been awarding military contracts mainly as a way to enrich himself rather than to properly supply the army. Cameron's replacement, Edwin M. Stanton, cleaned up the department. Freely intervening in matters of military strategy, the president also regularly removed unsuccessful generals, even when he liked them personally or when they were popular with the public.

Lincoln's ability to make the decisions that he thought were right and then endure whatever criticism followed came paired with a keen sense of political timing. He worked by making a series of small decisions that tended to open the way for bigger ones. Lincoln's handling of the Fort Sumter crisis, for example, allowed the president to portray the South as an aggressor, thus enabling him to call for state troops to put down the rebellion. He would move toward emancipation in the same way. Such a combination of skills, along with the genuine emergency presented by the war, helped Lincoln to become the most powerful and innovative president of the nineteenth century.

Jefferson Davis, by contrast, seemed more ill-suited for his office as the war dragged on. He intervened in military strategy, as did Lincoln, but his choices tended to be ineffective or worse. Playing favorites with his generals and fighting with his subordinates, Davis's pride would not permit him to let insults pass, and he had little patience for those he disliked. The Confederate Cabinet, which for political reasons included neither opponents of secession nor its most outspoken advocates, proved weak relative to Lincoln's. Limited by the Constitution to a single, six-year term, Davis had little practical incentive to build alliances, leaving him politically isolated over time.

Davis also proved reluctant to delegate authority, and his government consequently gave little attention to the challenges that emerged on the home front as the South's social order unraveled. The decentralized nature of the Confederacy compounded his difficulties. Southern governors regularly invoked states' rights doctrine to oppose such Confederate national policies as conscription.

The Confederate Cabinet including President Jefferson Davis, Vice President Alexander Hamilton Stephens, Attorney General Judah P. Benjamin, Secretary of the Navy Stephen M. Mallory, Secretary of the Treasury C.S Memminger, Secretary of War Leroy Pope Walker, Postmaster John H. Reagan, and Secretary of State Robert Toombs. 1861.

Despite his long list of pre-war accomplishments, the struggle ultimately overwhelmed Davis. The advantage of national leadership thus went to the Union, but like the other factors thus far discussed, Lincoln's ability was by no means the sole factor in bring about the North's victory.

Diplomacy During the Civil War

A key to victory for both sides lay in international diplomacy. Confederate leaders correctly viewed diplomatic recognition by Great Britain, France, and other European powers as an important step toward establishing their new republic. Insisting that the Civil War was a strictly domestic affair, Lincoln and Seward worked laboriously to keep these European nations neutral. As with most other important factors dealing with the war effort, the North and the South in the diplomatic realm possessed both advantages and disadvantages. The northern electorate's relative discomfort with slavery tended to be more in line with European public sentiment, which had long turned against the institution. But European governments in the 1860s were largely monarchies, thus public opinion had limited impact. A number of Lincoln's tactics, such as blockading southern ports, raised questions as to whether the conflict was merely a domestic affair. Any distaste toward slavery, moreover, had to be weighed against the fact that the South possessed a valuable commodity—cotton. Control of that vital resource gave the Confederacy a great deal of potential leverage in international diplomacy.

Confederate leaders placed high hopes in cotton. "You dare not to make war on cotton," Senator James Henry Hammond of South Carolina told his northern colleagues a few years before secession. "Cotton is king." What he meant was that factory systems in the North and in Europe were so dependent on the South's staple that they could not afford to isolate themselves. A war on cotton threatened economic depression abroad, leading to closed shops and protests from angry displaced workers. Hammond and other southern leaders had a point. Southern cotton accounted for more than half of U.S. exports in 1860. Those exports provided nearly all of the cotton used by factories in France and Russia and three-quarters of the fiber consumed in Great Britain.

As the war began, the Confederate government implemented **"King Cotton Diplomacy"** in an effort to pressure European powers for recognition. Although southern leaders acted reasonably given their region's power in the world cotton market, the strategy backfired as it ran afoul of a number of unintended consequences. First, the South experienced a few bumper crops during the 1850s. European textile manufacturers—who were quite aware of the potential for instability in the U.S.—had thus built up stockpiles that provided a cushion from the shock. Second, the factory owners searched for and cultivated replacement sources of cotton (an understandable reaction given the drop in southern exports of the staple from nearly four million bales in 1860 to almost nothing in 1862). By the war's end, a defeated South would reenter the world cotton market, not as a dominant producer but as one major player among several others including Egypt and India.

Although the limits of cotton as a diplomatic tool had become clear by mid-war, northern military and diplomatic strategy prevented the Confederacy from correcting itself. The Union's key tool lay in its blockade. One of the early military strategies considered by the Lincoln administration was the **"Anaconda Plan"** proposed by venerable General Winfield Scott. The strategy called for the Union to blockade southern ports while simultaneously advancing down the Mississippi River—a process that would slowly squeeze the South into submission. The plan was ultimately rejected in favor of a more aggressive approach, but the blockade became a major feature of the war effort. The Union ultimately built enough ships to effectively limit trade along the southern coast, with the exception of several successful swift craft known as "blockade runners." When Confederate leaders decided to bring cotton back to market, the blockade largely stopped them (except for a few hundred thousand bales exported through Texas to ports in northern Mexico). It continued to deprive the South of sorely needed imports.

General Winfield Scott

Map 16.2 The Anaconda Plan

The Union blockade, however, posed a diplomatic problem. According to international law, the tactic constituted an act of war among countries. Lincoln, meanwhile, continued to assert that the federal government was not engaged in a formal war because such a declaration would amount to tacit recognition that the South was an independent nation. He insisted that his government was putting down a domestic rebellion. If that were the case, however, a blockade was not a legal tactic, and foreign powers need not respect it. Nevertheless, the British government overcame internal divisions among its high officials and ultimately decided to adhere to the blockade's provisions anyway, remaining neutral throughout the conflict. Again, this was not an inevitable turn of events. Relations between the U.S. and Great Britain became quite tense in late 1861 when a U.S. Navy frigate stopped a British mail packet vessel, the *Trent*, off the northern coast of Cuba, removing two Confederate diplomats in violation of international law. Though a few politicians on both sides of the Atlantic talked seriously about the potential for war, cooler heads prevailed, and Lincoln eventually ordered the release of the Confederate emissaries. In these dealings, the president's ambassador to the United Kingdom, **Charles Francis Adams** (the son of a president and grandson of another) proved to be a great asset, working effectively with the aristocratic members of England's foreign policy establishment. Though Lincoln succeeded in securing European neutrality, the true key to stopping the southern independence movement lay in producing clear-cut victories on the battlefield, yet significant Union military successes were rare during the first year of the conflict.

A sketch of a group of Zouaves, April 17, 1862.

The War Begins in Earnest

The Confederate firing upon Fort Sumter created a public clamor for war in both the North and the South. Both sides expected the conflict to be short-lived. Lincoln responded to the fort's surrender by calling up 75,000 troops for ninety days of service, although later calls would demand more soldiers and longer terms of service (usually three years). Volunteers poured forth from all around the North, and distinctive regiments formed in communities throughout the region. Wealthy New Yorkers organized, as did Irish and German immigrants, and Ohio farmers. These new soldiers brought with them essentially no military experience and a wide array of uniforms—ranging from blue, to gray, to red, to multi-colored "Zouave" stylings that copied outfits worn by famed units in the French military. Organizing and equipping these troops—numbering 700,000 by 1862—with standardized gear took time. Meanwhile, volunteers also poured into the Confederate ranks. By Lincoln's first call, the South had already mobilized 60,000 men, and the Confederate Congress had authorized a total force of 100,000. Like their Yankee counterparts, Confederate armies also required organization and equipment—a process that produced inevitable delays. Meanwhile, the northern and southern publics both clamored for the one big battle that would force the other side to capitulate. That did not happen. Within a year, the Union and Confederacy would find themselves locked in a struggle with no end in sight. Although the Union won numerous strategically important battles in the West and at sea, its forces failed—at times spectacularly—in the politically important Eastern Theater centered in the area between Washington, D.C. and the Confederate capital of Richmond, Virginia.

The First Battle of Bull Run (Manassas)

As the Union army prepared for battle, Lincoln debated his strategic options. Despite persistent calls from the northern press to move quickly and capture Richmond, supposedly to swiftly bring the conflict to an abrupt end, most military commanders and political leaders remained skeptical that the war would be short. General Scott's Anaconda Plan, for example, was designed to take time—the ultimate goal being to isolate the South, cut its economic ties to the rest of the world, and then wait for secessionist leaders to lose their legitimacy. Such a policy, Scott argued, would minimize wartime deaths and limit destruction while perhaps paving the way for a smooth reconciliation. Editors denounced this plan as too timid and demanded immediate action. Concerned that the terms of some of the initial recruits were about to expire, Lincoln proved sensitive to these demands and

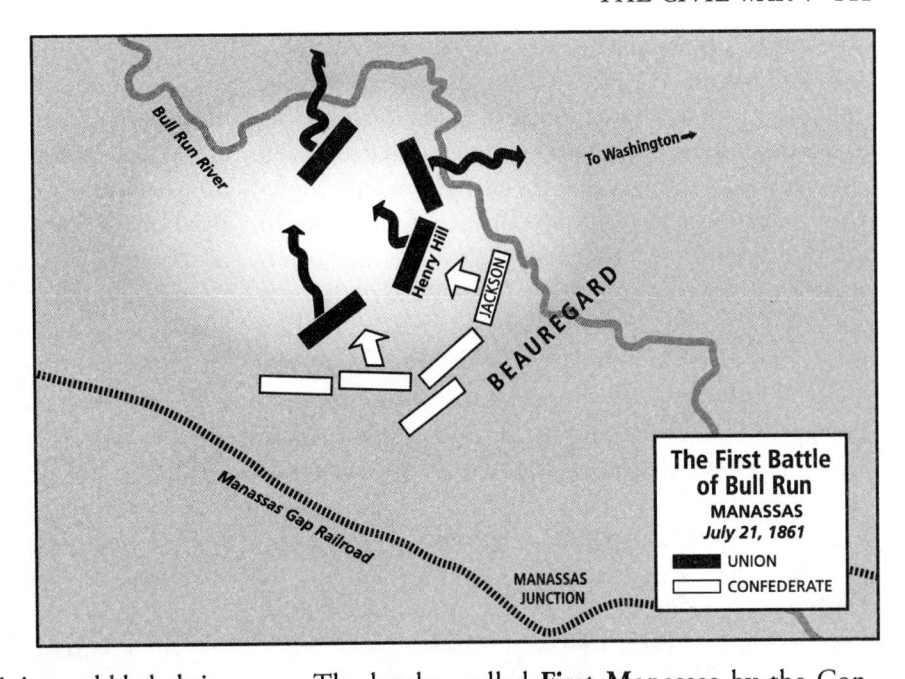

Map 16.3 The First Battle of Bull Run

hoped that an early victory in Virginia would help bring a rapid end to the war. Thus, he ordered General Irvin McDowell, commander of the 35,000 troops stationed in the Washington, D.C. area, to attack amassing Confederate forces assembling in northern Virginia.

McDowell, a career staff officer with no experience commanding troops in combat, decided to attack the 20,000 Confederate troops defending Manassas Junction (a railroad intersection located 25 miles southwest from the national capital). His objective was to force rebel troops to withdraw deeper into Virginia, thus making Washington less vulnerable to attack. The general's battle plan seemed sound in theory, but its execution required experienced troops and officers. When McDowell told Lincoln that his forces were not ready, the president responded by reminding him that both sides were "all green alike." He thus pressed forward with 30,000 men, although delayed supply wagons, a continuous need to organize newly-arrived troops, and his soldiers' lack of familiarity with marching slowed his advance. By the time Union troops arrived at Manassas Junction, the Confederate commanding officer, General **P.T.G. Beauregard**, was prepared to meet the attack. McDowell's slow march, combined with intelligence provided by the South's spies in Washington, had provided plenty of advanced notice. Beauregard reinforced the positions that he anticipated McDowell planned to attack and summoned General Joseph E. Johnston to bring his force of 11,000 soldiers from Harpers Ferry to reinforce him. McDowell took Beauregard's new positioning in stride and revised his plan accordingly. In anticipation of Johnston's movements, he ordered General Robert H. Patterson to tie down Johnston's forces. Patterson, however, failed in his mission, and Johnston's troops soon joined the fight.

The battle—called **First Manassas** by the Confederacy (who tended to name battles after the nearest settlement) or **First Bull Run** by the Union (who often named battles after the nearest body of water)—took place on July 21, 1861 when McDowell sent 10,000 troops against a weak point in the Confederate lines. Although enemy fire and their own officers' inexperience slowed their advance and hampered their coordination, Union troops initially drove the Confederates from their positions, forcing them into retreat. Then, the battle turned against them as Colonel (soon to be General) Thomas J. "Stonewall" Jackson earned his nickname by rallying his troops and stopping the Union advance. Both sides spent the afternoon slugging it out until Beauregard gained access to Johnston's troops and ordered a counterattack. Advancing with a vicious scream—the famous "rebel yell"—that terrified McDowell's men, the Confederates pushed the exhausted Union forces back. Their retreat quickly turned into a panicked flight as many soldiers dropped everything they carried, even fleeing through crowds of spectators who had come from Washington to watch the battle (one northern congressman in the chaotic scene was actually captured by advancing Confederate troopers). The First Battle of Bull Run thus ended in a humiliating Union defeat.

The battle produced a number of important consequences. In theory, the South's victory opened the way for a Confederate advance toward Washington, which, if attempted, might have ended the war more quickly in the South's favor. In July 1861, however, both Johnston and Beauregard believed that their forces were in no condition for an immediate follow-up on their victory. Their troops were disorganized and out of supplies, rainy weather made travel difficult, and McDowell immediately began positioning fresh troops between Manassas and Washington. The Confederate triumph did succeed in slowing Union efforts to invade Virginia, bolstering southern confidence and instilling a deep-seated suspicion among Union soldiers that perhaps the Confederates were simply superior warriors. In the North, although the defeat proved jarring, Lincoln and his supporters responded with renewed resolve. Immediately following the battle, Lincoln placed **General George B. McClellan** in command of federal troops in Washington. Over the next few days, the president signed bills authorizing the enlistment of a million men for three-year terms. What proved to be an agonizingly long war had just begun.

McClellan Takes Command

Lincoln's promotion of George McClellan, who would soon demonstrate himself to be a lackluster commander on the battlefield, made much sense in mid-1861. Born in Pennsylvania and educated at West Point (where he graduated second in his class), McClellan had enjoyed successful military and civilian careers by the time he rejoined the United States Army. He served as an engineering officer during the Mexican War, taking from the experience a deep appreciation of flanking maneuvers and siege tactics. McClellan also admired General Scott's efforts to avoid alienating civilian populations and the strict enforcement of discipline among his troops. Following the war, he taught at West Point and undertook various observation missions in Europe. McClellan left the service in 1857 to work as the president of two railroad companies—a job that gave him a great deal of logistical experience. His list of accomplishments gave McClellan a considerable amount of confidence. "I can do it all," he told Lincoln when the president expressed concerns about the general's increasing workload.

That quip would become a glaring overstatement, but Lincoln's new general did succeed in completely reorganizing the main federal army. McClellan combined the forces that had been under McDowell's command with a number of troops in Virginia to form the Army of the Potomac. Retraining his soldiers from scratch, he drilled his men constantly and reviewed their progress regularly, a process that built up morale. The general enforced discipline, coming down hard against drunkenness and absences without leave. McClellan fortified the capital behind a network of fortifications protected by heavy artillery. As press reports lauded his changes, he reveled in his newfound prestige, telling his wife in a letter that he was so esteemed that he could be named dictator if he wished.

Beyond his ego, McClellan had one major failing: he almost never believed his force was ready to face the enemy. The general's concern brought a regular series of delays and quickly generated tensions with Lincoln and other military commanders. (Lincoln commented once that he believed McClellan suffered from a "perpetual case of the slows.") The general and Winfield Scott quickly became embroiled in an argument over whether to follow the Anaconda Plan or McClellan's idea to build an invasion force of greater than a quarter-million men to crush the South in one massive campaign. McClellan won the dispute; Scott resigned, and by November 1861, McClellan was general-in-chief of the Union's armies. McClellan's relationship with Lincoln became very tense. The general, politically a Democrat, held the president in low regard, casually describing him as a "baboon" and "gorilla" in letters to his wife. Once when Lincoln came to see him at his residence, McClellan decided to go to bed rather than meet his commander-in-chief. In response to what he regarded as McClellan's foot dragging, Lincoln drew up his own plans to attack Virginia and ordered offensive operations to begin in February 1862. McClellan countered with a long critique and finally presented his own plans—the first he had ever submitted in writing. Lincoln deferred to his general because at least he had received a commitment to attack. Even so, McClellan would not begin moving until mid-March 1862, and he did so with his characteristic caution.

The War in the West

Although McClellan's Army of the Potomac made little headway in the East, which, because it contained both capitals, was the most politically important theater of the war, Union forces had considerable success in the strategically critical Western Theater. There, armies fought for control of the continent's major rivers, which provided access to numerous potential targets. Union control of the Mississippi River especially would effectively split the Confederacy in two. In addition to producing a few early victories, the West became the proving grounds that groomed the Union commanders who would ultimately win the war, especially **Ulysses S. Grant**. Like McClellan, Grant had been an officer in the regular army who had returned to civilian life. Yet his career—whether military or civilian—had not been nearly as impressive. Grant graduated in the middle of his class at West Point. He served as a quartermaster during the Mexican War, earning recognition for bravery and skilled horsemanship delivering dispatches under fire. After the war, he attained the rank of captain and assigned to a remote northern California post when rumors of heavy drinking forced his

Lincoln visited McClellan to urge the general to take action.

resignation. Grant then spent most of the 1850s failing at a variety of civilian jobs. Working in a relative's tannery when the war began, he promptly volunteered, taking an assignment training new soldiers while lobbying for a field command. Grant ultimately received one, attaining the rank of colonel and, along with other commanders such as **William Tecumseh Sherman** and Phillip Sheridan, developed the aggressive tactics that would secure Union victory.

Although Grant achieved some minor victories by the end of 1861, his successes in early 1862 elevated his reputation as an outstanding offensive commander. In February 1862, Grant coordinated his force with naval gunboats and captured Fort Henry, a Confederate outpost that controlled access to the Tennessee River (mastery of this waterway cut off Memphis, Tennessee from the rest of the state and opened a route into northern Alabama). About a week later, Grant's forces surrounded nearby Fort Donelson, which protected the Cumberland River and provided direct access to the farms and vital manufacturing centers near Nashville, Tennessee. With these triumphs, Grant secured his reputation as an aggressive field officer. When Fort Donelson's commander asked for surrender terms, Grant offered none, "except uncondi-

tional and immediate surrender." The strategy paid off, as the force of about fifteen thousand capitulated. Grant received a promotion to major general, and the press joked that the "U.S." in his initials stood for "unconditional surrender."

Grant's next major battle demonstrated the new general's ability to recover from setbacks and to drive his men to ultimate victory in the face of horrific conditions. Having secured control of two important waterways, Grant moved his army, now numbering nearly 50,000 men organized into six divisions, southward down the Tennessee River. His goal was to secure control of the railways running through western Tennessee. By the beginning of April, Grant's men had set up camp next to **Shiloh** Church, a small establishment in southern Tennessee near the borders of Alabama and Mississippi. Grant left the position largely unfortified and focused on drilling his soldiers. (He had a reputation for focusing more on what he planned to do rather than what the enemy intended to do against him.) Consequently, the Confederate Army of Mississippi, under the command of General Albert Sidney Johnston, took the Union troops by surprise on the morning of April 6, 1862. The Confederate attacking force turned out to be somewhat

The General's Wife

One of the men leading the fight at Shiloh was 40-year-old Brigadier General William H. L. Wallace, the newly appointed head of the Second Division of the Union army. He wrote to his wife that he had been ill and prayed for the "strength and wisdom to enable me to do my whole duty toward the country in this her hour of peril." He also described his longing to see her and his family once again and his hope that the war would end. His wife, Ann, twelve years his junior, was so moved by his letters that she decided to go south from Illinois to visit him, despite warnings that she would not be allowed through.

She had known her husband since she was a child when, as a young lawyer, he visited her father, a very successful attorney. He had taken a lively interest in the bright little girl, suggesting books to read, watching her play, and chatting with her. When he returned from service in the Mexican War, he discovered that she had become a delightful young woman of fifteen. He announced his love to her and asked her to marry him when she was sixteen. They wed shortly after her eighteenth birthday. After so many years, it seemed to her that he should not face illness and danger alone. "It seems wrong to enjoy every comfort of a good home and you sick in a tent." She wrote him. "Is it indeed my duty to stay so far back and wait so anxiously?"

She arrived by steamboat on April 6, 1862. As she prepared to walk to her husband's headquarters, a captain suggested that he should go there first to see how great a distance it was. She could hear the increasingly loud sounds of firing. When the captain returned, he told her that the battle had begun, and she would not be able to see her husband until it ended. So she waited anxiously on the steamboat. Later that night, a friend from her home in Illinois came to see her. "It is an awful battle," he kept repeating. Finally, he revealed that her husband had been hit by enemy fire. Grief-stricken, she could not sleep and spent the night helping to take care of the many wounded she found all around her.

Her spirits revived the following morning when the news came that her "Will" had been found still alive. Despite a horrible wound on his head, she was able to squeeze his hand and detected a glimmer of recognition. She stayed by his side as he was sent to a hospital where, at first, his condition seemed to improve. Then he began to fail and, three days later, he died. Ann later wrote that she was grateful that at least he didn't die by himself on the battlefield and that she could spend his last few days with him.

disorganized—because Johnston and one of his major subordinates, General P.T.G. Beauregard, had not coordinated their battle plans—but they mounted a punishing assault nonetheless, leading some new Union recruits to retreat. Other units faced nearly complete destruction. Grant and his subordinates had not expected any attack that day. Still recovering from a fall off his horse, Grant did not reach the front until a few hours after the fighting began. General Sherman, however, stepped into the fray and appeared all along the front to rally his troops. Even so, by the end of the day, the Union army was forced to fall back two miles from its original position. Grant remained undeterred. When Sherman remarked that they had had "the devil's own day," the general simply replied, "Yes. Lick 'em tomorrow."

And he did. During the previous day's fighting, Albert Sidney Johnston had been killed, depriving the South of one of its best generals. Fresh Union troops arrived as well, giving them a numerical advantage not immediately apparent to southern commanders like Beauregard. By the days end, the Union army had forced its enemy to withdraw from the field. The battle proved costly in terms of human life. With nearly 25 percent of the combatants for each side either killed or wounded, the Battle of Shiloh produced more American casualties than the total number lost in combat during the American Revolution, the War of 1812, and the Mexican War combined. The battle convinced Grant that defeating the Confederacy would be a long and bloody task. His performance at the beginning of the battle, combined with the unprecedented number of casualties, raised questions about his abilities as a commander. Lincoln, however, rejected calls for his removal—"I can't spare this man; he fights." Grant followed his victory at Shiloh by capturing the railroad junction at Corinth, Mississippi before moving against Vicksburg, Mississippi, which by the end of 1862 became the last Confederate defensive position along the Mississippi River.

The War at Sea

The Union commanders in the Western Theater were not the only ones to secure major gains for the North. Union naval commanders quickly made headway against the Confederates along the coasts and the high seas. The Union Navy, in fact, dominated conflicts at sea, despite impressive efforts on the part of the Confederacy to break its power.

The *Monitor* and the *Merrimack*

The *Virginia*, originally the warship *Merrimack*, was scuttled when the Union abandoned the Norfolk naval yards.

As the Union worked to tighten its blockade, Flag Officer **David Farragut**, a Virginian who opposed secession and kept his post in the U.S. Navy, sailed his fleet into New Orleans and captured the city in April 1862. (A move that left Vicksburg isolated.) Congress responded by elevating him to the newly created rank of admiral.

Because the Confederacy began the war with no navy and did not have the shipbuilding capacity to match the Union, Southerners concentrated on building a few highly powerful vessels. Most notably, they bolted iron plating onto the wooden hull of the *Merrimack*—a scuttled U.S. Navy frigate—to construct the world's first "ironclad." Outfitted with concealed cannons and a battering ram, Confederates hoped that the modified vessel, renamed the *C.S.S. Virginia*, could sink wooden blockade ships with impunity as cannon balls harmlessly bounced off its reinforced metal frame. The *Virginia* performed as planned on March 8, 1862, when it emerged unscathed after destroying two Union frigates and running another aground in Hampton Roads at the mouth of the James River. The U.S. Navy, however, had already developed its own ironclad, the *U.S.S. Monitor*, which arrived in the Hampton Roads area the next day. The two ships then fought each other to a standstill, leaving both crews deafened from the sound of cannonballs striking their ships' iron plating. Although the battle ended inconclusively, the North had negated the *Virginia's* impact and soon built another fifty ironclads. (Confederates scuttled the *Virginia* in mid-May when the Union regained control of its base in Norfolk, Virginia.) During the war, Southerners also experimented with prototypes for torpedoes and submarines. They also contracted with the British shipbuilders John Laird Sons and Company to construct specialized ramming vessels ("Laird Rams") to destroy Union blockaders and to build swift "commerce raiders" (most famously the **C.S.S. Alabama**) to harass northern merchant ships. Union diplomats finally convinced the British government to put a stop to this practice by 1863, and the U.S. Navy remained the dominant force on the water.

McClellan and the Peninsular Campaign

While commanders at sea and in the West pushed forward, George McClellan continued dragging his feet. The general had reorganized, resupplied, and trained a powerful army which did not move. Lincoln pressed him, at one point even relieving him from post as general-in-chief so he could concentrate on what the president hoped would

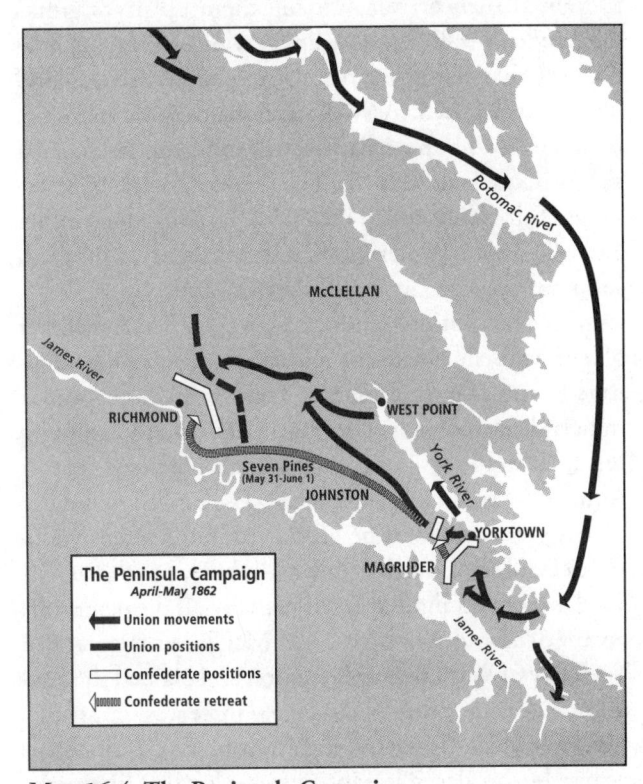

Map 16.4 The Peninsula Campaign

be a frontal assault on Richmond. McClellan, however, opted for an indirect, less heavily defended route. In March 1862, he moved the Army of the Potomac by water from Washington, D.C. to the Virginia peninsula flanked by the York River, the Chesapeake Bay, and the James River. From this staging area, he planned to move westward against Richmond, but the logistics involved produced delays. Moving his force and its equipment required four hundred ships and took several weeks. Meanwhile, McClellan continued to exercise excessive caution. By early April, McClellan had 100,000 men in position facing only 17,000 Confederates on the peninsula after most its defenders withdrew to protect Richmond. Rather than overwhelming the rebels, McClellan ordered a siege. He had been duped by the Confederate commander, John Magruder, who deceptively marched his small force back and forth, deployed fake cannons, and spread false rumors to create the illusion that he commanded far more soldiers than he actually possessed. Lincoln pressed McClellan to attack, but the general waited until his artillery was fully in place. When finally ready to attack, McClellan learned that Magruder's troops had completely withdrawn from the peninsula.

The Army of the Potomac then slowly moved toward Richmond, but upon arrival at his destination McClellan believed his men were outnumbered and thus refused to attack Confederate forces under the command of General Joseph E. Johnston. McClellan called for reinforcements, but General Thomas "Stonewall" Jackson prevented their arrival by tying them up in Virginia's Shenandoah Valley following a series of dizzying maneuvers that left the larger Union force divided and ultimately defeated. As McClellan maneuvered his forces in an effort to besiege Richmond, Johnston launched a surprise attack on May 27. The resulting Battle of Seven Pines (Fair Oaks) ended inconclusively, but the conflict left McClellan shaken and Johnston badly wounded, soon replaced by General **Robert E. Lee**.

Lee's promotion transformed the conflict. A member of Virginia's elite related by marriage to George Washington's family, Lee would soon become one of the greatest military leaders of his generation. McClellan thought him unsuited to the task of command and predicted that he would be a timid leader. Instead, Lee proved willing to accept great risks, and he quickly took the offensive. In the **Seven Days' Battle** (June 25–July 1), Lee drove McClellan from Richmond and eventually off the peninsula. As the Union general fell back, McClellan telegraphed Secretary of War Edwin M. Stanton and blamed the government for his defeat "because my force was too small." He also stated: "You have done your best to sacrifice this army," but an alert telegraph operator left that line out of his message. In August 1862, a frustrated Lincoln ordered McClellan to withdraw from a defensive position on the peninsula and return to Washington. He then reduced the size of McClellan's command by transferring three corps from his army to General John Pope's Army of Virginia.

Stalemate

Although he had been successful in the Western Theater, Pope—a career officer from Kentucky—proved to be no match for Lee and his force, the Army of Northern Virginia. Pope's troops operated in the Shenandoah Valley, charged with protecting the capital and relieving pressure on McClellan while he remained on the peninsula. Thus, in August 1862, Lee faced two large Union forces: the withdrawing Army of the Potomac, which lay to the east of Richmond, and Pope's Army of Virginia situated to the north. Lee decided to strike before the two units could link up. With McClellan tamed, the Confederate general went after Pope, who Lee believed to be indecisive. Lee split his force, ordering "Stonewall" Jackson to flank Pope's army from behind, a feat that Jackson performed well. His troops captured a major Union supply depot at Manassas Junction, which drew Pope's full attention. The Union commander committed the majority of forces to an attack on Jackson, but as he did so, Lee slammed his army into one of Pope's relatively unprotected flanks. The ensuing battle, **Second Bull Run** (or Manassas)

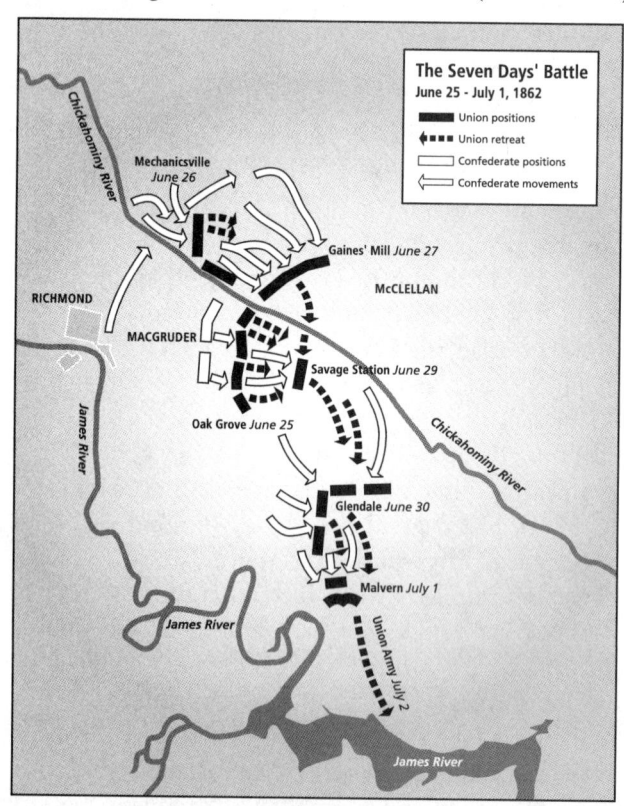

Map 16.5 The Seven Days' Battle

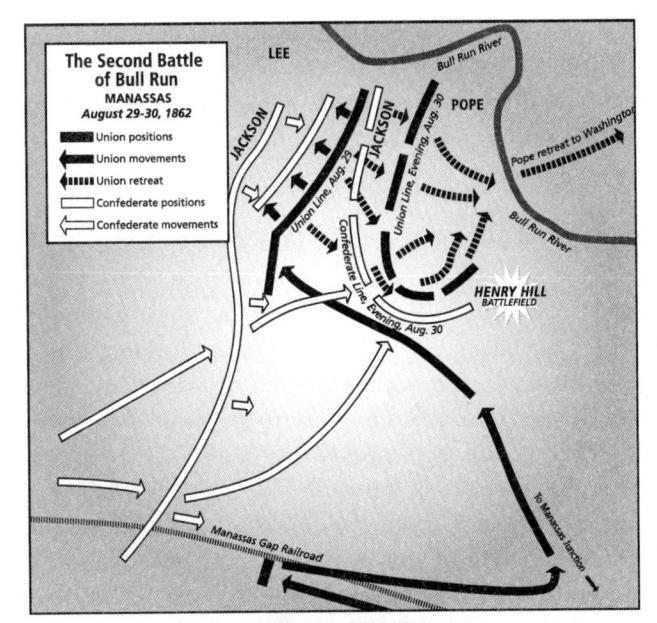

Map 16.6 The Second Battle of Bull Run

fought August 28–30, 1862, resulted in a Union defeat with heavy losses. The Confederate victory created an impression that Lee was unstoppable. Lincoln responded to Pope's failure by sending him to Minnesota where he would spend the remainder of the war contending with the Sioux Nation. The Army of Virginia was then merged with the Army of the Potomac, still under the command of McClellan.

In spite of his limitations as a field commander, George McClellan would prove that Lee was beatable at the **Battle of Antietam** (Sharpsburg), fought on September 17, 1862. Lee planned to follow up his victory at Second Bull Run with an invasion of the northern states, which would allow him to capture needed supplies and maybe create a demand for peace that would influence upcoming congressional elections. To carry out these goals, Lee again split his command. His main force moved northward through western Maryland, while the other moved against the federal arsenal at Harpers Ferry (located in present-day West Virginia at the convergence point with the borders of Virginia and Maryland). McClellan, however, had been tipped off. One of Lee's subordinates had inadvertently dropped his copy of the invasion plans, which were soon discovered by Union scouts. Upon receiving this information, McClellan responded by sending the Army of the Potomac to crush Lee's divided force, but his troops were somewhat delayed moving through mountainous terrain while being harassed by smaller Confederate units. By the time McClellan caught up to Lee, the latter had gathered most of his forces near Sharpsburg, Maryland. The fighting resulted in the war's bloodiest singe day—actually the bloodiest day in all American military history. A quarter of Union soldiers engaged

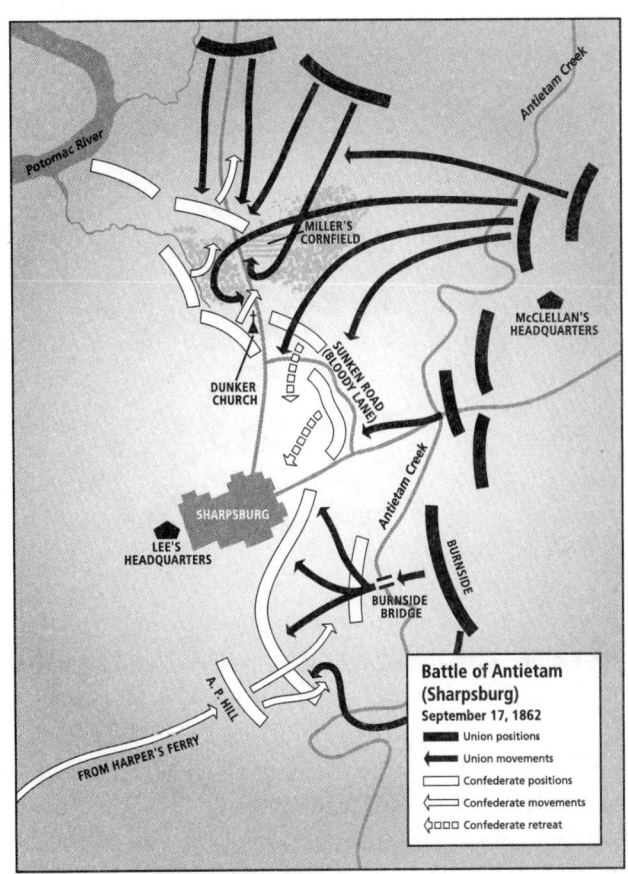

Map 16.7 Battle of Antietam

in the battle were casualties, while a third of Confederate soldiers were killed or wounded. The battle itself was a tactical draw. Lee's losses, however, forced him to withdraw from Maryland, so the Union claimed victory. Lincoln by this point had become completely disillusioned with McClellan. The general's forces had outnumbered Lee's army nearly two-to-one, and he passed on several opportunities during the battle to crush the enemy. Most disappointingly, McClellan neglected to pursue Lee back into Virginia. The president finally removed McClellan from his command, replacing him with General Ambrose Burnside.

Although Burnside was a popular corps leader, he proved to be an ineffective army commander. Eager to provide the president with the rapid type of offensive that he had been demanding from McClellan, Burnside amassed a huge force of 115,000 men and boldly advanced toward Richmond. Confederate defenders under Lee found time to dig in outside Fredericksburg, Virginia while Burnside's forces were delayed waiting for the arrival of pontoon bridges to allow them to cross the nearby Rappahannock River. When they finally engaged Lee at the Battle of Fredericksburg on December 13, 1862, Burnside's men faced an enemy entrenched in solid positions on high ground. The Confederates drove back wave after wave of Union assaults, seven in all. Ambrose's men

Tending the wounded on the battlefield of Antietam,

suffered more than 12,600 casualties while Lee lost less than half that amount. "It is well that war is so terrible," Lee commented as he watched the fighting, "or we should grow too fond of it." The defeat left Union morale shaken. "All think Virginia is not worth such a loss of life," wrote one Union soldier in a letter to home. "Why not confess that we are worsted," he continued, "and come to an agreement?" Lincoln, who described himself as being in "a worse place than Hell," removed Burnside but faced renewed questions about his leadership. Rumors swirled that his cabinet would be reorganized—Salmon P. Chase, in fact, tried to use the defeat as a way to force Seward out of the cabinet. Lincoln outmaneuvered him, and Chase felt compelled to offer his resignation (which the president refused to accept).

By the end of 1862, Union war prospects looked bleak. Although it had won significant battles of the high seas and in the West—victories that removed Confederate forces from Kentucky and almost all of Tennessee—the fighting between Washington and Richmond had brought nothing but defeat and frustration. A succession of Union commanders had no luck defeating the Confederacy as Lee's Army of Northern Virginia proved thus far to be the dominant force in the Eastern Theater. As the war raged, significant transformations were taking place in both the North and the South. The astonishing numbers of casualties, although inviting doubts about Lincoln's abilities as a war leader, opened the way for a transformation in northern war aims from a fight solely to save the Union to one also including the death of slavery. Lee's success, in fact, ironically put the survival of slavery at greater risk, as Lincoln and his cabinet reached the conclusion that emancipation was a necessary war measure. Even so, the end of the war remained a long way off, and Union victory at the end of 1862 was far from certain.

WARTIME TRANSFORMATIONS

By the end of 1862, the Civil War had already brought significant changes to the North and South. The fighting over the previous months produced an astonishing number of casualties. Reflecting on the Battle of Shiloh—in which the casualties surpassed 23,000—Grant wrote that one could "walk across the clearing in any direction stepping on dead bodies without a foot touching the ground." Sherman remarked that "the scenes on this field would have cured anybody of war." Shiloh proved to be just the beginning. The Seven Days Battles brought an additional 36,000 casualties; Second Bull Run, 25,000; Antietam, 23,000; and Fredericksburg, 18,000. Troops fighting in Tennessee closed out the year at the Battle of Stones River (December 31, 1862), which resulted in another 19,000 killed and wounded. Soldiers wrote home describing the bodies—mangled, swollen, decapitated—they had seen in the aftermath of battles. Numerous soldiers returned home as amputees. And future battles would bring more casualties. Chancellorsville in May 1863 cost nearly 30,000; Gettysburg a few months later brought more than 50,000; Chickamauga took almost

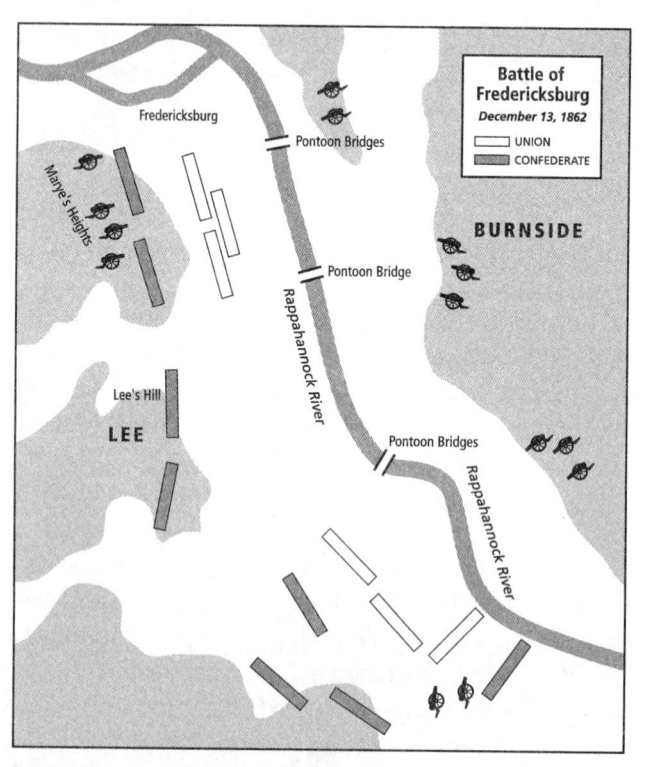

Map 16.8 Battle of Fredericksburg

35,000 casualties. Historians have long claimed the total number Civil War deaths exceeded a half million, with the most likely estimate being around 620,000. A recent approximation based on comparisons of census data taken from before and after the war, however, argues that the traditionally-cited number is too low because military records, especially those from the South, undercounted the number of casualties. The new estimate, which seems to be gaining rapid acceptance among historians, raises the total number of deaths to around 750,000. Whatever the exact figure, however, the scale of the Civil War, in terms of mobilization and total casualties unleashed a host of transformations throughout government and society.

The Civil War and State Power

Wartime demands significantly altered the role of government for both adversaries. Indeed, the war made a number of actions possible that had been politically feasible. Republicans in Congress, for example, took advantage of secession to drive through a number of measures that had been blocked by southern opposition in the 1850s. Before the end of 1862, Congress enacted a Homestead law, which offered farmers an opportunity to claim 160 acres of land if they actually live on the property and made substantive improvements. Congress also raised tariffs, authorized a transcontinental railroad, created a national banking system, and established land grant colleges. Such policies would ultimately provide a legal and social foundation for an industrializing economy, but the most sweeping transformations proved to be more directly tied to the war effort.

Both the Confederate and Union governments passed **conscription laws** to address their manpower demands. In April 1862, the Confederate Congress passed the first draft law in American history. The U.S. government reciprocated the following year. For the most part, the intent of these law was to use the threat of the draft to encourage men to enlist voluntarily and the vast majority of soldiers in both armies continued to be volunteers. Even so, the policies generated significant hostility from the public on both sides. Each law allowed individuals the option of hiring a substitute, giving rise to the popular assertion that the conflict was a "rich man's war, but a poor man's fight." A great deal of scholarship has worked to debunk that claim, as there are plenty of examples of wealthy people heading off to the front. Substitution, moreover, gave officials the option of keeping skilled people in civilian life where their work—such as in food production and manufacturing—were critical to sustaining the war effort. Still, the perception remained that the policy was manifestly unfair to the poor, especially in the case of the Confederate law that, for a while, permitted planters with twenty or more slaves to stay home and manage their plantations.

Another considerable expansion of state power—especially in the Union—involved the suppression of civil liberties. Although Lincoln willingly endured Democratic Party opposition (the Democrats actually gained 32 House seats in the 1862 congressional elections), the president had his limits. Lincoln worried a great deal about Maryland which, although its legislature voted not to secede, had enough hostile elements within the state to cause him to take drastic measures there. Losing control of Maryland would result in the nation's capital being surrounded by hostile territory, and in early April, Confederate sympathizers in Maryland attempted to thwart a Massachusetts unit's efforts to reach Washington. Likewise, states like Kentucky, with its long border along the Ohio River, offered huge potential disadvantages to the Union war effort if they fell into Confederate hands. Thus, in late April 1862, Lincoln ordered the suspension of the writ of **habeas corpus** and authorized warrantless arrests of citizens (though the Constitution seemed to imply that only the legislative branch could curtail *habeas corpus*, Congress sanctioned Lincoln's actions in early 1863). During the course of the war, 30,000-50,000 citizens, most residing

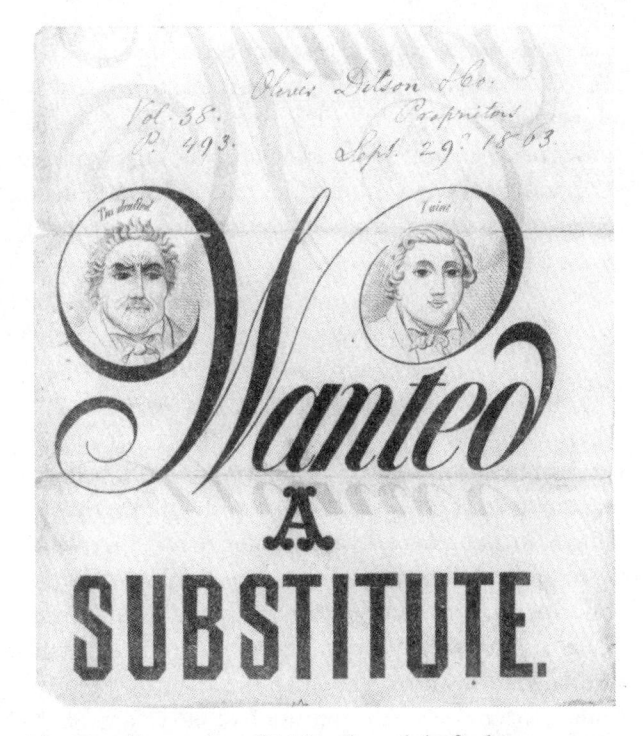

The Enrollment Act of 1863 allowed drafted men to purchase an exemption or to furnish a "substitute" in lieu of their own service. This illustration dramatizes the unfairness of the measure to the economically disadvantaged showing the bust of one man, "I'm drafted" in contrast to that of an obviously more well-to-do young man, "I ain't." 1863.

in the Border States or active war zones, were incarcerated at one time or another. The president personally ordered very few arrests. Instead, he and his subordinates gave vague dictates to military officers and federal marshals to arrest those accused of giving aid and comfort to the enemy or otherwise engaging in "disloyal practices." In the vast majority of the cases, those arrested were not detained for their political speech. A major exception was ex-Congressman Clement Vallandigham, one of the "Copperhead" leaders whose opposition to the war had crossed the line to open disloyalty. (Though General Burnside, not Lincoln, ordered Vallandigham's arrest in May 1863, the president eventually deported him to the Confederacy. He returned to the North unmolested a year later.) By far, most were arrested for trading or communicating with the enemy, blockade running, undertaking fraudulent sales to the U.S. government, selling alcohol to Union soldiers, and hindering the draft or voluntary enlistments. Lincoln firmly believed his power to be a short-term war measure. In an 1863 open letter, he professed seeing little chance "that the American people will, by means of military arrest during the rebellion, lose the right of public discussion, the liberty of speech and the press, the law of evidence, trial by jury, and Habeas Corpus, throughout the indefinite peaceful future . . . any more that . . . a man could contract so strong an appetite for emetics during temporary illness, as to persist in feeding upon them through the remainder of his healthful life." Although the policies of conscription and the suppression of civil liberties proved temporary, they nevertheless represented some of the most aggressive uses of power by a national government in American history.

Emancipation

The most far-reaching exercise of state power, emancipation, by no means proved to be temporary. Before the war, only radicals and fear-mongers seriously believed that the federal government possessed authority under the Constitution to end slavery in the states. Faced with potential trouble in the slaveholding Border States and opposition from a northern electorate that was not particularly sympathetic toward African Americans, Lincoln worked hard in the early phases of the war to keep the conflict focused on the preservation of the Union. As he wrote Horace Greeley, editor of the widely read *New York Tribune*, "My paramount object in this struggle is to save the Union. . . . What I do about slavery, and the colored race, I do because I believe it helps to save the Union; and what I forbear, I forbear because I do not believe it would help to save the Union." By the time of his letter to Greeley, however, Lincoln had privately concluded that the saving of the Union required ending slavery.

Lincoln's effort to keep the war focused on preserving the Union proved to be politically problematic. Slavery's role in bringing about secession was no secret. Confederate leaders, such as Vice President Alexander Stephens of Georgia, freely admitted that slavery formed a "cornerstone" of their government, and the South had acted to fix a wrong turn made by Thomas Jefferson when he declared that "all men are created equal." Abolitionists and Radical Republicans also saw the war as inseparable from slavery. Frederick Douglass, however, insisted that the price of secession had to be emancipation. Some Union commanders ordered their soldiers to free any slaves found in the areas under their control. Lincoln moved cautiously. He floated the possibility of gradual emancipation and colonization to border state politicians (with no success) and avoided sudden moves that might alienate Unionists in those areas. He even ordered his commanders not to free slaves in their jurisdictions while reserving the right to order emancipation in the future.

Events on the ground, however, ran ahead of the president. Slavery unraveled as Union armies pushed into the South, and enslaved Southerners—perhaps as many as 500,000—left their plantations and followed Union troops. By 1862, Union policy, influenced by commanders and politicians who saw no good in turning slaves back to their labor might sustain Confederate resistance, moved to accommodate this movement. Federal law initially defined such runaways as "**contrabands**" and forbade

Fugitive slaves—"Contrabands"—came into the union lines and were employed as laborers. Contrabands on Mr. Foller's farm, Cumberland. May 14, 1862.

returning them to the South. Within a matter of months, Congress had moved from that point to confiscation, a policy that freed the slaves of anyone who supported the Confederate war effort. By this time, Congress, with Lincoln's support, had imposed a compensated emancipation on the District of Columbia.

By the summer of 1862, Lincoln himself was ready to connect the war effort directly to emancipation. In July, he shared with his cabinet a draft of the **Emancipation Proclamation,** an executive order ending slavery in all areas not under Union control by a specific date (ultimately January 1, 1863). His proclamation transformed the nature of the war. No longer would the conflict be solely concerned with preserving Union—although that goal remained significant. The war now also became a war to end slavery. Militarily, the promise of freedom would hopefully induce slaves to run away to Union lines if an opportunity presented itself, further weakening the Confederate war effort. When Lincoln presented the document, however, his cabinet advised caution, suggesting that he wait for a significant Union victory before releasing the order to the public. Otherwise, in the wake of McClellan's unsuccessful Peninsular Campaign, Lincoln could be open to the charge that he acted out of desperation, a move that might bring the South some sympathetic European support. Lincoln agreed, waiting until Lee's retreat after the Battle of Antietam to issue the proclamation.

News of the Emancipation Proclamation brought a mixed response among abolitionists. Some criticized its limited nature since the document only promised to legally end slavery in the areas of Confederate control. Others, however, viewed the presidential order as the first step toward full emancipation and helped to fulfill its promise to transform the meaning of the war.

The proclamation's authorization for the use of African-American soldiers further cemented the idea that the Civil War was becoming a crusade for freedom in a very literal sense. Even before Lincoln had issued his order, Secretary of War Stanton began enlisting former slaves from the sea islands of South Carolina, overturning a federal prohibition on black soldiers in place since 1792. Service in the Union Army struck at the heart of the southern slave regime. Abolitionist leader Frederick Douglass regarded that as a good reason to enlist. "Every negro-hater and slavery lover in the land," he wrote in 1863, "regards the arming of negroes as a calamity and is doing his best to prevent it." One good way to deal with an enemy, he continued, was to "find out what he does not want and give him plenty of it." Military service also provided African Americans with an opportunity to claim a right to citizenship:

It has been the fashion in this country,—even in some of our northern cities,—to assault and mob colored citizens, for no other reason than the ease with which it could be done. We have it in our power to do something towards changing this cowardly custom. When it is once found that the black man can give blows as well as take them, more congenial employment will be found than pounding him. The black man, in arms to fight for the freedom of his race, and the safety and security of the country, will give his countrymen a higher and better revelation of his character. We have asked . . . for a chance to fight the Rebels; to fight against slavery and for freedom. That chance is now given us.

Ultimately 178,000 African Americans served in the war. Many did so at great cost, as 37,000 died in the conflict—a greater proportion of deaths than those suffered by their white counterparts. Black soldiers served in segregated units and endured unequal pay (until 1864) while often performing monotonous support work such as garrison duty. By 1863, however, African-American troops began making significant military contributions after Major Robert Gould Shaw's 54th Massachusetts Regiment made headlines after a gallant but ultimately unsuccessful attack on Fort Wagner, which protected the Charleston, South Carolina harbor. Ultimately, black soldiers and sailors gave Union commanders an incredible boost in manpower and many performed well in battle (twenty-five African Americans won Congressional Medals of Honor during the Civil War for outstanding feats of valor on land and at sea). Confederate troops reacted viciously to the use of black soldiers and sometimes killed the ones they captured on the spot. The **Fort Pillow Massacre** demonstrated how far such resentment could go. In April 1864, Confederate forces under the command of **General Nathan Bedford Forrest** (who later served for a time as the main leader of the postwar Ku Klux Klan) overran the fort's garrison then captured and killed over two hundred of the black troops who had defended the post.

Everyday Life during Wartime

As the fighting raged, the war transformed many aspects of everyday life for both civilians and soldiers. At home, the economics of daily life became more challenging. In the North, inflation pushed prices up 80 percent over the course of the war. While wages failed to keep pace, labor unrest—strikes punctuated with the rapid use of strike breakers—followed. Southerners had an even more difficult time. Hemmed in by the blockade and burdened with a flood of paper money, the southern economy faced rapid inflation. Prices increased by 9,000 percent. Shortages of goods, such as salt and coffee, were common. Basic staples, such as butter and flour, cost a small fortune.

Economic and social tensions in both regions also generated a number of riots. Shortages of food in the South brought a wave of bread riots in Alabama, North Carolina, and even in the Confederate capital of Richmond. The largest riot, however, occurred in the North. In July 1863, economic discontent combined with resentment toward conscription and emancipation produced the **New York City Draft Riots**. The incident began when a crowd of largely Irish, working-class protestors, especially outraged by the draft law's provision allowing individuals to purchase an exception for $300 (a year's salary for the average worker), stormed a draft office. Four days of rioting followed, and much of the violence targeted New York City's free black community. New York's Colored Orphan Asylum was burned to the ground. Although the children escaped, the riots resulted in the deaths of over 100 people, including ten African Americans who were lynched. Militia and regular army soldiers eventually arrived to restore order in the city.

Everyday life remained challenging for soldiers as well. Although they endured harrowing battles, soldiers spent much time on the march and even more in camps, where life was monotonous and potentially deadly. Camps were often unsanitary and frequently lacked fresh drinking water, leading to soldiers succumbing to such diseases as typhoid and dysentery. Food quality also tended to be poor (over the course of the war, this improved for Union soldiers while becoming even worse for Confederate troops.)

Soldiers' medical needs quickly overwhelmed the capabilities of military physicians. Crowded camps filled hospitals with soldiers exposed for the first time to the measles and mumps, joining their comrades suffering from typhus and dysentery. Combat created soldiers wounded by devastating new weapons. In earlier wars, soldiers used muskets—weapons with a relatively short range (about 100 yards), slow rate of fire, and not much accuracy. Tactics built around those weapons led soldiers to fire massive volleys at one another (timed so that some soldiers were firing as others reloaded) before moving in to fight at close quarters with bayonets. Early in the Civil War, however, new weapons with rifled barrels could be loaded much more rapidly and fired accurately up to 800 yards, but Union and Confederate battlefield tactics did not change as rapidly as the technology, resulting in massive casualties. Those who were not killed outright, like Corporal Jonathan Allison, often lost a limb in surgical procedures designed to stop the spread of infection. Such men became, in Allison's words, "the living monuments of the . . . cruel and bloody Rebellion."

Some soldiers faced capture. Initially, the Union and Confederate armies agreed to exchange their respective prisoners of war. (Neither side possessed the capacity to house the number of captives that battles between such large forces made possible.) That system broke down when Confederate officials refused to recognize black soldiers as legitimate prisoners of war. Both sides then kept prisoners in crowded and unsanitary prison camps. Southern camps, which like the rest of the South, suffered from a lack of food and medicine, became particularly horrid places to be held. At **Andersonville**, Georgia, the worst of all camps of the era, thirteen thousand men died during their internment. The war thus touched almost

The War in America: the Conscription in New York. Blindfolded men are drawing slips from a cylinder. 1865.

Thirteen thousand prisoners died at the Confederate prison camp at Andersonville, Georgia.

every aspect of American life, and the experience left deep scars—both physically and socially—that would take a long time to fade.

Women on the Home Front

War also brought new roles for women. In the North, thousands of women served as nurses. Many women participated in the work of the United States Sanitary Commission, the chief agency through which northern women helped the war effort. Volunteer workers ran its thousands of auxiliaries, collecting clothing, food, and medicine. "Sanitary Fairs" were organized whose fundraising strategies included lavish galas that benefited directly from the growing economic inequality accelerated by the war, which helped to provide cleaner camps, healthier diets, and improved medical care for Union soldiers. Such work expanded female influence in the public sphere and built upon work carried out by women in the antebellum reform movements. Elizabeth Cady Stanton and Susan B. Anthony founded the National Women's Loyal League, enabling them to continue the struggle for the abolition of slavery and securing women's rights in the context of the war effort. Northern women took over many of the remaining male jobs in teaching and, for the first time, gained positions in government offices and stores, as a result of the wartime manpower shortages. Many of these women, whose husbands and fathers were away in the army, would have been destitute without these new jobs.

Just like the women in the North, southern women likewise found new roles thrust upon them. They formed patriotic societies and collected supplies for the soldiers. But they suffered far worse shortages and more severe losses of manpower, resulting in greater hardships. Wealthy women ran plantations—some of the largest economic enterprises in the nation before the war. Plantation mistresses often had to manage their slaves at a time when slavery was disintegrating. As stealing, dawdling, and even sabotage by restless slaves was increasing, soldiers exhorted their wives to take charge. "You may give your Negroes away," one weary mistress wrote her husband in 1864, "I cannot live with them another year alone." Poor women often became saddled with heavy field work while their male relatives went off to fight. As in the North, women also found work as teachers. In Richmond, many women nicknamed "government girls" found work in offices of the Confederate bureaucracy.

Many women, North and South, suffered the loss of their husbands, lovers, and sons and had to learn to make do without them. "I have not read my bible since Charlie died, " one bereft southern woman wrote, "My tears and feelings seem frozen. I know, I feel but one thing, I am alone, utterly desolate."

Women on the Battlefield

Not only did women do most of the work in volunteer civilian agencies like the Sanitary Commission, but thousands also worked as nurses in army hospitals. Florence Nightingale in the 1854 Crimean War had elevated the nursing profession, previously defamed as menial or morally dubious. Many still worried that the rough and bloody atmosphere of a military hospital was no place for a gentle, respectable young woman. The Union appointed

Clara Barton was called, "the true heroine of the age, the angel of the battlefield." She later founded the American Red Cross.

the famed reformer **Dorothea Dix** as superintendent of nurses. She insisted that her nurses be over thirty years old, "plain in appearance," and unadorned by jewelry. Eventually, 3,200 women met these requirements and served as northern army nurses, the first professional nurses in American military history. Perhaps the most famous of them, "Mother Bickerdyke," crusaded tirelessly to improve the health of the soldiers and won the admiration and respect of the normally ornery General Sherman.

Others were volunteers on the battlefield. A small, pretty woman in a bonnet and a bright red bow named **Clara Barton** arrived at Antietam with a wagonload of bandages and medicine. She worked tirelessly through the battle comforting the wounded and aiding the surgeons. One of the latter called her, "the true heroine of the age, the angel of the battlefield." She continued her efforts through most of the war. Later, she worked to identify the remains of the POWs at Andersonville and, eventually, founded the American Red Cross. "Michigan Bridget" Divers who attached herself to her husband's cavalry regiment became famous for her courage and coolness under fire in removing wounded men from the battlefield. She also picked up a fallen soldier's weapon and fought alongside the men.

At least one woman, **Mary Walker**, served as a surgeon in the Union army. When the Confederates captured the pants-wearing Walker, they expressed astonishment "at the sight of a thing that nothing but the debased and depraved Yankee nation could produce." Walker was awarded the Medal of Honor for her battlefield and prison camp medical services. (It was rescinded by Congress two years before her death in 1917 and restored in 1977.)

The Confederate army was slower to allow "decent" white women to serve as nurses. At first, only slave women performed this task in army hospitals. Eventually, however, white women from "good families" volunteered and were authorized to work as nurses. One of the southern surgeons admitted he preferred the women to the "rough country crackers" who had been performing that duty and who did not "know caster oil from a gun rod."

Black women helped the Union army by working as laundresses and unofficial nurses. Hundreds of others hid Union soldiers and helped them to escape. Some were punished for bringing food to Union prisoners. Susie

**Mary Walker,
between 1911 and 1917.**

King Taylor, who had learned how to read and write, was recruited by Union officers when she was 14 years old to teach freed slaves. She married a black sergeant and served alongside him as a nurse and laundress. She also confided, "I learned to handle a musket very well while in the regiment, and could shoot straight and often hit the target." Harriet Tubman not only worked as a nurse and cook for the Union army, she also served as a spy, utilizing her "invisibility" as a black woman to learn important information about troop movements.

Several other women operated as spies for both sides, including society hostess, Rose O'Neal Greenhow, a close friend of former president James Buchanan. She was arrested and deported to England, only to drown in a shipwreck trying to smuggle gold to the Confederacy. **Belle Boyd** carried messages and spied for Stonewall Jackson. She later made quite a career for herself on stage, recounting her dramatic adventures.

Both in the North and the South (although more in the former) there were a number of women who dressed as men and fought in the war. The best research has uncovered 150 women soldiers. Several of these were

Belle Boyd

promoted to sergeant, a few to lieutenant, and one even became a captain. Albert D.J. Cashier, whose real name was Jennie Hodgers, fought in numerous battles from 1862 to 1865. After the war, she collected a pension for disabled soldiers and was active in the Grand Army of the Republic, the Union veterans' organization. Her sex was not discovered until 1911 when she broke her leg and had to be treated by a physician.

While the efforts of these soldiers are interesting, the work of the women nurses had greater significance in advancing the professional status of nursing in America. After the war, nursing veterans started training programs, wrote textbooks, and even administered hospitals. Nursing became an important profession for women although the job description continued to include such menial activities as cleaning, doing laundry, and cooking for patients.

THE TURNING POINTS OF 1863

Gettysburg

In 1863, the war's momentum fundamentally changed. Although the end of the conflict remained far off, the Union achieved two crucial victories at Gettysburg, Pennsylvania and Vicksburg, Mississippi that turned the tide forever in its favor. Those victories did not come

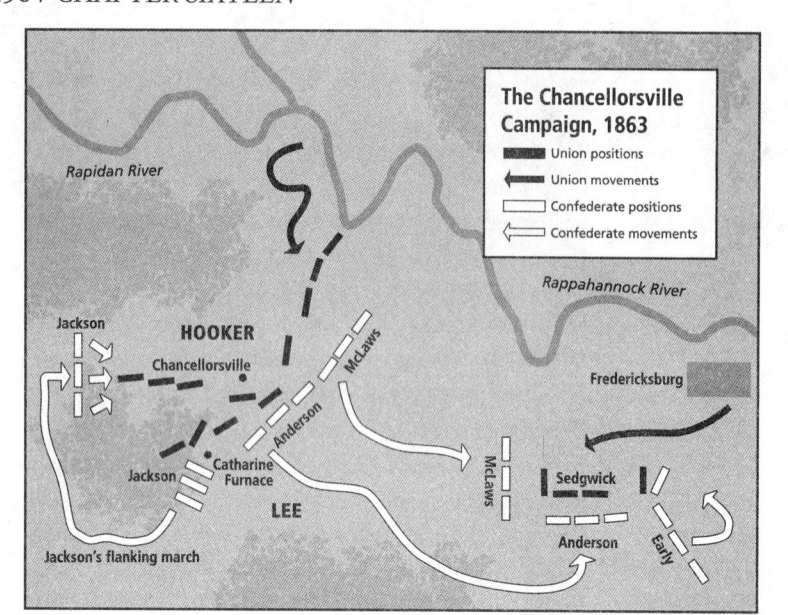

Map 16.9 The Chancellorsville Campaign

quickly. After the Battle of Fredericksburg, Lincoln replaced Burnside with General Joseph Hooker, an aggressive corps commander. The president did not hold Hooker in high regard, particularly because the general was reputed to favor establishing a dictatorship. Lincoln gave him the command anyway. "Only those generals who gain successes, can set up dictators," Lincoln wrote to Hooker. "What I now ask of you is military success, and I will risk the dictatorship." In the spring of 1863, Hooker took a force of 125,000 men across the Rappahannock River in a flanking maneuver designed to move behind Lee. Anticipating Hooker's movements, Lee moved to intercept the Army of the Potomac in a heavily-wooded area near Chancellorsville, Virginia. Though outnumbered two-to-one, Lee skillfully used his knowledge of the local terrain to his advantage, even dividing his forces further by sending Stonewall Jackson to strike at Hooker's right flank. Jackson's surprise attack combined with Lee's frontal assault wilted the Union lines. Although the Union troops rallied, they ultimately retreated after bearing over 17,000 casualties. By comparison, Lee lost 13,000 men, none more important than Stonewall Jackson who died of wounds received when accidentally shot in the dark by a nervous Confederate sentry after returning from a reconnaissance mission. Despite this major blow to the Confederate high command, the **Battle of Chancellorsville** (April 30—May 6, 1863) is considered a masterpiece by military historians. To this day, war colleges cite Lee's masterpiece as a textbook example of how an aggressive general can use the terrain to negate numerical disadvantages.

Robert E. Lee decided to capitalize on his victory at Chancellorsville by invading Pennsylvania and destroying the Army of the Potomac on Union soil. Moving into Pennsylvania would relieve pressure on Richmond

The Death of Stonewall Jackson

In the moonlight on May 2, in an area filled with smoke, General Stonewall Jackson was riding with a small contingent of his men. He was looking for a route in the Wilderness to be able to block any Union retreat. As he headed back to Confederate lines, the noise of his horses led a startled North Carolina brigade to fire wildly. "You are firing at your own men," one of Jackson's officers shouted. A major with the brigade responded, "It's a lie! Pour it into them boys!" The volley killed four of the men in the group. Three of the bullets hit Jackson, two shattering his left arm. Staff members tried to shield him with their bodies. As they carried him back, they fell, dropping him on his mutilated shoulder and recommencing the severe arterial bleeding. As was common with such injuries, the doctor was forced to amputate his arm.

Informed of the grim news, a dismayed General Lee declared, "He has lost his left arm, but I have lost my right." Still, Lee believed that Jackson would recover, "God will not take him from us now that we need him so much." At first, Lee appeared to be right, as Jackson seemed to be recovering at a country house where he had been taken by ambulance. On the morning of May 7, however, Jackson complained of a sharp pain in his side, and the doctors realized that pneumonia had set in. His wife arrived that day and warned him that he was dying. "My wish is fulfilled," he responded, "I have always desired to die on Sunday." On Sunday, May 10, after desperately gasping for breath Jackson died, murmuring, "Let us cross over the river and rest under the shade of the trees."

and allow the Army of Northern Virginia to live off the land in an area that had not been a scene of regular fighting. If successful, Lee's plan would also make Lincoln's government appear weak, bolster peace sentiment in the North, and hasten an end to the war. Though Hooker moved his forces between Lee's army and Washington, D.C., Lincoln did not believe Hooker was moving rapidly enough to intercept Lee's invading army and soon replaced him with General George G. Meade, who caught Lee as Confederate forces concentrated at Gettysburg, Pennsylvania. The next three days of fighting would largely determine the final outcome of the war.

On the first day, Lee's forces held the edge, but Meade's men were able to retreat to the high ground overlooking the town. By the second day, additional troops from each army arrived on the scene, and the Union had tightened its defenses. Though outnumbered, Lee launched massive attacks on Meade's fortified flanks, but units at each position, fighting desperately, managed to hold their ground. On the third day, Lee made one final attempt to break through the Union lines. Believing in the ability of his men to do whatever he asked of them and determined to make Gettysburg the decisive battle of the war, Lee boldly (many would later say foolishly) launched one final massive frontal assault on the Union center—the ill-fated "Pickett's Charge"—which resulted in over 10,000 casualties before the attack dissipated before a withering fire of rifle and cannon fire. Fought between July 1 and July 3, 1863, the **Battle of Gettysburg** became the bloodiest battle of the entire war. Lee lost over 23,000 men, almost one-third of his army. Though victorious, Meade also lost over 23,000 men totally one-fourth of his fighting force. As a result of the heavy casualties sustained, the general (to Lincoln's great dismay) chose not to pursue Lee's battered army when the defeated general reluctantly ordered his men to retreat on the Fourth of July.

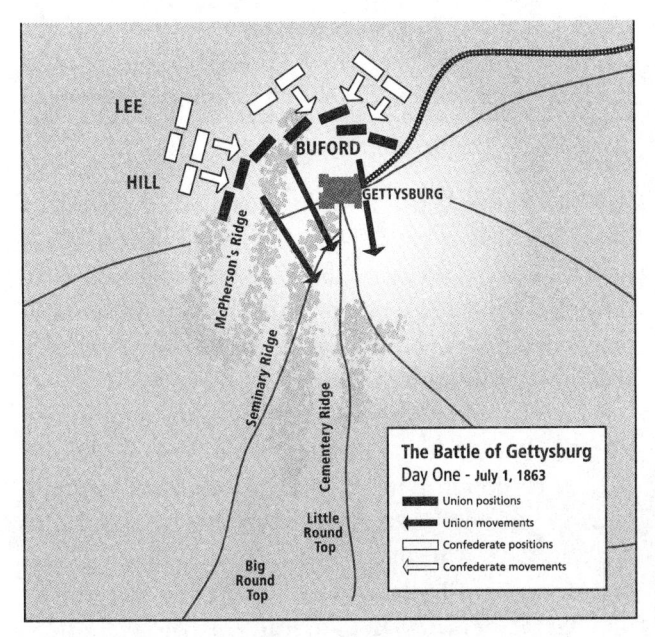

Map 16.10 Battle of Gettysburg, Day One

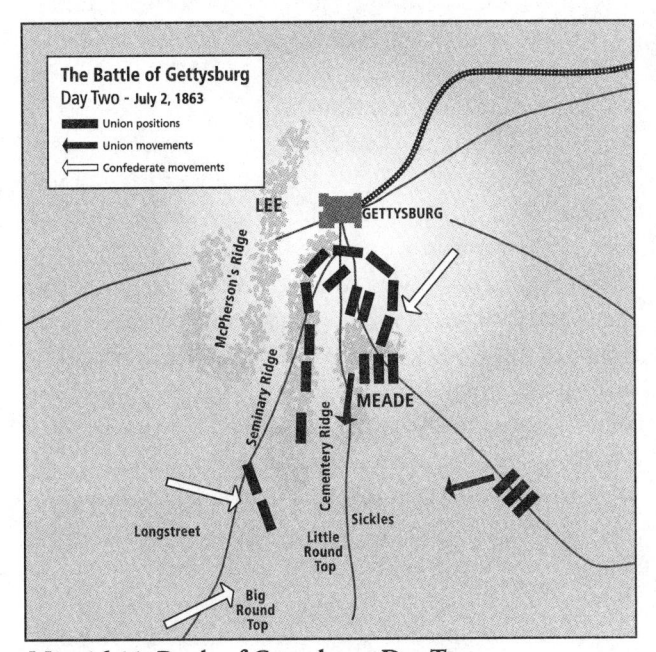

Map 16.11 Battle of Gettysburg, Day Two

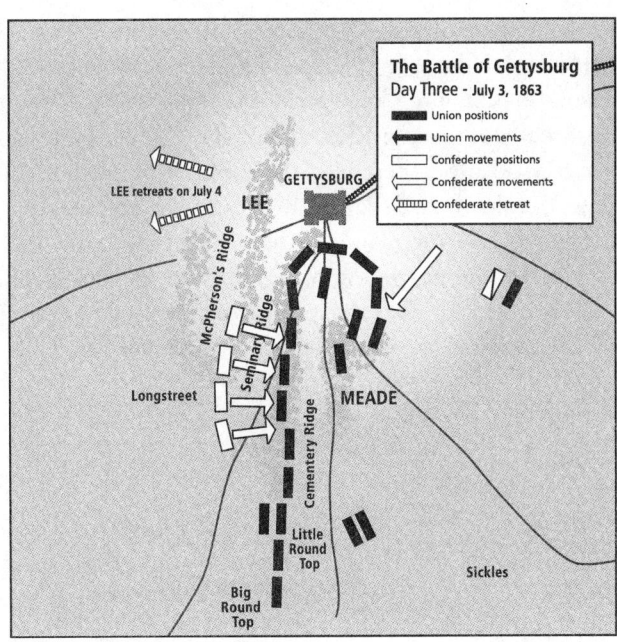

Map 16.12 Battle of Gettysburg, Day Three

The Vicksburg Campaign

On the very day that Lee retreated from Gettysburg, the Confederate defenders of Vicksburg, Mississippi, surrendered to Ulysses Grant's army. The general had been trying to capture the fortified city since March 1863, proceeding against the city through a process of trial and error, embracing a new approach after the preceding one failed. By the end of April, Grant had managed to get his troops onto Vicksburg's side of the Mississippi River. He then moved inland so he could attack the city from behind (along the way he captured the state capital of Jackson). The general's assaults on Vicksburg toward the end of May, however, inflicted heavy losses on his troops while failing to breech the city's defenses, so Grant ordered a siege on May 25. Confederate defenders held on for over forty days, but Grant's position kept them cut off from reinforcements, and their supplies dwindled. On July 4, 1863, Vicksburg surrendered, and Grant captured an army of nearly 30,000 troops. The Union now had complete control of the Mississippi River. Lincoln, who had questioned Grant's strategy, promoted Grant to major general and sent him a letter of apology. "I now wish to make the personal acknowledgement," the president wrote, "that you were right, and I was wrong."

By 1863, momentum in the war had definitely shifted. Union victories at Gettysburg and Vicksburg placed the South on the defensive. Lee would never again have a chance to push into Union territory, and Grant's achievement had cut the Confederacy in half. The meaning of the war had also undergone a significant shift. Although Lincoln initially had worked to present the conflict as a struggle to save the Union, he had come to link the war to a higher purpose—the protection and expansion of freedom. In his **Gettysburg Address,** delivered as part of a dedication for a cemetery for Union soldiers who

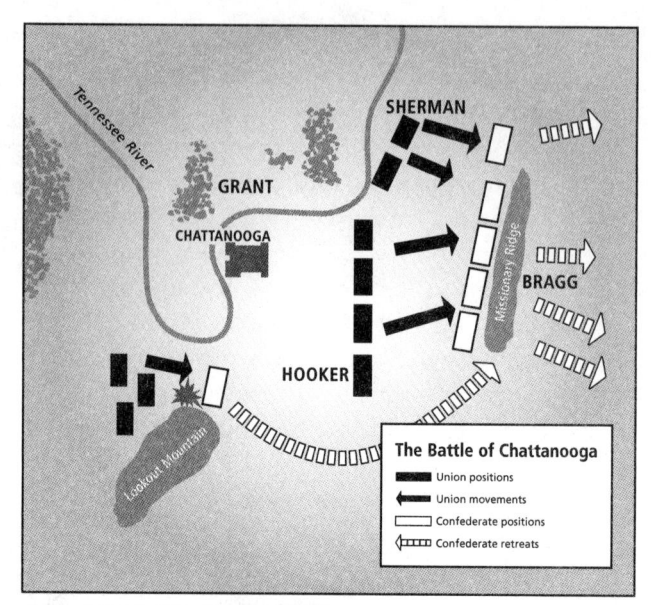

Map 16.14 The Battle of Chattanooga

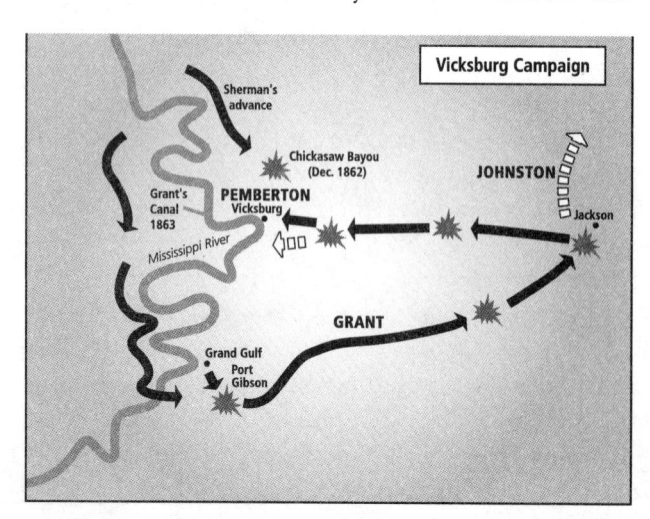

Map 16.13 Vicksburg Campaign

had died in that battle, Lincoln noted that "these dead . . . have not died in vain." They, and others like them, had died for a cause; they gave their lives so "that this nation, under God, should have a new birth of freedom—and that government of the people, by the people, for the people, shall not perish from the earth."

Even so, the end of the war lay in the distant future. Meade's decision not to pursue Lee into Virginia permitted Lee an opportunity to regroup and gather strength. Grant, moreover, paroled the troops that he captured in Vicksburg, allowing them to return home. Keeping them as prisoners of war would have slowed down his forces, plus Grant hoped that the return of defeated troops would sap Confederate morale. Instead, many former prisoners joined new units; some of them even returned to battle in time to fight Grant's force again at the **Battle of Chattanooga** in eastern Tennessee. Indeed, southern resolve remained strong. Confederate forces in Tennessee defeated a Union army under the command of General William Rosecrans at the Battle of Chickamauga (September 19–20, 1863). The fighting, which resulted in over 35,000 casualties combined, forced Union troops to retreat into Chattanooga where the Confederates placed them under siege. Grant, now in command of all Union troops in the West, soon arrived to save them. His forces managed to open supply lines to the besieged city. The fighting culminated toward the end of November when Grant's troops broke the siege and forced the Confederate forces out of Tennessee. As it settled into its winter quarters, the Union army was now positioned to push its way into the Deep South. Grant had earned his way to the top. When the fighting picked up again, Grant would be commander-in-chief of the Union Army. Lincoln had found his man.

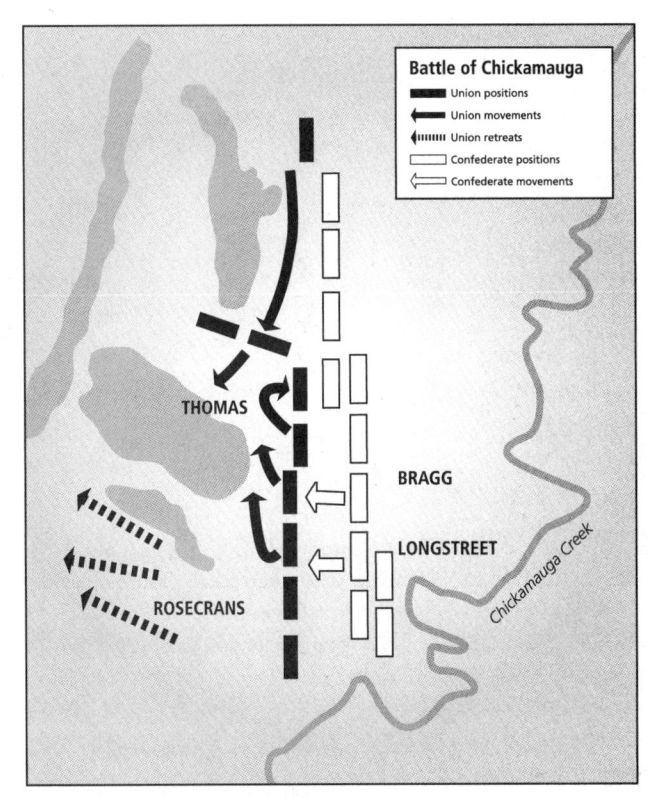

Map 16.15 Battle of Chickamauga

TOWARD UNION VICTORY

Although the Union had won significant victories in 1863, the war remained far from over. The situation did not look good for the Confederacy, of course, after its crippling losses at Gettysburg and Vicksburg. Despite criticism of the Davis administration and the state of the war effort from the Confederate press, southern resolve remained firm. The Confederate armies still contained experienced soldiers, albeit in reduced numbers, that remained very capable in the field. Southern military objectives still sought recognition of Confederate independence, but the strategy now centered on holding out long enough to turn northern public opinion against the war. Such an effort required dragging the conflict well into 1864 so that antiwar sentiment could undermine the Republicans' prospects in the election of 1864. Faced with such opposition, the Union military, now under the command of Ulysses Grant, responded by conducting the war in a way designed to undermine the South's own willingness to carry on the struggle.

Grant versus Lee

Unlike his predecessors, Grant did not allow himself to be intimidated by Robert E. Lee, who had become a larger than life figure in the minds of many commanders in the war's Eastern Theater. He ultimately instructed his subordinates to concentrate on what they might do against Lee rather than what he might do against them. Grant employed a straightforward strategy: "Find out where your enemy is. Get at him as soon as you can and keep moving on." He described this strategy as "simple enough," but it probably worked in 1864 and 1865 for two primary reasons. One involved the position of Union forces. Although the Army of the Potomac had failed to dislodge Lee's Army of Northern Virginia from the Richmond area, Union forces under the command of William T. Sherman (one of Grant's most trusted subordinates) were ready to push from Tennessee into the Deep South. Grant planned to trap Lee between his and Sherman's armies and crush him. The second reason stemmed from the North's relative abundance of men and equipment. Grant could "keep moving on" because he could replace whatever he lost after any particular battle. Lee could not. (Grant also had accepted as early as Shiloh that defeating the South would entail a great deal of bloodshed.) Grant's approach soon put Lee on the defensive—but his troops paid a high price.

Grant and Lee first faced off at the **Battle of the Wilderness** (May 5–7, 1864). Breaking with previous generals, Grant shifted the focus in the East from capturing Richmond to destroying Lee's army, and he gathered a force of over 100,000 men to accomplish the task. An outnumbered Lee, whose army amounted to only 61,000 soldiers, forced the Union fight in a largely uninhabited area covered with thick underbrush near the site of the Battle of Chancellorsville. The terrain in this location—the Wilderness of Spotsylvania—deprived Grant of his superior numbers and reduced the effectiveness of his artillery. The next three days of fighting resulted in a costly draw. Grant's suffered more than 17,000 casualties while Lee lost over 11,000 men before the Union general broke off the attack.

Rather than withdrawing after the Battle of the Wilderness, however, Grant kept moving as he planned to maneuver around the Army of Northern Virginia and force Lee to fight in terrain more hospitable to his forces. Grant planned to take control of a nearby crossroads, which would effectively place his army between Lee and Richmond—a shift that would surely draw the Confederate commander out of the Wilderness. Unfortunately, Union forces did not move quickly enough to prevent some of the Confederates from beating them to the crossroads and entrenching. The ensuing **Battle of Spotsylvania Court House** lasted from May 8 to May 21. Nearly two weeks of sporadic fighting brought another 32,000 casualties (over 18,000 of them among Grant's men) while the Union tried to break the Confederate defenses. Again,

This photograph of Grant at Cold Harbor was taken by the famous Civil War photographer Mathew Brady.

the Union commander broke off the attack and attempted to maneuver for a better position. When Grant's forces captured a crossroads at **Cold Harbor**, which lay about ten miles outside of Richmond, reinforcements for both sides arrived and the Confederate defenders quickly constructed a seven-mile line of defenses. The subsequent fighting lasted from May 31 to June 12, with much of the heaviest fighting occurring on a June 3 frontal assault by Grant's troops. The combat produced little but dead and wounded bodies for the Union, with casualties numbering nearly 13,000 (compared to a little over 4,500 for Lee's forces). Grant regretted his decision, later stating: "No advantage whatever was gained to compensate for the heavy loss we sustained."

Grant pressed on, shifting his objective from defeating Lee in the field—although the previous month of fighting had reduced the size of Lee's army by over 45 percent—to putting pressure back on Richmond. He now moved against Petersburg, a city that served as Richmond's principle source of supplies. With this maneuver, Grant effectively pinned Lee down because the fall of Petersburg would rapidly produce the fall of Richmond and the Confederacy's retreat. Lee's forces responded by digging in, forcing Grant's forces (after an assault on the city failed) to besiege to the city. Soon, the two armies sat deployed in more than 30 miles of trenches and engaged in fighting that anticipated the type of warfare later seen in France during World War I. The siege lasted from June 1864 to March 1865. The war in the East had stalled again.

The Election of 1864

On August 23, 1864, while Grant maintained the siege against Petersburg, Lincoln asked the members of his cabinet to endorse a sealed memorandum without reading the contents. The document contained the president's prediction that "this Administration will not be reelected" and a pledge to "cooperate with the President elect as to save the Union between the Election and the inauguration." Lincoln won the election of 1864, but the outcome, as his memo demonstrated, was far from certain. Although Grant's aggression against Lee ultimately won the war, few Northerners could see that result in the summer of 1864. What citizens saw instead was a general—many in the press called him a butcher—who in the space of a month had produced 60,000 casualties before getting stopped by Lee. To make matters worse, a Confederate unit under the command of General Jubal Early came within five miles of Washington in July 1864. There was no real threat to the city, but many northern observers had concluded that the quickest way to end the war entailed voting Lincoln out of office.

Although deeply divided among themselves, northern Democrats united against Lincoln. Since the outbreak of the fighting, the party was divided into war and peace factions. War Democrats, like Governor Horatio Seymour of New York, sought a negotiated peace that would bring the South back into the Union without further bloodshed. Peace Democrats, led at the convention by politicians such as Clement Vallandigham (who had returned from Canada after his failed effort to run for governor of Ohio *in absentia*), advocated peace at all costs. These two factions struck a compromise and nominated General George B. McClellan, a War Democrat, and Thomas H. Seymour, a Peace Democrat and one-time governor of Connecticut. Peace Democrats also wrote the party platform, despite McClellan's outspoken support for continuing the war effort until the South agreed upon reunification (the ex-general opposed the Emancipation Proclamation, arguing that it served as an impediment to reunion). Grant's high casualties against Lee's forces in Virginia strengthened McClellan's support among the public.

Meanwhile, the Republican Party became divided as the war dragged on. Radical Republicans, who were beginning to push for constitutional amendments to consolidate the gains made on behalf of emancipation, remained critical of Lincoln for moving too slowly. Some even bolted the party and temporarily rallied around the possible candidacy of John C. Frémont. Lincoln did little to ingratiate himself to the Radicals. Indeed, he dropped his Vice President Hannibal Hamlin (a Radical Republican from Maine) in favor of **Andrew Johnson**, a War Democrat from Tennessee. Johnson, a former U.S. Senator who refused to resign when his state seceded and presently was serving as the military governor of Tennessee, represented a political fusion in the Upper South and Border States between War Democrats and moderate Republicans. Lincoln hoped that such support would secure his re-election.

Although Lincoln eventually won the election, his victory was far from certain. By the fall of 1864, however, events began to shift in his favor. Frémont, whatever his criticism of Lincoln, reacted with horror to the Democratic Party's peace platform, which he believed threatened to restore slavery to the Union. Rather than stay in the election and risk a McClellan victory, he pulled out of the race. Without Frémont splitting the Republican vote, McClellan had little chance of winning. Lincoln received 55 percent of the popular vote and 212 of 233 Electoral College votes. What clinched the president's victory, however, had less to do with Frémont's decision to withdraw than with General William Sherman's victories in the Deep South.

General Sherman on the March

While Grant led the fight against Lee in Virginia, General William T. Sherman, his trusted subordinate, moved an army of nearly 100,000 men from Tennessee into northern Georgia. His goal was to crush the Confederate force under the command of General Joseph E. Johnston and to capture Atlanta—a strategically important city. Sherman's success in securing Atlanta followed by his destruction of large portions of the Georgia plantation belt would ultimately undermine southern morale and hasten the end of the war.

Although his force outnumbered Johnston's, Sherman hoped to avoid a frontal assault against his enemy. Instead, he proceeded by moving his forces along the Confederate flanks. Such maneuvers forced Johnston to either fight from a disadvantaged position or to vacate to a better location. Johnston tended to opt for the latter course, a tendency that Jefferson Davis found highly troubling. This strategy allowed Sherman to move toward Atlanta with a minimal number of casualties, but he did not always adhere to his strategy. At the **Battle of Kennesaw Mountain** (June 27, 1864), Sherman ordered a frontal attack because he thought Johnston had stretched himself out too thin in the course of his maneuvers. He was wrong, and the Confederates quickly fought him off, inflicting about 3,000 casualties in just a few hours of fighting, while only suffering 1,000 casualties themselves. Like Grant, Sherman did not allow defeat to stop him. By early July, the Union general had forced Johnston to withdraw to Peachtree Creek (a site three miles outside of Atlanta). Johnston planned to assault Union troops as they crossed the creek, but Davis removed him from command and replaced him with John Bell Hood, a general who the Confederate president hoped would be more aggressive.

Hood, largely followed the plans of his predecessor, except he attacked after the Union troops crossed Peachtree Creek. His attack hit the Union lines hard, but they withstood the assault, forcing the Confederates to fall back. A few days later, Hood tried again at the **Battle of Atlanta** (July 22, 1864) to drive Sherman from the vicinity, this time by sending troops around the Union general's rear flank. The effort failed, and the Confederate forces suffered heavy casualties (nearly 8,500 to the Union's 3,641). Sherman responded by placing the city under siege, a process that took time because his troops had to gain control of the rail line supplying the city. Cavalry raids failed to do the job, so Sherman ultimately moved his entire army to capture the line. After Hood pulled his troops out of Atlanta, the city surrendered on September 2, 1864. Sherman notified Lincoln on September 3, and the news probably saved the president's election as many Northerners felt that the fall of Atlanta meant that the war would soon be over.

Though General Hood ordered all public buildings and property to be destroyed before Confederate troops withdrew, William Sherman made the devastation of Atlanta complete by torching most of the city before following up on his victory with his famous "**March to the Sea**" (November 15—December 21, 1864) during which he advanced his army 250 miles from Atlanta to Savannah along the Atlantic Coast. As they moved, Sherman's troops lived off the land. Union officers were ordered to destroy or confiscate any property that could be used to support the rebellion. The march left a path of devastation in its wake. Soldiers took 5,000 horses, 4,000 mules, 13,000 cattle, nearly 5,000 tons of corn, and over 5,000 tons of fodder. They also destroyed 300 miles of rail line and a great number of bridges. Overall, the destruction amounted to $100 million (well over one billion in current dollars). Sherman embarked on this march for a number of reasons. He wanted to undermine southern civilians' willingness and capability to support the war. He also wished to demonstrate that the Confederacy was powerless to stop his army. Although he faced resistance along the route, and both Grant and Lincoln had doubts about his strategy, Sherman reached Savannah before December 25. "I beg to present you as a Christmas gift," Sherman telegraphed the president when he arrived, "the City of Savannah."

The War Ends

By the beginning of 1865, the Union was positioned for victory with General Grant beginning the new year besieging Lee's forces at Petersburg and General Sherman poised to march northward from Savannah to help crush Lee's army. The Confederacy's days were clearly numbered.

Sherman's army began their trek toward Virginia in January 1865 with an overland campaign through the

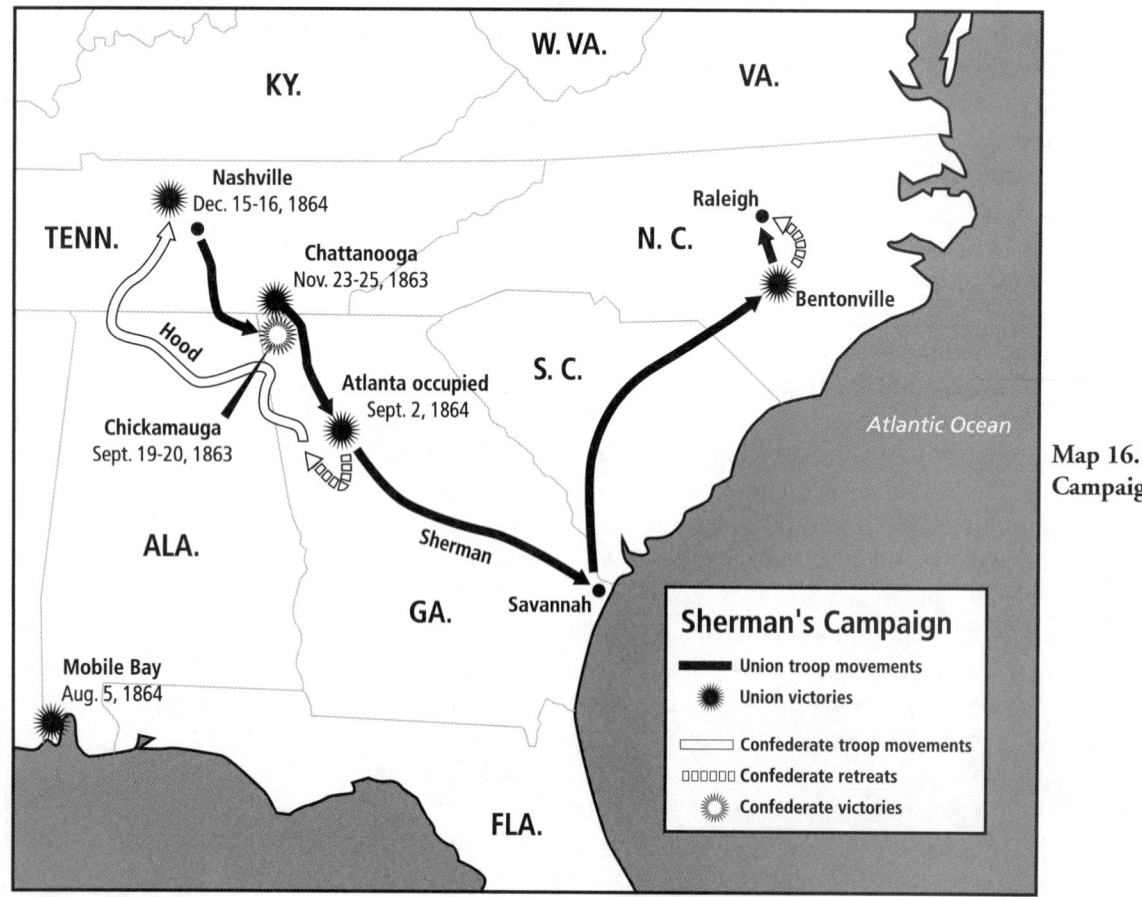

Map 16.16 Sherman's Campaign

especially as it moved through South Carolina, the state in which the war began—would undermine southern morale. Sherman divided his 60,000 men (although the number of men grew to nearly 90,000 by the end of the war) into three groups whose movements had been planned to confuse the enemy. By mid-February, Sherman had forced the surrender of Columbia, the state capital of South Carolina. Union troops had stripped the city of valuables and left it burning (although who started the fires remains a matter of dispute). Less than a week after Columbia's surrender, the vital port of Wilmington, North Carolina also capitulated. Sherman later defeated Johnston at the Battle of Bentonville (March 19–21), a rout of smaller Confederate forces that left little opposition between Sherman and Virginia.

As Sherman moved northward, Grant kept the pressure on Lee at Petersburg. A winter in the trenches had left the 50,000 Confederate defenders in poor shape. Disease and desertion had further thinned their ranks. Supplies ran short, and Lee's efforts to break the Union's pressure had failed. By the end of March, Lee found himself facing not only Grant, but also a force under the command of **General Phillip S. Sheridan**, who had just completed a Sherman-style march through the Shenandoah Valley. Sherman too was on his way with another army. Lee made one final effort to break the Union siege and regain the

Sherman left Atlanta in ruins, 1864

Carolinas. Union troops were able to move through the region as easily as they had rampaged through Georgia. Along the way, he hoped that the impact of his march—

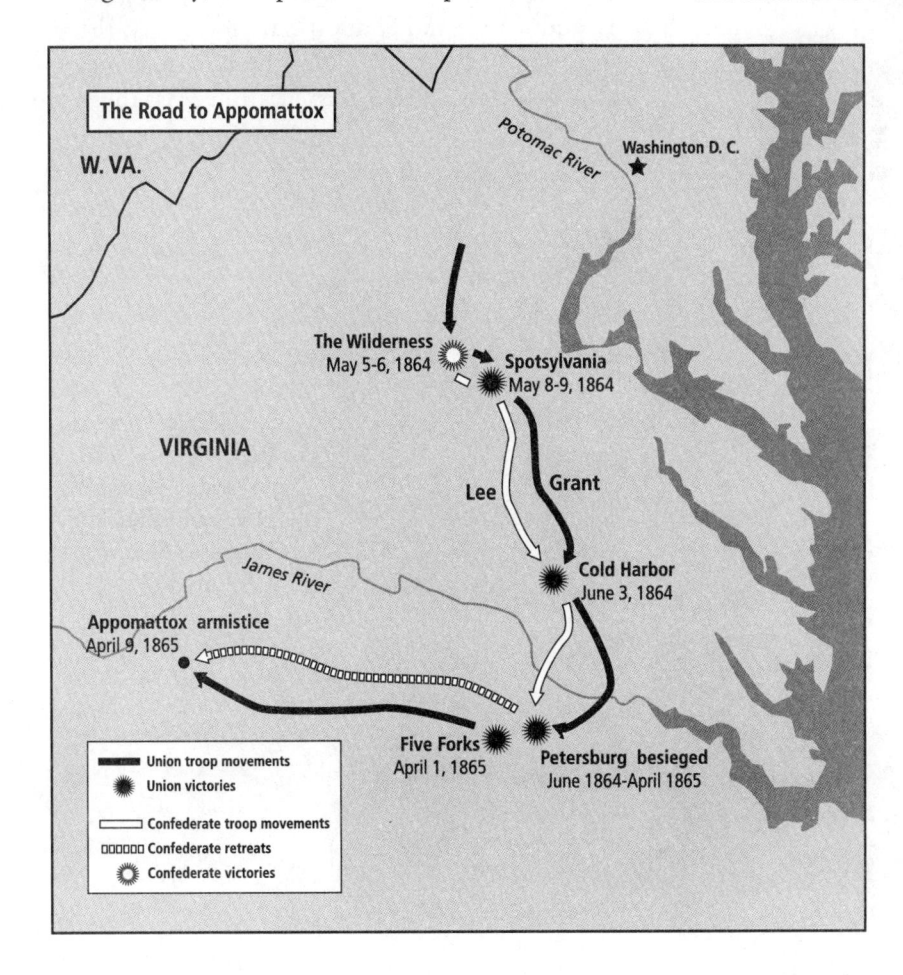

Map 16.17 The Road to Appomattox

initiative on March 25. He failed with his troops suffering 4,000 casualties while Grant's army, which itself suffered around 1,000 casualties moved into a better position.

On April 1, Union troops broke through the Confederate lines. Both Petersburg and Richmond surrendered on the following day. Jefferson Davis fled the city, although Union troops would capture him about a month later. Lee too evacuated the city, hoping that he could join the Confederate forces that were still fighting in North Carolina. But as Grant had done before the Siege of Petersburg, he again pursued Lee with tenacity. Within days, Lee's efforts to escape had failed, and his army was surrounded on nearly all sides by Union troops. Reluctantly, but to avoid needless bloodshed, Lee surrendered to Grant at **Appomattox Court House** on April 9, 1865. A few weeks later, General Johnston surrendered to Sherman in North Carolina. Though sporadic skirmishing continued for another month among die-hard Confederates and those yet to hear the news of Lee and Johnston's surrenders, the war had finally come to an end.

ENDINGS, BEGINNINGS, AND CONTINUATIONS

As the war entered its final few weeks, Lincoln delivered his brief Second Inaugural Address, which looked solemnly to the nation's future. The conflict, he noted, now progressed in a manner that was "reasonably satisfactory and encouraging to all." He made no predictions but had "high hopes for the future." Lincoln then moved to a discussion of slavery, which all observers at the outset of the conflict "knew...was somehow the cause." Neither side, however, could have predicted "that the cause of the conflict might cease with or even before the conflict itself should cease." Both had sought "a result less fundamental and astounding." Yet, the struggle proved to be bigger than either side—perhaps one that could be explained only by trying to discern divine will:

> The Almighty has His own purposes. "Woe unto the world because of offenses; for it must needs be that offenses come, but woe to that man by whom the offense cometh." If we shall suppose that American slavery is one of those offenses which, in the providence of God, must needs come, but which, having continued through His appointed time, He now wills to remove, and that He gives to both North and South this terrible war as the woe due to those by whom the offense came, shall we discern therein any departure from those

Confederate General Robert E. Lee (left) and Union General William Tecumseh Sherman (right)

Table 16.1 — Major Battles of the Civil War, 1861 - 1865

Battle or Campaign	Date	State	Outcome
Battle of Fort Sumter	April 12, 1861	South Carolina	Confederate victory; first battle of American Civil War
First Bull Run	July 21, 1861	Virginia	Confederate victory that bolstered southern confidence
Fort Henry / Fort Donelson	February 6, 1862 / February 11-16, 1862	Tennessee	Union victory that gave the North control of strategic river systems
Battle of Shiloh	April 6-7, 1862	Tennessee	Union victory
Seven Days Battles	June 25-July 1, 1862	Virginia	Standoff; halted Union General McClellan's advance on Richmond in the Peninsula Campaign
Second Bull Run	August 29-30, 1862	Virginia	Confederate victory
Antietam	September 17, 1862	Maryland	Standoff; halted Lee's first advance into the North
Fredericksburg	December 13, 1862	Virginia	Confederate victory that revived morale of Lee's army
Chancellorsville	April 30-May 6, 1863	Virginia	Confederate victory; Confederate General Thomas "Stonewall" Jackson killed
Gettysburg	July 1-3, 1863	Pennsylvania	Union victory; halted second Confederate advance into the North
Vicksburg	May 18-July 4, 1863	Mississippi	Union victory; Union gained complete control of the Mississippi River
Chattanooga	August – November 1863	Tennessee	Union victory
Chickamauga	September 19-20, 1863	Georgia	Confederate victory
Battle of Fort Pillow	April 12, 1864	Tennessee	Confederate victory; Confederate troops under General Nathan B. Forrest massacres black soldiers
Battle of the Wilderness	May 5-7, 1864	Virginia	Standoff; Union and Confederate forces suffer huge losses; Union General Grant continues advance toward Richmond
Battle of Spotsylvania Court House	May 8-21, 1864	Virginia	Standoff; Union and Confederate forces suffer huge losses
Cold Harbor	May 31-June12, 1864	Virginia	Confederate victory; Lee repulses Grant
Battle of Petersburg	June 9, 1864	Virginia	Confederate victory; Beauregard defeats Butler
Battle of Kennesaw Mountain	June 27, 1864	Georgia	Confederate victory; Johnston repulses Sherman
Battle of Atlanta	May-September, 1864	Georgia	Union victory; Union General Sherman captures Atlanta
Sherman's March to the sea	November 16-December 21, 1864	Georgia	Union victory; Sherman's forces destroy southern infrastructure along a wide path
Battle of Bentonville	March 19-21, 1865	North Carolina	Union victory; Sherman defeats Confederates
Appomattox Court House	April 9, 1865	Virginia	Lee was surrounded and surrendered formally to Grant

John Wilkes Booth

divine attributes which the believers in a living God always ascribe to Him? Fondly do we hope, fervently do we pray, that this mighty scourge of war may speedily pass away. Yet, if God wills that it continue until all the wealth piled by the bondsman's two hundred and fifty years of unrequited toil shall be sunk, and until every drop of blood drawn with the lash shall be paid by another drawn with the sword, as was said three thousand years ago, so still it must be said "the judgments of the Lord are true and righteous altogether."

Lincoln, however, did permit himself briefly to consider the future. "With malice toward none… let us strive on to finish the work we are in, to bind up the nation's wounds,…to do all which may achieve and cherish a just and lasting peace among ourselves and with all nations."

With that brief statement, Lincoln summed up the magnitude of the conflict and offered a hint of vision for the post-war Reconstruction era. Most significantly, the war brought an end to slavery. By the end of 1865, the United States would ratify the **Thirteenth Amendment,** which placed Lincoln's wartime policy of emancipation on firm constitutional footing. The conflict also fundamentally transformed both the North and the South. The North emerged from the war as an economic powerhouse and the region's interests were now firmly wedded to

Bioterrorism

The threat of bioterrorism did not originate in the twenty-first century. During the Civil War southern sympathizers concocted a plan to spread the dreaded disease of yellow fever in northern cities. At the time, there was no known treatment for yellow fever, which spread rapidly through cities causing swift death after the victims bled through their noses and mouths and threw up black dried blood.

In 1864 a mysterious doctor, Luke Blackburn, arrived in Bermuda where a yellow fever epidemic was decimating the population. For a month he devotedly cared for the sick and dying, declining to accept any money for his efforts. His real motive, however, was to obtain clothing, blankets, and sheets contaminated by victims of yellow fever. He filled three trunks with these items, many stained with black vomit, and tried to ship them to Canada. From there, he planned to bring them to New York where he expected to start an epidemic.

A spy, who informed the United States consul about Dr. Blackburn's nefarious schemes, thwarted the plot. Despite the efforts of a Confederate spy to warn the keeper of the clothing, a Mr. Swan, that the conspiracy had been uncovered, Mr. Swan was caught "preparing to burn the damaging articles" and sent to prison. The plot was revealed in the North on the same day that Lincoln was assassinated. Dr. Blackburn, called the "fever fiend" by northern newspapers, was charged with murder but was not prosecuted due to insufficient evidence. He later returned to his home state of Kentucky where he was elected governor in 1879. He resumed his medical practice there and became known for his courageous work in fighting yellow fever with disinfectants and quarantines.

Ironically, the plot (and another similar one) would never have worked. In 1901 it was discovered that infected mosquitoes, rather than people, spread yellow fever.

national policy. The war left the South economically devastated—it would not recover for decades—and politically weakened, although it was by no means rendered impotent. As he delivered that address, Lincoln and Congress were already engaged in the process of developing a plan for Reconstruction, and Lincoln may have favored a strategy that would have rapidly restored the South to the Union.

Whatever Lincoln may have planned, however, he had no chance to carry them out. Less than a week after Lee's surrender to Grant at **Appomattox Court House**, **John Wilkes Booth**, a Confederate sympathizer from a prominent Maryland acting family, assassinated Lincoln while he relaxed watching a comedic play in a Washington, D.C., theater. The difficult work of Reconstruction would then fall into the hands of the recently selected Vice President Andrew Johnson and Republicans in Congress. Johnson would prove to be a starkly different leader than his predecessor. Though a Unionist, the new president was also a Southerner who carried a deep hostility toward both planters and free blacks. Had Johnson and Congressional Republican leaders agreed on Reconstruction policies, then the transition to peacetime would have been much smoother, but their disagreements would add to the tumult of the postwar period.

As Johnson and his contemporaries prepared to move forward, they faced a continuation of a variety of lingering issues. One involved the persistent bad blood between veterans of the war. Although Lincoln had suggested "malice toward none" and "with charity for all," memories of the war would endure in both regions. Soldiers, like the amputee Jonathan Alison, gave up a great deal in the war, and they struggled with the idea of a rapid reunion with those they considered rebels and traitors. Debates over the place of African Americans in American society would also continue. Although the Civil War brought an end to slavery in the United States, what freedom meant remained an open question—and one that would not be settled for decades to come.

Chronology

1861   Confederate States of America formed and Jefferson Davis named president.
Firing on Fort Sumter begins Civil War.
Lincoln calls up militia and suspends *habeas corpus*.
Union blockades the Confederacy.
Trent incident endangers U.S.-British relations.
First Battle of Bull Run.

1862   The *Monitor* battles the *Merrimac*.
Battle of Shiloh.
Second Battle of Bull Run.
Battle of Antietam.
Battle of Fredericksburg.
Confederacy institutes military draft.
Homestead Act passed.
Morrill Land Grant College Act passed.
Union Pacific Railroad chartered.

1863   Lincoln issues Emancipation Proclamation.
Congress enacts military draft.
Battle of Chancellorsville.
Battle of Gettysburg and surrender of Vicksburg.
New York City antidraft riots erupt.
Food riots break out in the South.

1864   Battle of the Wilderness.
Siege of Petersburg.
Sherman's "March to the Sea" through Georgia.
Lincoln reelected.

1865   Lee surrenders at Appomattox.
Thirteenth Amendment abolishes slavery.
Lincoln assassinated.

Review Questions

1. What were the relative advantages held by the North and the South in the Civil War and the weaknesses suffered by each side?

2. What challenges did the Union and the Confederacy face in manning, funding and supplying their armies, and what was the reaction to conscription in each region?

3. What factors shaped the attitude of European powers towards the American Civil War?

4. What issues shaped how and when Abraham Lincoln issued the Emancipation Proclamation?

5. How did perceptions of President Lincoln vary and evolve during the course of the Civil War?

Glossary of Important People and Concepts

Charles Francis Adams
Andersonville
"Anaconda Plan"
Battle of Antietam
Appomattox Courthouse
Clara Barton
Pierre Gustave Toutant Beauregard
John Wilkes Booth
Belle Boyd
First Battle of Bull Run
Second Battle of Bull Run
Battle of Chancellorsville
Chattanooga Campaign
Battle of Cold Harbor
Copperheads
C.S.S. Alabama
Jefferson Davis
Dorothea Dix
Emancipation Proclamation
David Farragut
Nathan Bedford Forrest
Gettysburg Address
Habeas corpus
Thomas J. "Stonewall" Jackson
Andrew Johnson
Abraham Lincoln
March to the Sea
Phillip S. Sheridan
William Tecumseh Sherman
Thirteenth Amendment
Mary Walker

SUGGESTED READINGS

Iver Bernstein, *The New York City Draft Riots* (1990).
Bruce Catton, *The Civil War* (1985).
David Donald, *Lincoln* (1995).
―― *Charles Sumner and the Coming of the Civil War* (1981).
Joseph Glatthaar, *Forged in Battle: The Civil War Alliance of Black Soldiers and White Officers* (1990).
Herman Hatttaway, *Shades of Blue and Gray* (1997).
Elizabeth Leonard, *Yankee Women: Gender Battles in the Civil War* (1994).
Glenn Lindend and Thomas Pressly, *Voices From the House Divided* (1995).
Leon Litwack, *Been in the Storm So Long: The Aftermath of Slavery* (1979)
William McFeely, *Grant* (1981).
James McPherson, *Abraham Lincoln and the Second American Revolution* (1990).
―― *Battle Cry of Freedom* (1988).
―― *For Cause and Comrades* (1998).
―― *The Negro's Civil War* (1965).
Mayo, Louise, *The House Divided: America in the Era of Civil War and Reconstruction* (2009).
Reid Mitchell, *The Vacant Chair: The Northern Soldier Leaves Home* (1993).
Mark Neely, *The Fate of Liberty: Abraham Lincoln and Civil Liberties* (1991).
―― *The Last Best Hope of Earth: Abraham Lincoln and the Promise of America* (1993).
Stephen Sears, *George B. McClellan: The Young Napoleon* (1988).
Wendy Hamand Venet, *Neither Ballots nor Bullets: Women Abolitionists and the Civil War* (1991).
Ronald C. White Jr., *Lincoln's Greatest Speech: The Second Inaugural* (2002).
Bell Wiley, *The Life of Billy Yank* (1952).
―― *The Life of Johnny Reb* (1943).
Garry Wills, *Lincoln at Gettysburg* (1992).
C. Vann Woodward, ed., *Mary Chestnut's Civil War* (1982).

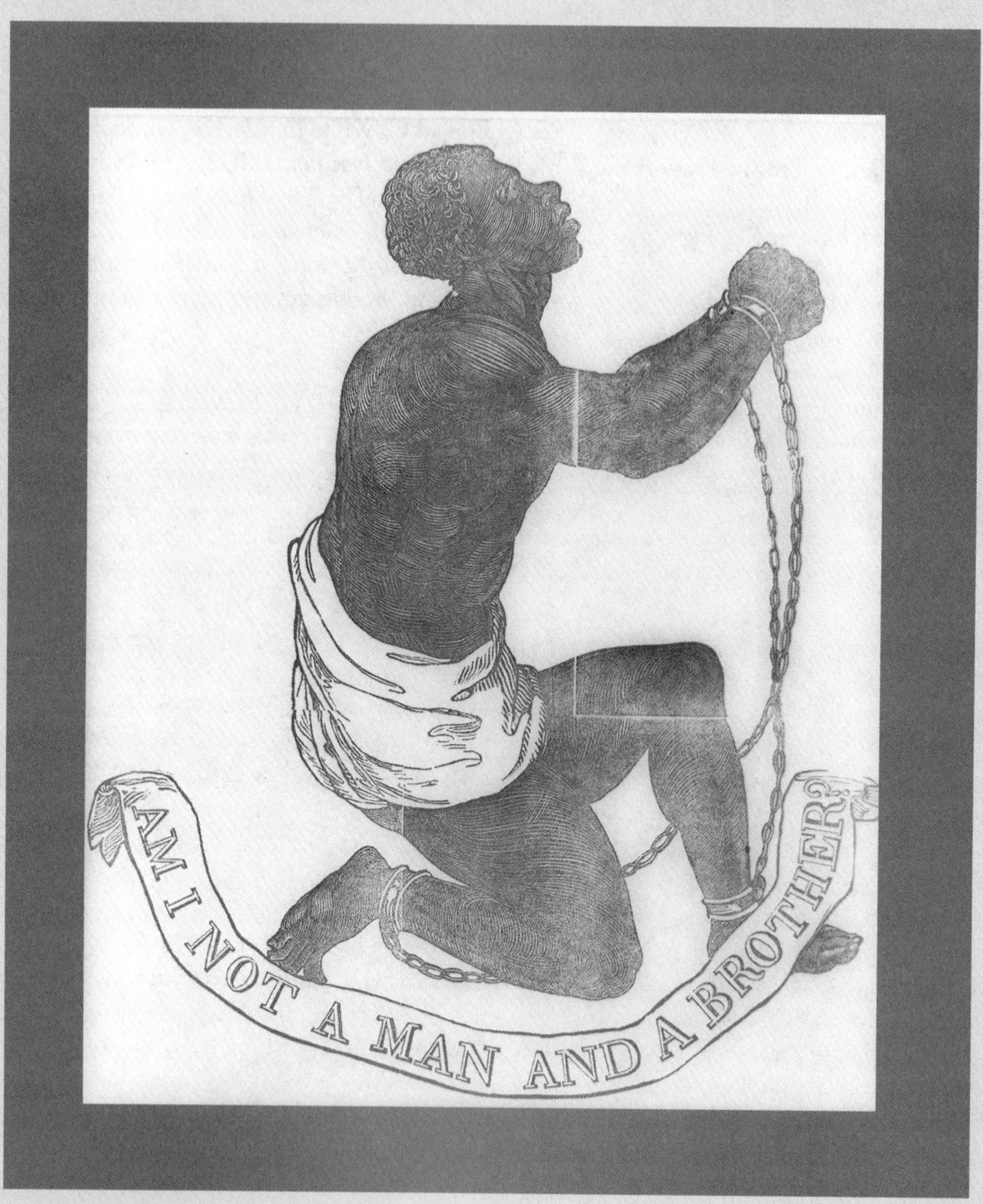
AM I NOT A MAN AND A BROTHER?

Chapter Seventeen

RECONSTRUCTION: The Turning Point That Never Turned

In April 1864, one year before Abraham Lincoln's assassination, wealthy South Carolina slave owner and rice planter Robert Allston died of pneumonia. His daughter, Elizabeth, was bereft of "terrible desolation and sorrow." As the Civil War raged on around her, Elizabeth and her mother tried to maintain their many rice plantations. With Yankee troops ravaging their way through coastal South Carolina in the late winter of 1864-65, Elizabeth's grieving for the loss of her father turned to "terror" for she was certain that the Union soldiers would ransack her plantation and inflict "all manner of mischief and unspeakable behavior" upon her and her mother and even their slaves. Union soldiers did indeed pillage their home, looking for liquor and hidden valuables as well as encouraging the slaves to have their way with the Allston's furniture and other household goods. Some slaves did take such items from the "Big House" to their slave cabins, but after the soldiers had left, returned them to the Allston house. However, before they left, the Yankee soldiers did give the keys to crop barns to the semi-free slaves.

When the war was over, the widow Adele Allston took an oath of allegiance to the United States and secured a written order from the local Union general in command for her former slaves to give back the keys. She and Elizabeth made plans to return in the early summer of 1864 to begin anew the family plantation, thereby reestablishing white authority of their black labor force, which although now free was supposed to continue to work for the Allston family per the orders of the Union army of occupation. Mrs. Allston was assured that although their former slaves were free and could even now possess firearms as a "means to a livelihood, no outrage has been committed against whites except in the matter of property." To the Allstons, property was the key issue, and the possession of the keys to the barns, Elizabeth wrote, would be the "test case" of whether former slaves or their former masters would control land, labor and its fruits, and even subtle aspects of interpersonal relations.

No doubt the Allston women returned to their estate, Nightingale Hall, with much trepidation, not knowing how they would be greeted by their former slaves. To their surprise and relief, a pleasant reunion took place, for many of the slaves had always liked the women and had remained loyal to the family throughout slavery and the war. The Allston women knew all of their slaves' names, greeted them accordingly, inquired after their children, and caught up on the affairs with whom they had lived closely for many years. To their further delight, a trusted foreman handed over the keys to the barns. Such an interesting scene of harmony and the display of good will of blacks towards whites and vice versa was more common than not in the South in the war's and emancipation's immediate aftermath.

However, not every black-white encounter was "sunshine and roses" at the Allstons' plantations in the South Carolina Low Country. At Guendalos, a plantation owned by a son absent during the war fighting with the Confederacy, the Allston women encountered a very different scene. Apparently the son was not nearly as kind to his slaves, who resented their master intensely for his often cruel treatment and were now ready to ventilate their rage on the Allston women. As their carriage arrived and moved toward the crop barns, an armed group of angry former slaves menaced the women's buggy as it slowly drove toward the barns. The women politely asked for the keys to the barns from a former black driver, Uncle Jacob, but as he was about to hand the women the keys, the other freedmen shouted "Ef yu gie up de key, blood'll flow." Uncle Jacob slipped the keys back into his pocket. The other freedmen "would be damned" if they would relinquish barns full of rice and corn put there by black labor. The Allston women then proceeded to the Big House, where they locked themselves in as best they could. Through the night freedmen who had threatened the Allston women sang freedom songs and danced while waving hoes, pitchforks, and guns to discourage anyone from going into town for help. Two "loyal" freedmen, however, managed to escape the celebration and made it to town to find some Union soldiers who they convinced to come to the plantation and rescue the Allston women. The two freedmen returned and told their fellows that the Yankee soldiers were on their way and that they would be most upset with what had taken place. Early the next morning, the women were awakened by a knock at the front door. Adele slowly opened the door, and there stood Uncle Jacob. Without a word, he gave her the keys.

The story of the keys reveals many of the human ingredients of the Reconstruction era. Despite defeat and surrender, southern whites were determined to regain control of both their land and labor—their former slaves. Despite sporadic, half-hearted attempts by federal officials to redistribute wealth in the South by destroying the prewar landed elite and giving their land to the freedmen, throughout Reconstruction, law, property titles, and federal enforcement remained on the side of the former "slaveocracy." The Allston women were friendly, even solicitous of their slaves in a very maternalistic way, insisting on the restoration of the deferential relationship that had existed before the war. In short, both Adele and Elizabeth both feared and cared about their slaves' well-being particularly as it affected their own future. The freedmen likewise revealed mixed feelings toward their former masters. At different plantations they demonstrated a variety of emotions: anger, loyalty, love, resentment, and pride. Even at Guendalos, respect was paid to the person of the Allstons but not to their property and crops. The freedmen's actions indicated that what they wanted was not revenge for generations of bondage but economic independence and freedom.

In this encounter between former slaves and their mistresses, the role of northern officials, particularly that of the United States Army, is also revealing. The Union soldiers literally and symbolically gave the keys of freedom to the blacks but did not stay around long enough to guarantee that freedom, and such would be the case throughout most of Reconstruction relative to the freedmen protection of both his person and economic and civil rights. Although encouraging the freedmen to plunder the Allston's estate and take possession of the crops, they then disappeared, leaving the ultimate decision to engage in such activity up to the freedmen. The soldiers' retreat demonstrated to freedmen that in the end, they would be on their own to find a way through a very changed existence. Indeed, Uncle Jacob appeared to grasp the limits of northern help, handing the keys to land and liberty back into the hands of whom he prophetically or instinctually knew his future fate in the South would ultimately lie. The Guendalos freedmen knew that if they wanted to ensure their freedom, they had to do it themselves.

A major theme of the immediate postwar years is the story of what happened to the conflicting goals and dreams of three groups as they sought to form new social, economic, and political relationships during the Reconstruction era. Amid devastation and divisions of class and race, white Southerners sought to put their lives back together again while black Southerners attempted to establish themselves as a respected free people. Meanwhile, northern whites, with varying degrees of motivation, commitment, humanity, and success, tried to help the freedmen achieve a life of social and economic independence as well as a respect for their rights as human beings and citizens. The interplay of these three groups guaranteed that the Reconstruction era would be divisive, leaving a mixed legacy of human gains and losses.

THE CONFEDERACY'S DEFEAT

The Civil War presents one of the greatest paradoxes in United States history. For forty years (1820-1860), white Americans debated slavery, sometimes violently and never without acrimony. Yet, rarely if ever, did their arguments reflect any genuine humanitarian concern for the plight of the millions of African Americans in bondage. Even many abolitionists worried more about the sin and stigma of slavery upon the nation's image than about the institution's barbarity. White Americans were divided not on the morality of slavery but on the institution's political and economic ramifications. Such little regard for the slaves' condition reflected an inherent and prevailing racism among the majority of northern whites, including a good number of even the most zealous of abolitionists.

RECONSTRUCTION: *The Turning Point That Never Turned* / 473

Five generations lived on Smith's Plantation, Beaufort, South Carolina, 1862.

Although condemning slavery on moral and religious grounds and recognizing and valuing African Americans as human beings, many abolitionists nonetheless believed blacks to be innately inferior to whites. Such underlying racist sentiments among even abolitionists helped to reinforce the ghettoization and marginalization of the thousands of free blacks already living in the North in 1860. For the majority of them, daily life was not that much better than it had been in bondage; the only appreciable difference was that at least one was "free" and no longer chattel. Thus, when pushed by other northern whites on the issue of post-emancipation assimilation of the freedmen, abolitionists either dodged the issue or advocated a deportation/colonization agenda. Such a position by those who were supposedly the African Americans' greatest champions for manumission were at the same time opposed to integration and equality for black Americans as their more overtly racist counterparts. Such northern white racism towards African Americans shaped the course of Reconstruction.

Since the nation's official beginning in 1787 with the enactment of the Constitution and over the course of the next seventy-three years, the political elite avoided confrontation and the potential disruption of the Union by promulgating a series of compromises on the slavery expansion issue. However, by the late 1850s, the political leadership at that time proved incapable of finding common ground to forge another compromise. By 1860, southern whites, led by the "slaveocracy," concluded that their inalienable right to "property" (their slaves) was no longer secure in the Union and thus seceded, declaring that the Union that had been created in 1787 had been subverted by a "black Republican" Party determined not only to abolish slavery but also to abrogate states' rights, which to southern slave owners meant the right to own slaves and to take their property anywhere they deemed essential for their "pursuit of happiness." Therein lies part of the paradox of the Civil War: a conflict caused by slavery yet became the nation's greatest bloodbath ignited by secession. In the end, the United States convulsed in bloody conflict, not to end the blight of human bondage but to preserve the Union—for an abstract entity rather than for the liberation of human beings.

Reinforcing this theme was the fact that the majority of northern whites were as racist in their attitudes and treatment of the free blacks in their communities as their white southern counterparts. Indeed, by 1860, significant numbers of northern whites had come to despise the "Black Republicans" for their position on slavery while denying civil rights to the black people in their own states. Secession, however, united northern whites. In the northern white mind, secession and slavery were mutually exclusive issues: the former tied to the sanctity of nationhood, with the latter associated with a race of inferior people, not worth a blood sacrifice. Nonetheless, an interesting coalition formed in the North during the war years that helped to guarantee a Union triumph. Unionists and antislavery men put aside their differences and joined forces, for both knew they could not obtain their respective objectives without the other. Both opposed secession and agreed that the Union must be preserved. Unionists, however, did not see the abolition of slavery and the preservation of the Union as symbiotic. Yet, the Unionists knew they could not defeat the secessionists without antislavery support, and abolitionists knew they would not see the end of slavery without Unionist support, nor without defeating the Confederacy. Thus an uneasy alliance formed between the two groups. The Union victory put an end to the coalition, for the two allies no longer needed one another. Most importantly, the Confederacy's defeat transformed the issue of union into a question of race, and the freedmen (ex-slaves) had few northern supporters and thus were doomed almost from the beginning of Reconstruction to a life of continued servility, oppression, poverty, illiteracy, terror, and, all too frequently, an early death. Whenever a successful coalition dissolves after a war because of dissension among the victors, the vanquished, if shrewd and united, almost always find an opportunity to reassert or reclaim their power, often in a greater, more dominating form than before the conflict. That was precisely what the white South was able to accomplish by the end of Reconstruction.

RECONSTRUCTION'S OVERARCHING ISSUES

Without question, the emancipation of four million African Americans from bondage presented both white and black Americans with Reconstruction's most pressing issue. There was simply no consensus among whites, and even among some blacks, about the possible place of freed people in a reconstructed United States. Both black and white leaders, including Abraham Lincoln, wondered, if not doubted, whether different races could ever peacefully co-exist, let alone be willing to accept each other as equal citizens. Also vexing, especially for white Northerners, was the question of how southern whites, particularly those who had aided and encouraged the slaveholders' rebellion, were to be treated. Should they be punished—executed or imprisoned, permanently disenfranchised or their property confiscated? On what terms should the Confederate or rebellious states return to the Union? And finally, what would be the powers of the states and of the national government in a reconstructed Union?

The Civil War cost $6.5 billion, not including the pensions for wounded and elderly soldiers and widows and orphans of the conflict (by 1890 such payments represented 40 percent of the federal budget). That amount of money would have been more than enough in 1861 for the Lincoln administration to buy the freedom of all four million southern slaves from their masters, which, after all, was what Lincoln had advocated all along—"emancipation with compensation." Moreover, there would have been enough money left over to give each African-American family 40 acres and a mule and some cash. The breaking up of rebel plantation estates and parceling out that land to freedmen in 40-acre allotments was the Radical Republican's initial vision and agenda for the South's economic reconstruction. However, the plan was never implemented.

Although Reconstruction would affect every aspect of southern life, its most dramatic and enduring impact was social—the daily working out by black and white, male and female, and rich and poor of how they were to treat each other in these changed times. In some instances these social dramas reflected old ties sundered or renewed, as when former slaves drifted back to the plantation after having enjoyed freedom for a few weeks, looking for work or someone to provide for them as "old massa" had for years. Sometimes the bonds were reversed: a freedmen bringing food to a former master who was now steeped in poverty, a white man being hauled before a black judge, African Americans defending their homes with rifles, a black militia instead of a white slave patrol, or interracial crowds of Union League supporters celebrating Independence Day. Other transformations were smaller: freedmen driving newly bought buggies or poor black and white children attending school together. Of such seemingly insignificant changes revolutions are made; against such dread reordering, the forces of reaction launch their strongest battalions. So it would be in the Reconstruction of the South.

Reconstruction unleashed unforeseen conflicts that propelled events along a startling revolutionary path. The dialectic between conservatism and revolution, along with the desire for order and for freedom, defined Reconstruction in terms of its successes and failures. In the beginning, only one certainty prevailed: thousands of black

Abraham Lincoln

Southerners eagerly awaited its advent while thousands of their white counterparts dreaded its inaugural.

WARTIME AND PRESIDENTIAL RECONSTRUCTION

Abraham Lincoln

No history of **Reconstruction** would be complete, or accurate, without a discussion of **Abraham Lincoln**'s views and policies, no matter how ambiguous, conflicting, inconsistent, and half-hearted they might have been. Although Lincoln is considered to be the nation's greatest president because he successfully held the country together through its most perilous ordeal, he nonetheless had flaws, especially when it came to the issue of race, which became Reconstruction's most critical dynamic. Perhaps the first question that must be asked regarding Lincoln and his racial views is: Was Lincoln a racist himself? The answer is a qualified "yes." As he declared during the 1858 Illinois Senate race in one of his debates with Stephen Douglas, "I am not, nor ever have been in favor of bringing about in any way the social and political equality of the white and black races; that I am not, nor ever have been in favor of making voters or jurors of Negroes, nor of qualifying them to hold office, nor to intermarry with white people . . . . there is a physical difference between the white and black races, which I believe will forever forbid the two races living together on terms of social and political equality. And inasmuch as they cannot so live, while they do remain together there must be the position of superior and inferior, and I as much as any other man am in favor of having the superior position assigned to the white man."

If the above statement is taken at face value, then Lincoln was indeed a "white supremacist," holding the same racial attitudes at that time as the majority of his fellow white citizens. But was Lincoln's racism simply "political"; that is, was he expressing such views in order to win votes? Four years earlier a different Lincoln is revealed, one who recognized that color prejudice was a totally irrational basis for determining race relations. "If A can prove conclusively that he may of right enslave B—why may not B snatch the same argument, and prove equally, that he may enslave A? You say A is white and B is black. It is *color* then; the lighter having the right to enslave the darker? Take care. By this rule, you are to be the slave to the first man you meet with a fairer skin than your own. You do not mean *color* exactly? You mean the whites are *intellectually* the superiors of the blacks, and therefore you have the right to enslave them? Take care again. By this rule, you are to be slave to the first man you meet with an intellect superior to your own. But you say, it is a question of *interest*; and if you make it your interest, you have the right to enslave others. Very well. And if he can make it his interest, he has the right to enslave you."

Unfortunately for posterity, Lincoln never publicly stated this lean and muscular bit of reasoning. Had he done so, the racist label would have been expunged, especially when coupled with his public declaration that both he and his party (the Republicans) considered slavery as "a wrong . . . a moral, social, and political wrong." Thus, at best, Lincoln, like many of his white contemporaries, was ambiguous about race in America. Lincoln, without question, believed blacks to be people, human beings, albeit "inferior" but nonetheless members of the human race entitled to their freedom. To enslave them and strip them of their humanity and reduce them to property was, as he publicly announced, morally, socially, and politically wrong, particularly in a country that proclaimed to the world in 1776 that "all men are created equal." To Lincoln, this included "men of color" as well.

Although publicly condemning human bondage and acknowledging the slaves' humanity, Lincoln was not willing to engage in a clash of arms to rid the nation of chattel slavery. From the moment that the first salvos were fired, Lincoln believed that the Civil War was unequivocally about preserving the Union, and thus the slavery issue became of much lesser importance. He made this point very clear in a letter to newspaper publisher Horace Greeley in August 1862. "My paramount objective is to save the Union, and is not either to save or destroy slavery. If I could save the Union without freeing any slave, I would do it; and if I could save it by freeing all the slaves, I would do it; and if I could save it by freeing some and leaving others alone, I would also do that. What I do about slavery and the colored race, I do because I believe it helps to save this Union." Interestingly, the Emancipation Proclamation, though at this point unannounced, was already in his desk, the result of his conclusion that such an act would help the Union cause by giving Yankee soldiers and northern whites hopefully something more tangible to fight for than an abstraction—the Union—while simultaneously crippling the Confederate war effort by depriving it of valuable labor. Thus for reasons political and strategic, Lincoln "freed the slaves" in the states still in rebellion against the United States on January 1, 1863.

As the man who issued the Emancipation Proclamation and as the key leader in securing congressional adoption of the **Thirteenth Amendment**, Lincoln could certainly be called the "Emancipator," albeit a reluctant one. No sooner did the Emancipation Proclamation go into effect than Lincoln initiated "phase two" of his manumission agenda—the colonization of freedmen outside the United States in Haiti, in Panama, or elsewhere in the Western Hemisphere in which could be found countries with all-black populations. Could such an initiative be further proof of Lincoln's inherent racism? Perhaps, for it appears that Lincoln had thought about this idea for quite some time as part of his overall emancipation plan. He tested black receptivity to his scheme in August 1862 when he invited to the Oval Office a group of already free African Americans, some of whom had been interested in colonization, to confer with him about such a prospect. Usually a man with great sensitivity to others' feelings, Lincoln on this occasion seemed hard-hearted and insensitive. Observing that whites and blacks were of different races, he said further, "your race suffers greatly and we of the white race suffer from your presence. Even when you cease to be slaves, you are yet far removed from being on an equality with the white race. On this broad continent, not a single man of your race is made the equal of a single man of ours. I cannot alter it if I could. It is a fact. It is better for us both to be separated." He then proceeded to describe to them the attractions of an area in Colombia (the future country of Panama) made available for such purposes by the Colombian government, which at the time needed to populate the isthmus. Lincoln urged them to emigrate there as soon as possible.

Again, if Lincoln's words are taken at face value, then he most definitely was a racist. However, Lincoln's racist rhetoric and callousness could also be interpreted as an awkward attempt at humanitarianism. By painting such a bleak and cruel picture of post-emancipation for freedmen, perhaps Lincoln was trying to impress upon African Americans a harsh reality few could envision. In effect, what Lincoln was trying to say to his black audience was that America was for whites only and that the overwhelming majority of white Americans, including himself, subscribed to that racist premise and thus a post-Civil War United States would be anything but a safe haven for freedmen. By encouraging emigration, Lincoln hoped to save blacks from the oppression, violence, and anguish that would become part and parcel of their everyday life in the South for the next 100 years.

Entirely separate from the harshness of telling African Americans that they were to pursue their new life as a free people in some place other than the land of their birth, Lincoln's plan was completely unrealistic: the United States had neither the facilities to colonize four million human beings nor a place to which it could send them. At the existing procreation rate, no less than five hundred black Americans were being born in the United States every day, it would thus be logistically impossible to "colonize" (deport) the African-American population as rapidly as it was increasing. Moreover, increasing numbers of black leaders, abolitionists, and many Republicans objected to Lincoln's policy, rightly arguing that such action would punish the victims of racial prejudice rather than its perpetrators. Blacks were Americans. Why should they not have the rights of American citizens instead of being urged to leave the country?

Nonetheless, Lincoln actually got a colonization experiment into operation in April 1863, when a group of 453 freedmen settled on Cow Island (Île à Vache), off Haiti. Predictably, they suffered and died from smallpox, malaria, and poisonous insects. They were unable to sustain themselves because of infertile soil, and in March 1864, a Navy transport arrived and took 368 survivors back to the United States. Despite the dismal failure of the Cow Island experiment, Lincoln, to his death, continued to believe that African-American emigration was the solution to the "Negro issue" if the nation hoped to avoid generations of bitter, vicious, and tragic race relations. Lincoln's dream of colonization prevented any significant public discussion about the hard question of the position of former slaves in American society.

Although addressing the freedmen issue, Lincoln made the re-assimilation of southern *whites* his priority, especially those white Southerners whose loyalty to the Confederacy had been lukewarm. He believed these people would become the foundation for his overall objective for a rapid restoration of the Union. Lincoln's desire for leniency for southern whites became a divisive issue not only within the Republican Party but also among northern whites, many of whom believed *all* southern whites were guilty of secession and should be punished accordingly. For the moment, however, Lincoln prevailed on this issue with the promulgation of his Proclamation of Amnesty, which offered a presidential pardon to all southern whites (excluding Confederate government officials and high-ranking military officers) who took an oath of allegiance to the United States and accepted the abolition of slavery. More importantly, in any state where the number of white males aged 21 or older who took this oath equaled 10 percent of the number of 1860 voters, that group could establish a state government, which Lincoln promised he would recognize as legitimate, and that state could reenter the Union, as if it had never left.

Lincoln's so-called Ten Percent Plan outraged many Republicans, who rightly claimed that Lincoln's amnesty policy favored former Confederates at the freedmen's expense. To this opposition, Lincoln's plan smacked of betrayal and hypocrisy, for it rewarded "traitors" to the country with a complete restoration of their political rights while denying such rights to black men who had fought *for* the Union. Further incensing these Republicans was Lincoln's Proclamation of Reconstruction, which allowed ex-Confederate landowners and former slaveholders to establish labor regulations and other measures to control the freedmen's labor, so long as they recognized manumission and made minimal provisions for their ex-slaves' education.

The freedmen issue was not the only source of conflict between Lincoln and some Republicans. The question of which branch of government—executive or legislative—should have authority and control over the Reconstruction process also caused rancor. In Lincoln's mind, it should be the president. Lincoln based this prerogative on his belief that he had been engaged for four years in suppressing an insurrection, which according to Lincoln's interpretation of the Constitution was clearly an executive, not legislative, responsibility. Moreover, Lincoln never asked Congress for a "declaration of war," only the right to use force to suppress an internal rebellion, the exact term he used in April 1861 when he called for 75,000 volunteers to join the United States Army for six months. Thus, in Lincoln's mind, no state of war existed between North and South because a war can only be fought between two "legitimate" nations. In Lincoln's view, the Confederate States of America never existed as a legitimate nation because no state has the Constitutional right to secede from the Union. Based on such an interpretation of his executive powers, Lincoln assumed the right to reorganize the South and guide it back into the Union largely on his own authority as commander-in-chief.

Many congressional Republicans thought otherwise. They interpreted Lincoln's call for volunteers to suppress rebellion not to be an executive order but a declaration of war, which only Congress can approve. By sanctioning Lincoln's call for troops, Congress believed a state of war existed between the United States of America and another political entity, the Confederate States of America. If that were the case, then the legislative branch, not the executive branch, should have authority over Reconstruction, for only Congress can declare war, not the president; he can only ask for such a proclamation. Disturbing these Republicans most was Lincoln's apparent states' rights disposition. By insisting that secession was illegal, that the southern states had never actually left the Union, Lincoln appeared to be asserting that the southern states thus maintained their right to govern their own affairs. Such a rendering was completely unacceptable to hardline Republicans who rejected any notion that the rebellious states had the right to immediately reclaim their **Antebellum** status without retribution for their treason. Congressional Republicans believed that the only way to avoid such an insult to the Union dead was to challenge Lincoln's interpretation of the crisis by defining the Civil War as a war rather than a rebellion. If that conception prevailed, they, not the president, would have the Constitutional right of jurisdiction over Reconstruction, thus guaranteeing punishment of Confederates for their treasonous acts. This controversy coupled with the debate over the status of the freedmen destined the two branches of government for a showdown for power. Such a confrontation, however, would not occur until the ascendancy of Andrew Johnson to the presidency.

Radical Republicans and Reconstruction

Those within the party who opposed Lincoln's agenda became known as the "**Radicals Republicans.**" Contrary to Lincoln, these men, led by Charles Sumner of Massachusetts in the Senate and Thaddeus Stevens of Pennsylvania in the House, believed not only that the white South must be punished for secession and rebellion but for the sin of slavery as well. To the Radicals, it was quite obvious and simple what should be done in the South in the war's aftermath: all white Southerners, regardless of status, should be punished for their treason, either by their property confiscated or disfranchisement, or both. Appropriated rebel land should then be given to freedmen to help them to establish themselves. The Radicals feared that Lincoln's lenient policies would result in the old ruling class being restored to power. To prevent that possibility, Radicals Republicans proposed that freedmen be given the right to vote, which, they

John Wilkes Booth

believed, would ensure a genuine nucleus of loyal supporters in the South.

The Radicals countered with their own plan, the **Wade-Davis Bill** (named for Senator Benjamin Wade of Ohio and Representative Henry Winter Davis of Maryland), which required white Southerners to take a much more stringent loyalty oath (the "**iron clad oath**") as well as requiring 50 percent rather than Lincoln's 10 percent of the population to swear allegiance to the Union. Surprisingly, the Wade-Davis Bill made no provision for black enfranchisement, the result of the Radicals being a minority within the Republican Party at that time (1864). The majority of congressional Republicans were moderates and conservatives, cool to the idea of black voting rights and thus were more inclined to support Lincoln's agenda rather than that of the Radicals. With such a coalition behind him, Lincoln killed the Wade-Davis Bill with a pocket veto (whereby a bill passed at the end of a congressional session fails to become law if it is not signed by the president).

Although upset with Lincoln, the Radicals were loyal Republicans and thus united with their more moderate comrades to ensure Lincoln's and their party's victory and control of both the White House and Congress. By the spring of 1865, the Confederacy's collapse was only a matter of weeks, setting the stage for a compromise between Lincoln and Congress on a policy for the postwar South. Two days after Lee's surrender to Ulysses S. Grant at Appomattox, Lincoln promised that he would soon announce a more thorough Reconstruction agenda, which he intimated would include provisions for black enfranchisement and stronger guarantees to protect their civil rights.

Tragically for the entire nation, no one will ever know what Lincoln had in store for the South or for four million African Americans. On April 14, 1865, as Lincoln and his wife watched a play at Ford's Theater in Washington, a rebel fanatic actor named John Wilkes Booth shot Lincoln at close range in the back of the head, leaped to the stage, and escaped. Lincoln never recovered consciousness, dying early the next morning.

Booth was part of a larger conspiracy of rebel zealots, which almost succeeded in beheading the national executive branch in one, coordinated fatal blow. While Booth murdered Lincoln, his two compatriots, Lewis Powell and George Atzerodt, were supposed to kill Secretary of State William Seward (Powell's target) and Vice President Andrew Johnson (Atzerodt's assigned victim). Atzerdodt got drunk and backed down. Powell came close to succeeding with his knife, but a heavily-wounded Seward fought off his attacker enough to survive. Powell was later hanged with the other conspirators. After a long and frantic search, Booth was captured and killed in a Virginia barn. The assassin's bullet lost a hero for the North, a potential ally for fair and equal opportunity for African Americans, and a leader who called for "charity toward all" and "malice toward none" for southern whites.

ANDREW JOHNSON AND RECONSTRUCTION

Between 1865 and 1868, the United States confronted one of the greatest political crises of its history—the battle between President Andrew Johnson and Congress over Reconstruction. The struggle resulted in profound changes in the nature of citizenship, the structure of constitutional authority, and the meaning of American freedom.

Booth's bullet elevated to the presidency a man who still thought himself a Democrat and a Southerner: Andrew Johnson of Tennessee. Originally from North Carolina of poor white heritage, Johnson rose to power in Tennessee politics as a Jacksonian populist, championing the cause of the small, non-slaveholding farmers, shopkeepers, and artisans of East Tennessee against the planter elite of the state's central and western regions who controlled Tennessee politically. True to his Jacksonian core, Johnson was equally suspicious and hostile toward banks, corporations, bondholders, and New Englanders. He fervidly opposed the Whig/Republican policy of government participation in, and promotion of, the

Andrew Johnson, 1866.

nation's economic development. Johnson's enemies list included not only the plantation aristocracy but also the "bloated, corrupt aristocracy" of the commercial-industrial economy emerging in the Northeast. A devoted Unionist, Johnson was the only senator from a seceding state not to support the Confederacy. For his loyalty, the Republicans in 1864 rewarded him with their party's vice-presidential nomination, hoping that his presence on the ticket would attract the votes of northern pro-war Democrats and Upper South yeoman Unionists.

Although many Radicals believed that Johnson would be too "soft" on his white southern brethren, such concerns faded quickly as the new president displayed an enmity toward "the stuck up [slaveholding] aristocrats" that shocked at times even the most passionate of Radicals. In Johnson's mind it was clear from the start that it was the South's slaveholding elite who had been responsible for secession and war. Thus the time had come to punish these "traitors. Traitors must be impoverished; they must not only be punished, but their social power must be destroyed."

The Radical Republicans delighted in Johnson's harsh rhetoric. His rantings against the slaveocracy seemed to convey that he was in agreement with the Radicals on the type of reconstruction policy to be pursued—one that would disenfranchise former Confederates but would enfranchise the freedmen. With Johnson's support, the Radicals envisioned the creation of a coalition between the freedmen and the small minority of southern white Unionists. Together they would become the basis for a new southern political order; naturally they would become Republicans, the party of Union and emancipation. Once such a coalition took power in the southern states, they would pass laws to provide civil rights and economic opportunity for African Americans. Not incidentally, these new Republicans would also strengthen the party nationally by ending the Democrats' domination over the southern states.

Much to the Radicals' and even some moderate Republicans' dismay, Johnson proved hostile to the party's vision of the freedmen's place in society. Although earlier proclaiming to be black Tennesseans "Moses," leading them out of bondage, Johnson never embraced the liberal tenets of the antislavery ideology. Indeed, Johnson had once owned slaves himself. To Johnson, the Civil War concerned combating secession and destroying the power of those responsible—the planter elite; it was never a crusade to end slavery. In 1866, a black delegation led by Frederick Douglass visited with Johnson to urge the president to include provisions for black suffrage in his reconstruction agenda. Johnson parried their arguments and afterwards remarked to his secretary: "Those damned sons of bitches thought they had me in a trap! I know that damned Douglass; he is just like any other nigger, and he would sooner cut a white man's throat than not."

Johnson clearly was a racist, sharing with his white brethren, North and South, a firm belief in white supremacy. Johnson and other non-slaveholding white Southerners may have despised the slaveocracy, but it was not because they owned slaves. It had been their possession of disproportionate political power that had caused such dislike.

This ideology even took hold in the North, which saw the Democratic Party aggressively champion white supremacy, resulting in the party's ability to attract the Irish, southern Midwest "Butternuts" (white Southerners who migrated to the southern areas of free states such as Indiana, Illinois, and Ohio), and unskilled laborers to its camp. These people believed blacks to be inferior, and no matter how poor they might be, these white people were still better than blacks. Like their southern non-slaveholding counterparts, they feared emancipation because it would render their whiteness meaningless.

To many Republicans' further consternation, Johnson, like Lincoln, believed Reconstruction (which he preferred to call "restoration") to be primarily an executive function. He also believed in Lincoln's theory of "indestructible states"—that the rebellion had been one of individuals, not states, and although the individuals might be punished, the states retained all their constitutional rights. Given such conflicting views about who should control the reconstruction agenda and what the priorities were to be, it would only be a matter of time before the inevitable occurred: a nasty showdown between the president and a Republican-dominated Congress.

Johnson's Reconstruction Policy

In May 1865, Johnson fired the opening salvo in his war with congressional Republicans when he issued two proclamations on his own initiative. The first provided for a blanket amnesty and restitution of property (except slaves, of course) to all who would take an oath of allegiance. Excluded from Johnson's general pardon were Confederate civil and diplomatic officials, army officers above the rank of colonel, state governors, and all persons owning taxable property valued at $20,000 or more. Johnson was true to his word that he would punish those most responsible for having caused the war—the stuck-up aristocrats. In his second edict, beginning with North Carolina, Johnson personally appointed provisional governors for the former Confederate states, directing them to call elections for delegates to draft new state constitutions. Only those white men who had received amnesty and had taken the oath of allegiance could vote. The state conventions were to draft constitutions that abolished slavery, nullified secession, and repudiated all debts incurred by the state while it was a member of the Confederacy (on the grounds that, secession being illegal, all indebtedness acquired in its behalf was null and void). Johnson's policy was clear. He excluded both the freedmen and upper-class whites from the Reconstruction process. The new political foundation for the "restored South" would be those white yeomen and artisans who had remained loyal Unionists in alliance with those who now proclaimed their fidelity.

Johnson outraged the Radical Republicans by his complete disregard for the freedmen and by his blatant slight of Congress. It appeared that Johnson was not only a dedicated white supremacist but also intent on usurping power to the executive branch by arrogating taking complete control of Reconstruction. In hopes of rallying northern opinion to their side, the Radicals bombarded voters with speeches, pamphlets, and editorials, all declaring that the president's policies would inevitably lead to the restoration of the old power structure in the South, minus only slavery.

None of the southern conventions made any provision for black suffrage in their new constitutions. Johnson made no more gestures in the direction of black enfranchisement. He stated that voting qualifications were a state matter and that it was beyond his constitutional right to interfere. Johnson's refusal to push any further for even a limited black suffrage not only alienated moderate Republicans but encouraged southern defiance on other issues as well.

The Black Suffrage Issue in the North

The Radical cause for black enfranchisement in the South received a devastating blow in the fall of 1865 when Connecticut, Minnesota, and Wisconsin held referendums on whether to amend their respective constitutions to allow the right to vote to the few black men in their states. Everyone knew that in some measure the referendums' outcomes would reveal much about northern white racial attitudes. The Democrats in these states engaged in their usual race-mongering and black-baiting with the result that the amendments were defeated in all three states. Republicans in those states voted overwhelmingly for allowing black men the right to vote. Most contemporaries interpreted the election outcomes as a northern white mandate against black suffrage. Southern whites were delighted with the results, for in their mind the amendments' defeat was confirmation that their northern white brethren were just as determined to keep the United States "a white man's country." Perhaps more importantly, the defeat of black suffrage in the North only further emboldened southern whites to flagrantly defy Johnson's Reconstruction mandates.

Southern Defiance

Not only did the southern state constitutional conventions reject black enfranchisement in any capacity, but some even balked at ratifying the Thirteenth Amendment and at repudiating the Confederate debt. Once again, throughout the South could be heard disparaging anti-Northern rhetoric and deprecating and mocking of all things "Yankee." It sounded and felt like 1861 all over again. White, neo-Confederate paramilitary units appeared, terrorizing blacks and their white sympathizers. Johnson seemed to encourage such activities by his own rhetoric and refusal to address such reprisals.

Compounding Johnson's troubles with white violence perpetrated on freedmen was the issue of presidential pardons. This particular matter caused more immediate acrimony between the president and congressional Republicans than any other controversy. After all his bluster about punishing southern traitors, Johnson had reversed himself by the fall of 1865, issuing special pardons to 13,500 ex-Confederates and restoring all property and political rights to them. The majority of these individuals were the stuck-up aristocrats who he had vowed he would impoverish and destroy only a few months earlier. What had caused this transformation in Johnson's attitude and behavior, from one who spoke menacingly about the crime of treason to one who now spoke of forgiveness? Johnson was a Southerner and had no more liking for the Radical Yankee ethos than the majority of his southern brethren. Moreover, his exchanges and encounters with the Radicals during the summer and fall of 1865 convinced him that his real friends were his southern white compatriots, including the very individuals that he once personally despised and publicly lambasted. They praised his policies and flattered his ego, while the Radicals chastised him openly and moderates expressed their concerns in private. Reveling in his power over these once-haughty aristocrats who had deprecated him as a humble tailor, Johnson waxed eloquent on his "love, respect, and confidence" toward southern whites for whom he now felt "forbearing and forgiving." Perhaps more important was the outpouring of support by northern Democrats, many of whom disingenuously whispered in his ear that he would be their party's choice in the 1868 election if he could manage to reconstruct the South in such a way that would maintain the Democratic majority there.

To the Republicans' further dismay, under the new state constitutions established by Johnson's policy, southern voters elected hundreds of former Confederates to state offices. Northerners were even more outraged by the election to Congress of nine ex-Confederate congressmen, seven former Confederate state officials, four generals, four colonels, and the selection of Confederate Vice President Alexander H. Stephens to the U.S. Senate by the new Georgia legislature. For Republicans, it appeared that the rebels, unable to capture Washington in war, were about to do so in peacetime.

The Black Codes

As many Radicals feared, no sooner did southern whites reclaim their governments than they passed the infamous "**black codes**," reflecting not only devotion to white supremacy but a determination as well to reduce the freedmen to a condition of virtual re-enslavement. The freedmen were excluded from juries and voting and could not testify against whites in court. Also forbidden was interracial marriage, and blacks suffered much harsher punishment than whites for certain crimes. Most states passed vagrancy laws, subjecting to forced labor on a plantation any unemployed freedmen. Blacks could not lease land and any black youth whose parents could not adequately provide for his or her care was apprenticed to a white man.

The black codes outraged Republicans who could not believe this latest manifestation of southern white arrogance and brazenness. For many Republicans the codes were the last straw in their war with Andrew Johnson, whom they held responsible for this latest insult to the Union dead.

LAND AND LABOR IN THE POSTWAR SOUTH

Although blatantly racist and oppressive, the black codes were designed to address a legitimate problem. Emancipation plunged black-white relations into a world of uncertainty, fear, and hostility with whites especially bitter toward their former slaves. In much of the South, the Yankee army had physically destroyed the southern landscape and antebellum economy. Burned-out plantations, fields gone to seed, railroads without tracks or bridges, and rolling stock marked the effects of total war visited upon the South by the invading Federal armies. Over half of the South's livestock was gone as well as much of its sustainable land, compounding already serious food shortages; possible starvation loomed for both white and black Southerners. Lawlessness was also rampant with roaming bands of hungry ex-rebel soldiers and black vagabonds looking for food and shelter often engaging acts of violent crime to survive. The war ended early enough in the spring to allow the planting of at least some crops but who would plant and cultivate them? The South had lost one-quarter of its white farmers in war, and the slaves had been freed.

Despite such struggles, life went on. Soldiers' widows and their children plowed and planted; masters without slaves and their wives calloused their hands for the first time. Former slave owners now had to ask their former chattels if they would be willing to work the land for wages or shares of the crop, and many freedmen readily agreed to such a changed capital-labor relationship. Plantation life and economy was all they had known for generations. Many freedmen, however, wanted nothing to do with their former masters, choosing instead to get as far away from the old plantation as possible. Thousands migrated to the nearest city or town in search of work rather than return to the painful memory of bondage. Some wandered aimlessly, simply enjoying freedom as long as they could until getting hungry or "disciplined" by roaming white vigilante groups. Nonetheless, for the majority of freedmen, true emancipation meant never returning to the plantation. As a black preacher told his congregation, "You ain't, none of you, gwinter feel rale free till you shakes de dus' ob de ole plantashun offen yore fee an an' goes ter a new place why you kin live out o'sight o' de gret house." (dialect in original source).

The Freedmen's Bureau by A.R. Waud.
A man representing the Freedmen's Bureau stands between armed groups of white Americans and African Americans. 1868.

The Freedmen's Bureau

Attempting to bring a semblance of order and stability to the South was the United States Army and the **Freedmen's Bureau**. Tens of thousands of United States troops remained in the South as an occupation force, establishing martial law in the ex-Confederate states until civil government could be restored. Perhaps more important to the history of Reconstruction was the Freedmen's Bureau (the agency's official name was the Bureau of Refugees, Freedmen, and Abandoned Lands) created by Congress in March 1865. This particular federal initiative marked the first time in the history of the Republic that the national government established an agency to protect and promote the socio-economic welfare of its citizens. Although the Bureau's primary purpose was to safeguard the freedmen from white reprisals, whether legal, physical, or from whatever form such retaliation might take, white Southerners too benefited from this program. The Bureau issued food rations to 150,000 people daily in 1865, one-third of them to whites.

The Bureau's commissioner, General Oliver O. Howard, established his headquarters in Washington. In each former slave state, an army general was assigned as assistant commissioner and directed his field operatives from the state's capital or largest city. The majority of the Bureau's 550 local agents were junior officers from middle-class northern backgrounds. Some took genuine interest in their charges' well-being, displaying a sincere belief in equality, while others were simply marking time until something better in the civilian world came along. Sadly, the officers of the latter disposition often displayed toward the freedmen the same racist attitudes and general disdain for blacks as their southern white counterparts. The Bureau also appointed some civilian agents, including a few African Americans. Although the number of agents was too few to reach every corner of the South, these agents—backed by the army's occupation troops—nevertheless had considerable potential power to transform postwar southern labor relations.

Once it became clear that the federal government intended no massive land redistribution for the freedmen's benefit, the Bureau then focused its energies on trying to forge a new relationship between planters and freedmen. The agents' main objective was to encourage (or require) planters and laborers to sign written contracts that specified the amount and kind of work to be done, the wages to be paid, and other conditions of employment. Wages

This print depicts African Americans gathered outside the Freedmen's Bureau in Richmond, Virginia. The Bureau is issuing rations to the old and sick. 1866.

agreed upon ranged from eight to fifteen dollars a month, plus room and board, and sometimes work clothes and equipment and even medical care. Freedmen were paid either in cash or a share of the crop. Because of a shortage of money, planters preferred to pay laborers with a percentage of the crop, which would not be paid until after harvest. Such a contract ensured worker loyalty by creating a relationship in which both planter and freedmen had a vested interest in getting the crops out of the ground. Thus, one of the Bureau's principal tasks was to protect freedmen from potential exploitation as its agents adjudicated thousands of complaints registered by black workers against their employers not only for abuse but for violation of contracts as well. Because southern state courts would never give freedmen a fair hearing, General Howard urged Congress to revise the original bill to empower the Bureau to establish special courts to function as military tribunals until Congress declared the rebellious states restored to the Union. Johnson vetoed the new mandate, but the Radicals in Congress would not be deterred and worked to override the president's rejection. With usually only one agent acting as judge and jury, these "special courts" remained in existence until 1868.

Southern whites, particularly the antebellum elite, came to despise the Bureau, denouncing it as a "curse," a "ridiculous folly," and a "vicious institution." Interestingly, such remarks reflected not so much a hatred of the Bureau for what it did but, rather, for what it symbolized—conquest and emancipation. Planters insisted they could "make the nigger work" if meddling Bureau agents would only leave them alone. In reality, such complaints and denunciations were unfounded. More often than not, the Bureau proved to be more of a planter ally than a manifestation of emancipation and alleged white degradation. Agents got idle freedmen back to work by enforcing contracts whose terms favored employers rather than workers. Reflecting sensitivity to criticism in both the northern and southern press that the Bureau was promoting a welfare ethic among freedmen, many Bureau officers would cut off rations to able-bodied blacks to force them to work. While publicly vilifying the Bureau, privately planters admitted that without it the postwar labor situation would have been even more chaotic. Indeed, in late 1865, the Bureau helped to suppress a possible insurrection among freedmen when they learned that they were not going to receive their anticipated **"forty acres and a mule."** In response to the news, thousands of freedmen throughout the South refused to sign contracts for the next year. To the Bureau fell the unhappy task of disabusing the freedmen about land redistribution and compelling them to sign contracts. In 1867, a Bureau official assessed the contract system: "It has succeeded in making the Freedman work and in rendering labor secure & stable—but it has failed to secure the Freedman his just dues or compensation."

The Issue of Land for the Landless

Naturally, freedmen wanted land for themselves rather than having to work for former masters or other whites. The majority of freedmen believed that only ownership of their own land would make them truly free. For most former slaves, however, purchasing land was impossible. Few had money, and if they had, even the most destitute whites often refused to sell or even rent land to them for fear of having African Americans being anything other than subservient and dependent. Thus, freedmen looked to the federal government to help gain true independence from continued white control. The hope for "forty acres and a mule" was no delusion of ignorant minds. By June 1865, the Freedmen's Bureau had appropriated almost 500,000 acres of plantation lands along the Georgia and South Carolina coastal areas and had settled in those areas nearly 10,000 black families. General William T. Sherman also gave freedmen captured horses and mules so they could work the land. Elsewhere in the South, Freedmen's Bureau agents took it upon themselves to reallocate to freedmen nearly a million acres of abandoned or confiscated land in their respective areas.

Such initiatives by Union generals and Bureau agents raised expectations throughout the South that all freedmen would soon be given their own land by a massive confiscation and redistribution plan being formulated in Washington. Such was precisely the agenda envisioned by Thaddeus Stevens of Pennsylvania and other Radical Republicans who advocated the appropriation of land owned by wealthy former Confederates and allocating forty acres of this land to each adult freedman. The remainder was to be sold to finance war pensions and repay the war debt.

Unfortunately, Andrew Johnson and Congress dashed such hopes. Johnson's amnesty and pardon proclamation restored all property to their original owners, and Congress failed to pass effective legislation that would have allowed for even abandoned land to be turned over to freedmen. Commissioner Howard, however, refused to comply with Johnson's edicts. Howard considered the amnesty proclamation inapplicable to abandoned or confiscated property, which he interpreted as being "set apart [for use] by refugees and freedmen." Johnson believed otherwise, ordering Howard to restore property to all pardoned Confederates, but Howard ordered his agents to stall and delay as long as possible property restoration to rebels, hoping to retain as much land as possible until Congress met in December. Howard hoped Congress would challenge the president on this issue and allow for the freedmen's possession of at least some of the land under Bureau control.

In February 1866, Congress passed an addendum to the Freedmen's Bureau Bill that allowed for those freedmen given land along the Georgia and South Carolina coastal areas to keep the land for three years. But Johnson vetoed the bill, and Congress failed to pass it over the veto. In July 1866, Republicans finally managed to pass a revised bill over the president's veto, but the new law called for the displacement of freedmen from Georgia and South Carolina proper to those states' respective offshore islands. Worse, the dispossessed freedmen now had to purchase the government-held land on those islands, albeit at a price below market value. Only 2,000 displaced black families were able to purchase the offshore land. The new policy marked a sad ending to the high hopes of 1865. By the end of 1866, nearly all the arable land once controlled by the Freedmen's Bureau had been returned to its ex-Confederate owners.

Perhaps to atone for such betrayal, Congress passed the Southern Homestead Act soon after its earlier measure had displaced Georgia and South Carolina freedmen. Similar in design and purpose to the 1862 **Homestead Act** for the Great Plains area (the former "Great American Desert"), this law set aside 44 million acres of public land in five southern states (Alabama, Arkansas, Florida, Louisiana, and Mississippi) to be parceled out in 80-acre allotments to black settlers. If they improved the land over a five-year period, then, as stipulated in the 1862 act, it was theirs for the keeping, free of charge. In order to ensure that the land designated in these states went to freedmen and white Unionist, the law forbade anyone who had supported the Confederacy from settling in the specified areas. Generous in conception, the Southern Homestead Act was largely a failure in practice. Typically, most of the remaining public land in these states was marginal at best, and few freedmen possessed enough money to purchase seed, tools, livestock, and building materials to improve the land. Consequently, fewer than 7,000 freedmen relocated to these states, and only 1,000 of these homesteaders were able to fulfill the requirements for final ownership. Thus, meaningful land reform did not become part of Reconstruction, and with such a failure came the inevitable return of the majority of freedmen to a status of quasi-bondage (debt peonage) in the form of sharecropping and tenant farming.

THE ORIGINS OF RADICAL RECONSTRUCTION

It was only a matter of time before the growing schism between Andrew Johnson and the Republican-dominated 39th Congress would escalate into an outright power struggle over who should control the Reconstruction process. However, not until the Radicals gained dominance within the party did a full-fledged assault on the president become a certainty. As long as Republicans were divided along Radical, moderate, and conservative alignments, Johnson's Reconstruction policies would prevail. However, once Republicans put aside their differences and united in a determination to oppose Johnson and agree on the course Reconstruction should take, then the president's days as an effective leader would indeed be numbered.

What goodwill existed between Republicans and the president began to evaporate when Johnson vetoed two bills to protect the freedmen. The first extended the life of the Freedmen's Bureau, expanded its legal powers, and authorized the agency to build and support schools. The second bill defined the freedmen's civil rights and gave federal courts appellate jurisdiction in cases concerning these rights.

Johnson knew his veto would alienate the moderates and move him toward an alliance with the Democrats, who held mass rallies in support of the president's veto. After one such gathering, the celebrants marched to the White House where Johnson feted the crowd with one of the most remarkable presidential speeches ever delivered. Johnson denounced the Radicals as traitors who did not want the Union restored. He also told the crowd that the Radicals were plotting his assassination, comparing them to Judas and himself to Christ. "If my blood is to be shed because I vindicate the Union and the preservation of this government in its original purity and character, let it be shed; let an altar to the Union be erected, and then if it is necessary, take me and lay me upon it, and the blood that now warms and animates my existence shall be poured out as a fit libation to the Union."

The president's behavior mortified many Americans. "Was he drunk?" they asked. Radicals could now declare to their moderate colleagues "I told you so!" The final straw for moderate and Radical Republicans came with Johnson's veto in March 1866 of a civil rights bill for freedmen, initiated by the moderate leader Lyman Trumbull of Illinois. The measure defined freedmen as United States citizens and guaranteed their rights to own or rent property, to make and enforce contracts, and to have access to the courts as parties and as witnesses. Interestingly, Trumbull's initiative did not call for black enfranchisement, or mandate that African Americans sit on juries, or require integrated schools and public accommodations. Republicans therefore expected Johnson to sign this moderate bill despite his states' rights convictions. Even his cabinet was unanimous in urging the president to sign the measure.

Like his earlier veto, this one also provoked Democratic euphoria and Republican condemnation. Democratic editors rejoiced that Johnson did not believe "in compounding our race with niggers, gipsies [sic], and baboons." If Johnson's objective with his vetoes had been to isolate the Radicals while forging a moderate/conservative coalition in support of his policy, he had badly miscalculated just how far moderates were willing to go to obtain at least a modicum of rights for the freedmen.

The Fourteenth Amendment

Johnson had thrown down the gauntlet with his veto of the Freedmen's Bureau and Civil Rights bills. Congressional Republicans, led by the Radicals, did not hesitate to pick it up, pushing through Congress in June 1866 the **Fourteenth Amendment** to the Constitution. (It would take an additional two years before the requisite two-thirds of the states ratified the amendment). The measure defined all native-born and naturalized persons, including African Americans, as American citizens and prohibited the states from denying any such individual from the "privileges and immunities" of citizenship and from depriving "any person of life, liberty, or property without due process of law." The initiative further mandated that states enfranchise black males or they would forfeit a proportionate number of congressional seats and electoral votes. Another section barred a significant number of ex-Confederates from holding federal or state offices while repudiating the Confederate debt. All of the bill's stipulations were to be enforced by Congress by "appropriate legislation."

White Southerners and Democrats naturally denounced the bill as one more manifestation of Radical vengeance on men who had already suffered enough for their sins. Radical Republicans countered by declaring the measure did not go far enough to punish traitors and prevent their political resurgence. Radicals and abolitionists also decried the bill for not making fiat in all states black enfranchisement. The bill penalized southern states from denying black suffrage but allowed northern states to do so with impunity because their black population was too small to make a difference in the basis of representation. Abolitionists condemned the bill as a "swindle," a "wanton betrayal of justice and humanity."

For the moment, the Radical Republicans accepted the amendment as the best they could get while hoping that future events would move the country toward universal African-American male suffrage. Despite Radical and abolitionist lamentations, the Fourteenth Amendment had far-reaching consequences—the initiative became the most important constitutional provision for defining and enforcing civil rights in the nation. Unlike the first ten amendments (the Bill of Rights), which imposed restrictions on federal power, the Fourteenth Amendment greatly expanded federal authority to prevent state violations of civil rights. To the joy of the Radicals, the bill also greatly expanded African-American rights (at least on paper), while curtailing ex-Confederates' political power. That is why Johnson and his Democratic supporters, with their states' rights, proslavery mentality, opposed it.

The 1866 Congressional Elections

In many ways the 1866 congressional elections were a referendum on the Fourteenth Amendment, which the Republicans made the centerpiece of their party's platform. Since moderates still held sway in the party, they offered Southerners a carrot: any ex-Confederate state that ratified the amendment would be declared "reconstructed," and its representatives and senators could then take their respective congressional seats. Tennessee accepted this overture, ratified the amendment, and seated its representatives and senators. Johnson, believing he could still stem the congressional Republican tide against him by rallying southern and northern Democrats to his position, unwisely counseled other southern legislatures to reject the amendment, and they did so. Johnson then prepared for an all-out campaign to gain a pro-administration northern majority in the congressional elections by cobbling together a coalition of a few conservative Republicans, border-state Unionists, and Democrats. The new alliance called itself the **National Union Party**. No sooner was the coalition formed than the Democratic tail soon began to wag the National Union dog, thus dooming from the outset the party's chances of victory at the polls. Northern voters remained suspicious of Democrats, many of whom still believed the party had betrayed the country by opposing the war. Also, adversely affecting Johnson and his coalition was the ongoing violence against freedmen, which resulted in vicious race riots in New Orleans and Memphis, where white mobs rampaged against freedmen and their white allies, killing 80 blacks, among them several former Union soldiers. The endemic violence against African Americans only served to confirm the Republican contention that without greater federal protection and intervention in the South, African Americans were doomed to a life of perpetual fear, proscription, and terror.

Perhaps the National Union Party's greatest liability was Andrew Johnson, who in a speech in St. Louis soon after the melees in New Orleans and Memphis, blamed Republicans for provoking the white mobs while expressing no regret for the victims. In a whistle-stop tour of the North, Johnson engaged in shouting contests with hecklers and traded insults with hostile crowds. The substance of his speeches never varied: the South was loyal; the real traitors were the Radicals, who were bent on revenge, further polarizing the nation. Furthermore, he, Andrew Johnson, was willing to give his life if necessary for the salvation of the Union and the Constitution. In virtually every speech, Johnson closed by comparing himself to Jesus and his Republican adversaries to Judas. The National Union Party was embarrassingly routed at the polls, with the Republicans sweeping the election and gaining a 3-to-1 majority in the next Congress. Southern intransigence and the condoning of the wanton, often violent, persecution of the freedmen coupled with Johnson's tacit, if not blatant, approval of both actions accomplished what the Radicals alone could not achieve: the conversion of moderates to black suffrage and the congressional takeover of the Reconstruction process.

Above, a satirical cartoon by Thomas Nast that blames the Democratic Party for anti-black violence in the South. Nast mocks what he sees as the three wings of the Democratic Party. From the left, Nast depicts an Irish immigrant, a Confederate soldier and a greedy Wall Street investor. The three stand on a dead African-American soldier from the Union Army. In the background, black schools and orphanages are in flames. This illustration appeared in an 1868 edition of *Harper's Magazine*.

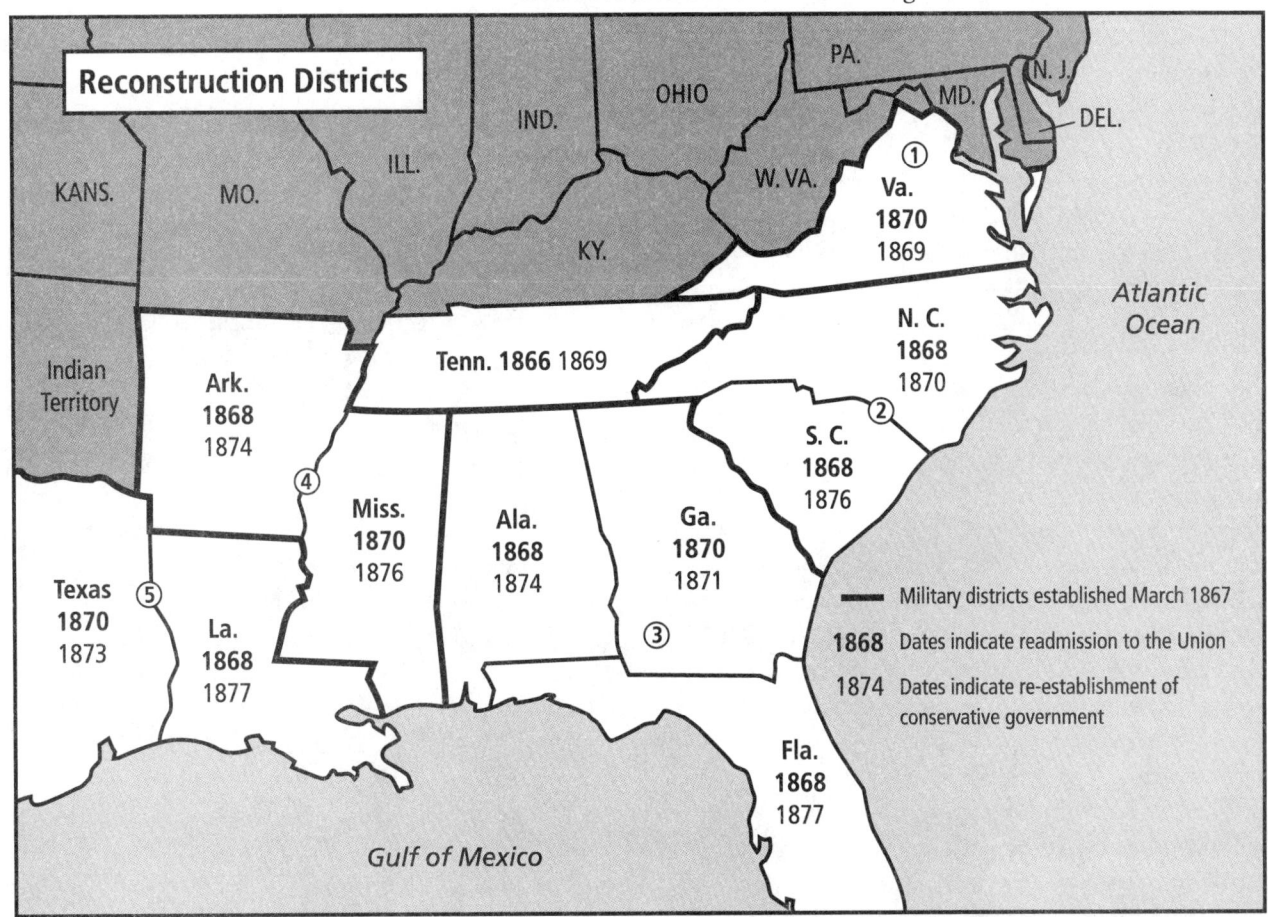

Map 17.1 Reconstruction Districts

The Reconstruction Acts of 1867

No sooner did the Republicans gain control of Congress with the Radicals in the ascendancy, than the history of the post-war South took yet another turn, one that many southern whites to this day would come to despise. As far as the Radicals and many of their once-moderate allies were concerned, the South had yet to be properly reconstructed; nor had southern whites sufficiently atoned for their sins of slavery and secession—treason. Until that reformation occurred, the South would have to be placed under martial law, for not only the freedmen's protection but for those white Southerners who had remained loyal to the Union. Thus, the **Reconstruction Acts of 1867** divided the ten southern states into five military districts under the authority of a Union general and whose sub-commanders in the states in his district were to register voters for the election of delegates to new constitutional conventions. *All* adult males over the age of 21 were to be enfranchised to vote in those elections. However, the act disenfranchised (for these elections only) those former Confederates who were disqualified from holding office under the not-yet-ratified Fourteenth Amendment, which translated to fewer than 10 percent of all eligible white male voters. The act further stipulated that all new state constitutions had to ratify the Fourteenth Amendment as well as guarantee equal civil and political rights to all citizens, regardless of race. Until that occurred, the state's congressional representatives would not be seated.

The Radical Republicans believed that the reduction of ex-Confederate states to the status of "conquered territories" would bode well for their larger vision and agenda for southern Reconstruction. They hoped that such a condition would allow time for the Freedmen's Bureau, freedmen's aid societies, northern soldiers and settlers, and northern money to flow into the South to help elevate and educate the freedmen and protect them from white reprisals. The Radicals believed that until the southern rebels felt the heavy hand of national power and presence, they would continue to resist all attempts at reformation.

The 1867 Reconstruction Acts reflected a true revolution—"the maddest, most infamous revolution in history," according to many southern whites. Just a few years earlier white Southerners had been masters of four million slaves and leaders of an independent Confederate nation. Now they had been stripped of political power and their former slaves not only freed but politically

The White Backlash During Presidential Reconstruction:
The 1866 Race Riots in Memphis and New Orleans

Throughout the Reconstruction era the majority of white Southerners refused to accept any notions of treating freedmen with any degree of dignity and respect for their person, let alone entertain any possibility of accepting them as equals, either before the law or in any social context. Indeed, white Southerners during the decade after the Civil War repeatedly engaged in violent reprisals against any attempts by freedmen to assert the political and civil rights guaranteed them by the federal government. A few weeks after Congress passed the 1866 Civil Rights Act, white citizens in the cities of Memphis and New Orleans made it clear that they would not accept the federally-mandated decree by unleashing a several-days-long reign of violent terror on those cities' respective black residents.

In Memphis, the black population had multiplied four times since the end of the war, as former slaves left the Tennessee countryside in hopes of better opportunities in the city. As the black population in Memphis increased, so did white fears and hostility. "Would to God they were back in Africa, or some other seaport town," declared the Memphis Argus, "anywhere but here." Interestingly, Andrew Johnson's proscriptive policies toward the old Tennessee elite succeeded in their ousting from power in Memphis, but their replacements, aggressive parvenu Irish politicians, proved to be just as racist and as oppressive of blacks as the old guard. Not surprisingly, the city's new political leaders turned blind as tensions between white and blacks escalated, resulting in numerous incidents of physical assaults by whites (by both Irish and WASP residents) on the freedmen. It was only a matter of time before such conflicts would produce the incident that would spark a full-scale riot. On May 1, 1866, two hack drivers—one white and one black—had a traffic accident, and when the police arrived, they, of course, arrested the black driver, even though the run-in was not his fault. A group of black veterans tried to prevent the arrest, which attracted white bystanders who proceeded to attack the veterans. The former soldiers fought back, and within minutes the "Memphis Riots" had begun. Over the course of the next three days, rampaging whites burned hundreds of black homes, churches, and schools. Five black women were raped, and nearly fifty people, all but two of them black, were killed.

Three months later, the same racial violence occurred in New Orleans. As was happening throughout the South during Presidential Reconstruction, both state and municipal governments were coming under the control of ex-Confederates, who were not about to protect the freedmen from white reprisals. However, the New Orleans massacre had more explicitly political dimensions. For decades, the city had a well-established free black population. By 1866, they had not only become the most vociferous advocates for black political and civil rights, but for all those disillusioned with the presidential reconstruction agenda, which by that year had completely abandoned any civil rights initiatives for freedmen. A group of white and black Radicals issued a call to bring the state's 1864 constitutional convention back into session in hopes of bringing the issue of black political and civil rights to the forefront of the state's reconstruction program. This black-white radical alliance called for enfranchising the freedmen while disenfranchising all "rebels," as well as for turning out the members of the current state government regime of ex-Confederates and establishing an entirely new state government composed of the free black elite in conjunction with the white Radicals. The convention was scheduled to meet on July 30, 1866.

However, as the delegates convened, white mobs set out to stop them. Led by the city's police and firemen, consisting mostly of ex-Confederates, they first attacked a parade of about two hundred blacks who were marching to the Mechanic's Institute to support the delegates. When the mob reached the convention hall, deadly violence ensued. They assaulted the building, busting through its doors, shooting and killing delegates as they tried to escape through the windows. The slaughter continued, even though many attendees raised the white flag of surrender. As one Union veteran who witnessed the massacre reported, "the wholesale slaughter and the little regard paid to human life" were worse than anything he had seen in battle. When the mob finally dispersed, thirty-four blacks and three white supporters had been killed, and another hundred had been injured.

News of the Memphis and New Orleans melees quickly filtered north, becoming explosive political issues, which the Radicals exploited to further discredit Andrew Johnson and his reconstruction policies. Johnson, not known for his political savvy, played into the Radicals' hands. In late August 1866, Johnson undertook an unprecedented political campaign tour designed to generate voter hostility toward Congress, particularly the Radicals, whom he blamed for the calamities in New Orleans and Memphis. At one point during one of his tirades, he suggested that Radical Congressman Thaddeus Stevens should be hanged. Republicans charged in turn that Johnson's own policies *had been responsible for the massacres—his blatant racist attitudes toward blacks and his lack of concern for their well-being encouraged the vicious attacks. His obvious disdain for the freedmen had revived both white racism and white rebelliousness, both of which were unleashed upon the black citizens of New Orleans and Memphis.*

The 1866 congressional elections thus became a referendum on competing visions of what American democracy should mean. For Andrew Johnson, "democracy" meant government by local majorities, which meant white supremacy. For African Americans and a growing number of Republicans, genuine democracy could only be constructed on a firm foundation of equal civil and political rights. Northern voters overwhelmingly rejected the president's notion of democracy, and as the **New York Times** *declared, the results "clearly, unmistakably, decisively" reflected "Congress and its policy." The 1866 congressional elections also brought an overwhelmingly Republican majority to both houses of Congress, giving the party a veto-proof hold on both the House and Senate, and perhaps even more damaging to Johnson, the incidents in Memphis and New Orleans, radicalizing many former moderate Republicans, convincing them that Andrew Johnson and his policies were making a mockery of both democracy and of the Union dead. Radical Reconstruction was about to begin.*

empowered as well. The "Old South" was (temporarily) vanquished, and the Radicals could not have been more delighted, for as they argued correctly, the revolution that began in 1863 with emancipation would never be realized as long as the old master class retained economic and social preeminence.

Despite Radical hopes that all would go smoothly with the presence of federal troops, southern whites continued to breathe defiance and refused to cooperate. Although white reprisals on the freedmen somewhat abated, thousands of white Southerners who were eligible to vote refused to do so, hoping that their non-participation would delay the process long enough for northern voters (the majority of whom were as racist as their southern brethren) to come to their senses and elect Democrats to Congress to reverse this "mad revolution."

Literate freedmen, white southern unionists, and northern white emigrants organized Union leagues to inform and mobilize new black voters into the Republican Party. Southern Democrats contemptuously labeled southern white Republicans as "**scalawags**" and northern migrants as "**carpetbaggers**." It was obvious to the southern "loyalists" (to the Lost Cause) that the Radicals intended to use the new black registrants and their white allies to gain control of the upcoming constitutional conventions. Since white Republicans were a minority in the South, the key to establishing such regimes in the southern states was the black vote. Thus, to prevent blacks from registering and voting, whites engaged in all manner of terrorist activities against freedmen, officially sanctioning such reprisals with the organization of the **Ku Klux Klan** in Pulaski, Tennessee in 1867. Although the Klan's terrorizing of blacks and whites who supported the Radical agenda would not become a serious problem until the early 1870s, the fact that such an organization emerged rather early in Reconstruction reflected white determination to resist any changes in the socio-political order that the war had brought.

With their huge majority, congressional Republicans were confident that could stymie the president's capacity to thwart the enactment of the new Reconstruction mandates. However, as commander in chief of the army and as head of the branch of government charged with executing the laws, Johnson still retained great power to frustrate the implementation of Congress's stipulations. Johnson made clear his intention to do so. Indeed, the president did all he could to try to stop the Radical momentum, encouraging southern whites to obstruct and delay voter registration and the election of convention delegates. Never in the history of the Republic had these two branches been more bitterly at odds.

Johnson's plan in obstructing the congressional agenda was to retard the process until 1868, in the hope that northern voters would repudiate the Radicals' program and elect him president on a Democratic ticket. Encouraging Johnson in this direction were the off-year state elections, held in the fall of 1867, which saw Republicans take a beating at the polls in several northern states, especially where they endorsed referendum measures to enfranchise black males. After the elections results, however, such Democratic euphoria was destined to be short-lived. There was no way the Radical Republicans would allow Johnson to prevail on these crucial issues. Many were willing to go to any extreme necessary to defeat the president, even if it meant removing him from office. Increasing numbers of Radicals concluded that the South's proper Reconstruction would never come about as long as Andrew Johnson was President of the United States. They thus put forth a concerted effort to impeach the president and remove him from office, hoping to replace him with the Radical Republican President pro tempore of the Senate, Benjamin Wade of Ohio.

The Senate court of impeachment for the trial of Andrew Johnson. 1868.

THE IMPEACHMENT OF ANDREW JOHNSON

The Radicals' drive to rid themselves of the "Johnson nuisance" began with the passage of the 1867 **Tenure of Office Act**, which required Senate approval of the president's removal of any cabinet members. Johnson naturally vetoed the bill, rightly declaring it to be unconstitutional. In Johnson's view, the act violated presidential authority and prerogative: the right of presidential appointment of cabinet members. Although all such individuals selected by the president had to be approved by the Senate, once confirmed, the president could remove them at his discretion.

Adding to the sensitivity of this particular showdown was the fact that through the course of the war, Lincoln had greatly expanded presidential power, ranging from the unprecedented issuance of executive orders to the suspension of the writ of *habeas corpus*, all in the name of national security and crisis. Indeed, Lincoln perhaps became the most notorious executive violator of civil liberties and other usurpations of constitutional authority. As a result, during Lincoln's presidency, Congress increasingly found itself becoming subservient to the executive branch. In the eyes of many Radicals, Johnson's obstructionism provided the perfect opportunity (or excuse) to reverse such an imbalance in national power, which they contended Johnson (not Lincoln) had so egregiously upset. In reality, however, the Radical Republicans simply used such arguments to mask their own personal antipathy toward Johnson's "copperheadedness" and obvious pro-southern and anti-freedmen sentiments. Although Johnson brought upon himself much of the Radicals' scorn and opposition with his arrogance and self-righteousness, nonetheless, he did not warrant impeachment; constitutionally none of his actions could be considered "Treason, Bribery, or other high Crimes and Misdemeanors." The Radicals, however, asserted that impeachment was not a criminal proceeding but rather a means of punishing a public official for "grave misuse of his powers, or any mischievous nonuse of them—for any conduct which harms the public or perils its welfare." In the Radical view, Johnson's obstructionist policies and his consorting with rebels to oppress the freedmen and restore the political status quo antebellum had most definitely harmed the public welfare. To substantiate their position, Radicals pointed to Johnson's wholesale pardons of ex-rebels, his open defiance of Congress, his intimation that Congress was an illegal body, his disgraceful public speeches, and his complicity by inaction in the New Orleans and Memphis riots.

The Radical Republicans believed Johnson had demonstrated no intention of enforcing the law in good faith and thus wanted to begin impeachment proceedings immediately. Moderates, however, feared that impeachment might make Johnson a martyr. Unfortunately for Johnson, he allowed his petulance and arrogance to get the better of him, and to the Radicals' delight, he took their "bait" (the Tenure of Office Act) and fired the last member of his cabinet, Secretary of War Edwin Stanton, who supported congressional Reconstruction. To try to stave off a full-fledged Radical assault on his administration, Johnson attempted to mollify Republicans with the appointment of General Ulysses S. Grant as interim Secretary of War. Grant was the most popular man in the North, and, despite a personal aversion to politics, Republicans were determined to make him their standard-bearer in 1868. However, some Radicals worried that Grant's acceptance of the position reflected his support for the president's policies. To their great relief, it did not. Indeed, Grant had urged Johnson not to remove Stanton, and he only accepted the position so he could serve as a buffer between Johnson and the army to prevent Johnson from doing more mischief. Grant, for example, refused Johnson's request to replace the more zealous, "Radically-inclined" commanders of the military districts, such as Grant's best friend, General William T. Sherman, of the Louisiana-Texas district, with more willing individuals. Grant refused and eventually resigned from the office, turning the reigns of power back to Stanton. In the meantime, Johnson took the initiative to replace Sheridan and other generals with men of a more moderate disposition, especially toward southern whites. As predicted, these moves outraged the Radicals, for Johnson's actions further encouraged the growing southern resistance to Reconstruction. By February 1868, both moderates and Radical Republicans had had enough; the House voted to impeach Johnson by a vote of 126-47. All 47 opposition votes were Democratic. The official reason for impeachment was Johnson's violation of the Tenure of Office Act. The real reason was Johnson's stubborn defiance of three-quarters of Congress on the most important issue before the nation—Reconstruction.

Under the Constitution, impeachment by the House does not remove an official from office. The process is more like a grand jury indictment that must be tried by a petit jury—the Senate, which sat as a court to try Johnson on the impeachment charges brought by the House. If convicted by a two-thirds majority of the Senate, Johnson would be removed from office, and president pro tempore of the Senate, Benjamin Wade, a Radical, would become president.

Tension filled the Senate chambers as Johnson's impeachment trial began on March 4, 1868. The trial proved to be long and complicated, which boded well for Johnson by allowing passions to cool. A plus for Johnson was also his defense counsel, which included some of the best lawyers in the country: Henry Stanbery, the attorney general; William M. Evarts, a future secretary of state; and Benjamin R. Curtis, a former Supreme Court justice, who had written the principal dissenting opinion in the *Dred Scott* case. During the trial these men demonstrated greater legal acumen than their opponents. These counselors

"Farewell, a long farewell, to all my greatest."
The caricature shows Andrew Johnson dressed as a king crying. 1869.

argued that a government official can be impeached only for criminal offenses that would be indictable in ordinary courts—Johnson had committed no crime by seeking to test the constitutionality of the Tenure of Office Act. In short, they exposed the act's technical ambiguities that raised doubts about whether Johnson had actually violated it.

To counter these assertions, the prosecution argued that to allow a president to disobey a law in order to test it in court would set a dangerous precedent. Regardless of whether Johnson was guilty of any crime, the impeachment trial was a political maneuver. To the Radicals and their supporters, Johnson had been impeached and was now on trial for two years of relentless opposition to the Republican reconstruction vision and agenda. Perhaps most important, Johnson's impeachment reflected the culmination of the long power struggle between the legislative and the executive branches, which as alluded earlier, began with the Lincoln administration. In many ways, Congress, not Johnson, had become the abusers and usurpers of power. Many moderates and the American public feared the creation of a precedent by which a two-thirds majority of Congress could remove any president who happened to disagree with them. In short, despite public and partisan disgust with Johnson, neither moderate Republicans nor the American people wanted to emasculate or disgrace the executive branch.

Behind the scenes moderates and other anti-impeachment coalitions worked to get Johnson to concede on some of the key Reconstruction issues that had caused the crisis. Apparently, the president understood the gravity of his predicament and responded positively to such overtures. He conducted himself with dignity and restraint during the trial. He gave no more self-righteous, emotionally-charged, irrational speeches or interviews. Most importantly, he promised to enforce the Reconstruction Acts. As a further sign of conciliation (even capitulation), Johnson appointed General John M. Schofield as Secretary of War, an individual acceptable to all factions. Johnson's willingness to reach such accords with Congress portended well for his acquittal. However, such a prospect remained in doubt until the very end. The final roll call took on the dimensions of high drama; not until West Virginia's Senator Peter G. Van Winkle, near the end of the alphabet, voted nay did it become clear that Johnson had been acquitted by one vote short of the necessary two-thirds majority. The final tally was 35-19. Had Van Winkle voted yes, Andrew Johnson would have become the first president in United States history to have been removed from office. Johnson remained on his best behavior for the rest of his term. Congressional (Radical) Reconstruction proceeded without any further presidential hindrance. A crisis that had shaken the constitutional system to its foundation ended without any fundamental alteration of that system.

THE SOUTHERN RESPONSE TO THE RECONSTRUCTION ACTS

Much to the surprise and disappointment of many Radicals, prominent ex-Confederates advised their white compatriots to accept the inevitable—defeat and the end of slavery—and comply with the laws. The thinking of such members of the antebellum elite was that cooperation with the congressional mandates would allow them to influence the process in a moderate direction, especially when it came to the freedmen issue. Many of these individuals still possessed their sense of pre-war paternalism and saw themselves as the freedmen's natural protectors and benefactors who knew what was best for their people. They certainly believed they knew their "negroes" better than any alien Yankee intruders, whom they believed (somewhat correctly) were only using the freedmen as political pawns to remake the South into a Republican majority. The old elite thus organized interracial political meetings and barbecues at which they urged the freedmen to vote Democratic with their fellow white Southerners in order to keep out the Yankees.

This convergence approach became known as the **New Departure**, and it became part of a persistent effort in postwar southern politics led mainly by former Whigs to create a moderate third force independent of both Democrats and Republicans. These New Departure advocates believed in enfranchising the freedmen as well as guaranteeing them their full civil rights. That is not to suggest such individuals believed in equality. They were all committed racists, but, nonetheless, they believed that it was wrong to wage aggressive war on the freedman, strip him of his basic constitutional rights, ostracize him, humiliate him, and rob him of elemental human dignity. To the proponents of convergence, African-American degradation was not a necessary corollary of white supremacy. As prominent antebellum attorney William Pitt Ballinger of Texas told a friend, although freedmen were "in our power," whites, particularly those of Ballinger's class, were their "custodians. We should extend to them as far as possible, all civil rights that will help them to be decent and self-respecting, law-abiding, and intelligent citizens. If we do not help elevate them they will surely bring us down." As far as Ballinger (and other New Departure proponents) was concerned, it was time for white Southerners "to bury the past and move forward." Southern whites had to accept "the fact of the negro's right to vote," and thus white reprisals of "intimidation and violence" toward freedmen must end. By downplaying the race issue, Ballinger and his compatriots hoped convergence would attract black votes, for African Americans would realize that their true guardians were patricians, like himself, and not the Radicals. The New Departure movement also hoped to win the support of moderate and conservative white Republicans once they became convinced that the postwar South's true leaders had accepted the accomplished facts of the war.

Unfortunately, Ballinger's and others' pleas for moderation and accommodation went unheard. The majority of white Southerners rejected the legitimacy of Reconstruction or the permanence of black suffrage. Even among many of its supporters, the New Departure was less of a genuine commitment to the democratic revolution manifested in Reconstruction than a strategy for mollifying Northerners about the southern Democratic Party's intentions. Most northern whites knew that in their hearts few of their southern brethren accepted black civil and political equality.

Assisting Republicans in mobilizing black voters was the Freedmen's Bureau and the Union League, which together were capable of overwhelming any efforts by the convergers to draw black voters away from the Republican Party. Some Bureau agents served simultaneously as Union League officials and, in their military capacity, as supervisors of voter registration under the Reconstruction Acts. These partisan activities gave white Southerners another reason to condemn the Bureau—not only did it intervene in their labor relations with the freedmen but now it was helping to rally these workers into an alien political party. As Republican success in wooing black voters to the Grand Old Party became clear, many southern whites, including some convergers, began to change their tune about accommodation. Yet, many remained sanguine that somehow or other Andrew Johnson or the northern Democrats could reverse the process and overthrow the Radicals. All such hopes, however, were dashed with Johnson's impeachment proceedings, which turned Johnson into one of the lamest of duck presidents in the Republic's history. The way was now clear for the final implementation of congressional Reconstruction.

THE COMPLETION OF FORMAL RECONSTRUCTION

Under the mandates established by the Reconstruction Acts of 1867, the southern states held their constitutional conventions during the winter and spring of 1867-68. Hostile whites, especially those who had been disenfranchised by the **iron-clad oath**, derisively referred to the gatherings as the "Bones and Banjoes Conventions" and the Republican delegates, many of whom were black, as "ragamuffins and jailbirds, baboons, monkeys, and mules." In a typical denunciation, Louisiana conservatives labeled the new charter written by the state convention as a "base conspiracy against human nature. It is the work of ignorant negroes cooperating with a gang of white adventurers." No doubt the Republican Party dominated the assemblages, comprising 75 percent of the delegates attending the ten state conventions. About one-quarter of those Republicans were relocated northern whites ("Carpetbaggers"), 45 percent were native southern whites ("Scalawags"), and about 30 percent were African Americans. Only in South Carolina were blacks in the majority. In Louisiana 50 percent of the attendees were African Americans, while in Texas only 10 percent of the delegates were freedmen. Regardless of their number, the black delegates constituted the elite of their race. At least half of them had been free before the war, and most of those who had been slaves belonged to the upper strata of the slave community. About four-fifths of all the black delegates were literate. Their predominant occupations were clergymen, teachers, artisans, and independent yeoman farmers. Contrary to white backlash propaganda, very few were former field hands or unskilled, illiterate laborers.

Much to the consternation of the **white backlash**, the delegates produced some of the most progressive state constitutions in the nation. In all ten states of the former Confederacy, universal male suffrage was enacted, putting the South ahead of most northern states in this most controversial issue. Some of the constitutions disfranchised certain classes of ex-Confederates for several more years, but by 1872, all such restrictions had been lifted. Ironically, the removal of such disqualifications allowed for southern whites by the early 1870s to redeem their states, that is, a return to white supremacy and political control by the antebellum elite. For the first time in southern history a mandated public school system was established for both races. Though the constitutions permitted segregated schools, formal education of any kind for African Americans represented a great step forward. Most of the constitutions expanded the state's responsibility for social welfare beyond anything previously known in the South. Some constitutions established state boards of public charities, and several of them enacted badly needed prison reforms and reduced the number of capital crimes. Such welfare expansion naturally had to be paid for, and thus property taxes increased significantly. Alleged exorbitant taxation became the initial rallying cry of the "Redeemers."

Despite the increases, most states provided homestead exemptions that assisted small landowners by exempting from taxation real and personal property up to $2,000 or $3,000 from attachment for debts. Although some of the Radical attendees urged confiscating the land of disfranchised ex-Confederates, no convention promulgated such a decree. Only the South Carolina convention made any gesture in this direction, authorizing the state land commission to buy abandoned property at market value and resell it in small tracts (mostly to freedmen) on liberal terms.

Reactionary whites opposed these new charters and worked assiduously to defeat ratification. Most southern whites could not believe that their northern brethren would abandon them at this crucial hour, allowing the Radicals to impose "Negro rule" on the South. So determined were southern whites to defeat ratification that they resorted to violent intimidation and terrorizing of black voters, whom they believed were the key to Republican ascendancy. Naturally leading this crusade was the KKK, which made it first serious appearance and forays during these elections. However, the main conservative tactic was to boycott the polls. If enough whites could be persuaded or coerced to stay home, the vote in favor of ratification might fall short of a majority of registered voters. In some states, such as Alabama, such a ploy initially worked. By the close of 1868, seven ex-Confederate states had ratified their constitutions and elected new legislatures that also ratified the Fourteenth Amendment, which became part of the Constitution the following summer. The newly elected representatives and senators from those seven states took their seats in the House and Senate.

Despite having neutralized Andrew Johnson and establishing (at least for the moment) Republican rule in the South, many party members were reluctant to take the final step of readmission. Causing them the greatest uneasiness was the reduction of federal troops, which would result as soon as self-government had been restored. Moreover, it would only be a matter of time before disfranchised whites regained the ballot, and, once they had, the days of Republican control would end soon thereafter. Moreover, the various Republican coalitions that had written the state constitutions, and subsequently took control, were fragile at best. During the ratification process, the vulnerability of its black constituents to intimidation became apparent. With troop presence on the decline, what would prevent a Democratic resurgence in the South and the certain dismantling of the new constitutions, black suffrage, and all the other reforms established? But political necessities and realities dictated readmission, and, whether the Radicals liked it or not, those southern states which had complied with all congressional mandates had to be readmitted to the Union. Northern voters wanted an end to the contention, for the majority no longer wanted to think about nor cared about the Negro problem. In the minds of most northern whites, Reconstruction appeared to be completed. Events, however, would soon demonstrate that it had barely begun.

THE FIRST GRANT ADMINISTRATION

The Election of 1868

Just as the 1864 presidential election had been a referendum on Republican war policies, so the 1868 contest reflected yet another mandate on Reconstruction. Initially however, it appeared that the financial question might supersede Reconstruction as the central campaign issue. The origins of this issue went back to the wartime legislation promoted by Lincoln, which made legal tender paper money called "**greenbacks**," while simultaneously creating a host of national banks through which this currency flowed throughout the northern economy. The flood of greenbacks into the economy resulted in inflation, causing an 80 percent cost of living increase in the North from 1861-1865. Such an acceleration fell gradually but steadily after the war was over. With the suspension of specie payments and the adoption of greenbacks in 1862, the United States went off the gold standard, though it still used gold for international trade.

After the war, Secretary of the Treasury Hugh McCulloch, a "hard-money" advocate (a believer in specie/gold as the only legitimate currency for a nation to circulate), pursued a policy of returning the nation's monetary system to the gold standard by slowly retiring greenbacks while bringing the remainder in circulation to par with gold. By 1867, McCulloch had reduced the value of greenbacks in circulation to $319 million and the gold premium stood at 140 ($140 greenbacks were required to buy $100 in gold). McCulloch's policies, however, caused deflation and a postwar recession, and those economic sectors hurt by the secretary's agenda blamed the contraction of greenbacks for their plight. Alarmed, Congress forbade further greenback reduction in 1868. The issue created a

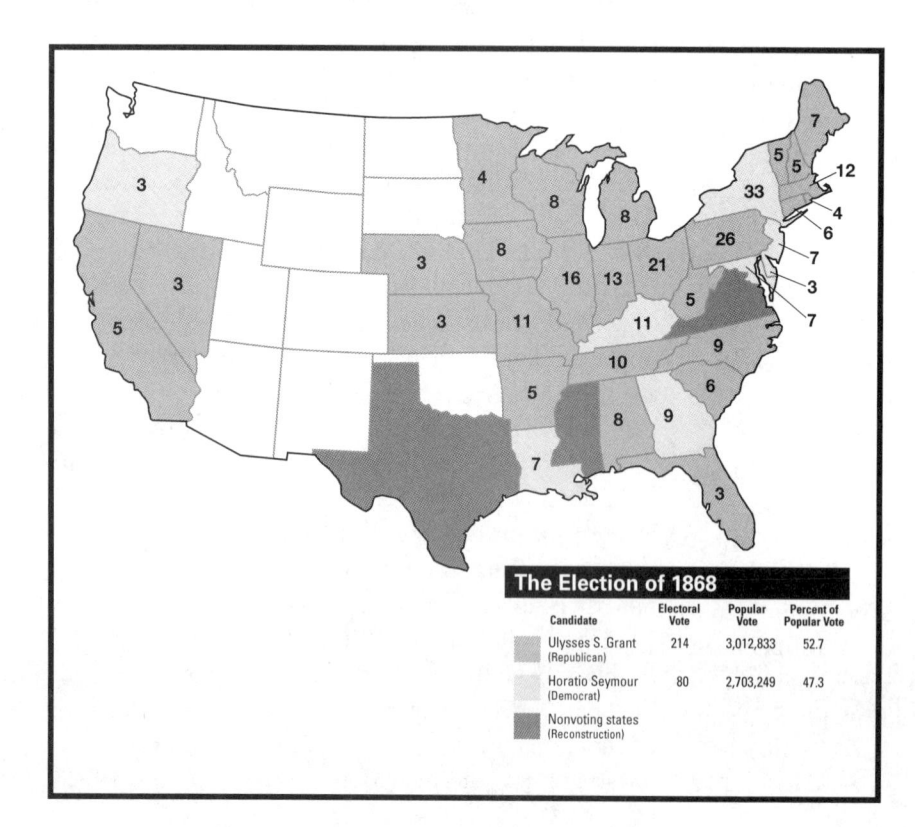

Map 17.2 The Election of 1868

new sectional alignment: East against West (the West was still an overwhelmingly rural and agrarian region) as both western Democrats and Republicans opposed contraction, which hit the Western states' economy harder than the Northeast, whereby bankers, financiers, and industrialists all favored contraction and the return to the gold standard. Western farmers and other debtors favored soft money, for they would be repaying debts with depreciated currency if the greenbacks continued in circulation. Moreover, such individuals favored greenbacks as legal tender because it was cheap money that inflated prices for farm goods. A return to a strict gold standard would negate such a boon for farmers and other debtors.

Led by Ohio party leader Senator George H. Pendleton, western Democrats attempted to make the monetary question a major campaign issue. Pendleton, a leading candidate for his party's presidential nomination, favored making greenbacks the nation's legal tender, replacing gold but keeping the new currency on a gold standard. The Pendleton Plan found its way into the Democratic platform, but when the party turned to New Yorker Horatio Seymour, a "**gold bug**," as its standard bearer, this plank became a dead letter as Reconstruction and the candidates' war records took center stage. The monetary debate was not dead. Indeed, once Reconstruction had ended, this particular issue reignited, rivaling at times in intensity and partisanship the North-South slavery debate of the antebellum period.

As the 1868 election neared, the Republican nominee became a foregone conclusion: General-in-Chief of the Army and Union war hero, **Ulysses S. Grant**. Only one issue continued to mar Republican unanimity: the problem of black suffrage in the northern states. Radicals insisted it must be a central feature of the party's platform while moderates believed it essential to downplay the crusade, fearing of alienating northern white voters, the majority of whom had made it clear in various state elections that they adamantly opposed black enfranchisement. In the end, the moderates agreed to impose black suffrage on the ex-Confederate states while allowing the "question of suffrage in all the loyal [northern] States to properly belong to the people of those States." This hypocrisy outraged abolitionists and Radicals, who denounced this "mean-spirited, foolish, and contemptible" plank.

The Democrats initially had an abundance of candidates, including Andrew Johnson, whom, it was quickly realized, possessed too many political liabilities to become a viable contender. The other possibilities—George Pendleton of Ohio, Thomas Hendricks of Indiana, and General Winfield Scott Hancock—all had supporters, but as the convention progressed and ballot after ballot had been cast, one by one they all fell by the wayside, ultimately leaving the "dark horse," Horatio Seymour of New York, as the last man standing, whom party officials had to hustle out of the hall to prevent him from declining the nomination. In the end, Seymour reluctantly accepted his party's dubious honor of running against Grant.

The Democratic platform naturally condemned the Reconstruction Acts as "a flagrant usurpation of power, unconstitutional, revolutionary and void." The platform also demanded "the abolition of the Freedmen's Bureau, and all political instrumentalities designed to secure negro supremacy." It was clear the Democrats hoped to win by engaging in **race-baiting**, negrophobia, and the promotion of white solidarity and supremacy with its southern colleagues. In this approach, vice-presidential candidate Frank Blair of Missouri became the party's mouthpiece. In his famous Brodhead Letter, Blair set his party's campaign agenda. "There is but one way to restore the Government and the Constitution, and that is for the President-elect to declare these [Reconstruction] acts null and void, compel the army to undo its usurpations at the South, disperse the Carpet-bag governments, and allow white people to reorganize their own governments." Implicitly Blair and his party were calling for a counterrevolutionary movement to overthrow the southern Republican governments, and the only way to achieve such a goal was to terrorize and suppress southern Republican voters. The Klan naturally heard Blair's and the Democrats' call to arms, and during the election, the Klan and similar white backlash terrorist organizations unleashed upon both white and black pro-Republican supporters and voters violent mischief and murder. In Louisiana alone between April and November 1868, more than a 1,000 persons, mostly blacks, were killed. Such intimidation by the Klan and other white paramilitary organizations did help the Democrats carry Louisiana and Georgia, but their activities hurt the party in the North by lending substance to Republican charges that Rebels (ex-Confederates) and Copperheads (white Northerners, mostly Democrats, who had sympathized with the South before and during the war) were trying to achieve by terrorism what they had failed to accomplish by war.

In the end, Grant won handily, receiving 55 percent of the northern vote, virtually the same proportion as Lincoln had in 1864. Seymour carried only three northern states, Oregon, New Jersey, and New York, as well as three border/former slave states, Delaware, Maryland, and Kentucky, and two of the eight reconstructed ex-Confederate states, Georgia and Louisiana, giving him 80 electoral votes to Grant's 214.

The Fifteenth Amendment

During the year after Grant's election, Congress focused on the unfinished task of Reconstruction by working assiduously on a constitutional amendment to enfranchise African-American males in every state, not just southern freedmen. Without such an amendment, the future of black suffrage would become a farce, especially in the southern states where the Democrats were destined to regain control. Moreover, the inequity of mandating black suffrage in the South while allowing northern states the option disturbed many Republicans, for their party's lassitude on the issue smacked of racism and hypocrisy.

With such sentiments motivating their efforts, the Republican-dominated Congress passed the **Fifteenth Amendment** on February 26, 1869, marking the highpoint of Reconstruction's constitutional achievements. The amendment prohibited states from denying the right to vote on grounds of race, color, or previous condition of servitude. Its purpose was not only to prevent any future revocation of black suffrage by the reconstructed states but also to extend equal suffrage to the border states and to the North. Within four months of congressional passage, seventeen Republican legislatures then in session ratified the amendment, and the four Democratic counterparts in session predictably rejected it. It remained uncertain where enough votes could be won among the eleven more states when their respective legislatures met in the fall. Fortunately, the Republicans had an opportunity to mitigate the chances of defeat by mandating in the still unreconstructed states of Virginia, Mississippi, and Texas that if they hoped to be readmitted, their legislatures had to ratify both the Fourteenth and Fifteenth Amendments. All three states complied and were restored to the Union in 1870. Georgia remained the lone ex-Confederate state still unreconstructed. However, after several months of interesting maneuvers and behind-the-scenes deals, Georgia rejoined the Union and ratified the Fifteenth Amendment, giving the two-thirds majority required. With Georgia's ratification the Fifteenth Amendment became part of the Constitution on March 30, 1870. Many Republicans believed the amendment represented the last great point that remained to be settled on the issues of the war. Now the nation could focus on the other issues long neglected because of preoccupation with sectional strife. Even since Texas's annexation a quarter-century earlier, the Republic had scarcely a moment's respite from this tension. "Let us have done with Reconstruction," pleaded the *New York Tribune* in

First African American Senator and Representatives in the 41st and 42nd Congress of the United States, by Currier and Ives, 1872.
(Left to right) Senator Hiram Revels of Mississippi, Representatives Benjamin Turner of Alabama, Robert DeLarge of South Carolina, Josiah Walls of Florida, Jefferson Long of Georgia, Joseph Rainey and Robert B. Elliot of South Carolina.

April 1870. "The Country is tired and sick of it. LET US HAVE PEACE."

Another motivating factor for many politicians to support the Fifteenth Amendment was to silence the outcry among northern white women, the "suffragettes," who had been lobbying for the right to vote for decades. Congress never anticipated the suffragette outrage when the Fourteenth Amendment passed, not only making citizens of ex-slaves but also automatically giving them the right to vote at age 21. Even black females allegedly had this right for the amendment made no specific mention of gender. Such legislation incensed the suffragettes, for not only were they white (a good number of these women were racists) but also had never been property (chattel) in the same sense as the freedmen. To give an ex-slave such privileges while white women continued to languish as non-citizens in this capacity was simply unacceptable to the suffragettes. Thus, in many ways the Fifteenth Amendment was a sort of "throw-away" piece of legislation, designed to clarify who was specifically eligible to now vote in this country: all adult *males*, 21 years or older, regardless of *race, color*, or *previous condition of servitude*. Since *gender* was not mentioned, it was to be naturally *assumed* that women, regardless of color, were to be excluded from the franchise. No doubt suffragettes felt duped and betrayed, especially by the Radicals whose talk of supposed equality for all smacked of hypocrisy and political opportunism, especially at the expense of white women. Thus the promulgation of the Fifteenth Amendment reflected that when it came to the extension of full-fledged citizenship to white women, few, if any, white males were ready to go that far. Even in the most revolutionary of times, American white male chauvinism continued unabated.

Grant in the White House

Few presidents in American history entered the White House with more prestige and goodwill than Ulysses S. Grant. Now that Reconstruction was supposedly over, Republican supporters were eager to focus on other pressing issues such as the currency and related financial problems, civil service reform, and foreign policy, an area that had been particularly neglected because of sectional strife and civil war. Unfortunately, rather than solving or ameliorating these problems, Grant's inexperience and errors in judgment coupled with the venality of some of his associates not only worsened many of these issues but created a whole new set of troubles for the president as well. Compounding these domestic difficulties was the ongoing insolvable problems of Reconstruction, all of which ultimately dashed the hopes of many Americans that the hero of the War of the Rebellion would be the nation's messiah. In short, the Grant years were plagued by scandals, corruption, and graft that seemed to pervade his administration from top to bottom from the moment he took office.

Within months of his first term, Grant had to deal with an attempt by two of the Gilded Age's most notorious Wall Street buccaneers, Jay Gould and Jim Fisk, to corner the gold market. Prompting Gould and Fisk to try such shenanigans was Congress's passing of the **Public Credit Act**, which allowed for the redemption of all government bonds in gold or its equivalent and the pledging to bring greenbacks to par with gold at the earliest practicable period. In the meantime, the price of gold fluctuated, creating the perfect opportunity for speculators such as Gould and Fisk, both of whom had previously made a killing among capitalist titans (Gould and Fisk against Cornelius Vanderbilt) for control of one of the nation's most important railroad lines, the Erie. With their profits from this venture, Gould and Fisk hoped to corner the gold market by buying as much gold as possible when the market price reached its lowest point, which they were certain it would soon because of the uncertain, fluctuating nature of the nation's overall financial system.

Much to their chagrin, the government (the Treasury) sold only specified amounts monthly, which greatly limited the amount of the bullion Gould and Fisk could buy at one time. Not to be deterred, the corsairs found an ally in the White House in Abel R. Corbin, the president's brother-in-law, who introduced Grant to Gould and Fisk, who convinced the president to suspend the monthly sales allotment and simply let as much gold be sold on the open market as possible. Gould told the president that such a free-wheeling policy of allowing the price of gold to rise would benefit the nation, especially the farmers by lowering the dollar price of wheat in European markets, thereby increasing exports. Grant was noncommittal, but his brother-in-law assured Gould that the government would suspend restricted gold sales. No sooner did the Treasury lift the limitations on gold sales than Gould and Fisk began buying every ounce of gold in sight, driving up the premium to 144. By late September 1869, the price of gold had risen to 162. Grant saw that he had been hoodwinked by Gould and Fisk and immediately ordered the Treasury to stop gold sales and then only sell $4 million each month thereafter. Grant's action caused a quick tumble in the gold market, which settled at 133, leaving scores of brokers and speculators ruined. Gould avoided disaster by selling at the top of the market, and his sidekick Fisk simply repudiated several of his contracts. Although acting promptly upon learning the truth of Gould's schemes, the gold fiasco nonetheless tainted Grant's image as being an individual susceptible to nepotism and cronyism.

Sadly for Grant, the Gould-Fisk escapade was only the beginning of a wave of scandals and corruption that sullied his White House years. The president's private secretary, Orville Babcock, became involved in the infamous "**Whiskey Ring**," a network of distillers and revenue agents that bilked the government of millions of excise tax dollars on whiskey while amassing fortunes. In one scandal, it was proved that Grant's Secretary of War William Belknap (who was subsequently impeached) had been accepting bribes from men whom he had appointed as agents on Indian reservations—in effect selling government posts at a price that the agent would recover by cheating the Indians.

Although honest himself, Grant appeared to have an indiscriminate reverence for wealth, and he seemed quite blind to the effect of having the president associate with rich, unscrupulous looters and market manipulators such as Jay Gould and Jim Fisk. Grant was also too trusting of subordinates. He appointed many former members of his military family, as well as several of his wife's relatives, to offices for which they were scarcely qualified. However, not all of the era's scandals emanated from the White House; this was an era notorious for corruption at all levels of government with the infamous **Tammany Hall** "Ring" of Democratic "Boss" William Marcy Tweed of New York City leading the way. Tweed and his associates may have stolen more money from New York City taxpayers than all the federal agencies combined, and the New York legislature was famous for the buying and selling of votes. The Tweed Ring used the simple device of taking whatever funds they wanted from the municipal treasury on the pretext of paying for goods and services that were never ordered and never received. In one day they helped themselves to $14 million by this uncomplicated method.

Perhaps the most notorious and widely publicized scandal of the era was the **Crédit Mobilier Affair**, which much to Grant's relief involved Congress and not members of his administration. This particular debacle pertained to the building of the Union Pacific Railroad. When the railroad company was organized, it did not manage the construction of its own road; rather, it farmed out the line's building to a construction company named somewhat fancifully and pretentiously the Credit Mobilier of America. Although such an arrangement was not unusual, quite legitimate in fact, what made this particular deal suspect was the fact that the railroad company's directors had organized the construction company. Then in their capacity as railroad directors they awarded themselves, as contractors, the contracts to build a cheaply constructed road at exorbitant prices. In this way they could easily siphon off government grants, leaving the railroad company almost bankrupt but themselves wealthy. Now all these rascals had to do was avoid any government inquiry into their shenanigans, which they did by distributing shares of construction company stock to targeted, susceptible, influential members of the House of Representatives, including its Speaker, soon-to-be vice president, Schuyler Colfax, to keep them from becoming too vigilant. The influence-peddling was eventually exposed and became the first clear illustration that the public received of what can happen when a group of insiders gains control of a wealthy enterprise that they do not own. The separation of ownership and control marked a new trend in American capitalist development and became over the next several decades an unfortunate hallmark of Gilded Age politics and economics.

What accounted for this explosion of corruption in the postwar decade, which one historian has called "The Era of Good Stealings"? The expansion of government

A cartoon depicts President Ulysses S. Grant as a circus acrobat being pulled down by several figures in his administration implicated in the "Whiskey Ring" scandal. Multiple scandals marred Grant's presidency. Illustration from an 1880 edition of *Puck* magazine.

contracts and the bureaucracy during the war created new opportunities for the unscrupulous, compounded by a general relaxation of tensions and standards following the intense sacrifices of the war years. In other words, for four long, bloody years, white Americans (especially those in the North) seemed to have adhered to a comparatively rigid moral and ethical code, one that placed a premium on the virtues of self-sacrifice, frugality, and altruism, all for the good of a greater cause. Now that the cause had ended, with the Union preserved and slavery abolished, so ended four years of pent-up emotional and material self-deprivation. Americans were now eager to embrace the new industrial order the war had wrought, especially in the North, and with such change came opportunities for one to not only enjoy a life of material abundance but in the process become rich as well. Enterprises such as railroad construction became the consummate symbolic example of the get-rich-quick mentality and greed that took hold of many post-war Americans, satirized by Mark Twain and Charles Dudley Warner in their 1873 novel *The Gilded Age*, which gave its name to the era. In many ways, post-Civil War American culture produced attitudes, behaviors, and values not unfamiliar to Americans of the late twentieth and early twenty-first centuries: an ethos of crass materialism, hedonistic self-indulgence, and a passion to accumulate monetary wealth regardless of how ethical the endeavor or how detrimental the affects on others.

Civil Service Reform

As a result of the endemic corruption, a civil service reform movement emerged to try to cleanse an inefficient government bureaucracy that had become rife with malfeasance, cronyism, and nepotism—in many ways the inevitable result of decades of the spoils system initiated by Andrew Jackson's administration of the late 1820s. Beginning with Jackson and through Grant, the victorious party in an election rewarded party loyalists with federal appointments, usually at the lower bureaucratic level such as postmasters, customs collectors, and the like. Even when a party was out of power, the possibility of appointment helped to maintain the party faithful. The spoils system politicized the bureaucracy and staffed it with unqualified personnel who spent more time working for their party than for the government. Such were the realities and conditions on which reformers focused a harsh light—into the dark corners of corruption previously obscured by the sectional conflict, war, and reconstruction. Although much of the corruption may have been exaggerated by reformers for publicity purposes, plenty was nonetheless there to warrant serious investigation and rectification.

Reformers were mainly well-educated northeastern professionals, and many came from some of the nation's most pedigreed families. Most of them were Republicans, cut from the old Conscience Whig cloth of the party. They admired the incorruptible efficiency of the British civil service and wanted to emulate that system. Professional politicians on both sides of the aisle, however, looked askance at such notions. To them, patronage was the lifeblood of democracy and had been since the days of the "Jacksonian revolution." They accused the reformers of being elitists and ridiculed them as dilettantes trying to play at the serious business of nitty-gritty American politics.

Civil service reformers wanted to separate the bureaucracy from politics by mandating competitive examinations for the appointment of civil servants. This movement gained momentum during the 1870s and finally achieved success in 1883 with the passage of the **Pendleton Act**, which established the modern structure, system, and procedure for positions within the civil service. When Grant took office, he appeared to share the sentiments of the civil service reformers. Several of his cabinet officials—Secretary of the Treasury George Boutwell, Secretary of the Interior Samuel D. Cox, and Attorney General Rockwood Hoar—inaugurated examinations for certain appointments and promotions in their respective departments. Grant also named a civil service commission headed by the editor of *Harper's Weekly* and a leading reformer, George William Curtis. Unfortunately too many of Grant's contemporaries opposed reform. They simply found the spoils system too personally beneficial to do away with. Patronage was the grease of the political machines that kept them in office and all too often enriched them and their political chums. They managed to subvert reform, sometimes using Grant as an unwitting ally and turning many reformers against the president. Thus, much to the disappointment of the reformers, a thoroughgoing reform of the spoils system was not achieved in the 1870s.

Foreign Policy Issues

Although the Grant administration's focus was domestic rather than foreign, there were significant foreign policy developments and issues during these years, some of which added to Grant's woes. One such setback was the **Santo Domingo Affair**, an attempt by the Grant White House to annex the island nation of Santo Domingo (present-day Dominican Republic). Such a move by the administration reflected a resurgent American nationalism and the concomitant momentary revival of Manifest Destiny, led ironically by post-war Republicans, not Democrats, as had been the case in the past. Leading the rejuvenated expansionist spirit was Secretary of State William Seward, the individual most responsible for the U.S. purchase of Alaska from Russia in 1867. Seward had also earlier attempted to purchase the Virgin Islands from Denmark, for the Civil War had demonstrated the need for a U.S. naval base in the Caribbean. The Senate killed this treaty but not the idea of U.S. expansion into the Caribbean.

To the surprise of many and to the dismay of many others, President Grant was as keen on American expansion as his secretary of state. Grant too was interested in promoting a U.S. presence in the Caribbean and thus when approached by wily Dominican dictator, Bonaventura Baez, who wanted the United States to acquire his country as a means to bolster his power against insurgent movements, Grant jumped at the opportunity to acquire the island nation. So too were unsavory land speculators, commercial developers, mercenaries, promoters of fabulous gold and silver mines, and naval officers who wanted a Caribbean base and dreamed of a canal built across modern-day Panama. For Grant the acquisition of the Dominican Republic represented the opportunity for the United States to bring peace and stability to a country of chronic revolutions, develop its rich resources, open the gateway for the extension of beneficent American influence throughout the region, and initiate the Isthmian canal project. Grant hoped to make the annexation the showpiece foreign policy achievement of his administration.

Grant let his enthusiasm for the scheme get the better of him, as he committed one political blunder and diplomatic faux pas after another throughout the negotiation process, beginning with his peremptory ordering of the purchase without first lining up key political support among his cabinet and Congress. Without consulting either group, Grant sent his private secretary, Orville Babcock, to the island nation in July 1869 to open negotiations. The overzealous Babcock did more than discuss the possibilities of acquisition. He brought back a treaty of annexation. After the irregularities of the procedure had been pointed out by Cabinet members, Grant, determined to have Santo Domingo, regardless of having violated a multitude of diplomatic protocols, sent Babcock back to Santo Domingo with State Department authorization to renegotiate the agreement properly. Baez agreed to the terms, and Babcock returned with a treaty that made Santo Domingo a U.S. territory and declared her 120,000 people to be American citizens, all at a bargain price of $1.5 million. Santo Domingans unanimously approved annexation. In January 1870, Grant proudly submitted the treaty for Senate ratification. In effect, he handed the Senate an unwelcomed, distasteful *fait accompli*, which incensed Senate leaders of both parties.

Leading the anti-annexation movement in the Senate were Charles Sumner of Massachusetts and Carl Schurz of Missouri. Along with other senators from both sides of the aisle, Schurz and Sumner castigated the corrupt promoters who had bought up land in expectation of windfall profits from annexation. Schurz and Sumner invoked the traditional Whig/Republican hostility to expansion with Schurz questioning the wisdom of incorporating a new mixed-blood Catholic people into an American population that already had more than enough trouble with racial issues. "These islands by climate, occupation, and destiny belong to the colored people," Sumner declared. "We should not take them away. No greed of land should prevail against the rights of this race."

Outraged by Sumner's and Schurz's opposition as well as their criticism of his high-handedness, Grant went on a personal rampage, dismissing or sending out to political pasture as many of Sumner's and Schurz's allies as fast as he possibly could. Grant's counterattack yielded little favorable results except to alienate a growing number of Republicans from the administration. On June 30, 1870, the Senate defeated the treaty by a tie vote of 28-28, with nineteen Republicans joining nine Democrats in opposition. Open warfare now erupted between Grant and Sumner, becoming increasingly savage as the months wore on.

The Santo Domingo affair seriously divided the Republican Party. Both the president and senators had demonstrated traits of petty vindictiveness. Sumner's vain ego and righteous moralism seemed to grow more excessive with age. To the senator's friends, however, Grant's vendetta seemed to be an attack on the idealism that had made the Republican Party great. They feared that the party, under Grant's lack of leadership and general personal fortitude, was fast falling into the hands of spoilsmen and opportunists. By 1871, a new noun, "**Grantism**," had entered Washingtonian verbiage. It became a catch-all term for all the things the old Republicans believed were wrong with postwar America: spoilsmanship and corruption in government; crude, vulgar taste and anti-intellectualism in culture; dishonesty in business; and a boundless materialism and a get-rich-quick acquisitiveness that was becoming more and more to define a new American creed. This breach between old and new Republicans would split the party in the 1872 election, giving rise to the Liberal Republican movement.

The Grant administration also had to reckon with Great Britain and Mexico over events that were in a sense unfinished business from the war itself. One involved the French-supported empire of Austrian archduke Maximilian in Mexico. The other concerned the United States's claims against Great Britain for having permitted the construction and outfitting, as well as a safe haven, for the Confederate commerce raider, the *Alabama*, which ravaged the U.S. merchant marine during the war.

At the beginning of the U.S. Civil War, the Mexican government had defaulted on its debts to Britain, Spain, and France. All three nations agreed to use force if necessary to collect what they were owed, but they also agreed that none would attempt to gain peculiar advantage from the situation. The French emperor, Napoleon III, however, had no intention of fulfilling his pledge, for he saw a grand opportunity to begin the resurrection of his uncle's empire (Napoleon I), which he believed he was destined to achieve. In secret negotiations with the ruling Habsburgs of the Austro-Hungarian empire, Napoleon III arranged for the archduke Maximilian to become emperor of Mexico with French support. Great Britain and Spain knew nothing of this deal. In 1862, the creditor nations invaded Mexico, driving into exile into the northern Mexican mountains and deserts its president, Benito Juarez. By 1863 England and Spain had grown weary of the whole affair and withdrew their troops, leaving France in charge of future operations. Napoleon could not have asked for a more perfect scenario to implement his scheme. French armies occupied Mexico City a month before the Battle of Gettysburg, and, shortly afterward, a hand-picked group of wealthy, conservative, anti-Juarez Mexican landowners, Catholic clergy, and military officers offered Maximilian the throne as Emperor of their country, which the Austrian accepted in 1864. In reality, Maximilian was barely the emperor of Mexico City, for all around him were the Juarista republican insurgents.

The Lincoln administration was greatly upset by this blatant violation of the Monroe Doctrine, and Congress responded by voting angry resolutions. But there was little the United States could do at the moment, embroiled as Secretary of State William Seward stated, "in a struggle for our own life." Both Lincoln and Seward knew, however, that the French invasion portended ill for national security. Indeed, the French invasion, occupation, and the establishing of an empire represented the most serious direct threat to American security since the War of 1812. Both Lincoln and Seward were biding their time. After Lee's surrender, and with Lincoln's death, the job of getting the French out of Mexico fell to Seward, who began to pressure Napoleon, gently at first, to leave Mexico. When such nudging failed, Seward became more aggressive and bellicose, demanding in February 1866 that France set a date to get out of Mexico or U.S. troops would be sent into Mexico to drive them out. Napoleon knew Seward was serious. Moreover, all of Europe knew that the Union Army had fought itself into being one of the best armies in the world and could have easily crushed the French forces in Mexico, which would have become a most humiliating defeat for a supposed great European power. Thus, in April 1867, Napoleon agreed to begin the withdrawal process. Aside from U.S. pressure, by that time Napoleon had found his venture more costly and unpopular than he had anticipated.

Maximilian remained in Mexico, regarding himself as a Mexican and a legitimate ruler. For such a delusion, he paid with his life at the hands of a Mexican firing squad in June 1867. Apparently the Mexicans did not see Maximilian in the same light as he saw himself. During all these developments, Seward never invoked the Monroe Doctrine, but Napoleon's withdrawal from Mexico was perhaps the most important victory it ever scored.

The second piece of war-related unfinished business was the damage claims against Britain for losses caused by the C.S.S. *Alabama* and other Confederate commerce raiders (the *Florida* and the *Shenandoah*) built in British shipyards. This particular issue should have been settled quickly, for the British were in a conciliatory mood, admitting that the building of such ships had violated the principles of neutrality. The British also feared the possibility of American retaliation—that the United States might allow an enemy of England to build commerce raiding ships in American ports that would attack Brit-

Charles Sumner of Massachusetts - great senator and statesman, a champion of civil and political equality.

ish merchant marines. Complicating negotiations were a cluster of other issues as well: a dispute about possession of the San Juan Islands off Vancouver; questions about Canadian-American fishing rights; Irish-American aid to Irish revolutionists; and, most of all, a lingering American desire for the United States to annex all or part of Canada. Because of these issues, negotiations did not begin until 1869.

No sooner did talks begin than Senator Charles Sumner blasted the negotiations, declaring Britain financially accountable not only for destroyed American merchant ships but also for prolonging the war by two years, for according to Sumner (and some others), after Gettysburg and Vicksburg, it was only British support that enabled the Confederacy to continue fighting. He proposed astronomical damages—far greater, in fact, than Germany would soon impose on France at the end of the Franco-Prussian War. Sumner's tirade caused negotiations to break off, and for two years strained relations existed between the U.S. and Great Britain. Newspapers on both sides of the Atlantic traded bellicose threats.

Thanks to the skillful handling by Secretary of State Hamilton Fish, the impasse was finally broken when the Grant administration agreed to the Treaty of Washington (1871), which called for submitting the dispute to an international arbitration commission comprised of the United States, Britain, Switzerland, Italy, and Brazil. By a 4-1 vote (Britain dissenting) the arbitrators declared that the British government had failed to exercise due diligence to prevent the building and arming of the Confederate raiders and awarded the United States $15.5 million for the damages done by these ships.

The events leading to the Treaty of Washington also resolved another long-festering issue affecting relations between Britain and the United States: the status of Canada. The seven separate British North American colonies were especially vulnerable to U.S. desires for annexation. Indeed, so angered were many Northerners toward Britain for the Confederate raiders' depredations, that they demanded that England relinquish her Canadian provinces as payment for these damages. Such bellicosity strengthened Canadians' loyalty to Britain as a counterweight to American aggression. In 1867, Parliament passed the British North American Act, which united most of the Canadian colonies into a new and largely self-governing Dominion of Canada.

Further strengthening Pro-British Canadian nationalism were the actions of the Irish American Fenian Brotherhood, a secret society organized during the Civil War dedicated to the overthrow of British rule in Ireland. The Fenians believed that a U.S. invasion and acquisition of Canada would go far toward achieving an independent Ireland. Three times from 1866 to 1871, Fenians, composed mainly of Irish American ex-Union army veterans, crossed the U.S.-Canadian border, only to be driven back after light skirmishes. The Fenian invasions intensified Canadian anti-Americanism, complicating the negotiations leading to the 1871 Washington Treaty. However, the successful conclusion of that treaty cooled American-Canadian tensions, leading to resolutions of disputes over American commercial fishing in Canadian waters. U.S. troops prevented further Fenian raids, and American demands for annexation of Canada also dissipated as well. The easing of these tensions helped to usher in a prolonged period of peaceful relations between the U.S. and Canada, who share a 3,500-mile border with the United States that remains the longest unfortified frontier in the world.

The purchase of Alaska from Russia, the result of Secretary of State William Seward's astuteness, taking advantage of a financially hard-pressed Russian government that had overextended itself in the far Pacific Northwest, was not recognized as a major event. Through diplomatic back-channels, Seward found out that Russia would be interested in selling Alaska to the United States and jumped at the possibility, settling on the negotiated price of $7.2 million. For Seward, the Alaska purchase represented a grand opportunity to increase U.S. ports on the Pacific, which would further facilitate the nation's trade possibilities with the Far East, even potentially with Russia. To the commercial-minded Seward, Russia's present backwardness made it a perfect market for America's burgeoning manufacturing enterprises to dump their surplus goods. When the public found out about "Seward's Folly," the secretary was chastised in the press and in government circles for having purchased this frozen wasteland. Some congressmen even had to be bribed to vote for the appropriation. Despite the criticism, Seward persevered, certain that some day his folly would be worth far more than the purchase price to the United States. The treaty was ratified in 1867, the payment voted in 1868, and then Alaska was put away and forgotten, unexplored and unknown, until the 1897 Klondike Gold Rush, which turned out to be the greatest in American history, yielding more gold than all other such finds combined.

THE WHITE BACKLASH CONTINUES

No sooner did Republican regimes come to power in the South than southern whites were determined to bring them down. Always ready to help in such crusades was the Ku Klux Klan, whose terrorist acts reached a crescendo in 1870 and 1871. Although keeping freedmen subjugated was the Klan's priority, members also believed it their mission to destroy the Republican Party by terrorizing its voters and, if necessary, murdering its leaders. No one knows the number of politically motivated killings that occurred in the South during Reconstruction, but it was certainly in the hundreds, if not in the thousands, with African Americans easily comprising the lion's share of victims. In one notorious incident, the "Colfax Massacre" in Louisiana (April 18, 1873), a confrontation between black militia and armed whites left three whites and nearly one hundred blacks dead, with the majority of the latter shot down in cold blood after they had surrendered. In some states, most notably Arkansas and Tennessee, Republicans formed state militias to protect themselves and successfully suppressed Klan raids and other terrorist activities. But in most of the southern states the militias were outgunned and outmaneuvered by ex-Confederate veterans who had joined the Klan. Some Republican governors were reluctant to use black militia against white guerrillas, fearing that such an encounter could spark a racial bloodbath as happened at Colfax.

No matter what the Republican governments did, they appeared to be losing the battle with the Klan, whose popularity among white Southerners seemed to be increasing daily. It was time to seek federal help. In 1870 and 1871, Congress enacted three laws intended to enforce the Fourteenth and Fifteenth Amendments with federal marshals and troops if necessary. Interference with voting rights became a federal offense, and any attempts to deprive another person of civil or political rights became a felony. The third law, popularly called the Ku Klux Klan Act, gave the president the power to suspend the writ of *habeas corpus* and send in federal troops to suppress armed resistance to federal law.

Although virtually handed by Congress carte blanche to deal with the Klan as forcefully as warranted, Grant showed restraint, sensitive to charges of being a military despot. He suspended the writ of *habeas corpus* in only nine South Carolina counties. Nevertheless, there and elsewhere federal marshals backed by troops arrested thousands of suspected Klansmen. Federal grand juries indicted more than three thousand, and several hundred defendants pleaded guilty in return for suspended sentences. To clear congested court dockets so that the worst offenders could be tried quickly, the Justice Department dropped charges against nearly two thousand others. About six hundred Klansmen were convicted. Most received fines or light jail sentences, but sixty-five went to a federal penitentiary for terms of up to five years.

The 1872 Presidential Election

The crackdown on the Klan helped to bolster Grant's image, especially among the Radicals and even among a still strongly supportive northern white majority, many of whom remained in a vindictive mood toward white Southerners. However, within the GOP a dissident group had emerged to challenge Grant's reelection.

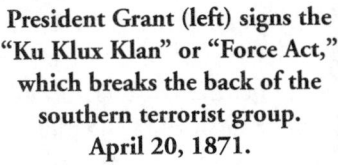

President Grant (left) signs the "Ku Klux Klan" or "Force Act," which breaks the back of the southern terrorist group. April 20, 1871.

Disillusioned with his record on civil service reform, disgusted with the scandals and corruption that seemed to have infected his White House, and disturbed with his consorting with Robber Barons such as Jim Fisk and Jay Gould served to alienate the more high-minded, righteous purists within the party. These disgruntled Republicans broke with the party and organized a splinter group, calling themselves the Liberal Republicans, who believed that in alliance with the Democrats they could defeat Grant. Their slogan became "Anything to beat Grant." With Democratic approval and support, this fusion party nominated Horace Greeley, the famous editor of the *New York Tribune*, who, ironically, had been a Democratic nemesis for decades. The Liberal Republican-Democratic coalition called for a new policy of conciliation toward southern whites rather than continued military intervention as the only way to achieve peace in the region. The party's platform thus denounced Grant's supposed "bayonet rule" in the South, and Greeley urged fellow Northerners to put the issues of the Civil War behind them and to "clasp hands across the bloody chasm which has too long divided" North and South.

Much to the party's chagrin, most northern voters were still not prepared to trust either Democrats or southern whites. Powerful anti-Greeley lampoons by political cartoonist Thomas Nast showed Greeley shaking the hand of a Klansman dripping with blood of a murdered black Republican. Nast's most famous cartoon portrayed Greeley as a pirate captain bringing his craft alongside the ship of state while ex-Confederate leaders, armed to the teeth, hid below waiting to board it. To no one's surprise, Grant swamped Greeley by over a million popular votes. Republicans carried every northern state and ten of the sixteen southern and border states. In the Electoral College, Grant received 286 votes to Greeley's 66. Southern blacks enjoyed more freedom in voting than they would enjoy again for a century. But this apparent triumph of Republicanism and Reconstruction proved to be short-lived.

The Panic of 1873

President Grant had but one year to bask in the rays of his resounding victory over Horace Greeley. The following September, the worst economic decline in the Republic's history to date rocked both the Grant administration and the American people, ushering in close to a decade of hard times for millions of Americans. Most importantly, the panic proved to be the death knell for Reconstruction. Northern whites, now distracted and consumed by a more pressing economic crisis, simply lost what little interest or passion they had left for Reconstruction and turned away from the cause, wanting an end to issues and concerns that had never really affected their daily lives in the first place. Economic survival now became the order of the day for the majority of northern whites, and with such preoccupation came the abrupt end for sustaining either the freedmen's rights or for the Republican regimes established to defend those rights and reform the South.

The U.S. economy had grown at an unprecedented rate since recovering in 1867 from a mild postwar recession. As many miles of new railroad track (35,000) were laid down in eight years as in the preceding thirty-five. The first transcontinental railroad had been completed on May 10, 1869, when a golden spike was driven at Promontory Point, Utah Territory, linking the Union Pacific and Central Pacific. But it was the construction of a second transcontinental line, the Northern Pacific, that precipitated a Wall Street panic in 1873 and plunged the economy into a five-year depression and a ten-year general downturn.

Ironically, the hero of Civil War finance, Jay Cooke, was the main culprit. Cooke's banking firm, fresh from its triumphant marketing of Union war bonds, took over the Northern Pacific in 1869. Despite government land grants and loans, the company had not yet laid a single mile of track. Cooke pyramided every imaginable kind of equity and loan financing to raise money to begin laying rails west from Duluth, Minnesota. Other investment firms did the same as a fever of speculative financing swept the country. In September 1873, the pyramid of paper collapsed. Cooke's firm was the first to go under.

Horace Greeley, c. 1872.

The swearing-in of President Ulysses S. Grant for his second term, March 4, 1873.

Like dominoes, hundreds of banks and businesses also collapsed. By 1875, over 18,000 railroad related enterprises had failed. Northern unemployment rose to 14 percent, and hard times set in across the region.

RETREAT FROM RECONSTRUCTION

It is almost a given in American politics that the party responsible or blamed for economic hard times will most certainly lose and usually big in the forthcoming election. That axiom proved true in the 1870s as the Democrats made large gains in the 1874 congressional elections, winning a majority of House seats for the first time in eighteen years. Compounding Republican woes, the Panic of 1873 caused northern public opinion to turn against Republican policies in the South, believing continued support for the Republican governments to be a waste of valuable money and effort that could be put to better use trying to ameliorate the northern economic crisis. When the Liberal Republican-Democratic coalition in 1872 clamored against bayonet rule and carpetbag corruption in the South, their braying at the time fell mostly on deaf ears. However, by 1874, those charges found increasingly receptive northern audiences. Intraparty battles among southern Republicans enabled Democratic Redeemers (along with the use of terror and violence) to regain control of several southern state governments, which became an almost inevitable outcome once southern whites regained their right to vote. No sooner did that occur than they simply voted the scalawags, carpetbaggers, and freedmen out of office, and if they resisted, they would be visited by the Klan or one of the many other white backlash organizations that had emerged to overthrow "negro rule" and restore white supremacy.

Well-publicized corruption scandals, especially in Louisiana, also discredited Republican leaders. Although malfeasance was probably no worse in southern states than in many parts of the North, southern postwar poverty made waste and extravagance seem worse and gave the reform impulse an extra impetus. Southern white Democrats pointed to the corruption as confirmation of the Negroes alleged inherent depravity, incompetence, and ignorance—their complete unfitness to participate in political life. The only reason they had gained political office was because they had been placed there by the scalawags and carpetbaggers who, in reality, had only used them for their own political aggrandizement.

Northerners grew increasingly weary of what seemed the endless turmoil of southern politics. From the beginning of Reconstruction, most northern whites had never had a very strong commitment to racial equality, and they were increasingly willing to let white supremacy restore

A Thomas Nast cartoon, "Worse than Slavery" from *Harper's Weekly* in 1874, portrays the sinister alliance of violent terror organizations—the so-called "White League" and the Ku Klux Klan—that bullied and murdered African Americans in the South during Reconstruction. Armed with guns and knives, the two groups shake hands above a frightened family of freedman. A lynched African American looms in the background. Such organizations sought to frighten away African Americans from seeking an education or exercising their just-won right to vote.

itself in the South. Also motivating many northern whites was the fact that beginning in the 1870s, and over the course of the next four decades, the North would be inundated with millions of southern and eastern European immigrants. About 30 million such individuals came to the United States from 1870-1910. Never before had so many from Europe come to the United States, and, more importantly, they had not come from those regions of Europe. The United States had always been for White Anglo-Saxon Protestants, and now WASP America was about to be overwhelmed by Italians, Poles, Czechs, Slovaks, Greeks, and a whole host of swarthy individuals whom white Americans believed to be ethnically, if not racially, inferior to them and thus a threat to the American way of life. Moreover, these new immigrants not only represented an ethnic and racial menace but a religious problem as well, for the majority were Catholic, or Orthodox, or, horror of all horrors, many were Jews. Not only was the United States a white man's country, but it was Christian as well. To most Anglo-Saxon Americans that meant Protestant. As a result of immigration, a peculiar bond of white solidarity began to take shape between northern and southern whites with the former now declaring they understood southern whites' negro problem, for now Northerners had a similar immigrant problem. In the minds of many northern whites, they could not in good conscience continue to force black equality upon their southern brethren if they were unwilling to accept immigrant equality. Thus, by the mid-1870s, as northern whites became increasingly obsessed with their immigrant issue, they were no longer willing to support Republican governments in the South that forced negro rule on their poor, beleaguered white comrades. As immigrants flooded northeastern cities, Anglo-Saxon Northerners found the Fifteenth Amendment's ambiguous wording a very effective tool to disenfranchise the immigrants, whom they feared would become the unsuspecting pawns of big city bosses and their local henchmen and lackeys. Interestingly, the Republicans, more than the Democrats, used the amendment for such purposes, thus becoming the party of an often vicious nativism.

With the loss of northern white support, it was no surprise that by 1875 only four southern states remained under Republican control: South Carolina, Florida, Mississippi, and Louisiana. In those states white Democrats had revived paramilitary organizations under various names: White Leagues (Louisiana), Rifle Clubs (Mississippi), and Red Shirts (South Carolina). Unlike the Klan, these terrorist squads operated openly. In Louisiana they fought pitched battles with Republican militias in which scores were killed. When Grant sent troops to Louisiana to quell the violence, both northern and southern whites cried out against military rule. The protest grew even louder when soldiers marched into the Louisiana legislature in January 1875 to expel several Democratic legislators after a contested election in which voter fraud was committed along with the terrorizing of black voters away from the polls. Liberal Republicans, such as Carl Schurz, delighted in such events, for such Republican reprisals only helped fuel the fires of northern discontent with Republican rule in the South, which Schurz and others wanted to end.

Southern resistance leaders were quick to sense that the tide was turning in their favor. By 1874, the Redeemers had regained control of Texas, Arkansas, and Alabama, leaving Radical control of only four states—Florida, Louisiana, South Carolina, and Mississippi. Only the first three had black majorities, which allowed the Republican regimes to hang on by a thread for a few more years. In Mississippi, however, whites did not hesitate to institute a reign of terror on African Americans to regain power. That violence became a key to their return to control of the state, for even with all whites voting Democratic, the party could still be defeated by the 55 percent black majority. Economic coercion against black sharecroppers kept some freedmen away from the polls, but overt violence became the most effective means. Democratic rifle clubs (code for terrorist paramilitary groups) showed up at Republican rallies, attended mostly by black voters, provoked riots and then shot down in cold blood as many freedmen as possible in the ensuing melees.

The Grant administration had washed its hands of Reconstruction. It had finally succumbed to the antifederal intervention sentiment of the majority of northern whites, thus dooming one of the last Republican regimes in the South to being violently overthrown. All Mississippi Redeemers had to do now was persuade the 10 to 15 percent of white voters still calling themselves Republicans to switch to the Democrats. The Mississippi Plan worked like a charm. In five of the state's counties with large black majorities, the Republicans polled 12, 7, 4, 2, and 0 votes, respectively. When the Democratic legislature met the following January 1875, the Democrats took complete control of the state.

The 1876 Presidential Election

The various scandals of the Grant administration, along with those occurring in northern cities and states as well as in many southern states under Republican rule, ensured that reform would be the leading issue in the year's presidential race. In this centennial year of the nation's birth, Americans wanted to present their nation as the beacon of virtue, justice, righteousness, and morality for all to behold. Although the reality of the last two decades could not have been further from the truth, Americans nonetheless believed they could find their way back to such an image if they chose the right president to lead them in the right direction. Thus, both major parties gave their presidential nomination to governors who had earned reform reputations in their respective states: Democrat Samuel J. Tilden of New York and Republican Rutherford B. Hayes of Ohio.

Democrats entered the campaign as the favorites for the first time in two decades. They based their optimism on the belief that they could put together an electoral majority of solid South Democrats, disaffected northern Republicans (Liberal Republicans) and by carrying New York and two or three other big northern states, hopefully Ohio and Indiana or Illinois, where Grantism and Radical Reconstruction had caused Republican Party splits. So desperate for victory, the Democrats even openly supported the Mississippi Plan in the South, encouraging their southern white counterparts to continue their violent rampages against blacks and the use of other terrorist tactics to keep freedmen from the polls and voting Republican.

When the returns were in, Tilden had won the popular vote by 252,000 but had lost in the Electoral College by one vote, 185-184. The result, screamed the Democrats,

Rutherford B. Hayes

was fraudulent "Negro-Carpetbag-Scalawag" voting in the three unredeemed southern states of Florida, Louisiana, and South Carolina. Tilden had carried all the rest of the southern states, including all the border states, as well as West Virginia. In the North, he captured New York, New Jersey, Indiana, and Connecticut. Unfortunately for the Republicans, the Democratic accusations of fraud were more than likely correct. Obvious voter irregularities popped up in several Louisiana parishes and in other districts in both Florida and South Carolina where two years earlier many of those same districts and parishes had returned sizeable Democratic majorities and now they had miraculously gone Republican. The opposite also had occurred: in 1874, a Louisiana parish had recorded 1,688 Republican votes, but in 1876, Republicans only tallied one brave vote, the result of obvious voter intimidation by whites of both black and white Republicans. The Democrats refused to yield, continuing to shout fraud and even threatened an armed march on Washington. The country now faced a serious constitutional crisis because the document offered no clear guidance on how to deal with such a scenario. The only point of clarity was that a concurrence of both houses of Congress was required to count the electoral votes of the states, but with a Democratic-controlled House and a Republican-dominated Senate an impasse would surely be the result. To break the deadlock, Congress created a special electoral commission consisting of five House members, five senators, and five Supreme Court justices split evenly between the two parties.

The commission discovered that even in three disputed southern states, Tilden had won a majority, but an estimated 250,000 southern Republicans had been terrorized away from the polls. In a genuinely fair and free election, the Republicans might have carried Mississippi and North Carolina, as well as the three disputed states. After three months of wrangling, threats, and outright nastiness among partisans of both parties, the electoral commission issued its ruling. By a strict party vote of 8-7, the commission awarded all the disputed states to Hayes, but the Democrats refused to accept the decision and began a House filibuster to delay the final electoral count beyond the inauguration date of March 4. Such a move would throw the election into the House, an eventuality that threatened to bring anarchy. To avoid such a cataclysm, behind the scenes less-partisan Democrats and Republicans negotiated a compromise. To these individuals, preventing another North-South showdown was essential so the country could proceed with the business of economic recovery and development. Thus,

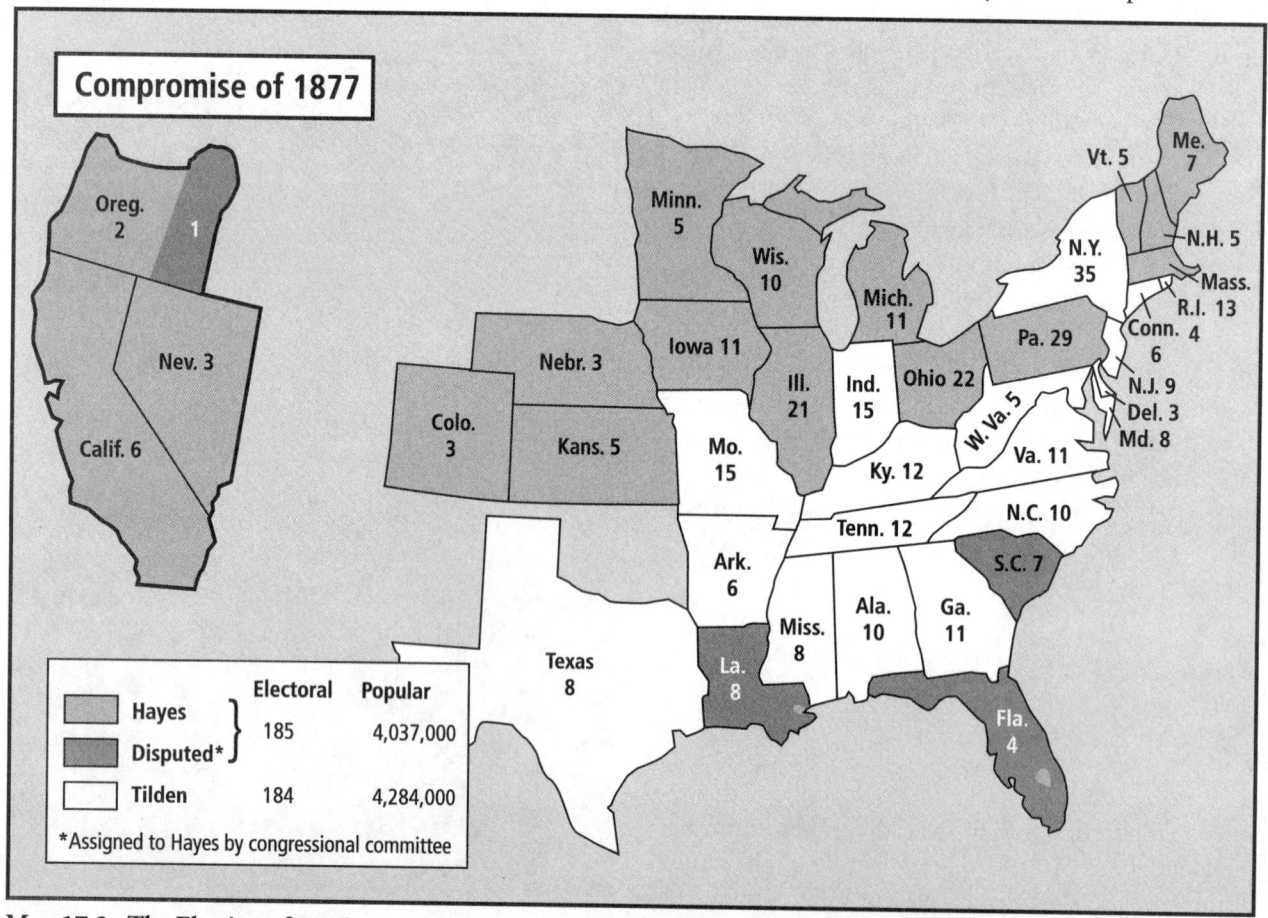

Map 17.3 The Election of 1876

Hayes promised his support for federal appropriations to rebuild war-destroyed levees on the lower Mississippi River and federal aid for a southern transcontinental railroad. Hayes' lieutenants also hinted at the appointment of a Southerner as Postmaster General, who would have a considerable amount of patronage at his disposal. Most important, Hayes signaled that he fully supported the end of bayonet rule, which meant he would withdraw from South Carolina, Florida, and Louisiana, and anywhere else in the South federal troops still resided, allowing a return of complete power to southern whites. In return for his pledge, Hayes asked for and received promises from white Southerners and their respective Democratic state government officials that freedmen would receive fair treatment and respect for their constitutional rights. Such promises were easier to make than to keep, as future years would reveal.

As a result of the backroom negotiations, the Democratic filibuster collapsed, and Hayes was inaugurated on March 4, 1877. No sooner did he take office than ex-Confederate David Key of Tennessee became Postmaster General. The South received more federal money in 1878 for improving its infrastructure than it had ever received before, and federal troops left the capitals of South Carolina and Louisiana. Old abolitionists and Radical Republican warhorses denounced Hayes as a traitor to his party, as well as having sold out the freedmen.

Chronology

1863 Lincoln issues Proclamation of Amnesty and Reconstruction.
Lincoln proposes his Ten Percent Plan

1864 Congress passes stringent Wade-Davis Bill.

1865 Freedmen's Bureau established.
Civil War ends.
Lincoln assassinated (April 14).
Andrew Johnson succeeds to the presidency.
Black Codes enacted by southern legislatures.
Thirteenth Amendment.

1866 Fourteenth Amendment.
Congress passes Civil Rights Act and Freedmen's Bureau Act over Johnson's veto.
Ku Klux Klan founded.
Republicans triumph in congressional elections despite Johnson's efforts.
Southern Homestead Act.

1867 Congressional Reconstruction Act.
U. S. purchases Alaska from Russia.
Congress passes Military Reconstruction Acts, Tenure of Office Act.

1868 President Johnson is impeached but acquitted.
Fourteenth Amendment ratified.
Ulysses S. Grant elected president.

1869 Ratification of the Fifteenth Amendment.

1870 Last four southern states admitted to the Union.
Enforcement Act.

1871 Ku Klux Klan Act.

1872 Grant re-elected president.

1873 Financial panic leads to five-year depression.

1875 Whiskey Ring scandal further discredits Grant administration.
Civil Rights Act.

1876 Disputed presidential election of Hayes vs. Tilden.

1877 Electoral commission awards presidency to Rutherford B. Hayes.

Review Questions

1. Describe Lincoln's Reconstruction plan. What were Lincoln's views on race?

2. How did the Radicals' plan differ from Lincoln's? Who were the "Radicals," and how did they perceive the defeated white South? What was their view of how the freedmen should be treated?

3. Describe the white South "backlash" led by the KKK and other white terrorist organizations against Radical Reconstruction.

4. As a result of the collapse of the Radical regimes, what happened to the freedmen in the aftermath of the Radicals' downfall?

5. What led to Andrew Johnson's impeachment ordeal? Why and how did Johnson alienate the Radicals as well as northern whites?

Glossary of Important People and Concepts

Black Codes
"carpetbaggers"
Crédit Mobilier Affair
Fifteenth Amendment
"Forty Acres and a Mule"
Fourteenth Amendment
Freedmen's Bureau
"Gold Bug"
Ulysses S. Grant
"Grantism"
"Greenbacks"
Homestead Act of 1862
"Iron-clad oath"
Ku Klux Klan
Abraham Lincoln
National Union Party
New Departure
Pendleton Act
Pendleton Plan
Presidential Reconstruction
Public Credit Act
Race-baiting
Radicals Republicans
Reconstruction Acts of 1867
Santo Domingo Affair
"scalawags"
Tammany Hall
Tenure of Office Act of 1867
Thirteenth Amendment
Wade-Davis Bill
"Whiskey Ring"
White backlash

SUGGESTED READINGS

Edward L. Ayers, *The Promise of the New South: Life After Reconstruction* (1992).

Dan T. Carter, *When the War Was Over: The Failure of Presidential Reconstruction in the South, 1865-1867* (1985).

LaWanda Cox, *Lincoln and Black Freedom* (1981).

Richard Nelson Current, *Those Terrible Carpetbaggers* (1988).

W.E. B. DuBois, *Black Reconstruction in America* (1935).

Laura Edwards, *Gendered Strife and Confusion: The Political Culture of Reconstruction* (1997).

Barbara J. Fields, *Slavery and Freedom on the Middle Ground: Maryland During the 19th Century* (1985).

Eric Foner, *Reconstruction: America's Unfinished Revolution, 1863-1877* (1988).

——, *A Short History of Reconstruction* (1990).

George Frederickson, *The Black Image in the White Mind* (1971).

William Gillette, *Retreat From Reconstruction, 1869-1879* (1980).

Herbert Gutman, *The Black Family in Slavery and Freedom, 1750-1925* (1976).

Steven Hahn, *A Nation Under Our Feet: Black Political Struggles in the Rural South From Slavery to the Great Migration* (2003).

William Hesseltine, *Lincoln's Plan of Reconstruction* (1960).

Harold Hyman, *A More Perfect Union: The Impact of the Civil War and Reconstruction on the Constitution* (1973).

Jacqueline Jones, *Labor of Love, Labor of Sorrow: Black Women, Work, and the Family from Slavery to the Present* (1985).

Leon Litwack, *Been in the Storm So Long: The Aftermath of Slavery* (1979).

William S. McFeely, *Grant: A Biography* (1981).

——, *Frederick Douglass* (1990).

Eric McKitrick, *Andrew Johnson and Reconstruction* (1960).

James McPherson, *Ordeal by Fire* (1992).

Michael Perman, *Emancipation and Reconstruction, 1862-1879* (1987).

Benjamin Quarles, *Lincoln and the Negro* (1962).

George C. Rable, *There Was No Peace: The Role of Violence in the Politics of Reconstruction* (1984).

Roger L. Ransom and Richard Sutch, *One Kind of Freedom: The Economic Consequences of Freedom* (1977).

Heather C. Richardson, *Greatest Nation of the Earth: Republican Economic Policies During the Civil War.* (1997).

——, *The Death of Reconstruction: Race, Labor, and Politics in the Post-Civil War North* (2001).

John C. Rodrigue, *Reconstruction in the Cane Fields: From Slavery to Free Labor in Louisiana's Sugar Parishes, 1862-1880* (2001).

Willie Lee Rose, *Rehearsal for Reconstruction: The Port Royal Experiment* (1964).

Theodore Rosengarten, *All God's Dangers: The Life of Nate Shaw* (1974).

Mark W. Summers, *Railroads, Reconstruction, and the Gospel of Prosperity: Aid Under the Radical Republicans* (1984).

Hans L. Trefousse, *Andrew Johnson* (1989).

——, *The Radical Republicans: Lincoln's Vanguard for Justice* (1969).

Joel Williamson, *The Crucible of Race* (1984).

C. Vann Woodward, *Origins of the New South, 1877-1913* (1951).

——, *The Strange Career of Jim Crow* (1974).

APPENDIX A

Declaration of Independence

Congress, July 4, 1776

When, in the course of human events, it becomes necessary for one people to dissolve the political bonds which have connected them with another, and to assume, among the powers of the earth, the separate and equal station to which the laws of nature and of nature's God entitle them, a decent respect to the opinions of mankind requires that they should declare the causes which impel them to the separation.

We hold these truths to be self-evident: That all men are created equal; that they are endowed by their Creator with certain unalienable rights; that among these are life, liberty and the pursuit of happiness; that, to secure these rights, governments are instituted among men, deriving their just powers from the consent of the governed; that whenever any form of government becomes destructive of these ends, it is the right of the people to alter or to abolish it, and to institute new government, laying its foundation on such principles, and organizing its powers in such form, as to them shall seem most likely to effect their safety and happiness. Prudence, indeed, will dictate that governments long established should not be changed for light and transient causes; and accordingly all experience hath shown that mankind are more disposed to suffer, while evils are sufferable, than to right themselves by abolishing the forms to which they are accustomed. But when a long train of abuses and usurpations, pursuing invariably the same object, evinces a design to reduce them under absolute despotism, it is their right, it is their duty, to throw off such government, and to provide new guards for their future security. Such has been the patient sufferance of these colonies; and such is now the necessity which constrains them to alter their former systems of government. The history of the present King of Great Britain is a history of repeated injuries and usurpations, all having in direct object the establishment of an absolute tyranny over these states. To prove this, let facts be submitted to a candid world.

He has refused his assent to laws, the most wholesome and necessary for the public good.

He has forbidden his governors to pass laws of immediate and pressing importance, unless suspended in their operation till his assent should be obtained; and, when so suspended, he has utterly neglected to attend to them.

He has refused to pass other laws for the accommodation of large districts of people, unless those people would relinquish the right of representation in the legislature, a right inestimable to them, and formidable to tyrants only.

He has called together legislative bodies at places unusual, uncomfortable, and distant from the depository of their public records, for the sole purpose of fatiguing them into compliance with his measures.

He has dissolved representative houses repeatedly, for opposing, with many firmness, his invasions on the rights of the people.

He has refused for a long time, after such dissolutions, to cause others to be elected; whereby the legislative powers, incapable of annihilation, have returned to the people at large for their exercise; the state remaining, in the mean time, exposed to all the dangers of invasions from without and convulsions within.

He has endeavored to prevent the population of these states; for that purpose obstructing the laws for naturalization of foreigners; refusing to pass others to encourage their migrations hither, and raising the conditions of new appropriations of lands.

He has obstructed the administration of justice, by refusing his assent to laws establishing judiciary powers.

He has made judges dependent on his will alone, for the tenure of their offices, and the amount and payment of their salaries.

He has erected a multitude of new offices, and sent hither swarms of officers to harass our people and eat out their substance.

He has kept among us, in times of peace, standing armies, without the consent of our legislatures.

He has affected to render the military independent of, and superior to, the civil power.

He has combined with others to subject us to jurisdiction foreign to our constitution, and unacknowledged by our laws, giving his assent to their acts of pretended legislation:

For quartering large bodies of armed troops among us;

For protecting them, by a mock trial, from punishment for any murder which they should commit on the inhabitants of these states;

For cutting off our trade with all parts of the world;

For imposing taxes on us without our consent;

For depriving us, in many cases, of the benefits of trial by jury;

For transporting us beyond seas, to be tried for pretended offenses;

For abolishing the free system of English laws in a neighboring province, establishing therein an arbitrary government, and enlarging its boundaries, so as to render it at once an example and fit instrument for introducing the same absolute rule into these colonies;

For taking away our charters, abolishing our most valuable laws, and altering fundamentally the forms of our governments;

For suspending our own legislatures, and declaring themselves invested with power to legislate for us in all cases whatsoever.

He has abdicated government here, by declaring us out of his protection and waging war against us.

He has plundered our seas, ravaged our coasts, burned our towns, and destroyed the lives of our people.

He is at this time transporting large armies of foreign mercenaries to complete the works of death, desolation and tyranny already begun with circumstances of cruelty and perfidy scarcely paralleled in the most barbarous ages, and totally unworthy the head of a civilized nation.

He has constrained our fellow-citizens, taken captive on the high seas, to bear arms against their country, to become the executioners of their friends and brethren, or to fall themselves by their hands.

He has excited domestic insurrections among us, and has endeavored to bring on the inhabitants of our frontiers the merciless Indian savages, whose known rule of warfare is an undistinguished destruction of all ages, sexes, and conditions.

In every stage of these oppressions we have petitioned for redress in the most humble terms; our repeated petitions have been answered only by repeated injury. A prince, whose character is thus marked by every act which may define a tyrant, is unfit to be the ruler of a free people.

Nor have we been wanting in our attentions to our British brethren. We have warned them, from time to time, of attempts by their legislature to extend an unwarrantable jurisdiction over us. We have reminded them of the circumstances of our emigration and settlement here. We have appealed to their native justice and magnanimity, and we have conjured them, by the ties of our common kindred, to disavow these usurpations, which would inevitably interrupt our connections and correspondence. They, too, have been deaf to the voice of justice and of consanguinity. We must, therefore, acquiesce in the necessity which denounces our separation, and hold them, as we hold the rest of mankind, enemies in war, in peace friends.

We, therefore, the representatives of the United States of America, in General Congress assembled, appealing to the Supreme Judge of the world for the rectitude of our intentions, do, in the name and by authority of the good people of these colonies, solemnly publish and declare, that these United Colonies are, and of right ought to be, FREE AND INDEPENDENT STATES; that they are absolved from all allegiance to the British crown, and that all political connection between them and the state of Great Britain is, and ought to be, totally dissolved; and that, as free and independent states, they have full power to levy war, conclude peace, contract alliances, establish commerce, and do all other acts and things which independent states may of right do. And for the support of this declaration, with a firm reliance on the protection of Divine Providence, we mutually pledge to each other our lives, our fortunes, and our sacred honor.

JOHN HANCOCK

BUTTON GWINNETT
LYMAN HALL
GEO. WALTON
WM. HOOPER
JOSEPH HEWES
JOHN PENN
EDWARD RUTLEDGE
THOS. HEYWARD, JUNR.
THOMAS LYNCH, JUNR.
ARTHUR MIDDLETON
SAMUEL CHASE
WM. PACA
THOS. STONE
CHARLES CARROLL OF CARROLLTON
GEORGE WYTHE
RICHARD HENRY LEE
TH. JEFFERSON
BENJ. HARRISON

THOS. NELSON, JR.
FRANCIS LIGHTFOOT LEE
CARTER BRAXTON
ROBT. MORRIS
BENJAMIN RUSH
BENJA. FRANKLIN
JOHN MORTON
GEO. CLYMER
JAS. SMITH
GEO. TAYLOR
JAMES WILSON
GEO. ROSS
CAESAR RODNEY
GEO READ
THO. M'KEAN
WM. FLOYD
PHIL. LIVINGSTON
FRANS. LEWIS
LEWIS MORRIS

RICHD. STOCKTON
JNO. WITHERSPOON
FRAS. HOPKINSON
JOHN HART
ABRA. CLARK
JOSIAH BARTLETT
WM. WHIPPLE
SAML. ADAMS
JOHN ADAMS
ROBT. TREAT PAINE
ELBRIDGE GERRY
STEP. HOPKINS
WILLIAM ELLERY
ROGER SHERMAN
SAM'EL HUNTINGTON
WM. WILLIAMS
OLIVER WOLCOTT
MATTHEW THORNTON

APPENDIX B

The Constitution of the United States of America

PREAMBLE

We the people of the United States, in order to form a more perfect union, establish justice, insure domestic tranquility, provide for the common defense, promote the general welfare, and secure the blessings of liberty to ourselves and our posterity, do ordain and establish this Constitution for the United States of America.

ARTICLE I.—THE LEGISLATIVE ARTICLE

Section 1. All legislative powers herein granted shall be vested in a Congress of the United States, which shall consist of a Senate and a House of Representatives.

House of Representatives: Composition, Qualification, Apportionment, Impeachment Power

Section 2. The House of Representatives shall be composed of members chosen every second year by the people of the several States, and the electors in each State shall have the qualifications requisite for electors of the most numerous branch of the State Legislature.

No person shall be a Representative who shall not have attained to the age of twenty-five years, and been seven years a citizen of the United States, and who shall not, when elected, be an inhabitant of that State in which he shall be chosen.

Representatives and direct taxes shall be apportioned among the several States which may be included within this Union, according to their respective numbers, *which shall be determined by adding to the whole number of free persons, including those bound to service for a term of years and excluding Indians not taxed, three-fifths of all other persons.* The actual enumeration shall be made within three years after the first meeting of the Congress of the United States, and within every subsequent term of ten years, in such manner as they shall by law direct. The number of Representatives shall not exceed one for every thirty thousand, but each State shall have at least one Representative; *and until each enumeration shall be made, the State of New Hampshire shall be entitled to choose three, Massachusetts eight, Rhode Island and Providence Plantations one, Connecticut five, New York six, New Jersey four, Pennsylvania eight, Delaware one, Maryland six, Virginia ten, North Carolina five, South Carolina five, and Georgia three.*

When vacancies happen in the representation from any State, the Executive authority thereof shall issue writs of election to fill such vacancies.

The House of Representatives shall choose their Speaker and other officers; and shall have the sole power of impeachment.

Senate Composition: Qualifications, Impeachment Trials

Section 3. The Senate of the United States shall be composed of two Senators from each State, *chosen by the legislature thereof,* for six years; and each Senator shall have one vote.

Immediately after they shall be assembled in consequence of the first election, they shall be divided as equally as may be into three classes. The seats of the Senators of the first class shall be vacated at the expiration of the second year, of the second class at the expiration of the fourth year, and of the third class at the expiration of the sixth year, so that one-third may be chosen every second year; and if vacancies happen by resignation or otherwise, during the recess of the legislature of any State, the Executive thereof may make temporary appointments until the next meeting of the legislature, which shall then fill such vacancies.

---

*Passages no longer in effect are printed in italic type.

No person shall be a Senator who shall not have attained to the age of thirty years, and been nine years a citizen of the United States, and who shall not, when elected, be an inhabitant of that State for which he shall be chosen.

The Vice President of the United States shall be President of the Senate, but shall have no vote, unless they be equally divided.

The Senate shall choose their other officers, and also a President *pro tempore*, in the absence of the Vice President, or when he shall exercise the office of President of the United States.

The Senate shall have the sole power to try all impeachments. When sitting for that purpose, they shall be on oath or affirmation. When the President of the United States is tried, the Chief Justice shall preside: and no person shall be convicted without the concurrence of two-thirds of the members present.

Judgment in cases of impeachment shall not extend further than to removal from the office, and disqualification to hold and enjoy any office of honor, trust or profit under the United States; but the party convicted shall nevertheless be liable and subject to indictment, trial, judgment and punishment, according to law.

Congressional Elections: Time, Place, Manner

Section 4. The times, places and manner of holding elections for Senators and Representatives shall be prescribed in each State by the legislature thereof; but the Congress may at any time by law make or alter such regulations, except as to the places of choosing Senators.

The Congress shall assemble at least once in every year, and such meeting *shall be on the first Monday in December, unless they shall by law appoint a different day.*

Powers and Duties of the Houses

Section 5. Each house shall be the judge of the elections, returns and qualifications of its own members, and a majority of each shall constitute a quorum to do business; but a smaller number may adjourn from day to day, and may be authorized to compel the attendance of absent members, in such manner, and under such penalties, as each house may provide.

Each house may determine the rules of its proceedings, punish its members for disorderly behavior, and with the concurrence of two-thirds, expel a member.

Each house shall keep a journal of its proceedings, and from time to time publish the same, excepting such parts as may in their judgment require secrecy; and the yeas and nays of the members of either house on any question shall, at the desire of one-fifth of those present, be entered on the journal.

Neither house, during the session of Congress, shall, without the consent of the other, adjourn for more than three days, nor to any other place than that in which the two houses shall be sitting.

Rights of Members

Section 6. The Senators and Representatives shall receive a compensation for their services, to be ascertained by law and paid out of the treasury of the United States. They shall in all cases except treason, felony and breach of the peace, be privileged from arrest during their attendance at the session of their respective houses, and in going to and returning from the same; and for any speech or debate in either house, they shall not be questioned in any other place.

No Senator or Representative shall, during the time for which he was elected, be appointed to any civil office under the authority of the United States, which shall have been created, or the emoluments whereof shall have been increased, during such time; and no person holding any office under the United States shall be a member of either house during his continuance in office.

Legislative Powers: Bills and Resolutions

Section 7. All bills for raising revenue shall originate in the House of Representatives; but the Senate may propose or concur with amendments as on other bills.

Every bill which shall have passed the House of Representatives and the Senate, shall, before it become a law, be presented to the President of the United States; if he approve he shall sign it, but if not he shall return it with objections to that house in which it originated, who shall enter the objections at large on their journal, and proceed to reconsider it. If after such reconsideration two-thirds of that house shall agree to pass the bill, it shall be sent, together with the objections, to the other house, by which it shall likewise be reconsidered, and if approved by two-thirds of that house, it shall become a law. But in all such cases the votes of both houses shall be determined by yeas and nays, and the names of the persons voting for and against the bill shall be entered on the journal of each house respectively. If any bill shall not be returned by the President within ten days (Sundays excepted) after it shall have been presented to him, the same shall be a law, in like manner as if he had signed it, unless the Congress by their adjournment prevent its return, in which case it shall not be a law.

Every order, resolution, or vote to which the concurrence of the Senate and House of Representatives may be necessary (except on a question of adjournment) shall be presented to the President of the United States; and before the same shall take effect, shall be approved by him, or being disapproved by him, shall be repassed by two-thirds of the Senate and House of Representatives, according to the rules and limitations prescribed in the case of a bill.

Powers of Congress

Section 8. The Congress shall have power
To lay and collect taxes, duties, imposts and excises, to pay the debts and provide for the common defense and general welfare of the United States; but all duties, imposts and excises shall be uniform throughout the United States;
To borrow money on the credit of the United States;
To regulate commerce with foreign nations, and among the several States, and with the Indian tribes;
To establish an uniform rule of naturalization, and uniform laws on the subject of bankruptcies throughout the United States;
To coin money, regulate the value thereof, and of foreign coin, and fix the standard of weights and measures;
To provide for the punishment of counterfeiting the securities and current coin of the United States;
To establish post offices and post roads;
To promote the progress of science and useful arts by securing for limited times to authors and inventors the exclusive right to their respective writings and discoveries;
To constitute tribunals inferior to the Supreme Court;
To define and punish piracies and felonies committed on the high seas and offenses against the law of nations;
To declare war, grant letters of marque and reprisal, and make rules concerning captures on land and water;
To raise and support armies, but no appropriation of money to that use shall be for a longer term than two years;
To provide and maintain a navy;
To make rules for the government and regulation of the land and naval forces;
To provide for calling forth the militia to execute the laws of the Union, suppress insurrections, and repel invasions;
To provide for organizing, arming, and disciplining the militia, and for governing such part of them as may be employed in the service of the United States, reserving to the States respectively the appointment of the officers, and the authority of training the militia according to the discipline prescribed by Congress;
To exercise exclusive legislation in all cases whatsoever, over such district (not exceeding ten miles square) as may, by cession of particular States, and the acceptance of Congress, become the seat of the government of the United States, and to exercise like authority over all places purchased by the consent of the legislature of the State, in which the same shall be, for erection of forts, magazines, arsenals, dock-yards, and other needful buildings;—and
To make all laws which shall be necessary and proper for carrying into execution the foregoing powers, and all other powers vested by this Constitution in the government of the United States, or in any department or officer thereof.

Powers Denied to Congress

Section 9. *The migration or importation of such persons as any of the States now existing shall think proper to admit shall not be prohibited by the Congress prior to the year 1808; but a tax or duty may be imposed on such importation, not exceeding $10 for each person.*

The privilege of the writ of habeas corpus shall not be suspended, unless when in cases of rebellion or invasion the public safety may require it.

No bill of attainder or ex post facto law shall be passed.

No capitation, or other direct, tax shall be laid, unless in proportion to the census or enumeration herein before directed to be taken.

No tax or duty shall be laid on articles exported from any State.

No preference shall be given by any regulation of commerce or revenue to the ports of one State over those of another; nor shall vessels bound to, or from, one State, be obliged to enter, clear, or pay duties in another.

No money shall be drawn from the treasury, but in consequence of appropriations made by law; and a regular statement and account of the receipts and expenditures of all public money shall be published from time to time.

No title of nobility shall be granted by the United States; and no person holding any office of profit or trust under them, shall, without the consent of the Congress, accept of any present, emolument, office, or title, of any kind whatever, from any king, prince, or foreign state.

Powers Denied to the States

Section 10. No State shall enter into any treaty, alliance, or confederation; grant letters of marque and reprisal; coin money; emit bills of credit; make anything but gold and silver coin a tender in payment of debts; pass any bill of attainder, ex post facto law, or law impairing the obligation of contracts, or grant any title of nobility.

No State shall, without the consent of the Congress, lay any imposts or duties on imports or exports, except what may be absolutely necessary for executing its inspection laws: and the net produce of all duties and imposts, laid by any State on imports or exports, shall be for the use of the treasury of the United States; and all such laws shall be subject to the revision and control of the Congress.

No State shall, without the consent of Congress, lay any duty of tonnage, keep troops or ships of war in time of peace, enter into any agreement or compact with another State, or with a foreign power, or engage in war, unless actually invaded, or in such imminent danger as will not admit of delay.

ARTICLE II.—THE EXECUTIVE ARTICLE

Nature and Scope of Presidential Power

Section 1. The executive power shall be vested in a President of the United States of America. He shall hold his office during the term of four years, and, together with the Vice President, chosen for the same term, be elected, as follows:

Each State shall appoint, in such manner as the legislature thereof may direct, a number of electors, equal to the whole number of Senators and Representatives to which the State may be entitled in the Congress; but no Senator or Representative, or person holding an office of trust or profit under the United States, shall be appointed an elector.

The electors shall meet in their respective States, and vote by ballot for two persons, of whom one at least shall not be an inhabitant of the same State with themselves. And they shall make a list of all the persons voted for, and of the number of votes for each; which list they shall sign and certify, and transmit sealed to the seat of government of the United States, directed to the President of the Senate. The President of the Senate shall, in the presence of the Senate and House of Representatives, open all the certificates, and the votes shall then be counted. The person having the greatest number of votes shall be the President, if such number be a majority of the whole number of electors appointed; and if there be more than one who have such majority, and have an equal number of votes, then the House of Representatives shall immediately choose by ballot one of them for President; and if no person have a majority, then from the five highest on the list said house shall in like manner choose the President. But in choosing the President the votes shall be taken by States, the representation from each State having one vote; a quorum for this purpose shall consist of a member or members from two-thirds of the States, and a majority of all the States shall be necessary to a choice. In every case, after the choice of the President, the person having the greatest number of votes of the electors shall be the Vice President. But if there should remain two or more who have equal votes, the Senate shall choose from them by ballot the Vice President.

The Congress may determine the time of choosing the electors, and the day on which they shall give their votes; which day shall be the same throughout the United States.

No person except a natural-born citizen, *or a citizen of the United States at the time of the adoption of this Constitution*, shall be eligible to the office of President; neither shall any person be eligible to that office who shall not have attained to the age of thirty-five years, and been fourteen years a resident within the United States.

In case of the removal of the President from office or of his death, resignation, or inability to discharge the powers and duties of the said office, the same shall devolve on the Vice President, and the Congress may by law provide for the case of removal, death, resignation, or inability, both of the President and Vice President, declaring what officer shall then act as President, and such officer shall act accordingly, until the disability be removed, or a President shall be elected.

The President shall, at stated times, receive for his services a compensation, which shall neither be increased nor diminished during the period for which he shall have been elected, and he shall not receive within that period any other emolument from the United States, or any of them.

Before he enter on the execution of his office, he shall take the following oath or affirmation: —"I do solemnly swear (or affirm) that I will faithfully execute the office of President of the United States, and will to the best of my ability preserve, protect, and defend the Constitution of the United States."

Powers and Duties of the President

Section 2. The President shall be the commander in chief of the army and navy of the United States, and of the militia of the several States, when called into the actual service of the United States; he may require the opinion, in writing, of the principal officer in each of the executive departments, upon any subject relating to the duties of their respective offices, and he shall have power to grant reprieves and pardons for offenses against the United States, except in cases of impeachment.

He shall have power, by and with the advice and consent of the Senate, to make treaties, provided two-thirds of the Senators present concur; and he shall nominate, and by and with the advice and consent of the Senate, shall appoint ambassadors, other public ministers and consuls, judges of the Supreme Court, and all other officers of the United States, whose appointments are not herein otherwise provided for, and which shall be established by law: but the Congress may by law vest the appointment of such inferior officers, as they think proper, in the President alone, in the courts of law, or in the heads of departments.

The President shall have power to fill up all vacancies that may happen during the recess of the Senate, by granting commissions which shall expire at the end of their next session.

Section 3. He shall from time to time give to the Congress information of the state of the Union, and recommend to their consideration such measures as he shall judge necessary and expedient; he may, on extraordinary occasions, convene both houses, or either of them, and in case of disagreement between them, with respect to the time of adjournment, he may adjourn them to such time as he shall think proper; he shall receive ambassadors and other public ministers; he shall take care that the laws be faithfully executed, and shall commission all the officers of the United States.

Section 4. The President, Vice President and all civil officers of the United States shall be removed from office on impeachment for, and on conviction of, treason, bribery, or other high crimes and misdemeanor.

ARTICLE III.—THE JUDICIAL ARTICLE

Section 1. The judicial power of the United States shall be vested in one Supreme Court, and in such inferior courts as the Congress may from time to time ordain and establish. The judges, both of the Supreme and inferior courts, shall hold their offices during good behavior, and shall, at stated times, receive for their services a compensation which shall not be diminished during their continuance in office.

Jurisdiction

Section 2. The judicial power shall extend to all cases, in law and equity, arising under this Constitution, the laws of the United States, and treaties made, or which shall be made, under their authority;—to all cases affecting ambassadors, other public ministers and consuls;—to all cases of admiralty and maritime jurisdiction;—to controversies to which the United States shall be a party;—to controversies between two or more States;—*between a state and citizens of another state*;—between citizens of different States;—between citizens of the same State claiming lands under grants of different States, and between a State, or the citizens thereof, and foreign states, citizens or subjects.

In all cases affecting ambassadors, other public ministers and consuls, and those in which a State shall be party, the Supreme Court shall have original jurisdiction. In all the other cases before mentioned, the Supreme Court shall have appellate jurisdiction, both as to law and fact, with such exceptions, and under such regulations, as the Congress shall make.

The trial of all crimes, except in cases of impeachment, shall be by jury; and such trial shall be held in the State where said crimes shall have been committed; but when not committed within any State, the trial shall be at such place or places as the Congress may by law have directed.

Treason

Section 3. Treason against the United States shall consist only in levying war against them, or in adhering to their enemies, giving them aid and comfort. No person shall be convicted of treason unless on the testimony of two witnesses to the same overt act, or on confession in open court.

The Congress shall have power to declare the punishment of treason, but no attainder of treason shall work corruption of blood, or forfeiture except during the life of the person attained.

ARTICLE IV.—INTERSTATE RELATIONS

Full Faith and Credit Clause

Section 1. Full Faith and credit shall be given in each State to the public acts, records, and judicial proceedings of every other State. And the Congress may by general laws prescribe the manner in which such acts, records and proceedings shall be proved, and the effect thereof.

Privileges and Immunities; Interstate Extradition

Section 2. The citizens of each State shall be entitled to all privileges and immunities of citizens in the several States.

A person charged in any State with treason, felony or other crime, who shall flee from justice, and be found in another State, shall on demand of the executive authority of the State from which he fled, be delivered up, to be removed to the State having jurisdiction of the crime.

No person held to service or labor in one State, under the laws thereof, escaping into another, shall, in consequence of any law or regulation therein, be discharged from such service or labor, but shall be delivered up on claim of the party to whom such service or labor may be due.

Admission of States

Section 3. New States may be admitted by the Congress into this Union; but no new State shall be formed or erected within the jurisdiction of any other State; nor any State be formed by the junction of two or more States, or parts of States, without the consent of the legislatures of the States concerned as well as of the Congress.

The Congress shall have power to dispose of and make all needful rules and regulations respecting the territory or other property belonging to the United States; and nothing in this Constitution shall be so construed as to prejudice any claims of the United States, or of any particular State.

Republican Form of Government

Section 4. The United States shall guarantee to every State in this Union a republican form of government, and shall protect each of them against invasion; and on application of the legislature, or of the executive (when the legislature cannot be convened) against domestic violence.

ARTICLE V.—THE AMENDING POWER

The Congress, whenever two-thirds of both houses shall deem it necessary, shall propose amendments to this Constitution, or, on the application of the legislatures of two-thirds of the several States, shall call a convention for proposing amendments, which, in either case, shall be valid to all intents and purposes, as part of this Constitution, when ratified by the legislatures of three-fourths of the several States, or by conventions in three-fourths thereof, as the one or the other mode of ratification may be proposed by the Congress; *provided that no amendment which may be made prior to the year one thousand eight hundred and eight shall in any manner affect the first and fourth clauses in the ninth section of the first article*; and that no State, without its consent, shall be deprived of its equal suffrage in the Senate.

ARTICLE VI.—THE SUPREMACY ACT

All debts contracted and engagements entered into, before the adoption of this Constitution, shall be as valid against the United States under this Constitution, as under the Confederation.

This Constitution, and the laws of the United States which shall be made in pursuance thereof; and all treaties made, or which shall be made, under the authority of the United States, shall be the supreme law of the land; and the judges in every State shall be bound thereby, anything in the Constitution or laws of any State to the contrary notwithstanding.

The Senators and Representatives before mentioned, and the members of the several State legislatures, and all executive and judicial officers, both of the United States and of the several States, shall be bound by oath or affirmation to support this Constitution; but no religious test shall ever be required as a qualification to any office or public trust under the United States.

ARTICLE VII.—RATIFICATION

The ratification of the conventions of nine States shall be sufficient for the establishment of this Constitution between States so ratifying the same.

Done in Convention by the unanimous consent of the States present, the seventeenth day of September in the year of our Lord one thousand seven hundred and eighty-seven and of the Independence of the United States of America the twelfth. In witness whereof we have hereunto subscribed our names.

GEORGE WASHINGTON
President and Deputy from Virginia

New Hampshire
JOHN LANGDON
NICHOLAS GILMAN

Massachusetts
NATHANIEL GORHAM
RUFUS KING

Connecticut
WILLIAM S. JOHNSON
ROGER SHERMAN

Virginia
JOHN BLAIR
JAMES MADISON, JR

South Carolina
J. RUTLEDGE
CHARLES G. PINCKNEY
PIERCE BUTLER

New York
ALEXANDER HAMILTON

New Jersey
WILLIAM LIVINGSTON
DAVID BREARLEY
WILLIAM PATERSON
JONATHAN DAYTON

Pennsylvania
BENJAMIN FRANKLIN
THOMAS MIFFLIN
ROBERT MORRIS
GEORGE CLYMER
THOMAS FITZSIMONS
JARED INGERSOLL
JAMES WILSON
GOUVERNEUR MORRIS

Delaware
GEORGE READ
GUNNING BEDFORD, JR.
JOHN DICKINSON
RICHARD BASSETT
JACOB BROOM

Maryland
JAMES MCHENRY
DANIEL OF ST. THOMAS JENIFER
DANIEL CARROLL

North Carolina
WILLIAM BLOUNT
RICHARD DOBBS SPRAIGHT
HU WILLIAMSON

Georgia
WILLIAM FEW
ABRAHAM BALDWIN

THE BILL OF RIGHTS
The first ten Amendments (the Bill of Rights) were adopted in 1791.

AMENDMENT I.—RELIGION, SPEECH ASSEMBLY, AND PETITION

Congress shall make no law respecting an establishment of religion, or prohibiting the free exercise thereof; or abridging the freedom of speech, or of the press; or the right of the people peaceably to assemble, and to petition the government for a redress of grievances.

AMENDMENT II.—MILITIA AND THE RIGHT TO BEAR ARMS

A well-regulated militia being necessary to the security of a free State, the right of the people to keep and bear arms shall not be infringed.

AMENDMENT III.—QUARTERING OF SOLDIERS

No soldier shall, in time of peace, be quartered in any house without the consent of the owner, nor in time of war, but in a manner to be prescribed by law.

AMENDMENT IV.—SEARCHES AND SEIZURES

The right of the people to be secure in their persons, houses, papers, and effects, against unreasonable searches and seizures, shall not be violated, and no warrants shall issue but upon probable cause, supported by oath or affirmation, and particularly describing the place to be searched, and the persons or things to be seized.

AMENDMENT V.—GRAND JURIES, SELF-INCRIMINATION, DOUBLE JEOPARDY, DUE PROCESS, AND EMINENT DOMAIN

No person shall be held to answer for a capital, or otherwise infamous crime, unless on a presentment or indictment of a grand jury, except in cases arising in the land or naval forces, or in the militia, when in actual service in time of war or public danger; nor shall any person be subject for the same offense to be twice put in jeopardy of life or limb; nor shall be compelled in any criminal case to be a witness against himself, nor be deprived of life, liberty, or property, without due process of law; nor shall private property be taken for public use without just compensation.

AMENDMENT VI.—CRIMINAL COURT PROCEDURES

In all criminal prosecutions, the accused shall enjoy the right to a speedy and public trial, by an impartial jury of the State and district wherein the crime shall have been committed, which district shall have been previously ascertained by law, and to be informed of the nature and cause of the accusation; to be confronted with the witnesses against him; to have compulsory process for obtaining witnesses in his favor, and to have the assistance of counsel for his defense.

AMENDMENT VII.—TRIAL BY JURY IN COMMON LAW CASES

In suits at common law, where the value in controversy shall exceed twenty dollars, the right of trial by jury shall be preserved, and no fact tried by a jury shall be otherwise reexamined in any court of the United States, than according to the rules of the common law.

AMENDMENT VIII.—BAIL, CRUEL AND UNUSUAL PUNISHMENT

Excessive bail shall not be required, nor excessive fines imposed, nor cruel and unusual punishments inflicted.

AMENDMENT IX.—RIGHTS RETAINED BY THE PEOPLE

The enumeration in the Constitution, of certain rights, shall not be construed to deny or disparage others retained by the people.

AMENDMENT X.—RESERVED POWERS OF THE STATES

The powers not delegated to the United States by the Constitution, nor prohibited by it to the States, are reserved to the States respectively, or to the people.

PRE-CIVIL WAR AMENDMENTS

AMENDMENT XI.—SUITS AGAINST THE STATES
[Adopted 1798]

The judicial power of the United States shall not be construed to extend to any suit in law or equity, commenced or prosecuted against one of the United States by citizens of another State, or by citizens or subjects of any foreign state.

AMENDMENT XII.—ELECTION OF THE PRESIDENT
[Adopted 1804]

The electors shall meet in their respective *States*, and vote by ballot for President and Vice President, one of whom, at least, shall not be an inhabitant of the same State with themselves; they shall name in their ballots the person voted for as President, and in distinct ballots the person voted for as Vice President, and they shall make distinct lists of all persons voted for as President, and of all persons voted for as Vice President, and of the number of votes for each, which lists they shall sign and certify, and transmit sealed to the seat of the government of the United States, directed to the President of the Senate;—the President of the Senate shall, in the presence of the Senate and House of Representatives, open all the certificates and the votes shall then be counted;—the person having the greatest number of votes for President shall be the President, if such number be a majority of the whole number of electors appointed; and if no person have such majority, then from the persons having the highest numbers not exceeding three on the list of those voted for as President, the House of Representatives shall choose immediately, by ballot, the President. But in choosing the President, the votes shall be taken by States, the representation from each State having one vote; a quorum for this purpose shall consist of a member or members from two-thirds of the States, and a majority of all the States shall be necessary to a choice. And if the House of Representatives shall not choose a President whenever the right of choice shall devolve upon them, before *the fourth day of March* next following, then the Vice President shall act as President, as in the case of the death or other constitutional disability of the President.

The person having the greatest number of votes as Vice President shall be the Vice President, if such a number be a majority of the whole number of electors appointed; and if no person have a majority, then from the two highest numbers on the list the Senate shall choose the Vice President; a quorum for the purpose shall consist of two-thirds of the whole number of Senators, and a majority of the whole number shall be necessary to a choice. But no person constitutionally ineligible to the office of President shall be eligible to that of Vice President of the United States.

CIVIL WAR AMENDMENTS

AMENDMENT XIII.—PROHIBITION OF SLAVERY
[Adopted 1865]

Section 1. Neither slavery nor involuntary servitude, except as a punishment for crime whereof the party shall have been duly convicted, shall exist within the United States, or any place subject to their jurisdiction.

Section 2. Congress shall have power to enforce this article by appropriate legislation.

AMENDMENT XIV.—CITIZENSHIP, DUE PROCESS, AND EQUAL PROTECTION OF THE LAWS
[Adopted 1868]

Section 1. All persons born or naturalized in the United States, and subject to the jurisdiction thereof, are citizens of the United States and of the State wherein they reside. No State shall make or enforce any law which shall abridge **the privileges or immunities** of citizens of the United States; nor shall any State deprive any person of life, liberty, or property, without **due process of law**; nor deny to any person within its jurisdiction the **equal protection of the laws**.

Section 2. Representatives shall be apportioned among the several States according to their respective numbers, counting the whole number of persons in each State, excluding Indians not taxed. But when the right to vote at any election for the choice of Electors for President and Vice President of the United States, Representatives in Congress, the executive and judicial officers of a State, or the members of the legislature thereof, is denied to any of the male inhabitants of such State, being twenty-one years of age and citizens of the United States, or in any way abridged, except for participation in rebellion, or other crime, the basis of representation therein shall be reduced in the proportion which the number of such male citizens shall bear to the whole number of male citizens twenty-one years of age in such State.

Section 3. No person shall be a Senator or Representative in Congress, or Elector of President and Vice President, or hold any office, civil or military, under the United States, or under any State, who, having previously taken an oath, as a member of Congress, or as an officer of the United States, or as a member of any State legislature, or as an executive or judicial officer of any State, to support the Constitution of the United States, shall have engaged in insurrection or rebellion against the same, or given aid or comfort to the enemies thereof. Congress may, by a vote of two-thirds of each house, remove such disability.

Section 4. The validity of the public debt of the United States, authorized by law, including debts incurred for payment of pensions and bounties for services in suppressing insurrection or rebellion, shall not be questioned. But neither the United States nor any State shall assume or pay any debt or obligation incurred in aid of insurrection or rebellion against the United States, or any claim for the loss or emancipation of any slave; but all such debts, obligations and claims shall be held illegal and void.

Section 5. The Congress shall have power to enforce, by appropriate legislation, the provisions of this article.

AMENDMENT XV.—THE RIGHT TO VOTE
[Adopted 1870]

Section 1. The right of citizens of the United State to vote shall not be denied or abridged by the United States or by any State on account of race, color, or previous condition of servitude.

Section 2. The Congress shall have power to enforce this article by appropriate legislation.

AMENDMENT XVI.—INCOME TAXES
[Adopted 1913]

The Congress shall have power to lay and collect taxes on incomes, from whatever source derived, without apportionment among the several States, and without regard to any census or enumeration.

AMENDMENT XVII.—DIRECT ELECTION OF SENATORS
[Adopted 1913]

Section 1. The Senate of the United States shall be composed of two Senators from each State, elected by the people thereof, for six years; and each Senator shall have one vote. The electors in each State shall have the qualifications requisite for electors of (voters for) the most numerous branch of the State legislatures.

Section 2. When vacancies happen in the representation of any State in the Senate, the executive authority of such State shall issue writs of election to fill such vacancies: Provided, that the Legislature of any State may empower the executive thereof to make temporary appointments until the people fill the vacancies by election as the Legislature may direct.

Section 3. This amendment shall not be so construed as to affect the election or term of any Senator chosen before it becomes valid as part of the Constitution.

AMENDMENT XVIII.—PROHIBITION
[Adopted 1919; Repealed 1933]

Section 1. *After one year from the ratification of this article the manufacture, sale, or transportation of intoxicating liquors within, the importation thereof into, or the exportation thereof from the United State and all territory subject to the jurisdiction thereof, for beverage purposes, is hereby prohibited.*

Section 2. *The Congress and the several States shall have concurrent power to enforce this article by appropriate legislation.*

Section 3. *This article shall be inoperative unless it shall have been ratified as an amendment to the Constitution by the legislatures of the several States, as provided by the Constitution, within seven years from the date of the submission thereof to the States by the Congress.*

AMENDMENT XIX.—FOR WOMEN'S SUFFRAGE
[Adopted 1920]

Section 1. The right of citizens of the United States to vote shall not be denied or abridged by the United States or by any State on account of sex.

Section 2. The Congress shall have power to enforce this article by appropriate legislation.

AMENDMENT XX.—THE LAME DUCK AMENDMENT
[Adopted 1933]

Section 1. The terms of the President and Vice President shall end at noon on the 20th day of January, and the terms of the Senators and Representatives at noon on the 3rd day of January, of the years in which such terms would have ended if this article had not been ratified; and the terms of their successors shall then begin.

Section 2. The Congress shall assemble at least once in every year, and such meeting shall begin at noon on the 3rd day of January, unless they shall by law appoint a different day.

Section 3. If, at the time fixed for the beginning of the term of the President, the President-elect shall have died, the Vice President-elect shall become President. If a President shall not have been chosen before the time fixed for the beginning of his term, or if the President-elect shall have failed to qualify, then the Vice President-elect shall act as President until a President shall have qualified; and the Congress may by law provide for the case wherein neither a President-elect nor a Vice President-elect shall have qualified, declaring who shall then act as President, or the manner in which one who is to act shall be selected, and such persons shall act accordingly until a President or Vice President shall have qualified.

Section 4. The Congress may by law provide for the case of the death of any of the persons from whom the House of Representatives may choose a President whenever the right of choice shall have devolved upon them, and for the case of the death of any of the persons from whom the Senate may choose a Vice President whenever the right of choice shall have devolved upon them.

Section 5. Section 1 and 2 shall take effect on the 15th day of October following the ratification of this article.

Section 6. This article shall be inoperative unless it shall have been ratified as an amendment to the Constitution by the Legislatures of three-fourths of the several States within seven years from the date of its submission.

AMENDMENT XXI.—REPEAL OF PROHIBITION
[Adopted 1933]

Section 1. The eighteenth article of amendment to the Constitution of the United States is hereby repealed.

Section 2. The transportation or importation into any State, Territory, or Possession of the United States for delivery of use therein of intoxicating liquors, in violation of the laws thereof, is hereby prohibited.

Section 3. This article shall be inoperative unless it shall have been ratified as an amendment to the Constitution by conventions in the several States, as provided in the Constitution, within seven years from the date of submission thereof to the States by the Congress.

AMENDMENT XXII.—NUMBER OF PRESIDENTIAL TERMS
[Adopted 1951]

Section 1. No person shall be elected to the office of President more than twice, and no person who has held the office of President, or acted as President, for more than two years of a term to which some other person was elected President shall be elected to the office of President more than once. But this article shall not apply to any person holding the office of President when this article was proposed by the Congress, and shall not prevent any person who may be holding the office of President, or acting as President, during the term within which this article becomes operative from holding the office of President or acting as President during the remainder of such term.

Section 2. This article shall be inoperative unless it shall have been ratified as an amendment to the Constitution by the legislatures of three-fourths of the several States within seven years from the date of its submission to the States by the Congress.

AMENDMENT XXIII.—PRESIDENTIAL ELECTORS FOR THE DISTRICT OF COLUMBIA [Adopted 1961]

Section 1. The District constituting the seat of Government of the United States shall appoint in such manner as the Congress may direct:
A number of electors of President and Vice President equal to the whole number of Senators and Representatives in Congress to which the District would be entitled if it were a State, but in no event more than the least populous State; they shall be in addition to those appointed by the States, but they shall be considered for the purposes of the election of President and Vice President, to be electors appointed by a State; and they shall meet in the District and perform such duties as provided by the twelfth article of amendment.

Section 2. The Congress shall have power to enforce this article by appropriate legislation.

AMENDMENT XXIV.—THE ANTI-POLL TAX AMENDMENT
[Adopted 1964]

Section 1. The right of citizens of the United States to vote in any primary or other election for President or Vice President, for electors for President or Vice President, or for Senator or Representative in Congress, shall not be denied or abridged by the United States or any State by reason of failure to pay any poll tax or other tax.

Section 2. The Congress shall have power to enforce this article by appropriate legislation.

AMENDMENT XXV.—PRESIDENTIAL DISABILITY, VICE-PRESIDENTIAL VACANCIES
[Adopted 1967]

Section 1. In case of the removal of the President from office or his death or resignation, the Vice President shall become President.

Section 2. Whenever there is a vacancy in the office of the Vice President, the President shall nominate a Vice President who shall take office upon confirmation by a majority vote of both Houses of Congress.

Section 3. Whenever the President transmits to the President pro tempore of the Senate and the Speaker of the House of Representatives his written declaration that he is unable to discharge the powers and duties of his office, and until he transmits to them a written declaration to the contrary, such powers and duties shall be discharged by the Vice President as Acting President.

Section 4. Whenever the Vice President and a majority of either the principal officers of the executive departments or of such other body as Congress may by law provide, transmit to the President pro tempore of the Senate and the Speaker of the House of Representatives their written declaration that the President is unable to discharge the powers and duties of his office, the Vice President shall immediately assume the powers and duties of the office as Acting President.

Thereafter, when the President transmits to the President pro tempore of the Senate and the Speaker of the House of Representatives his written declaration that no inability exists, he shall resume the powers and duties of his office unless the Vice President and a majority of either the principal officers of the executive department{s} or of such other body as Congress may by law provide, transmit within four days to the President pro tempore of the Senate and the Speaker of the House of Representatives their written declaration that the President is unable to discharge the powers and duties of his office. Thereupon Congress shall decide the issue, assembling within forty-eight hours for that purpose if not in session. If the Congress, within twenty-one days after receipt of the latter written declaration, or, if Congress is not in session, within twenty-one days after Congress is required to assemble, determines by two-thirds vote of both Houses that the President is unable to discharge the powers and duties of his office, the Vice President shall continue to discharge the same as Acting President; otherwise, the President shall resume the powers and duties of his office.

AMENDMENT XXVI.—EIGHTEEN-YEAR-OLD VOTE
[Adopted 1971]

Section 1. The right of citizens of the United States, who are eighteen years of age or older, to vote shall not be denied or abridged by the United States or by any State on account of age.

Section 2. The Congress shall have power to enforce this article by appropriate legislation.

AMENDMENT XXVII.—VARYING CONGRESSIONAL COMPENSATION
[Adopted 1992]

No law varying the compensation for the service of the Senators and Representatives shall take effect until an election of Representatives shall have intervened.

APPENDIX C

PRESIDENTIAL ELECTIONS

Year	Name	Party	Popular Vote	Electoral College Vote
1789	George Washington	Federalist		69
1792	George Washington	Federalist		132
1796	John Adams	Federalist		71
	Thomas Jefferson	Democratic-Republican		68
1800	Thomas Jefferson	Democratic-Republican		73
	John Adams	Federalist		65
1804	Thomas Jefferson	Democratic-Republican		162
	Charles C. Pinckney	Federalist		14
1808	James Madison	Democratic-Republican		122
	Charles C. Pinckney	Federalist		47
1812	James Madison	Democratic-Republican		128
	George Clinton	Federalist		89
1816	James Monroe	Dmocratic-Republican		183
	Rufus King	Federalist		34
1820	James Monroe	Democratic-Republican		231
	John Quincy Adams	Democratic-Republican		1
1824	John Quincy Adams	Democratic-Republican	108,740	84
	Andrew Jackson	Democratic-Republican	153,544	99
	William Crawford	Democratic-Republican	46,618	41
	Henry Clay	Democratic-Republican	47,136	37
1828	Andrew Jackson	Democrat	647,286	178
	John Quincy Adams	National Republican	508,064	83
1832	Andrew Jackson	Democrat	687,502	219
	Henry Clay	National Republican	530,189	49
	Electoral votes not cast			2
1836	Martin Van Buren	Democrat	765,483	170
	William Henry Harrison	Whig	550,816	73
	Hugh White	Whig	146,107	26
	Daniel Webster	Whig	41,201	14
	Total for the 3 Whigs		739,795	113
1840	William Henry Harrison	Whig	1,274,624	234
	Martin Van Buren	Democrat	1,127,781	60
1844	James K. Polk	Democrat	1,338,464	170
	Henry Clay	Whig	1,300,097	105
1848	Zachary Taylor	Whig	1,360,967	163
	Lewis Cass	Democrat	1,222,342	127
	Martin Van Buren	Free-Soil	291,263	
1852	Franklin Pierce	Democrat	1,601,117	254
	Winfield Scott	Whig	1,385,453	42
	John P. Hale	Free-Soil	155,825	
1856	James Buchanan	Democrat	1,832,955	174
	John Fremont	Republican	1,339,932	114
	Millard Fillmore	Whig-American	871,731	8

1860	Abraham Lincoln	Republican	1,865,593	180
	John C. Breckinridge	Democratic	848,356	72
	Stephen Douglas	Democrat	1,382,713	12
	John Bell	Constitutional Union	592,906	39
1864	Abraham Lincon	Unionist (Republican)	2,206,938	212
	George McClellan	Democrat	1,803,787	21
	Electoral votes not cast		81	
1868	Ulysses S. Grant	Republican	3,013,421	214
	Horatio Seymour	Democrat	2,706,829	80
	Electoral votes not cast		23	
1872	Ulysses S. Grant	Republican	3,596,745	286
	Horace Greeley	Democrat	2,843,446	
	Thomas Hendricks	Democrat		42
	Benjamin Browns	Democrat		18
	Charles Jenkins	Democrat		2
	David Davis	Democrat		1
1876	Rutherford B. Hays	Republican	4,036,572	185
	Samuel Tilden	Democrat	4,284,020	184
	Peter Cooper	Greenback	81,737	
1880	James A. Garfield	Republican	4,453,295	214
	Winfield S. Hancock	Democrat	4,414,082	155
	James B. Weaver	Greenback-Labor	308,578	
1884	Grover Cleveland	Democrat	4,879,507	219
	James G. Blaine	Republican	4,850,293	182
	Benjamin Butler	Greenback-Labor	175,370	
	John St. John	Prohibition	150,369	
1888	Benjamin Harrison	Republican	5,447,129	233
	Grover Cleveland	Democrat	5,537,857	168
	Clinton Fisk	Prohibition	249,506	
	Anson Streeter	Union Labor	146,935	
1892	Grover Cleveland	Democrat	5,555,426	277
	Benjamin Harrison	Republican	5,182,690	145
	James B. Weaver	People's	1.029,846	22
	John Bidwell	Prohibition	264,133	
1896	William McKinley	Republican	7,102,246	271
	William J. Bryan	Democrat	6,492,559	176
	John Palmer	National Democratic	133,148	
	Joshua Levering	Prohibition	132,007	
1900	William McKinley	Republican	7,218,491	292
	William J. Bryan	Democrat	6,356,734	155
	John C. Wooley	Prohibition	208,914	
	Eugene V. Debs	Socialist	87,814	
1904	Theodore Roosevelt	Republican	7,628,461	336
	Alton B. Parker	Democrat	5,084,223	140
	Eugene V. Debs	Socialist	402,283	
	Silas Swallow	Prohibition	258,536	
	Thomas Watson	People's	117,183	
1908	William Howard Taft	Republican	7,675,320	321
	William J. Bryan	Democrat	6,412,294	162
	Eugene V. Debs	Socialist	420,793	
	Eugene Chafin	Prohibition	253,840	

1912	Woodrow Wilson	Democrat	6,296,547	435
	William Howard Taft	Republican	3,486,720	8
	Theodore Roosevelt	Progressive	4,118,571	86
	Eugene V. Debs	Socialist	900,672	
	Eugene Chafin	Prohibition	206,275	
1916	Woodrow Wilson	Democrat	9,127,695	277
	Charles E. Hughes	Republicn	8,533,507	254
	A.L. Benson	Socialist	585,113	
	J. Frank Hanly	Prohibition	220,506	
1920	Warren Harding	Republican	16,143,407	404
	James M. Cox	Democrat	9,130,328	127
	Eugene V. Debs	Socialist	919,799	
	P.P. Christensen	Farmer-Labor	265,411	
	Aaron Watkins	Prohibiton	189,408	
1924	Calvin Coolidge	Republican	15,718,211	382
	John W. Davis	Democrat	8,385,283	136
	Robert La Follette	Progressive	4,831,289	13
1928	Herbert Hoover	Republican	21,391,993	444
	Alfred E. Smith	Democrat	15,016,169	87
	Norman Thomas	Socialist	267,835	
1932	Franklin D. Roosevelt	Democrat	22,809,638	472
	Herbert C. Hoover	Republican	15,758,901	59
	Norman Thomas	Socialist	881,951	
	William Foster	Communist	102,785	
1936	Franklin D. Roosevelt	Democrat	27,752,869	523
	Alfred M. Landon	Republican	16,674,665	8
	William Lemke	Union	882,479	
	Norman Thomas	Socialist	187,720	
1940	Franklin D. Roosevelt	Democrat	27,307,819	449
	Wendell Willkie	Republican	22,321,018	82
1944	Franklin D. Roosevelt	Democrat	25,606,585	432
	Thomas E. Dewey	Republican	22,014,745	99
1948	Harry S. Truman	Democrat	24,179,345	303
	Thomas E. Dewey	Republican	21,991,291	189
	Strom Thurmond	Dixiecrat	1,176,125	39
	Henry Wallace	Progressive	1,157,326	
	Norman Thomas	Socialist	139,572	
	Claude A. Watson	Prohibition	103,900	
1952	Dwight D. Eisenhower	Republican	33,936,234	442
	Adlai Stevenson II	Democrat	27,314,992	89
	Vincent Hallinan	Progressive	140,023	
1956	Dwight D. Eisenhower	Republican	35,590,472	457
	Adlai Stevenson II	Democrat	26,022,752	73
	T. Coleman Andrews	States' Rights	111,178	
	Walter B. Jones	Democrat		1
1960	John F. Kennedy	Democrat	34,226,731	303
	Richard M. Nixon	Republican	34,108,157	219
	Harry Byrd	Democrat		15
1964	Lyndon B. Johnson	Democrat	43,129,566	486
	Barry Goldwater	Republican	27,178,188	52

Year	Candidate	Party	Popular Vote	Electoral Vote
1968	Richard M. Nixon	Republican	31,785,480	301
	Hubert H. Humphrey	Democrat	31,275,166	191
	George Wallace	American Independent	9,906,473	46
1972	Richard M. Nixon	Republican	47,170,179	520
	George McGovern	Democrat	29,171,791	17
	John Hospers	Libertarian		1
1976	Jimmy Carter	Democrat	40,830,763	297
	Gerald R. Ford	Republican	39,147,793	240
	Ronald Reagan	Republican		1
1980	Ronald Reagan	Republican	43,904,153	489
	Jimmy Carter	Democrat	35,483,883	49
	John Anderson	Independent candidacy	5,719,437	
1984	Ronald Reagan	Republican	54,455,074	525
	Walter F. Mondale	Democrat	37,577,137	13
1988	George Bush	Republican	48,881,278	426
	Michael Dukakis	Democrat	41,805,374	111
	Lloyd Bentsen	Democrat		1
1992	Bill Clinton	Democrat	43,727,625	370
	George Bush	Republican	38,165,180	168
	Ross Perot	Independent catdidacy	19,236,411	0
1996	Bill Clinton	Democrat	45,628,667	379
	Bob Dole	Republican	37,869,435	159
	Ross Perot	Independent catdidacy	7,874,283	0
2000	George W. Bush	Republican	49,820,518	271
	Albert Gore Jr.	Democrat	50,158,094	267
	Ralph Nader	Green Party	7,866,284	
2004	George W. Bush	Republican	62,040,610	286
	John Kerry	Democrat	59,028,439	251
	Ralph Nader	Green Party	463,653	
2008	Barack Obama	Democrat	66,882,230	365
	John McCain	Republican	58,343,671	173
2012	Barack Obama	Democrat	60,459,974	332
	Mitt Romney	Republican	57,653,982	206

APPENDIX D

Members of the Supreme Court of the United States

Chief Justices	State App't From	Appointed by President	Service
Jay, John	New York	Washington	1789-1795
Rutledge, John*	South Carolina	Washington	1795-1795
Ellsworth, Oliver	Connecticut	Washington	1796-1799
Marshall, John	Virginia	Adams, John	1801-1835
Taney, Roger Brooke	Maryland	Jackson	1836-1864
Chase, Salmon Portland	Ohio	Lincoln	1864-1873
Waite, Morrison Remick	Ohio	Grant	1874-1888
Fuller, Melville Weston	Illinois	Cleveland	1888-1910
White, Edward Douglass	Louisiana	Taft	1910-1921
Taft, William Howard	Connecticut	Harding	1921-1930
Hughes, Charles Evans	New York	Hoover	1930-1941
Stone, Harlan Fiske	New York	Roosevelt F.	1941-1946
Vinson, Fred Moore	Kentucky	Truman	1946-1953
Warren, Earl	California	Eisenhower	1953-1969
Burger, Warren Earl	Virginia	Nixon	1969-1986
Rehnquist, William H.	Virginia	Reagan	1986-2005
Roberts, John G., Jr.	Maryland	Bush, G. W.	2005-

Associate Justices			
Rutledge, John	South Carolina	Washington	1790-1791
Cushing, William	Massachusetts	Washington	1790-1810
Wilson, James	Pennsylvania	Washington	1789-1798
Blair, John	Virginia	Washington	1789-1796
Iredell, James	North Carolina	Washington	1790-1799
Johnson, Thomas	Maryland	Washington	1791-1793
Paterson, William	New Jersey	Washington	1793-1806
Chase, Samuel	Maryland	Washington	1796-1811
Washington, Bushrod	Virginia	Adams, John	1798-1829
Moore, Alfred	North Carolina	Adams, John	1799-1804
Johnson, William	South Carolina	Jefferson	1804-1834
Livingston, Henry Brockholst	New York	Jefferson	1806-1823
Todd, Thomas	Kentucky	Jefferson	1807-1826
Duvall, Gabriel	Maryland	Madison	1811-1836
Story, Joseph	Massachusetts	Madison	1811-1845
Thompson, Smith	New York	Monroe	1823-1843
Trimble, Robert	Kentucky	Adams, J. Q.	1826-1828
McLean, John	Ohio	Jackson	1829-1861
Baldwin, Henry	Pennsylvania	Jackson	1830-1844
Wayne, James Moore	Georgia	Jackson	1835-1867
Barbour, Philip Pendleton	Virginia	Jackson	1836-1841
Catron, John	Tennessee	Jackson	1837-1865

*ActingChief Justice; Senate refused to confirm appointment.

McKinley, John	Alabama	Van Buren	1837-1852
Daniel, Peter Vivian	Virginia	Van Buren	1841-1860
Nelson, Samuel	New York	Tyler	1845-1872
Woodbury, Levi	New Hampshire	Polk	1845-1851
Grier, Robert Cooper	Pennsylvania	Polk	1846-1870
Curtis, Benjamin Robbins	Massachusetts	Fillmore	1851-1857
Campbell, John Archibald	Alabama	Pierce	1853-1861
Clifford, Nathan	Maine	Buchanan	1858-1881
Swayne, Noah Haynes	Ohio	Lincoln	1862-1881
Miller, Samuel Freeman	Iowa	Lincoln	1862-1890
Davis, David	Illinois	Lincoln	1862-1877
Field, Stephen Johnson	California	Lincoln	1863-1897
Strong, William	Pennsylvania	Grant	1870-1880
Bradley, Joseph P.	New Jersey	Grant	1870-1892
Hunt, Ward	New York	Grant	1873-1882
Harlan, John Marshall	Kentucky	Hayes	1877-1911
Woods, William Burnham	Georgia	Hayes	1880-1887
Matthews, Stanley	Ohio	Garfield	1881-1889
Gray, Horace	Massachusetts	Arthur	1882-1902
Blatchford, Samuel	New York	Arthur	1882-1893
Lamar, Lucius Quintus C.	Mississippi	Cleveland	1888-1893
Brewer, David Josiah	Kansas	Harrison	1889-1910
Brown, Henry Billings	Michigan	Harrison	1890-1906
Shiras, George, Jr.	Pennsylvania	Harrison	1892-1903
Jackson, Howell Edmunds	Tennessee	Harrison	1893-1895
White, Edward Douglass	Louisiana	Cleveland	1894-1910
Peckham, Rufus Wheeler	New York	Cleveland	1896-1909
McKenna, Joseph	California	McKinley	1898-1925
Holmes, Oliver Wendell	Massachusetts	Roosevelt T.	1902-1932
Day, William Rufus	Ohio	Roosevelt T.	1903-1922
Moody, William Henry	Massachusetts	Roosevelt T.	1906-1910
Lurton, Horace Harmon	Tennessee	Taft	1910-1914
Hughes, Charles Evans	New York	Taft	1910-1916
Van Devanter, Willis	Wyoming	Taft	1910-1937
Lamar, Joseph Rucker	Georgia	Taft	1911-1916
Pitney, Mahlon	New Jersey	Taft	1912-1922
McReynolds, James Clark	Tennessee	Wilson	1914-1941
Brandeis, Louis Dembitz	Massachusetts	Wilson	1916-1939
Clarke, John Hessin	Ohio	Wilson	1916-1922
Sutherland, George	Utah	Harding	1922-1938
Butler, Pierce	Minnesota	Harding	1923-1939
Sanford, Edward Terry	Tennessee	Harding	1923-1930
Stone, Harlan Fiske	New York	Coolidge	1925-1941
Roberts, Owen Josephus	Pennsylvania	Hoover	1930-1945
Cardozo, Benjamin Nathan	New York	Hoover	1932-1938
Black, Hugo Lafayette	Alabama	Roosevelt F.	1937-1971
Reed, Stanley Forman	Kentucky	Roosevelt F.	1938-1957
Frankfurter, Felix	Massachusetts	Roosevelt F.	1939-1962
Douglas, William Orville	Connecticut	Roosevelt F.	1939-1975
Murphy, Frank	Michigan	Roosevelt F.	1940-1949

Byrnes, James Francis	South Carolina	Roosevelt F.	1941-1942
Jackson, Robert Houghwout	New York	Roosevelt F.	1941-1954
Rutledge, Wiley Blount	Iowa	Roosevelt F.	1943-1949
Burton, Harold Hitz	Ohio	Truman	1945-1958
Clark, Tom Campbell	Texas	Truman	1949-1967
Minton, Sherman	Indiana	Truman	1949-1956
Harlan, John Marshall	New York	Eisenhower	1955-1971
Brennan, William J., Jr.	New Jersey	Eisenhower	1956-1990
Whittaker, Charles Evans	Missouri	Eisenhower	1957-1962
Stewart, Potter	Ohio	Eisenhower	1958-1981
White, Byron Raymond	Colorado	Kennedy	1962-1993
Goldberg, Arthur Joseph	Illinois	Kennedy	1962-1965
Fortas, Abe	Tennessee	Johnson L.	1965-1969
Marshall, Thurgood	New York	Johnson L.	1967-1991
Blackmun, Harry A.	Minnesota	Nixon	1970-1994
Powell, Lewis F., Jr.	Virginia	Nixon	1972-1988
Rehnquist, William H.	Arizona	Nixon	1972-1986**
Stevens, John Paul	Illinois	Ford	1975-2010
O'Connor, Sandra Day	Arizona	Reagan	1981-2006
Scalia, Antonin	Virginia	Reagan	1986-
Kennedy, Anthony M.	California	Reagan	1988-
Souter, David H.	New Hampshire	Bush, G. H. W.	1990-2009
Thomas, Clarence	Georgia	Bush, G. H. W.	1991-
Ginsburg, Ruth Bader	New York	Clinton	1993-
Breyer, Stephen G.	Massachusetts	Clinton	1994-
John Roberts	Maryland	Bush, G. W.	2005-
Alito, Samuel A., Jr.	New Jersey	Bush, G. W.	2006-
Sonia Sotomayor	New York	Obama	2009-
Elena Kagan	New York	Obama	2010-

Notes: The acceptance of the appointment and commission by the appointee, as evidenced by the taking of the prescribed oaths, is here implied; otherwise the individual is not carried on this list of the Members of the Court. Examples: Robert Hanson Harrison is not carried, as a letter from President Washington of February 9, 1790 states Harrison declined to serve. Neither is Edwin M. Stanton who died before he could take the necessary steps toward becoming a Member of the Court. *Chief Justice Rutledge is included because he took his oaths, presided over the August Term of 1795, and his name appears on two opinions of the Court for that Term.

[The foregoing was taken from a booklet prepared by the Supreme Court of the United States.]

**Elevated.

APPENDIX E
ADMISSION OF STATES INTO THE UNION

State	Date of Admission	State	Date of Admission
1. Delaware	December 7, 1787	26. Michigan	January 26, 1837
2. Pennsylvania	December 12, 1787	27. Florida	March 3, 1845
3. New Jersey	December 18, 1787	28. Texas	December 29, 1845
4. Georgia	January 2, 1788	29. Iowa	December 28, 1846
5. Connecticut	January 9, 1788	30. Wisconsin	May 29, 1848
6. Massachusetts	February 6, 1788	31. California	September 9, 1850
7. Maryland	April 28, 1788	32. Minnesota	May 11, 1858
8. South Carolina	May 23, 1788	33. Oregon	February 14, 1859
9. New Hampshire	June 21, 1788	34. Kansas	January 29, 1861
10. Virginia	June 25, 1788	35. West Virginia	June 20, 1863
11. New York	July 26, 1788	36. Nevada	October 31, 1864
12. North Carolina	November 21, 1789	37. Nebraska	March 1, 1867
13. Rhode Island	May 29, 1790	38. Colorado	August 1, 1876
14. Vermont	March 4, 1791	39. North Dakota	November 2, 1889
15. Kentucky	June 1, 1792	40. South Dakota	November 2, 1889
16. Tennessee	June 1, 1796	41. Montana	November 8, 1889
17. Ohio	March 1, 1803	42. Washington	November 11, 1889
18. Louisiana	April 30, 1812	43. Idaho	July 3, 1890
19. Indiana	December 11, 1816	44. Wyoming	July 10, 1890
20. Mississippi	December 10, 1817	45. Utah	January 4, 1896
21. Illinois	December 3, 1818	46. Oklahoma	November 16, 1907
22. Alabama	December 14, 1819	47. New Mexico	January 6, 1912
23. Maine	March 15, 1820	48. Arizona	February 14, 1912
24. Missouri	August 10, 1821	49. Alaska	January 3, 1959
25. Arkansas	June 15, 1836	50. Hawaii	August 21, 1959

APPENDIX F

POPULATION GROWTH

Year	Population	Percent Increase
1630	4,600	
1640	26,600	478.3
1650	50,400	90.8
1660	75,100	49.0
1670	111,900	49.0
1680	151,500	35.4
1690	210,400	38.9
1700	250,900	19.2
1710	331,700	32.2
1720	466,200	40.5
1730	629,400	35.0
1740	905,600	43.9
1750	1,170,800	29.3
1760	1,593,600	36.1
1770	2,148,100	34.8
1780	2,780,400	29.4
1790	3,929,214	41.3
1800	5,308,483	35.1
1810	7,239,881	36.4
1820	9,638,453	33.1
1830	12,866,020	33.5
1840	17,069,453	32.7
1850	23,191,876	35.9
1860	31,443,321	35.6
1870	39,818,449	26.6
1880	50,155,783	26.0
1890	62,947,714	25.5
1900	75,994,575	20.7
1910	91,972,266	21.0
1920	105,710,620	14.9
1930	122,775,046	16.1
1940	131,669,275	7.2
1950	151,325,798	14.5
1960	179,323,175	18.5
1970	203,302,031	13.4
1980	226,542,199	11.4
1990	248,718,301	9.8
2000	281,421,906	13.1
2010	308,745,538	9.7

GLOSSARY OF IMPORTANT PEOPLE AND CONCEPTS

Act of Toleration (1649): The granting by the second Lord Baltimore (Cecilius Calvert) of religious toleration to all Christians living in Maryland.

Adams, Abigail (1744-1818): The wife and perhaps most influential advisor of John Adams (the first vice president and second president of the United States) and mother of the sixth president John Quincy Adams.

Adams, Charles Francis (1807-1886): The grandson of one president (John Adams) and the son of another (John Quincy Adams), Charles Francis Adams served as the American ambassador to Great Britain during the critical Civil War years (1861-1865) and is widely credited with persuading that not nation to intervene in the conflict.

Adams, John (1735-1826): Massachusetts lawyer and politician who served as a member of the Second Continental Congress and on the committee that drafted the Declaration of Independence, and who later won election as the first vice president and second president of the United States.

Adams-Onís Treaty of 1819: Treaty by which Spain finally ceded Florida to the U.S. for $5 million, which was payment to American citizens for damages done to them by marauding Seminoles. Treaty also established the boundaries of the Louisiana Purchase with Spain along its Borderland territories all the way up to the 42nd parallel in the Pacific Northwest. For such terms the U.S. agreed to relinquish its demands for Texas.

Adams, Samuel (1722-1803): Massachusetts politician who served in the First Continental Congress in Philadelphia in 1774 and the Second Continental Congress in 1776, where he signed the Declaration of Independence. He was a cousin of the nation's second president, John Adams.

Adena and Hopewell: mound building cultures of Native Americans that existed in the Ohio River Valley from about 100 B.C. to about 700 A.D.

African Methodist Episcopal Church: Founded by the Rev. Richard Allen (1760-1831) in Philadelphia in 1816, this African American sect originated among members of the Free African Society, established in 1787.

"Age of Prophecy": A revival movement among Native American tribes in the trans-Appalachian regions to the Mississippi River to try to preserve their way of life against the white onslaught into the area. The propagators of the movement were accommodationists; that is they believed armed resistance to be futile and that co-existence with whites was possible and perhaps the only way to survive.

Alabama: A Confederate commerce raider constructed in Liverpool, England, that attacked Union merchant ships and navy vessels, including the *USS Hatteras*, between 1862-64 before being sunk in battle by the *USS Kearsarge* near the Port of Cherbourg, France.

Albany Plan of Union: Plan put forth in 1754 by Massachusetts Governor William Shirley, Benjamin Franklin and others calling for an intercolonial union to manage defense and Indian affairs.

Alien Act: Part of a two-pronged High Federalist attempt to destroy their opposition, the Democratic-Republican Party, by curtailing immigrant voting potential by extending the naturalization period from 5 to 14 years, thus effecting the Jeffersonian party by denying it of the future citizens' vote.

Allen, Ethan (1738-1789): A Vermont politician and military leader who organized resistance to British rule in his home state. In the late 1760s, Ethan Allen led a militia called the Green Mountain Boys.

American Anti-Slavery Society: The first national abolitionist organization established in 1833.

American Colonization Society: An anti-slavery organization founded in 1817 by anti-slavery reformers, calling for a gradual emancipation and removal of freed blacks to Africa.

American Crisis: A series of pamphlets written by Thomas Paine and published in installments beginning on December 19, 1776, encouraging continued armed resistance against the British.

American Female Moral Reform Society: Organization founded in 1839 by female reformers that established homes of refuge for prostitutes and petitioned states criminalize adultery and seduction of women.

American (Know Nothing) Party: A nativist political organization that came together in New York in 1843 but rose to prominence in response to the influx of immigration to the United States after 1845.

American System: The name Clay gave his economic program for the country's post-war development, which called for government funding and promotion of the nation's infrastructure, a national bank, and protective tariffs to help promote domestic manufacturing.

Amerindians: A term anthropologists use to describe the approximately 2,000 cultures of native people that inhabited North and South America at the time of contact with Europeans.

Amistad: A Spanish ship taken over in June 1839 by 53 African slaves on board who sought freedom and a return to their African homeland.

"Anaconda Plan": The original war plan to crush the Confederate rebellion, devised by Union General-In-Chief Winfield Scott in 1861. It called for a major thrust by ground troops along the path of the Mississippi Valley to bisect the southern states and a naval blockade of southern ports to deprive the Confederacy of badly needed manufactured supplies and revenue from cotton sales.

Andersonville: A Confederate military prison in Sumter County, Georgia where about 25 percent of just under 50,000 Union prisoners, or about 13,000, died from hunger, disease, and exposure to unsanitary conditions in just 14 months from February 1864 to the end of the Civil War the next spring.

Andros, Edmund: Imperious governor of the Dominion of New England who enforced James II's will over an especially harassed and targeted Puritan New England, whom James especially despised, holding the sect responsible for his father's death.

Antebellum: Term used by historians to describe the pre-Civil War period (1820-1860) in United States history. It is especially applicable to the pre-war South.

Anthony, Susan B. (1820-1906): A feminist leader from Massachusetts who spent much of her life promoting women's suffrage, the abolition of slavery, and temperance.

Antietam, Battle of: The bloodiest single-day battle in American history, fought between the Union and Confederate armies on September 17, 1862 near Sharpsburg, Maryland, and resulting in a total of 23,000 casualties (including 3,654 dead). The battle ended the first unsuccessful Confederate invasion of the North.

Anti-Masonic Party: Formed in 1827 in opposition to the presumed power and influence of the Masonic order.

Antinomianism: The belief that faith alone was all that was necessary for salvation; that demonstrable, outward signs of "grace" did not prove one had been saved.

Appomattox Courthouse: Near the site of the last battle fought by Robert E. Lee's Army of Northern Virginia against Union Gen. Ulysses S. Grant, the courthouse became the scene of Lee's surrender April 9, 1865.

Arnold, Benedict (1741-1801): An American general during the Revolutionary War who switched sides and ended up a British officer by the end of the conflict.

Asiento: Allowed England to participate in the provisioning of African slaves to Spanish colonial possessions annually as well as permission of one British merchant ship to trade at Spanish ports per year.

Associated Press: Established in 1846 when five New York City newspapers pooled their financial resources to pay for a Pony Express route from the city to Alabama

Articles of Confederation: The first formal constitutional document for the United States of America, approved by the states in 1781. It established a Congress with each state delegation casting one vote—but no separate president or executive branch agencies, no national judiciary, and no grant of authority to the Congress to levy its own taxes or compel the states to provide funds.

Aztecs: a group of Native Americans that developed a highly sophisticated civilization in central Mexico.

Bacon, Nathaniel: Unscrupulous, power-hungry aristocratic leader of the Bacon Rebellion, who not only led the rebellion, but was also able to exploit and articulate the freedmen's grievances and unite them around a common cause.

Bacon's Rebellion: After years of growing acrimony between the planter elite of Virginia and the colony's freedmen. Rebellion brought about the end of indentured servitude in the Chesapeake. African slavery would be the permanent labor force on the tobacco plantations.

Bank of the United States: Part of the Hamiltonian agenda to assert greater governmental control over the new Republic's economy and finances by establishing a national bank that would print and back a national currency and regulate other banks as well as make loans to individuals and companies, especially those for manufacturing enterprises.

Bank War: The controversy over renewing the charter of the Second Bank of the United States during the administration of President Andrew Jackson.

"Barbadian Connection": Refers to the emigration to the Carolinas by former English Barbadian sugar planters, whom the Carolina proprietors believed would be able to rapidly turn their colonial venture into a profitable staple-producing enterprise.

Barbary Pirates: North African corsairs operating out of Tripoli who harassed both European and U.S. shipping in the Mediterranean.

Barnum, P.T. (1810-1891): An American entertainment producer and creator of the most popular 19th-century circus called "The Greatest Show on Earth." Barnum became famous for featuring bizarre acts at his shows and pulling off often fraudulent publicity stunts.

Bartolomé de Las Casas: Spanish priest who protested the enslavement of Native Americans in a book entitled *The Destruction of the Indies*.

Barton, Clara (1821-1912): An American nurse, humanitarian, and (in 1881) the founder of the American Red Cross, noted for her heroic services for the Union military during the Civil War.

Beauregard, Pierre Gustave Toutant (1818-1893): The Louisiana-born commander of Confederate forces at the Battle of Fort Sumter in South Carolina, the encounter that started the American Civil War.

Beecher, Catherine (1800-1878): An education pioneer who urged a broader-based education for girls and young women, the hiring of women as public school teachers and improvement of teacher training.

Benevolent Empire: Term used to describe the coalition of religious political reformers in the early and mid-19th century who sought to spread Protestant Christianity and were dedicated to the restoration of moral order.

Benjamin, Judah (1811-1884): Born a British citizen in the West Indies, Benjamin served as an important civilian leaders of the Confederate States of America during the Civil War.

Berkeley, Sir William: Imperious royal governor of Virginia at the time of Bacon's Rebellion. Berkeley served as Virginia's governor for over 30 years.

Biddle, Nicholas (1786-1844): President of the Second Bank of the United States from 1823 to 1836, Biddle supported the attempts of Henry Clay and Daniel Webster to re-charter the bank years before its expiration in 1836.

Bill of Rights: An addendum to the original Constitution that guaranteed individuals liberties. Such guarantees became the first ten amendments to the Constitution.

Black Codes: Laws passed by the newly-elected southern white governments during presidential reconstruction (under the Johnson administration) that virtually re-enslaved southern blacks, making a mockery of the war's purpose, especially in the eyes of Radical Republicans and many northern whites.

Black Hawk War: A Native American war of resistance to forced relocation west of the Mississippi by the U.S. government, led by Sauk and Fox war chieftain Black Hawk.

Blackburn, Luke (1816-1887): A Kentucky physician and politician accused of plotting biological warfare against the North during the Civil War.

"Bleeding Kansas": A term describing the violence surrounding the settlement of Kansas. The term encompassed the activities of the border ruffians of Missouri, the actions of John Brown, and the attack by Preston Brooks on Charles Sumner on the floor of the U.S. Senate.

Booth, John Wilkes (1839-1865): The child of renowned stage actor Junius Brutus Booth, and the brother of famed Shakespearean actors Edwin and Junius Booth, who on April 14, 1865 assassinated President Abraham Lincoln.

"Border Ruffians": A 1850s term describing people who entered Kansas from western Missouri with the intent of intimidating antislavery settlers.

Boston Associates: Boston industrial entrepreneurs led by Lowell who built factory towns around the greater Boston area for textile production.

Boston Massacre: A violent confrontation between an angry street mob and a group of British soldiers on March 5, 1770. The crowd began throwing snowballs containing rocks, and the terrified soldiers panicked, and fired into then. Five died, including Crispus Attucks, a man of African and Native American heritage. Six others suffered injuries.

Boston Tea Party: A protest action against the British Parliament's 1773 Tea Act carried out by a group of Massachusetts colonists December 16, 1773. Protestors dumped 342 containers of tea worth approximately $18,000 into Boston Harbor.

Bowery: A street and a neighborhood in the southern end of Manhattan in New York City. The Bowery represents the oldest street on Manhattan Island, becoming an upscale residential, shopping and entertainment district, but went into decline beginning in the 1830s, when it served as home to brothels, flop houses and saloons.

Boyd, Belle (1843-1900): A Confederate spy born in what is now West Virginia, she provided information on Union troop movements to Confederate generals Thomas "Stonewall" Jackson and Turner Ashby.

Braddock, Edward: British general sent by King and Parliament to drive the French out of the Ohio River Valley. Accompanying Braddock's 3,000 British regulars on this mission was a contingent of 2500 colonial militia, commanded by George Washington.

Bradford, William: Leader of the Plymouth Colony and progenitor of the Mayflower Compact, which in effect, granted all male colonists the right to participate in the colony's governance.

Brandywine Creek, Battle of: A major battle of the American Revolution in which British General Sir William Howe led a combined force of British regular troops and Hessian mercenaries to victory over the Continental Army led by George Washington on September 11, 1777 near Chadds Ford, Pennsylvania.

Brant, Joseph (also known as Thayendanegea) (1743-1807): A war chief of the Mohawk tribe (one of the Six Nations of the Iroquois), who led a company of "Volunteers" in raids and campaigns against settlements, militias, and the Continental Army in Iroquois country and the Ohio region.

British East India Company: A joint-stock company that received a royal charter in 1600. It operated its own military force which dominated much of the Indian subcontinent and which enjoyed monopoly privileges, with little government interference, in many commodities such as tea throughout the British Empire.

Brown, John (1800-1859): A white abolitionist who became convinced that slavery would only end through violence. In 1856, John Brown and his sons killed a family of proslavery settlers in Kansas. Three years later, Brown unsuccessfully attempted to start a slave revolt by capturing the federal arsenal at Harpers Ferry, Virginia (now West Virginia). He was captured and executed for treason, but many northerners regarded him as a martyr.

Brown, William Wells (1814-1884): A former slave who escaped and became an abolitionist and writer who traveled extensively as a speaker through the United States and Europe.

Bubonic Plague: a disease that devastated Europe in the 14th century, killing about one-third of the continent's population during the 1360s and 1370s.

Buchanan, James (1791-1868): A Pennsylvania politician who served as president from 1857 to 1861.

Bull Run, First Battle of: The first major battle of the Civil War, fought on July 21, 1861, which resulted in a Confederate victory and shattered northern overconfidence that the Union forces would win a quick and easy victory over the South.

Bull Run, Second Battle of: Civil War battle fought in northern Virginia, between Aug. 28-30, 1862 as part of Confederate Gen. Robert E. Lee's offensive march against Union Commanding Gen. John Pope on the same terrain where the First Battle of Bull Run was fought. Confederate forces won, but were unable to destroy Pope's army.

Bunker Hill, Battle of: British General Thomas Gage's armies faced encirclement by Massachusetts militiamen who occupied the high ground overlooking the Boston peninsula and, after receiving reinforcements, he decided to risk an assault on American troops led by Colonel William Prescott on ridgetops called Bunker Hill and Breed's Hill on June 17, 1775. The British scored a Pyrrhic victory, suffering more than 1,000 dead and wounded and failing to crush the American will to fight. The British government relieved Gage of his command, replacing him with General William Howe.

Burgoyne, John (1722-1792): British general who commanded forces in Canada in 1776 and 1777, known as "Gentleman Johnny" for his stylish and expensive tastes, who in 1777 was forced to surrender after the Battle of Saratoga.

Burned-Over District: The counties of Western New York south of the Adirondack Mountains that were the scene of repeated religious revivals in the first four decades of the 19th century where religious revivals and Pentecostal movements took place.

Burr, Aaron: Democratic-Republican candidate in presidential election of 1800, who surprisingly garnered enough electoral votes to throw the election to the House of Representatives, where Jefferson won enough votes to become president while Burr became vice-president.

Cabot, John: a Venetian sea captain who explored North America for England in 1497 and 1498 in search of the Northwest Passage.

Cahokia: the largest city known to have exited in Mississippian culture. It contained about 80,000 people in what is today Illinois.

Calhoun, John C. (1782-1850): A South Carolina politician known for his articulate defense of the southern states' rights and slavery.

California Gold Rush: The worldwide mass migration to California following the discovery of gold on the Sacramento Valley estate owned by John Sutter (1803-1880). .

Calvert, George (Lord Baltimore): English, Catholic proprietor/founder of Maryland. Maryland became the first English colony to be owned by an individual and his heirs.

"carpetbaggers": Name given to all northern whites who migrated south allegedly to take advantage of a prostrated southern people and economy. Most carpetbaggers were northern male and female school teachers who came to the South to help educate the freedmen, not unscrupulous, opportunists.

Chancellorsville, Battle of: Fought between April 30 and May 6, this Civil War battle in Northern Virginia was part of an offensive launched by Union Gen. John Hooker designed to bypass massed Confederate forces in Fredericksburg in part of a general campaign to capture the southern capital in Richmond.

Charleston, Siege of (April 1-May 12, 1780): The engagement that began the British military offensive in the Southern states (in 1780-1781) and the largest single military defeat for Continental forces during the war.

Chase, Salmon (1808-1873): An Ohio politician known for his abolitionist political organization. In the 1850s, he became a leader of the Republicans and played a leading role in articulating the new party's antislavery arguments.

Chattanooga Campaign: A series of Civil War battles in October and November 1863 during which Union Maj. Gen. Ulysses S. Grant dislodged Confederate forces from southeastern Tennessee and was given the command of Union forces on the Western Front.

***Cherokee Nation v. Georgia* (1831):** The United States Supreme Court in 1831 ruled that, because the Cherokees were not a foreign nation but a "domestic dependent nation" and had a relationship to the U.S. like a "ward to its guardian" that the Cherokees did not have standing to argue their case in the federal courts.

Chesapeake, Battle of the (Sept. 5, 1781): The decisive naval battle of the American Revolution, between British and French fleets seeking control of the mouth of Chesapeake Bay in which the French maintained control of Chesapeake Bay, making possible the siege of Yorktown that ended the Revolutionary War.

Chestnut, Mary (1823-1886): Daughter of Stephen Decatur Chestnut, who served as a U.S. House member and senator from South Carolina and governor, she became the most famous diarist and recorder of southern politics and society during the Civil War. Her diary was published after the Civil War as *Mary Chestnut's Civil War*.

Children's Aid Society: A charitable organization dedicated to helping orphans and other impoverished children, established in New York in 1853 by Charles Loring Brace (1826-1890).

Clay, Henry (1777-1852): A Kentuckian member of Congress, speaker of the House, senator, and secretary of state who played an instrumental role in forging the Missouri Compromise and the Compromise of 1850. Clay would be a principal founder of the Whig Party, formed to oppose Democratic President Andrew Jackson.

Clinton, Henry (1730-1795):): A general appointed commander-in-chief of the British forces in North America in 1778, who led a successful invasion of South Carolina in 1779, and captured Charleston in 1780, but waited too long to dispatch his fleet to rescue General Charles Cornwallis in Yorktown, Virginia, resulting in the decisive British defeat there October 17, 1781.

Columbus, Christopher: an Italian sailor who accidentally "discovered" North and South America when he was sailing westward across the Atlantic looking for a water route to Asia.

Clovis Point: a tool that was far superior to European and Asian choppers and scrapers developed by Native Americans of the Paleo-Indian period.

Cold Harbor, Battle of: A Civil War battle fought May 31-June 12, 1864 as part of northern Gen. Ulysses S. Grant's "Wilderness Campaign" in central Virginia that inflicted heavy casualties on southern Gen. Robert E. Lee's Army of Northern Virginia and led to the siege of the Confederate capital at Richmond.

Colt, Samuel (1814-1862): An American inventor from Connecticut who developed a cost-effective means of mass-producing revolvers and in numerous other ways modernized gun manufacturing.

Columbian Exchange: a term used to describe the exchange of animal and plant life between the Old and New Worlds that was sometimes deliberate and sometimes inadvertent.

Common Property Doctrine: An alternative to the Wilmot Proviso articulated by John C. Calhoun and asserting that all federal territory should be opened to slavery.

***Common Sense*:** A provocative pamphlet written by radical journalist and author Thomas Paine and published in January 1776 that bluntly characterized King George III as a tyrant, argued the 13 North American colonies should seek independence from Great Britain, and urged the colonists to think of themselves as belonging to a single American nation.

Compass: an important navigational instrument invented by the Chinese that contained a magnetic needle that always pointed toward the north.

"Connecticut Compromise": The key agreement worked out, in early July 1787, between delegates from large and small states at the Constitutional Convention in Philadelphia, over the allocation of representatives in the two houses of the proposed national legislature and the division of powers between the two houses.

Constitution of the United States: The charter establishing a new national government, defining its institutions (branches), and specifying their legal powers and responsibilities. After ratification was accomplished in 1788, the new federal government began operating under the terms of the Constitution in early 1789.

Constitutional Convention: The political convocation held in Philadelphia between May 14-September 17, 1787 that drafted the United States Constitution.

Constitutional Union Party: A short-lived political organization that emerged during the presidential election of 1860, mainly of former Whigs, of Southerners who emphasized allegiance for the Union.

Continental dollar: A unit of paper money first issued by the Second Continental Congress in 1775, as a means of payment for army expenses and other costs incurred by the Congress.

Convention of 1818: Another accord for the purpose of rapprochement between England the U.S. whereby both nations agreed to the 49th parallel as the northern boundary of the U.S.-controlled Louisiana territory all the way to the Pacific while setting up a system of "joint-occupation" of the Oregon Territory.

Copperheads: Northern Democrats who supported the South during the Civil War and demanded an immediate peace agreement with the Confederate government.

Cornwallis, Lord Charles (1738-1805): British general who served as commander of the British army in the South after the conquest of Charleston in 1780, but allowed his forces to be trapped between the Americans and the French in the 1781 Battle of Yorktown. He surrendered his large forces, ending the American Revolution with a defeat for Great Britain and independence for the United States.

Corrupt Bargain (1824): The deal made between Henry Clay and John Quincy Adams during the House vote to determine who would become 7th president of the U.S.—Andrew Jackson or John Quincy Adams. Clay agreed to throw his support to Adams if Adams would appoint him Secretary of State.

Cotton: A soft, fluffy staple fiber that grows in a boll and a profitable crop whose labor demands were satisfied through the exploitation of enslaved African Americans.

Cortina, Juan (1824-1892): The child of a prosperous cattle rancher in the state of Tamaulipas, Mexico near the Texas border. Best remembered for his capture of Brownsville, Texas, in 1859.

Cortés, Hernán: Spanish conquistador who subdued the Aztec empire.

Cowpens and Guilford Courthouse, Battles of: A pair of major Revolutionary War battles fought, respectively, on January 17 and March 15, 1781, in South and North Carolina that resulted in strong American victories that effectively ended the British attempt to seize control of the two states.

Crandall, Prudence (1803-1890): A Rhode Island Quaker, teacher and proponent of providing education for African Americans.

Crédit Mobilier Affair: A Grant administration scandal involving the siphoning off of millions of dollars in government funds to a "dummy company" to build the Union Pacific Railroad. In order to cover up their fraud, the railroad company owners sold bogus stock to greedy Congressmen, who believed they could make a quick buck.

Cromwell, Oliver: English Puritan who led Parliament's forces during the English civil war of the 1640s. Eventually defeated the king's army, responsible for Charles I's execution, and became Lord Protector of England in 1654, transforming England into a republican commonwealth as well as creating "Great Britain," which included Scotland, Ireland, and Wales.

Currency Act (1764): A law passed by the British Parliament that aimed to prevent American colonists from paying debts to British merchants in depreciated colonial currency but required payment in gold or silver coins.

***Dartmouth College v. Woodward*:** One in a series of post-war landmark cases of the John Marshall Supreme Court in which the court's ruling reflected the Federalist position of the power of the federal government over that of the states—*McCulloch v. Maryland*.

Davis, Jefferson (1808-1889): A Mississippi politician who at various times served as congressman, United States senator, secretary of war, and, during the Civil War, as president of the Confederate States of America. An ardent believer in white supremacy and slavery.

Day, Benjamin (1810-1889): The New York newspaper publisher who ushered in the era of the penny press in publications like the *New York Sun*.

de Tocqueville, Alexis (1805-1859): French author and historian whose four-volume book *Democracy in America* (published between 1835 and 1840) still ranks as one of the most perceptive portraits of American social and political life in the early 19th century.

de Vimeur, Jean-Baptiste Donatien, comte de Rochambeau (1725-1807): A French general who served as the commander-in-chief of the French armies in North America sent to aid the American Continental Army during the Revolutionary War and who played a key role in the Battle of Yorktown.

Declaratory Act: A declaration adopted in March 1766 by the British Parliament upon the repeal, after American protests, of the Stamp Act. The Declaratory Act proclaimed that the Parliament held "full power and authority" to make any laws binding the colonies "in all cases whatsoever."

Deere, John (1804-1886): The inventor, in 1837, of the steel plow, which replaced the more fragile and less powerful wooden and cast-iron plows. By 1857, his factory was producing 10,000 plows a year.

Deerfield, Massachusetts: Although the French and Indian wars did not involve massive numbers of troops and large-scale fighting, they nonetheless were vicious and brutal in nature, as witnessed by the French and Indian attack on the Massachusetts settlement of Deerfield during the European War of the Spanish Succession (1702-1713, in which French and Indian forces killed 50 men, women, and children, took 100 townsfolk as prisoners, and burned the town to the ground.

Deganawida, Chief: Native American leader who formed the five Iroquois Nations into a confederacy to regulate the economy and control violence and warfare in 1451.

Deism: The "religion" of many of the Enlightenment philosophes, who believed in a Supreme Being (God) but not in Christianity. Moreover, deists maintained that divine intervention did not rule the universe; that God had removed himself from temporal affairs and that it was man's duty to God and himself to discover God's natural laws that governed the universe.

Democratic Party (1832 --): The oldest political party in the United States, the Democrats can trace their origins to Thomas Jefferson's Republican Party, which formed in the 1790s.

Democratic Republicans: Party name assumed by the opponents of Hamilton and his followers. Leaders became Thomas Jefferson and James Madison, and eventually the party's ideology became that of Jeffersonianism.

Dias, Bartolomeu: sailor who rounded the Cape of Good Hope and saw the Indian Ocean for the first time.

Dickinson, John (1732-1808): A Philadelphia lawyer who became a political leader during the Revolutionary War era who, even though he had consistently opposed separation from Great Britain, enlisted in the American military when the war started.

Dix, Dorothea (1802-1887): : A social reformer who served as the Union Army's Superintendent of Female Nurses during the Civil War (1861-1865), she devoted much of her life to humanizing the treatment of the insane.

Dominion of New England: Created by James II to impose tighter royal control over England's North American empire, especially the New England colonies, whom James perceived as potentially the most dangerous to royal authority.

Dorr War: An 1841 uprising in Rhode Island against the existing state constitution, which limited the right to vote to freeholders (those with at least $134 in property.)

Douglas, Stephen (1813-1861): An Illinois politician who emerged a prominent Democratic politician in the 1850s. Douglas embraced the popular sovereignty position, which he defended in his successful bid for reelection to the U.S. Senate in 1858 (in which he defeated Abraham Lincoln) and his unsuccessful run for the presidency in 1860 (in which he lost to Lincoln).

Douglass, Frederick (1818?-1895): An escaped slave who became an eloquent leader in the abolitionist movement. His classic 1845 memoir, *Narrative of the Life of Frederick Douglass, an American Slave*, energized the Northern anti-slavery forces.

***Dred Scott* Case**: An 1857 Supreme Court decision that held African Americans were not citizens of the United States and that Congress possessed no power to limit slavery's expansion into the federal territories. Republicans used the case as evidence that a Slave Power Conspiracy had captured the federal government.

Dueling (*Code duello*): The code of conduct governing dueling, drawn up in England and generally honored in America in the 1700s and early 1800s. A form of one-on-one combat, originally involving swords but by the early 19th century using pistols, dueling occurred when men believed their honor had been insulted and the offending parties refused to apologize.

"Free Labor": An antebellum Republican shorthand for what made the North superior to the South. The phrase denoted the ability of northerners to choose their own employers, places of residence, and political views.

Edwards, Jonathan: Perhaps the most famous of the Great Awakening's evangelical preachers, who delivered "fire and brimstone" sermons with such passion that people reacted physically to the imagery presented in his emotion-charged perorations. Although a firm believer in delivery God's message to all for salvation, Edwards was nonetheless a devoted Puritan, whose theology remained orthodox.

Emancipation Proclamation: A decree issued by President Abraham Lincoln that declared free as of January 1, 1863 all slaves living in territory still in rebellion against the Union.

Embargo Act (1807): Jefferson pushed through Congress the Embargo Act which forbade all American ships from leaving US ports while denying foreign vessels access to American ports and trade. In effect, Jefferson cut off all trade with the outside world certain such action would devastate the belligerents' economies.

Emerson, Ralph Waldo (1803-1882): The son of a Unitarian minister, Emerson was an author, anti-war activist and leader of the Transcendentalist movement, which argued that humans were innately good but could become corrupted through institutions like the church and government. In essays like "Nature" and "Self Reliance," Emerson stressed the need for intellectual independence from majority opinion and derided the American emphasis on materialism.

Encomienda System: A system designed to meet labor shortages in which the Spanish government rewarded Conquistadors by giving them title to vast tracts of land and allowing them to enslave Native Americans.

English Test Act (1704): Required all Englishmen to adhere to Anglican supremacy and orthodoxy, stripping all dissenters of their political and civil rights.

Enlightenment (The "Age of Reason): An eighteenth-century philosophical movement that emphasized the use of reason to reevaluate previously held doctrines.

Erie Canal: This canal provided the first relatively rapid transportation across the Appalachian Mountains. Construction began on July 4, 1817, with German and Irish immigrants comprising a large percentage of the labor pool. Much of the digging was done by shovel and by horses pulling plows. Finished on October 25, 1825, the canal cost $7 million and greatly reduced the time and expense of transporting goods.

"Errand into the Wilderness": The belief according to historian Perry Miller, among the Great Migration Puritans that they had come to the New World on a mission for God; to establish a purified church and godly community—"a City Upon a Hill"—that would inspire their countrymen in England to reform the Anglican church and save the nation from God's wrath.

Excise Tax: A tax placed by the government in order to raise revenue on a specific domestic product or products. The first excise tax, which was also part of the Hamiltonian agenda, was on whiskey.

Fallen Timbers, Battle of: The U.S. Army under the command of General "Mad Antony" Wayne defeated the tribes at Fallen Timbers near present-day Toledo, Ohio, driving them out of area, further west.

Farragut, David (1801-1870): Considered the most gifted admiral in the Union Navy during the Civil War. A Southerner, he remained loyal to the Union. He was the first U.S. Navy officer to earn the rank of first rear admiral, vice admiral and admiral.

Federalist Papers: A series of 85 essays written by James Madison, Alexander Hamilton and John Jay in defense of the proposed United States Constitution, then being considered for ratification by the states.

Federalists: Supporters of the Constitution who favored its ratification.

Field, Cyrus (1819- 1892) and Peter Cooper (1791-1883): American businessmen who organized the laying of the undersea transatlantic telegraph cable from Ireland to Newfoundland, Canada.

Fifteenth Amendment: A Reconstruction-era amendment that bars states from interfering with the right to vote based on "race, color, or previous condition of servitude."

Fillmore, Millard (1800-1874): A New York politician, who succeeded Zachary Taylor to the presidency following his death in 1850. As president, Fillmore supported the provisions of the Compromise of 1850 and signed each one into law.

Finney, Charles Grandison (1792-1875): A fiery evangelical Christian preacher who played a leading role in the religious revivals that began in the first decade of the 19th century and peaked in the 1830s and 1840s. Finney rejected the strict Calvinist doctrine that God predestined who would be saved and who would be damned. Finney preached that God wanted all to achieve salvation.

Five Civilized Tribes: The Indian peoples—Cherokee, Choctaw, Chickasaw, Creek and Seminole—originally living in the Southeastern United States (in Georgia, Alabama, Mississippi, Tennessee and Florida) deemed to be "civilized" by their white neighbors. These Indians developed written languages, published books and newspapers, ended communal ownership of property and divided land into lots owned by individuals. They enslaved African Americans, and many adopted Christianity.

Five Points: a New York neighborhood famous for its poverty, brothels, and violence.

Forrest, Edwin (1806-1872): One of the leading Shakespearean actors in the United States in the first half of the 19th century. He performed frequently on stages in small towns in Pennsylvania, Ohio and Kentucky before making a hit playing the title character in *Othello* in New York in July 1826.

Forrest, Nathan Bedford (1821-1877): A Confederate cavalry officer responsible for one of the worst war crimes during the American Civil War, the Fort Pillow Massacre.

Fort Mims Massacre: A Red-Stick attack in northern Alabama on a white settlement in which Creek warriors, with the help of black slaves, killed at least 247 men, women, and children during the War of 1812, which saw some of the most brutal encounters occur between white and red Americans.

Fort Pillow Massacre: One of the worst war crimes in the American Civil War, committed by a cavalry division led by General Nathan Bedford Forrest against captured African-American troops in Henning, Tennessee. Forrest's men captured the Union-held Fort Pillow, manned by 557 northern soldiers, including 262 African Americans. Some historians estimate that Confederate soldiers slaughtered up to 300 African American soldiers after they had surrendered and given up their weapons.

Fort Quebec: a French trading post on the St. Lawrence River established by Samuel de Champlain in 1608.

Fort Wagner, Battle of: A Civil War battle fought in July 1863 over the control of a key approach to Charleston, South Carolina that convinced President Abraham Lincoln to support African American suffrage at least for war veterans, and which won greater support for the Emancipation Proclamation, effective the previous January, abolishing slavery in rebel territory.

"Forty Acres and a Mule": A radical Republican proposal during Reconstruction to destroy the pre-Civil war plantation/slave-owning elite by confiscating their property and redistributing it to freedmen in allotments of 40 acres. Radicals hoped to create a black independent yeoman farming class.

Fourier, Charles (1772-1837): A French philosopher who supported women's equality and whose ideas represented a primitive version of socialism. He advocated a living wage for all workers and financial support for those who couldn't earn adequate income. Fourier inspired a number of utopian communes, such as Utopia, Ohio, the Oneida community in New York and the La Reunion settlement in modern-day Dallas.

Fourteenth Amendment: A Reconstruction-era amendment passed in 1866 that officially made the freedmen U.S. citizens while prohibiting the states from denying such individuals all the rights and privileges guaranteed any citizen of the United States.

Franklin, Benjamin (1706-1790): A Pennsylvania politician, author, scientist, and diplomat who would be present for many of the most important events in early American history, including the writing of the Declaration of Independence, the negotiation of the peace treaty with Great Britain ending the Revolutionary War, and the writing of the United States Constitution.

Fredericksburg, Battle of: A Civil War battle fought in Virginia between December 11 and 15, 1862, that resulted in heavy Union casualties and ended a Union drive toward the Confederate national capital in Richmond.

Free Soil Party: A third party made up of antislavery Whigs and Democrats that organized in 1848 in reaction to both parties selection of presidential candidates. The Free Soil favored closing all territory to slavery.

Free Soil Position: A policy proposal in the 1840s and 1850s, most famously articulated in the Wilmot Proviso, that all federal territory be closed to slavery.

Freedmen's Bureau: First federally-sponsored and funded welfare agency created during Reconstruction to help the freedmen adjust to their new status while providing education, protection, and other services. The Bureau was staffed with junior Union army officers and under the directorship of the U.S. Army and General O.O. Howard.

Freeman, Elizabeth (?—1829): An African American woman who sued for her freedom in Massachusetts following the American Revolution, and won. Her case led to the disappearance of slavery in Massachusetts.

French and Indian War (1754-1763): The last of the Anglo-French colonial wars and the first in which the fighting began in North America. The war ended with France's defeat and loss of its North American empire.

Frobisher, Martin: an English explorer who brought back iron pyrite (fool's gold).

Fulton, Robert (1765-1815): An engineer and inventor often mistakenly believed to be the inventor of the steamboat, Fulton actually was the first person to put a workable design to the test. Fulton tested the first steamboat he constructed, the *Clermont*, on the Hudson River in New York in 1807.

"Gag Rule": A rule implemented in the United States House of Representatives in May 1836 at the behest of the Southern delegation. It required that all anti-slavery petitions be automatically tabled without debate.

Gage, Thomas (1721-1787): A British Army general in command in Massachusetts, and the colony's last royal governor, at the beginning of the American Revolution. Gage was quickly relieved of his position after achieving only mixed results in the battles of Lexington and Concord in April 1775 and winning a victory of questionable value at the cost of high casualties at Bunker and Breed's hills in June that same year.

Garnet, Henry Highland (1815-1882): A former slave, minister, and fierce advocate of abolitionism, Garnet in 1843 pleaded for slaves to rise up against their masters, even if this resulted in bloodshed.

Garrison, William Lloyd (1805-1879): An anti-slavery journalist who in 1831 began publication of *The Liberator*, an anti-slavery newspaper that continued publication through the end of the Civil War in 1861.

Gates, Horatio (1727-1806): An American general during the Revolutionary War (1775-1783) who won a major victory against the British in the Battles of Saratoga in 1777, suffered a crushing defeat in the Battle of Camden in 1780 and was considered a rival to the Continental Army's commander, George Washington.

Genêt, Citizen Edmund: French Girondist emissary sent by the revolutionary republican government to enlist American aid for France's war effort in Europe, disregarding with blatant contempt the official U.S. position of neutrality.

George III (1738-1820): The British monarch during the time of the American Revolution who supported the policies of prime ministers like Frederick North who sought to relieve Britain's budget crisis by shifting some of the costs of empire to the barely-taxed American colonists.

Germain, Lord George (1716-1785): British politician who served as secretary of state for America (1775-1781) in the government headed by Lord North and an uncompromising advocate of the military reconquest of the American states.

Gettysburg Address: Speech delivered by President Abraham Lincoln November 19, 1863 at the dedication of the national cemetery at the scene of the Battle of Gettysburg that had resulted in a Union victory July 1-3 that year. Many consider The Gettysburg Address, which connected the Civil War to a long struggle for human freedom that dated back to the American Revolution, a rhetorical and literary masterpiece.

Gettysburg, Battle of: Widely considered the turning point of the Civil War, this battle was fought July 1-3 near Gettysburg, Pennsylvania, ending with Union General George Meade halting an invasion of the North mounted by the commander of the Army of North Virginia, Robert E. Lee, inflicting high casualties and forcing a Confederate retreat.

Gilbert, Sir Humphrey: the driving force behind England's overseas explorations under Elizabeth I. He, like Cabot, wanted to find a Northwest Passage.

Glorious Revolution: Parliamentary insurrection in 1688 against James II's attempt to rule England as an absolute monarch. The event marked the end of the English monarchy's power, establishing England as a constitutional monarchy.

Godey's Lady's Book: A monthly magazine aimed at women that for years enjoyed the highest circulation in the country. It was published by Louis A. Godey (1804-1877) in Philadelphia between 1830 and 1878. The magazine included news, poems, short stories, and fashion designs that women could make at home.

"Gold Bug": Democrat or Republican politicians in the late 19th century who favored keeping all U.S. currency backed by gold.

Goodyear, Charles (1800-1860): An inventor who developed a technique to vulcanize rubber. He earned a patent for this process in the United States in 1844 and in Europe in 1851. The Goodyear Tire Company was named after him, but the inventor's family never owned shares of the corporation.

Grant, Ulysses S. (1822-1885): General-in-chief of the Union Army by the end of the American Civil War (1861-1865), Grant won credit for the North's victory and was able to ride his popularity to two terms in the White House (1869-1877). Lee surrendered at Appomattox Courthouse in Virginia on April 9, 1865. Three years later Grant won election as president.

"Grantism": Refers to government officials acting in a corrupt, unethical way. Derives from the many scandals that erupted during the Grant administration from 1869 to 1877.

Great Awakening: Tremendous religious revival that emerged during the colonial period. It was a movement against the traditional Puritan theology of predestination. Salvation was now open to all and God's message was delivered in a most passionate and direct way to all those wanting his grace and redemption; evangelism became the most important feature of this revival.

Great Famine of 1845: A humanitarian disaster caused by a disease affecting the Irish potato crop. The potato blight would result in the death of one million men, women and children.

"Great Migration": The name given to the 14,000 plus Puritans who came to New England in the 1630s and 1640s, fleeing persecution and eventual civil war in their homeland. Migrants were not Separatists but "mainstream" Puritans who formed the Massachusetts Bay Company, obtained a charter from the king (Charles I) and migrated to New England beginning in 1630. They initially had no intention of staying permanently in the New World.

Greeley, Horace (1811-1872): Publisher of the *New York Tribune* beginning in 1841, Greeley's newspaper was one of the first of the so-called "penny dailies" that aimed at a mass circulation.

"Greenbacks": Paper currency printed by the federal government during the Civil War to finance the northern war effort. Their issue caused widespread, exorbitant inflation in the North while taking the dollar off the gold standard.

Greene, Nathanael (1742-1786): A major general in the Continental Army who became Washington's most trusted subordinate, and later won fame in his own right for his command of the Continental Army in the Southern states.

Grenville, Sir George (1712-1770): Brother-in-law of William Pitt the Elder, who served as British Secretary of State and most powerful government minister during the French and Indian War (1754-1763), Grenville served as prime minister from 1763-1765. It was his administration that pushed through the Parliament the Stamp Act in February 1765.

Grimké Sisters: Sarah (1792-1873) and Angelina (1805-1879) were born and raised on a plantation owned by their slave-owning father but became notable abolitionists and advocates for women's rights.

Guinea: a area along the western coast of Africa where most slaves who were sent to the Americas came from.

Gutenberg, Johann: a resident of Mainz, Germany who is credited with inventing the modern printing press that used moveable type.

Habeas corpus: The constitutional right through which a prisoner can ask a court to be released unless the jailing authority presents sufficient grounds to justify continued detention.

Hamilton, Alexander (1757-1804): Leading American statesman and politician after 1789 whose early career included key contributions to the Continental Army and the ratification of the Constitution.

Hamiltonianism: The personal political and economic philosophy of the first Secretary of the Treasury Alexander Hamilton. Hamilton used his position to strengthen the powers of the central government by having the government play a direct role in the nation's economic development.

Hancock, John (1737-1793): A Massachusetts politician and the first and most visible signer of the Declaration of Independence.

Hartford Convention 1814: A gathering of anti-war, rabid anti-Republican High Federalist New Englanders, the party's regional bastion, at Hartford, Connecticut, to protest not only the war but also Republican policies, which they believed reflected the Republican desire to destroy the Federalist Party.

Hawthorne, Nathaniel (1804-1864): A fiction writer from Massachusetts who authored *The Scarlet Letter* and *The House of the Seven Gables*.

Hayne-Webster Debate: A legislative battle between Senators Daniel Webster of Massachusetts and Robert Y. Hayne of South Carolina in 1830 over the sale of public land in the West and the effect this had on the supply of labor in different regions in the country. The debate turned into an argument over states' rights.

Headright System: In order to attract more settlers to Jamestown for tobacco growing, the Virginia Company offered 50-acre land grants as incentives to newcomers. Those already living in the colony received two head-rights if they agreed to grow tobacco rather than other crops on their farms or engage in other enterprises.

Hector, Charles, comte d'Estaing (1729-1794): The French admiral who commanded the fleet sent to assist the United States in the American Revolution whose fleet and marines captured Grenada and St. Vincent in the Caribbean July 4, 1779.

Henry, Patrick (1736-1799): A Virginia planter, attorney, riveting speaker and fierce advocate of American independence in the 1770s. Henry opposed the Constitution adopted in 1787, believing it violated the principle of states' rights.

Henry the Navigator, Prince: Portuguese leader who supported efforts to explore parts of the world previously unknown to Europeans.

Hessians: The popular name given to German mercenaries fighting for the British Army during the American Revolutionary War (1775-1783).

"High" Federalists: The Federalist party split into two factions, with the more rabid and ultra-Hamiltonians being called the High Federalist.

***H.L. Hunley*:** A Confederate submarine, built in Mobile, Alabama, in 1863, that became the first such vessel to battle and sink a warship.

Hodgers, Jennie, aka Albert D.J. Cashier: (1843-1915): One of more than 400 documented cases of women posing as men and fighting in the Civil War.

Homestead Act: A law passed by the United States Congress in 1862 that allowed farmers to obtain 160 acres of public land for free, as long as they cultivated it for five years. Farmers also had the option of buying the land for $1.25 an acre if they cultivated it for six months.

Horseshoe Bend, Battle of (March 1814): Decisive U.S. victory over the Creeks, which saw over 800 Creeks slaughtered by General Andrew Jackson's Tennessee militia and their pro-assimilation Choctaw and Cherokee allies. Battle proved to mark the end not only of Tecumseh's confederation, but along with the Indian defeat at the Thames, the end of Indian military power east of the Mississippi River.

House of Burgesses: In 1619 the Virginia Company granted Jamestown colonists the right to form a legislative assembly, which its elected members called the House of Burgesses. The meeting of this body represented the first gathering in the New World of an elected representative government, even though the majority of Burgesses were members of the plantation elite.

House of Delegates: Maryland's counterpart to Virginia's House of Burgesses; a representative legislative body Lord Baltimore had also been forced by circumstances to grant by the Protestant majority in his colony. The House assumed all political power and law-making rights, which Baltimore relinquished in exchange for retaining absolute control over land distribution.

House of Stuart: England's new ruling dynastic house which assumed the crown upon Elizabeth Tudor's death in 1603. The new royal family was Scottish and not well received by the English aristocracy. The first Stuart king was James I (James VI of Scotland and Elizabeth's cousin)

Howe, William (1729-1814): The general who took over the position of commander-in-chief of the British forces in the American Revolution (1775-1783) from Thomas Gage but who resigned after being unable to defeat George Washington after three years in the position.

Hudson, Henry: An English sea captain who explored and claimed for the Netherlands the Delaware Bay, New York, the Hudson River, and Hudson Bay.

Huguenots: French citizens who had converted to Protestantism during the 16th century but during the reign of Louis XIV became a persecuted minority and many decided to flee to New World sanctuaries such as the Carolinas.

Hutchinson, Anne: Perhaps the most legendary of Puritan New England's dissenters, who challenged the fundamental tenets of the Puritan faith, most notably predestination.

Hutchinson, Thomas (1711-1780): A businessman and Massachusetts politician who stayed loyal to the British government during the American Revolutionary War. Hutchinson served as acting governor of Massachusetts from June to August of 1760 and as governor from 1769 to 1774.

Impressment: A more serious affront to American neutrality by the Royal Navy: The forced abduction of American sailors from American vessels into the British Navy. Typical policy of the British navy during times of war to ensure the manpower needs of their most important fighting force: the navy. The US regarded such action as a flagrant and contemptuous disregard for American neutrality.

Impressment Act of 1863: A highly controversial law passed by the Confederate Congress in March 1863 that allowed the military to seize from farmers flour, corn, meat, wood for fuel, slaves and other supplies, with compensation for the owners as low as 50 percent below market value.

Inca: A sophisticated Native American civilization in modern Peru that developed a social welfare system to care for the physically handicapped, the mentally ill, and individuals suffering from chronic illnesses.

Indentured Servitude: Indentured servants were poor, dispossessed Englishmen, desperate for work, who contracted with the Chesapeake planters to come to Virginia and work for a specific time until they had fulfilled their debt obligation to their planter-employer. Once the contractual obligations had been met, the individual became "free."

Indian Removal Act of 1830: A law adopted by Congress that gave the president authority to negotiate treaties with Indian nations living east of the Mississippi for their removal and settlement west of the river. Those who chose to remain east of the river would become citizens of the state in which they lived, thereby eliminating tribal authority. Motivated by white greed for land and resources and by anti-Indian racism, the law supposedly provided for peaceful migration, but the so-called "Civilized Tribes" in the American Southeast would be removed at bayonet point.

Industrial Revolution: The period from the late 1700s to just after the Civil War in which the United States transformed from an agricultural economy to one increasingly urban and technologically advanced.

"Intolerable Acts": A series of harsh laws passed by the British Parliament in 1774 in response to the Boston Tea Party. Also known as the "Coercive Acts," these measures closed Boston Harbor to all commerce until the colonists compensated the East India Company for the destroyed tea; rewrote the Massachusetts Bay Colony's charter in order to expand the royal governor's limited powers, and limited town meetings to once a year; and moved the trials to England for royal officials charged with crimes.

"Iron-clad oath": An oath of allegiance all southern white males had to swear in which they promised that they in no way aided or abetted the Confederate cause. If able to take such an oath, they could vote and run for office in state elections. The oath was used by Radical Republicans to disenfranchise southern whites of suspect loyalty to the Union and likely to support the Democratic Party.

Jackson, Rachel Donelson (1767-1828): The wife of military leader and politician Andrew Jackson who became an issue in the 1828 presidential race. During the bitter 1828 presidential election between Jackson and the incumbent, John Quincy Adams, pro-Adams forces smeared Rachel as both an adulteress and bigamist.

Jackson, Thomas J. "Stonewall" (1824-1863): A veteran of the Mexican-American War (1846-1848), Jackson was renowned as a brilliant commander in the Confederate Army during the Civil War (1861-1865).

Jacobs, Harriet (1813-1897): Born a slave, Jacobs would later author a searing memoir of her experiences in North Carolina, including warding off the sexual advances of her married master, in the autobiography *Incidents in the Life of a Slave Girl*.

Jamestown: Name given by the Virginia Company to their colony founded in 1608 on the James River in present-day Virginia. Named after King James I of England, who had granted the company their charter.

Jay's Treaty (1795): After several years of dealing with British violations of American neutrality, Washington believed it was time to try to negotiate a settlement so sent John Jay, Chief Justice of the Supreme Court to England. Jay was only able to secure the most modest of British concessions and a guarantee of no war "in the immediate future" between the two nations.

Jefferson, Thomas (1743-1826): A Virginia politician, inventor, writer, principal author of the Declaration of Independence, the founder of the Republican Party (which later evolved into the Democratic Party), the second vice president and third president of the United States.

Jenkins, Robert: English merchant who was caught violating the trading decree's stipulations and had his ear cut off as punishment. The incident provided the government with the excuse it had long been waiting for to declare war on Spain. In 1739 the War of Jenkins's Ear began between England and Spain, and colonials from both nations were involved in North America.

Jeremiah, Thomas (? – 1775): A free African American man executed in South Carolina on August 18, 1775 after being accused of plotting a slave revolt.

Johnson, Andrew (1808-1875): A pro-Union but anti-black-suffrage Tennessee politician who served in the U.S. House, the Senate, as governor of his home state, as vice president under Abraham Lincoln and, following Lincoln's murder in April 1865, as president from 1865-1869. Johnson became president the night of April 14, 1865 when John Wilkes Booth assassinated Abraham Lincoln.

Johnston, Albert Sidney (1803-1862): One of the smartest and most talented generals in the Confederate Army, he died during the Battle of Shiloh in Tennessee in April 1862.

Junto Society of Philadelphia: Similar to the famous salons, that became the gathering places for Europe's Enlightenment intelligentsia, Franklin and his equally progressive friends developed such a community in Philadelphia, which by the middle of the 18th century, was not only colonial America's most populous city, but thanks to its Quaker heritage, the most tolerant and welcoming of new ideas and their free expression.

Kansas-Nebraska Act: A law drafted by Stephen Douglas, passed by Congress, and signed by President Franklin Pierce that organized the territory that became the states of Kansas and Nebraska. Controversy surrounded this law because it repealed the Missouri Compromise restriction, and the reaction against that repeal brought about the organization of the Republican Party.

King Philip's War: The bloodiest Anglo-Indian conflict in American colonial history, ironically one of the few initiated by Native Americans. The Wampanoag chief Metacom (whom the English called "King Philip") led his tribe against the Puritans in 1675 and because the Puritans did not expect such an uprising, Metacom's braves succeeded in winning many encounters and each victory brought new Indian allies. Eventually the Puritans defeated Metacom and his forces, the result of Puritan alliances with other tribes, ironically the Pequot.

Kitchen Cabinet: President Andrew Jackson's unofficial advisors, mostly newspaper editors and the president's friends from his home state of Tennessee. The term has come to mean anyone in the president's inner circle who does not hold a cabinet post but who provides counsel to the White House.

Knox, Henry (1750-1806): One of the most gifted of the American officers during the War of Independence (1775-1783) who made valuable contributions in almost every important battle of the conflict.

Ku Klux Klan: A white supremacist group that aimed to destroy the Reconstruction-era Republican Party in the South, to force the withdrawal of Union troops from the region, and terrify African Americans into not voting or demanding better working conditions.

La Salle, René-Robert Cavelier, Sieur de: French explorer and colonizer who hoped to extend France's presence in North America into the Southwest, territory claimed but not colonized by Spain.

Lecompton Constitution: A document that tried to bring Kansas into the Union as a slave state. The entire process was riddled with fraud, and the effort was defeated—despite the support of President Buchanan—by the combined efforts of Stephen Douglas and the Republicans. Kansas would ultimately enter the Union as a free state in 1862.

Lee, Charles: (1732-1782): A native of England, a mercenary and a controversial American general during the Revolutionary War (1775-1783) who wanted to replace George Washington as commander of the American Army and would be fired by him for insubordination after the Battle of Monmouth Courthouse in 1778.

Lee, Robert E. (1807-1870): For three years the commander of the Army of Northern Virginia during the American Civil War (1861-1865), Lee ranks as one of the finest military minds in American history although his high-risk tactics often placed his men at high risk. He became one of the top-ranking Confederate generals. He won engagements such as the Second Battle of Bull Run, the Seven Days' Battles, and Chancellorsville. He surrendered to Union General-in-Chief Ulysses S. Grant on April 9, 1865.

Legal Tender Act (1862): A law passed by the U. S. Congress during the Civil War that allowed the U.S. government to use paper currency rather than gold and silver to pay off debts.

Lewis and Clark Expedition: Soon after Jefferson purchased Louisiana he authorized the Lewis and Clark expedition, whose mission it was to thoroughly assess what the U.S. had bought; the territory's scientific and commercial value, the still hoped-for Northwest Passage.

Lexington and Concord, Battles of: The first military engagements of the American Revolutionary War. The battles marked the outbreak of open armed conflict between Great Britain and its thirteen colonies in North America.

Liberty Party: The first antislavery party, formed in 1840.

Lincoln, Abraham (1809-1865). An Illinois politician who served as president from 1861 to his assassination in 1865. Before 1860, Lincoln, a successful lawyer, served a single term in the House of Representatives in the 1840s but his stance against the Mexican American War ended his career in the House. In 1858, he lost a contest for the Senate to Stephen Douglas, but then defeated Douglas in the 1860 presidential election. As president, Lincoln shepherded the United States through a bitter Civil War. He was assassinated shortly after the war ended by a prosouthern sympathizer.

Lincoln, Benjamin (1733-1810): A Massachusetts farmer who served as Major General during the American Revolution (1775-1783) who, after taking part in the key American victory in Saratoga in the fall of 1777 was named to lead American forces in the South in 1778.

Locke, John: One of the Enlightenment's most important political philosophes, whose work greatly inspired America's future revolutionary leaders. Especially influential were Locke's ideas in his *Theory of Government*, in which he justified rebellion against a government when it becomes corrupted and degenerates into a tyranny.

Locofoco Party: The name applied to the radical wing of the Democratic Party from 1835 to the mid-1840s. Locofocos opposed tariffs and state banks, supported laissez-faire economic policies, backed unions and opposed the printing of paper currency.

London or Virginia Company: The consortium of private merchant/capitalists who formed a joint stock company to try to establish a mainland colony in North America. Their enterprise was for personal and collective profit, not for the greater glory of God and King.

Long Island, Battle of (Aug. 27, 1776): The first major battle between the Continental Army, under General Washington, and the British army commanded by General William Howe, and the largest battle of the war in numbers of troops engaged.

Louis XIV: Perhaps the most powerful monarch in all of French monarchial history, whose aggressive foreign policy of French continental expansion precipitated several European war among the great powers that reverberated across the Atlantic to North America, which saw several frontier conflicts erupt between English, Spanish, and French colonials.

Louis XVI (1754-1793): The French monarch at the time of the American Revolution (1775-1783) who decided to support the American struggle against Great Britain and who would be executed during the French Revolution (1789-1799). French participation in the American struggle proved critical, in terms of loans Louis' regime provided the rebel government and military support provided in the decisive victory against the British in the Battle of Yorktown in 1781.

Louisiana Purchase (1803): The greatest purchase/acquisition of foreign territory in US history. Jefferson purchased from France for $15 million all of French Louisiana, doubling the size of the United States. Jefferson initially had serious personal, political, and constitutional reservations about the purchase but eventually overcame all such qualms by reassuring himself and the American people that the acquisition of Louisiana would guarantee for generations to come his agrarian republic.

Lovejoy, Elijah (1802-1837): A Maine native, minister and abolitionist newspaper publisher assassinated for his anti-slavery views. In 1833, he began publishing the *St. Louis Observer*, which ran articles critical of slavery.

Lowell, Francis Cabot: American who toured English factory towns before the War of 1812 and copied the machines he saw in operation, bringing such knowledge back to the U.S.

Macon's Bill Number 2: Passed by the Madison administration in 1810, which allowed for the resumption of trade with France and Great Britain but allowed the president to re-impose sanctions on whichever country refused to respect US neutrality, while authorizing trade with the other. Madison hoped such a measure would prevent war, which was likely by 1810 with either France or Great Britain.

Magellan, Ferdinand: Spanish explorer who found an ocean route to Asia and led the first expedition to circumnavigate the earth.

Malthus, Thomas: English political economist who maintained that the world's population would eventually outstrip the world's food supply causing global famine and all manner of socio-political problems. Malthus believed England was headed for such a catastrophe if population growth was not checked. Malthus' dire predictions affected Thomas Jefferson, who used Malthus' forecast to further convince Americans of the necessity of remaining an agricultural economy and society.

Mann, Horace (1796-1859): The leader of the Common School movement, which aimed at providing every child a tax-supported basic education. Mann believed that social conflicts, poverty and class divisions would fade with the spread of education to the masses. A democratic society, he said, depended on a well-educated population. He also urged states to institute formal teacher training at so-called Normal Schools, an effort that bore fruit in his home state in 1838 when Massachusetts began to create such public institutions.

March to the Sea: Union Gen. William Tecumseh Sherman's offensive through Georgia to the Atlantic Ocean during the Civil War in 1864 in which, by destroying cities, railroads lines, and farms, he hoped to demonstrate to Southerners that the Confederate government could not protect them. The March concluded in Savannah on December 21. Sherman's "total war" tactics had the intended effect: Southerners suffered because of food and fuel shortages and men began to desert the Confederate Army because they feared what was happening to their families living in the path of Sherman's forces.

Marshall, John: Marshall was chief justice of the Supreme Court from 1801-1835 and during his tenure he established the all-important concept of judicial review. The Marshall Court, in a series of landmark decisions, further strengthened the balance of power within the federal government and thus the system of checks and balances. The Marshall Court in an overwhelming majority of cases heard decided in favor of the federal government over the states.

Mason, George (1725-1792): A Virginia politician active in the resistance against Great Britain's Stamp Act in 1765 and a supporter of American independence who participated as a delegate in the Constitutional Convention in 1787.

Mather, Cotton: Boston Puritan pastor who embraced the Enlightenment's scientific, rationalist probing of common phenomenon such as diseases. Mather was one of the first colonial Americans to urge inoculation for small pox with a weakened strain of the deadly contagion to help individuals develop stronger immunity to the disease.

Mayan: an educated people who created the first system of writing in North and South America, developed a system of complex mathematics, and studied astronomy. They discovered the number zero long before Europeans and could accurately calculate the beginning of solar eclipses

McClellan, George (1826-1885): Appointed general-in-chief for the Union Army in November 1861, early in the American Civil War, McClellan became famous for his skills in organizing and drilling his troops but infamous for his indecision and his reluctance to put his forces into battle.

McCormick, Cyrus (1809-1884): The inventor of the mechanical harvester, which used features of other men's designs, first patented in 1834. He began manufacturing his model three years later and opened a large factory to produce his machine in Chicago in 1847.

McGuffey Readers: A widely used 19th-century schoolbook aimed at teaching primary-grade children how to read along with moral virtues like honesty, thrift and hard work. The editor, William Holmes McGuffey (1800-1873), began producing the readers in 1835. There were eventually six levels of readers, the higher-level books providing portions of classics in Western literature to teach children reading comprehension.

Melville, Herman (1819-1891): A former sailor turned author who wrote such classics as *Moby Dick: or, The Whale* (1851) and *Billy Budd* (published posthumously in 1924), works that satirized American self-righteousness, zealotry, and obsession with wealth.

Mercantilism: The dominant economic theory among the European imperial powers of the 17th and 18th centuries. Mercantilism maintained the importance of colonies as vital additions or augmentations to a nation's overall wealth and power. Colonies thus, at all times, were to be subservient to the needs of the mother country, especially in the providing of valuable raw products or resources, and as markets for the mother country's manufactured goods.

Middle Passage: Name given by slave traders to the journey on slave ships from Africa to the New World. Without question the most brutal and inhumane treatment of slaves occurred during this phase of their bondage, where onboard the ships the slaves suffered from all manner of unimaginable deprivation and cruelty, from which hundreds would die on every "passage."

Miller, William (1782-1849): An evangelist active in upstate New York and beyond who gathered followers in the 1830s and 1840s after he announced he had discovered, by careful reading of Bible prophecy, that the second coming of Jesus Christ would happen between March 21, 1843 and March 21, 1844.

Minstrelsy: A form of entertainment popular from the 1840s until the civil rights era in the mid-20th century in which white performers would sing, dance and tell jokes while portraying African Americans and wearing "blackface" makeup. The stage shows would mock black dialect and black music and would sometimes touch on current political controversies and celebrities.

Missouri Compromise: The first in a series of several compromises to come in an attempt to avoid civil war over the issue of slavery expansion. Missouri was admitted as a slave state along with Maine as a free state, thus preserving the balance of power in the Senate. All territory above Missouri, above the parallel 36 30 was to be free; territory below Missouri's southern boundary was assumed to be open to slavery by Southerners. At the time of the compromise the land belonged to Spain. From this point forward the nation's political leaders and parties would avoid or postpone civil war by seeking compromises to the slavery issue and the larger tensions of sectionalism slavery was causing.

Missouri Compromise Restriction: A federal policy established in the 1820s that prohibited the expansion of slavery north of 36°-30' latitude (essentially the southern border of the state of Missouri). Although many northerners, especially those who would be attracted to the Republican Party, regarded the restriction as almost a sacred compact, Congress repealed this it in 1854, and the Supreme Court ruled it unconstitutional in 1857. Those decisions exacerbated sectional conflict.

Missouri Crisis: The first in a 40-year series of sectional showdowns between the North and the South over the issue of slavery expansion, the result of the rapid westward move of Americans at the time as well as South's market revolution with cotton production. Causing the tension was that Missouri was above the Old Northwest Ordinance of 1787 line (the Ohio River) which declared the region closed to slavery. Moreover, Missouri's entry into the Union as a slave state would upset the balance of power in the Senate; prior to Missouri territories had entered the Union as states in pairs, one slave, one free, thus preserving the balance.

Monitor* and the *Merrimac: The two innovative ironclad ships that battled in the Chesapeake Bay March 9, 1862, during the American Civil War.. In 1861, the Confederate Navy had recovered a sunken United States steamship called the *Merrimac*, covered it with iron plates for protection and mounted on it six nine-inch guns and four heavy rifles They renamed the *Merrimac* the *Virginia*. Confederate leaders hoped that the innovation of ironcladding might allow them to block the damaging naval blockade the Union had maintained that was strangling the southern economy.

Monmouth Court House, Battle of: The final, indecisive battle in the North during the American Revolution (1775-1783) fought on June 28, 1778 in Pennsylvania. That night, with both sides having lost hundreds of dead and wounded, and with the American side holding the battlefield, the British troops slipped away and resumed their march to New York City. The battle was inconclusive, but to the Americans it felt like a victory. A court martial later convicted Lee of insubordination and ended his service in the Continental Army.

Monroe Doctrine: Promulgated by the Monroe administration and largely the handiwork of Secretary of State John Quincy Adams, that declared the US to be not only opposed to any attempts by the European powers to reclaim or expand their New World empires but that the US spoke for all the nations of the Western Hemisphere. Any attempt by any "outside" powers to expand their empire would be met with harsh reprisals from the US. At the time few of the great European powers took the US threats seriously, dismissing such bravado as bluster. However, with Great Britain's support of the Doctrine, none of the other European powers attempted to reclaim or expand their presence in the New World.

Morgan, Daniel (1736-1802): An American general during the War for Independence (1775-1783) who played a vital role in the Continental Army's victories in the Battles of Saratoga in 1777 and the Battle of Cowpens, South Carolina in 1781. Morgan served a term in the United States House of Representatives from 1797 to 1799 as a Federalist.

Mormonism: The religious ideas laid out between the 1820s and the 1840s by Joseph Smith, who claimed to have received revelations from angels who led him to discover gold plates in the hills of New York State written in an ancient language that he translated into *The Book of Mormon*. Smith's followers would establish the Church of Jesus Christ of Latter-day Saints. Mormons believe that Joseph Smith was a divinely inspired prophet, and that the *Book of Mormon* is the word of God on equal standing with the Bible.

Morris, Robert (1734-1806): Leading Philadelphia merchant, financier, and political figure who supported the resistance to the Stamp Act, served in the Second Continental Congress as a Pennsylvania delegate, and signed the Declaration of Independence and the Constitution. Morris profited during the Revolution by organizing naval raids on British merchant ships, but he also helped sustain the Continental Army with his own funds.

Morrison v. White: A Supreme Court case that revealed the ambiguities of racial categories as they related to slavery. James White bought a slave woman, Jane Morrison, in Louisiana in 1857, who quickly escaped and filed a lawsuit in Jefferson Parish seeking her freedom. Morrison was blonde and blue-eyed, and her attorneys argued that she was illegally held as a slave because, based on her appearance, she was white. Louisiana defined as black any person who had 1/16th African American ancestry,, but Morrison argued that she had no discernible "black" traits and didn't act like a black person supposedly would. The Louisiana jury consisted mostly of non-slave owners, and they deadlocked. A new trial was held, and White got it moved to New Orleans. This jury decided that Morrison was white and therefore free, but the state Supreme Court overturned the verdict. A third jury, in 1862, deadlocked again, but another trial was never held as the Civil War continued until 1865. The Emancipation Proclamation and the 13th Amendment to the U.S. Constitution, abolishing slavery, rendered the issue of Morrison's status as a slave moot.

Samuel Morse: Invented of the telegraph in 1836, which allowed Americans to spread information across many parts of the nation almost instantaneously. The system involved the transmission and reception of electrical impulses along a connected wire using a standard code.

Motier, Gilbert du, Marquis de Lafayette (1757-1834): French nobleman who, as a young military officer and an enthusiastic supporter of American independence, served General Washington and the Continental Army during the Revolutionary War (1775-1783), endured the hardships of Valley Forge, the Continental Army's winter camp from December 1777 to June 1778, successfully lobbied the French government to increase its financial aid to the U.S. military, and played a major role in the American victory at the Battle of Yorktown. He made a triumphant tour of the United States in 1824 and 1825 in which he was celebrated as a hero. He was buried in Paris, his grave covered with soil from Bunker Hill in memory of his role in the American Revolution.

Mott, Lucretia (1793-1880): A Quaker woman committed to equal rights for women, opposed to slavery, and supportive of temperance and prison and school reform. Mott and Elizabeth Cady Stanton helped organize the Women's Rights Convention in Seneca Falls, New York, in 1848. The convention called for women's suffrage and issued a statement proclaiming, "all men and women are created equal." After the Civil War, Mott worked tirelessly for African American suffrage.

Napoleonic Wars (1804-1815): The "second phase" of the wars of the French Revolution, which were referred to as the "Napoleonic Wars" after Napoleon Bonaparte had seized control of the French government in a coup and eventually became "emperor of the French" (1804) and thus France's conflicts with the rest of the European powers from 1805 on became known as the Napoleonic Wars.

National Republicans: Those Jeffersonian Republics who became neo-Federalist in the years after the end of the War of 1812. By 1824 presidential election, it had become clear that the Republican consensus had factionalized; that the "party" had split into two increasingly hostile factions, the neo-Federalist "National Republicans" and those who remained loyal to Jeffersonian agrarianism, the Republicans.

National Union Party: A third-party coalition formed by conservative Republicans, northern Democrats, and other Unionists to represent a compromise between the Radical Republicans and the Democrats while supporting Andrew Johnson's policies.

National Women's Loyal League: A pro-Union organization formed during the Civil War on May 14, 1863 by Susan B. Anthony and Elizabeth Cady Stanton that lobbied for an amendment to the United States Constitution that would abolish slavery in all U.S. states and territories. Women suffragists dominated the group. They set aside their battle for women's equality to focus on abolition and they collected the signatures of 400,000 Americans urging passage of an anti-slavery amendment. In 1865 the Thirteenth Amendment, which abolished slavery, was enacted. With the amendment's passage, the league disbanded, and women, armed with valuable experience in organizational planning and public speaking, returned to the battle for suffrage. The League considered its work successfully completed with the ratification of the Thirteenth Amendment, which abolished slavery, in December 1865.

Navigation Acts: A series of trade regulation measures, passed by Parliament beginning in 1660, to be applied to England's overseas colonies designed to enforce mercantile policies. Acts were formulated to ensure that all colonial trade benefited England at all times, mandating, for example, that all colonial goods be shipped on English-made ships manned by three-fourths English sailors. Acts also stipulated that certain colonial goods, "enumerated" goods, must go directly to England, such as timber, naval stores, tobacco, and sugar.

Negro Act: Passed by Carolina slaveowners in the aftermath of the Stono Rebellion, which decreed that blacks were to henceforth have minimal interaction with other Carolina slaves; they could possess firearms, earn money or become literate. Such restrictions were designed to prevent future insurrections, at least in the mind of Carolina planters/slaveowners.

Neo-Federalist: Those post-war political leaders such as Henry Clay, who were Jeffersonian Republicans but because of the revelations the war brought about the nation's economic underdevelopment, many former Republicans morphed into what were called "neo-Federalist" because they embraced Hamiltonian ideas relative to government participation in the nation's development.

New Departure: A coalition movement by moderate and liberal southern whites in the late 1860s to find a middle ground between white backlash extremism and the Radical Republicans supposed agenda of black equality. New Departure advocates believed in treating freedmen fairly, decently, and enfranchising them as well. They nonetheless remained white supremacists.

New Lights: Those colonial Protestant ministers who embrace the theology and evangelism of the Great Awakening, insisting that they were not challenging the fundamental of Calvinist or Puritan orthodoxy but rather opening up the potential for salvation to all mankind. New Lights also maintained that formal seminary training in Protestant theology was not necessary to spread God's work and redemption.

New Orleans, Battle of (January 1815): A decisive American War of 1812 victory over British troops in January 1815 that ended British hopes of gaining control of the lower Mississippi.

New York City Draft Riots of 1863: A mostly Irish-immigrant protest against conscription in New York in July 1863 that escalated into a racial riot that had to be quelled by federal troops.

Newburgh Conspiracy: An abortive plot by officers in the Continental Army in 1783 to overthrow the Confederation Congress and establish a military government headed by George Washington or, if he refused, General Horatio Gates, if promised bonuses were not paid.

Non-Intercourse Act (1809): Before leaving office, Jefferson repealed the precipitous Embargo Act, replacing the measure with the Non-Intercourse Act, which allowed US to resume trade with all nations but England and France. If, however, those two nations rescinded their edicts against US shipping, the US would resume trade with them as well.

North, Lord Frederick (1732-1792): A British Prime Minister deeply loyal to King George III and serving before and during the American Revolution (1775-1783). A personal friend of the king, Lord North tried unsuccessfully to be a moderating influence as tensions between the British government and the American colonists escalated in the early 1770s.

Nullification Crisis: A conflict between South Carolina's political leadership and President Andrew Jackson over a tariff law, which went into effect in 1832, imposing taxes on foreign-made goods.

Oberlin College: The first American college or university to admit women and African Americans.

Oglethorpe, James: Georgia's philanthropic/humanitarian proprietor/founder who convinced George II to establish a colony between Spanish Florida and the Carolinas that would not only serve as a buffer between the two empires but also to become a place of refuge for England's poor; put export them and put them to work rather than in prison. Oglethorpe also hoped his colony would become a "mission" to proselytize the Protestant faith among the Indians and slaves.

Ohio Company: A private company owned and financed by wealthy Virginia planters, among them George Washington, who wanted to acquire the Ohio River Valley area for both tobacco cultivation and land speculation, as well as to penetrate the lucrative Indian fur trade of the region.

Old Lights: Name given to those conservative members of colonial Protestant sects opposed to the Great Awakening, its message of salvation open to all and they were especially contemptuous of the evangelical style of preaching.

Olive Branch Petition: Written largely by John Dickinson declaring the unchanging loyalty of the American colonists to the king, but demanded that the Parliament cease what the Congress saw as oppressive measures like the so-called "Intolerable Acts." The king never responded to the petition.

Olmsted, Frederick Law (1822-1903): A journalist also considered the founder of American landscape architecture who designed many important American outdoor sites His 1857 book, *Journey Through Texas*, revealed the harshness and cruelty of the "peculiar institution" and the deep class division in that state before the Civil War.

Oneida Community: A utopian settlement established in 1848 by socialist John Humphrey Noyes and his followers in upstate New York.

Opechancanough: Powhatan's brother who succeeded Powhatan as chief of the Algonquian Confederacy, and who was determined to rid the Chesapeake of the English menace.

Orders in Council: British decrees authorizing the British navy to seize any foreign ships attempting to trade with French, which resulted in the seizure of scores of US merchant ships caught trading with French West Indian possessions. Suffice to say US merchant ship owners as well as the Washington administration were outraged by such illegal actions.

Osceola (1804?-1838): A military leader of both white and Native Americans who directed the resistance of the Seminole Indians during the Second Seminole War (1835-1842) to the U.S. Army's attempts to remove that people from their land in Florida.

Ostend Manifesto: A proposal by American diplomats stationed in Europe to acquire Cuba, by purchase or conquest, to provide more territory for the United States.

Otis, James, Jr. 1725-1783): A Massachusetts politician and lawyer and an early advocate of American independence who coined the phrase, "Taxation without Representation is Tyranny," which became a rallying cry of the American resistance to British authorities in the 1760s and 1770s.

Owen, Robert (1771-1858): A Welsh drapes manufacturer who tried to end some of the worst excesses of the Industrial Revolution, including limiting child labor to only those age 10 and older, limiting working hours for the older children, and providing them an education. He established a commune called New Harmony in Indiana.

Paine, Thomas (1737-1809): Radical pamphleteer and author of *Common Sense*, advocate of American independence and supporter of the French Revolution.

Panic of 1819: The first "depression" in American economic history caused by the decline of European demand for American goods in the aftermath of the Napoleonic Wars.

Panic of 1837: An economic crisis caused by loosely regulated state banks and reckless land speculation that sparked a major recession.

Parochial schools: Church-sponsored schools opened as an alternative to public education, particularly by Catholics as early as the 1700s.

Patent medicines: Originally referring to 18th- and 19th-century medicines whose manufacturers had obtained patents, the term came to refer to concoctions containing vegetable extracts, various narcotics, and alcohol. By the end of the 19th century, state and federal laws like the Pure Food and Drug Act (1906) put an end to such products by requiring labeling of ingredients and banning claims that could not be verified.

Paternalism: Term used by historians to describe the changed relations of the master-slave beginning in the 1820s. Postwar slaveowners believed that if they treated the slaves with a modicum of decency and respect for their humanity that they would be more "cooperative" and thus more productive laborers. Thus beginning in the 1820s slave life improved materially and physically—better food, clothing, free time, etc. which slave holders believed would also create "happier," less recalcitrant slaves. Slaves became part of their owners' "families," which required a more solicitous attitude and treatment of slaves.

Paul, Francois Joseph, Comte de Grasse (1722-1788): Admiral who led the French naval forces in the decisive Battle of the Chesapeake that helped seal off one of British General Charles Cornwallis' escape routes for the decisive Battle of Yorktown that ended the American Revolution.

Penn, William: A former aristocrat and son of one of England's most decorated naval heroes, Penn converted to the Quaker faith in 1667 and emerged as one of the faith's most important leaders after Fox. Because of his court connections, Penn was able to obtain from Charles II a charter to establish a colony in North America to be a refuge for his persecuted Quaker brethren. Penn received the most generous charter in English colonial history; an expanse of territory larger than England.

Peggy Eaton Affair: The daughter of a Washington tavern owner, Margaret O'Neall Timberlake "Peggy" Eaton (1799-1879) played a central role in a sex scandal during the administration of Andrew Jackson in 1829. She had been married to a sailor named John Timberlake, and rumors started that during his many lengthy trips at sea she had cheated on him, driving Timberlake to suicide. She soon married Senator John Eaton of Tennessee, a close friend of President Jackson. Jackson named Eaton his secretary of war. Her scandalous background led the other Cabinet wives, led by Vice President John C. Calhoun's spouse, Floride, to shun her.

Pendleton Act: One of the most broad-sweeping reform measures of the federal government's civil service system, passed in 1883, which established the modern procedure for positions within the federal bureaucracy.

Peninsula Campaign: A failed northern offensive during the Civil War, launched in 1862. Union General George McClellan proposed to reach the Confederate capital of Richmond through bypassing the southern defenders entrenched in northern Virginia. According to his plan, Navy ships would transport more than 100,000 Union soldiers to Urbana on the Rappahannock River.

Pequot War: First in a series of conflicts between Puritan New Englanders and their Native American neighbors. Puritan militia slaughtered over 400 innocent Pequot women, children and old men in this "war." Even the Puritans Indian allies were shocked by the Englishmen's ferocious brutality in annihilating the Pequot.

Perry, Commodore Oliver Hazard: Commander of U.S. naval forces on the Great Lakes, who secured the lakes for the U.S. by defeating a British fleet at Put-In Bay in September 1813. Control of Lake Erie prevented the British from supplying their troops in the Northwest.

Petersburg, Siege of: A Civil War battle fought from June 9, 1864 to March 25, 1865 which involved the extensive use of trench warfare to the east and the south of Petersburg, Virginia. Lee finally withdrew his troops and abandoned both Petersburg and Richmond, leading to his attempt to unite his troops with other southern forces in North Carolina, which ended with his surrender to General Grant at Appomattox Courthouse.

Philipsburg Proclamation: An announcement of British policy relating to slaves in the South, issued on June 30, 1779, by General Sir Henry Clinton, the British commander, as part of his preparations for the campaign to reconquer the southern states. Clinton proclaimed that loyal subjects of the King could keep their slaves, but that slaves taken from owners who were participating in the rebellion would be sold off—and that slaves escaping from rebel owners would serve in the British army.

Philosophes: The name assumed by the Enlightenment's intellectual creators and followers.

Phrenology: A pseudo-science popular in the early 19th century based on the idea that various "organs" within the brain housed different "faculties" such as creativity or aggression and that these organs were located underneath the scalp. Their relative sizes caused the unique bumps that mark a person's head. A trained phrenologist supposedly could tell how intelligent, honest or reliable a person was by massaging the skull and interpreting its topography.

Pierce, Franklin (1804-1869): A New Hampshire politician who served as president from 1853 to 1857. Support for the South—especially the Ostend Manifesto and the Kansas-Nebraska Act—marked his presidency, and Pierce became distinguished as a "northern man with southern principles" by his critics.

Pinckney's Treaty (1795): The United States secured a favorable treaty with Spain relative to American neutrality (which Spain recognized), the U.S.-Florida border, American settlement of the old Southwest, and perhaps most important, American right to navigate the Mississippi River and the right of deposit at New Orleans of American goods for transshipment.

Pitt, William: One of England's great prime ministers, who took charge of his majesty's government and war effort in 1757, completely changing the British war focus and ultimately bringing victory and the greatest empire in world history to Great Britain. Pitt believed ultimate British victory would result in defeating the French where they were the weakest: in their colonial possessions world-wide.

Pizarro, Francisco: Spanish conquistador who subdued the Inca empire.

Planters: An individual owning a plantation was known as a planter. Planters comprised only 12 percent of slave owners, but held over half of the slaves in the region.

Popular Sovereignty: An alternative to the Wilmot Proviso asserting that settlers in the federal territory should decide whether a territory should be open or closed to slavery. The most prominent proponents of this position were Senators Lewis Cass and Stephen Douglas.

Powhatan: Leader of the indigenous Algonquian tribes that lived in the Chesapeake area and who had formed a large Indian confederacy to keep other tribes out of the area. Powhatan hoped to form a trading partnership and possible military alliance with the English at Jamestown. Smith was receptive to such arrangements.

Praying Towns: Name given to those Indian communities whose inhabitants had converted to Christianity and thus were to be exempt or protected from Puritan reprisals. Very few Puritans, even among the clergy, believed in "saving" the Indians of the region; most wanted to wipe them away.

Presidential Reconstruction: The period from 1863 to 1866 which saw the executive branch rather than Congress was responsible for Reconstruction of the South at the end of the Civil War.

Predestination: The Calvinist/Puritan tenet (indeed, perhaps the essence of Calvinism) that God had predetermined every soul for either salvation or damnation, and that there was nothing the individual could do to change God's mind.

Princeton, Battle of (January 3, 1777): Clash between the Continental Army and British units in and around Princeton, New Jersey resulting in a minor American victory. Washington's triumph at the Battle of Princeton further demonstrated the Continental Army's abilities and reinforced the impact of the Battle of Trenton on patriot morale.

Property Qualifications: Up to the 1820s, most states in the union extended the right to vote and to hold elective office to only those native-born or naturalized white men 21 and older who owned a certain amount of property or paid a certain amount of taxes.

Public Credit Act: Law passed in 1869 that allowed for the redemption of all government bonds in gold, while pledging to bring greenbacks (paper currency) on par with gold as well.

Puritans: One of the most important and largest groups of English migrants coming to North America in the 17th century, whose proved to be pivotal in the shaping of the American creed.

Quakers (The Society of Friends): Perhaps the most radical Protestant sect to emerge in Reformation/Civil War England. Founded by George Fox in the 1640s, Quakers believed more in a way of living in the temporal world than in any specific religious doctrine. For their "strange" beliefs, the Quakers became, along with English Catholics, one of the most proscribed Christian sects in English history.

Quantrill, William (1837-1865): The leader of a lethal band of Confederate guerillas, before the Civil War, Quantrill had alternated between working as a schoolteacher and life as a gambler, horse thief and murderer. His band, known as "Quantrill's Raiders," numbered no more than a dozen men who assassinated and robbed Union troops and Northern sympathizers along the Missouri-Kansas state line.

Queenston Heights, Battle of: No sooner did the War of 1812 begin (June of that year) than the War Hawk vision of invading and conquering Canada was implemented. All attempts at taking Canada away from Great Britain were dashed, as the British army, Canadian militia and their Indian allies defeated all U.S. invasion attempts.

Race-baiting: Politicians use of race as a campaign issue, exploiting white racism and fear of black equality.

Radicals Republicans: Opposed to President Abraham Lincoln and Andrew Johnson's Reconstruction policies from 1863-1868. The Radicals believed the South should be punished for their "treason" and that the freedmen should become full-fledged United States citizens and their new status protected by the federal government.

Raleigh, Sir Walter: Sir Humphrey Gilbert's stepbrother who attempted to establish an English colony at Roanoke Island, off the coast of modern North Carolina.

Randolph, Edmund (1753-1813): Virginia politician who, at the 1787 Constitutional Convention, proposed the so-called "Virginia" or "large state" plan for organizing a new United States Congress. A peculiar oversight marked Randolph's "Virginia Plan": he didn't call for giving the Congress the power to impose and collect taxes, perhaps the most serious flaw in the Articles. Randolph refused to sign the Constitution, however, because he feared that the presidency had been given too much power.

Reconstruction Acts of 1867: Represented the end of Presidential Reconstruction and the beginning of Congressional or Radical Reconstruction. These laws restarted the political process in the South, with the 10 unreconstructed southern states divided into five military districts administered by Army generals.

"Red Sticks": Creek Indian prophets who allied with Tecumseh and believed in his Pan-Indian movement as the best way to hold off white America from taking over the lands and destroying the Native American way of life.

Redemptioners: A quasi-form of indentured servant whereby passage to America was paid by someone upon arrival, and the individual thus became "bonded" to the payee until the passage was paid. If the emigrant could not find such a sponsor, then he was auctioned off to become an indentured servant, to the highest bidder.

Reformation: a religious upheaval during the 1500s that shattered the religious unity of Europe.

Renaissance: a flowering of knowledge in the fourteenth and fifteenth centuries that led to development of new technology important in overseas navigation and exploration.

Republican agrarianism: The essence of Jeffersonian ideology which maintained that if Americans hoped to retain the republican ideal of democracy and public virtue, then it was imperative for the United States to remain a nation of independent yeoman farmers and rural communities; the antithesis of the Hamiltonian vision.

Republican Party: A political organization that emerged in response to a growing belief among antebellum northerners that the federal government and Democratic party had been captured by a politicians who wanted to force the expansion of slavery throughout the United States. The party focused on the non-extension of slavery in the 1850s and on keeping the South in the Union in the 1860s.

Restoration: Period in English history when the monarchy in the form of Charles II (Stuart) returned but Parliament made it clear that henceforth the king would rule with Parliament and that autocracy or absolutism had died with his father on the scaffold in 1649. Charles' reign (the Restoration) saw England expand in North American with the establishing of colonies in the uninhabited area between Virginia and New England; the "Middle Colonies" of New York, Pennsylvania, Delaware, and New Jersey.

Revolution of 1800: Jefferson's triumph in the 1800 election, which many Americans hailed as a moment of redemption for democratic republican government; that now the "spirit of 1776" would be made real and that the despotism of the Federalists was over and power returned to where it rightfully belonged, to the people.

Revolutions of 1848: The wave of liberal and radical political uprisings, also known as "the spring of nations," that began in Italy and France and swept across the European continent in 1848.

Rhode Island: Colony founded by Williams and his followers in 1644. Colony gained a reputation in New England as a refuge for dissenters and other unwanted individuals from the area's other colonies. Ironically Rhode Island helped the mainstream Puritan colonies to maintain their orthodoxy by providing a "dumping ground" for their nonconformists.

Rhode Island System: Early manufacturing capitalists such as Slater wanted to avoid being stigmatized by the Jeffersonians of creating horrible factory towns rife with poverty, blight, and class tensions. So, Slater and other early industrialists moved their operations to rural areas, creating "factory villages" which employed local farm women and children or providing outwork to such individuals. At the same time Slater and others rented land to local farmers for them to provide food for their factory workers.

Ross, John (1790-1866): The leader of the Cherokee people beginning in 1827 who tried to assimilate his people to white culture as a means of preserving his nation's land and resource rights in their native Georgia and Alabama.

Royal African Company: An English joint-stock company authorized by the Crown to engage in the African slave trade with the New World. The Crown granted the company a monopoly on the importing of slaves to all of England's New World colonies, both mainland and West Indies.

Rose, Ernestine (1810-1892): The daughter of an Orthodox rabbi, Rose, an atheist, became a follower of Robert Owen and labored for the National Women's Suffrage Association for three decades. Rose also fought for the abolition of slavery. She battled state laws that handed a wife's property over to her husband upon marriage and that gave men exclusive legal guardianship over children. In 1848, the New York state legislature extended some property rights to women.

Rush-Bagot Agreement (1817): First in a series of agreements between Great Britain and the US to establish a rapprochement after decades of fear, suspicion, and hostility. The accord recognized the Great Lakes as the natural boundaries between the US and British Canada while completely demilitarizing the lakes.

Salem Witch Trials: People were executed for being "witches," the result of the resentment and hostility that had emerged in Salem and other Massachusetts towns born of economic frustration, especially among young males, who believed their economic advancement and security (land ownership) was being stymied by widowed landowners and others. Conservative Puritan leaders believed the presence of witches reflected the sinful behavior of many community's inhabitants and thus God had allowed the devil and minions to come to that community.

Santo Domingo Affair: The attempt by the Grant administration in 1869 to annex the present-day country of the Dominican Republic.

Saratoga, Battles of (Sept. 19 and Oct. 7, 1777): The first large-scale, strategically crucial military victory of American forces over a British army. The American victory sustained the patriot cause and led directly to French intervention in the war.

"scalawags": A pejorative term given during the Reconstruction Era in the 1860s and 1870s to southern whites who had supported the Union during the Civil War and the Republican Party during Reconstruction.

Scott, Winfield (1786-1866): The commander of the United States Army during the Mexican-American War between 1846-1848. His military renown led to his nomination for president by the Whig Party in 1852, in which Democrat Franklin Pierce soundly defeated him.

Second Bank of the United States: Chartered in 1816, the Second BUS had even more direct regulatory power over the nation's fiscal and monetary policies than the original bank. The principal purpose of the Second BUS was the same as the first: to help stimulate economic growth while simultaneously stabilizing the nation's financial and monetary system.

Second Continental Congress: Delegates from the colonies that convened in May 1775 after the outbreak of fighting in Massachusetts between British and American forces.

Second Great Awakening: Series of religious revivals in the first half of the nineteenth century which showed great emotionalism in large public meetings.

Sedition Act: The other proscription measure pushed through Congress by the High Federalist to destroy the Democratic-Republican Party by denying its members the right of free speech and press to criticize the Federalist party. The act set jail terms and fines for persons who advocated disobedience to federal law or who wrote, printed, or spoke out against any person or policy of the federal government.

Seneca Falls Convention of 1848: A women's rights gathering held July 19-20, attended by Lucretia Mott, Elizabeth Cady Stanton, Frederick Douglass and other leading feminists of the mid-19th century to "discuss the social, civil and religious condition and rights of women." Stanton authored a *Declaration of Sentiments* that demanded women receive the right to vote.

Separatists: English Puritans who believed the Church of England was beyond redemption and thus to avoid its corruption, true believing Calvinists (Puritans) must separate themselves completely from its popery and Catholic sinfulness. This particular sect of Puritans left England, ultimately establishing the first Puritan colony in North America at Plymouth in present-day Massachusetts. Also became known as the Pilgrims.

Sequoyah (1770?-1843): The child of a British father and a Cherokee mother, Sequoyah reached adulthood illiterate, but in 1821 he devised a written language for the Cherokee language that uses 86 characters. The Cherokee Nation adopted Sequoyah's system, which had a character for every syllable in the language, in 1825.

Seward, William (1801-1872): A New York politician known for his strong antislavery views. He served as governor of New York and then moved on to the U.S. Senate where he would become a leading figure in the new Republican Party in the 1850s. His stature in the party led to his appointment as Secretary of State in the Lincoln administration.

Shakers: Members of the United Society of Believers in Christ's Second Appearing, a sect that split off from the Quaker religion. The name comes from the herky-jerky motions the faithful make when they are supposedly filled with the Holy Spirit.

Samuel Slater: The Englishmen who brought (stole) the blueprints of English inventor Richard Arkwright's steam-powered spinning machine for woolen and cotton textiles, to the US, which in turn stimulated the beginning of the Northeast's "industrial revolution."

Shaw, Robert Gould (1837-1863): Shaw would lead one of the most famous African-American fighting units in the Civil War (1861-1865).

Shays's Rebellion (1786-1787): An armed rebel group of debt-ridden farmers that attacked the federal arsenal at Springfield, Massachusetts But on February 2, 1787 in Petersham, Massachusetts, a militia organized by the state governor attacked and scattered the rebels. Hundreds were indicted and eighteen "ringleaders," including Shays, were sentenced to death for treason, although only two were ultimately hanged.

Sheridan, Phil (1831-1888): A Union major general during the Civil War (1861-1865) who successfully drove the Confederates out of Virginia's fertile Shenandoah Valley and destroyed farm land in an offensive in August 1864 that aimed to cut Robert E. Lee's Army of Northern Virginia from food supplies.

Sherman, William Tecumseh (1820-1891): One of the most perceptive and innovative generals in the Union Army during the Civil War, William T. Sherman embraced total war tactics during his "March to the Sea" across Georgia to the Atlantic Ocean in 1864. Sherman believed that undermining the morale of Southern civilians would be a key to Northern victory, so he directed his men to live off the land and to take food supplies from the Confederate-owned farms they seized and to destroy what couldn't be taken.

Shiloh, Battle of: A bloody defeat for the Confederacy during the Civil War on April 6-7, 1862. The Union victory opened up the path of the Union Army to northern Mississippi.

"Slave Power": A theory, most fully developed by Republicans in the 1850s, that a conspiracy of slaveholders had captured the federal government and were using its power to expand slavery into the West, and perhaps into the North.

Smalls, Robert (1839-1915): A South Carolina man who during the Civil War, as a slave, gained control of a Confederate transport steamship and piloted it successfully from Charleston to a Union port.

Smith, Adam and *The Wealth of Nations*: Smith, a member of the "Scottish Enlightenment" of the late 18th century, published in 1776, what became "the textbook" for free market capitalism. Indeed, Smith is considered "the father of capitalism."

Smith, Captain John: Member of the original 104 settlers who established Jamestown who survived the first winter and eventually took charge of the colony. The other colonists came to resent because Smith imposed a harsh regimen of work and discipline for the sake of survival. Had Smith not imposed his will, colony would have self-destructed and England might have given up on establishing a North American colony.

Smith, Joseph (1805-1844): The founder of the Church of Jesus Christ of Latter-day Saints or the Mormon religion.

Sons of Liberty: Originally called The Loyal Nine, this group of Boston merchants and artisans formed in the summer of 1765 to organize opposition to the Stamp Act.

Spiritualism: The belief that the universe is not limited to material objects and that it is possible to speak to the dead and other spirit beings. Such beliefs became faddish in the early and mid-19th century and led to Mary Todd Lincoln (1818-1882) holding séances in the White House to communicate with her deceased sons.

Spoils System: The practice of removing political opponents from positions in the federal government and replacing them with loyal party members.

Squanto and Massasoit: Pokanoket Indian leaders who forged an alliance with the Pilgrims in order to have Pilgrim assistance in freeing their tribe from Narragansett domination. The "Indians" of American mythology responsible for helping the Pilgrims survive their "starving times," and thus honored with a "thanksgiving" feast hosted by the Pilgrims in the fall of 1621, out of which emerged the mythology of the "first Thanksgiving;" a celebration of alleged red-white harmony, cooperation, and peace.

Stamp Act: A highly controversial tax passed by the British Parliament on March 22, 1765 to help the government pay down its large debt from the French and Indian War. The Stamp Act required all legal documents, newspapers, magazines, playing cards, and other printed materials be made with paper stamped in London and distributed in the colonies by tax collectors.

Stanton, Edwin (1814-1869): An Ohio politician and lawyer who served as attorney general (1860-1861) under President James Buchanan and who became secretary of war under Presidents Abraham Lincoln (1861-1865) and Andrew Johnson (1865-1869). During the Civil War (1861-1865), Stanton cleaned up much of the corruption that marked the process by which Department of War awarded contracts for military supplies.

Stanton, Elizabeth Cady (1815-1902): An abolitionist advocate of women's suffrage who was from New York, Stanton authored the "Declaration of Sentiments" adopted at the Seneca Falls Convention in 1848 that called for women to have the right to vote.

"Starving Time": Name given to the winter of 1609-1610 when 440 out of 500 Jamestown colonists died, the result of Powhatan's having cut off the colony's food supplies and killing livestock new colonists had brought over from England. The episode was so devastating that the surviving colonists (60) decided to return to England but the arrival of new emigrants convinced them to stay.

Steuben, Frederich Wilhelm Von (1730-1794): Prussian officer hired by the American Continental Army who professionalized that force, teaching them European drills, precision marching and providing discipline, during the long, bitter winter the soldiers spent in Valley Forge in the winter of 1778. The Baron also wrote a comprehensive set of training instructions and standard regulations, which was published by Congress in 1779 and served as the U.S. Army's official manual until 1812.

Stono Rebellion: A major slave insurrection among South Carolinian slaves, assisted by the Spanish promise of arms and sanctuary, against the colonies' rice planting elite. Rebellion was crushed but henceforth South Carolina rice planters enforced strict slave codes on all their bondsmen.

Strong, George Templeton (1820-1875): A lawyer, American diarist and co-founder of the Sanitary Commission, which provided nursing care for Union soldiers during the Civil War (1861-1865).

Sugar Act: A tax passed by the British Parliament April 5, 1764 in an attempt to offset the debt the British government ran up during the French and Indian War (1754-1763).

Sunset Laws: Laws passed in the 19th century in states like New Jersey, Massachusetts and Rhode Island, closing polls at sunset in order to keep workers, who worked shifts of 12 or more hours, from voting. The term also refers to provisions in laws that require a regulation, statute or agency to expire at a certain date unless reauthorized by a legislature.

Tallmadge Amendment: Proposal of New York congressmen James Tallmadge during the Missouri crisis which stipulated that upon admission as a slave state, Missouri would begin the process of gradual emancipation and that no more slaves would be allowed into the state.

Tammany Hall: The name given to a powerful, corrupt New York City political machine. William Marcy Tweed ruled over Tammany Hall, controlling the city's Democratic Party and the municipal government from behind the scenes from 1863 to 1871.

Tappan Brothers: Arthur (1786-1865) and Lewis (1788-1873) Tappan were wealthy businessmen and influential abolitionists. Making a fortune by importing silk from Asia, the Tappan Brothers funded an anti-slavery newspaper *The Emancipator* and sought to integrate churches in their native New York. Unlike many abolitionists, the Tappan brothers opposed extending political rights to women.

Tariff of 1816: The first "real" protective tariff passed in US history, which raised the duties on many foreign manufactured and raw good to 35 percent ad-valorem. Such protectionism would eventually lead to sectional discord as the South will come to oppose what it will perceive as "Yankee favoritism" by the federal government.

Tarleton, Banastre ((1754-1833): A brilliant but vicious British cavalry officer who in one infamous incident at Waxhaws, South Carolina May 29, 1780, ordered his men to cold-bloodedly kill 113 American prisoners who had surrendered. Since Tarleton had given no quarter to his defenseless prisoners, American militias would often shout "Tarleton's Quarter" when they subsequently butchered British or Loyalists troops who surrendered. .

Taylor, Susie King (1848-1912): An African-American educator in Georgia during the Civil War. The daughter of slaves, Taylor lived with her grandmother in Savannah, Ga., and received an informal education from two underground schools that violated Georgia's strict laws against educating African Americans. Union troops gained control of Georgia's Sea Islands in 1862 and Taylor escaped to St. Simon Island in April of that year. The Union Army appointed her to teach at a Freedmen's Bureau school, making her the first African American educator employed at a Georgia campus.

Tecumseh: Shawnee Indian, who along with his brother the Prophet, forged the largest Indian confederation in US history against white America. Tecumseh's efforts at promoting a Pan-Indian movement proved successful as he united all the tribes from the Great Lakes to the Gulf of Mexico along the Mississippi River Valley. To Tecumseh co-existence with whites was delusional. The British aided Tecumseh in his cause, which only fueled the War Hawk clamor for war against the British.

Telegraph: By 1836 allowed Americans to spread information across many parts of the nation almost instantaneously. The telegraph transmitted and received electrical impulses along a connected wire using a standard code

Temperance Movement: The drive, beginning in the early 19th century, to eliminate alcohol from American life. Temperance crusaders blamed alcohol abuse for poverty, workplace injuries, crime and spousal and child abuse. The temperance movement would culminate in the ratification of the 18th Amendment to the United States Constitution, implementing Prohibition nationwide, in 1920.

Tenure of Office Act of 1867: Bill passed by Radical Republican-controlled Congress designed to further strip President Andrew Johnson of his power by making it illegal for him to remove any cabinet member without Senate approval. Johnson defied the act by attempting to fire Secretary of War Edwin M. Stanton, which became the pretext for Johnson's impeachment and Senate trial in 1868.

Thames, Battle of the: October 1813 in which American General William Henry Harrison defeated Tecumseh's Indian allies and in which the Indian leader was killed, precipitating the rapid collapse of his Pan-Indian movement and confederation. Tecumseh's death proved to be a serious blow to the British, who soon lost their Indian allies from the Great Lakes down the Mississippi River valley.

Thirteenth Amendment: Ratified in December 1865, the Thirteenth Amendment prohibited slavery or any form of involuntary servitude except as punishment in the United States. President Abraham Lincoln (1861-1865) and Congressional Republicans supported this amendment because they feared that the archconservative Supreme Court might rule that Lincoln's Emancipation Proclamation was unconstitutional. President Andrew Johnson (1865-1869) made ratification of this amendment a condition for former Confederate states to be readmitted to the Union, though he proved unwilling to enforce this requirement.

Thoreau, Henry David (1817-1862): A former schoolteacher, abolitionist and philosopher. He wrote *Resistance to Civil Government or Civil Disobedience* (published in 1849) in which he argued that a moral person has an obligation to resist unjust laws.

"Three-Fifths Compromise": The key agreement worked out, in August 1787, between delegates from northern (some antislavery) states and southern (slaveholding) states, at the Constitutional Convention in Philadelphia. Three-fifths of the slave population was added to the population of free people to be used in allocating representatives by state in the lower house of Congress.

Tidewater: The coastal river areas in the South where the region's staples such as tobacco and rice were grown and where the great planters of such commodities lived.

Tories: One of the names given to Americans who remained loyal to the British crown during the War for Independence (1775-1783).

Townshend Acts: A series of taxes and other laws proposed by the British Chancellor of the Exchequer Charles Townshend in 1767 that imposed new import duties on an odd selection of goods for which colonial consumers relied on the import trade: lead, paint, glass, paper, and tea. The Townshend Duties were meant to cover salaries for royal governors and magistrates.

Townshend, Charles (1725-1767): The British Chancellor of the Exchequer from 1766-1767 whose so-called "Townshend Acts" aimed to increase the government's tax revenues from the 13 American colonies. These Acts only increased tensions between the Americans and the British government and helped pave the way to the War of Independence.

Trail of Tears: The United States government had, for years, been attempting to force Indians living in Georgia and Alabama to leave their traditional lands and relocate to territories set aside for them west of the Mississippi. The Indian Removal Act of 1830 authorized the president to carry out this ethnic cleansing. President Martin Van Buren sent a 7,000-man military force under General Winfield Scott to round up the Cherokees and prod them at bayonet point out of Georgia. Soldiers arrived during the winter of 1838 and gave Cherokees mere minutes to gather their families and possessions before they were forced to march westward. About a quarter succumbed to exposure, exhaustion and disease.

Transcendentalism: The philosophical, literary, and political movement arising in the 1830s and 1840s and exemplified by the works of Henry David Thoreau and Ralph Waldo Emerson. Transcendentalists believed in the inherent worth of every individual, opposed slavery and believed that an authentic life was one lived in harmony with nature and not concerned with the acquisition of material things.

Treaty of Alliance (1778): One of two agreements between American negotiators and the government of King Louis XVI of France, initialed in Paris on Feb. 6, 1778 (the other involving commercial ties). The Treaty of Alliance established a military alliance between France and the United States, committed the French to support "the liberty, sovereignty, and independence absolute and unlimited" of the United States, and provided that neither side would make a peace agreement with Britain without the consent of the other.

Treaty of Ghent (December 1814): City in Belgium where U.S. and British officials signed the accord ending the War of 1812.

Treaty of Greenville: Miami and Shawnee signed a treaty with the U.S. ceding two-thirds of their land to the U.S. in what is today Ohio and southeastern Indiana.

Treaty of Paris (1783): Agreement between Great Britain and the United States, signed in Paris on Sept. 3, 1783, formally ending the war and stating British recognition of American independence.

Tredegar Iron Works: A foundry in the Confederate capital of Richmond, Virginia. Opened in 1837, the Tredegar plant produced artillery, steam locomotives, the iron plating for the *Merrimac* (also known as the *Virginia*, the first ironclad ship in America), and a high-caliber, rail-mounted siege cannon.

***Trent* Affair** Britain almost declared war on the United States in 1861 when an American ship stopped a British vessel, the *Trent*, arresting and removing two Confederate diplomats, James M. Mason and John Slidell. The British government saw this as an act of aggression and a violation of its neutrality in the Civil War. Secretary of State Charles Francis Adams skillfully calmed British officials and arranged for the release of Slidell and Mason.

Trenton, Battle of (Dec. 26, 1776): Attack by Continental Army forces on the Hessian garrison at Trenton, New Jersey, resulting in a small but decisive victory that re-energized the Continental Army after a demoralizing succession of defeats and retreats. In a broader sense, it helped restore confidence in Washington's leadership and hope for the eventual success of the cause of American independence.

Trollope, Frances (1779-1863): A British writer who in 1832 authored the travelogue *Domestic Manners of the Americans*, in which she mocked Americans for their alleged vulgarity, materialism and self-righteousness, but especially for their moral hypocrisy. She also harshly critiqued the slaughter of Native Americans and the theft of their land by the United States. Her 1836 anti-slavery novel, *Jonathan Jefferson Whitlaw*, is widely considered an inspiration for Harriet Beecher Stowe's 1852 novel *Uncle Tom's Cabin*.

Truth, Sojourner (1797?-1883): A former slave, Christian evangelist, and supporter of abolition and women's rights who, after the Civil War, called for the government to distribute public land to freedmen as compensation for their unpaid labor under slavery. She also preached against the death penalty.

Turner, Nat (1800-1831): The leader of a major slave revolt in Southhampton County, Virginia, in August 1831.

Tubman, Harriet (1820-1913): An escaped slave who became a leading abolitionist, a "conductor" on the Underground Railroad, and a spy for the Union during the Civil War (1861-1865). After the war, she battled for African-American voting rights and for women's suffrage and used the funds from an 1869 authorized biography, *Scenes from the Life of Harriet Tubman*, to establish the Harriet Tubman Home for the poor.

***Uncle Tom's Cabin*:** An antislavery novel written by Harriet Beecher Stowe in 1852. The novel sold enormously well and helped distribute abolitionist arguments beyond the ranks of the already converted.

Underground Railroad: A secret network of abolitionists, free blacks and escaped slaves who assisted African Americans escaping bondage in the South 1840s and 1850s. "Conductors" directed slaves to safe houses where they could eat, rest and hide from slave patrols, and provided them disguises and the quickest routes to free territory.

United States Sanitary Commission: A private relief agency, commissioned by the United States Congress during the Civil War and directed by author and landscape architect Frederick Law Olmsted that provided nursing, medical supplies, clothing, and food to soldiers and their families.

Valley Forge: Site in eastern Pennsylvania, roughly 30 miles from Philadelphia, selected by General Washington for the Continental Army's winter quarters in 1777-1778, and re-membered from then on for the suffering of soldiers during the winter. Diseases common to military camps—such as typhoid and dysentery—killed hundreds of weakened men. Ultimately Valley Forge became a symbol of perseverance as well as suffering, but the army endured many of the same problems each winter for the rest of the war.

Van Buren, Martin (1782-1862): A New York politician and the most important organizer of the Democratic Party in the 1830s. He became President Andrew Jackson's must trusted political advisor. He served as secretary of state and as vice president (during Jackson's second term) before winning election as president in 1836.

Vesey, Denmark (1767?-1822): A former slave in South Carolina who led a major slave revolt in Charleston, South Carolina in 1822. Eventually authorities arrested 131 slaves for complicity in the plot, with 67 convicted and 35 hanged, including Vesey on July 2, 1822.

Vicksburg, Siege of: A military engagement, from May 18-July 4, 1863, considered a major turning point in the Civil War, that allowed Union Gen. Ulysses S. Grant to split the Confederacy in half and to give the North control of the Mississippi River.

Vikings: people from Scandinavia led by Leif Erickson who established colonies in Canada long before Columbus "discovered" the New World.

Virginia Resolves: Resolutions authored in 1765 by Patrick Henry, a member of the state's House of Burgesses, that denounced the Stamp Act, a law imposed by the British Parliament.

"Virginia Dynasty": The phrase used to describe the succession of presidents from Virginia. Four out the nation's first five presidents were all Virginians, the only exception being John Adams and then his son John Quincy Adams, both of whom hailed from Massachusetts. Most important, was the fact that throughout the antebellum period the South dominated White House, beginning with the "Virginia Dynasty."

Voltaire: Perhaps the most famous and legendary of the Enlightenment philosophes, whose books, essay, satires, and writings on the excesses and abuses of monarchial power and the repressive doctrines of orthodox Christianity were the most harmful to human progress and decency.

Wade-Davis Bill: The Radical Republicans' counter-proposal to President Abraham Lincoln's "10 percent plan." Lincoln's plan would have allowed a former Confederate state to be eligible for readmission to the Union once 10 percent of the number of voters in that state who participated in the 1860 presidential election swore loyalty to the Union. The Radicals' proposal called for all southern whites to take an "iron-clad" oath that they had never taken up arms against the United States government before they would be eligible to vote or hold office. The Radicals also proposed requiring 50 percent of a state's white population to swear their allegiance to the United States before that state would be eligible for re-admission.

Walker, David (1785-1830): An African American abolitionist who in 1829 published his anti-slavery pamphlet *Appeal to the Colored Citizens of the World*, a document that called for African American slaves to use any method, including violence, to win their freedom. Walker also harshly criticized the American Colonization Society, which advocated relocating freed American slaves to Africa. "America is more our country than it is the whites' -- we have enriched it with our blood and tears," Walker wrote.

Walker, Mary (1832-1919): An abolitionist, temperance advocate and campaigner for women's suffrage who served as a surgeon and alleged spy for the Union during the Civil War and became the only woman to date to receive the Congressional Medal of Honor.

Waltham System: Labor system/force used by the Boston Associates in their various factory towns. Lowell and company used exclusively young, single, rural women as their principal workforce.

War Hawks: Name given to those Congressmen, primarily from the South and West, who agitated for war against Great Britain to uphold national honor.

Washington, George (1732-1799): The commander of the American Continental Army during the Revolutionary War and the first president of the United States. Washington participated in the First and Second Continental Congresses, which aimed to coordinate resistance to British tax policies in all of the colonies. He vigorously supported the Constitution's ratification, which took place by 1789. He was elected president unanimously and took office April 30, 1789.

Webster, Daniel (1782-1852): Member of the United States House, senator and secretary of state under presidents William Henry Harrison, John Tyler and Millard Fillmore, Webster ran three unsuccessful campaigns for president in the first half of the 19th century.

Webster, Noah (1758-1843): A lexicographer who produced in 1806 *A Compendious Dictionary of the English Language*, the first American dictionary.

Whig Party: Followers of President Andrew Jackson (served 1829-1837) formed the modern Democratic Party by the 1832 White House race, holding national conventions, and adopting positions on specific issues. By the middle of the decade, Jackson's opponents, including Daniel Webster and Henry Clay, formed an opposition coalition that came to be known as the Whig Party.

Whiskey Rebellion: A 1794 uprising among western Pennsylvania farmers against Hamilton's excise tax on "spirits," which they believed to be "illegal."

White backlash: The refusal of southern whites during the Reconstruction Era from 1863-1877 to accept the defeat of the Confederacy, the end of slavery, black equality, and federal occupation. Also refers to the violent insurgency of some southern whites against Reconstruction policies through groups like the Ku Klux Klan.

Whitefield, George: Evangelical English disciple of Methodism founder John Wesley, who came to the colonies to preach a similar message to that of Edwards; that the ability to be saved was now an individual matter and that God no longer predestined your ultimate fate. Evangelical preachers such as Whitefield and Edwards found their greatest audiences among the colonies' lower classes.

Whitman, Walt (1819-1892): A notable journalist and poet from New York whose 1855 collection of poems, *Leaves of Grass*, shocked contemporary readers with its frank celebration of the human body and sexuality. His use of free verse in poetry was considered innovative.

Willard, Emma (1787-1870): A teacher who promoted female education, Willard headed an academy for women in Vermont before establishing her own school for girls in Troy, New York in 1821. Willard believed that girls needed the same well-rounded education given boys, including courses in science and math.

Williams, Roger: The first among several dissenters who emerged within the first decade of the Puritans' presence in New England. Williams, a minister, had been a "closet" Separatist, whose true sentiments emerged after coming to Massachusetts. He began preaching his "heresy," which challenged, on a variety of levels, the colony's quasi-theocratic structure. Most disturbing to the colony's governors and elders was Williams' advocacy of religious toleration and the separation of church and state.

Wilmot Proviso: A rider to an appropriations bill proposed by Representative David Wilmot of Pennsylvania at the beginning of the Mexican-American War. The Proviso stated that any territory acquired from Mexico should be closed to slavery. The proposal reopened sectional conflict.

Winthrop, John: Leader of the Massachusetts Bay colony and responsible for holding the saints together through some very challenging early years. Winthrop was governor from the moment the Puritans sailed until his death in 1649.

Worcester v. Georgia (1832): A case filed by the Rev. Samuel Worcester, in which the United States Supreme Court vacated the conviction of Samuel Worcester and held that the Georgia criminal statute that prohibited non-Indians from being present on Indian lands without a license from the state was unconstitutional.

XYZ Affair: Adams's attempt at negotiation resulted in the "XYZ Affair" as the insult to the U.S. was called after French officials attempted to extort $250,000 from the U.S. before France would even begin discussion. The U.S. emissaries refused to pay, feeling insulted and returned home.

Yancey, William (1814-1863): An Alabama politician, member of the United States House of Representatives and then, during the Civil War, a member of the Confederate Senate, William Yancey became the most vociferous of the so-called "fire-eaters," pro-slavery extremists who advocated the secession of Southern states from the Union.

Yorktown, Siege of (Sept. 28-Oct. 19, 1781): The decisive military engagement of the war in the South, which led directly to the British decision to accept the independence of the United States. The loss of Cornwallis' army of some 7,000 men was the final blow to the British war effort in North America.

Young, Brigham (1801-1877): An early convert to Mormonism in 1823, Young acted as a missionary for the Church of Jesus Christ of Latter-day Saints. By 1841, he ranked second in authority within the church only to the founder of Mormonism, Joseph Smith.

Index

A

Abolitionists, 373
Absolutism, 77
Act of Toleration, 40
Adams, Abigail, 161
Adams, Charles Francis, 440
Adams, John, 153, 158, 159, 210, 243
    as vice president, 228
    election of 1796, 243
Adams, John Quincy,
    appeal for Amistad Africans, 374, 392
    defense of Jackson, 312
    election of 1824, 311
    gag rule, 373
    Secretary of State, 294, 297
Adams-Onís Treaty of 1819, 295
Adams, Samuel, 152, 155, 157
Adena Indians, 5
African Methodist Episcopal Church, 219, 349
Alabama, 501
Alamo, 386
Alaska, 502, 503
Albany Plan of Union, 133
Albermarle Sound, 61
Algonquians, 7-8, 34, 93
Alien Acts, 245
Allen, Ethan, 159, 173
Allison, Jonathan M., 431
Ambrister, Robert, 312
Amendment,
    Fifteenth, 496–498, 503, 506, 507
    First, 245, 373
    Fourteenth, 485, 487, 493, 497, 503
    Ninth, 230
    Second, 230
    Tenth, 230, 245
    Third, 230
    Thirteenth, 164, 480
    Twelfth, 218, 243, 312, 327
American Anti-Slavery Society, 372, 374, 376
American Colonization Society, 372
American Female Moral Reform Society, 363
American Prohibitory Act, 160
American Red Cross, 454
American Renaissance, 367
American system of manufacturing, 278-280, 347
Amistad, 374, 392
Ampudia, Pedro de, 396
Anaconda Plan, 439, 440
Anderson, Robert, 432, 433
Andersonville, 452
André, Major John, 192
Andros, Edmund, 105
Anglo-Powhatan War, 38

Annapolis Convention, 210
Anthony, Susan B., 377-378
Antietam, Battle of, 447
Anti-federalists, 215
Antigua, 41
Anti-Masonic Party, 323
Anti-slavery movement, 371–372
Appomattox Court House, 464
Arbuthnot, Alexander, 312
Arista, Mariano, 395
Arkwright, Richard, 285
Army of the Potomac, 442
Arnold, Benedict, 159, 186, 192
Articles of Confederation, 206
Astor, John Jacob, 253
Atahualpa, 19
Atlanta, Battle of, 462
Attucks, Crispus, 153
Atzerodt, George, 478
Austerlitz, Battle of, 263
Austin, Moses, 296
Austin, Stephen F., 296
Aztec civilization, 3-4

B

Babcock, Orville, 498, 500
Backus, Isaac, 127
Bacon, Nathaniel, 45
Bacon's Rebellion, 44, 120
Baez, Bonaventura, 500
Balboa, Vasco Nuñez de, 18
Ballinger, William Pitt, 492
Baltimore and Ohio (B&O), 345
Bank of the United States, 233
Barbados, 41, 58
Barbary Pirates, 263
Barnburner, 409
Barnum, P.T., 351
Barracoons, 52
Barrow, Bennet H., 290
Barton, Clara, 454
Baseball, 342
Batts, Nathaniel, 61
Bear Flag Revolt, 395
Beauregard, P.T.G., 441, 444
Beaver Wars, 93
Beckley, John, 243
Beecher, Henry Ward, 418
Belknap, William, 498
Bell, John, 425
Benevolent Empire, 362
Benton, Thomas Hart, 309
Bentonville, Battle of, 463
Berkeley, Lord John, 94
Berkeley, Sir William, 45
Bernard, Governor Francis, 150
Biddle, Nicholas, 324
Bill of Rights, 217, 230
Binn, John, 316
Bioterrorism, 466
Birney, James G., 373
Blackbeard, 62
Black codes, 481

Black Death, 9
Black Republicans, 474
Blackwell, Captain John, 100
Blackwell, Elizabeth, 378
Bladensburg, Battle of, 270
Blair, Frank, 495
Bleeding Kansas, 418
Blithedale Romance (Hawthorne), 368
Bloomer, Amelia, 378
Bonaparte, Napoleon, 255
Bonnet, Stede, 62
Boone, Daniel, 210
Booth, John Wilkes, 467, 478
Border Ruffians, 418
Boston Manufacturing Company, 285
Boston Port Act, 155
Boston's Quincy Market, 289
Boston Tea Party, 155
Boutwell, George, 499
Bowdoin, Governor James, 209
Bowleg's Town, 312
Boyd, Belle, 455
Boylston, Dr. Zabdiel, 123
Braddock, Edward, 134
Bradford, William, 78
Brahmins family, 287
Brandenburg Stone, 14
Brandywine Creek, Battle of, 187
Brant, Mohawk Joseph, 190
Bray, Dr. Thomas, 63
Brazil, 50
British East India Company, 154
British Hudson Bay Company, 383
British North American Act, 502
British taxes,
    Currency Act, 148
    Declaratory Act, 152
    Townshend's Revenue Act 152
    Stamp Act, 149
    Sugar Act, 147
    Tea Act, 154
Brock, General Isaac, 269
Brodhead Letter, 495
Brook Farm, 369
Brooks Brothers, 289
Brooks, Preston, 418, 419
Brown, John, 418, 423
Brown, Moses, 285
Brown University, 127
Bubonic Plague, 9
Buchanan, James, 399, 407, 418, 432
Bucktail Faction, 314
Buena Vista, Battle of, 396, 436
Bull Run, First, Battle of, 440–441
Bull Run, Second, Battle of, 446
Bull, William, 121
Bunker Hill, 158
Burgoyne, General John, 186
Burke, Edmund, 189
Burned Over District, 323
Burnside, Ambrose, 447
Burr, Aaron, 243, 247, 254
Butler, Andrew, 419

563

Butler, Pierce, 418
Butternuts, 479

C

Cabot, John, 21
Cadamosto, Alvise da, 15
Calendar development, 4
Calhoun, John C., 267, 279, 311, 313, 319, 392, 406, 407, 410
Callendar, James, 245
Calvert, Cecilius, 40
Calvert, George, 39
Calvinism, 74
Calvin, John, 11
Cameron, Simon, 437
Canada, 502
Canals, 345
Candide (Voltaire), 124
Cane Ridge revival, 256
Caravels, 13
Caribbean islands, 41
Carib people, 20
Carleton, Sir Guy, 198
Carolina,
  beginning of, 58
  deerskin trade network, 60
  Indian slaves, 60
  indigo production, 61
  rice production, 60
Carpetbaggers, 489, 493
Carroll, Charles, 148
Carteret, Sir George, 94
Cartier, Jacques, 23
Cass, Lewis, 409
Caucus (Boston), 149
Cayugas, 7
Cayuses, 384
Central Pacific Railroad, 504
Champlain, Samuel de, 23
Chancellorsville, Battle of, 456
Charles II (King of Spain), 130
Chase, Salmon, 416, 417, 424, 436
Chase, Samuel, 259
Cheavis, Langdon, 310
Cherokee Indians, 2, 7, 239
  written language, 330
Chesapeake,
  colonies, founding of, 32
  indentured servants, 43
  slavery beginning of, 44
  tobacco planters, 43–45
Chestnut, Mary, 354
Cheyenne Indians, 3
Chichimec people, 20
Chickamauga, Battle of, 458
Chickasaw Indians, 7
Chin, Julia, 327
Choctaw, 7, 239
Church of England, 11
Cinque, Joseph, 392
Citizens: A Chronicle of the French Revolution (Schama), 179
Civil Disobedience (Thoreau), 368

Civilizations,
  Adena, 5
  Aztecs, 3
  Hopewell, 5
  Incas, 4
  Mississippian, 5
Civil Service Reform, 499–500
Civil War,
  Anaconda Plan, 439, 440
  Andersonville prison camp, 452
  Appomattox Court House, 464
  Army of the Potomac, 442
  Battle of Atlanta, 462
  Battle of Antietam, 447
  Battle of Bentonville, 463
  Battle of Buena Vista, 436
  Battle of Bull Run, First, 440–441
  Battle of Bull Run, Second, 446
  Battle of Chancellorsville, 456
  Battle of Chickamauga, 458
  Battles of Cowpens, 193
  Battle of Fredericksburg, 447, 456
  Battle of Gettysburg, 457
  Battle of Kennesaw Mountain, 461
  Battle of Spotsylvania Court House, 459
  Battle of the Wilderness, 459
  contrabands, 450
  Emancipation Proclamation, 451
  Fort Donelson, 443
  Fort Henry, 443
  Fort Pillow Massacre, 451
  King Cotton Diplomacy, 438
  March to the Sea, 462
  northern advantages, 434
  Pickett's Charge, 457
  southern advantages, 434
  Winfield Scott, 439
Clarendon Code, 97
Clark, George Rogers, 190
Clark, William, 262
Clay, Henry, 267, 278, 299, 311, 314, 391, 397, 313
  American Colonization Society, 372
Clermont (steamboat), 280
Clinton, DeWitt, 271, 281, 323
Clinton, General Henry, 189
Clinton, George, 239
Clipper ships, 345
Clovis, discovery of, 3
Coahuila y Tejas, 386
Coercive Acts, 155
Colfax Massacre, 503
Colfax, Schuyler, 498
Colleton, Sir John, 58
Colonies,
  economy of, 118
  Great Awakening, 124–125
  immigration in, 119–120
  indentured servitude, 119
  King William's War, 130
  Negro Act, 122
  Proclamation of 1763, 138
  Rationalism thought of, 123

  Redemptioners, 119
  Security Act, 121
  Stono Rebellion, 121
  War of the Spanish Succession, 130
Columbian Exchange, 24
Columbia University, 129
Columbus, Christopher, 1, 15
Comanche, 384
Committees of safety, 156
Common property doctrine, 407
Common Sense (Paine), 145, 161
Communitarians, 369
Compass, invention of, 12
Compromise Tariff of 1833, 323
Conciliatory Proposition, 172
Conduct Unbecoming: Gays and Lesbians in the U.S. Military (Shilts), 170
Confederate States of America, 432-440
Congregationalists, 371
Connecticut Compromise, 213
Conquistadors, 18
Conscience Whigs, 410, 499
Conscription, 437
Constitutional Convention, 211
Constitutional Union Party, 425
Continental Army, 159
Contrabands, 450
Convention of 1818, 295
Convention of Free People of Color, 375
Coode, John, 41
Cooke, Jay, 504
Cooper, Sir Anthony Ashley, 58
Copperheads, 436, 495
Corbin, Abel R., 497
Cornwallis,, Lord Charles, 175
Corps of Discovery, 262
Cotton, John, 88
Cotton press, 292
Cotton Whigs, 410
Council for the Indies, 19
Covenant Chain, 105
Cow Island, 476
Cowpens, Battles of, 193
Cox, Samuel D., 499
Crandall, Prudence, 366
Crawford, William, 311
Creek Indians, 7, 240, 269
Creek War, 310
Creoles, 20
Cricket clubs, 342
Crittenden Compromise, 432
Crittenden, John J., 432
Crockett, Davy, 309
Cromwell, Oliver, 84, 90
Cuba, 41, 415
Currency Act, 148
Curtis, Benjamin Robbins, 420, 491
Curtis, George William, 499

D

Dale, Sir Thomas, 35
Dare, Virginia, 31
d'Arouet, François-Marie (Voltaire), 124

Dartmouth, 129, 366
Dartmouth College v. Woodward (1816), 281
Davis, Henry Winter, 478
Davis, Jefferson, 424, 436
Dawes, William, 157
Deane, Silas, 179
De Bow, James, 293
"Declaration of Sentiments and Resolutions," 377
Declaratory Act, 152
Deere, John, 347
Deganawida, Chief, 7
Deism, 124
Delano, Columbus, 407
de La Warr, Lord, 34
de Leon, Alonso, 66
de León, Juan Ponce, 18
Democratic Party, beginning of, 300
Democratic Republicans, 228, 243
Deposit Act of 1836, 326
Descartes, René, 92
Deseret, state of, 370
de Vimeur, Jean-Baptiste Donatien, comte de Rochambeau 190
Dias, Dinis, 15
Dickens, Charles, 364
Dickinson, Charles, 309
Dickinson, John, 159
Dinwiddie, Robert, 133
Directory, 244
Discovery (ship), 33
Dix, Dorothea, , 365
Dominican Republic, 499
Dominion of New England, 107
Donelson, Rachel, 308
Dorchester Heights, 160
Dorr, Harbottle, 151
Douglass, Frederick, 349, 423, 450, 451, 479
  abolitionist, 374
  and women's suffrage, 378
  anti-slavery leader, 375
Douglas, Stephen, 407, 412
  denouncing Sumner, 419
Drake, Sir Francis, 22, 31, 36
Dred Scott, 491
Duane, William, 245
Dueling, 353
Dunbar, Jesse, 163
Dutch West India Company, 93
Dyer, Mary, 96

E

Early, Jubal, 461
Eaton, John H., 318
Edict of Nantes, 11
Edwards, Jonathan, 125
Elastic clause, 218
Election,
  of 1796, 243; of 1800, 247;
  of 1804, 262; of 1808, 264;
  of 1812, 271; of 1816, 294;
  of 1820, 278; of 1824, 313;
  of 1828, 315–317; of 1832, 327;
  of 1836, 327; of 1840, 391;
  of 1844, 393; of 1848, 410;
  of 1852, 413; of 1856, 419;
  of 1860, 423; of 1864, 460;
  of 1866, 486; of 1868, 494;
  of 1872, 500, 503; of 1874, 505;
  of 1876, 507
Electoral College, 218
Eliot, Reverend John, 102
Elizabethan Settlement, 74
Emancipation Proclamation, 451, 476
Embargo Act (1807), 264
Emerson, Ralph Waldo, 367– 368, 406
English Test Act of 1704, 119
Enlightenment, 122, 371
Enrollment Act of 1863, 449
Enslin, Lt. Gotthold Frederick, 171
Ericson, Leif, 13
Erie Canal, 345, 280
Erie Railroad, 497
Eries, 8
Erik the Red, 13
Essay Concerning Human Understanding (Locke), 123
Essay on the Principle of Population (Malthus), 257
Ethiopian Regiment, 160, 192
Evarts, William M., 491
Excise tax, 233, 240
Experiments and Observations on Electricity (Franklin), 123
Exploration,
  Africans,
    importation of, 23
  Dutch, 93– 95
  English, 21, 33–34, 39–41, 58–59
  France, 23, 64–68
  Netherlands, 23
  Portugal, 14
  prior to Columbus, 13
  Spanish, 33–35

F

Faithful Narrative of the Surprising Work of God, A (Edwards), 126
Fallen Timbers, 239
Farragut, David, 445
Federalist Papers, 217
Federalists, 215
Federalists Party, 237
Feminist movement, founding of, 375
Ferdinand of Aragon, 10
Ferguson, Major Patrick, 193
Fillmore, Millard, 412
Finney, Charles Grandison, 362, 372
Finn, Mike, 341
First Continental Congress, 156
Fish, Hamilton, 502
Fisk, Jim, 497– 499
Five Civilized Tribes, 329
Five Points, 343

Fletcher v. Peck (1810), 259
Flexner, James Thomas, 169
Flogging, 55
Forrest, Nathan Bedford, 451
Fort Donelson, 443
Fort Duquesne, 133
Fort Henry, 443
Fort Mims Massacre, 269
Fort Necessity, 133
Fort Niagara, 191
Fort Orange, 93
Fort Pillow Massacre, 451
Fort Snelling, 405
Fort Ticonderoga, 159
Fort Toulouse, 67
Fort Washington, 174
Founding Brothers: The Revolutionary Generation (Ellis), 221
Founding Fathers, 180
Fourier, Charles, 369
Fox, Charles James, 172
Fox, George, 95
Francis, Charles, 410
Franklin, Benjamin, 122, 124, 134, 145, 237, 197
  ambassador to France, 170, 179
Frederick II (Frederick the Great, Prussia) 136
Fredericksburg, Battle of, 447, 456
Freedmen's Bureau, 482– 485, 492
  special courts, 483
Freeman, Elizabeth, 219
Freeport Doctrine, 423
Free Society of Traders, 99
Free Soil Party, 374, 409
Frémont, John C., 395, 418, 461
French and Indian War. 132– 133
French Revolution, 237
Frieze, Jacob, 347
Frobisher, Martin, 22
Fugitive Slave Act (1850), 375
Fugitive Slave Bill, 412
Fugitive Slave Law, 432
Fulton, Robert, 280

G

Gadsden Purchase, 398
Gage, General Thomas, 155
Gag Rule, 322, 373
Gama, Vasco da, 15
Garnet, Henry Highland, 375
Garrison, William Lloyd, 213, 321
  abolitionist, 372–377
Gates, General Horatio, 186, 192
Genêt, Edmond, 238
George IIII (King), 172
Germain, George, 172
Gerry, Elbridge, 214, 244
Gettysburg, Battle of, 457
Gettysburg Address, 458
Gibbons v. Ogden (1824), 282
Giddings, Joshua, 397, 406, 416
Gilbert, Sir Humphrey, 22

566 / INDEX

Gilded Age, The (Twain and Warner), 499
Glorious Revolution, 108
Gnadenhutten Massacre, 191
Godspeed (ship), 33
Goodrich, Samuel, 248
Gordon, Thomas, 124
Goree, Jordan, 292
Gorgas, General Josiah, 434
Gould, Jay, 497–499
Granada, 15
Grant, Ulysses S., 395, 435, 442, 491, 495–497
   and civil service reform, 499
   at Appomattox, 478
   election of 1868, 494
   election of 1872, 503
   first administration, 497–499
   foreign policy issues of, 499–501
   Panic of 1873, 504
Grasse, François Joseph Paul, Marquis de Grasse-Tilly, Comte de, 195
Graves, Admiral Thomas, 195
Great Awakening, 124–126,
Great Britain's Order in Council, 263
Great Migration, 79
Great Serpent Mound, 5
Greeley, Horace, 421, 475, 504
Greenbacks, 434, 494
Greene, General Nathanael, 187, 193
Greenhow, Rose O'Neal, 455
Green, John Sitgreaves, 431
Greenland, 13
Green Mountain Boys, 159, 173
Greensted, William, 48
Grenville, Lord, 138, 147
Grimké, Angelina, 376
Grimké, Sarah, 376
Griswold, Roger, 245
Guilford Court House, 193
Guinea, 24
Guy Fawkes Day, 163

H

Haiti 222, 476
Half-Way Covenant, 125
Hamilton, Alexander, 196, 212, 246
   Bank of the United States 233
   financial program, 231
   New York legislature, 210
   Report on Manufactures 233
   Report on Public Credit, 232
   Secretary of the Treasury, 229–231
   Whiskey Rebellion, 240
Hamilton, Henry, 190
Hammond, Charles, 316
Hammond, James Henry, 438
Hancock, John, 152, 157, 176, 209
Hancock, Winfield Scott, 495
Handsome Lake, 266
Hard-money advocate, 494
Harmar, Josiah, 239
Harrington, James, 124

Harrison, William Henry, 239, 267, 270, 326
Hartford Convention, 271
Harvard, 366
Hat Act, 119
Hawkins, Benjamin, 266
Hawkins, John, 22
Hawthorne, Nathaniel,
   short stories and novels, 368–369
Hayes, Rutherford B., 507
Headright system, 37, 40
Heenan, John, 342
Hemings, Sally, 220
Hendricks, Thomas, 495
Henry, Patrick, 149, 156, 175, 212, 217, 219
Henry VIII (King of England), 11
Herjolfsson, Bjarni, 13
Hermitage, 308
Herrera, José Joaquín de, 394
Hessians, 171
Hiawatha, 8
Hicks, Elias, 278
Hieroglyphic writing, 3
Higginbotham, Don, 170
Hispaniola, 41
Hoar, Rockwood, 499
Hodgers, Jennie, 455
Holmes, Oliver Wendell Jr., 431
Homestead Act of 1862, 262, 484
Homestead law, 449
Hood, Admiral Sir Samuel, 195
Hood, John Bell, 461
Hooker, Joseph, 456
Hopewell Indians, 5
Horseshoe Bend, Battle of, 270, 310
House of Burgesses, 37
House of Delegates, 40
House of the Seven Gables (Hawthorne), 368
House of Trade, 19
Houston, Sam, 386, 388
Howard, Oliver O., 482
Howe, Colonel William, 158
Hudson, Henry, 93, 23
Huguenots, 11
Hull, William, 269
Humanism, 12
Hurons, 8
Hutchinson, Anne, 88
Hutchinson, Thomas, 149, 155

I

Immediate, Not Gradual Abolition (Heyrick), 278
Inalienable rights, 230
Incas, 19
   civilizations of, 4
Indentured servants, 43, 146
Independent Treasury Act, 391
Indian Removal Act, 330
Institutes of the Christian Religion (Calvin), 11
Intolerable Acts, 155

Inventing the People: The Rise of Popular Sovereignty in England and America (Morgan), 144
Irish American Fenian Brotherhood, 502
Iron Act, 119
Ironclad, 445
Iron clad oath, 478
Iroquois, 93, 133
Iroquois Confederacy, 8
Iroquois Federation, 239
Irving, Washington, 342
Isabella of Castille, 10

J

Jack, Gullah, 320
Jackson, Andrew,
   and Rachel Donelson, 308
   attempted presidential assassination of, 309
   early years, 306–307
   election of 1824, 311
   election of 1828, 315–316
   Florida expedition, 295
   Force Bill, 323
   Horseshoe Bend, battle of, 270
   Indian Removal Act, 330
   kitchen cabinet of, 319
   military service of, 308
   Old Hickory, 309
   Petticoat Affair, 319
   Specie Circular, 326
   spoils system, 318
   Tariff of Abominations, 313
   veto power use, 318
   War of 1812 and, 309–310
Jacksonian democracy, 306
Jackson, Thomas "Stonewall," 435, 441
Jacobs, Harriet, 349
Jamaica, 41
Jamestown, 46
Jay, John, 217, 241
Jay's Treaty, 241
Jefferson, Thomas, 124, 156
   agrarian republic of, 257
   as Secretary of State, 228
   declaration writing, 162
   Democratic Republican, 228
   election of 1796, 243
   election of 1800, 247
   Embargo Act (1807), 264
   Lewis and Clark Expedition, 262
   Louisiana Purchase, 260
   Non-Importation Act, 263
   Non-Intercourse Act, 264
   political philosophy, 255
   presidency of, 252–259, 254–261
   purging the government, 255
   rivalry with Alexander Hamilton, 236
   strict constructionist, 236
   Tripoli war, 263
Jenkins, Robert, 130
Jeremiah, Thomas, 160
Johann Gutenberg, 12

Johnson, Albert Sidney, 443
Johnson, Andrew, 461
　as president, 478–479
　　impeachment proceedings of, 490–492
　　presidential pardons of, 480
　　Reconstruction policy, 480–481
　　views toward slavery, 479
Johnson, Richard Mentor, 327
Johnson, William, 321
Johnston, Joseph E., 441, 461
Jolliet, Louis, 65
Juarez, Benito, 501
Judicial review, 259
Judiciary Act (1789), 230
Judiciary Act (1801), 248, 258
Junto Society of Philadelphia, 122

K

Kansas-Nebraska Act, 416
Kaskaskia outpost, 190
Kearny, Stephen W., 395
Kemble, Francis Anne, 354
Kennesaw Mountain, Battle of, 461
Key, David, 509
Key, Francis Scott, 270
King Cotton Diplomacy, 438
King George's War (1744-48), 131
King Philip's War, 103
King, Rufus, 212, 294
Kings Mountain, 193
King William's War (1689-1697), 130
Kitchen cabinet, 319
Klondike Gold Rush, 502
Know-Nothing Party, 416
Knox, Colonel Henry, 176, 229
Ku Klux Klan, 502
　beginning of, 493
　Ku Klux Klan Act, 503
　organization of, 489

L

Labrador, 22
Lafayette, Marquis de, 179
Lamar, Mirabeau B., 388
Lane, Ralph, 31
La Salle, Cavelier, Rene Robert, 65
Las Casas, Bartolomé de, 20
Lateen sail, 13
Laud, William, 90
Lawrence, Richard, 309
Lawrence Taliaferro, 405
League of Armed Neutrality, 191
Leaves of Grass (Whitman), 368
Lee, Charles, 178, 189
Lee, Robert E., 423, 435
　Mexican American War, 395
Leisler, Jacob, 109
Le Moyne, Jean Baptiste, 66
Le Moyne, Pierre, 66
Lenni Lenape area, 105
Letters From an American Farmer (Crevecoeur), 234
Lewis and Clark expedition, 385

Lewis Cass, 408
Lewis, Meriwether, 262
Liberal Republicans, 504
Liberator (Garrison), 372
Liberia, nation of, 372
Liberty Party, , 373
Lincoln, Abraham,
　colonization of blacks, 476
　Emancipation Proclamation, 476
　expanding presidential power, 490
　House of Representative, 397
　preserving the Union, 475
　Proclamation of Reconstruction, 477
　racial views of, 475–476
　rise of, 421
　Ten Percent Plan, 477
　views on slavery, 417
　views toward southern whites, 476
Lincoln-Douglas Debates, 422
Lincoln, General Benjamin, 192
Locke, John, 92, 123, 144, 162
Locomotives, 345
London Company, 32
Longfellow, Henry Wadsworth, 419
Longhouse, 8
Long Island, Battle of, 174–175
Lords Committee of Trade and Plantations, 107
Lost Cause, 489
Louisiana Purchase, 260–262
Louis XIV (France), 129, 130
Louis XVI (King), 188
L'Ouverture, Toussaint, 261
Lovejoy, Elijah, 373
Lowell, Francis Cabot, 285
Lowndes, William, 267
Loyal Nine, 149, 150
Luther, Martin, 10, 11
Lyceums, 367
Lyon, Mary, 366
Lyon, Matthew, 245

M

Macon, Nathaniel, 299
Macon's Bill No. 1, 265
Macon's Bill No. 2, 265
Madeira, 50
Madison, James, 228
　anti-federalist, 235
　as Secretary of State, 259
　election of 1808, 264
　Father of the Constitution, 230
　Macon's Bill No. 1, 265
　Macon's Bill No. 2, 265
　member of Virginia legislature, 210
　National Road, 279
　presidency of, 264–266
　War of 1812, 267–269
Magellan, Ferdinand, 18
Magnum, Willie Person, 326
Malaria, 33
Mali Empire, 51
Malthus, Thomas, 257

Manifest Destiny, 390, 499
Mann, Horace, 366
Mansa Musa, 51
Marbury v. Madison (1803), 259
Marbury, William, 259
March to the Sea, 462
Marcy, William L., 318
Marion, Francis, 193
Market Revolution, 315
Marquette, Jacques, 65
Marshall, John, 244, 281, 330
　as Chief Justice, 254, 259
　Cohens v. Virginia, 283
　Dartmouth College v. Woodward, 281
　Fletcher v. Peck (1810), 259
　Gibbons v. Ogden, 282
　judicial review, 259
　Marbury v. Madison (1803), 259
　McCulloch v. Maryland, 282
Martinique, 50
Martin, Luther, 217
Maryland, founding of, 39
Mason, George, 214, 217
Mason, John, 102
Massachusetts, cod fishing industry, 84
Massachusetts Bay Colony, 79, 79–81
Massachusetts Circular Letter, 152
Massachusetts Government Act, 155
Massasoit, 79
Mather, Cotton, 123
Mather, Increase, 104
Maximilian, 501
Maya, 3, 19
Mayflower Compact, 78
Mayhews, Thomas 102
McClellan, George B., 442, 461
McCormick, Cyrus, 347
McCulloch, Hugh, 494
McCulloch v. Maryland (1816), 282
McDowell, Irvin, 441
McIntosh, Ebenezer, 150
McLean, John, 420
McLoughlin, John, 389
Meade, George G., 457
Meigs, Montgomery, 434
Melungeons, 32
Melville, Herman, 368
Memphis race riots, 486
Mercantilism, 86, 106
Mercenaries,
　during Revolutionary War, 171
Merrimack (ironclad), 445
Mestizo, 20
Metacom, 103
Methodists, 371
Mexican American War,
　consequences of, 398–399
　major conflicts, 395–397
　opposition to, 397
　Treaty of Guadalupe Hidalgo, 397
Miami Indians, 132, 239
Middle Passage, 52
Mims, Samuel, 269

Minutemen, 157
Mississippi Plan, 507, 507–508
Missouri, 299
Missouri Compromise, 298
Mittelberger, Gottlieb, , 73
Moby Dick (Melville), 368
Mohawk Indians, 7, 105, 2
Monitor (ironclad), 445
Monmouth Courthouse, 190
Monroe Doctrine, 278, 296–297, 501
Monroe, James,
    election of 1816, 294
    Monroe Doctrine, 296
    National Road, 279
Montcalm, Louis-Joseph de, 134
Monterrey, Battle of, 396
Montgomery, General Richard, 159
Monticello, 257
Moore, James, 64
Moors, 10, 15
Morgan, Brigadier General Daniel, 193
Mormons, , 370–371
Mormon Trail, 389
Morrison, Jane, 355
Morris, Robert, 253
Morrissey, John, 342
Morse, Samuel F.B., 346
Mother Bickerdyke, 454
Mott, Lucretia, 377
Mound Builders, 5, 9
Mountain Meadows Massacre, 399
Mt. Holyoke Female Seminary, 366
Mulattoes, 20
Munro, George, 134
Murray, John, 156
Muskogean Indians, 7, 8

N

Napoleon III, 501
Naseby, Battle of, 90
Nashoba, 369
Nast, Thomas, 504
Natchez Indians, 7
Natchez Trace, 280
National Union Party, 486
Nativism, 416
Nauvoo, 370
Navaho Indians, 8
Navigation Act, 107, 118
Necessary Evil: A History of American Mistrust of Government, A (Wills), 170
Negro Act, 122
Negro Fort, 312
Negro Seaman Act, 321
Nemattanew, 38
Nepotism, 499
Netherlands, 77
Neville, General John, 240
Newburgh Conspiracy, 208
New Departure, 492–495
New England,
    land and labor of, 82
New England Emigrant Aid Company, 418

New Hate: A History of Fear and Loathing on the Populist Right, The (Goldwag), 163
New Jersey Plan, 213
New Lights, 126
New Netherland, 93–94
New Orleans, race riots, 486
New Orleans, Battle of, 271
New York, 94
New York City, 289
New York City Draft Riots, 452
Nicholson, Francis, 107, 109
Nicola, Colonel Lewis, 208
Ninety-five Theses (Luther), 11
Non-Importation Act, 263
Non-Intercourse Act, 264
Norsemen, 13
North Carolina, 61
    Albermarle Sound, 61
    pirating, 62
Northern Pacific Railroad, 504
North, Lord Frederick, 172
North Star (Douglas), 375
Northup, Solomon, 374
Northwest Ordinance, 219
Northwest Passage, 21
Notes on the State of Virginia (Jefferson), 220, 234
Noyes, John Humphrey, 370
Number zero, 3

O

Oberlin College, 366
Obsidian, 4
Oglethorpe, James, 63, 131
Ohio Company, 133
Old Hickory, 309
Old Lights, 126
Olive Branch Petition, 159
Oliver, Andrew, 150
Oliver, Peter, 153
Oneida, New York, 370
Oneidas, 7
Onondagas, 7
Opechancanough, 38
Opium, 117
Orders in Council, 239
Ordinance of Nullification, 323
Oregon Trail, 383, 384
Osceola, 331
Osgood (ship), 73
Ostend Manifesto, 415
O'Sullivan, John, 390
Oswald, Richard, 197
Otis, James, 150
Owenite experiment, 369
Owen, Robert, 369

P

Paine, Thomas, 145, 161, 173, 188, 390
Paleo-Indians, 3
    mound builders, 5
Palmer, William A., 324

Palo Alto, Battle of, 395
Panic of 1819, 310
Panic of 1837, 387
Panic of 1857, 423
Panic in 1873, 504–505
Paramilitary units,
    Confederate, 480, 495
Paredes, Mariano, 394
Parker, Captain John, 157
Parliament, 151
Patents, 346
Paternalism, 290
Paterson, William, 213
Patriots, 163
Patronage, 499
Patterson, Robert H., 441
Pawnee Indians, 2
Peace of Hubertusburg, 137
Peck, Jedediah, 245
Pendleton Act (1883), 499
Pendleton, George H., 495
Penitentiaries, 365
Penn-Meade trial, 97
Pennsylvania,
    constitution of, 98
    founding of, 95–96
    Frame of Government, 98
    government in, 97
    immigrants in, 98
    judicial system and penal code, 98
    Quakers in, 95–96
    religious toleration of, 98
Pennsylvania Abolition Society, 219
Penn, William, 41, 95–96
Penny press, 316
Pequot War, 101–102
Perceval, Sir John, 63
Perkins School for the Blind, 364
Perry, Commodore Oliver Hazard, 269
Petition of Right, 90
Petticoat Affair, 319
Petuns, 8
Phalanxes, 369
Philadelphia Free Produce Society, 278
Philip IV (King of Spain), 130
Philipsburg Proclamation, 192
Phillips, Wendell, 375
Phrenologists, 351
Pica, 147
Pickett's Charge, 457
Pierce, Franklin, 413
Pierce, William, 212
Pilgrims, 77
Pinckney, Charles, 213
Pinckney, Charles Cotesworth, 244, 247, 262, 264
Pinckney, Elizabeth Lucas, 61
Pinckney, Thomas, 241
    election of 1796, 243
Pitt, William, 135
Pizarro, Francisco, 19
Plymouth Colony, 77–79
Plymouth Plantation, 77

Pocahontas, 35
Pocket veto, 478
Political Party System,
    rise of, 235
Polk, James K., 393
Polo, Marco, 12
Polygamy, , 384, 370
Polygenesis, 329
Polygyny, 50
Pope's Day, 150
Popular sovereignty doctrine, 408
Population,
    between 1790-1860, 342
    urban areas of, 343
Porter, Peter B., 267
Powell, Lewis, 478
Powhatan, 34
Praying towns, 102
Predestination, 76
Prescott, Colonel William, 158
Preston, Captain Thomas, 153
Prince Henry the Navigator, 10, 14
Princeton University, 127
Printing press, 12
Prize fighting, 341
Proclamation of 1763, 138
Proclamation of Amnesty, 477
Proclamation of Reconstruction, 477
Promontory Point, 504
Prophetstown, 266
Public Credit Act, 497
Puebla, 397
Pueblo Indians, 6–10
Puerto Rico, 41
Puritanism, 74
Puritans, 75
Put-in-Bay, Battle of, 269

Q

Quakers, 95–97, 371
    and slavery, 219, 221
Quebec Act, 155
Quebec, Battle of, 136
Queenston Heights, Battle of, 269
Quetzalcoatl, 4, 19

R

Race-baiting, 495
Radicalism of the American Revolution, The
    (Wood), 143
Radical Republicans, 436, 477
Raleigh, Sir Walter, 23, 31–32,
Randolph, Edmund, 212, 214, 229
Randolph, John, 267, 313
Rationalism, 123
Raynal, Abbé Guillaume, 179
Rebels, 495
Reconstruction,
    Andrew Johnson and, 478–480
    issues of, 474
    presidential, 475–477
    Radical Republicans and, 477, 485–489
    retreat from, 505–507
    white backlash, 502
Reconstruction Acts of 1867, 487–488, 493
    southern response, 492–493
Redcoats, 170
Redeemers, 493, 505
Redemptioners, 119
Red Shirts, 506
Red Sticks, 269, 310
Reformation, 10
Reform movements,
    abolitionists, 373
    pre-Civil War, 363
    public education, 365
    rehabilitation, 364
    temperance, 363
Reign of Terror, 237
Remond, Charles Lenox, 375
Renaissance, 11
Renegade History of the United States, A
    (Russell), 182
Report on Manufactures (Hamilton), 233
Report on Public Credit (Hamilton), 232
Resaca de la Palma, Battle of, 395
Reservations, 400
Revere, Paul, 153, 157
Revivalism, 362–363
Revolutionary War,
    Battle of Long Island, 173
    Battle of Princeton, 176
    Battles of Cowpens, 193
    France support, 188
    Guilford Court House, 193
    Treaty of Paris, 197
    War in the North, 185
    War in the South, 191–193
    War in the West, 190
    War on the Frontier, 190
Reynolds Arcade, 289
Rhode Island, 88
Rhode Island System, 285
Rifle Clubs, 506
Ritner, Joseph, 324
Roanoke Island, 23, 31, 32
Rolfe, John, 35, 38
Rosecrans, William, 458
Rose, Ernestine, 377
Ross, John, 266, 329, 332
Royal African Company, 49
Rubber, 347
Rush-Bagot Pact (1817), 295
Rush, Benjamin, 328
Rutgers University, 129

S

Sabbatarians, 363
Sacagawea, 262
San Jacinto, Battle of, 386
San Juan Islands, 502
Santa Anna, Antonio López de, 386, 395
Santo Domingo Affair, 499
Savannahs, 60
Scalawags, 489, 493

Scarlet Letter (Hawthorne), 368
Schofield, John M., 492
Schurz, Carl, 500, 507
Scientific Revolution, 122
Scott, Dred, 405
Scott, Winfield, 331, 396, 413, 439
Second Bank of the United States, 279, 310
Second Continental Congress, 158, 175, 188, 206
Second Great Awakening, 256, 362–363
Security Act, 121
Sedition Act, 245
Seminole War, 311–312
Seminole War, Second, 331
Seneca Falls convention, 377
Senecas, 7
Separatists, 77
Sequoyah, 330
Seven Years' War, 137
Sevier, John, 308
Seward, William, 406, 409, 424, 436, 478, 500
Seymour, Horatio, 495
Seymour, Thomas H., 461
Shakers, 369
Sharecropping, 484
Shaw, Gould, 451
Shawnee, 239
Shays, Captain Daniel, 209
Shays' Rebellion, 209
Sheridan, Phillip, 443, 463
Sherman, William Tecumseh, 443, 459, 461, 484, 491
Shifting cultivation, 50
Shoe production, 289
Silesia, 137
Silk Road, 12
Simms, Thomas, 413
Sinners in the Hands of an Angry God (Edwards), 125
Sioux, 384
Slater, Samuel, 285
Slaveocracy, 473
Slave Power conspiracy, 374
Slavery,
    expansion of cotton production and, 290
    impact on Africa, 56
    Indian slaves, 60
    organization of labor, 290
    origins of, 49–53
    paternalism and, 290–291
    Potuguese trade, 49
    slave codes, 57
    Spanish trade, 50
Slidell, John, 394
Smallpox,
    colonial contraction of, 123
Smith, John, 34, 78
Smith, Joseph, 370, 389
Smith, William Loughton, 221
Society of Friends. See Quakers
Songhai kingdom, 51

INDEX

Sons of Liberty, 151, 152
Southern Homestead Act, 484
Spanish Armada, 32
Spanish Inquisition, 10
Specie Circular, 326
Spiritualists, 351
Spoils system, 318, 499
Spotsylvania Court House, Battle of, 459
Squanto, 78
Stanbery, Henry, 491
Stanton, Edwin M., 434, 437, 490
Stanton, Elizabeth Cady,
   women's suffrage, 377–378
Staple Act, 107
Stark, John, 186
Statute for Religious Freedom (Jefferson), 200
St. Clair, Arthur, 239
St. Dominque, 50
Steamboats, 345
Stephens, Alexander, 406, 416, 450, 481
Stevens, Thaddeus, 436, 477, 484
St. Kitts, 41
St. Leger, Colonel Barry, 186
Stockton, Richard, 175
Stockton, Robert F., 395
Stoddard, Solomon, 125
Stone, Barton W., 256
Stone, Lucy, 378
Stono Rebellion, 121–122
Stowe, Harriet Beecher, 414
Strict constructionists, 236
Strutt, Jedediah, 285
Stuart dynasty, 75
Stuart, J.E.B., 423
Subscription lists, 153
Suffragettes, 497
Sugar Act, 147
Sumner, Charles, 416, 418, 477, 419, 500
Susan Constant (ship), 33
Sweatshops, 289

T

Tallmadge Amendment, 298
Tallmadge, James, 298
Tammany Hall, 498
Taney, Roger, 336, 420
Tappan, Arthur, 362
Tappan, Lewis, 362, 374
Tariff of 1816, 279
Tariff of Abominations, 313, 320
Tarleton, Banastre, 192, 307
Tarleton's Quarter, 192
Taylor, Susie King, 454
Taylor, Zachary, 394, 395, 409
Tea Act, 154
Tecumseh, 266
Teepees, 8
Telegraph, 346, 347
Temperance, 362, 363
Tenant farming, 484
Tennent, Gilbert, 127
Tennessee, 486

Tenochtitlan, 4
Ten Percent Plan, 477
Tenskwatawa (The Prophet), 266
Tenure of Office Act, 490
Teotihuacan, 4
Thanksgiving, 79
The Destruction of the Indies (Las Casas), 20
Thoreau, Henry David, 397
   transcendentalist, 367–368
Thornton Affair, 394
Tilden, Samuel J., 507
Timberlake, Margaret "Peggy" O'Neale, 318
Timbuktu, 50
Tippecanoe, Battle of, 267
Tobacco,
   cultivation of, 26
   labor of, 36
Tocqueville, Alexis de, 362, 374
Tomochichi, 63
Toombs, Robert, 406, 407
Tories, 163, 193
Tory, 185
Towards a More Perfect Union: Virtue and the Formation of the American Republic (Withington), 163
Townshend, Charles, 152
Townshend Revenue Act, 152
Trail of Tears, 332–333
Transcendentalism, 367
Transportation Innovations, 345
Treaty of Easton, 137
Treaty of Ghent, 271
Treaty of Greenville, 239
Treaty of Guadalupe Hidalgo, 397, 408
Treaty of Paris, 137, 197
Treaty of Ryswick, 130
Treaty of Tordesillas, 16
Treaty of Utrecht, 130
Treaty of Washington (1871), 502
Tredegar Iron Works, 434
Trenchard, John, 124
Tripoli, 263
Trist, Nicholas, 398
Troup, George M., 267
Troy Female Seminary, 366
Trumbull, Lyman, 485
Truth, Sojourner, 349, 361
   black abolitionist, 374–377
Tubman, Harriet, 349, 455
   anti-slavery leader, 376
Turner, Nat, 321, 353
Tuscarora, 61
Tweed, William Marcy, 498
Twiggs, David, 432
Tyler, John, 391

U

Uncle Tom's Cabin (Stowe),, 414
Underground Railroad, 374
Underhill, John, 102
Unionists, 474, 480
Union Jack, 198

Union League, 489, 492
Union Pacific Railroad, 498, 504
Unitarians, 96
United States Sanitary Commission, 453
Utah territory, 398

V

Vagrancy laws, 481
Vallandigham, Clement, 450
Valley Forge, 169, 188
Van Buren, Martin, 406, 409
   Jackson supporter, 313
Van Winkle, Peter G., 492
Vanderbilt, Cornelius, 497
Verrazzano, Giovanni da, 23
Vesey, Denmark, 320
Vespucci, Amerigo, 17
Victoria, Guadalupe, 386
Vikings, 13
Vincennes outpost, 190
Virginia Company. See London Company.
Virginia (ironclad), 445
Virginia Plan, 212
Virginia Resolves, 149
Virgin Islands, 500
von Steuben, Baron, 170
Voting Rights Act of 1965, 164

W

Wade, Benjamin, 478, 489, 490
Wade-Davis Bill, 478
Walden (Thoreau), 368
Waldseemuller, Martin, 18
Walker, David, 375
Walker, Mary, 454
Walker, Robert J., 421
Walker, William, 423
Wampanoag, 101
Wampum, 101
War of 1812,
   Battle of Queenston Heights, 269
   invasion of Canada, 268
   isues of, 267–269
   Put-in-Bay, Battle of, 269
   Tecumseh's last stand, 269
   Treaty of Ghent. 271
War of Jenkins's Ear (1739-1744), 131
War of the Spanish Succession (1702-1713), 130
Warner, Charles Dudley, 499
Washington, George, 124, 133, 158
   Jay's Treaty, 241
   military leader, 158
   Native American troubles, 239–240
   presidency of, 228–231
   two-term limit, 242
   western frontier troubles, 240–241
   Whiskey Rebellion, 240
Washington Societies, 363
Wayne, "Mad Anthony," 239
Wealth of Nations, The (Smith), 231
Webster-Ashburton Treaty (1842), 392
Webster, Daniel, 281, 326, 392, 398

Weld, Theodore, 321, 372, 373
Westo War, 60
West Point, New York, 171, 255
Westward movement,
  epidemic diseases, 384
  missionaries expectations, 383
  Mormons, 389
  Oregon, 384
  Texas, 386
  Texas Republic, 387
Whig Party, 193, 390
  formation of, 325
  idealogy of, 325
  post Civil War, 492
Whiskey Rebellion, 233, 240
Whiskey Ring, 498
Whitefield, George, 126, 128– 129

White, Hugh Lawson, 326
White, John, 31
White Leagues, 506
Whitman, Walt, 368
Whittier, John Greenleaf, 370
Wilderness, Battle of the, 459
Willard, Emma, 366
Williamson, Captain David, 191
Williams, Roger, 87
Wilmot, David, 406
Wilmot Proviso, 406
Wilson, James, 211
Winthrop, John, 81, 87, 390
Wirt, William, 324
Wolfe, General James, 136
Women's Rights Movement, beginning of, 377

Women's Temperance Association, 378
Wool Act, 119
Wright, Frances, 369

X

XYZ Affair, 244

Y

Yamasees, 60
Yates, Robert, 212
Yazoo Land Company, 259
Yeo, John, 41
Young America, 413, 415
Young, Brigham, , 389, 370